Balambangan Banggi Mapun

SULU SEA

SOUTH CHINA SEA

F

Natuna Besar

Natuna Is

Tarakan

Maratua

Sarawak

MALAYSIA

nbelan Is

Borneo

Kalimantan

Karimata Is

elitung

Laut

JAVA SEA

INDONESIA

Matasiri

Makassar Strait

Wallace's Line

Karimunjawa Is

Bawean

Masalembu

Kangean Is

Madura

Java

BALI SEA

Bali

Lombok

Nusa
Penida

Sumbawa

Lesser Sundas
(Nusa Tenggara)

Birds of the Indonesian Archipelago

Greater Sundas and Wallacea

James A. Eaton,
Bas van Balen,
Nick W. Brickle,
Frank E. Rheindt

Birds of the Indonesian Archipelago

Greater Sundas and Wallacea

James A. Eaton,
Bas van Balen,
Nick W. Brickle,
Frank E. Rheindt

Colour plates by

Richard Allen
Norman Arlott
Hilary Burn
Clive Byers
John Cox
Martin Elliott
Alan Harris
Ren Hathway
Mark Hulme
Àngels Jutglar
Francesc Jutglar
Ian Lewington
Toni Llobet
Alex Mascarell

Oriol Massana
Dave Nurney
Douglas Pratt
David Quinn
Chris Rose
Lluís Sanz
Brian Small
Lluís Solé
Juan Varela
Etel Vilaró
Jan Wilczur
Ian Willis
Martin Woodcock
Tim Worfolk

Illustrations
For contributions by family, see CONTENTS:

RA — Richard Allen
NA — Norman Arlott
HB — Hilary Burn
CB — Clive Byers
JC — John Cox
ME — Martin Elliott
AH — Alan Harris
RH — Ren Hathway
MH — Mark Hulme
ÀJ — Àngels Jutglar
FJ — Francesc Jutglar
IL — Ian Lewington
TL — Toni Llobet
AM — Alex Mascarell

DN — Dave Nurney
DP — Douglas Pratt
DQ — David Quinn
CR — Chris Rose
LS — Lluís Sanz
BS — Brian Small
LSo — Lluís Solé
JV — Juan Varela
IV — Ilian Velikov
EV — Etel Vilaró
JW — Jan Wilczur
IW — Ian Willis
MW — Martin Woodcock
TW — Tim Worfolk

Second Edition: February 2021

© Lynx Edicions – www.lynxeds.com
   Lynx Edicions®: Alada Books, S.L.
© Texts: Eaton, J.A., van Balen, B., Brickle, N.W. & Rheindt, F.E.

Recommended citation:
Eaton, J.A., van Balen, B., Brickle, N.W. & Rheindt, F.E. (2021). *Birds of the Indonesian Archipelago. Greater Sundas and Wallacea.* Lynx Edicions. Barcelona.

Project co-ordinator: Arnau Bonan-Barfull
Cover design: Susanna Silva
Interior book design: Xavier Ruiz
Layout: Oriol Cabrero

Cover illustration by Ilian Velikov
Wallace's Standardwing (*Semioptera wallacii*)

Printed and bound in Barcelona by Índice Arts Gràfiques
Legal Deposit flexi bound: B 3028-2021
Legal Deposit hardcover: B 867-2021
ISBN flexi bound: 978-84-16728-44-2
ISBN hardcover: 978-84-16728-43-5

CONTENTS

ACKNOWLEDGEMENTS

Many people have – in one way or another – helped with the preparation of this book, including (in alphabetical order) Panji Gusti Akbar, Per Alström, Hidayat Ashari, Mikael Bauer, Pratibha Baveja, Alex Berryman, Mark Bezuijn, David Bishop, Carlos Bocos, Andy Boyce, Arjan Brenkman, Ryan Burner, Heru Cahyono, Robert Chong, Serene Chng, Les Christidis, Nigel Collar, Rohan Clarke, Emilie Cros, Shashank Dalvi, Edward Dickinson, Paul Dimus, David Donsker, David Edwards, Boas Emmanuel, Dave Farrow, Freddy Hambuwali, Gabriella Fredriksson, Tim Forrester, Frank Gill, Gwee Chyi Yin, Robert Hall, Paul Holt, Muhammad Iqbal, Mohammad Irham, David James, Kamalludin, Chaiyan Kasorndorkbua, Joseph Kelly, Ben King, Kanitha Krishnasamy, Hery Kusumanegara, Frank Lambert, Geraldine Lee, Jessica Lee, Bryan Lim, Iwan "Londo" Febrianto, Gabriel Low, Simon Mahood, Clive Mann, Adam Miller, Simon Mitchell, John Mittermeier, Pete Morris, Mike Nelson, Ng Chin Wei, Dominic Ng, Elize Ng, Nathaniel Ng, Peter Ng, Vincent Nijman, Fransisca Noni, Richard Noske, Agus Nurza, Darren O'Connell, Wesley Pangimangen, Politarius, Colin Poole, Dewi Malia Prawiradilaga, Pamela Rasmussen, Ceisar Riupassa, Craig Robson, Philip Round, Keren Resha Sadanandan, Antoni Saputra, Richard Schodde, Fred Sheldon, Chris Shepherd, Sang Sigar, Keita Sin, Rob Sinke, Soekarja Somadikarta, Morten Strange, Vinno Soemarlan, Subandi, Sumaraja, Suparno, Tang Qian, Rob Tizard, Tedi Wahyudi, David Wells, Olva Winerungan, Roland Wirth, Melody Wu, Pete Wood, Tan Hui Zhen, Yeo Siew Teck, Dennis Yong, Yong Ding Li, Khaleb Yordan and numerous others that may have inadvertently been omitted but should have been listed here. We thank them all.

We would like to thank the personnel at Lynx Edicions for their tireless work in the design and production of this guide, in particular Arnau Bonan-Barfull for his expertise in editing the species accounts text, along with Amy Chernasky, Xavier Ruiz and Josep del Hoyo. A field guide is only as good as its drawings. We wish to thank the army of artists at Lynx Edicions for their beautiful illustrations for this field guide, specifically Francesc Jutglar, Juan Varela and Oriol Massana and a special thank you to Alex Mascarell for his patience and producing so many wonderful new figures. Their patience and indulgence with our numerous requests at re-drawing were highly appreciated.

This guide presents considerable new information on the taxonomy, distribution, identification and general biology of birds within the region. This is only possible thanks to the work of untold legions of birdwatchers, field workers and lab ornithologists, both professional and amateur, that publish their findings in journals, trip reports, on email lists and discussion forums, on photo and bird sound archives or on social media. Without the collective effort of this community, our knowledge about the birds of the Indonesian archipelago would not be where it is today. We would like to recognise these contributions and encourage anyone visiting or working within the region to continue to add to our knowledge in this way.

The world's major museum collections are a main repository of ornithological material and knowledge. A book such as this one would have been impossible without recourse to specimens and DNA material of birds at museums throughout the world. We wish to thank Mark Adams at the British Natural History Museum (UK), Dewi Malia Prawiradilaga and Irham Mohammad at the Museum Zoologicum Bogoriense (Indonesia) and Steven van der Mije at the Naturalis Museum (Netherlands) for allowing us broad access to their collections. Other museum collections and their curators and collections managers are also warmly acknowledged for having – in one way or another – contributed to this work, including (but not limited to) the American Museum of Natural History (USA), the Raffles Collection at the Lee Kong Chian Natural History Museum (Singapore), the Smithsonian Institution (USA), the Field Museum in Chicago (USA), the Muséum d'Histoire Naturelle (France), the Australian Museum (Australia), the Senckenberg Museum (Germany), and Museum Victoria (Australia).

There are several people who have contributed disproportionately to this book, and we would like to single them out for the knowledge and support they have provided. They include Dave Bakewell, Colin Trainor, Philippe Verbelen and Robert Hutchinson. All of them have contributed greatly both to this book, and to ornithology in the region generally.

Finally, we thank our families and friends for their help and support, both in producing this book, and for all the years of birding in the region that came before it!

James A. Eaton is very grateful to his parents John and Roz Eaton for unconditional support and encouragement to pursue his birding dream from such an early age, from the UK to Indonesia, to his Grandmother, for planting the seeds of his birding career, handing him a copy of Benson's *The Observer's Book of Birds*, and Nancy Gibson for her unconditional support.

Bas van Balen would like to thank Like, Leonie and Gerrit for their patience and understanding during the many weeks and months of his absence; posthumous thanks to his parents Herman en Bep van Balen for tolerating his ornithological aspirations, and grandfather Gerrit whose bird volume of *Brehm's Life of Animals* had imprinted in him a life-long passion for birds.

Nick W. Brickle would like to thank Anna, Robert and Alex Brickle for their support and encouragement in writing this book, for tolerating his birdwatching obsession in general, and for following that obsession to Indonesia for so many years! Also to his parents Norma and Barrie Brickle for unreserved encouragement and support from the very beginning.

Frank E. Rheindt is deeply grateful to Ng Chin Wei for her unwavering, unconditional support in his ornithological work throughout the years, and would like to thank his parents Ditta and Erwin Rheindt for letting him pursue his dream in the field from the earliest years of his life.

Here we are again. Just a little over four years since the publication of the first edition of *The Birds of the Indonesian Archipelago* an updated edition is now ready to head to the printers. This fully revised, second edition describes all 1,456 bird species known to occur across the Indonesian archipelago, including 628 endemics, 106 vagrants, four introduced species and ten species yet to be formally described by the end of 2020. This is a turbulent shift from the first edition, published in 2016, which described 1,417 species, including 601 endemics, 98 vagrants, eight introduced species and 18 species yet to be formally described. The rise in the total number of species is due to new records since 2016 and taxonomic changes, which have increased the number of endemics by 27, totalling 43% of all species recorded in the archipelago. The reduction in the number of undescribed species reflects continuing vivid taxonomic research within the region that has seen ten species formally described between the first and second editions, eight of them discovered and/or (co-) described by one of us (Rheindt *et al.* 2020a; Irham *et al.* 2020; Ng *et al.* 2018; Prawiradilaga *et al.* 2017), along with our description of seven more subspecies in the region (Rheindt *et al.* 2020a; Ng *et al.* 2017; Rheindt *et al.* 2017). Alas, only one undoubted undescribed species has been discovered since the first edition was published (Selayar Leaf Warbler; Eaton & Rheindt 2017).

The seven years of research leading up to the publication of the first edition were a tortuous battle and a real labour of love, as thousands of hours were spent uncovering snippets of information in historical publications, unravelling multiple ornithological mysteries and myths, and researching the status of even the most common species on hundreds of islands. The four years leading to the second edition were no less eventful: since the first edition was published, we have learnt so much additional novel information, not only from our own research and fieldwork but from others, who, with the first edition in hand, were able to report novelties that had previously been ignored. Myriads of new island records, corrected island inventories and distribution updates have come to our attention or were formally published, in numerous instances by ourselves (e.g., Rheindt *et al.* 2020b; O'Connell *et al.* 2020; Rheindt *et al.* 2019; Chiok *et al.* 2019; Asari *et al.* 2018; Eaton & Rheindt 2017; Eaton 2017). Pooling all this new information, we have produced what we believe is an even more authoritative, accurate and wholesome treatise of the birds of the Indonesian archipelago.

With the passage of time, there has been a concomitant advancement in taxonomic insights, changing our understanding of so many taxa. As field guide authors, we were particularly susceptible to criticisms from academia that many of our novel taxonomic arrangements in the first edition – which were based on our own data and knowledge – were unsubstantiated by the peer-reviewed literature. In this context, we are proud to have used these past four years to formally publish some of our bioacoustic, genomic and morphological data on a large part of our novel taxonomic arrangements in peer-reviewed journals, including novel taxonomic insights into **pied starlings** (Baveja *et al.* in press), **hill mynas** (Ng *et al.* in press), **Black-winged Mynas** (Sadanandan *et al.* 2020), **pittas** (Yue *et al.* 2020; Ericson *et al.* 2019), **robins** (Ng *et al.* 2020), various **babblers** and **bulbuls** (Cros *et al.* 2020; Cros & Rheindt 2017), various **Barusan** endemic taxa (Rheindt *et al.* 2020a), **flowerpeckers** (Rheindt & Eaton 2019), **owls** (Gwee *et al.* 2019a; Gwee *et al.* 2017), **jungle-flycatchers** (Gwee *et al.* 2019b; Garg *et al.* 2018), **plovers** (Sadanandan *et al.* 2019),

white-eyes (Lim *et al.* 2019; Rheindt & Eaton 2018), **leaf-warblers** (Alström *et al.* 2018; Berryman & Eaton 2020), **swiftlets** (Rheindt *et al.* 2017), **fantails** (Ng *et al.* 2017) and **cuckoo-doves** (Ng *et al.* 2016a, b). More of this kind of taxonomic research is in the works and will hopefully see the light of day soon, including on redshanks, junglefowl, swiftlets, shortwings and, of course, additional work on white-eyes and leaf-warblers.

Having already done 'the hard yards' with the more well-known species for the first edition, we have specifically concentrated on lesser-known species for the second edition, especially with regards to identification. Much effort has been placed into an expansion of the "Similar Species" (SS) sections of each species account to educate the reader as to how to identify even the trickiest of species in a single field guide. James and Frank, in particular, spent countless hours discussing the finer points of identification of white-eyes, bulbuls, plovers and many other troublesome groups. Frank, with immense help by James, has gone through each single species account to make sure that details on identification, ecology, status and taxonomy are updated to the best of our knowledge. James undertook the Herculean task of completely overhauling the maps, which – for the first time in this edition – we consider largely reliable not only for the bigger, more well-known islands, but also the smaller and more obscure archipelagos (e.g. Lingga, Banyak, Batu etc). The microscopic detail would have been difficult to fully appreciate in the single, archipelago-wide map design of the first edition so we have invested additional time into developing additional map frames depicting a magnified representation of three regions: Greater Sundas, Wallacea and Lesser Sundas.

Bas has been indispensable with his encyclopaedic knowledge on historic records not only of obscure species, but also of some of the most widespread and mundane species at an admirable level of detail. We have worked with Arnau Bonan-Barfull and Oriol Cabrero from Lynx Edicions to produce an improved layout of plates, switching the sequence of many species accounts as much as the taxonomic order allowed, to enable as many similar and region-specific species as possible to be depicted on the same plate. Thanks to Alex Mascarell and Francesc Jutglar, we have nearly 500 improved figures and 325 entirely new figures compared to the first edition, with a massive expansion of our panels of flight depictions including ducks, pigeons, waterbirds, raptors and hornbills. In coordination with Alex we have added and corrected details in hundreds of illustrations, leading to a substantially improved alignment with the text.

Nick, assisted by Bas and James, has been working behind the scenes on the complicated task of producing an Indonesian language version of the field guide, and once that is published and distributed, we will feel our work is done. Teamwork and friendship is something needed for such a project and we feel all the richer for it. We have attempted to create a perfect field guide that can truly be used beyond the borders of the region it covers, the Indonesian archipelago.

We sincerely hope that our blood, sweat and tears (and intensely heated taxonomic debates) have not all been in vain, and you, the reader, will find this work informative, educational and above-all-else, enjoyable. The only way such a revision could have taken place, in our busy schedules, was if something like a global pandemic took over our everyday lives and disrupted our usual work patterns. Serendipitously, that is exactly what happened.

The region comprises over 17,000 islands stretching in an arc along the Equator over almost 5,000 km, but occupies only around 1% of the world's land surface. It is amongst the most biodiverse regions on Earth, but remains one of the least studied. The birds found in the Indonesian archipelago represent approximately 13% of all the world's described bird species. Of these 43% are endemic to the region, and more species continue to be described.

In this field guide we build on the work of many others: from the earliest historic explorers through the pioneering work that led to the first field guides, to the most recent advances in identification and taxonomy. We present the most up-to-date state of knowledge on the region's birds, treated for the first time as a whole in a single volume.

Geographic Limits

The Indonesian archipelago as here defined encompasses the biogeographic regions of the Greater Sundas (Sumatra, Borneo, Java and Bali) and Wallacea (Sulawesi, the Moluccas and the Lesser Sundas), plus all satellite islands. Therefore, the term "Indonesian archipelago", as used in our book, is not a political but a biogeographic attribute. This book includes areas currently outside the political boundaries of the Republic of Indonesia (Brunei, East Timor and the Malaysian states of Sarawak and Sabah), while it excludes two provinces of the Republic (West Papua and Papua).

The north-western boundary of the region is defined by the Malacca and Singapore Straits and the South China Sea. These bodies of water divide Sumatra and Borneo from mainland South-east Asia. All satellite islands that territorially lie within the Republic of Indonesia, including the Riau archipelago, the Natuna and the Anambas Island groups, are included in the guide, while territorial possessions of neighbouring countries (Tioman Island, Singapore and Nicobar Islands) are not included despite their close biogeographic affinity.

The north-eastern boundary is formed by the Sulu and Sulawesi Seas that separate Borneo and Sulawesi from the Philippines. Included are all satellite islands that form part of the territorial limits of Sabah, Sarawak and Indonesia, including Banggi, Sangihe and Talaud, while territorial possessions of the Philippines (Balabac, Palawan, Tawi-Tawi) are excluded.

The western and southern boundary of the region is formed by the Indian Ocean and the Timor and Arafura Seas that separate the Indonesian archipelago from Australia. Satellite islands that territorially form part of Indonesia or East Timor are included, while those that form part of Australian territory, such as Christmas Island and the Ashmore Reef, are excluded.

The eastern boundary is defined by the continental shelf of New Guinea and runs along the distinct biogeographic boundary known as Lydekker's Line. Wallacean island groups surrounded by deep-sea trenches, including Halmahera, Morotai, Seram, Seram Laut, Kai and Tanimbar are included in this guide. On the other hand, nearby island groups that lie on the Papuan continental shelf, including Kofiau, Misool, Raja Ampat and Aru, as well as a few smaller islands in the close vicinity of the Papuan shelf, such as Gebe and Gag, are excluded. While all of these islands politically lie within the Republic of Indonesia, together with half the island of New Guinea itself, the birds of these areas are not considered in this book as they form part of an unrelated avifauna that is better treated separately along with the birds of New Guinea as a whole.

EARTH HISTORY AND BIOGEOGRAPHY
(by Frank E. Rheindt)

Geology

Lying between the Eurasian, Australian, Philippine and Pacific plates, the Indonesian archipelago has a complex geologic history. The meeting of continental plates contributes to making the archipelago one of the most tectonically dynamic and volcanic regions on Earth. Around three quarters of the volcanoes in the region belong to the Sunda Volcanic Arc that stretches over 3,000 km from north Sumatra through Java and Bali to the Banda Sea. Other areas of high volcanic activity include the regions of north Sulawesi, Sangihe and Halmahera.

There are few other regions in the world that have seen such precipitous changes and developments in land distribution and land formation within the last few million years. Modern research, especially by Robert Hall and colleagues, has shown that the eastern Indonesian archipelago, and in particular Sulawesi and the Moluccas, are the site of ongoing tectonic upheaval, with island shapes and land connections constantly being re-drawn by the collision and grinding of plates with one another. If one were to look at a world map from, say, five million years ago, the shape of most continents and islands on the planet would look familiar, whereas the eastern Indonesian archipelago presented a very different geography, with Sulawesi just having completed formation from its four aggregate parts, and the Northern Moluccas still far removed from their current location and within tight grasp of the Papuan Vogelkop Peninsula. The speed with which the geographic environment of this area continues to change has contributed to its biological complexity, and DNA research into birds and other groups is just starting to uncover amazing parallels between patterns of gene flow and Earth history.

Sea Level Fluctuations

The world's climate is undergoing constant change and fluctuation. The Quaternary period in particular, which covers the past ~2.6 million years, has seen the coming-and-going of 20–30 global glaciations recurring at roughly regular intervals of 50,000–100,000 years. Prior to that, during the previous epoch, the Pliocene, the Earth was a much hotter and more stable place. Quaternary ice ages have repeatedly led to expanding glaciation across wide swathes of the colder parts of the planet, especially in the northern hemisphere, while drops in temperature and fluctuations in precipitation have caused frequent changes in the distribution of plant and animal communities worldwide. However, biological communities in the world's continental shelf regions (of which the Indonesian archipelago is the largest) have been impacted by glaciations in an important additional way: at the peak of an ice age (the 'glacial maximum'), much of the Earth's oceanic water freezes around the poles, leading to global drops in sea level by up to ~120 m, whereas during warm periods between ice ages (the 'interglacial maximum') sea levels rise back to original conditions. The current millennium is thought to be close to an interglacial maximum, but sea levels were >100 m lower as little as ~18,000 years ago during the last glacial maximum.

The Indonesian archipelago is characterised by extensive shelf areas of shallow sea, especially (but not exclusively) in its western part. During glaciations and global drops in sea level, enormous areas of land form across the archipelago and lead to connections between land masses we now see as islands. In our region, Quaternary sea level fluctuations are one of the most important biogeographic factors, and bathymetry (research into sea depths) has become a useful tool for ornithologists to predict faunal connections between islands across the region (Figure 1).

While we have known about the effects of Quaternary glaciations for a while now, there are two aspects about them that are still in-sufficiently appreciated in the ornithological community: (1) their fre-quency, and (2) their recency. As regards their frequency, Quaternary drops in sea level have recurred so many times, and for such extend-ed periods of time, that it is almost biogeographically inappropriate to think of some land masses as 'islands'. Land masses such as Sumatra and Java have been connected to the Asian mainland far more often – and for longer – than they have been separated as islands. Modern humans' perception of these regions as islands is based on our existence during a less typical era (the peak of an interglacial) that is marked by their brief severance from mainland Asia before they become reconnected only a few thousand years later. As regards the recency of drops in sea level, the last glacial maximum occurred as

little as 18,000 years ago, but land connections in particularly shallow shelf areas would have been even younger by a few thousand years. Modern humans walked from the Malay Peninsula to Sumatra and Java, or from Sulawesi to Buton. Animals and plants from these land masses would have been closely connected, too.

Wallace's Line

In biogeographic terms, the region comprises two halves split by an iconic biological boundary, the name of which com-memorates one of the region's greatest explorers: Sir Alfred Russel Wallace. This line separates the Asian continental shelf in the west from the more easterly Wallacea, a region of deep-sea islands (again named after Wallace) that is tucked in between the Asian and Australo-Papuan continental shelves and is characterised by an avifauna of mixed Asian and Australo-Papuan descent. Without a knowledge of the dis-tribution of deep-sea trenches or shallow shelf water, it was Wallace who first identified the difference in the mammals and birds of the island of Bali to those of the island of Lombok situated only 21 km to the east. In his book *The Malay Archipelago* he says "In Bali we have Barbets, Fruit thrushes and Woodpeckers; on passing over to Lombok we see these no more, but on Lombok we have an abundance of Cockatoos, Honeysuckers, and Brush-turkeys which we do not see in Bali or further west." Recognising similar differences between the wildlife of Borneo and Sulawesi, he drew a line between islands that was later named by Huxley as 'Wallace's Line'. Subsequent explora-tion by Richard Lydekker identified a similar distinction between the birds and mammals of Wallacea and those of New Guinea, with the latter being defined by species that were purely of an Australo-Pap-uan origin while the former exhibits a pronounced Asian element. This line subsequently became known as 'Lydekker's Line' and now forms the eastern boundary of the region covered by this guide.

Expanding on these distinctions further, the Indonesian archi-pelago can broadly be described as having four geographically distinct regions: west of Wallace's Line lie the Greater Sundas, whereas Wallacea to the east of Wallace's Line comprises the Lesser Sundas, Sulawesi and the Moluccas. Below these regions are considered in greater detail:

The Greater Sundas

The Greater Sundas comprise the islands that lie on the Sunda Shelf. This area is essentially an extension of the Malay Peninsula and the South-east Asian mainland, and at most times during the Pleistocene has formed its own 'Sundaic subcontinent' (sometimes referred to as 'Sundaland'). However, at other times (such as now) the Greater Sundas constitute an archipelago consisting of some of the largest islands on Earth. The main islands in this group, Sumatra, Borneo, Java and Bali, all have mountains over 3,000 m, with the highest being Mt Kinabalu on Borneo at 4,095 m (see table below).

The continental Asian nature of the Greater Sundas is reflected in the bird families found here, which are of a typically South and South-east Asian ('Oriental') affinity. The constant land connec-tions among the Greater Sunda Islands are also reflected in their relatively high species diversity (deep-sea islands are much more isolated and have a lower diversity) and their low levels of ende-mism. By taxonomic standards of the 1980s and 1990s, the num-ber of bird species endemic to each of the major Greater Sunda Islands is almost an order of magnitude lower than the level of endemism on comparable deep-sea islands in the region (such as Sulawesi), although modern taxonomic standards have considera-bly increased the number of Greater Sundaic island endemics.

The Greater Sundas are roughly divided into two bio-geographic sub-regions: (1) **Sundaic rainforest**: characterised by rich, lush tropical forest and found on Sumatra, Borneo and westernmost Java. This region is extremely similar with and biogeographically

Figure 1.

Bathymetric and topographic map comprising most of our region (minus easternmost parts, such as Kai). Green shades denote various elevations of currently exposed land. Blue shades denote various depths of current sea and ocean. Yellow and ochre shades denote areas currently submerged by shallow sea (=shelf) but exposed as land at various periods during Quaternary glaciations in the last ~2 million years. At glacial maxima, such as during the 'Last Glacial Maximum' (LGM) at 18,000–21,000 years ago, the ex-tent of land was greatest, leading to the formation of the Sundaic subcontinent that has repeatedly been connecting Borneo, Java, Sumatra, Bali and the South-east Asian mainland. Note also the smaller but equally important land connections between various Wallacean islands (such as Sumbawa and Flores, or Sula Islands and Banggai Islands) (modified from Sathiamurthy & Voris 2006).

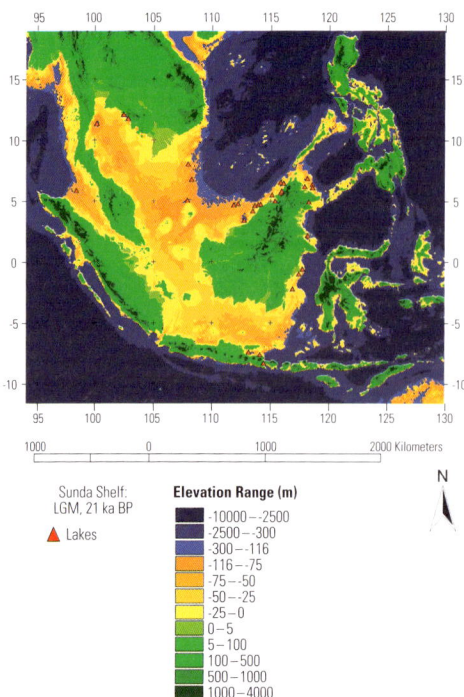

connected to the adjacent Sundaic forests of the Malay Peninsula and the Philippine island of Palawan. (2) **Monsoonal forest and savannah**: generally much drier and found on Bali, most of Java, and small pockets of southern Borneo. This latter sub-region is characterised by an avifauna better adapted to seasonal rainfall and more arid environments, and shares a surprising proportion of species with similar monsoonal forest and savannah regions in Cambodia, Vietnam and central and northern Thailand. These faunal similarities between distant regions are a testament to periodically recurring **monsoonal and savannah corridors** that have connected the biomes of Java with those of central Thailand and Cambodia at various times during the glacial formation of the Sundaic subcontinent. The exact extent and Quaternary timing of these savannah corridors is still largely unknown. Mountains in both the 'Sundaic rainforest' and the 'monsoonal' sub-regions of the Greater Sundas are invariably shrouded in exuberant montane forests, which often have a sizeable endemic element.

While the shared affinity of animals and plants on islands such as Sumatra and Borneo has been recognized since the earliest historic explorations, their commonalities have – at times – been exaggerated at the expense of cryptic biological diversity. For example, minor plumage differences between Sumatran, Bornean and sometimes Javan populations of rainforest understorey birds, such as babblers and bulbuls, have in the past typically been accommodated at the subspecies level. However, modern bioacoustic and DNA data frequently indicate deeper divisions than previously anticipated. Keeping in mind that these rainforest species have had opportunities for gene flow between Sumatra, Borneo and Java as recently as "yesterday" (evolutionarily speaking, i.e. ~10,000–18,000 years ago), some of the deep DNA and vocal differences could not have been maintained if these populations really chose to interbreed with one another. In many cases, as we now must infer, there was no gene flow between island populations despite land connections between them, indicating that distinct island populations have passed the species threshold. Thanks to this important realization, we are currently witnessing a renaissance in the avian taxonomy of the Greater Sundas: just as scientists are dividing up populations of South American antbirds (Thamnophilidae) into many dozens of additional species along the lines of Amazonian tributaries, Asian ornithology is getting ready to separate out its babblers, bulbuls and many other Greater Sundaic rainforest birds along the lines of Quaternary islands.

One region in the Greater Sundas stands out like a faunal oddball for reasons that nobody has been able to expound so far. The avifauna of the Malaysian state of **Sabah** on the island of Borneo is surprisingly distinct and consists of a large number of endemics not shared with neighbouring Bornean areas of Kalimantan, Brunei and Sarawak. The geographic boundary of this distinct Sabah region, while incompletely charted, is uncannily congruent with the political boundary of Sabah, as if humans had modelled political boundaries after biological zones of endemism. Why Sabah should have such a unique fauna is one of the biggest remaining biogeographic puzzles of modern times: its lowlands are perfectly contiguous with adjacent Sarawak and Kalimantan, with no known barrier. Some suggest that Sabah's endemic birds are the old Bornean endemic stock, while Kalimantan and Sarawak are overrun by immigrant populations from Sumatra and the Malay Peninsula every time there is a land connection. However, the latter explanation is incompatible with a pattern in which dozens of bird complexes from different families share roughly the same contact zone between a form from Sabah and a form from the remainder of Borneo.

Whenever the sea drops and exposes land between Sumatra and Borneo, birds would be able to colonise this new land from both sides. However, the modern distribution of species and subspecies on some of the existing satellite islands between Borneo and Sumatra indicates that this colonisation may not have been symmetrical. The island of Bangka, while only 12 km off the coast of Sumatra, is inhabited by a surprising number of Bornean (not Sumatran) species and subspecies, while the opposite is true for the Riau archipelago despite its comparable geographic position.

While largely continental in nature, the Greater Sundaic region does include a number of **satellite islands surrounded by deep sea** that do not form part of the Sundaic subcontinent. One is **Maratua**, off the coast of East Kalimantan (Borneo), which harbours a couple of birds at or close to the species boundary that were previously recognised as mere subspecies. The other group of deep-sea satellite islands comprises what is commonly known as the 'West Sumatran Islands', for which we are here resurrecting the historic name "**Barusan Islands**". These islands extend from Simeulue in the north, through Nias and the Mentawai group, to Enggano in the south.

The Barusan Islands have a comparatively sizeable endemic element (although this was insufficiently recognised in former taxonomic treatments). Most of the Barusan endemics are restricted to particular islands or island groups, but the existence of a few pan-Barusan endemic forms (shared across the group) suggests that a number of species may have adapted to a dispersive small-island lifestyle, shunning the Sumatran mainland for a variety of possible reasons. Importantly, not all Barusan Islands are equally isolated, and – again – bathymetry and knowledge of sea depths are important tools at gauging their significance for bird endemism. For instance, Simeulue and – in particular – Enggano are the most isolated larger land masses in the Greater Sundaic region, while Siberut is equally isolated from Sumatra but regularly forms a larger paleo-island with neighbouring Pagi and Sipora Islands and shares most of its birds with the latter two. Even some of the smallest Barusan Islands can show a bird-endemic element so long as they are surrounded by deep sea and have not been connected to other islands during glaciations: such is the remarkable case of Babi and Lasia Islands (close to Simeulue), which harbour a highly distinct taxon of *Hypothymis* monarch although they are no greater than 7 km in diameter. Historic collectors such as Harry Oberholser also emphasized the significance for subspecific endemism of some of the other small Barusan Islands, such as the Batu or the Banyak Island groups, although some of the described subspecies from these islands may not withstand modern scrutiny considering that both the Batu and Banyak groups are continental in nature and connected with Sumatra by a shallow shelf. The biggest member of the Barusan Islands, Nias, is also the one with the most intense history of human settlement and the highest degree of habitat degradation. It is characterised by a surprisingly low degree of endemism at or near the species level – at least at current taxonomic knowledge. The reason for this impoverished endemism on Nias is unclear because its topography with hills rising to 800 m would provide some of the richest opportunities for endemism among the Barusan Islands. However, although not reflected in most bathymetric maps, fine-scale data on sea depths do show that a narrow ridge of land may extend from Sumatra across the Banyak Islands to Nias at glacial maxima, with only a small ~3 km portion disconnected by sea. This would suggest that Nias is the least isolated of the larger Barusan land masses.

The Sulawesi Region

On the eastern side of Wallace's Line, in the heart of Wallacea, lies what is arguably the most complex island in the world: Sulawesi. Although only ~110 km from Borneo, it couldn't be a more different place in biological terms. Much of Sulawesi is mountainous, with the highest peak being Gunung Rantemario at 3,440 m. Not surprisingly – given its odd shape – Sulawesi is an amalgamation of land masses that converged to form one island only ~10–5 million years ago. Its south-western peninsula is of Greater Sundaic geologic origin (although it has never been connected to the Greater Sundas through Pleistocene land bridges), while its south-eastern, eastern and northern peninsulas are of Australo-Papuan and Pacific origin. Sulawesi continues to accrete additional land from the east: the Banggai Islands (now only 12 km away) will doubtless make Sulawesi's shape even odder once they dock onto it in the not-too-distant geologic future, and the Sula Islands and Northern Moluccas may follow at some point.

Given that Sulawesi's different peninsulas have been merged for millions of years now, its immense species-level endemism – consisting of far more than 100 endemics by any taxonomic standard – is largely shared across the whole island. Nevertheless, there is an important element of endemism particular to each peninsula, and this element is becoming larger and more thoroughly recognised with increasing study of bioacoustics and DNA. Some of the most iconic Sulawesi endemics (whether it be kingfishers or terrestrial songbirds) may well be divided up into 3–4 species, if they haven't been already, once researchers have completed their painstaking molecular, bioacoustic and morphological work.

Sulawesi is the largest Wallacean land mass. As such, it harbours some of the most ancient endemics of Wallacea. The great majority of Wallacean endemics are relatively young and derived from either Asian or Australo-Papuan stock. But Sulawesi is home to a number of unique Wallacean species and/or radiations with uncertain or obscure affinities to either side, and even though their closest relatives are increasingly being revealed through DNA, it is becoming clear that the last common ancestor connecting them to other birds lived many million years ago. Some of these ancient Sulawesi forms include *Hylocitrea*, *Malia*, and *Heinrichia* amongst others.

The Sulawesi Region includes a number of satellite islands of varying character. Some of them are part of the modern Sulawesi Shelf and are frequently connected with the Sulawesi mainland – except during brief interglacial maxima such as now. These land masses include the sizeable islands of Buton and Muna at the south-eastern tip of Sulawesi, and are of lesser biogeographic interest because of their lack of endemism. Another group of satellites, the Togian Islands, are sandwiched between the northern and eastern Sulawesi peninsulas. They have a surprising element of endemic bird species given their biogeographic connection to the eastern peninsula through a narrow but distinct Quaternary land bridge. Yet other satellites are surrounded by deep sea and essentially form sub-regions of endemism of their own. Among the deep-sea satellites is a northern group (Talaud, Sangihe, Siau), an eastern group (Banggai, Sula), a south-eastern group (Wakatobi, Tukangbesi), and a southern group (Tanahjampea, Kalao, Kalaotoa, Salayar).

The northern group of Sulawesi satellites is one of the historically best-explored groups of small islands in Wallacea. The most remote, low-lying Talaud Islands, are biogeographically part of the Philippines, although they are politically part of Indonesia and we include them in the region covered by this book. Apart from a number of proper island endemics, the Talaud Islands add several Philippine birds to our region's tally. The volcanic and – by now – heavily degraded island of Sangihe, on the other hand, has a distinct Sulawesi character coupled with the presence of a number of island endemics, some of them at lower and some at higher elevations. Even the tiny unconnected island of Siau, with its destructive volcano, has a small number of endemic bird taxa.

The eastern group of deep-sea satellites comprises the Banggai Islands (with Peleng its largest member) and the Sula Islands (with Taliabu its largest representative). These islands are a stepping stone connector to the more easterly Moluccas and already comprise some Moluccan elements. As mentioned above, the Banggai and Sula groups are on a direct geologic trajectory to docking onto the eastern Sulawesi peninsula. Peleng is a mere 12 km away from Sulawesi now, but the sea in between is deep and land has never connected the two. On the other hand, the sea between the Banggai and Sula groups, although ~80 km wide, is sufficiently shallow to allow for land connections during glacial maxima. This explains the sizeable element of endemism that is shared between Banggai and Sula, especially among lowland-inhabiting species. The island-specific endemics on these groups are often montane. Thorough ornithological exploration on these islands has been recent, and they have produced one of the highest global totals of new bird species descriptions in modern times.

The south-eastern group of Sulawesi's deep-sea satellites comprises the Wakatobi Islands, historically better known as Tukangbesi. As with the Sula and Banggai Islands, the Tukangbesi group has only recently been explored in greater detail, with one species discovery awaiting write-up. The Tukangbesi Islands consist of four main islands which are strung out like a chain of pearls. While they are isolated from Sulawesi as a whole, each of the main Tukangbesi Islands is also isolated from one another by deep sea.

The southern group of Sulawesi satellites includes some of the best-explored small island groups in Wallacea, with a long history of visitation by historic collectors and very little modern work in contrast. The state of the habitat is so degraded in modern times that a number of endemic bird taxa described historically have already vanished. Each of the four main islands in this group (Kalao, Kalaotoa, Salayar, Tanahjampea) is surrounded by deep sea and unconnected to any of the other islands. Even so, these land masses share a sizeable element of dispersive small-island specialists (oftentimes with Lesser Sundaic, not Sulawesi, affinities), probably because each of them has been too unstable to foster a sizeable endemic element of its own.

The Lesser Sunda Islands

The Lesser Sunda Islands are now often known under their Indonesian name Nusa Tenggara ('South-eastern Islands'). Their English name is somewhat misleading in that they do not actually form part of the Sundaic subcontinent (or 'Sundaland'), being separated from it by the narrow 21 km deep-sea strait between the islands of Bali and Lombok which forms Wallace's Line. From Lombok onwards, the Lesser Sundas form an eastward linear chain of islands over 1,000 km across Sumbawa, Flores, Pantar, Alor, Wetar to Romang and Damar, which is joined by a parallel, more southerly near-linear chain of islands from Sumba through Sawu, Rote, Timor, Moa to Babar. Our biogeographic definition of the Lesser Sunda Islands differs from Indonesia's political delimitation of Nusa Tenggara, with many of the eastern Lesser Sundas politically included in Indonesia's Moluccan provinces. While all Lesser Sundas are dry, seasonal and monsoonal, there is a southward gradient to increased aridity from Lombok to the more arid Rote and from Babar to the more arid Timor, respectively. The Lesser Sundas are typically of volcanic origin or formed from uplifted coral, or a combination of both. Those of volcanic origin typically include high mountains, with the highest peak within the region being Mt Rinjani on Lombok at 3,726 m.

Endemism is high among the birds of the Lesser Sundas. Many of the lowland families present show affinities to Australia while there is also a large degree of evolutionarily recent invasions of Greater Sundaic birds, especially in the montane avifauna. Peculiarly, many of the Greater Sundaic invaders show a present-day distribution that skips several intervening islands. For instance, a few Greater Sundaic bird groups have outliers in Timor and/or Flores while there are no modern records on Sumbawa or Lombok. Rather than far-distance dispersal, this odd distributional pattern suggests a history of widespread pre-historic extinction, especially in species restricted to montane forests that can easily be wiped out on individual islands by single volcanic eruptions.

Again, present-day land connections are not as good a predictor for patterns of Lesser Sundaic endemism as land bridges of the past. The western members of the Lesser Sundas, from Lombok through Sumbawa, Flores and Adonara to Lembata (formerly Lomblen), are all connected through shallow shelf areas that form land bridges during glaciations. This explains their pronounced shared element, with only very few single-island endemics mostly restricted to Flores or Lombok. At the eastern extension of this large paleo-island, Lembata is only ~11 km from the twin island of Pantar–Alor, yet a deep sea trench between Lembata and Pantar accounts for a mixed avifaunal element on Pantar and Alor; the latter two islands are inhabited by some species from the western Lesser Sundas, others from Timor, and yet others endemic. The easterly extension of this chain is then characterised exclusively by deep-sea islands (Atauro, Wetar, Romang and Damar) with levels of endemism high (on large Wetar) or moderate (on the remaining smaller islands).

The southerly chain in the Lesser Sundas (from Sumba through Timor to Babar) exhibits much less extensive Pleistocene connectivity. Virtually all the larger members of this chain are surrounded by deep sea, accounting for a pronounced endemic element on all of them, proportional to island size. Timor is by far the largest Lesser Sundaic island, but also the driest; this latter aspect may have limited its evolutionary potential somewhat, but even so it has evolved the greatest number of single-island endemics across the Lesser Sundas, followed by the smaller (but still sizeable) Sumba. But even the smaller deep-sea islands in the southern chain, such as Sawu, Rote, Babar, Kisar and Moa, have a certain endemic element, sometimes subspecific and sometimes at the species level, depending on island size and distance to other islands.

The Moluccas

Now often known by their Indonesian name, Maluku, the Moluccan Islands have enjoyed the interest of historic explorers for a long time. The Moluccan Islands are sandwiched between the Sulawesi Region and the New Guinea Shelf and comprise over 1,000 islands of both volcanic and non-volcanic origin. Overall species diversity is relatively low, as is typical for deep-sea islands, but endemism is extremely high. Our biogeographic delimitation of the Moluccas is incongruent with political divisions in Indonesia: we here divide them into a northern, central and southern group.

The Northern Moluccas are one of the most fascinating island groups in Indonesia. They are one of the modern land masses with the most turbulent geologic and Earth historic background, and recent research shows that they have moved into the Wallacean Region at a relatively fast pace within the last 2–5 million years, having come from north of the Papuan Vogelkop Peninsula. This geologic background may explain that the Northern Moluccas are the only island group in the region covered by this book that is inhabited by birds-of-paradise. The Northern Moluccas are divided into two parts: (1) Obi, and (2) Halmahera and satellites.

Obi is a mid-sized oval island, only ~86 km in length but rising to above ~1,500 m. Historically somewhat neglected, detailed exploration of its highlands has only recently been completed, with new subspecies and perhaps species descriptions awaiting publication. Continuing scrutiny of bioacoustic and DNA data seems to indicate that Obi populations of many shared endemics with Halmahera are in fact quite distinct in their own right.

Dominating the Northern Moluccas is Halmahera, the largest Moluccan island, although relatively low-lying and devoid of a pronounced montane species element commensurate with its size. Halmahera has a good number of island endemics, although an equally good number of endemics is shared with its satellites. Foremost amongst Halmahera's satellites is Bacan, which is connected with Halmahera by shallow shelf and Quaternary land bridges, but which also hosts the highest Northern Moluccan mountain, Mt Sibela (2,120 m), providing it with a pronounced endemic element. The second most important Halmahera satellite, Morotai, is less high (~1,300 m) but a bit more isolated, with the ~15 km strait that separates it from Halmahera narrowing to a handful of kms during glacial times. This narrow severance has been sufficient to reward Morotai with endemism of its own.

No less important than the Northern Moluccas is the collection of islands we here define as the Central Moluccas. They consist of two disconnected giants, Buru and Seram, the latter replete with its impressive collection of satellites. Both Buru and Seram have an amazing array of montane endemics as they rise to almost 2,500 m (Buru) or slightly above 3,000 m (Seram). Their classification as Central Moluccas is one of geographic convenience as they share a very small common endemic element. Seram's satellites are all connected to the main island by Quaternary land bridges, but some of them are narrow; this is what may have led to some low degree of endemism on two satellites, namely Boano and Ambon (the latter now known as the main transport hub and former seat of the capital of the Moluccas).

A pearly string of tiny deep-sea islands extends between the Central Moluccas and the Kai Islands. The latter consist of the low-lying twins Greater Kai and Little Kai (Kai Besar and Kai Kecil). They are dry, but given their isolation they do show a pronounced endemic element of mixed character, partly Moluccan, partly Lesser Sundaic and partly Australo-Papuan. Further south, the Tanimbar Islands are a bit greater in size, equally low-lying, and at the terminus of the two Lesser Sundaic island chains. They are home to a surprising number of endemics plus a near-endemic element shared with the easternmost Lesser Sundas. In this book, we define the Kai and Tanimbar Islands as the Southern Moluccas although the Tanimbars' inclusion as part of the Lesser Sundas by other biological treatises makes just as much sense.

The tiny Banda Islands are geographically set in between the Lesser Sundas and the Moluccas, but much closer to the latter. Despite their minute size, they have attracted ample historic attention from spice traders, and their great isolation has bestowed them with a moderate endemic element.

TOPOGRAPHY, CLIMATE, AND HABITATS
(by James A. Eaton)

Climate

The Indonesian archipelago straddles the Equator and therefore has a predominantly tropical climate. Temperatures are generally stable, with variations across the day exceeding those across the year. Daytime temperatures in the coastal plains average around 28°C year-round, with a steady decrease as the land rises. Night time temperatures in the high mountains can drop close to 0°C. Humidity is generally stable at around 70–90%. Daylight hours also change little across the year, with the shortest day only around 45 minutes shorter than the longest.

Prevailing wind patterns interact with local topography to produce significant variations in rainfall throughout the archipelago. In general, western and northern parts of the archipelago (the Greater Sundas) experience the most precipitation, with annual rainfall often

in excess of 2 m. The heaviest rainfall is in the 'wet season', between October and February, and is associated with monsoon winds
blowing north and east from the Indian Ocean. Further south and
east, particularly in East Java and the Lesser Sundas, annual rainfall
is lower at around 1 m per year, and more seasonal with a distinct
dry season between April and September, caused by prevailing
wind flows from continental Australia. Within the Moluccas rainfall
patterns are more complex depending on local wind patterns, but
in general the northern and central Moluccas receive more rainfall
during the northern summer months, while in the south rainfall is
heavier in the northern winter, similar to the Lesser Sundas.

Habitats

For such a huge region, there are actually relatively few stable and
well defined habitat types. Most are variations of forest habitat,
reflecting the fact that until recent times almost the entire archipelago was essentially blanketed in tropical forest, with differences in the plant communities largely generated by altitude and
rainfall. Although modern humans (*Homo sapiens*) have been in
the region for more than ~50,000 years, and other hominid groups
have co-existed with them until only ~12,000 years ago, sweeping
changes in the distribution of terrestrial habitat have only come
about in modern times (the last ~150 years). During this period,
intensified agriculture and urbanisation have led to the creation of
new man-made habitat types which often lack a well-developed or
specialised bird fauna. Some of the main habitat types include:

- **Lowland tropical rainforest (from sea-level to around
  800 m)**: lowland tropical rainforest is one of the richest ecosys-
  tems on Earth, supporting the greatest diversity of plants, birds,
  mammals and insects, including many specialists and regional
  endemics. Lowland rainforests in the region are dominated by
  one tree family (Dipterocarpaceae), and are therefore often
  characterised as 'dipterocarp rainforests'. Sadly, pristine lowland rainforest is now one of the most threatened habitats in the
  region, and few genuinely intact examples remain.
- **Lowland peat swamp forest**: this important sub-type of
  lowland rainforest is found mainly in coastal areas of southern
  Kalimantan, Sarawak, Brunei and eastern Sumatra, where dipterocarp forest grows on a deep layer of swampy peat. This type
  of forest is usually less diverse than lowland forest on mineral
  soils, but supports a number of important specialised species.
- **Sub-montane and montane forest (>800 m)**: as altitude rises,
  temperature, tree height and plant diversity tend to drop, but
  precipitation levels increase, laying the foundation for a pronounced change in plant community. At higher elevations (above
  1,000 m on smaller islands and many isolated hill tops near the
  coast, but >2,000 m on larger mountains), trees start to become
  stunted and the amount of lichens, mosses and other epiphytes
  increases. The birds of montane forest are typically specialised
  and display some of the highest levels of endemism because of
  the isolated nature of mountain ranges. On a number of islands,
  highly specialised montane forest types occur, such as tropical
  montane pine forests in north Sumatra, rhododendron forests
  on Lombok and eucalypt forests on Timor. At the very highest
  altitudes, above 2,000–3,000 m (depending on island size and
  position), alpine-like scrubland and meadows replace trees.
- **Deciduous (monsoonal) forest**: this forest type is typically
  found in the south and east of the region – East Java east to
  Tanimbar – where rainfall is lower and more seasonal. During
  the dry season, some trees will shed their leaves. Birds in these
  forests are thought to display a more stringent seasonal breeding phenology and some even migrate away to avoid the peak of
  the dry season.

- **Heath forest (*kerangas*)**: mainly found on Borneo, in areas
  with acidic sandy soils (often near peat swamp areas), heath
  forests are often stunted, with a thick underbrush supporting
  many mosses. Bird diversity is typically poor, but some specialist
  species can be found.
- **Grasslands**: across the region, grassland is often the result of
  forest clearance. However, in parts of Sulawesi, eastern Java
  and western Bali, there are several areas of natural savannah,
  such as in Baluran, Alas Purwo and Bali Barat National Parks,
  that support a specialist dry grassland avifauna. Extensive alpine
  areas can also support natural grasslands, although these are
  mostly of limited extent in our region (e.g. Mt Leuser in northern
  Sumatra). Elsewhere, clearings and man-made grasslands
  support relatively few species.
- **Mangroves**: most of the region's shallow and muddy estuaries
  would naturally have supported mangrove forests. However,
  many now have been degraded and lost – being cut for firewood
  and converted to fish ponds – with few large areas now remaining. Where mangrove still remains it typically supports a number
  of specialist birds.
- **Freshwater swamps, rivers and lakes**: across the region there
  are many areas of wetlands, ranging from the small to the
  huge; from the near pristine to the highly disturbed. As would
  be expected, wetland habitats often support an abundance of
  specialised birdlife.
- **Farmland and plantations**: wherever people are found, so is
  agriculture. This can range from small-scale subsistence farms
  through century-old rice paddies to vast, modern commercial
  plantations of oil palm and rubber. Few of these man-made
  habitats have any kind of specialised bird fauna associated with
  them; rather they may be home to a number of habitat general-
  ists able to adapt to rapid change.
- **Seas**: around 80% of the archipelago consists of open sea,
  dotted with small isolated islets. These areas are home to both
  resident and migratory seabirds passing between the Indian
  and Pacific Oceans. The seas within the region remain un-
  der-watched and there is no doubt much still to be learnt about
  seabird migration throughout the archipelago.

Highest mountains on the region's larger islands

Island	Highest mountain	Elevation (metres)
Borneo	Kinabalu	4,095 m
Sumatra	Kerinci	3,800 m
Java	Semeru	3,676 m
Bali	Agung	3,142 m
Sulawesi	Rantemario	3,440 m
Lombok	Rinjani	3,726 m
Sumbawa	Tambora	2,851 m
Flores	Mandasawu	2,350 m
Sumba	Wanggameti	1,225 m
Timor (East Timor)	Tatamailau	2,986 m
Seram	Binaya	3,027 m
Buru	Kapalatmada	2,700 m
Halmahera	Gamkonora	1,560 m
Bacan	Sibela	2,111 m
Obi	Unnamed peak	1,611 m
Kai Besar	Daab	736 m
Tanimbar	Labobar	340 m

CONSERVATION
(by Nick W. Brickle)

The Indonesian archipelago is spectacularly diverse in terms of wildlife. In addition to birds, it is home to over 500 mammal species, 1,000 species of amphibians, 2,000 species of 'reptiles', 8,000 species of fish, 25,000 species of flowering plants and a mind-boggling 250,000 species of insect (almost a third of all the world's insect species). The region also tops the global charts for endemism – for the number of species found here and nowhere else.

Politically the region is dominated by the nation of Indonesia, home to over 250 million people: the world's fourth highest human population. This population is spread across around 6,000 inhabited islands, ranging in size from Sumatra, Borneo and Java, to the smallest atolls (and meaning that 11,000 of the region's islands have no permanent human presence at all).

With so much wildlife, and so many people sharing the same islands, conflicts for resources are inevitable: rapid development and population growth are competing for the same space. Despite the pressure, the battle is far from lost, and there are many reasons to remain optimistic. To date only few bird species are thought to have become extinct from the region – Javan Lapwing *Vanellus macropterus* many decades ago, and several others only recently, including Maratua Shama *Copsychus barbouri*, Sangihe White-eye *Zosterops nehrkorni* and Javan Pied Starling *Gracupica jalla*. However, many more are considered endangered, including many species threatened by virtue of being found only on one or two small islands, and several species haven't been seen for many years: Siau Scops Owl *Otus siaoensis*, was collected over 150 years ago with no further sightings! However, there is always hope: after over 170 years, the Black-browed Babbler *Malacocincla perspicillata* was sensationally rediscovered in South Kalimantan in 2020.

Habitat Loss

The vast majority of the region's wildlife relies on natural tropical forest, and it is the threat to this forest that most commonly puts the region in the headlines. As recently as 1950 forests covered over 80% of the land area within the region. By 2013 it had fallen to around 50%. While the area lost is staggering, the area remaining is also staggering. With almost 100 million hectares of forest thought to remain, Indonesia alone is still thought to have the third most tropical forest of any country (FWI/GFW 2002; UNORCID 2015).

The main cause of deforestation has been commercial exploitation. Repeated cycles of logging and, more recently, massive-scale conversion to monoculture plantations, including in particular oil palm and acacia, are to blame. This rise in commercial exploitation has been matched by small-scale deforestation caused by a bourgeoning rural population, increased access and the growing demand for farmland. Lowland forests have been the most affected, and in some areas have almost been lost totally outside of protected areas.

Despite all this loss, not all forests are threatened. Within the region around 1/3 of the remaining forests (30 million ha, an area equivalent in size to Germany or Texas) are included within a vast network of national parks and nature reserves spread across many islands. However, the management of these parks is in the hands of authorities that only number a few thousand staff, which stretches resources to the limit.

Hunting and Wildlife Trade

Habitat loss is not the only threat to the wildlife of the region. Hunting and wildlife trade are also a massive problem, operating as a vast, international, multibillion-dollar commercial enterprise, with terrestrial and marine animals and plants being traded for food, medicines, skins, souvenirs and pets. Species trapped and traded, often in massive volumes, include tiger, rhino, elephant, orangutan, bears, pangolins, bats, rodents, almost any species of bird, snakes, turtles, marine and freshwater fish, sharks, coral, orchids, fragrant timber and many, many more. Indonesia alone is considered to be the largest exporter of wildlife, both legal and illegal, within Southeast Asia. Of the more than 170 species of birds and mammals listed by IUCN (2020) as endangered in Indonesia, overexploitation is identified as the principal threat in over one third. In the case of the reptiles listed in the same category, overexploitation is identified as the principal threat for all species. Amongst the birds, the domestic (rather than international) trade is the main threat to most species, particularly songbirds, with many formerly common species declining rapidly within otherwise stable habitat, including national parks. Once trapped, such species are traded legally within Indonesia, and demand remains high. Species most affected by this domestic trade include White-rumped Shama *Copsychus malabaricus*, Oriental Magpie-robin *C. saularis*, Straw-headed Bulbul *Pycnonotus zeylanicus*, Javan White-eye *Zosterops flavus* and several thrush, starling and parrot species. In many accessible areas, these species have effectively already become extinct. At the same time, the international trade on ivory has led some species, such as the Critically Endangered Helmeted Hornbill *Rhinoplax vigil*, to be locally extinct in much of its former range in the space of just five years.

While Indonesia and other countries in the region have systems of laws to control wildlife hunting and trade, enforcement is typically weak and under-resourced. Public and political will to address the issues is often lacking, and both the capacity and motivation of responsible authorities is often low.

Future hope

The future is not all bleak. While many threats remain, there are signs that others may finally be receding. An old generation of politicians, some of whom knew nothing other than short-term exploitation, are slowly being replaced by a younger generation that have been educated in concepts of conservation and sustainable use. This is already having its effect within government, with recent drives to reduce the damaging effects of corruption and more carefully plan and limit commercial and small-holder expansion into natural forest areas. Industry also appears to be responding to commercial pressure to curtail their most damaging practices. The role that forest protection and restoration plays in mitigating global climate change is also being recognised more fully, and initiatives are underway to see forest resources properly valued in this light. Public attitudes to wildlife are also slowly changing, and with it, it is hoped, a reduction in the demand for traded wildlife will follow.

For bird conservation in particular, the region is experiencing something of a boom in younger generations taking up birdwatching, bird photography and issues of bird conservation – ably assisted by a profound love of social media!

What can you do?

The easiest way to support conservation within the region is simply to visit: try and come as often as possible, stay as long as possible, and in doing so spend as much money as possible. Visiting areas in order to see and photograph birds living in the wild creates a value for that resource that is not lost on local people or local governments. While visiting areas try to talk to people and explain why you are visiting. Make sure people understand you want to see live birds in the wild rather than catch or buy them. Try and use local guides, stay in local hotels, eat in local restaurants. After your visit write to local people and local authorities and thank them. Publicise your visit so others will follow.

You can also help by thinking carefully about the products you purchase that have originated in the region, particularly those agricultural commodities that are behind some of the most rampant deforestation. This all helps to incentivize the companies involved to improve their ways, and appears to be yielding results. If you are lucky enough to have money to invest, likewise think carefully about where it goes and put pressure on the financial backers of exploitative industry to divest. Pick your politicians carefully on the basis of the commitments they will make to support the countries of the region in addressing deforestation and wildlife trade.

Finally consider supporting organizations that are actively trying to promote conservation in the region, especially local ones. The future of conservation in the Indonesian archipelago ultimately lies in the hands of the 250 million people that live there, and any support you can offer them will go a long way.

ORNITHOLOGICAL HISTORY
(by Bas van Balen)

The history of ornithological exploration and study within the Indonesian archipelago spans the centuries. In this section we give a brief overview of work across the ages, presented in chronological order.

Pre-Modern Era

The first written record of an Indonesian bird is that of a talking Common Hill Myna *Gracula religiosa*, described by a Chinese historian of the Tang Dynasty (7–10th Century AD). However, a far older oral history of ornithological knowledge must have been present amongst the first human inhabitants, including the Austronesian tribes who came later from Taiwan via the Philippines around 4,000 years ago. They are the ancestors of the majority of modern Indonesians and their use of blowpipes, traps and snares would have enabled them to hunt many species of bird. Some of these ancient trap and snare designs remain in remarkably universal use throughout the archipelago today. Other devices that attest to a thorough knowledge of avian vocalizations are the bamboo whistles designed to lure birds into shooting distance.

Birds have also entered cultural folklore in other ways. The Dayak people, natives of Borneo, consider the Brahminy Kite *Haliastur indus* as the major omen bird, with trogons, Rufous Piculet *Sasia abnormis* and spiderhunters amongst the lesser omen birds. Details of their behaviour and in particular vocalizations determine the progress of hunting parties. The first arrivals in autumn of northern migrants such as Eastern Yellow Wagtails *Motacilla tschutschensis* have been the signs to plant rice.

Artistic expressions of the role birds have played in human life are found throughout the archipelago. In the 9th century temples of Prambanan and Borobudur on Java, cockatoos, peafowl, owls and various songbirds can be identified in the stone sculptures. A crested eagle was the model of the mythical Garuda, which has now become Indonesia's national symbol, and in the ikat cloths of Sumba, cockatoos are a popular motif.

With around 457 living languages spoken in the region, ornithological interest is also reflected in a huge variety of local bird names. Lists of 50–70 or more names for as many different bird species can be found in a single local dialect, and on Borneo champions mastering up to 300 different names have been known. Many names are euphonious onomatopoeias (i.e. words imitating the sound of the object), e.g., the Sundanese *cangkurawok* or *cangkurileung* for two species of bulbul. Others describe particular habits or plumage characters. Thomas Horsfield provided some of his newly described species with locally derived scientific names: *enca*, *meninting*,

Prinia, and *manyar* are examples of the Javan language that became scientific names of a crow, kingfisher, a genus of prinias and a weaver. In the old days, including local bird names in ornithological publications was common practice, and remains rewarding today, not only as a way to document rapidly disappearing languages, but also as a useful tool when discussing birds with local people, where a local name may elicit more reaction than a picture in a book. In these modern times, with the replacement of many local languages by Bahasa Indonesia, species of commercial value have a common Indonesian name throughout the region, such as Common Hill Myna (*beo*), White-rumped Shama (*murai batu)*, Oriental Magpie-robin (*murai*) and Chestnut-capped Thrush *Geokichla interpres* (*anis kembang*).

1602–1799 Verenigde Oostindische Compagnie (VOC)

Few bird studies were undertaken in the 17th and 18th centuries. At this time the Dutch East India Company (VOC) ruled a large part of the archipelago and allowed little room for non-profitable work. Moreover, the use of maps was considered a crime, whilst venturing away from the few reinforced fortresses and trading posts was considered desertion and vagabondry punishable by penal servitude in chains. Nevertheless, in 1781 Baron Friedrich von Wurmb, secretary of the 'Bataviaasch Genootschap van Kunsten en Wetenschappen' [Batavian Society of Arts and Sciences], produced the first detailed descriptions of Javan birds, such as Brahminy Kite and Grey-headed Fish-eagle *Icthyophaga ichthyaetus*. Other information from this period is sparse but includes books written by François Valentijn (allegedly using information from Rumphius's unpublished notes), and other French authors such as Comte de Buffon and L.J.P. Vieillot, who described the collections of their countrymen De Bougainville, Sonnerat and De Labillardière from the Moluccas, Sulawesi and Java.

1800–1820

The 19th century commenced with expeditions by the French naturalist Nicolas Baudin to Timor and Java, but ornithological research experienced a real boost with the arrival in 1800 of the American Thomas Horsfield. He stayed on Java until 1806 and compiled a list of more than 200 bird species. Today, 73 of the species and 10 of the genera he described are still recognised.

During a brief period of British rule within the region (1811–1824), Sir Stamford Raffles, lieutenant governor of Java and later Bengkulu, supported various collecting expeditions. This included the 1819 expedition of the French naturalist Pierre-Médard Diard to Sumatra, who, to the chagrin of his employer, sent his collections to Paris. Raffles's support also extended to the work of Professor C.G.C. Reinwardt, who arrived in 1816 on Java and spent five years collecting many specimens and artefacts, a large part of which was lost in a series of shipwrecks. Reinwardt produced an unpublished list of 407 bird species for Indonesia, including a number of undescribed taxa, while Raffles himself produced a list of 168 for Sumatra.

1820–1850

In 1820, the Natural History Commission of Batavia was established, instigated by the enthusiasm of the English naturalists in the previous era. The first two naturalists, Johan Coenraad van Hasselt and Heinrich Kuhl, under contract by the commission for 4–6 years, succumbed to exhaustion within a few years after their arrival on Java; they were replaced by H. Boie, H.C. Macklot and Salomon Müller. Boie made notes on birds around Bogor, and was particularly keen on bird vocalizations. His plans to write a book on the avifauna of Java never came to pass because of his death in 1827 and the loss of all his notes during a Chinese revolt in 1832, when Macklot was murdered. The Commission had proved to be disappointingly ineffective, aggravated by untimely deaths of four of its naturalists who succumbed to tropical disease, exhaustion and manslaughter, and was dissolved in 1850 after 30 years of existence. The only testimony of its members' hard work were the published letters sent from the Indies to Temminck and ~2,000 bird skins, of which only a part had been examined and described by the latter in the *Nouveau Receuil de Planches coloriés d'Oiseaux*. Ironically, Müller, who was initially appointed as assistant taxidermist, was the only commission member who survived to conduct expeditions and write up findings.

1850–1900

This was a period of extensive exploration, with the publication of several weighty travelogues in bulky multivolume books. One famous explorer was H.A. Bernstein, who started in 1855 as a medical doctor near Bogor, but his interest in biology led him to collect nests and eggs, about which he published several important papers. In 1859 he was appointed by the Natural History Museum of Leiden, Netherlands (now Naturalis National Biodiversity Centre), as a travelling naturalist and, in this role, collected birds in the Moluccas and Papua until his death in 1865.

Another famous explorer from this period was Alfred Russel Wallace. Although not primarily an ornithologist, he collected many birds new to science across the archipelago spanning from Sumatra to Papua in the years between 1854 and 1862. His name is still commemorated in 18 scientific bird names, a dozen of which occur in the region, and 20 common names, amongst which Wallace's Standardwing *Semioptera wallacii* of Halmahera is perhaps the best known. During his travels in the region he also independently conceived of the concept of evolution by natural selection, and defined the biogeographic concept of 'Wallace's Line'. His classic travel book *The Malay archipelago* has gone through many editions and reprints, and has been translated into eight languages. He is considered the father of modern biogeography.

Other notable explorers from this period in history include C.B.H. von Rosenberg, who travelled and collected in New Guinea, Sumatra, Sulawesi and the Moluccas and reported his findings in his 1878 travelogue *Der Malayische Archipel*, which included descriptions of 13 new bird species. Dr A.G. Vorderman was also active from 1880 to 1900 and published about birds he had collected during his travels to Java, Lombok, Sulawesi and the Moluccas. He also published works on the collections made by the Belgian A. Colffs on Sumatra and the Swede Carl Bock on Kalimantan. Meanwhile, Henry Forbes wrote *A Naturalist's Wanderings in the Eastern archipelago* (1885), followed in 1887 by a book in which the same wanderings were seen through the eyes of his wife Anna Forbes. W. Doherty and A.H. Everett, both working for Lord Rothschild at the British Museum of Natural History, mainly visited Sulawesi, East Java and the Lesser Sundas between 1887 and 1897. Their collections were described by Ernst Hartert in a number of papers in *Novitates Zoologicae*.

Tommaso Salvadori managed to publish *Uccelli di Borneo* in 1874, based on Beccari's and Doria's bird collections from north Borneo, and *Ornitologia della Papuasia e delle Molucche*, in 1880–1882, based on the collections by Beccari, d'Albertis, Bruijn and Doria. Pioneering work on Mt Kinabalu was undertaken in 1887 by John Whitehead, who laid the base for our knowledge of Bornean montane avifauna by adding 59 species to the island's list, all described in his beautiful folio-sized book *Exploration of Mount Kina Balu* (1893). Elsewhere on Borneo Dr A.W. van Nieuwenhuis undertook several journeys across the island, described in his book *Dwars door Borneo* (1900). His collection of more than 200 species was described by Johann Büttikofer, one of his travel mates, and Otto Finsch.

Further east in Sulawesi the Swiss brothers Paul and Fritz Sarasin travelled through much of the island in 1893–1896, and again

1902–1903. They accumulated an important bird collection with many new species, and published the account of their journey in *Reisen in Celebes* (1905). A publication by Meyer & Wiglesworth entitled *Birds of Celebes and Neighbouring Islands* (1898) was also largely based on the Swiss brothers' specimens.

Due to a lack of interest from sponsors, the attempt by Hermann Schlegel (Natural History Museum of Leiden) to publish a book of the birds of Indonesia failed after the first three richly illustrated family accounts (pittas, kingfishers, birds of prey), printed between 1863 and 1866.

1900–1942

In 1901 the Zoological Museum at Bogor was established; its first director, J.C. Koningsberger, published a first volume on birds of Java, followed by the second volume in 1909. Meanwhile the exploration of Indonesia's avifauna continued, but became more fine-tuned and targeted at particular islands or mountain groups. The wealthy William Louis Abbott was an American physician preferring the exploration of offshore islands to running a medical practice; from 1899–1907 he collected on numerous islands off west Sumatra, Borneo and north Java.

Max Bartels and his three sons Max, Ernst and Hans collected mainly in west Java in the first four decades of the 20th century; their names are commemorated in such taxonomic monikers as *bartelsorum*, *bartelsi*, *ernsti*, and *maxi*. They published numerous papers and left many unpublished field notes, together with a huge egg and skin collection deposited in Naturalis National Biodiversity Centre. Also publishing works on Javan birds was the little-known but meritorious German planter August Spennemann. He described the biology of many species observed on Java between 1915 and 1940, published in 46 papers in German and Dutch journals. Similarly, the Japanese Nagamichi Kuroda visited Java, Bali and Lombok twice in the 1920s, leading to his publication of the two-volume *Birds of the Island of Java*, with a number of beautiful colour plates and a state-of-the-art summary of the region's ornithology.

Herbert C. Robinson, director of the Federated Malay States Museum in Kuala Lumpur, collected together with C. Boden Kloss on Mt Kerinci in 1914. Robinson went to Java in 1916, Kloss in 1920, and they co-authored an important paper on their collection in *Treubia*, which would become one of the most important journals for ornithological contributions from Indonesia in the years to come.

Further east, one of the most spectacular discoveries made by Ernst Stresemann during the *Freiburger Molukken-Expedition* in 1910–1911 was the Bali Starling *Leucopsar rothschildi*, collected during an unintended three-month delay on Bali. This bird was amongst 350 skins belonging to 127 taxa. Further east again, Gerd Heinrich's quest for the Snoring Rail *Lewinia plateni* during his collecting journey on Sulawesi and Halmahera in 1930–1932 (described in his book *Der Vogel Schnarch*) produced 5,000 skins, with a fair number of new genera, species and subspecies. His findings were published by Stresemann in *Vögel von Celebes* with much attention to Heinrich's biological field notes, and including the description of the enigmatic "Heinrichia" *Heinrichia calligyna*, all three currently recognised races of which were discovered by Heinrich. Likewise, Bernard Rensch's expedition in 1927 to the Lesser Sundas resulted in a considerable increase of known bird species.

In 1915, the 620-page bird volume of *De Dierenwereld van de Insulinde* by Johan Hendrik van Balen was published and became – despite its shortcomings – the foremost handbook and guide for ornithologists visiting the archipelago for many years to come. Astonishingly, the author had worked on this book for 25 years without ever having been in the region.

In 1929, Andries Hoogerwerf arrived as a taxidermist and excellent photographer at the Bogor Museum, but would soon be one of the most productive ornithologists in the area. The results of his expeditions to Mount Leuser, Ujung Kulon (Java), Bawean, and his accounts on seabirds of Gunung Api, heronries in Java, and trips around Jakarta and Bogor were published in short notes and lengthy papers alike. Towards the end of the period, *Irena*, the ornithological Journal for the Dutch-Indies, was launched. Its first issue of 28 pages, with papers on the birds of the Tengger Mountains by J.G. Kooiman and on the breeding of Cinnamon Bittern *Ixobrychus cinnamomeus*, was also the very last because of the outbreak of war.

In 1932 Tom Harrisson joined the Oxford University Expedition to Sarawak and stayed active long after World War II, especially in the Kelabit highlands, contributing numerous bird papers.

1942–1950 Second World War and aftermath

Although ornithological activities in the region were at a low during this period, interesting contributions were provided by L. Coomans de Ruiter. Before 1942 he was active in West Kalimantan, then during the Japanese occupation (1942–1945) he compiled detailed bird observations from three different prisoner of war camps in South Sulawesi. Nine ornithologists who were active before 1942, however, did not survive to the end of the war, amongst them Max Bartels Jr and Spennemann.

Andries Hoogerwerf, who had secured most of the Bartels collection from total destruction during the Japanese occupation, published three illustrated books on the birds of the Bogor Botanical Gardens and Cibodas, and on the zoology of Java. He also published numerous other papers on new bird taxa in the Bogor Museum collection. Shortly after the war, Jean Delacour published the *Birds of Malaysia* (1947). This was the first comprehensive affordable bird book that included the Greater Sundas.

1950–1975

During the post-war period Javan birds received ample attention. Gerlof Mees collected data in west Java that led to his detailed review of the Indo-Australian Zosteropidae in 1957–1969.

Henri J.V. Sody continued his field studies and published papers on birds of Javan teak forest.

The Krakataus and other islands off Java were the subject of taxonomic and avifaunal surveys undertaken by Hoogerwerf, as organized by the Kebun Raya Bogor. The production of an illustrated book on the birds of Java was also initiated by Hoogerwerf, but it did not get beyond 1–2 printed proof pages and a typescript.

The Sarawak Museum (Kuching, Malaysia) was especially active during this period, organising collection trips to various destinations in north Borneo. In particular its curator T. Harrisson, multitalented anthropologist with a special interest in birds, produced much material for E. Smythies's *Birds of Borneo*, a monumental work that appeared in 1960 and was completely revised by G.W.H. Davison in 1999. Pfeffer made a large collection, described in several papers and in his book *Bivouac à Bornéo*.

Further east in Flores the missionaries Erwin Schmutz and Jilis A.J. Verheijen collected bird specimens and a host of zoological, distributional, and ethno-ornithological data, spanning the period 1946–1993.

In the 1960s the first Indonesian large-scale banding studies were carried out on Pulau Dua: 31,676 birds of 35 species were banded by Soekarja Somadikarta and his assistants.

1975–1990 New exploration

In 1975 the first comprehensively illustrated bird guide for South East Asia (King *et al.* 1975) became available. It did not extend to cover the Indonesian archipelago but was used enthusiastically

by birdwatchers nevertheless! This in turn helped contribute to a growing tide of birdwatching tourists arriving on the archipelago, producing desk-published trip reports, which have nowadays become readily available on the internet. Around this time surveys, in particular those undertaken by Food and Agricultural Organization teams in the framework of the National Conservation Plan for Indonesia in 1979–1982, resulted in reports with contemporary bird lists for hitherto unsurveyed areas, in turn generating more interest amongst visiting birdwatchers.

In 1975–76 *Kukila*, Journal of the Indonesian Bird Association, was launched and revived by Derek Holmes and Soekarja Somadikarta in 1985; the same year the first *Bulletin of the Oriental Bird Club* (later *BirdingASIA*), and in 1986, *Forktail*, the bird club's journal, were launched. British Ornithologists' Union checklists of Wallacea (White & Bruce 1986) and Sumatra (van Marle & Voous 1988) constituted the first major annotated compilations of the Indonesian avifaunal regions, with updates in *Kukila*.

Bird records from Brunei, which had remained largely unexplored hitherto, were collected by various field ornithologists, such as Derek Holmes and in particular Clive Mann, who compiled an annotated checklist of the sultanate's avifauna (Mann 1987). Later the ornithology of Sabah and of Borneo were described by Sheldon *et al.* (2001) and Mann (2008), respectively.

1990–present New Technologies

The widespread use of modern DNA sequencing techniques in the late 1980s and 1990s started to bring about a steady and unstoppable re-organisation of our understanding of avian taxonomy. Birds of the Indonesian archipelago were not necessarily the first candidates to benefit from increased taxonomic insight, but the continuing expansion of DNA sequencing, coupled with the application of novel Next-Generation Sequencing methods that allow to generate genome-wide sequence data, has by now revolutionised our insights into the taxonomy and evolution of many birds in the region.

Our knowledge of migratory pathways has increased in parallel to the number of birdwatchers reporting from the region, together with specific studies including leg-flagging waders and raptors equipped with satellite transmitters. Our knowledge of forest birds has increased as a result of numerous studies and environmental impact assessments associated with the increase in agricultural and mining expansion. These studies have produced valuable data on the distribution and status of forest birds in the region.

Photographic techniques have improved considerably, while entry-level equipment costs have fallen (mainly through the advent of 'digiscoping'). The result has been a profusion in the availability of high quality photographs of many of the region's birds. Camera trapping has also become more widely used, leading to an increased knowledge of some very shy ground living forest birds. Sound recordings of many of the region's birds have become widely and freely available, and the equipment to both record and play back bird calls has become cheaper and more robust. The combination of these factors has brought about a new chapter in our knowledge of the vocalizations of the region's birds. Field guides, in particular the Indonesian version of MacKinnon and Phillipps's (1993) *Field Guide to the Birds of Borneo, Sumatra, Java and Bali*, and Coates and Bishop's (1997) *The Birds of Wallacea*, have provided an enormous impetus to birdwatching in Indonesia. Along with the development of the internet and social media such as Facebook, bird clubs in Indonesia are booming now, and the contributions of young ornithologists are increasing in quantity and quality. Numerous websites store local avifaunistic information, photos, and local activities on Pontianak, Baluran NP, Semarang, Jakarta, Bandung, Yogyakarta etc., whereas the website of Burung Nusantara offers visiting and local ornithologists a wealth of up-to-date information on destinations, conservation action, bird news and links to before-mentioned local sites. The Atlas Burung Indonesia, published in 2020, is based on bird records from throughout Indonesia collected on the Burungnesia on-line database website between 2006 and 2020. Annotated checklists, richly illustrated with photos, have been locally produced for a number regions (e.g., Semarang), national parks (e.g., Baluran, Bali Barat), etc.

Websites such as the Oriental Bird Club's www.orientalbirdimages.org, Birds of the World (birdsoftheworld.org) and xeno-canto.org have rendered visual and aural identification substantially easier, while Cornell's ebird website (ebird.org) and app have allowed for detailed citizen science record keeping, and a better understanding of the regional status of species. Ornithological papers, especially the older ones, are nowadays much more accessible as many can be downloaded for free from a number of websites, such as the Biodiversity Heritage Library (http://biodiversitylibrary.org).

The Indonesian Ornithologists' Union was established in 2004, successor of the Indonesian Ornithological Society, which initially had an avicultural component. *Kukila* was adopted as its club journal. It offers an international and local forum, has endorsed field studies into the dispersal of avian influenza and the design of an atlas project for birds. To date it has hosted five ornithological conferences, organized in collaboration with universities. The region is also aptly covered by the *Journal of Asian Ornithology*, which often features publications on conservation, taxonomy and field ornithology.

TAXONOMY AND SYSTEMATICS
(by Frank E. Rheindt)

Family Sequence

The world's birds are divided into roughly 250 families, 107 of which are represented in the region covered by this field guide. In this book – as in many other field guides – species are arranged according to affinity to bird families and not according to other criteria, such as the islands they inhabit. We feel that a taxonomic arrangement of species is not only the biologically sensible thing to do, but also has great practical relevance. Most readers would probably like to see all similar drongos (*Dicrurus*) on one page rather than across various sections of the book, even though this practice may – at times – arrange multiple species on a page that do not geographically overlap in nature.

While the practice of placing family members together is fairly uncontroversial, the chronological family sequence different field guides have followed over the years has created substantially more discussion. Many field guides of the 1980s and 1990s invariably started off with a medley of pelagic bird families at the beginning, followed by large wading birds, waterfowl, birds of prey, landfowl and the remaining non-passerine bird families, with the perching birds (passerines) at the end. This 'classic field guide sequence' was based on our systematic knowledge of the day, but has since been superseded in many field guides by various adjustments that reflect new morphological and phylogenetic insights. Most notably, modern field guides usually start off with ratites (cassowaries and relatives), then waterfowl and landfowl, in recognition of overwhelming evidence that "chickens and ducks" are an extremely ancient clade distantly related to all other birds on Earth.

A constant trickle of new phylogenetic information has continued to promote adjustments to the way in which bird families are correctly arranged to reflect natural relationships. This has put a burden on birdwatchers and ornithologists who may be dealing with multiple guides for different regions that each follow a distinct family sequence. In the field, when the successful identification of a bird can be a matter of a few seconds, it is of utmost importance for the user to be able to locate a particular species account quickly. Continuing changes to family sequence, even between different editions of the same field guide, have therefore caused a growing amount of discontent and elicited calls for a 'unified sequence' (usually some random variation of the 'classic sequence') to be followed by all field guides.

As avid field birders, we empathise with observers' frustration about having to learn different family sequences for each guide they use. However, we regard calls for following a specific sequence of the past as unworkable. Firstly, there is no widely followed 'unified family sequence' available at the moment. Secondly, we believe it would be wrong to follow an older sequence in the full knowledge that some of its elements reflect an outdated understanding of phylogenetic relationships. In this book, therefore, we strive to follow the most recent insights on bird systematics while causing as little disruption to traditional sequence as possible.

The skeleton of our family sequence is provided by decades of modern morphological and phylogenetic research that has resulted in the detailed understanding we now have of birds' interrelationships, culminating in the seminal publication of whole-genomic data by Jarvis *et al.* (2014), whose work we largely follow in the rough arrangement of family groupings (=orders). While the new arrangement may cause some initial sighs among birdwatchers, it is the one that is likely to be followed by most field guides well into the future, as our latest insights are derived from whole genomes, with no more unsequenced DNA left to be added to the puzzle. Therefore, after the turbulent 2000s and early 2010s, we anticipate a period of calm and stability in the way bird families are arranged in field guides in the decades to come, with only minor additional adjustments possible (for example regarding the exact placement of doves). We hope that readers will embrace this family sequence as one to learn for their future enjoyment of other field guides as well.

Genus Arrangements

Scientific names serve stability and assign each species to a genus it shares with closely related species. Hence, the name *Pycnonotus plumosus* conveniently conveys that its bearer, the Olive-winged Bulbul, is closely related to other bulbuls sharing the genus name *Pycnonotus*. Instability and frustration arise when the usage of scientific names changes over time. The following is a summary of how we have dealt with genus-level arrangements and name changes of birds in this book. There are two types of changes of scientific name usage as compared to traditional usage: (1) obligatory ones and (2) arbitrary ones.

An obligatory change may arise when a name that had been in usage for a long time turns out to be technically incorrect or younger as compared to an older name that should have enjoyed priority. One such case is the Javan Crocias *Laniellus albonotatus*, in most previous books known by its superseded name *Crocias albonotatus*. Readers who are interested in the complex and intricate rules by which zoological nomenclature (or name-giving) is governed are referred to the Code of the International Commission of Zoological Nomenclature (freely available online at iczn.org). In this book, we have tried to follow the latest nomenclatural insights on bird names to ensure that readers are exposed to the most updated standard. Another way in which obligatory name changes arise is when new (often genetic) information reveals that a particular species is not, in fact, part of the genus it has usually been placed in. This happened to the Chestnut-necklaced Partridge *Tropicoperdix charltonii*, which has recently been shown to be fairly unrelated to the *Arborophila* partridges it is usually associated with.

Arbitrary changes to name usage are different in nature. They refer to instances in which scientists decide to divide a former genus into several smaller ones (=genus splitting), or to unite several former genera into a larger one (=genus lumping). Given our ever increasing knowledge of species relationships, the practice of genus splitting has become much more prevalent than genus lumping of late. The important issue to realise, however, is that these changes are arbitrary and reflect the personal preferences of usage of some scientists over those of others. In this book, we have intended to remain as conservative as possible with regard to arbitrary name changes. A good example is the large gull genus *Larus*, which has traditionally comprised approximately 50 species, a number considered unwieldy by many taxonomists. With recent phylogenetic studies demonstrating finer-scale relationships among gull species, the genus has been separated into as many as five smaller genera, although the genetic support for some of these smaller genera has been questionable as of 2020. In cases like this, we have opted to maintain the old, equally correct (or possibly even more correct) treatment of retaining all gulls in one genus *Larus*. Proponents of small genera advocate that separation into narrower units conveys more information about the relationships of species. However, the opposite argument can be made that information goes lost as species are divided into ever smaller, ever more meaningless genera, while using names like *Larus* in the traditional sense has an unequivocal appeal to birdwatchers and ornithologists alike.

"Genus Paraphyly": to Split or Not to Split

Many of the recent changes to scientific name usage have not fallen neatly into either the arbitrary or obligatory category. Complications often arise when new knowledge (mostly genetic, but also bioacoustic) conclusively demonstrates that a genus – as recognized at the time – should actually include members of another genus, too (=paraphyly), in order to reflect true biological relationships. A good example is the well-known genus *Accipiter* (sparrowhawks and goshawks). When recent genetic information indicated that harriers (*Circus*) are embedded within *Accipiter* hawks, meaning that some *Accipiter*s are more closely related to harriers than to other *Accipiter*s, an obligatory name change was required, but taxonomists had an arbitrary choice between different types of change: (1) either all *Accipiter*s and harriers are united into one big genus, namely *Accipiter*; or (2) the old *Accipiter* is split into two or more smaller genera. Unsurprisingly, in the case of these hawks, most biologists agree on a split (which – alas – has been carried out in this book) because of the dramatic differences in body shape and biology of harriers and sparrowhawks. However, it is important to note that in other cases, the choice is not as clear, and personal preference rather than some inherent biological truth dictates the way genera are arranged.

In cases of paraphyly where the choice whether to split or not to split is not as straightforward as in *Accipiter* hawks, we often decided to steer against the modern current of genus splitting and remain conservative. For instance, *Calidris* is a perfectly good genus comprising a homogenous group of sandpipers, and our book's treatment ignores recent advances to split the genus into smaller ones only because there happens to be an unusual 'extraneous' species, the Ruff (here *Calidris pugnax*), embedded within it. Similar treatments include that of the leaf-warblers as one genus (*Phylloscopus*) rather than 4–6 genera, as some modern treatments would have it, or the retention of numerous bulbuls in *Pycnonotus* despite some authors' preference for multiple genera.

Some cases of newly-discovered paraphyly result in inconvenient but necessary changes that obliterate popular and familiar names. A great illustrative case is that of the green barbets, which had long been divided into two genera, *Psilopogon* (for the Fire-tufted Barbet)

and the well-known *Megalaima* (for all the dozens of other Asian green barbet species). With new phylogenetic insights, we know that the Fire-tufted Barbet is, in fact, not a sister species to all other green Asian barbets, but is embedded within them. As *Psilopogon* (and not *Megalaima*) is the older name, all barbets must now be referred to by the former, unfortunately removing the latter name which had become such a household item in Asian ornithology.

English Group Names

With dozens of recent cases in which genetic and bioacoustic evidence has demonstrated unexpected relationships in the region's birds, we feel that English group name changes are frequently in order. Examples are the old 'Raffles's Malkoha' (now Rhinortha *Rhinortha chlorophaea*), which is not a malkoha (*Phaenicophaeus*) and should hence no longer be called one; or the old 'Crimson-headed Partridge' (now Bloodhead *Haematortyx sanguiniceps*), which is actually a primitive peacock-pheasant; or the former 'Crested Jay' (now Jay Shrike *Platylophus galericulatus*), which is a basal shrike.

We know that some readers may have initial misgivings about certain group name changes in cases where they feel that the misleading nature of an old name is worth maintaining for the sake of stability. Our outlook on this is different: while English names, even misleading ones, are well-entrenched in Western countries, especially those in which English is spoken as a mother tongue, they have a much briefer history in the Indonesian archipelago. With the publication of this field guide as, we hope, a major new milestone in Indonesian field ornithology, we hope to establish a coherent and helpful set of English-language names for many species that are otherwise obscure or covered by few other regional field guides. Our hope is for these new, phylogenetically consistent names to simplify English name usage and to facilitate an easy intuitive understanding of the birds' actual affinities.

We sometimes felt the need to carry out more sweeping changes to whole group names in English, especially when bioacoustic knowledge indicated strong support for DNA-based genus rearrangements. Some of these include:

1) Some of the former cuckooshrikes (*Coracina*) are now known to be more closely related to trillers (*Lalage*). This bipartition of cuckooshrikes makes complete bioacoustic sense, which is now reflected in the expansion of the traditional name 'cicadabird'.
2) Members of the genus *Pteruthius* (former shrike-babblers) do not look nor sound nor behave like babblers, and are in fact members of the vireo family. We feel this is the right time in Asian ornithology to eliminate a singularly unhelpful vernacular name by slightly adjusting it to 'shrike-vireo'. The fact that the latter name is already in circulation for other members of the vireo family in the Neotropics should not be in the way. The use of identical English group names for distantly related members of a family has wide precedence (see 'sandpiper').
3) The 'flycatchers' of the genus *Myiagra* are actually monarchs. Re-adjusting their English name accordingly is relatively straightforward and creates intuitive names with little chance of confusion.
4) With increased phylogenetic insight, we now know that several species variably referred to as white-eyes, dark-eyes and ibons are unexpectedly united in a single genus formerly known as *Heleia*. By now, it has become clear that *Heleia* is the junior name to an older moniker, *Apalopteron*, which therefore enjoys priority. Given that eye colour ("white eye", "dark eye") has been inconsistent as a taxonomic group name, what better English name is there for this new clade than the pleasing-sounding 'Heleia' which some of them had been classified under for so long?

5) The inconspicuous but fascinating 'bush warblers', long avoided by generations of ornithologists, actually fall out in two unrelated clades: one with melodious-sounding members of the undergrowth, the true bush warblers (*Horornis* etc.), and the other with cryptic, hard-to-see members with insect-like sounds that happen to be closely related to Eurasian grasshopper warblers (*Locustella*). Changing this latter group's English name to grasshopper warbler is consistent and intuitive (although a mouthful).

6) A last example we would like to mention here is the supreme confusion that has reigned in English name usage of certain Oriental groups of true flycatchers.

   a) *Cyornis*, a genus with largely blue males, has been aptly known as the 'blue-flycatchers' whereas the name 'jungle-flycatchers' has been reserved for *Rhinomyias*, a much drabber group thought to be unrelated to *Cyornis*. Molecular evidence now indicates that both genera are intricately intertwined, with blue species being sister species of drab ones and vice versa. In hindsight, anyone familiar with these birds in the field will find this arrangement sensible as their high-pitched, metallic, tinkling songs are all similar. To reflect this cohesion, a single name, 'jungle-flycatcher', is in order.

   b) To complicate things further, genetic data have shown that one jungle-flycatcher (former Streak-breasted Jungle-Fly-catcher *Rhinomyias additus* from Buru) is related to the genus *Eumyias*. Many recent treatments have taken this as evidence of a single case of mistaken genus affinity, but bioacoustic evidence points at a biological truth that is even more fascinating: numerous 'blue-flycatchers' (former *Cyornis*) and 'jungle-flycatchers' (former *Rhinomyias*) from eastern Indonesia share with members of *Eumyias* a continuous, endless, reeling warble that sets them apart from the tinkling, metallic sounds of true jungle-flycatchers. All these species require to be assigned to *Eumyias*, which now – with its larger composition – is best referred to as 'warbling-flycatchers'.

Species Concepts

The textbook definition of a species that most of us will be familiar with from high school is a simplified rendition of what has been known as the 'Biological Species Concept' (=BSC): "two populations belong to different species if they don't interbreed" (or some variation thereof). Since its inception during the Biological Synthesis of the 1960s and 1970s, the BSC has served as the main species concept in biology until the 'Species Concept Wars' broke out in the 1980s. Some scientists became increasingly disenchant-ed with the BSC because of its perceived failure to make predic-tions about populations that do not live in contact with each other. Would those populations interbreed or would they not? This has led to the formulation of dozens of alternative species concepts, including versions of the Phylogenetic Species Concept (PSC) that attained a considerable ornithological following in the 1990s and 2000s, although never succeeding in displacing the primacy of the BSC. The most widely used version of the PSC classifies any two populations as different species so long as they differ in at least one fixed character, no matter how insignificant (such as a single DNA base-pair difference in some unimportant gene). For regions such as the Indonesian archipelago, the implementation of such a species concept would be highly consequential: the vast majority of island subspecies and even unnamed island populations would require elevation to species level, possibly creating many thou-sands of new species of questionable biological significance.

It is with great joy that we have witnessed the Species Concept Wars subside in the 2010s. Although they helped biologists discuss the nature of the species, they have also been a great distraction from more important biological work. As the waters have calmed, proponents of various species concepts have joined in the literature to realize that – in the end, and despite our inability to find a perfect defi-nition – a species is still always going to be the same simple concept that even a child can grasp. This decade has seen biologists find the commonalities rather than the differences in their species concepts and emerge with a 'Unified Species Concept'. It is this Unified Species Concept, defined by character cohesion and gene flow, that we are striving to follow in the species-level taxonomy of this guide.

Species Taxonomy

Avian taxonomy in the last few decades has been defined by a widespread push towards species splits. The ~8000 bird species recognized in the 1980s have since grown to more than 11,000, and most of this growth is due to the practice of splitting large, polytypic species into multiple, more narrowly defined ones. The thrust of these new species splits has come from two new sources of information: (1) bioacoustics, and (2) phylogenetics. But the ability of scientists to publish results has not kept pace with the avalanche of new vocal and genetic data flowing in every week. This has led to a large number of 'grey splits' that are widely proposed and followed although they are not backed up by scientifically reviewed publications.

In this new era, field guide authors such as ourselves are in a particular predicament. Some authors opt to implement splits that have not been formally published, a practice that exposes them to widespread criticism and accusations of 'field guide splitting' from some but not all corners of academia. Other authors choose to follow well-established checklists that may be lagging behind in actual knowledge about splits. For the present guide, the second option has not really been viable because our book deals with a region that is not the focus of any of the well-known and reputable regional checklist committees, such as the NACC in North America and the SACC in South America. Our own field and lab-based knowledge of the region's birds has equipped us with an awareness of numerous subspecies or populations that require to be elevated to the species level, and it would be a waste if we failed to implement those splits because of some ill-advised adherence to an outdated Asian checklist. Indeed, as of the completion of this second edition (2020), and since the publication of the first edition in 2016, some 25 species splits have already been adopted in major ornithological checklists based on our own peer-reviewed publications, with more set to follow.

Having said this, there were numerous cases in which evidence for a species split is suggestive but not conclusive. In these cases, it was still important for us to draw the readers' attention to pos-sibilities of deep differentiation and future splitting. This is why we have introduced a special account category in this field guide called the 'limbo split' in which we direct the readers' attention to possible splits by assigning them common English names within the respective species account and putting them into bold-face like so: **'Javan Broadbill'** *Eurylaimus javanicus*. Limbo splits are possible splits that have either been mentioned in the literature but we feel that support is weak or insufficient, or they have generally not been mentioned in the previous literature and we feel that potential for splitting is considerable.

A multitude of genetic data has been published on Indonesian birds in the last ten years, but much of this has come in the form of mitochondrial DNA (mtDNA), whose sole use for species delimita-tion is controversial. While mtDNA divergences of ~3% and more can be suggestive of species-level differences, these predictions are not always borne out. So while mtDNA is often mentioned in the taxonomy sections as a criterion for a split or limbo split, we only implement splits based on mtDNA in combination with real biological data. There are many cases in which deep divergences in mtDNA been found in the absence of supporting vocal or plumage characters (e.g. Pied Triller *Lalage nigra* or Lesser Green Leafbird *Chloropsis cyanopogon*), prompting us to flag the mtDNA divergence in the form of a potential 'limbo split'. In other cases, such as numerous bulbuls and babblers, there is suggestive vocal data (often in addition to deep mtDNA divergences) in need of more rigorous analysis, again prompting us to flag these populations as limbo splits only, not as full splits. This practice ensures that the visiting or local birdwatcher is alerted to possible future splits in her quest to enjoy as many Indonesian birds as possible.

Subjectivity in taxonomy

Despite all the strict adherence to our own criteria, there will always be a few taxonomic 'tough nuts', which – as some readers may opine – have defied our best intentions at sober and impartial taxonomic classification. After all, in the absence of perfect data, species-level classification remains a subjective task no matter which method is employed.

USING THE FIELD GUIDE

Explanation of accounts

Each species account is given in the following format:
- **Name**: common English names are followed by the scientific name in italics. An 'E' following the name indicates that the species is an endemic to the region (rather than to any particular political entity). 'V' states the species is a vagrant to the region. An 'I' states the species is introduced to the region.
- **Size**: 'L' denotes length in centimetres. Where relevant, 'WS' denotes wingspan in centimetres. WS measurements should however be treated with caution, as this is not a measurement that is typically recorded by field researchers, and cannot accurately be measured from museum specimens. In Pandionidae, Accipitridae and Falconidae the wingspan/body length ratio is also included, following WS.
- **Extralimital Range**: for species that also occur outside the region, brief notes indicate the general range.
- **Taxonomy**: for polytypic species the number of described subspecies that occur within and outside the region is given. For those subspecies that occur within, the geographic range is given in parentheses. Where relevant, additional taxonomic notes are provided.
- **Habitat and habits**: a brief description is provided of a species' general abundance in the region and its preferred habitat. Where relevant, notes are also provided on general habits, especially where these can assist identification.
- **Identification (ID)**: unless otherwise stated, the initial description is either of the nominate race, or that first listed. Adult plumages are generally listed before immature or juvenile plumages. Additional notes are provided on sex-specific, sub-specific and/or seasonal differences as appropriate.
- **Vocalizations (Voc)**: vocalizations are described for almost all species, typically based on a description of the song, followed by any calls. For some non-breeding migrants that are very unlikely to be heard singing, only call is given. The speed of delivery is stated as n/s (notes per second) where appropriate. For some species, such as seabirds, ducks and swifts, vocalizations are not transcribed as they are unlikely to aid field identification.
- **Similar Species (SS)**: additional notes are given in cases where another species may cause confusion in identification.
- **Alternative Names (AN)**: where other common English names are, or have been, in use, such alternative names are stated. However, we do not provide spelling variants or alternative names that differ only slightly from the name employed.

Map key

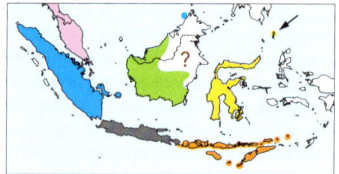

Resident/present all-year round: used to indicate areas where the species is generally present year-round, although this does not preclude the possibility of erratic or dispersive movements, or even partial migration.

Breeding visitor: used to indicate zones habitually occupied for breeding, but where the species is not normally present outside the breeding season.

Migrant/Visitor: Northern summer/Austral winter visitor (May–Sep) or Northern winter/Austral summer visitor (Sep–Apr): indicates zones where a species does not normally breed, or where breeding is suspected but has not definitely been recorded; thus, these colours should not be interpreted exclusively as summer and winter distributions, a regular practice in many bird guides, especially in temperate zones.

Circular blue spots indicate where the species has occurred only as a vagrant.
   On the maps of a few species, the only area shaded is blue; this means that in these species, usually seabirds, the general zone occupied is known, but the breeding grounds have not yet been located.

Passage migrant: indicates areas used by a species only when moving between breeding and non-breeding ranges; if the status is not certain due to limited data, the species is mapped as a blue winter/non-breeding visitor.

Introduced: populations that are either wholly or partially the result of introduction events by humans, both deliberately introduced or the product of escapes from captivity. We have attempted to conservatively map only those populations that are, or appear to be, self-sustaining, or have regular, repeated sightings in the same area and breeding behaviour has been observed.

Extinct/historical records only: indicates where a species has been previously confirmed but is now either known to be extinct or is only known from historical times (usually over 50 years) with no modern records.

highlighting presence on certain small islands.

highlighting an area where the species may have been collected historically, but its status is uncertain as the exact provenance of the specimen or accuracy of the record has been questioned. It can also highlight an area where a species might be expected to occur but lacks confirmation.

Bird Topography

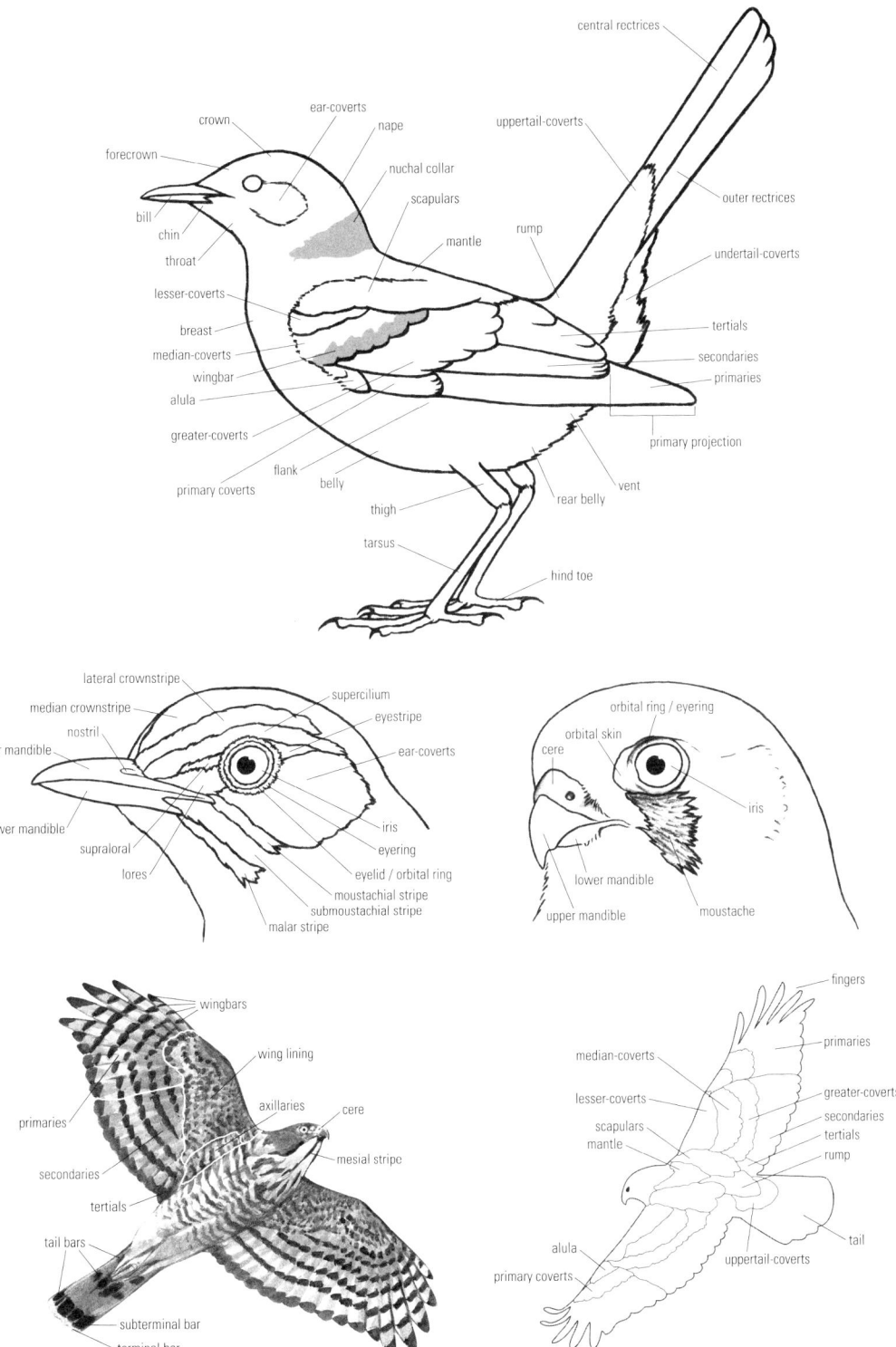

central rectrices
uppertail-coverts
outer rectrices
undertail-coverts
ear-coverts
crown
nape
forecrown
nuchal collar
scapulars
bill
chin
mantle
rump
throat
lesser-coverts
tertials
breast
secondaries
median-coverts
primaries
wingbar
alula
greater-coverts
primary projection
flank
primary coverts
belly
vent
rear belly
thigh
tarsus
hind toe

lateral crownstripe
supercilium
median crownstripe
eyestripe
nostril
ear-coverts
upper mandible
lower mandible
iris
supraloral
eyering
lores
eyelid / orbital ring
moustachial stripe
submoustachial stripe
malar stripe

orbital ring / eyering
orbital skin
cere
iris
lower mandible
upper mandible
moustache

wingbars
wing lining
axillaries
cere
primaries
mesial stripe
secondaries
tertials
tail bars
subterminal bar
terminal bar

fingers
primaries
median-coverts
lesser-coverts
greater-coverts
secondaries
scapulars
tertials
mantle
rump
alula
tail
primary coverts
uppertail-coverts

Abbreviations

E	east	S Mol	Tanimbar, Kai (Kai Kecil and Kai Besar), and surrounding islands
S	south		
N	north	Sul	Sulawesi
W	west	M	male
C	central	F	female
Aus	Australasia	Ad/ad	adult
MPen	Thai-Malay Peninsula	br	breeding plumage
Phil	Philippines	non-br	non-breeding plumage
NZ	New Zealand	Juv/juv	juvenile
NG	New Guinea	Imm/imm	immature
GS	Greater Sundas (Sumatra, Borneo, Java, Bali and surrounding islands)	sec	seconds
		n/s	notes per second
Sum	Sumatra	km	kilometres
Bor	Borneo	m	metres
Jav	Java	cm	centimetres
LS	Lesser Sundas (Lombok to Babar, including Sumba, Timor, Flores and surrounding islands)	I	Island
		Is	Islands
Mol	Moluccas	L	Lake
N Mol	Halmahera, Morotai, Obi, Bacan, and surrounding islands	R	River
		Mt	Mount
C Mol	Seram, Buru, Ambon, and surrounding islands	Mts	Mountains

ABOUT THE AUTHORS

James A. Eaton: co-founder and guide for Birdtour Asia, has been leading and pioneering birdwatching tours throughout the region since 2005. Having travelled, birded, sound recorded and photographed birds extensively throughout Asia over the past 20 years this field guide is the culmination of that time. With a particular interest in little-known taxa and exploring the most remote areas to enhance what is known about the least-known species in the region, as a consequence he has discovered numerous undescribed species, along with developing birding tourism infrastructure. In addition, devoting much of his time researching the bird trade for conservation NGOs, James has a PhD studying taxonomically cryptic species and their conservation status and a member of several IUCN specialist groups including the Asian Songbird Trade Group.

Bas (Sebastianus) van Balen: active in Indonesia ever since his two years of student fieldwork in West Java in 1979-81; freelance ornithologist and consultant for a large number of international and local conservation NGOs and universities throughout Indonesia. Co-editor of *Kukila*, the Journal of Indonesian Ornithology, from its early days, subject editor of the *Journal of Asian Ornithology*, and keen recordist of bird sounds, many of which have been made available at xeno-canto.org.

Nick W. Brickle: long-time Indonesia resident, birdwatcher and conservationist from 1992 onwards. Has travelled extensively across the region in pursuit of birds and while working for a number of conservation NGOs. Co-founder of Burung-Nusantara, the Indonesian birdwatching website. Co-editor of *Kukila*. Continues to work in Indonesia focused on creating new protected areas, on initiatives to reduce deforestation and forest degradation within the commercial forestry sector and on the restoration of degraded forest areas.

Frank E. Rheindt: ornithologist, former bird guide and currently associate professor and dean's chair at the National University of Singapore with a focus on avian phylogenetics and conservation genetics. Travelled Indonesia since 1998. Published dozens of articles on birds in the region based on DNA and field data. Co-described a dozen novel bird species, some of which he discovered himself. Global leader on bird taxonomy, serving as commissioner and councillor in the International Commission on Zoological Nomenclature and as chair of the taxonomic team of the Working Group on Avian Check-listing of the International Ornithologists' Union. After exploring some of the most seldom-visited islands on earth, seeing >8000 species by age 40, he is now concentrating on conservation genomic work, including as co-chair of the IUCN Specialist Group on Asian Songbird Trade. Editor-in-chief of the *Journal of Asian Ornithology* and associate/subject editor for three more journals.

SPECIES ACCOUNTS

CASUARIIDAE
Cassowaries
1 species in region (1 introduced)

Huge, long-necked, flightless birds with prominent casques. Secretive within forest, often detected by their large three-toed footprints and faecal mounds.

Southern Cassowary *Casuarius casuarius* I

L 130–170 cm. Aus. Monotypic. Seram; introduced. Uncommon in primary forest, <1200 m. Flightless, shy and inconspicuous. Presence often revealed by footprints and droppings. **ID** Huge and unmistakable. **Ad** black body; blue and red bare skin on neck and head; high casque on crown. **Imm** smaller and duller. **Imm** buff with dark brown stripes. **Voc** Hollow booming, grunts, rumbling, roars and coughs. Also stamps feet.

ANSERANATIDAE
Magpie Goose
1 species in region

Large, primitive atypical goose-like birds, now placed in their own family. Inhabit shallow wetland habitats where often found in large flocks.

Magpie Goose *Anseranas semipalmata* V

L 75–90 cm. Aus. Monotypic. Records from Banda (May 1988), Yamdena (Nov 2017), Rote (Nov 2019). Shallow wetlands. **ID** Large. **Ad** black-and-white goose-like bird with distinct knobbed head; orange bare parts. In flight, shows contrasting black outerwing and white wing coverts. **Imm** duller with black parts edged grey-brown. **Voc** Very vocal honking, in flight and while feeding.

ANATIDAE
Ducks and Geese
20 species in region

A large diverse family of medium sized waterbirds. Typically with a stocky build, short legs and short, flattened bills. Occupy a wide range of aquatic habitats, feeding by dabbling and diving.

Spotted Whistling-duck *Dendrocygna guttata*

L 43–50 cm. Aus, Phil. Monotypic. Nomadic, with some local breeding, in lakes, rivers, marshes, coastal mudflats and mangroves. Singly to small flocks. Mostly feeds actively by night, dabbling and diving; often perches in trees by day. **ID Ad** generally brown with greyish face; dark eyestripe and dark crown extending to back of neck; distinct white spots on flanks. In flight, head held low; broad, rounded wings; black underwing; uniform brown upperwing. **Imm** paler; flanks more streaked than spotted. **Voc** Coarse nasal whistle "whu-wheouw-whee", "whee-ow" or "ziow", often given in flight. **SS** Lacks chestnut upperwing coverts shown by Wandering and Lesser Whistling-ducks.

Wandering Whistling-duck *Dendrocygna arcuata*

L 43–61 cm. Aus, Phil. 3 ssp, 1 in region: *arcuata* (Indo Archipelago, Phil). Breeds locally. Generally scarce but locally common in LS and Sul, in lakes, rivers, marshes, coastal mudflats and mangroves. Singly to small flocks. Mostly feeds actively by night, dabbling and diving, seldom perches in trees. **ID Ad** dark brown upperparts, white uppertail-coverts; chestnut underparts and head, paler throat; dark brown crown and hindneck; distinctive white flank plumes (not always visible in flight). In flight, head held low; broad, rounded black wings with chestnut upperwing coverts. **Imm** more uniform; weaker reddish underparts and lacks broad pale back feathers. **Voc** High-pitched twittering "pwit-wit-tit-t-t-t" or nervous, descending "wit-wit-wit" and whistles, often given in flight. **SS** From smaller Lesser Whistling-duck by white (not chestnut) uppertail-coverts and distinct flank plumes. In flight Lesser's trailing edge to chestnut upperwing coverts shows bluish contrast with black flight feathers in good light (all-black in Wandering). See also Spotted and Plumed Whistling-ducks.

Lesser Whistling-duck *Dendrocygna javanica*

L 38–40 cm. S–SE–E Asia. Monotypic. Locally common in GS, scarce in LS. Usually found in small parties in lakes, marshes, wet rice fields, coastal mudflats and mangroves. Feeds by grazing, dabbling and diving. Occasionally roosts in trees. **ID Ad** similar to Wandering Whistling-duck, but has ill-defined cream feathering on flanks, not plumes, and uppertail-coverts chestnut not white. In flight, head held low; broad, rounded black wings with chestnut restricted to lesser and median upperwing coverts and bluish greater coverts, tertials and base of secondaries. **Imm** slightly duller; blacker crown. **Voc** Whistled "cheewirLEE", "hee-tieuw" or "tjieuw", often in flight. **SS** See larger Wandering and Spotted Whistling-ducks.

Plumed Whistling-duck *Dendrocygna eytoni* V

L 40–45 cm. Monotypic. Aus. Vagrant Rote (4 in Oct 2018). Freshwater and brackish wetlands. **ID/SS** From Wandering Whistling-duck by much paler, greyer head, lacking capped appearance; long, wispy white flank plumes that rise above the body when in water; pale iris; pink (not black) feet. In flight, large, rounded dark brown wings with paler brown underwing coverts. **Imm** paler with narrower, less distinct breast barring.

Green Pygmy-goose *Nettapus pulchellus*

L 30–36 cm. Aus. Monotypic. Swamps, marshes, lakes and rivers, particularly with floating vegetation in which it feeds. Singly or small flocks. **ID** Small. Dark green upperparts and heavily barred flanks. In flight, large, gleaming white secondary patch on dark wings. **M** dark green head and neck with white throat and cheek patch. **Imm/F/M eclipse** has cheeks, neck and throat pale grey. **F** with narrow whitish supercilium. **SS** Fem Cotton Pygmy-goose has long, broad (not narrow) supercilium, browner upperparts and paler neck. In flight, Green has white patch on secondaries versus narrow white trailing edge in female Cotton and white in primaries of male Cotton.

Cotton Pygmy-goose *Nettapus coromandelianus*

L 31–38 cm. Aus, S–SE Asia. 2 ssp, 1 in region: *coromandelianus* (S–SE Asia to NG). Status as resident unclear. Scarce on lakes, ponds, marshland and wet rice fields, particularly with floating vegetation. **ID M** white with black cap, dark green back and breast band; in flight, short rounded wings with broad white flash through base of primaries to tertials, contrasting with black coverts. **Imm/F/M eclipse** less contrasting; browner crown and upperparts; black eyestripe from bill base; dusky flanks; in flight, dark wings with white trailing edge to secondaries. **SS** See Green Pygmy-goose.

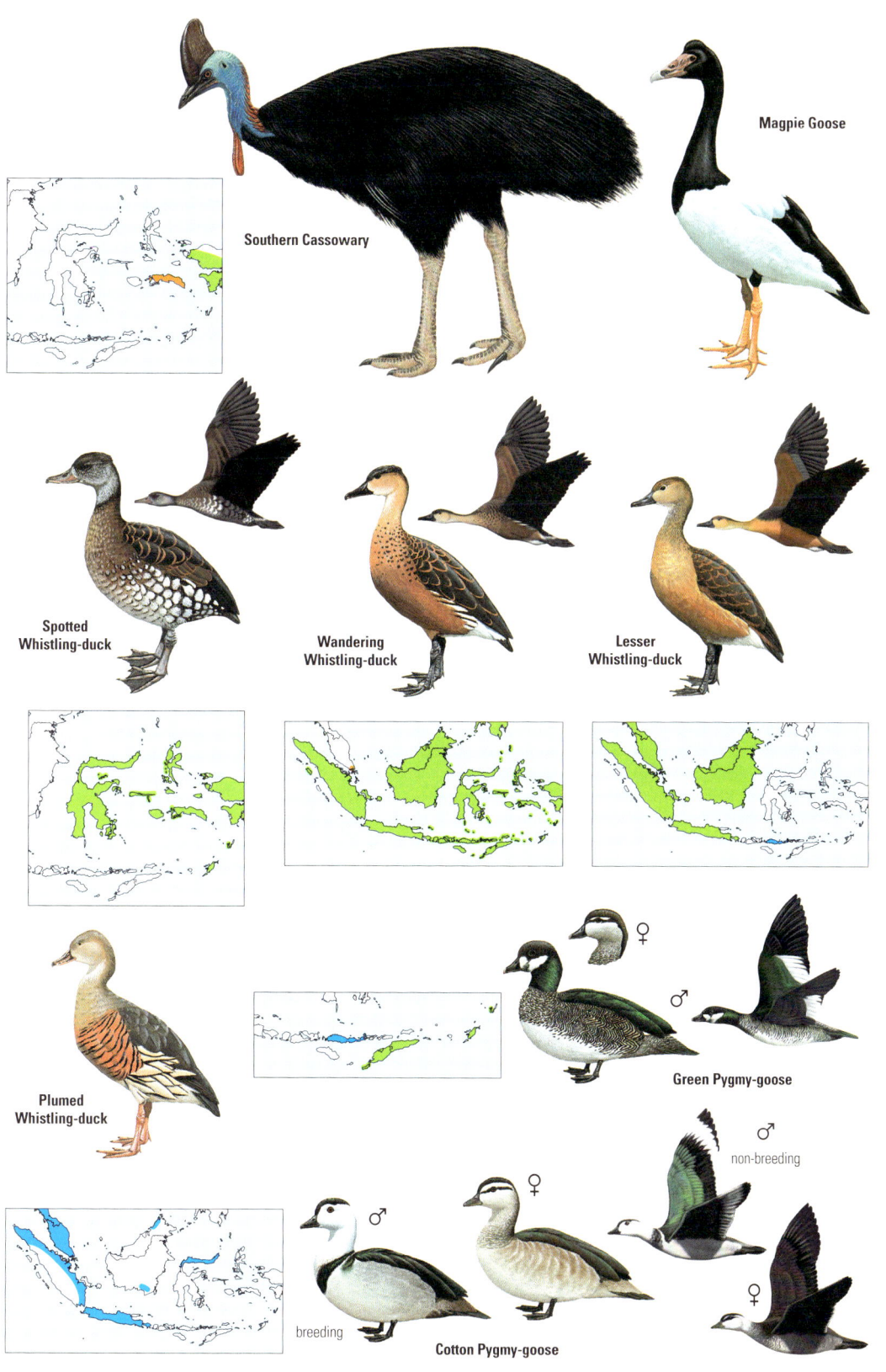

Southern Cassowary

Magpie Goose

Spotted
Whistling-duck

Wandering
Whistling-duck

Lesser
Whistling-duck

Plumed
Whistling-duck

Green Pygmy-goose

♀

♂

♂
non-breeding

breeding

♀

Cotton Pygmy-goose

♀

Radjah Shelduck *Radjah radjah*

L 49–61 cm. Aus. 2 ssp, 1–2 in region: *radjah* (Mol, NG); *rufitergum* (N Aus; one vagrant to Timor, 1882, probably this ssp). Uncommon migrant. May breed locally. Lakes, ponds, rivers, marshland, coastal mudflats and mangroves. Feeds by dabbling in shallow water. **ID Ad** large with wholly white head, dark wings, back and neck band. In flight, distinctive white upperwing-coverts and white trailing edge; white underwing with black primaries. Ssp *rufitergum* more reddish-brown dorsally. **Imm** has duller upperparts and dirty white plumage. **Voc** In display **M** hoarse whistle "peek-peek-..." and "peeEE", **F** harsh rattle "krre-krre-...".

Eurasian Wigeon *Anas penelope* ▣

L 42–50 cm. Breeds Palaearctic; wintering to S. Monotypic. Rare visitor to N Bor, vagrant N Sul. Lakes, rivers and coastal lagoons. **ID** Medium-sized, with short neck, large rounded head and small bill. **M** has chestnut head with cream-yellow forehead flash; grey bill with extensive black tip; black rear-end with pointed tail; grey body with pinkish breast; in flight, pale underwing with whitish coverts; upperwing has large white covert patch above dark green speculum; large white belly patch. **F/M eclipse** dark rufous brown with extensive mottling; in flight, all dark-grey upperwing. **SS** Fem told from fem teals, Mallard and Garganey by more rufous plumage tone, small grey bill with large, rounded head.

Chinese Spot-billed Duck *Anas zonorhyncha* ▣

L 58–63 cm. Monotypic. Breeds NE Asia; winters to E Asia. Vagrant to Sabah (2 each in Nov 2018 and Jan 2020). Freshwater and brackish wetlands, often associating with other ducks. **ID** Distinctive face pattern: black crown, facial stripe through eye and black line from gape towards eye creating a 'smiley face' appearance; broad yellow tip to black bill; dark brown body with pale fringes on flanks; purplish-blue speculum bordered by thin white tertial line; orange feet; in flight shows contrasting white underwing coverts with black outerwing. **Imm** generally duller overall but shows all distinctive features of Ad. **SS** Pacific Black Duck has similar facial pattern but lacks yellow bill tip and has straight (not upcurved) 'smile line' continuing behind eye; Pacific Black often has green (not bluish) speculum. From other *Anas* ducks by striking face and yellow bill tip; note underwing pattern in flight.

Mallard *Anas platyrhynchos* ▣

L 50–60 cm. Holarctic; wintering to S. 2 ssp, 1 in region: *platyrhynchos* (most of range). Vagrant to N Bor. Lakes, ponds, rivers, wet rice fields and coasts. **ID** Large stocky duck with large yellow to orange bill. In flight largely white underwing with dusky primaries; upperwing with dark blue speculum bordered white. **M** green head, narrow white collar and chestnut breast; rest of body generally grey. **F/M eclipse** streaked brown with darker crown and eyestripe; paler underparts; in flight shows brown belly. **SS** Most other fem ducks in region have dark (not orange) bill. Fem teals and Garganey smaller and smaller-billed. Fem Northern Pintail more slender and long-necked with smaller, bluish bill. See also Eurasian Wigeon. Extralimital **Gadwall** *Anas strepera* (Holarctic, wintering to S) likely to occur N Bor; **M** all-grey plumage with black bill and rear; **F** as Mallard but smaller; neatly-delimited black upper ridge along orange bill; both sexes with diagnostic white (not blue) speculum and dark belly in flight.

Pacific Black Duck *Anas superciliosa*

L 47–60 cm. Aus. Monotypic. Fairly common resident in E. Rare on Sum, vagrant to Bor. Lakes (including mountain lakes), ponds, marshland and wet rice fields. Pairs to small flocks. **ID** Large, generally dark brown, with conspicuous pale and black stripes on face; orange feet. In flight shows contrasting white underwing-coverts; large green/purple speculum bordered black, with very narrow white fringes. **Voc** (i) Repeated nasal "raeb"; (ii) far-carrying, deep "quack". **SS** See Garganey and Chinese Spot-billed Duck.

Northern Pintail *Anas acuta* ▣

L 51–76 cm. Holarctic; wintering to S. Monotypic. Rare visitor to N Bor, single records from Sum (1992), Jav (1933), Talaud (Nov 2014). Lakes, marshland, wet rice fields and coastal lagoons. **ID** Medium-sized, slim, elegant duck with long neck and tail. In flight, white trailing edge to secondaries. **M** chocolate head, white neck stripe, greyish body and long black tail; in flight, grey underwing. **F/M eclipse** similar to Mallard, but plainer head, small grey bill, pointed tail and long, narrow neck; in flight, brownish underwing. **SS** More slender and long-necked than smaller fem teals and Garganey. See also Mallard. In flight, note brownish underwing and grey feet.

Eurasian Teal *Anas crecca* ▣

L 34–38 cm. Palaearctic; wintering to S. Monotypic. Rare visitor to N Bor. Lakes, rivers, marshes and coast. **ID** Small, compact, with round head and small bill. **M** chestnut head with long green eye patch; grey body; cream patch on sides of black undertail-coverts; in flight, broad white bar along secondary bases; speculum green proximally, turning black on secondaries. **F/M eclipse** black crown and narrow eyestripe with indistinct brown supercilium; brown body with dark scalloping, especially on flanks; dark bill sometimes with orange at base of lower mandible; in flight has whitish underwing coverts contrasting with dusky remaining wing; upperwing shows diffuse green speculum turning black on outer secondaries, bordered white; pale belly. **SS** See Garganey, Eurasian Wigeon, Sunda Teal, Mallard and Northern Pintail.

Radjah Shelduck

Eurasian Wigeon
♂
♀

Chinese Spot-billed Duck

Mallard
♂
♀

Gadwall
♂

Pacific Black Duck

Northern Pintail
♂
♀

Eurasian Teal
♂
♀

Sunda Teal *Anas gibberifrons* E

L 37–47 cm. Monotypic. Formerly included Grey Teal, forming an expanded '**Grey Teal**' *Anas gibberifrons*, but now usually split because of coloration and forehead shape. Museum specimens from E of range (Sulawesi, Rote-Wetar) exhibit some morphological admixture with Grey Teal, suggesting that a future re-merger of these two forms may be necessary, and field photographs appear to show mostly pure gibberifrons-type birds, perhaps due to recent re-expansion from Jav-Bali. Uncertain status on Sum, rare on Bor (now breeds Sabah), but fairly common in east of range. Small to large flocks in marshland, lakes, rivers, mangroves and coastal mudflats, with a preference for brackish water. Occasionally perches in trees. **ID** Generally dark grey-brown, with paler throat and darker crown and back; grey feet. In flight, large white, triangular leading edge to dark speculum and narrow white trailing edge; underwing shows squarish, gleaming white axillary patch, greater coverts either wholly dark or tipped white producing narrow white line; brown belly. **M** has bulging forehead. **Voc** (i) "peek" and grunts in display; (ii) typical duck call when flushed. **SS** See Grey Teal. Greyer and less stripy-headed than fem Garganey and Eurasian Teal.

Grey Teal *Anas gracilis* V

L 37–47 cm. Aus. 2 ssp, 1 in region: *gracilis* (most of range). Vagrant to region: sightings from W+E Timor, with specimens from Kai Kecil, Ambon, Timor, Rote and Java. Habitat as Sunda Teal. Birds have been recorded in flocks of Sunda Teal. **ID/SS Ad** as fem Sunda Teal and difficult to separate unless seen well or together. Generally paler and greyer (less brown, particularly on breast), slightly larger, no bulging forehead and smaller spots on flanks and breast. Best identified in flight as underwing shows extensively white axillaries with broad white band extending outwards along proximal two thirds of greater coverts and onto base of secondaries, creating impression of a large white triangle; Sunda Teal, in contrast, has much smaller squarish white patch centred around axillaries, with either no white band extending outwards or at most a faint line of white feather tips. Grey Teal lacks the stripy head of fem Garganey.

Garganey *Spatula querquedula*

L 37–41 cm. Palaearctic; wintering to S. Monotypic. Scarce to rare migrant throughout. Marshland, coastal lagoons and wet rice fields. **ID** Green speculum broadly bordered white on both sides; thick blackish leading edge on underwing contrasting with whitish underwing coverts; grey feet. **M** generally dark brown with prominent white eyestripe and grey flanks; in flight, pale blue upperwing-coverts above speculum; square white belly and dark brown breast. **F/M eclipse** streaked brown with heavily scalloped flanks; dark bill; paler supercilium, darker eyestripe and crown; white belly; in flight, eclipse M has dull grey upperwing coverts. **Voc** Rattling call, sounding buzz-like when given by dense flocks from a distance. **SS** Eclipse male told from Eurasian Teal by silvery-grey forewing, obvious in flight. All plumages from Eurasian Teal by broad white trailing edge to secondaries and more obvious supercilium and facial pattern. See also other teals, Mallard, Eurasian Wigeon and Northern Pintail. F/M eclipse from larger Pacific Black Duck by less bold head pattern, supercilium not as conspicuous in front of eye, eyestripe brown (not black), and paler, browner body.

Northern Shoveler *Spatula clypeata* V

L 44–52 cm. Holarctic; wintering to S. Monotypic. Vagrant N Bor. Lakes, ponds, marshland and coastal lagoons. **ID** Unmistakable, large, spatulate bill. **M** green head, white breast and large chestnut flank patch; orange feet; in flight, conspicuous bright chestnut belly; whitish axillaries; grey-blue upperwing coverts; green speculum has large white leading edge, but black trailing edge. **F/M eclipse** similar to fem Mallard, but smaller and spatulate bill obvious; in flight, as M. **SS** In flight, note unique speculum pattern, which features a white leading edge and black trailing edge; only F dabbling duck in region with blue-grey upperwing coverts.

Hardhead *Aythya australis*

L 45–60 cm. Aus. Monotypic. Rare visitor. Has bred E Jav. Lakes, ponds and marshes. **ID** Uniformly dark brown with white belly and undertail-coverts. In flight, white underwing with narrow black trailing and leading edges; upperwing shows gleaming, broad white wingbar across secondaries and primaries. Iris white in **M**, dark-brown in **F**. **SS** See Tufted Duck.

Tufted Duck *Aythya fuligula* V

L 40–47 cm. Palaearctic; wintering to S. Monotypic. Recorded N Bor, N Sul, Talaud. Lakes, ponds and coast. Prefers open water, where dives. **ID** Small, compact; iris yellow. In flight, white underwing with narrow black trailing and leading edges; upperwing shows gleaming, broad white wing bar across secondaries and inner primaries, becoming dusky on outer primaries; white belly. **M** distinctive black-and-white plumage and tuft on head; **M eclipse** browner, flanks greyer. **F** generally dark brown with paler belly and short tuft on head; often shows white around base of bill. **SS** Fem from Hardhead by yellow (not white or dark-brown) iris, tuft on head, white on face (if present) and generally lack of white on undertail-coverts; in flight white wing bar is dusky (not white) towards outer primaries.

White-winged Duck *Asarcornis scutulata*

L 66–81 cm. S–SE Asia. Monotypic. Now rare in swamp forest and slow-running forest rivers of Sum; less often peat swamp. Formerly Jav but not recorded since 1930s. Singly or small family groups. Largely nocturnal, flying to and from roosting locations at dawn and dusk. **ID** Large; generally dark with variable amounts of white. Typically body all-dark with black speckling on white head and neck; however in region head, neck, breast, and even belly, flanks and mantle can be wholly white; mucky orange bare parts. In flight, gleaming white upperwing coverts and primary coverts; dark outerwing; gleaming white axillaries; dull blue-grey speculum. **Voc** Flight call a distinctive series of "honk", two-syllable "honk-onk" or "hew". **M** calls slightly higher-pitched.

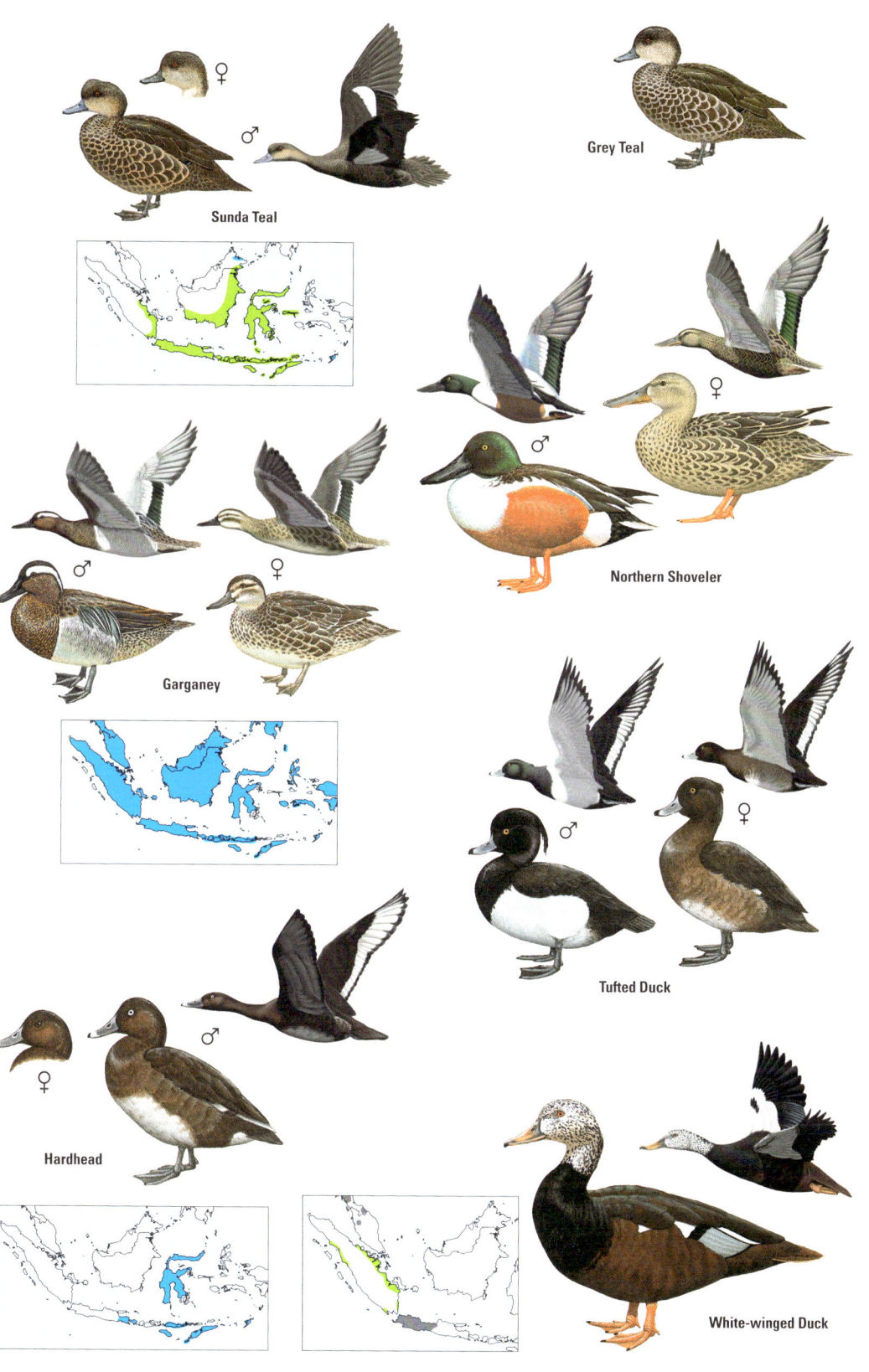

Sunda Teal

Grey Teal

♀

♂

Garganey

♂

♀

Northern Shoveler

♂

♀

Tufted Duck

♂

♀

Hardhead

♀

♂

White-winged Duck

MEGAPODIIDAE
Megapodes

8 species in region

Medium to large terrestrial birds with strong legs. Generally secretive within forested habitat. Typically construct large nesting mounds or breed communally on beaches or volcanically heated soil. Some species are good dispersers, colonising small offshore islands. Eggs are often harvested unsustainably, leading to massive declines throughout range.

Maleo *Macrocephalon maleo* **E**

L 55–60 cm. Monotypic. Now local and scarce in primary and degraded forest. Singly, pairs or small groups (<5). Nests communally on sandy beaches and volcanically-heated soil. Many former nesting grounds now abandoned due to over-collection of eggs. **ID** Large. **Ad** with distinctive brown-black upperparts and pink-white underparts; bill and bare facial skin variably pink and yellow; horny casque on crown. **Imm** smaller; head pattern duller, and lacking casque. **Voc** Bizarre, drawn-out, tremulous yelp, "waaaoou", trailing off towards end, lasting 2 sec, regularly repeated; primarily early morning.

Moluccan Scrubfowl *Eulipoa wallacei*

L 34 cm. Mol to Misool I. Monotypic. Very local and uncommon in primary and secondary forest, <1500 m. Breeds communally on sandy beaches or clearings, usually visited at night. Shy and elusive. **ID** Grey-brown head and breast contrast with white belly and vent; nape, mantle and wings olive-brown with broad chestnut bands across wings and mantle. **Voc** (i) Noisy crowing or loud wailing series; (ii) irregular rapid series of sharp nasal "kep" or "kew"; (iii) also "kyouw kouw" or "kouw-kouw-kouw-kouw" or "KOOK-kook-ook (ook)"; no duetting known.

Tabon Scrubfowl *Megapodius cumingii*

L 31–44 cm. Phil, E Indonesia. 6–7 ssp, 4 in region: *cumingii* (Is off N Bor; Palawan); *gilbertii* (Sul); two ssp, *sanghirensis* (Sangihe, Siau) and *talautensis* (Talaud), look and may sound distinct and perhaps better treated as a separate species '**Sanghihe Scrubfowl**' *M. sanghirensis*. Taxonomy poorly known; more ssp may need to be elevated to species level. Scarce to locally common within primary and degraded, especially coastal, forest; on Sul <2000 m, in N Bor restricted to offshore islands and adjacent coastal forest. Shy and elusive. Builds nesting mounds or buries eggs within tree roots. **ID** Back and wings rich olive-brown; underparts, neck and head dark grey; legs blackish to dark-red; prominent red facial skin. Ssp *gilbertii* is smaller, and has warmer brown (often cinnamon-hued) upperparts. Ssp *sanghirensis* larger than previous two, with more chestnut upperparts; *talautensis* largest in size, and even darker chestnut to rich maroon on upperparts, with almost plumbeous-black underparts. **Voc** Long mournful whistle (4–5 sec), rising then descending: "kyoooooooooooooo", higher-pitched version sounding like a miaow of a cat in distress; no duetting known; often calls at night.

Sula Scrubfowl *Megapodius bernsteinii* **E**

L 30 cm. Monotypic. Local and scarce within primary and degraded forest and coastal scrub, <500 m. Singly, pairs or small family groups. Shy and terrestrial, when flushed often perches in mid-canopy. Builds large nesting mounds. **ID** Uniform, dark, rich chestnut brown, occasionally paler brown on head and/or crown; legs dark red-orange. **Voc** In duet, one bird produces a high screeching 3-note "wa-wuU-waa", while the other bird produces a knocking sound, lasting ~4 sec.

Tanimbar Scrubfowl *Megapodius tenimberensis* **E**

L 30–43 cm. Monotypic. Often erroneously included with Orange-footed, but DNA shows it to be closely related to Tabon Scrubfowl. Scarce in primary and secondary forest, more numerous on offshore, forested islets. Singly or pairs. Shy and inconspicuous. Builds large nest mounds. **ID** Olive-brown wings and back; grey underparts; pale grey head with sparse feathering, prominent red facial skin and no crest; legs blackish-red. **Voc** Accelerating series of 5–10 notes "wee-wee-wee-wedo-wedo-wedo...", often in duet, 5 n/2 s.

Dusky Scrubfowl *Megapodius freycinet*

L 34–41 cm. Mol to W Papuan Is. 3 ssp, 1 in region: *quoyii* (N Mol). Taxonomy see Forsten's. Scarce to locally common in forested areas, <1000 m. Shy and terrestrial. Singly, pairs or small family groups. **ID** Uniformly dark brown with short crest, dark grey-black legs and indistinct red facial skin. **Voc** Laughing, rising then descending "keyouououorr" followed by "keyou keyou" from partner.

Forsten's Scrubfowl *Megapodius forsteni* **E**

L 30–39 cm. 2 ssp: *forsteni* (Seram, Ambon); *buruensis* (Buru). Often erroneously included with Orange-footed. Closely related to (and often considered conspecific with) Dusky, which it resembles in plumage, bare parts and mtDNA. Scarce to locally common in primary and secondary forest, coastal scrub and mangrove, often on small offshore islets, <1900 m. Builds large nest mounds. Shy, terrestrial. Singly or pairs. **ID** Dark brown wings and mantle; dark grey underparts and neck; blackish crown, short crest; legs dark orange-red to paler olive. Ssp *buruensis* larger and greener on upperparts. **Voc** Loud high-pitched and guttural screeches, including "ga-ga-ga...", "ugk-ugk-ugk..."; often calls at night.

Orange-footed Scrubfowl *Megapodius reinwardt*

L 37–45 cm. Aus. 5 ssp, 1 in region: *reinwardt* (LS, Kai, NG). Taxonomy see Tanimbar and Forsten's. Fairly common in primary and secondary forest, coastal scrub, mangroves, often on small offshore islets, <1000 m. Builds large nest mounds. Shy, terrestrial. Singly or pairs. **ID Ad** olive-brown wings, rump and lower back contrasting with grey underparts, neck and upper back; head with brownish crown and crest and variable indistinct red facial skin; legs orange, varying from bright to dull. **Imm** smaller with wholly dark olive plumage. **Voc** Loud high-pitched and guttural screeches, including "ga-ga-ga...", "ugk-ugk-ugk..."; often calls at night.

Maleo

Tabon Scrubfowl
cumingii

Moluccan Scrubfowl

Sula Scrubfowl

Tanimbar Scrubfowl

Dusky Scrubfowl

Forsten's Scrubfowl
forsteni

Orange-footed Scrubfowl

PHASIANIDAE
Pheasants and allies
28 species in region

A large family of medium to large terrestrial birds, typically with stout bodies, robust legs, short wings and often long tails. Secretive ground feeders, usually in dense forest. Often distinctly vocal. Some highly ornate in colouration.

Long-billed Partridge *Rhizothera longirostris*
L 30–35 cm. Sundaic. Monotypic. For taxonomy see Dulit Partridge. Scarce and local in primary and mature secondary forest, <1300 m. Terrestrial, extremely shy, but may fly to low branch if flushed. Singly or pairs. **ID** Rufous face and underparts, darker crown; upperparts mottled brown and black; long, stout, decurved bill. **M** has broad grey breast band, rump and uppertail-coverts; some pale shaft streaks on mantle. **F** lacks grey breast band and rump. **Imm** as fem but duller, with pale streaking on throat, breast and mantle and indistinct dark barring on flanks. **Voc** Monotonous, fast 2-note piping "kan-king", often in duet, repeated incessantly. **SS** Ferruginous Partridge is smaller, with extensive black-and-white barring on flanks and black spots on wings. See also Dulit Partridge.

Dulit Partridge *Rhizothera dulitensis* **E**
L 30–35 cm. Monotypic. No longer considered conspecific with Long-billed based on pronounced plumage differences. Collected from four mountain locations, Murud, Dulit, Batu Song and Kinabalu, from lower montane forest, 900–1200 m; presumably more widespread. Poorly known (collected between 1895–1937), no recent records. **ID** As Long-billed but shows grey-white belly (not rufous), darker upperparts, and more vermiculated greater secondary coverts and secondaries. **M** shows broader grey breast band than Long-billed. **F** as Long-billed, but rufous underparts confined to upper breast grading into grey-white belly. **Imm** as fem but duller, with pale streaking on throat, breast and mantle and indistinct dark barring on flanks. **Voc** Undescribed but presumably similar to Long-billed. **SS** For separation from Long-billed, see ID. Ferruginous is smaller, with extensive black-and-white barring on flanks and black spots on wings. **AN** Hose's Partridge.

Roulroul *Rollulus rouloul*
L 25 cm. Sundaic. Monotypic. Uncommon to fairly common but shy in primary and mature secondary forest, <1300 m. Terrestrial. Singly, pairs or small groups (<15), scattering noisily when disturbed. **ID** Small rotund partridge with red orbital skin and red legs. Plumage can appear all dark in poor light. **M** metallic blue-green with red crest and white spot on forehead. **F** green with rufous wings and slate-grey head. **Imm** as fem but duller and greyer. **Voc** Upslurred high-pitched whistle, easily imitated, with down-slurred ending, "swee", lasting 1.5 sec, repeated every 1 sec. **AN** Crested Partridge.

Ferruginous Partridge *Caloperdix oculeus*
L 23–27 cm. Sundaic. 3 ssp, 2 in region: *borneensis* (Bor); *ocellatus* (Sum). Uncommon and patchily distributed in primary and secondary forest and bamboo, <1200 m. Usually singly or pairs. **ID** Head, neck and breast bright rufous; belly and throat paler; dark line through eye. Sides of breast, flanks and mantle barred black-and-white in *borneensis* or black-and-buff in *ocellatus*. Wings paler brown with distinct black spots; rump and uppertail-coverts blackish with rufous barring. **Voc** Series of ~40 ascending notes, lasting 6 sec, ending abruptly with 2–5 harsh notes "pip-pip-pip-pipipipipipipip... duit-duit", given singly or as a duet. **SS** Barring on flanks, breast and mantle, and spotting on wings separate from all other partridges.

Black Partridge *Melanoperdix niger*
L 24–27 cm. Sundaic. Monotypic. Rare and local, few recent records, in primary and mature secondary forest, especially peat swamp, <200 m, though known from <1100 m in kerangas forest. Terrestrial, shy and little known. **ID** Small with thick black bill and blue-grey legs. **M** uniformly black. **F** chestnut brown, with slightly paler throat, belly and undertail-coverts, and prominent black barring on scapulars. **Imm** as fem, but with white spotting on underparts and less obvious scapular barring. **Voc** "whirr-wirr-a", lasting 1 sec, reminiscent in pitch and quality of Bock's Hawk-cuckoo opening sequence. **SS** Fem differs from all other partridges in stubby bill shape and overall chestnut colouration (especially mantle).

Roll's Partridge *Arborophila rolli* **E**
L 28 cm. Monotypic. Very different from Sumatra and White-faced; the three no longer considered conspecific. Uncommon in submontane and montane forests of N Sum south to Batak Mts and Simalungun, 500–2000 m. Terrestrial. Singly or small groups. **ID** Head black with brown forehead and nape, white lores and cheek spots and some white on throat; underparts rich buff, becoming off-white on belly; flanks heavily barred black and white; upperparts brown with fine black barring; wings brown with chestnut-and-black spotting. Bill black. **Voc** (i) Even series of <70 "wu" notes per ~20 sec gradually increasing in volume; (ii) a disyllabic "whur-hu", often in duet of similar intensity and increasing volume. **SS** From Chestnut-necklaced by red (not green) legs, much blacker head markings and bold barring on flanks. See also Red-billed.

Sumatran Partridge *Arborophila sumatrana* **E**
L 28 cm. Monotypic. Taxonomy see Roll's. Locally uncommon in submontane forest of Sum S of Batak Mts and Simalungun, 500–1500 m. Terrestrial. Singly or small groups. **ID** As Roll's Partridge but breast grey, with black nape (olive-brown crown and nape in **F**), white cheek spot. **Voc** As Roll's. **SS** From Chestnut-necklaced by red (not green) legs, much blacker head markings and bold flank bars. See also Red-billed.

Bornean Partridge *Arborophila hyperythra* **E**
L 27 cm. 2 ssp: *erythrophrys* (Mt Kinabalu); *hyperythra* (other Bor mts). Fairly common resident in (sub-) montane forest, 600–3000 m. Terrestrial. Singly or small groups. **ID** Head reddish brown with blackish crown, nape and eyestripe extending onto neck: blue-grey supercilium and ear patch (often missing in *erythrophrys*, though racial differences apparently not discrete). Bill black; legs pink; breast reddish-brown becoming whitish on belly and undertail-coverts; flanks heavily spotted black-and-white; upperparts dark brown with fine black barring on back and rump, and black spots on wings. **Voc** As White-faced but often starts with 2-note "whur-hu", then switching to single note "wu" mid-way in series. **SS** Superficially similar to Ferruginous, but separated by pink legs, distinct head pattern and lack of black-and-white scaled upperparts. From Sabah Partridge by red (not green) legs, black-and-white polka dot pattern on flanks, and lack of black-and-white scaling across lower breast. **AN** Red-breasted Partridge.

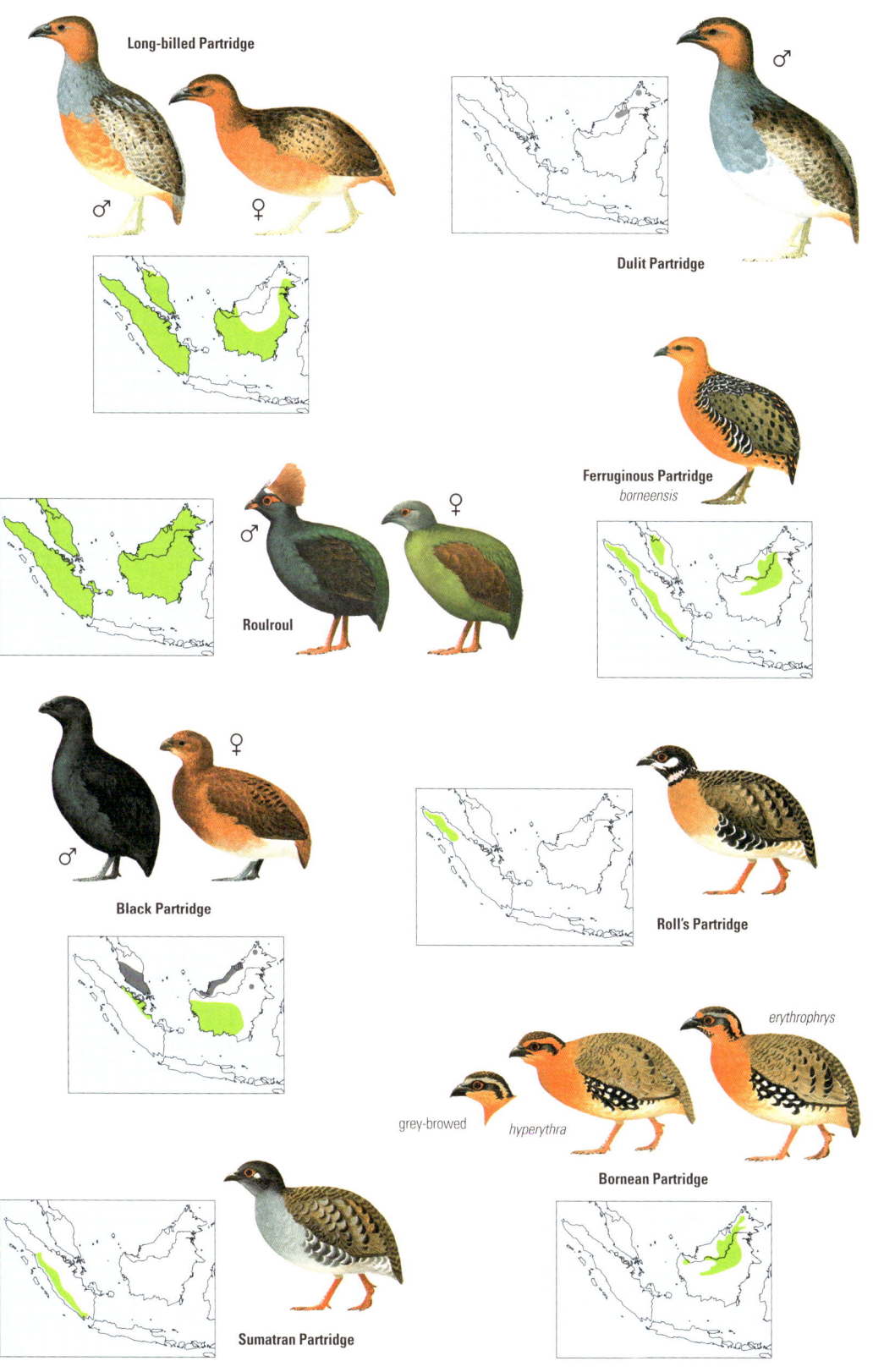

Long-billed Partridge

♂ ♀

Dulit Partridge

♂

Ferruginous Partridge
borneensis

Roulroul

♂ ♀

Black Partridge

♂ ♀

Roll's Partridge

grey-browed *hyperythra* *erythrophrys*

Bornean Partridge

Sumatran Partridge

Red-billed Partridge *Arborophila rubrirostris* E

L 29 cm. Monotypic. Fairly common in montane forest, 900–2500 m. Terrestrial. Singly or small groups. **ID** Bright-red bill and legs. Head black, or black with white throat, lores and fine supercilium; broad reddish-brown breast band spotted white; belly grey-white, marked with black; flanks black fringed with white giving scaly appearance; upperparts dark brown with fine black scales and spots. **Voc** (i) Series of disyllabic "wa-hu" notes, shorter and slower than Roll's and Sumatran, ~11 n/9 s; (ii) also a duet with one bird producing the same "wa-hu" notes and the other a downslurred single "owh" note of similar intensity. **SS** From other partridges on Sum by combination of red bill and legs, blackish head and broad reddish-brown breast band.

Chestnut-bellied Partridge *Arborophila javanica* E

L 28 cm. 3 ssp: *javanica* (W Jav); *bartelsi* (WC Jav); *lawuana* (EC Jav). Fairly common resident. Montane forests, extending E to Mt Semeru; 900–3000 m, rarely to 300 m. Terrestrial. Singly, pairs or small groups. **ID Ad** chestnut flanks and belly contrasting with grey breast; back and rump finely barred; wings brown with chestnut and black spotting. Black lores, eyestripe and neck; rufous-orange throat, cheeks and forehead; brown crown and nape. Ssp *bartelsi* has face showing less black and more rufous-orange; *lawuana* shows more black on nape and neck. **Imm** may have rufous on face replaced with off-white; underparts dull brown. **Voc** (i) Even series of <70 "wu" notes per ~20 sec gradually increasing in volume; (ii) a disyllabic "whur-hu", often in duet of similar intensity and increasing volume.

White-faced Partridge *Arborophila orientalis* E

L 28 cm. Monotypic. Taxonomy see Roll's. Scarce in montane forest of E Jav extending west to Yang Highlands, 500–2200 m. Terrestrial. Singly or small groups. **ID** White face and throat; dark crown extending to nape and hindneck; thin, dark eyestripe. Body predominantly uniform grey; wings have chestnut feather lining. **Voc** As Chestnut-bellied. **AN** Grey-breasted Partridge.

Chestnut-necklaced Partridge *Tropicoperdix charltonii*

L 26–32 cm. Sundaic. 2 ssp, 1 in region: *atjenensis* (Sum). Previously considered conspecific with Sabah Partridge and extralimital Tonkin Partridge *T. tonkinensis*. Rare, last recorded Lampung district, 1939. Forest, <300 m. Terrestrial. Singly or pairs, presence usually betrayed by vocalisations. **ID** Generally brown with unmarked chestnut upper breast band bordered above by black-speckled collar; white throat; speckled supercilium; orange ear patch; red orbital skin and gape; dark bill; back and wings finely barred; breast and flanks with variable dark scaling; belly buff. **Voc** (i) Series of two vibrating notes every 6 s, culminating in loud scolding: "tweo-tweo-tweo-tweo-tweo-tweo TCHIRRA-TCHWIU-TCHIRRA-TCHWIU-TCHIRRA-TCHWIU..."; sometimes only the opening series is given; (ii) single, "urh" at 2 n/s when in close proximity. **SS** See Roll's, Sumatran and Red-billed Partridges from higher elevations.

Sabah Partridge *Tropicoperdix graydoni* E

L 26–32 cm. Monotypic. For taxonomy see Chestnut-necklaced Partridge. Locally uncommon in forest; <300 m. Terrestrial. Singly or pairs, presence usually betrayed by vocalisations. **ID** Similar to Chestnut-necklaced but paler bill; blackish orbital skin, off-white ear patch, white supercilium; black lower throat; lower breast generally more dark-barred; darker chestnut upper belly. **Voc** (i) Slowly accelerating series of vibrating notes (~15 n/12 s) culminating in loud scolding: "tu-tu-tu-tu-tu-tu-tututututututu TCHIRRA-TCHWIU-TCHIRRA-TCHWIU-TCHIRRA-TCHWIU..."; sometimes only the opening series is given; (ii) a tremulous evenly-paced "pee-yoo" at ~8 n/10 s lasting for <2 min. **SS** See Bornean Partridge.

Green Peafowl *Pavo muticus*

L 180–250 cm (M), 100–110 cm (F). SE Asia. 3 ssp, 1 in region: *muticus* (Jav, formerly MPen). Formerly widespread on Jav, but now largely restricted to E. Very locally common in dry open forest, savanna and occasionally teak plantations. Terrestrial and shy, usually found close to water. Rarely takes flight except to roost in trees. **ID M** unmistakable large greenish peacock, with long tail extensions during breeding season. **F** smaller; similar to male in general colouration, but has vermiculated, not plain, tertials; lacks train. **Imm** duller with extensively barred outerwing. **Voc** (i) Far-carrying "kee-ouw"; (ii) softer "ouwooooooh-ouwood-... kokokokokoko"; (iii) softer "eeeeeehay..., eeeeeehay-who".

Great Argus *Argusianus argus*

L 150–200 cm (M), 74–75 cm (F). Sundaic. 2 ssp: *argus* (Sum, MPen); *grayi* (Bor). Fairly common in primary and mature secondary forest interior; <1000 m (Sum), <1800 m (Bor). Terrestrial and shy. Usually one male with several fem or singly. Male clears patches of forest floor as display ground to perform elaborate peacock-like display. **ID** Large, long tail. Bare cobalt-blue skin on head and neck (duller in **F**); stubbly crest. Underparts rufous-brown; upperparts brown, spotted buff. Ssp *grayi* has breast more orange, upperparts greyer and spotted white. **Voc** (i) Loud "KWOW" repeated every 1.5 sec for <2 min, typically changing halfway from downslurred to upslurred; (ii) very loud "KA-WOO" repeated occasionally, usually from ~2 m diameter display ground while displaying.

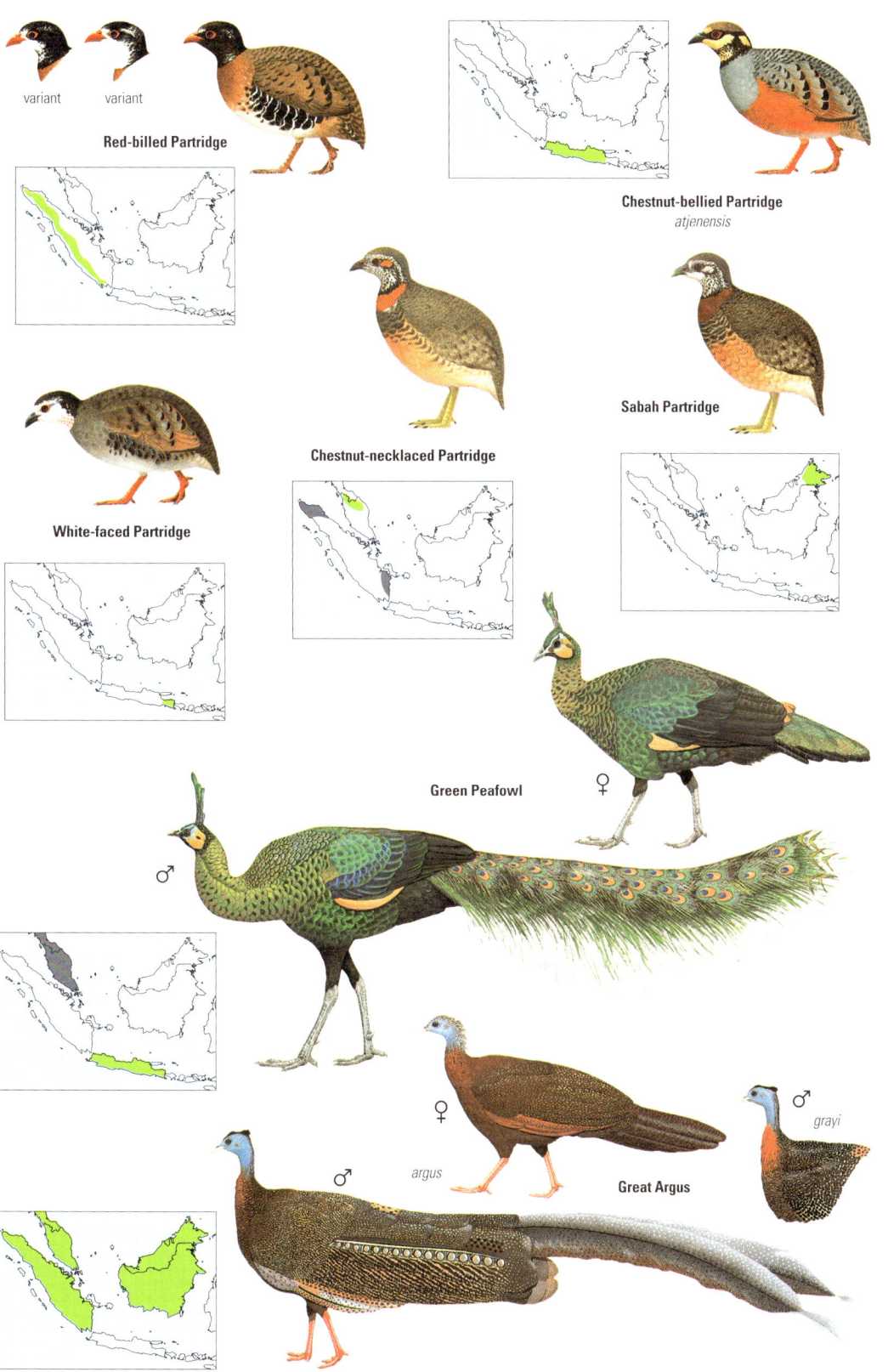

variant

variant

Red-billed Partridge

Chestnut-bellied Partridge
atjenensis

Sabah Partridge

Chestnut-necklaced Partridge

White-faced Partridge

Green Peafowl

♀

♂

♀

argus

♂

grayi

Great Argus

Sumatran Peacock Pheasant *Polyplectron chalcurum* E

L 65 cm (M), 46 cm (F). 2 ssp: *chalcurum* (S–C Sum); *scutulatum* (N Sum). Uncommon in primary submontane and montane forest, also forest edge, 800–1800 m. Terrestrial. Shy within dense undergrowth. Singly. **ID** Elegant dark rusty-brown pheasant, finely barred black apart from head and neck. Ssp *scutulatum* has more distinctly barred upperparts. **M** has long tail with metallic violet-blue panels on outermost feathers. **F** as male, but tail shorter and metallic panels smaller and less distinct. **Imm** as fem, but lacks metallic panels on tail. **Voc** Loud, harsh dry "OW-OW-ow", lasting 1.5 sec, often missing the last note. Also a single loud harsh "WAK". **AN** Bronze-tailed Peacock Pheasant.

Bornean Peacock Pheasant E
Polyplectron schleiermacheri

L 50 cm (M), 35 cm (F). Monotypic. Rare and local in primary and tall secondary forest, favouring alluvial forest, <200 m, reported to <1000 m. Recent sightings only from a handful of sites across Kalimantan and camera-trap footage from two areas in Sabah. Terrestrial and very shy, usually encountered singly. **ID M** distinctive blackish underparts becoming iridescent blue-green on sides of breast, contrasting with white throat and central breast stripe; red orbital skin; bushy crest; back, wings and tail with large blue and green ocelli. **F** duller brown; whitish throat; less distinct ocelli. **Imm** similar to fem, but smaller. **Voc** Far-carrying rising eerie "hor-hoor", lasting 1.5 sec. Calls: (i) harsh "WIRR", lasting 0.5 sec; (ii) snappy double-note "kekeck", lasting 0.4 sec.

Bloodhead *Haematortyx sanguiniceps* E

L 23–27 cm. Monotypic. A dwarf pheasant formerly thought to be a partridge. Fairly common in hill forest, 1000–2000 m, rarely 185–3000 m. Terrestrial. Singly or small groups. **ID M** head, neck, breast and undertail-coverts crimson-red; rest of body sooty-black. **F** as male, but red parts duller rufous-brown. **Imm** as fem but breast dark with some rufous spotting and darker crown. **Voc** Startling, loud "chewee-too", lasting 1 sec, repeated regularly as a series, usually in duet. **AN** Crimson-headed Partridge.

Brown Quail *Synoicus ypsilophorus*

L 17–22 cm. Aus. 10 ssp, 2 in region: *raaltenii* (Flores–Tanimbar); *pallidior* (Sumba, Sawu). Complex internal taxonomy; may consist of multiple species-level lineages. Locally common in grassland and scrub, especially near wetlands. Shy and inconspicuous. Runs or flies short distances when flushed. Usually singly or small groups (<20). **ID** Generally warm rufous-brown and grey. **M** *raaltenii* has mantle and wing-coverts rufous brown with grey feather centres, and bright tawny chestnut underparts; head paler with dark crown, eyestripe and ear-coverts; pale crown stripe. M *pallidior* similar, but with blackish crown, grey-toned underparts, blackish vermiculations on flanks and pale shaft streaks on upperparts. **F** similar to male but duller. **Imm** similar to fem but often with more spotting and barring. **Voc** Squeaky 2-note "eye-wee", lasting 0.5 sec, repeated irregularly. Contact calls include various quiet squeaks such as "uwee". **SS** See Blue-breasted Quail and buttonquails.

Blue-breasted Quail *Synoicus chinensis*

L 12–15 cm. S–E–SE Asia, Phil to Aus. ~6 ssp, 1 in region: *lineatus* (Phil, GS, LS, Sul). Locally fairly common in dry and wet grasslands, scrub, cultivation and clearings, <1200 m. Shy and inconspicuous. Runs or flies short distances when flushed. Usually singly or small groups (<10). **ID M** distinct black 'bridle' enclosing white malar patch and white crescent on throat; forehead, face, neck, breast and flanks grey-blue; belly rufous-brown; upperparts and wings brown mottled buff and black. **F** head rufous brown, whiter on throat and with darker crown, eye and malar stripes; breast and underparts buff-brown, barred darker; upperparts similar to male, sometimes with pale shaft streaks. **Imm** as fem but more heavily streaked above and below. **Voc M** calls are a diagnostic whistle "tee-yew" or "tee-tee-yew", and a quiet, snore-like "waaaa", lasting ~2 sec. Also a single-note "peeuw", lasting 0.5 sec. **SS** Fem Blue-breasted is smaller than Brown Quail, has much more obvious barring on underparts and more subdued brownish overall colouration (less bright grey-and-chestnut). See also buttonquails. When flushed, Blue-breasted lands distinctively with upright body-axis unlike Brown Quail and buttonquails. **AN** Asian Blue Quail, King Quail.

Red Junglefowl *Gallus gallus*

L 65–78 cm (M), 41–46 cm (F). S–SE Asia. 5 ssp, 2 in region: *spadiceus* (Sum, mainland SE Asia); *bankiva* (Jav–Bali); populations on Sul, LS and Bor are introduced and largely composed of individuals of domesticated origin. Fairly common in primary, secondary and disturbed forest, scrub and occasionally cultivation, up to 900 m in Sum, to 3000 m in Jav. Terrestrial. Singly or small groups. **ID** Subspecific traits are eroding through frequent interbreeding with (semi-) feral birds of captive stock. **M** (*spadiceus*) often has white ear lobe; reddish-orange neck hackles and rump plumes; dark metallic green tail, back and underparts; red comb and wattles; *bankiva* usually has less white on ear lobe; neck hackles rounded, shorter and redder. **F/Imm** brown with pale buff-yellow edging and streaking on head, neck and underparts; flight feathers and tail dark-brown mottled rufous. **Voc** Loud, raucous "errch-KRROO-doo", lasting ~1.5 sec, higher-pitched than domestic chicken with last syllable cut short, though *bankiva* more hoarse "AH-oh-oww". **SS** Often resembles domestic chickens, and widely interbreeds and intergrades with them, but truly wild populations have a constant male and fem plumage type and never exhibit colour variation of captive stock. See also Green Junglefowl.

Green Junglefowl *Gallus varius* E

L 65–75 cm (M), 42–46 cm (F). Monotypic. Fairly common in primary, secondary and degraded forest, scrub, savanna and occasionally cultivation, <2400 m. Terrestrial. Occurs singly to small groups (≤12). **ID M** head, neck, back and rump blackish fringed blue-green or yellow; wings glossy blue-black, fringed orange-red; tail glossy blue-black; underparts blackish; comb and wattles green, red, purple and yellow; comb without serrations. **F/Imm** dull brown; upperparts with pale shaft streaks; tail blackish; wings and tail edged buff giving somewhat barred appearance; throat white. **Voc** Loud, harsh "CHEW-a-AAAR", much harsher than Red Junglefowl, lasting 1 sec. Contact and alarm calls include repeated cackling "wok" and "kak". **SS** Fem separated from Red Junglefowl by buff barring to wings and tail.

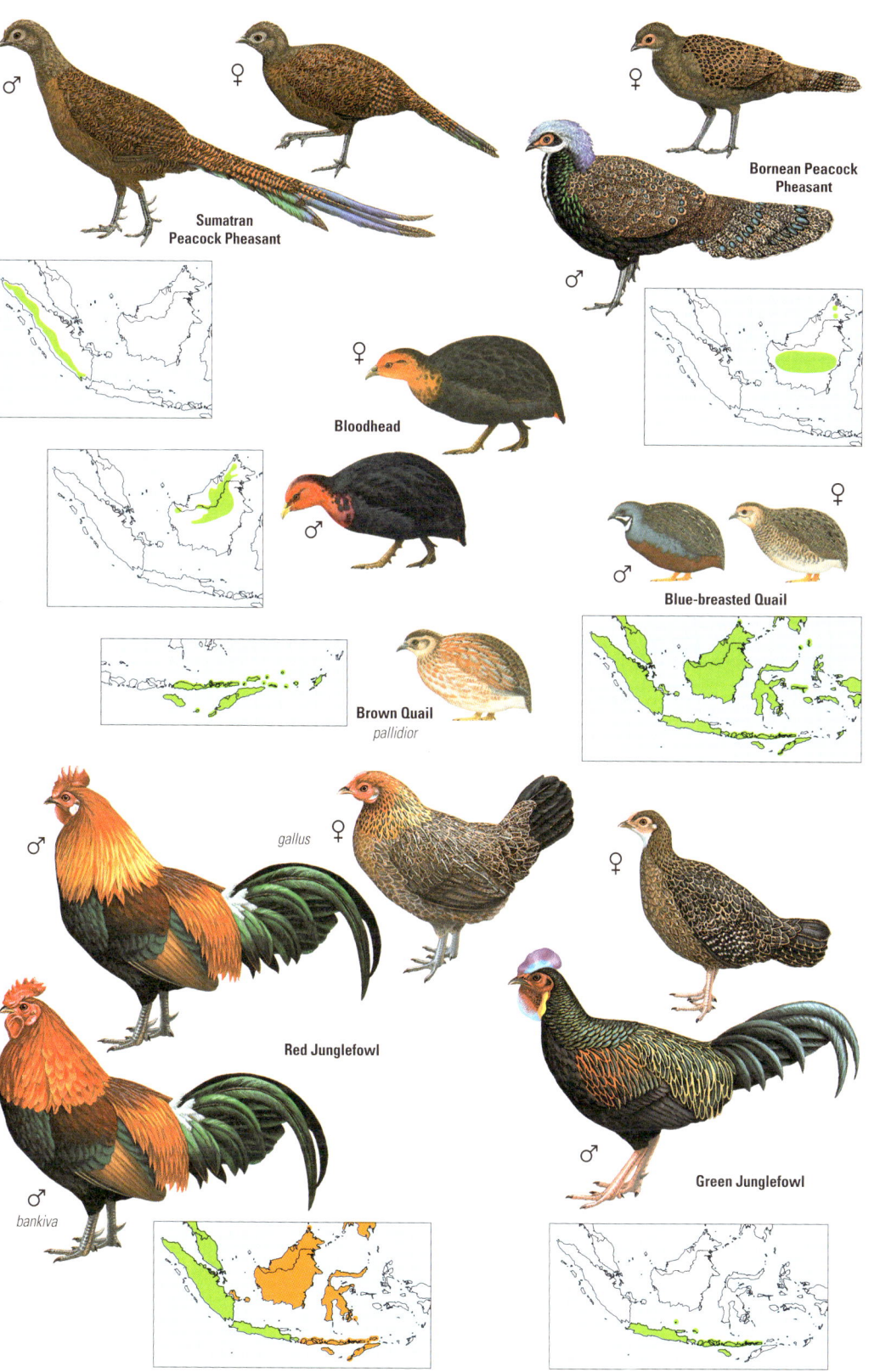

Sumatran Peacock Pheasant

Bornean Peacock Pheasant

Bloodhead

Blue-breasted Quail

Brown Quail
pallidior

Red Junglefowl
gallus
bankiva

Green Junglefowl

Salvadori's Pheasant *Lophura inornata* [E]

L 46–55 cm. 2 ssp: *inornata* (S–C Sum); *hoogerwerfi* (N Sum). Ssp *hoogerwerfi* sometimes treated as distinct species, '**Hoogerwerf's Pheasant**', based on relatively limited plumage differences. Uncommon in montane forests, 800–2200 m. Shy and terrestrial. Usually singly. **ID** Red bare facial skin with yellow post-ocular dot; whitish bill. **M** wholly blue-black with broad metallic blue fringes. **F** wholly rufous-brown with pale feather shafts and pale buff streaking on neck, breast, flanks and mantle; *hoogerwerfi* more uniform, showing less distinct pale feather shafts and no obvious streaking. **Voc** Performs a wing-whirring display, audible at close range; (i) excited, repeated "oo-cha", 2 n/s; (ii) *Polyplectron*-like grating notes "grr-grr-grr"; (iii) quiet, repeated "bub" or "keep". **SS** See Malayan Crestless Fireback.

Malayan Crestless Fireback *Lophura erythrophthalma*

L 47–50 cm (M), 42–44 cm (F). Sundaic. Monotypic. Previously considered conspecific with Bornean Crestless Fireback. Very local and scarce in low-lying, damp primary and mature secondary forest, especially peat swamp, <300 m. Shy and terrestrial, usually in pairs or small groups (<6). **ID M** almost wholly purple-black, but finely vermiculated whitish on mantle, wings and sides of breast; lower back and rump rich chestnut; tail rich cinnamon-buff; red facial skin. **F** almost wholly black with blue-green gloss on wings and body. **Imm** feathers fringed buff. **Voc** Low "tak-takrow"; also vibrating, throaty "purr"; loud "kak" in alarm. **SS** Fem Malayan Crestless from male Salvadori's Pheasant by stocky build, less glossy plumage, dark (not pale-horn) bill, lack of a yellow postocular spot, and tail usually held cocked; note elevation.

Bornean Crestless Fireback *Lophura pyronota* [E]

L 47–51 cm (M), 42–44 cm (F). Monotypic. For taxonomy see Malayan Crestless Fireback. Very local and scarce in low-lying, damp primary and mature secondary forest, especially peat swamp, <500 m. Also frequents naturally stunted heath scrub on poor soil. Shy and terrestrial, usually in pairs or small groups (<6). **ID M** upperparts, neck and breast grey, finely vermiculated; breast streaked white; underparts glossy blue-black, including lower rump, with small reddish patch on lower mantle; tail rich cinnamon-buff; red facial skin. **F** almost wholly black with blue-green gloss on wings and body. **Imm** feathers fringed buff. **Voc** Low "tak-takrow"; also vibrating, throaty "purr"; loud "kak" in alarm.

Malayan Crested Fireback *Lophura rufa*

L 65–70 cm (M), 56–57 cm (F). Sundaic. Monotypic. Often considered conspecific with Bornean Crested Fireback because of hybrid specimens (sometimes named '*macartneyi*') historically reported and collected in Lampung and Jambi (Sum) close to Bangka, where Bornean occurs. There is little modern information on hybrid populations in S Sum, but well-studied populations in S Lampung are mostly pure *L. rufa*. Uncommon in primary and mature secondary forest, <600 m. Shy and terrestrial. Usually singly or small groups (<15). **ID** Semi-erect crest on head. **M** generally blue-black, with coppery-red rump, white central tail feathers, white flank streaks; blue facial skin. **F/Imm** predominantly rufous-brown; throat whitish; pale edging to feathers on breast and flanks; blue facial skin less extensive than on male. **Voc** Wing-whirring display, audible at close range. Calls include guttural "UKHH" in alarm, and quiet "keep" or "chek" when in groups.

Bornean Crested Fireback *Lophura ignita* [E]

L 65–70 cm (M), 56–57 cm (F). 2 ssp: *ignita* (S Bor, Bangka); *nobilis* (N Bor). For taxonomy see Malayan Crested Fireback. Uncommon in primary and mature secondary forest, <1300 m. Shy and terrestrial, usually singly or small groups (<6). **ID M** as Malayan Crested Fireback but lower breast and flanks bright chestnut, and central tail feathers rufous-buff (not white). **F** as Malayan Crested Fireback but tail feathers finely vermiculated blackish, not rufous-brown. Ssp *nobilis* smaller. **Voc** As Malayan Crested Fireback. **SS** See Bulwer's Pheasant.

Bulwer's Pheasant *Lophura bulweri* [E]

L 77–80 cm (M), 55 cm (F). Monotypic. Poorly known. Scarce and local in primary and mature secondary forest, <1300 m, mainly >300 m. Appears to prefer slopes and ridges. Usually singly or pairs. Nomadic. Follows Bearded Pigs in search of food. **ID M** shining black body; white arching tail; blue facial skin (extended into a hammer shape during display). **F/Imm** chestnut-brown, finely vermiculated black; blue facial skin. **Voc** Territorial call is a harsh, penetrating "uw-EEhoo", similar in quality to Sumatran Peacock Pheasant. **SS** Fem and Imm told from Bornean Crested Fireback by plain brown underparts (feathers not edged white), lack of crest, brown (not blackish) tail, and overall duller brown plumage.

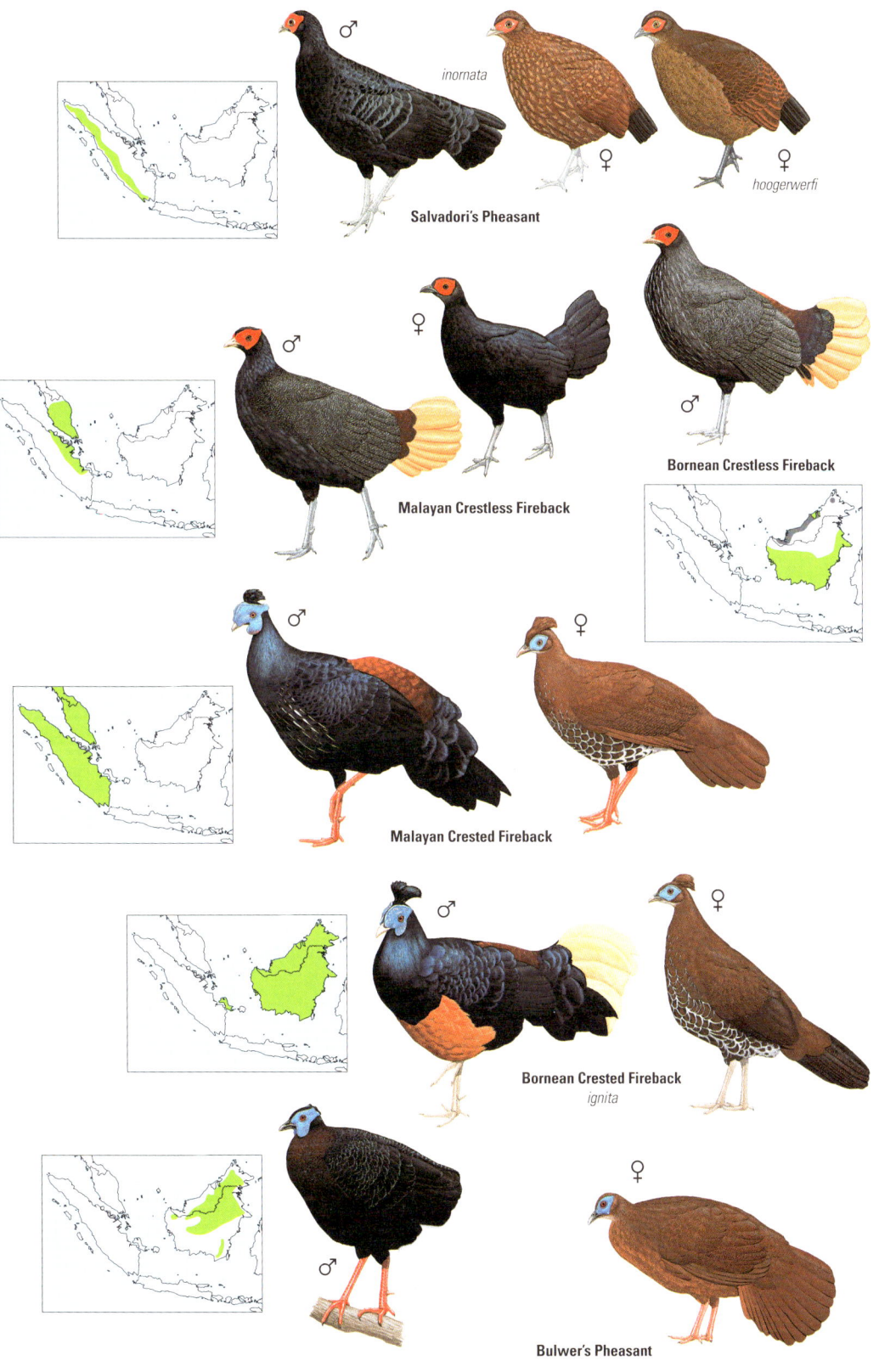

inornata

♂

♀

♀

hoogerwerfi

Salvadori's Pheasant

♂

♀

Bornean Crestless Fireback

Malayan Crestless Fireback

♂

♀

Malayan Crested Fireback

♂

♀

Bornean Crested Fireback
ignita

♂

♀

Bulwer's Pheasant

PODICIPEDIDAE
Grebes
3 species in region

Small dabbling and diving waterbirds with pointed bills, lobate feet and short tails. Inhabit a variety of wetlands, open water and coastal habitats.

Little Grebe *Tachybaptus ruficollis*

L 23–29 cm. Africa, Eurasia to NG. 9 ssp, 4 in region, but few records of migrants racially identified: *poggei* (E–SE Asia, presumably this form wintering sparsely N Sum and N Bor); *philippensis* (Phil, recent colonist to N Bor); the two ssp *tricolor* (Mol, Sul, Banggai, Sula, NG) and *vulcanorum* (Jav to Tanimbar, probably this form on Kai), along with extralimital ssp *collaris* (Melanesia), often considered separate species, '**Tricoloured Grebe**' *T. tricolor*, based on morphology. Ponds, lakes and swamps with open water. Dives to feed. Singly or small dispersed groups. **ID** Small, squat, rounded, tailless grebe. Iris usually yellow in *poggei* and *philippensis* and dark red-brown in *tricolor* and *vulcanorum*. The latter two ssp have a distinctly longer, more massive bill. **Ad br** has conspicuous yellow rictal patch; the two N migrant forms have dark-brown crown, nape and upperparts as well as rich chestnut cheeks and neck (ssp *poggei* has more blackish upper throat than *philippensis*), underparts grey-buff to white (on average lighter in *poggei* than in *philippensis*), with 'fluffy' white rear end. Ssp *tricolor* and *vulcanorum* similar but have black, not whitish belly (with throat patch larger in *vulcanorum* than in *tricolor*). **Ad non-br** has cheeks buffy-white, underparts and foreneck grey-buff to white. Some *poggei* are known to retain breeding plumage through winter. **Juv** cheeks and neck whitish, streaked black. **Voc** Rapid series of high-pitched chattering "ke-ke-ke-ke", rising to wavering trill "kiri kiri kiri kirirriri". **SS** See Australasian Grebe.

Australasian Grebe *Tachybaptus novaehollandiae*

L 23–27 cm. Aus. ~5 ssp, 2 in region: *fumosus* (Talaud, Sangihe); *novaehollandiae* (Aus, Jav–Tanimbar, NG, scattered localities across Mol). No recent records for *fumosus*, perhaps extinct. Uncommon resident and migrant on ponds, lakes and swamps with open water. Dives to feed. **ID/SS** As Little Grebe, but has pale iris and white wing stripe visible in flight. Ssp *fumosus* is smaller and longer-billed. **Ad br** as Little Grebe but shows black throat with chestnut restricted to cheeks and sides of neck only. **Ad non-br/Imm** as sympatric forms of Little Grebe (*tricolor/vulcanorum*), but less buffy on cheek. **Voc** Series of clear rapid trills, occasionally as duet, sounding shriller than Little.

Great Crested Grebe *Podiceps cristatus*   V

L 46–51 cm. Palaearctic, Africa, Aus. 3 ssp, 1 in region: *australis* (Aus). One record on Kai (Oct 1981). Ponds, lakes with open water, estuaries and coasts. **ID** Large, long-necked, tailless grebe. **Ad** has unmistakable black and orange head plumes; dark brown upperparts, whitish grey underparts. **Juv** duller, lacks head plumes, with black streaks on white face. **Voc** (i) Noisy, far-carrying "kuwaa"; (ii) rolling "craa-ahrr"; (iii) wooden "breck-breck-breck".

COLUMBIDAE
Pigeons
83 species in region (2 introduced)

A large family of small to medium-sized stocky frugivores or granivores with short bills. Typically strong fliers, often in search of fruit. Occupy a wide variety of arboreal and terrestrial habitats.

Domestic Pigeon (Rock Pigeon) *Columba livia*   I

L 33 cm. Native to Palaearctic, adjacent Africa and S Asia. 9 ssp. Domesticated form introduced worldwide. In region, domesticated for consumption and kept as pets. Escapees throughout region forming flocks and populations in villages, towns and cities, some self-sustaining, others return to owners to roost. **ID** Highly variable, but most birds resemble grey plumage of wild form, others having random patches of white, brown and black in plumage. Some birds appear unicoloured. **Voc** Soft, guttural "oo-roo-coo". **SS** Mostly white individuals may resemble Pied or Silver-tipped Imperial Pigeons, but they rarely if ever show identical black wing or tail markings. Unusual colour morphs may accidentally resemble other pigeon species, but note that Domestic Pigeon flocks usually contain variety of colour morphs.

Silvery Woodpigeon *Columba argentina*   E

L 34–38 cm. Monotypic. Formerly also found on Riau, Lingga, Anambas, Natuna and Karimata, but recently only recorded from Banyak, Simeulue, Nias, Babi and Siberut. Has undergone a catastrophic decline. Mangroves and woodland in hills and lowlands of small islands, formerly occasionally straying to mainland. Generally solitary or pairs, often sits for prolonged periods in mid-canopy. **ID** **Ad** very pale grey with black primaries and secondaries; tail grey on basal half, black distally; green iridescence on hindneck; reddish orbital skin; bill brownish at base, yellowish-green tip; legs pink (probably breeding male) to fleshy greyish. In flight shows white base to under-primaries. **Imm** sandy-buff breast and buff edging to feathers. **Voc** Undescribed. **SS** Pied Imperial Pigeon lacks reddish orbital skin, has bluish-horn bill with black tip (not dark-brown bill with pale-yellowish tip), has bluish-grey (not pink to fleshy-greyish) legs, often has a yellowish-white rather than greyish overall hue, and a rounder head; in flight, Pied Imperial shows black base to primaries on underwing (but can be difficult to see) and appears heavier and longer-necked with broader wings.

Metallic Pigeon *Columba vitiensis*

L 37–41 cm. Aus, Phil. 8 ssp, 3 in region: *metallica* (Sumba, Flores to Tanimbar); *griseogularis* (main Phil, Is off NE Bor including Mantanani, Sipadan, Maratua); *halmaheira* (Talaud, Banggai–Mol, NG, Melanesia). Ssp *metallica* sometimes considered monotypic species '**Metallic Pigeon**' based on plumage, with remaining taxa separated into '**White-throated Pigeon**' *C. vitiensis*. Here considered conspecific because all forms sound similar and *griseogularis* has intermediate plumage. Favours all types of woodland, from small islands to montane forest, <2700 m. Nomadic. Often sits for prolonged periods of time in mid-canopy. **ID** Large, heavy, all dark. Body has variable amounts of iridescent green, purplish on neck and crown; orange orbital skin; bill tipped yellow with red base. Throat and auriculars white in *halmaheira*, light greyish in *griseogularis* and dark-grey in *metallica*. **Voc** Deep, variable, far-carrying 2-note "wuO-hoo", lasting 1.5–2.5 sec, second note tailing off and inaudible at distance. **SS** See Timor Imperial Pigeon.

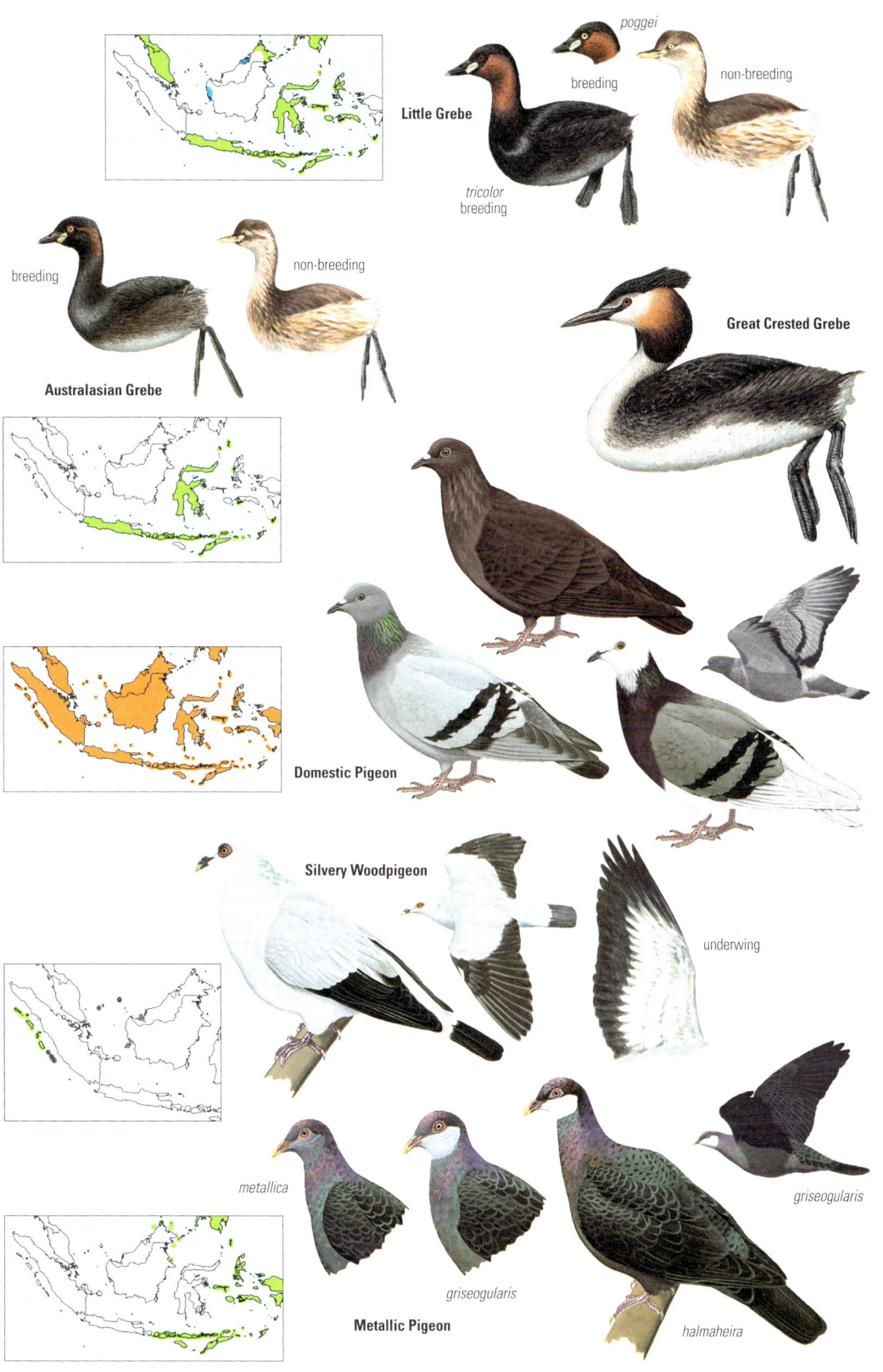

Little Grebe

poggei

breeding

non-breeding

tricolor breeding

breeding

non-breeding

Australasian Grebe

Great Crested Grebe

Domestic Pigeon

Silvery Woodpigeon

underwing

metallica

griseogularis

griseogularis

Metallic Pigeon

halmaheira

Sunda Collared Dove *Streptopelia bitorquata* **E**

L 30–33 cm. Monotypic. Formerly lumped with Philippine Collared Dove. Fairly common in open areas including cultivated and urban areas, mangroves, predominantly coastal lowlands. Usually on or near ground, flying up when disturbed. **ID** Quite rounded, short-tailed. **Ad** black hindcollar with white trim, grey crown, brown upperparts and uppertail; rest of body pinkish-grey becoming white on vent. In flight, wing feathers black. Outer tail feathers black with white terminal band creating distinct tail pattern. **Imm** duller; still showing black, unmarked hindcollar. **Voc** Soft, throaty "rra-RARRR-ru", lasting 2 sec. **SS** Slimmer Spotted Dove has scalloped upperparts and spotted hindcollar; in flight has longer tail and more white on outer tail. See also Red Collared Dove.

Philippine Collared Dove *Streptopelia dusumieri* **I** **V**

L 30–33 cm. Phil. Monotypic. See Sunda Collared Dove for taxonomy. Vagrant or escape N Bor; Kuching (Nov 1957), Sandakan (1870s), Si Amil (2 in Sep 1962). Open areas, including cultivated and urban areas, mangroves, predominantly coastal lowlands. **ID** Similar to Sunda Collared Dove but duller and paler; grey reaching from crown onto auriculars and neck; hindneck collar less distinct and lacks noticeable white trim. Less white on tips of outer tail feathers. **Voc** Soft "Wa-wu-WAA", lasting 1.5 sec. **SS** Slimmer Spotted Dove has scalloped upperparts, longer tail with more white on outer tail and spotted hindneck. See also Red Collared Dove.

Red Collared Dove *Streptopelia tranquebarica* **V**

L 20–23 cm. S–SE–E Asia, Phil. 2 ssp, 1 in region: *humilis* (SE–E Asia, Phil). Recorded Sabah (Nov 2018, Oct 2019). Open countryside, scrub, dry woodland. **ID** Compact, short-tailed. **M** head bluish-grey, rusty body with black hindcollar; bluish-grey rump and uppertail. **F** drab brown overall with black hindcollar. **Imm** rusty edges to flight feathers. **Voc** Soft, throaty "croodle-oo-croo", repeated regularly. **SS** From Sunda and Philippine Collared Doves by smaller size and thinner hindcollar (lacking Sunda's white trim). Male Red Collared has much more rusty (not earthen-brown) back than Sunda and Philippine, while female Red Collared is more uniform brown overall and lacks the other two species' contrast between grey crown and pinkish breast.

Eastern Spotted Dove *Spilopelia chinensis*

L 27–30 cm. SE–E Asia, Phil. 2 ssp, 1 in region: *tigrina* (GS, LS, SE Asia, Phil). No longer includes Western Spotted Dove *S. suratensis* from S Asia. Common in urban areas, open countryside, forest edge. Usually on or near ground, rarely flies far even when disturbed. **ID** Slim, long-tailed. Spotted hindcollar, greyish crown; buff-pink underparts and neck; scalloped brown wings and back. In flight shows white distal parts of outer rectrices, fans tail just prior to landing. **Imm** lacks hindcollar; more uniform upperparts. **Voc** Soft "wu huuu-croo[-huk]". **SS** See Sunda and Philippine Collared Doves.

Zebra Dove *Geopelia striata*

L 21 cm. SE Asia, Phil. Monotypic. Generally uncommon, rare on Jav, in open countryside, gardens, scrub and cities. Behaves like a tiny Spotted Dove but with rapid flight, usually close to or on ground. **ID M** heavily barred upperparts; face tinged-bluish-grey, orbital skin pale blue-grey. In flight shows white outer tail feathers, lined black. **F** barring extends further down underparts; less blue on head. **Imm** buffier; barring less distinct. **Voc** Soft rolling notes, starting with 4–6 rapid notes, followed by 4–10 slower notes "k'k'k'k'roor hoo hoo hoo hoo hoo hoo", lasting 1–2.5 sec, regularly repeated. **SS** Barred Dove barred across entire underparts, more conspicuous orange (not blue) orbital skin and deep chestnut rather than light-chestnut underwing-coverts. Note vocalisations.

Barred Dove *Geopelia maugeus* **E**

L 22–25 cm. Monotypic. Common in open countryside, gardens, scrub and cities. **ID** Like Zebra Dove but with yellow-orange orbital skin and more extensive barring on underparts across entire breast and belly. Sexes similar. **Imm** buffier; barring less distinct. **Voc** Disyllabic "wa-waa", lasting 0.3 sec, monotonously repeated at ~2–3 sec intervals. **SS** See Zebra Dove.

Wetar Ground Dove *Alopecoenas hoedtii* **E**

L 27 cm. Monotypic. Highly localised, little-known on Timor, with recent records from East, but very locally fairly common on Wetar in forest, particularly riverside forest, <250 m, known to 900 m. **ID M** light-blue head becoming white on breast; strongly demarcated chocolate-brown belly; rufous-brown upperparts and tail. **F** uniform rufous-brown, head and neck slightly more rufous than rest of body. **Imm** undescribed. **Voc** (i) Deep "ho-hooW", lasting 0.6 sec, repeated every 2 sec; (ii) hollow single-note "hooW", lasting 0.3 sec.

Sulawesi Ground Dove *Gallicolumba tristigmata* **E**

L 32–35 cm. 3 ssp: *tristigmata* (N–NC Sul); *bimaculata* (SW Sul); *auripectus* (SC–SE Sul). Scarce in primary forest, rarely secondary, <2100 m. Singly, pairs; primarily terrestrial, rarely perches up, even when flushed. **ID Ad** dark brown wings, mantle and tail, outer tail feathers greyish; head and breast greyish, becoming white to belly with yellowish breast spot; yellow forecrown, green rear-crown with a purple hindneck-band. Ssp *bimaculata* and *auripectus* have purple neck band divided into two patches on side of neck, latter having more golden-yellow rather than buffy-yellow breast patch. **F** slightly duller. **Imm** mainly brownish overall with rusty edges to feathers. **Voc** Deep "whoo-whoo-whoo…", monotonously repeated. **SS** Asian Emerald Dove and Stephan's Dove share similar habits and habitat but plumage very different (e.g. green wings).

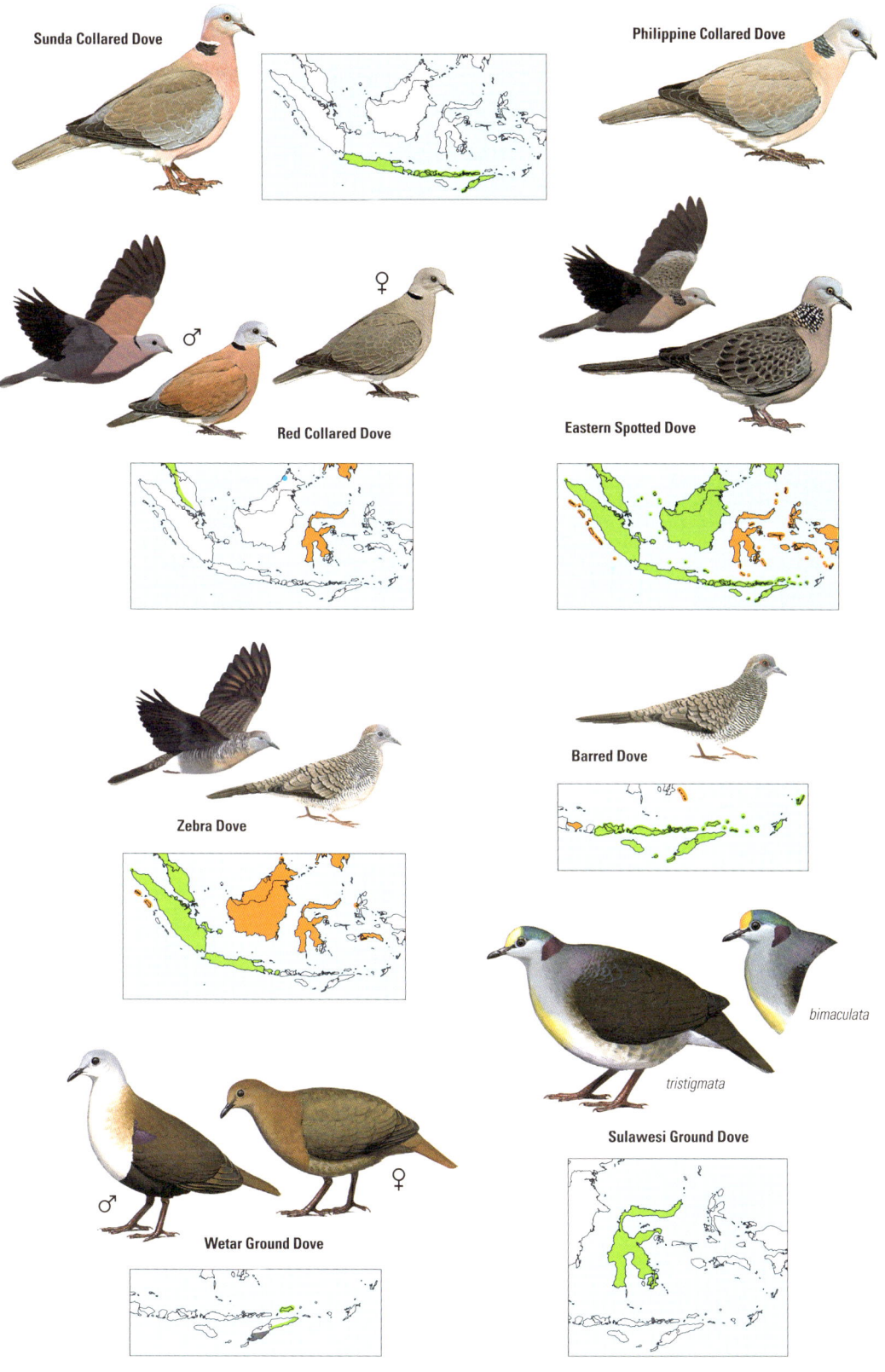

Sunda Collared Dove

Philippine Collared Dove

♂ ♀

Red Collared Dove

Eastern Spotted Dove

Zebra Dove

Barred Dove

bimaculata

tristigmata

Sulawesi Ground Dove

♂ ♀

Wetar Ground Dove

Amboina Cuckoo Dove *Macropygia amboinensis*
L 34–37 cm. NG, Melanesia, Mol. 12 ssp, 2 in region: *amboinensis* (C Mol); *keyensis* (Kai). Depending on taxonomic treatment, previously considered to include some or all of the following nine species and additional extralimital species and then called '**Brown Cuckoo Dove**' or '**Slender-billed Cuckoo Dove**' *M. amboinensis*, but morphological and vocal differences dictate a break-up into multiple species as here proposed. Fairly common in all types of woodland and forest edge. **ID M** all rufous-brown (lighter below, more chocolate brown on upperparts) with light barring on breast, scalloping on back and iridescent hindcrown. M *keyensis* has grey crown and nape and is more extensively barred down to vent. **F** lacks iridescent hindcrown and has barring on head and neck as well; *keyensis* more strongly barred on crown and hindneck but less strongly on breast. **Voc** Series of rapid, single-note "wua-wua-wua...", 4 n/s in *amboinensis* and 3 n/s in *keyensis*.

Sulawesi Cuckoo Dove *Macropygia albicapilla* ⬛E
L 34–37 cm. 4 ssp: *albicapilla* (Sul and satellites); *sanghirensis* (Sangihe, Talaud); *atrata* (Togian); *sedecima* (Sula). See Amboina Cuckoo Dove for taxonomy. Fairly common in all types of woodland and forest edge, <2000 m. **ID** Similar to nominate Amboina Cuckoo Dove but smaller, shows more white on underparts, and **M** shows grey cap with white forecrown. Ssp *atrata* larger and darker above and below; *sanghirensis* also darker above and more boldly barred on breast; *sedecima* **M** has brownish tinge to grey crown and is more cinnamon above and darker below than *albicapilla* while **F** more strongly barred above than *albicapilla*. **Voc** 2-note "puk-hooa", lasting 0.7 sec, regularly repeated. First note sometimes absent or inaudible at distance.

Sultan's Cuckoo Dove *Macropygia doreya*
L 34–37 cm. NG to N Mol. 3 ssp, 1 in region: *albiceps* (N Mol). See Amboina Cuckoo Dove for taxonomy. Fairly common in all types of woodland and forest edge. **ID** Similar to Amboina Cuckoo Dove but head, throat and breast more rusty or pink with almost no barring. **Voc** Hollow, 2- to 3-note "wu-haa" or "wu-hu-haa", lasting 0.7 sec, rapidly repeated in short series.

Timor Cuckoo Dove *Macropygia magna* ⬛E
L 38–39 cm. Monotypic. See Tanimbar and Amboina Cuckoo Doves for taxonomy. Fairly common (scarce and local W Timor) in tall monsoon and gallery forest, <1000 m. Prefers to stay in canopy, sitting for long periods. **ID** Pale rufous body, upperparts slightly darker; tail long and unbarred. **M** dark barring on upper- and underparts. **F** underparts unbarred. **Voc** Distinctive 3-note "whua-whu-whu", lasting 1.5 sec, repeated every few seconds <5 times before pausing. **SS** Eucalypt Cuckoo Dove is much smaller, unbarred and differs considerably in vocalisations.

Tanimbar Cuckoo Dove *Macropygia timorlaoensis* ⬛E
L 38–39 cm. Monotypic. Previously considered conspecific with Flores Sea and Timor Cuckoo Doves but all three sound and look different. See also Amboina Cuckoo Dove for taxonomy. Fairly common in primary and secondary forest, forest edge and plantations. **ID** Like Timor Cuckoo Dove but colder brown above, pale grey below, lacking strong rufous tones; barring on underparts and head thicker and denser, with barring on mantle; tail is broader but slightly shorter. **Voc** 2-note "whua-wooo", lasting 1.5 sec, first note short and upslurred, second longer and softer, repeated every few seconds.

Flores Sea Cuckoo Dove *Macropygia macassariensis* ⬛E
L 40–42 cm. 2 ssp: *macassariensis* (Salayar, Tanakeke); *longa* (Tanahjampea, Kalao, Kalaotoa). See Tanimbar and Amboina Cuckoo Doves for taxonomy. Fairly common in primary and secondary forest, forest edge. **ID** Greyish overall, lacking rufous tones. Pale head and underparts finely barred and contrasting with darker upperparts; greyish-brown tail with broad pale terminal band. Ssp *longa* distinctly larger. **Voc** 2-note "whuUUA-waa", lasting 3 sec, first note hoarse, upslurred, second shorter and softer.

Barusan Cuckoo Dove *Macropygia modiglianii* ⬛E
L 32–37 cm. 3 ssp: *modiglianii* (Nias); *hypopercna* (Simeulue); *elassa* (Mentawai). See Philippine and Amboina Cuckoo Doves for taxonomy. Fairly common in primary, secondary and degraded forest. **ID Ad** very similar to Parzudaki's Cuckoo Dove but slightly larger. Ssp *hypopercna* largest, with darker rump; *elassa* smaller and less reddish overall, with more brownish tail. **Imm** less bright, slightly mottled, lacking iridescence. **Voc** Series of 3-note "ho-ho-hoooo", lasting 1.1 sec, regularly repeated. First 2 notes quiet and short. **SS** On Simeulue, different-sounding Little Cuckoo Dove is smaller, narrower-tailed and generally shows black breast mottling (although can be indistinct in male).

Enggano Cuckoo Dove *Macropygia cinnamomea* ⬛E
L 30–37 cm. Monotypic. See Philippine and Amboina Cuckoo Doves for taxonomy. Common in woodland, forest edge. **ID Ad** uniform bright cinnamon plumage with scaled appearance. **Imm** undescribed. **Voc** Series of 3-note "wo-hoo-hoooo", lasting 1.2 sec, regularly repeated; first note quiet and short, second slightly longer.

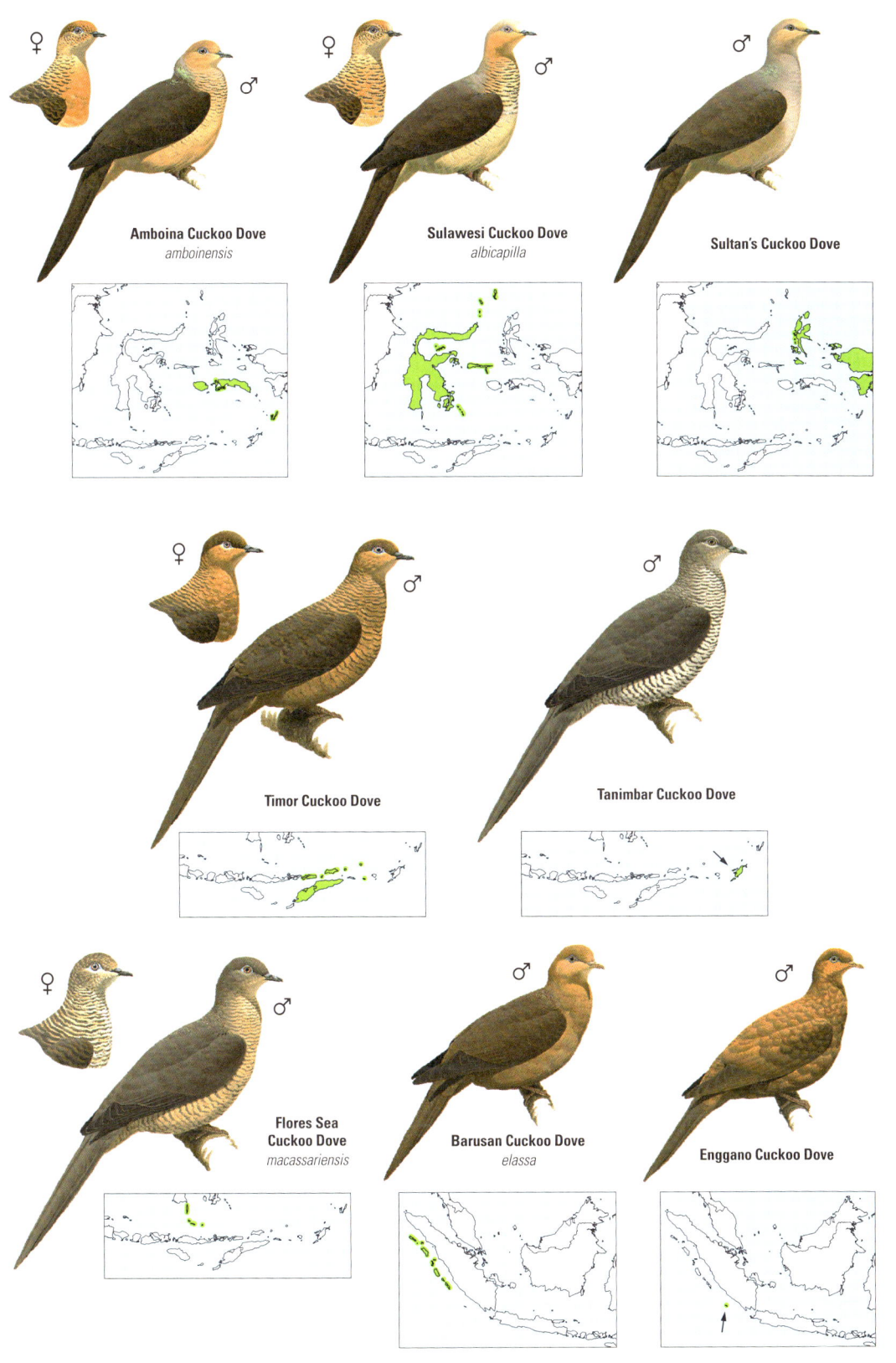

Amboina Cuckoo Dove
amboinensis

Sulawesi Cuckoo Dove
albicapilla

Sultan's Cuckoo Dove

Timor Cuckoo Dove

Tanimbar Cuckoo Dove

Flores Sea Cuckoo Dove
macassariensis

Barusan Cuckoo Dove
elassa

Enggano Cuckoo Dove

Parzudaki's Cuckoo Dove *Macropygia emiliana* ![E]

L 30–37 cm. 2 ssp: *emiliana* (Jav–Flores); *megala* (Kangean). See Philippine and Amboina Cuckoo Doves for taxonomy. Uncommon in woodland, plantations, degraded forest, <1500 m. Usually feeding low in trees and scrub. **ID** Rich purple iridescence on neck. **M** rich reddish-brown, completely lacking barring; upperparts slightly darker brown. In flight appears dark-reddish with dark underwing. **F** has hindneck and upper mantle barred dark. Ssp *megala* larger, with flight feathers warmer, less dark-brown. **Voc** Series of 2-note, hollow "ho-hoooa", lasting 0.7 sec, rapidly repeated. **SS** Parzudaki's sounds distinct and always lacks Little Cuckoo Dove's breast spotting, but silent individuals can be difficult to tell from Little Cuckoo Dove's largest, plainest and darkest ssp *orientalis* in LS: Parzudaki's is a more massive bird with a wider tail and vent and a longer bill, and male Parzudaki's probably always has a more extensive iridescent neck patch. Also see Barred Cuckoo Dove.

Philippine Cuckoo Dove *Macropygia tenuirostris*

L 37–38 cm. Phil, Taiwan, Bor. ~4 ssp, 1 in region: *borneensis* (Bor). Ssp *borneensis* previously united with Enggano, Barusan and Parzudaki's Cuckoo Doves into '**Ruddy Cuckoo Dove**' *M. emiliana* but bioacoustics and plumage suggest break-up of the latter and inclusion of *borneensis* with Philippine *tenuirostris*. See also Amboina Cuckoo Dove for taxonomy. Locally fairly common (uncommon in Sabah) in primary, secondary and degraded forest, <1400 m. **ID Ad** very similar to Parzudaki's Cuckoo Dove but slightly larger with more greenish iridescence on neck and darker chestnut crown contrasting with face. **Imm** less bright, slightly mottled, lacking iridescence. **Voc** Series of 3-note "ho-ho-woooo", lasting 1.1 sec, regularly repeated. First 2 notes barely audible at range. **SS** Little Cuckoo Dove spp *nana* is smaller, has paler cinnamon-buff (not reddish-brown) underparts, and shows strong black mottling on breast.

Little Cuckoo Dove *Macropygia ruficeps*

L 27–30 cm. SE Asia. 8 ssp, 5 in region: *ruficeps* (Jav, Bali); *simalurensis* (Simeulue); *sumatrana* (Sum); *nana* (Bor); *orientalis* (Lombok–Flores). For taxonomy, see Eucalypt Cuckoo Dove. Fairly common in hill and montane forest, also forest edge, lightly wooded cultivation, 300–2500 m (sea level on Simeulue). **ID** Small. **M** underparts paler than (and contrasting with) darker upperparts; faint black mottling on breast. **F** paler overall, lacks iridescent hindneck, breast more heavily mottled black. Ssp *orientalis* larger and darker below, largely lacks black mottling on breast; *sumatrana* and *nana* darker above with strong dark mottling on upper breast (particularly pronounced in *sumatrana*); *simalurensis* with richer chestnut wing-coverts. **Imm** uniformly mottled, lacking iridescence. **Voc** Soft monotonous, upslurred "wup-wup-wup...", 2 n/s. **SS** Barred Cuckoo Dove is larger, heavily barred overall (especially on tail), lacks bright tones. Also see Parzudaki's, Philippine and Barusan Cuckoo Doves.

Eucalypt Cuckoo Dove *Macropygia sp.* ![E]

Undescribed species usually subsumed within Little Cuckoo Dove but vocally extremely distinct. Known from Sumba, Alor and Timor; presumably also Wetar and Pantar. **ID** Like ssp *orientalis* of Little Cuckoo; plumage differences insufficiently known. **Imm** undescribed. **Voc** Single, repeated, slightly inflected (Sumba) to distinctly inflected (Timor, Alor) "whooh, whooh, whooh", 6 n/10 s, higher-pitched than *Ptilinopus* fruit doves. **SS** See Timor Cuckoo Dove. Note, Parzudaki's Cuckoo Dove does not occur within range of Eucalypt.

Barred Cuckoo Dove *Macropygia unchall*

L 37–41 cm. S–SE–E Asia. 3 ssp, 1 in region: *unchall* (Sum–Flores, MPen). Uncommon in submontane forest, occasionally plantations, 800–3000 m. **ID** Slim, elongated body. **M** head and underparts pale brown, often with indistinct barred appearance; greenish iridescent hindneck; wings and long tail chocolate brown, heavily barred. **F/Imm** heavy barring also on head and underparts. **Voc** Deep "wu-OO", every 1–2 sec. **SS** Parzudaki's Cuckoo Dove lacks barring, is reddish in overall colour and has different call. Also see Little Cuckoo Dove.

White-faced Cuckoo Dove *Turacoena manadensis* ![E]

L 36–40 cm. Monotypic. For taxonomy, see Solilongan Cuckoo Dove. Uncommon in primary, secondary and degraded forest, forest edge, <800 m. **ID Ad** moderately long, broad tail; all slaty-black body; white face; red orbital skin and some green/purple iridescence on hindneck. **Imm** duller, face suffused with grey. **Voc** Harsh "wok-wo-wo", lasting 0.7 sec, regularly repeated. **AN** Sulawesi Black Pigeon.

Solilongan Cuckoo Dove *Turacoena sulaensis* ![E]

L 36–39 cm. Monotypic. Previously lumped with White-faced Cuckoo Dove but sounds spectacularly different. Uncommon in primary, secondary and degraded forest, forest edge, <900 m. **ID Ad** as White-faced Cuckoo Dove but face dirty-white with less extensive white throat. **Imm** duller, face suffused with grey. **Voc** Long series of notes, initially an accelerated stutter then becoming louder and slower "w-w-w-w-w-w-WHoo-Whoo-Whoo-Whoo-Whoo-Whoo", lasting 2–3 sec.

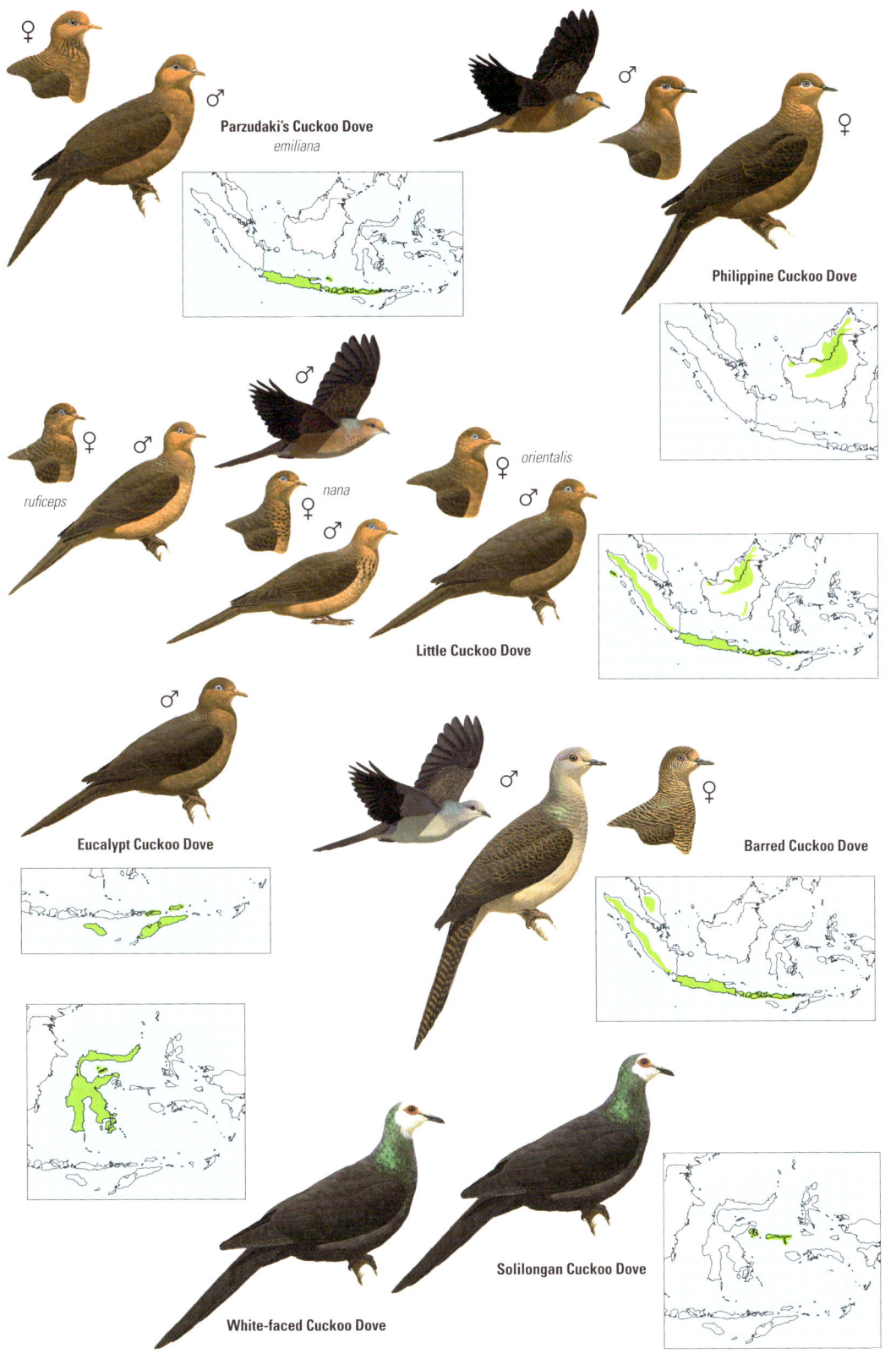

Parzudaki's Cuckoo Dove
emiliana

Philippine Cuckoo Dove

ruficeps

nana

orientalis

Little Cuckoo Dove

Eucalypt Cuckoo Dove

Barred Cuckoo Dove

Solilongan Cuckoo Dove

White-faced Cuckoo Dove

Black Cuckoo Dove *Turacoena modesta* `E`

L 39 cm. Monotypic. Uncommon on Timor, Rote, fairly common on Wetar in primary, secondary and degraded forest, forest edge, <1800 m. **ID Ad** uniform slaty-black with moderately long, broad tail; yellow orbital skin and green/purple iridescence on hindneck. **Imm** duller, lacking yellow orbital skin and iridescence. **Voc** Series of medium-pitched, upslurred notes "hoo-woo", starting slowly and accelerating rapidly until it becomes just a single note "woo", lasting 6–8 sec. Very similar to Rose-crowned Fruit Dove but slightly lower-pitched. **AN** Timor Black Pigeon.

Great Cuckoo Dove *Reinwardtoena reinwardti*

L 47–53 cm. NG to Mol. 3 ssp, 1 in region: *reinwardti* (Mol). Uncommon in middle–upper canopy of primary, secondary and gallery forest, <3300 m. **ID** Big, heavy and long-tailed. **Ad** whitish underparts; red orbital skin; chestnut upperparts and tail. **Imm** sooty brown with chestnut wash to upperparts. **Voc** Series of fast loud, clear "wook-woo" notes, lasting 0.6 sec, 3 n/2 s.

Nicobar Pigeon *Caloenas nicobarica*

L 32–35 cm. SE Asia–Aus, Phil. 2 ssp, 1 in region: *nicobarica* (most of range). Nomadic. Now rare on small, offshore islands throughout, though present on some larger islands. Found in wooded areas, mangroves, degraded habitat, <700 m. Rarely recorded along coast of larger islands. Terrestrial, singly or pairs, often flushed from the ground, flying a short distance. **ID Ad** large, all dark with white undertail-coverts and tail; head, neck, hackles and wings have a strong golden-green/blue gloss. **Imm** lacks gloss, browner, no neck hackles. Tail is dark for several years. **Voc** (i) Harsh, guttural, barking "ko-RRAU"; (ii) low reverberating "rrr-rrr-rrr..."; (iii) very deep, drawn-out "woooow", lasting 1 sec. **SS** Can be confused with scrubfowl when flushed, especially dark-tailed imm, but adult has conspicuous white tail.

Asian Emerald Dove *Chalcophaps indica*

L 23–27 cm. S–SE–E Asia, Phil, Aus. 6 ssp, 1 in region: *indica* (most of range). See Pacific Emerald Dove for taxonomy. Common in all types of woodland, including plantations, <1800 m. Terrestrial feeder, perches up to call (<3 m). **ID M** metallic green upperparts; white to light greyish crown; vinous-pink underparts and neck; black/grey rump bands. In fast, rapid flight through forest, shows prominent black/grey rump contrasting with emerald-green wings and grey head. **F** much browner, lacks white shoulder patch and has reduced white crown. **Imm** quite barred, almost lacking green on upperparts but rump bands visible. **Voc** Deep, soft "tik-whoOO", lasting 1 sec. First note barely audible at distance. **SS** See Stephan's Dove and Sulawesi Ground Dove.

Pacific Emerald Dove *Chalcophaps longirostris*

L 23–27 cm. Aus. 4 ssp, 1 in region: *timorensis* (Timor–Kai). Now separated from Asian Emerald Dove based on plumage. Common in all types of woodland, including plantations, <1800 m. **ID** As Asian Emerald Dove but completely lacks white on forehead and crown; underparts darker, slightly browner. **Voc** Deep, quite harsh "hu-whoo", lasting 1 sec. **SS** See Stephan's Dove.

Stephan's Dove *Chalcophaps stephani*

L 24–25 cm. Aus. 3 ssp, 2 in region: *stephani* (Kai, NG); *wallacei* (Sul, Sula). Uncommon in all types of woodland, <1200 m, but usually replaces Asian and Pacific Emerald Doves in forest interior. **ID M** reddish-brown body; green wings; white forecrown; buff-black rump bands; reddish-brown tail; red legs. M *wallacei* darker below, rustier rump and grey-violet gloss on head and breast. **F** slightly duller; greyish forecrown; reduced green on wing. **Imm** green-brown wings; blackish barring on body. **Voc** Series of deep, monotonous "hoo" notes rising in volume, up to 30 n/10 s. **SS** Asian and Pacific Emerald Doves sound different, have green (not reddish-brown) mantle and lesser coverts, paler body, grey-black (not buff-black) rump bands, blackish (not reddish-brown) tail and pinkish (not red legs). Male Asian Emerald Dove additionally has wholly pale crown. Also see Sulawesi Ground Dove.

Sumatran Green Pigeon *Treron oxyurus* `E`

L 30–34 cm. Monotypic. Uncommon in primary and secondary hill forest, 350–1900 m, rarely to 3000 m. **ID** Dark green mantle, paler underparts and head; bluish-green orbital skin and lores; greyish hindneck and pale orange breast patch pale orange undertail-coverts; pointed tail. **F/Imm** lacking orange breast patch and greyish hindneck; yellow-and-green undertail-coverts. **Voc** Typical whining, but well-structured musical duets "hu-wa-hu-wa-huu-waa-hu-wa...". **SS** Easily told from Wedge-tailed by bold, clown-like, glowing yellow-green spectacles, yellowish (not whitish) undertail-coverts, pointed (not wedge-shaped) tail and lack of male chestnut shoulder. **AN** Green-spectacled Green Pigeon.

Wedge-tailed Green Pigeon *Treron sphenurus*

L 30–33 cm. S–SE Asia. 5 ssp, 2 in region: *korthalsi* (Jav–Lombok); *etorques* (Sum). Uncommon in montane forest, >1400 m, generally replacing Sumatran Green Pigeon at higher elevations. **ID M** chestnut shoulder patch; yellowish-green underparts and broad orange breast patch (absent in *etorques*); bluish-grey orbital skin largely inconspicuous; orange undertail-coverts. **F** lacks chestnut shoulder patch and orange breast patch; white-and-green undertail-coverts. **Imm** duller, slightly darker. **Voc** Long and high, with rolling introduction "pruu-uah-po puu...". **SS** See Sumatran Green Pigeon.

Black Cuckoo Dove

Great Cuckoo Dove

Nicobar Pigeon

stephani

wallacei

Stephan's Dove

Asian Emerald Dove

Pacific Emerald Dove

♀

Wedge-tailed Green Pigeon
korthalsi

Sumatran Green Pigeon

Cinnamon-headed Green Pigeon *Treron fulvicollis*

L 25–27 cm. Sundaic. 4 ssp: *fulvicollis* (Sum and E satellites, MPen); *melopogenys* (Nias, probably this ssp Mentawai); *oberholseri* (Natuna); *baramensis* (Bor). Uncommon in swamp and peat-swamp forest, open tall scrub, <200 m. Regularly in flocks (<40) on open branches and snags in late afternoon, as other *Treron* species. **ID M** light chestnut upperparts, head and breast with greyish lower belly; orange undertail-coverts; broad terminal band. Ssp *oberholseri* larger and perhaps more greenish-tinged on belly; *melopogenys* reported to be smaller than nominate but perhaps indistinct; *baramensis* darker chestnut overall with greyish belly reaching lower breast. **F/Imm** superficially similar to most other *Treron* though greyish cast on mantle, crown and nape; red-based, grey-tipped bill; green-and-whitish undertail-coverts. **Voc** Typical *Treron* musical whining; similar to "wee-wo-eew-wooo-yooee…"; often several birds calling in unison or duets; relatively flat with no sudden inflections, contrasting with Thick-billed. **SS** Fem is similar to some other *Treron*. Thick-billed Green Pigeon shows eyering and all other *Treron* lack red bill base.

Little Green Pigeon *Treron olax*

L 21–22 cm. Sundaic. Monotypic. Fairly common in primary and secondary forest, visiting forest edge and parks in search of fruit, <1400 m. **ID** Small; pale iris. **M** chestnut mantle; bluish-grey hood; orange breast patch; dark tail, reddish undertail-coverts. **F** grey crown; dark green mantle; green-and-whitish undertail-coverts. **Imm** darker, less grey on crown. **Voc** Whining "weee-yoo-ee-wu-weee-ee…", lacking any sudden inflections; more whining, significantly higher-pitched than Cinnamon-headed and other *Treron* species. **SS** Fem from other *Treron* species by combination of pale iris, contrastingly grey cap and lack of orbital skin.

Pink-necked Green Pigeon *Treron vernans*

L 23–28 cm. SE Asia, Phil. Monotypic. Fairly common in coastal mangroves, parks, plantations, wooded areas, <1200 m. **ID** Slaty-grey uppertail with black subterminal and narrow ashy-grey terminal band. Undertail blackish with narrow pale-grey terminal band; chestnut undertail-coverts. **M** grey head, pinkish neck band wrapping around hindneck; orange breast patch, green mantle. **F** rather uniform green, slightly paler underparts; greyish-tinged head. **Imm** greyer above with brownish-tipped flight feathers; greenish-yellow undertail-coverts. **Voc** Typical *Treron* calls but harsher, louder than Little Green Pigeon, also nasal rattles and gargles with multiple accelerating opening notes "gr-gr-grrr-ga-ga-ga" and rasping "krrk, kraak…". **SS** The bland female is the standard confusion species in disturbed habitats across most of region; see other *Treron* species, but particularly Orange-breasted, Barusan and Flores Green Pigeons.

Orange-breasted Green Pigeon *Treron bicinctus*

L 29 cm. S–SE Asia. 4 ssp, 1 in region: *javanus* (Jav, Bali). Uncommon in coastal savanna, scrub and lightly wooded areas, <200 m. **ID** Undertail blackish with broad pale-grey terminal band. Uppertail has broad ashy-grey terminal band followed by narrower black subterminal band and slaty-grey uppertail (the two bands being interrupted by uniform slaty-grey central tail feathers); chestnut undertail-coverts **M** greyish nape, broad orange and pinkish breast patch. **F** green breast. **Imm** no grey on nape. **Voc** Very similar to Pink-necked: starting with a long-drawn siren-like whistle, followed by some gurgling notes and ending on 2, 3 or more rasping notes "ko-WRRROOOK" or "kreew". **SS** In both sexes, similar Pink-necked Green Pigeon always has narrow rather than broad pale terminal tail band (on upper and undertail), with uppertail bands rarely interrupted. Male Pink-necked has pink neck band wrapping around hindneck. Fem Pink-necked rarely shows as much grey on nuchal area.

Thick-billed Green Pigeon *Treron curvirostra*

L 24–31 cm. S-SE Asia, Phil. 2 ssp: *curvirostra* (most of range); *pegus* (Nias). For taxonomy see Barusan. Fairly common in forest including lightly wooded areas, <1500 m. **ID** Light bluish-grey crown; broad bright bluish-green orbital skin; distinctive two-toned bill whitish-yellow with red base; vent green-and-white; chestnut undertail-coverts. **M** chestnut mantle. **F** green mantle. **Imm** duller and greyer. Ssp *pegus* larger; paler underparts. **Voc** Similar to Little Green Pigeon though much lower-pitched, with short inflected notes "woo-wee-wooee-wee…"; also similar to Grey-cheeked Green Pigeon but slightly higher-pitched. **SS** For fem see Cinnamon-headed Green Pigeon.

Barusan Green Pigeon *Treron hypothapsinus* `E`

L 28–31 cm. Monotypic. Often considered conspecific with Thick-billed Green Pigeon but separated based on strong morphological and vocal differences. Outlying population on Babi Island appears admixed with Thick-billed Green. Fairly common in forest. **ID** Pale iris with no orbital skin. Bill base grey, but outlying Babi population has small red chip on bill base. Plumage like Thick-billed but paler yellowish-green underparts. **Imm** undescribed. **Voc** Typical *Treron* musical whining, but mainly comprises long, flat notes, some with a sudden mid-note upward inflection, each series lasting <9 s. **SS** Female told by combination of pale iris, lack of orbital skin and lack of red bill base (except on Babi).

Grey-cheeked Green Pigeon *Treron griseicauda* `E`

L 25–26 cm. 5 ssp: *griseicauda* (Jav, Bali); *sangirensis* (Sangihe, Talaud); *wallacei* (Sul and satellites); *pallidior* (Kalao, Tanahjampea, Kalaotoa); *vordermani* (Kangean). Fairly common in forest and lightly wooded areas, mangroves, villages, <2500 m. **ID** Bluish-grey crown and face with broad yellowish-green orbital skin; white-and-cream vent; chestnut undertail-coverts. **M** chestnut mantle. **F** green mantle. Ssp *vordermani* yellowish neck and purplish wash to breast; *wallacei* and *sangirensis* more orange on side of breast, the latter duller overall and less yellowish-green on underparts. Ssp *pallidior* larger, stronger-billed, paler. **Imm** lacks orbital skin. **Voc** More nasal, lower-pitched than Thick-billed, "arh-wee-woo-wee-wooee-uuhh…".

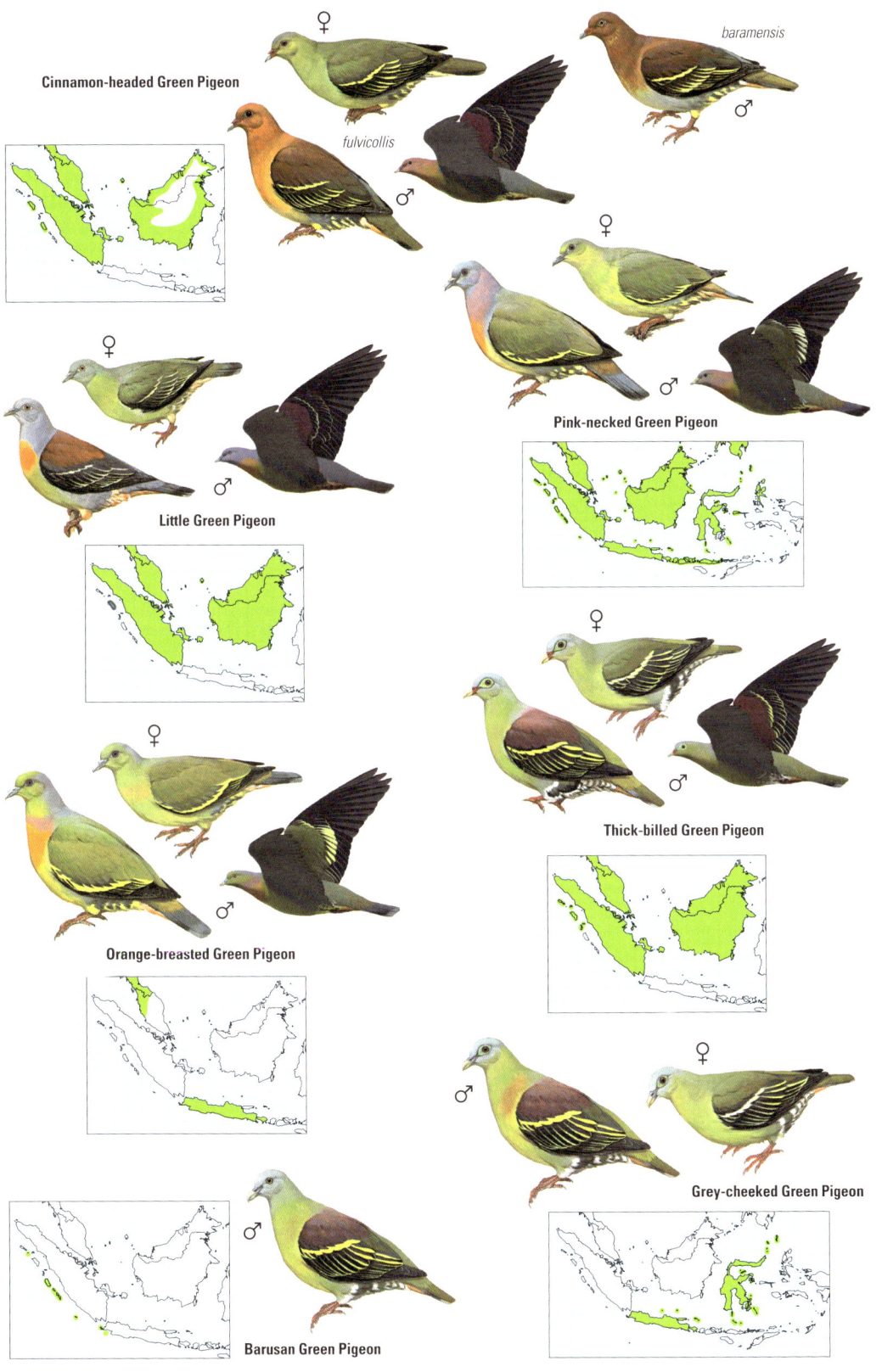

Cinnamon-headed Green Pigeon

fulvicollis

baramensis

Pink-necked Green Pigeon

Little Green Pigeon

Orange-breasted Green Pigeon

Thick-billed Green Pigeon

Grey-cheeked Green Pigeon

Barusan Green Pigeon

Large Green Pigeon *Treron capellei*

L 35–36 cm. Sundaic. Monotypic. Scarce in primary and mature secondary lowland forest, <1300 m. Usually in small groups (<10), historically in big flocks (>300). **ID** Large with massive bill; yellow feet. **M** upperparts green, slightly darker than grey-tinged head; yellow-fringed wing feathers reduced to inner wing; large orange breast patch; chestnut undertail-coverts. **F/Imm** paler, reduced breast patch; white-and-green undertail-coverts. **Voc** Harsher and deeper than other *Treron*: "hu-wu-ooa-ha". Also grunts and grumbles "hu-wa, grk...", almost hornbill-like in quality. **SS** From all other *Treron* by larger size and yellow feet (unique in region). In flight *Ducula*-like, appearing long-necked with slower wing beats.

Buru Green Pigeon *Treron aromaticus* `E`

L 28 cm. Monotypic. Previously considered part of the extralimital Pompadour Green Pigeon *T. pompadora* complex. Scarce in primary and degraded forest, tall trees in villages, <300 m. Only *Treron* on Buru. **ID M** dark chestnut mantle with bluish band across upper mantle; bluish crown and pale iris. **F** all-green mantle. **Imm** presumably similar to fem. **Voc** Typical *Treron* musical whining comprising long notes interspersed with short, higher-pitched notes.

Sumba Green Pigeon *Treron teysmannii* `E`

L 28 cm. Monotypic. Lowland forest and lightly wooded areas, <800 m. Only *Treron* on Sumba. **ID M** chestnut mantle with green shoulder patch; white-and-green undertail-coverts. **F** green mantle and whitish wing markings. **Imm** slightly duller, greyer. **Voc** Typical *Treron* sounds, "wa-yooee-waa-wee-waa...", with additional grunt-like sounds.

Flores Green Pigeon *Treron floris* `E`

L 28 cm. Monotypic. Uncommon in forest, including lightly wooded areas, coastal scrub and villages, <1000 m. **ID M** greyish-green mantle, slightly darker than rest of body; bluish-grey forecrown; green undertail-coverts feathers broadly fringed white. **F** mantle colour as rest of body. **Imm** blackish bill. **Voc** Distinct from other *Treron* but similar in structure, less whining, more guttural "uww-waa-err-waa-uwww-wa...". **SS** Fem Pink-necked lacks grey crown and has chestnut undertail-coverts and narrow (not broad) terminal band on undertail.

Timor Green Pigeon *Treron psittaceus* `E`

L 28 cm. Monotypic. Local and scarce in E Timor, likely extirpated from W Timor and few recent records from Rote and Atauro, in primary, secondary and monsoon lowland forest, <700 m. Only *Treron* on Timor. **ID M** green overall; prominent pale blue orbital skin; slight greyish-tinge to neck and mantle. **F** whitish wing markings. **Imm** slightly duller, lacks orbital skin. **Voc** Whining, nasal "uw-wha-uw-wha-grr-waa...", similar to other *Treron*. **SS** Imm Rose-crowned Fruit Dove is all-green but shows yellow-fringed feathers and is smaller in size.

Jambu Fruit Dove *Ptilinopus jambu*

L 22–28 cm. SE Asia. Monotypic. Nomadic, travelling long distances in search of fruit. Uncommon in all types of woodland including city parks and mangroves, <1800 m. **ID M** head crimson with white eyering; white underparts with pink breast patch; upperparts wholly green. **F/Imm** with dull purple suffusion to face, otherwise head to breast green, belly white. **Voc** Repeated, soft "hoo", very similar to Asian Emerald Dove but without the opening "tik" note.

Black-backed Fruit Dove *Ptilinopus cinctus* `E`

L 34 cm. 5 ssp: *cinctus* (Timor, Wetar, Romang); *albocinctus* (Bali–Flores); *everetti* (Pantar, Alor); *lettiensis* (Leti, Moa, Luang, Sermata, Teun); *ottonis* (Damar, Babar, Nila). Fairly common in forest and wooded areas, <2000 m. **ID M** yellowish wash on head and breast; black upperparts with paler terminal tail band; black breast band; yellow belly and vent. **M** *ottonis* greenish rump, less well-defined terminal tail band; *lettiensis* whiter, broader terminal tail band; *everetti* more creamy-white head and neck, fine greyish vermiculations on chest and neck; *albocinctus* lacks yellow tinge altogether, replaced with pale bluish-grey on head and neck. **F** slight speckling on nape in all races. **Imm** yellowish fringes to dark upperpart feathers and dirty-grey speckling on head, underparts not as bright. **Voc** Single deep "WHUU", repeated every ~3–5 sec. When excited, produces rapid succession of this single note.

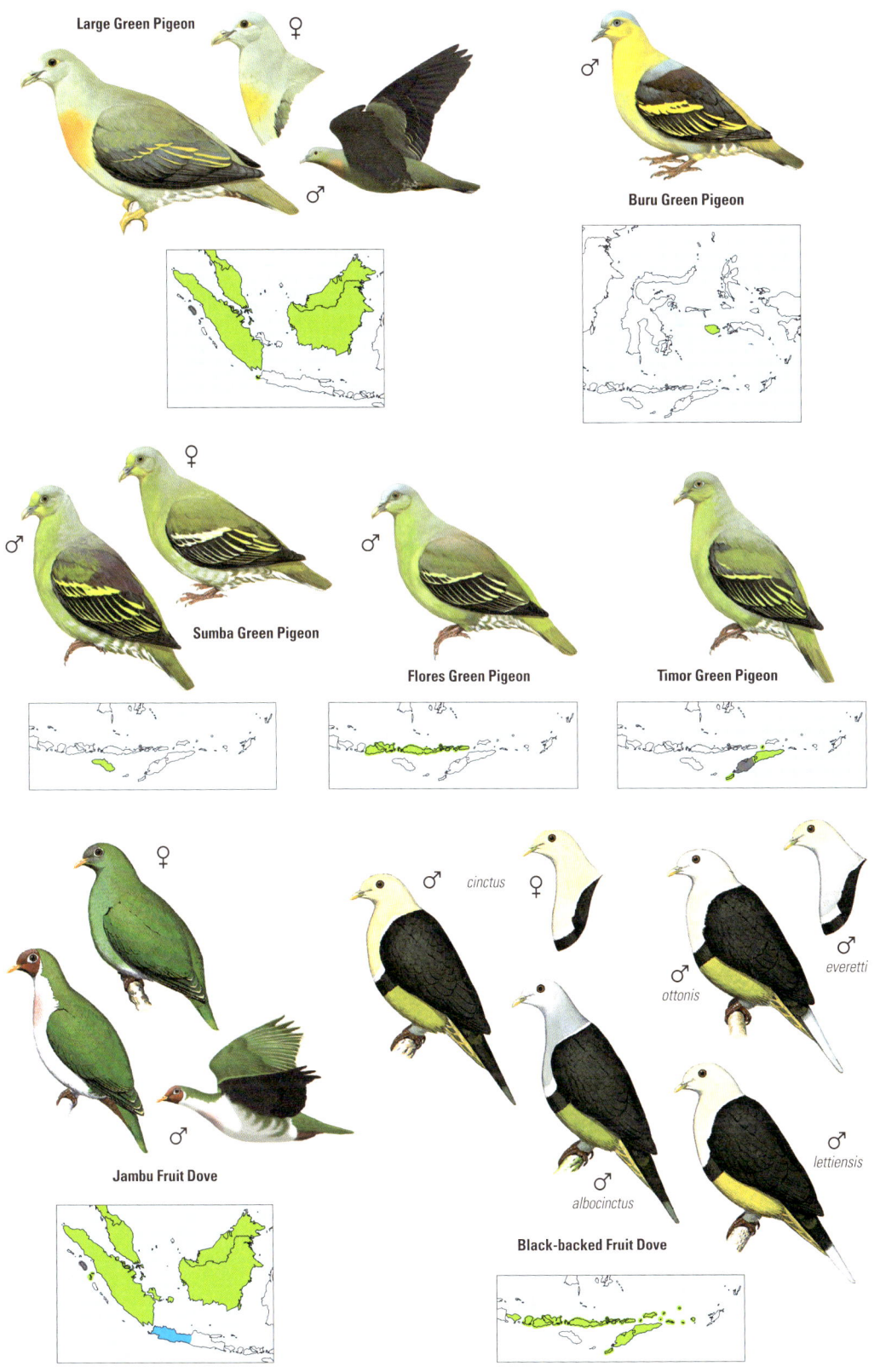

Large Green Pigeon

♀

♂

Buru Green Pigeon

♂

♀

Sumba Green Pigeon

♂

♂

Flores Green Pigeon

Timor Green Pigeon

♀

Jambu Fruit Dove

♂

♂ *cinctus* ♀

ottonis

♂ *albocinctus*

♂ *everetti*

♂ *lettiensis*

Black-backed Fruit Dove

Red-naped Fruit Dove *Ptilinopus dohertyi* E

L 35 cm. Monotypic. Uncommon in primary and secondary forest patches. **ID Ad** pinkish-hued head and breast with crimson nape patch; rest of body dark green, purple and blue. **Imm** head and breast have greenish feathers, rest of body has yellow fringes to dark feathers, paler belly. **Voc** Single, deep "wuHU", repeated every ~3 sec. When excited, can produce a rapid succession of this single note.

Pink-headed Fruit Dove *Ptilinopus porphyreus* E

L 29 cm. Monotypic. Montane forest, 1200–2300 m. **ID M** striking deep pink head; green upperparts; grey belly with black-and white breast bands. **F** duller, breast bands less clear and head a dull pink. **Imm** predominantly green with yellow fringes to most feathers. **Voc** Single, deep "WUU", repeated every ~3 sec. When excited, can produce a rapid succession of notes, slow at first, accelerating towards the end.

Red-eared Fruit Dove *Ptilinopus fischeri* E

L 35–37 cm. 3 ssp: *fischeri* (N Sul); *centralis* (C–SE Sul); ssp *meridionalis* (S Sul) sometimes divided as monotypic species but appears clinal through intermediate *centralis*. Uncommon in montane forest, 1000–3000 m. **ID Ad** head white becoming grey on breast and hindneck; red ear patch connected by black nape band; belly golden-yellow; bright green upperparts; dark iris. Ssp *centralis* dark-grey mantle and hindneck; *meridionalis* wholly dark-grey wings and mantle, lacks yellow on belly, has orange eye. **Imm** duller with less well-defined ear patch, lacking black band on hindneck. **Voc** Single, deep "WHUP", repeated every ~3–5 sec.

Oberholser's Fruit Dove *Ptilinopus epius* E

L 33–36 cm. Monotypic. Previously considered conspecific with Banggai and Sula Fruit Doves as '**Maroon-chinned Fruit Dove**' *P. subgularis*. Local and uncommon in primary and secondary lowland forest, <800 m. **ID Ad** green upperparts; grey head and underparts with maroon chin and undertail-coverts; large buff breast patch. **Imm** greener on head and breast, markings less pronounced. **Voc** Series of ~5–12 single notes "whoop-whoop-whoop...", ~3–5 n/s.

Banggai Fruit Dove *Ptilinopus subgularis* E

L 33–36 cm. Monotypic. See Oberholser's Fruit Dove for taxonomy. Fairly common in primary, secondary and degraded forest patches. **ID Ad** similar to Oberholser's Fruit Dove but reduced breast patch; maroon on chin often reaching around bill base. **Imm** greener on head and breast, markings less pronounced. **Voc** Series of ~20 single notes "whoop-whoop-whoop...", ~7–8 n/s.

Sula Fruit Dove *Ptilinopus mangoliensis* E

L 33–36 cm. Monotypic. See Oberholser's Fruit Dove for taxonomy. Uncommon in primary, secondary and degraded forest patches. **ID Ad** similar to Oberholser's but lacks breast patch, greenish nape and underparts with broad yellowish feather-tips. **Imm** undescribed. **Voc** Series of ~6–18 single notes "whoop-whoop-whoop...", delivered in quick succession, ~3 n/s.

Scarlet-breasted Fruit Dove *Ptilinopus bernsteinii* E

L 28–29 cm. 2 ssp: *bernsteinii* (Halmahera, Ternate, Bacan); *micrus* (Obi). Uncommon in primary and degraded forest. **ID M** green upperparts fading to greyish head; scarlet lower breast patch and rich buff belly. Ssp *micrus* smaller with shorter tail. **F** lacks breast patch, has greener head. **Imm** undescribed. **Voc** Deep, hollow "uw-uuWH", repeated every ~8 sec.

Wallace's Fruit Dove *Ptilinopus wallacii*

L 24–28 cm. Aru into Banda Sea. Monotypic. Fairly common in primary and degraded secondary forest, forest edge, <300 m. **ID M** grey mantle with golden-fringed feathers, grey head and breast, scarlet crown; white lower breast band, orange belly, grey-and-green undertail-coverts. **F** orange belly less intense; grey head tinged green. **Imm** whole body diffused with green fringing. **Voc** (i) Single deep, drawn-out "wuu", repeated every 3 sec; (ii) faster series of 4–8 "wuu-wuu-wuu..." at 4 n/5 s.

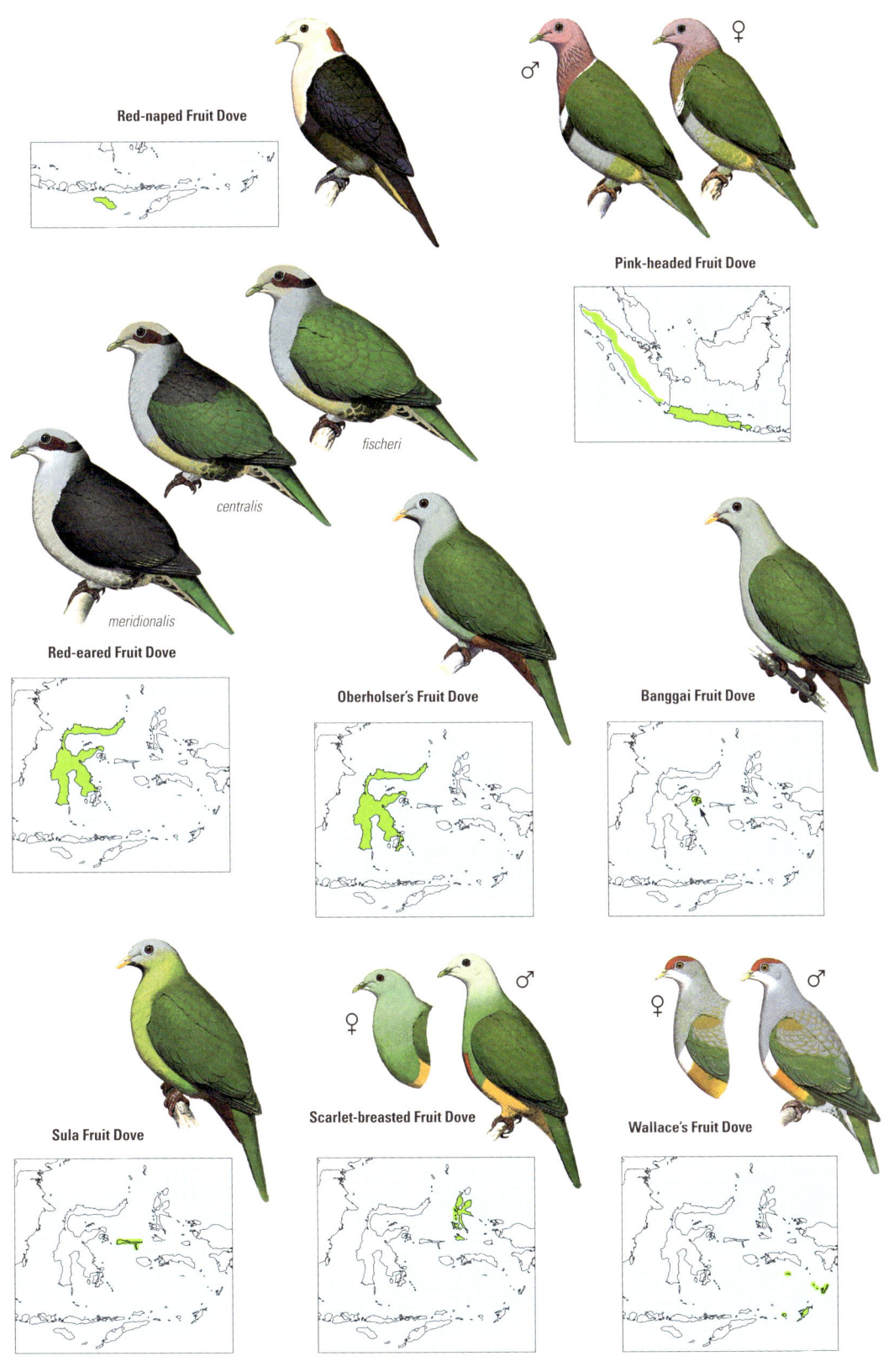

Red-naped Fruit Dove

Pink-headed Fruit Dove

♂

♀

fischeri

centralis

meridionalis

Red-eared Fruit Dove

Oberholser's Fruit Dove

Banggai Fruit Dove

Sula Fruit Dove

Scarlet-breasted Fruit Dove

♀

♂

Wallace's Fruit Dove

♀

♂

Superb Fruit Dove *Ptilinopus superbus*

L 21–24 cm. Aus. 2 ssp: *superbus* (Mol, Aus); *temminckii* (Sul, Selayar; on Sula and Banggai probably this ssp). Based on plumage, the two races sometimes divided into separate species, '**Western Superb Fruit Dove**' *P. temminckii* and '**Eastern**' *P. superbus*. Fairly common in primary and degraded secondary forest, forest edge, <1600 m. **ID M** beautifully marked: purple crown turning into reddish nape, purple speckling and band on breast, green-and-white belly and vent, upperparts green with black spotting. M *temminckii* has more purple on breast and yellow wash on white of belly. **F** all-green with whitish throat, white on vent and small black nape patch. F *temminckii* has purple crown spot and lacks black nape patch. **Voc** ~6 single notes increasing in pace "uwwh-uwwh-uwwh...", ending abruptly, repeated every ~10 sec. **SS** See fem White-bibbed and Black-naped Fruit Doves.

Rose-crowned Fruit Dove *Ptilinopus regina*

L 22–24 cm. Aus. 5 ssp, 3 in region: *flavicollis* (Flores–Alor, Sawu, Rote, Semau, W Timor); *xanthogaster* (Banda, Kai, Damar, Sermata, Babar, Teun, Nila, Tanimbar, Aru); *roseipileum* (E Timor, Wetar, Romang, Kisar, Moa, Leti). Research into boundary between different-looking *flavicollis* and *roseipileum* on Timor required to verify whether there is clinal variation or a discrete species break. Common in primary and degraded secondary forest, forest edge, <1000 m. **ID** (*flavicollis*) **M** green upperparts; greyish-green head and breast with crimson forecrown bordered yellow; orange underparts with small crimson breast patch. **F** duller. Ssp *roseipileum* paler, with more rosy-silver breast patch and forecrown (front of forecrown often white); *xanthogaster* all greyish-silver forehead and breast patch with no rose. **Imm** generally green in colouration but with yellow-fringed feathers, particularly on wings. **Voc** (i) Series of slowly accelerating disyllabic "uw-wu, uw-wu" notes becoming a rapid series of single "wu" notes, lasting ~7 sec; (ii) series similar in frequency but much slower, "uw-whu-whu-uw-whu-whu-uw-whu", lasting ~12 sec.

Blue-capped Fruit Dove *Ptilinopus monacha*   **E**

L 16–18 cm. Monotypic. Fairly common in primary and secondary forest and forest edge, <750 m. **ID M** all-green with blue forecrown bordered yellow, blue lower breast patch and yellow undertail-coverts. **F** forecrown lacks yellow border; no breast patch. **Imm** yellow fringes to flight feathers. **Voc** Slow monotonous disyllabic "who-oo" occasionally accelerating towards the end. **SS** See Black-naped Fruit Dove.

White-bibbed Fruit Dove *Ptilinopus rivoli*

L 22–26 cm. Aus. 5 ssp, 1 in region: *prasinorrhous* (Mol, W NG Is), which probably deserves treatment as monotypic species '**Small-island Fruit Dove**' morphologically distinct from taxa in NG highlands and Melanesia. Small-island specialist occurring in primary and tall secondary forest near sea level but also frequents montane forest <1300 m. **ID** Yellow gape line. **M** all-green with maroon forecrown and belly patch; broad white breast band; black blotches on mantle. **F** all-green plumage. **Imm** yellow fringes to flight feathers. **Voc** Deep single note "whuu", repeated every 2–3 sec. **SS** From fem Superb Fruit Dove by yellow gape line, lack of white on vent and throat, and lack of black nape patch. See also Black-naped Fruit Dove.

Claret-breasted Fruit Dove *Ptilinopus viridis*

L 20–21 cm. Aus. 6 ssp, 1 in region: *viridis* (C Mol). Common in primary, secondary forest, including forest edge, <1200 m. **ID M** green body with grey blotches on upperparts, blue forecrown and throat, yellow eyering, yellow undertail-coverts and large claret patch from throat to breast. **F** head pattern less distinct and claret patch reduced in size. **Imm** head pattern and claret patch reduced further; yellow fringes to flight feathers. **Voc** Series of ~10 accelerating disyllabic "wu-hoo", at 2 n/s.

Grey-headed Fruit Dove *Ptilinopus hyogastrus*   **E**

L 20–23 cm. Monotypic. Common in primary and degraded secondary forest, forest edge, <1000 m. **ID Ad** green plumage; broad grey-blue markings on mantle and wings; wholly blue-grey head; purple belly patch; light iris; yellow undertail-coverts. **Imm** undescribed. **Voc** Drawn-out "wuoooow", lasting 2.5 sec, starting softly, becoming louder.

Carunculated Fruit Dove *Ptilinopus granulifrons*   **E**

L 20–23 cm. Monotypic. Uncommon and local in primary and degraded secondary forest, forest edge, <550 m. **ID M** similar to Grey-headed Fruit Dove but yellowish edging to purple belly patch, dark iris and a set of protuberant fleshy knobs at base of bill. **F** pale iris. **Imm** undescribed. **Voc** As Grey-headed Fruit Dove.

Black-naped Fruit Dove *Ptilinopus melanospilus*

L 21–27 cm. Phil, Wallacea, Jav, Bali. 5 ssp: *melanospilus* (Sul, Togian); *bangueyensis* (islands off NE Bor, Phil); *xanthorrhous* (Talaud, Sangihe, Doi); *chrysorrhous* (Banggai, Sula, Obi); *melanauchen* (Jav–Alor, Sumba, Java Sea and Flores Sea Is). Common in primary and degraded secondary forest, forest edge, <1600 m. **ID** Light iris. **M** green body; silver-grey head with black nape and yellow chin; vent golden-yellow, undertail red. M *melanauchen* (S of nominate) and *bangueyensis* (N of nominate) are both lighter green above and more lemon-yellow on vent; *chrysorrhous* more yellowish-green above and deep orange-yellow on vent; *xanthorrhous* slightly larger than others, resembles nominate but with orange-tinged vent. **F** wholly green plumage with slight yellow eyering. **Imm** yellow fringing to flight feathers. **Voc** Deep, bouncing "wu-woo", "oouup" or "oouup-wu", repeated every 2–3 sec. **SS** Fem best told from Superb Fruit Dove by all-green plumage (no black crown/nape patch, no white on throat and vent). Similar fem White-bibbed Fruit Dove has yellow gape line. Fem Blue-capped has yellow (not green) vent and blue forecrown patch.

Sombre Pigeon *Cryptophaps poecilorrhoa*   **E**

L 46 cm. Monotypic. Uncommon in montane and hill forest, 950–2300 m. Shy and solitary, favours lower and midstorey. Does not fly above the canopy. **ID M** dark-brown upperparts with pale tail tips; head and breast dark grey with red orbital skin, brownish-grey hindneck; belly barred brown-and-buff. **F** head and breast with diffused pinkish hue, brown fringes to breast feathers. **Imm** undescribed. **Voc** Very deep, resonant "uwww", lasting 1 sec, repeated every 3–5 sec.

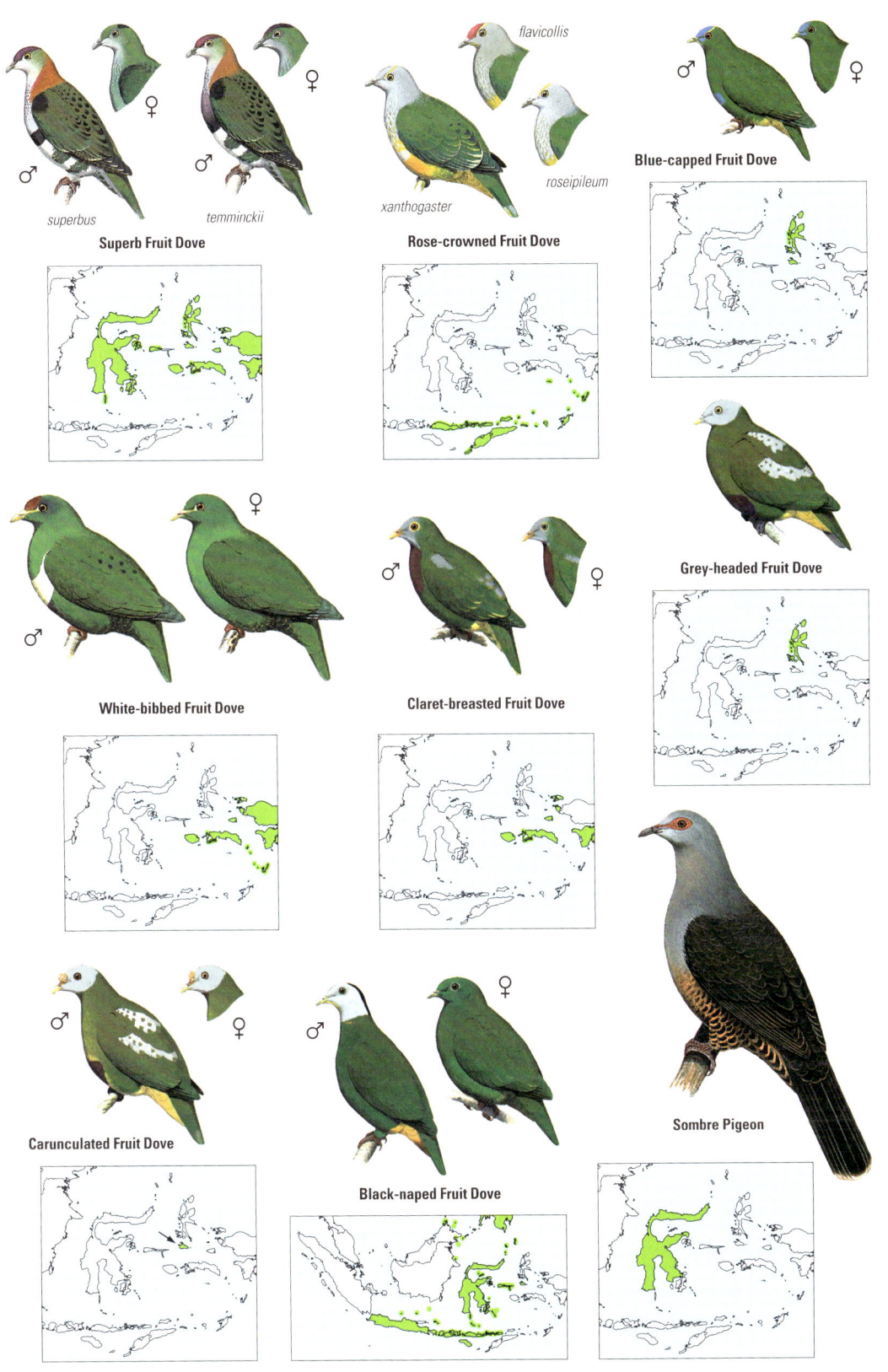

superbus　　　*temminckii*

Superb Fruit Dove

flavicollis

xanthogaster　　　*roseipileum*

Rose-crowned Fruit Dove

Blue-capped Fruit Dove

Grey-headed Fruit Dove

White-bibbed Fruit Dove

Claret-breasted Fruit Dove

Carunculated Fruit Dove

Black-naped Fruit Dove

Sombre Pigeon

Papuan Mountain Pigeon *Gymnophaps albertisii*

L 33–36 cm. NG, Melanesia, Bacan. 2 ssp, 1 in region: *exsul* (Bacan), which is disjunct and biogeographically unusual though modestly differentiated in morphology. Uncommon in montane forest, 900–1500 m. **ID Ad** upperparts, tail and head dark greenish-grey; large red orbital skin with chestnut cheek patch; breast greyish-white, belly rufous, vent grey, pale terminal tail bar. **Imm** dark brown upper breast; forehead chestnut. **Voc** Produces whirring whistle with wings, lasting 4–5 sec (NG data).

Buru Mountain Pigeon *Gymnophaps mada*　E

L 33–39 cm. Monotypic. No longer considered conspecific with Seram Mountain Pigeon based on plumage. Uncommon in montane and hill forest, 700–2100 m, occasionally to coastal lowlands. Singly, pairs, congregates at fruiting trees. **ID M** silky grey-green upperparts, grey hindneck and crown; red orbital skin and orange bill; white throat and breast grade into vinaceous-pink belly. **F** darker orbital skin. **Imm** duskier breast. **Voc** A deep, gruff "wuooo", lasting 1.5 sec, is presumed to be this species, but requires confirmation.

Seram Mountain Pigeon *Gymnophaps stalkeri*　E

L 33–39 cm. Monotypic. See Buru Mountain Pigeon for taxonomy. Uncommon in montane and hill forest, 1200–2300 m but occasionally down to 300 m. Singly, pairs, congregates at fruiting trees. **ID Ad** similar to Buru Mountain Pigeon but whole underparts to chin are deep buffish-vinaceous. **Imm** darker overall. **Voc** Undescribed.

White-bellied Imperial Pigeon *Ducula forsteni*　E

L 42–52 cm. Monotypic. Fairly common in primary and secondary hill forest, most common 800–1600 m, recorded sea level–2200 m. **ID M** emerald to golden-green including neck band, tail and nape; pale-grey head, red orbital skin; white belly, chestnut vent and broad grey band across tail. **F** darker head and belly. **Imm** undescribed. **Voc** Very deep, resonant, far-carrying "oo-uumm", lasting 1 sec, repeated every 5 sec.

Grey-headed Imperial Pigeon *Ducula radiata*　E

L 36–39 cm. Monotypic. Uncommon in primary and secondary montane forest, 1600–2200 m, rarely 100–2400 m. **ID M** grey head and underparts with rusty flanks and vent; dark purple hindneck fading to bronze mantle and green wings and tail with grey subterminal tail band. **F** hindneck bronze and head and underparts slightly darker grey. **Imm** brownish-grey head; underparts and hindneck. **Voc** Undescribed, possibly soft grumbling.

Moluccan Imperial Pigeon *Ducula perspicillata*

L 42 cm. Kofiau (Papua), Mol. Monotypic. Previously united with different-looking Seram Imperial Pigeon into '**Spectacled Imperial Pigeon**' *D. perspicillata*. Fairly common in primary and secondary forest and edge, <1400 m. **ID Ad** mid-grey underparts; distinct broad white eyering; green upperparts including hindneck with deep blue outerwing and tail. **Imm** duller than Ad. **Voc** (i) Single, very deep "wooHOOoo", lasting 1.5 sec; (ii) 5–20 deep, descending "UH-uh-uh-uh-uh...", 3 n/s.

Seram Imperial Pigeon *Ducula neglecta*　E

L 42 cm. Monotypic. See Moluccan Imperial Pigeon for taxonomy. Primary and secondary forest and edge, <1100 m. **ID Ad** differs from Moluccan Imperial Pigeon by much paler grey head and hindneck, indistinct white eyering, brighter green upperparts. **Imm** duller than Ad. **Voc** (i) Deep growling "grwhoOWW", lasting ~1 sec, repeated every 3–8 sec; (ii) 5–15 deep, descending "UH-uh-uh-uh-uh...", 2 n/s.

Papuan Mountain Pigeon

Buru Mountain Pigeon

Seram Mountain Pigeon

White-bellied Imperial Pigeon

Grey-headed Imperial Pigeon

Moluccan Imperial Pigeon

Seram Imperial Pigeon

Cinnamon-bellied Imperial Pigeon *Ducula basilica* E

L 36–42 cm. 2 ssp: *basilica* (N Mol); ssp *obiensis* (Obi) sometimes separated as monotypic species based on minor differences in plumage hue. Fairly common in primary and secondary forest, edge and wooded cultivation, <1100 m. **ID M** pinkish head and breast, cinnamon belly; greyish hindneck; upperparts and tail green with broad light-grey terminal tail band. M *obiensis* has rusty patch on darker grey hindneck; deeper cinnamon belly. **F** slightly duller in both races. **Imm** undescribed. **Voc** Deep, coarse, growling "oo-wowwwwh", lasting 3 sec.

Elegant Imperial Pigeon *Ducula concinna*

L 43 cm. Aru to Wallacea. Monotypic. Small-island specialist, fairly common in primary and secondary forest and edge, plantations, <850 m. **ID Ad** silky-grey head (with small white frontal area) and underparts, dark green upperparts, dark blue outerwing and tail; deep chestnut vent; prominent yellow iris. **Imm** duller than Ad. **Voc** (i) Very deep, drawn-out, growling "ooowwwhhh", repeated every 3–5 sec; (ii) contact calls include a rough, nasal "grrk" and "huk". **SS** See Grey, Pink-headed and Green Imperial Pigeons. **AN** Blue-tailed Imperial Pigeon, Yellow-eyed Imperial Pigeon.

Grey Imperial Pigeon *Ducula pickeringii*

L 40 cm. Phil to Bor satellites and Talaud. Monotypic. Small-island specialist. Uncommon in primary, secondary and coastal monsoon forest. **ID Ad** head, neck and underparts pale grey with subtle pinkish hue; darker bronzy-grey upperparts and uppertail; pale greyish-pink vent, light undertail. Some variants can be deeper salmon-pink on head and underparts. **Imm** slightly darker underparts. **Voc** Deep growling disyllabic "o-oow", sometimes dropping the first note, repeated every 2–5 sec. **SS** Elegant Imperial has yellow (not dark) iris. Green Imperial *intermedia* on Talaud has buff-hued nape patch contrasting with more greyish head and neck (never shown by Grey Imperial). Both Green and Elegant Imperial Pigeons are much more vivid green or blue on upperparts, with darker vent than Grey.

Spice Imperial Pigeon *Ducula myristicivora* V

L 41–43 cm. W NG Is. Monotypic. Previously included extralimital Geelvink Imperial Pigeon *D. geelvinkiana*. Single record, Widi (1883). Occurs in variety of wooded areas on small islands. **ID** Iris brown. **Ad** pale grey head and underparts (belly with pink hue); green upperparts; dark blue tail and chestnut vent; black enlarged knob-like cere. **Imm** lacks enlarged cere; vent paler. **Voc** High-pitched, upslurred "crrruooo" or "urwoow".

Green Imperial Pigeon *Ducula aenea*

L 40–47 cm. S–SE–E Asia, Phil. ~13 ssp, 6 in region: *polia* (GS, Lombok–Alor, MPen); *consobrina* (Mentawai, Nias, Babi, Lasia, Simeulue); *palawanensis* (Banggi, Palawan); *intermedia* (Talaud); based on strong plumage differences, *oenothorax* (Enggano) and *paulina* (Sangihe, Sul, Togian, Banggai, Sula) each sometimes divided into monotypic species, '**Enggano Imperial Pigeon**' and '**Paulina's Imperial Pigeon**', respectively. Common in variety of forest types including primary and degraded forest patches, mangroves, <1000 m. **ID Ad** head, neck, breast and belly pale grey pink; upperparts iridescent green; vent chestnut; undertail brown; iris dark red; bill blue-grey; feet red. Ssp *palawanensis* has darker, bluer uppertail; *consobrina* lacks pink hue on head, has darker chestnut vent and more sharply delineated border between neck and back;

oenothorax has light-grey head and neck, darker pink-vinaceous breast and greenish-bronzy vent; *intermedia* blue-and-green back (with little iridescence), dark mahogany vent, black undertail, buff hue to nape; *paulina* shows prominent rusty nape and richer iridescent upperparts. **Imm** less metallic upperparts. **Voc** Several calls include: (i) very deep, repeated "wah-whhoo", "wah-wah-wah", "wah-wahroo" or "wuu-WHUU"; (ii) purring "krrhoo". **SS** On Talaud, *intermedia* is told from the larger Elegant Imperial Pigeon by its dark-red (not yellow) eye, more pinkish (less silver-grey) underparts, greyer underwings, green (not blue) uppertail, and a lack of the white frontal area of Elegant Imperial Pigeon. Also see Mountain, Dark-backed, Pink-headed and Grey Imperial Pigeons.

Pink-headed Imperial Pigeon *Ducula rosacea* E

L 39–44 cm. Monotypic. Fairly common in primary and secondary forest and edge, plantations. Small-island specialist, also found in coastal forest on some larger islands. **ID Ad** salmon-pink head and underparts with greyish cast to nape and collar; upperparts greyish-green, blackish-green upper and undertail; red to brown iris with pale greyish orbital skin; chestnut vent. **Imm** with buffish fringes to feathers. **Voc** (i) Series of 5 very deep, far-carrying "WHOoo-whoo-whoo-whoo-whoo", repeated at irregular periods; (ii) very deep, far-carrying "whoo". **SS** Similar to *polia* Green Imperial Pigeon but darker tail, less vivid green upperparts, more of a greyish cast to collar contrasting with pinkish-hued head. From Elegant Imperial Pigeon by dark iris, less vivid green upperparts and pink hue to head and underparts.

Mountain Imperial Pigeon *Ducula badia*

L 43–51 cm. S–SE Asia. 3 ssp, 1 in region: *badia* (GS, MPen). Species no longer includes Nilgiri Imperial Pigeon *D. cuprea* from peninsular India. Fairly common, though rare on Jav, in foothills and montane forest <2500 m, occasionally visits coastal lowlands. **ID Ad** pale iris; head and underparts mid-grey, buffish belly and broad red orbital ring; maroon brown upperparts becoming greyer towards tail; pale grey terminal tail band; bill red with pale tip. In flight shows dark underwing. **Imm** duller, rusty-brown underparts. **Voc** Very deep, far-carrying "uh-WROO-WROO" or "uh-WROO", repeated after long intervals. **SS** See Dark-backed Imperial Pigeon. In flight from Green Imperial Pigeon by pale terminal tail band.

Dark-backed Imperial Pigeon *Ducula lacernulata* E

L 39–45 cm. 3 ssp: *lacernulata* (W Jav); *williami* (E Jav, Bali); *sasakensis* (Lombok–Flores). All three sometimes divided into separate species based on peculiar geographic leapfrog pattern in head colouration, but more research required. Uncommon, but locally fairly common, in forested foothills and mountains, 500–2500 m, rarely to lowlands. Nomadic, often found in mid-canopy, not shy. **ID Ad** dark-brown upperparts and tail with pale terminal band; pinkish-grey underparts to throat with chestnut wash to vent; bluish tinge to head and hindneck; blackish bill; dark iris. Ssp *williami* lacks bluish tinge to head; *sasakensis* only shows bluish tinge on crown and hindneck. **Imm** undescribed. **Voc** (i) Ssp *lacernulata* and *williami* produce very loud, far-carrying "uw-UW-UW" or "uw-UW", repeated every few sec; (ii) *sasakensis* produces a deeper, even "uw-uw", and "uw-UW-UW-UW", much lower in frequency. **SS** From Mountain Imperial Pigeon by all-dark bill, dark iris, lack of maroon tones to upperparts, contrast between bluish-grey head and pinkish-grey throat and breast, and contrast between chestnut vent and pinkish-grey belly. In flight from Green Imperial Pigeon by pale terminal band.

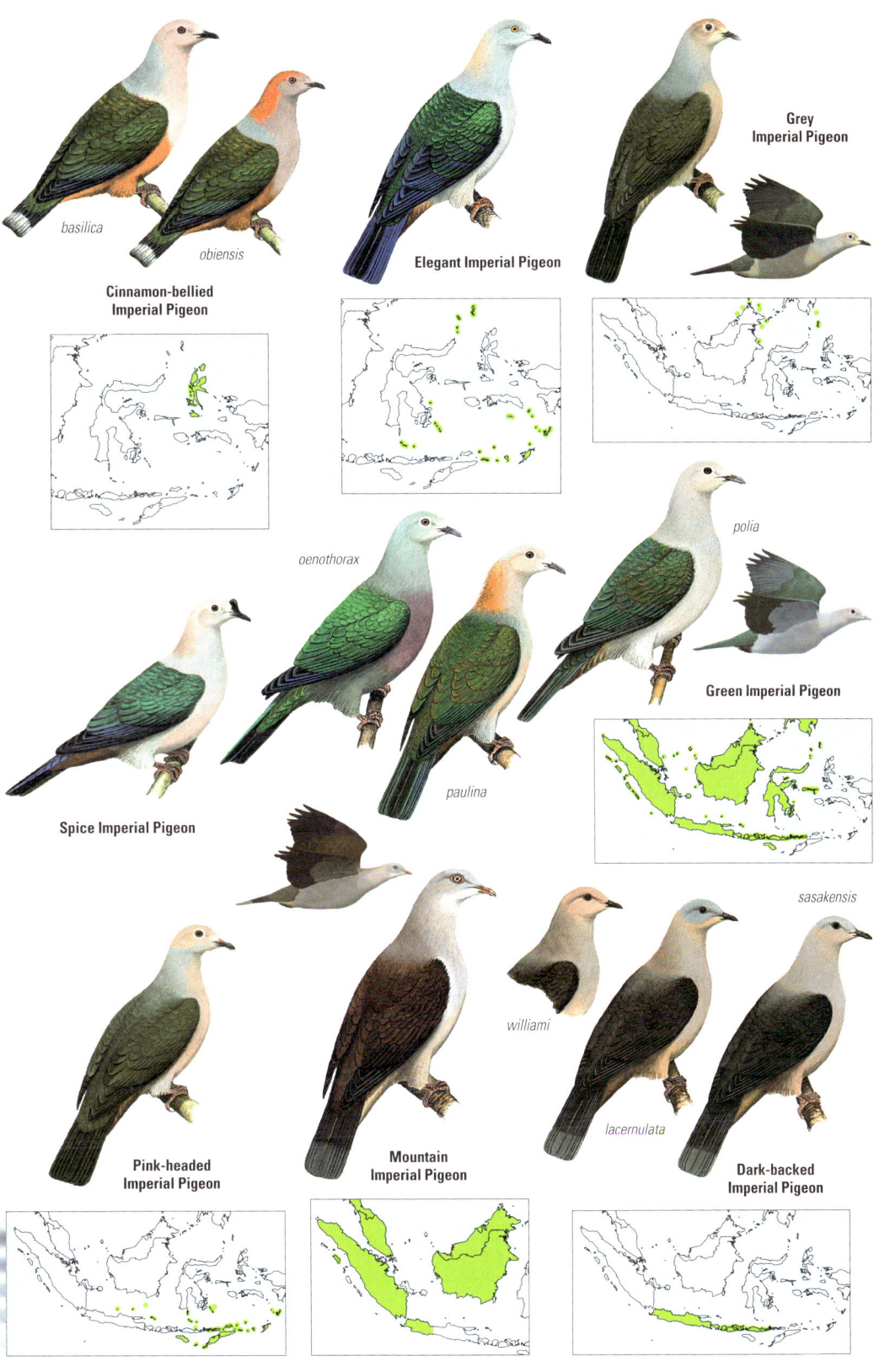

basilica

obiensis

Cinnamon-bellied Imperial Pigeon

Elegant Imperial Pigeon

Grey Imperial Pigeon

oenothorax

polia

paulina

Green Imperial Pigeon

Spice Imperial Pigeon

sasakensis

williami

lacernulata

Pink-headed Imperial Pigeon

Mountain Imperial Pigeon

Dark-backed Imperial Pigeon

Timor Imperial Pigeon *Ducula cineracea* **E**

L 39–45 cm. 2 ssp: *cineracea* (Timor); *schistacea* (Wetar). Fairly common in E Timor, scarce in W Timor in montane forest, >800 m. On Wetar fairly common, including lowlands. Singly or pairs, not known to flock. Rarely perches conspicuously, favouring canopy interior. **ID** Rather sombre-looking. **Ad** yellow iris and all blackish bill. Dark-grey to dark-brown upperparts; dark-greyish hindneck and head; purplish-grey underparts; cream vent. Ssp *schistacea* darker underparts, hindneck, head and throat. **Imm** shows rufous-buff fringes to tail and flight feathers. **Voc** Series of 15–25 rapidly-uttered, quivering "hu-hu-hu...", lasting 1–2.5 sec, 15 n/10 s, at constant pitch. **SS** Metallic Pigeon is darker overall, glossed green and purple, has two-toned, yellow-tipped bill and dark eye. Note vocalisations.

Pied Imperial Pigeon *Ducula bicolor*

L 35–42 cm. SE Asia, Phil to Aus. Monotypic. A distinct form '*melanura*' overlaps with standard birds in Mol and has been treated as distinct species but probably only constitutes colour morph. Small-island specialist, common, often abundant, favouring mangroves, coconut plantations and coastal forest. Rarely strays to mainland of larger islands except Seram and Sul, where can occur <1300 m. **ID Ad** distinctive pied appearance. White plumage can be tinged yellowish; black restricted to outer wing and tail. Reputed '*melanura*' has whole tail black (proximal portion of outer tail feathers white in standard birds) and can show black on vent. **Imm** white areas diffused grey, can show buffish fringes to feathers. **Voc** Various deep, hollow calls, both single notes "uwH", and disyllabic calls "uw-uwh", often repeated after short intervals. **SS** See Silvery Woodpigeon and Silver-tipped Imperial Pigeon.

Silver-tipped Imperial Pigeon *Ducula luctuosa* **E**

L 37–48 cm. Monotypic. Locally fairly common in coastal forest, forest edge and occasionally plantations and mangroves, <500 m. Flocks, especially around fruiting trees. **ID/SS Ad** similar to Pied Imperial Pigeon, but wing feathers silvery-grey with black edges (not all-black); Pied Imperial has white tertials whereas Silver-tipped has tertial pattern identical to other wing feathers; Silver-tipped has black markings on vent (rare in Pied). **Imm** greyer, with buffish fringes. **Voc** Deep, far-carrying, booming "HWOO", lasting 0.7 sec, sometimes up to 15 notes in quick succession, gradually tailing off.

CUCULIDAE
Cuckoos
50 species in region

Small to medium-sized, typically with long tails and short bills. Inhabit a variety of forest and open habitats. Typically arboreal in habit, but some species predominantly terrestrial. Many species are brood parasites of other species.

Rhinortha *Rhinortha chlorophaea*

L 32 cm. Sundaic. Monotypic. Formerly considered a malkoha, but now known not to be closely related. Fairly common in dense mid-storey vegetation in forest, second growth, plantations and heath scrub, <1000 m **ID M** all-rufous (lighter on breast) except for black grey-barred tail (with white tip) and greyish vent and belly. **F** rufous belly, upperparts and tail (with black subterminal and white terminal band); grey breast, head and upper back. **Imm** narrower white tail tip, **F** is buff on throat. **Voc** (i) Series of 3–7 slow cat-like descending notes, not unlike a trogon, with first 1–2 notes often longer and more emphatic than following ones, this call is sometimes initiated by 1–2 lower-pitched notes; (ii) rarer calls include single "meows", often similar in quality to elements of main call; (iii) rising, fast "hoo-chit-chit-kreee". **AN** Raffles's Malkoha.

Red-billed Malkoha *Phaenicophaeus javanicus*

L 42 cm. Sundaic. 3 ssp: *javanicus* (Jav); *pallidus* (Sum, Bor, MPen); *natunensis* (Natuna). Despite similar appearance, *javanicus* from Java has quite distinct mtDNA. Uncommon in high trees in drier forest, edge, woodland and plantations, <1300 m. **ID Ad** grey above with bluish-green gloss on back and wings; white tail tips; rufous throat and underparts except for wide grey breast bar; blue eyering, red bill. Ssp *pallidus* has lighter grey breast band; *natunensis* has least well-defined breast band. **Imm** has narrower white tail tip. **Voc** (i) Rapidly quavering "queh-gueh-heh-heh-heh-heh-heh-heh..."; (ii) unobtrusive "took"; (iii) "ga-gar" given at 1–3 sec interval; (iv) down-slurred, low-pitched whistle.

Chestnut-bellied Malkoha *Phaenicophaeus sumatranus*

L 40–41 cm. Sundaic. Monotypic. Local in overgrown plantations, forest, peat swamps and mangroves, <1200 m. **ID Ad** blue-green upperparts and tail, the latter tipped white; head and breast dark-grey; belly and vent rufous; light-green bill, red orbital skin. **Imm** smaller white tail tips. **Voc** (i) Thin high-pitched "mew"; (ii) rapid series "kokokokokok...", like a knocking sound. **SS** Chestnut (not black) belly, more orange orbital skin and smaller white tail tips distinguish this species from Black-bellied and the larger Green-billed Malkohas, but all three traits can be difficult to judge in the field. With good views, nostril shape is diagnostic: elongated and parallel to facial skin in Chestnut-bellied, elongated but vertical in Black-bellied, and dot-shaped in Green-billed.

Black-bellied Malkoha *Phaenicophaeus diardi*

L 38 cm. Sundaic. 2 ssp: *diardi* (Sum, MPen); *borneensis* (Bor). Locally fairly common in tangles in forest, bamboo and swamp forest, <1200 m, rarely 1700 m. **ID Ad** blue-green upperparts, white tail tip, otherwise all dark-grey becoming black on belly; red orbital skin around eye is delimited by black line, bill light-green. Ssp *borneensis* smaller, greener below. **Imm** less green and more sooty on wings, and less white on tail tips. **Voc** (i) "pwew-pwew"; (ii) gruff "gwaup" or "gwagaup"; (iii) loud "pauk". **SS** On Sum, Green-billed is larger, has lighter-grey head and pale (not black) outline of red orbital skin. Green-billed has dot-shaped nostril while Black-bellied has elongated vertical nostril. Also see Chestnut-bellied Malkoha.

Green-billed Malkoha *Phaenicophaeus tristis*

L 50–58 cm. S–SE Asia. 6 ssp, 2 in region: *elongatus* (Sum); ssp *kangeangensis* (Kangean) poorly known, perhaps distinct. Common in dense foliage in forest edge and woodland, <1800 m. **ID Ad** green wings and tail; large white tips to long tail; rest of body grey, with dark tone on belly, greenish tinge on back; red orbital skin bordered by almost white outline, green bill. Ssp *kangeangensis* reported to have white tail tip nearly twice as large and yellow tinged breast. **Imm** less green overall, no white outline of red orbital skin and less white in tail tip. **Voc** (i) Single, oriole-like "OUW", regularly repeated; (ii) clucking "chock" notes, sometimes ending in a faster gruff "kokokokok...". **SS** See Black-bellied and Chestnut-bellied Malkohas.

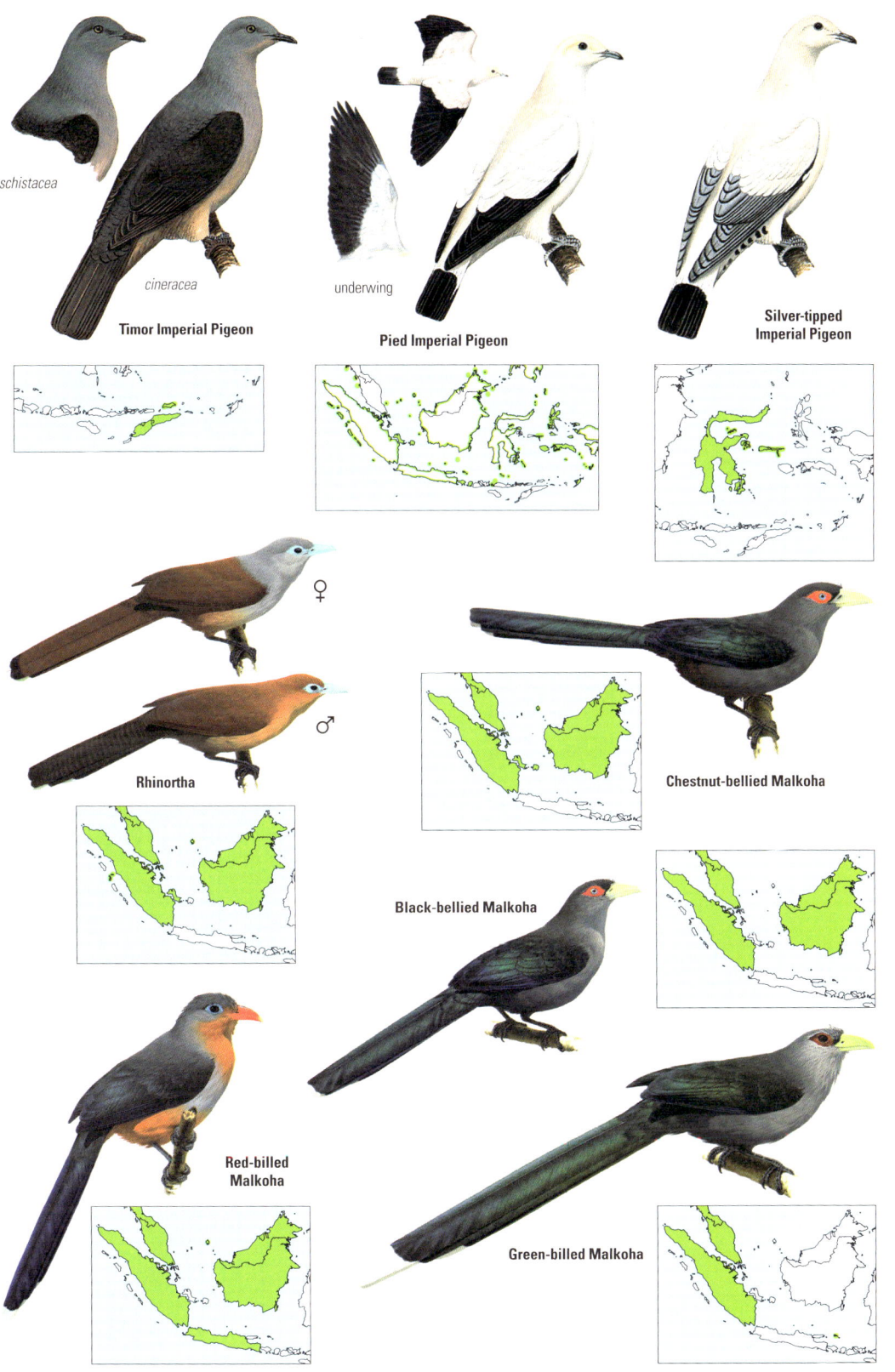

schistacea

cineracea

Timor Imperial Pigeon

underwing

Pied Imperial Pigeon

Silver-tipped Imperial Pigeon

♀

♂

Rhinortha

Chestnut-bellied Malkoha

Black-bellied Malkoha

Red-billed Malkoha

Green-billed Malkoha

Chestnut-breasted Malkoha *Phaenicophaeus curvirostris*
L 42–49 cm. Sundaic, Palawan. 5 ssp, 4 in region: *curvirostris* (W–C Jav); *singularis* (Sum, MPen); *deningeri* (E Jav, Bali); *microrhinus* (Bor, Bangka, Natuna). See Mentawai Malkoha for taxonomy. Common in thickets and dense foliage in forest, edge, peat swamps, <1100 m. **ID Ad M** rufous underparts; glossy-green back and tail with broadly vinaceous tail tip; head grey, red orbital skin; upper and tip of lower mandible pale green, rest of bill red to black; pale blue eye. Ssp *deningeri* has paler rufous underparts; *singularis* has darker vinaceous underparts becoming blackish on belly, black on bill replaced by red; *microrhinus* as latter but even darker reddish-brown underparts and broader rufous tail tip. **F** orange-yellow eye. **Imm** less bare facial skin and dark-grey bill. **Voc** (i) Utters a slow, clucking "kuk, kuk, ..." or a faster "kok-kok-krok"; (ii) in alarm, harsh cat-like "miaou"; (iv) loud giggling crescendo "kekekekekeke".

Mentawai Malkoha *Phaenicophaeus oeneicaudus* `E`
L 42–49 cm. Monotypic. No longer considered conspecific with Chestnut-breasted Malkoha based on pronounced plumage differences. Fairly common in thickets and dense foliage in forest, edge. Singly, pairs or small groups (<5); joins mixed feeding flocks. **ID Ad** differs from *singularis* Chestnut-breasted Malkoha by shorter, all green tail, dark green belly and darker chestnut breast. **Imm** undescribed. **Voc** Clucking "kok", regularly repeated.

Sulawesi Malkoha *Rhamphococcyx calyorhynchus* `E`
L 53 cm. 3 ssp: *calyorhynchus* (N–E–SE Sul, Togian); *meridionalis* (S–C Sul); *rufiloris* (Buton, Muna). Fairly common in forest, edge, riverine growth, scrub and woodland, <1650 m. **ID Ad** purple wings and tail, maroon-rufous back; breast and throat rufous; belly, crown and face dark grey with red orbital skin; swollen bill has upper mandible yellow with black tip, lower mandible red. Ssp *meridionalis* paler on crown and underparts; *rufiloris* has red (not grey) lores. **Imm** rufous suffusion on crown, brown cast to belly and blackish bill not as swollen. **Voc** Characteristic nasal rattle "wuwaaa" that accelerates, then dies away, while rising and falling in pitch. **AN** Yellow-billed Malkoha.

Channel-billed Cuckoo *Scythrops novaehollandiae*
L 60 cm. Aus. 3 ssp, 2 in region: *novaehollandiae* (breeds Aus; winters to E Wallacea, but breeds at least Buru, Flores and Sumba); *fordi* (Sul and satellites to Sula). Woodland, edge and mangroves. Conspicuous in flight, otherwise rarely seen. **ID** Large; hornbill-like. **Ad** grey plumage, whiter on the belly, with broad black subterminal tail band, narrow white tail tip, black scaling on back and black barring on vent and lower belly; facial skin red; bill tip pale, but grey base. Ssp *fordi* larger. **Imm** buffier above with more pronounced barring below. **Voc** Variable: (i) loud guttural screams "krrrRRROW"; (ii) melodious screams, often likened to bubbling trumpet "KLOH-oo KLOH-oo KLOH-oo", often as a duet.

Chestnut-winged Cuckoo *Clamator coromandus*
L 38–46 cm. Breeds S–SE–E Asia; winters S–SE Asia, Phil. Monotypic. Scarce migrant in thick low growth in woodlands, scrub, cultivation and mangroves. Singly, often feeds on or close to ground. Shy. **ID Ad** black tail, back and crest; nape and underparts white; throat and upper breast rusty; wings chestnut. **Imm** black back and head replaced by dark-brown, often with rufous-buff feather edges; tail dark-brown with buff tip. **Voc** Mostly silent in region. Song: loud, 2-note mechanical "creech-creech". Call: loud descending cackling rattle.

Drongo Cuckoo *Surniculus lugubris*
L 23–25 cm. S–SE-E Asia, Phil. ~7 ssp, 2 in region: *lugubris* (SE Asia, GS, Palawan); *musschenbroeki* (Sul, Banggai, Sula, N Mol). Taxonomy confused: *musschenbroeki* often separated as monotypic species '**Moluccan Drongo Cuckoo**' or—along with three extralimital races—as part of '**Philippine Drongo Cuckoo**' *S. velutinus*, but vocal, plumage and genetic evidence underwhelming. Moreover, recent treatments suggest additional species, '**Fork-tailed Drongo Cuckoo**' *S. dicruroides*, but current plumage, vocal and genetic evidence would reject such a treatment at least for SE Asia (although perhaps not for S Asia). More research required. Open habitats and forest, <1300 m. **ID Ad** all glossy black; white bars on vent and white stripe on underwing; tail slightly forked. Ssp *musschenbroeki* has velvet-purple sheen to head. **Imm** black with white spotting mainly on head, wings and breast. **Voc** (i) Easily remembered series of 6–9 (in *musschenbroeki* <12) whistles rising evenly up the scale "one-two-three-four-five-six"; in *musschenbroeki* sometimes, not always, rendered with harsher quality; (ii) harsh, rising "krree-krree-krree...". **SS** Resembles certain drongos, but told by slim body, white vent barring, smaller bill and tail shape.

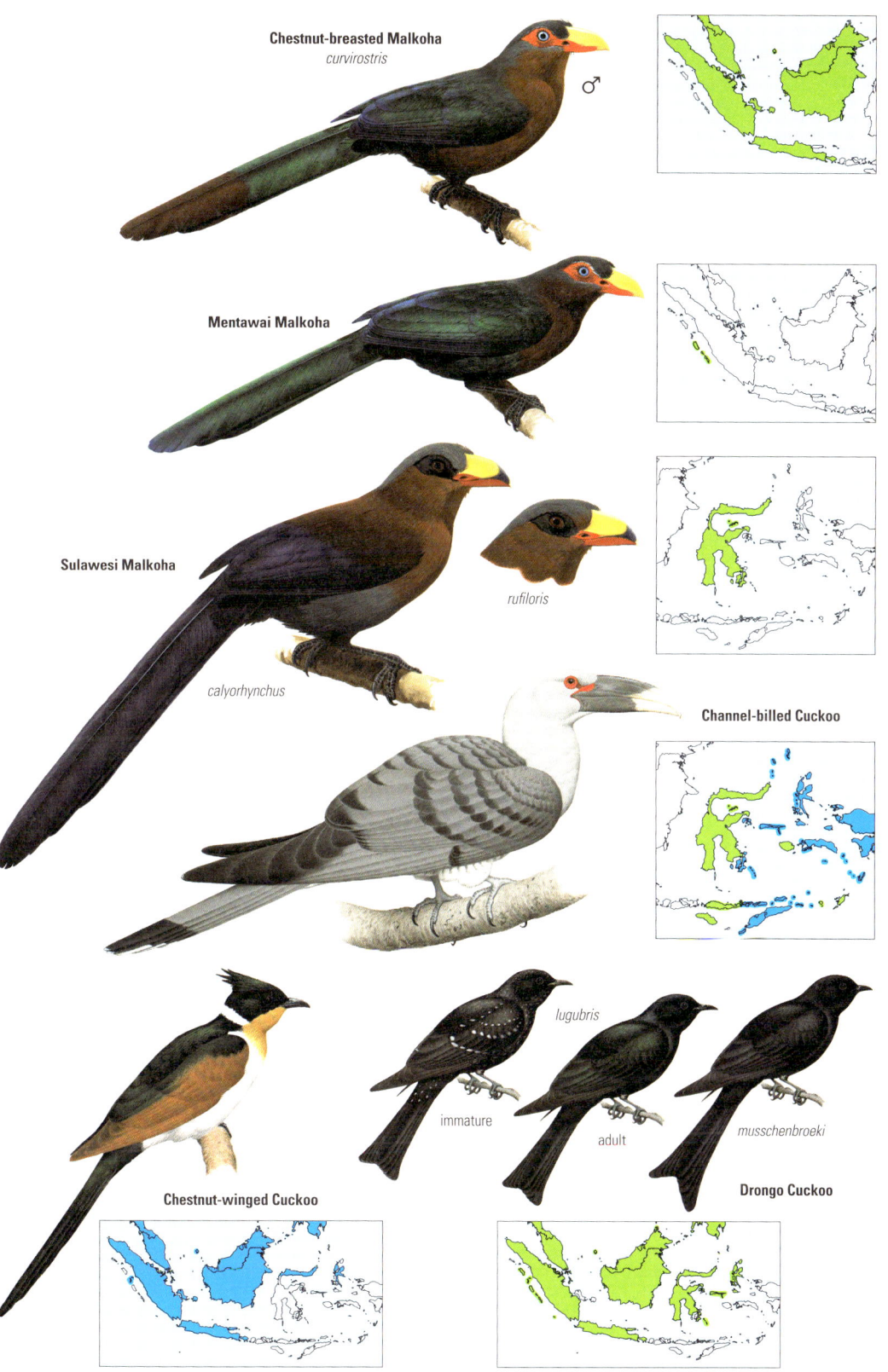

Chestnut-breasted Malkoha
curvirostris
♂

Mentawai Malkoha

Sulawesi Malkoha

rufiloris

calyorhynchus

Channel-billed Cuckoo

lugubris

immature

adult

musschenbroeki

Chestnut-winged Cuckoo

Drongo Cuckoo

Sulawesi Cuckoo *Cuculus crassirostris*   E

L 34 cm. Monotypic. Scarce in forest, edge, <1500 m. Extremely secretive, seldom-seen. **ID Ad** two plumages, possibly sex-related: (i)
grey-brown to brown above with unpatterned wings; head grey with
yellow eyering; tail banded black and rufous with black subterminal
band and light tip; underparts and throat (extending up the neck
sides) white with black barring; (ii) wholly buff underparts including
chin with very little barring; richer rufous upperparts. **Imm** white
underparts with heart-shaped spotting, black head; rufous-grey back;
pied undertail barring. **Voc** Far-carrying, descending, somewhat
melodious "keh-kah-koo" mostly given at dawn and dusk or in the
dark, third note can be faint or silent. **SS** Brown back contrasting
with grey head and barred or buff breast distinguish it from other
Cuculus cuckoos on Sul.

Indian Cuckoo *Cuculus micropterus*

L 32–33 cm. S–SE–E Asia, Phil. 2 ssp: *micropterus* (breeds S–SE–E
Asia; winters SE Asia to GS, Phil); *concretus* (resident SE Asia to
GS). Fairly common resident and migrant, mostly in lowland and hill
forest canopy, but occasionally in more disturbed or open habitat,
<2000 m. **ID Ad** grey-brown back and tail; outer-tail with white
bars; wide black subterminal tail band; head, throat and breast grey
(breast rufous in **F**); eyering yellow to grey; belly white with widely-
spaced black bars. Ssp *concretus* smaller and darker, but there is
overlap. **Imm** extensive rufous and white feather tips on back and
tail; white crown feathers and black mask. **Voc** 4-note, loud, hollow
"one-more-bot-tle" with penultimate note slightly higher-pitched;
repeated incessantly. **F** also gives loud hurried bubbling. **SS** More
widely-spaced barring on underparts and browner wings than other
Cuculus cuckoos; the only *Cuculus* in range with wide black subterminal tail band.

Sunda Cuckoo *Cuculus lepidus*

L 29–30 cm. Sundaic. 2 ssp: *lepidus* (Sum–Wetar, MPen); despite
only limited differentiation in plumage, *insulindae* (Bor) differs
consistently in voice and could be separated as monotypic species
'**Kinabalu Cuckoo**'. Population from LS (especially Flores–Sumbawa) may also be vocally distinct. Also see Himalayan Cuckoo
for taxonomy. Fairly common resident in montane forest, >900 m,
to sea level on Timor. **ID Ad** slaty-grey upperparts, tail and head;
yellow eyering; light-grey throat; broadly-spaced black bars on white
underparts, vent with rufous suffusion sometimes reaching to belly
(usually more intense in *insulindae*, but with overlap). **Hepatic
morph** (**F** only): densely barred black; rufous upperparts, tail and
crown; white underparts and throat. **Imm** grey-brown with extensive
white barring. **Voc** 3–4 note "hoop, hoop-hoop(-hoop)", first note
higher-pitched, 2–3 last notes at lower, even frequency. Some birds
in LS (at least Flores–Sumbawa) often give a distinctly slower 3-note
rendition of this call, at almost half the pace, "hoop hoop-hoop". Ssp
insulindae invariably gives more even-spaced, 3-note "hoop hoop
hoop" with all notes at equal frequency. **F** of all populations rarely
utter "quick-quick-quick". **SS** Larger wintering Oriental and Himalayan Cuckoos greatly resemble Sunda but rarely range into uplands.
They are vocally distinct but mostly silent in region. In comparison,
Sunda is darker overall with wider bars (both morphs), more intense
rufous suffusion to vent and sometimes belly (grey morph). Also see
Indian Cuckoo.

Common Cuckoo *Cuculus canorus*   V

L 32–33 cm. Breeds Palaearctic; winters Africa, S–SE Asia. 4ssp,
1 in region: presumed *canorus* (most of range). Specimen, female
hepatic morph, Air Besar Island in Jakarta Bay, W Jav (Jan 1923).
On passage could turn up anywhere. **ID/SS Ad** Very similar to

Oriental and Himalayan Cuckoos, on average, has thinner, less
distinct underparts barring and paler upperparts. Has pale, yellow
(not dark brownish) eye, but beware subadults in all three species
with darker eyes. In flight, leading edge of underwing coverts on
Common is clearly barred and background colour pure white, while
Oriental and Himalayan show a plain or indistinctly barred leading
edge often with a warm buff wash, but much overlap. Only reliable
feature is underwing primary pattern, also applying to **Hepatic
morph** and **Imm**, clearly visible on flight photos: P10 (outermost
primary) Oriental/Himalayan has < 6 pale bars vs Common > 5;
P9: Oriental/Himalayan < 7 bars vs Common > 7; P8: Oriental/
Himalayan < 7 bars vs Common > 8. Vast majority of Oriental and
Himalayan have total of 19 bars or fewer on P8/9/10, whereas
Common nearly always >20. For separation from other *Cuculus*, see
Oriental and Himalayan.

Himalayan Cuckoo *Cuculus saturatus*

L 32–33 cm. Breeds S–E Asia; winters to SE Asia, Phil. Monotypic.
No longer considered conspecific with Sunda and Oriental Cuckoos
mainly based on vocalisations. Uncommon migrant throughout,
but exact E extent of winter range uncertain due to confusion with
Oriental, specimens only known from GS. Winters in open habitat
and woodland, rarely forest, mostly in lowlands. **ID Ad** much like
smaller Sunda Cuckoo but paler overall, with narrower underparts
barring and a fainter, creamier warm-toned suffusion to vent (and
sometimes belly). **Hepatic morph** (**F** only): very similar to Sunda
Cuckoo but lighter rufous overall with narrower black barring. **Imm**
probably not safely distinguishable from Sunda and Oriental. **Voc**
Similar to nominate Sunda, but much lower-pitched: 4–5 note "hoop,
hoop-hoop-hoop(-hoop)" with first note at higher pitch. Rarely calls
in region. **SS** Not safely identified from longer-winged Oriental
Cuckoo except by voice or measurements. Also see Sunda and
Indian Cuckoos.

Oriental Cuckoo *Cuculus optatus*

L 32–33 cm. Breeds Palaearctic; winters SE Asia, Phil, NG, Aus.
Monotypic. See Himalayan Cuckoo for taxonomy. Uncommon
migrant in woodland and forest. Abundance increases towards E,
with specimens from throughout Wallacea, also Java and Nias,
whereas Himalayan Cuckoo only in GS. **ID Ad** longer-winged than
Himalayan Cuckoo, but otherwise nearly identical in appearance
and only distinguishable with certainty vocally and biometrically.
Imm probably not safely distinguishable from Himalayan. **Voc** Rarely calls in region. Distinct equal-pitched double-hoot "hoop-hoop";
sometimes introduced by 3–6 hoots "huhuhuhuhu hoop-hoop".
F rarely utters "quick-quick-quick". **SS** See Himalayan, Indian and
Sunda Cuckoos.

Moustached Hawk-cuckoo *Hierococcyx vagans*

L 26 cm. SE Asia. Monotypic. Type specimen from W Jav but no
confirmed sightings since. Uncommon in forest (especially alluvial),
<900 m. Singly or pairs; shy; favouring lower to mid-storey. **ID Ad**
brown upperparts with faint light-brown barring on wings; cap grey;
throat and cheek white with dark moustache; underparts white with
distinct black streaks; tail grey with two narrow interior and one
wide subterminal black bar; light tail tip. **Imm** brown crown. **Voc**
(i) Disyllabic, subdued, hollow "TOO-TOO", regularly repeated; (ii)
series of dozens of "tchoo" or "TCHOOdoo" notes, initially repeated
at same frequency and interval, then rising in pitch and speed until
reaching plateau, when speed slows down and pitch stays even.
SS Characteristic moustache (including Imm), brown back colour,
distinct tail pattern and lack of black chin distinguish it from Malaysian, Northern and Whistling.

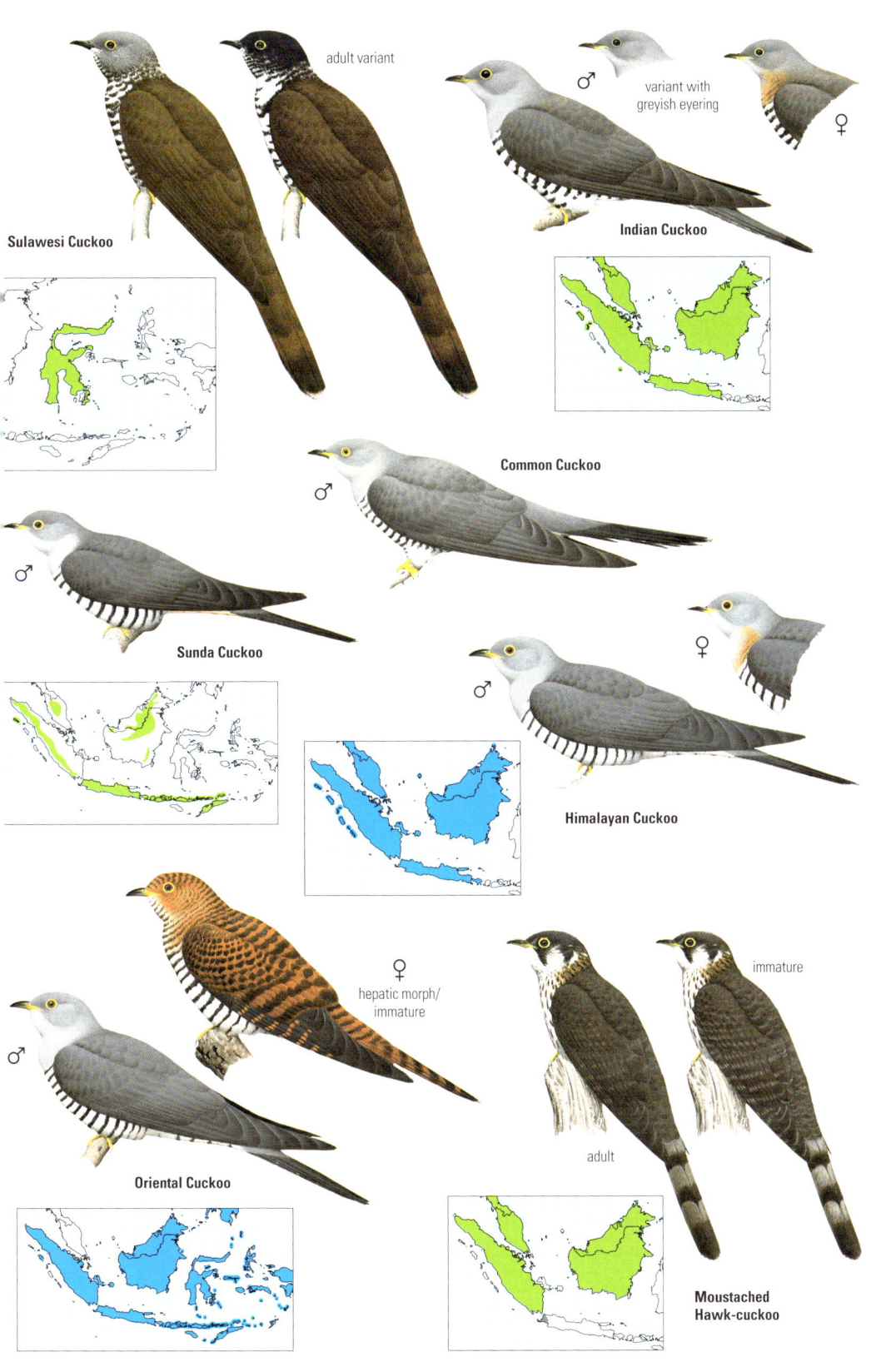

Sulawesi Cuckoo

adult variant

♂ variant with greyish eyering ♀

Indian Cuckoo

Common Cuckoo

♂

♂ **Sunda Cuckoo**

♂ ♀

Himalayan Cuckoo

♂

♀ hepatic morph/ immature

immature

adult

Oriental Cuckoo

Moustached Hawk-cuckoo

Northern Hawk-cuckoo *Hierococcyx hyperythrus*

L 30 cm. Breeds E–NE Asia; winters Phil to C–E Indonesia, Palau. Monotypic. See Malaysian Hawk-cuckoo for taxonomy. Scarce migrant, but probably overlooked in montane forest and edge. **ID** Dark bill with bright yellow at least on base. **Ad** like Whistling but lacks obvious underparts streaking, replaced by uniform pinkish-red; fine grey streaks on underparts sometimes visible at close range on sub-adult birds; medium to large white nape patch and tertial patch. **Imm** distinctive hooded appearance; extensive black chin patch; large white nape and tertial patches; pencil-thin black streaking on white underparts; brownish-grey upperparts with indistinct rufous barring. **Voc** Rarely calls in region: (i) high-pitched, strident "joo-ichee", regularly repeated; (ii) chattering "pipipijujujupipipip", reaching a crescendo, lasting 3–4 sec. **SS** See Moustached, Large, Bock's, Malaysian and Whistling. **AN** Rufous Hawk-cuckoo.

Malaysian Hawk-cuckoo *Hierococcyx fugax*

L 28–30 cm. Sundaic. Monotypic. Previously united with Philippine *H. pectoralis*, Whistling and Northern Hawk-cuckoos into '**Hodgson's Hawk-cuckoo**' *H. fugax*, but vocal and plumage differences dictate separation. Uncommon in forest and edge, <1400 m. **ID** Bill dark with bright yellow at least on base. **Ad** rich brown back often with small white tertial patch; grey-brown head; yellow eyering; obvious white nape patch; tiny black chin; white underparts and loral mark above bill base; narrow, dark brown streaks on underparts; tail grey with three narrow interior and one wide subterminal black band; tail tip rufous. **Juv** much darker on back and crown. Later, **Imm** like Ad but indistinct rufous barring on back; spotted white chin. **Voc** (i) Series of monotonous, high-pitched, shrill disyllabic "pe-pwit" given at regular intervals; (ii) single "pe-pwit" followed by rapid series of equal-pitched notes, gradually increasing then decreasing in a non-uniform pattern in which higher and lower-pitched notes alternate, "teh-teh-teh-teh-TIT-teh-teh-TEE-tit-tit-TEE-tit-tit-TEEE-tit-tit-teh-teh-teh...", ~25 n/2.5 s. **SS** Wintering Ad Whistling and Northern are greyer above with strong rufous or pink tones to underparts and distinct white tertial patch (indistinct in Malaysian). Imm identification more challenging: Whistling has dark-brown streaks on underparts like Malaysian, but streaks outlined warm-rufous (not against white background). Malaysian often has extensive white nape patch that is absent or smaller in Whistling (but large in Northern); white chin with fine spotting, whereas Whistling shows small black smudge and Northern extensively black. Penultimate tail bar in Whistling and Northern narrower than Malaysian's, and rufous-toned in Northern (versus grey in Malaysian). See also Moustached, Bock's and Large Hawk-cuckoos.

Whistling Hawk-cuckoo *Hierococcyx nisicolor*

L 28–30 cm. Breeds S-E–SE Asia; winters SE Asia. Monotypic. For taxonomy see Malaysian Hawk-cuckoo. Uncommon migrant mainly to montane forest and edge, but also passes through lowlands. **ID** Bill dark with bright yellow at least on base. **Ad** grey back and head; yellow eyering; white line from above bill base to throat; chin greyish; small or absent white nape patch; large white tertial patch; tail grey with three narrow interior and one wide subterminal black band; rufous tail tip; white underparts variably streaked rufous. **Imm** with rufous barring on upperparts; dark-brown underpart streaks outlined by rufous tones. **Voc** Rarely calls in region: (i) similar to Malaysian, "pe-pwit"; (ii) excited high-pitched, shrill, rising then falling "trrrtititititititirrrtrrr", ~32 n/3 s. **SS** On Bor and Sul overlaps

with wintering Northern Hawk-cuckoo, which has uniform salmon-pink (not streaked rufous) underparts and larger nape and tertial patches in Ad. Imm Northern has more extensive black chin; lacks rufous outline of black breast streaks; has large nape patch (indistinct in Whistling) and always seems to show rufous-toned narrow penultimate tail bar (often grey in Whistling). Also see Malaysian, Large, Bock's and Moustached Hawk-cuckoos.

Large Hawk-cuckoo *Hierococcyx sparverioides*

L 38–40 cm. Breeds S–SE–E–NE Asia; winters S–SE Asia, Phil. Monotypic. Formerly included Bock's but apparently more closely related to extralimital Common Hawk-cuckoo *H. varius*. Uncommon migrant in wide variety of woodlands, scrub, mangrove and cultivation across lowlands. **ID** Bill mostly black with yellow base to lower mandible; no white nape or tertial patches. **Ad** rich brown above; tail brown with black bars and subterminal band; light tail tip; head grey; yellow eyering; dark smudge on chin; rufous throat and upper breast with black streaks; white underparts with black bars on belly. **Imm** has black throat stripe splitting into two diagonal lines; less rufous on breast; underparts all streaked (more bar-like on flanks); brown upperparts narrowly barred rufous, strongly contrasting with grey head. **Voc** Rarely calls in region. Characteristic "brain-fe-ver" call given incessantly at dawn, dusk and into the night, repeated with rising pitch and speed until reaching frantic climax. **SS** Bock's only occurs in highlands, is smaller with darker grey head colouration in front of eye, greyer (less contrasting) mantle, has less or no streaking on throat and breast, and sounds different (but Large rarely calls in region). Imm Bock's lacks diagonally bifurcating throat stripe of Imm Large, has fewer streaks on breast, and clearer bars on belly; greyer, less brown upperparts and lacks bright-warm nape patch frequently present on Imm Large. Imm Large superficially resembles smaller Malaysian (Imm and ad), Whistling (Imm) and Northern (Imm), and is most easily told by more intensely wedge-like or bar-like spots on belly and by all-dark bill with – at most – limited yellow near bill tip, compared to bright yellow bill bases in the latter three. Also Imm Large almost always lacks white patches on nape and tertials characteristic of the other species. Moreover, Malaysian has more even tail bars than Large.

Bock's Hawk-cuckoo *Hierococcyx bocki*

L 30–32 cm. Sundaic. Monotypic. See Large Hawk-cuckoo for taxonomy. Distinct vocalisations suggest that Bornean population is a cryptic, unnamed novel taxon, '**Penan Hawk-cuckoo**'. Uncommon in montane forest and edge, >1000 m. **ID** Black bill with limited yellow at base; no white nape or tertial patches. **Ad** like larger Large Hawk-cuckoo, but has greyer (less brown) upperparts (no contrast with grey head); brighter, redder throat and breast. **Imm** very similar to larger Large Hawk-cuckoo but more adult-like underparts pattern with bars across belly at early age and a few broad streaks on breast; greyish-brown, not brown upperparts; lacks diagonally bifurcating throat stripe. **Voc** Predominantly heard in rainy season: (i) Bor: loud series of level-pitched, trisyllabic "pit-piwet...", mainly at dawn and dusk; (ii) Sum and MPen: series of 8–15, disyllabic "pee-hee" rising in pitch and delivery speed to a climax, lasting ~20 sec. Less tremolo than in Large. **SS** See Large, the main confusion species. Imm Bock's told from Malaysian (ad/Imm), Whistling (Imm) and Northern (Imm) mainly through barred (not streaked) belly, all-dark bill (lacking extensive yellow base) as well as lack of white nape and tertial patches. **AN** Dark Hawk-cuckoo.

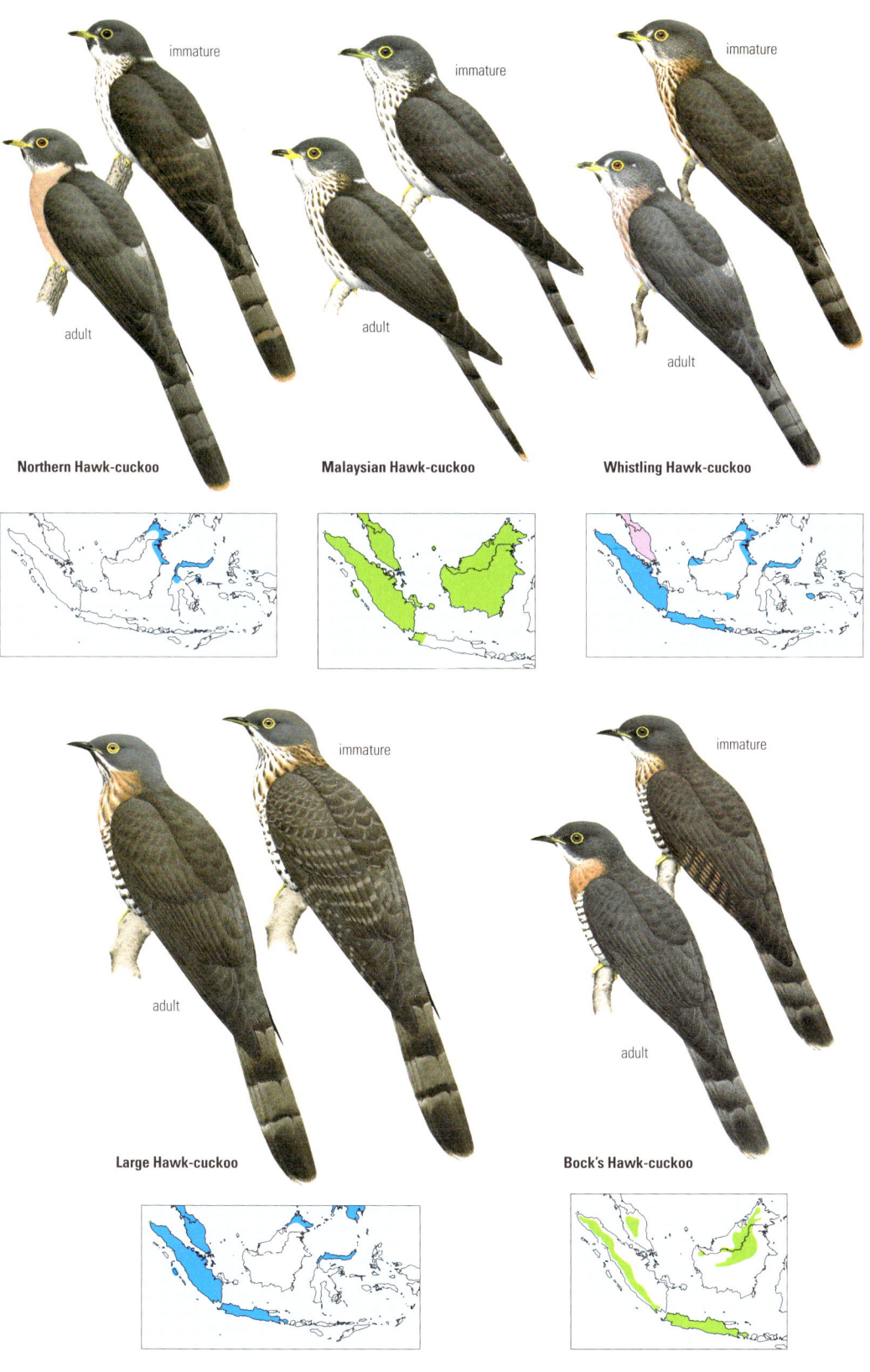

Northern Hawk-cuckoo

Malaysian Hawk-cuckoo

Whistling Hawk-cuckoo

Large Hawk-cuckoo

Bock's Hawk-cuckoo

Pallid Cuckoo *Cacomantis pallidus*

L 31 cm. Aus. Monotypic. Rare migrant in open habitats. In region known Aug-Oct. **ID Ad** underparts off-white; upperparts and crown light-grey; inconspicuous yellow eyering, black eye line curves down to neck sides; tail black with dense white barring. **Imm** variable amounts of blackish mottling with primarily white wing-coverts, sometimes showing thick black breast streaking. **Voc** Mellow series of 7–18 ascending whistles in quick but decelerating succession, with first note often higher than second: "tit-tu-tu-tu tu terr terr tee". **SS** Imm stages confusing, but their irregular mottling and lack of neat black barring eliminate other ad and imm *Cacomantis* and *Cuculus* cuckoos.

Banded Bay Cuckoo *Cacomantis sonneratii*

L 22 cm. S–SE Asia, Palawan. 4 ssp, 2 in region: *fasciolatus* (Sum, Bor, Palawan); *musicus* (Bali, Jav). Uncommon in forest, edge, <1500 m. **ID Ad** rufous upperparts, tail, crown and cheek; white underparts and supercilium; fine wavy bars across whole body; black subterminal tail band and white tail tip. Ssp *musicus* lighter rufous and less densely barred. **Imm** whiter face, white tips to crown and back feathers, less regular underparts barring. **Voc** (i) 4-note "tu-ti-fru-tee" on descending scale, sounding agitated, faster and higher-pitched than Indian Cuckoo; (ii) series of 2–4 long notes, then lower note followed by 2 higher ones "pee-pui-pee", repeated <6 times at increasing speed and frequency, then abruptly stopping. **SS** Note unique supercilium.

Plaintive Cuckoo *Cacomantis merulinus*

L 18–23 cm. SE Asia, Phil. 4 ssp, 3 in region: *merulinus* (Phil, Sul), *threnodes* (Sum, Bor, MPen); *lanceolatus* (Jav, Bali). Common in lowlands; open woodlands to cultivation, towns, rarely to 2000 m. **ID Ad** brownish-grey upperparts, grey head and breast; buff-rufous belly; tail blackish with outer tail barred white. Ssp *threnodes* browner above, more intense rufous on belly reaching onto lower breast; *lanceolatus* paler overall, with pale-grey breast extending further down and merging into pale rufous-buff belly. **Hepatic morph** (F only) all-rufous but belly white with black barring, and back with extensive black mottling or barring. **Imm** either all-grey with white bars on belly, or has rufous upperparts with brown barring and streaking, and white underparts with black barring. **Voc** (i) Hurried, fading "fee-fee-fee-fee-fee-feefeefee" descending in pitch; (ii) so-called 'brainfever call', an ascending 3-note "fee-fa-FEE" gradually accelerating as it is repeated. **SS** Sunda and Sulawesi Brush Cuckoos are larger with rufous (not grey) breast, and darker overall on most islands. Both Sunda and Sulawesi Brush Cuckoos generally inhabit less open habitat than Plaintive. Immatures of all three species are doubtfully distinguishable but Plaintive is probably paler overall. Hepatic morphs are difficult and often variable, but Plaintive is frequently warmer rufous or cinnamon overall, with finer, less coarse black barring on underparts, wider pale undertail bars, and with more distinct buff/rufous barring on uppertail (in Sunda/Sulawesi Brush, dark undertail bars are wider than the pale ones, while uppertail mostly only has rufous lateral notches).

Sunda Brush Cuckoo *Cacomantis sepulcralis*

L 21–27 cm. SE Asia, Phil. 2 ssp, 1 in region: *sepulcralis* (Sum–Alor, Sumba, Bor, MPen, Phil). Traditionally merged with Sulawesi Brush Cuckoo (as '**Rusty-breasted Cuckoo**' *C. sepulcralis*), often additionally with Australian and sometimes Moluccan Brush Cuckoos (as '**Brush Cuckoo**' *C. variolosus*), but all four separated on basis of various combinations of consistent plumage and vocal differences. Fairly common in forest, edge, mangroves. **ID Ad** brown wings merging into grey head; underparts uniformly rufous (barred light-grey in most F) except for grey chin; tail black with light tip

and white notches on outertail; distinct yellow eye ring. **Hepatic morph** (F only) rufous upperparts with dark brown bars, and all-white underparts with even black bars. **Imm** similar to rufous Imm Plaintive Cuckoo but perhaps darker overall. **Voc** (i) Series of 6–20 melancholy, even-pitched, slightly upward-inflected notes "whee-whee-whee..."; (ii) brain-fever call similar to Plaintive but hoarser "fee-fa-WEE..." (last note slightly inflected), accelerating, becoming more agitated. **SS** See Plaintive and Australian Brush Cuckoos.

Sulawesi Brush Cuckoo *Cacomantis virescens* E

L 21–27 cm. Monotypic. See Sunda Brush for taxonomy. Fairly common in forest, edge. **ID Ad** differs from Sunda Brush Cuckoo in darker, more greenish-brown upperparts, darker rufous belly, distinct grey throat; longer tail. May have rare **F hepatic morph** and **Imm** as in Sunda Brush. **Voc** (i) Series of 6–20 melancholy, even-pitched notes, similar to Sunda Brush but consistently higher-pitched and deflected "feew-feew-feew..." at faster delivery; (ii) an accelerating "fee-fa-FEEW" series ('brainfever call'), seemingly identical to Sunda Brush, although delivered faster, with the last note deflected not inflected. **SS** See Plaintive Cuckoo.

Moluccan Brush Cuckoo *Cacomantis aeruginosus* E

L 24 cm. 2 ssp: *aeruginosus* (C Mol); *heinrichi* (N Mol). Ssp *aeruginosus* formerly included in Australian Brush Cuckoo, sometimes along with Sunda Brush and Sulawesi Brush, but sounds identical to *heinrichi*. See Sunda Brush Cuckoo for taxonomy. Fairly common (scarce on Halmahera) in forest, more numerous in uplands. **ID Ad** closely resembles allopatric Sulawesi Brush Cuckoo, but paler overall, especially on back, with less of a greenish sheen, and less distinct grey throat. **Voc** 'Locomotive call', constitutes a unique rapid series of 10–30 staccato piping whistles, accelerating and rising in the beginning, then steady and rapid and ultimately decelerating and dropping. Also gives fast-paced renditions of the 'brainfever call' and the simple repetitive call typical of other 'brush cuckoos', but much less commonly and at faster delivery than sympatric Australian Brush. **SS** Australian Brush overlaps on all islands but often inhabits more open habitat, has shorter and less graduated tail, paler grey reaching from head onto breast (versus dark-grey head contrasting with vividly rufous lower breast), paler brown-grey (not greenish-brown) upperparts (especially in migrant *variolosus*, less so in resident *major*), and indistinct greyish-lime (not bright yellow) eye ring. Note vocalisations.

Australian Brush Cuckoo *Cacomantis variolosus*

L 21–27 cm. Aus. 8-9 ssp, 4-5 in region: *variolosus* (breeds Aus; migrates to Wetar, Flores, Mol, NG); *infaustus* (NG; Watubela, Kai, Seram Laut); *major* (N Mol); *tymbonomus* (Timor, Rote, Wetar); Tanimbar population possibly undescribed ssp. For taxonomy also see Sunda and Moluccan Brush Cuckoos. Fairly common in forested and open habitats. **ID Ad** brown-grey back merges into medium to light-grey head and breast; belly pale rufous; indistinct greyish-lime eye ring; tail black with light tip and white notches on outertail. Ssp *infaustus* smaller with darker brown upperparts, more vividly rufous underparts, and a rufous-grey suffusion on breast. Population on Tanimbar lacks grey breast suffusion, rufous throat and breast contrasting strongly with grey head. Ssp *major* intermediate in size and paleness between *variolosus* and *infaustus*. Ssp *tymbonomus* very pale overall, with earthen-brown upperparts (and grey suffusion to crown) as well as off-white underparts, mostly lacking any warm tones; often with faint vestigial barring on flanks even in adult plumage. **Hepatic morph** (F only) and **Imm** indistinguishable from Sunda Brush. **Voc** (i) Series of 6–20 simple melancholy notes, similar to Sunda and Sulawesi Brush Cuckoos and delivered at intermediate pace between the latter two species, but consistently

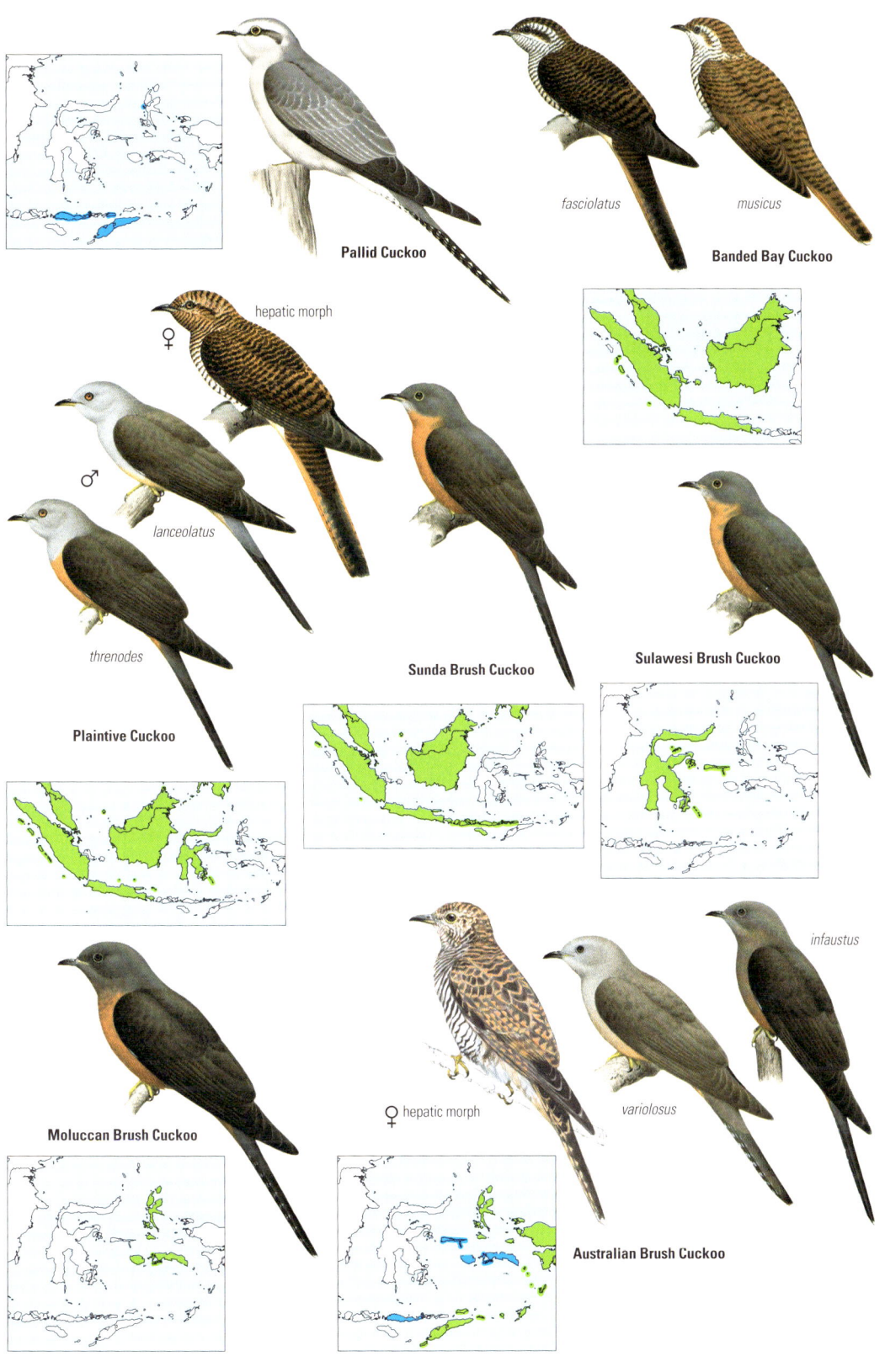

Pallid Cuckoo

fasciolatus

musicus

Banded Bay Cuckoo

hepatic morph

♀

♂

lanceolatus

threnodes

Plaintive Cuckoo

Sunda Brush Cuckoo

Sulawesi Brush Cuckoo

Moluccan Brush Cuckoo

♀ hepatic morph

variolosus

infaustus

Australian Brush Cuckoo

exhibiting both an initial inflection and final deflection, "fweew-fweew-fweew..."; the series of notes is usually level but can be strongly descending, especially in ssp *tymbonomus*; (ii) an accelerating "fee-fa-FWEEW" series, as Sunda Brush, although the last element is deflected towards the end. **SS** In C-N Mol, see Moluccan Brush Cuckoo. Migrant ssp *variolosus* differs from Sunda Brush in greyish-lime (not yellow) eye-ring, much paler brown upperparts, paler grey on head reaching down to breast and much paler rufous remaining underparts (versus intensely-rufous lower throat to vent in Sunda Brush). Note vocalisations (Australian Brush commonly sings in winter quarters).

Horsfield's Bronze-cuckoo *Chrysococcyx basalis*
L 17 cm. Breeds Australia; winters NG to SE Asia. Monotypic. Austral migrant, more common in LS; open woodland, mangroves and scrub, rarely inland. **ID Ad** bronze-brown upperparts and crown; white supercilium and blackish-grey eyestripe; whitish underparts with finely dark-streaked throat and coarsely-barred neck-sides and flanks; tail blackish, but outer tail feathers rufous along basal two thirds; upperparts have light feather margins that create scaly appearance; wing feathers also have unique light margins. **Imm** duller; upperparts more greyish. **Voc** (i) Flowerpecker-like "zee-zee-zee..." repeated every 0.5 sec, sometimes accelerating; (ii) single "pisuh" repeated every ~1.5 sec. **SS** From other bronze-cuckoos by combination of strong dark eyestripe, rufous outer tail, incomplete barring on underparts.

Shining Bronze-cuckoo *Chrysococcyx lucidus*
L 17 cm. Aus. 4 ssp, 1 in region: *plagosus* (breeds Australia; winters LS, NG). Uncommon migrant, recorded Feb–Oct in forest, mangroves, scrub and plantations. **ID Ad** upperparts and tail bronzy brownish-green to green, but crown always brownish; underparts white with dark barring often extending to throat. Green-backed birds often have all-white face (including lores) with fine black barring; brownish-backed birds often have olive cheek and narrow whitish supercilium. **Imm** duller, barring restricted to flanks. **Voc** (i) Series of ascending whistles, "fay?-fay?-fay?..." 20 n/10 s; (ii) descending "pweu", 10 n/6 s. **SS** Little Bronze often has red eyering. In region of overlap, 'Gould's' (*jungei, poecilurus*) has more brownish-bronze back colouration and more rufous colour on tail. 'Banda' (*rufomerus*) quite similar, especially females which lack red eyering, but Shining has brown crown contrasting with green back while 'Banda' has dark-green (almost black) crown and more bronze-green back. Also see Horsfield's Bronze-cuckoo.

Little Bronze-cuckoo *Chrysococcyx minutillus*
L 15–16 cm. SE Asia–Aus, Phil. 11 ssp, 6 in region. Based on plumage, often subdivided into ≤3 species in our region, the first two of which also contain extralimital ssp: (a) '**Malaysian Bronze-cuckoo**' (*albifrons* group; also MPen) includes *albifrons* (Jav, Sum, Mentawai) and *aheneus* (Bor, S Phil); (b) '**Gould's Bronze-cuckoo**' (*poecilurus* group) includes *poecilurus* (NG, Australia, Mol) and *jungei* (Sul, Banggai, Flores–Alor; unnamed populations in Timor and Wetar may belong here); (c) '**Banda Bronze-cuckoo**' (*rufomerus* group) includes *rufomerus* (Romang–Damar) and *salvadorii* (Babar). However, variation among groups appears clinal, current genetic evidence inconclusive, and no known vocal differences. See also Pied Bronze-cuckoo for taxonomy. Uncommon in wide array of lowland habitats, occasionally into the mountains, especially on Sul (>2000 m). **ID Ad** distinct eyering (**M** red; **F** yellow). Generally green or brownish-bronze upperparts, crown and tail (some ssp with rufous outer tail) and white underparts with dark barring; pale supercilium. The westernmost form, 'Malaysian' *albifrons*, is all green-backed and snowy-faced but becomes successively less white-faced and more

bronzy-backed towards east via *aheneus*, climaxing in the brownish-bronze upperparts, dingy supercilium and rufous outer tail feathers of 'Gould's' *jungei*. Continuing east, populations revert to a Malaysian-like plumage via 'Banda' *rufomerus* (with its greener upperparts) to *salvadorii*, which is very similar to 'Malaysian' *albifrons* but may have minor introgressed characters from Pied Bronze-cuckoo (such as partial white wing patch). Poorly known on Mol: birds reported from Seram are typical for bronzy-backed 'Gould's' *poecilurus* but others reported from Halmahera are green-backed, have indistinct barring on underparts and much white in wing, almost appearing intermediate towards Pied Bronze-cuckoo. **Imm** is duller and greyer above and has bars restricted to flanks. **Voc** (i) Melodious fast level trill lasting ~5 sec, often deflected towards the end; (ii) series of 3–7 deflected "tew" notes, descending in pitch, often with slight pause between last and penultimate note. **SS** See Horsfield's and Shining Bronze-cuckoos and fem Violet Cuckoo.

Pied Bronze-cuckoo *Chrysococcyx crassirostris*
L 15–16 cm. Monotypic. Sometimes subsumed under Little Bronze-cuckoo but vocally and morphologically distinct. Usually ssp *salvadorii* of Little is included in Pied Bronze-cuckoo based on erroneous rendition of plumage characters in the literature, but vocal and plumage evidence from modern population on Babar rejects such a placement. Uncommon in wide array of dense woodland vegetation. **ID Ad** distinct red eyering (**M** only). Deeply green-backed and green-tailed with entire face blackish-green (concolorous with crown) and a large white wing patch; all-white underparts lack barring (**M**) or barred on flanks only (**F**). **Imm** unknown. **Voc** 3 descending "tew-tew-tew", lasting 0.8 sec.

Black-eared Bronze-cuckoo *Chrysococcyx osculans*
L 20 cm. Aus. Monotypic. Rare migrant, recorded Jul, Sep, Nov. Open dry scrub, rarely in well-vegetated areas. **ID Ad** upperparts and crown uniform grey (with slight gloss); tail blackish-grey with white tip, pale rump; conspicuous broad white supercilium and black eyestripe; underparts white. **Imm** more buff-tinged below, less pronounced facial markings. **Voc** Melancholy, whistled "peer", often repeated in succession. Courtship call: repeated "peeowit-peeoweer".

Asian Emerald Cuckoo *Chrysococcyx maculatus*
L 17 cm. S–SE–E Asia. Monotypic. Rare migrant; forest and gardens. **ID** Bill yellow to orange with black tip. **M** bright glossy green upperparts, head and breast; white belly with dark bars. **F** crown buff; throat and underparts white with dense dark barring. **Imm** extensive rufous on back and more buffy underparts with rufous or bronzy barring. **Voc** Presumably silent in region: (i) descending 3–4 "kee-kee-kee"; (ii) sharp "chweek" in flight. **SS** Violet Cuckoo upperparts but can appear greenish in harsh light, note bill colour.

Violet Cuckoo *Chrysococcyx xanthorhynchus*
L 16 cm. SE Asia, Phil. 2 ssp, 1 in region: *xanthorhynchus* (SE Asia to GS, Palawan). Uncommon in forest, usually in canopy. **ID M** violet upperparts, head and breast; yellow bill with red base and eyering; belly white with black bars. **F** greenish-bronze upperparts and crown; white face and underparts with dark barring; dark bill; outer tail barred rufous. **Imm** rufous barred upperparts. **Voc** (i) Disyllabic "qui-víck, qui-víck, qui-víck" during undulating flight between tree crowns; (ii) descending trill preceded by triple-note "seer-sa-seer, see-see-see-swee-swee-swee". **SS** Fem resembles Little Bronze-cuckoo but has bronzier upperparts (especially crown), more densely-barred supercilium, and indistinct dark (or incipient red, in imm M) rather than distinct yellow/red eye-ring. Also see Asian Emerald.

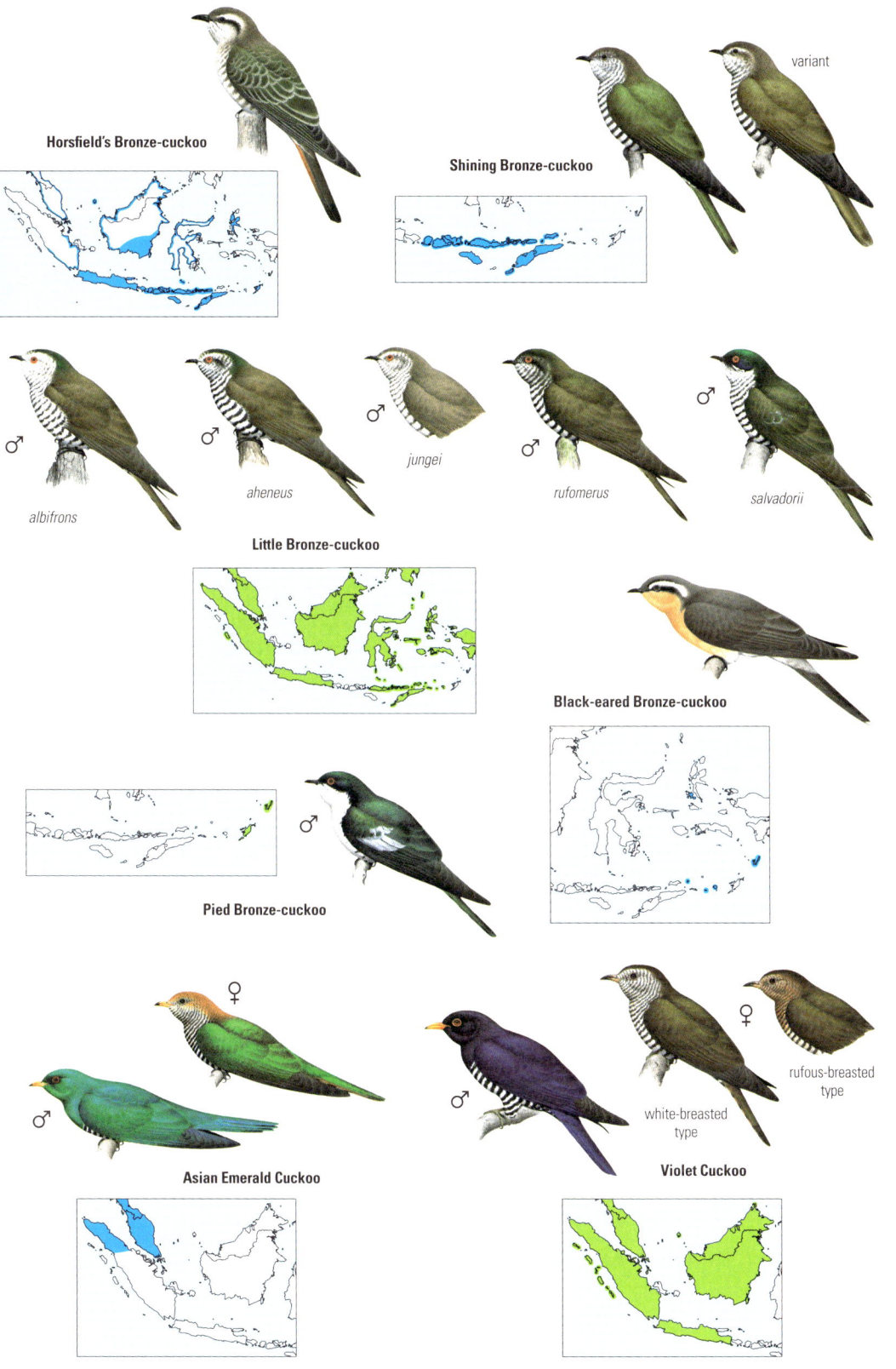

Horsfield's Bronze-cuckoo

Shining Bronze-cuckoo

variant

♂ *albifrons*

♂ *aheneus*

♂ *jungei*

♂ *rufomerus*

♂ *salvadorii*

Little Bronze-cuckoo

Black-eared Bronze-cuckoo

♂

Pied Bronze-cuckoo

♀

♂

Asian Emerald Cuckoo

♂

white-breasted type

♀

rufous-breasted type

Violet Cuckoo

Asian Koel *Eudynamys scolopaceus*

L 39–46 cm. S–SE–E Asia, Phil. 8 ssp, 5 in region: *chinensis* (E–SE Asia; winters to Bor); *malayanus* (SE Asia, GS, Lombok–Flores); *simalurensis* (Simeulue, Babi); *mindanensis* (Phil, islands N of Sul); *corvinus* (N Mol). Some treatments include Pacific Koel, others also Black-billed Koel, within this species, but differences in bare parts colouration, fem plumage and small but consistent vocal distinctions suggest treatment as separate species. The geographically disjunct *corvinus* is little known; here included with Asian Koel (not Pacific Koel as in other treatments) based on fem and Imm plumages, but its bare parts colouration perhaps more closely resembles Pacific Koel and its voice is unique, possibly warranting status as monotypic species '**Sultan's Koel**'. Some authors include Pacific Koel ssp *orientalis* in present species (leaving Pacific Koel as *E. cyanocephalus*), but *orientalis* and Asian Koel differ substantially in plumage, rejecting such a treatment. Further taxonomic study required. Woodlands, edge, cultivation and villages; rarely enters closed forest or uplands, <1200 m. Shy, rarely perches in exposed position, concealing itself in dense foliage when calling. **ID** Green bill (probably black in *corvinus*); red iris. **M** all-black. **F** geographically variable; *chinensis* dark brown above with white spots and bars (or streaks on crown), white below with dark-brown streaks on throat/breast and bars on belly; *malayanus* has white parts washed rufous, with the smaller *simalurensis* showing larger rufous markings above; *mindanensis* (N of Sul) and *corvinus* (E of Sul) have all white replaced by rufous and exhibit narrower belly barring. **Imm** generally blackish-brown; in *malayanus* and probably *chinensis* with lighter markings. **Voc** (i) Loud "ko-WEEW", the second element inflected, then deflected, often given in accelerating series at increasing pitch; in *corvinus*, the call is more monosyllabic, only showing a slight final deflection, distinctly sounding like "WEEEW"; (ii) rapidly delivered, melodious 8–10 note "wrrick wrrick wrrick…" or less burry "glick glick glick…", or more hollow "kweow kweow kweow…", all of which can be even-pitched or rising.

Black-billed Koel *Eudynamys melanorhynchus* 🄴

L 36–44 cm. 2 ssp: *melanorhynchus* (Sul and satellites); *facialis* (Sula). Treated as distinct from closely-related Pacific Koel although more research needed on exact affinity of latter's ssp *orientalis*, which may be more closely related to Black-billed. See also Asian Koel for taxonomy. Fairly common in primary and secondary forest, edge. **ID** Black bill, red iris. **M** all-black; *facialis* reported to have irregular white markings, but possibly due to individual variation. **F** variable: may approach **M** in plumage, or with buffy-white underparts, dark bars and white moustachial line; upperparts range from all-black to rufous black-barred. **Imm** mostly black. **Voc** (i) Loud accelerating series at increasing pitch, starting off as "ko-WEEW" (the second element deflected as in Asian Koel), but notes gradually losing final inflection and becoming like Pacific Koel's "hoo-WEE" towards the end; (ii) rapidly delivered melodious 8–10 note "wrrick wrrick wrrick…", or less burry "glick glick glick…", or more hollow "kweow kweow kweow…", all of which can be even-pitched or rising.

Pacific Koel *Eudynamys orientalis*

L 39–46 cm. Aus. 9 ssp, 3 in region: *orientalis* (C Mol); *picatus* (Sumba, Wetar, Timor–Tanimbar, Alor, Kai); *subcyanocephalus* (Australia; winters NG and S Mol). Ssp *subcyanocephalus*—along with extralimital ssp—sometimes divided into '**Australian Koel**' *E. cyanocephalus* based on plumage. For taxonomy also see Asian and Black-billed Koels. Uncommon resident and migrant. Mostly in woodlands and cultivation in lowlands. **ID** Red iris. **M** all-black; bill black (at least in *orientalis*) or blue-grey (at least in *subcyanocephalus*). **F** geographically variable; *orientalis* most often has black head and throat with light moustachial streak, rich uniform rufous underparts, and brown upperparts with rufous spots and bars; *picatus* has buff underparts with thick black bars; *subcyanocephalus* underparts whiter with narrower and more regular bars. **Imm** all-rufous (never all-black), sometimes with dark bars on under or upperparts and dark cap or ear patch. **Voc** Call repertoire very similar to Asian Koel, but the main call is inflected (not deflected) towards the end: "HooWEE?, HooWEE?…".

Timor Coucal *Centropus mui* 🄴

L 65 cm. Monotypic. Often merged with extralimital Pheasant Coucal *C. phasianinus* (Aus); doubtless closely related, but looks very different. Restricted to Los Palos region in E Timor, inhabits monsoon forest, edge, fragmented stunted forest, <500 m. Singly or pairs, quite shy but vocal. **ID Ad** uniform whitish with dusky lores and forecrown; wings and tail rufous-brown with whitish-buff barring. **Imm** undescribed. **Voc** Song, often in duet: (i) series of slow, hollow "boop" notes, lasting 3–5 sec, at 2 n/s; (ii) very similar to Greater Coucal "water bottle" call, series of "boop" notes, becoming more emphatic then fading out, and frequently initiated by singlets or doublet, lasting <10 sec. Call: harsh "kheeup".

Kai Coucal *Centropus spilopterus* 🄴

L 60 cm. Monotypic. Often merged with extralimital Pheasant Coucal *C. phasianinus* (Aus) and shares similar mtDNA, but looks distinct. Common, inhabits forest patches, edge, gardens and woodlands. Singly or pairs, quite shy but vocal. **ID Ad** all-black with greenish gloss; red iris; black bill; light barring on primaries. **Imm** is barred buff on upperparts. **Voc** Song: (i) series of slow, hollow "boop" notes, lasting 4–6 sec, at 3 n/s; (ii) long even-pitched series "boop-boop-boop…", accelerating, descending and fading off at end while rising in pitch, lasting <6 sec. Call: series of hoarse, harsh "chk" notes.

Asian Koel

♂ ♀ *chinensis* ♀ *mindanensis*

dark variant

Black-billed Koel
melanorhynchus

♂ ♀ resembling ♂

♀ variants

Pacific Koel

♂ ♀ *orientalis* ♀ *subcyanocephalus*

Timor Coucal

Kai Coucal

Short-toed Coucal *Centropus rectunguis*

L 38–43 cm. Sundaic. Monotypic. Scarce in closed-canopy forest (often floodplain or peat swamp), <600 m. Singly or pairs in dense forest understorey, shy, difficult to observe. Largely terrestrial. **ID Ad** all-black with purplish to greenish gloss, except for chestnut wings and back; iris red; bill black. **Imm** rufous upper head, rufous back with black bars and tail black with fine white bars; underparts buff, dark-brown or black with fine white bars. **Voc** Series of sombre "boop, boop boop boop…", sometimes even-pitched but more often descending, usually repeated 4–7 times or more. Greater Coucal gives similar calls, typically but not always higher-pitched; however, Short-toed's call is often slower and often has the first note separated by longer break. **SS** Greater Coucal extremely similar but prefers forest edge. The two species can meet in good forest along rivers and logging roads. Greater is larger, proportionately longer-tailed, has a fiercer red eye (versus dull-red) and a longer, straighter culmen (slopes down immediately in Short-toed). With excellent views, neck and nape of Short-toed show more greenish (versus purplish) gloss and give more ruffled scaled impression. Imm Short-toed has black barring on mantle and unbarred wings (reverse in imm Greater). Lesser Coucal has less rufous on wings and mantle, often has buff mantle streaks and brown eyes, and prefers grasslands.

Greater Coucal *Centropus sinensis*

L 47–52 cm. E–S–SE Asia, Phil. 6 ssp, 2 in region: *bubutus* (GS, Palawan); ssp *kangeangensis* (Kangean) has a distinct morph alongside typical birds; further study required. Common but shy inhabitant of wide array of habitats, especially cultivation, gardens, stream sides, secondary forest and villages, rarely enters good forest. **ID Ad** all-black with purplish gloss, except for chestnut wings and back; iris red; bill black. Ssp *kangeangensis* is considerably smaller with duller black underparts. **Buff morph** (ssp *kangeangensis* only) with head and body pale buff, tail grey, alongside commoner typical birds. **Imm** buff barring on head and tail, black barring on wings and brown (often white-barred) underparts. **Voc** (i) Characteristic "water bottle" call, series of many "boop" notes, often changing pitch or becoming more emphatic, then fading out, frequently initiated by singlets, doublet or short series of "boop"s, often in duet; (ii) harsh "skaah" and "tok, tok" notes. **SS** Larger than Lesser Coucal, with brighter wings and back, and lack of white mantle streaks. Also see Short-toed and Javan Coucals.

Javan Coucal *Centropus nigrorufus*　　　　　**E**

L 46 cm. Monotypic. Scarce and local, inhabits coastal swamps, estuaries, mangroves, adjacent palm vegetation and tall grass. Shy, rarely vocalises, but often sits up in early morning. **ID Ad** all black with purplish sheen, except for rufous edges of variable size to carpal and outerwing; black bill; red iris. **Imm** identical. **Voc** Similar to Greater Coucal's series of "boop" notes, but level-pitched, lasting 3–4 sec, at 4 n/s. Also gives characteristic cackle. **SS** Told from larger Greater Coucal by black back and wing markings. Lesser Coucal is much smaller, lacks distinct rufous-black wing pattern, always lacks red iris and often looks white-streaked on mantle. **AN** Sunda Coucal.

Lesser Coucal *Centropus bengalensis*

L 31–34 cm. S–SE–E Asia, Phil. 6 ssp, 3 in region: *javanensis* (MPen, GS to W Phil); *sarasinorum* (Sul and satellites, Sula, LS); *medius* (Mol, except Kai). Common in secondary growth, especially grasslands. **ID Ad br** is dull black with pale rufous wings; white inconspicuous streaks often visible all over body, especially mantle; dark iris. Ssp *sarasinorum* slightly larger; *medius* larger still. **Imm** and some **Ad non-br** have rufous wings, black tail, brown upperparts and head with black and light streaks, and light buff underparts with dark bars on belly, flanks, rump and lower back. **Imm** has upperparts paler (more rufous) and barring and streaking more extensive (including wings). **Voc** (i) Mechanical disyllabic "koo-kook" or trisyllabic "koo-kuk-kuk", sounding like a knock on a cask, often given in a series or duet, with notes much shorter and less hollow than other typical coucal notes; (ii) alarm calls "krah, krah"; (iii) series of more typical hollow coucal notes "pok, pok, pok, po, po-po-po-po-po…". **SS** Imm or non-br birds may resemble other imm coucals, but always much smaller, and often much streakier and less uniform dark. Also see Greater, Short-toed and Javan Coucals.

Goliath Coucal *Centropus goliath*　　　　　**E**

L 62–70 cm. Monotypic. Common in undergrowth to midstorey of forest, woodland, edge and regrowth. Regularly sits out, more conspicuous than other coucal species. **ID Ad** all black except for white wing patch. A rare **pale morph** is white with a buffy head. Some other birds have irregular white markings on black plumage. **Imm** chestnut white-streaked head and breast; other (older?) individuals also resemble Ad but are browner overall with barred head and underparts. **Voc** (i) Lower-pitched than most other coucals, a deep "boo" note repeated persistently at about 2 n/s; (ii) harsh "TSOW" or "TSOW-kuk" in alarm.

Bay Coucal *Centropus celebensis*　　　　　**E**

L 44–50 cm. 2 ssp: *celebensis* (N Sul, Togian); *rufescens* (E–S–C Sul, Muna, Buton). Fairly common in forest, edge and thick regrowth. Unlike many other coucals, creeps around in lianas and thickets like a malkoha. **ID Ad** all rufous-chestnut, but much greyer on upper back and crown; greyish bill. Ssp *rufescens* more rufous overall, especially on back and crown. **Imm** lighter on throat and breast. **Voc** Characteristic "water bottle" song: series of hollow "hoo" notes, often becoming shorter and speeding up, then slowing down again; usually at even pitch for entire segments, but pitch can change between segments. One bird frequently incites other birds to join for a duet. Solitary birds give repeated "wheeze".

Short-toed Coucal

Greater Coucal

kangeangensis
buff morph

bubutus

Javan Coucal

immature

Lesser Coucal

celebensis

Goliath Coucal

rufescens

Bay Coucal

Bornean Ground-cuckoo *Carpococcyx radiceus* 🟩E

L 60 cm. Monotypic. Scarce within lowland primary and tall secondary forest, particularly alluvial, <500 m. Terrestrial. Highly territorial pairs, shy. Usually runs away when disturbed. Follows herds of pig and macaque to feed. **ID Ad** head, chin and throat glossy purple-black; back and wing-coverts green with purple gloss, rump dark rufous with black bars; wings and tail coppery violet; neck sides and breast band grey, rest of underparts mostly white finely barred dark; green bill and orbital skin. **Imm** browner on head and throat; underparts more rufous and only barred on flanks; upperpart feathers may partly have rufous edges. **Voc** Often calling from perch 1–5 m off ground when calling. (i) Start-up call is a loud, deep cooing "purr", lasting 0.5 sec, repeated every 1.5 sec for several minutes before turning to next call type; (ii) loud low-pitched, far-carrying guttural "pook-poo", lasting 1.2 sec, the second note falling, continually repeated every 5 sec, for up to an hour at times, often in duet; (iii) sharp pig-like snortle "khrrkh" in alarm.

Sumatran Ground-cuckoo *Carpococcyx viridis* 🟩E

L 55 cm. Monotypic. Rare in primary hill forest, 400–1400 m (may be overlooked in N Sum). Terrestrial. Highly territorial pairs, shy. Usually runs away when disturbed. **ID Ad** crown black becoming green on hindcrown; upper back, wings and tail green (the latter two shading into black); lower back and rump rufous with fine black bars; chin black; throat and breast dull green; belly buff with dark barring; multicoloured orbital skin and coral-green bill. **Imm** mostly all rufous with fine dark bars; less extensive orbital skin. **Voc** Often calling from perch 1–3 m off ground, pumps tail when calling. (i) Deliberate hollow, 3-note whistle of 2 even notes interrupted by a lower note: "quee-oh-wee", lasting 1.5 sec; regularly repeated, often in duet; also produced as descending, quick succession in advertising call. Call carries far and can be delivered at much lower pitch and gruff quality. (ii) Loud "TZZICK-K", like two metal bars clapped against each other with a slight echo; (iii) Scolding "KEAOWW".

HEMIPROCNIDAE
Treeswifts
3 species in region

Large, branch-perching swifts with long wings and long forked tails. Often conspicuous within canopy of forest and edge habitat, making sallying flights to catch flying insects.

Whiskered Treeswift *Hemiprocne comata*

L 15–17 cm. Sundaic, Phil. 2 ssp, 1 in region: *comata* (Bor–Sum, MPen). Fairly common in primary and secondary forest, tall plantations, locally tall mangroves, <1200 m. Perches on exposed bare branches in mid-high canopy, making short sallies; does not soar above canopy. Singly or pairs, rarely congregates. Flight jerky with stiff wingbeats. **ID** Compact; long tail with shallow fork. **M** mostly olive-bronze body, glossy dark-blue wings and head, white belly, tertials and long supercilium and moustachial stripes; rufous ear-coverts. **F** dark-blue ear-coverts. **Imm** finely barred brown, grey and white. **Voc** (i) Shrill chattering "she-she-she..."; (ii) shrill "chew" or "e-chew".

Moustached Treeswift *Hemiprocne mystacea*

L 28–31 cm. Aus. 6 ssp, 1 in region: *confirmata* (N–C Mol, Aru). Fairly common in primary and secondary forest, tall plantations, locally tall mangroves, <1600 m. Perches on exposed bare branches in high canopy, making long sallies; regularly soars. Singly, pairs or small groups (<20). **ID** Slim; long body and tail with very deep fork. **M** mostly grey body; dark-blue wings, tail and crown; white tertial tips, supercilium and moustachial stripes; small rufous ear-covert patch. **F** grey ear-coverts. **Imm** barred rufous-buff head and back, rufous white body. **Voc** Squeaky, high-pitched "wee-wee-wee..." and "chew-chew-chew...".

Grey-rumped Treeswift *Hemiprocne longipennis*

L 21–25 cm. SE Asia. 4 ssp: *longipennis* (Jav–Lombok, Kangean); *harterti* (Sum–Bor, MPen, Sulu); *perlonga* (W Sum Is); *wallacii* (Sul to Sula). Fairly common in primary and secondary forest, tall plantations, locally tall mangroves, <1600 m. Perches on exposed bare branches in high canopy, making long sallies; regularly soars. Singly, pairs or small groups (<10). Deep, slow wingbeats; languid flight rarely at speed. **ID** Slim; long body and tail with very deep tail fork. **M** green-glossed upperparts with long, upward crest to forehead; grey rump and underparts; orange ear-coverts. **F** ear-coverts dark-green. Ssp *wallacii* larger; *harterti* darker underparts; *perlonga* slightly larger than nominate with darker underparts and rump. **Imm** rufous-fringed upperparts and white-edged flight feathers. **Voc** Surprisingly vocal: (i) harsh, piercing "kik-kik-kik..."; (ii) staccato tern-like "e-chit-chew"; (iii) disyllabic "too-eet".

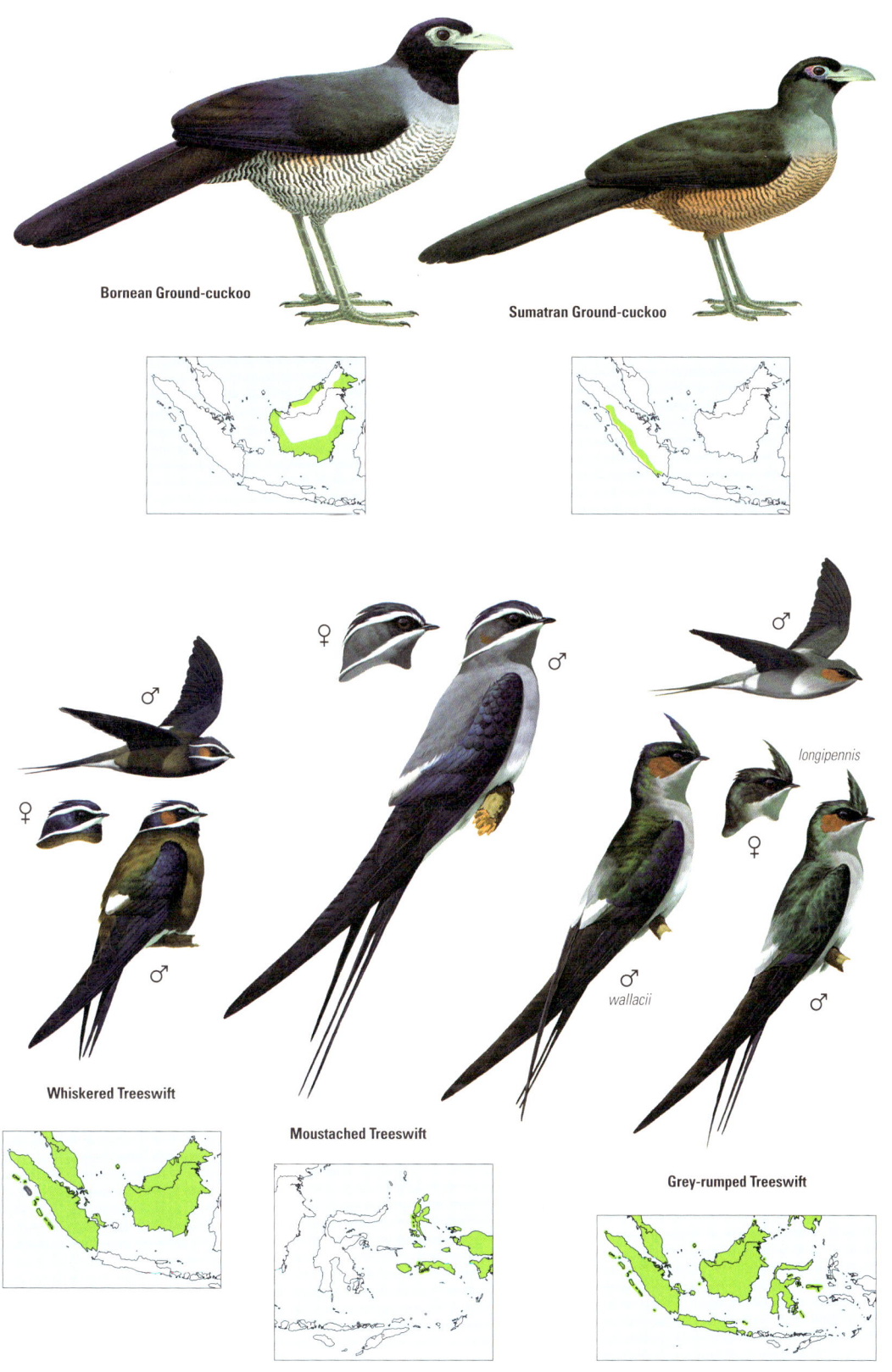

Bornean Ground-cuckoo

Sumatran Ground-cuckoo

♂

♀

♂

♀

♂

longipennis

♀

♂

wallacii

♂

Whiskered Treeswift

Moustached Treeswift

Grey-rumped Treeswift

23 species in region

Small to medium-sized, highly aerial insectivores, often found feeding in large loose flocks. Some species nest communally within caves or on buildings, others in tree cavities. Spend most of their lives on the wing, only landing to nest. One genus (*Aerodramus*) capable of echolocation and produces poorly-understood series of high-pitched squeaks and clicks.

Silver-rumped Spinetail *Rhaphidura leucopygialis*

L 11 cm. Sundaic. Monotypic. Fairly common over primary, secondary and degraded forest, <1500 m. Singly or small groups (<20), particularly during wet weather when flocks feed lower in clearings and along rivers and roads. **ID** Robust; short, square tail; broad paddle-shaped wings, pinching in at base. **Ad** glossed dark-blue body, silvery-white rump to tail. **Imm** lacks gloss. **AN** Silver-rumped Needletail.

House Swift *Apus nipalensis*

L 15 cm. S–SE–E Asia, Phil. 4 ssp, 2 in region: *furcatus* (Jav, Bali; probably this ssp spreading east through LS); *subfurcatus* (Bor–Sum, MPen, Phil; perhaps this form spreading east through Sul and Mol). No longer included with extralimital Little Swift *A. affinis* based on body structure and potential sympatry. Locally common over variety of habitats, including breeding in city buildings, towns, cliffs and feeding over surrounding countryside and forest, <1500 m. Highly gregarious. **ID** Chunky-looking; broad, rounded white rump and clearly-defined white throat; square-ended tail with slight tail notch. Ssp *subfurcatus* blacker overall, shallower tail fork. **SS** See Pacific Swift.

Pacific Swift *Apus pacificus*

L 17–18 cm. Breeds N–E Asia; winters SE Asia, Phil, Aus. 2 ssp: *pacificus* (breeds N Asia; winters SE Asia to Aus); *kurodae* (breeds E Asia; winters SE Asia, Phil). No longer includes three extralimital Asian species (*A. cooki, A. salimali, A. leuconyx*) based on consistent, stable plumage differences. Locally fairly common over variety of habits, forming large flocks during passage, recorded Sep–early May. **ID** Large, rakish structure; long, pointed wings and deeply forked, long tail; black body with clearly defined white throat and rump; underparts strongly scaled whitish. Ssp *kurodae* throat greyish, less well-defined and rump patch slightly narrower. **SS** House Swift is smaller, more compact, has broader shorter wings, a shallower tail fork, a more rounded rump patch and a less direct flight style. **AN** Fork-tailed Swift.

Asian Palm Swift *Cypsiurus balasiensis*

L 13 cm. S–SE Asia, Phil. 4 ssp, 2 in region: *bartelsorum* (Jav, Bali) and *infumatus* (Bor–Sum, mainland SE Asia; perhaps this form recently spreading through Sul), combined with extralimital *pallidior* (Phil), sometimes separated from nominate *balasiensis* (S Asia) as '**Eastern Palm Swift**' *C. infumatus* based on contact in NE India with limited intergradation. Locally common over villages, towns, open countryside and cultivation; breeds in fan palms and thatched roofs, <1500 m. Highly gregarious. **ID Ad** long, slender wings and body; long, deeply-forked tail; brownish-grey body, slightly paler rump and underparts. Ssp *infumatus* darker, especially on rump. **Imm** tail less deeply forked. **Voc** Distinct nervous "TEETtereeTEET". **SS** From *Aerodramus* swiftlets by much longer and thinner body, faster flight and longer, deeply-forked tail.

Giant Swiftlet *Hydrochous gigas*

L 16 cm. Sundaic. Monotypic. Uncommon over submontane forest, often around waterfalls, 700–2000 m, rarely down to 200 m. Usually in fast-moving large groups, <80, hawking over forest, particularly ahead of weather fronts. Breeds on small ledges within spray of waterfall. Flight usually direct and fast, regularly soars. **ID Ad** large, *Apus*-like silhouette with long, barrel-chested body, broad-based wings and noticeable tail notch. No contrast between upper- and underparts. **Imm** undescribed. **SS** Smaller *Aerodramus* swiftlets have more rounded wings without noticeable broad base, flap more often and appear slower in flight. **AN** Waterfall Swiftlet.

Ameline Swiftlet *Aerodramus amelis*

L 13 cm. Phil. 2 ssp, 1 in region: ssp *palawanensis* (Palawan; off Sabah coast at least on Balambangan) is sometimes separated from extra-limital nominate form as monotypic '**Palawan Swiftlet**'. The two formerly united with Uniform Swiftlet but not closely related. **ID/SS** Very similar to Uniform Swiftlet, which does not breed in its offshore nesting caves off Sabah. Ameline reported to have 'capped' appearance because of pale face, but it is questionable whether a stray to the coast of the Bornean mainland would be identifiable in the field from Uniform or Black-nest. The only other swiftlet sharing its offshore nesting caves, the smaller Edible-nest, has paler rump and underparts on average, but may only be safely identifiable by being observed on its white nest. **AN** Grey Swiftlet.

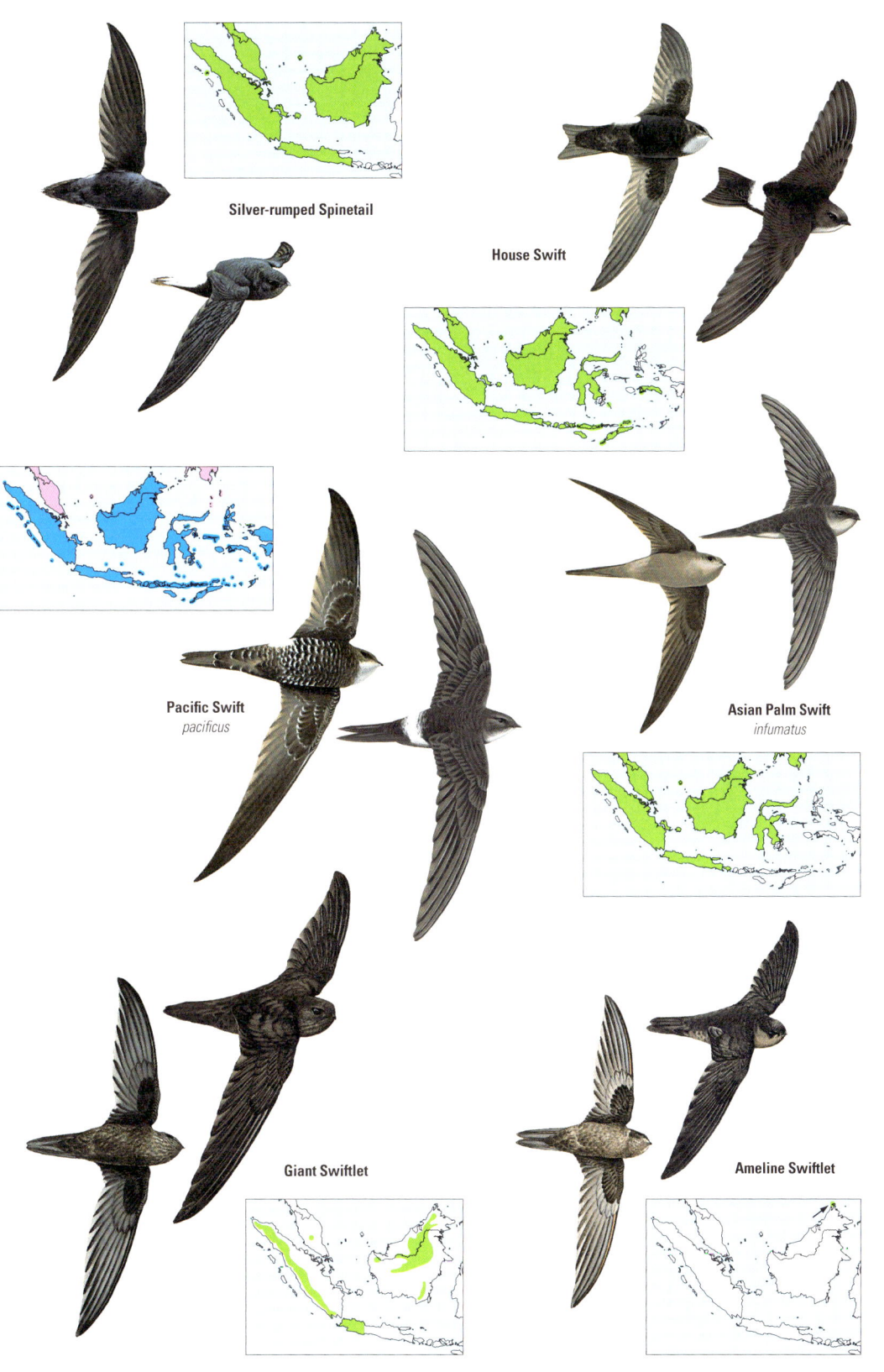

Silver-rumped Spinetail

House Swift

Pacific Swift
pacificus

Asian Palm Swift
infumatus

Giant Swiftlet

Ameline Swiftlet

Seram Swiftlet *Aerodramus ceramensis* E

L 11 cm. Monotypic. Often united with Halmahera and Sulawesi Swiftlets into '**Moluccan Swiftlet**' *A. infuscatus*, but all three display non-clinal differences in plumage. Fairly common over forest, cultivation and villages. Highly gregarious, flocking with congeners. **ID** Round-winged; slightly paler underparts to upperparts; broad dirty-white rump; obvious tail notch. **SS** Uniform Swiftlet is slightly larger and lacks obvious pale rump. See also Glossy Swiftlet.

Halmahera Swiftlet *Aerodramus infuscatus* E

L 11 cm. Monotypic. For taxonomy see Seram Swiftlet. Fairly common over forest, cultivation and villages. Highly gregarious, flocking with congeners. **ID** Round-winged; brown-grey body with slightly paler underparts; broad greyish rump; obvious tail notch. **SS** Uniform Swiftlet is slightly larger with generally darker rump concolorous with back. However, Uniform's rump often appears paler than rest of body in bad viewing conditions, and views from above or against background below horizon are usually needed for conclusive identification. See also Glossy Swiftlet.

Sulawesi Swiftlet *Aerodramus sororum* E

L 11 cm. Monotypic. For taxonomy see Seram Swiftlet. Common over forest, cultivation and villages. Highly gregarious, flocking with congeners. **ID** Round-winged; brown-grey body with slightly paler underparts, particularly belly; broad greyish-white rump; obvious tail notch. **SS** Uniform and widely introduced Edible-nest Swiftlets are slightly larger with generally darker rump (concolorous with back in Uniform; often pale but more diffuse, less narrow and well-defined in Edible-nest). See also Glossy Swiftlet and Asian Palm Swift.

Uniform Swiftlet *Aerodramus vanikorensis*

L 12–13 cm. SE Asia to Aus. ~18 ssp, 8 in region: *aenigma* (N–C–SE Sul, Banggai, Sula); *heinrichi* (S Sul); *moluccarum* (C–S Mol, probably this form in Tanimbar); *waigeuensis* (N Mol, W Papuan Is); the GS ssp *salangana* (Jav), *aerophilus* (W Sum Is), *maratua* (Maratua) and *natunae* (Bor–Sum) are usually treated as separate species '**Mossy-nest Swiftlet**' *A. salangana*, but we follow classical treatment as subspecies of Uniform Swiftlet based on identical nest, extremely minor plumage differentiation and lack of considerable genetic divergence. For the same reasons, extralimital Pacific taxa *bartschi* and *sawtelli*, which are often treated as separate species, are here included with Uniform. See also Ameline Swiftlet for taxonomy. Fairly common over variety of habitats adjacent to breeding caves. Highly gregarious, flocking with congeners. Echolocates in nesting caves where it builds nests out of mossy material interwoven with saliva. **ID** (*salangana*) Uniform blackish-brown upperparts and slightly paler, dusky underparts; slight tail notch. Ssp *aerophilus* slightly smaller with deeper tail notch; *maratua* also slightly smaller and averages paler; *natunae* averages longer-winged and with feathered tarsi. Eastern ssp *aenigma* uniform brownish-grey with slight tail notch, underparts and rump slightly paler than blue-green tinged upperparts; *heinrichi* slightly paler below than previous, green-glossed above; *moluccarum* has pale suffusion around eye and more pronounced fringing on undertail-coverts; *waigeuensis* darker than *aenigma* but with paler throat and breast. **SS** Field identification from Edible-nest and Black-nest Swiftlets is virtually impossible away from nesting caves where birds can be seen on their mossy (as opposed to white or black) nests. In hand, 'Mossy-nest' always has dark rami (=barb stems) on back feathers whereas Edible-nest often has whitish rami (exposed by blowing on back surface), while Black-nest has larger wing measurements. Smaller

Collocalia swiftlets have contrastingly white belly, more intense blue/green gloss, bat-like flight and often fly lower. See also Giant, Ameline, Volcano, Halmahera, Sulawesi and Seram Swiftlets and Asian Palm Swift.

Black-nest Swiftlet *Aerodramus maximus*

L 12–14 cm. Sundaic. 3 ssp, 2 in region: *lowi* (most of GS); *tichelmani* (SE Bor). Abundant over variety of habitats adjacent to breeding caves. Highly gregarious, flocking with congeners. Echolocates in nesting caves where it builds blackish nests out of feathers and other material interwoven with saliva. **ID** Uniform blackish-brown upperparts and paler brown underparts; often with slightly paler greyish rump, slight tail notch. Ssp *tichelmani* smaller. **SS** The smaller Uniform (which see for more details) and Edible-nest Swiftlets are virtually indistinguishable in the field unless seen on their mossy or white (as opposed to blackish) nests. Smaller *Collocalia* swiftlets have contrastingly white belly, blue/green gloss, bat-like flight and often fly lower. See also Giant, Volcano and Ameline Swiftlets and Asian Palm Swift.

Edible-nest Swiftlet *Aerodramus fuciphagus*

L 12 cm. SE Asia, Phil. 8 ssp, 7 in region: *fuciphagus* (Jav–Sumbawa, Flores Sea Is); *dammermani* (Flores–Alor); *micans* (Sumba–Timor, presumed this ssp to Babar); *perplexus* (Maratua); *vestitus* (Bor–Sum, MPen); the two northern ssp *germani* (coasts of mainland SE Asia, offshore N Bor and W Phil) and *amechanus* (Anambas) sometimes separated as '**Germain's Swiftlet**' *A. germani*, or as '**Brown-rumped Swiftlet**' *A. inexpectatus* (with extralimital ssp *inexpectatus* from Andamans and Nicobars), but genetic differentiation is minimal and plumage turn-over between *germani* and *vestitus* is bridged clinally through ample intra-colony plumage variation in MPen and Bor. Locally abundant over variety of habitats adjacent to breeding caves and man-made breeding houses. Echolocates in caves (or breeding houses) where it builds highly-prized white nests mostly made of saliva. Commercial colonies now being established all across region for farm breeding, leading to mixing of subspecies. Highly gregarious, flocking with congeners. **ID** Uniform blackish-brown upperparts and paler brown underparts, paler rump can appear concolourous with upperparts; notable tail notch. Ssp *dammermani* apparently with even paler rump; *micans* paler and greyer; *perplexus* purple sheen to remiges and rectrices, and only slight rump contrast; *vestitus* blackest above, only slight rump contrast; *amechanus* much paler rump than nominate; *germani* the palest-rumped form. **SS** See Black-nest and Uniform Swiftlets, which are virtually unidentifiable away from nest. Smaller *Collocalia* swiftlets have contrastingly white belly, blue/green gloss, bat-like flight and often fly lower. See also Giant, Volcano, Sulawesi and Ameline Swiftlets and Asian Palm Swift.

Volcano Swiftlet *Aerodramus vulcanorum* E

L 14 cm. Monotypic. Breeds along rim of active volcano craters in Jav; known from six localities spread across the island, where fairly common. Usually found flying over breeding craters though during poor weather found over forest below craters, >2400 m. **ID** Notable tail notch; underparts and rump slightly paler than upperparts. **SS** Extremely similar to Uniform, Black-nest and Edible-nest Swiftlets, but has deeper tail notch; the latter three unlikely to be found around its high-elevation volcano crater haunts. Smaller Linchi Swiftlet has contrastingly white belly, blue/green gloss, bat-like flight and often flies lower. See also Giant Swiftlet and Asian Palm Swift.

Seram Swiftlet

Halmahera Swiftlet

Sulawesi Swiftlet

Uniform Swiftlet
salangana

Black-nest Swiftlet
lowi

Volcano Swiftlet

fuciphagus

vestitus

germani

Edible-nest Swiftlet

Linchi Swiftlet *Collocalia linchi* E

L 9–10 cm. 3 ssp: *linchi* (Jav, Madura, Bawean); *ripleyi* (Sum); *dedii* (Bali, Lombok). Population on Nusa Penida resembles *linchi* although geographically adjacent to *dedii*. Does not include extralimital Christmas Island Swiftlet *C. natalis* based on latter's divergent plumage colouration. See also Bornean Swiftlet for taxonomy. Abundant over all habitats. Ssp *ripleyi* thought to occur in mountainous and hilly areas only. Bat-like flight, often low to ground; continual fast flapping, constantly changing direction, rarely glides. **ID** Small-bodied. **Ad** white belly and lower breast contrasting with rest of blackish body; pale base to rectrices; mantle glossed green, not easily discernible. Naked hind-toe. Ssp *ripleyi* shorter tail and darker undertail-coverts; *dedii* longer wings and tail. **Imm** lacks gloss, pale-fringed flight feathers. **SS** On Sum, challenging to separate from Plume-toed; the latter is not only found in hilly terrain and has bluer body gloss, which is impossible to judge on most flying birds and perhaps only diagnosable on some birds perched on nest. Linchi held in hand can be told by naked hind-toe (versus hind-toe with feather tuft on Plume-toed). See also Uniform, Black-nest, Edible-nest and Volcano Swiftlets. **AN** Cave Swiftlet.

Bornean Swiftlet *Collocalia dodgei* E

L 8–9 cm. Monotypic. Formerly included with Linchi but there are fairly deep mtDNA and some mensural differences. Currently only known from four localities, >1300 m, including Mt Kinabalu and Crocker Range but probably found throughout the mountains of Bor. **ID Ad** green-glossed crown and mantle; gleaming white belly extends to breast; naked hind-toe. **Imm** undescribed. **SS** Challenging to separate from Plume-toed, the latter also occurring at lower elevations but with broad overlap. Flocks seen around highest rocky parts of Mt Kinabalu likely attributable to Bornean, although further down the slope in forest both species possible. Plume-toed slightly larger overall, perhaps darker breast on average and with bluish (not greenish) mantle gloss, but field reliability of these characters is questionable with colour change due to incidence of light and photo flash. Bornean held in hand can be told by naked hind-toe (versus hind-toe with feather tuft on Plume-toed). See also Uniform, Black-nest and Edible-nest Swiftlets.

Glossy Swiftlet *Collocalia esculenta*

L 9–10 cm. Aus. 17 ssp, 4 in region: *esculenta* (C–S Sul – C–S Mol, Aru; probably this form on Tanimbar); *manadensis* (N Sul–Talaud); *minuta* (Tanahjampea, Kalao); *spilura* (N Mol). In region, no longer includes the genetically divergent Tenggara, Plume-toed and Drab Swiftlets. Common over cities, mangroves, forest and cultivation, <2000 m. Often forms flocks, frequently feeding at or below canopy, usually lower than *Aerodramus*. Flight bat-like, fast, erratic flapping with constant change of direction. **ID Ad** dark green-glossed mantle; pure white underparts except upper breast; broad white tail spot on rectrices. Ssp *manadensis* mantle tinged green-blue, more contrasting breast demarcation; *minuta* smaller; *spilura* dull green-blue mantle, sooty-brown underparts with only belly whitish. **Imm** pale fringes to flight feathers; less glossy. **SS** From larger, brownish *Aerodramus* swiftlets by strong blue/green overall gloss, contrast between white belly and dark breast, and more erratic, bat-like flight action.

Tenggara Swiftlet *Collocalia sumbawae* E

L 8–9 cm. 2 ssp: *sumbawae* (Sumbawa, Flores); ssp *sumbae* (Sumba) is deeply diverged genetically and may warrant treatment as monotypic '**Sumba Swiftlet**'. For taxonomy also see Glossy. Common in all habitats. Flight similar to small bat: fast, shallow wing-beats, often just over and inside forest. **ID Ad** bluish-green glossed mantle and wings; extensive white underparts to lower breast; small white spots on rectrices; no hindclaw feathering. Ssp *sumbae* bluish-glossed mantle and faint white edging on rump. **Imm** undescribed. **SS** See larger Edible-nest.

Plume-toed Swiftlet *Collocalia affinis*

L 9–10 cm. Sundaic, Andamans, Nicobars. 5 ssp, 3 in region: *cyanoptila* (Bor–Sum, MPen); *oberholseri* (Batu, Mentawai); *vanderbilti* (Nias). For taxonomy see Glossy. Common over cities, mangroves, forest and cultivation, <2000 m. Often forms flocks feeding at or below canopy, usually lower than *Aerodramus*. Flight bat-like, fast, erratic flapping with constant change of direction. **ID Ad** dull glossed blue-green mantle; chocolate-brown throat and breast, mottled lower breast, white belly; feathered hind-toe and dark tail. Ssp *oberholseri* shows green-tinged mantle; *vanderbilti* deep-blue mantle. **Imm** pale fringed flight feathers. **SS** See Bornean, Linchi, Edible-nest, Black-nest and Uniform Swiftlets.

Drab Swiftlet *Collocalia neglecta* E

L 8–9 cm. 2 ssp: *neglecta* (Timor, Rote); *perneglecta* (Sawu, Pantar–Babar). For taxonomy see Glossy. Common in all habitats. Flight similar to small bat: fast, shallow wing-beats, often just over and inside forest. **ID Ad** as Glossy but mantle matt-brownish, lacking gloss, and white belly reaches upper breast. Ssp *perneglecta* greenish-glossed mantle. **Imm** undescribed. **SS** See larger Uniform and Edible-nest.

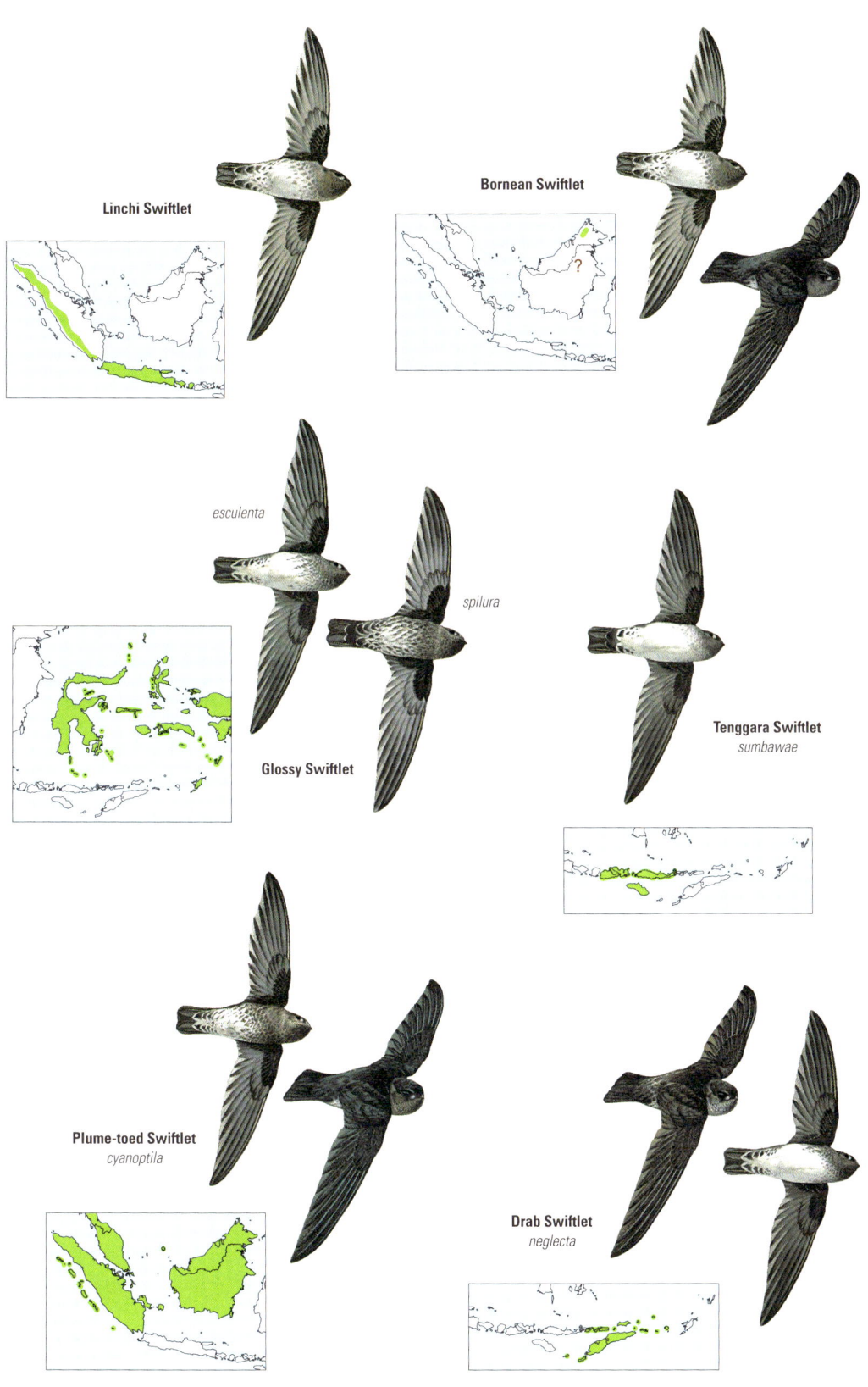

Linchi Swiftlet

Bornean Swiftlet

esculenta

spilura

Glossy Swiftlet

Tenggara Swiftlet
sumbawae

Plume-toed Swiftlet
cyanoptila

Drab Swiftlet
neglecta

White-throated Needletail *Hirundapus caudacutus*
L 19–20 cm. Breeds Himalaya–NE Asia; winters Aus. 2 ssp: *caudacutus* (breeds N-NE Asia; winters to Aus); the rare ssp *nudipes* (breeds Himalaya; wintering grounds poorly known; two specimens W Jav, Nov 1922; flocks observed SE Sul, Dec 2017, Jan 2020) probably best considered monotypic species '**Himalayan Needletail**' based on plumage differences. Fairly common migrant Sep–Nov, Mar–Apr, occasional records Dec–Feb. Variety of habitats but particularly over mountain passes, sometimes in large flocks. Fast gliding flight with loud swooshing sound; often soars. **ID** Large; powerfully built. **Ad** all dark with clearly defined white throat and forehead, large white 'saddle' and white V on flanks and undertail. Ssp *nudipes* lacks white lores; less distinct, browner mantle with darker blue-glossed upperparts. **Imm** greyish-brown forehead, V on underparts with blackish marks. **SS** Silver-backed has less clearly defined, smaller white throat and saddle; additionally differs from ssp *caudacutus* by lack of white on forehead. Larger Brown-backed has even less white on saddle and lacks white on throat. Purple Needletail lacks white on throat and saddle altogether; on underwing shows broad white fringes to greater coverts.

Silver-backed Needletail *Hirundapus cochinchinensis*
L 20 cm. S–SE–E Asia. 2 ssp: *cochinchinensis* (breeds E Himalaya, northern SE Asia, Hainan, Taiwan; winters SE Asia, Sum, Jav); *rupchandi* (breeds C Himalaya; winters SE Asia, Sum, Jav). Recorded Sep–Apr. Uncommon over variety of habitats, usually over forest in small flocks, <20. Fast gliding flight with loud swooshing sound; often soars. **ID Ad** all dark with ill-defined whitish-grey throat; greyish-white saddle; white V on flanks and undertail. Ssp *rupchandi* slightly paler below with darker throat, but probably not identifiable in the field. **Imm** white V has blackish marks. **SS** See White-throated. Larger Brown-backed lacks pale throat and has less contrasting saddle.

Brown-backed Needletail *Hirundapus giganteus*
L 25 cm. S–SE Asia, Palawan. 2 ssp, 1–2 in region: *giganteus* (GS, MPen, Palawan); ssp *indicus* (southern S Asia, mainland SE Asia) is possible vagrant to GS. Variety of habitats, usually over forest in small flocks, <30. Fast gliding flight with loud swooshing sound; often soars. **ID Ad** all dark except pale brownish saddle and white V on flanks and undertail. Ssp *indicus* white lores. **Imm** white V has blackish marks. **SS** See White-throated and Silver-backed.

Purple Needletail *Hirundapus celebensis*
L 25 cm. Sul–Sula, Phil. Monotypic. Uncommon over variety of habitats, usually over forest, <2000 m, often in flocks (<100). Fast gliding flight with loud swooshing sound; often soars. **ID** Large; powerfully-built. **Ad** white V on flanks and undertail; purple-glossed mantle; underwing shows broad white fringes to greater coverts. **Imm** white V has blackish marks; lacks gloss on upperparts. **SS** See White-throated.

AEGOTHELIDAE
Owlet-nightjars
1 species in region
Small, cryptically coloured, with distinct owl-like facial appearance and upright stance. Crepuscular or nocturnal within forest habitat; arboreal. Presence usually revealed by call.

Moluccan Owlet-nightjar *Aegotheles crinifrons* `E`
L 29 cm. Monotypic. Fairly common in primary and secondary forest and edge, <1800 m. Perches upright in mid-storey. **ID Ad** polymorphic: brown and rufous morphs with intermediates. Slim and long-tailed; finely vermiculated upperparts; underparts paler, variably spotted dark. **Imm** undescribed. **Voc** (i) Usually 4–5 upslurred notes producing a descending, squeaky laughter "whaa-ha-ha-ah", lasting ~1.8 sec, sometimes fewer or more notes; (ii) scolding "keow", lasting 0.3 sec.

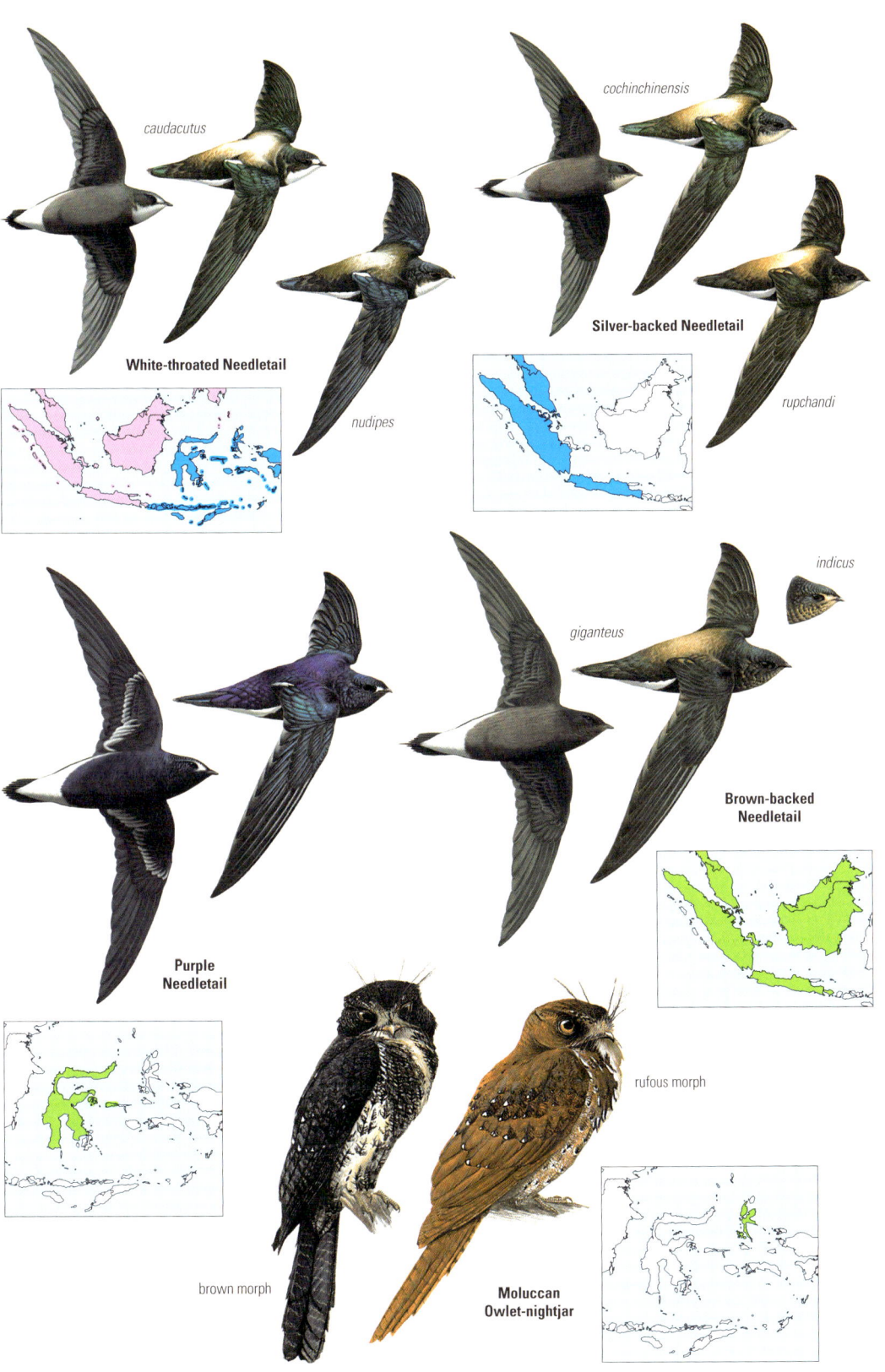

caudacutus

White-throated Needletail

nudipes

cochinchinensis

Silver-backed Needletail

rupchandi

giganteus

indicus

Brown-backed Needletail

Purple Needletail

brown morph

rufous morph

Moluccan Owlet-nightjar

Small to medium-sized, cryptically coloured, with stocky bodies, large eyes and extremely wide mouths. Crepuscular or nocturnal within forest habitat; arboreal. Often quite vocal but shy and unobtrusive, frequently remaining motionless for long periods.

Gould's Frogmouth *Batrachostomus stellatus*

L 23–27 cm. Sundaic. Monotypic. Uncommon in primary and secondary forest, <500 m, rarely <900 m. **ID** Polymorphic. **Ad** rufous and dark morphs with intermediates. Brown scalloping on whitish underparts; white spots on wing-coverts; protruding bill; shortish tail. **Imm** more uniform; dark-barred upperparts. **Voc** (i) Eerie, whistled "wooah-weo", lasting 1 sec, first note drawn-out, last note descending; (ii) 3–5 yapping, rapid "wek" notes; (iii) <5 descending, tremulous "weeeh" notes; (iv) forceful "weeeoh". **SS** Best told by voice, but most silent Gould's individuals separated from Sunda and Blyth's by more uniformly scalloped underparts (versus irregular markings), lacking distinct breast band and not usually showing the latter two species' typical white diamond-shaped breast spots contrasting with background. Occasional Gould's (usually rufous morph, possibly always females) reported with all-red underparts and a few contrasting white diamond spots on breast would be difficult to separate from equivalent plumages of fem Blyth's and Sunda without vocalisations. Limited elevational overlap with different-sounding Sumatran and Bornean Frogmouths, but silently perched Sumatran and Bornean individuals can be told but their shorter tail, much longer facial whiskers and more distinct white scaly diamond pattern on underparts.

Sumatran Frogmouth *Batrachostomus poliolophus*   E

L 20–23 cm. Monotypic. See Bornean Frogmouth for taxonomy. Uncommon in primary and secondary forest, rarely edge, 1200–2000 m, rarely down to 600 m. **ID M** slightly scalloped white underparts with dark-brown breast and dark line down centre of belly; upperparts unmarked, warm brown with large white spots on coverts and scapulars; whitish supercilium with long, shaggy bristles protruding from face. **F** brighter rufous; indistinct collar; more uniform underparts with scalloped belly. **Imm** uniform rufous-brown, slightly paler underparts. **Voc** (i) Descending whistled "wawawawa", lasting 3–4 sec; (ii) 4–15 loud, forceful "woo-ra" notes, at 1 n/s; (iii) various shrieking, haunting whistles. **SS** Blyth's and Sunda longer-tailed. Fem Blyth's and Sunda more uniformly rufous underneath with large white markings; male Blyth's and Sunda darker with untidy barred and spotted underparts; both sexes never as extensively scalloped underneath as either sex of Sumatran. Also see Gould's. **AN** Pale-headed / Short-tailed Frogmouth.

Bornean Frogmouth *Batrachostomus mixtus*   E

L 20–23 cm. Monotypic. Formerly united with Sumatran into '**Short-tailed Frogmouth**' *B. poliolophus*, but differs in plumage and vocalisations. Scarce in primary and secondary forest, 900–2400 m, rarely down to 300 m. **ID M** dark-brown with broad white nuchal collar and supercilium; scapulars and coverts with bold white spots; heavily scalloped white belly delimited from more 'messy' brown-and-white pattern on breast by a noticeable brown neck-lace across lower breast. **F** brighter rufous; indistinct collar; less white on wing-coverts; rufous underparts with irregular white breast spots. **Imm** as F but fewer white markings on underparts. **Voc** (i) Descending whistle lasting ~4 sec; (ii) succession of short whistles lasting <1 sec; (iii) tremulous whistle, lasting 1.3 sec; (iv) 2-note whistle "wirrr-hu", lasting 1.2 sec, sometimes second note absent; (v) 5–10 bubbly chattering notes, lasting ~1.5 sec.

SS Longer-tailed Blyth's and Sunda Frogmouths from generally lower elevations similar: fem Blyth's has more well-defined white diamond necklace as opposed to Bornean's more irregular white diamond spots on breast; larger fem Sunda can be very similar in colouration but often has dark marks on undertail coverts and more boldly patterned, noticeably longer tail. M Bornean has unmarked, brighter brown breast feathers and white scalloped belly with neat, narrowly-fringed feathers whereas M Blyth's appears messier due to small scalloped feathers with dark marks at tip and small dark marks on brown breast feathers. Larger M Sunda told from Bornean by blackish-brown, not brighter brown, overall plumage colouration (except in S-SE Kalimantan) and by similar underparts pattern to Blyth's. Also see Gould's.

Javan Frogmouth *Batrachostomus javensis*   E

L 20–23 cm. Monotypic. Formerly included Blyth's and Palawan Frogmouth *B. chaseni* (Palawan) but all three differ vocally and—less so—in plumage. Fairly common in forest, edge and tall plantations, <2200 m. **ID M** dark brown, lacking white markings on wings and tail except narrow nuchal collar; boldly scalloped breast. **F** rufous with bold white breast spots. **Imm** similar but plainer and paler rufous. **Voc** (i) ~10 excited, sharp laughing "wha-ha-ha-ha...", 10 n/1.3 s; (ii) growling "KWAHa", immediately followed by 1–4 high-pitched, whining "twoowa"; (iii) 4-note, high-pitched shrieking "towee-towee-towee-towee", 4 n/5 s; (iv) slightly descending whistle, tailing off "peeeyoo", lasting 2.6 sec.

Blyth's Frogmouth *Batrachostomus affinis*

L 21–23 cm. SE Asia. 2 ssp, 1 in region: *affinis* (Bor, Sum, MPen). Extralimital ssp *continentalis* (mainland SE Asia except MPen) sometimes separated as monotypic '**Indochinese Frogmouth**' but vocal differences minor. See also Javan Frogmouth for taxonomy. Status on, and around Sum uncertain, only specimens from Aceh and Bintan with no confirmed sight records. Uncommon in primary and secondary forest, <1700 m. **ID M** brownish-grey upperparts, lightly barred and spotted; thin white nuchal collar; underparts whitish with belly heavily scalloped and broad brown breast band with small dark markings. **F** rufous; prominent white spots on scapulars and breast (but not belly), white nuchal collar; belly paler. **Imm** similar but plainer and paler rufous. **Voc M**: (i) tame growl "gwaa", lasting 0.5 sec; (ii) short, whistled "teooo", slightly downslurred, lasting 0.8 sec. **F**: (i) laughing "grra-ga-ga-ga", lasting 1 sec; (ii) short, yapping "yap". **SS** See Sunda, Sumatran, Gould's and Bornean.

Sunda Frogmouth *Batrachostomus cornutus*   E

L 25–28 cm. 3 ssp: *cornutus* (Sum), *adspersus* (Bor–Bangka); taxonomic status of ssp *longicaudatus* (Kangean) uncertain, possibly more closely related to Javan, study of unknown vocalisations required. Recently discovered population on Mentawai may be undescribed ssp. Possible intra-Bornean variation requires study, as male specimens from Banjarmasin area of S Kalimantan and photographed birds from SE Kalimantan differ in plumage from elsewhere in Bor. Apparent vocal differentiation between Sumatra and Borneo also requires further research. Fairly common in secondary forest and edge, also plantations, particularly along coast, <1000 m. **ID M** (*adspersus*) as Blyth's but plumage blackish-brown with white-speckled mantle and crown; tail pale-barred with black borders; in Banjarmasin area, at least, much paler, browner overall; *cornutus* browner overall, less speckling on crown and mantle, lacks black border on tail bars; *longicaudatus* less contrasting plumage, less white on forehead and collar, and longer-tailed. **F** *adspersus* very similar to smaller, sympatric Blyth's but white breast markings more extensive, reaching lower belly; *cornutus* possibly less rufous, and with more distinct tail barring than *adspersus*. **Imm** paler,

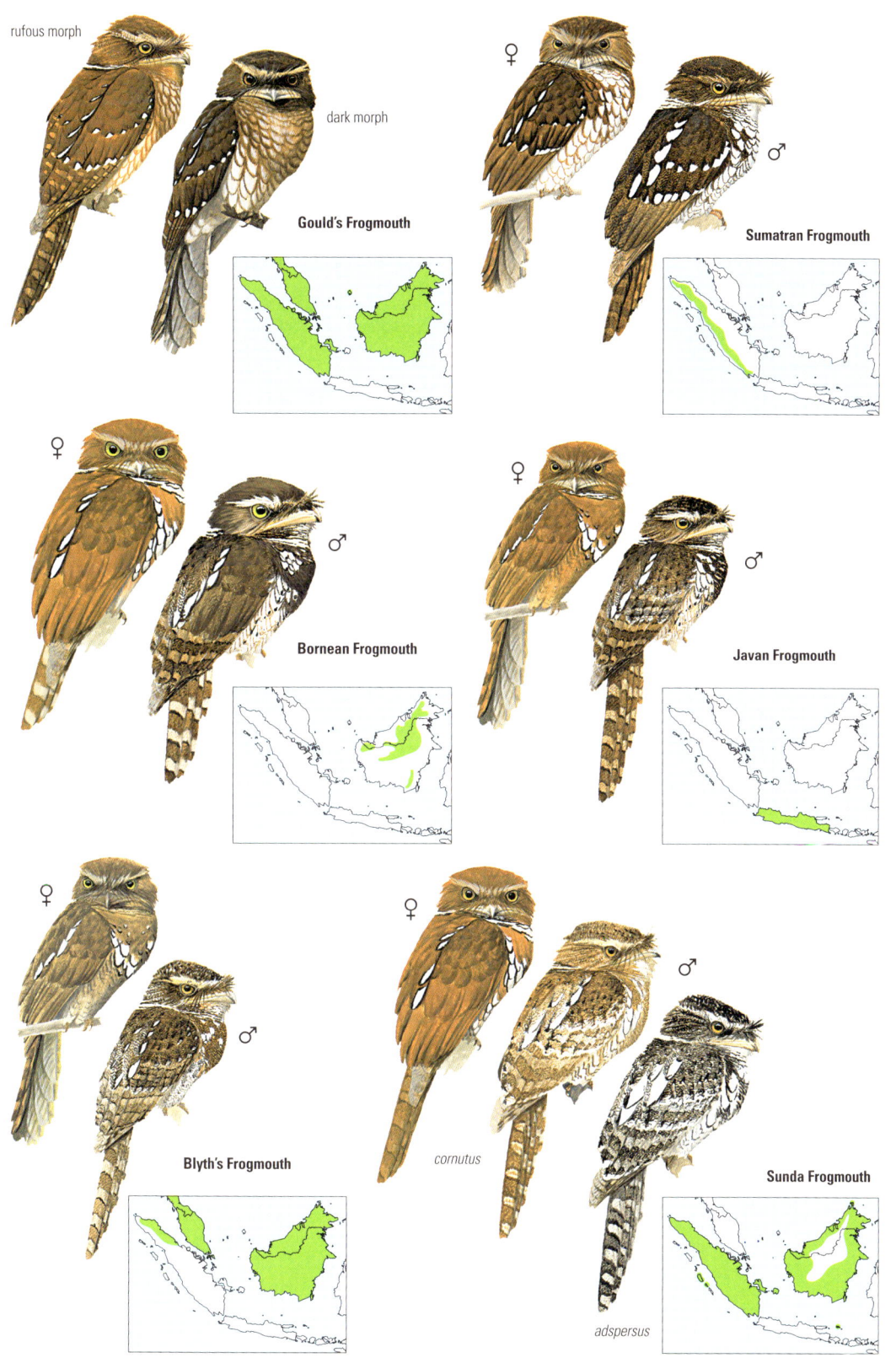

rufous morph

dark morph

Gould's Frogmouth

♀

♂

Sumatran Frogmouth

♀

♂

Bornean Frogmouth

♀

♂

Javan Frogmouth

♀

♂

Blyth's Frogmouth

♀

♂

cornutus

Sunda Frogmouth

adspersus

buffier and more vermiculated overall. **Voc** (i) Slightly descending stretched-out whistle, tailing off "peeeyoo", lasting 2 sec, very similar to Javan; (ii) short, downslurred note "peyoo", lasting 0.2 sec; (iii) <11 growling "graa" notes, 11 n/8.5 s; (iv) several laugh-like "waa" notes in quick succession, 5 n/2.2 s. **SS** Blyth's is very similar (best separated by voice) but smaller with shorter tail. Male Blyth's shows indistinct, hard-to-discern barring on belly (lacking on Sunda) and brown overall plumage tone, whereas Sunda in most areas of Bor has more blackish-greyish overall tone. Fem Blyth's has less extensive white spotting on underparts largely restricted to breast, not reaching belly. Also see Bornean, Sumatran and Gould's.

Large Frogmouth *Batrachostomus auritus*
L 39–42 cm. Sundaic. Monotypic. Scarce in lowland primary and secondary forest, <300 m. **ID** Large. **Ad** large white droplets on wing-coverts; barred outerwing and tail with slightly speckled breast. **Imm** paler, no nuchal collar or covert spots. **Voc** Song: series of 4–8 loud hollow, tremolo "prrrroh", lasting 1 sec each. Call: (i) excited, low growling "oow-OP"; (ii) very harsh, wild scolding and screeches. **SS** See Dulit.

Dulit Frogmouth *Batrachostomus harterti*   `E`
L 34–37 cm. Monotypic. Local in submontane forest in the Kelabit Highlands and neighbouring ranges, ~600–1230 m. **ID Ad** very similar to Large Frogmouth in shape, size and general plumage characters. Hexagonal white spots on wing-coverts, black spots on scapulars, thin white nuchal collar with clearly barred outerwing and tail. **Imm** undescribed. **Voc** (i) Series of 1–8 loud trumpeting, monotonous "whoooooaah", lasting 1–1.5 sec; (ii) series of excited "ee-Woop, ee-Woop...", each couplet lasting 0.3 sec, at 3–4 n/s. **SS** Large Frogmouth generally occurs at lower elevations and sounds different. Silent Large individuals separable on combination of larger size and often paler body, with more droplet-shaped (less hexagonal) wing-covert spots, and often less distinct barring on throat, belly and rear-crown. Underside of primaries often extensively barred on Large, less so on Dulit.

CAPRIMULGIDAE
Nightjars
12 species in region
Small to medium-sized crepuscular nightbirds. Found within forest and open-country habitats, elegantly feeding aerially above trees and vegetation, often while calling. Cryptically coloured so as to remain hidden while roosting or nesting on the ground or trees.

Spotted Nightjar *Eurostopodus argus*
L 27–35 cm. Aus. Monotypic. Austral winterer recorded Jul–Sep. Rare in open woodland, savanna, grasslands. Roosts on ground in clearings and open areas. **ID** Rufous ear-coverts, large white throat patch; greyish upperparts with black and buff markings. In flight shows white primary patch. **Voc** Unlikely to be heard in region: (i) ascending series of 6–8 "whaw" notes increasing in tempo, followed by <25 bubbling "gobble" notes, lasting <5 sec; (ii) ascending series of 40–60 clucking "cluck" notes, followed by 4–40 deep "whaw" notes, lasting 7–12 sec. **SS** Smaller Large-tailed and Timor have white moustachial stripe, more pronounced wing-covert spots and, in flight, white outertail tips.

Satanic Nightjar *Eurostopodus diabolicus*   `E`
L 26 cm. Monotypic. Uncommon in clearings, openings and tracks through primary forest, 1000–2500 m, rarely down to 250 m. Roosts on the ground in small clearings. **ID M** undescribed but very similar to **F**, which has blackish body with white and rufous speckles, silvery-grey scapulars and 'horns', buff band around throat; tiny white primary patch. **Imm** undescribed. **Voc** (i) Rapid succession of 1–10 "whee" notes, at 6 n/5 s, regularly repeated; (ii) <40 rapid "chee" notes, 8 n/s. **AN** Diabolical Nightjar, Heinrich's Nightjar.

Malaysian Eared-nightjar *Lyncornis temminckii*
L 25–28 cm. Sundaic. Monotypic. Fairly common in primary and secondary forest and edge, <1100 m. Usually hawks above canopy in graceful flight. Roosts on ground or low perch, <2 m. **ID Ad** dark overall with thin white throat but otherwise rather uniform with contrasting mottled grey crown and horns; no white in wing or tail. **Imm** paler upperparts, less heavily vermiculated. **Voc** 3-note, easily imitated whistle "tit wee-oow", lasting 1 sec, regularly repeated, often when hawking above canopy. **SS** Only nightjar in range to hawk above the canopy.

Great Eared-nightjar *Lyncornis macrotis*
L 31–40 cm. S–SE Asia, Phil. 5 ssp, 2 in region: *macropterus* (Sul–Sula, Talaud, Sangihe); the restricted ssp *jacobsoni* (Simeulue) is part of the western ssp group from mainland Asia which is sometimes separated as a distinct species '**Monsoon Eared-nightjar**' *L. cerviniceps* based on geographical disjunction and plumage differences (leaving the nominate group as '**Pacific Eared-nightjar**'). Fairly common in primary and secondary forest and edge, <1750 m. Usually hawks above canopy in graceful, leisurely flight. Roosts on ground or low perch, <2 m. **ID** Dark appearance. **Ad** uniform dark brown upperparts, greyish crown and 'horns', rufous face and white band across throat connecting to buffy nuchal collar; underparts paler, finely barred; no white in wing or tail. Ssp *jacobsoni* smaller; chestnut upperparts, blackish underparts. **Imm** undescribed. **Voc** 2-note, easily imitated "PIP PEEOOOW", lasting 2.5 sec, though short introductory note often absent. **SS** Only nightjar in range to hawk above the canopy.

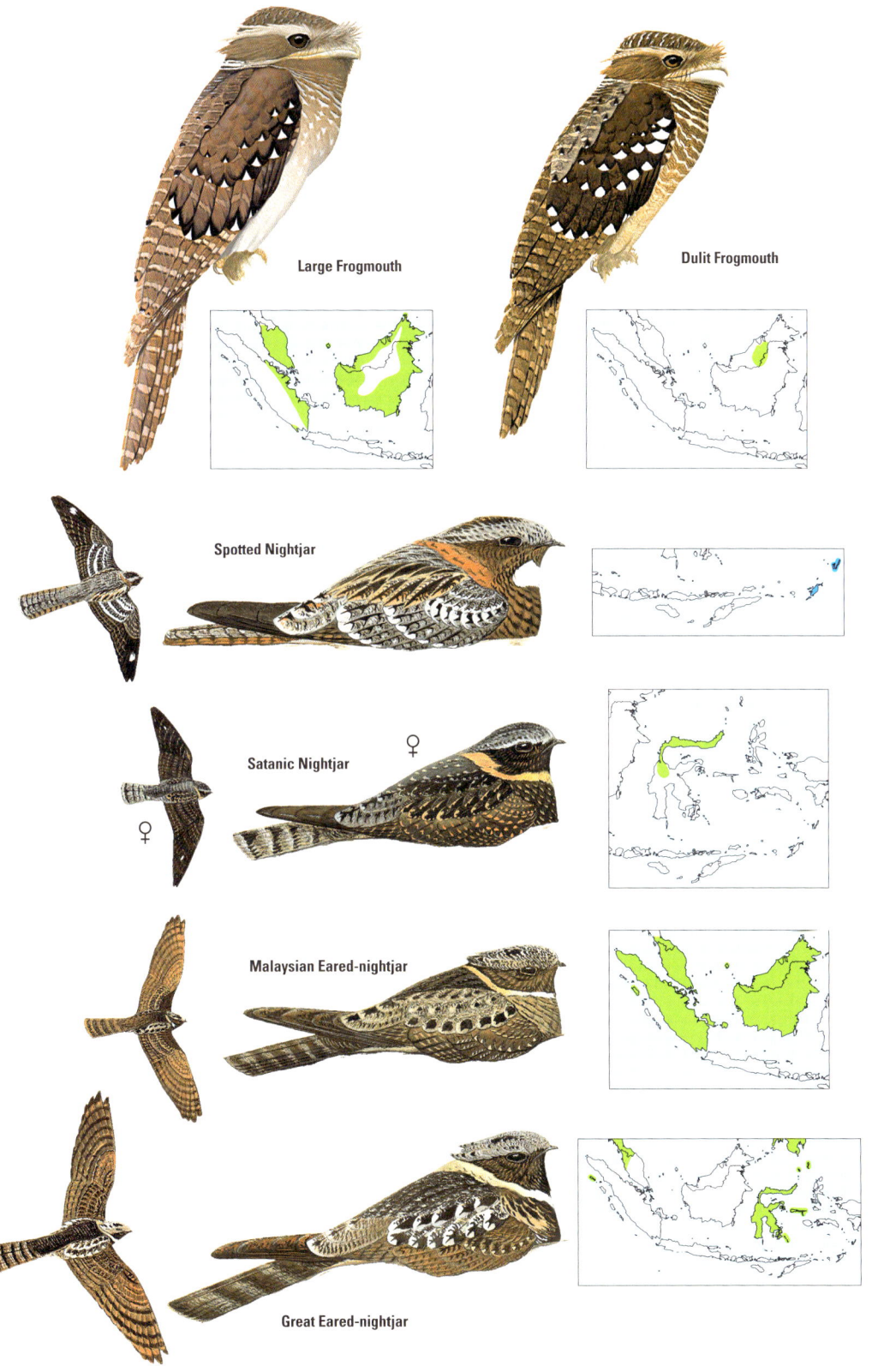

Large Frogmouth

Dulit Frogmouth

Spotted Nightjar

Satanic Nightjar ♀

♀

Malaysian Eared-nightjar

Great Eared-nightjar

Grey Nightjar *Caprimulgus jotaka*
L 28–32 cm. Breeds NE–E–SE–S Asia; winters E–SE Asia, Phil.
2 ssp, 1 in region: *jotaka* (breeds NE–E Asia; winters to SE Asia,
Phil). Previously considered conspecific with Jungle Nightjar *C. indicus* (S Asia) and Palau Nightjar *C. phalaena*. Uncommon in primary
and secondary forest and edge, <3300 m, predominantly >900 m.
Roosts on tree branches, >2 m. **ID** Rather uniform greyish upperparts
with bold buff wing-covert spots, whitish moustachial stripe and
spots either side of throat; tail extends just beyond wings; in flight
has white (**M**) or buff (**F**) primary patch and complete white terminal
band on undertail. **Imm** less heavily marked crown; more strongly
barred mantle; broadly white-tipped; paler wing-coverts and tertials.
Voc Similar to Salvadori's, series of rapid "tok" notes but slightly
lower-pitched and slower, 8 n/1.5 s. Regularly heard in region.
SS Silent migrants hawking overhead often conclusively identifiable
from all other species in region through unique white terminal
undertail band, especially on spread tail. Large-tailed has longer tail,
distinct rufous ear-coverts and more contrasting scapular and covert
spots; white base to rictal bristles (black in Grey). Smaller Bonaparte's lacks white primary patch in wings, has distinct triangular
white throat patch, shows narrow rufous covert barring (not broad
buff covert spots) and has shorter tail not protruding beyond wings.
Much smaller Salvadori's is quite similar in colouration but has plain
buff covert spots (Grey shows dark markings on buff spots) and tail
not extending beyond wings. Savanna lacks thin white moustachial
stripe, and has either full outertail feathers white (not only tips) or
lacks pale tail marks altogether; Savanna's plumage is generally
warmer grey and buff, not cold and steel-grey.

Large-tailed Nightjar *Caprimulgus macrurus*
L 25–29 cm. S–SE Asia to Aus, W Phil. 6 ssp, 4 in region: *macrurus*
(Jav–Lombok, presumed this form on Sumbawa and Flores Sea Is.);
bimaculatus (Sum and E satellites, mainland SE Asia); *salvadorii*
(Bor, Sulu); ssp *schlegelii* (Mol, NG, Aus; presumed this form on
Leti–Tanimbar) is oddly disjunct from other ssp. Common in wide
variety of habitats; forest, edge, scrub, mangroves, <1500 m. Roosts
on ground or low perch, <1 m. **ID** Tail extends well beyond wings;
rufous lesser-coverts contrast with buff-spotted coverts; thick buff
line along scapulars; silvery-grey crown contrasting with rufous ear-coverts and white moustachial stripe and throat. In flight white (**M**)
or buff (**F**) primary-patch and outertail tips. Ssp *bimaculatus* larger;
salvadorii more blackish upperparts, whitish edges to wing-coverts,
and less rufous underparts; *schlegelii* upper- and underparts darker
and less buff, crown coarsely speckled. **F** less contrasting head
pattern; fewer buff spots on wing coverts. **Imm** duller and tawnier.
Voc Single "chok", continually repeated every 0.5–1 sec, sometimes
becoming more rapid. Occasionally produces low grunt when
agitated. Calls from low perch, ground or in flight. **SS** See Spotted,
Savanna and Grey Nightjars. Both Salvadori's and Bonaparte's are
smaller, tail not extending beyond wings; Bonaparte's has rufous
barred wing coverts (with no buff spotting).

Timor Nightjar *Caprimulgus* sp.　　　　　　　　　　　　**E**
L 25 cm. Subject to taxonomic description. Previously considered
conspecific with *schlegelii* Large-tailed Nightjar but distinct vocalisations. Uncommon and local in forest and edge, <1400 m. Roosts
on ground or low perch, <1 m. **ID Ad** very similar to *schlegelii* Large-tailed Nightjar but possibly smaller and slimmer. **Imm** undescribed.
Voc Rapid series of 10–50 "chok" notes, 10 n/2.5 s. **SS** See Spotted
and Savanna Nightjars.

Mees's Nightjar *Caprimulgus meesi*　　　　　　　　　　**E**
L 25–29 cm. Monotypic. Fairly common in forest, edge, scrub,
mangroves, <1000 m. Roosts on ground or low perch, <1 m. **ID Ad**
probably indistinguishable from *schlegelii* Large-tailed Nightjar.
Imm undescribed. **Voc** Sharp, 2-note "chow-chow", lasting 0.7 sec,
regularly repeated, sometimes several notes repeated in quick
succession from perch and in flight. **SS** See Savanna Nightjar.

Sulawesi Nightjar *Caprimulgus celebensis*　　　　　　　**E**
L 24–30 cm. 2 ssp: *celebensis* (N–C–SE Sul, Buton); *jungei* (Sula,
Banggai). Uncommon in lowland forest, edge, scrub, mangroves.
Roosts on ground or low perch, <1 m. **ID Ad** very similar to Large-tailed but less variegated, smaller white wing and tail spots. Sexes
similar. Ssp *jungei* smaller white tips to tail. **Imm** undescribed. **Voc**
6–8 notes eventually trailing-off "tok-tok-tok-tr-tr-tr-tr-tr", lasting
~1 sec, like a bouncing ping-pong ball. **SS** See Savanna Nightjar.

Savanna Nightjar *Caprimulgus affinis*
L 20–26 cm. S–SE–E Asia, Phil. 10 ssp, 5 in region: *affinis* (GS–
Lombok, MPen); *propinquus* (Sul); *undulatus* (Sumbawa–Flores);
kasuidori (Sawu, Sumba); *timorensis* (Alor, Timor, Rote, Kisar, Leti).
Common in grassland, rocky areas, mangroves, coastal scrub and
urban areas with flat roofs for breeding. Roosts on ground in open
areas, and on flat-topped buildings. **ID** Rather uniform greyish-buff
with fine black barring and white speckling; buff nuchal collar and
scapular spots; underparts buff, barred blackish; underwing-coverts
plain buff; white (**M**) or buff (**F**) primary patch; **M**'s white outertail
absent in **F**. Ssp *propinquus* paler, smaller black markings, and
underparts barred on upper belly only; *undulatus* paler, more evenly
coloured vermiculated upperparts and more narrowly marked
underparts; *kasuidori* greyer and paler, underparts more coarsely
barred, less white in outertail; *timorensis* as *kasuidori* but less grey,
buffier. **Imm** paler. **Voc** Loud "chWEEP", lasting 0.3 sec, regularly
repeated. Calls from ground, roof tops and in flight. **SS** Large-tailed,
Timor, Mees's and Sulawesi Nightjars are longer-tailed and have
rufous (versus grey) ear-coverts, more pronounced moustachial
stripe and pronounced pale scapular and wing-covert barring (Savanna's wing-coverts tipped buff). See also Grey, Bonaparte's and
Salvadori's.

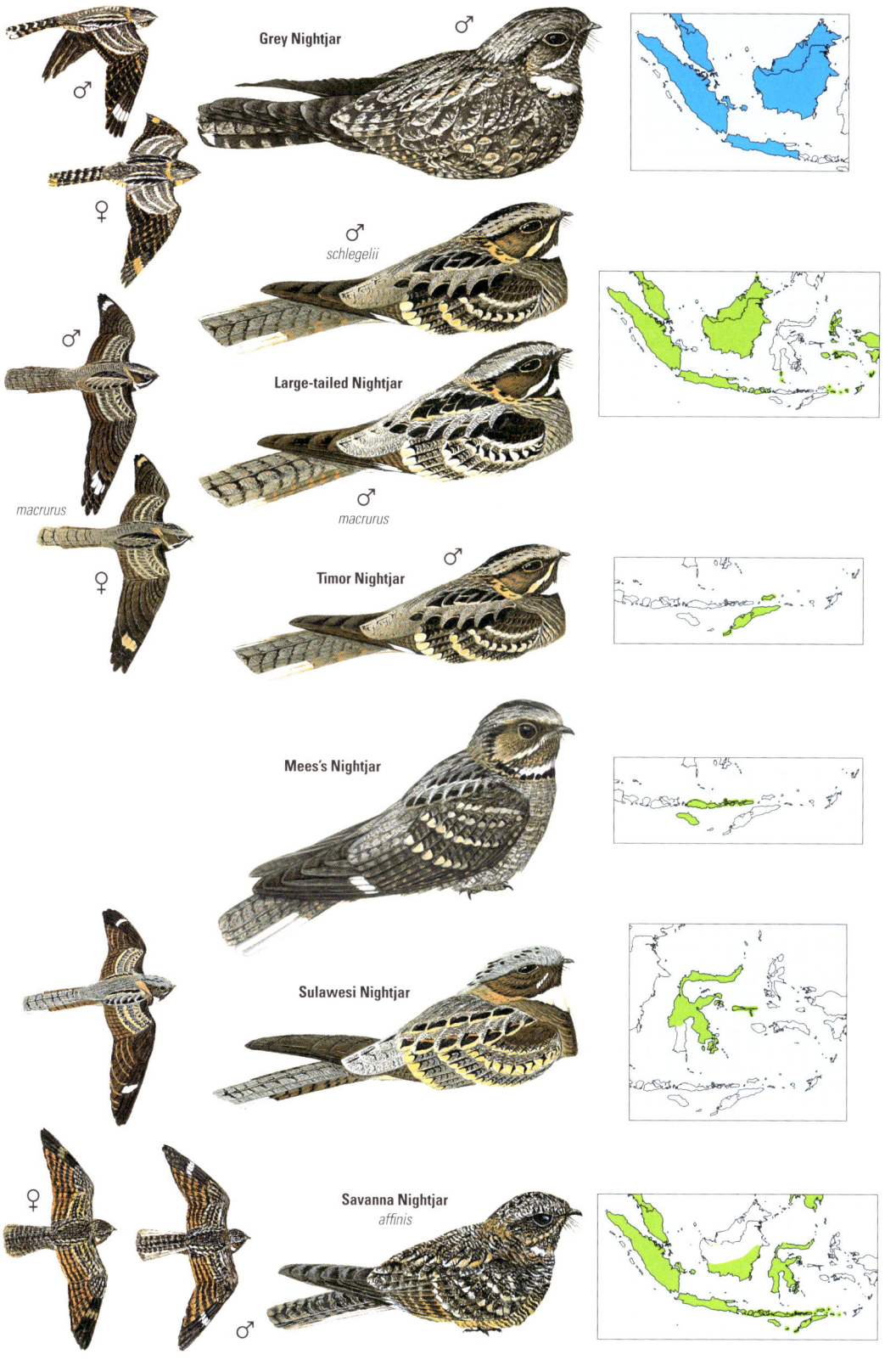

Grey Nightjar ♂

♂

schlegelii

Large-tailed Nightjar

macrurus

♂ macrurus

♂

♀

Timor Nightjar ♂

Mees's Nightjar

Sulawesi Nightjar

♀

Savanna Nightjar
affinis

♂

Bonaparte's Nightjar *Caprimulgus concretus* E

L 21–22 cm. Monotypic. Rare and very local in primary, secondary and heath forest, <500 m. Favours areas of stunted growth on poor or flooded soil and large natural vegetated clearings within forest. Roosts on ground or on low perch, often in thick tangles, < 2m. **ID** Compact; wings at least as long as tail; all-dark; upperparts, head and breast neatly barred rufous; underparts barred whitish; well defined white throat and thin white moustachial. In flight lacks white on wings but **M** white tips to outertail (absent in **F**). **Imm** undescribed. **Voc** Bizarre, low, mournful "wa-ouuu", lasting 1–1.5 sec, first note sometimes missing. **SS** Savanna and Salvadori's Nightjars have pale wing markings in flight and lack Bonaparte's distinct white throat and moustachial. Savanna male additionally has white outertail (Bonaparte's male only has white tips). Also see Grey and Large-tailed.

Salvadori's Nightjar *Caprimulgus pulchellus* E

L 19–22 cm. 2 ssp: *pulchellus* (Sum); *bartelsi* (Jav). Scarce and local in montane and submontane forest, 800–2100 m. Favours clearings and tracks within forest, rarely in open areas. Roosts on ground or on low perch, often in thick tangles, < 3m. **ID** Compact proportions: tail extends only to wing tip. Underparts barred grey-and-buff, grey crown with black streaks along centre; rufous nuchal collar; darker rufous ear-coverts with white patch either side of throat; upperparts spotted and barred buff-and-rufous. In flight small white (**M**) or buffy (**F**) primary patch and outer tail tips. Ssp *bartelsi* has streaky area on crown extending further outwards and lacks distinct nuchal collar. **Imm** undescribed. **Voc** Series of <100 rapid "tok-tok-tok...", 8 n/s, often calling from canopy perch, rarely low. **SS** Savanna (usually very different habitat) is superficially similar but lacks pale tail tips (or has entire outertail white in male), and has grey (not rufous) cheek patch. See Grey, Bonaparte's and Large-tailed Nightjars.

RALLIDAE
Rails, Crakes and Coots
27 species in region

A diverse family of small to medium-sized terrestrial or aquatic birds, occupying a range of wetland and forest habitats. Many species are shy and skulking, while others are more conspicuous. Many have loud distinctive calls.

Talaud Rail *Gymnocrex talaudensis* E

L 33–35 cm. Monotypic. Uncommon and very shy in dense, damp understorey of primary and degraded lowland forest; also recorded in marshy areas at forest edge. **ID Ad** head, breast chestnut; black belly and green-olive upperparts; yellow bill, pinkish or yellow legs and blue bare skin behind eye. **Imm** undescribed. **Voc** Series of >15 deep, thumping gulps "ump-ump-ump...", at 2 n/s.

Blue-faced Rail *Gymnocrex rosenbergii* E

L 30 cm. Monotypic. Uncommon in dense, damp understorey of primary, secondary and degraded lowland forest, <1800 m. Usually runs away from observer, tail cocked. **ID Ad** bright rufous upperparts and black underparts and head with cobalt blue bare skin behind eye. **Imm** undescribed. **Voc** Series of gulping "uw-uw-uw...", at ~13 n/s. When running away makes clucking noises.

Bare-eyed Rail *Gymnocrex plumbeiventris*

L 30–33 cm. Aus. 2 ssp, 1 in region: *plumbeiventris* (N Mol, NG). Scarce in dense, damp understorey of primary and degraded lowland forest, also marshy areas and scrub at forest edge. **ID Ad** head, breast chestnut; grey underparts and green-olive upperparts; greenish bill, red legs and pinkish bare skin behind eye. **Imm** undescribed. **Voc** (i) Loud barking call, can be followed by bizarre, trumpeting "woooo-wooot"; (ii) loud, gulping "ump-ump-ump...".

Barred Rail *Gallirallus torquatus*

L 33–35 cm. Phil to NG. 5 ssp, 4 in region: *torquatus* (islands off NE Bor, Phil); *celebensis* (Sul and satellites); *sulcirostris* (Banggai, Sula); *kuehni* (Tukangbesi). Fairly common resident in open grassland, scrub, ricefields, swamps, marshes, damp areas, and inside forest, <1000 m. **ID Ad** distinctive rich brown upperparts to crown (darker olive brown in *kuehni*, more reddish in *sulcirostris*); black underparts barred white; chestnut breast band (missing in *celebensis*, *sulcirostris* and *kuehni*); thick white cheek stripe (longer in *sulcirostris*). **Imm** underparts buffish; whitish throat. **Voc** (i) Loud "OG-OG-OG...", 4 n/s; (ii) loud, discordant harsh croaking, in duet, "EUW-EUW-EUW...". Often mixing both call types while dueting.

Buff-banded Rail *Gallirallus philippensis*

L 25–33 cm. Aus, Phil. 5–15 ssp, 2 in region: *philippensis* (Bor, Sul and satellites, Bali, LS, Phil; perhaps this ssp on Buru); *mellori* (Mol, Kai, Gunungapi, S NG, Australia). Ssp taxonomy confused; more study needed, but only two ssp in region recognized here because of great individual variation. Uncommon in open grassland, scrub, ricefields, swamp, marsh, damp areas, <3600 m. **ID Ad** dark-red bill; light-grey supercilium, brown cap, rufous from lores to nape; greyish underparts with black-and-white barring on flanks and belly; black-and-brown mottled upperparts with white spotting. Ssp *mellori* has a rufous to pale-ochraceous breast band (darker and more distinct on Kai and Gunungapi, paler northwards within region), but *philippensis* rarely shows traces of pale breast band as well. On Buru, birds resembling both ssp have been found. In region, white spotting on upperparts of *mellori* is more extensive on Kai, less extensive northwards. **Imm** face pattern less distinct, darker bill. **Voc** Mostly at dawn and dusk: (i) irregular sudden harsh squeak "SIP"; (ii) metallic "PIP" or "SIP"; (iii) harsh, loud nasal scream "KREEK". **SS** Slaty-breasted Rail lacks supercilium and has white barring (not spotting) on upperparts. Also see Eastern Water and Lewin's Rails.

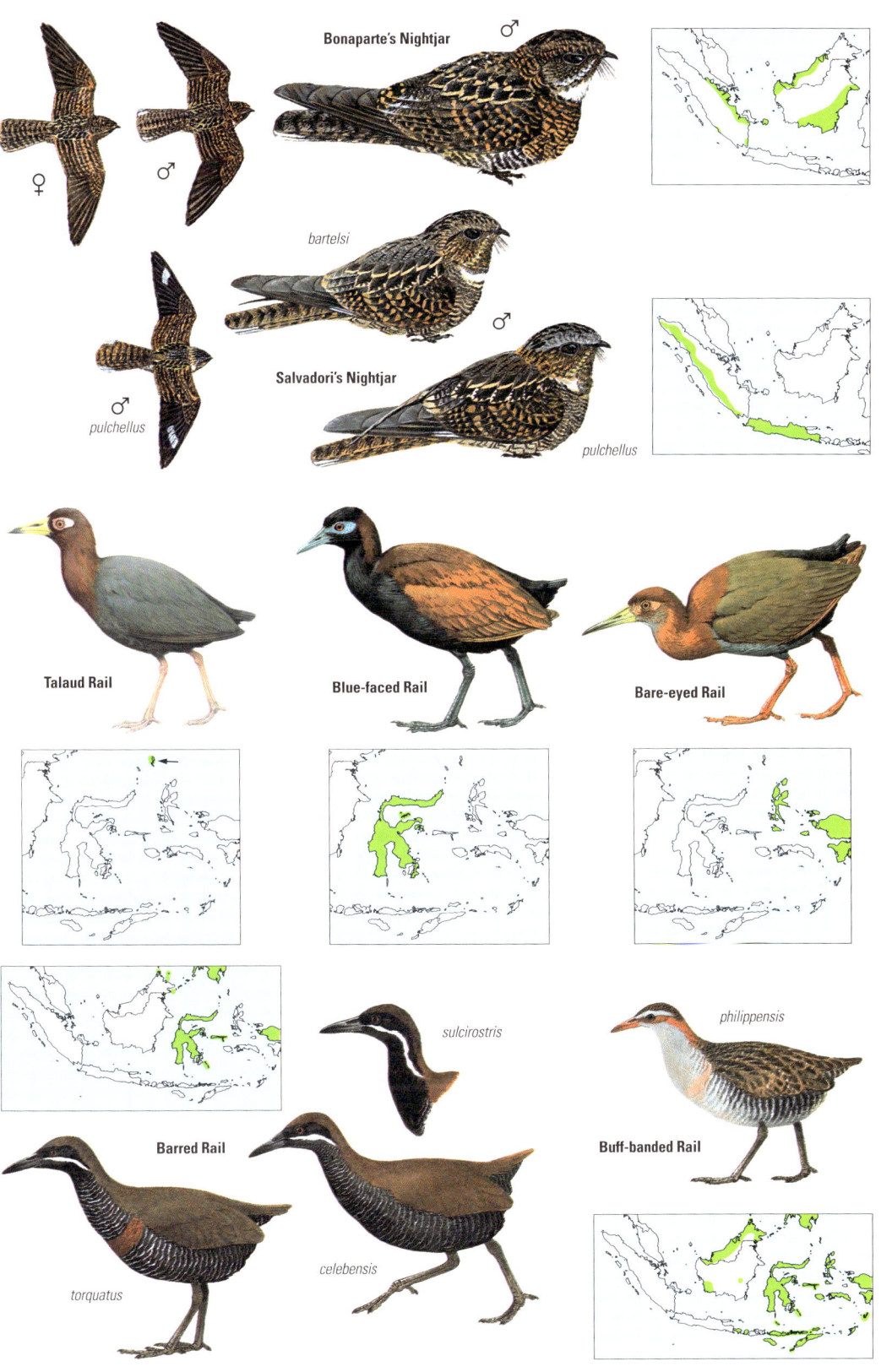

Bonaparte's Nightjar ♂

♀ ♂

bartelsi

♂

Salvadori's Nightjar

pulchellus

♂

pulchellus

Talaud Rail

Blue-faced Rail

Bare-eyed Rail

sulcirostris

philippensis

Barred Rail

Buff-banded Rail

torquatus

celebensis

Invisible Rail *Gallirallus wallacii* **E**

L 35 cm. Monotypic. Scarce, and very local, in dense swampy thickets and damp forest, especially sago swamp, also edge. Singly or pairs, flightless but fast runner, extremely shy. **ID** Vaguely reminiscent of black oystercatchers *Haematopus*. Broad black body, appearing tailless with red bare parts. **Voc** Very loud, raucous "WAK-WAK-WAK...", at 3–5 n/s, in bouts lasting <1 min often while making a "tuk-tuk-tuk..." noise with its wings. **AN** Drummer Rail.

Slaty-breasted Rail *Lewinia striata*

L 25–30 cm. S–SE–E Asia, Phil. ~7 ssp, 2 in region: *striata* (N Bor, Phil, N–NC Sul); *gularis* (most of GS, Flores, mainland SE Asia; reported vagrants from Lombok and—probably this ssp—Sawu). Uncommon in wetlands including meadows, marshes, ricefields, mangroves, ditches, <1500 m. Perhaps only migrant to Sul and Flores (Mar, Aug–Oct). **ID M** rufous crown and nape; grey underparts and black-white barred belly; dark-brown upperparts barred and spotted white. **F** duller underparts and more white on belly. Overall paler *gularis* shows greyish lores. **Imm** streaked upperparts and crown, paler underparts. **Voc** (i) Repeated, sharp "kek-kek-kek..."; (ii) sharp, high "pip-pip-pip...". **SS** Smaller Lewin's Rail lacks white barring and spotting on upperparts. See Buff-banded and Eastern Water Rails.

Lewin's Rail *Lewinia pectoralis*

L 18–27 cm. Aus. 7 ssp, 1 in region: *exsul* (Flores). Known from four specimens, last recorded 1959, ssp *exsul* has important plumage differences from extralimital forms and may well be an endemic species, '**Flores Rail**'. Outside region, inhabits freshwater and saline marshes, wet thickets, cultivated areas. **ID M** quite darkish overall, dull uniformly rufous crown (*exsul* lacks black crown streaks) and dark olive-brown upperparts (less red than in extralimital forms) with dark streaking; uniformly grey breast (*exsul* lacks black breast pattern) and black-and-white barred flanks and belly. **F/Imm** insufficiently known, but based on other ssp, Imm may be darker and lack rufous crown. **Voc** Unknown for *exsul*, but Australian birds give repeated loud "crek" followed by rasping grunts lasting <30 sec; also repeated, metallic "jik" like two coins struck together. **SS** Larger Buff-banded Rail shows prominent face pattern. See also similar Slaty-breasted Rail.

Snoring Rail *Lewinia plateni* **E**

L 30 cm. Monotypic. Rare and shy in dense, damp understorey of primary and secondary forest, <1300 m. **ID** Flightless. Long, robust bill; tailless, hump-backed appearance with relatively long, S-shaped neck; heavy-legged. **M** rufous hindneck; reddish-brown wings; grey face, mantle and underparts with pied barred belly and white chin. **F** less white chin, nape more rufous. **Imm** undescribed. **Voc** (i) Distinctive, low "hmmm" lasting 0.8 sec, hence the English name. **AN** Platen's Rail.

Eastern Water Rail *Rallus indicus* **V**

L 25–28 cm. Breeds E Palaearctic; winters to SE Asia, Phil. Monotypic. Previously considered conspecific with Western Water Rail *R. aquaticus*. Recorded N Bor; Sarawak (Dec 1956) and Brunei (Sep 1980, Mar 1988, Jan 1990, Aug 1991). Wetlands including meadows, marshes, ricefields, ditches, particularly with muddy margins, <2000 m. **ID Ad** black-and-buff mottled upperparts, crown and eyestripe; dull-greyish supercilium and underparts; belly and flanks barred black-and-white; reddish bill with black culmen. **First winter** browner and scaled breast. **Voc** Unlikely to be heard in region: series of loud, piping "kwee" notes, lasting 0.2 sec, repeated

every 0.3 sec. **SS** Slaty-breasted Rail lacks supercilium, has brighter crown and white-barred upperparts. Buff-banded Rail shows more pronounced head pattern with distinct rufous nape, has white spotting on upperparts, and has heavier barring extending further up on underparts. **AN** Brown-cheeked Rail.

Red-necked Crake *Rallina tricolor*

L 23–30 cm. Aus. Monotypic. Presumed resident, but most records Jun–Sep (Mol, Talaud) and Nov–Dec (Damar, Tanimbar); wet, swampy areas in lowland forest, dense thickets in secondary habitat, <700 m, rarely to 1250 m. Very secretive, presence usually betrayed by call. **ID Ad** two-toned rallid: dark chestnut head and breast, near-black upperparts and underparts, barring on belly indistinct; bill yellow-green, legs black. **Imm** uniform dark olive brown. **Voc** (i) Territorial call: harsh, penetrating, descending "nark-nak-nak..."; (ii) repeated "tock"; (iii) soft "plop" contact notes. **SS** Both Red-legged and Slaty-legged Crakes are paler with conspicuous black-and-white barred belly, brown (not blackish) upperparts.

Red-legged Crake *Rallina fasciata*

L 23–25 cm. SE Asia, Phil. Monotypic. Uncommon resident and migrant in primary, secondary and degraded lowland forest, dense cultivated areas, also marshes and other water courses, <800 m. Locally dispersive, recorded on Timor only in wet season. **ID M** white belly with thin black bars, boldly barred wing-coverts and bright red legs; bill blackish-green. **F** narrower black bars on underparts. **Imm** poorly defined wing barring, darker head and brownish legs. **Voc** (i) Series of 6–9 staccato notes "UH-UH-UH...", given mainly at night; (ii) sharp "hiccup" followed by shrill rattles reeling down in scale for ~2 sec, similar to Ruddy-breasted; (iii) quavering nasal "brrr'ay" contact call. **SS** See Band-bellied, Red-necked and Slaty-legged Crakes.

Slaty-legged Crake *Rallina eurizonoides*

L 21–25 cm. S–SE–E Asia, Phil. 7 ssp, 2 in region: *telmatophila* (breeds mainland SE Asia; winters to Sum and W Jav); *minahasa* (Sul, Banggai, Sula). Vagrant to N Bor; Labuan (Sep 2018), Brunei (Jun 2020). Uncommon resident (*minahasa*) and migrant (*telmatophila*) in primary, secondary and degraded lowland forest, also marshes and other water courses, <800 m. **ID Ad** uniform dark-brown upperparts; black underparts with thin white barring; rufous head, breast. Ssp *minahasa* has lighter rufous throat and narrower white barring on underparts. **Imm** dark olive-brown head and underparts. **Voc** (i) repeated "kek-kek-kek...", often given at night; (ii) low "krrr" in alarm; (iii) long, drumming "krrrrrr-kraa-kraa-kraa..."; (iv) loud, clear "OG OG", lasting 1 s. **SS** Red-legged has red (not slaty) legs and bold wing barring. See also Red-necked Crake.

Baillon's Crake *Zapornia pusilla*

L 17–19 cm. Old World. 6 ssp, 2 in region: *pusilla* (C–E Palaearctic; winters to Jav, N Bor, probably this spp to LS, N Sul, Mol); *mira* (E Bor). Breeding recorded from Belitung (1949) and Jav (1930), ssp unknown. Based on potentially clinal plumage differences, *pusilla* sometimes divided from other races as separate species, '**Eastern Baillon's Crake**', with *mira* either included in it or divided as monotypic '**Bornean Baillon's Crake**'. Scarce resident and migrant in marshes, damp grassland, paddyfields. Secretive. **ID** Intricate pattern on upperparts. **Ad** brown eyestripe produces grey supercilium, more distinct in **F**; throat and breast paler in smaller *mira*. Bare parts greenish. **Imm** very pale underparts, lacking bluish tone, darker bill. **Voc** Song: creaky, rattling "krrr-krrr-krrr...", <30 n/1.3 s. Call: includes soft "kik" and harder "tac".

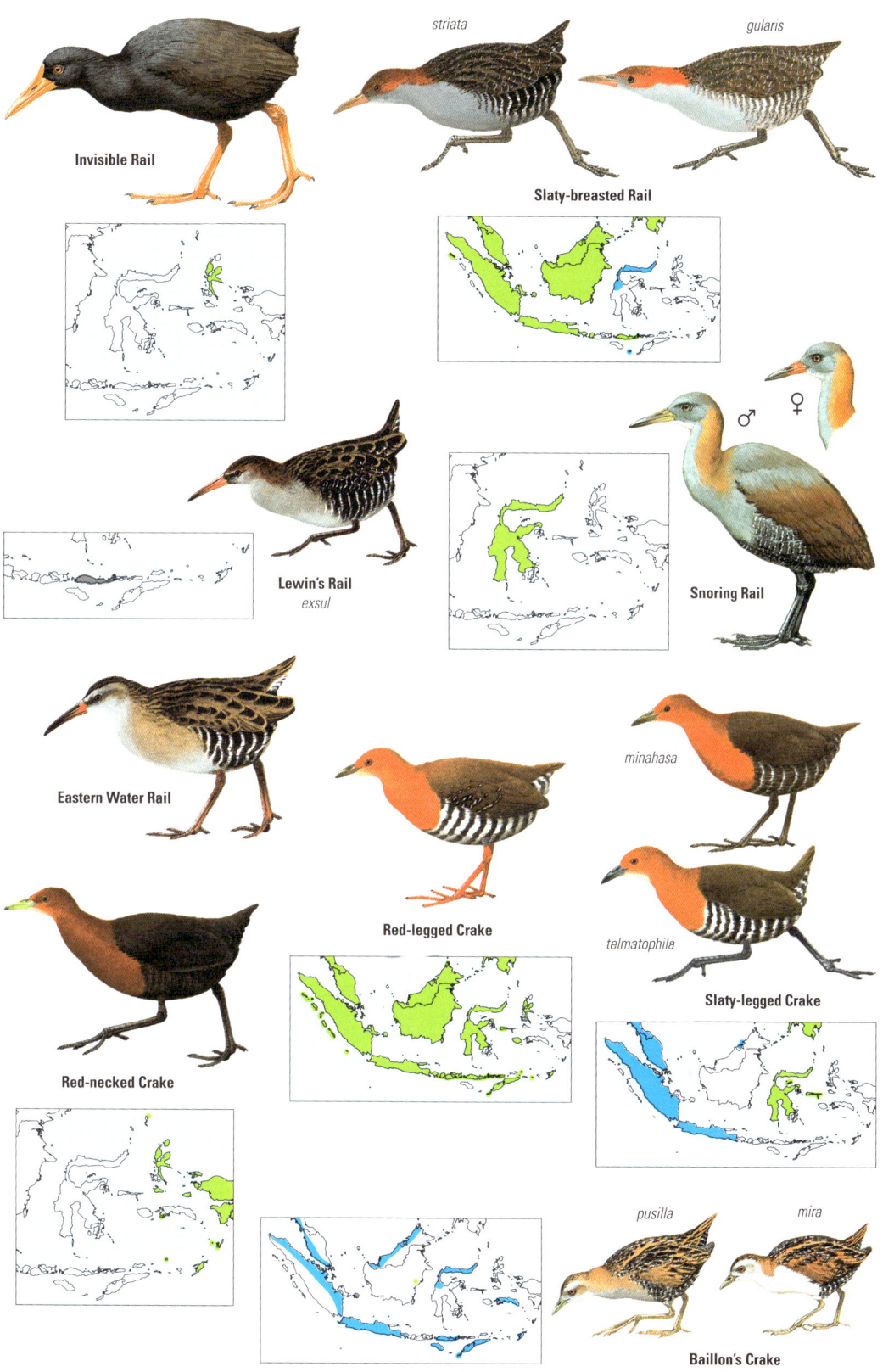

Invisible Rail

striata *gularis*

Slaty-breasted Rail

Lewin's Rail
exsul

Snoring Rail

Eastern Water Rail

Red-legged Crake

minahasa

telmatophila

Slaty-legged Crake

Red-necked Crake

pusilla *mira*

Baillon's Crake

Ruddy-breasted Crake *Zapornia fusca*

L 21–23 cm. S–SE–E Asia, Phil. 4 ssp, 2 in region: *fusca* (Sundaic, LS, Sul, S Asia, Phil); *erythrothorax* (NE-E Asia; winters S to GS). Uncommon in marshes, damp grassland, paddyfields. **ID M** olive-brown upperparts and cinnamon underparts; greenish bill and red legs. **F** generally paler with whitish throat. Ssp *erythrothorax* has lighter underparts; barring on undertail difficult to see. **Imm** darker upperparts but whitish underparts and face. **Voc** ~30 shrill rattles reeling down in scale lasting 1.5 sec, similar to Little Grebe. Also a soft "chuck" when foraging. **SS** See Band-bellied Crake.

Band-bellied Crake *Zapornia paykullii*

L 20–22 cm. Breeds NE Asia; winters SE Asia. Monotypic. Rare in marshes, damp grassland, paddyfields and forest edge. Solitary, very secretive. **ID/SS Ad** whitish throat and greenish bill; red legs. Very similar to Red-legged Crake but has thicker beak, less boldly barred wing-coverts, less extensive underparts barring not reaching as far up the belly, and upperparts more olive-brown, extending to nape and crown, contrasting more with the underparts. From Ruddy-breasted Crake by more extensive and well-defined belly barring reaching further up and presence of wing barring (often indistinct). **Imm** paler head and breast, legs browner. **Voc** Song: ~14 loud, rolling "brr" notes lasting ~1 sec.

Spotless Crake *Zapornia tabuensis*

L 15–18 cm. Aus, Phil. 3 ssp, 1 in region: *tabuensis* (most of range). May only be non-breeding visitor outside Timor. Freshwater and saline wetlands with dense vegetation. Very secretive. **ID** Tiny and dark. **Ad** dark brown upperparts contrasting with dark grey-blue underparts; deep-red eye and legs. **Voc** Rapid series of <50 "wer" notes, repeated regularly.

White-browed Crake *Poliolimnas cinereus*

L 15–20 cm. SE Asia, Phil, Aus. Monotypic. Fairly common in marshes, particularly with floating vegetation, mangroves, grasses, damp areas. Ventures out to feed more often than other crakes. **ID** Slim, long-legged. **Ad** distinctive black-and-white face pattern, streaked upperparts and soft grey underparts; greenish-yellow bare parts with red bill base. **Imm** more washed out, paler bare parts with no red at bill base. **Voc** Bubbling and squeaky, often in duet, similar to the noise of squeaky toys. Also nasal "hee" in alarm.

Watercock *Gallicrex cinerea*

L 43 cm (M), 36 cm (F). S–SE–E Asia, Phil. Monotypic. Uncommon resident (GS) or migrant (Sul, LS) in marshes, waterside vegetation, scrub and cultivation including paddyfields. Shy and secretive, occasionally perches out in low vegetation at dusk. **ID** Heavy, especially in flight, with long, dangling legs. **M br** all dark, with scalloped upperparts; bill yellow with red shield and red legs. **M non-br** all brown with lightly barred underparts and scalloped upperparts; yellowish bare parts. **F/Imm** similar to male non-br but smaller. **Voc** Song: repeated "ogh" every 1 sec. Call: nasal "krey". **SS** Much larger than Common and Dusky Moorhens, and with erect comb in black male breeding plumage. Structure and jizz similar to Purple Swamphen but note bill.

Sulawesi Bush-hen *Amaurornis isabellina* 🟩E

L 35–40 cm. Monotypic. Fairly common in riparian scrub, grass, cultivation and forest edge, <800 m. Singly, pairs or small groups (<10), quite shy; regularly flicking tail. **ID Ad** olive-brown upperparts and cinnamon-rufous underparts; greenish bill and olive legs. **Imm** browner, less rich overall. **Voc** Loud cacophony of various sharp screeches: "tak-tak…", "ee-uwh" and "wa-wa-wa…". Also utters calls similar to White-breasted Waterhen but drier, often given in duet. **AN** Isabelline Bush-hen.

Plain Bush-hen *Amaurornis olivacea*

L 30 cm. Phil, Talaud. 2 ssp, 1 in region: *magnirostris* (Talaud), which is usually considered monotypic species '**Talaud Bush-hen**' but is virtually identical in voice and very similar in plumage to slightly smaller nominate form from Phil. Uncommon in damp, dense under-storey in primary and degraded forest, particularly swampy areas with rattan. In region, less common in marshy, rank vegetation at forest edge. Singly or pairs, very shy. **ID Ad** very dark with striking robust, pale-green bill; upperparts dark-brown; underparts dark blue-grey with olive legs. **Imm** undescribed. **Voc** Series of 4–25 loud grating, barking "gra-gra-gra…", ~2 n/s. **SS** Smaller Pale-vented Bush-hen is extremely similar. Best told by voice, shorter bill in which nostril is almost halfway towards tip (versus massive bill with nostril only a third towards tip), darker and more blackish eye (versus piercing red eye) and – with good views – rufous (not blackish) vent. Pale-vented Bush-hen inhabits forest edge and marshes (rarely entering forest interior).

Pale-vented Bush-hen *Amaurornis moluccana*

L 23–30 cm. Aus. 4 ssp, 1 in region: *moluccana* (Sangihe, Talaud, Mol, Sula, Tanimbar, NG). Uncommon in forest edge, marsh, swampy areas, rank vegetation, cultivation. Singly or pairs, shy. **ID Ad** dark olive-brown upperparts; rufous vent with greyish face and breast. **Imm** browner with whitish throat. **Voc** (i) Loud, scolding growls and cackles; "keuw-keuw…", "gog-gog-gog…", "gokoo-gokoo-gokoo…", rather monotonous compared to White-breasted Waterhen; usually several individuals calling together; (ii) loud "WHA-WHA-WHA" from single birds; (iii) quiet bubbling "waduwaduwadu" followed by a crescendo-like, noisy, awkward, ear-splitting "EE–KO-EE–KO-EE–KO…", often in duet; (iv) loud, single "TIT" when alarmed. **SS** See Talaud Bush-hen. **AN** Rufous-tailed Bush-hen.

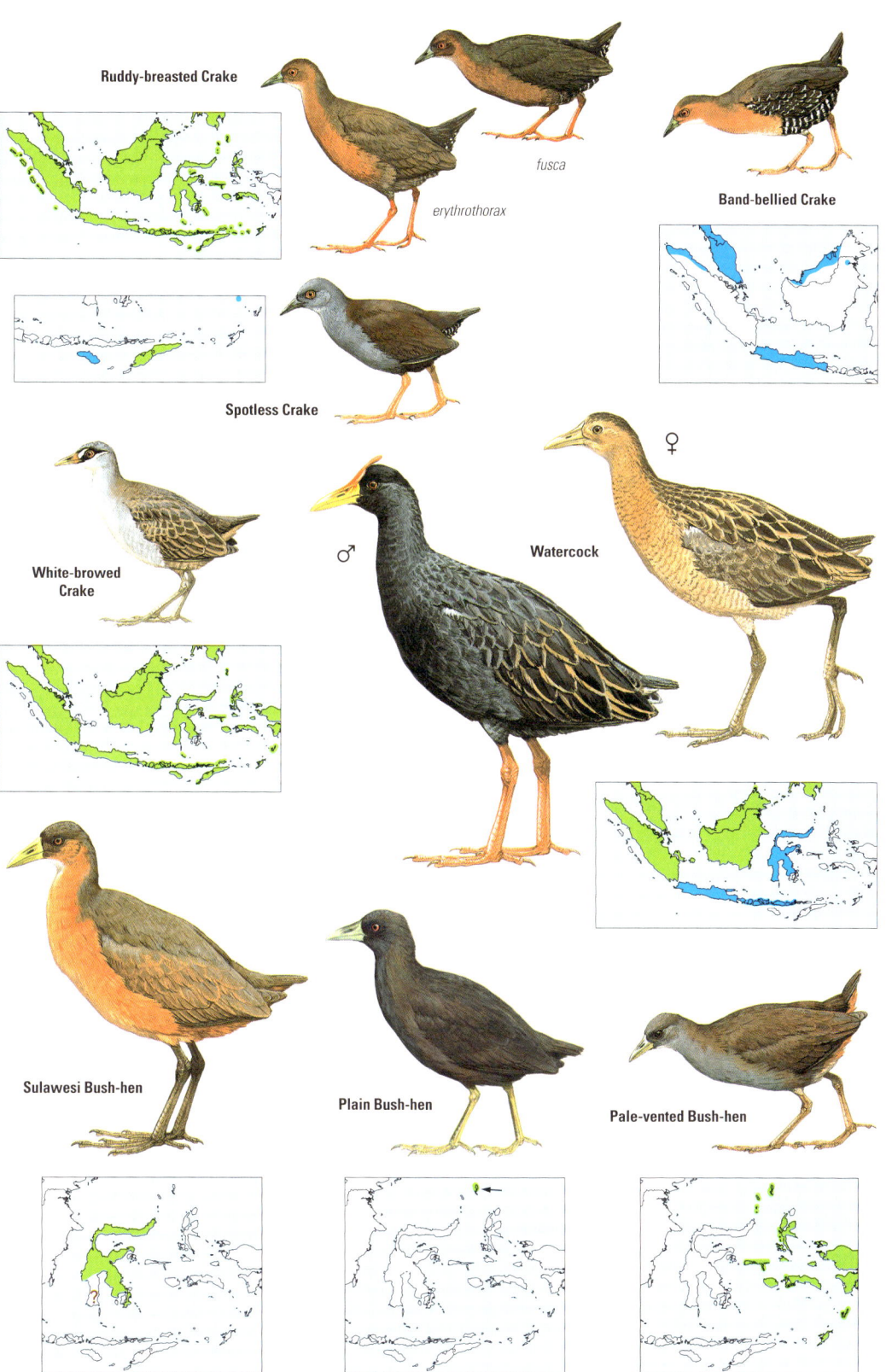

Ruddy-breasted Crake

fusca

erythrothorax

Band-bellied Crake

Spotless Crake

White-browed Crake

♂

♀

Watercock

Sulawesi Bush-hen

Plain Bush-hen

Pale-vented Bush-hen

White-breasted Waterhen *Amaurornis phoenicurus*
L 28–33 cm. S–SE–E Asia, Phil. 4 ssp, 2 in region: *phoenicurus* (GS, Talaud, Sangihe, Phil, S–SE–E Asia); *leucomelana* (Sul and satellites, LS, Sula, C-N Mol). Fairly common in marshes, vegetated water margins, scrub, mangroves, forest edge. Solitary, pairs or family groups. **ID Ad** distinctive pied appeareance with rufous washed undertail. **F** slightly smaller, and – in *leucomelana* – with variable amounts of slate-grey on ear-coverts and lores, and more extensive dark colouration on neck and flanks. **Imm** duller; upperparts more olive-brown and underparts washed buff. **Voc** Very loud calls, often in duet, comprising grunts, croaks, bubbles and chuckles, followed by monotonous "kru-ak-kru-ak...".

Purple Swamphen *Porphyrio porphyrio*
L 38–50 cm. Old World. ~12 ssp, 4 in region: *indicus* (GS, S Sul); *viridis* (N Sum; migrant and recent resident); *samoensis* (N–C–SE Sul, LS, Mol, NG, Melanesia); *pulverulentus* (Phil; vagrant to Talaud). Most populations of *samoensis* in region comprise individuals with partial *indicus*-like characters (often separated as *melanopterus*), making Wallacea a potential zone of intergradation. Ssp *viridis* locally intergrading with *indicus* and probably expanding. Based on plumage, complex often divided into 3–7 species (i.e. regionally '**Sunda Swamphen**' *P. indicus*, '**Australasian Swamphen**' *P. melanotus* (includes *samoensis*), '**Philippine Swamphen**' *P. pulverulentus,* '**Grey-headed Swamphen**' *P. poliocephalus* (includes *viridis*)). However, most populations intergrade in plumage, and defined groups do not sort into separate mtDNA clusters. More research needed. Uncommon in densely vegetated marshes, damp long grasses, and fringes of open water. **ID** Large and heavy. **Ad** large red bill and legs; red frontal shield flat except in *viridis*, which has two raised lateral ridges. Ssp *indicus* has blackish upperparts and head contrasting with brilliant-blue to greenish-turquoise underparts and wing-coverts and white undertail-coverts. Ssp *samoensis* similar but smaller; underparts darker blue; more extensive black on head and uniform blackish wings; bare parts darker red; *pulverulentus* as previous but head and neck uniformly blue, concolorous with underparts, and back and scapulars chestnut-olive; *viridis* with pale grey head and cobalt-blue to blackish wings. **Imm** grey, with duller bare parts. **Voc** Noisy: (i) loud, raucous "grek"; (ii) drawn-out duck-like "kraak"; (iii) goose-like "urrh". **SS** See Watercock.

Common Moorhen *Gallinula chloropus*
L 30–38 cm. Old World. 5 ssp, 1 in region: *orientalis* (MPen, Andamans, GS to Timor, Sul, Phil, Palau). No longer includes Common Gallinule *G. galeata* (America). Locally common in marshes and open water with vegetated fringes, freshwater wetlands. **ID Ad** dark slate-brown, white undertail-coverts and flank line; bill and shield red, tipped yellow; greenish-yellow legs. **Imm** much paler brown, particularly face and breast; bill greenish. **Voc** Song: loud "brrruk" or "kark". Call: (i) loud "kittick" or "keh-keh"; (ii) various other clucking and chattering calls. **SS** See Dusky Moorhen and Watercock.

Dusky Moorhen *Gallinula tenebrosa*
L 35–40 cm. Aus. 3 ssp, 1 in region: *frontata* (Sul, Sula, C Mol, Sumbawa to Timor, NG; formerly SE Bor). Local and scarce in marshes and open water with vegetated fringes. **ID/SS Ad** similar to Common Moorhen but lacks white flank line (although can show traces of it) and has more reddish legs and feet. **Imm** uniform greyish-brown, dark bill and blotched red-yellowish legs; much darker than Imm Common Moorhen. Also see Watercock. **Voc** Variable clucking and chattering including "krurk, krruk-uk-uk", "krek, krok", much higher-pitched and piercing than Common Moorhen. Also trumpeting "WERR".

Common Coot *Fulica atra*
L 36–39 cm. Old World. 4 ssp, 2 in region: *atra* (Palaearctic, S Asia; winters to Phil and SE Asia; vagrant N Bor); *lugubris* (bred Jav in 1940s; now known from Bali, LS, NG; record on Buru probably this ssp). Rare visitor and resident. Open water with submerged and fringing vegetation. **ID/SS Ad** All black with white bill and frontal shield. In flight shows white on secondaries. Ssp *lugubris* smaller, often with shield appearing larger. **Voc** (i) Sharp, loud "kowk" or "pyee"; (ii) nasal trumpeting "pep ee-yew" regularly repeated.

HELIORNITHIDAE
Finfoots
1 species in region
Medium-sized grebe-like bird of undisturbed waterways and lakes, usually within dense, marginal vegetation. Swims semi-submerged and occasionally perches on logs or low branches.

Masked Finfoot *Heliopais personatus* **V**
L 52 cm. SE Asia. Monotypic. Rare migrant, now in steep global decline and increasingly unlikely to re-appear in region: last record on Sum in Dec 2009, single records W Jav (1984) and Sarawak (Feb–May 2004). Shy and secretive, along slow-flowing forest rivers and mangrove waterways. Swims partly submerged with head-bobbing motion. Perches on low overhanging branches or emergent logs. **ID** Grebe- or cormorant-like in appearance. Upperparts grey-brown, becoming paler grey on hindneck and rear crown; underparts buff, becoming white on belly; bill stout and yellow; legs pale green. **M** forehead, face and throat black, bordered by white line. **F/Imm** has throat and centre of foreneck white.

phoenicurus

♀

leucomelana

White-breasted Waterhen

indicus

viridis

pulverulentus

Purple Swamphen

Common Moorhen

Common Coot
atra

Dusky Moorhen

♂

♀

Masked Finfoot

BURHINIDAE
Thick-knees
1 species in region
Large and stocky with strong legs and bill. In region usually found on sandy beaches or estuaries.

Beach Thick-knee *Esacus magnirostris*
L 53–57 cm. SE Asia to Aus, Phil. Monotypic. Widespread but uncommon throughout, rare in W. Sandy beaches and estuaries. Singly, pairs or small groups (<10). Partly nocturnal. **ID** Large with very stout bill and striking black, white and brown plumage. Upperparts plain brown with blackish covert bar and grey coverts; head black with white supercilium and throat; breast buffy and rest of underparts white. In flight shows bold black-and-white wing-panel. **Voc** Song: mournful, wailing "wee-loo", often heard at night. Call: metallic "clip".

RECURVIROSTRIDAE
Stilts and Avocets
3 species in region
Elegant medium-sized waders with distinct black and white plumage, long legs and long, narrow bills. Found in a wide variety of wetland habitats both inland and on coast.

Pied Stilt *Himantopus leucocephalus*
L 35–40 cm, **WS** 67–83 cm. Aus; winters N to Phil. Monotypic. Here considered different species from Black-winged Stilt and extralimital stilts on the basis of plumage. Many records from the region do not separate forms, making a full understanding of status difficult. Breeding population seems to have recently expanded north and westwards to Sabah, Sum and MPen. Shallow coastal and inland wetlands, rice fields and fish ponds. **ID** Slender with long, thin black bill and very long flesh-pink legs. **Ad** has all black back, wings and characteristic black hindneck patch narrowing towards nape (**F** with brownish tinge to black colouration); underparts, rump and wedge on back all white. **Imm** reddish base to bill; black parts on head and neck often lacking or, if present, browner and extending to forecrown (as in Black-winged Stilt). **Voc** Rather slow, low-pitched, puppy-like "yelp". **SS** See Black-winged Stilt.

Black-winged Stilt *Himantopus himantopus*
L 35–40 cm, **WS** 67–83 cm. Palaearctic, Africa, S–SE–E Asia. Monotypic. For taxonomy see Pied Stilt. Status uncertain in region as few records separate the forms. On current knowledge, known to breed N Sum and recently W Jav, northern winterer elsewhere; possibly expanding range. Shallow coastal and inland wetlands, including rice fields and fish ponds. **ID/SS Ad** similar to Pied Stilt, but often has entirely white head and neck, occasionally variable amounts of black on crown, ear-coverts and nape (browner in **F**), but lacking the characteristic shape of Pied's hindneck patch, though a small number of individuals can show variable shape of hindneck patch. Both wing length and tarsus <9% longer than Pied. **Imm** probably not safely told from Pied Stilt. **Voc** High-pitched, sharp "kyik", quickly repeated.

Pied Avocet *Recurvirostra avosetta* V
L 42–45 cm, **WS** 67–77 cm. Old World. Monotypic. Recorded Sarawak (Jan 2009), Sabah (Dec 2011, Dec 2015, Jan 2016, Jan 2019) and SE Sum (Jun 2014). Shallow brackish water or inland wetlands, often scything bill from side to side in water. **ID Ad** large, slender, long-legged wader with distinctive upturned bill. Predominantly white with black crown and nape, black bands on mantle and coverts and black outer primaries; legs blue-grey; bill black. **Imm** white plumage tinged buff, black plumage duller and browner. **Voc** Emphatic, piping "kluit".

HAEMATOPODIDAE
Oystercatchers
3 species in region
Small family of medium-sized shorebirds with distinctive pied or black plumage and long orange-red bills. Noisy, typically found in coastal wetland habitats but also recorded inland.

Pied Oystercatcher *Haematopus longirostris*
L 49–51 cm, **WS** 85–95 cm. Aus. Monotypic. Erratic local visitor, but possibly resident on some islands. Single vagrant record from Bali. Mudflats, estuaries, sandy coasts. **ID Ad** distinctive black and white plumage; red-orange bill, red iris and eyering; pinkish legs. In flight short white wingbar only appears across secondaries, not primaries, and does not meet trailing edge of wing. **Imm** as Ad but back and wings brownish. Plumage quickly replaced by Ad type. **Voc** Loud, piping "pleep", and a rapid "pee-pee-pee...". **SS** See Eurasian Oystercatcher.

Sooty Oystercatcher *Haematopus fuliginosus* V
L 46–49 cm, **WS** 100 cm. Aus. 2 ssp, 1 in region: *ophthalmicus* (N Australia), which is sometimes considered monotypic species '**Spectacled Oystercatcher**' based on distinct eye morphology. Single record from Bali (Apr 1997). Rocky coasts and stony and sandy beaches. **ID Ad** entirely sooty black with red bill and pink legs; iris red with fleshy orange eyering. **Imm** bill, eye and eye ring duller. **Voc** Similar to Pied, but more mournful.

Far Eastern Oystercatcher *Haematopus osculans* V
L 40–47 cm, **WS** 72–86 cm. NE-E Asia. Monotypic. Traditionally included with Eurasian Oystercatcher *H. ostralegus* (W-C Palaearctic) but phylogenetic data indicate it is more closely related to other oystercatcher species. Recorded from Sarawak (Jan 2006, Nov 2006–Feb 2007) and N Sum (Feb 2018). Beaches, mudflats, also inland lakes, fields and wet grasslands. **ID/SS** As Pied Oystercatcher but wingbar extends across primaries and secondaries and joins with trailing edge of wing. **Voc** Calls include a downslurred loud, piping "KLEew", abrupt "KLEEP".

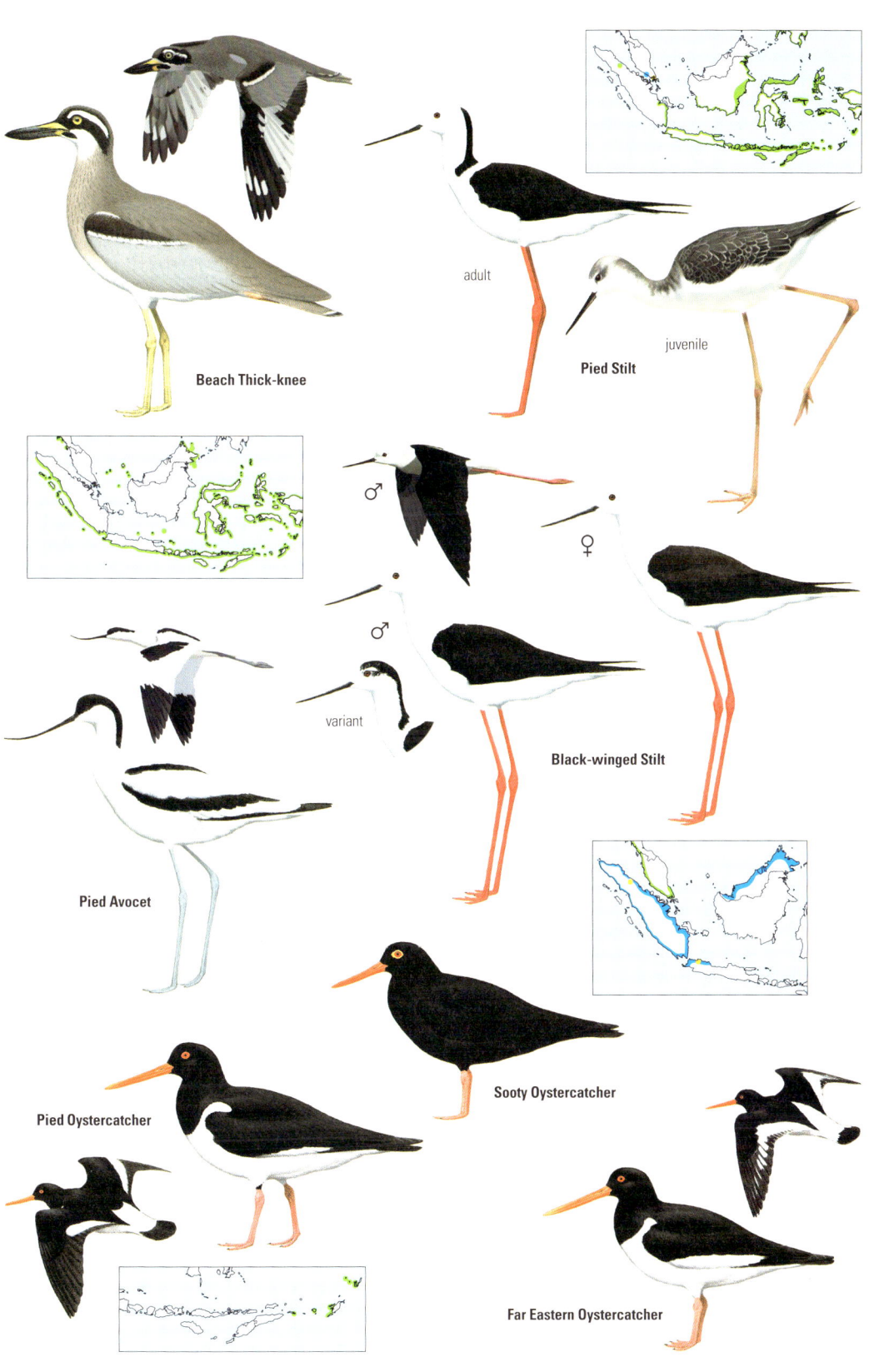

Beach Thick-knee

Pied Stilt

adult

juvenile

♂

♀

♂

variant

Black-winged Stilt

Pied Avocet

Sooty Oystercatcher

Pied Oystercatcher

Far Eastern Oystercatcher

CHARADRIIDAE
Plovers
21 species in region

A large family of small to medium-sized shorebirds, mostly migratory and gregarious. Typically found in coastal wetland habitats but also occur inland, away from water, in fields.

Pacific Golden Plover *Pluvialis fulva*

L 23–26 cm. Breeds E Palaearctic to Alaska; winters to S. Monotypic. Fairly common in variety of habitats; coastal mudflats, lagoons, inland fields and burnt areas. Usually in flocks. **ID** Slender, long-legged; upright stance. In flight shows weak wingbar. **Ad br** black face and underparts with broad white side-stripe down to lower flanks; upperparts mottled gold-and-black. **Ad non-br/Imm** black upperparts mottled gold-and-buff; greyish-buff breast; dark cap contrasting with white supercilium; warm buff face. **Voc** Excited, bisyllabic "choo-it". **SS** See Grey and Oriental Plovers. Also see Buff-breasted Sandpiper.

Grey Plover *Pluvialis squatarola*

L 27–31 cm. Breeds Holarctic; winters to S. Monotypic. Fairly common migrant; mudflats, beaches, pools. Singly or small groups. **ID** In flight shows white rump, prominent white wingbar and diagnostic black axillaries. **Ad br** black face and underparts, white side-stripes to upper flanks; marbled upperparts. **Ad non-br** very pale, greyer, more uniform; indistinct supercilium on plain face with large black eye; mottled upperparts; whitish underparts with diffused breast streaking. **Imm** buffier upperparts. **Voc** Mournful "pee-uu-ee". **SS** Larger and more heavily built than Pacific Golden, with shorter legs, heavier bill, diagnostic black (not light) axillaries, and an overall greyer colouration (but beware of buffy Imm Grey Plover with golden-tinged impression). **AN** Black-bellied Plover.

Grey-headed Lapwing *Vanellus cinereus*

L 34–37 cm, **WS** 75 cm. Breeds E Asia; winters S–SE Asia, Phil. Monotypic. Rare; small number of records from N Bor, N Sul and N Sum. Grassland, marshes, open agricultural ground. **ID** Large. Bill yellow with black tip. Striking wing pattern in flight: black primaries contrasting with white rump and secondaries and brown coverts. **Ad br** head and neck uniformly grey, becoming darker on breast to form blackish breast band; back and upperwing-coverts olive-brown; tail white with black subterminal band. **Ad non-br** duller, with browner head and neck. **Imm** grey feathering replaced by dull brown; upperparts finely edged buff. **Voc** Repeated series of shrill, metallic, loud "CHEE-INK".

Javan Lapwing *Vanellus macropterus* **E**

L 27–29 cm. Monotypic. Jav, with single record from S Sum. Not reliably recorded since 1939 and now extinct. Formerly occupied coastal marshes, rice fields and fish ponds. **ID Ad** distinctive dark plumage with long yellow legs and yellow facial wattles. Head and belly patch sooty black; breast, wing-coverts and back dark brown; rump, tail, vent and underwing-coverts white; tail with broad black band; flight feathers black (above and below). Wings show black spurs. **Imm** Undescribed. **Voc** (i) Trumpet-like "tet tet tet"; (ii) rattling "tretretretretret"; (iii) agitated "krihhh" in flight.

Red-wattled Lapwing *Vanellus indicus*

L 32–35 cm. SW–S–SE Asia. 2–4 ssp, 1 in region: *atronuchalis* (SE Asia), which is sometimes considered monotypic species '**Black-necked Lapwing**' because of distinct head colouration. Rare, but slowly expanding into region from MPen. Vagrant, Brunei (Mar 2014). Marshy wetlands, dry grassland and agricultural fields. **ID** Bold black-and-white head markings with red wattles and base of bill and yellow legs distinctive. **Ad br** black head, neck and breast with white ear-spot and narrow white cervical collar; back and wing-coverts olive-brown; in flight shows black flight feathers separated from brown coverts by white wing bar; rump and tail white with black subterminal band; underparts and underwing-coverts white. **Ad non-br** as Ad br but black head becomes duller and browner. **Imm** as Ad non-br but chin and throat white. **Voc** Song: nasal "KWAY-kuwick", often interspersed with phrases of alarm call. Call: grating alarm (often given by several individuals simultaneously) harsh, rapid "kek-kek-kek...", or "kerrek-kerrek-kerrek...".

Masked Lapwing *Vanellus miles*

L 33–37 cm. Aus. 2 ssp, 1 in region: *miles* (N Australia, NG), sometimes considered a separate species, '**Northern Masked Lapwing**', from ssp *novaehollandiae* (SE Australia, NZ) based on plumage and bare-part morphology. Irregular migrant. Vagrant to Jav (1 record). Grassland and open agricultural fields. **ID Ad** large and distinctive with white head and underparts, small black cap, conspicuous yellow bill and wattles, and pink-red legs. Rump and tail white with black subterminal band; upperparts uniformly grey-brown. In flight black flight feathers contrast with brown coverts on upperwing and white coverts on underwing. **Imm** grey upperparts barred darker and edged buff. **Voc** Loud, grating "GRA-GRA-GRA...", monotonously repeated.

Northern Lapwing *Vanellus vanellus* **V**

L 28–31 cm, **WS** 82–87 cm. Breeds Palaearctic; winters to S. Monotypic. Vagrant, Brunei (Jan 1976, Dec 1986, Nov-Dec 2007). Grassland, open agricultural fields, coastal marshes. **ID** Bold green, black and white colouration with distinctive long wispy crest. Moth-like flight with broad rounded wings. Outermost primaries tipped white; rump and tail white with broad black subterminal band. **Ad br** upperparts dark green with metallic sheen; bold black-and-white face pattern (more striking in **M** than **F**) with black throat, crown and breast band; crown extends to long thin crest; rest of underparts white except for buff undertail-coverts. **Ad non-br** head pattern duller, throat and chin white; wing-coverts edged buff. **Imm** shorter crest. **Voc** Rising, shrill "fweEIT", sometimes falling at the end.

Red-kneed Dotterel *Erythrogonys cinctus* **V**

L 17–19 cm. Monotypic. Aus. Vagrant, Rote (Aug 2018). Freshwater wetlands and lake edges, less tolerant of brackish wetlands. **ID M** boldly patterned; black head and broad breast band contrast with broad, white throat; rufous flanks; mid-brown upperparts and white belly; pink base to both bill and legs. In flight shows broad white trailing edge and white underwing coverts contrasting with black remainder of wing. **F** duller; less striking; crown and mask browner. **Imm** mid-brown upperparts contrasting sharply with white underparts; hint of black mask; pink base to lower mandible. **SS** Black-fronted Dotterel less striking; has red eyering, white supercilium and brown (not black) crown; scalloped upperparts and lacks rufous flanks; narrower breast band.

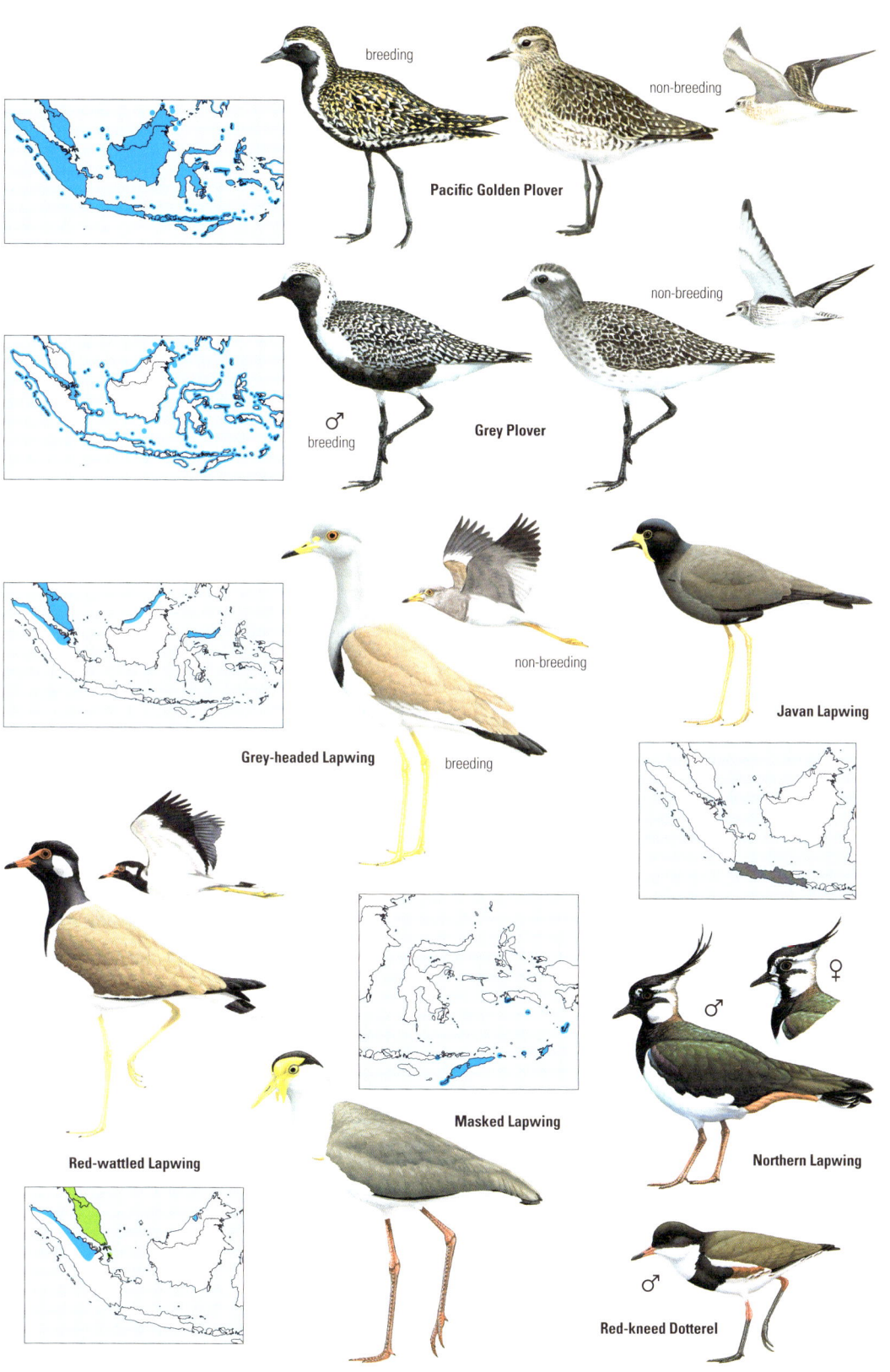

breeding

non-breeding

Pacific Golden Plover

non-breeding

♂ breeding

Grey Plover

non-breeding

Javan Lapwing

Grey-headed Lapwing

breeding

Red-wattled Lapwing

Masked Lapwing

♂   ♀

Northern Lapwing

♂

Red-kneed Dotterel

Oriental Plover *Anarhynchus veredus*

L 22–25 cm, **WS** 46–53 cm. Breeds C–E Asia; winters Aus. Monotypic. Regular but local migrant and winter visitor in dry open grassland, playing fields, recently burnt areas. On migration can be found in estuaries and wetlands. Usually in small groups (~5–30). **ID** Slim, elegant-looking, with long yellowish legs; long pointed primaries. In flight shows dark underwing and uniform upperwing with feet projecting beyond tail. **M br** creamy-white face and throat, rufous breast with black lower edge and white belly; hindcrown to tail mid-brown. **F br** reddish-brown breast without black lower edge; brownish face with white supercilium and throat. **Ad non-br** brownish head, breast and upperparts with broad whitish supercilium and paler nape giving capped appearance. **Imm** as Ad non-br but with pale-fringed upperparts. **Voc** (i) Brief, stony "dzhup"; (ii) short, piping "klink-klink". **SS** In flight, similar shaped Pacific Golden Plover has more contrasting underparts and slimmer, longer proportions. From Tibetan, Siberian and Greater Sand Plovers told by more uniform buff face, complete broad buff breast band, supercilium starting from around the eye (not extending to bill base), and longer, yellowish (not grey/black) legs.

Tibetan Plover *Anarhynchus atrifrons*

L 18–21 cm, **WS** 45–58 cm. Breeds C Asia; winters Africa to SE Asia. 3 ssp, 2 in region: *atrifrons* (breeds Himalaya to S Tibet; winters S Asia to Sum); *schaeferi* (breeds E Tibet to S Mongolia; winters SE Asia at least to GS). Often merged with Siberian Plover into '**Lesser Sand Plover**' *A. mongolus* but here split based on plumage and breeding ecology. Common on coastal mudflats, sand bars. In large flocks; some birds over-summer in region. **ID** Quite thin long bill; grey-black legs. In flight white wingbar across secondaries to outer primaries. **Ad br** black mask and white throat bordered by broad orange band extending to upper flanks; *schaeferi* shows thinner breast band, can show traces of a pair of white spots on forehead. **Ad non-br** (Sep–May) lacks rufous and black; white underparts to throat; brown ear-coverts, white supercilium, unmarked flanks. **Imm** has pale-fringed upperparts. **Voc** (i) Soft trill "prrit"; (ii) sharper "kip-ip". **SS** Smaller Kentish and White-faced Plovers show white hindcollar. See Oriental and especially Greater Sand Plover for tricky identification from those species. Siberian Plover is challenging to distinguish and not all individuals can be identified outside breeding: on average, Siberian has shorter legs and shorter, stubbier bill than smaller Tibetan. Breeding Siberian has more rufous (not orange) breast band and always has distinct white on forehead, often showing black outline of white throat. In winter and Imm plumage, Siberian often has distinct combination of darker upperparts, darker lores, a more complete breast band, a shorter white supercilium and darker ear-coverts than crown, whereas Tibetan is usually paler overall, with less contrasting ear-coverts, shorter breast tabs and a longer supercilium. Flanks in ~60% of Siberian show brown mottling always absent in Tibetan. Siberian's underwing shows darker bases to greater primary and secondary coverts.

Siberian Plover *Anarhynchus mongolus*

L 18–21 cm, **WS** 45–58 cm. Breeds NE Asia; winters SE–E Asia to Aus. 2 ssp: *mongolus* (breeds E Siberia; winters E Asia to Aus); *stegmanni* (breeds Pacific Siberia; winters E Asia through Phil to Aus). In GS, only few records from Sarawak and Jav, but regular from Bali eastwards. For taxonomy see Tibetan Plover. Common on coastal mudflats, sand bars. In large flocks; some birds over-summer in region. **ID** Quite short, stubby bill; grey-black legs. In flight white wingbar across secondaries to outer primaries. **Ad br** black mask and white throat bordered by thin black line (often absent in *stegmanni*) and by broad deep rufous breast band extending to upper flanks; extensive white on forehead (split into two spots in *stegmanni*). **Ad non-br** (Sep–May) lacks rufous and black; white underparts to throat; dark brown ear-coverts and lores, long breast band, short white supercilium; often with some brown markings on flanks. **Imm** has pale-fringed upperparts. **Voc** (i) Soft trill "prrit"; (ii) sharper "kip-ip". **SS** Kentish and White-faced Plovers show white hindcollar. See Oriental Plover, Greater Sand Plover and Tibetan Plover for difficult identification. **AN** Mongolian Plover.

Greater Sand Plover *Anarhynchus leschenaultii*

L 22–25 cm, **WS** 53–60 cm. Breeds C–SW Asia; winters Africa to Aus. 3 ssp, 1 in region: *leschenaultii* (breeds C Asia; winters S Asia to Aus). Fairly common on coastal mudflats, sand bars; prefers sandier areas than Tibetan and Siberian Plovers. In small groups. When feeding, generally slower than Siberian and Tibetan Plovers, with more deliberate, longer pauses. **ID/SS** Very similar to Siberian and especially Tibetan Plovers but larger, heavier; has longer legs; bill thicker, more bulbous at tip and often longer (especially compared to Siberian). At most angles, less steep forehead than Siberian and Tibetan, with position of eye more central (further from the bill than in Siberian and Tibetan); greenish (not blackish) legs. **Ad br** less black on head than Siberian or Tibetan; breast band narrower and paler rufous to orange, more sharply delimited below; orange/rufous colour not extending to flanks, but—on average—extending further onto hindneck and crown than in Tibetan and Siberian (but beware worn fall plumage in which Tibetan and Siberian can also have orange/rufous extending onto crown); usually has a pair of small white spots on forehead intermediate in size between Siberian and Tibetan. **Ad non-br** (Aug–Mar) and **Imm** (with pale-fringed upperparts) lack rufous and black head and breast pattern; variably distinct white supercilium; best separated on jizz and structure (see above), especially from small-billed Siberian which sometimes has unique dark flank spots and much darker Imm plumage, but less easily from the structurally more similar Tibetan. Also see Oriental Plover. **Voc** Trilling "kuriri", "trrt" or "prrit", slightly deeper than Siberian and Tibetan.

Red-capped Plover *Anarhynchus ruficapillus*

L 14–16 cm, **WS** 27–34 cm. Aus. Monotypic. Locally common resident and perhaps migrant; coastal habitats, including sandy areas, mudflats and salt pans. Usually in pairs or small groups. **ID** In flight shows thin white wingbar. **M br** short white supercilium; black lores, frontal bar, and lateral breast patches; bright rufous crown and nape; uniform brown upperparts, black legs and bill. **F br** duller face pattern, brownish crown, black replaced by pale rufous wash. **Ad non-br** less rufous on head. **Imm** has buff-fringed upperparts. **Voc** Hard, squeaky "twiwk". **SS** From Malaysian, Kentish, White-faced and Javan Plovers by lack of white nuchal collar. Some non-descript fem/non-br Javan have obscure nuchal collar, resembling Red-capped Plover, but at least traces of nuchal collar usually visible.

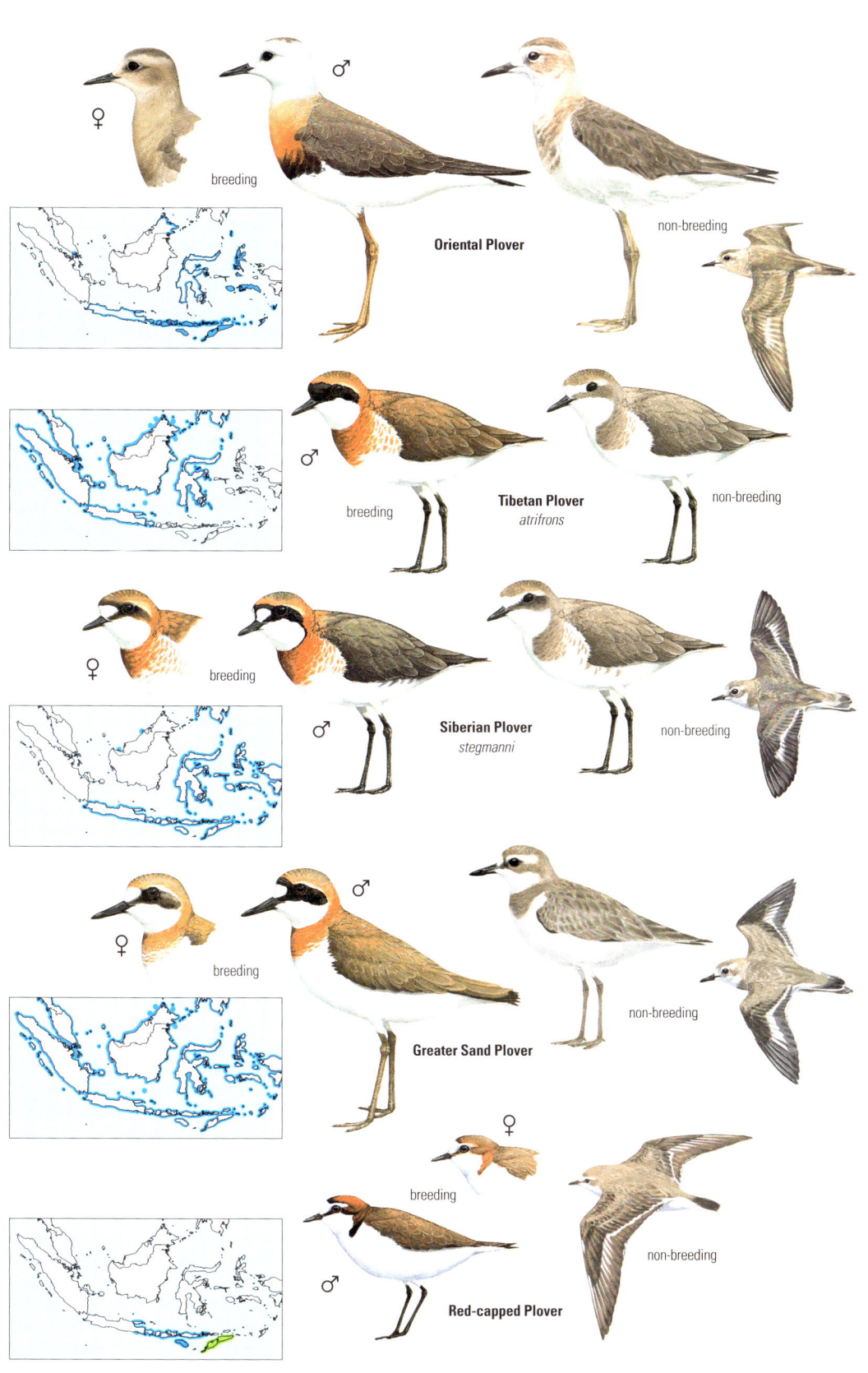

breeding

non-breeding

Oriental Plover

♀

♂

breeding

non-breeding

Tibetan Plover
atrifrons

♂

♀

breeding

♂

Siberian Plover
stegmanni

non-breeding

♀

breeding

♂

non-breeding

Greater Sand Plover

♀

breeding

♂

Red-capped Plover

non-breeding

Malaysian Plover *Anarhynchus peronii*
L 14–16 cm. SE Asia, Phil. Monotypic. Increasingly local on sandy beaches, sand dunes and shallow bays. Usually in pairs. Reluctant to fly. **ID** Short-billed; long, pale-pinkish legs; diagnostic mottled upperparts. In flight shows prominent white wingbar. **M** short white supercilium; black frontal bar; black breast patch extending onto hindneck collar; black eyestripe rarely reaching bill; rufous crown washed with brown; white nuchal collar. **F** black replaced by buff wash. **Imm** less rufous than fem. **Voc** Soft, excited "twik". **SS** Black collar fully connecting across nape (in male) and mottled upperparts separate from Kentish, White-faced, Javan and Red-capped Plovers.

Kentish Plover *Anarhynchus alexandrinus*
L 15–18 cm, **WS** 42–45 cm. Palaearctic; wintering Africa to Phil. 3 ssp, 2 in region: *alexandrinus* (breeds Palaearctic; wintering S to GS); *nihonensis* (breeds Japan and Taiwan; wintering S to Phil, Bor and, rarely, LS, Sul and Mol). No longer considered conspecific with Snowy Plover *A. nivosus* (Americas). Also see White-faced Plover for taxonomy. Common on coastal mudflats and sand bars. In small flocks. **ID** Black legs (paler, more flesh-coloured on average in *nihonensis*). Short black bill (longer in *nihonensis*). In flight white wingbar. **M br** black frontal bar, black lateral breast patches and eyestripe (including lores); white nuchal collar; rufous crown and nape; *nihonensis* with duller crown and longer breast patches. **F/Ad non-br** white nuchal collar, no black in plumage, more uniform brown head and upperparts. **Imm** as Ad non-br but pale-fringed upperparts. **Voc** (i) Rattling trill "trrrt"; (ii) hard, gritty "kurrt"; (iii) hard, buzzy "tzit". **SS** See Tibetan, Siberian, Malaysian, White-faced, Red-capped and Javan Plovers.

White-faced Plover *Anarhynchus dealbatus*
L 15–18 cm, **WS** 42–45 cm. Monotypic. No longer considered con-specific with Kentish Plover based on distinct plumage and genomic signature. Scarce winter visitor along sandy coastline, less frequent-ly muddy edges. Singly, small groups (<6), often mixing with Kentish Plovers. **ID** Flesh-coloured legs. Short, broad-based black bill. In flight extensive white wingbar. **M br** black frontal bar, short black lateral breast patches; white lores, broad supercilium and broad nuchal collar; orange crown; sandy-brown upperparts. **F/Ad non-br** white nuchal collar, no black in plumage, more uniform brown head and upperparts. **Imm** as Ad non-br but pale-fringed upperparts. **Voc** Call: high-pitched "tip" or "tee". **SS** In M breeding plumage, straightforward to tell from Kentish Plover by white (not black) lores; less extensive black markings behind eye; more extensive white forehead with reduced black crown; paler, more orange crown; and more reduced lateral breast patches. Fem and non-br challenging to separate from Kentish, best done in direct comparison (as is often possible), with White-faced showing paler upperparts (similar to Malaysian but without the latter's distinct markings) and a longer, broader wingbar in flight. Also see Tibetan, Siberian, Malaysian, Red-capped and Javan Plovers.

Javan Plover *Anarhynchus javanicus*
L 15 cm. Monotypic. Locally common; beaches, shrimp ponds, mudflats and wetlands by coast. Appears to be expanding range. Usually in pairs to small flocks (<10). **ID** Long, flesh-coloured legs; long, thin, black bill; slender proportions. In flight shows white wingbar. **M br** warm-buff lateral breast patches, often with blackish suffusion; buff ear-coverts to hindcrown; blackish frontal bar and lores; narrow white nuchal collar often washed buff; mid-brown upperparts and crown. **F/Ad non-br** brown lores; often buff ear-coverts; white supercilium extending behind eye. **Imm** pale-fringed upperparts. **Voc** (i) Rattling trill "trrk-trrk"; (ii) rolling "rrrrer-rer-rer"; (iii) squeaky, short "put". **SS** Warm buff ear-coverts and lateral patches separate males and bright females from Kentish and White-faced, but many non-descript females and immatures which have not yet developed warm head colouration will be nearly identical to Kentish. Also see Red-capped and Malaysian Plover.

Little Ringed Plover *Charadrius dubius*
L 14–17 cm, **WS** 42–48 cm. Breeds Palaearctic, S–SE Asia, Phil and Aus; winters Africa to SE Asia. 3 ssp, 1–2 in region: *curonicus* (breeds Palaearctic; winters Africa to SE Asia), *dubius* (Phil, NG, possibly Wallacea). Locally common migrant to lowland wetlands, particularly sandy margins with sparse vegetation, scarcer on coast (*curonicus*). The occurrence of resident *dubius* in Wallacea is possible but requires confirmation. **ID** Slender proportions, less 'full' breast than similar species; short, pointy black bill with a pink (less often pale-yellow) base and long, dull legs. In flight shows uniform upperwing. Ssp *curonicus* slightly larger with shorter, all-black bill and much brighter yellow (sometimes orange-tinged) legs. **Ad br** broad yellow orbital ring; black mask, lores and band over white forecrown; white nuchal collar; black breast band wrapping around collar; *curonicus* has less broad orbital ring and less extensive black forecrown band. **Ad non-br** plumage exists in *curonicus* only: face pattern less distinct with black replaced by dark-brownish, incom-plete breast band. **Imm** as Ad non-br but with buff supercilium, speckled buff forecrown and pale-fringed upperparts. **Voc** Short, sharp "piu", sometimes extended to "p-p-piu". **SS** See Common Ringed and Long-billed Plovers.

Common Ringed Plover *Charadrius hiaticula*
L 19 cm. Breeds Palaearctic; winters Africa to W Asia. 3 ssp, 1 in region: *tundrae* (breeds C–E Palaearctic; winters Africa to W Asia). Several records from N Bor and Jav on coastal mud and sand flats, which it favours in winter. Singly to large groups. **ID** Orange legs. In flight shows broad white wingbar. **Ad br** orange bill with black tip; broad black breast band; lacks eyering. **Ad non-br** more diffuse broad breast band; duller facial pattern; dull orange base to lower mandible. **Imm** all-dark bill, legs less brightly orange; buff-fringed upperparts. **Voc** Mellow, rising "too-lee". **SS** Larger and more robust than Little Ringed with presence of wingbar and lack of eyering; leg colour tells these species apart in W Palaearctic but is only slightly more orange in Common Ringed compared to locally wintering E Asian populations of Little Ringed. See also Long-billed Plover.

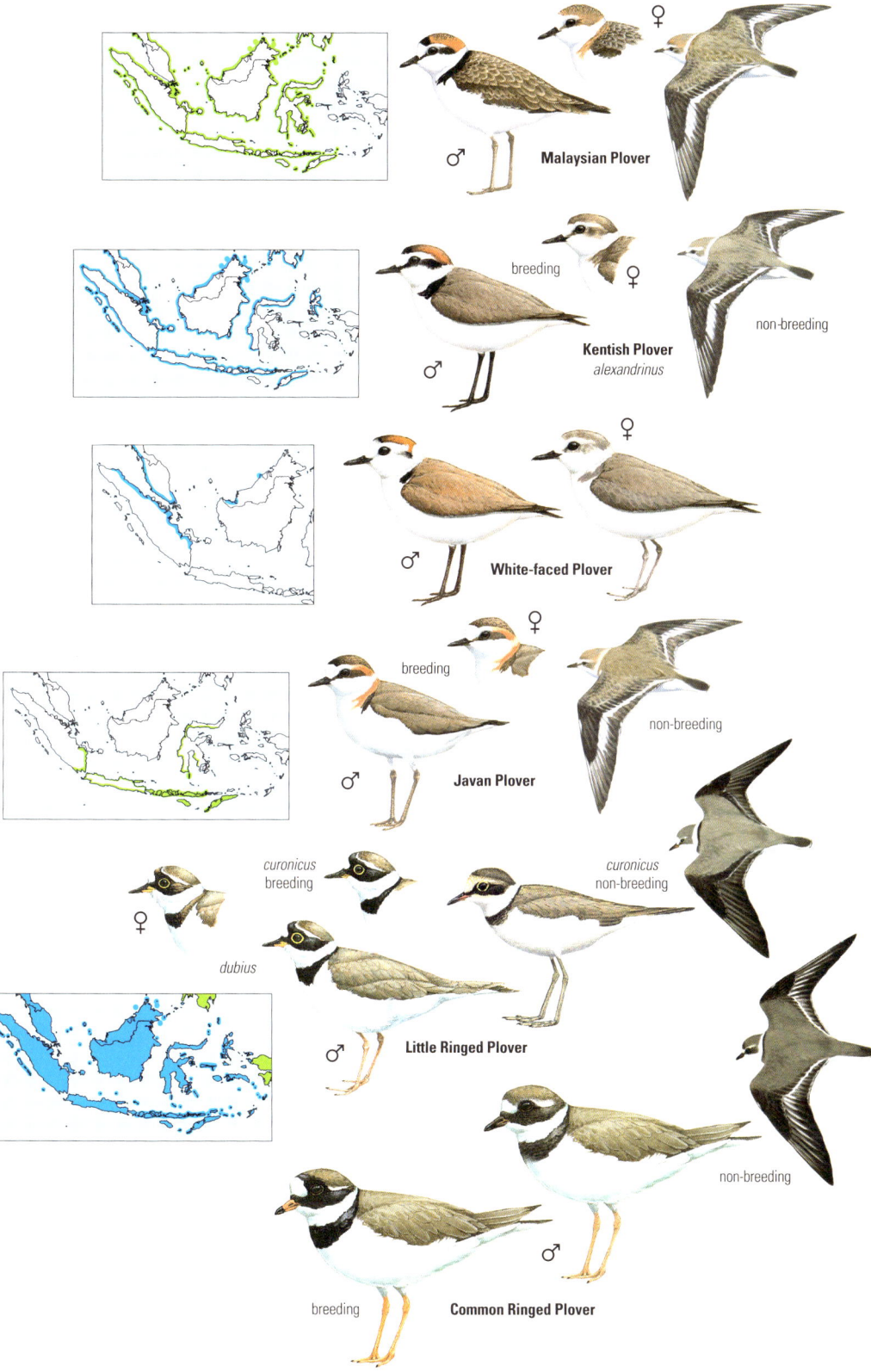

Malaysian Plover

♀

♂

breeding

non-breeding

Kentish Plover
alexandrinus

♀

♂

♀

♂

White-faced Plover

♀

breeding

non-breeding

♂

Javan Plover

curonicus
breeding

curonicus
non-breeding

♀

dubius

♂

Little Ringed Plover

non-breeding

breeding

Common Ringed Plover

♂

Long-billed Plover *Charadrius placidus* V

L 19–21 cm. Breeds Himalaya to NE Asia; some disperse to coastal E Asia and N Indochina. Monotypic. Vagrant to Brunei, though photographic evidence lacking (Jan 1982, Jan 1983, 2 birds Mar 1990). Outside region prefers rivers and streams with shingle, adjacent fields. Usually in pairs and small groups (<5). **ID** Long and slender, with pinkish-yellow legs and long black bill (often showing orange or pink base to lower mandible). In flight shows narrow white upperwing bar. **Ad br** white forehead and supercilium, black forecrown band, duller dark-brown ear-coverts and lores, black breast band narrows markedly in centre; ghosts an obsolete yellow eyering. **Ad non-br** duller breast band and facial pattern but retains black frontal shield. **Imm** has round-ended, buff supercilium; complete greyish-brown breast band with upper edge black. **Voc** Clear, rising "pewee", sometimes rapidly repeated. **SS** Longer-legged, longer-billed and more slender than Little Ringed Plover ("Little") and Common Ringed Plover ("Common"), with less vividly yellow/orange leg tones for each equivalent age group; in Ad br, duller blackish lores do not connect above bill base. Obsolete eye ring never pronounced as in Little. Long-billed always shows wingbar (absent in Little). Ad Long-billed always has black frontal shield contrasting with duller lores; in Little and Common, frontal shield disappears in non-br, while during breeding lores and ear-coverts share same black colour. Long-billed's breast band often narrows at centre more significantly than Ringed Plovers'. Long-billed's breast band is diagnostically bicolored (upper margin black, lower sides greyish-brown) except in Ad br (nearly all-black) and Imm before Sep (diffuse); this is especially helpful to ID imm birds without frontal shield from equivalent Ringed Plovers with broader all-brown breast bands. Imm Long-billed has distinct buffy rear supercilium (in Imm Common white and extending across eye to forehead; in Imm Little absent). Imm Little usually has buffish suffusion/mottling on forehead (all-white in Imm Long-billed).

Black-fronted Plover *Charadrius melanops* V

L 16–18 cm. Aus. Monotypic. Two records: Sumba (Aug 2015), Rote (Aug 2017). Margins of freshwater or brackish wetlands, particularly sandy margins with sparse vegetation. Singly, pairs or small groups. **ID Ad** red orbital ring; black eyestripe, lores, forecrown and breast band contrasting sharply with white supercilium and broad throat; brown upperparts with buff fringes and purplish scapulars; red bill with black tip; orange legs. In flight shows contrasting underwing: white underwing-coverts and black outerwing. **Imm** less contrasting face pattern, white forecrown; lacks orbital ring. **Voc** Short, emphatic "pit".

ROSTRATULIDAE
Painted-snipes
1 species in region

Small, unobtrusive wader with distinctive colouration. While largely crepuscular or nocturnal in habit, they may also be active by day, typically within reedy or grassy wetland habitats with adequate vegetation to hide. Reversed sexual dimorphism and parenting.

Greater Painted-snipe *Rostratula benghalensis*

L 23–28 cm, **WS** 50–55 cm. Africa, S–SE–E Asia, Phil. Monotypic. Uncommon to scarce local resident and apparent migrant in parts of range. Freshwater and coastal swamps and marshes, also rice fields and wet grassland. **ID** Stocky with long decurved bill and greenish-grey legs. Shows reverse sexual dimorphism with **F** more brightly and boldly marked. **F** upperparts rich chestnut; head, neck and breast

maroon; prominent white 'braces' (becoming buff towards rear) and white 'tear drop' eyering; bill pinkish-orange at base, black at tip. **M** smaller and duller with buff edging on wings and buff-coloured eyering; bill pinkish-grey at base, black at tip. **Imm** similar to male but wing-coverts greyer. **Voc** Song: series of low, slow "koh-koh-koh...", given at night from ground or in circular flight. Call: explosive "twick-twick". **SS** Sightings in LS should be checked for potential vagrant **Australian Painted-snipe** *R. australis* (Australia), no longer included in this species. Australian separated by slightly larger size, shorter legs and bill, longer wings, generally less chestnut on breeding females head and neck, as well as round (rather than flat) barred spots on tail (fem) and wing-coverts (male).

JACANIDAE
Jaçanãs
3 species in region

Medium-sized, crake-like waterbirds with long legs and extremely long toes. Found in wetland habitats where they feed by walking on floating and emergent vegetation. Often shy and unobtrusive. Polyandry (with one female tending a harem of males) has led to reversed sexual dimorphism.

Pheasant-tailed Jaçanã *Hydrophasianus chirurgus*

L 31–58 cm. S–SE–E Asia, Phil. Monotypic. Uncommon migrant. Swamps, wetlands, lakes and ponds with emergent vegetation. **ID Ad br** very long, drooping black tail; black underparts; brown mantle, scapulars and inner-coverts; rest of wing white (except for black tips to outer wing) creating a distinctive white panel in folded wing; face and foreneck white, separated from golden-yellow hindneck by narrow black line. **Ad non-br** shorter tail; wing-coverts brownish; underparts white apart from poorly defined black-brown breast band; crown and hindneck blackish with golden-yellow restricted to sides of neck. **Imm** buff edging to back and wing-coverts; dull-white sides of neck; less distinct breast band; chestnut cap. **Voc** Song: mellow bell-like "KU-wuul". Call: (i) rapid, purring "hrrrt"; (ii) loud, mewing "dew-w". **SS** See Bronze-winged Jaçanã.

Comb-crested Jaçanã *Irediparra gallinacea*

L 21–24 cm. Phil to Aus. Monotypic. Widespread but generally rare resident, locally common S Sul. Swamps, wetlands, lakes and ponds with emergent vegetation. **ID Ad** brown wing and mantle; black breast, hindneck and cap contrast with white belly; face, throat and foreneck white tinged golden-yellow; prominent pink-red comb. In flight black flight feathers and tail contrast with brown coverts and mantle. **Imm** duller; cap chestnut brown, not black; lacks black breast band. **Voc** Squeaky "pee-pee-pee". **SS** See Bronze-winged Jaçanã.

Bronze-winged Jaçanã *Metopidius indicus*

L 28–31 cm. S–SE Asia. Monotypic. Formerly uncommon migrant, now rare. Swamps, wetlands, lakes and ponds with emergent vegetation. **ID Ad** glossy black apart from brownish wing-coverts and mantle and rufous tail, rump and vent; long white supercilium behind eye; small red shield on forehead. **Imm** hindneck and rear eyestripe black, becoming chestnut on crown; tiny white loral stripe; foreneck and breast buff; lower breast and belly white. **Voc** (i) Loud, screeching "WHIRTT", regularly repeated; (ii) short, wheezy "scrit-scrit-scrit...". **SS** Buffy breast, white loral stripe and black rear eyestripe separate Imm Bronze-winged from Imm Comb-crested Jaçanã. Lack of diffuse blackish breast band and pale neck-sides separate it from Imm Pheasant-tailed Jaçanã.

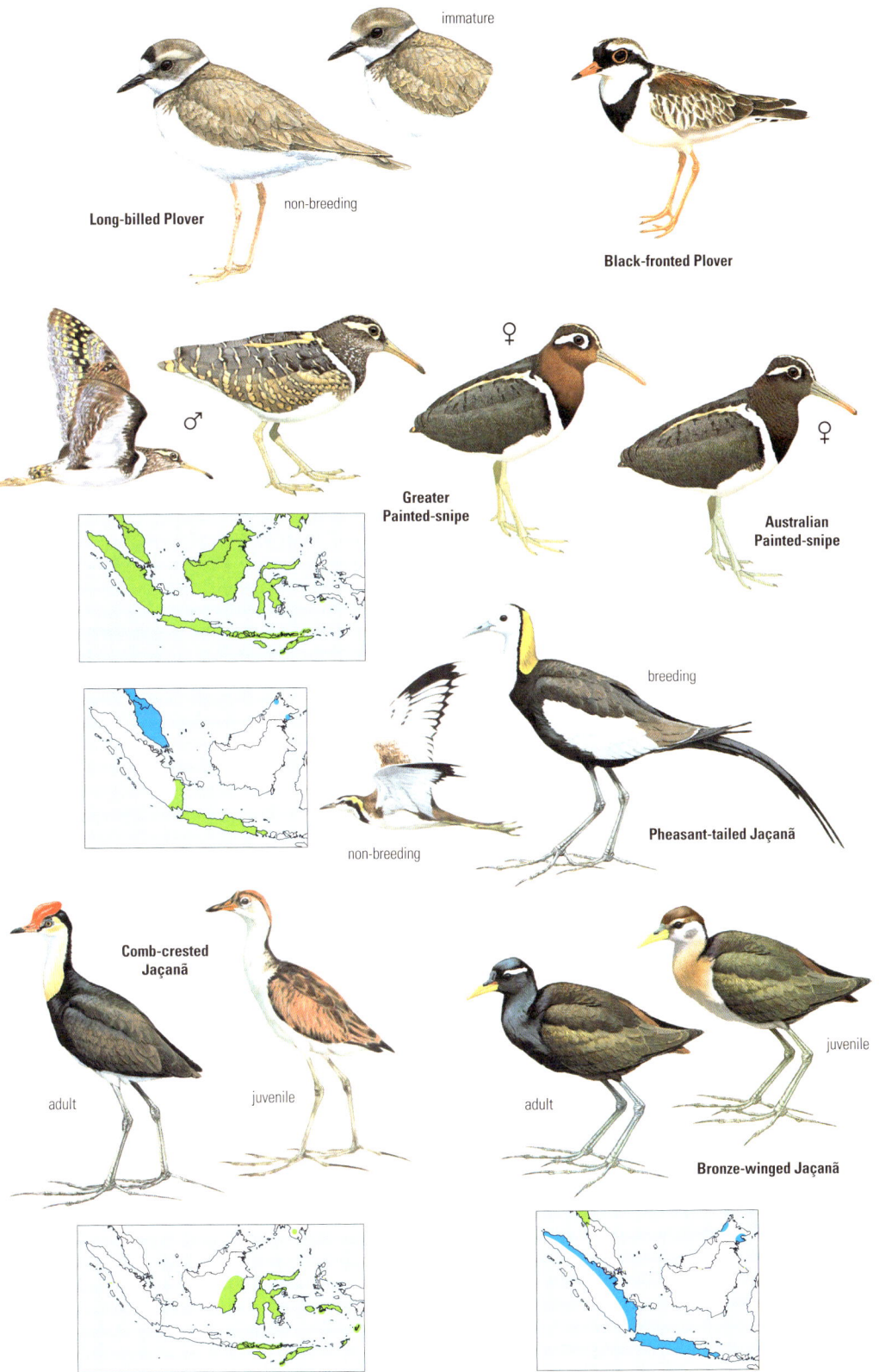

immature

Long-billed Plover

non-breeding

Black-fronted Plover

♂

♀

Greater
Painted-snipe

♀

Australian
Painted-snipe

breeding

non-breeding

Pheasant-tailed Jaçanã

Comb-crested
Jaçanã

adult

juvenile

adult

juvenile

Bronze-winged Jaçanã

SCOLOPACIDAE
Sandpipers and Snipes
44 species in region

A large and diverse family of small to medium-sized shorebirds, ranging from cosmopolitan migrants found in large flocks in coastal wetlands to secretive nocturnal inhabitants of dense upland forest.

Red-necked Phalarope *Phalaropus lobatus*
L 16–20 cm, **WS** 30–38 cm. Breeds N Holarctic; winters at sea in Pacific and Indian Oceans. Monotypic. Common migrant and winterer, occasionally in large flocks. Common at sea in E but also regular in W. Generally pelagic when not breeding, but occasionally coastal and also regular on migration in wetlands in highland with ancient cultivation (e.g. Bario in Sarawak). Swims on water. **ID** Small and elegant. Needle-like black bill; legs black. **F br** wings and back dark grey with orange bands on mantle and scapulars; head, neck and sides of breast blackish-grey with bright red sides to neck; throat, belly and narrow supercilium white. **M br** duller, with less contrasting red sides to neck. **Ad non-br** pale grey upperparts with white edging and darker feather centres; white head, neck and underparts; black eye patch and variable amounts of black on crown. **Imm** dark brown back and wings with paler buff edging; hindneck and crown streaked brown; warm buff wash to foreneck and breast; rest of underparts white. **Voc** Short, sharp "chep". **SS** See Red Phalarope.

Red Phalarope *Phalaropus fulicarius*   `V`
L 20–22 cm, **WS** 37–43 cm. Breeds N Holarctic; winters at sea in E Pacific and Atlantic Oceans. Monotypic. Recorded Sarawak (Oct 1968), Jav (Apr–May 2008), off N Obi (Oct 2016). Generally pelagic when not breeding. Occasionally in coastal wetlands, particularly after storms. Swims on water. **ID** Larger and stockier than Red-necked Phalarope. Bill stout and short with black tip and yellow base when breeding. **F br** rufous-red underparts, breast and neck; black cap and white cheek patch; wings and back black with broad buff-orange edging. **M br** as fem but with variable white markings on red underparts. **Ad non-br** uniformly pale grey upperparts and hindneck; head, neck and underparts white with black eye patch and variable black on rear of crown. **Imm** back and wings blackish with broad pale edging; underparts, head and neck white with black eye-patch and crown. **Voc** High-pitched, metallic "pit". **SS** In Ad non-br/Imm plumages from Red-necked Phalarope by larger, stockier size and thicker, less needle-like bill, often with pale base. Adult non-br Red has a paler unmarked grey mantle compared to Red-necked's dark, stripy mantle, but immatures of both species have dark upperparts with pale edges and stripes that can look similar to each other.

Terek Sandpiper *Xenus cinereus*
L 22–25 cm, **WS** 57–59 cm. Breeds Palaearctic; winters from Africa to Aus. Monotypic. Common migrant throughout. Some birds linger year-round. Coastal mudflats, sandbanks and lagoons. **ID** Short-legged, stocky with long, upturned bill; legs yellowish. **Ad br** grey-brown upperparts with black bar on shoulder; underparts white; white trailing edge to wing visible in flight. **Ad non-br** duller with less prominent black bar. **Imm** darker brown with pale fringes to upperparts giving scaled appearance. **Voc** 2–5 short, whistled "pwee-wee-wee".

Common Sandpiper *Actitis hypoleucos*
L 19–21 cm, **WS** 38–41 cm. Breeds Palaearctic; winters Africa to Aus. Monotypic. Common migrant throughout with records year-round. Coastal mudflats, sandbanks, wetlands, inland marshes,

rivers, ponds and wet rice fields. Singly, pairs or small groups. Flight flickering with down-turned wings interspersed with stiff-winged glides. Constantly bobs tail. **ID** Small brown-and-white wader with distinctive horizontal stance, bobbing motion and white wedge formed between closed wing and grey-brown sides of breast. Bill dark grey; legs dull grey-green to yellow. **Ad br** white eyering and supercilium; upperparts glossy brown with faint pale feather edging. **Ad non-br** plainer upperparts and less prominent brown sides to breast. **Imm** more scaled appearance to wing-coverts and mantle caused by pale edging and darker subterminal bars. **Voc** Series of rapid, high-pitched whistled "swee-swee-swee...".

Green Sandpiper *Tringa ochropus*
L 21–24 cm, **WS** 57–61 cm. Breeds Palaearctic; winters to S. Monotypic. Rare migrant. Typically in freshwater wetlands, ponds, rivers and wet rice fields, usually singly or small flocks. **ID** Stocky with brown-black upperparts and white underparts. Bill blackish; legs dark green; wings uniformly dark in flight. **Ad br** heavily streaked breast; sparse white spotting on dark upperparts; dark loral bar with white supraloral patch and narrow white eyering. **Ad non-br** upperparts plainer with even less prominent spotting and paler breast streaks. **Imm** as Ad non-br but breast streaking more prominent. **Voc** Clear, ringing whistled "tlueet-wit-wit". **SS** From Wood Sandpiper by darker upperparts with sparser spotting, darker breast appearing like uniform extension of upperparts, and dark (not pale) underwings. See also Imm Grey-tailed Tattler.

Grey-tailed Tattler *Tringa brevipes*
L 24–27 cm, **WS** 60–65 cm. Breeds E Siberia; winters SE Asia to Aus, Phil. Monotypic. Common migrant in E, scarcer in W. Some birds apparently oversummer. Frequents rocky coastlines, including coral flats, sand and shingle beaches, as well as mudflats and inland lakes. Singly or small flocks. **ID** Upperparts uniformly ash-grey; short yellow legs and blackish bill often with yellow base; prominent white supercilium extending beyond eye and dark loral stripe. **Ad br** white underparts with dark grey barring. **Ad non-br** lacks barring on underparts but shows grey wash to sides of breast and flanks. **Imm** upperparts show pale spotting. **Voc** Clear, double-whistled "pyu-ee". **SS** Imm with spotted back may recall Green Sandpiper but larger, longer-billed, greyer-backed, with more intensely yellow-coloured legs and lack of breast streaks.

Spotted Redshank *Tringa erythropus*   `V`
L 29–32 cm, **WS** 61–67 cm. Breeds Palaearctic; winters Africa to SE Asia. Monotypic. Vagrant. Only recent confirmed records from N Sum (Sept 2010, Oct 2010) and Sabah (Mar and May 2019). Coastal and inland wetlands, mudflats, wet rice fields. **ID** Long-legged and elegant. Bill black with red on base of lower mandible, long and narrow with slightly down-curved tip. In flight shows uniformly coloured wings without prominent white wingbar or trailing edge, finely grey-barred rump and white oval patch on back. **Ad br** entirely black with white spotting on wings and mantle; white eyering; legs blackish-red. **Ad non-br** pale grey upperparts with faint spotting; white underparts with greyish wash to breast; prominent white supercilium and dark loral bar; legs red. **Imm** as Ad non-br but darker and browner with more prominent spotting on upperparts; underparts faintly barred grey. **Voc** Loud, emphatic "choo-IT". **SS** Most easily told from Common Redshank by lack of prominent white wingbar. Otherwise very similar though Spotted has longer bill and legs, with a more prominent supercilium extending behind eye. Red legs distinguish from most other similar sandpipers.

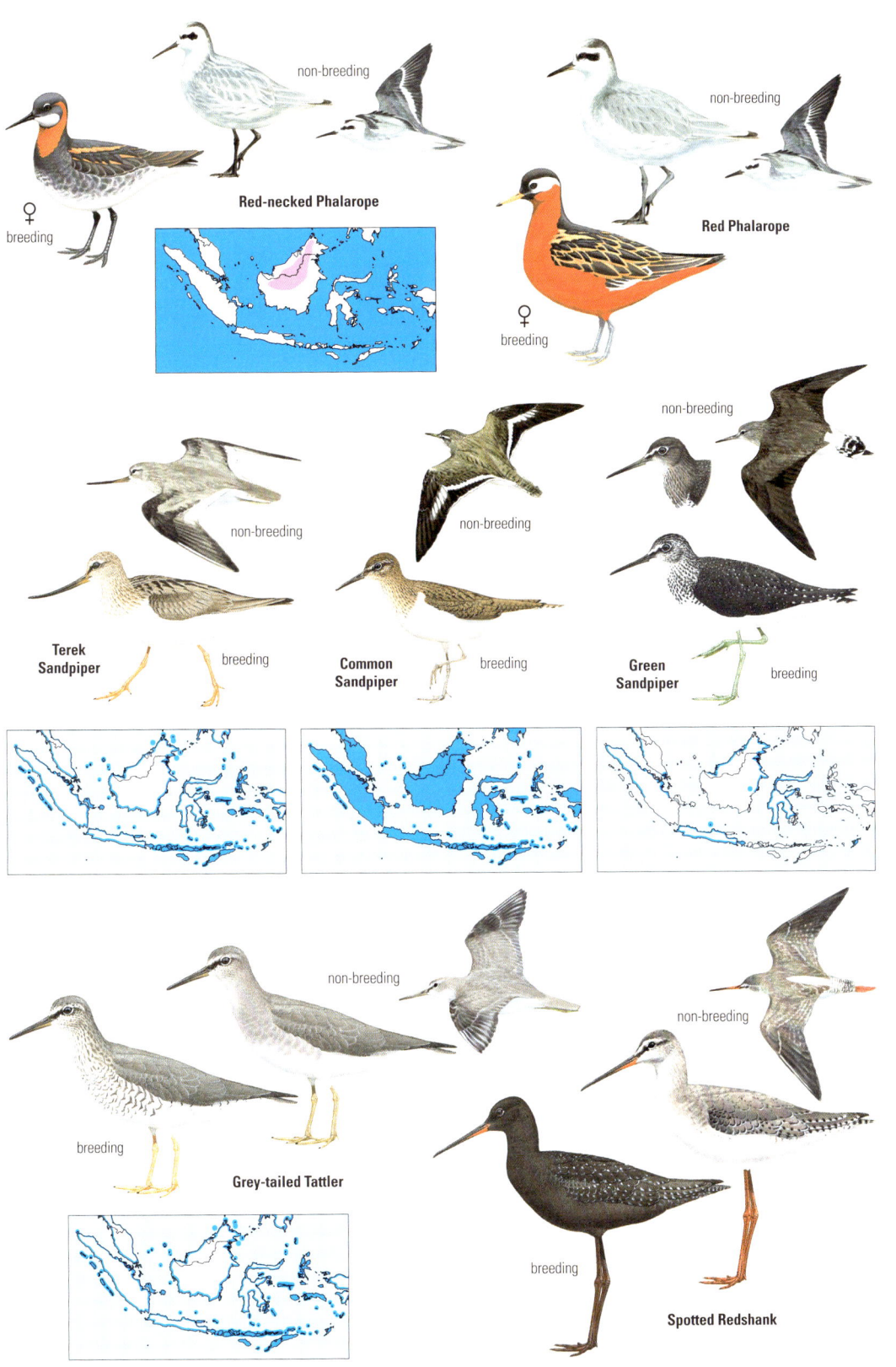

Red-necked Phalarope

non-breeding

♀ breeding

Red Phalarope

non-breeding

♀ breeding

Terek Sandpiper

non-breeding

breeding

Common Sandpiper

non-breeding

breeding

Green Sandpiper

non-breeding

breeding

Grey-tailed Tattler

non-breeding

breeding

non-breeding

breeding

Spotted Redshank

Common Greenshank *Tringa nebularia*

L 30–35 cm, **WS** 68–70 cm. Breeds Palaearctic; winters Africa to Aus. Monotypic. Locally common migrant throughout in coastal and inland wetlands, wet rice fields, sandbanks and mudflats. Usually singly or small flocks. **ID** Stout-bodied with long, slightly upturned greyish bill, blacker at tip. Long, grey-green legs. In flight shows uniformly dark wings with white rump and white wedge extending up back; tail whitish with faint barring. **Ad br** back and wings grey-brown with white edging and darker centres to feathering; head, neck and upper breast with heavy black streaks and spots. **Ad non-br** paler with less prominent streaking. **Imm** browner with pale buff fringing to upperparts. **Voc** Trisyllabic, far-carrying whistled "tyew-tyew-tyew". **SS** Smaller Marsh Sandpiper is more slender and has thinner, straighter, more needle-like bill. See also Nordmann's Greenshank.

Nordmann's Greenshank *Tringa guttifer*

L 29–32 cm. Breeds E Siberia; winters SE Asia. Monotypic. Very rare but apparently regular migrant. Coastal and inland wetlands, wet rice fields, sandbanks and mudflats. Usually singly or small flocks (<20). **ID** Stocky, short-necked; short yellow legs; stout, slightly upturned bill. In flight shows white tail, rump and wedge extending onto back; white underwing coverts and short leg projection. Slight supercilium **Ad br** wings and back dark grey-brown spotted and fringed white; head and upperneck white with heavy grey-brown streaks and blotches, and slightly contrasting darker crown and lores; breast and flanks with prominent blackish spots; black bill. **Ad non-br** pale grey upperparts, hindneck and head, with pale white feather edging on back and wings; underparts clean white; yellowish base to bill. **Imm** as Ad non-br but darker and browner with buff feather edging; strongly bicoloured bill, yellow-grey at base, blackish distal half. **Voc** Trilled "kwee". **SS** Marsh Sandpiper is smaller, more slender, longer-legged; has thinner, straighter, more needle-like bill. Nordmann's is slightly smaller than Common Greenshank, with much shorter, brighter yellow-green legs and more contrasting yellowish (vs greyish) bill base in non-breeding plumage; in flight shows white (not dark) underwing coverts and largely white uppertail (barred in Common). **AN** Spotted Greenshank.

Lesser Yellowlegs *Tringa flavipes*

L 23–25 cm, **WS** 59–64 cm. Breeds Nearctic; winters to Neotropics. Monotypic. Single records from N Sum (Sep 1983) and Flores (Sep 2003). Typically in freshwater and coastal wetlands, mudflats and sandbanks. **ID** Elegant. Long yellow legs. Slim, straight bill, grey-brown at base, blacker towards tip. **Ad br** dark grey-brown wings and back with prominent white spotting; head and neck heavily streaked grey-brown; faint white supercilium and dark loral bar; underparts, tail and rump white. **Ad non-br** paler with less prominent spotting and streaking. **Imm** as Ad br but paler, browner, with more prominent buff spots on upperparts. **Voc** High-pitched, clear, whistled "tew". **SS** Most similar to smaller Wood Sandpiper. Lesser Yellowlegs lacks an obvious supercilium, is longer-billed and usually has much more yellow-coloured legs. Told from most other similar sandpipers by combination of yellow legs and strongly spotted upperparts. Identification should also eliminate vagrant **Greater Yellowlegs** *T. melanoleuca* (Americas; as yet unrecorded in region), which is larger, more heavily built, and has longer, heavier, slightly upturned bill that is usually twice the length of head, while Lesser's bill is only up to 1.5 times the head length.

Marsh Sandpiper *Tringa stagnatilis*

L 22–26 cm, **WS** 55–59 cm. Breeds Palaearctic; winters Africa to Aus. Monotypic. Locally common migrant throughout. Coastal and inland wetlands, wet rice fields, sandbanks and mudflats. Usually singly or small flocks. **ID** Graceful grey-and-white wader. Long yellow-green legs; thin, needle-like grey-black bill. In flight shows white rump and wedge extending up back; tail white with indistinct dark barring. **Ad br** grey-brown back and wings spotted black with white edging; head and neck finely streaked blackish; breast and flanks with blackish chevrons. **Ad non-br** upperparts pale grey with faint white edging; white supercilium contrasts with slightly streaked crown; underparts including foreneck and breast white. **Imm** may be browner and show darker feather fringes on wings and back. **Voc** High-pitched, ringing "kyew". **SS** See Common and Nordmann's Greenshanks.

Wood Sandpiper *Tringa glareola*

L 19–23 cm, **WS** 56–57 cm. Breeds Palaearctic; winters Africa to Aus. Monotypic. Common migrant throughout. Typically in fresh-water wetlands including wet rice fields, lakes and marshes. Singly or small flocks. **ID** Medium-sized brown-and-white, rather elegant wader. Straight blackish bill; long yellow-green legs. In flight shows prominent white rump and white tail with faint dark barring. **Ad br** upperparts dark brown, boldly speckled white; head, neck and breast streaked brown, flanks with some brown barring; conspicuous white supercilium and pale throat. **Ad non-br/Imm** upperparts browner, with less conspicuous spotting; head, neck and breast with less distinct streaking; white supercilium still prominent. **Voc** Rapid, high-pitched "chiff-if-if". **SS** See Green Sandpiper and Lesser Yellowlegs.

Common Redshank *Tringa totanus*

L 27–29 cm, **WS** 59–66 cm. Breeds Palaearctic; winters Africa to Aus. Here considered monotypic: plumage variability apparently related to phenology and polymorphisms. Common migrant throughout. Coastal and inland wetlands, wet rice fields, sandbanks and mudflats. Occasionally very large flocks. **ID** Medium-sized wader with bright orange legs and orange-black bill. Distinctive broad, white trailing edge to wings and white wedge extending up back visible in flight. **Ad br** brown upperparts with some pale and dark feather edging; head, neck, breast and flanks streaked and spotted brown. **Ad non-br** paler grey-brown above; streaking on head, neck and underparts replaced with grey-brown wash. **Imm** upperparts browner with buff spotting; head, neck, breast and flanks streaked and spotted brown; legs paler orange to yellow. **Voc** (i) Emphatic, clear whistled "tew"; (ii) downslurred "tew-huhu". **SS** See Spotted Redshank.

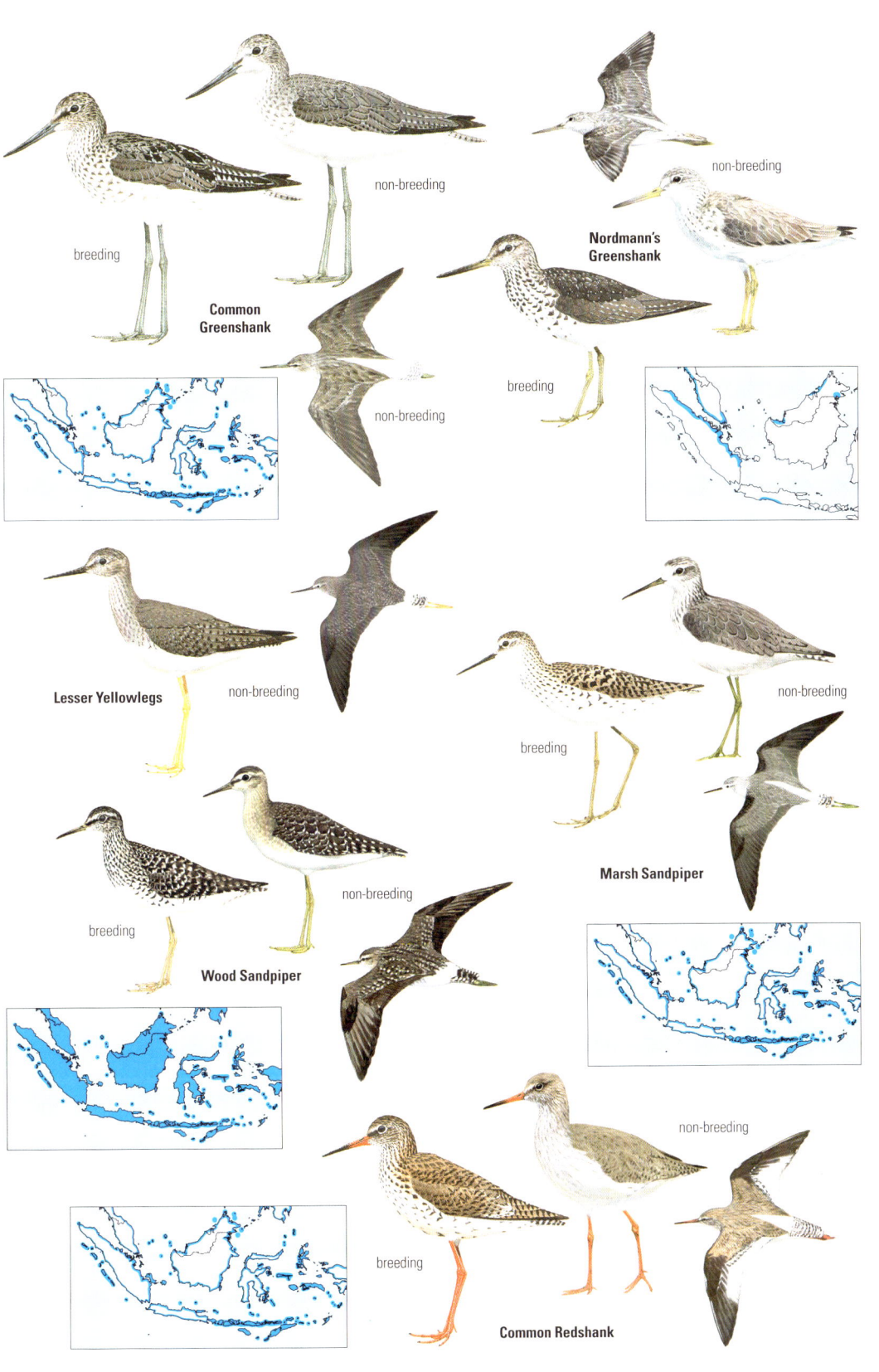

non-breeding

breeding

**Common
Greenshank**

non-breeding

**Nordmann's
Greenshank**

non-breeding

breeding

Lesser Yellowlegs

non-breeding

breeding

non-breeding

Marsh Sandpiper

breeding

non-breeding

Wood Sandpiper

non-breeding

non-breeding

breeding

Common Redshank

Ruddy Turnstone *Arenaria interpres*
L 21–26 cm, **WS** 50–57 cm. Breeds Holarctic; winters to S. 2 ssp, 1 in region: *interpres* (breeds Palaearctic; winters S to Africa to E Pacific). Common migrant throughout. Rocky coasts, mudflats, sandbanks. Generally solitary or small flocks. **ID** Small, chunky wader with black, white and red-brown plumage. Short black bill, short red legs. In flight shows striking dark and white pattern on wings, rump and back. **M br** rufous-orange upperparts, white head and underparts with complex and variable black markings on head, neck and breast. **F br** duller; head more brown than white. **Ad non-br** upperparts duller with pale edging and lacking bright chestnut; head and neck brownish with pale throat; variable black markings on neck and breast as Ad br. **Imm** upperparts more uniformly brown with buff edging; head and neck streaked brown with pale throat and black breast patches. **Voc** (i) Short, staccato "tuk-tuk-tuk…"; (ii) short, yelping "kew".

Sanderling *Calidris alba*
L 20–21 cm, **WS** 35–39 cm. Breeds Holarctic; winters to S. Monotypic. Common migrant throughout. Typically on sandy beaches, but also coastal wetlands and mudflats. Often runs along tideline. Singly or small flocks. **ID** Stocky with short black legs and bill. Underparts white. In flight shows black flight feathers and primary coverts contrasting with broad white wingbar. **Ad br** upperparts, head and breast predominantly chestnut with paler edging and dark streaks and spots; variable patches of white on head. **Ad non-br** upperparts, hindneck and crown very pale grey with contrasting dark carpal patch usually prominent; rest of body white. **Imm** wings and back blackish with white edging and spots; head, neck and breast pale with buffish wash and fine dark streaking on crown, ear-coverts and breast. **Voc** Short, emphatic "plit", regularly repeated. **SS** Size separates it from smaller stints, especially Red-necked Stint in similar breeding plumage. With experience, tidal running habits instantly give away identity of typically-behaving individuals.

Little Stint *Calidris minuta* □V
L 12–14 cm, **WS** 28–31 cm. Breeds Palaearctic; winters to Africa to S Asia. Monotypic. Confirmed from Brunei (Apr–Jun 1982), consequently now several recent records from Sarawak and Sabah, Indonesian records confined to Bali (Dec 2017) and N Sum (Oct 2019). Found in coastal and inland wetlands, mudflats and sandbanks. **ID** Small and dumpy with short, straight, black bill and short black legs. Prominent white wingbar in flight. **Ad br** wings and back brown-black with orange and white edging; prominent white 'braces' on mantle; head, neck and undefined breast band washed rufous with extensive whitish throat; breast lightly streaked black. **Ad non-br** plain grey-brown upperparts, hindneck and head, with darker feather centres on wings and back; white supercilium and unstreaked white underparts, breast and foreneck. **Imm** as Ad br but less extensive rufous wash and dark streaking on face and neck, and prominent white supercilium contrasting with darker rufous crown; white 'braces' at edge of mantle usually obvious. **Voc** Sharp, high-pitched "stit". **SS** In non-breeding and Imm plumages very similar to Red-necked Stint: Little is longer-legged, shorter-winged, hunch-backed and has a slightly longer, drooping bill. It typically has a smaller, rounder head that is held upright in a vertical round-bodied posture, rather than Red-necked's big-headed, neckless, horizontal posture. Non-breeding Little has, on average, broader dark feather centres on back, but is difficult to identify without some lingering feathers from breeding plumage. Imm Little has darker cap, more conspicuous (often 'split') supercilium behind eye, more streaks/spots on neck sides, darker-centred wing-coverts and scapulars with well-marked pale edges (vs plain coverts, contrasting with well-marked scapulars), and more conspicuous 'braces' on back than

Red-necked. From other sandpipers by combination of black legs and minute size. In br plumage, white, not rufous throat, and rich chestnut fringes to dark-centred coverts and tertials giving strikingly bright appearance, while Red-necked often shows chestnut on tertials, rarely on coverts.

Red-necked Stint *Calidris ruficollis*
L 13–16 cm, **WS** 29–33 cm. Breeds E Palaearctic; winters SE Asia to Phil and Aus. Monotypic. Very common migrant throughout. Coastal marshes, mudflats, sandflats, occasionally also inland wetlands. Often present in large flocks. **ID** Small, dumpy, with relatively long wings. Short black bill and legs. In flight shows prominent white wingbar and narrow dark line through otherwise white rump. **Ad br** rufous-red head and upper breast with darker, streaked crown; back and wings mostly rufous and black with paler edging; underparts white with some black spotting on lower breast. **Ad non-br** pale grey upperparts with fine dark streaks, grey wash to sides of breast; underparts white. **Imm** wings and back blackish with pale and rufous edging and indistinct white 'braces'; head and neck streaked grey-brown with grey-brown wash on sides of breast. **Voc** High-pitched, squeaky "chriit". **SS** See Sanderling and Little Stint. From Long-toed and Temminck's Stints best told by black (not greenish) legs.

Temminck's Stint *Calidris temminckii*
L 13–15 cm, **WS** 34–37 cm. Breeds N Palaearctic; winters S to Africa to Phil. Monotypic. Scarce but regular visitor to Bor. Typically in freshwater pools, marshes and flooded grassland, but also coastal wetlands and mudflats. Usually singly or small flocks. **ID** Small brown-and-white wader with pale green-yellow legs and short blackish bill. **Ad br** brown upperparts with pale fringing and darker centres to scapulars; head, neck and breast grey-brown with fine dark streaking. **Ad non-br** plain grey-brown upperparts, head, neck and breast; whiter throat and white underparts. **Imm** buff edging and dark shaft streaks on wings and back. **Voc** Dry trilling "tirrr-tirr-tirr…" regularly repeated. **SS** From Long-toed Stint by much plainer upperparts lacking the pale feather margins creating scaly pattern, especially in Imm and breeding plumages. From other sandpipers by combination of small size and pale leg colour.

Long-toed Stint *Calidris subminuta*
L 13–16 cm, **WS** 26–31 cm. Breeds E-C Palaearctic; winters S Asia to Aus. Monotypic. Scarce to locally common migrant throughout. Typically in freshwater wetlands, flooded grassland, muddy pools and wet rice fields, but occasionally coastal lagoons. Usually singly or small flocks. **ID** Small and slender with yellow-green legs and short blackish bill, paler at base. **Ad br** wings and back blackish with rufous edging; neck and sides of breast buff with fine dark streaking; prominent white supercilium contrasting with rufous, dark-streaked crown. **Ad non-br** wings and back dark grey-brown with darker feather centres; head, neck and breast finely streaked grey. **Imm** as Ad br but brighter and usually shows white 'braces' on mantle. **Voc** Trilling "chirp". **SS** See Temminck's and Red-necked Stints. From other sandpipers by combination of small size and pale leg colour.

Spoon-billed Sandpiper *Calidris pygmaea* □V
L 14–16 cm, **WS** 35–38 cm. Breeds E Palaearctic; winters SE Asia. Monotypic. Single record Aceh, Sum (Oct 2018). Coastal wetlands, mudflats, estuaries, favouring tideline. Mixes with Red-necked Stint, Curlew and Broad-billed Sandpipers. **ID** Unique spatulate bill. **Ad br** rusty-red face, throat and supercilium; black inner wing feathers fringed rufous; less contrasting outerwing; white underparts; black legs. **Ad non-br** upperparts, hindneck, crown and ear-coverts plain

> > >

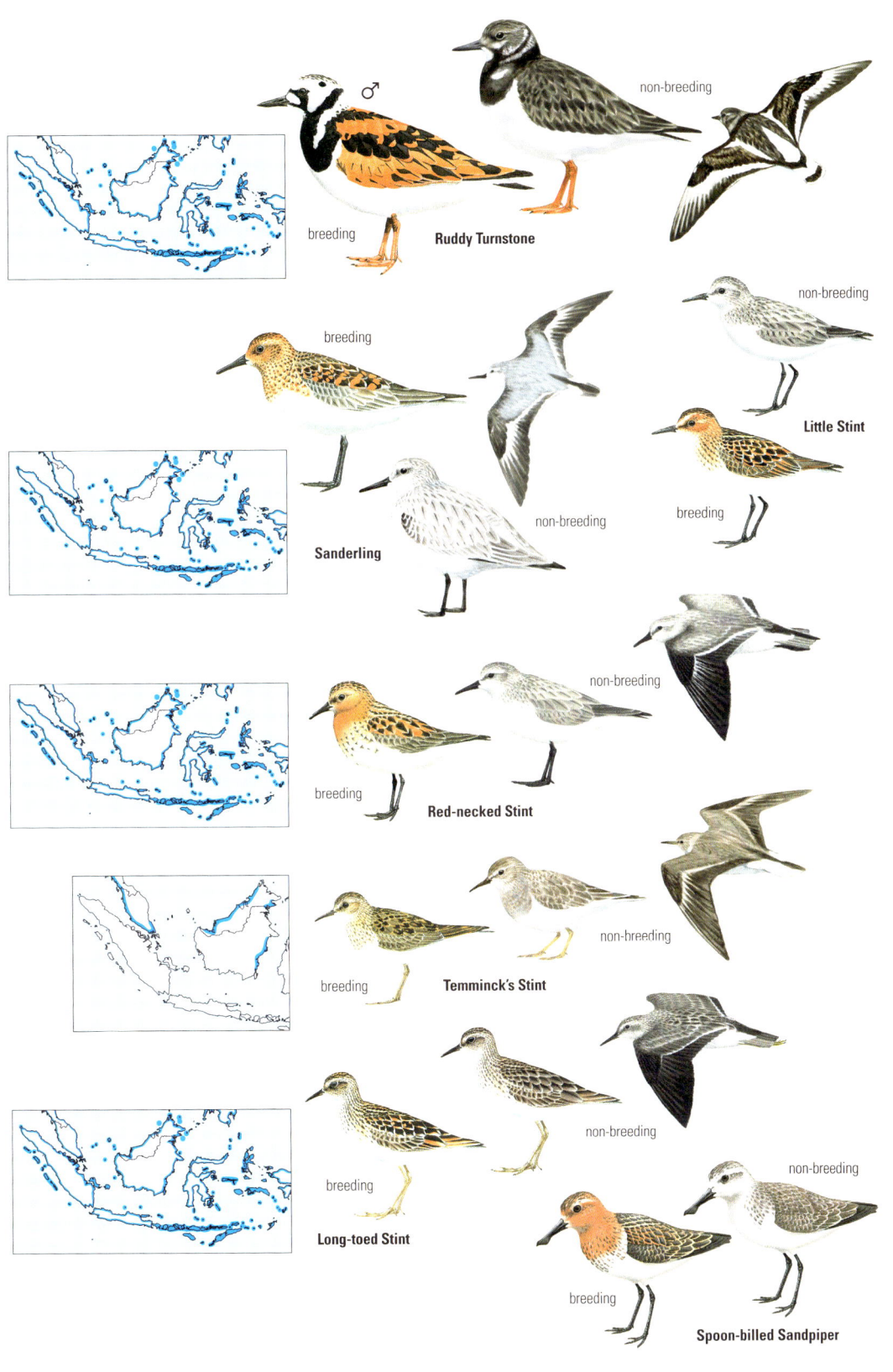

non-breeding

breeding ♂

Ruddy Turnstone

breeding

non-breeding

non-breeding

Little Stint

Sanderling

breeding

non-breeding

breeding

Red-necked Stint

non-breeding

breeding

Temminck's Stint

non-breeding

breeding

Long-toed Stint

non-breeding

breeding

Spoon-billed Sandpiper

grey with fine dark streaks and pale fringed feathers; prominent, broad white supercilium; underparts and forecrown white. **Imm** as Ad non-br but wing feathers darker-centered; crown blackish-rufous; buff-tinged face and neck. **Voc** Short "puree" or shrill "wheet". **SS** Unique spatulate bill separates it from other *Calidris*, along with constant shovelling feeding action, less probing like other species.

Curlew Sandpiper *Calidris ferruginea*
L 18–23 cm, **WS** 38–41 cm. Breeds C-E Palaearctic; winters Africa to Aus. Monotypic. Common passage migrant throughout, recorded year-round. Coastal and inland wetlands, mudflats, sandbanks, often in large numbers. **ID** Medium-sized with distinctive long, black, droop-tipped bill and black legs. In flight shows prominent white rump. **Ad br** head and underparts rusty-red except for white under-tail; scapulars and back blackish with white and chestnut spotting; wing-coverts paler grey. **Ad non-br** upperparts, hindneck, crown and ear-coverts plain grey with fine dark streaks; prominent white supercilium; underparts white. **Imm** warmer brown tone above with pale edging and buff wash on breast and sides of neck. **Voc** Trilling, bouncy "churrip". **SS** In flight or with raised wings, white rump separates from Dunlin and Broad-billed Sandpiper. Dunlin also has shorter legs and wings and shorter, less drooping bill. Curlew Sandpiper lacks Broad-billed's distinctive split supercilium (though the latter can be hard to see in non-breeding Broad-billed).

Dunlin *Calidris alpina* V
L 16–22 cm, **WS** 33–40 cm. Breeds Holarctic; winters to S. 6–10 ssp, probably 1 in region: *sakhalina* (breeds E Palaearctic; winters to E Asia). Records from Brunei (Sep 1989), E Kalimantan (Oct 1991), Sarawak (Jan 2020). Typically in coastal and inland wetlands, mudflats and sandbanks. **ID** Stocky and large-headed with shortish, thick, black down-curved bill. Legs green-black. In flight conspicuous white wingbar. **Ad br** back and scapulars rufous with dark centres; wing-coverts plainer grey; head and neck greyish with fine dark streaks, crown darker and more rufous; white underparts with prominent and distinctive black belly patch. **Ad non-br** pale grey wings, back and head; pale edging to wing-coverts; sides of breast with faint dark streaks. **Imm** blackish-brown wings and back with paler edging to coverts; head and neck washed buff and streaked black; diagnostic blackish-brown spotting on flanks and sides of belly. **Voc** Harsh, buzzy, rolling "chrreet". **SS** Black markings on underparts (when present in Imm and Ad br) separate from all other sandpipers. In non-breeding plumage, Broad-billed Sandpiper has more white edging on upperparts and typically shows characteristic split supercilium. See also Curlew Sandpiper.

Broad-billed Sandpiper *Calidris falcinellus*
L 16–18 cm, **WS** 34–37 cm. Breeds N Palaearctic; winters Africa to Aus. 2 ssp, 1 in region: *sibirica* (breeds C-E Palaearctic; winters SE Asia to Aus). Uncommon migrant throughout. Coastal and inland wetlands, mudflats, wet rice fields, sandbanks and beaches. **ID** Smallish with short, grey-green legs; relatively long, droop-tipped blackish bill. **Ad br** blackish wings and back with pale-orange and white feather edging and usually prominent white 'braces' on mantle; head, neck and breast heavily streaked, darkest on crown and ear-coverts; distinctive white 'split' supercilium. **Ad non-br** pale grey upperparts with narrow dark shaft streaks and occasionally a dark carpal patch; head, neck and breast much paler and less prominently streaked than in breeding plumage, but split supercilium usually still visible. **Imm** as Ad br but broader buff fringes to feathering on back and wings. **Voc** Buzzing trill "brre-eet", regularly repeated. **SS** See Dunlin and Curlew Sandpiper. Split supercilium separates it from other similar-sized sandpipers but can be hard to see in non-breeding.

Buff-breasted Sandpiper *Calidris subruficollis* V
L 18–20 cm. Breeds E Siberia, N America; winters S America. Monotypic. Dry grasslands, ploughed fields, saltmarshes, rarely mudflats. Single record, Bali (Jan–May 2015). Singly, or small flocks on migration (<10), feeding like a plover with occasional run and stops. **ID Ad** uniformly warm buff. Short, pointed, black bill; rounded head with pale ring around black, beady eye; long yellow legs; small black spots on breast sides, streaked crown and scalloped upperparts; primaries project well beyond tertials. In flight shows white underwing and lacks wing-bar and foot projection. **Imm** paler below, more scalloped above. **Voc** Quiet "greet" in flight. **SS** Ruff much larger, with longer neck and legs, longer tertials with little primary projection, lacks spotted breast sides, duller, more olive legs and with a more upright feeding posture; in flight Ruff shows white wing-bar and rump sides. Pacific Golden Plover has shorter, thicker bill, and darker legs.

Pectoral Sandpiper *Calidris melanotos* V
L 19–23 cm, **WS** 37–45 cm. Breeds C-E Palaearctic and Nearctic; winters mainly to Neotropics but occasional visitor to Old World. Monotypic. Records from E Timor (Nov 2004), Jav (Oct 2012), Bali (Aug 2015), Siberut (Sep 2017), Ambon (Oct 2019). Passage and wintering birds favour freshwater wetlands, less commonly coasts. **ID** Stocky with upright stance and pot-bellied appearance. Greenish legs; bill slightly down-curved with dark tip and yellowish base. **Ad br** wings and back brown-black with extensive chestnut, buff and white edging; neck and breast heavily streaked black, demarcated from white belly by distinct, straight line. **Ad non-br** greyer, but retains clear demarcation between chest and belly. **Imm** narrower rufous fringes to upperparts and prominent white 'V' on mantle. **Voc** harsh "kreeek" or "tirrp–tirrp". **SS** Pectoral is told from Sharp-tailed by longer neck; less distinct supercilium broader in front of eye versus behind eye (giving Sharp-tailed a rufous-capped appearance on flatter crown); noticeably longer bill, drooping at tip, with more extensive pale base; and a sharply demarcated, cleanly streaked breast band with white belly (versus variably marked breast with warm background colour in Imm Sharp-tailed or "messier" breast with chevron markings on flanks in adult Sharp-tailed). From Ruff by clearly demarcated breast band.

Sharp-tailed Sandpiper *Calidris acuminata*
L 17–22 cm, **WS** 36–43 cm. Breeds E Palaearctic; winters Aus. Monotypic. A rare passage migrant in W, more common to E. Coastal lagoons, wetlands, mudflats and sandbanks, but also inland wetlands and wet rice fields. Typically small to large flocks. **ID** Sturdy with yellow-green legs and short, slightly down-curved bill, blackish toward tip, paler at base. **Ad br** wings and back brown-black with extensive chestnut, buff and white edging; neck and breast buff with dark streaking; rufous crown with dark streaking contrasts with white supercilium and gives a distinctive 'capped' appearance; underparts white with darker chevrons on flanks. **Ad non-br** duller and greyer above; less distinct streaking on neck, breast and flanks; usually retains some rufous on crown. **Imm** similar to Ad br but with warmer buff wash to breast and less prominent streaking. **Voc** Clear, piping "cheep", often doubled, and repeated, or "trrt". **SS** See Pectoral Sandpiper. Larger Imm Ruff is less streaked on breast and flanks and has much longer legs.

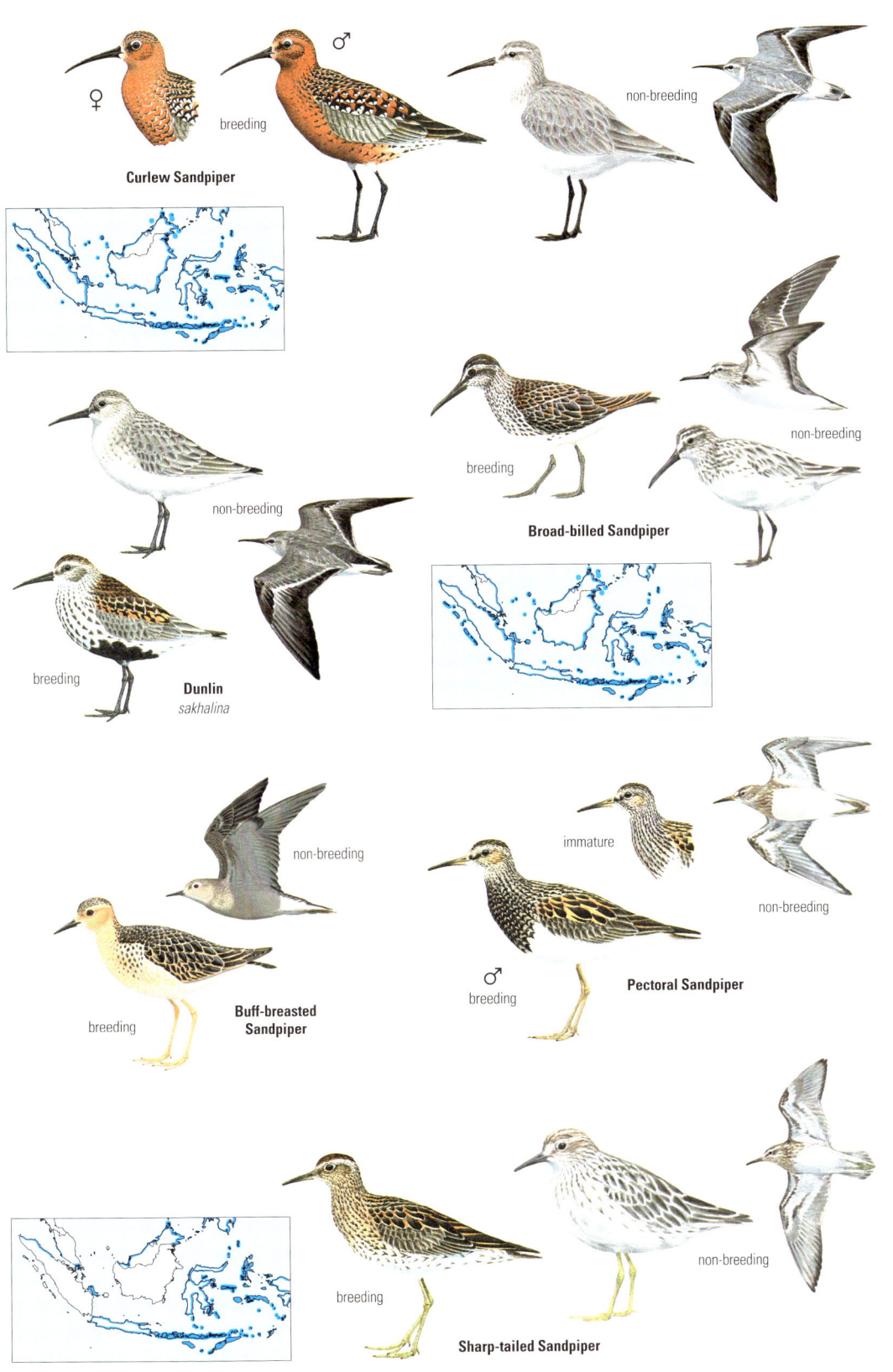

Curlew Sandpiper

♀ breeding

♂ breeding

non-breeding

Dunlin
sakhalina

non-breeding

breeding

Broad-billed Sandpiper

breeding

non-breeding

non-breeding

Buff-breasted Sandpiper

non-breeding

breeding

immature

Pectoral Sandpiper

♂ breeding

non-breeding

Sharp-tailed Sandpiper

breeding

non-breeding

Ruff *Calidris pugnax*
L 20–32 cm, **WS** 46–60 cm. Breeds Palaearctic; winters S to Africa to S Asia, rarely to Aus. Monotypic. Rare but regular migrant, most often recorded N Sum, N Bor but could occur anywhere. Typically in coastal and freshwater wetlands, flooded grassland, mudflats and sandbanks. **ID** Large, erect-standing, with long green, orange or red legs and short brown, pink or yellow bill (varies seasonally). Sexually dimorphic, with **M** usually ~20% larger than **F**. **M br** unmistakable with large erectile ear-tufts and neck ruff, variably coloured white, black or rufous (with intergrades); rest of upperparts blackish mottled rufous; underparts white, barred black. **F br** lacks ear-tufts and ruff; upperparts blackish with white, buff and chestnut edging; belly white. **Ad non-br** grey-brown wings and back with darker centres and pale buff edging giving scaled appearance; crown, hindneck and sides of breast washed grey-brown; rest of underparts white. **Imm** dark-brown wings and back with broad buff edges and darker centres giving distinctive scaled appearance; head and breast washed buff; rest of underparts white. **Voc** Rarely calls, even when disturbed; shrill "hoo-ee". **SS** See smaller Pectoral, Buff-breasted and Sharp-tailed Sandpipers. **AN** Reeve (for females only).

Great Knot *Calidris tenuirostris*
L 26–28 cm, **WS** 62–66 cm. Breeds NE Palaearctic; winters S Asia to Phil and Aus. Monotypic. Scarce but regular migrant throughout. Typically coastal wetlands, mudflats, sandbanks and estuaries. Solitary or small flocks. **ID** Stocky sandpiper with blackish bill, slightly decurved at tip, and dull grey-green legs. In flight darker primary coverts contrast with rest of wing and back; rump white. **Ad br** upperparts generally dark-grey fringed whitish, with some chestnut feathering on scapulars; head, neck, breast and flanks heavily streaked and spotted blackish. **Ad non-br** paler grey upperparts with less prominent streaks on head, neck and breast; flanks usually retain some darker spotting. **Imm** upperparts as Ad non-br but usually with more contrasting pale fringes and dark centres. **Voc** Double whistled "queet-queet". **SS** Stockier, larger and plumper than most comparable sandpipers, but see similar Red Knot.

Red Knot *Calidris canutus*
L 23–25 cm, **WS** 45–54 cm. Breeds Holarctic; winters to S. 6 ssp, 2 in region: *piersmai* (breeds NC Palaearctic; winters to W Aus); *rogersi* (breeds NE Palaearctic; winters to E Aus). Scarce migrant throughout, with *piersmai* more common in W and *rogersi* more common in E. Coastal wetlands, mudflats, sandbanks and estuaries. Solitary or small flocks. **ID** Stocky with short blackish bill and short green-grey legs. Ssp *piersmai* slightly smaller than *rogersi*. In flight thin white wingbar contrasts with uniformly dark flight feathers and paler grey coverts. **Ad br** red-orange face, neck, breast, flanks and belly (paler orange extending further to rear belly in *rogersi*); crown and hindneck grey-brown, streaked dark grey; upperparts greyish mottled with black, white and some orange feathering. **Ad non-br** plain grey upperparts with pale fringes; head, neck and breast greyish with fine dark streaks. **Imm** somewhat browner with more prominent pale and dark fringing to upperparts. **Voc** Short, nasal but soft "whet-whet". **SS** Non-breeding Great Knot is larger, longer-billed, has white rump and darker-mottled breast and tail. All other comparable non-breeding sandpipers are smaller and less plump and stocky.

Common Snipe *Gallinago gallinago*
L 25–27 cm, **WS** 44–47 cm. Palaearctic; winters S to Africa to Phil. 2 ssp, 1 in region: *gallinago* (most of range). Locally common migrant, but rare away from N Bor; possibly overlooked. Coastal and inland wetlands, wet grassland, rice fields. Usually flushes with towering, erratic zig-zag flight, sometimes dropping to cover again quickly. **ID** Cryptically coloured head and body. **Ad** head with dark crown and eyestripe broken up by buffish supercilium, cheek bar and median crown stripe; back and wings mottled brown with two broad buff-white lines on mantle and broad buff to white fringes to scapulars; outer tail feathers almost as broad as central tail feathers. In flight, extensive pale bars on underwing and prominent white trailing edge to secondaries. **Imm** has coverts fringed buff. **Voc** Abrupt, longish scratching "crraahtch", or disyllabic "kha-atch", usually when flushed on take-off. **SS** Extremely similar to Pintail and Swinhoe's Snipe. Separated with difficulty. Best told by thinner bill base, less bulging white loral stripe, white trailing edge to wing (in flight), pale underwing (in flight or with raised wings) and generally more contrasting plumage (more blackish background colour contrasting with whitish stripes and fringes). Moreover, at rest Common shows fairly uniform-dark median wing-coverts with prominent white tips (as opposed to brown-and-buff barred median wing-coverts with a less prominent pale tip in Swinhoe's and Pintail). Common's face pattern usually incorporates prominent pale and dark cheek bars (versus a blander face lacking pronounced cheek bars in the other two species), and the whitish-buff scapular fringes (at rest) are broad on outer webs and narrow on inner webs (as opposed to narrow on both inner and outer webs in the other two species). Common Snipe has outer tail feathers of normal and equal width (unlike the unusually thin feathers of the other two species), but this can only be seen when the tail is spread.

Pintail Snipe *Gallinago stenura*
L 25–27 cm, **WS** 44–47 cm. Breeds C-E Palaearctic; winters E Africa to Phil. Monotypic. Common migrant to GS, rare to E (Sul, LS). Coastal and inland wetlands, wet grassland, rice fields. Flight when flushed less erratic, more direct than Common, but less heavy than Swinhoe's. **ID/SS** Extremely similar to Common and especially to Swinhoe's Snipe, and separated with difficulty. See Common Snipe for most salient differences from that species. Best told from Swinhoe's by series of 6-9 narrow, pencil-like outertail feathers (as opposed to feathers becoming successively wider towards centre), but this trait only visible close-up when preening with spread tail. Other, less reliable, marks from Swinhoe's include long foot projection (in flight) and often thinner legs, but only identifications based on outer tail feathers should be considered reliable. **Voc** When flushed, a squeaky, nasal "kwerrk", quite duck-like in character. Also gives a drier "chert"-like vocalisation similar to Swinhoe's, probably higher-pitched, but extent to which ID can be based on this is uncertain.

Swinhoe's Snipe *Gallinago megala*
L 27–29 cm, **WS** 47–50 cm. Breeds C-E Palaearctic; winters S Asia to Aus. Monotypic. Uncommon migrant, locally common in E, rarer in W, but confirmed from as far W as Sum. Status not well understood due to identification difficulties. Coastal and inland wetlands, wet grassland, rice fields. Flight when flushed heavier, slower and less erratic than the other two snipe species; drops to cover more quickly on average. **ID/SS** Extremely similar to Common and especially to Pintail Snipe. Separated with difficulty. See those two species for most salient differences. **Voc** Calls less frequently when flushed than other *Gallinago* snipes: sneeze-like, rasping "chert", similar to other *Gallinago* species but shorter than call of Common. Uncertain whether this call is always identifiably lower-pitched than certain calls given by Pintail.

♂
non-breeding

rufous bird

♀
breeding

non-breeding

Ruff   grey bird

non-breeding

breeding

Great Knot

non-breeding

breeding

Red Knot
rogersi

Common Snipe

Pintail Snipe

Swinhoe's Snipe

Eurasian Woodcock *Scolopax rusticola*　[V]

L 33–35 cm, **WS** 56–60 cm. Breeds Palaearctic; winters to S. Monotypic. One record from Sabah (Apr 1999), and unconfirmed reports from Brunei (1978–1982). May be more widespread but overlooked. Winters in damp forest in lowlands and hills, often near streams. On migration in wider variety of forest and scrubby habitat. **ID** Large, thick-set, cryptically-coloured brown, buff, chestnut and black; buff edging to scapulars and wing-coverts; often shows pale-greyish stripes at sides of mantle; paler underparts and underwing-coverts lightly barred grey-brown; underside of tail feathers tipped white; crown and nape show broad dark transverse bands. **Voc** When disturbed gives abrupt, repeated "chikky".

Sunda Woodcock *Scolopax saturata*　[E]

L 29–31 cm. Monotypic. No longer considered conspecific with Papuan Woodcock *S. rosenbergii* as plumage and behaviour quite distinct and probably not closely related. Scarce in montane forests, 1500–3000 m. On ground in damp forest with dense understory, often tame if encountered, and may quickly land again if flushed. Performs roding display after dusk and before dawn for 10-20 minutes, using the same flight circuit every ~5 minutes, occasionally perching in low to mid-canopy to call before continuing to next perch. **ID** Small and dark with chestnut-and-black upperparts (lacking pale edging); head, throat and breast brown, belly white, all strongly barred brown-black; crown and nape show broad dark transverse bands; underside of tail feathers tipped white; underwing very dark. **Imm** undescribed. **Voc** Loud three-part song, given from regular display perches, beginning with short, low growl "grrrr" followed by explosive sneeze "churrrr" and a drawn-out staccato grunt "do-do-do-do-do-do", lasting ~9 sec in total.

Sulawesi Woodcock *Scolopax celebensis*　[E]

L 30–35 cm. 2 spp: *celebensis* (at least C Sul), *heinrichi* (N Sul). Poorly known resident of damp montane forest, 800–2500 m. Display flight not described. Has been flushed from trail sides in day time. **ID** Large with blackish upperparts speckled reddish-brown; face and underparts dark-buff with no barring except on flanks; crown and nape show broad dark transverse bands; underside of tail feathers tipped white; underwing closely barred dark brown, contrasting with paler belly and breast. Ssp *heinrichi* shorter bill. **Imm** undescribed. **Voc** Undescribed.

Moluccan Woodcock *Scolopax rochussenii*　[E]

L 32–35 cm. Monotypic. Only recent records from Obi, locally fairly common in primary and secondary forest, <400 m, particularly swampy forest. A single historical specimen purported from Bacan requires verification. Roding display flight at dusk and dawn around clearings, Mar–Nov, at least. Not known to perch while roding. **ID** Large and bulky with long stout bill; upperparts blackish with bold buff spots and edging; underparts bright ochre-buff, lacking any barring except on flanks; crown and nape show broad black transverse bands; underside of tail feathers tipped white; underwing blackish with narrow buff barring, contrasting with paler belly and breast. **Imm** undescribed. **Voc** During post-dusk and pre-dawn display flight gives 8–11 loud, hard metallic "tit-tit-tit…", 8 n/0.5 s, regularly repeated.

Long-billed Dowitcher *Limnodromus scolopaceus*　[V]

L 24–30 cm, **WS** 46–52 cm. Breed E Palaearctic to Nearctic; winters S to N Neotropics. Monotypic. Recorded Bali (Dec 1982), Sabah (Apr 1996), Sarawak (Jan 2020). Coastal and freshwater wetlands, mudflats. **ID** Large and stocky snipe-like wader with long straight bill and yellow-green legs. In flight shows narrow white wingbar and white patch from rump to centre of back. **Ad br** head and underparts largely rich rufous, with dark barring on flanks and breast; back and wings blackish with white edging and chestnut spots; bill black with variable amounts of greenish-grey at base. **Ad non-br** pale grey upperparts with fine pale edging on wing-coverts; head, neck and breast washed grey; throat and supercilium white. **Imm** similar to Ad non-br but shows paler grey head often contrasting with buff-washed breast; mantle and scapulars blacker with chestnut edging. **Voc** Short, shrill "yip". **SS** Extremely similar to **Short-billed Dowitcher** *L. griseus* (New World), which is unrecorded in the region but may occur as a vagrant; further references should be consulted for separation criteria. From larger Asian Dowitcher best told by green legs and less massive bill.

Asian Dowitcher *Limnodromus semipalmatus*

L 33–36 cm, **WS** 59 cm. Breeds C–E Palaearctic; winters S Asia to Aus. Monotypic. Locally common (E Sum, Jav) or scarce (Bor) migrant; few records from E. Mudflats. **ID** Stocky with stout, straight, all-black bill and black legs. In flight shows narrow wingbar and pale rump. **Ad br** underparts, head and neck rufous-brown; lacks obvious white supercilium but usually shows small pale loral spot; wings and back dark-brown with rufous edging. **Ad non-br** uniformly pale grey-brown above with paler fringes on wings and back and mottled dark barring on underparts, neck and head; white supercilium more prominent. **Imm** more prominent pale buff edging on wings and back, buffish wash to breast and fine dark streaking on head and neck. **Voc** Yelping "chep-chep". **SS** Smaller than Bar-tailed Godwit with all-black, straight bill. See also Long-billed Dowitcher.

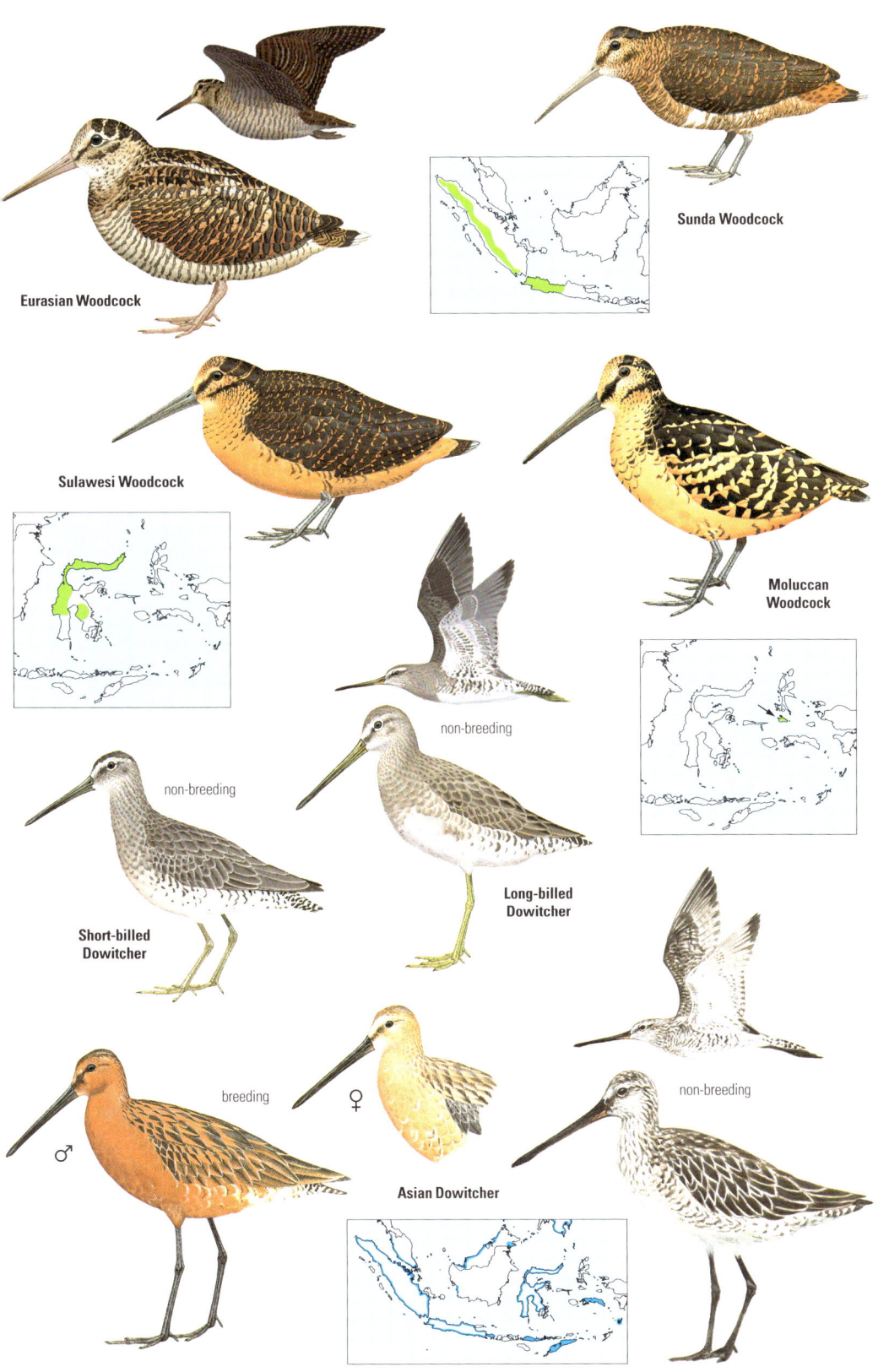

Eurasian Woodcock

Sunda Woodcock

Sulawesi Woodcock

Moluccan Woodcock

non-breeding

Short-billed Dowitcher

non-breeding

Long-billed Dowitcher

breeding ♀

♂

non-breeding

Asian Dowitcher

Black-tailed Godwit *Limosa limosa*

L 36–44 cm, **WS** 70–82 cm. Breeds Palaearctic; winters S to Africa to Aus. 3 ssp, 1 in region: *melanuroides* (breeds E Palaearctic; winters S Asia to Aus). Generally uncommon to scarce migrant throughout, locally more common on E coast of Sum. Mudflats, beaches, wet grassland, wetlands. **ID** Large, long-necked wader with long straight bill, dark at tip, pinkish at base. In flight shows prominent white wingbar and rump contrasting with black flight feathers and tail. **Ad br** rufous head, neck, breast and belly (slightly paler in **F**); crown streaked darker, contrasts with white supercilium; heavy black barring on lower breast, flanks and belly; vent and undertail white; mantle and scapulars blackish with grey and rufous edging; wing-coverts grey with pale edging; legs black. **Ad non-br** plain grey upperparts, neck, head and breast; fine white and black edging to wing-coverts and back; fine black streaking on neck and breast; retains indistinct white supercilium; legs grey-green to black. **Imm** warm orange wash to breast and neck. **Voc** Rapid, squeaky "vee-vee-vee", and "vah-it". **SS** See Bar-tailed Godwit.

Bar-tailed Godwit *Limosa lapponica*

L 37–41 cm, **WS** 70–80 cm. Breeds Palaearctic to Alaska; winters S to Africa to Aus. 5 ssp, 3 in region: *baueri* (breeds Alaska; winters Aus); *anadyrensis* (breeds E Palaearctic; winters Aus); *menzbieri* (breeds C Palaearctic; winters SE Asia to Aus). Generally an uncommon to scarce migrant throughout, locally more common on E coast of Sum. Few records identified to ssp, but *baueri* and *anadyrensis* probably more common in E and *menzbieri* in W. Mudflats, beaches, wet grassland, wetlands. **ID** Large with long, straight, slightly upcurved bill (longest in *menzbieri*, shortest in *baueri*), dark at tip, pinkish at base. In flight grey-brown wings lack any white wingbars. Rump white with barring, faintest in *menzbieri*, intermediate in *anadyrensis* and heaviest in *baueri*. Tail with dark barring. **M br** rufous underparts, breast, head and neck; dark-streaked crown contrasting with white supercilium; wings and back brown-black with grey and chestnut-buff edging; legs black. **F br** usually rufous plumage replaced by paler buff-brown. **Ad non-br** duller plain grey-brown wings and back with pale edging and fine dark shaft streaks; head, neck and breast washed grey with fine dark streaks; white supercilium less distinct; legs dark grey. **Imm** wings and back dark brown-black with contrasting pale edging; neck and breast washed buff and finely streaked; belly whitish. **Voc** Lower-pitched than Black-tailed, "kek-kek-kek". **SS** Lacks Black-tailed Godwit's contrasting wing and tail pattern in flight. See also Asian Dowitcher.

Little Curlew *Numenius minutus*

L 28–32 cm, **WS** 68–71 cm. Breeds C-E Palaearctic; winters Aus. Monotypic. Vagrant to W of Wallace's Line (Bor, Jav, Bali), scarce but more regular passage migrant to E (Mol, LS), recorded mainly Sep–Nov, occasionally to March. Short grasslands and wetlands. **ID** Smallest Asian curlew. Bill relatively short, decurved at tip, brown with pinker base to lower mandible; legs green-grey. **Ad** wings and back blackish-brown with pale edging and spotting; head, neck and breast buff with fine dark streaking; head has dark eyestripe and lateral crown-stripes divided by pale buff supercilium and central crown stripe. **Imm** narrower buff fringes to wing-coverts. **Voc** 3-note chattering whistled "tet-tet-tet". **SS** Much smaller and more golden-tinged than Eurasian Whimbrel, with slimmer, shorter and less curved bill.

Eurasian Whimbrel *Numenius phaeopus*

L 40–46 cm, **WS** 76–89 cm. Breeds Palaearctic; wintering to S. 3–5 ssp, 1-2 in region: *variegatus* (breeds E Siberia; winters SE Asia to Aus), *rogachevae* (breeds C Siberia, winters to S-SE Asia, Sumatra and satellites). Common migrant throughout. Mudflats, beaches, wetlands. **ID** Compact, with relatively short decurved brown bill, pinker at base. Legs blue-grey; wings brown-black with whitish edging; back and rump white, heavily barred black in *variegatus* but less heavily so in *rogachevae*; tail heavily barred; head, neck and breast white-buff with fine dark streaks; head distinctly striped with dark eyestripe and lateral crown-stripes divided by pale buff supercilium and central crown stripe. **Voc** Loud, piping, whistled "hu-hu-hu-hu-hu-hu-hu". **SS** See Little Curlew.

Far Eastern Curlew *Numenius madagascariensis*

L 53–66 cm, **WS** 110 cm. Breeds E Palaearctic; winters SE Asia to Aus. Monotypic. Uncommon migrant throughout. Mudflats and beaches. **ID** Largest curlew in region with very long, brown-grey, downcurved bill (longer in **F** than **M**). Buff-brown throughout, with dark streaking and barring on wings, back, rump and tail; finer streaking on head, neck and breast; legs blue-grey. **Voc** Similar to Eurasian's "coor-lee" but deeper, flatter and longer. **SS** See Eurasian Curlew.

Eurasian Curlew *Numenius arquata*

L 50–60 cm, **WS** 80–100 cm. Breeds Palaearctic; winters to S. 3 ssp, 1 in region: *orientalis* (breeds C–E Palaearctic; winters S to S Asia to Phil). Locally common migrant in W, less common in E. Mudflats, beaches, wet grassland, wetlands. **ID** Large, rather pale grey-brown curlew with long, decurved, grey-brown bill, pinker at base; blue-grey legs. In flight shows white wedge extending from rump onto back. **Ad** wings and mantle grey-brown with darker feather centres and barring; head, neck, breast and flanks lightly washed buff with fine dark streaking; belly and vent white. **Imm** more strongly washed buff on head and neck. **Voc** Far-carrying, fluty "coor-lee". **SS** From larger Far Eastern Curlew best told by shorter bill, and in flight by white wedge on back and white underwing-coverts.

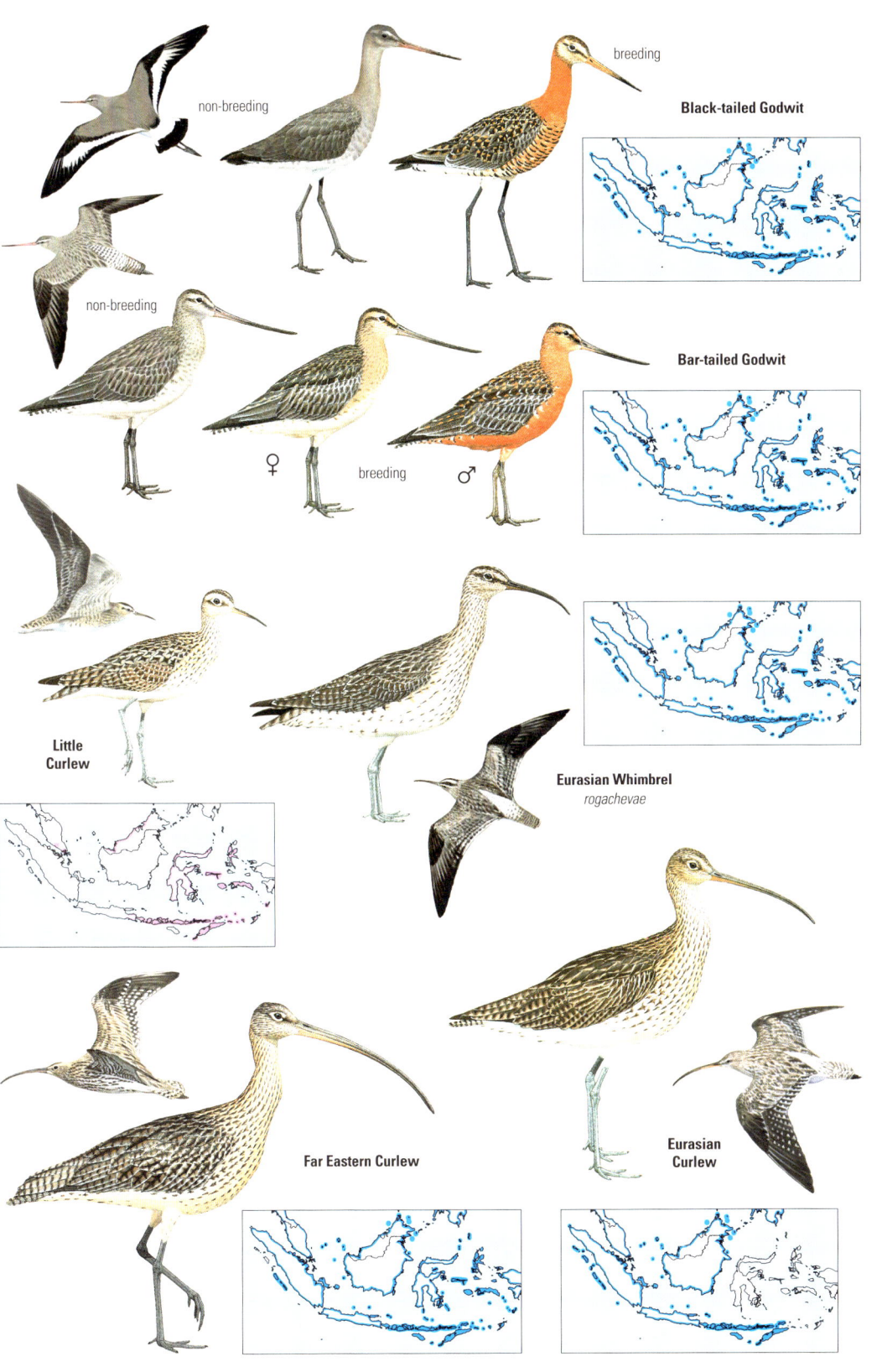

non-breeding

breeding

Black-tailed Godwit

non-breeding

♀

breeding ♂

Bar-tailed Godwit

Little Curlew

Eurasian Whimbrel
rogachevae

Far Eastern Curlew

Eurasian Curlew

TURNICIDAE
Buttonquails
4 species in region

Small, stocky, terrestrial birds, found singly of in small groups usually within open or grassland habitats. Cryptically coloured, shy, and typically silent, they can be difficult to observe unless flushed. Polyandry (one female tending a harem of males) has led to reversed sexual dimorphism and parenting.

Small Buttonquail *Turnix sylvaticus*
L 13–16 cm. Africa, S Palaearctic, S–SE Asia, Phil. 9 ssp, 1 in region: *bartelsorum* (Jav, Bali). Species often divided into African '**Kurrichane Buttonquail**' *T. sylvaticus* and Asian '**Small Buttonquail**' *T. dussumier*. Scarce in grasslands and low-intensity, dry cultivation. Solitary, pairs or small groups (<5); easily flushed, flying <50 m, keeping low to the ground. **ID** Bluish bill, dull pinkish legs. **M** streaked mid-brown upperparts with spotted, open facial expression; white throat, rufous breast and whitish belly and undertail. In flight shows contrasting upperparts and whitish undertail. **F** stronger rufous breast and flanks with darker upperparts. **Imm** smaller and more heavily spotted. **Voc** F song, largely given at night (extralimital): series of "hooo" notes lasting 1 sec; slower, longer and more mournful than Barred Buttonquail. **SS** Barred Buttonquail is barred across breast and has rufous belly and undertail. Barred Buttonquail also has a yellow (not bluish) bill and yellow (not pinkish) legs. In flight Barred shows less contrasting upperwing.

Red-backed Buttonquail *Turnix maculosus*
L 12–16 cm. Aus. 14 ssp, 7 in region: *maculosus* (Rote, Timor, Wetar, Kisar, Moa); *beccarii* (Sul, Togian, Muna, Tukangbesi); *floresianus* (Sumbawa–Alor); *kinneari* (Peleng); *obiensis* (Obi, Kai, Babar); *savuensis* (Sawu); *sumbanus* (Sumba). Ssp taxonomy confused and requires study. Uncommon in rank grassland, cultivation, light scrub, <2400 m. **ID** Yellow feet and bill (although upper mandible tinged greyish in M). **M** similar to Small Buttonquail but greyer, less well-marked mantle; rufous wash to face and nape. **F** strong rufous wash to face, breast and undertail, with rusty collar. Ssp *savuensis* paler on back than nominate, *beccarii* and *obiensis* darker on back (with *beccarii* having a finer pattern of yellowish-rusty bars and speckling), all three ssp with less pronounced collar, while *floresianus* darker on back than nominate and more rusty on underparts; *sumbanus* lacks rufous collar altogether and has greyer upperparts; larger and dark-backed *kinneari* shows broad rusty collar and rusty underparts. **Imm** much darker overall, lacking pale upperwing-coverts. **Voc** F song: subdued "oom", repeated more regularly and note more upslurred than Barred. **SS** The larger Barred Buttonquail always shows strongly barred breast and throat with no rufous wash, and less-marked upperparts. See also Sumba Buttonquail.

Barred Buttonquail *Turnix suscitator*
L 15–17 cm. S–SE–E Asia, Phil. 17-18 ssp, 4 in region: *suscitator* (Sum–Bali); *baweanus* (Bawean); *rufilatus* (Sul and satellites); ssp *powelli* (Lombok–Alor) most distinct and often considered monotypic species, '**Dusky Buttonquail**'. Fairly common in rank grassland, cultivation, scrub, bamboo thickets, secondary growth, <2400 m. **ID** Bright yellow bare parts. **M** boldly patterned head and upperparts, heavily barred breast with rufous washed belly to undertail; breast barring much coarser in *powelli* and *baweanus*; rufous belly and vent less intense in *rufilatus* and *baweanus*, and almost lacking in *powelli*. **F** strikingly marked with black throat, much reduced in *powelli* and *baweanus*, and absent in *rufilatus* (replaced by breast barring). **Imm** more buff-coloured with spotted underparts. **Voc** F song, mainly given at night: series of rising "ooo" notes, ~30 n/20 s, increasing in volume before ending abruptly. **SS** See Red-backed and Small Buttonquail.

Sumba Buttonquail *Turnix everetti*   **E**
L 14 cm. Monotypic. Fairly common in grassland, less so in paddyfields, particularly coastal areas. Solitary, pairs or small groups (<5); easily flushed, flying <50 m, keeping low to the ground. **ID** Uniquely in range, has thick, conical, bluish-grey bill. **Ad** upperparts heavily streaked; pale iris; rufous wash on breast and lower flanks (stronger in **F**), pale undertail-coverts and belly. In flight shows contrasting pale upperwing-coverts to all-dark outerwing and streaked mantle. **Imm** undescribed. **Voc** Undescribed. **SS** Best told from Red-backed by thick, conical, bluish (not thin, decurved yellowish) bill and pinkish (not yellow) legs. Lacks the rufous tones on face and nape of female Red-backed, but male Red-backed lacks these, too. Both sexes of Red-backed always show strong black polka dots on breast sides and flanks, often all the way to lower flanks, while Sumba Buttonquail is largely plain here, at most with limited black barring extending in from flanks. Brown and Blue-breasted Quails much heavier and darker in flight, usually calling.

GLAREOLIDAE
Pratincoles
2 species in region

Elegant medium-sized wader-like birds with long wings and short legs and bills. Strong and graceful fliers. Typically found within open grassland habitats, often near coasts or rivers.

Australian Pratincole *Stiltia isabella*
L 22–24 cm. Aus. Monotypic. Vagrant to GS. Scarce migrant in E, but regular and locally common S Mol, E LS. Singly to large flocks in grasslands, open fields and coastal wetlands. Forages on ground and occasionally hawks for insects with swallow-like flight. Stands upright, often bobbing up and down. Runs with hunched posture. **ID** Slender and elegant with very long wings. In flight underwing shows black coverts and axillaries contrasting with silvery secondaries and inner primaries, while upperwing shows contrast between dark outerwing and paler innerwing and back. **Ad br** upperparts, head and breast uniformly sandy-rufous; dark chestnut patch on fore-belly can appear blackish; rear belly, undertail and rump white; tail white with wide black band; dark lores and white throat; bill short and orange-red with black tip. **Ad non-br** duller in colour; chestnut belly patch reduced or absent; bill duller grey. **Imm** pale buff edging to upperparts. **Voc** Loud, whistled "chirrup".

Oriental Pratincole *Glareola maldivarum*
L 23–24 cm, **WS** 59–64 cm. Breeds E Palaearctic, S–SE–E Asia, Phil; winters S to Aus. Monotypic. Widespread and locally common migrant in GS, scarcer to E, where usually recorded Sep–Dec. Has bred N Bor and N Sum. Singly to large flocks in grasslands, open fields and coastal wetlands. Hawks for insects with swallow-like flight, occasionally feeds on ground. **ID** More compact and darker brown than Australian Pratincole. In flight shows forked tail and chestnut underwing-coverts. **Ad br** upperparts dullish brown; head, neck and breast warmer buff; throat paler and outlined by narrow white and black line and black lores; belly, undertail and rump white; tail with broad black band; bill blackish with some red at base. **Ad non-br** duller with less well-defined throat markings; bill uniformly black. **Imm** pale buff edging to upperparts. **Voc** Tern-like, hard, repeated "chik".

Small Buttonquail

Red-backed Buttonquail

maculosus

suscitator

powelli

Sumba Buttonquail

rufilatus

Barred Buttonquail

Australian Pratincole

non-breeding

breeding

Oriental Pratincole

Large, diverse family that includes the elegant terns and noddies and more robust stocky gulls. Mostly strong-flying, they mainly inhabit a variety of coastal and marine habitats, breeding colonially on islets, but some occur inland.

Brown Noddy *Anous stolidus*

L 40–45 cm, **WS** 79–86 cm. Pantropical. 4–5 ssp, 1 in region: *pileatus* (Indian Oc, W–C Pacific Oc). Uncommon in W, locally common in E. Breeds Gunung Api, Manuk and possibly islets off Sum and Bor. Generally pelagic, but often seen in inshore waters. Flight tern-like, glides or flaps on slow wingbeats close to the sea with wings held slightly forward. **ID Ad** brown body and head with white crown sharply demarcated at lores; wing-coverts paler than flight feathers; underwing pale with dark margins giving two-toned appearance at sea. **Imm** white crown replaced with grey or lacking. **Juv** back and wing-coverts edged pale. **SS** Large size (bigger than Bridled Tern) and heavier bill demarcate from Black and Lesser Noddies. Also, Brown Noddy has two-toned, brown appearance (with pale upper and underwing-coverts), distinct from one-toned smoky-black plumage of Lesser and Black Noddies. Lesser Noddy has pale lores.

Black Noddy *Anous minutus*

L 35–39 cm, **WS** 66–72 cm. Tropical Pacific and Atlantic Oceans. 7 ssp, 1–2 may occur in region: *worcesteri* (breeds Sulu Sea); perhaps *minutus* (breeds S Pacific Oc to E NG). Formerly considered conspecific with Lesser Noddy but separated because of plumage and genetic divergence. Rare migrant to Indonesian waters (Bor, Sum, LS), but no records have been assigned to ssp. Most birds in region are probably *worcesteri*, although LS records may pertain to *minutus*. May formerly have bred off Belitung and Karimunjawa. Disperses widely over sea outside breeding season. Flight as Brown Noddy but somewhat faster and more fluttering with lighter jizz. **ID Ad** small (smaller than Bridled Tern), uniformly dark with fine bill; body and wings dark brown; white crown sharply demarcated from lores, merging to grey at nape. Ssp *worcesteri* has darker, greyer tail. **Imm** white crown sharply demarcated from darker nape. **Juv** with pale edging on wing-coverts and back. **SS** See Brown and Lesser Noddy.

Lesser Noddy *Anous tenuirostris* ⟨V⟩

L 30–34 cm, **WS** 58–63 cm. Breeds tropical Indian Oc. 2 ssp, probably only 1 in region: *melanops* (E Indian Oc). Single sight record off W Jav (Aug 2010). Closest known breeding ground at Ashmore Reef. Pelagic. **ID Ad** similar in general size, appearance and habits to Black Noddy. Forehead and crown white (with pale lores) merging evenly into darker grey nape. **Imm** cap browner or lacking. **SS** Lesser lacks sharply demarcated black lores of Black Noddy. See also Brown Noddy.

White Tern *Gygis alba* ⟨V⟩

L 28–33 cm, **WS** 70–87 cm. Pantropical. 4 ssp, 1 in region: *candida* (tropical Pacific and Indian Oceans). Rare vagrant, scattering of records: off N Jav (Oct 1884), Weh, N Sum (100 in Jul 1956, 1 in Sept 1956, 10 in Jul 1957), Ternate (dead, March 1989), E of Sumbawa (Aug 1993). Pelagic. **ID Ad** only all-white tern. Bill black (with blue base in breeding), slightly upturned. **Imm** dusky ear-coverts and greyish-buff wash to nape, back and wing-coverts; outer primaries show dark shafts.

Heuglin's Gull *Larus heuglini* ⟨V⟩

L 51–65 cm, **WS** 124–150 cm. Breeds NC Palaearctic; winters to E Africa to E Asia. 2 ssp, 1 in region: *taimyrensis* (breeds NC Palaearctic; winters SE–E Asia). Confused taxonomy. Often included with Lesser Black-backed Gull *L. fuscus* (W Palaearctic). Ssp *taimyrensis* sometimes not recognised; alternatively, *taimyrensis* is increasingly classified as monotypic eastern species '**Taimyr Gull**' differing from the more westerly Heuglin's Gull *L. heuglini* in plumage. Recorded from Wetar (Oct 2008), Batam (Nov 2011), W Kalimantan (Jan 2013) and Sabah (Oct 2017). Non-breeding birds inhabit coasts and estuaries. **ID** Large grey and white gull. Heavy orange bill with red spot at gonys; orange to pale yellow legs; pale iris. **Ad br** white head and underparts; slaty grey mantle and upperwings; outer primaries broad black with small white tips. **Ad non-br** shows variable dark smudging on head and nape. **1st winter** variable brown edging to head, nape and flanks; mantle and upperwings mottled brown; primaries, secondaries and primary coverts black-brown. **2nd winter** upperparts begin to show ad-type grey feathers; paler underparts and head. **SS** See Black-tailed and Slaty-backed Gulls. Separating large vagrant gulls requires careful examination. While Heuglin's Gull is one of the most likely vagrants, **Vega Gull** *L. vegae* (breeds E Palaearctic; winters to E Asia) is also possible. Further literature should be consulted before an identification is confirmed.

Slaty-backed Gull *Larus schistisagus* ⟨V⟩

L 55–68 cm, WS 145–150cm. Monotypic. Breeds NE Asia, winters to E Asia. Single record of imm in 1st winter, Lombok (Feb 2016). Coastline, estuaries, harbours, mudflats. Singly or mixed with other gull species. **ID/SS Ad non-br** structurally larger, more angular head shape than Heuglin's; short primary projection; darker-mantled with bubble-gum pink legs; pale iris; fine brown head markings, more so around eye. Easiest to identify in flight; wing-tip black with white mirrors to tenth primary, pale inner webs to primaries and large white tongue in mid-primaries, forming 'string of pearls' connecting with broad white trailing edge to wing (Heuglin's and Vega show white mirrors only on 2 outermost primaries, lacking pale inner webs); broad white trailing edge. **1st winter** from Vega and Heuglin's Gulls by much more uniform, darker plumage with no apparent streaking; paler head to upper breast, often shows dark eye-patch, streaked crown set off by pale hind collar; typically, blotchy, dark belly; almost unpatterned greater coverts (distinctly barred in Heuglin's and Vega); all-dark, uniform underwing with pale underside to primaries (generally paler in Heuglin's with barred axillaries and lesser coverts but black underside of primaries); upperwing shows two-toned pattern on outer primaries and relatively plain greater coverts; wholly dark tail; well barred rump (white with dark spotting in Heuglin's and even less spotting in Vega). **2nd winter** largely white head and underparts with dark grey starting to appear on mantle; only large, dark-mantled gull with bubble-gum pink legs, already shows pale eye and pale bill base.

Black-tailed Gull *Larus crassirostris* ⟨V⟩

L 44–48 cm; **WS** 126–128 cm. Monotypic. E Asia. Vagrant to Sabah (Nov 2013). Inhabits sea coasts and estuaries. **ID** Medium-sized grey and white gull with broad black sub-terminal band to tail in all plumages. Bill broad and long, yellow with black sub-terminal band and red tip; legs yellow-green (**Ad**) or flesh-coloured (**Imm**). **Ad br** white with slaty-grey upperwings and black primaries showing narrow white tips. **Ad non-br** dusky grey-brown streaks on head and nape. **Imm** dark brown all over with pale feather edging and blackish flight feathers. White vent and rump. **SS** Separated from other gulls within range by black tail band in Ad, and black tail band contrasting with white rump and brown body in Imm.

Brown Noddy

Black Noddy

melanops

Lesser Noddy

tenuirostris

immature

White Tern

adult

1st winter

non-breeding

1st winter

Heuglin's Gull

breeding

non-breeding

immature

non-breeding

breeding

Slaty-backed Gull

Black-tailed Gull

Silver Gull *Larus novaehollandiae* V

L 38–41 cm, **WS** 91–96 cm. Aus. 2 ssp, 1 in region: *forsteri* (N Australia, Melanesia; probably this ssp vagrant to our region). Two records from Bali (Oct 2009, Aug 2010). Usually inhabits sea coasts and estuaries but often found far inland on lakes, ponds and waterways. **ID** Small gull with red (**Ad**) or blackish (**Imm**) bill and legs. Iris white (**Ad**) or brown (**Imm**). **Ad** pale grey mantle and upperwing; broad black primary ends showing 2–3 white 'mirror' patches and narrow white tips; white base to outer primaries and coverts. **Imm** head white, variably dusky brown on nape; back, mantle and innerwing-coverts scalloped brown; primary pattern resembles Ad but feathers tipped black (not white); tail with black sub-terminal band. **SS** From all other gulls in range by combination of small size, clean white head and primary pattern.

Black-headed Gull *Larus ridibundus*

L 37–43 cm, **WS** 94–110 cm. Breeds Palaearctic; winters to Old World tropics. Monotypic. Rare but seemingly regular winter visitor. Inhabits inland lakes, waterways, estuaries and coasts. **ID** Small, dainty gull with long slender dark red bill, with black tip in non-breeding birds. Legs dark red, paler in non-breeding birds. **Ad br** dark brown hood with broken white eyering; pale grey back and upperwings with distinctive white outer primaries; all primaries have narrow black tips on upperwing. **Ad non-br** brown hood replaced by dark ear-covert smudge. **Imm** shows variable brown scalloping on back; brown tertials and wing-coverts; broad black trailing edge and reduced white on outer primaries; tail shows broad black subterminal band. **Voc** Wintering birds usually silent, but occasional screeched "kyaar" or "krreearr". **SS** Must be distinguished with care from **Brown-headed Gull** *L. brunnicephalus* (breeds C Asia; winters S–SE Asia; likely to appear N Sum). Brown-headed Gull differs by bigger size, heavier bill, and distinct wing-tip pattern: Ad shows white base to outer primaries and coverts, broad black tips to outer primaries with white 'mirror' patch on outer 2–3 primaries; imm shows even more black on upperwing, with broad black trailing edge and black outer primaries.

Sabine's Gull *Xema sabini* V

L 30–36 cm, **WS** 80–91 cm. Circumpolar, wintering south of Equator. Monotypic. Recorded off W Sum (Oct 1984). Mainly pelagic, occasional near coasts during storms. **ID** Small elegant gull with forked tail and distinct tricoloured wings. **Ad br** dark grey hood, black bill with yellow tip. **Ad non-br** partial grey hood. **Imm** brown mantle, nape, sides of breast and wing-coverts, black subterminal band on tail, and lacks white tips to primaries; bill black. **SS** Separated from other pelagic gulls and terns by size and contrasting upperwing pattern of black outer primaries, white inner primaries and secondaries, and grey/brown coverts and back.

Sooty Tern *Onychoprion fuscatus*

L 43–45 cm, **WS** 86–94 cm. Pantropical. 2–7 ssp, 1 in region: *nubilosus* (tropical Pacific and Indian Oceans). Uncommon in W, scarce to locally common in E (breeds Gunungapi; Jun–Aug). Highly pelagic, rarely seen close to shore. Often found in flocks with other seabirds. Light, buoyant flight, usually low over water, hovering, and dipping down to take food from water's surface; rarely plunge-dives. **ID Ad** upperparts and upperwings uniformly black; white forehead only extends to above eye; black crown and nape joins with black back; underparts white with dark primaries. **Imm** entirely sooty-brown except for white vent and undertail; back and wing-coverts edged buff, gradually being replaced by paler feathers. **SS** From Bridled by broader wings and broader body, with less languid flight

action; white forecrown patch not extending over eye. Underside of primaries all dark, compared to pale with dark tips on Bridled. Sooty usually lacks white nuchal collar of Bridled. Sooty's upperparts look all-black, whereas Bridled has more brownish upperparts with contrasting black trailing edge of secondaries in good light. Imm can be confused with noddies but lacks pale crown.

Grey-backed Tern *Onychoprion lunatus* V

L 35–38 cm, **WS** 73–76 cm. Tropical Pacific. Monotypic. Collected from Halmahera (1863, 1950). Largely pelagic but also found in inshore waters, resting on sand bars, shingle, and even on boats. **ID Ad** resembles Bridled Tern but paler grey mantle. Wings and rump dark grey-brown, contrasting with pale grey mantle; black cap with white supercilium extending beyond eye; pale cervical collar separates crown from mantle. **Imm** head pattern less clearly defined; back and wing-coverts fringed buff. **SS** Ad from Bridled by much paler mantle and upperwing contrasting sharply with black crown; Imm and Ad both have narrower trailing edge on underwings, especially on tertials and primaries. From ad Aleutian by much narrower white forehead.

Bridled Tern *Onychoprion anaethetus*

L 35–38 cm, **WS** 76–81 cm. Pantropical. 4 ssp, probably only 1 in region: *anaethetus* (E Asia, Phil, Indonesia to Aus). Common; pelagic but also in inshore waters, often in large flocks and with other species, breeds locally on rocky islets. Light, buoyant flight, usually low over water, hovering, and dipping down to take food from water's surface; rarely plunge-dives. **ID Ad** similar to Sooty Tern but smaller, with white forehead patch much narrower and extending beyond eye, and less uniformly black on upperparts. Black cap separated from dark brown wings and back by narrow pale nuchal collar; underparts off-white. **Imm** back and wing-coverts edged buff, contrasting with darker flight feathers; head pattern less clearly defined. **SS** See also Sooty and Grey-backed Terns.

Aleutian Tern *Onychoprion aleuticus*

L 33–38 cm, **WS** 76–81 cm. Breeds E Palaearctic to Alaska; winters to SE Asia. Monotypic. Scarce migrant (Sep–Apr). Generally pelagic but known to approach inshore waters, regularly found perched on flotsam (wood, man-made materials etc). Flight action similar to Common Tern though seldom plunge-dives. **ID** Underwing shows distinctive broad black trailing edge on secondaries (and outer primaries), with white inner primaries. **Ad br** wings and mantle pale grey contrasting with white rump and black cap; white forehead patch extends behind eye as in Bridled Tern; underparts pale grey; black bare parts. **Ad non-br** black crown reduced to less distinct patch behind eye and on nape with extensive white forecrown reaching above eye. **Imm** mantle and wing-coverts buff with pale edging; underparts white washed buff on flanks and sides of breast; crown mostly dull brown, not black; white forehead patch absent. **SS** From Common and longer-billed Roseate Terns in all ages by diagnostic black underwing trailing edge to secondaries (Common non-br usually shows black trailing edge to primaries). Perched non-br looks most similar to Common Tern, but has completely black legs and bill (Common non-br sometimes has reddish bill base or legs). Ad Aleutian lacks Common's distinct black shoulder bar; imm Aleutian usually only shows black on shoulder when wing coverts also still show black. Non-br Aleutian's black rear crown usually less extensive, with eye usually unconnected or contrasting via white eyering (in Common, eye often engulfed by black rear crown and not contrasting). Note short bill. See also Grey-backed and Black-naped Terns.

Silver Gull

immature

breeding

immature

non-breeding

Black-headed Gull

breeding

breeding

Sabine's Gull

immature

non-breeding

immature

non-breeding

Grey-backed Tern

breeding

adult

Sooty Tern

immature

non-breeding

breeding

adult

immature

Aleutian Tern

Bridled Tern

White-winged Tern *Chlidonias leucopterus*

L 22–24 cm, **WS** 66 cm. Breeds Palaearctic; winters to S. Monotypic. Common migrant to coasts, estuaries, inland water bodies and wetlands. Flight buoyant, shallow and leisurely, low over water, often quickly changing direction, dipping to surface-feed, does not plunge-dive. Often perches on posts. **ID Ad br** black head, mantle and underparts (except for white undertail), contrasting markedly with white upperwing-coverts, rump and tail; flight feathers silvery-grey; underwing-coverts black contrasting with silvery-grey outer-wing. **Ad non-br** black colouration replaced by white except for 'headphones'-like black ear-covert patch and variable black on rear of crown; upperwings dull grey with dark leading edge to coverts (forming a dark shoulder patch when perched) and dark outer primaries and primary tips; underwing pale grey, sometimes retaining some black feathering on coverts. **Imm** brown scalloped mantle that contrasts with paler wing and whitish rump and tail. **SS** Black on underwing-coverts diagnostic when present. Non-br/Imm similar to Whiskered but has distinctly shaped black ear patch and dark rear crown, and darker leading edge to upperwing-coverts. From other terns by head pattern, dark-grey upperwing, short tail and feeding habits. At rest, wings project well beyond tail.

Whiskered Tern *Chlidonias hybrida*

L 25–26 cm, **WS** 69 cm. Old World. 3 ssp, 2 in region: *hybrida* (breeds Palaearctic; winters Africa to SE Asia, mainly Oct–May); *javanicus* (breeds Aus; winters SE Asia and Phil, mainly May–Oct). Common migrant year round in freshwater wetlands and water bodies, also coastal wetlands and lagoons. Flight buoyant, shallow and leisurely, low over water, more direct than White-winged, dipping to surface-feed, does not plunge-dive. Often perches on posts. **ID** Small grey 'marsh tern' with short notched tail. **Ad br** pale grey wings and mantle, outer primaries and primary tips darker; solid black cap, contrasting whitish cheeks and chin; greyish underparts becoming blackish towards belly; bill and legs dark red. Ssp *javanicus* lighter grey wings, darker underparts becoming blackish from breast. **Ad non-br** black crown becomes white at lores and forehead, streaked rear crown, merging with black smudge around and behind eye, looking like a diffuse, widening post-ocular stripe; bill and legs black; underparts white. **Imm** mantle and wing-coverts with black-and-buff scalloping. **SS** See White-winged Tern. From Common and Little Terns by head pattern, dark-grey upperwing, short tail and feeding habits. At rest, wings project well beyond tail.

Little Tern *Sternula albifrons*

L 20–28 cm, **WS** 50–55 cm. Old World. 3-6 ssp, 1 in region: *sinensis* (breeds E Palaearctic; resident S–SE Asia to Aus). Locally common resident and migrant along coasts, estuaries, sandy beaches, occasionally inland wetlands. Flies with rapid, jerky wingbeats, frequently hovers, bill facing down, and plunge dives. **ID** Very small, slender. **Ad br** wings, back and rump pale-greyish white, contrasting with black outer primaries (with white shafts); white tail, black cap and white forehead patch; underparts white; bill yellow with black tip; legs yellow-orange. **Ad non-br** lores and crown white with black restricted to post-ocular patch extending to nape; inner forewing dusky grey, visible as dark shoulder patch on perched bird; bill and legs blackish. **Imm** crown streaked brown; back and wing-coverts show dark subterminal feather edging. **SS** From marsh terns (genus *Chlidonias*) and Common Tern by small size, short tail more deeply forked than marsh terns but less deeply forked than Common, and rapid, jerky flight action with sudden hover-and-dives. The extremely similar extralimital **Saunders's Tern** *S. saundersi* (breeds W Indian Ocean; possible W Sum) has a white forecrown not forming super-cilium and browner legs in Ad br.

Roseate Tern *Sterna dougallii*

L 35–43 cm, **WS** 76–79 cm. Cosmopolitan. 5 ssp, 1 in region: *gracilis* (Indian Oc to E China Sea and W Pacific Oc). Uncommon migrant (from Aus May–Oct; from N Oct–May) and scarce resident throughout, breeding locally on isolated rocky islets. Predominantly pelagic. Breeds on isolated rocky islets. Flight rapid with shallow, stiff wingbeats (more elegant than Common), hovering and diving. **ID** Elegant, pale, long-tailed with long pointed bill. **Ad br** very pale wings and mantle; outer primaries show black shafts, outer-veins and narrow black tips; rump and tail all white with very long tail streamers; glossy black cap; underparts white with rosy tint; black bill with variable deep-red at base (sometimes leaving black only at tip); short red legs. **Ad non-br** forecrown becomes white; bill and legs black. **Imm** cap all brownish-black; back and wing-coverts scalloped black-and-buff; legs and bill black. **SS** Whiter above and below than Ad Common Tern, with longer bill and tail with no black on outer tail. In region, Roseate is seen far more often in breeding plumage than Common. Lacks Common's distinct broad dark under-wing trailing edge to primaries. Unlike Common, imm Roseate never exhibits red on legs or bill. See also Aleutian, Gull-billed and Black-naped Terns.

Black-naped Tern *Sterna sumatrana*

L 30–32 cm, **WS** 61 cm. Indian Oc to E China Sea and W Pacific Oc. Monotypic. Locally common resident. Coastal. Breeds on isolated rocky islets, on ledge just above sea. **ID** Elegant white plumage with black bill and legs; deeply forked tail. **Ad** black patch extends in line from behind eye to nape; crown, rump, tail and underparts pure white; wings and mantle pale grey except for black edge to outer-most primary. **Imm** nape and rear-crown mottled dark grey-brown; mantle and coverts scalloped black and buff; base of bill sometimes yellowish. **SS** Resembles Ad non-br Common, Aleutian and Roseate Terns, but smaller, with much less diffuse, more narrow and well-defined crown pattern, and much whiter appearance. Imm Roseate very similar to Imm but has dusky, not white, lores.

Common Tern *Sterna hirundo*

L 32–38 cm, **WS** 72–83 cm. Cosmopolitan. 4 ssp, 2 in region: *longipennis* (breeds E Palaearctic; winters SE Asia to Aus); *tibetana* (breeds C Asia; winters E Indian Oc). Common migrant. Some birds remain year-round. Most records *longipennis*, but *tibetana* fairly common in GS (much scarcer to E). Predominantly coastal, occasionally on inland water bodies. **ID** Elegant grey and white tern with long, narrow wings and longish, deeply-forked tail. Bill is long and heavy-set (shorter and thinner in *tibetana*). **Ad br** black crown; white cheeks, tail and rump; grey mantle, upperwings and underparts; outermost tail feathers have grey-black outer web; dark outermost primaries form panel on wing, dark primary tips form broad, diffused trailing edge to underwing; bill and legs black. Ssp *tibetana* lighter grey above and off-white (not grey) below; red (not black) legs and bill with narrow black tip. **Ad non-br** as Ad br except white on forehead, dark carpal bar on wing and paler underparts; bill and sometimes legs turn more blackish. Ssp identification on non-breeders must rely on bill shape and not always possible. **Imm** wing-coverts and back feathers edged dark; in flight shows dark carpal bar, darker bar across secondaries, more pronounced dark tips to primaries. Most Imm *tibetana* have (dark-) reddish legs and bill base. **SS** See Aleutian, Gull-billed, Whiskered, Roseate and Black-naped Terns. Extralimital **Arctic Tern** *Sterna paradisaea* (breeds Circumpolar, winters Antarctica) possible through region on migration. Ad br from Common by distinct, narrow black underwing trailing edge to primaries (not diffused); longer tail; shorter, all red bill and legs; shorter neck and more rounded head. Ad non-br black bill; white rump and tail (grey in Common). Imm lacks conspicuous dark carpal and secondary bars.

non-breeding

breeding

White-winged Tern

immature

non-breeding

breeding

Whiskered Tern

immature

adult

Saunders's Tern

immature

adult

Little Tern

immature

adult

immature

adult

with all-red bill

Roseate Tern

immature

adult

Black-naped Tern

breeding

non-breeding

Common Tern

longipennis

breeding

immature

Gull-billed Tern *Gelochelidon nilotica*

L 35–43 cm, **WS** 86–103 cm. Cosmopolitan. 6 ssp, 2 in region: *affinis* (E Palaearctic; winters to SE Asia, May–Oct); ssp *macrotarsa* (Aus; seasonal in LS and Mol, mostly Oct–May) sometimes considered monotypic species '**Australian Gull-billed Tern**' based on morphology. Common migrant. Mostly coastal, but occasionally inland wetlands. Flight slow and deliberate, dipping to feed from water, also hovers and dives. **ID** Large and gull-like, with short, stout black bill and notched tail. Ssp *affinis* ~20% smaller, with shorter legs and thinner bill. **Ad br** upperparts uniformly pale grey; primaries darker grey, with blackish tips forming dark trailing edge (more obvious on underwing); full glossy black cap extending to nape; underparts white; legs black. **Ad non-br** paler above and black cap replaced by rounded dark smudge through and behind eye; *macrotarsa* shows larger, square-ended black ear-coverts; paler grey back and wings contrasting with white (not grey) rump and uppertail. **Imm** crown streaked brownish and mantle and wing-coverts mottled buff-brown. **SS** Larger than Roseate and Common Terns with thicker, shorter black bill and shorter tail; quite gull-like in Ad non-br and Imm plumage, with white crown and relatively confined black ear-coverts.

Caspian Tern *Hydroprogne caspia*

L 48–59 cm, **WS** 127–140 cm. Cosmopolitan. Monotypic. Rare migrant, mostly coastal, but occasionally inland wetlands. Gull-like flight, plunge-dives from great height. **ID** Largest tern. Huge red bill, large head and short forked tail give front heavy appearance. **Ad br** glossy black crown; pale grey back and wings with darker primaries (blackish from below). **Ad non-br** black crown becomes streaked white. **Imm** bill paler, and wings and back mottled brown. **SS** Large size and thick red bill separates it from all other terns.

Great Crested Tern *Thalasseus bergii*

L 43–48 cm, **WS** 99–109 cm. Africa to E Asia and Aus. 4–5 ssp, 1 in region: *cristatus* (E–SE Asia to Aus). Common migrant and scarce resident, breeds on Spratley Is. Coastal and pelagic. Graceful, strong flight action with deep wingbeats, usually quite high over sea; plunge-dives. **ID Ad br** white forehead and lores; black crown extending to shaggy crest on nape; wings, back, rump and inner tail feathers uniformly slate-grey; outer primaries darker; underparts white; bill yellow or yellow-green; legs black. **Ad non-br** white forehead extends in streaks to crown, black restricted to nape and behind eye. **Imm** dark feather edging on mantle and wing-coverts, darker centres to flight feathers and dark carpal bar; bill dull greenish yellow; legs brown. **SS** See Lesser and Chinese Crested Terns.

Lesser Crested Tern *Thalasseus bengalensis*

L 38–43 cm, **WS** 89–94 cm. N-W Africa, Indian Oc to W Pacific. 3 ssp, 2 in region: *bengalensis* (Red Sea, Indian Oc); *torresii* (breeds GS to Aus; wanders to W Pacific and E Indian Oceans). Uncommon migrant and local resident. Most birds in region are *torresii*, but *bengalensis* may be regular at least in W GS. Coastal and pelagic. Flight more graceful and buoyant than larger Great Crested Tern. **ID Ad br** black crown extends from bill base to indistinct shaggy crest at nape; upperparts grey, darker primaries; diagnostic bright orange bill; legs black. Ssp *torresii* slightly larger, darker upperparts. **Ad non-br** white forehead extends in streaks to crown, black restricted to nape and behind eye; bill duller-orange. **Imm** dark edging to mantle and coverts, dark primaries and dusky secondary bar, but lacks pronounced carpal bar. **SS** Lacks white forehead of larger, darker-mantled Great Crested Tern in Ad br, and has bright orange (not yellow-green) bill. Also see Chinese Crested Tern.

Chinese Crested Tern *Thalasseus bernsteini*   **V**

L 38–42 cm, **WS** 94 cm. Breeds coastal E China; winters to S. Monotypic. Probably extremely rare but regular winter visitor, five previous records: Sarawak (1890, 1891, 1913), Halmahera (1861) and Seram (single wintering bird, Oct-Mar, 2010-2019). Coastal, including rocky offshore islets, in association with Great Crested Terns. **ID** Large, slender with diagnostic orange bill with black tip. **Ad br** black cap extending from base of bill to nape; back and wings pale grey, contrasting with darker primaries; rump and inner tail feathers uniformly grey with back. **Ad non-br** white forehead and lores extend in streaks to crown, black restricted to nape and behind eye. **Imm** shows dark edging to mantle and coverts. **SS** Resembles Lesser and Great Crested Terns but told by distinct bill pattern in all plumages; gleaming whiter upperparts apparent even at distance.

4 species in region

Medium to large seabirds. Strong-flying and largely pelagic in habits. Kleptoparasitic - often feeding by stealing food from other seabirds. Frequently attracted to boats.

South Polar Skua *Stercorarius maccormicki*   **V**

L 50–55 cm, **WS** 127–140 cm. Breeds Antarctic but ranges to N Atlantic and N Pacific Oceans in austral winter. Monotypic. Vagrant off Weh, N Sum (May 1958), Malacca Straits, N Sum (May 1958), off SE Sum (Jul 1984) and N Bor (1976, Jun 1983, Feb 1992) but records not conclusively separated from similar **Brown Skua** *S. [antarcticus] lonnbergi*, which may also occur. Mostly pelagic when non-breeding, often attracted to boats, will prey upon smaller seabirds or kleptoparasitise larger species. Direct, purposeful flight. **ID** Large, heavy-set. Polymorphic with pale, dark and intermediate morphs. Prominent white flash at base of dark primaries in all plumages. **Ad pale morph** upperparts and wings cold greyish-brown; underparts and head pale grey-brown to whitish; hindnape paler mimicking partial collar; sides of neck with variable yellow streaking. **Ad dark morph** body and wings uniformly cold dark-brown; paler area around base of bill. **Imm** as Ad dark morph but greyer with more prominent pale edging to body and wing feathers; chin and throat often paler than rest of head; hindneck often pale grey-buff mimicking pale collar. **SS** From other skua species by large size, build, more extensive white flashes on base of primaries (upper- and underwing), and contrasting light-dark colouration with pale hindnape collar (in pale and intermediate morphs). Brown Skua from sub-antarctic waters is larger, thicker-billed, mostly lacks lighter colouration around base of bill; shows uniformly warm-brown plumage with distinct pale streaking on nape and body. Imm South Polar Skua can be difficult to separate from Brown Skua, but is colder brown overall, often with pale colouration around base of bill, and has thinner bill. Careful description should be sought. See also Pomarine Skua.

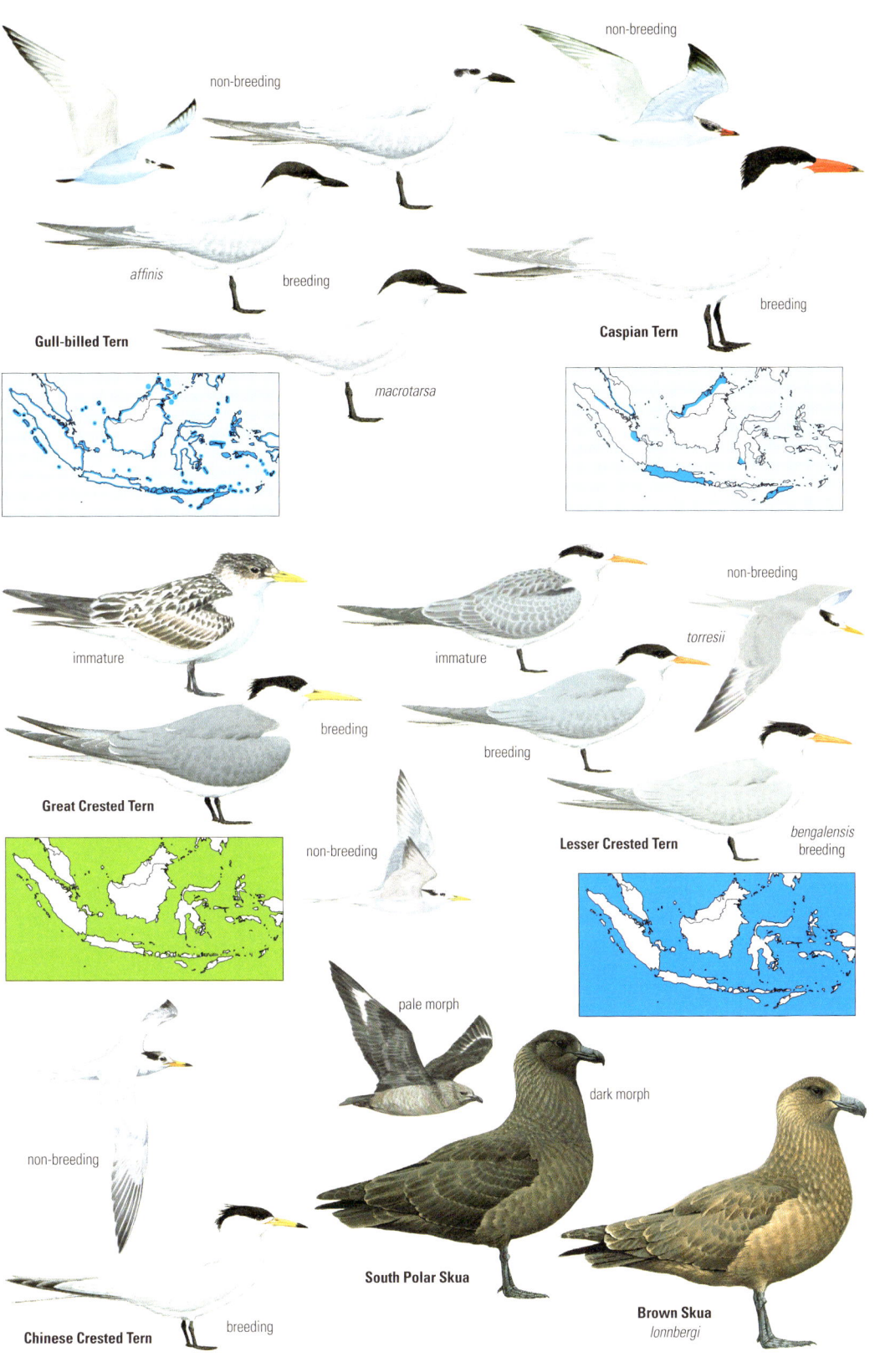

non-breeding

non-breeding

affinis

breeding

Gull-billed Tern

macrotarsa

breeding

Caspian Tern

immature

breeding

Great Crested Tern

non-breeding

immature

breeding

torresii

non-breeding

Lesser Crested Tern

bengalensis
breeding

pale morph

dark morph

non-breeding

breeding

Chinese Crested Tern

South Polar Skua

Brown Skua
lonnbergi

Pomarine Skua *Stercorarius pomarinus*

L 42–58 cm, **WS** 115–138 cm. Breeds N Holarctic; winters to S. Monotypic. Uncommon migrant; generally pelagic, occasionally coastal. Scavenger and kleptoparasite. Strong, purposeful flight, like a large gull. **ID** Large, barrel-chested, intermediate in size between South Polar and Arctic Skuas. Polymorphic. All plumages show pale upper- and underwing flash formed by white base to outer primaries (appearing as 'double patch' on underwing) and pale bill with dark tip. Breeding birds show diagnostic elongated spoon-like central tail feather. **Ad pale morph** prominent dark cap, mottled dark breast band (sometimes incomplete or lacking), pale belly and yellow-white hindneck forming pale collar; remaining upperparts and wings black-brown. Non-breeding birds duller throughout. **Ad dark morph** entirely black-brown apart from pale wing flash. **Imm** variable from uniformly dark chocolate brown to pale brown, with paler edging on upperparts and wings and extensive buff barring especially on flanks, vent, underwing and rump. **SS** South Polar and Brown Skuas in any plumage always much larger, lack pronounced barring (but Brown may be extensively streaked) and have more extensive white wing flash. Ad Pomarine, when lacking tail 'spoons', best separated from Arctic Skua by heavier build (larger head, broader neck and chest), broad-based wings, 'double flash' (not single flash) on underwings and more prominently two-toned bill. Imm Pomarine differs from Arctic in same features as Ad, but additionally has more prominent, colder brown barring on vent, underwings, rump and nape; underwing often appears lighter than belly (usually vice versa in Arctic), head often darker, with less distinct pale collar; reddish Imm morph is rare in Pomarine but common in Arctic. Also see Long-tailed Skua.

Arctic Skua *Stercorarius parasiticus*

L 37–51 cm, **WS** 102–125 cm. Breeds N Holarctic; winters to S hemisphere. Monotypic. Uncommon migrant (less numerous than Pomarine and Long-tailed); generally pelagic but often recorded inshore and coastal. Scavenger and kleptoparasite. Flight purposeful, falcon-like, with short dashes and glides. **ID** Smaller than Pomarine Skua and less barrel-chested with smaller, more triangular head. Polymorphic with pale and dark morphs. **Ad pale morph** dark cap, separated from base of bill by pale patch; underparts pale grey; darker tabs on sides of breast, rarely forming a complete band; sides of neck and nape pale grey, washed yellow; wings and back dark brown with contrasting distinctive white flash on base of outermost 3–5 primaries (appearing as 'single patch' on underwing); underwing otherwise dark; breeding birds show elongated, pointed central tail feathers, but often lacking. **Ad dark morph** all dark brown, with slightly contrasting darker cap; wings and upperparts as pale morph. **Imm** dark to cinnamon reddish-brown with pale buff edging on upperparts and wings; underparts variably barred, but lacks pronounced barring on vent and underwing; upperwing retains white flash as in Ad. **SS** See South Polar, Pomarine and Long-tailed Skuas.

Long-tailed Skua *Stercorarius longicaudus*

L 35–53 cm, **WS** 105–117 cm. Breeds N Holarctic, winters to S hemisphere. Monotypic. Uncommon migrant; generally pelagic but occasionally recorded inshore. Scavenger and kleptoparasite. Flight buoyant and tern-like; less purposeful than Arctic and Pomarine. **ID** Slender and more elegant than Arctic Skua with more delicate, two-toned bill and proportionately longer and thinner wings. **Ad br** very long central tail feathers; pale grey mantle, rump and inner wing-coverts contrasting with blackish outerwing, secondaries and tail; white wing flash limited to upperwing shafts of two outermost primaries, appearing more as a line than a patch; neat, black cap; rest of head pale yellow fading into white breast and light-brown lower belly and vent. **Ad non-br** shorter central tail feathers, less distinct dark cap and shows barring on rump and vent. **Imm dark**

morph all blackish except for single white underwing flash and white barring on vent, axillaries and rump. **Imm pale morph** similar but has white, unbarred belly, very pale head and extensive cold barring on underwing, rump, vent and flanks. Intermediate morphs occur, but never reddish. **SS** Ad Long-tailed distinct from larger and thicker-billed Arctic and Pomarine even when central tail feathers are missing: never shows underwing flash and has contrasting paler upperwing-coverts. Imm thinner-billed and slimmer than Arctic and Pomarine and never occurs in reddish morph; from Arctic additionally by two-toned bill, upperwing flash restricted to outermost 2–3 primaries, and usually stronger barring on vent, rump and underwing; from Pomarine additionally by single (not double) underwing flash and much slimmer, tern-like jizz.

PHAETHONTIDAE
Tropicbirds
3 species in region

Elegant, predominantly white seabirds, typically displaying distinctive elongated tail streamers. Pelagic in habit; generally only approach coasts when breeding. Often flying high over sea; feed by plucking food from the sea surface.

White-tailed Tropicbird *Phaethon lepturus*

L 38–40 cm, **WS** 89–96 cm. Pantropical. 4–6 ssp, 3 in region: *lepturus* (Indian Oc, Jav–LS); *dorotheae* (W Pacific, possibly this ssp present in E of region); *fulvus* (Christmas I breeder; recorded off W Sum). Pelagic unless breeding. Breeds on cliffs. Fast buoyant flight, often high above sea. Regularly sits on sea. **ID Ad** white with black eyestripe, black outer primaries and bar on inner wing; tail with long white central streamers; bill orange-yellow. Ssp *dorotheae* smaller, but not separable at sea. Ssp *fulvus* washed golden-buff, but this polymorphism sometimes also occurs in other ssp. **Imm** white with dark barring on upperparts and wing-coverts; outer primaries mainly black as Ad. **SS** Black outer primaries distinguish from Red-tailed in all plumages. See also Red-billed Tropicbird.

Red-tailed Tropicbird *Phaethon rubricauda*

L 46 cm, **WS** 104 cm. Tropical Pacific and Indian Oceans. Probably monotypic. Uncommon but regularly recorded in E (breeds Manuk, Gunungapi). Nests on ground. Occasionally seen off Indian Oc coast of Jav–Sum but otherwise scarce in W. Pelagic. Flight more laboured than White-tailed Tropicbird and rarely attracted to ships. **ID Ad** generally white with black eyestripe, red bill and long red central tail streamers; scapular tips and primary shafts black. **Imm** as Imm White-tailed Tropicbird, but lacks extensive black on outer primaries. **SS** See White-tailed and Red-billed Tropicbirds.

Red-billed Tropicbird *Phaethon aethereus* **V**

L 46–50 cm, **WS** 99–106 cm. E Pacific, NW Indian Oc, and Atlantic. 3 ssp, 1 presumed in region: *indicus* (NW Indian Oc; sometimes considered monotypic species '**Arabian Tropicbird**' because of plumage differences). Single record from Flores Sea, east of Kalaotoa (Nov 2011). Pelagic. **ID Ad** black outer primaries and black eyestripe. Birds most likely to straggle into region (ssp *indicus*) have orange bill, not to be confused with much redder bill in Red-tailed Tropicbird. Long white tail streamers. Distinct barring on back, rump and wing-coverts separate from all other tropicbirds. **Imm** lacks tail streamers; bill orange-yellow with black tip; back and wing-coverts finely barred black; outer primaries black; distinct black eyestripe. **SS** Larger, with slower, more deliberate flight than White-tailed Tropicbird, and lighter jizz than similar-sized Red-tailed Tropicbird. Imm Red-billed similar to White-tailed but more densely barred on upperparts and more conspicuous black eye-line forming nuchal collar. Black primary patches distinguish from Red-tailed in all plumages.

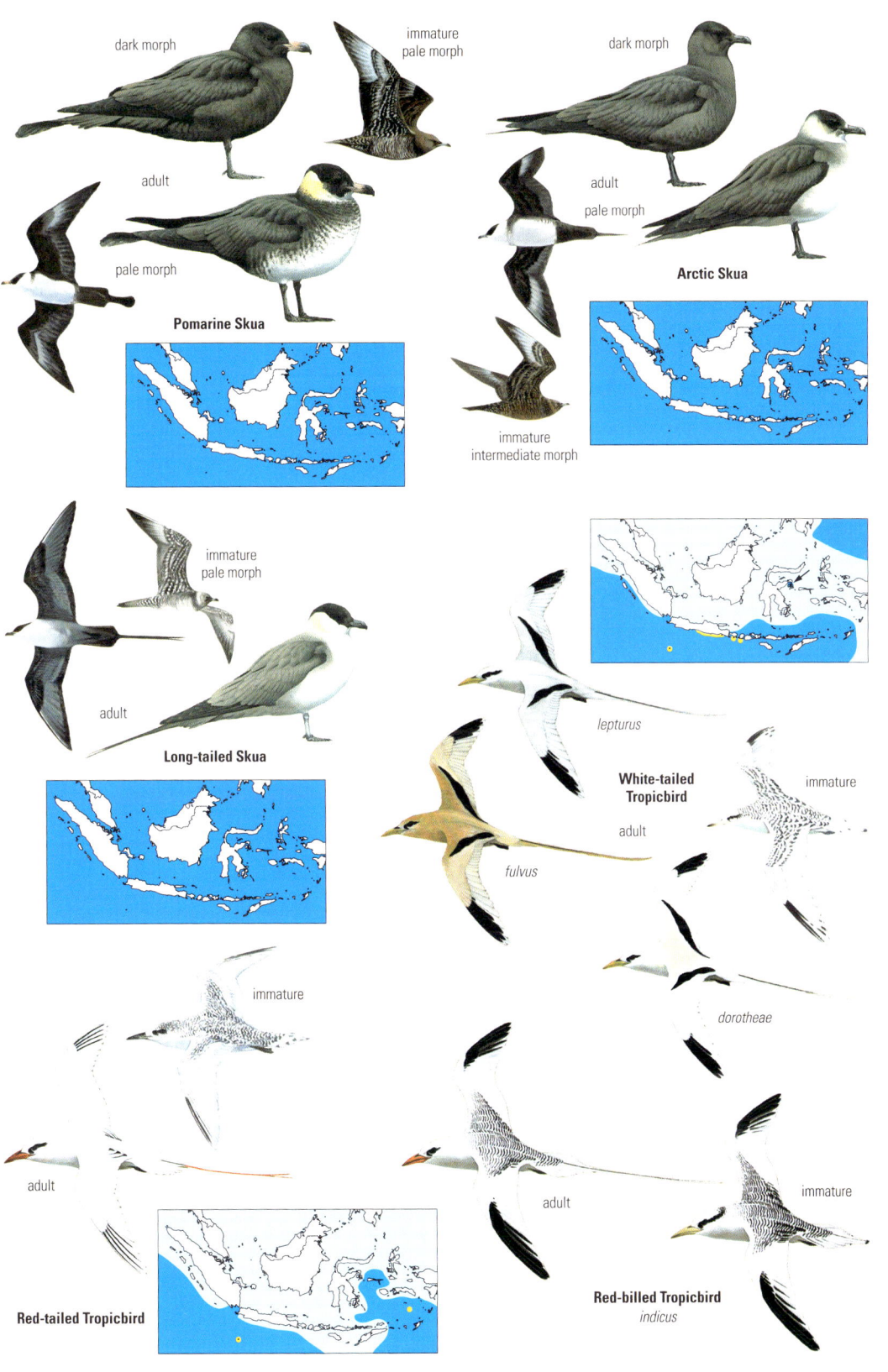

dark morph

immature
pale morph

dark morph

adult

adult

pale morph

pale morph

Arctic Skua

Pomarine Skua

immature
intermediate morph

immature
pale morph

lepturus

adult

**White-tailed
Tropicbird**

immature

adult

fulvus

immature

dorotheae

Long-tailed Skua

immature

adult

adult

immature

adult

Red-billed Tropicbird
indicus

Red-tailed Tropicbird

PROCELLARIIDAE
Shearwaters, Petrels and allies
15 species in region
A large family of small to medium sized oceanic seabirds. Includes the strong-flying, long-winged shearwaters and larger, bulkier petrels. Almost all are birds of the open ocean, rarely close to land. Often follow boats or are attracted to fish waste discarded from fishing vessels. Feed by plucking food from the ocean surface or diving to catch fish and other prey.

Cape Petrel *Daption capense* V
L 35–42 cm, **WS** 80–91 cm. Southern Oc. 2 ssp: *capense* (circumpolar around Antarctic; '**Antarctic Cape Petrel**'); based on distinct plumage ssp *australe* (sub-antarctic NZ; '**Snares Cape Petrel**') may deserve species recognition. Vagrants reach north beyond equator. Sight record from Banda Sea (Mar 1876) of unknown taxon. Often following ships. Flight typically stiff flaps interspersed by glides; occasionally soars in high arcs; swims with an upright posture. **ID** Medium-sized, stocky with distinctive black-and-white upperparts and white underparts; mantle and inner upperwing predominantly white, outer upperwing predominantly black with a distinctive white panel. Ssp *australe* has more black on inner upperwing and mantle. **AN** Cape Pigeon, Pintado Petrel.

Hawaiian Petrel *Pterodroma sandwichensis* V
L 43 cm, **WS** 97–98 cm. Central Pacific Oc; breeds Hawaii. Monotypic. No longer considered conspecific with extralimital Galápagos Petrel *P. phaeopygia*. Single specimen collected near Ternate (Apr 1862). Pelagic, usually solitary. Typical *Pterodroma* flight of soaring arcs and glides. **ID** Long, pointed wings and long tail. Forehead, throat and cheeks white, contrasting with black hood that extends below eye and onto sides of neck; broad black 'M' across upperwings in fresh plumage (upperparts more uniformly dark in worn birds); underwing white with black trailing edge, broad black wing tip and black leading edge ending in prominent black 'tick mark'. **SS** In the Indian Oc, Barau's Petrel is smaller, with paler upperparts, typically with less black on underwing and a smaller 'tick mark'. In Pacific Oc, **White-necked Petrel** *P. cervicalis* (unrecorded in region but a potential vagrant) is paler overall with a much smaller 'tick mark'.

Barau's Petrel *Pterodroma baraui* V
L 38 cm, **WS** 96 cm. Tropical Indian Oc; breeds Réunion. Monotypic. Sight record at sea off Enggano (Jul 1985). Also recorded Christmas I (Aus). Pelagic, usually solitary. Typical *Pterodroma* flight of soaring arcs and glides with wings usually held forward and slightly bowed. **ID** Long wings, long tail and narrow body. White forehead and cheeks contrast with dark grey-black cap that extends over eye, grey sides of neck, mantle and scapulars, becoming darker toward rump and tail; upperwing with black-brown 'M' that does not cross back; underwing white with dark trailing edge, wider to tip, and dark leading edge to outerwing ending in a prominent black 'tick mark' at carpal. **SS** See Hawaiian Petrel.

Tahiti Petrel *Pseudobulweria rostrata* V
L 39 cm, **WS** 84 cm. Breeds tropical Pacific Oc; non-breeders disperse widely, including to Indian Oc. Monotypic. Uncommon, but regularly recorded near Ashmore Reef (Aus), and exceptional record of 56 south of Babar in Oct 2017, suggesting it could occur anywhere in region. Pelagic, usually solitary. Flight usually low over water with languid wingbeats and occasional dynamic soaring in stronger winds. **ID** Large petrel with long narrow wings, held at right angle, and long tail. Head, throat, upper breast and upperparts uniformly dark brown; rest of underparts white with variable brown feathering on flanks and thighs and a dark border to white undertail; underwing dark brown with a silvery central pane visible if viewed well. **SS** See Beck's Petrel. Pale morph Kermadec Petrel *P. neglecta* and Herald Petrel *P. heraldica* (both Pacific Oc and currently unrecorded in region) appear shorter-winged and generally paler brown, with a pale panel on the outer underwing.

Beck's Petrel *Pseudobulweria becki* V
L 30–34 cm, WS 84–89cm. Monotypic. Bismarck Archipelago and Solomon Is, non-breeders reach Geelvink Bay, West Papua. Vagrant Molucca Sea, off Obi (1 in Oct 2019). **ID/SS** Extremely similar to larger Tahiti Petrel, but flight quicker, more manoeuvrable, less languid; quicker, snappier wingbeats and buoyant glides. In the absence of direct size comparisons with other seabirds, any records should be accompanied by detailed documentation.

Antarctic Prion *Pachyptila desolata* V
L 25–27 cm, **WS** 58–66 cm. Breeds Southern Oc (Dec–Mar); non-breeders disperse north in sub-antarctic waters and occasionally beyond. Probably monotypic. Single record of a moribund bird on SW coast of Jav (1938). Pelagic, highly gregarious in its range. Flight erratic with rapid wingbeats and short glides on bowed wings. **ID** Grey-and-white with prominent dark 'M' across upperwings. Face pale with darker mask and crown and broad white supercilium; dark grey half-collar on neck; narrow dark tip to tail; bill blue, large and broad. **SS** Difficult to impossible to separate at sea from a number of other prion (*Pachyptila*) species that may occur as vagrants. Care should be taken to record head and neck colouration, exact colour and structure of bill and extent of dark in tail. Consult specialist seabird literature. **AN** Dove Prion.

Streaked Shearwater *Calonectris leucomelas*
L 48 cm, **WS** 122 cm. Breeds NW Pacific; winters to tropical waters including Indian Oc. Monotypic. Fairly common, with most records from across region typically Jul–Nov, but possible year-round. Pelagic, singly to large flocks. Typical shearwater flight of flap-flap-glide close to water on slightly bowed wings with occasional dynamic soaring in stronger winds. **ID** Large with long broad wings held forward in flight, long neck and small head. Face white (not always obvious at distance) with variable dark streaking grading to brown-grey nape, neck and half-collar, looking pale at distance; mantle and upperwings grey-brown with pale tips giving a scaly appearance, and an indistinct darker 'M' formed by darker flight feathers and greater-coverts (more obvious when fresh); underparts white; underwing white with dark brown flight feathers and dark smudges on leading edge of outer wing; bill horn-coloured. **SS** Pale morph Wedge-tailed Shearwater smaller and lacks white on face.

capense

Cape Petrel

australe

Hawaiian Petrel

White-necked Petrel

Antarctic Prion

Beck's Petrel

Tahiti Petrel

Barau's Petrel

Streaked Shearwater

Flesh-footed Shearwater *Ardenna carneipes* V

L 46–48 cm, **WS** 110–120 cm. Breeds S Indian and Pacific Oceans (Nov–Feb); migrates to N. Monotypic. Several sightings off W coast of Sum and possibly off Jav/Bali. Pelagic, but sometimes recorded inshore. Leisurely 'flap-flap-glide' flight. **ID** Large, all-dark, heavy-looking shearwater with long broad wings and rounded tail. Bill heavy and distinctly pink-coloured, noticeable from considerable range; underwing can appear paler in centre in some lights; legs pink, but not always visible. **SS** Compared to Short-tailed and Wedge-tailed Shearwaters, Flesh-footed is larger, heavier built and has larger, clearly pink bill. The same differences apply to extralimital Sooty Shearwater *A. grisea* (see under Short-tailed).

Short-tailed Shearwater *Ardenna tenuirostris* V

L 40–45 cm, **WS** 95–100 cm. Pacific and S Indian Oceans; in recent years regularly recorded off W coast of MPen and in waters around Batam (peaking in May), suggesting unknown migration route. Monotypic. Pelagic. Typical shearwater flight of 'flap-flap-glide'. **ID** Rounded head; narrow, slightly rounded wings and short, thin bill; tail stumpy and either square or slightly rounded; plumage entirely dark chocolate-brown except for slightly paler underwing-coverts; head sometimes slightly darker than rest of body. **SS** Head more rounded, bill shorter (without overlap), and underwing-coverts rarely as pale as in similar **Sooty Shearwater** *A. grisea* (Pacific and Atlantic Oceans; unrecorded in region). See larger Wedge-tailed, Flesh-footed and smaller Heinroth's Shearwaters.

Wedge-tailed Shearwater *Ardenna pacifica*

L 46–47 cm, **WS** 97–99 cm. Tropical Pacific and Indian Oceans. Monotypic. Uncommon; regularly recorded in region, typically Jul–Nov. Pelagic. Singly or small groups. Leisurely 'shearwatering' flap-flap-glide flight. **ID** Long broad wings, long wedge-shaped tail and long slender dark bill (latter can appear pale in some lights); legs and feet variably dark to flesh-coloured. Polymorphic. **Dark morph** dark-brown all over, but worn birds may show paler tips to mantle and upperwing-coverts. **Pale morph** brown above with indistinct darker 'M' on upperwing, dark cap and tail; underparts white; underwing white with dark trailing edge and tip and variably dark smudging in centre. **SS** Short-tailed Shearwater and extralimital Sooty Shearwater (see under Short-tailed) have shorter tail and typically a silvery panel on underwing. See also Streaked and Flesh-footed Shearwaters, Bulwer's and Jouanin's Petrels.

Tropical Shearwater *Puffinus bailloni* V

L 31 cm, **WS** 69 cm. Pacific and Indian Oceans. 3–6 ssp, 1 in region: *dichrous* (breeding in Pacific, including on Palau). Known from several off Morotai and Halmahera (Aug 1945) and E of Kalaotoa (Oct 2016). Typical shearwater flight of 'flap-flap-glide' close to sea surface. **ID** Relatively small black-and-white shearwater with short, broad, rounded wings and blue-black legs. Upperparts, including upperwings, tail, head (to level of eye), neck and half-collar all sooty-black; underparts white, with contrasting dark undertail-coverts and wide dark margin to underwing; white 'tabs' extend upwards from underparts to the sides of the rump. **SS** Seasonal sightings (~Mar/Apr) of aggregations of shearwaters in Australian waters bordering Timor Sea have tentatively been identified as **Arabian Shearwater** *Puffinus persicus* (breeding in NW Indian Oc). Like Arabian, these birds differ from Tropical in having pink (not blue) legs, browner (less black) upperparts, an almost complete lack of white rump 'tabs', and the presence of dark marks on the underwing-coverts (especially around axillaries). However, the extent of dark marks on the underwing of these birds is less extensive than in true Arabian, calling into question their identification. Any sighting of Tropical-type shearwaters in regional waters should be carefully documented. See also Heinroth's and Hutton's Shearwaters.

Hutton's Shearwater *Puffinus huttoni* V

L 36–38 cm, **WS** 72–78 cm. Breeds NZ (Oct–Dec); non-breeders circumnavigate Australia, passing through Timor Sea far offshore, S of Rote. Monotypic. Pelagic. Singly or small groups. Flight low and fast with rapid wingbeats and short glides. **ID** Medium-sized shearwater with long wings, long body and neck, flat head, broad tail and pink legs. Upperparts, breast collar and most of head blackish brown (only chin sticks out as distinctly white); underparts white; underwing generally white with dark trailing edge and tip, variable dark markings in centre of outer wing, predominantly brown centres to inner wing and brown 'armpit'. **SS** Larger than Tropical and Arabian (see under Tropical) Shearwaters, with dark extending much further down the breast side and cheek (well below the eye). Additionally told from Tropical by browner (less black) upperparts colouration, pink (not blue) legs and the lack of distinct white tabs on rump sides.

Heinroth's Shearwater *Puffinus heinrothi*

L 27 cm, **WS** 59 cm. Breeds Melanesia, occasionally strays to N NG coast. Monotypic. Recorded Flores Sea (2 E of Bonerate, Oct 2011), at sea off W Taliabu (70+ in Nov 2012; 12 in Nov 2015), off Lombok (May 2015), off N Mangole (209 in Mar 2017), off N Lomblen (Oct 2018). Possibly migrant but breeding in region should not be ruled out. Flutters low over water, usually singly or small groups. **ID** Sooty-brown, with variable but always conspicuous silvery underwing bar. Can show pale chin and belly; distinctive long, slender bill; pink feet do not extend beyond tail tip; long, thin neck gives skinny appearance in flight; diagnostic pale marginal covert-bar on underwing. **SS** From Short-tailed Shearwater by small size, short stubby wings, often paler belly, weak flight and longer bill. From extralimital Christmas Shearwater *P. nativitatis* (C Pacific) by paler underwing, smaller size, rounder wings and longer bill. From Tropical and Arabian Shearwaters by browner plumage and largely dark underparts.

Bulwer's Petrel *Bulweria bulwerii*

L 26–28 cm, **WS** 67 cm. Circumtropical. W Pacific Oc breeders disperse widely, including to Indian Oc. Monotypic. Fairly common throughout, more so to E. Most records Jun–Nov. Pelagic, usually alone. Flight is storm-petrel like, buoyant, erratic; in stronger winds may flap and glide more determinedly. **ID** Medium-sized with long pointed wings and long wedge-shaped tail. Generally sooty brown, apart from pale ulnar bar on upperwing visible at considerable range; with moult feathering on chin and face can become paler; bill short, stout, black. **SS** Brown Noddy similar in size, but lacks the pale wingbar and has a longer bill. In Indian Oc, Jouanin's Petrel is larger, heavier, broader-winged and has a less pointed tail, a stronger, less hurried flight, larger bill and less obvious ulnar bar only visible in strong light. From dark morph Wedge-tailed Shearwater by small size and flight pattern.

Jouanin's Petrel *Bulweria fallax* V

L 31 cm, **WS** 79 cm. NW Indian Oc (breeds Socotra, May–Sep) but prone to long-distance vagrancy with records from NW Aus. Monotypic. Known from single observation at sea W of Enggano (Jul 1984). Pelagic, rarely seen near land and rarely follows boats. Flight with bowed wings close to the water; may flap almost continuously in light winds, and soar in high arcs in moderate winds. **ID** Medium-sized, round-headed, long-winged and long-tailed petrel. Entirely dark brown apart from faint paler ulnar bar on upperwing; tail bluntly rounded, although can appear more pointed/stepped with moult; stout black bill, held downwards **SS** See Bulwer's Petrel. From dark morph Wedge-tailed Shearwater by size and flight pattern.

Flesh-footed
Shearwater

Short-tailed Shearwater

dark morph

Wedge-tailed Shearwater

pale morph

Tropical Shearwater

Arabian Shearwater

Hutton's Shearwater

Heinroth's Shearwater

Bulwer's Petrel

Jouanin's Petrel

OCEANITIDAE
Southern Ocean Storm-petrels
2 species in region

Small, oceanic seabirds with distinctive fluttering flight, often paddling their feet in the water to disturb prey as they fly slowly above the surface. Rarely seen near coasts, they are birds of the open ocean, often being attracted to boats.

Wilson's Storm-petrel *Oceanites oceanicus*
L 15–19 cm, **WS** 38–42 cm. Breeds Southern Oc, wintering to N. 3 ssp, 1 presumed in region: *exasperatus* (breeds Antarctica in Nov–Apr; migrates to tropical oceans and into N hemisphere). Regularly recorded in waters in region, including Sum, Jav, LS and Mol. Pelagic. Singly or small to large groups. Swallow-like flight at sea, often with legs pattering on water while foraging; attracted to fishing boats and bait. **ID** Small and dark with paler wing crescents and prominent white rump extending onto sides of vent; legs black with diagnostic yellow webs to feet (difficult to see); feet project beyond tail in flight. **SS** Extralimital **Leach's Storm-petrel** *Hydrobates leucorhous* (N Pacific and Atlantic Oceans, may straggle to NE of region) shows white rump typically longer than is wide, and not extending onto sides of vent. Extralimital **Black-bellied Storm-petrel** *Fregetta tropica* (Southern Oc, may straggle to S and W of region) distinguished by white belly with black central stripe and white underwing.

White-faced Storm-petrel *Pelagodroma marina*
L 18–21 cm, **WS** 42–43 cm. Tropical and sub-tropical seas, mainly in S hemisphere. 5–6 ssp, 1 presumed in region: *dulciae* (W–S Aus). Several records from Indian Oc coast of Sum and LS and single record off Batam. Pelagic. Bounding, erratic flight with periods of flapping interspersed with short glides on bowed wings; often patters feet on water while foraging; solitary to large groups. **ID** Bicoloured with distinctive face pattern and white underparts; long rounded wings and long legs projecting beyond tail.

HYDROBATIDAE
Northern Ocean Storm-petrels
2 species in region

Small oceanic seabirds with predominantly all-dark appearance. Strong fliers that migrate through the waters of the region. Typically seen singly on the open ocean, but may pass close to land in large, loose groups when on migration routes. Rarely attracted to boats.

Swinhoe's Storm-petrel *Hydrobates monorhis*
L 18–21 cm, **WS** 45–48 cm. Breeds off Japan/Korea (Jul–Aug); winters in N Indian Oc. Monotypic. Regularly recorded migrant (May, Aug–Dec), rarer E of Wallace's Line (likely under-recorded). Pelagic, usually solitary and not attracted to boats, but on migration large, loose groups can pass close to land. On passage flight is typically strong and direct. **ID** Medium-sized, all dark with pale wing crescent. Can show white bases to primaries on upperwing. **SS** Matsudaira's Storm-petrel is similar in appearance but larger, shows more deeply forked tail (often impossible to assess in flight), and – on average – shows a more extensive white patch on upperwing primaries. With experience, flight style is best mark: Matsudaira's slow, purposeful flight with stiff, non-angled wings versus Swinhoe's tern-like, more erratic flight that often includes sudden banks and arcs with interspersed fluttering.

Matsudaira's Storm-petrel *Hydrobates matsudairae*
L 24 cm, **WS** 56 cm. Breeds off Japan (Jan–Jun); winters to tropical Indian Oc. Monotypic. Rare migrant in E (Jul–Nov) but has been recorded as far W as Sunda Straits. Pelagic, usually solitary. Flight can be strong and deliberate, or show more leisurely 'flap-flap-glide' progression. **ID** Large, all-dark with paler wing crescent; usually has pale base to primaries forming a noticeable white patch on upperwing. **SS** See Swinhoe's Storm-petrel.

PHALACROCORACIDAE
Cormorants and Darters
6 species in region

Medium to large, long-necked birds of coastal and inland wetlands. Swim semi-submerged and dive to catch fish. Often seen near water perched in trees drying wings after foraging.

Little Black Cormorant *Phalacrocorax sulcirostris*
L 61 cm, **WS** 81 cm. Aus. Monotypic. Widespread throughout E, locally common on N coast of Jav, spreading west along Sum coast. Ponds, lakes, waterways, estuaries and coasts. **ID** Bill grey-black; bare facial skin blue-grey; greenish-blue eyes. **Ad br** blackish-brown with green or purple gloss; small white plumes can form tuft behind eye; wing-coverts paler edged black giving scaly appearance. **Ad non-br/Imm** uniformly dull brown. **SS** See Little Cormorant.

Great Cormorant *Phalacrocorax carbo*
L 77–94 cm, **WS** 121–149 cm. Old World, Aus. 4–6 ssp, 2 in region: *sinensis* (Palaearctic; wintering to S; irregular visitor to N Sum and N Bor, where has formerly bred); ssp *novaehollandiae* (Aus, recorded from Kai Kecil, Oct 1981) sometimes considered separate species, '**Australian Great Cormorant**', based on differences in breeding display characters. A single record from Bali may relate to either form. Lakes, ponds, inland waterways, estuaries and coasts. **ID** Large cormorant. **Ad br** largely black plumage with green gloss; prominent white flank and throat patches, yellow facial skin and greyish bill; usually shows extensive white plumes on side of head and neck. Ssp *novaehollandiae* differs in having white plumes restricted to small patch on sides of neck. **Ad non-br** generally duller. **Imm** dull brown, with extensive white on underparts, replaced by brown with age.

Little Pied Cormorant *Microcarbo melanoleucos*
L 58–63 cm, **WS** 84–91 cm. Aus. 3 ssp, 1 in region: *melanoleucos* (Aus to E Indo Archipelago). Widespread and locally common in E. Occasional in E Jav. Vagrant to Bor. Lakes, ponds, inland waterways, estuaries and coasts. **ID Ad** easily identified in all plumages by white underparts and contrasting black upperparts, hindneck and crown; bill yellow. **Imm** black in crown extending below level of eye.

Little Cormorant *Microcarbo niger*
L 56 cm, **WS** 90 cm. S–SE Asia. Monotypic. Formerly common coastal bird on Jav, now scarce. Freshwater ponds, lakes, marshes and waterways. **ID** Very small cormorant. Bill dull yellowish; eyes dark brown. **Ad br** wholly blackish-green, with some narrow white plumes on head. **Ad non-br** blackish-brown with variable white on throat and neck. **Imm** similar to Ad non-br but duller brown. **SS** Ad br from Little Black Cormorant by small size, uniformly coloured wing-coverts, yellowish bill. Imm and Ad non-br by whiter throat and neck, dark-brown eyes and yellowish bill. In all ages, from Little Black by distinct head shape with short beak and steep forecrown.

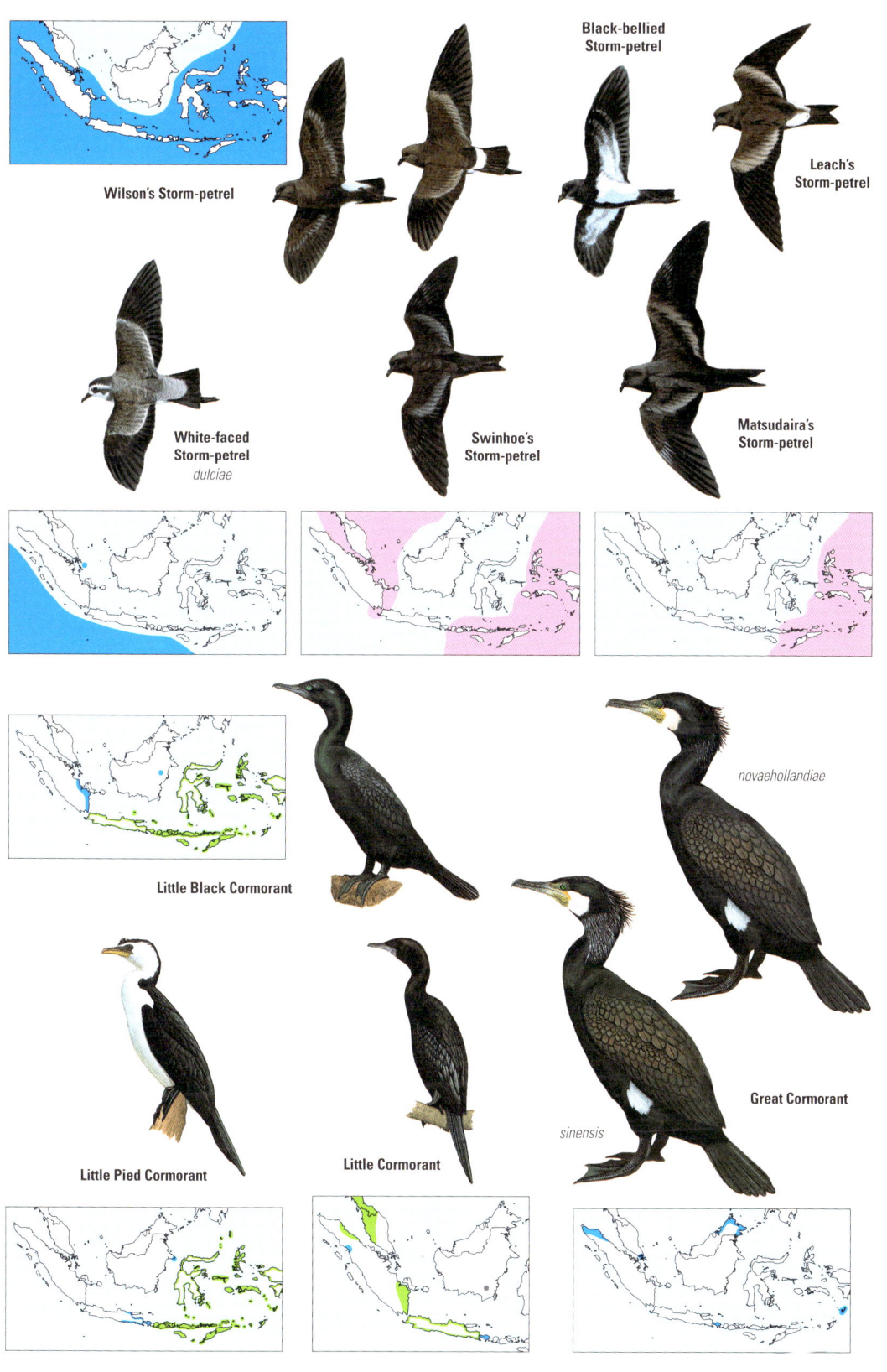

Wilson's Storm-petrel

Black-bellied Storm-petrel

Leach's Storm-petrel

White-faced Storm-petrel
dulciae

Swinhoe's Storm-petrel

Matsudaira's Storm-petrel

Little Black Cormorant

novaehollandiae

Little Pied Cormorant

Little Cormorant

Great Cormorant

sinensis

Oriental Darter *Anhinga melanogaster*

L 88–94 cm. S–SE Asia, Phil. Monotypic. Formerly considered conspecific with other darters (including Australian), but here separated on plumage and molecular differences. Fairly common resident GS, Sul. Occasional non-breeding visitor LS. Lakes, ponds, marshes and waterways, <1500 m. Swims low in water, often with body submerged. **ID** Long snake-like neck and dagger-shaped bill. **M** black body and underparts; wings with long, white covert plumes; head and neck can show large extents of brown, always with narrow white stripe extending down neck. **F** paler buff-white throat and underparts. **Imm** browner and paler below. **SS** See Australian Darter.

Australian Darter *Anhinga novaehollandiae*

L 86–92 cm. Aus. 2 ssp, 1 presumed in region: *novaehollandiae* (Australia into Wallacea). For taxonomy see Oriental Darter. Scarce and local visitor to lakes, ponds, marshes, waterways and coasts. **ID/SS** As larger Oriental Darter but **M** shows black head and neck with wider, shorter white stripe down neck and usually with more limited rusty chestnut foreneck and breast patch. Unlike Oriental, **F/Imm** are generally very pale on entire underparts and never show contrast between a black lower breast and a pale-brown foreneck/upper breast.

SULIDAE
Boobies

4 species in region

Large pelagic seabirds with long wings and dagger-like bills. Feed by plunge diving for fish. Breed on isolated coasts and islands and forage in coastal waters or open oceans. Breeding populations in region have undergone precipitous declines following human interference.

Masked Booby *Sula dactylatra*

L 81–92 cm, **WS** 152 cm. Pantropical. 4–5 ssp, 1 in region: *personata* (E Indian Oc, W–C Pacific). Occasional records from Mol, LS (breeds Gunungapi), scarce elsewhere, has been recorded from Malacca and Sunda Straits. Pelagic unless breeding; unlikely to be seen from coast. Feeds by plunge diving. **ID** Bill yellow (duller in **F** and **Imm**). **Ad** wholly white body and head; wings white above and below with black primaries, secondaries and some black tips to scapulars; tail black; bare facial skin blue-black; legs and feet variably grey to olive-yellow. **Imm** wholly brown head separated from brown back by narrow white hindcollar; tail and upperwings dark brown; mantle and lesser-coverts with pale feather tips giving more sandy-brown appearance; underparts white. **SS** Imm from Brown Booby by presence of white hindcollar. Ad from extralimital **Australasian Gannet** *Morus serrator* (Australia, potential vagrant) by black-tipped scapulars and lack of yellow on head. See also Red-footed Booby.

Brown Booby *Sula leucogaster*

L 64–74 cm, **WS** 132–150 cm. Pantropical. 4 ssp, 1 in region: *plotus* (Indian Oc, W–C Pacific). Common across E and occasional to locally common in W; ground nester; breeding on Kakabia, Gunungapi, Manuk, Suanggi at least (mainly Mar–Sep). Pelagic but often feeds inshore and roosts on offshore rocks. Singly or small groups, occasionally large flocks. Plunge dives for food. **ID Ad** head, neck, upper breast, back, upperwing and tail uniformly dark brown; underparts white, with clear-cut division from brown upper breast; underwing white with brown margins; bill, facial skin and legs yellow to yellowish-green. **Imm** as Ad but bill and facial skin greyish, underparts and underwing often tinged brown. **SS** See Masked Booby.

Red-footed Booby *Sula sula*

L 66–77 cm, **WS** 91–101 cm. Pantropical. 3 ssp, 1 in region: *rubripes* (Indian Oc, W–C Pacific). Commonly seen in E; tree-nester; breeds Sarege, Kakabia, Moromaho, Gunungapi, Manuk, Suanggi (mainly Mar–Sep); uncommon to scarce in W. Pelagic unless breeding. Singly to large groups. **ID Ad** legs red; bill pale blue, occasionally pink or orange towards base. Polymorphic. **White morph** white body and head, often with yellow-golden cast; white upperwing-coverts with black primaries and secondaries; underwing similar to upperwing but with black carpal patch; tail white, but black-tailed morph occurs. **Brown morph** entirely brown-grey with occasional yellowish cast to head. **Brown-white morph** brown wings with white rump, tail, rear belly and undertail-coverts and either brown or white head, neck and underparts. Intermediate morphs with black tail also possible. **Imm** (all morphs) brownish overall; blackish bill; yellow-grey legs. **SS** From Masked Booby by leg colour, blackish carpal patch on underwing and white tail (if present). Imm Red-footed lacks white hindcollar of Masked; most Imm Brown Boobies show ghost of Ad pattern with sharply delimited dark breast, never shown by Red-footed.

Abbott's Booby *Papasula abbotti*

L 71 cm. Breeds Christmas I but formerly more widespread. Monotypic. Several records off Indian Oc coast of Jav and Sum, including Sunda Strait. Several records in S–C Mol, as far as Kofiau, since 1985 may represent unknown dispersal. Pelagic, has been observed perched on flotsam. Flies with slow flaps and glides. Distinctive jizz with large head, long neck and narrow wings. **ID Ad** head and underparts white; rump white with black spots; mantle and back mostly black, with narrow white strip extending from hindneck to rump; upperwings black with white leading edge and some white edging to coverts and inner primaries; underwing white with black tip; tail black; bill blue-grey (**M**) or pinkish (**F**), facial skin blue-black; legs grey. **Imm** as Ad, but duller, with grey bill.

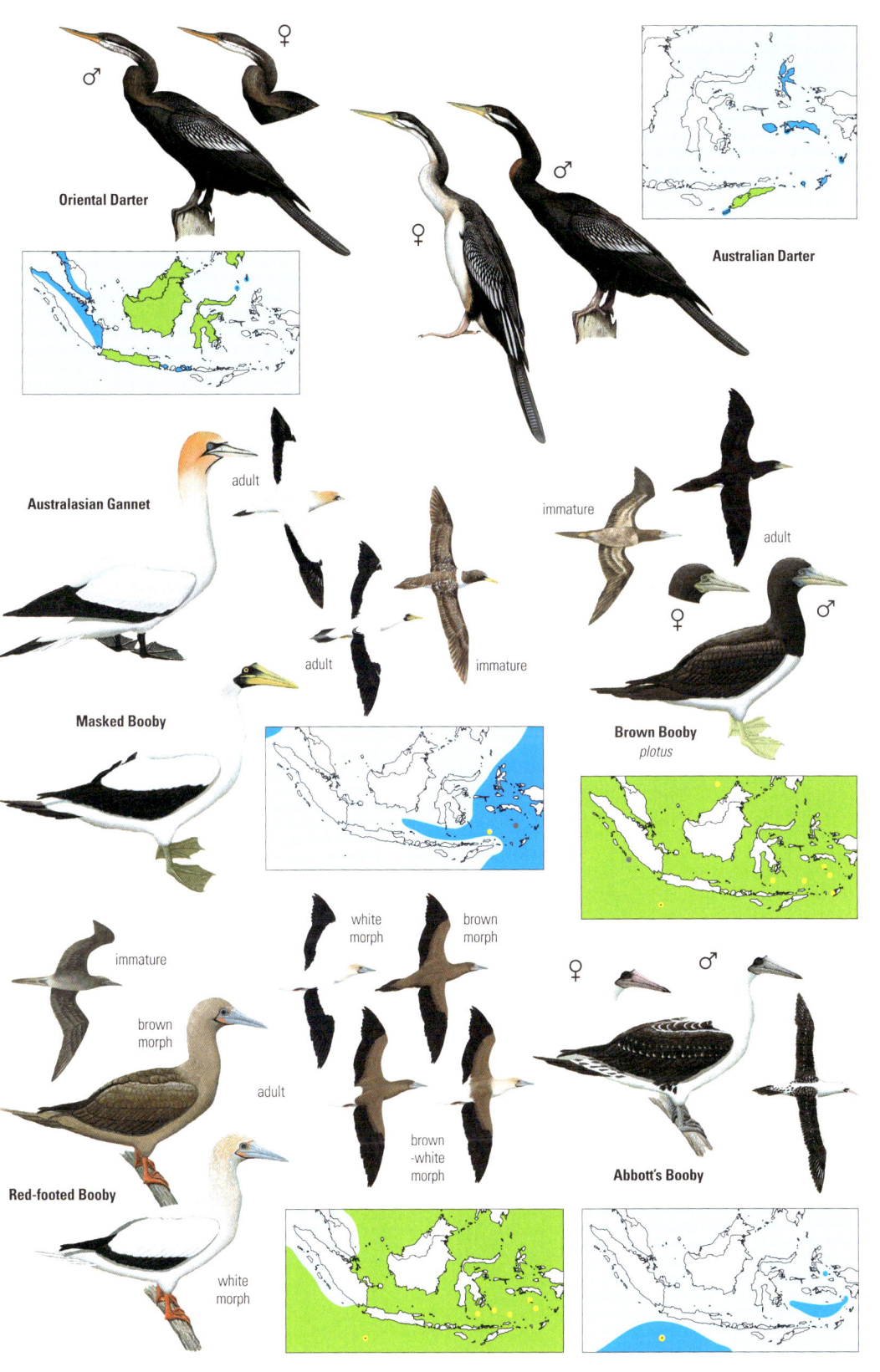

Oriental Darter

Australian Darter

♂ ♀

♀ ♂

Australasian Gannet

adult

immature

adult

Masked Booby

immature

adult

adult

immature

♀ ♂

Brown Booby
plotus

immature

brown
morph

adult

white
morph

brown
morph

brown
-white
morph

♀ ♂

Red-footed Booby

white
morph

Abbott's Booby

Large, elegant seabirds with long curved wings, long, deeply forked tails and long bills. Found in pelagic and coastal habitats, kleptoparasitic or picking food from the sea. Almost always remain airborne, only coming to roost occasionally on coastal fish traps or isolated islands with trees.

Christmas Frigatebird *Fregata andrewsi*

L 89–100 cm. Breeds Christmas I. Monotypic. Fairly common GS, rare in E. Generally pelagic, but occasionally inshore. Usually singly or small groups, but large accumulations of roosting birds often present in Jakarta Bay. Sometimes together with Lesser Frigatebird. **ID** Plumage highly variable with age and sex. **M** wholly black apart from white, oval to squarish belly patch and red gular pouch (not often visible). In all other plumages, a pair of parallel-sided white axillary 'spurs' is often present (though sometimes not); these 'spurs' typically extend anteriorly from the centre of the white breast/belly patch, usually connecting with belly patch well behind the black breast band or breast 'tabs' (=variable black lateral spots forming half-collar or incomplete breast band). **F** black head and throat and a hexagonal white breast-and-belly patch (convex at rear). **Imm** as fem but has variable breast 'tabs'; head white to yellow-buff, often mottled black. **Juv** as Imm but head less mottled, breast 'tabs' often form complete band in the form of two lobes joining at centre; usually shows prominent whitish (not buff) alar bar on upperwing-coverts. **SS** In all age/sex combinations, Christmas is larger than other frigatebirds, with broader wings and a bulkier, longer bill (although Great Frigatebird comes close and perhaps not distinguishable by size alone). Ad fem Christmas best distinguished by large white breast patch reaching onto belly (with convex rear end). Plumages of all Juv/imm frigatebirds similar and confusing: in Juv plumage, when breast band is fully developed, its lower edge is usually straight in Lesser (forming base of triangular belly patch) and concave in Great (forming side of oval belly patch), while Christmas has a distinct two-lobed breast band. In this plumage and later ones (when breast band shrinks into breast 'tabs'), Christmas also told from Lesser by position of axillary 'spurs', when present, at sides of hexagonal belly patch, not at front of triangular patch, and from Great by shape of 'spurs' (usually extending well onto underwing, not as blunt and stopping short of underwing). In imm plumage, breast 'tabs' can be missing, making identification rely solely on shape and orientation of axillary 'spurs': triangular and outward-angled in Lesser, absent (or blunt and short) in Great, and parallel-sided and angled anteriorly in Christmas. Occasional imm Christmas in this plumage may lack spurs and then almost indistinguishable from Great. Juv Christmas also told by presence of a whitish (not buff) upperwing bar, but this can be hard to see.

Great Frigatebird *Fregata minor*

L 86–100 cm, **WS** 206–230 cm. Pantropical. 2–5 ssp, 1 in region: *minor* (Indian Oc to SW Pacific Oc). Widespread resident; more common in E. Breeds Kakabia, Moromaho, Gunungapi, Manuk. Formerly bred several locations in W. Generally pelagic, but often soars along coasts. Usually singly or small groups but occasionally roosting in large groups on small offshore islands. **ID** Highly variable with age and sex. **M** the only all-black frigatebird (apart from indistinct red gular pouch). All other plumages usually lack white axillary 'spurs' or only show weak, blunt 'spurs' (not reaching underwing) radiating out from sides of oval white breast/belly patch. **F** white breast patch, concave at rear so as to avoid most of belly; black head with off-white (not black) throat. **Imm** similar to fem but has head buff to whitish; belly white and forming oval white 'breast-and-belly patch' but black mottling sets in with age, leading to black belly of Ad plumages. **Juv** as Imm but with broad blackish breast band delimited from oval-shaped white belly patch by concave dividing line. **SS** See Christmas Frigatebird. Distinctly larger than Lesser (in direct comparison). Fem told from Lesser by off-white throat and usual absence of axillary 'spurs'. When breast band is fully developed, Juv told from Lesser by oval (not triangular) white belly patch in part caused by concave (not straight) lower edge of breast band. In this plumage, Great also told from Lesser by blunter, much shorter axillary 'spurs' (if present at all) angling out from side of oval white patch (not from front of triangular white patch). In imm plumage, when breast band or rudimentary breast 'tabs' are absent, presence and shape of axillary 'spurs' becomes crucial for identification: Lesser always has much longer, triangular 'spurs'.

Lesser Frigatebird *Fregata ariel*

L 71–81 cm, **WS** 175–193 cm. Pantropical. 3 ssp, 1 in region: *ariel* (E Indian Oc and W–C Pacific). Locally common throughout. Suspected to breed on Uma (Karimata, Bor) and Popaja (N Sul), but unconfirmed; also possible breeder on Gunungapi. Generally pelagic, but often soars along coasts, or even over land. Usually singly or small groups but occasionally roosting in large groups on small offshore islands. **ID** Highly variable with age and sex. All plumages have triangular white axillary 'spurs' angled outwards. **M** otherwise all black (apart from difficult-to-see red gular pouch). **F** white breast patch, concave at rear so as to avoid most of belly; black head and throat. **Imm** as Ad but has head buff to whitish and variable white mottling on belly. **Juv** as Imm with broad, straight blackish breast band; triangular white belly patch with white axillary spurs extending outward from front corners. **SS** See larger Christmas and Great Frigatebirds.

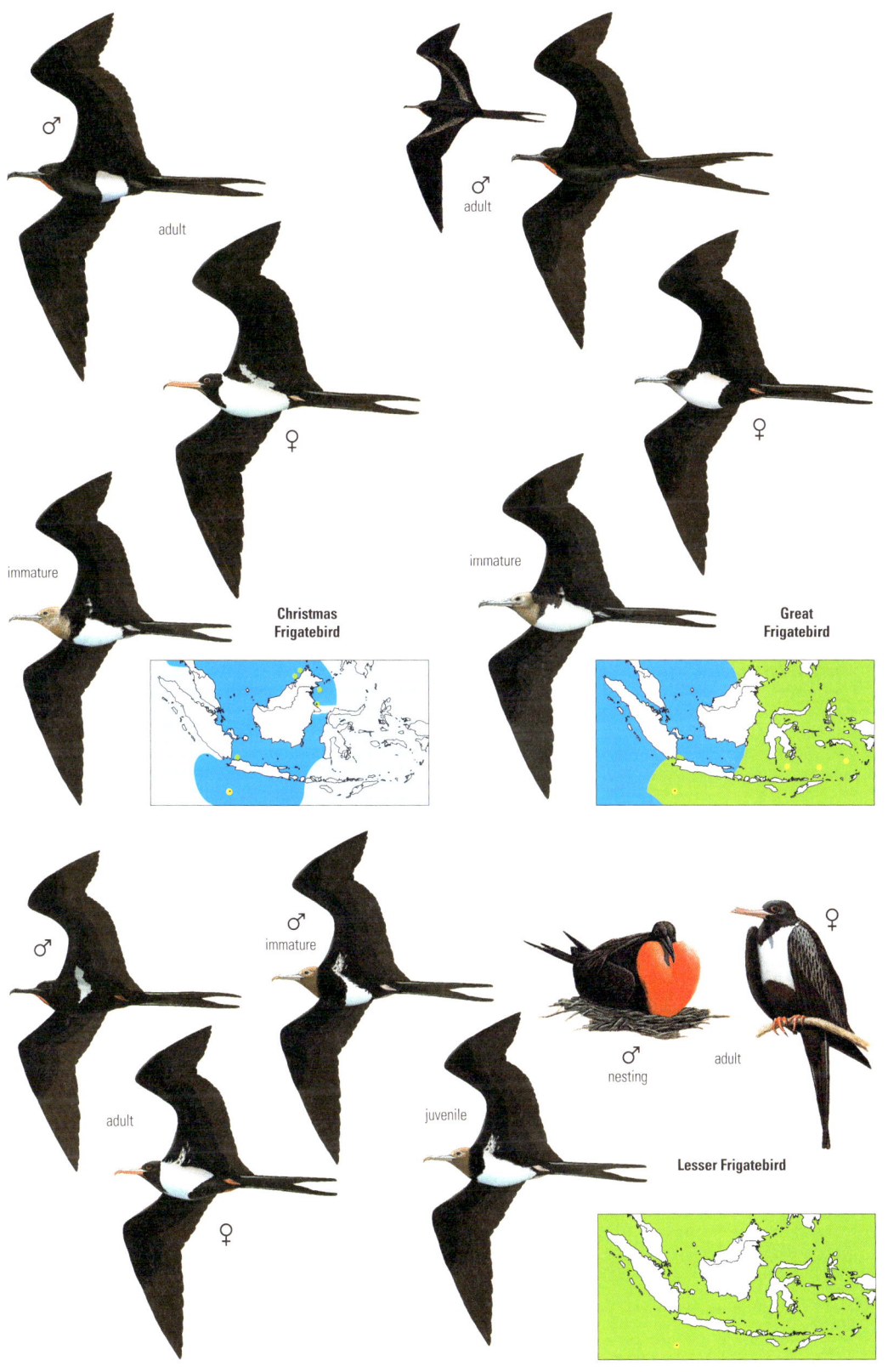

♂

adult

♀

immature

Christmas Frigatebird

♂

adult

♀

immature

Great Frigatebird

♂

immature

♂

adult

♀

juvenile

♂ nesting

adult ♀

Lesser Frigatebird

6 species in region

Large, long-necked, long-billed waterbirds found in a variety of coastal and inland wetland habitats, including forest wetlands. Typically feed by probing in shallow water or marshland. Often seen perched or roosting in high trees.

Glossy Ibis *Plegadis falcinellus*

L 55–65 cm, **WS** 88–105 cm. Cosmopolitan. Monotypic. Locally common resident Jav. Scarce but possible resident Sul. Vagrant elsewhere in region. Freshwater lakes, wetlands, wet rice fields, grasslands, coastal mudflats and mangroves, <1350 m. **ID** Relatively small all-dark ibis. **Ad br** deep chestnut with purple and green gloss and metallic green wings; feathering around base of bill white. **Ad non-br/Imm** duller with white streaking on head and neck.

Black-headed Ibis *Threskiornis melanocephalus*

L 65–76 cm. S–SE–E Asia. Monotypic. Was an occasional migrant to N Bor, last recorded 1975 (6 records between Oct–Feb). Formerly locally common resident Sum and N Jav but now rare. Coastal swamps, grassland and wet rice fields. Usually solitary or small groups. **ID** Large ibis with black legs and bill. In flight bare pink skin on 'arm' visible on underwing. **Ad** all white with naked black skin on head and neck. **Ad br** shows loose ruff of white feathers on lower neck, elongated grey scapulars and tertials and occasional yellow wash to underparts. **Imm** as Ad but head and hindneck feathered grey and rest of neck feathered white.

Australian Ibis *Threskiornis molucca*

L 65–75 cm. Aus. 2 ssp, 1 in region: *molucca* (Aus, Mol). Uncommon migrant to S Mol. Apparently resident on Seram, at least. Found in wide variety of open habitats but particularly swamps, grassland, coastal mudflats, lakes and ponds. **ID Ad** similar in appearance to Black-headed Ibis but bare black skin restricted to upper neck and head; long, loose black tertial plumes overhang tail. **Imm** similar to Ad but with sparse white feathering on head and neck and shorter bill.

White-shouldered Ibis *Pseudibis davisoni*

L 60–85 cm. SE Asia. Monotypic. Rare, recent confirmed records only from Mahakam R catchment in E Kalimantan. Older records and recent unconfirmed reports from Barito R catchment in C Kalimantan and Sarawak. Forested rivers and streams in lowlands. **ID** Large ibis with long decurved yellow-grey bill and red legs. **Ad** generally brown-black with bluish wash to wings; on head bare black skin bordered by band of bare white skin from chin to nape; wings show white patch on lesser-coverts, sometimes only visible in flight. **Imm** duller and browner than Ad.

Royal Spoonbill *Platalea regia*

L 74–81 cm. Aus. Monotypic. Uncommon but widespread migrant E of Jav. Formerly bred in W Jav but now absent. May breed locally on Mol. Freshwater and coastal wetlands, mudflats and mangroves. **ID** Large, predominantly white spoonbill with black legs and black bill; black facial skin extends from forehead around eye to upper chin. **Ad br** long white nape plumes (sometimes tinged yellow) and variable yellowish band on lower breast; black facial skin broken by a small patch of red on forehead and small crescent of yellow skin above eye. **Ad non-br** lacks yellow breast patch and nape plumes. **Imm** additionally lacks red and yellow facial marks and shows narrow black tips to primaries in flight. **SS** Smaller Imm Black-faced Spoonbill is extremely similar but has slightly less extensive black facial skin. Adults are easier: apart from slightly less extensive facial skin, Black-faced never shows red or yellow patches on face as in Royal. Breeding Black-faced has shorter nape plumes. Extralimital **Yellow-billed Spoonbill** *P. flavipes* (Aus), possible in LS and Mol, shows pinkish-buff facial skin, legs and bill in all plumages.

Black-faced Spoonbill *Platalea minor*   Ⓥ

L 60–79 cm, **WS** 110 cm. E–SE Asia. Monotypic. Single record from Brunei (Jan–Apr 1985). Wintering birds inhabit wetlands, coastal marshes, lakes and mudflats. **ID** Predominantly white spoonbill with black legs, black (**Ad**) or greyish (**Imm**) bill and black facial skin extending from forehead around eye to base of bill. **Ad br** yellowish band on lower breast and fairly long white nape plumes (sometimes tinged yellow). **Ad non-br** lacks yellow breast band and plumes. **Imm** as Ad non-br but additionally shows narrow black tips to primaries in flight. **SS** See Royal Spoonbill. Larger extralimital **Eurasian Spoonbill** *P. leucorodia* (Palaearctic), possible vagrant to GS, particularly N Bor, similar but lacks black facial skin, leading to eye being almost completely engulfed by white feathering; Ad non-br/Imm Eurasian has only tip of bill pale (vs distal third in Black-faced).

Glossy Ibis

Black-headed Ibis

Australian Ibis

White-shouldered Ibis

Royal Spoonbill

Black-faced Spoonbill

CICONIIDAE
Storks

5 species in region

Large, long-necked and long-legged waterbirds with dagger-like bills. Often seen soaring high on large wings. Occupy a variety of habitats from remote forested wetlands to dry open country. Feed on a variety of small ground-living prey caught by probing in shallow wetland vegetation.

Asian Woollyneck *Ciconia episcopus*

L 75–91 cm. S–SE Asia to Phil. 2 ssp: *episcopus* (S–SE Asia, Phil; migrates to N Sum), *neglecta* (Jav–Flores, Sul). Previously considered conspecific with extralimital African Woollyneck *C. microscelis* but split based on pronounced plumage differences. Uncommon resident and migrant. Open swamps, flooded fields, rice fields, grassland and dry crops. Occasionally on coasts. **ID** Relatively small stork with blackish bill tinged red towards tip, blue-grey facial skin (more extensive in *neglecta*) and dull red legs. In flight has all black underwing and chest, contrasting with white belly. **Ad** predominantly greenish-purple glossed black plumage and black cap; neck and vent contrastingly white. **Imm** as Ad but black parts of plumage duller brown; bare parts duller. **SS** See Storm's Stork.

Storm's Stork *Ciconia stormi*

L 75–91 cm. Sundaic. Monotypic. Single previous record from Jav (1920). Scarce and local in wetlands, streams and ponds within undisturbed lowland forests, including secondary forest and peat swamp, in singles and pairs. Often seen circling high over forest in mid-morning thermals, sometimes in small numbers (< 10). Solitary tree nester in undisturbed areas of forest. **ID** Relatively small stork with red legs, striking red bill and orange-yellow facial skin surrounding eye and black cap. In flight all black underwing. **Ad** predominantly black, apart from white vent and neck; black extends onto sides of neck. **Imm** black parts duller brown and bare parts duller. **Voc** Crow-like "krauu" when taking off. **SS** In flight, similar to Asian Woollyneck but has black underneck, and more rounded (less square-ended) wings.

Black-necked Stork *Ephippiorhynchus asiaticus* [V]

L 110–137 cm, **WS** 190–218 cm. S–SE Asia, Aus. 2 ssp, 1 in region: single record of a skull recorded in Jav in 1908 probably relates to *australis* (Aus). Found in coastal and freshwater wetlands, rivers, lakes, beaches and mudflats. **ID** Very large distinctive stork with striking black-and-white plumage and long straight bill. In flight white wings with black band through greater coverts. **Ad** white with black head, neck, wing stripe and tail; bluish-green sheen to head and neck in good light; legs red. **Imm** dull brown; black legs.

Milky Stork *Mycteria cinerea*

L 95–100 cm. SE Asia. Monotypic. Widespread and rare, but very locally common resident Sum, Jav and S–SE Sul. Occasional vagrant Bali, LS. Nesting colonies suffer from high human predation. Coastal and freshwater wetlands, mudflats, sandbanks, estuaries, wet rice fields, rivers, lakes in both forested and open areas. Usually solitary or small groups, occasionally large flocks. Populations in MPen and Singapore now constitute mixture of released and/or escaped Milky Storks, extralimital Painted Storks *M. leucocephala* (S-SE Asia), and their hybrids, which may in time appear in Sum. **ID** Large, predominantly white stork with black flight feathers and tail; large, heavy, slightly drooping bill. In flight shows contrasting white coverts and black outerwing. Black feathers on wing coverts and/or breast and pink flush on tertials indicate signs of Painted Stork admixture. **Ad br** bright red facial skin, bright yellow bill and red legs. **Ad non-br** bare parts duller. **Imm** head, neck and upperparts greyish-brown. **SS** See Asian Openbill. From other storks in flight by white underwing coverts.

Asian Openbill *Anastomus oscitans* [V]

L 68–81 cm, **WS** 145–149cm. Monotypic. Vagrant Batam (thousands, Dec 2019), Riau, Sum (several, Aug 2020) and N Sum (hundreds, Sep-Nov 2020); with recent rapid southward expansion through MPen in the wake of introduction of Golden Apple Snail *Pomacea canaliculate*, a crop-pest, Openbill likely to become frequent visitor to Sum. Open country, rice fields, wetlands, suburban areas. Forms large flocks, often soaring high. **ID** Diagnostic "cleft beak". **Ad br** largely white plumage with black wings and lores; broad, horn-coloured bill; pink legs. In flight all-black tail and outerwings, contrasting with pale underwing coverts; black inner greater coverts on upperwing. **Non-br/imm** plumage distinctly 'dirty' greyish. **SS** Larger Milky Stork has conventional yellow stork bill (not horn-coloured and cleft) and diagnostic red facial skin. In flight Openbill's leg projection equals tail length, while Milky's is 2-3 times longer. With practice, distant Milky can be told by massive wingspan and long protruding neck, while Openbill has shorter, less spread-out primary fingers and wings of a roughly equal width as neck. Openbill shows black (not white) inner greater coverts on upperwing. From all other storks in flight by pale underwing coverts.

Lesser Adjutant *Leptoptilos javanicus*

L 123–129 cm. S–SE Asia. Monotypic. Scarce to locally common in coastal and freshwater wetlands, mudflats, mangroves, estuaries, wet rice fields, rivers, lakes. Found in open and forested habitats, usually solitary or small groups. Flies with neck retracted like a heron. **ID** Very large with distinctive bare yellowish skin on head and neck and huge horn-coloured bill; wings and back uniformly black; underparts uniformly white. In flight huge black, parallel-sided wings with white inner lesser coverts on underwing; yellow neck pouch visible from some distance. **Ad br** narrow white edging to scapulars, tertials and inner greater-coverts; bare skin on head redder in colour. **Imm** duller with downy feathering on head and neck.

Asian Woollyneck

Storm's Stork

adult ♀

♂

immature

Black-necked Stork

Milky Stork

non-breeding

Asian Openbill

Lesser Adjutant

ARDEIDAE
Herons, Egrets and allies
24 species in region

Large family of long-necked, long-legged waterbirds with long dagger-like bills. Closely associated with wetland habitats where they stab at prey in shallow water or vegetation. Some species are highly conspicuous while others are cryptically coloured and shy, hiding within vegetation. One mostly white subgroup, the so-called 'egrets', don unusual plumes and exhibit brightly-coloured tracts of bare skin (on legs, face and bill) during breeding season, lasting only few weeks of the year, but are most often seen in their common non-breeding attire.

Eurasian Bittern *Botaurus stellaris* [V]

L 64–80 cm. **WS** 100–130 cm. Africa, Eurasia. 2ssp, 1 in region: *stellaris* (breeds Palaearctic, winters to S). Recorded from Brunei (Jan-Mar 1987), S Sum (Oct 1978), Sabah (Feb 1985, Jan 2020). Extensive reedbeds, marshes, thick grassy areas, ditches; fresh and brackish water. Despite size, inconspicuous and highly secretive, usually found when flying low over marshland and reedbeds, or flushed up. **ID** Cryptic brown plumage finely spotted and vermiculated; broad black moustachial stripe on warm-brown face, white throat and black crown; greenish-yellow bare parts; in flight only feet extend beyond tail; densely barred wing with paler-brown upper-wing coverts. **Voc** Call: single, nasal, hoarse, slightly downslurred "argh", sometimes repeated, in flight. **SS** Imm Black-crowned and Rufous Night Herons have strong white spotting on wings, lack black moustachial stripe. In flight both appear smaller, slighter, with faster wingbeats and have plain, unbarred flight feathers.

Yellow Bittern *Ixobrychus sinensis*

L 30–40 cm, **WS** 45–53 cm. S–E–SE Asia, Phil, Aus. Monotypic. Widespread migrant and resident. Solitary and secretive within reedbeds, rice fields, swampy lakes and pond margins, <1500 m. **ID** In flight blackish-brown flight feathers contrast strongly with pale buff wing-coverts and back. **M** blackish cap, tawny-brown hindneck and upper back; underparts pale buff. **F** similar but cap dark grey-brown and some streaking on back and neck. **Imm** heavily streaked brown above and below. **Voc** Song: slow repeated "wo...wo... wo...". Call: staccato "kik kik" when flushed. **SS** Perched ad Yellow has less contrasting pale wing covert patch and is much buffier and paler, less maroon or chestnut on upperparts than M Schrenck's, but occasionally bright Yellow Bitterns can be confusing: M Schrenck's always has sharp division between rufous upperparts and pale-buff breast, whereas bright Ad Yellow Bittern has rufous-buff upperparts slowly blending into off-white underparts. In flight, Schrenck's has uniformly pale underwing, lacking Yellow Bittern's contrasting black flight feathers (while both share contrasting black upperwing contrast). Yellow Bittern never shows pale-spotted appearance of Fem or Imm Schrenck's and Cinnamon.

Schrenck's Bittern *Ixobrychus eurhythmus*

L 33–39 cm, **WS** 55–59 cm. Breeds E Asia; winters to S. Monotypic. Now rare migrant. In region, forest edge, secluded, dark swampy areas, tiny wetlands, rarely open areas and large wetlands. Solitary and secretive. **ID M** blackish crown, tail and flight feathers; maroon to dark chestnut face, hindneck, back and rump; pale buff wing-coverts form prominent contrasting patch; underparts whitish-buff. **F/Imm** neck, back, tail and wings heavily spotted white with less prominent or absent buff wing patch; white underparts heavily streaked brown. **Voc** Song (often at night): a repetitive "woo woo woo...", twice as fast as Yellow's, rarely given in region. Call: low, gruff "wek" in flight. **SS** See Cinnamon and Yellows Bitterns. **AN** Von Schrenck's Bittern.

Cinnamon Bittern *Ixobrychus cinnamomeus*

L 40–41 cm. S–SE–E Asia, Phil. Monotypic. Common migrant and resident. Reedbeds, rice fields, swampy lake and pond margins. Solitary and secretive. **ID M** upperparts and wings uniformly bright orange-cinnamon; underparts pale buff with some black streaking on flanks. **F** dark-brown crown and upperparts becoming warmer brown on flight feathers; upperparts (but not head) finely spotted buff; whitish to buff underparts heavily streaked brown. **Imm** as fem but colder brown overall, with heavier, whiter spotting on upperparts. **Voc** Song (often given at night or dawn): a soft repeated "kok kok kok..."; secondary song an even series of deep "aaa aaa" notes. Call: when flushed sharp "kwok" or frog-like "kik kik kek", less harsh than Yellow. **SS** In flight, Schrenck's has contrasting black (not bright rufous) flight feathers on upperwing, but Fem and especially Imm of both species can be extremely similar when perched, unless flight feathers are partly exposed: Schrenck's has larger white spots above, at least on mantle against a darker-maroon background, while on Cinnamon spotting is often buffier, less contrasting and less well-defined. Cinnamon has bright reddish tertials, which – when seen on perched bird from behind – become the safest ID mark. Also see Yellow Bittern.

Black Bittern *Ixobrychus flavicollis*

L 54–66 cm, **WS** 80 cm. S–SE-E Asia, Phil, Aus. 3 ssp, 2 in region: *flavicollis* (S–SE-E Asia, GS, Sul, Phil); *australis* (Aus, Mol, LS). Uncommon resident (Sul, Mol, perhaps GS) or scarce migrant (GS, LS). Solitary and secretive inhabitant of wooded streams, swamps, mangroves and reedbeds. **ID** Stocky. **M** uniformly black but yellowish throat and upper breast with heavy brown streaking; *australis* has throat and breast white with brown streaking and yellow restricted to sides of neck only. **F** black upperparts tinged brown; dark chestnut ear-coverts. **Imm** with pale buff edging to upperparts. **Voc** Song: a mellow, booming "BOoOUHh" at 15 sec intervals. Repeated short "nyuk".

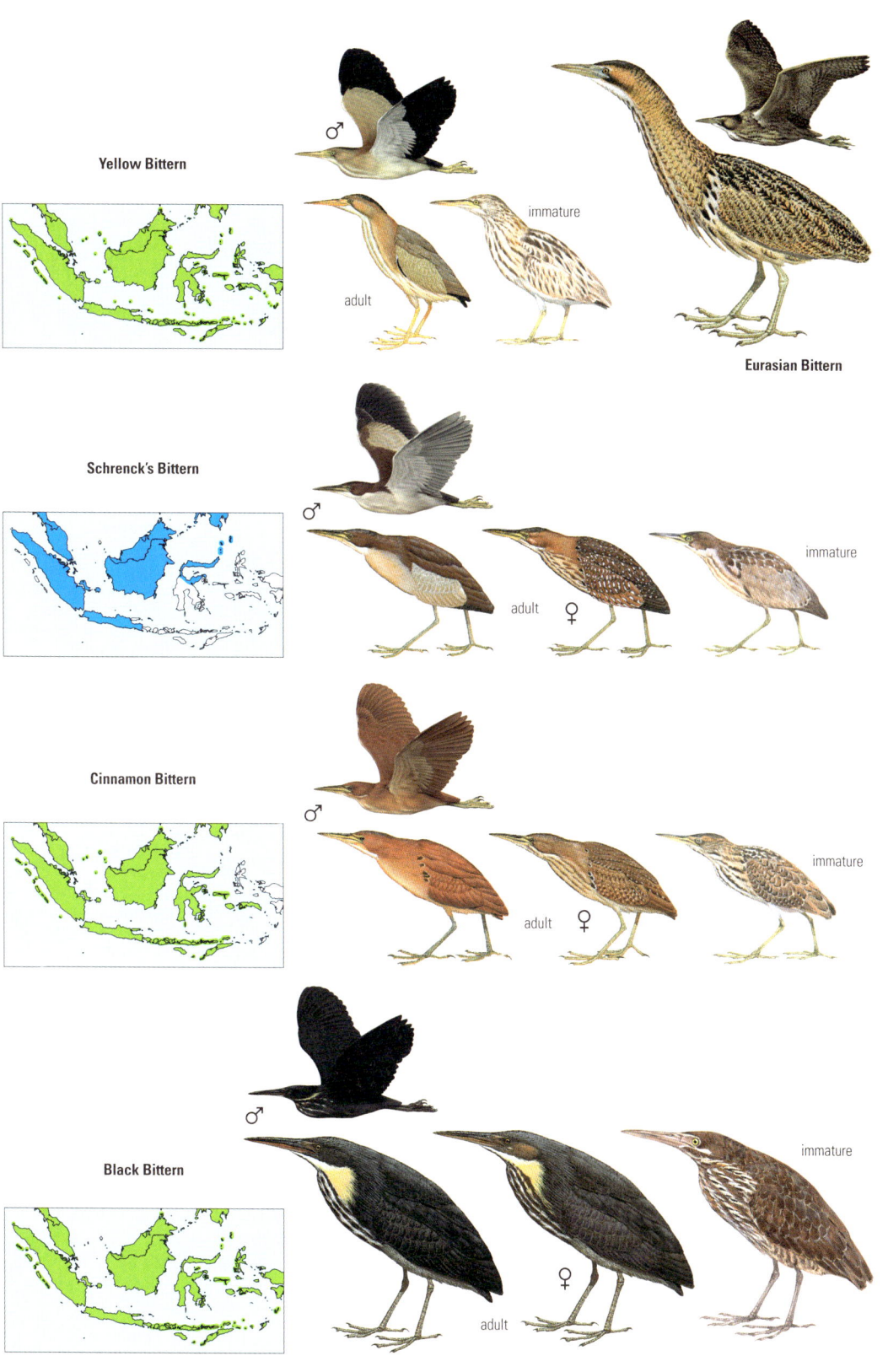

Yellow Bittern

Eurasian Bittern

adult

immature

Schrenck's Bittern

adult ♀

immature

♂

Cinnamon Bittern

adult ♀

immature

♂

Black Bittern

immature

♂

adult ♀

Striated Heron *Butorides striata*

L 35–48 cm, **WS** 52–60 cm. Cosmopolitan species with pronounced but complicated regional variation. If divided into regional species, as is probably appropriate, Indonesian birds would belong to the Old World '**Little Heron**' *B. atricapillus* (including African populations) or the Asian '**Mangrove Heron**' *B. javanica*. 15–30 ssp, 4 in region: *javanica* (SE Asia, GS, Sul, Phil, Taiwan, LS to Tanimbar); *spodiogaster* (Andamans, Nicobars, W Sum Is.); *moluccarum* (Mol); *amurensis* (E Asia; wintering to GS and N Sul). More races may need to be recognized in region (see ID), additional research required. Common resident and migrant. Mangroves, rivers, lakes, ponds, coasts, exposed coral flats and wet rice fields, <1200 m. Typically shy and solitary, usually keeping close to dense cover. **ID** Small, stocky, dark-coloured heron with long, straight black bill and short, yellow-green legs. **M** black crown and nuchal crest; black gape stripe running below eye; cheeks and throat variably white; rest of body grey with pale edging to mantle and wing-coverts; *spodiogaster* and *amurensis* darker grey overall with more contrasting white throat. **F** as male but generally browner in tone. In both sexes, wintering *amurensis* larger than other ssp, but there is overlap. Ssp *moluccarum* has buffier-brown cast to underparts than *javanica* (even in **M**), but birds on LS and Tanimbar ("*steini*") are intermediate. **Imm** generally brown with paler, heavily streaked underparts and white spotting on wing-coverts. **Voc** Loud explosive "kyawk" when flushed. Advertising call low-pitched "chyooow". **AN** Mangrove Heron, Green Heron, Green-backed Heron, Little Heron.

Black-crowned Night Heron *Nycticorax nycticorax*

L 58–65 cm, **WS** 90–100 cm. Cosmopolitan (except Aus). 4 ssp, 1 in region: *nycticorax* (Old World). Locally common. Forages nocturnally in wetlands, ponds, streams and mangroves. Nests and roosts communally in noisy colonies. **ID** Medium-sized, stocky heron with large head, short bill and short neck. **Ad** black crown, nape and back; long white nuchal plumes; forehead and chin white; underparts white to pale grey; wings darker grey. **Imm** white underparts heavily streaked brown; rest of body dull brown with heavy white spotting on upperparts and fine white streaking on head. **Voc** Coarse, nasal "quark" in flight, often at night. **SS** See Rufous Night Heron and Eurasian Bittern.

Rufous Night Heron *Nycticorax caledonicus*

L 55–59 cm, **WS** 95–110 cm. Phil to Aus. 6 ssp, 2 in region: *manillensis* (Phil, Bor; possibly vagrant to N Sul); *australasiae* (Jav and Sul E to Aus). Widespread but uncommon resident, probably also occasional migrant. Known to hybridise with Black-crowned Night Heron. Generally nocturnal, foraging in swamps, ponds, lakes, forest-lined rivers, mangroves etc. **ID** Slightly smaller than Black-crowned Night Heron but otherwise similar in build. **Ad** generally rich rufous brown throughout (darker in *manillensis* than in *australasiae*) apart from paler whitish belly and distinctive black cap and nape. **Imm** white underparts heavily streaked brown; rest of body brown, often darker on crown and nape, with heavy white spotting on upperparts and fine white streaks on head. **Voc** Similar to Black-crowned, loud peevish "kyok" or "kwok" in flight, often at night. **SS** Imm Black-crowned Night Heron very similar; often indistinguishable. Imm Black-crowned usually has orangish-yellow (sometimes pure yellow) eyes, Imm Rufous probably always yellow, never orangish. Imm Rufous tends to have more reddish/cinnamon-hued tone to wing-coverts, as opposed to a uniform cold-brown tone to entire wings, but this mark is not constant. Rufous also tends to develop blackish contrast on cap earlier, starting in imm white-spotted stage, while Black-crowned often (not always) retains white-streaked, brown cap for longer, but younger immatures of both species indistinguishable in this mark. See also Eurasian Bittern. **AN** Nankeen Night Heron.

Japanese Night Heron *Gorsachius goisagi* ⬛V

L 49 cm, **WS** 87 cm. Breeds E Asia; winters to Phil. Monotypic. Recorded Brunei (Oct 1985, Nov 1988), Halmahera (Dec 1874), N Sul (Feb 1885), Sabah (Apr 2010, at 1110 m), Mantanani off Sabah (Nov 2018). Streams in mature forest. Nocturnal, skulking and elusive. **ID** Small, stocky, short-necked, short-billed heron. **Ad** head and sides of neck brown with purple tinge; rest of upperparts duller brown with fine dark vermiculations; underparts paler with faint brown mottling and barring as well as strong black streaks down the centre of body; bill grey; lores yellow-green, or blue when breeding. In flight shows chestnut tips to black primaries; upperwing coverts and tertials chestnut. **Imm** similar to Ad but lacks rufous tones and has blackish crown and fine white streaking/spotting on neck and breast. **SS** See Malayan Night Heron.

Malayan Night Heron *Gorsachius melanolophus*

L 47–51 cm. Breeds S–SE-E Asia, Phil; winters to S. 2 ssp, 1 in region: *melanolophus* (most of range). Scarce migrant to GS, with additional records as far E as Mol, indicating it's a largely overlooked migrant to most of region, with breeding confirmed on Peleng (Oct 2020). Wooded streams and rivers, forest and edge. Nocturnal, skulking and elusive. **ID/SS** Similar in build to Japanese Night Heron but with longer, less stout bill. **Ad** as Japanese but shows black crown with prominent nuchal crest (absent in Japanese); face warm buff-brown (purple-tinged in Japanese); bright blue lores (usually, but not always, greenish in non-br Japanese); more distinct brown barring and mottling on underparts than Japanese. In flight shows white (not chestnut) tips to black outermost primaries. **Imm** as Imm Japanese but extensively white-spotted upperparts, especially on crown and nape (vs finer, buffier vermiculations and spotting, never white in Japanese), giving more striking appearance (vs overall browner, vermiculated look of Japanese); crown and nape can start to show black feathers from young age (Japanese never shows black here); yellowish lores and orbital skin can show traces of blue in Malayan.

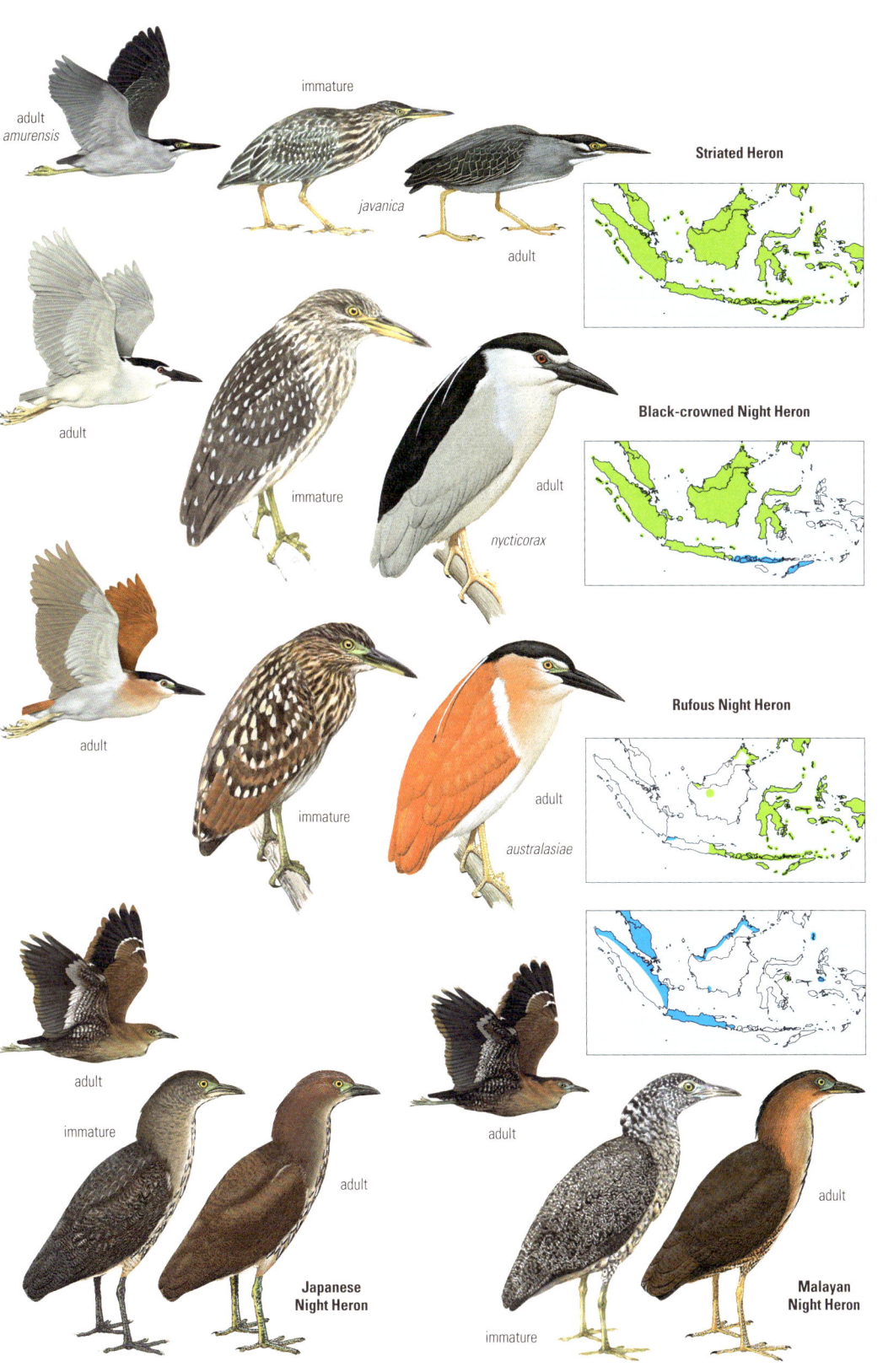

adult
amurensis

immature

Striated Heron

javanica

adult

adult

Black-crowned Night Heron

immature

adult

nycticorax

adult

Rufous Night Heron

immature

adult

australasiae

adult

immature

adult

adult

adult

**Japanese
Night Heron**

immature

adult

**Malayan
Night Heron**

Chinese Pond Heron *Ardeola bacchus*

L 42–52 cm, **WS** 79–90 cm. Breeds E Asia; winters to SE Asia–Phil. Monotypic. Rare migrant. Freshwater swamps, wet rice fields, ponds and streams. Usually solitary or small flocks. **ID** Small heron with bittern-like appearance when foraging; wings, rump and tail white. **Ad br** head, neck and breast rich dark chestnut with prominent nape plumes; mantle grey-black; legs yellow to pinkish-orange. **Ad non-br/Imm** chestnut parts turning whitish with heavy grey brown streaking; mantle dull brown; legs dull yellow-green. **SS** See Javan Pond Heron.

Javan Pond Heron *Ardeola speciosa*

L 45 cm. SE Asia, Phil. 2 ssp, 1 in region: *speciosa* (Phil, GS, Sul, W LS). Common (Jav, Bali) to locally common (Bor, Sum, Sul, W LS) resident. Freshwater swamps, wet rice fields, coastal lagoons, estuaries, mudflats, mangroves, lakes, rivers and ponds, <1350 m. **ID** white wings, rump and tail. **Ad br** head and neck sandy-yellow becoming richer chestnut towards lower breast; prominent nape plumes; mantle grey-black. Legs yellow to pinkish-orange. **Ad non-br/Imm** head, neck and breast whitish with heavy grey-brown streaking, mantle dull brown; legs dull yellow-green. **Voc** Occasionally a soft "hoo-hoo". **SS** Ad non-br may be inseparable from non-breeding Chinese Pond Heron, which often has slightly larger bill.

Grey Heron *Ardea cinerea*

L 84–102 cm, **WS** 155–175 cm. Old World. 4 ssp, 1 in region: *jouyi* (E–SE Asia, Phil). Widespread migrant and resident. Freshwater and coastal swamps, rivers, estuaries and rice fields. Breeds in conspicuous colonies but otherwise usually solitary, <900 m. **ID Ad** head, neck and breast white with black eyestripe extending to form small nuchal crest; foreneck and breast streaked black; wing-coverts, back and tail grey with contrasting darker grey-black flight feathers conspicuous in flight. **Imm** white feathering replaced by dull grey; crown blackish. **Voc** In flight a loud, harsh "kah-AHRK".

Purple Heron *Ardea purpurea*

L 70–90 cm, **WS** 110–145 cm. Old World. 4 ssp, 1 in region: *manilensis* (S–SE–E Asia, Phil). Common resident and migrant throughout. Freshwater swamps, reedbeds, wet rice fields, lakes, ponds, rivers, mangroves, coasts, <1500 m. **ID** Large with long slender neck. **Ad** generally grey and chestnut with prominent black stripes on head and neck and paler throat and foreneck. **Imm** duller and predominantly rufous brown. **Voc** In flight as Grey Heron, but shorter, less resonant "krrek".

Great-billed Heron *Ardea sumatrana*

L 114–115 cm. SE Asia, Phil to Aus. Monotypic. Uncommon, predominantly coastal, including beaches, rocky coasts, reefs and lagoons. Occasionally also inland along forested rivers and coastal swamps. Usually solitary. **ID** Very large grey-brown heron with large blackish bill and dark legs. **Ad br** uniformly grey-brown with small nuchal crest, hackles on foreneck and plumes on back; belly paler grey-brown. **Ad non-br** plumes and hackles reduced or absent. **Imm** uniformly rufous brown; lacks crest, plumes and hackles. **Voc** Song: series of loud, deep, resonant roars "hwurHUHhur'hur", usually at night. Call: loud, harsh croak when flushed.

White-necked Heron *Ardea pacifica*   ☑V

L 76–106 cm, **WS** 147–160 cm. Aus. Monotypic. Single record on Yamdena (Oct 2013). Freshwater wetlands, occasionally also salt and brackish water. Usually alone. **ID** All white head and neck; dark grey bill and legs; prominent white patch on shoulder of wing, visible in flight and at rest. **Ad br** back and wings sooty black; breast and belly grey-brown, streaked white; lanceolate maroon plumes on back and (less pronounced) on breast. **Ad non-br** like Ad br but has greyish spotting forming a line down foreneck. **Imm** more heavy dark spotting on neck and lanceolate plumes absent. **Voc** Usually silent; utters guttural croaking sounds if alarmed. **SS** From Imm Pied Heron by larger size, presence of white wing patches and bare part colouration.

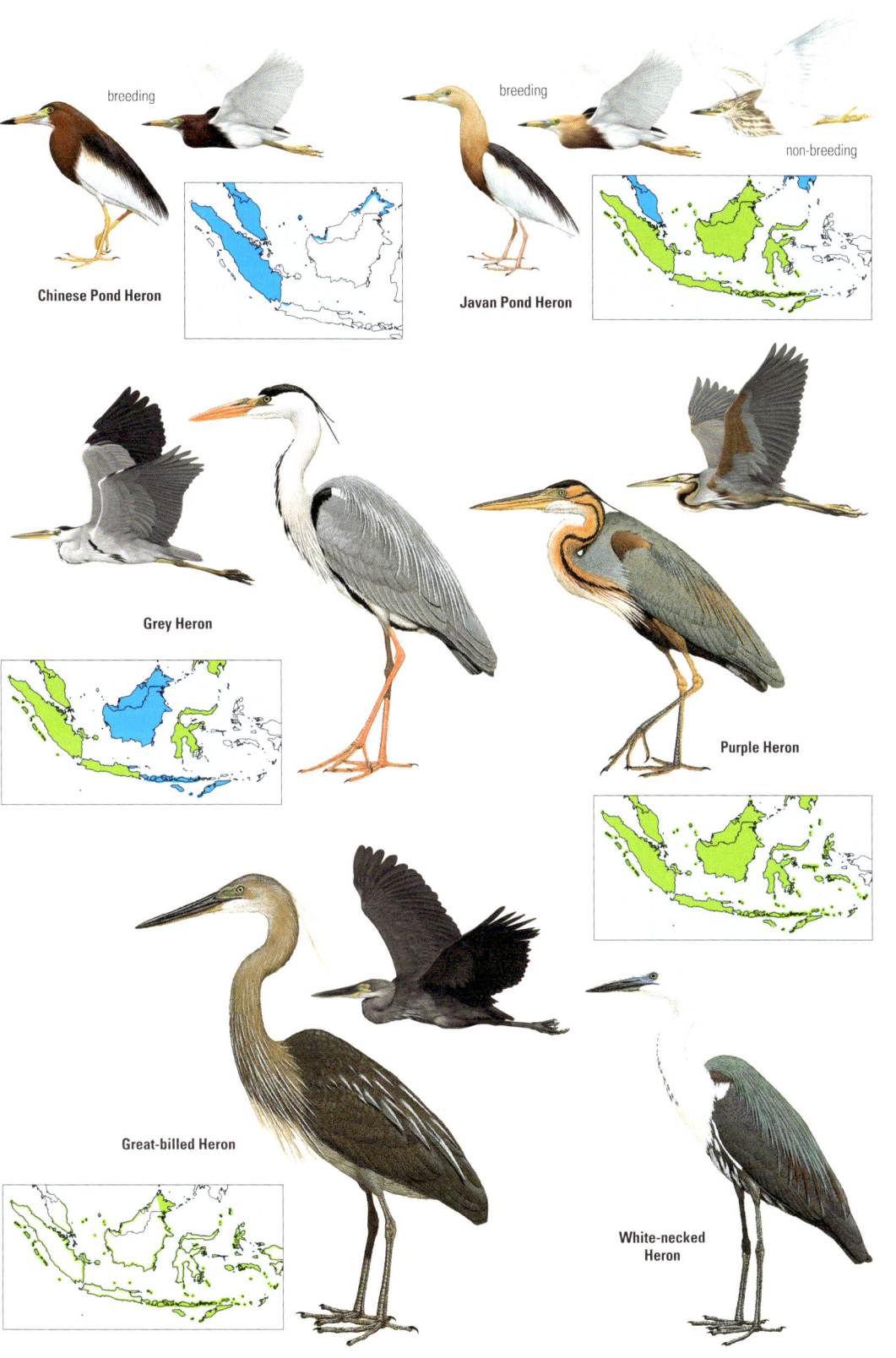

breeding

non-breeding

Chinese Pond Heron

Javan Pond Heron

Grey Heron

Purple Heron

Great-billed Heron

White-necked Heron

Great Egret *Ardea alba*

L 80–104 cm, **WS** 140–170 cm. Cosmopolitan. 4 ssp, 1 in region: ssp *modesta* (S-E-SE Asia to Aus) sometimes considered monotypic species '**Eastern Great Egret**' because of differences in breeding attire. Widespread migrant and local breeder in coastal swamps, mangroves, mudflats, lakes and wetlands. **ID** Large, with a long, S-shaped neck. Long bill briefly black in breeding plumage, otherwise yellow; lores greenish; gape line extends to rear of eye; legs black, or with pink tibia in breeding season. **Ad br** shows lacy plumes on lower back. **Voc** (i) Raucous "rraah"; (ii) hoarse, rattled crow-like "keraaaa-keraaaa"; (iii) rarely short "kok". **SS** See Intermediate Egret. **AN** Great White Egret.

Intermediate Egret *Ardea intermedia*

L 65–72 cm, **WS** 105–115 cm. Africa, S–SE–E Asia to Aus. 3 ssp, 2 in region: *intermedia* (S–SE–E Asia to W Indo Archipelago); *plumifera* (Aus to E Indo Archipelago). The three races often divided into three species (*plumifera* then called '**Plumed Egret**') due to pronounced differences in breeding bare parts colouration. Geographic distribution of taxa in C Indonesia still insufficiently known; non-breeders may overlap. Widespread migrant and local breeder in W, uncommon migrant in E. Freshwater and coastal wetlands, wet rice fields and mudflats, <1300 m. **ID** Medium-sized, halfway between Great and Cattle. Bill relatively short, yellow; black bill tip often present for most of the year in *intermedia* but usually absent in *plumifera*. Bill briefly turns black (or orange-red in *plumifera*) in breeding season; lores greenish-yellow; gape line does not extend beyond eye; legs black (with reddish tibia in *plumifera* during breeding). **Ad br** has lacy plumes on back and lower breast but not neck. **Voc** Various discordant sounds especially during breeding season. **SS** Very similar to Great Egret, but identifiable with experience. Smaller than Great, but often appreciable only in direct comparison with identical posture. Intermediate's neck on average shorter, not as S-shaped. Intermediate's gape line does not reach behind eye as in Great. Black tip to yellow bill often present year-round in Intermediate (ssp *intermedia*), usually absent in Great (or of very small extent), but can be identical at start or end of breeding season; also note that Intermediate's ssp *plumifera* usually lacks black bill tip also. Bill proportions may be best mark: bill is roughly 1–1.5 times the length of the remaining head in Intermediate, but usually about twice the length in Great. Compared to Intermediate, the smaller, slimmer coastal-dwelling Pacific Reef and non-br Chinese Egrets have longer, more dagger-like bill (much thinner at base), greenish (not black) legs and less yellow bill; Pacific Reef additionally has much shorter tibia. See also Cattle Egret.

Cattle Egret *Ardea ibis*

L 46–56 cm, **WS** 88–96 cm. Cosmopolitan. 2 ssp, 1 in region: ssp *coromanda* (S–SE–E Asia to Aus) often considered a monotypic species '**Eastern Cattle Egret**' because of breeding plumage differences. Common resident and migrant throughout. Grassland, cultivation, freshwater swamps, marshes and rice fields, <1600 m. Often in large flocks associating with cattle. Groups fly to roosts or colonies in neat lines (perhaps more so than other egrets). **ID** Small, stocky with short neck, legs and bill; chin feathering forms characteristic 'jowl'. **Ad br** white with bright rusty orange head, neck, upper breast and back; bill yellow with reddish base; legs pinkish orange. Breeding plumage is seen only during few weeks of the year. **Ad non-br** all white; bill uniformly yellow; legs dark grey, green or black. **Voc** Short, gruff "guwaa". **SS** Intermediate Egret is larger, longer-necked, longer-billed, mostly has black tip to yellow bill and often blacker legs.

Chinese Egret *Egretta eulophotes*

L 65–68 cm. Breeds E Asia; winters to SE Asia–Phil. Monotypic. Uncommon to rare migrant. Coastal mudflats, rocky coasts and sandbanks. Distinctive crouched foraging posture, energetically chasing and lunging at prey. **ID** Medium-sized egret, similar in size to Little Egret but usually shows proportionately thicker neck and shorter legs, with stout and symmetrically dagger-shaped bill. **Ad br** shows shaggy crest on crown and nape, blue-grey lores, yellow-orange bill, reddish at base; black legs with yellow toes. **Ad non-br** (most of year) and **Imm** blackish bill with yellow base to lower mandible and below nostril of upper mandible; typically dark greyish-yellow lores; greenish-yellow legs with varying amounts of black on tarsus. **SS** Chinese looks intermediate in shape between longer-legged, slimmer-billed Little and shorter-necked, shorter-legged, stouter, more dagger-billed Pacific Reef Egret. Combination of black legs, yellow bill and yellow 'shoes' is diagnostic during breeding. Shaggy crest often still present in non-br, also diagnostic (always absent in Pacific Reef, and restricted to two filamentous plumes in Little). Otherwise non-br Chinese best told from Little and Pacific Reef by aggressive facial expression caused by downward kink (versus straight line) along upper edge of loral skin. Colour combination of facial bare parts on non-br egrets is key: Chinese has greyish-yellow lores combined with dark brown bill and orange-yellow bill base (often extending to entire lower mandible), Little ssp *nigripes* has bright-yellow lores combined with thin black bill and yellow or whitish lower mandible base, Little ssp *garzetta* has greyish lores combined with thin black bill and whitish lower mandible base, and Pacific Reef has variably coloured but often all-yellow, heavy bill. Chinese has steeper forecrown, while head peaks more towards rear on Little. See also Intermediate Egret. **AN** Swinhoe's Egret.

Little Egret *Egretta garzetta*

L 55–65 cm, **WS** 88–106 cm. Old World to Aus. 3 ssp, 2 in region: *garzetta* (Old World; common migrant in W Indo Archipelago); eastern ssp *nigripes* (NG; common migrant and local resident throughout Indo Archipelago, spreading west through Sum) exhibits pronounced differences in bare parts colouration and sometimes separated as '**Black-footed Egret**' *E. nigripes* (incl. extralimital ssp from Aus), but intermediate individuals seen at least in N Sul region and in mixed N Sum breeding colonies. Extent of interbreeding requires further investigation. Coastal and freshwater wetlands, rivers, lakes, mudflats and wet rice fields, <1500 m. **ID** Slender, delicate, medium-sized; snow-white plumage. Loral skin greyish to greyish-pink (*garzetta*) or yellow (*nigripes*). Slender black bill; base of lower mandible white (sometimes yellow in *nigripes*), can turn pale pink in both ssp during breeding. **Ad br** shows two elongated nape plumes; lacy breast and lower back plumes; black legs (with yellow 'shoes' only in *garzetta*). **Ad non-br** (most of the year) and **Imm** have legs from bluish-green to black with yellow 'shoes' (*garzetta*) or from greenish-yellow to blackish with greenish tibia and yellow soles (*nigripes*). **Voc** Gargling "bloob-bloob … bloob-bloob…" when courting. Crow-like calls when quarrelling. **SS** See Chinese and Pacific Reef Egrets.

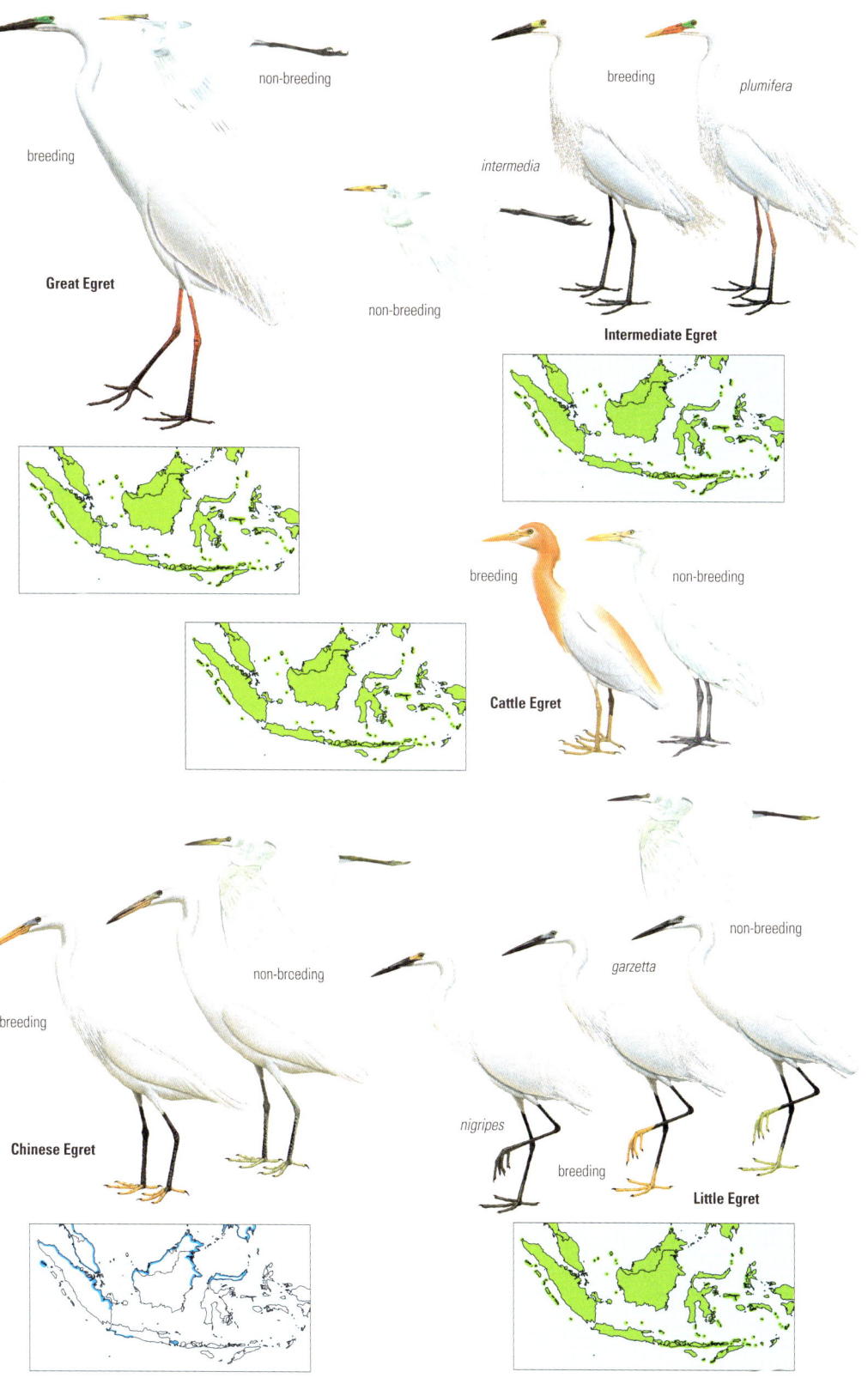

non-breeding

breeding

Great Egret

breeding

intermedia

non-breeding

plumifera

Intermediate Egret

breeding

non-breeding

Cattle Egret

non-breeding

breeding

Chinese Egret

non-breeding

garzetta

nigripes

breeding

Little Egret

Pacific Reef Egret *Egretta sacra*

L 58–66 cm, **WS** 90–100 cm. E-SE Asia to Aus. 2 ssp, 1 in region: *sacra* (most of range). Locally common throughout. Rocky and sandy coasts, offshore islands and exposed coral flats where forages by creeping and lunging at prey. **ID** Medium-sized egret with short, thick neck and rounded wings; bill long, narrows evenly from thick base; relatively short, thick, yellow-green legs with brighter yellow toes. Dimorphic plumage. **Dark morph** almost entirely blue-grey with some white on chin; bill dark yellow-grey. **White morph** entirely white; bill colour shows seasonal and probably sexual variation but often pale yellow with dark culmen. **Imm** may be intermediate with heavy grey flecking on neck, back and wing-coverts. **Voc** Occasional insignificant screech. **SS** Imm/non-br Little Egret is slimmer, more elegant, with taller black legs only exceptionally greenish, and a bill that is thinner, shorter and usually much blacker. See also Chinese and Intermediate Egrets. In flight, short foot projection: no other white egret has only feet extending beyond tail.

Pied Heron *Egretta picata*

L 43–55 cm. Aus. Monotypic. Widespread but patchy resident and migrant in E. Known to breed in S Sul, and likely breeds Tanimbar. Freshwater and coastal swamps, lakes, rice fields, mangroves and tidal mudflats. **ID** Distinctive small black and white heron with yellow bill and legs. **Ad br** has nuchal plumes, white hackles on lower neck and lanceolate plumes on back. **Ad non-br** has hackles and plumes reduced. **Imm** head and neck white, with occasionally grey-brown wash to crown. **SS** See White-necked Heron.

White-faced Heron *Egretta novaehollandiae*

L 65–69 cm, **WS** 106 cm. Aus. Monotypic. Very locally common resident and migrant in LS, Mol. Occasional in Bali, rare elsewhere. Freshwater and coastal wetlands, rivers, ponds and wet rice fields, <1500 m. **ID** Medium-sized egret. Generally uniformly grey, with contrasting dark flight feathers, dark bill and yellow-green legs. **Ad** white forehead, face, chin and throat; chestnut plumes on lower breast. **Imm** as Ad but less white on forehead and face, and lacks plumes.

PELECANIDAE
Pelicans

3 species in region

Massive; long beak and a large throat pouch used for catching prey and draining water from the scooped-up contents before swallowing. Gregarious, found on large inland or coastal waters, or in groups on nearby land. In flight often soar.

Great White Pelican *Pelecanus onocrotalus* [V]

L 140–175 cm, **WS** 245–295 cm. Africa, Eurasia. Monotypic. At least 5 records Java (Jun-Aug, Nov; 1883-1993); single records Sum (1863) and Bali (Apr 1981). Lakes, large rivers and estuaries. **ID** Huge and distinct waterbird; bill yellow-orange. **Ad** predominantly white with contrasting black flight feathers. **Imm** duller grey-brown. **SS** From Spot-billed Pelican by large size, white (not black or dark-grey) tail, and a generally whiter appearance (Ad). Great White has a more black-and-white underwing contrast (Ad, Imm) versus a generally duskier wing with less black flight feathers in Spot-billed. Australian Pelican has black on tail, rump band, inner upperwing coverts and bold ulnar underwing bar; all these body parts are white on Great White Pelican. Australian also has bluish-grey (not pinkish to yellow) legs and small yellow ocular disk separated from beak (versus extensive, variably coloured bare facial skin connected with beak).

Spot-billed Pelican *Pelecanus philippensis* [V]

L 127–152 cm, **WS** 250 cm. S–SE Asia. Monotypic. Historically occasional winter vagrant to Sum (1907, winter 1981-82, March 1986) and W Jav (regularly recorded Apr-Oct until 1940s, last in 1992). Global population (especially in SE Asia) has plummeted in last few decades. Lakes, large rivers and estuaries. **ID** Smallish pelican; bill pink-dull yellow. **Ad** dull, off-white to grey plumage. **Imm** dull grey-brown. **SS** See larger Great White and Australian Pelicans.

Australian Pelican *Pelecanus conspicillatus*

L 152–183 cm, **WS** 244–260 cm. Aus. Monotypic. Regular migrant in E, occasionally irruptive, with flocks numbering well over 100. Irregular W to N coast of Jav. Single record Sum. Lakes, large rivers and estuaries, sometimes in large flocks. **ID** Huge, with predominantly black-and-white appearance; bill pinkish. **Ad** white body; upperwings black apart from white patch on outer coverts; black bands across rump and tail. **Imm** slightly duller, with black feathering replaced by dark brown. **SS** From smaller Spot-billed by black rump band (versus white rump), black-and-white (versus white) upperwing coverts, and black ulnar underwing bar (versus all-white underwing coverts). See also Great White Pelican.

Pacific Reef Egret

white morph

dark morph

Great White Pelican

adult

immature

Pied Heron

adult

immature

Spot-billed Pelican

adult

immature

White-faced Heron

Australian Pelican

PANDIONIDAE
Osprey
1 species in region

Large birds-of-prey with distinctive wing shape in flight. Feed by diving to catch fish from just below the water surface while still in flight. Found within a wide variety of open aquatic habitats, both on coast and inland.

Osprey *Pandion haliaetus*
L 50–66 cm, **WS** 127–174 cm/2.6. Cosmopolitan. 4 ssp, 2 in region: *haliaetus* (Palaearctic; winters S to W Indonesia, N Sul and Phil); *cristatus* (Aus W to Sul and Jav). Occasionally divided into multiple species based on mtDNA, plumage and structure, prompting monotypic treatment of *haliaetus* as '**Palaearctic Osprey**' and *cristatus* as '**Australasian Osprey**'. Scarce resident and migrant in coastal areas, but also inland lakes and rivers, <1000 m. Mostly singly. Slow shallow elastic wingbeats, arched wings when gliding/soaring. Aerial display involves undulating flight high up with dangling feet. **ID Ad M** white below and dark-brown above; short-tailed with long pointed wings; white fluffy crown; wide dark eyestripe; brown streaked gorget. **F** slightly larger with broader, more extensive streaks on breast-band. Ssp *cristatus* smaller with whiter head, narrower eyestripe and more pronounced gorget. **Imm** pale-scaled above; dirty crown. **Voc** (i) Series of staccato "kyep-kyep-..." slightly rising in pitch; (ii) plaintive, wheezy "wEELP". **SS** Sea-eagles, fish-eagles, and whitish morphs of hawk eagles and honeybuzzards are more compact with broader wings held more straight, and usually differ in various details of head colouration.

ACCIPITRIDAE
Kites, Hawks and Eagles
57 species in region

Large and diverse family of birds-of-prey, ranging in size from medium to very large. Occupy a diverse range of habitats from forest to open country, typically feeding by diving or swooping on prey. Many species are resident, while several are strongly migratory, often being encountered in large flocks at key migration points.

Black-winged Kite *Elanus caeruleus*
WS 31–37 cm, **L** 77–92 cm/2.3. Africa, S Palaearctic to NG. 2-4 ssp, 1 in region: *hypoleucus* (Indo Archipelago, Phil). Uncommon resident in open country, cultivation. Now rare on Jav. Graceful flight almost owl-like at low speed, with protruding head; long, pointed but broad-armed wings; often hovers and uses exposed perches. Frequently crepuscular. **ID Ad** large-headed, pale grey above with blackish shoulders; white below with variably dark black under-primaries; black-rimmed red eyes. **Imm** browner with streaky crown. **Voc** Usually silent: (i) high-pitched whistled, upslurred "week"; (ii) sharp, wheezy "kyeeek". **AN** Black-shouldered Kite.

Jerdon's Baza *Aviceda jerdoni*
L 40–49 cm, **WS** 80–117 cm/2.0. S–SE Asia, Phil. 5 ssp, 3 in region: *jerdoni* (SE Asia; winters to Sum where recently proven to breed); *borneensis* (Bor); the distinct-looking ssp *celebensis* (Sul, Banggai, Sula) can possibly be elevated to species level ('**Sulawesi Baza**') as in some respects intermediate between Jerdon's and Pacific Baza. Uncommon in lowland and hill forest, partly cleared areas, mangroves and *Albizia* plantations. Flies with soft, flexible wing-beats; wings V-shaped when gliding, flat when soaring; display with dive and upward swoops. **ID** Brownish kite with long, dark crest and short legs; yellow eyes (may be brown in **F**); all-dark bill; black mesial stripe on white throat (often indistinct in **F**); dark brown upperparts; unmarked vent; two narrow and one broad dark tail bars with white tail tip. **M** vividly chestnut-banded on underparts; chest and face unmarked pale-greyish becoming darker towards crown; **F** tawnier (less grey) head and chest and paler rufous bars on underparts. Ssp *borneensis* smaller with more rufous sides of head and neck in both sexes (lacking greyish). Ssp *celebensis* even smaller with bluish-grey face; dark blue-grey upperparts; rich chestnut breast with chestnut underpart bars thicker than white bars. **Imm** as fem but head and breast more streaked, underparts barring spottier, and tail bars of more even width (often showing fourth bar). **Voc** Plaintive mewing "pe-WEEoh"; in aerial display "kip-kip-kip...". **SS** Crested Goshawk has smaller, more protruding head with shorter crest, yellow (not dark) cere, shorter and narrower wings, even tail bands and much denser barring on underparts. Some Oriental Honeybuzzards have surprisingly similar colouration but are much larger, with unusual "dove-like" protruding head, a much shorter crest, and – on the underwing – with numerous fine bands in between the prominent bars on the flight feathers, creating a marbled or scaly background impression. Sunda Honeybuzzards (which are also much larger and differently-shaped, but with long crests) do not usually exhibit Jerdon's Baza's barred underparts colouration. With practice, Jerdon's Baza can be told in flight from all previous species by typical *Aviceda* wing shape with pinched-in wing base and broad-spread "fingery" flight feathers. Wallace's Hawk Eagle is more massive with shorter wings, longer and feathered tarsus and much denser underparts barring.

Pacific Baza *Aviceda subcristata*
L 35–46 cm, **WS** 80–105 cm/2.3. Aus. 13 ssp, 5 in region: *pallida* (Manawoka, Gorong, Kai); *reinwardtii* (Boano, Seram, Ambon, Haruku); *rufa* (Morotai, Halmahera, Ternate, Tidore, Bacan, Obi); *stresemanni* (Buru); *timorlaoensis* (LS to Tanimbar and islands off S Sul). Pronounced subspecific variation across range (in region especially *rufa*) suggests more than one species may be involved; more study needed. Uncommon in lowland forest, wooded cultivation, <550 m. Flies with slow, loose, shallow, but sometimes deeper beats; display constitutes upward flight with few deep laboured beats, brief stop and almost vertical dive, this repeated many times. **ID** (*stresemanni*) **Ad** point-crested with long broad wings and short legs; greyish-brown upperparts (perhaps browner in **F**); whitish throat, grey head and breast; bold dark bars (browner in **F**) on white belly; tail with two narrow interior, one broad subterminal bars. Ssp *reinwardtii* slightly smaller and darker above; *timorlaoensis* and the smaller, paler *pallida* are paler above with greyish-brown (**M**) or rufous-brown (**F**) belly bars (less conspicuous in *pallida*); *rufa* reddest, with rufous wash on neck and breast and with rufous-brown belly bars. **Imm** often more rufous and obscurely barred underparts than Ad. **Voc** High-pitched reedy, quick "HEE-chok", repeated at 1 n/s or faster.

♀ ♂ *haliaetus*

♂ *cristatus*

Osprey

Black-winged Kite

borneensis ♂

♂

♀ *jerdoni*

celebensis

Jerdon's Baza

♂

rufa

stresemanni

Pacific Baza

Black Baza *Aviceda leuphotes*
L 28–35 cm, **WS** 64–74 cm/2.2. S–SE–NE Asia; winters to S. 3 ssp, 1 in region: *syama* (SE–E Asia; winters S to Sum, Jav). Scarce in forest, various habitats on migration, <1500 m. Gliding and soaring on level wings. **ID Ad** chunky point-crested black hawk with white and chestnut on the wings; white underparts with black throat, upper breast and vent; variably brown bars on underparts (blacker towards breast, more rufous towards belly). In flight underwing and primary tips black, white primaries, grey secondaries. **Imm** as Ad with white and dark streaks. **Voc** Quavering plaintive "CHAWee-yee".

Sulawesi Honeybuzzard *Pernis celebensis*   **E**
L 50–58 cm, **WS** 110–125 cm/2.1. Monotypic. Uncommon resident in forest and partly cleared areas, <2000 m. Typical honeybuzzard flight with longish elastic wings. **ID** Small head, weak bill, long neck and long tail. **Ad** brown above; whitish throat with black mesial stripe; dark-streaked rufous breast; finely dark-and-white barred belly; typical honeybuzzard tail with 2–3 narrow interior and one wide subterminal dark bars. **Imm** paler overall with more (and more evenly wide) tail bars. **Voc** Mostly silent; single, plaintive "kyew"; 2-note high-pitched curlew-like, voice-cracking call, with intervals of several seconds to minutes. **SS** Striking plumage mimic of Sulawesi Hawk Eagle, but latter is told in all ages by stockier build, shorter wings, feathered legs, different vocalisations and a more intensely, evenly black-and-white barred tail. Oriental Honeybuzzard is longer-winged (in flight), often shows small erect crest (when perched) and – despite great variability – never really shows dark-streaked rufous breast in combination with such distinct, dense belly barring as in Sulawesi Honeybuzzard.

Oriental Honeybuzzard *Pernis ruficollis*
L 46–64 cm, **WS** 110–155 cm/2.4. Breeds S–E–NE–N Asia, Phil; winters SE Asia. 3 ssp, 2 in region: *orientalis* (breeds N–NE–E Asia; winters S to Phil, GS and LS); *ruficollis* (breeds S Asia into northern SE Asia; winters at least to Jav). Traditionally considered conspecific with Sunda Honeybuzzard as '**Crested Honeybuzzard**' *P. ptilorhynchus*, but different in DNA and morphology. Fairly common in forest, open wooded country, <1800 m. Small numbers of immatures summer in region, commonly so in LS. Wings mostly held level with deep, downward, elastic wingbeats. **ID** Tiny crest (often fully absent in *orientalis*). Yellow unfeathered legs. Ssp *orientalis* is slightly larger and has more pointed wings with distinctly longer primaries: the distal 'finger' portions of primaries make up 30–35% of wing length in *orientalis* as opposed to 20–25% in *ruficollis*. Variable plumage. **Ad** black bill, dark brown upperparts (blacker in *orientalis*); usually dark moustache and black gorget (more distinct in *orientalis*) bordering pale throat; underparts from whitish, creamy-buff to dark brown, mostly with dark streaks on breast and white-and-brown/rufous barring on belly (on average heavier in *orientalis*). **M** dark-brown eyes, grey face; black tail with broad central pale bar; underwing with black tips, broad black trailing edge and few rows of black banding on white flight feathers. **F** yellow eyes, browner face (with little grey); two narrow and one broad unevenly spaced dark tail bars, and underwing lacking distinct trailing edge but with more even banding on white flight feathers. **Ad** *ruficollis* in both sexes known to appear in rare **melanistic morph**, which is all-black apart from distinct pale throat and black-and-white pattern on tail and flight feathers. **Imm** with yellow eye, cere and base to black bill; plumage even more variable; underparts from whitish to dark brown; pale primary covert patch on upperwing; fine underwing

barring forms paler pattern on primaries and darker pattern on secondaries; has finer, more even tail barring than Ad. **Voc** Similar to Sunda but usually silent in region. **SS** Sunda Honeybuzzard's much longer flapping crest (absent or vestigial in Oriental) often visible when perched (in both Ad and Imm), and Sunda always has yellow/orange eye (dark in Ad M Oriental), but difficult to separate in flight: *orientalis* has much longer primaries than Sunda with a more conspicuous 'hand', but Oriental ssp *ruficollis* possibly not safely separable from Sunda on wing shape. Ad Sunda's underparts are generally all-brown with whitish "drop bars", never showing the pale background with or without dark breast streaking typical for Oriental. Unlike Oriental, imm Sunda probably never occurs in dark morph; imm Sunda overwhelmingly shows pale-contrasting head, but so do some imm Oriental Honeybuzzards. Rare melanistic morph of Ad *ruficollis* is almost identical to that of Sunda's ssp *torquatus*, making crest length imperative for identification. Imm from similarly-coloured imm hawk eagles (Blyth's, Wallace's, Changeable, Flores, Javan) by slimmer build, much longer (less rounded) wings lacking the distinct pinched-in wing base of hawk eagles, smaller (pigeon-like) head with much less massive bill, much smaller crest than some hawk-eagle species, and unfeathered legs. See also Jerdon's Baza, Eurasian Buzzard, Sulawesi Honeybuzzard, Imm Bonelli's Eagle and dark morph Booted Eagle.

Sunda Honeybuzzard *Pernis ptilorhynchus*
L 52–68 cm, **WS** 104–150 cm/2.0–2.2. Sundaic, Palawan. 3 ssp, 2 in region: *ptilorhynchus* (Jav); *torquatus* (Sum, Bor, MPen). For taxonomy see Oriental Honeybuzzard. Scarce in lowland forest and woodland, even entering suburban parks, <2100 m. Flight action and silhouette as in Oriental. Wings only held above horizontal during undulating, butterfly-like sky-dance. **ID** Long crest (slightly shorter in *torquatus*). Yellow unfeathered legs. Yellow or orange eyes. Extremely variable plumage with different morphs. **Ad** black bill. **Ad brown morph** rich rufous to dark brown above and below, with white "drop bars" on lower breast and belly; often creamy throat with or without black gorget and/or median stripe; in flight tail and flight feathers as in Oriental; ssp *torquatus* more variable in colouration, often duller above, more greyish on head and less clearly barred below. **Ad Tweeddale morph** occurs only in *torquatus* and closely mimics plumage of Blyth's Hawk Eagle: blackish body with white throat and bold white barring below. **Ad melanistic morph** all-black with blackish-brown underparts, sometimes showing white barring on belly. **Imm** with yellow base to black bill; creamy to buff-cinnamon below; pale forewings; usually whitish head with or without dark mask and crown. **Voc** High-pitched, screaming "KEE-yooo" and "YEeeewww". **SS** See extremely similar Oriental Honeybuzzard, also Eurasian Buzzard, Jerdon's Baza and dark morph Booted Eagle. Ad and imm mimic respective plumages of Mountain Serpent-Eagle and *Nisaetus* hawk eagles, such as Blyth's (mimicked by Tweeddale's morph and imm), Wallace's (mimicked by imm), Javan (mimicked by imm) and Changeable (mimicked by melanistic morph and imm); however, hawk eagles have a less pigeon-like head and neck with a more massive bill, a fatter build, shorter and more rounded wings characteristically pinched in at the base, and fully-feathered legs. Ad hawk eagles do not show the distinct uneven banding pattern of Sunda Honeybuzzard's undertail. When perched Wallace's, Javan and Blyth's Hawk Eagles have long, upright crest more erect than Sunda Honeybuzzard's, while Changeable Hawk Eagle lacks crest.

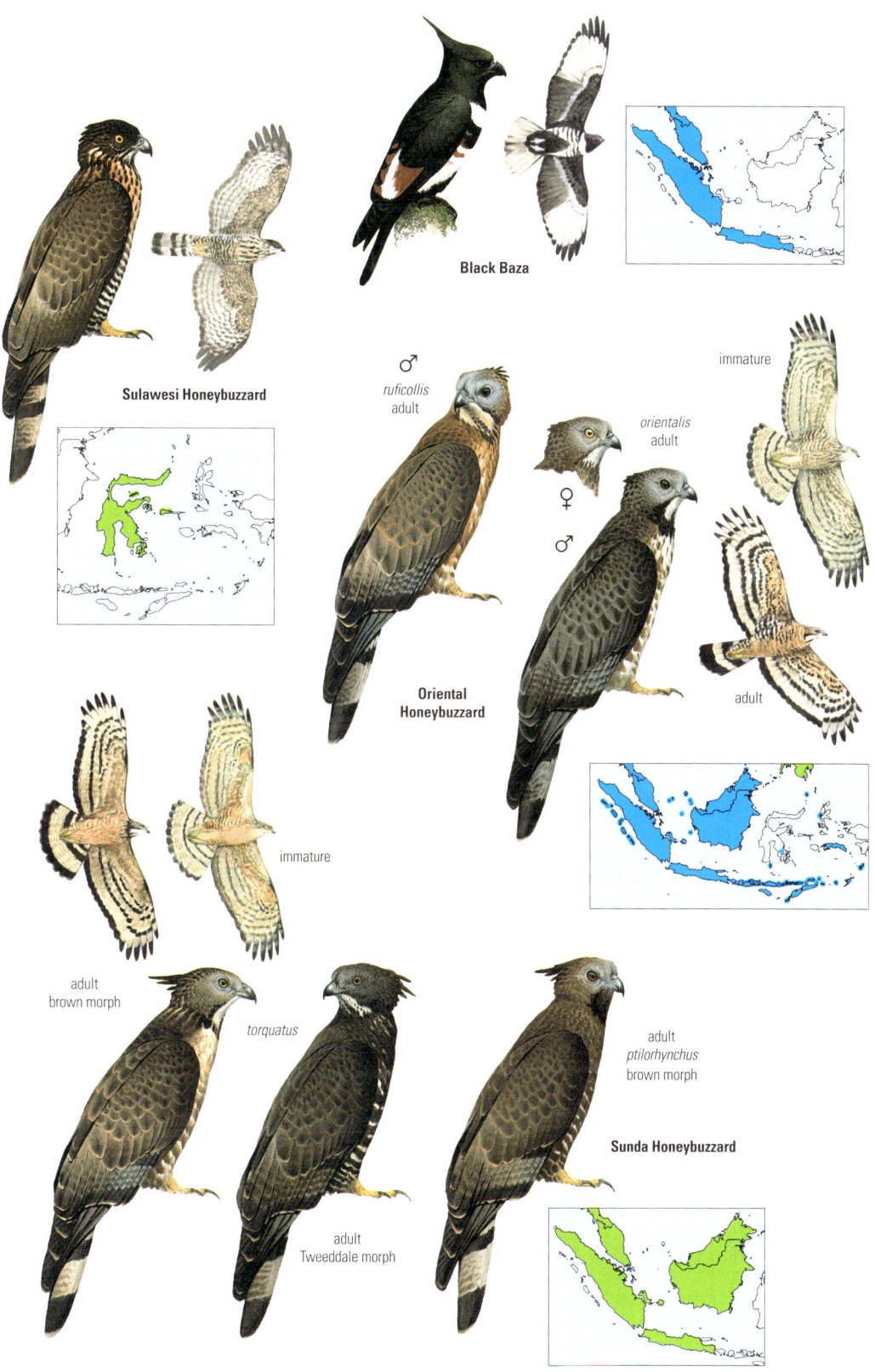

Sulawesi Honeybuzzard

Black Baza

♂
ruficollis
adult

orientalis
adult

♀

♂

immature

**Oriental
Honeybuzzard**

adult

immature

adult
brown morph

torquatus

adult
Tweeddale morph

adult
ptilorhynchus
brown morph

Sunda Honeybuzzard

Himalayan Griffon *Gyps himalayensis* [V]

L 103–110 cm, **WS** 260–289 cm/2.5–2.6. Breeds C–E Asia; non-breeders wander S–SE Asia. Monotypic. One record from Bintan, Riau (Dec 2007). Could occur in any open country habitat in N or W. **ID Ad** huge with thick pale bill, pale bare head and sandy buff body, white neck ruff; almost whitish underwing-coverts contrasting strongly with black flight feathers and tail. **Imm** head similar to Ad but body and underwing-coverts darkish brown with pale streaks. **SS** Records of a single vulture in N Sul in 1876 and of two birds in Brunei in Nov 1977 could refer to above species, or **White-rumped Vulture** *G. bengalensis* (**L** 75–85 cm, **WS** 205–220 cm; S–SE Asia; **Ad** blackish body, white rump and neck-ruff, strongly contrasting whitish underwing-coverts with black leading edge; **Imm** very similar to that of Himalayan Griffon but much smaller and slightly shorter-tailed; without size comparison the best mark is Imm White-rumped's all-black bill), or **Slender-billed Vulture** *G. tenuirostris* (**L** 80–95 cm, **WS** 196–258 cm; S–SE Asia; **Ad** sandy brown body and upper/underwing-coverts moderately contrasting with black flight feathers, indistinct pale neck-ruff, all-black head, bill and neck [although distal upper mandible can have pale sheen]; **Imm** very similar to Ad with pale down covering part of neck and head; all age groups best told from Ad Himalayan Griffon by smaller size, underwing-coverts sandy-brown [not whitish] and black head, neck and bill). **AN** Himalayan Vulture.

Sulawesi Serpent-eagle *Spilornis rufipectus* [E]

L 46–54 cm, **WS** 105–120 cm/2.2. 2 ssp: *rufipectus* (Sul and adjacent islands); *sulaensis* (Banggai, Sula). Singly; often perches on conspicuous treetops. Common in various forest types and adjoining grasslands, <2200 m. Soars with the wings held level. **ID Ad** dark with brown upperparts; dark-grey head; chestnut breast; white-and-brown barred belly; yellow facial skin and cere. In flight, broad and rounded dark wings with heavy brown, white and black speckling on underwing-coverts and black-and-white barring on flight feathers. Wings and tail show one diagnostic single, broad white subterminal band along trailing edge. Ssp *sulaensis* perhaps paler and smaller. **Juv** very different: white head and underparts with black eye mask, yellow facial skin (and often cere) and dark breast streaks; brown upperwings and heavy brown-mottled back; underwing-coverts lightly rufous with black streaks; underside of flight feathers and tail white with distinct dark bars. **Imm** becomes progressively darker. **Voc** Like Crested Serpent-eagle, a long-drawn "(ke)HEEeew", further a nervous, high-pitched "KlHihiw" or "keew kiwi". **SS** For those unfamiliar with typical serpent-eagle jizz, juv can be confused with various pale imm or light morph raptors, but face (dark mask, facial skin and cere) and dark breast streaks and back blotches diagnostic.

Crested Serpent-eagle *Spilornis cheela*

L 50–74 cm, **WS** 109–169 cm/2.2. S–SE Asia (including Palawan). ~20 ssp, 10 in region: *bido* (Jav, Bali); *malayensis* (MPen, Sum, Anambas); *pallidus* (N Bor) and *richmondi* (S Bor); many small-island races exhibit dwarfism and sometimes strikingly different plumage, incl. the following (in the region): *batu* (Batu) not usually split; *abbotti* (Simeulue) and *sipora* (Mentawai) often separated as '**Simeulue**' and '**Mentawai Serpent-eagles**', respectively; *asturinus* (Nias) often separated as '**Nias Serpent-eagle**';

baweanus (Bawean) sometimes separated as '**Bawean Serpent-eagle**'; *natunensis* (Natunas, Belitung) rarely separated as '**Natuna Serpent-eagle**'. More phenotypic and DNA data needed to clarify taxonomy. Common in forest, mangroves, plantations, <1200 m. Glides with level wings, soars in shallow V. **ID** (*bido*) Very dark brown body; black on (mostly flat) crest, tail, cheeks and some of wings; clearly white spotted shoulders and belly (sometimes forming bars); broad wings and medium-long tail; broad pale subterminal band in both underwing and tail; white along trailing edge in wing characteristic in flight. Ssp *malayensis* generally has brown of underparts clearly paler than upperparts, with white belly spots and bars often reaching onto lower breast; however, great individual variation exists, with some dark *bido*-like individuals seen as far N as MPen. Ssp *richmondi* is paler brown above than previous two with lighter rufous underparts and greyish cheeks; adjacent *pallidus* resembles *richmondi* but is larger and even paler overall. Ssp *batu* is smaller than adjacent *malayensis* and has much paler upper- and underparts with a generally greyish cast, especially in face. Ssp *asturinus* is probably the smallest Indonesian form, even tinier than adjacent *batu* with apparently no size overlap but otherwise similarly pale in plumage. To the north and south of pale *asturinus*/*batu* occur two dark forms, *abbotti* and *sipora*, both smaller than adjacent mainland *malayensis* but larger than *asturinus* (with *abbotti* slightly larger than *sipora*): *abbotti* often has fine blackish bars on dark-brown breast and perhaps a narrower pale subterminal tail and wing band, while *sipora* is the darkest form, almost lacking contrast between upper- and underparts. Ssp *baweanus* is smaller and much paler than adjacent *bido*, resembling *malayensis* in colouration but showing narrower white tail band. Ssp *natunensis* is smaller (with apparently no size overlap) than adjacent *pallidus* and darker on upper- and underparts, perhaps approaching *malayensis* in colouration. **Juv** very different: almost identical to juv of Sulawesi Serpent-eagle. **Voc** The most characteristic calls are "(ki-ki-) KLEEee(-ah-ah)" and a rising "ka-ka-ka-ka". **SS** In hilly Bor, see Mountain Serpent-eagle. For those unfamiliar with typical serpent-eagle jizz, juv can be confused with various pale imm or light morph raptors, but face (dark mask, facial skin and cere) and dark breast streaks and back blotches diagnostic.

Mountain Serpent-eagle *Spilornis kinabaluensis* [E]

L 55–58 cm, **WS** 118–129 cm/2.2. Monotypic. Montane forest; scarce in Sabah, fairly common in Sarawak and Kalimantan, 1100–2900 m, rarely down to 750 m. **ID/SS** Similar to Crested Serpent-eagle (limited overlap at mid-elevations with Crested ssp *pallidus*) but longer-winged. **Ad** darker overall, with all-black head, throat and upper breast (compared to pale face and throat in *pallidus*); Mountain's underparts dark maroon-red with white spotting confined to belly (not pale-buff with more extensive white spotting). Mountain has much broader white tail band reaching vent and redder underwing-coverts contrasting more with white wing band. In flight shows black (not brown) underwing coverts with white spotting. **Juv** undescribed and doubtfully distinguishable from Crested; however presumed **Imm** like Ad but with white-flecked crown and throat. **Voc** Complex call "quick-quick-quick-kele-heeeelleeeee", the latter also given singly; more drawn-out than similar calls of Crested Serpent-eagle. **An** Kinabalu Serpent-eagle.

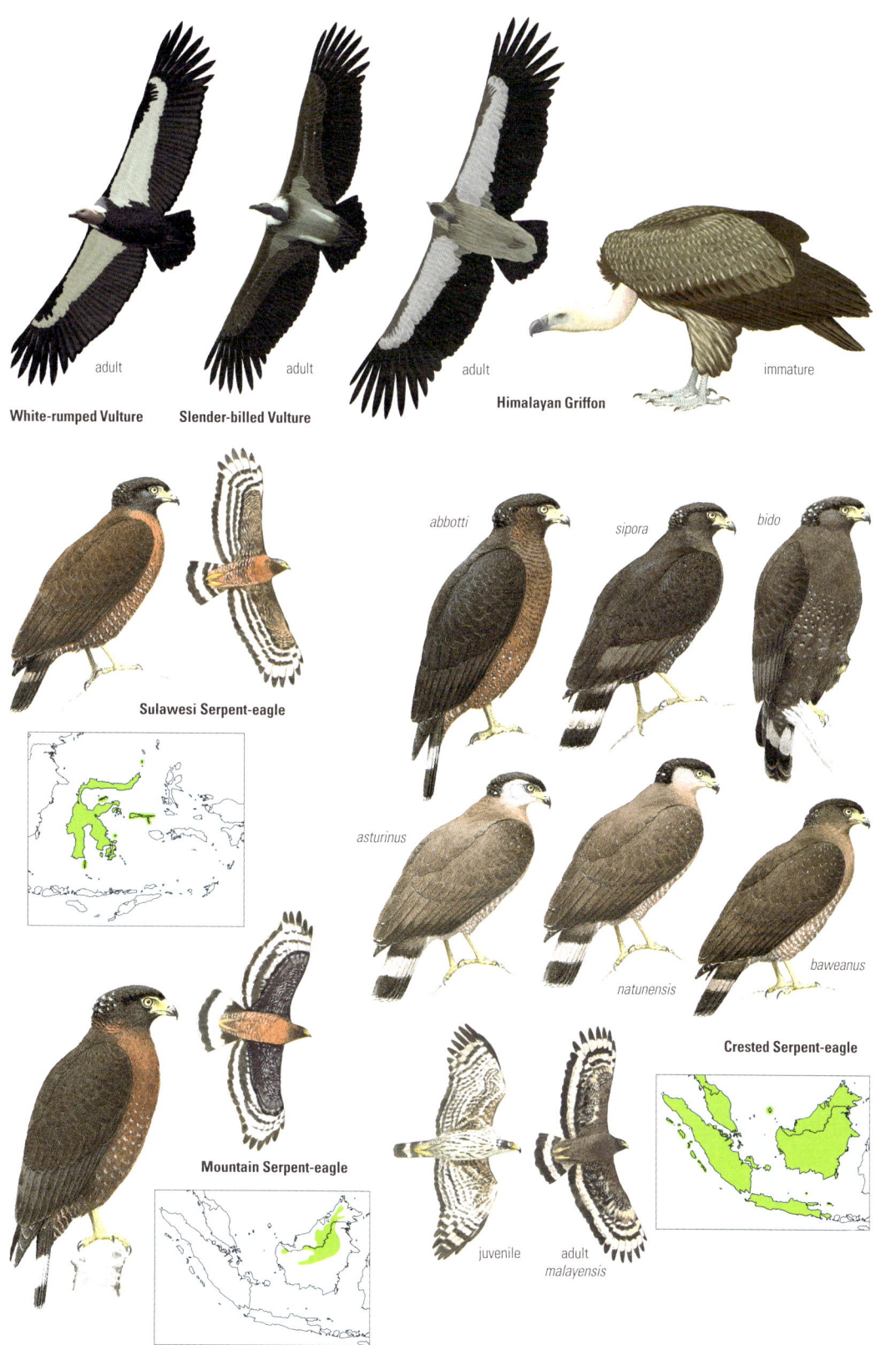

White-rumped Vulture
adult

Slender-billed Vulture
adult

adult

Himalayan Griffon
immature

abbotti

sipora

bido

Sulawesi Serpent-eagle

asturinus

natunensis

baweanus

Crested Serpent-eagle

Mountain Serpent-eagle

juvenile

adult
malayensis

Short-toed Snake-eagle *Circaetus gallicus*

L 62–70 cm, **WS** 166–188 cm/2.7. Breeds Palaearctic, S Asia, LS; N populations winter to Africa and S-SE Asia. 2 ssp, 1 in region: *sacerdotis* (LS). Uncommon resident, visitor to Bali, E Jav. Extralimital ssp *gallicus* (breeds Palaearctic, S Asia; winters to S-SE Asia) likely visitor to Sum as annual in MPen (including Singapore), but hitherto unreported. Woodland, open and coastal areas, <1500 m. Flies with slow heavy wingbeats, holds wings level or slightly raised when soaring and gliding; often hovers. **ID** Large-headed, stocky with large yellow eyes, all-dark bill and long wings. Ssp *sacerdotis* slightly smaller. **Ad** head, upperparts and upper breast pale greyish brown, darker in some individuals so as to confer a hooded look; white belly, undertail and underwings with variably dark, scattered barring (less distinct in *sacerdotis*). **Imm** paler overall with less distinct barring. **Voc** Gull-like "kyo-kyo-kyo...", "kee YOK", and plaintive "KYEE-ok". **SS** Much larger than Grey-faced Buzzard, with more barred underwing, all-dark bill, lack of rufous on breast and no mesial stripe. Compared to various imm and light morph hawk eagles, Short-toed is more extensively barred below (often including underwing) and usually has hooded appearance. See also Imm Bonelli's Eagle.

Bat Hawk *Macheiramphus alcinus*

L 47–51 cm, **WS** 95–120 cm. Sundaic, Sul, NG, Africa. 3 ssp, 1 in region: *alcinus* (MPen, Sum, Bor, Sul). Sometimes African *anderssoni* is split, leaving *alcinus* and *papuanus* (NG) as a narrower species, '**Asian Bat Hawk**'. Uncommon in wooded areas, often near bat and swiftlet caves. Crepuscular bat hunter. Cruising flight with slow wingbeats, fast and falcon-like in pursuit. **ID** Peregrine-like with long, broad-based and pointed wings and a short, square-cut tail. **Ad** all-black with white throat and black mesial streak. **Imm** browner with white below and dark breast band. **Voc** Usual call a rapid series of 5–11 high-pitched upslurred "kee" notes. **SS** See Peregrine Falcon.

Rufous-bellied Eagle *Lophotriorchis kienerii*

L 46–61 cm, **WS** 105–140 cm/2.3. S–SE Asia, Phil. 2 ssp, 1 in region: *formosus* (SE Asia, Phil). Uncommon in lowland and hill forests, mangroves, plantations, <1900 m (GS), <2400 m (Sul). **ID Ad** slightly crested; black upperparts; white throat and upper breast and dark-streaked chestnut belly and vent. In flight rufous wing lining and dark-barred grey wing and tail feathers. **Imm** dark greyish brown above, white below; white head with dark crown and eye mask creating white eyebrow appearance. **Voc** Plaintive but rapid "kee kee klikky heel", with upslurred end, reminiscent of whistling-duck; lower-pitched "whi HEE kek (kek)" with variations; **Imm**: protracted high-pitched "HEEEEeeee" dying off at the end. **SS** Imm Javan, Wallace's and Blyth's Hawk Eagles exhibit much longer crests and have tawny or buffy (not white) head and underparts lacking dark crown and eye mask. See also Imm Flores, Changeable and Sulawesi Hawk Eagles and Imm Bonelli's Eagle.

Black Eagle *Ictinaetus malaiensis*

L 65–80 cm, **WS** 148–182 cm/2.3. S–SE–E Asia. 2 ssp, 1 in region: *malaiensis* (SE–E Asia). Fairly common in primary and secondary forest, sometimes hunting over countryside villages, <2500 m. Glides with broad, paddle-shaped, fingered wings, with bulging secondaries; harrier-like in shallow V when foraging. Spectacular aerial displays of up to 400 m dives and undulating sky dances. **ID Ad** all black apart from fine pale tail bars and (sometimes) flight feather bars; small bill with yellow cere; feathered tarsus; wing tips exceed tail when perched. In flight shows long, pointed, 'fingered' primaries. **Imm** with tawny head, body and wing lining, all streaked dark; dark pale-barred underside of flight feathers and tail. **Voc** Single, high-pitched upslurred "kee", repeated in series; loud plaintive "klee-kee". **SS** Ad similar to dark morph Changeable Hawk Eagle, but latter has stable flight, much shorter wings lacking long pointed fingers and shows dark cere. See also Gurney's, Eastern Imperial and Greater Spotted Eagles.

Flores Hawk Eagle *Nisaetus floris*　**E**

L 60–80 cm, **WS** 140–160 cm/2.0. Monotypic. For taxonomy see Changeable Hawk Eagle. Rare in primary and tall secondary forest, occasionally hunts over degraded habitat, usually <1100 m. **ID Ad** dark brown above; barred tail with broad subterminal band; white underparts including wing lining; white head (sometimes with pale-brown suffusion on crown) with short crest, dark lores. In flight white underwing, black wing tips and white window at base of upperwing primaries. **Imm** very similar to Ad, upperparts paler brown. **Voc** Similar to Changeable. **SS** Imm Rufous-bellied Eagle has longer crest and longer, narrower wings, less clearly barred tail and a dark mask and crown (versus all-pale head). Also see Short-toed Snake-eagle, Imm Oriental Honeybuzzard and Imm Bonelli's Eagle.

Sulawesi Hawk Eagle *Nisaetus lanceolatus*　**E**

L 55–64 cm, **WS** 110–135 cm/2.1. Monotypic. Uncommon resident in forest and adjacent open country, <2300 m. **ID Ad** short crest; blackish above; grey tail with 3–4 blackish bars; black mesial stripe; rufous breast with strong black streaks; white abdomen barred dark brown or black. In flight barred wing lining, white-based primaries, three unevenly spaced tail bars. **Imm** white head (though lores can be black) and white underparts, otherwise dark brown above with variable white patches; tail barred dark-and-pale with 5–6 dark uppertail bars almost equally wide as pale bars; in flight appears white with thin bars on flight feathers and undertail. **Voc** Descending series of 4–10 notes, each lasting 0.5 sec, "kluuu-kluuu-kluuu..."; disyllabic note "klew-ICK" that may or may not precede this series; **Imm**: rapid series of ~10 "kee" notes. **SS** See Sulawesi Honeybuzzard. Imm resembles those of other eagles: Imm Rufous-bellied Eagle has dark mask, crown and flank patches, longer wings and shorter tail; Imm Changeable Hawk Eagle (which doubtfully occurs on Sul) is often larger and probably always shows much thinner dark uppertail bars.

Short-toed Snake-eagle

Bat Hawk

immature

adult

Black Eagle

adult

immature

Rufous-bellied Eagle

**Flores
Hawk Eagle**

adult

immature

Sulawesi Hawk Eagle

Javan Hawk Eagle *Nisaetus bartelsi* `E`

L 56–60 cm, **WS** 110–130 cm/2.0. Monotypic. Uncommon in hill and montane forest, and adjacent open country, <3000 m. **ID Ad** dark brown above; brown head with cheeks and nape often more rufous; long, black, white-tipped erect crest; greyish brown tail with four black bars; black moustache and mesial stripe; breast with black drop streaks; brown-barred belly, thighs and vent. In flight rusty-buff wing lining with dark streaks and greyish, darker-barred flight feathers. **Imm** dark brown above, edged whitish; pale buff head and underparts, including wing lining; five thin dark tail bars. **Voc** Sounding much like Blyth's: drawn-out "kleeee"; "seel-guk" near nest; **Imm**: shrill high-pitched "(ki)kiKI-HEEEeeee" repeated 2–3 times. **SS** See Imm *Pernis* honeybuzzards (especially Sunda Honeybuzzard, which may mimic Ad Javan Hawk Eagle). See also Imm Short-toed Snake-eagle, Rufous-bellied Eagle and Changeable Hawk Eagle.

Changeable Hawk Eagle *Nisaetus limnaeetus*

L 51–82 cm, **WS** 100–135 cm/2.0. Himalayas, Andamans, SE Asia, Phil. 3 ssp, 2 in region: *limnaeetus* (S–SE Asia, GS, Phil); *vanheurni* (Simeulue). Here treated as separate from genetically closely related Crested Hawk Eagle *N. cirrhatus* (S Asia) and Flores Hawk Eagle based on distinct morphology even in areas of (near-) contact. Possible occurrence on Sul based on single Imm specimen from SW Sul (shown to be genetically distinct from GS populations and Flores Hawk Eagle) that may or may not be mis-labeled. Fairly common in wooded country, cultivation; mainly lowlands, <1800 m. **ID** Polymorphic. Vestigial crest. **Ad light morph** upperparts dark brown, head buff streaked black; mesial stripe; white underparts with bold black streaks; abdomen and thighs barred rufous; four tail bars. Ssp *vanheurni* smaller; less bold breast streaks. **Imm light morph** whitish head and underparts, including wing lining; mottled brown and white upperparts; rump white. **Ad dark morph** (absent in *vanheurni*) all blackish brown, with darker terminal band; in flight dark wing lining contrasting with paler, barred flight feathers. **Imm dark morph** like Ad but often shows darker barring on underwing and tail. **Voc** Very vocal, piping, strident "whi-whi-whi-WHEEE" (3 sec, 1.6–2.6 kHz); flight call very similar to that of Crested Serpent-eagle, but stronger and less variable: "kewLEEK-LEEK". **SS** Imm Rufous-bellied Eagle has more pronounced crest, longer and narrower wings, less clearly barred tail and dark facial mask and crown (whereas head mostly all-white in Imm Changeable). Imm Wallace's, Javan and Blyth's Hawk Eagles have much longer crests and tawny-buff (not white) head and underparts. For some plumages also see Oriental and Sunda Honeybuzzards. For Imm see Short-toed Snake-eagle and (on Sul) Sulawesi Hawk Eagle. For dark morph see Booted, Black, Greater Spotted Eagle and possible vagrants under latter.

Blyth's Hawk Eagle *Nisaetus alboniger*

L 50–58 cm, **WS** 100–115 cm/2.0. Sundaic. Monotypic. Uncommon in hill and montane forest, 300–2000 m, occasionally lower. **ID Ad** black upperparts, including head and crest; tail black with broad greyish-white subterminal band; underparts with bold black-and-white pattern: black mesial stripe, bold black breast streaks, densely black-barred belly. In flight densely black-barred linings, thin-barred flight feathers; orange eye. **Imm** brown upperparts; tawny head; buff-tipped black crest; plain buff below; 4–5 tail bars. **Voc** In flight high-pitched, rapid "kek-keek kek-keek" or "spEEOo-oo" descending at the end. When perched gives short, high-pitched squeaks. **SS** Ad Wallace's Hawk Eagle has browner upperparts and paler, less distinct underpart patterning, with three black rather than one grey tail bars. Imm Blyth's ghosts Ad's broader, more greyish-white subterminal band on uppertail as it matures (on Wallace's always buffier, never grey-tinged). Starting from second year, Blyth's has distinct Ad black feathers appearing on upperparts. See also mimicking plumages of Sunda Honeybuzzard. For Imm, see Short-toed Snake-eagle, Oriental Honeybuzzard, Rufous-bellied Eagle and Changeable Hawk Eagle.

Wallace's Hawk Eagle *Nisaetus nanus*

L 45–49 cm, **WS** 95–105 cm/2.1. Sundaic. 2 ssp: *nanus* (Sum, Bor, MPen); *stresemanni* (Nias). Uncommon in riverine and lowland dipterocarp forest, mostly <500 m. **ID Ad** blackish brown above, edged paler; dark-streaked rufous-buff head with buff-tipped black crest; buff-brown tail with three black bars; creamy white below with dark mesial stripe, dark-brown breast streaks and dark brown bars on belly and legs (usually paler buff-brown on Bor). In flight with lightly dark-spotted rufous-buff wing linings, three fairly equal tail bars. **Imm** cream to pale buff (or all-white in *stresemanni*) underparts and head, except buff-tipped black crest. **Voc** Flat, piping "pit-weeee", lasting 1.4 sec. **SS** See Jerdon's Baza and Blyth's Hawk Eagle. For Imm see *Pernis* honeybuzzards, Short-toed Snake-eagle, Rufous-bellied Eagle and Changeable Hawk Eagle.

immature

adult

Javan Hawk Eagle

adult

light
morph

immature

dark morph

light morph

immature

adult

Changeable Hawk Eagle
limnaeetus

immature

adult

immature

adult

Blyth's Hawk Eagle

adult

Wallace's Hawk Eagle

Greater Spotted Eagle *Clanga clanga* [V]

L 59–71 cm, **WS** 157–179 cm/2.5. Breeds Palaearctic, winters Africa, S–SE Asia. Monotypic. Marshes with trees and forests near water, open country, paddyfields. Recorded S Sum (Dec 1988–Apr 1989) but probably regular in N Sum, as winter visitor along adjacent MPen coastline. **ID** Yellow cere. **Ad** dark brown with pale U on uppertail-coverts. In flight, appears bulky, compact and short-tailed with faint white carpal crescent on underwing and white bases of primaries on upperwing. **Imm** differs in having diagnostic white spots on upperwing-coverts (some forming white band) and creamy vent. Rare **Imm pale morph** '*fulvescens*' creamy buff with black tail and flight feathers. **Voc** Usually silent in winter quarters; series of musical, well-spaced yelping notes "kleEEP"; more plaintive, hoarse "waak-waak-waak, waAK-WAAK-KWAAK". **SS** Greater Spotted has relatively short, broad wings and much shorter tail than other all-black eagles (Changeable Hawk Eagle, Black Eagle and the following two vagrants). A single record in S Sum in Apr 1989 may have related to imm **Steppe Eagle** *Aquila nipalensis* (**L** 60–81 cm, **WS** 165–214 cm; C Palaearctic; winters to Africa and S–SE Asia; **Ad** all dark-brown with yellow nape patch; plumage best told from Greater Spotted by presence of fine black bands in secondaries and tail and black trailing edge to wing and tail; either lacks Ad Greater Spotted's white wing markings or obsolete; **Imm** intermediate in general colour between Greater Spotted's typical imm and '*fulvescens*', but with three bold pale bands across upperwing and bold white band across underwing). See also Eastern Imperial Eagle.

Eastern Imperial Eagle *Aquila heliaca* [V]

L 68–84 cm, **WS** 180–215 cm/2.6. Breeds Palaearctic; winters to Africa and S–SE–E Asia. Monotypic. Open country, paddyfields. Vagrant Lampung, Sumatra (Dec 2018). **ID/SS** Yellow cere. **Ad** resembles Ad Black Eagle, but with broader, parallel-sided wings and much more massive bill; white markings on scapulars, creamy vent and extensive creamy hindcrown to nape, grey tail with broad black terminal band; **Imm** resembles smaller '*fulvescens*' imm Greater Spotted, but heavily dark-streaked pale buff body (versus all-fulvescent body in Greater Spotted) and upperwing with two bold white wing bands to median and greater coverts and white trailing edge; underwing has pale grey panel to inner-primaries and black fingered primaries.

Gurney's Eagle *Aquila gurneyi*

L 74–86 cm, **WS** 165–185 cm/2.2. Aus. Monotypic. Scarce in lowland forests, usually <900 m. **ID** Large. **Ad** solid dark with longish wings and slightly wedge-shaped tail; grey-brown cere; yellow iris; greyish mottling at base of flight feathers and tail. **Imm** brown above with grey and buff marbling; tawny to buff head and underparts with brown streaks (especially on breast); grey-brown, dark-barred wings and tail; black-tipped primaries. **Voc** Moderately high, slightly nasal down-slurred piping, 1 n/s. **SS** Smaller, less massive Ad Black Eagle has paddle-shaped wings held more in V, yellow cere. Imm Black Eagle is more streaky on underparts and underwing-coverts, and has pale wing lining more contrasting with dark flight feathers.

Bonelli's Eagle *Aquila fasciata*

L 55–67 cm, **WS** 142–175 cm/2.5. W Palaearctic, S–SE–E Asia, LS. 2 ssp, 1 in region: *renschi* (Sumbawa–Tanimbar). Uncommon in primary and tall secondary forest, cultivation, <2000 m. Aerial displays include high circling and sky dance: plunging headlong with closed wings from great height, followed by rising and circling on stiff wings. **ID** Yellow cere. **Ad** dark-capped; dark brown upperparts; white patch on mantle; grey, faintly barred tail with broad blackish terminal band; white below with dark breast streaks, barred belly. In flight black wing lining and white leading edge of inner wing ('landing lights') diagnostic; dark-barred light-grey flight feathers with blackish trailing edge. **Imm** like Ad but much paler brown and less streaky below; brown wing lining; often still lacks terminal tail band. **Voc** Usually silent; repeated pairs of shrill, drawn-out notes; also series of short notes. **SS** Although pale, confusing Imm is browner below and usually has dark markings on wing lining compared to much whiter-looking Short-toed Snake-eagle, Flores Hawk Eagle and Imm Rufous-bellied Eagle. Pale Imm Oriental Honeybuzzards are only slightly smaller than Imm Bonelli's, but have slimmer build, less massive bill, small, pigeon-like head, unfeathered tarsus, usually more distinct and more irregular tail barring and lack dark markings on wing lining.

Booted Eagle *Hieraaetus pennatus* [V]

L 42–51 cm, **WS** 113–138 cm/2.7. Breeds W–C Palaearctic; winters Africa, S–SE Asia. Monotypic. Recorded Bali (Oct 1982), Bintan (Apr 1993), Batam (Oct 1993) and Jav (Oct 1999). Open countryside. **ID** Polymorphic. Feathered tarsus. **Ad** mid-brown upperparts, broadly edged buff; white 'landing lights' on anterior base of wing; bold pale panels on upperwing; white "U" on rump; greyish tail with dense but obsolete dark barring (often hardly visible; terminal bar slightly wider). **Pale morph** creamy-white head and underparts, with dark cheeks and variably dark-streaked head and breast; in flight white wing linings strongly contrast with black flight feathers. **Dark morph** dark brown (more rarely rufous-brown) on head, wing linings and underparts; black flight feathers create all-dark wing appearance. **Imm** similar to Ad. **Voc** Usually silent in winter quarters. **SS** Dark morph can be confused with other all-dark raptors but white "U" on rump and white 'landing lights' distinctive. In addition, pale upperwing panels separate from Changeable Hawk Eagle; feathered tarsus and less triangular tail shape separate from Black Kite; and feathered tarsus, pale upperwing panel and all-dark flight feathers and tail separate from dark Oriental and Sunda Honeybuzzards. See also Pygmy Eagle.

Pygmy Eagle *Hieraaetus weiskei*

L 38–48 cm, **WS** 112–126 cm/2.7. NG to Mol. Monotypic. No longer considered conspecific with Little Eagle *H. morphnoides* from Australia. Scarce in hill forest and edge. **ID** Polymorphic. Feathered tarsus. Uniformly dark-brown upperparts with streaked crown and cheeks; 7-8 dark tail bars. **"Booted Eagle morph"** (apparently unique to C Mol and Obi) with heavy black-and-white underwing contrast, seemingly identical to Booted Eagle pale morph on current knowledge. **Dark morph** (range-wide) chestnut-brown underparts with darker breast streaking; in flight dusky brown underwing with paler brown inner primary window. **Pale morph** (range-wide) white underparts with heavily brown-streaked breast and carpal area on underwing; white flight feathers with dense dark barring. **Imm** narrower pale outermost tail bands. **Voc** Loud, excited 2 or 3 note whistle, sometimes in accelerating series that drops in pitch. **SS** Imm Brahminy Kite is less robust, has unfeathered tarsus, and lacks distinct barring on flight feathers and tail. Black Kite (including imm) has more triangular, often slightly forked tail, unfeathered tarsus, and is much darker overall (including underwings) with less contrasting streaking and all-black flight feathers.

Greater Spotted Eagle

adult
immature

Steppe Eagle

immature

Eastern Imperial Eagle

adult
immature

Gurney's Eagle

immature
adult

Bonelli's Eagle

immature
adult
adult

Booted Eagle

light morph
dark morph

Pygmy Eagle

pale morph

White-bellied Fish-eagle *Icthyophaga leucogaster*

L 70–85 cm, **WS** 178–218 cm/2.6. S–SE Asia to Aus. Monotypic. Fairly common along coasts and islands, mangroves, lakes, swamps, <200 m, but locally <1700 m. Soars with wings in 'V' shape. **ID** Large. **Ad** white overall with grey wings and mantle. In flight, black flight feathers contrast with white wing linings; white wedge-shaped tail with black base. **Imm** mottled dark brown above, paler below; in flight shows extensive pale patch on underside of primaries, and white tail with variable dark subterminal bar (missing on older immatures). **Voc** Goose-like, upslurred "ank...ank...ank..." and faster duck-like "ka...ka...ka...". **SS** Other imm fish-eagles have shorter and rounder tails, and show contrasting primary spot only in some older individuals that already exhibit most adult traits. Imm Brahminy Kite is smaller with more uniformly-coloured, more squar-ish tail and a generally more chestnut-tinged body colour (especially on wing linings). Imm Brahminy also has different wing shape, with wings held forward and primaries diagonally pointed back. **AN** White-bellied Sea-eagle.

Lesser Fish-eagle *Icthyophaga humilis*

L 53–68 cm, **WS** 120–165 cm/2.4. S–SE Asia. 2 ssp, 1 in region: *humilis* (Sundaic, Sul, Buru). Uncommon along narrow undisturbed waterways, mangroves, <1500 m. **ID Ad** dark brown lower breast and upperparts gradually turning grey on mantle, wing coverts, scapulars and head; white belly and vent sharply demarcated from breast; all-dark wings with light flashes at base of primaries; dark tail with black terminal band. **Imm** has Ad's greyish and grey-brown body colour replaced with paler brown colour appearing mottled especially on upperparts with plain, whitish head; white feather bases on rump, pale undertail with dark terminal band; pale underwing with brown mottling on wing linings; white flight feathers mottled dark towards tips. **Voc** Series of 7–11 loud "kah-AW"; in flight, "yow (-HEEee)" and variations; often calls when soaring high. **SS** See imm White-bellied Fish-eagle. Larger Ad Grey-headed Fish-eagle has clear white (not dark) tail base, more uniformly rich-brown coloured wings and mantle contrasting with grey head (in Lesser wings and especially mantle more greyish-brown), much longer tail projection beyond wings, a larger and longer bill, and calls differently. Imm Grey-headed is more streaky (less mottled) overall, and has barred rather than mottled flight feathers. Imm Grey-headed also often lacks imm Lesser's contrast between white belly and brown breast (mimicking Ad plumage).

Grey-headed Fish-eagle *Icthyophaga ichthyaetus*

L 66–77 cm, **WS** 140–175 cm/2.2. S–SE Asia to Phil Monotypic. Uncommon along sea coasts, also swamps, forested waterways, <300 m. **ID Ad** dark brown breast and upperparts becoming grey on head and throat; white belly (sharply demarcated), vent and tail with broad black terminal band. **Imm** pale brown overall with white streaks (including wing linings); white flight feathers barred black; tail mottled light-and-dark with black terminal band, but quickly becoming more similar to Ad; can show white primary patch in older stages when large part of plumage Ad-like. **Voc** Repeated barking "eer-WUK" and owl-like "KYOOoow", both heard in flight and from perch; also calls at night. **SS** See Lesser Fish-eagle and imm White-bellied Fish-eagle.

Black Kite *Milvus migrans*

L 46–66 cm, **WS** 120–153 cm/2.4. Palaearctic to Aus. No longer includes Afrotropical resident taxa. 4–5 ssp, 2 in region: *affinis* (Sul and LS to Aus); *lineatus* (breeds E Palaearctic; winters S–SE Asia). Fairly common resident in open country in E (*affinis*); rare migrant N Sum, Bor, and vagrant Jav (*lineatus*). Graceful flight with slow deliberate beats. **ID Ad** dark-brown overall with slightly forked tail (sometimes appearing square-tipped). Larger, broader-winged *lineatus* is more rufous-tinged and has bluish cere and legs/feet; smaller *affinis* is less warm-brown and has yellow cere and legs/feet. Black cheek patch distinct in *lineatus*, often indistinct in *affinis*. In flight whitish patch at primaries (often obsolete in *affinis*). Ssp *lineatus* shows thin pale body streaking that is obsolete in *affinis*; belly and vent creamy-buff, lighter than rest of body in *lineatus*, but dark-brown and concolourous with breast in *affinis*. **Imm** colder dark-brown in both races with heavy cream streaking overall, espe-cially thick and pronounced in *lineatus*. **Voc** Whinnying, long-drawn gull-like "klee-ee-ee-ee-ee-ee" with down-slurred variations. **SS** See imm Brahminy Kite and dark morph Booted and Pygmy Eagles.

Brahminy Kite *Haliastur indus*

L 44–52 cm, **WS** 110–125 cm/2.4. S–SE–E Asia to Aus. 4 ssp, 2 in region: *girrenera* (Mol to Aus); *intermedius* (MPen, GS, LS, Sul, Sula, Phil). Common to scarce in mostly coastal, open areas and forest edge, but locally inland near rivers, lakes, <2400 m. Now rare on Jav. **ID Ad** chestnut brown overall with white head and breast (fine-ly dark-streaked in *intermedius*). In flight chestnut wing lining, paler flight feathers and black wing tips; distinctive S-shaped trailing edge to wing with primaries pointing back. **Imm** head and upperparts brown with paler edges; underparts paler streaky brown-and-white; tail uniformly grey to brown; in flight wing lining brown to chestnut, proximal wing feathers dark-grey, distal wing feathers mostly white, but with bold black wing tips. **Voc** Mewing, human baby-like "KIH-yeeEEeeh", mostly when perched; sometimes a repeated whistled call in flight. **SS** Black Kite has forked or strongly-angled tail, lacks strong chestnut tones (especially to wing lining) and never shows as much white on outer underwing as typical imm Brahminy. See dark morph Booted and Pygmy Eagles and imm White-bellied Fish-eagle. Note diagnostic wing shape.

immature

immature

immature

adult

adult

adult

**White-bellied
Fish-eagle**

**Lesser
Fish-eagle**

**Grey-headed
Fish-eagle**

affinis

lineatus

adult

immature

Black Kite

Brahminy Kite

White-eyed Buzzard *Butastur teesa* [V]

L 36–43 cm, **WS** 86–100 cm/2.3. S–SE Asia. Monotypic. Recorded SW Sul (Aug 2012, Sep 2014) in open, dry forest, cultivation. Status uncertain due to non-migratory extralimital range with no other vagrancy recorded E or S of Myanmar. **ID Ad** slim, slender appearance; white iris, yellow cere; white throat with wide black mesial stripe; white forehead and lores; uniformly chocolate-brown body with white-barred belly and paler upperwing-coverts; conspicuous long white thighs and orange-yellow legs. Wing tips almost reach tail tip when perched. In flight has brown underwing-coverts and white outerwing with inconspicuous barring and black-tipped primaries. Tail unmarked. **Imm** paler head with broad supercilium, darker eye; breast streaked; yellow legs. **Voc** Plaintive, mewing "pit-weer". **SS** Rufous-winged Buzzard lacks white forehead, white throat and dark mesial stripe; has darker upperwing-coverts contrasting with rufous outerwing and tail, and has underwing-coverts pale (not brown). Grey-faced Buzzard lacks white forehead, has more conspicuously barred underparts including thighs, shows darker upperwing-coverts, and, in flight, has pale (not brown) underwing-coverts.

Rufous-winged Buzzard *Butastur liventer*

L 35–41 cm, **WS** 84–91 cm/2.3. SE Asia. Monotypic. Scarce (Sul) to rare (Jav) in savanna and woodlands, <1200 m. In flight sparrowhawk-like with fast beats and glides, slim protruding head and long, narrow wings. **ID Ad** orange bill with black tip; light iris. Slender, greyish head and underparts becoming white on belly; rufous-brown upperparts (finely streaked black), tail and flight feathers. In flight, white wing lining and indistinctly barred tail and flight feathers. **Imm** similar to Ad but more brownish (less rufous or grey) and streakier overall, with white supercilium. **Voc** High-pitched double-note "kik, wEEee" similar to Grey-faced but with second note higher than first; long-drawn "oohihhHHHHehh!". **SS** Grey-faced Buzzard is larger, lacks rufous tones, has strongly barred belly and undertail, and black markings on white throat. See also White-eyed Buzzard.

Grey-faced Buzzard *Butastur indicus*

L 41–48 cm, **WS** 101–110 cm/2.4. Breeds E Asia; winters SE Asia, Phil. Monotypic. Uncommon (Sep–Apr) in forest, open areas, <1500 m. **ID** Smallish, slender. **Ad** black bill with wide orange base; light iris; greyish uppertail (with bold black bars) and head; white supercilium more pronounced in **F**. Greyish-brown upperparts (finely streaked black) and breast; white belly boldly barred brown (more so in **M**); white throat with black moustachial and mesial stripes. In flight pale whitish underwing and undertail with variably strong dark barring (on tail and flight feathers) and scaling (on wing lining). **Imm** similar to Ad but browner, lacks strong greyish tones; white underparts streaked dark-brown; broad white supercilium and submoustachial stripe encircle dark-brown face mask. **Voc** Loud "KIK, weeee" similar to Rufous-winged but with second note lower than first. **SS** See Short-toed Snake-eagle, Rufous-winged and White-eyed Buzzards.

Eurasian Buzzard *Buteo buteo* [V]

L 40–54 cm; **WS** 109–136 cm/2.6. Breeds Palaearctic S to Himalayas; winters Africa to SE Asia. ~14 ssp, 2 in region, both sometimes upgraded to species level: *vulpinus* ('**Steppe Buzzard**'; breeds W–C Palaearctic; winters Africa to S–SE Asia); ssp *burmanicus* (breeds NE Palaearctic; winters E–SE Asia) sometimes assigned to '**Eastern Buzzard**' *B. japonicus* along with extra-limital subspecies. Taxonomy confused, but substantial overlap in morphological characters and extremely limited mtDNA divergence advocate merger of all taxa into Eurasian Buzzard. Scarce migrant to Sum, Riau, rarely to Jav. Based on abundance in MPen, ssp *burmanicus* more common than *vulpinus*. Open country, forest edge. Regularly sits on prominent perches or soars low. **ID** Broad-winged and broad-tailed. Iris black in **Ad** and pale in **Imm**. Imm shows weaker black trailing edge. Polymorphic. Ssp *burmanicus* rich dark brown on upperparts and head; tail typically light-brown, unbarred (mostly Ad) or weakly barred (mostly Imm); white underparts typically show distinct brown flank patches contrasting with pale belly and vent and variable pale-brown mottling on breast and wing lining (from **pale** to **brown morph**), but pale birds more common; black carpal patches, white flight feathers (obscurely barred black on secondaries) with black tips (restricted to primaries in immatures). Ssp *vulpinus* often darker overall than *burmanicus*: **brown morph** of *vulpinus* more intensely brown on underparts, with solid brown wing lining, often with a pale breast 'bolt' coparating dark helly patch from upper breast streaking, brown mottling frequently reaching vent, more strongly barred tail, and broader black trailing edge to wing. Ssp *vulpinus* often occurs in unique **rufous morph**, with dark-brown of underparts and wing linings replaced by variable warm to rich rufous brown and less distinct tail barring. Rarer **dark morph** in *vulpinus* has blackish-brown body colour and wing linings, white flight feathers on underwing (with a thick black trailing edge in Ad). **Voc** Plaintive and loud "NYAAAarrh". **SS** Oriental and Sunda Honeybuzzards have more protruding head, longer tail, usually no carpal patches, different tail pattern, and elastic flight action. **AN** Common Buzzard.

immature

adult

White-eyed Buzzard

immature

adult

Rufous-winged Buzzard

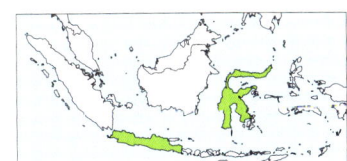

immature

adult

Grey-faced Buzzard

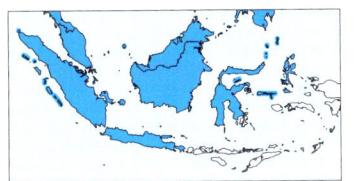

immature

burmanicus

vulpinus
immature

adult

Eurasian Buzzard

Western Marsh Harrier *Circus aeruginosus* [V]

L 48–56 cm, **WS** 115–145 cm/2.7. Breeds W-C Palaearctic; winters Africa to S Asia. 2 ssp, 1 in region: *aeruginosus* (most of range). Single specimen from N Sum (Dec 1914), unverified in modern times; re-examination needed to rule out Eastern Marsh as identification criteria were not well understood. Marshes and open country. **ID M** dark brown above; dark-streaked cream head and underparts becoming more densely streaked towards belly. In flight shows prominent black wingtips (both above and below), otherwise largely cream-white underwing with brown streaks on coverts, and un-barred grey upperwing with brown median and lesser-coverts and buff shoulders; tail light grey. **F** uniformly dark brown, edged rufous, with contrasting buff-cream crown, leading edge of wing-coverts, throat and (less obvious) breast patch. **Imm** as fem, but more restricted buff-cream areas, often restricted to forewing and crown. **SS** The unique, unstreaked, uniform dark-brown plumage and buff-cream head markings of fem and imm distinguish this species from all other harriers. Beware that some imm Eastern Marsh Harriers show similar pale anterior patches on an almost unstreaked dark body, but rarely in quite the same combination and intensity. In flight, confusing imm Eastern can always be told by large, greyish underwing primaries (dark-brown with narrow white crescent at primary base in Western). Western superficially resembles fem and imm of other co-occurring harrier species but has unmarked grey tail and distinctive black wing tips contrasting with unmarked grey upperwing field. **AN** Eurasian Marsh Harrier.

Eastern Marsh Harrier *Circus spilonotus*

L 48–56 cm, **WS** 115–145 cm/2.7. Breeds E Palaearctic; winters to SE Asia, Phil. Monotypic. Scarce migrant in marshes, paddyfields and open country, <2250 m. **ID M** head and breast streaked black-and-white at variable intensities; white belly; upperparts black with white edging. In flight black outer primaries (above and below) contrasting with white underwing and mostly grey upperwing (except for black-and-white mottled upperwing-coverts); uniformly grey tail. **F** brownish streaking on head, nape and breast becoming almost solid brown on belly and thighs; upperparts (including upperwing-coverts) brown with cream edging. In flight pale under-wing with brown streaking on underwing-coverts; black barring on flight feathers (both above and below) becoming less distinct or disappearing around the primary bases of underwing to form light window; variable white rump patch and brown-grey tail with black barring. **Imm** initially uniform, unstreaked brown with variable cream patches on head, breast and underwing-coverts and distinct white underwing patch at primary bases, with no barring; body grad-ually becomes paler (and greyer in male). Third winter birds combine Ad and imm traits. **SS** See Pied, Hen and Western Marsh Harriers.

Swamp Harrier *Circus approximans* [V]

L 50–60 cm, **WS** 118–145 cm/2.4. Aus. Monotypic. Recent record of long-staying individual from Sumba (2010–2013). Grasslands and marshes. **ID M** brown upperparts with pale edging; underparts and head whitish with variable brown streaking and facial disk; white rump; unbarred ash-grey tail; flight feathers (white on underwing and grey on upperwing) barred black. **F** similar but more rufous on underparts and with faintly barred tail. **Imm** uniform dark chocolate brown with pale nape, pale rump and pale underwing patch at primary bases; faintly barred tail. **Voc** short, thin "kyeow"; thin re-petitive call. **SS** Imm Spotted Harrier resembles Ad Swamp Harrier but has more rufous underparts, more conspicuously barred tail and a chestnut facial disk. **AN** Pacific Marsh Harrier.

Pied Harrier *Circus melanoleucos*

L 43–50 cm, **WS** 110–125 cm/2.5. Breeds E Asia; winters S–SE Asia, Phil. Monotypic. Uncommon migrant in open country, marshes and paddyfields. **ID M** striking pied plumage: black head, upper breast, mantle, back and outer primaries (above and below); white underparts and underwing; tail and upperwings grey with black median wing-coverts and white patch on lesser wing-coverts. **F** almost uniformly brown above (with some pale edging) and white below with brown streaking extending to lower breast; brown-and-white facial disk; tail grey-brown barred dark; white rump patch; in flight short-necked with striking upperwing characterised by pale lesser-coverts ("headlights") bordered by dark-brown median-coverts and back producing 'anchor' pattern, and grey flight feathers with black tips and variable dark barring; underwing pale with fine brown streaks on coverts and variable barring on flight feathers. **Imm** uniform dark rufous brown (including wing-coverts) although underparts can show variable brown streaking on whitish background with progressing age; usually shows distinctive pale nape patch, and in Imm F paler face; flight feathers on underwing pale with dark barring, but overall appearance of secondaries 'darkened'. **Voc** Occasional rapid "wek-wek-wek". **SS** Eastern Marsh exhibits equally confusing age- and sex-related plumage variability, but is larger overall, longer-necked, larger-headed, larger-billed and with more slender wings, and in some plumages best identified based solely on this. Male Ad Pied unmistakable but beware of male Ad Eastern Marsh individuals with extremely dense black overall barring, mimicking male Pied pattern. As compared to Ad fem Pied, Ad fem Eastern Marsh has brown (not grey-toned) upperside to flight feathers, a much more faintly barred or even unbarred tail, brown (not white) thighs and lower belly, and lacks distinct and well-defined 'headlights' at front of innerwing. The plumage of aging imm male Eastern Marsh individuals can appear almost identical to Ad fem Pied and must be separated with care (e.g. through the lack of strong "headlights" and lack of strong tail barring). First year Pied similar to some dark variants of Imm Eastern Marsh, but generally more rufous overall, with pale patches restricted to face and nape (whereas Eastern Marsh rarely has nape patch but often shows additional pale patches on shoulders and breast); in flight Imm Pied always shows black barring on white under-primaries and darker under-secondaries, whereas Eastern Marsh has unbarred white primary patch, attaining first barring when turning into Ad plumage. Also see Hen and Western Marsh Harriers.

immature

♀

adult

♂

Western Marsh Harrier

adult

♀

♂

Eastern Marsh Harrier

Swamp Harrier

♂
adult

adult

♀

Pied Harrier

adult

♂

immature

♀

adult

♂

Hen Harrier *Circus cyaneus* [V]

L 42–50 cm, **WS** 100–121 cm/2.4. Breeds Palaearctic, winters to E Asia. Monotypic. Traditionally considered conspecific with Northern Harrier *C. hudsonius* (N America) but here separated based on consistent plumage differences. Historical records from N Bor might not stand up to today's scrutiny. Grasslands and swamps. **ID M** grey with white belly and black outer primaries, dark trailing edge to wings; white rump. **F** almost uniform dark-brown upperparts and upperwing; pale panel on upperwing-coverts forms V in flight; underparts, wing linings and nape with variable brown streaking; distinct broad white eye crescents; strongly dark-barred tail and flight feathers on underwing (with especially thick secondary bars); white rump. **Imm** as fem, but rustier on underparts and underwing-coverts. **SS** Barred tail and flight feathers of fem and imm rule out imm Eastern and Western Marsh; older Eastern Marsh shows some barring on tail and flight feathers, but virtually never exhibits combination of uniform-brown upperparts with contrasting white rump, and has much less conspicuous facial disk. Fem Pied has grey background colour to tail and flight feathers (fem and imm Hen lack grey tones), lacks distinct eye crescents, lacks strong streaking on thighs and vent, does not have noticeably thicker secondary bars and has pale forewing panel ("headlights") in flight (not a pale V as in Hen). Imm Pied is much darker-bellied than any Hen Harrier plumage and also lacks pronounced eye crescents. Any Hen Harrier sighting in region should be documented and identified with specialist literature to rule out other possible vagrants (e.g. **Pallid Harrier** *C. macrourus*).

Spotted Harrier *Circus assimilis*

L 50–61 cm, **WS** 121–147 cm/2.4. Aus. Monotypic. Uncommon resident, but status uncertain on Taliabu and Timor due to paucity of records. In open country, ricefields, scrub, grasslands, <1100 m. Glides in shallow V. During sky-dance performs long series of steep undulations (while continuously flapping its wing) with zigzags, twists and turns, 100–200 m above the ground. **ID** Slender with long wings. **Ad** upperparts and upperwing-coverts blue-grey with white spotting/mottling; underparts and wing lining chestnut spotted with white; solid blue-grey nape and breast band; chestnut facial disk and shoulders; conspicuously barred tail and flight feathers. **Imm** rufous-buff overall, with fine brown streaks on breast and coarse dark-brown mottling on upperparts, nape and crown; facial disk, flight feathers and tail similar to Ad. In second year looks like Ad but is white-striped (not spotted) below. **Voc** Usually silent. Occasional short, shrill whistle and rapid chatter. **SS** See Swamp Harrier.

Eurasian Sparrowhawk *Accipiter nisus* [V]

L 28–40 cm, **WS** 56–78 cm/2.1. Breeds Palaearctic; winters to S. 6 ssp, 1 in region: *nisosimilis* (breeds E Palaearctic; migrates S). Single records N Bor (1895) and Jav (Feb 2013). Open woodlands. **ID** No mesial stripe; yellow to orange-yellow legs; yellow cere. Long, squared (sometimes notched) tail with 4–6 thick dark bars; short broad wings show six 'fingers' in flight. **M** with yellow-orange to red eyes; medium blue-grey upperparts, often with faint white supercilium, rufous cheeks; white underparts barred extensively rufous to brown, flanks usually completely rufous (often extending to breast), underwing with rufous-washed lining and heavily barred flight feathers. **F** yellow-eyed and larger with more distinct white supercilium, slate grey upperparts; white underparts and underwings, both with dense brown to grey barring. **Imm** browner above, and browner-barred below with breast bars sometimes appearing as speckles. **Voc** Main call a shrill cackling "keh-keh-keh...". **SS** In flight silhouette, only the differently coloured Crested Goshawk regularly shares six (versus five) primary 'fingers' within range. Otherwise most similar to Japanese, but appears longer-tailed, with shorter primary projection at rest. Male from all similar sparrow-

hawks by rufous cheek patch, additionally from male Japanese by usually lighter upperparts. Fem/imm lacks mesial stripe of Japanese and Besra, has more pronounced supercilium and usually greyer underparts barring (in Ad). Imm lacks the distinct breast streaking of similar imm sparrowhawks. See also Asian Shikra.

Rufous-necked Sparrowhawk [E]
Tachyspiza erythrauchen

L 26–35 cm, **WS** 47–65 cm/1.9. 2 ssp: *erythrauchen* (Morotai, Halmahera, Bacan, Obi); *ceramensis* (Buru, Seram, Ambon). Sometimes split into species-level '**Halmahera Sparrowhawk**' and '**Seram Sparrowhawk**', respectively, based on plumage differences. Uncommon in forest, <1400 m. Rarely soars though perches conspicuously after rain. **ID Ad** yellow to yellow-orange cere, iris and legs. Dark slate above with conspicuous rufous collar; faintly barred tail; whitish throat; breast rufous-pink with colour fading toward belly. **F** with slightly darker body. Ssp *ceramensis* is larger, blacker above; all greyish-white underparts with only faint rufous breast sides. **Imm** dark-brown above with thin rufous feather edging, densely barred tail, whitish below with thick dark-brown streaks to upper belly; *ceramensis* perhaps more broadly edged rufous above. **Voc** Ssp *erythrauchen*: rapid series of rather weak, forced, high-pitched, staccato notes (1–1.5 sec). Ssp *ceramensis*: rapid series of high-pitched "kik" notes, at 5 n/s; high-pitched "wheellee", repeated 2–3 times, 1 n/s. **SS** Ad of similarly-sized wintering Chinese lacks distinct hindcollar and has unique underwing pattern. Imm of Chinese has bars (not streaks) on belly and mimics Ad's unique underwing pattern. Meyer's Goshawk often has quite similar imm plumage but is almost twice the size, with massive bill. Imm of larger Varied and Halmahera Goshawks always show some extent of underparts barring (versus all streaking). Larger Ad Halmahera Goshawk lacks distinct rufous collar, has speckled throat and exhibits darker, more maroon underparts down to vent (versus rufous underparts that fade out toward belly). Ad Rufous-necked *ceramensis* told from larger Varied by distinct rufous collar and unmarked whitish underparts, but Ad *erythrauchen* closely mimics larger 'Grey-throated' Varied, and must be separated with care based on Varied's more uniformly rufous underparts (not fading out towards belly), longer, unbarred and more rounded tail, and paler upperparts. On Buru, possibility of larger imm Brown Goshawk should be considered (whose status on island is unclear); the latter shows barring or arrow-marking down to vent (versus whitish belly in imm Rufous-necked).

Halmahera Goshawk *Tachyspiza henicogramma* [E]

L 37–43 cm, **WS** 64–75 cm/1.7. Monotypic. Uncommon in primary and secondary forest, possibly with a preference for hill forest. Sits quietly in lower-mid storey or forest clearings; does not soar; hunts below canopy. **ID** Broad-winged, robust. Yellow to orange eyes, cere, and legs. **Ad** dark slaty above; inconspicuous black tail bars; deep maroon-chestnut below, faintly barred white on belly and lower breast; mottled throat. **Imm** dark brown above, white below with black-spotted throat, dark-barred breast grading into chestnut-barred abdomen; strongly barred tail. **Voc** Series of 8–10 upslurred screams, slightly accelerating at end, repeated at 5–6 sec intervals; series of 12–16 ascending whistles, last 6–8 wavering and more shrieking. **Imm**: 3 sec long series of 4 slightly upslurred "kwee" notes. **SS** Ad Varied distinguished by presence of variable rufous collar, plain tail, paler upperparts (especially head) and underparts. Imm Varied's breast more speckled or streaked rather than barred. Larger imm Meyer's is streaked, not barred, below. Smaller wintering Chinese has unique underwing pattern, orange (not yellow) cere; in imm plumage, has breast streaks (versus bars), whereas Ad lacks the solid maroon appearance on underparts. See also Rufous-necked Sparrowhawk. **AN** Moluccan Goshawk.

Pallid Harrier

immature

adult

♂

♀

♂

adult

Hen Harrier adult

♀

adult

Spotted Harrier

♀

♂

adult

♀

Eurasian Sparrowhawk

ceramensis adult

erythrauchen

immature

erythrauchen adult

adult

Rufous-necked Sparrowhawk

immature adult

adult

Halmahera Goshawk

Varied Goshawk *Tachyspiza hiogaster*

L 30–48 cm, **WS** 55–85 cm/1.8. Aus. 22 ssp, 8 in region: species shows considerable variation; genetic, vocal and morphological research may indicate presence of multiple species. Regional ssp here divided into four potential splits based on eye colour, size and plumage: '**Amboina Goshawk**' *T. hiogaster* incl. *hiogaster* (Seram, Ambon) and *pallidiceps* (Buru); '**Grey-throated Goshawk**' *T. griseogularis* consisting of *mortyi* (Morotai), *obiensis* (Obi) and *griseogularis* (Halmahera, Ternate, Tidore, Bacan); '**Tenggara Goshawk**' *T. sylvestris* (Sumbawa–Alor; monotypic), and '**Banda Goshawk**' *T. albiventris* consisting of *albiventris* (Kai) and *polionota* (Damar, Babar, Tanimbar). Extralimital Grey Goshawk *T. novaehollandiae* (Australia) and Christmas Island Goshawk *T. natalis* no longer included herein. Common in forest, woodland, cultivation, <1200 m. Frequents less open habitat than Brown Goshawk. Display flights swooping and circling while calling. **ID Ad** Eyes dark-red (*hiogaster* and probably *pallidiceps*), yellow ('Grey-throated'), orange ('Banda'), or black (*sylvestris*). Cere and legs yellow, but more orange at least on *sylvestris* and *hiogaster*. Ssp *sylvestris* uniquely smaller than all other forms. **M** dark slate above; grey and rounded tail with black bars; unbarred rufous underparts including throat; in flight with pale grey flight feathers. **F** browner above, paler below. For both sexes, *pallidiceps* similar but with plain tail; head to upper mantle and upper breast strikingly pale-grey, contrasting with darker grey upperparts and rufous underparts. 'Grey-throated' ssp similar to nominate but grey throat, plain tail and a variably obscure rufous hindneck collar; among 'Grey-throated' ssp, *mortyi* smaller and darker than *griseogularis*, with paler grey throat and more clear-cut rufous collar; *obiensis* paler than *griseogularis* with most distinct collar. Ssp *sylvestris* pale grey upperparts with ill-defined rufous collar; white underparts with even rufous barring (not reaching throat); tail plain and perhaps more squarish than other ssp. 'Banda Goshawk' even paler: *polionota* with barred tail and very subtle rufous barring on flanks and thighs; *albiventris* with plain tail and solid pink-hued underparts with white vent and wing lining. **Imm** much geographic variation: brown to blackish-brown above with rufous feather edges, white underparts marked with dark-brown splotches and (lower down) dropbars and arrow marks. Cere and legs yellow (sometimes orange). Eye colour black like Ad in *sylvestris*, but yellow in other ssp. Ssp *hiogaster* distinct, sooty-blackish upperparts and head with patchy white supercilium; underparts white with black bars on flanks. **Voc** Slight racial and regional variation; Tanimbar: series of rapid, excited, high-pitched, chattering "kik" notes. Flores: rising series of 5–15 weak, short, upslurred "kik" notes, accelerating then tailing off towards end. C–N Mol: series of 5–15 plaintive, slightly coarse, high-pitched, upslurred "hoooEE" notes at same pitch. **SS** See Brown, Halmahera and Meyer's Goshawk, and Rufous-necked Sparrowhawk. Outside LS, Ad Varied easily told from smaller wintering Chinese either by rufous collar or solid rufous underparts to vent, while imm Chinese separated from imm Varied by combination of unique underwing colouration and lack of strong rufous edging to upperparts. In LS, where Varied ssp *sylvestris* is unusually small, the latter two marks and black eye colour also serve to separate imm Varied from the yellow-eyed immatures of Chinese, Besra and Japanese. Regarding identification of adults in LS, Besra always has yellow to orange (versus black) iris, much darker upperparts, partly streaked (versus all-barred) breast, strongly barred (versus unbarred) tail and strong mesial streak. Ad Japanese is also much darker above with tail bars and mesial streak (especially in fem); male Japanese has much fainter, less extensive underparts barring and red (versus black) iris, while fem Japanese has yellow iris and cold-brown (not rufous) underparts barring. As compared to small Varied *sylvestris*, Ad Chinese has unique underwing pattern, with male additionally exhibiting rufous wash on breast (versus rufous bars on whole underparts), and fem showing yellow (versus black) iris and noticeable mesial streak. **AN** Variable Goshawk.

Brown Goshawk *Tachyspiza fasciata*

L 33–55 cm, **WS** 60–98 cm/1.8. Aus. 10 ssp, 7 in region: *fasciata* (S Aus; winters to Timor at least); *didimus* (N Aus; 5 specimens from Buru are probably post-breeding dispersers, possibly resident); *hellmayri* (Timor, Semau, Rote; in Alor possibly this ssp); *savu* (Sawu); *stresemanni* (Tanahjampea, Kalao, Bonerate, Kalaotoa, Madu, Tukangbesi); *tjendanae* (Sumba); *wallacii* (Lombok to Babar). Ssp may divide into multiple species-level lineages; more research needed. Locally fairly common in open monsoon forest, savanna, lightly wooded cultivation, <1800 m. Mostly silent aerial displays include undulating sky-dance, climbing with deep beats and fanned tail, closed-winged diving, brief circling etc. **ID** Yellow legs, cere and iris (but dark iris recorded from Juv at nest). **M** grey head, rufous hindcollar; slate brown above, thinly barred tail; underparts closely barred rufous-brown (conspicuously edged grey) and white. In flight with pointed wing tips, and longish rounded tail, finely barred wing lining and grey-barred flight feathers. **F** browner. All non-nominate ssp smaller and mostly lack grey edges on underparts barring: *tjendanae* has browner upperparts, whereas *didimus* has paler grey upperparts; *stresemanni* and slightly larger *wallacii* have dark-grey upperparts, darker vinous-rufous bars tending to merge on breast; *hellmayri* and *savu* resemble *wallacii* but show plain white abdomen and thighs, and revert to having grey edges to breast bars but not to ventral bars (with *savu* having narrower ventral barring). **Imm** mostly brown above with white supercilium; white below (*stresemanni* and possibly other races more buff below); most subspecies with contrast between brown streaks on breast and brown bars or arrow marks on belly to vent, but at least *hellmayri* mostly just streaked all the way to belly. **Voc** High "kik-kik-kik…" in 12+ thin rising notes; upslurred "mew", 1 n/s. **SS** Larger and more round-tailed than Besra (on Flores) and wintering Japanese and Chinese in all plumages. Ad quickly separated from these smaller species by presence of hindcollar and extensive underparts barring, whereas imm told from Besra, Japanese and Chinese by more heavily patterned belly and vent (mostly white in other species), with Chinese additionally having unique unmarked wing linings. Varied Goshawk ssp *pallidiceps* (on Buru) is unmistakably pale-headed in Ad plumage, but Imm plumage of both species on Buru insufficiently known, and best difference may be Brown's white supercilium and more intense bars on lower belly and vent (rather than arrow marks/splotches absent or vestigial in these parts). In LS, both Ad and Imm Varied (*sylvestris*) are smaller than Brown, have black (not yellow) iris, and have unbarred uppertail, but beware of very young Brown with dark iris or very young Varied with barred uppertail. On such individuals, Brown's white supercilium and heavier vent and lower belly markings are again best indication. On Buru, see also imm Rufous-necked Sparrowhawk.

sylvestris

immature

adult

griseogularis

adult

albiventris

pallidiceps

adult

hiogaster

immature

Varied Goshawk

griseogularis
immature

wallacii

hellmayri

adult

Brown Goshawk

fasciata

immature

Asian Shikra *Tachyspiza badia*

L 25–35 cm, **WS** 48–68 cm/1.9. C–S–SE Asia. 4 ssp, 1 in region: *poliopsis* (SE Asia; winters to Sum; recently found breeding in N Sum). No longer considered conspecific with African taxa *sphenura* and *polyzonoides*. Locally common migrant in open woodland and farmland in the lowlands, found nesting in cities. Aerial displays include soaring and high-and-low-circling, spiralling upward with flapping, tumbling and stooping at each other. Hunts from tree perches. In flight appears broad-bodied with short head projection, short wings with pronounced secondary bulge and long, rounded tail. Flies with deep, rapid wingbeats. **ID** Yellow legs and cere. Wings show five 'fingers' in flight. **M** pale to medium grey upperparts; faint mesial stripe; uppertail unbarred grey; undertail with 4–5 bars in centre and pale, unmarked outertail; breast and belly with dense, red bars; eyes red; vent white; wing lining white to lightly marked; outer underwing shows faint black bars, often grading into distinct blackish primary tips. **F** similar but larger; darker grey above, sometimes with brown tinge; darker mesial stripe; eyes yellow; stronger barring on underwing and undertail. **Imm** different: brown above, often with contrasting light-greyish head and chestnut ear patch; eyes yellow; strong mesial stripe; breast streaked with light-brown teardrops becoming bars on flanks and flight feathers; reddish streaks on leading edge of otherwise faintly marked wing lining; 4–5 strong bars on upper and undertail. **Voc** (1) Loud serial double-note "kerWIK" at 1 n/1–2 s; (2) "(PEE-)WHEEew" in series of 7–10, treeswift-like; (3) series of quickly-repeated even-pitched staccato notes, "kikik", 1 n/1–2 s. **SS** Long, floppy, rounded tail often helps separate from Chinese and Japanese in all plumages. Ad often lighter grey above than similar sparrowhawks: Ad Chinese has orange (not yellow) cere, more pointed wings with more contrasting black tips, and – in each sex – breast less clearly barred but more washed out, while Ad Japanese always lacks black wingtips and has stronger dark pattern on underwings and tail; male Eurasian is larger, slimmer, with six (not five) 'fingers', rufous-washed cheek, pale eyebrow, no mesial stripe and fully barred tail; Ad Besra is darker, with fully barred tail and streaked breast. When distinct tail shape not visible, imm Shikra is hard to identify: imm Chinese has orange (not yellow) cere and even less markings on wing linings, while Japanese has thinner mesial stripe and denser spotting on wing linings; imm Besra is very similar but usually has stronger mesial stripe, more contrasting underparts pattern, thicker uppertail bars and more densely spotted wing lining. The grey vs brown contrast between head and back in many imm Shikras is probably rarely seen in more uniformly coloured imm Besra, Japanese and Chinese. See also Crested Goshawk.

Chinese Sparrowhawk *Tachyspiza soloensis*

L 25–30 cm, **WS** 52–62 cm/2.1. Breeds E Asia; winters to SE Asia, Phil. Monotypic. Generally fairly common migrant (but rare in LS) in forest, edge, plantations, <1100 m. **ID** Orange cere; yellow to yellow-orange legs. Short tail with 4–6 dark, incomplete tail bands; long, pointed wings account for substantial primary projection; five 'fingers' in flight. **Ad** dark-grey upperparts; pale, generally unmarked underwing with substantial black wingtips. **M** lacks mesial stripe and has breast and wing linings washed pink; dark-red eyes. **F** larger with faint mesial stripe; wing linings and breast with a more orange tone, the latter showing the semblance of orange barring; yellow eyes. **Imm** different: dark brownish-grey above with often pronounced mesial stripe; brown-streaked breast, brown-barred belly; yellow eyes; underwing with pronounced barring on flight feathers often grading into black wingtips while wing linings almost entirely unmarked. **Voc** Generally silent; flat, but harsh "kik kik kik...", 11 n/2.4 s, quite different from other sparrowhawks. **SS** See Asian Shikra and Eurasian Sparrowhawk. In all plumages, Japanese

has spotted (not unmarked) wing linings, barred uppertail (unlike Ad Chinese), yellow (not orange) cere and lacks any black on wingtips. Imm Chinese tough to separate from imm Besra: the latter lacks any black on wingtip, has yellow (not orange) cere, more spotting on wing linings, thicker uppertail bars and often more contrasting underparts pattern and mesial stripe. See also Rufous-necked, Small, Vinous-breasted and Spot-tailed Sparrowhawks and Sulawesi, Crested, Varied and Brown Goshawks.

Japanese Sparrowhawk *Tachyspiza gularis*

L 23–30 cm, **WS** 46–58 cm/2.0. Breeds E Asia; winters to SE Asia, Phil. 2 ssp, 1 in region: *gularis* (most of range). Fairly common migrant in woodland and open country, <1200 m. **ID** Yellow cere; yellow to orange-yellow legs. In flight shows quite rounded wing shape with five 'fingers'; heavily barred flight feathers and densely spotted wing linings on underwing. Long primary projection; short tail squared, sometimes notched, with 4–5 medium-width bars. **M** dark slaty-grey above (with appearance of dark-slate cap); reddish washed-out barring below; faint mesial stripe; red iris. **F** larger and browner above with stronger mesial stripe, indistinct supercilium; extensive clear cold-brown barring below; yellow iris; somewhat hooded appearance created by grey-brown 'helmet' versus white throat. **Imm** dark brown above; white throat with narrow mesial stripe; yellow iris; thin white supercilium; rufous to brown teardrops on breast grading into bars and spots on flanks and belly. **Voc** Usually silent in winter; high-pitched descending "kee-kik-kik-kik-kik-kik", lasting 1.5 sec. **SS** See Asian Shikra, Chinese and Eurasian. Ad from Besra by lack of breast streaks and fainter mesial stripe, but imm difficult: imm Besra usually has thicker uppertail bars, more prominent underparts pattern, less densely spotted wing linings and stronger mesial stripe than imm Japanese. See also Small, Vinous-breasted and Spot-tailed Sparrowhawks and Sulawesi, Crested, Varied and Brown Goshawks.

Besra *Tachyspiza virgata*

L 24–36 cm, **WS** 42–65 cm/1.8. S–SE–E Asia, Phil. 11 ssp, 4–5 in region: *virgata* (Jav, Bali); *quinquefasciata* (Flores); *rufotibialis* (Bor); *vanbemmeli* (Sum); *affinis* (S–SE–E Asia wintering to MPen and likely to N Sum). Rare to uncommon in hill and montane forest, 300–3000 m. Usually flies below canopy, rarely soars. **ID** Yellow cere; yellow to orange-yellow legs; eyes yellow, in some males orange, strong mesial stripe on white throat. In flight shows short, rounded wing shape with five 'fingers', leading to short primary projection; underwing densely barred (on flight feathers) or spotted (on wing lining). Rather short, squared tail (except for long-tailed *affinis*) with 4–6 unusually thick black uppertail bars (thinner on undertail). **M** blackish-slate above; rufous flanks and breast, the latter heavily mottled centrally and black-streaked, grading into intense rufous bars and mottling on belly and thighs; vent white. **F** larger; underparts pattern usually less rufous, more brown; upperparts also more brown-tinged. Ssp *quinquefasciata* poorly known in life, said to have narrower, fainter uppertail bars and **M** with more hazel pattern on underparts; *rufotibialis* has **M** with richer rufous pattern on underparts (reaching lower down) with fewer black streaks; *vanbemmeli* has more creamy throat with less conspicuous mesial stripe, **M** more solid rufous underparts with inconspicuous barring; *affinis* longer-tailed and larger for each sex, also less dark-backed (more slate-grey in **M** and medium grey-brown in **F**) than other races. **Imm** brown above; underparts heavily streaked black and brown (on breast) or densely mottled and barred brown (on belly and flanks). **Voc** High-pitched, rather squeaky "kik-KYIK-KYIK-kyik-kyikyikyikyik", speeding up at end (1.5 sec, 1.5–2.2 kHz); wheezy "kyeellir", often preceding first call. **SS** See Asian Shikra, Crested, Varied and Brown Goshawks, Japanese, Chinese and Eurasian Sparrowhawks.

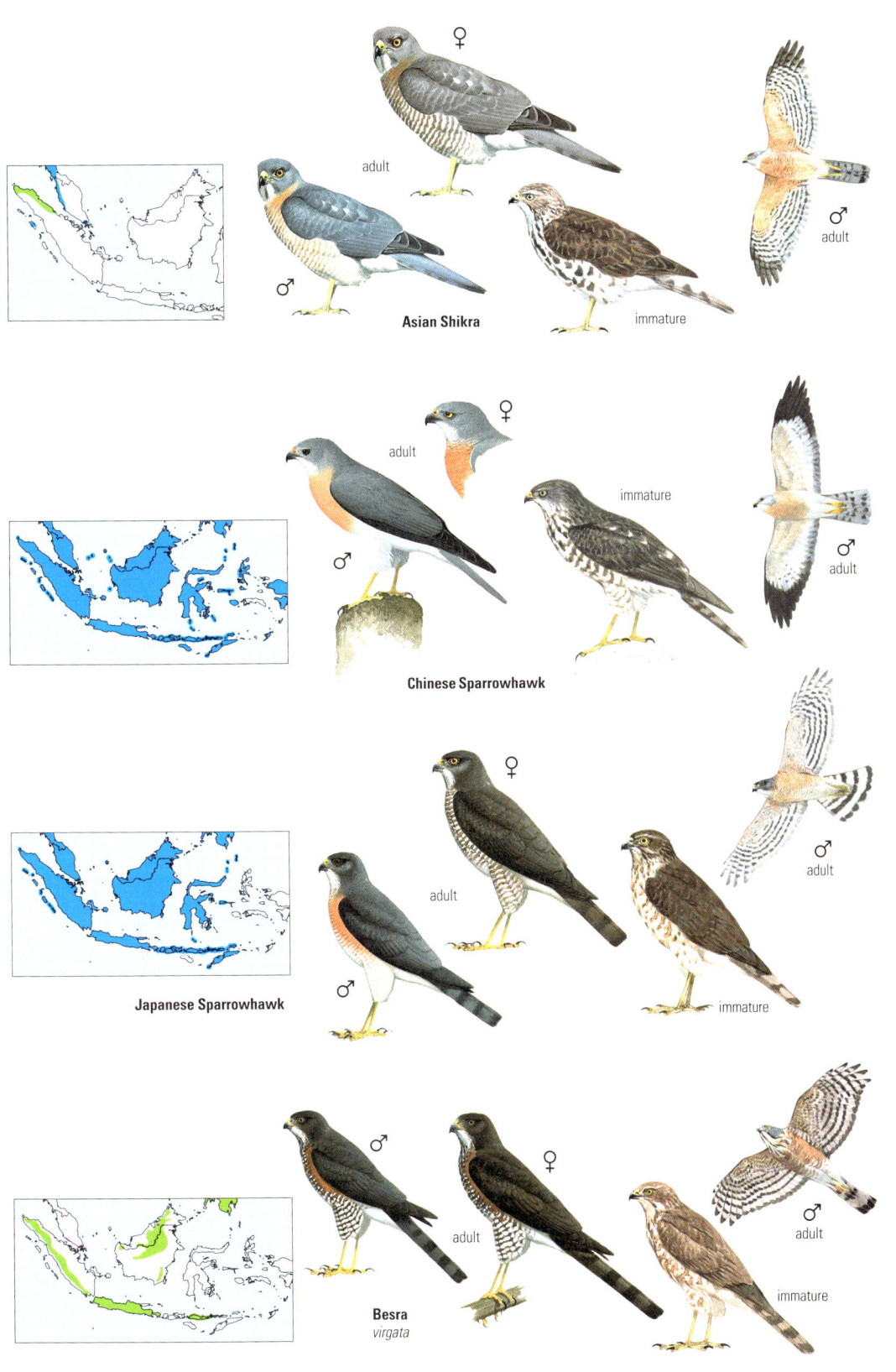

Asian Shikra

♀ adult

♂ immature

♂ adult

Chinese Sparrowhawk

adult ♀

♂ adult

immature

♂ adult

Japanese Sparrowhawk

♀ adult

♂

immature

♂ adult

Besra
virgata

♂

♀ adult

adult

immature

♂ adult

Vinous-breasted Sparrowhawk

Tachyspiza rhodogaster

L 26–33 cm, **WS** 46–62 cm/1.8. 3 ssp: *rhodogaster* (Sul); *butonensis* (Muna, Buton); *sulaensis* (Banggai, Sula). Uncommon in primary and tall secondary forest, rarely lightly wooded cultivation and mangroves, <2300 m. Usually flies below canopy, rarely soars. **ID** Legs, cere and eyes usually yellow (but see *sulaensis*). **M** slaty-grey upperparts, head and uppertail (the latter dimly barred black); white to greyish throat, thighs and vent; rest of underparts vinous; wing linings white or buffy, mottled grey. **F** larger, often with brownish tinge above, paler vinous breast, and more blackish-spotted under-wing. Ssp *butonensis* reported to have paler grey cheeks, paler vinous breast. Ssp *sulaensis* reported to have head sides tinged rufous and faint vinous nuchal collar, but neither of these traits found in the well-documented Peleng population, which appears smaller than nominate with more orange legs and eyes. **Imm** deep rufous above, boldly dark-spotted and barred; darker crown; creamy to whitish below with dark mesial stripe and heavy dark underparts streaking; underwing washed rufous with dense dark spotting (on wing linings) and barring (on flight feathers); thick black barring on rufous tail. **Voc** Rapid "hihihihihi", lower-pitched and less piercing than Small Sparrowhawk. **SS** See very similar Ad Small Sparrow-hawk. Ad Spot-tailed has dark (not yellow) eyes, very distinct white-spotted tail pattern, orange (not yellow) cere and less intense markings on underwing. Ad Chinese has cere orange (not yellow), distinct unmarked underwing with black tip (versus heavily marked underwing lacking black tip) and – in the more similarly-patterned male – dark (versus yellow) eyes. Male Japanese has eyes dark-red (versus yellow), faint mesial stripe, more barred (less washed-out) breast pattern and possibly more distinct black bars on tail. Distinct imm Vinous-breasted superficially resembles imm Sulawesi Gos-hawk but has distinct rufous-and-black back pattern and blacker (not warm-coloured) breast streaks.

Small Sparrowhawk *Tachyspiza nana*

L 23–28 cm, **WS** 44–54 cm/1.9. Monotypic. Uncommon in montane forest, >550 m. Sits quietly in lower-mid storey; does not soar; hunts below canopy. **ID** Tiny. Yellow cere; yellow (imm) to orange (Ad) eyes; yellowish-orange legs (yellower in imm). **Ad** has dark-grey upperparts and head; short, square, dimly barred dark-grey tail with three concealed white spots on upper side of outer feathers (usually only visible in hand); white throat; vinous breast and belly; thighs and vent white to light-grey. **Imm** plain rufous upperparts and tail (the latter with strong black bars), dusky head; white below, dark-streaked on breast and flanks. **Voc** Quite vocal: thin, high-pitched "kiliew" sometimes followed by very sharp, rapid "kik-kik-kik-kik-kik", higher-pitched than Vinous-breasted. **SS** Larger Ad Vinous-breasted extremely difficult to separate unless by voice: in hand, Vinous-breasted lacks obscure white outer tail spots of Small. In flight, Ad Vinous-breasted's underwing is more strongly mottled on wing linings and less strongly barred on flight feathers than Small; furthermore, Ad Vinous-breasted reported to have yellower (less orange) feet and eyes than Ad Small, but orange iris tone known from at least one Vinous-breasted ssp, so this trait may not

always hold. Ad Spot-tailed has longer, more rounded, white-tipped tail with 2–3 well-visible white spots, often exhibits whiter (less greyish) vent and thighs, has a conspicuous, more orange cere, less markings on underwing in flight, and blackish (versus yellow-orange) eyes. Imm Spot-tailed has dark (versus yellow) eyes, mostly black tail with white spots (versus rufous tail with black bars), orange to dark (versus yellow) cere, thinner streaking on breast and flanks and less boldly-patterned underwing. Ad Chinese has cere orange (ver-sus yellow); eyes dark (male) or yellow (fem) versus orange; longer, more pointed wing; and distinct unmarked underwing pattern with black tip (versus heavily marked underwing lacking black tip). Male Japanese has eyes dark-red (versus orange), faint mesial stripe, more barred (less washed-out) breast pattern and distinct black bars on tail. See also Sulawesi Goshawk. **AN** Dwarf Sparrowhawk.

Spot-tailed Sparrowhawk *Tachyspiza trinotata*

L 26–30 cm, **WS** 45–51 cm/1.7. Monotypic. Fairly common inside primary and tall secondary forest, dense mangrove, <1600 m. Usually perches quietly in mid-storey, rarely soars. **ID** Conspicuous orange-yellow legs and cere (the latter still colourless on young imm). Big, brown-black button-eye. Black tail (rufous-washed on sides in imm) has white tip and 2–3 white spots on inner webs, forming broken bars. **Ad** pale grey-blue head becoming darker on upperparts; pale vinous-washed breast; white belly. In flight, under-wing whitish with few bars on dark-tipped flight feathers. **Imm** bright rufous above, plain on upperparts but heavily dark-streaked on crown (rarely, mantle can be dark-spotted, too); off-white to pale rufous below with dark-streaked upper breast and flanks. **Voc** Quite frequent caller: (1) a deliberate, unhurried "hee", 4–6 times repeated; (2) a characteristic, decelerating, descending series of 5-8 "kek" notes; (3) weaker miaowing cry at longer intervals. **SS** See Small and Vinous-breasted. Male Chinese has longer, more pointed wings and lacks the white-spotted tail pattern. Male Japanese shows more distinct barring on breast, faint mesial stripe, a heavily patterned underwing without dark wingtips, a black-barred (versus white-spotted) tail and a more yellow cere.

Meyer's Goshawk *Astur meyerianus*

L 43–53 cm, **WS** 86–105 cm/2.0. Wallacea to Melanesia. Monotypic. Rare in forest and edge, predominantly found in uplands; occasionally perching conspicuously on open branches in canopy. **ID Ad** blackish above; white below with indistinct streaking and barring on breast and sides; brown eyes; black uppertail with lighter greyish bars; can show indistinct supercilium; dark grey cere. **Dark morph** entirely black with some white on nape. **Imm** dark brown above with rufous edging, rufous-buff below with sparse dark streaking; tail as Ad; in flight wing linings streaked and flight feathers barred. **Voc** Series of 8–10 clear, moderately high-pitched up-slurs (3 sec), answered by disyllabic, somewhat more strident and hurried "k-keh"; nasal upslurred "kyah". **SS** Smaller imm *hiogaster* Varied Goshawk has orange (not dark) cere, more distinct supercilium and generally broader bars restricted to outer flanks. See also imm Rufous-necked Sparrowhawk and Halmahera Goshawk.

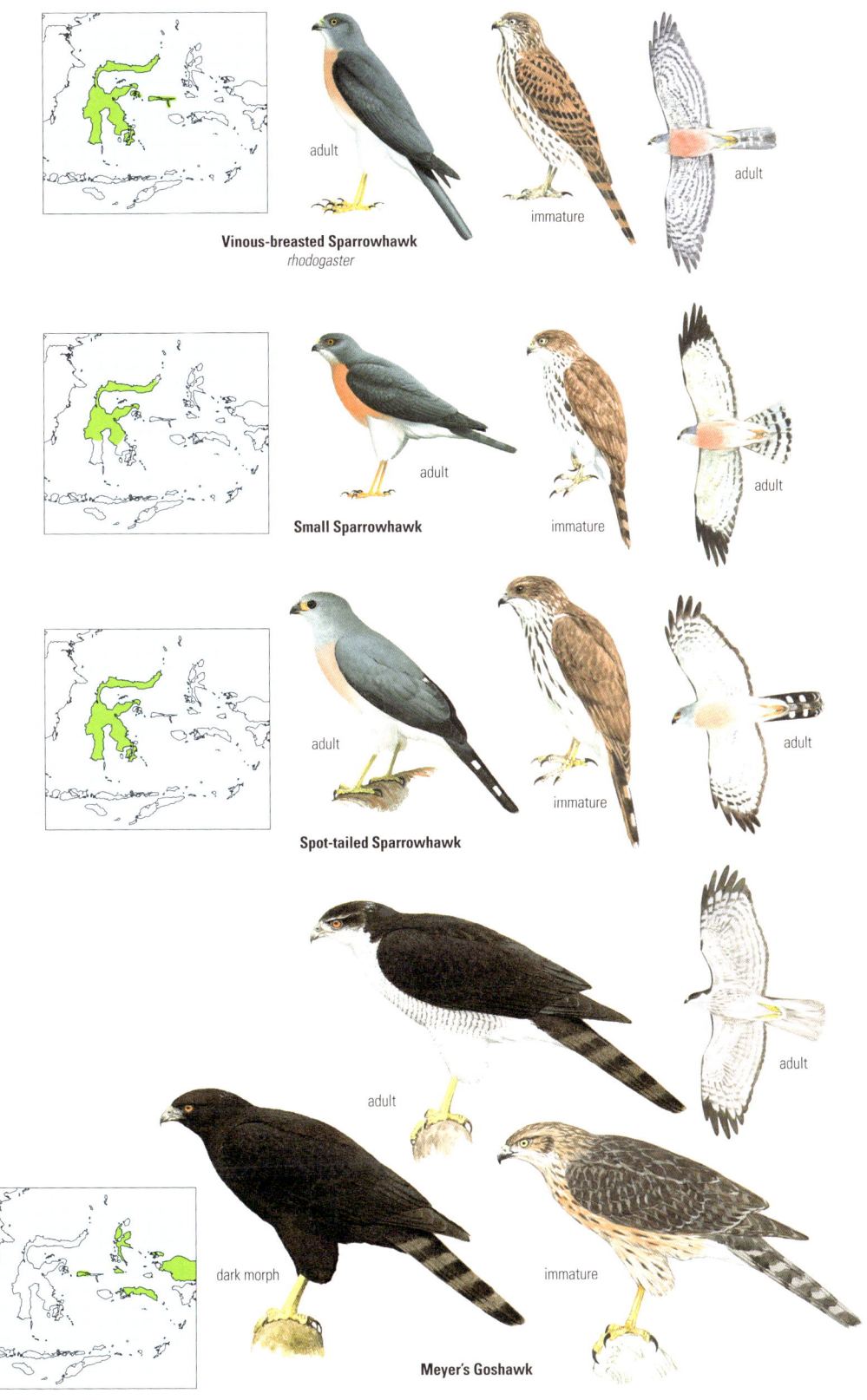

Vinous-breasted Sparrowhawk
rhodogaster

adult
immature
adult

Small Sparrowhawk

adult
immature
adult

Spot-tailed Sparrowhawk

adult
immature
adult

adult
adult

dark morph
immature

Meyer's Goshawk

Crested Goshawk *Lophospiza trivirgata*

L 30–46 cm, **WS** 54–79 cm/1.8. S–SE Asia, Phil. 11 ssp, 4 in region: *trivirgata* (Sum); *javanica* (Jav, Bali); *microsticta* (Bor); *niasensis* (Nias). This and Sulawesi Goshawk are unrelated to other sparrow-hawks and probably only mimic them in plumage and shape. Fairly common in many wooded habitats, even including city parks, <2000 m. During display, glides and flaps on winnowing wings and conspicuously puffs up undertail-coverts. **ID** Yellow cere; yellow to orange-yellow eyes and legs, the latter quite large; short crest can be hard to see; white throat with pronounced mesial stripe. Six 'fingers' in flight. Long tail with 4–5 quite thick black bars. **Ad** greyish above (larger **F** often brown-tinged on back and crown) with slaty head sides; rufous streaks on breast (often becoming solid rufous on breast sides) and rufous to brown bars on belly; vent contrastingly white. Ssp *javanica* is smaller for each sex, with darker back, possibly shorter crest; *niasensis* is still smaller and darker; *microsticta* smallest and more finely barred below. **Imm** upperparts browner; variably thick brown streaks and teardrops on underparts becoming fine bars on lower flanks, thighs and vent. **Voc** High-pitched, repetitive "wlee-wleeEE-wleeEE-chik-wleeEE-chik-wleeEE-chik-wleeEE"; soft-repeated high-pitched upslurred "wleeEEK". **SS** Multiple smaller sparrowhawk species (e.g. Besra, imm Shikra, imm Japanese, imm Chinese) have very similar plumage to Crested, but crest (when visible on perched bird) is diagnostic. In flight, Crested most easily told from confusion species by six (not five) primary 'fingers', but beware of moulting Crested with five fingers: full set of fingers on any of these species always features a diminutive outer-most primary that falls far short of black subterminal band of the second-outermost primary, while an incomplete set of five fingers on moulting Crested often features an unusually long outermost primary that reaches the black subterminal band of its neighbour. Ad Crested's unique puffed-up white vent is diagnostic when visible. Crested shows less barring and spotting on underwing than Besra and imm Japanese, but more than Chinese (the latter showing diagnostic black wingtips). Mesial stripe and underparts blotching of Crested thicker at least than Japanese. See also Jerdon's Baza.

Sulawesi Goshawk *Lophospiza griseiceps*   `E`

L 28–37 cm, **WS** 51–65 cm/1.8. Monotypic. For taxonomy see Crested Goshawk. Uncommon in forest, mangrove, and vicinity of villages, <2200 m. **ID** Yellow cere, legs and eyes. Small crest (often invisible). **Ad** slate-grey head contrasting with solid chocolate-brown upperparts and tail (the latter barred black); white throat with dark mesial stripe; white underparts coarsely streaked blackish-brown, heavily black-barred thighs; almost unmarked white wing linings. **Imm** similar but head concolourous with back; underparts streaking and barring rufous. **Voc** High-pitched, rather faint "kik-kik-kik…" (lasting 3 sec), slower than most other goshawks and sparrowhawks. **SS** Imm Small Sparrowhawk somewhat resembles Ad Sulawesi Goshawk, but is tiny, much redder on upperparts and lacks both mesial streak and contrasting grey head. Imm Sulawesi from imm Japanese and Chinese by longer tail and barring restricted to thighs (not reaching belly or flanks); Japanese additionally has heavily marked underwing (versus nearly unmarked wing linings), and Chinese additionally has orange (not yellow) cere and blackish underwing tips. See also imm Vinous-breasted.

TYTONIDAE
Barn Owls
5 species in region
Distinctive family of owls, with a characteristic facial pattern. Occupy a variety of habitats from open country to dense forest. Nocturnal in habit, they feed by silently pouncing on prey. By day, roosts in vegetation. Presence typically revealed by distinctive calls.

Eastern Barn Owl *Tyto javanica*

L 31-51 cm. S-SE Asia to Aus. 10-11 ssp, 6 in region: *javanica* (GS, MPen; presumably this ssp Lombok–Alor, Flores Sea Is); *delicatula* (Rote, Timor–Tanimbar, Aus); *sumbaensis* (Sumba, Sawu); based on darker plumage, smaller *nigrobrunnea* (Sula) often separated as monotypic '**Taliabu Masked Owl**', and larger *rosenbergii* (Sul, Togian, Buton, Selayar) and *pelengensis* (Peleng) often separated as '**Sulawesi Masked Owl**' *T. rosenbergii*, but both are geneti-cally and vocally similar to Eastern Barn. Eastern Barn sometimes merged into cosmopolitan '**Barn Owl**' *T. alba* with forms from other continents, but genetic differences pronounced and more research needed. Fairly common to locally scarce in forest clearings, edge, countryside and even in cities, <1800 m. Nests inside tree holes and buildings. Often seen hunting over fields and along hedges, with wings held in 'V'. Often perching conspicuously, including on rocks and roadside posts. **ID** All white underparts; rufous-and-grey upperparts with white and black specking; facial disc white. In flight has ginger-buff upperwing and uppertail, feet do not project beyond tail. Ssp *sumbaensis* slightly larger with whiter tail; *delicatula* shorter-tailed and lacks rufous tones on upperparts. Ssp *rosenbergii* largest and more variable: light or dark grey facial disc, grey crown, strong buff wash on black-spotted underparts can be restricted to flanks; dark-grey and buff upperparts; in flight upperwing wholly dark. Ssp *pelengensis* like previous but smaller, somewhat scaly-patterned underparts. Ssp *nigrobrunnea* smallest, with largely unmarked, dark-brown upperparts; underparts golden-brown with white speckles; greyish facial disc with rufous rim. **Imm** can show heavier spotting. **Voc** Long, harsh, ear-piercing screech, "cherrree", lasting ~0.5-0.9 sec, uttered both in flight and when perched, repeat-ed or irregular. **SS** See Grass and Minahasa Owls.

Grass Owl *Tyto capensis*

L 38–42 cm. Africa, S–SE–E Asia to Aus. 7 ssp, 1–2 in region: *longimembris* (S Asia to Aus; in region Sul, Flores and Sumba eastwards), and presumably this ssp or *amauronota* (Phil) recently recorded in Sabah and W Kalimantan. Sometimes separated from African ssp as '**Eastern Grass Owl**' *T. longimembris*, but genetic and morpho-logical differences minor. Rare and seldom seen in open grasslands and wetlands. Nests on ground, creating a tunnel and shallow depression. **ID** Long-legged, similar to Barn Owl but lower half of tarsi unfeathered; smaller eye. **Ad** upperparts darker than Barn Owl, with darker crown. In flight usually shows dark upperwing-coverts contrasting with outerwing, and dangling feet projecting beyond tail. Ssp *amauronota* slightly larger, greyer upperparts. **F/Imm** can show darker face and underparts. **Voc** Seldom calls: long, harsh screech, similar to Barn Owl but a little longer and lower-pitched, lasting 1 sec. Also other harsh screeches and wheezing sounds, usually when close to nest. **SS** Eastern Barn has larger eyes and feathered tarsus; in flight note Grass Owl's dangling foot projection beyond tail and contrasting upperwing pattern. Much smaller, large-eyed Minahasa Owl lives in forest interior and not known to overlap.

Minahasa Owl *Tyto inexspectata*   `E`

L 27–31 cm. Monotypic. Scarce in closed-canopy forest, 100–1800 m. Replaced by Eastern Barn Owl in more open areas and forest edge. **ID Ad** facial disc buff with darker crown and nape; underparts rich buff with small black spots on breast; wings dark, relatively plain with tiny white spots. **Imm** apparently paler underparts and browner upperparts. **Voc** Ear-piercing harsh hissing "shrrrrr" lasting ~1.6 sec. Much longer, harsher and lower-pitched than Eastern Barn. **SS** Eastern Barn Owl is larger, has grey or white (not buff) facial disc and usually more spotting on upper- and underparts, and grey (not rufous) crown. See also Grass Owl. **AN** Minahasa Masked Owl.

immature

adult ♂

Crested Goshawk

adult

Sulawesi Goshawk

delicatula

javanica

rosenbergii

nigrobrunnea

Eastern Barn Owl

Grass Owl

Minahasa Owl

Masked Owl *Tyto novaehollandiae*

L 31–47 cm. Aus. 11 ssp, 3 in region: *sororcula* (Tanimbar); *cayelii* (Buru); *almae* (Seram). The three ssp in region variably separated from others as '**Lesser Masked Owl**' *T. sororcula*, with *almae* often additionally afforded monotypic species status ('**Seram Masked Owl**'), and sometimes *cayelii* too ('**Buru Masked Owl**'). However, at least ssp *cayelii* and *sororcula* are genetically quite undifferentiated from all other ssp. Ssp *almae* is borderline distinct in mtDNA but here merged because plumage and vocal differences are extremely minor. Uncommon in secondary and primary forest, clearings and edge <1400 m, *almae* generally at higher elevations. Often along forested roads. **ID Ad** facial disc buff with pale-spotted rim; large grey-brown blotches and tiny dark spotting on white underparts; upperparts dark buff with black and tiny white spotting all over. Ssp *cayelii* slightly darker, duller upperparts; well-defined black tail bars; more buff facial disc though much individual variation and overlap with other ssp; *almae* buffier underparts, more well-defined black tail bars, but both traits with much individual variation based on existing photos. **Imm** undescribed in region. **Voc** Typical *Tyto* screech but longer than Eastern Barn, lasting ~1.3 sec, given intermittently, often in flight. **AN** Australasian Masked Owl.

Oriental Bay Owl *Phodilus badius*

L 22–29 cm. SE Asia. 3 ssp, 2 in region: *badius* (GS, MPen); *parvus* (Belitung). Recently split from Sri Lankan Bay Owl *P. assimilis* (S Asia). Uncommon in forest, edge, particularly with palms and lianas, <2300 m. Usually perching low to the ground. Powerful, large feet enable it to cling onto vertical lianas and trunks. **ID** Like a small *Tyto* but different jizz and habits. **Ad** rich chestnut upperparts with black and yellow spotting; paler underparts; elongated facial disc gives impression of ear-tufts; large, dark eyes. Ssp *parvus* larger white spots on upperparts. **Imm** paler, slightly streaked below. **Voc** Haunting series of 4–9 whining whistles "woo-woo-woe-woe-woe-woe", lasting 4–7 sec. First 2 notes loud with remaining notes tailing off. At a distance only first 2–3 notes can be heard. Sporadic caller, one night calling non-stop for hours, following night completely silent.

STRIGIDAE
Owls

45 species in region

A large family of small to medium-sized, primarily nocturnal birds. Most are inhabitants of forest, but some occupy sparsely wooded habitats. All feed by silently pouncing on prey on the wing or from perches. Usually found singly, they roost silently by day in vegetation where their often cryptic colouration makes them difficult to detect. Their presence is typically revealed by their distinctive calls.

Sunda Owlet *Taenioptynx sylvatica* **E**

L 15–17 cm. 2 ssp: *sylvatica* (Sum); *borneensis* (Bor). Traditionally considered conspecific with extralimital Collared Owlet *T. brodiei* (mainland Asia) but exhibits pronounced vocal and plumage differences. Uncommon in montane and submontane forest, 900–2700 m. Diurnal, usually in canopy. **ID Ad** speckled crown; streaked belly; buff barred upperparts; white-and-blackish imitation of face on nape; no obvious white on coverts. Ssp *borneensis* has white neck band. **Imm** unmarked; rufous crown to mantle, whitish spots on coverts. **Voc** Soft, mellow, evenly-pitched 7-note "toot, toot-toot, toot, too-too-too", lasting ~3 sec, repeated every 10–30 sec; calls throughout the day.

Javan Owlet *Glaucidium castanopterum* **E**

L 24 cm. Monotypic. Uncommon in primary and secondary forest, rarely plantations, <900 m, locally <2000 m. Mainly nocturnal, often vocal before dawn, sometimes through day. **ID Ad** indistinct facial disc; head, flanks and tail barred rufous-and-buff; broad white markings on scapulars, rufous on mantle and thick underpart streaking. **Imm** duller, lacks barring. **Voc** 15–50 throaty, barbet-like "coor-coor-coor...", lasting 8–30 sec; first 5–10 notes at 1 n/s speeding up into a rapid succession at 3 n/s, ending abruptly. Series of notes, starting with slow "kewkewkek..., kewkekkewkekkewkek..., kewkekikikikik...", last part excited, shrill, accelerating and rising, lasting ~12 sec.

Mentawai Scops Owl *Otus mentawi* **E**

L 22 cm. Monotypic. Common in forest, edge and plantations. Only *Otus* in range. **ID Ad** overall dark; dark-brown upperparts and head; dull rufous underparts with black streaks; dark eyes. **Imm** undescribed. **Voc** (1) Deep, throaty gruff "grrk" repeated every 0.4 sec; (2) inflected bellowing 2-3 note "woyk woyk", often in duets between lower-pitched male and higher-pitched female. **SS** Rufous (not white) underparts and dark eyes should separate it from any potential wintering Oriental Scops stray.

Simeulue Scops Owl *Otus umbra* **E**

L 16–18 cm. Monotypic. Fairly common in forest, edge and occasionally plantations. Only *Otus* on island. **ID Ad** uniform dark rufous-grey body with slight whitish barring on underparts, particularly belly. **Imm** undescribed. **Voc** Single "wher" or "wheru" often in duet; short series of lower-pitched staccato "whit-whert-whit-whit-whert...", lasting 4–7 sec, at 3 n/s, often in duet with main song.

Enggano Scops Owl *Otus enganensis* **E**

L 16–20 cm. Monotypic. Common in forest, edge and plantations. Only *Otus* on island. **ID Ad** dark-brown upperparts and head; white loral bristles; dark greyish face and dark rufous underparts. **Imm** undescribed. **Voc** Deep, throaty "grrr", repeated every 0.5 sec; louder 2-note "grr-ra", sometimes given in duet.

Mantanani Scops Owl *Otus mantananensis*

L 18 cm. Phil. 4 ssp, 1 in region: *mantananensis* (Mantanani). Small-island specialist. Found in various types of wooded areas on small islands. Only *Otus* in range. **ID Ad** prominent ear-tufts; black-rimmed facial disc; thick black streaks on breast; yellow eyes; big feet and claws. **Imm** pale, heavily barred dark-brown; underparts and crown plainer. **Voc** Series of deep, nasal "kwoak" notes, lasting 0.3 sec, often in duet.

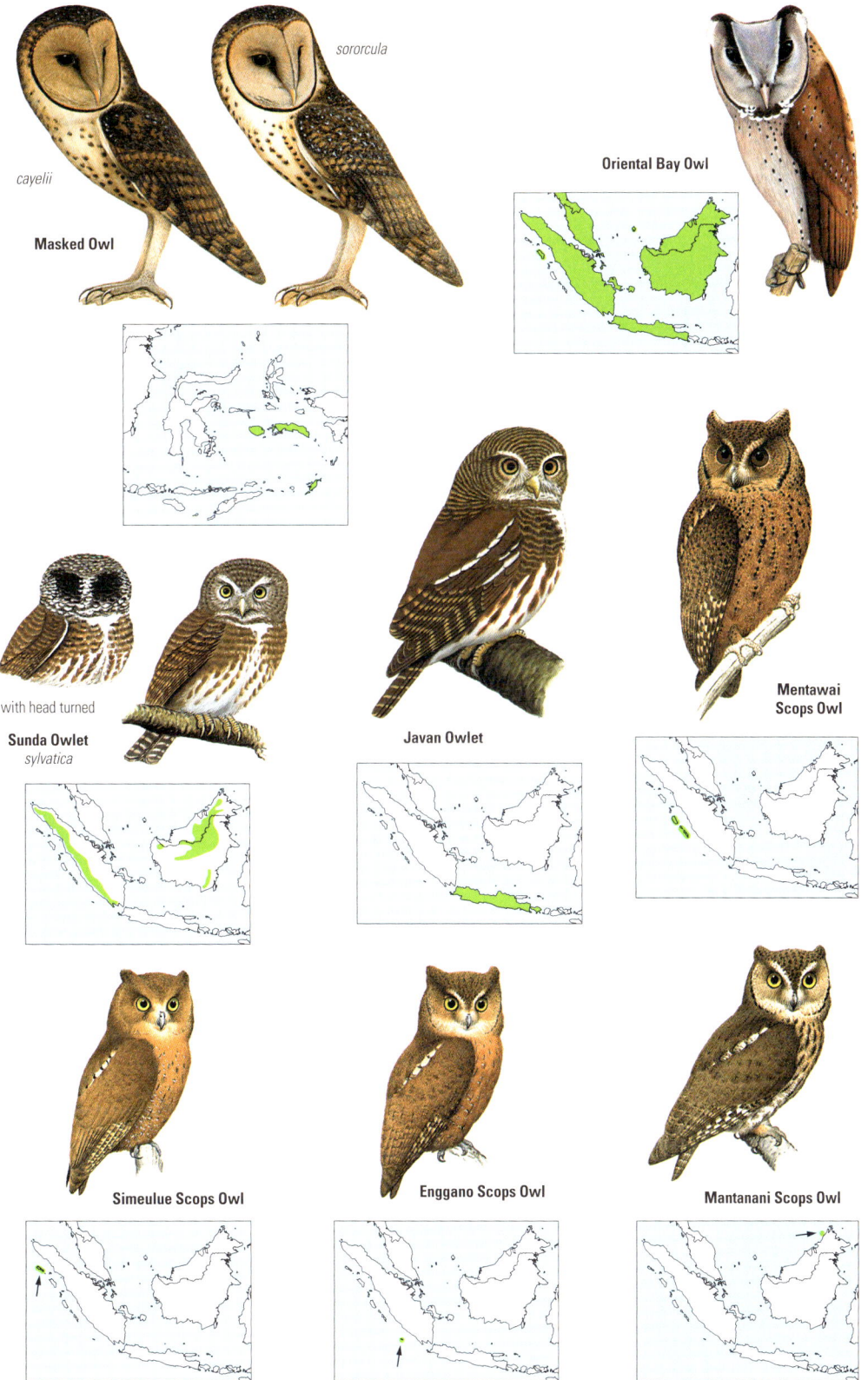

cayelii

sororcula

Masked Owl

Oriental Bay Owl

with head turned

Sunda Owlet
sylvatica

Javan Owlet

**Mentawai
Scops Owl**

Simeulue Scops Owl

Enggano Scops Owl

Mantanani Scops Owl

Oriental Scops Owl *Otus sunia* `V`

L 18–21 cm. Breeds S–SE–E–NE Asia, winters to region. 8 ssp, 1 in region: *malayanus* (breeds China; winters SE Asia). This ssp and two others breeding in temperate zone may need to be separated as '**Chinese Scops Owl**' *O. japonicus* based on vocal differences from subtropical forms. Recorded N Sum (Jan 1887, March 1974). Presumably scarce winterer and migrant in forest, edge, plantations and coastal scrub, but probably overlooked (given regular occurrence in Singapore). **ID** Polymorphic. **Ad** grey, grey-brown and rufous morphs have well-streaked and vermiculated underparts and conspicuous white markings on scapulars. Yellow eyes. **Imm** faint barring, less streaks on breast. **Voc** Unlikely to be heard in region: *malayanus* resonant 3-note whistle, "kroik-kroi-kroik", lasting 0.9 sec, repeated every 0.7 sec. **SS** Collared Scops has brown or orange (not yellow) eyes, paler ear-tufts, extensive white background colour to underparts pattern (versus grey, brown or reddish background at least to parts of breast barring in Oriental). Collared rufous morph is never as bright and chestnut as Oriental. Also see Rajah, Mountain and Mentawai Scops Owls.

Collared Scops Owl *Otus lempiji*

L 20–25 cm. S–SE–E Asia. 11 ssp, 4 in region: *lempiji* (S Sum–Bali, Bangka, Belitung, S Bor, Natuna); *hypnodes* (N–C Sum); *lemurum* (N Bor); isolated ssp *kangeanus* (Kangean) poorly known and requires investigation. Often united with Indian Scops Owl *O. bakkamoena* (S Asia) into a broadly-circumscribed '**Collared Scops Owl**' *O. bakkamoena*. On the other extreme, present species sometimes separated into '**Sunda Scops Owl**' *O. lempiji* (Sundaic; only this species in region) and '**Collared Scops Owl**' *O. lettia* from further north. All forms share similar mtDNA, but present treatment is based on unmistakeable vocalisations of Indian Scops, while vocal differences between 'Sunda Scops' and 'Collared Scops' *O. lettia* seem to occur over a geographic gradient across MPen. This species no longer includes ssp *ussuriensis*, which has been reassigned to Japanese Scops Owl O. *semitorques* (NE Asia). Fairly common in variety of habitats including city gardens, plantations, forest and edge, <1800 m, rarely to 2500 m. **ID Ad** polymorphic. Grey (rarest), brown and rufous morphs. Relatively long, pale ear-tufts contrasting slightly with face; upperparts relatively unmarked; underparts streaking sparse but prominent; eye colour usually dark brown but can be bright orange or even yellow. Ssp *hypnodes* overall darker, particularly rufous morph; *lemurum* overall more rufescent or reddish in each morph; *kangeanus* smaller and slightly paler. **Imm** bright brownish-buff, strongly vermiculated. **Voc** Male single, inflected "woyk", lasting 0.2 sec, usually repeated every 10–15 sec. Fem occasionally duets with a slightly higher-pitched "woik". **SS** See Reddish, Mountain, Rajah, Javan and Oriental Scops Owls.

Rajah Scops Owl *Otus brookii* `E`

L 22–25 cm. 2 ssp: *brookii* (Bor); ssp *solokensis* (Sum) is different in plumage, may differ vocally and should probably be afforded species status as '**Sumatran Scops Owl**', but the voice of *brookii* '**Bornean Scops Owl**' remains unknown. Scarce in montane forest, >1100 m. Usually perches low, rarely in canopy. **ID Ad** fierce-looking; dark-brown above; blackish-crown, white ear-tufts, brown-barred underparts with thick black streaking; orange eyes. Ssp *solokensis* shows darker underparts with heavier streaking, paler bill, less distinct nuchal collar. **Imm** *brookii* undescribed; *solokensis* rufous-tinged upperparts, vermiculated underparts. **Voc** Ssp *brookii* reported to utter a single, startling, monotonous call; *solokensis*: explosive barking "OWH" or "OWH-OWH", lasting 0.5 sec, irregularly repeated. **SS** See Mountain Scops. Among other light-eyed scops owls, *solokensis* is told from cold-brown morph of smaller wintering Oriental Scops by orange (not yellow) eyes and less uniform wings and back. Collared

Scops from more open habitat at lower elevation has darker brown eyes (beware pale reflection in torchlight!) and less strongly marked upper- and underparts; most conclusively separated by voice.

Javan Scops Owl *Otus angelinae* `E`

L 16–18 cm. Currently considered monotypic; a single specimen from E Jav, unknown in life, may differ from W Jav; further study required. Uncommon in primary montane forest, 1000–2500 m. Often perches low, occasionally clinging onto lianas. **ID Ad** similar to Collared Scops but thicker black streaks on breast, gleaming white ear-tufts, blacker crown and mantle, bright orange eyes, bigger feet. **Imm** darker, more vermiculated with yellowish undertail. **Voc** Distinctive shrill "weeeee", lasting 1 sec, at intervals of 5–20 sec; 2-note shrill "wee-wooww", first note rising, second note descending; explosive bark, similar to Rajah Scops Owl. **SS** Collared Scops is very similar, overlaps in Javan's lower elevational distribution, and shows considerable individual variation: generally (but not always) has less striking contrast between white ear-tufts and black crown; Collared underparts dominated by black fishbone streaks against fine black vermiculations in background (Javan tends to show black fishbone streaks against rufous-buff background with fine white bars); Collared eyes usually (but not always) darker, less orange; most conclusively separated by voice.

Reddish Scops Owl *Otus rufescens*

L 15–18 cm. Sundaic. 2 ssp, 1 in region: *rufescens* (GS). Uncommon in primary and secondary forest, <1100 m. **ID** Small, uniform rufous-brown with ear-tufts. **Ad** small; black spots over body, particularly breast; dark-brown eyes. **Imm** similar but less spotting. **Voc** Single "whoo", lasting 0.5 sec, tailing off towards the end, repeated every ~5 sec. **SS** Among dark-eyed scops owls, differs from Collared Scops in rufous underparts (Collared's red morph usually buff), all-dark ear-tufts (Collared usually has at least some pale feathers) and black-spotted, not streaked, breast, lacking vermiculations or fish-bone pattern.

Mountain Scops Owl *Otus spilocephalus*

L 18–20 cm. S–SE–E Asia. 8–9 ssp, 2–3 in region: *luciae* (Bor); *vandewateri* (Sum); '*stresemanni*' known from single specimen from Mt Kerinci (Sum) may only be a pale colour morph, but requires further study. Fairly common in montane forest, 900–2700 m. Notoriously difficult to locate when calling, often sits low and close to trunk or perched deep inside vegetation. **ID Ad** ill-defined ear-tufts, overall colouration varies from a warm rufous to grey; densely vermiculated underparts; thick white edges to scapulars; pale yellow eyes. Ssp *vandewateri* has prominent white collar; '*stresemanni*' rich rufous with white forehead, white speckles overall, no collar. **Imm** duller, more heavily barred. **Voc** Ventriloqual, high-pitched double whistle, like a hammer on an anvil, "pew-pew", lasting 0.8 sec, persistently at intervals of 5–10 sec; *vandewateri* occasionally calls with <7 whistles; *luciae* can also give a single-note "wheeer". **SS** Among light-eyed scops owls, lacks the strong dark streaks on underparts of both Oriental and the larger Rajah Scops. Rajah additionally has orange (not yellow) eyes. Collared Scops has darker brownish eyes (can appear light in torchlight but never bright yellow) and is also more streaked below.

Flores Scops Owl *Otus alfredi* `E`

L 19–20 cm. Monotypic. Scarce in montane forest, >700 m. **ID Ad** wholly rufous body with vermiculated, greyish underparts; facial disc reddish-rufous with yellow eyes; white edges to scapulars and ear-tufts; yellow feet. **Imm** uniform pale rufous with faint barring. **Voc** At dusk or when beginning to call, utters a distinctive, rapid series of "da-da-da-da-da-da", ~10 n/s, lasting 0.5–2 sec, later followed by a sharp, single note "Oop", lasting 0.1 sec. Often duets.

Oriental Scops Owl

grey-brown morph

rufous morph

Collared Scops Owl

brown morph

rufous morph

brookii

solokensis

Rajah Scops Owl

Javan Scops Owl

Reddish Scops Owl

vandewateri

luciae

'stresemanni'

Mountain Scops Owl

Flores Scops Owl

Moluccan Scops Owl *Otus magicus* E

L 21–23 cm. 7 ssp: *magicus* (Seram, Ambon); *bouruensis* (Buru); *morotensis* (Morotai); *leucospilus* (Halmahera, Bacan, Ternate); *obira* (Obi); *albiventris* (Sumbawa, Flores, Lembata); ssp *kalidupae* (Tukangbesi) sometimes erroneously placed under Sulawesi Scops but vocally clearly part of Moluccan. No longer considered to include extralimital Biak Scops Owl *O. beccarii*. See also Wetar Scops for taxonomy. Common in primary to degraded secondary forest, orchards, plantations, even villages, <1500 m. **ID Ad** grey, some birds show rufous wash, particularly around head. Dark mottling above and black streaks on underparts; dark rim around facial disc; fairly prominent ear-tufts; yellow eyes. Ssp *bouruensis* more uniform buffy-brown above, paler below; *morotensis* similar but generally darker, less spotted upperparts; *leucospilus* as previous but smaller more pale-faced; *obira* smaller than previous; *albiventris* smaller still with less-marked underparts; *kalidupae* pale grey-brown overall, finely patterned, feathering extends to top of toes. **Imm** similar but barred (not streaked) crown; less breast streaking. **Voc** Single, rough "croak", repeated every few seconds. Slight individual variation, some birds higher pitched than others. In flight or when excited can produce series of notes in quick succession. **SS** See Wallace's Scops.

Wetar Scops Owl *Otus tempestatis* E

L 20–21 cm. Monotypic. No longer included in Moluccan Scops based on distinct vocalisations. Common throughout; coastal, degraded forest to primary forest in hills. Only *Otus* on island. **ID** Polymorphic. Grey and rufous morph. **Grey morph** similar to Moluccan Scops but thick streaking on crown. Very different-looking **rufous morph** shows strong rufous barring on underparts and reduced streaking. Yellow eyes. **Imm** undescribed. **Voc** Series of 2–7 single gruff "wah", 6 n/5 s, sometimes at a faster pace.

Rinjani Scops Owl *Otus jolandae* E

L 20 cm. Monotypic. Fairly common in primary and degraded secondary forest, orchards, plantations, primarily >200 m. Only *Otus* on island. **ID Ad** as ssp *albiventris* of Moluccan Scops but upperparts warmer, more uniform and belly darker with more distinct barring. **Imm** undescribed. **Voc** Quite high-pitched, ascending "weera", lasting 0.4 sec, regularly repeated.

Wallace's Scops Owl *Otus silvicola* E

L 23–25 cm. Monotypic. Uncommon in primary and secondary forest, <1800 m. Favours upper canopy. **ID** Large. **Ad** dark-brown with blackish crown; thick breast streaking, yellow eyes. **Imm** paler, more rufous, strongly vermiculated with fewer markings. **Voc** Series of 5–10 loud, coarse single "POW" notes, lasting 0.3 sec each, repeated every ~1 sec. Series usually repeated after long intervals. **SS** Smaller Moluccan Scops is often greyer overall, and has extensive white background colour to underparts all the way to flanks, whereas Wallace's has white wedge extending up the mid-breast from belly while remaining breast and flanks have rich rusty background colour; most conclusively separated by voice.

Sula Scops Owl *Otus sulaensis* E

L 21 cm. Monotypic. Split from Sulawesi Scops Owl based on vocalisations. Fairly common in woodland and plantations throughout. Only *Otus* on island. **ID Ad** similar to Moluccan Scops but darker and more richly coloured with coarse markings. Ear-tufts concolourous with rest of head; yellow eyes. **Imm** lacks breast streaking, more vermiculated. **Voc** Rolling, 2-note "Ook-grrrrah", lasting 0.7 sec, regularly repeated.

Banggai Scops Owl *Otus mendeni* E

L 20 cm. Monotypic. Split from Sulawesi Scops Owl based on vocalisations. Fairly common in woodland and plantations throughout. Only *Otus* on island. **ID Ad** similar to Sulawesi Scops but more heavily streaked; facial disc grey-toned, indistinct dark-brown breast streaking; orange-yellow eyes. **Imm** lacks breast streaking, more vermiculated. **Voc** Tremulous "brrrrr", lasting ~1 sec, repeated regularly; 4–5 "euw" notes in flight.

Sulawesi Scops Owl *Otus manadensis* E

L 20 cm. Monotypic. For taxonomy see Moluccan, Sula and Banggai Scops Owls. Fairly common in primary to degraded secondary forest, <2500 m. **ID** Polymorphic. **Ad** brown and rufous morph, plumage variable. Fine black breast streaking; slight vermiculations over body; moderate-sized, whitish ear-tufts; yellow eyes. **Imm** similar but more barred, reduced streaking. **Voc** (i) Single "eehk", lasting 0.4 sec, repeated regularly, every 5–10 sec; (ii) single, inflected "plooek", lasting 0.3 sec; (iii) excited 6-note "woo-wooek-wooek-wooek-wooek-wooek", lasting 0.6 sec.

Siau Scops Owl *Otus siaoensis* E

L 19 cm. Monotypic. Single specimen collected Siau in 1866. Little forest remains on the island and has not been recorded despite searches in recent years. Only *Otus* on island, though beware potential migrant Oriental Scops Owl. **ID Ad** smaller, more uniform, short-winged and shorter-tailed than Sulawesi and Sangihe Scops. Prominent pale nuchal collar; breast streaked; belly barred. **Imm** undescribed. **Voc** Undescribed; a series of "uwh-uwh-uwh...", notes, 11 n/3.5 s, recorded at night, could be this species.

magicus

albiventris

kalidupae

Moluccan Scops Owl

rufous morph

Wetar Scops Owl

Rinjani Scops Owl

Wallace's Scops Owl

Sula Scops Owl

Banggai Scops Owl

brown morph

rufous morph

Sulawesi Scops Owl

Siau Scops Owl

Sangihe Scops Owl *Otus collari* **E**

L 19–20 cm. Monotypic. Fairly common in forest, mixed plantations, secondary growth. Only *Otus* on island. **ID Ad** dark greyish-brown upperparts; whitish eyebrows; grey underparts with black streaking. **Imm** undescribed. **Voc** Deflected whistle "twuu", lasting 0.6 sec, regularly repeated, sometimes in fast succession.

Barred Eagle Owl *Bubo sumatranus*

L 40–46 cm. Sundaic. 2 ssp: *sumatranus* (Bangka, Sum, MPen); *strepitans* (Bor, Jav, Bali). Uncommon in primary and secondary forest, well-wooded urban areas, plantations, <2000 m. **ID** Long ear-tufts usually held horizontally. **Ad M** dark, vermiculated upperparts with conspicuous white scapulars; dark barring on white underparts, denser on breast; yellow bill and feet; dark eyes. **F** larger; paler facial disc with distinctly darker edge, richer-brown upper-breast with less contrasting barring; narrower, more spotted barring on lower breast and belly. Ssp *strepitans* larger; barring stronger and denser below. **Imm** pure white body gradually becoming barred. **Voc** (i) Loud, far-carrying, deep "OOO-OWH", lasting 1.5 sec including 1 sec pause between notes, repeated regularly; sometimes only first note given; (ii) far-carrying mournful scream "whooa-who whoa wahooowa..."; (iii) single, deflected, far-carrying "ARHoo", lasting 0.5 s; (iv) peacock-like "ooo'eee"; (v) single "POWOO" or shorter "WOO"; (vi) long, loud, hornbill-like laughter, "ugh-ugh-ugh... ARH", lasting 3 s. Sometimes calls mid-morning and late afternoon. **SS** See Sunda Wood Owl.

Buffy Fish Owl *Bubo ketupu*

L 38–44 cm. SE Asia. 4 ssp, 3 in region: *ketupu* (MPen, most of GS); *pageli* (NW Bor); *buettikoferi* (Nias). Fairly common in forest, parks, plantations and wooded urban areas bordering streams, fish ponds and wetlands, <1600 m. **ID Ad** rich buff overall; broadly black-barred upperparts with white spots; underparts with thick black streaking; long ear-tufts; yellow eyes. Ssp *pageli* tinged rufous; *buettikoferi* smaller. **Imm** more rufous upperparts with less white spotting. **Voc** Single, repeated "POF", like somebody blowing over glass bottle; variety of hisses and screeches including "eeerhhh", lasting 0.8 sec, and shorter, less harsh "eeeuhh", lasting 0.6 sec. **SS** See Sunda Wood Owl.

Short-eared Owl *Asio flammeus* **V**

L 37–39 cm. Near-cosmopolitan. 11 ssp, 1 in region: *flammeus* (Holarctic). Vagrant to N Bor: Kuching (Nov 1910), Brunei (Jan 1976) and at sea, off Labuan (Sep 2014). Grassland, marshes, open areas, <1850 m. Diurnal, usually seen quartering fields at dusk like harrier, and sitting on fence posts and low bushes. **ID** Vertical, short whispy ear-tufts; very rounded head; facial disc forms radially streaked, broad circle; heavily streaked body; yellow eyes. In flight shows buff-orange upper primary patch and pale underwing with black bar at primary base. **Voc** Generally silent in region but can produce a short, sharp "yelp".

Spotted Wood Owl *Strix seloputo*

L 45–47 cm. SE Asia, Palawan. 3 ssp, 2 in region: *seloputo* (Jav, Sum, SE Asia); *baweana* (Bawean). Scarce in open forest, parks, plantations, mangroves, <1000 m. **ID Ad** plain, buff facial disc; prominent white spots on brown upperparts; white underparts with well-spaced dark bars; densely barred crown. Ssp *baweana* smaller, paler, with narrower bars. **Imm** prominently barred, with much white above. **Voc** Deep, forceful "WHO", lasting 0.2 sec, regularly repeated; rapidly repeated, rolling staccato "hoo-hoo-hoo...", lasting <5 sec. Often in duet, usually at dawn and dusk. **SS** See Sunda Wood Owl.

Sunda Wood Owl *Strix leptogrammica* **E**

L 45–50 cm. 7 ssp: *leptogrammica* (C–S Bor); *vaga* (N Bor); *chaseni* (Belitung); *bartelsi* (Jav); *myrtha* (Sum, presumably Mentawai); *nyctiphasma* (Banyak); because of vocal and morphological differences, the smaller *niasensis* (Nias) is sometimes considered a monotypic species '**Nias Wood Owl**'. Here separated from Brown Wood Owl *S. indranee* of mainland Asia based on vocalisations and plumage. Fairly common in primary and secondary forest, plantations, <1800 m. On Jav found only in montane forest, >800 m. **ID Ad** lower facial disk rufous, upper disk black; disk bordered by black on sides, rufous on brows; thick rufous upper breast band to collar largely unmarked; blackish-barred white underparts; lightly barred upperparts with whitish scapular markings. Ssp *vaga* slightly larger, duller (more greyish-brown), belly whiter, upperparts barring narrower and less well-defined; *bartelsi* paler facial disc, darker above (particularly nuchal collar), white throat patch; *chaseni* has darker, more contrasting crown, browner (less blackish) bars on body, brighter nuchal collar, more extensive, brighter rufous breast band, darker (dirty-buff) underparts; *myrtha* larger; *nyctiphasma* face and forehead lighter, belly darker, more rufescent, with less distinct barring; *niasensis* the smallest ssp, chest darker rufous, concolourous with face. **Imm** natal down pale buff, dark-rufous bars on upperparts and fainter underparts barring. **Voc** Deep, striking, single-note "WHO", lasting 0.4 sec, irregularly repeated. Ssp *niasensis* characteristically adds soft introductory note "oo-WHO", lasting 1 s in total, with **F** producing a higher-pitched "cow", rarely rendered multi-syllabically. **SS** From behind without facial view, Barred Eagle Owl less distinctly barred due to dark centres on narrower buff bars versus broader, plain buff bars on Sunda Wood; Buffy Fish Owl has broad, pale barring only on primaries and lacks white scapular markings. Spotted Wood Owl shows white speckling on wings, lacking buff barring altogether.

Sangihe Scops Owl

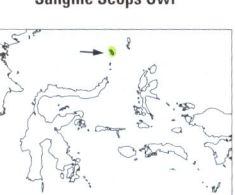

♂

Barred Eagle Owl

Buffy Fish Owl

Short-eared Owl

seloputo

Spotted Wood Owl

niasensis

leptogrammica

Sunda Wood Owl

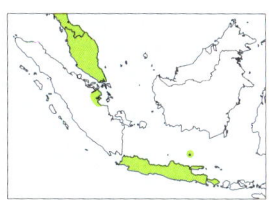

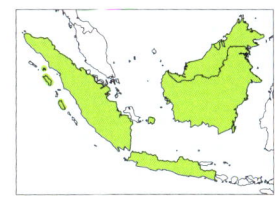

Brown Boobook *Ninox scutulata*

L 27–33 cm. S–SE–E Asia, Palawan. 9 ssp, 3–4 in region: *scutulata* (Sum, Bangka, MPen); *javanensis* (Jav–Bali); *borneensis* (Bor, Natuna); extralimital ssp *burmanica* (mainland SE Asia except MPen) very likely to winter into region (at least Sum) but difficult to ID in field. Previously included Northern and Chocolate Boobooks, but all three widely differ in voice and plumage. Fairly common in primary and secondary forest, edge, occasionally plantations and wooded parks, <1500 m. Usually in pairs. **ID Ad** brownish-grey head; chocolate-brown upperparts; white underparts with broad heart-shaped spotting; yellow eyes. Ssp *innominata* larger; *javanensis* smaller, rounder wings; *borneensis* also smaller, with underparts spotting showing tear drop shape as Northern Boobook. **Imm** paler upperparts, spotting more diffuse. **Voc** Loud, far-carrying "oo'OOP", lasting 0.5 sec, regularly repeated at >1 n/s, often in duet. Usually just after dusk and before dawn. **SS** See Northern Boobook. **AN** Brown Hawk Owl.

Northern Boobook *Ninox japonica*

L 29–33 cm. Breeds NE–E Asia; winters to SE Asia, Phil. 2 ssp: *japonica* (breeds at least Japan; winters to region, Phil); breeders on Taiwan constitute genetically distinct undescribed taxon probably including breeding populations in continental Asia, known to winter in Singapore and (probably this form) on Sum and perhaps Bor, restricting the winter range of *japonica* to the E of region; more research needed. For taxonomy also see Brown Boobook. Uncommon in forest, edge, occasionally plantations and wooded parks, <1500 m. **ID/SS** Conclusively told from resident Brown Boobook only by voice (though usually silent in region), longer wings (reaching tail tip, with fifth primary longer than second) and DNA. Confusion surrounds the use of the shape of spots on underparts for ID purposes: in mainland SE Asia to Sum, birds with preponderance of heart-shaped spots shown to correspond to Brown *scutulata* or *burmanica*, while predominance of tear-drop shaped spots corresponds to Northern Boobook (possibly the undescribed form from mainland Asia). However, further E the situation may be reversed, as Bornean ssp *borneensis* of Brown usually has tear-drop shaped spots, and wintering Northern *japonica* (at least in Wallacea, perhaps also Bor) can show a fair amount of heart-shaped spots, especially on belly. More research into subspecific variation needed. **Imm** similar to Ad. **Voc** Rarely heard in region. Loud, double "whoop-whoop" notes separated by ~0.4 sec, and repeated every ~0.7 sec, often in duet.

Chocolate Boobook *Ninox randi*

L 30–31 cm. Phil. Monotypic. For taxonomy see Brown Boobook. Scarce in primary and secondary forest, edge. **ID Ad** as Northern Boobook *scutulata*, though darker chocolate-brown overall and underparts spotting on average denser, appearing more streaked. **Imm** undescribed. **Voc** Series of 5–20 double "oowh-oowh" notes separated by ~0.2 sec, and repeated every ~0.4 sec, often in duet. **SS** Extremely difficult to identify from wintering Northern Boobook except by voice (the latter mostly silent in region but can be responsive). Chocolate often extensively streaked below (seemingly always with tear-drop shaped spots), sometimes so heavily that brown colour dominates on underparts, whereas Northern *japonica* on average has whiter underparts, sometimes with heart-shaped spots on belly; there is, however, overlap in intensity of underparts streaking. Northern can be greyish-tinged on head, although many are as chocolate-brown as Chocolate Boobook. Best difference may be tail: Northern almost always has distinct and often wide pale bars, while Chocolate has less distinct, often narrow pale bars.

Little Sumba Boobook *Ninox sumbaensis* `E`

L 23 cm. Monotypic. Uncommon in primary and secondary forest. **ID** Small. **Ad** dark-grey head; brown upperparts; white underparts barred rufous; whitish eyebrows; yellow eyes. **Imm** undescribed. **Voc** Single "poop", lasting 0.2 sec, repeated every ~4 sec. Usually in duet, presumably **F** being noticeably higher-pitched than **M**.

Great Sumba Boobook *Ninox rudolfi* `E`

L 30–36 cm. Monotypic. Uncommon in primary and secondary forest. **ID Ad** speckled grey head; white throat; brown upperparts and white underparts strongly barred rufous; dark eyes. **Imm** undescribed. **Voc** Choke-like, gruff "kok-kok-kok...", repeated at 3 n/s, sometimes for several minutes, rising in pitch when excited. Often in duet. **AN** Sumba Boobook.

Seram Boobook *Ninox squamipila* `E`

L 39 cm. Monotypic. Formerly included Buru, Halmahera and Tanimbar Boobooks but all four differ in combination of genetic, vocal and morphological characters. Fairly common in primary and secondary forest, <1400 m. **ID Ad** brownish-rufous upperparts and head; white underparts thinly barred rufous; dark eyes. **Imm** undescribed. **Voc** 50–80 rapid, low "wooh" notes at 7 n/s, often in duet.

Buru Boobook *Ninox hantu* `E`

L 25 cm. Monotypic. For taxonomy see Seram Boobook. Uncommon in primary and secondary forest, favouring uplands. **ID Ad** rufous upperparts, head and breast, with lightly rufous-barred white belly; yellow eyes. **Imm** undescribed. **Voc** 5–9 croaking notes, rather frog-like, "keh-keh-keh...", 6 n/s, often in duet.

Halmahera Boobook *Ninox hypogramma* `E`

L 36 cm. Monotypic. For taxonomy see Seram Boobook. Uncommon in primary and secondary forest, seems to be more numerous in uplands. **ID Ad** dark grey-brown upperparts and head; whitish eyebrows; thick rufous barring on underparts; yellow eyes. **Imm** undescribed. **Voc** Deep 2-note "oowh-ooowh", first note slightly shorter than second, ~0.3 sec between notes, repeated regularly. Often duets.

Tanimbar Boobook *Ninox forbesi* `E`

L 31 cm. Monotypic. For taxonomy see Seram Boobook. Fairly common in primary and secondary forest. **ID Ad** bright rufous upperparts, head and barring on underparts leading to whitish belly; yellow eyes. **Imm** undescribed. **Voc** Deep 2-note "oowh-ooowh", first note slightly shorter than second, ~0.2 sec between notes; repeated more regularly than similar Halmahera, both notes being slightly longer. Often duets.

scutulata

borneensis

Brown Boobook

Northern Boobook
japonica

Chocolate Boobook

Little Sumba Boobook

Great Sumba Boobook

Seram Boobook

Buru Boobook

Halmahera Boobook

Tanimbar Boobook

Southern Boobook *Ninox boobook*

L 28–36 cm. Aus. 6 ssp, 3 in region: *ocellata* (W–C Aus; this form thought to be on Sawu); *moae* (Moa, Romang, Leti, Sermata); *cinnamomina* (Babar). This species no longer considered to be part of Morepork *N. novaeseelandiae* (SW Pacific Is) based on genetic and vocal data. Formerly included Timor, Rote and Alor Boobooks, but that latter three separated because of vocalisations. Fairly common in primary and secondary forest, occasionally plantations and farmland. **ID Ad** rufous upperparts with white mottling; distinctly darker facial disc and paler rufous breast streaking; unbarred tail and outerwing. Ssp *moae* dark rufous crown and breast streaking, dark-grey facial disc; *cinnamomina* very distinct, rufous replaced by bright cinnamon. **Imm** more heavily streaked underparts. **Voc** Some racial variation; *ocellata* produces monotonous 2-note "boo-book", lasting 0.7 sec, regularly repeated, first note shorter than second; occasionally also one-note, tremulous "brook" at ~3 n/s; *moae* similar but slightly higher-pitched and shorter (~0.6 sec); *cinnamomina* slower, lower-pitched "boo-brook", lasting 1 sec; first note longer than second. **SS** Wintering Northern Boobook (probably occasionally reaches range of Southern) lacks extensive white mottling on upperparts and is much colder, darker brown overall, with darker, cleaner (less mottled) streaks on underparts.

Timor Boobook *Ninox fusca* E

L 30 cm. Monotypic. For taxonomy see Southern Boobook. Common in primary and secondary forest, occasionally plantations. **ID Ad** as Southern but rufous tones replaced by grey, with rufous restricted to underwing-coverts. Distinct white mottling on upperparts; indistinct grey facial disc; ill-defined barred tail and outerwing. **Imm** undescribed. **Voc** Jumpy, 2 or 3-note "woop-woop" or "woop-ee-woop" lasting ~0.6 sec, last note longer than first, repeated regularly. Rarely 4 notes. Often in duet. **SS** Told from wintering Northern Boobook by paler, greyer overall plumage and distinct white mottling on upperparts.

Rote Boobook *Ninox rotiensis* E

L 27 cm. Monotypic. For taxonomy see Southern Boobook. Scarce and little-known in primary and secondary forest, occasionally plantations. **ID Ad** as Timor Boobook but rufous-grey breast streaking more dense, giving mottled effect; head also shows rufous tone; well-defined barred tail and outerwing. **Imm** undescribed. **Voc** Deep, croaky 2-note "crok-crok", lasting ~0.5 sec, regularly repeated, though sometimes gives only one note, lasting ~0.15 sec, monotonously repeated. Throatier and lower-pitched than Southern and Timor. Often in duet. **SS** Potentially wintering Northern Boobook is colder brown overall, more neatly streaked below (no mottled effect) and lacks extensive white mottling on upperparts.

Alor Boobook *Ninox plesseni* E

L 30 cm. Monotypic. For taxonomy see Southern Boobook. Uncommon in primary and secondary forest, plantations and farmland with scattered trees, <1300 m. **ID Ad** similar to Timor Boobook but dense breast streaking less distinct; belly shows cross-barring, giving mottled impression; upperparts rufous-tinged with whitish mottling; underwing-coverts barred white-and-grey; barred tail and outerwing. **Imm** undescribed. **Voc** 5–20 notes "whoor-whoor-whoor..." rapidly repeated at 4 n/s. **SS** Wintering Northern Boobook is neatly streaked below (lacks mottled appearance on underparts) and lacks extensive white mottling on upperparts.

Ochre-bellied Boobook *Ninox ochracea* E

L 29 cm. Monotypic. Uncommon in primary and secondary forest, <1000 m. **ID Ad** dark grey-brown head and upperparts; rich rufous underparts; thin white eyebrow and white spotting on wing-coverts and scapulars; yellow eyes. **Imm** undescribed. **Voc** Throaty "wooow" or "woo-wooow" lasting 0.3 sec, regularly repeated, sometimes alternating between the two; often in duet.

Cinnabar Boobook *Ninox ios* E

L 22 cm. Currently monotypic; populations in C-SE Sul may belong to undescribed taxon with different underparts pattern but similar vocalisations; however, N Sul population variable in underparts, so distinction may not hold. Locally fairly common in montane forest, >1100 m. **ID Ad** uniform, dark rufous with slight barring on paler rufous breast; yellow eyes. Population in C-SE Sul shows scalloped belly. **Imm** undescribed. **Voc** 4-note call, delivered as couplets, "ka-da ka-da", lasting 0.7 sec, each couplet lasting 0.1 sec, separated by 0.5 sec break. Regularly repeated every 8–15 sec. C-SE Sul population delivers slower couplets, lasting 0.9 sec.

Togian Boobook *Ninox burhani* E

L 29 cm. Monotypic. Locally fairly common in primary and secondary forest, plantations and edge. **ID Ad** chocolate-brown upperparts and head with buff speckling; chocolate-mottled breast fading to whitish belly; yellow eyes. **Imm** undescribed. **Voc** (i) Throaty "raw", lasting 0.2 sec, repeated every 3–4 sec; (ii) 4-note "OOK-gr-ra-ra", emphasis on first note followed by 3 rolling notes, lasting 0.3 sec, repeated regularly. Often in duet. **SS** Wintering Northern Boobook colder brown overall with extensive streaking (not mottling) on underparts.

Speckled Boobook *Ninox punctulata* E

L 27 cm. Monotypic. Fairly common in primary and secondary forest, <1500 m, rarely higher. **ID Ad** dark-brown upperparts, breast and head with white speckling; white-lined facial disc; white belly; flanks barred brown; dark eyes. **Imm** undescribed. **Voc** (i) Excited chuckling lasting several seconds, "oor-oor-oor...", or "ay-ay-ay...", 6 n/s, often in duet; (ii) monotonous, chuckled "wa-wa-wa...", 4 n/s.

Barking Owl *Ninox connivens*

L 38–44 cm. Aus. 5 ssp, 2 in region: *rufostrigata* (N Mol); ssp *remigialis* (Kai Besar), known from single moulting imm specimen, previously considered ssp of Southern Boobook but included here, as modern *Ninox* population on Kai Besar sounds and looks like Barking Owl. Scarce in primary and secondary forest, <1000 m. **ID Ad** similar to Brown and Northern Boobook but larger, with paler, greyer head and white spots on upperparts. **Imm** similar to Ad; single moulting specimen of *remigialis* similar to *ocellata* Southern but wings less barred, earth-brown, lacking reddish tone. **Voc** (i) *rufostrigata*: 2-note, dog-like "woOW-woow", lasting 0.4 sec, regularly repeated, often in duet; very similar in *remigialis*, perhaps more excited, higher-pitched and shorter; (ii) cat-like "mioww", lasting 0.4 sec, irregularly repeated. **SS** Smaller wintering Northern Boobook has brown (not lighter grey) head and lacks extensive white spotting on upperparts.

Southern Boobook
ocellata

Timor Boobook

Rote Boobook

Alor Boobook

Ochre-bellied Boobook

Cinnabar Boobook

Togian Boobook

Speckled Boobook

Barking Owl

TROGONIDAE
Trogons
9 species in region

A distinctive family of brightly coloured forest-dwelling birds. Despite their appearance, they are unobtrusive in habits, typically moving from perch to perch within the mid-canopy and often sitting motionless between flights. Feed by pouncing to snatch prey from the ground or vegetation. Cavity nesters.

Red-naped Trogon *Harpactes kasumba*
L 32–34 cm. Sundaic. 2 ssp: *kasumba* (Sum, MPen); *impavidus* (Bor). Uncommon in primary and secondary forest, <600 m, rarely to 1200 m. Singly or pairs, sitting quietly in mid-storey. **ID M** black head and breast, red nuchal patch meeting bright-blue orbital skin; narrow white breast band and scarlet underparts; uniform cinnamon upperparts; unmarked white on undertail. Ssp *impavidus* slightly smaller. **F** greyish-olive head and breast; buffish underparts. **Imm** as fem but buff wing spotting; males gradually obtain patches of adult plumage. **Voc** Song: 3–6 rather subdued but harsh, evenly pitched notes, "kow-kow-kow..." at 4 n/2–3 s. Call: (i) hoarse, rolling "chierr"; (ii) loud "torrrr". **SS** Diard's not as striking, with dark undertail pattern; male Diard's with pinkish (not white) breast band and pinkish (not bright-red) nuchal band. Fem Diard's has reddish (not buff) underparts. Smaller Cinnamon-rumped lacks full orbital ring and male nuchal and breast bands; fem Cinnamon-rumped shows pale face patch.

Diard's Trogon *Harpactes diardii*
L 34 cm. Sundaic. 2 ssp: *diardii* (Bangka, Bor); *sumatranus* (Sum, MPen). Fairly common in primary and secondary forest, <600 m, rarely to 1200 m. Singly or pairs, sitting quietly in mid-storey. **ID M** blackish head and breast with maroon-tinged crown, pink nuchal band not meeting violet-blue orbital skin; pinkish breast band; scarlet underparts; cinnamon upperparts; dark markings on undertail. Ssp *sumatranus* generally lacks maroon crown. **F** and **Imm** brownish head and breast with pinkish-red underparts. **Voc** Song: slightly descending series of 10–15 notes, "koo-koo-koo...", at 5 n/s, faster and more penetrating than Red-naped. Call: (i) hoarse, rolling "chierr"; (ii) loud "turrr". **SS** See Red-naped and Red-headed Trogons. Unlike in smaller Cinnamon-rumped and Scarlet-rumped, Diard's head colour (in both sexes) reaches onto breast and ocular skin forms full ring (not only brow).

Cinnamon-rumped Trogon *Harpactes orrhophaeus*
L 25 cm. Sundaic. 2 ssp: *orrhophaeus* (Sum, MPen); *vidua* (Bor). Scarce in primary and secondary forest, <600 m (Sum), <1400 m (Bor). Singly or pairs, sitting quietly in understorey, generally feeding lower, less vocal and less conspicuous than other trogons. **ID M** black head with blue bill and eyebrow; scarlet underparts fading slightly to undertail-coverts; upperparts wholly cinnamon. Ssp *vidua* has barring on wings less dense. **F** brown head with large pale patch around eye and throat, underparts wholly yellowish-buff; *vidua* darker above, more chestnut on face. **Imm** head and breast show pale blotches. **Voc** Song: 3–4 weak, descending "taoop-taoop-taoop...", at 3 n/s, similar to Rhinortha. Call: (i) 2-note "er-owh"; (ii) scolding "turr". **SS** Male Scarlet-rumped smaller and slimmer with red (not cinnamon) rump. Fem Scarlet-rumped shows wholly dark head without pale face patch and reddish (not buff) belly. See also Diard's and Red-naped.

Scarlet-rumped Trogon *Harpactes duvaucelii*
L 23–24 cm. Sundaic. Monotypic. Fairly common in primary and secondary forest, <900 m, rarely to 1500 m. Singly or pairs, sitting quietly in mid-storey. **ID M** black head with blue bill and eyebrow; scarlet underparts and broad red rump on cinnamon upperparts. **F** paler, with dark-brownish head; cinnamon overall with pinkish belly and rump. **Imm** lacks pink tones; blotchy head and breast. **Voc** Song: stuttering, then accelerating series of 18–25 descending notes, "tyew-tyew-tyew-too-too-too-too...", lasting 2.5 sec, like a bouncing ball. Call: scolding "turr". **SS** See Cinnamon-rumped and Diard's.

Orange-breasted Trogon *Harpactes oreskios*
L 25–26 cm. SE Asia. 4 ssp: *oreskios* (Jav); *uniformis* (Sum, mainland SE Asia); *nias* (Nias); *dulitensis* (Bor). Upper lowland to submontane forest, unusually highly localised on Sum, 300–1500 m. Singly or pairs, sitting quietly in mid-storey. **ID M** olive-yellow head, blue orbital skin; yellowish underparts (to chin); chestnut upperparts with paler rump. Ssp *uniformis* lacks paler rump, with darker olive head extending to breast; *nias* darker-crowned and larger-billed than previous; *dulitensis* smaller with greener breast. **F** and **Imm** olive-grey head extending to breast. **Voc** Song: ~3–8 rather rapid, hard, whistled "tao-tao-tao..." at 4-6 n/s, slightly rising in pitch, sometimes only given as a series of triplets. Call: scolding "turr". **SS** See Sumatran and Javan Trogons.

Red-headed Trogon *Harpactes erythrocephalus*
L 31–35 cm. S–SE–E Asia. 9 ssp, 1 in region: *flagrans* (Sum). Fairly common in submontane forest, 500–1900 m. Singly or pairs, sitting quietly in mid-storey. **ID** Undertail largely white with black 'compartmental' boundaries. **M** dark red head and breast, white breast band; scarlet belly. **F** head and breast brown, concolourous with upperparts. **Imm** less red on underparts; head more rufescent. **Voc** Song: 8–15 well-spaced descending "tyowp-tyowp-tyowp...", lasting <4 sec, at 2 n/s. Call: coarse rattling "tewirr". **SS** Red-headed lacks the fine black vermiculations on undertail of fem Diard's and is more scarlet (less pink-hued) on underparts.

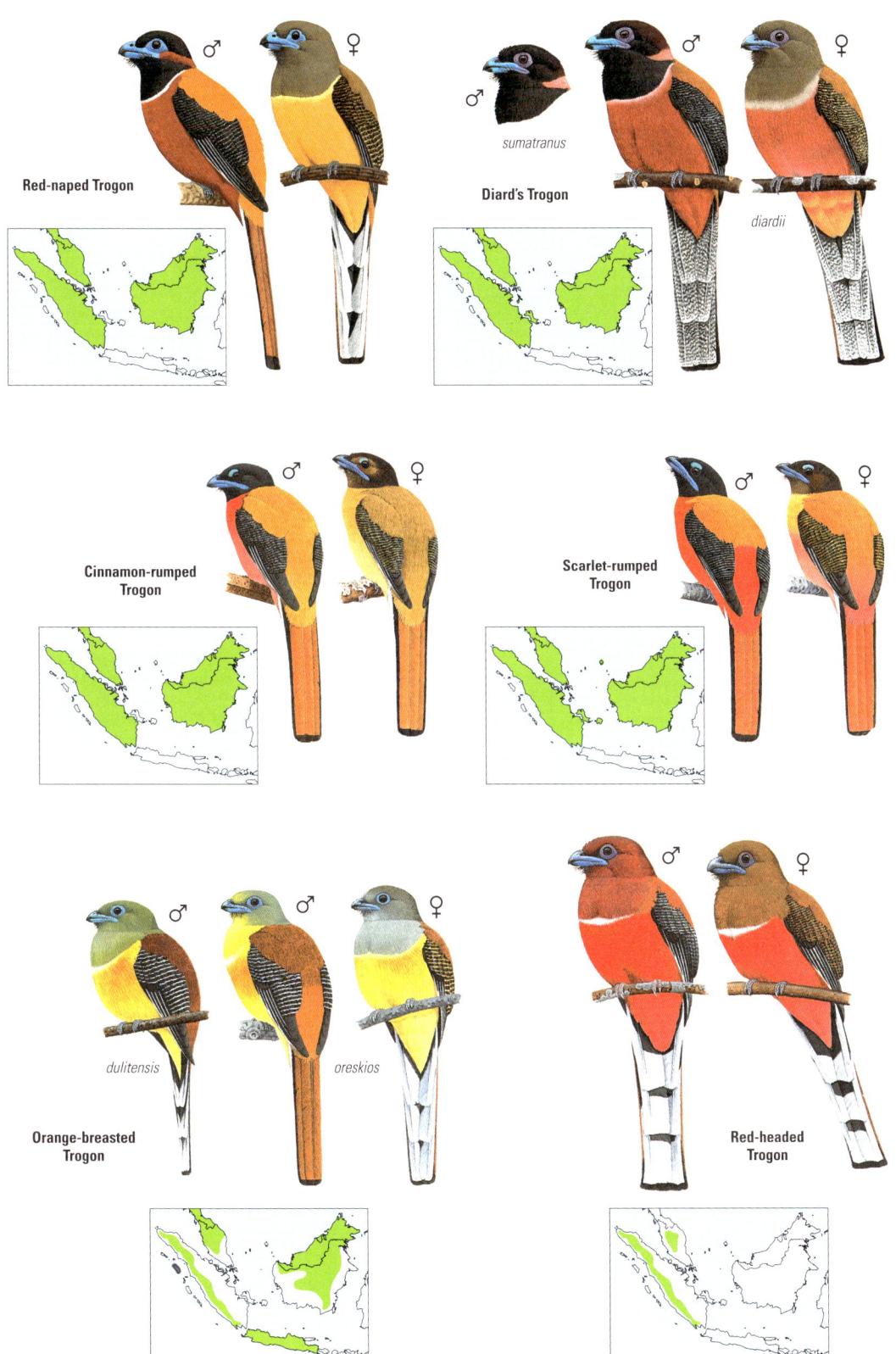

Red-naped Trogon ♂ ♀

Diard's Trogon ♂ *sumatranus* ♂ ♀ *diardii*

Cinnamon-rumped Trogon ♂ ♀

Scarlet-rumped Trogon ♂ ♀

Orange-breasted Trogon ♂ *dulitensis* ♂ *oreskios* ♀

Red-headed Trogon ♂ ♀

Whitehead's Trogon *Harpactes whiteheadi*   `E`

L 29–31 cm. Monotypic. Uncommon in montane forest, 900–1900 m. Singly or pairs, sitting quietly in mid-storey, occasionally joins feeding flocks, trailing at the back. **ID M** scarlet-red head and underparts; blue orbital skin; black throat fading to grey breast; back cinnamon. **F** red replaced by cinnamon. **Imm** similar to fem but darker; shorter tail. **Voc** Less vocal than other trogons. Song: 4–5 evenly-pitched strident whistled "whoop-whoop-whoop-whoop-whoop", at 4 n/6 s. Call: soft rolling "turrr" in alarm.

Javan Trogon *Apalharpactes reinwardtii*   `E`

L 34 cm. Monotypic. No longer considered conspecific with Sumatran Trogon. Scarce in submontane and montane forest, 900–2500 m. Singly or pairs, sitting quietly in mid-storey; often located by its whirring wings when flushed. **ID M** dull olive-green head with blue orbital skin and green gape; red bill; glossy greenish-blue upperparts, blue tail; yellow underparts with greyish-green breast band; rear flanks reddish. **F** reduced, paler reddish flanks and buffier wing markings. **Imm** less bright. **Voc** Song: long-drawn, hoarse but melodious, un-trogon-like note preceded by short introductory note, "oo-eeeeeee", main note rising slightly at end, lasting 1 s. Call: hoarse, rolling "chierr, chierr"; loud "turrr". **SS** Smaller Orange-breasted Trogon has chestnut (not green) upperparts; lacks green breast band; lacks striking red-billed facial pattern.

Sumatran Trogon *Apalharpactes mackloti*   `E`

L 30 cm. Monotypic. For taxonomy see Javan. Uncommon in submontane and montane forest, 700–2300 m. Singly or pairs, sitting quietly in mid-storey; often located by its whirring wings when flushed. **ID M** similar to larger Javan but has shorter tail, maroon rump and lacks red flanks. **F** buffier and narrower wing barring. **Imm** duller, with green rump; lacks mantle sheen. **Voc** Song: croaky, hoarse, un-trogon-like "wewe-wheer-oow", lasting 1.2 sec, repeated irregularly. Call: (i) hoarse, rolling "chierr, chierr"; (ii) loud "torrr". **SS** Smaller Orange-breasted Trogon has chestnut (not green) upperparts; lacks green breast band; lacks striking red-billed facial pattern.

BUCEROTIDAE
Hornbills

13 species in region

Large to very large denizens of forest and edge, often with huge bills and exaggerated casques. Their presence is often revealed by the sound of their wings flapping in flight or their far-carrying distinctive calls. Many species are becoming increasingly threatened by hunting and deforestation. Mainly frugivorous. Cavity nester, female blocks herself inside the cavity with the male feeding female and chick during nesting until fledging.

Knobbed Hornbill *Rhyticeros cassidix*   `E`

L 70–80 cm. Monotypic. Fairly common in primary and secondary forest, <1800 m. Often forms large roosting flocks (>100 s), though becoming smaller with habitat loss. **ID** Black body; white tail; yellow bill; blue gular pouch and facial skin. **M** large red casque and bill base; rufous head and breast. **F** smaller; black head. **Imm** less developed casque; darker bill. **Voc** Loud, double-note "OOW-RAA" and repeated "RAA-RAA-RAA...". **AN** Painted Hornbill.

Blyth's Hornbill *Rhyticeros plicatus*

L 65–85 cm. Aus. Monotypic. Fairly common in primary and secondary forest, <1500 m, rarely above. Usually in pairs or congregating at fruiting trees (<40). **ID** Black body; white tail; bluish-white gular pouch and facial skin; ivory bill with corrugated casque. **M** rufous head and neck; red bill base. **F** black head and neck, smaller bill. **Imm** smaller casque, darker bill. **Voc** Loud, repetitive "KOOK" or "OORH", lasting 0.2 sec. **AN** Papuan Hornbill.

Sumba Hornbill *Rhyticeros everetti*   `E`

L 55 cm. Monotypic. Uncommon in remaining patches of primary and secondary forest. Usually in pairs or congregating at fruiting trees (<10). **ID** All black; blue gular pouch; yellow bill with red base. **M** rich reddish head grading into buff neck. **F** all-black head and neck. **Imm** casque undeveloped. **Voc** ~5 slow introductory "ORG-GA-GA" followed by a loud, rapidly repeated "GA-GA-GA...", lasting <25 sec at 9 n/s.

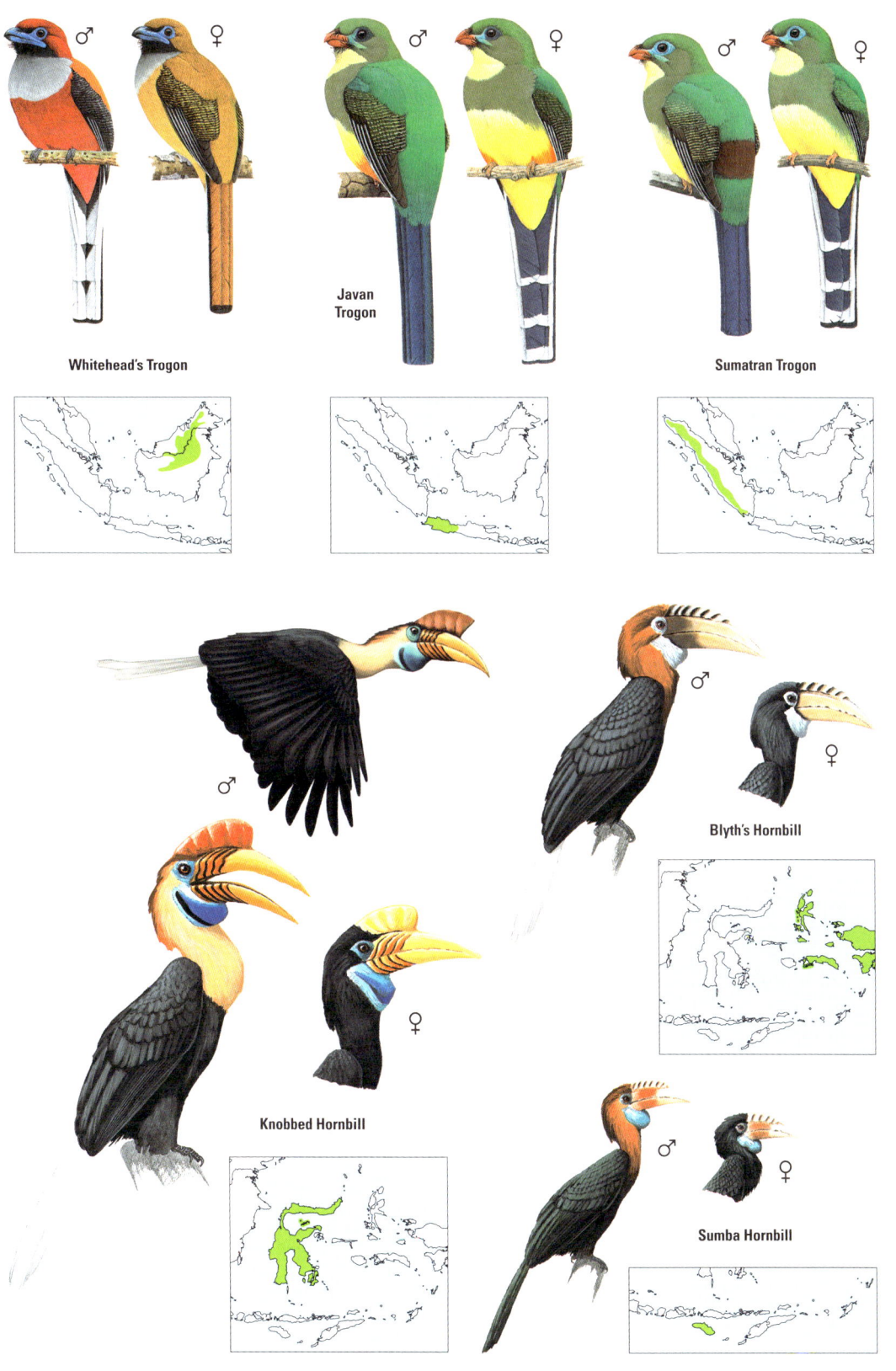

Whitehead's Trogon

Javan Trogon

Sumatran Trogon

Blyth's Hornbill

Knobbed Hornbill

Sumba Hornbill

Wreathed Hornbill *Rhyticeros undulatus*
L 75–85 cm. SE Asia. Monotypic. Fairly common in primary and secondary forest, <2600 m, favours foothills. Usually in pairs or congregating at fruiting trees (<50). Loud whooshing wing beats, often high above canopy. **ID** Black body; red orbital skin; shaggy hindneck; yellowish-horn corrugated bill. In flight, all black wings and white tail. **M** whitish face and breast; dark brown crown; bulging yellow gular pouch with dark line. **F** black head and breast; blue gular pouch. **Imm** casque undeveloped, uncorrugated bill with reddish base. **Voc** Loud "kok-kook-KEHK" and quiet "koohk". **SS** See Wrinkled.

Great Hornbill *Buceros bicornis*
L 95–105 cm. S–SE Asia. Monotypic. Scarce in primary and secondary forest, 500–2000 m, rarely lower. Pairs or small groups (<20); wary. **ID** Mostly yellow bill and neck, black breast and face; white belly. In flight, white tail with broad black central tail band, white trailing edge to wing and broad yellowish band across greater-coverts. **M** red eye. **F** smaller; with white eye. **Imm** small bill and casque; bluish eye. **Voc** Loud, hollow "GOK" and "OO-WOOK" often given in duet. In flight often a more stretched-out "UW-WAA".

Rhinoceros Hornbill *Buceros rhinoceros*
L 80–90 cm. Sundaic. 3 ssp: *rhinoceros* (Sum, MPen); *borneoensis* (Bor); *silvestris* (Jav). Uncommon in primary and secondary forest, <1400 m, now rare and local on Jav. In pairs; sometimes congregates in large numbers at fruiting trees (<30). **ID** Black body with white belly. In flight wings all back, white tail with broad black subterminal band. **M** red eye; pale-yellowish bill becoming bright red on up-curved casque. **F** smaller with smaller casque and whitish eye. **Imm** smaller with barely-developed casque. Ssp *borneoensis* smaller with shorter, broader, more sharply recurved casque; *silvestris* has broader black tail band and forward-facing casque. **Voc M** gives deep, loud "HOK" and **F** higher "HAK" often given in duet "HOK-HAK-HOK-HAK...". In flight often a more stretched-out "GER-ROK".

Helmeted Hornbill *Rhinoplax vigil*
L 110–120 cm. Sundaic. Monotypic. Scarce, now rare or locally extinct, requiring large tracts of undisturbed primary and secondary forest, <1500 m. Usually solitary or pairs, warier than other hornbills. Small groups only ever encountered at fruiting trees, where often joins Rhinoceros and Wreathed Hornbills. Its characteristic call usually betrays its presence. **ID** All dark with white belly, tail and rump; black subterminal band on tail including on elongated central feathers; red bare skin on face; short, yellow bill with reddish base and casque. In flight note tail shape and white trailing edge to wing. **M** red bare skin on throat and neck, white on smaller **F**. **Imm** casque less developed and shorter central tail feathers. **Voc** Song: amazing, loud, unmistakable series of well-spaced "HOOP" notes, quickening to "KE-HOOP", lasting 1–5 min, ending with a manic laughter, reaching a crescendo before tailing off, "KA-KA-KA...", lasting 3–6 sec, at <8 n/s. Audible from several kilometres. Call: (i) loud "KEK"; (ii) repeated tremulous, trumpeting "kakaka...", which is often produced in flight.

Wreathed Hornbill

Great Hornbill

♂ rhinoceros

♀

♂ silvestris

♂ borneoensis

Rhinoceros Hornbill

♂

♀

Helmeted Hornbill

Wrinkled Hornbill *Rhabdotorrhinus corrugatus*

L 65–70 cm. Sundaic. Monotypic. Locally scarce in primary and secondary forest, more numerous in swamp forest, <300 m, rarely above. Pairs, small groups or occasionally even larger groups (<20). Loud whooshing wing beats. Often flying slowly high over the forest or between forest patches. Congregates at fruiting trees, often with Rhinoceros Hornbills. **ID** Mostly black; yellow bill; blue facial skin. In flight, quite rounded all-black wings, pale buffish-stained tail with black base. **M** red bill base and casque; yellowish gular pouch, face and breast. **F** blue gular pouch, all-yellow bill and casque. **Imm** bill unridged with smaller casque lacking red. **Voc** Sharp, hollow, barking "KAH-KAH-KAH", lasting 0.6 sec, regularly repeated. **SS** Compared to larger Wreathed, flying Wrinkled shows buff-stained (not whitish) tail with black tail base and well-rounded wings. Compared to perched Wreathed, Wrinkled has yellower bill, blue (not red) orbital skin, lacks corrugations on upper mandible and males have red (not pale-horn) casque, black (not dark-brown) crown, and lack black mark on pouch.

Sulawesi Hornbill *Rhabdotorrhinus exarhatus* `E`

L 45 cm. 2 ssp: *exarhatus* (C–N Sul); *sanfordi* (S-SE Sul, Muna, Buton). Uncommon in primary and secondary forest, <650 m, rarely to 1000 m. Usually in small groups (<10) in mid-storey. **ID** Small; all black. **M** with yellow face, bill variably dark and pale-horn yellow with pinkish ridge; *sanfordi* with more extensive pink on upper mandible. **F** dusky-pinkish to blackish bill; *sanfordi* has pale creamy yellow ridges across lower mandible. **Imm** less-developed casque. **Voc** Trumpet-like double-note "EUOOW-EOOW".

White-crowned Hornbill *Berenicornis comatus*

L 75–80 cm. Sundaic. Monotypic. Scarce in primary and secondary forest, <1650 m. Less conspicuous than most other hornbills, usually in mid-canopy, in pairs or family groups (<5), can feed on ground. **ID** In flight all-white tail and trailing edge of wing. **M** white body with large shaggy crest; black upperparts and bluish facial skin. **F** all-black except crest, trailing edge of wing and tail. **Imm** brownish tinged body. **Voc** (i) Deep, resonant hooting series of 4–5 notes, "HO HOO-HOO-HOO-HOO...", lasting 1.5 sec, regularly repeated in quick succession; (ii) as previous but shortened to repeated 2 notes "HO-HOO", lasting 0.6 sec.

Bushy-crested Hornbill *Anorrhinus galeritus*

L 65–70 cm. Sundaic. Monotypic. Fairly common in primary and secondary forest, <1800 m. Usually in social, noisy groups (5–15). **ID** All dark. In flight all-black wings, brownish-grey basal two thirds to tail. **M** thick, drooping crest; pale-blue orbital and gular skin. **F** extensive yellow on distal two thirds of bill. **Imm** pinkish orbital skin; smaller, paler bill; browner plumage. **Voc** Noisy yelps and squeals "WAHA-WAHA-WAHA...", and "wirh-wirh-wirh", usually several birds calling at once. **SS** Male Bushy-crested from fem Black by pale-blue (not pinkish) orbital and gular skins and paler tail base (versus paler tail tip).

Oriental Pied Hornbill *Anthracoceros albirostris*

L 55–60 cm. S–SE Asia. 2 ssp, 1 in region: *convexus* (GS, MPen), sometimes considered a monotypic species '**Sunda Pied Hornbill**' based on distinct tail pattern. Fairly common in secondary forest, woodlands, plantations including oil palm, <700 m, avoids interior primary forest. Pairs or small groups (<15). **ID** Black with white belly and facial markings; in flight white undertail, primary tips and trailing edge to wing. **M** yellow bill with dark markings on casque. **F** smaller casque, more extensive black on bill. **Imm** much smaller casque. **Voc** Noisy, loud, high-pitched "KEK-KEK-KEK...", and "YIP-YIPYIP...".

Black Hornbill *Anthracoceros malayanus*

L 60–65 cm. Sundaic. Monotypic. Fairly common in primary and secondary forest, wooded areas, plantations including oil palm, <700 m. Pairs or small groups (<10). **ID** All black; in flight all-black wings and broad white terminal band. **M** bill and casque pale-yellow; variably shows broad white supercilium. **F** smaller blackish bill and casque; narrow pinkish facial skin. **Imm** pale-greenish bill; orange facial skin. **Voc** Distinctive harsh loud grating sounds "KYAAH-KYAAH-KYAAH...", and "OOG-OOG-OGRAA...". **SS** See Bushy-crested.

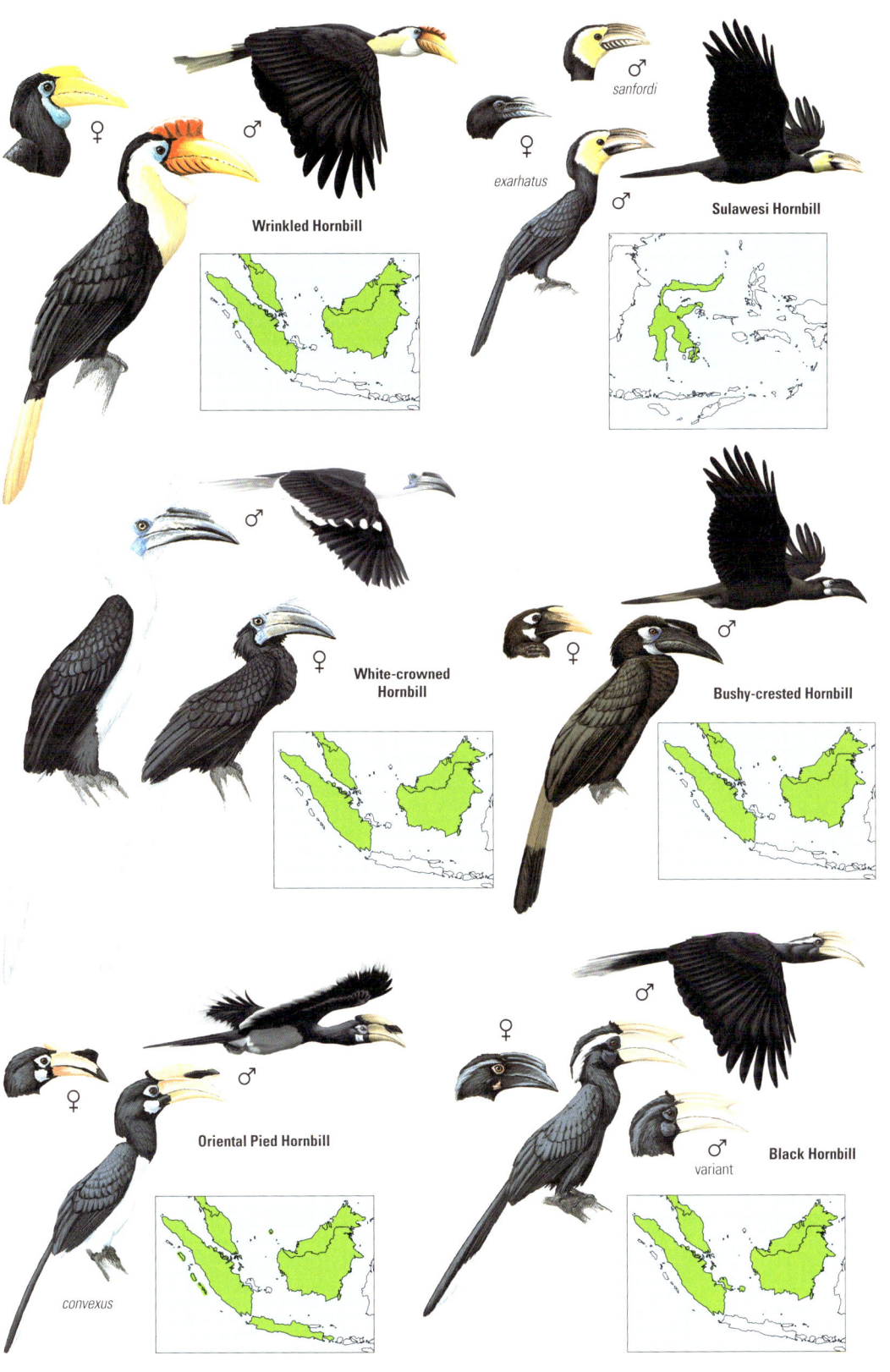

Wrinkled Hornbill

sanfordi

exarhatus

Sulawesi Hornbill

White-crowned Hornbill

Bushy-crested Hornbill

Oriental Pied Hornbill

convexus

Black Hornbill

variant

MEGALAIMIDAE
Asian Barbets
17 species in region

Small to medium-sized forest-dwelling birds. Typically green in overall appearance and highly arboreal in habits, often preferring the highest canopy of trees. Presence most easily revealed by their distinctive calls that may be uttered monotonously for long periods. They are often key frugivores in their habitats; generally solitary except at fruiting trees, where several species can congregate in large numbers. Cavity nesters.

Coppersmith Barbet *Psilopogon haemacephalus*
L 15–17 cm. S–SE Asia, Phil. 9 ssp, 2 in region: *delicus* (Sum); *roseus* (Jav, Bali). Common in open woodland, parks, plantations and urban areas, <2200 m. **ID** Green upperparts; pale underparts green-streaked. **M** red breast mark and forecrown, rest of face and throat yellowish-white with black eye-line, moustachial and rear auricular border. **F** less bright; face pattern less distinct. Ssp *roseus* yellowish-white areas on head in both sexes replaced by deep red. **Imm** paler bill, lacks red on head; streaky throat. **Voc** Incessant series of hollow "POP-POP-POP..." at 2 n/s. Reminiscent of the distant sound of a blacksmith hitting hammer on anvil.

Lineated Barbet *Psilopogon lineatus*
L 25–30 cm. S–SE Asia. 2 ssp, 1 in region: *lineatus* (Jav, Bali). Fairly common in all types of open lowland woodland including plantations, parkland, open country and clearings. **ID Ad** green upperparts and tail; otherwise brownish with broad pale head and breast streaking; broad yellow orbital ring and bill. **Imm** streaks more diffused. **Voc** (i) Loud, mellow "poo-TOK", lasting 0.5 sec, higher second note, repeated every 1–2 sec; (ii) rapid dry bubbling tremulous "woh-woh-woh...", 18 n/s; (iii) dry, bubbling, tremulous "wo'o'h-wo'o'h-wo'o'h-...", at 1 n/s.

Fire-tufted Barbet *Psilopogon pyrolophus*
L 29 cm. Sundaic. Monotypic. Introduced in W Jav. Fairly common in primary and secondary forest, 900–2100 m, rarely to 400 m. **ID Ad** striking head pattern: maroon nape, white forecrown, grey face, yellowish and black breast bands; yellowish bill with dark band; body green with yellowish tinge to underparts. **Imm** duller head pattern. **Voc** Cicada-like buzzing "zoo-zoo-zoo-ZOO-ZOO-ZOO...", lasting 5–7 sec, starting slowly before speeding up and rising in pitch, occasionally tailing off at end.

Brown-throated Barbet *Psilopogon corvinus*　　E
L 27 cm. Monotypic. Uncommon in primary and secondary forest, 800–2000 m. **ID Ad** brown head and yellow-streaked nape; green body. **Imm** duller, paler bill. **Voc** (i) 4–5 loud, hollow "WOOK-WOOK-WOOK-WOOK" notes lasting 0.6 sec, regularly repeated; (ii) rapid series of rolling "wok'wok'wok...", lasting 2–10 sec, at 7 n/s; (iii) loud "kukuak".

Black-banded Barbet *Psilopogon javensis*　　E
L 26 cm. Monotypic. Uncommon in primary and secondary forest, <1000 m, occasionally 1500 m. **ID** Green body. **Ad** yellow crown and moustachial; red throat and lores; black brow and eyestripe, extending down into breast band. **Imm** duller facial markings; paler bill. **Voc** (i) Loud, hollow couplets "tok-tok", lasting 0.2 sec, regularly repeated at 2 n/s; (ii) series starting with long-spaced "kook"s, gradually changing into faster "krook"s, not to be confused with similar but higher-pitched song of Javan Owlet.

Flame-fronted Barbet *Psilopogon armillaris*　　E
L 20–22 cm. 2 ssp: *armillaris* (Jav); *baliensis* (Bali). Common in primary and secondary forest, 600–2500 m, rarely lower. **ID** Green body. **Ad** forecrown, neck spots and breast mark yellowish-orange (darker orange in slightly larger *baliensis*); blue mid-crown to nape. **Imm** paler and duller markings. **Voc** (i) Loud, rolling "torrk-tork-torrrrrrrk", lasting 3–5 sec, occasionally second note shorter or absent; (ii) series starting with several "trrt" notes of up to 20 up-slurred "trewt"s, lasting up to 15 sec.

Blue-eared Barbet *Psilopogon australis*
L 16 cm. SE Asia. 7 ssp, 4 in region: *australis* (Jav, Bali); *duvaucelii* (Bor, Sum, Bangka, MPen); *gigantorhina* (Nias); *tanamassae* (Batu). Ssp *australis* often treated as monotypic '**Yellow-eared Barbet**' and the other three ssp as '**Black-eared Barbet**' *P. duvaucelii*, distinct from extralimital '**Blue-eared Barbet**' *P. cyanotis* based on pronounced plumage differences. However, 'Duvaucel's' and 'Blue-eared' exhibit a wide hybrid zone across northern MPen. More research needed. Fairly common in forest, woodland, occasionally parkland and cultivation, <1200 m, occasionally to 2000 m. **ID** Green body. **Ad** blue crown and throat, black band below throat, yellow ear-coverts framed black; black bill. Ssp *duvaucelii* black fore-crown and ear-coverts bordered red; *gigantorhina* as previous but larger bill; *tanamassae* as *duvaucelii* but broad zone of red below black throat band, golden olive underparts. **Imm** duller plumage; head largely green. **Voc** (i) Rapid, incessant, monotonous 2-note "ko-tek..." at 2 n/s; slightly lower-pitched and sometimes softer in *australis* than in other three ssp; (ii) series of strident whistled "pleow", repeated every 1 sec. **SS** See Bornean Barbet.

Bornean Barbet *Psilopogon eximius*　　E
L 15–16 cm. Monotypic. Fairly common in submontane forest, 700–1300 m, uncommonly 370–1700 m. **ID** Green body. **Ad** black throat and forecrown bordered red; blue ear-coverts and lores with distinctive yellow spot below eye; some birds show bluish throat and forecrown. **Imm** duller face pattern but yellow spot usually present. **Voc** Rapid, incessant "tok-tok-tok...", ~7 n/s, often whirring tail as it calls. **SS** Black-eared shows blue (not red) crown and black (not blue) cheek patch, also lacks yellow on face.

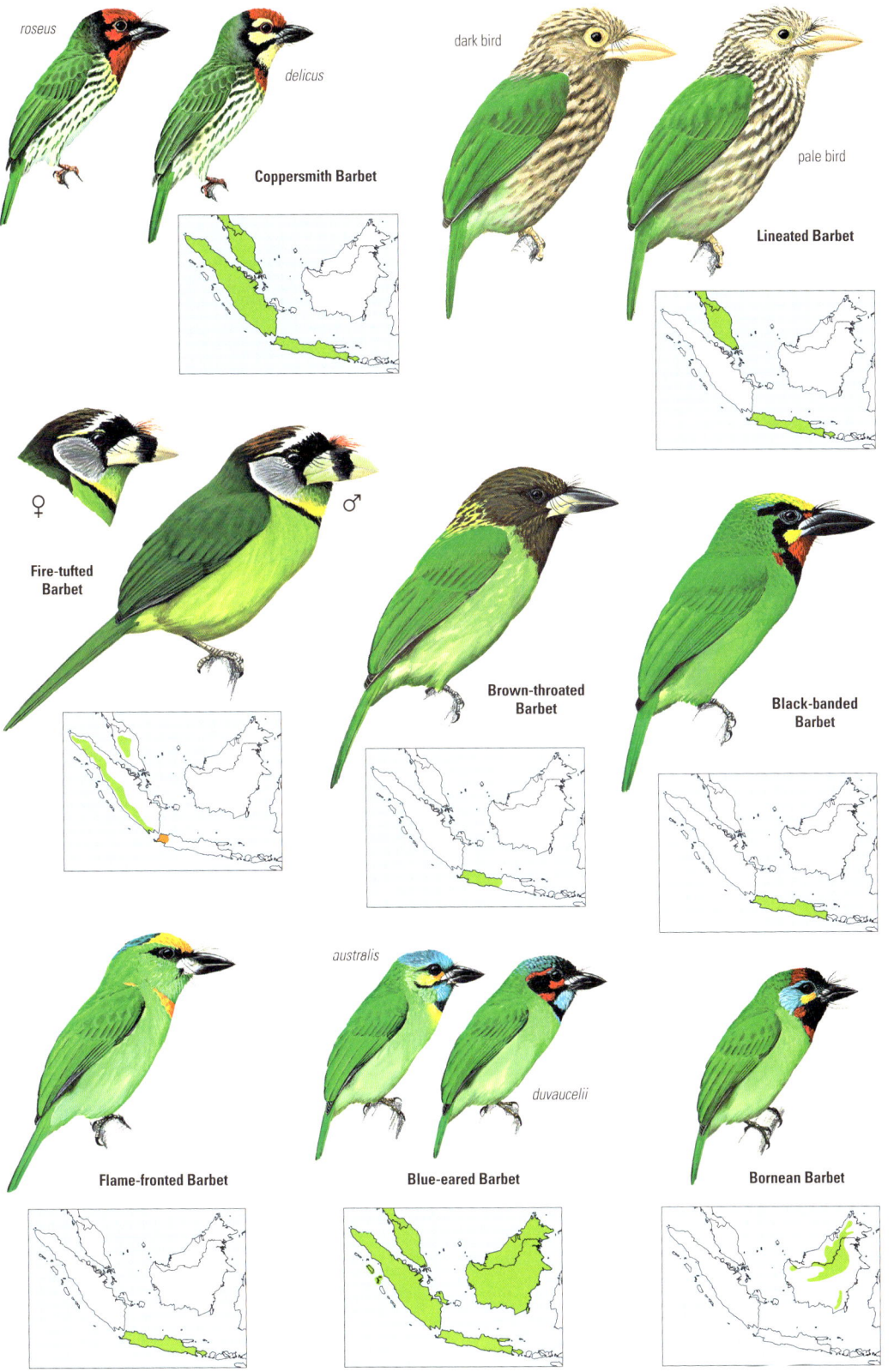

roseus

delicus

Coppersmith Barbet

dark bird

pale bird

Lineated Barbet

♀

♂

Fire-tufted Barbet

Brown-throated Barbet

Black-banded Barbet

Flame-fronted Barbet

australis

duvaucelii

Blue-eared Barbet

Bornean Barbet

Gold-whiskered Barbet *Psilopogon chrysopogon*

L 30 cm. Sundaic. 3 ssp, 2 in region: *chrysopogon* (Sum); based on deep mtDNA divergence, ssp *chrysopsis* (Bor) recently separated as monotypic '**Golden-faced Barbet**' but song appears identical to *chrysopogon* and plumage differences minor. Fairly common in primary and secondary forest, <1500 m; favours hills. **ID** Large and heavy-billed. **Ad** green body; broad yellow malar patch and forecrown, blue-speckled red crown and red lores, blackish-brown auriculars and throat. Ssp *chrysopsis* more intensely yellow fore-crown, strong blue suffusion on red crown and lilac-flecked blackish throat, darker ear-coverts; some birds with red spots on breast sides. **Imm** duller, paler bill. **Voc** (i) Loud, hollow, jumpy rapid "te'hoop-te'hoop-te'hoop...", at 3 n/s, continually repeated; (ii) deep, rapid trill "wooh'wooh'wooh...", lasting <2 sec, before breaking up into short series of "woo'who'who", lasting 1 sec, constantly repeated at various speeds.

Red-crowned Barbet *Psilopogon rafflesii*

L 26 cm. Sundaic. Monotypic. Scarce in primary and secondary forest, but locally fairly common in peat-swamp and kerangas forest and neighbouring plantations, <250 m, rarely to 800 m. **ID Ad** green body; wholly red crown, blue throat and supercilium, thick black eyestripe with red and yellow spots on side of throat; proportionate-ly longer bill than sympatric barbets. **Imm** much duller head pattern. **Voc** (i) Loud, low-pitched, slower "poop-poop" introduces series of "poop-poop-poop...", lasting <10 sec, at 4 n/s; (ii) Series of faster "pop'pop'pop'pop...", lasting <8 sec, at 9 n/s.

Red-throated Barbet *Psilopogon mystacophanos*

L 23 cm. Sundaic. 2 ssps: *mystacophanos* (Bor, Sum, MPen); *ampalus* (Batu). Fairly common in primary and secondary forest, <1200 m. **ID** Green body; red crown patch (larger in larger-billed *ampalus*). **M** yellow forecrown, red throat, blue cheek and thin black eyestripe. **F** greenish face with red spots on lores and upper breast side; *ampalus* bluer throat. **Imm** green head with yellowish forecrown and throat. **Voc** Slow, uneven series of "took-took-took...", at 2–3 n/s, often in short series of 3–5 notes, can last >2 min. Higher-pitched and more irregularly-spaced in delivery than Red-crowned and Gold-whiskered. **SS** Black-browed (from higher up the slope) has yellow (not red, green or blue) throat, more extensive blue on face and more yellow on crown. Fem resembles Mountain Barbet but has blue or green (not scaly buff-yellowish) forecrown and throat, less blue face and larger bill.

Black-browed Barbet *Psilopogon oorti*

L 22 cm. Sundaic. Monotypic. No longer includes Annam *P. anna-mensis*, Chinese *P. faber* and Taiwan Barbet *P. nuchalis*. Common in primary and secondary forest, 600–2400 m. **ID** Green body. **Ad** broad black supercilium, red forecrown, yellow crown and throat, blue face and lower throat; pale bill base. **Imm** duller head pattern. **Voc** Series of hollow, rolling "too-troock", at 1 n/s, a constant background sound in mountain forest. **SS** See Red-throated.

Mountain Barbet *Psilopogon monticola*   **E**

L 20–22 cm. Monotypic. Fairly common in primary and secondary forest, 600–1500 m, uncommonly 300–1800 m. **ID** Green body. **Ad** poorly marked facial pattern: red crown and neckside marks, bluish face and scaled buff-yellowish forecrown and throat; under-parts paler than other barbets. **Imm** duller head markings. **Voc** Incessant rapid "too-too-too...", at 5 n/s, followed by a 'rewinding' "too-rok", every 3–6 sec, with series continually repeated. **SS** See Red-throated.

Yellow-crowned Barbet *Psilopogon henricii*

L 21–23 cm. Sundaic. 2 ssps: *henricii* (Sum, MPen); *brachyrhynchus* (Bor). Uncommon in primary and secondary forest, <900 m. **ID** Green body. **Ad** yellow forecrown and side to crown; blue throat and crown spot; black lores; red nape patch. Ssp *brachyrhynchus* smaller and less bright; blue areas more violet; yellow crown less extensive. **Imm** duller face pattern; no yellow on crown. **Voc** (i) Loud, croaking "tok-tok-tok-tok-trrrrok", lasting 1.7 sec, similar to Golden-naped but slightly faster and higher-pitched; (ii) series of ~40 loud, tremulous "trrrrok" notes starting slow at 1 n/4 s, building in tempo to 2 n/s in final 2/3 of call, lasting ~40 sec. **SS** Limited elevational overlap with similar Golden-naped, which lacks yellow on crown and has golden (not red) nape patch.

Golden-naped Barbet *Psilopogon pulcherrimus*   **E**

L 20–22 cm. Monotypic. Common in montane forest, 1000–2000 m, uncommonly 600–3100 m. **ID** Green body. **Ad** extensive blue crown and throat, black lores, golden nape patch. **Imm** duller; lacks golden nape. **Voc** (i) Loud, rolling "tuk-tuk-trrrrruk", repeated regularly; (ii) long "prrrrt" trill, lasting 1–2 sec. **SS** See Yellow-crowned for both vocal and plumage differences.

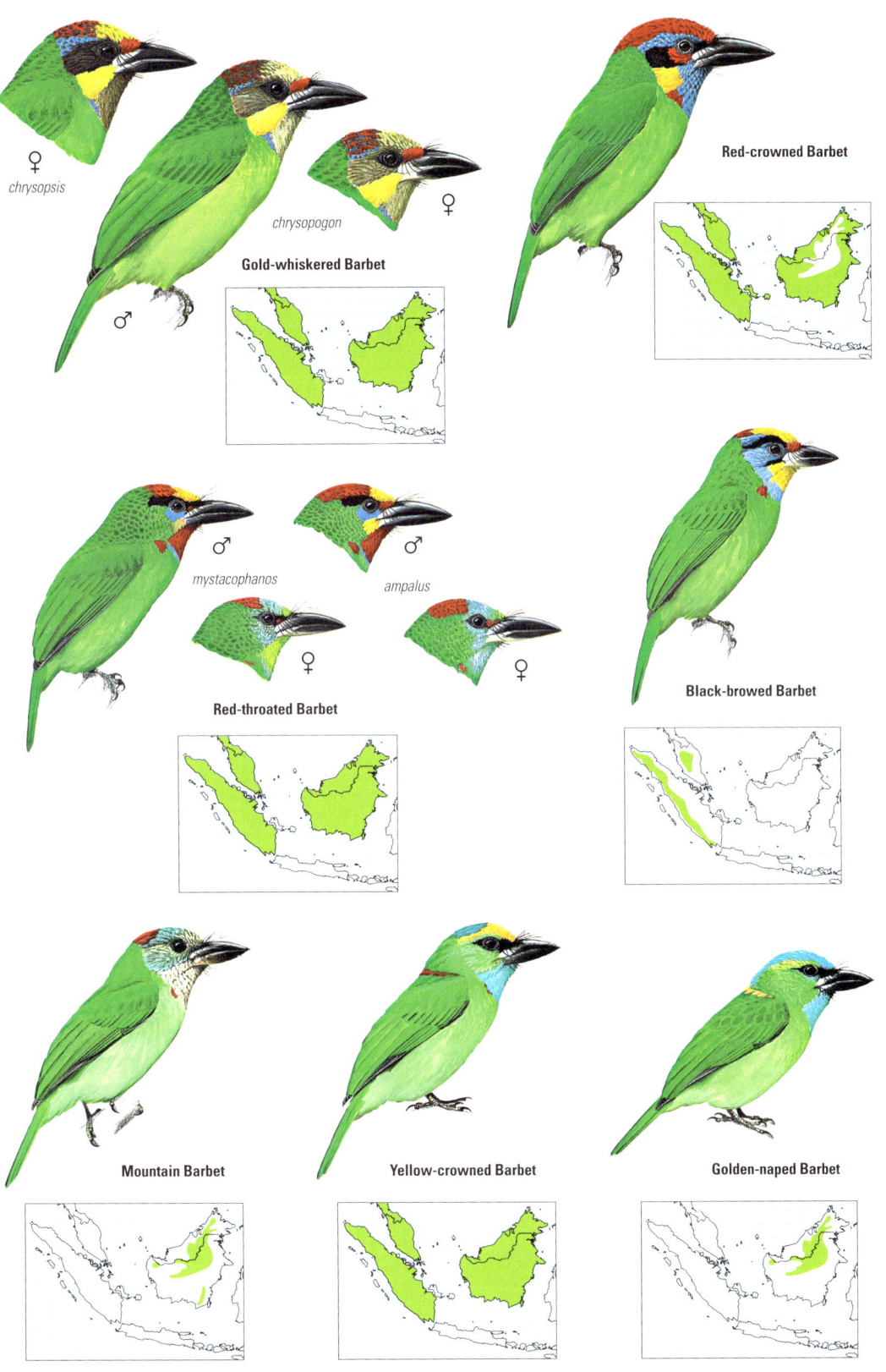

chrysopsis ♀

chrysopogon ♀

Gold-whiskered Barbet

Red-crowned Barbet

mystacophanos ♂

ampalus ♂

♀

♀

Red-throated Barbet

Black-browed Barbet

Mountain Barbet

Yellow-crowned Barbet

Golden-naped Barbet

Bornean Brown Barbet *Caloramphus fuliginosus* **E**

L 18 cm. 2 ssp: *fuliginosus* (C–S Bor); *tertius* (N Bor). For taxonomy see Malayan Brown. Fairly common in primary and secondary forest, <1300 m. Favours canopy; sometimes in small groups (<10). **ID** Brown upperparts; whitish underparts; rufous from face to lower breast (only to throat in *tertius*); red feet. **M** Blackish bill (perhaps dark-grey in *tertius*). **F** horn bill. **Imm** duller; less contrast. **Voc** Un-barbet-like thin, high-pitched "tseet tseet tseet...", regularly repeated; often several birds calling together.

Malayan Brown Barbet *Caloramphus hayii*

L 18 cm. Sundaic. Monotypic. No longer considered conspecific with Bornean Brown based on plumage and genetic evidence. Fairly common in forest, <1300 m. Favours canopy; sometimes in small groups (<10). **ID Ad** as Bornean Brown but paler head, lacking rufous throat/breast. **Imm** duller; less contrast. **Voc** As Bornean Brown.

INDICATORIDAE
Honeyguides
1 species in region

Forest species associated with honeybee nests, the surroundings of which they defend as territories over many years. Unobtrusive in habit, their presence is often revealed by their distinctive call.

Sunda Honeyguide *Indicator archipelagicus*

L 16 cm. Sundaic. Monotypic. Scarce in forest; associated with open-nesting honeybees (*Apis dorsata* and *A. florea*), <900 m, often keeps territory for several years in the same few trees, calling continuously, otherwise inconspicuous. **ID** Resembles many *Pycnonotus* bulbuls, nondescript but thick-billed (upper mandible black, lower pink), with dark-olive upperparts, paler underparts with narrow indistinct streaking; reddish eyes; pale undertail with darker outer feathers. **M** yellow shoulder patch. **F** lacks shoulder patch. **Imm** eyes brown. **Voc** Starts with a single cat-like "miaow", followed by a nasal rattle "miaow-krrrrwwww...", lasting ~4 sec, sometimes longer, repeated at irregular intervals. **SS** Some *Pycnonotus* bulbuls similar, but note Honeyguide's thick bicoloured bill, dark-olive colouration, contrasting undertail pattern, compact build and sometimes streaky underparts. **AN** Malaysian Honeyguide.

PICIDAE
Woodpeckers
26 species in region

Small to medium-sized birds with chisel-shaped bills. Typically feed by clinging to trunks and branches, drilling holes to find invertebrates. Many species have loud distinctive calls. Cavity nesters.

Speckled Piculet *Picumnus innominatus*

L 10 cm. S–SE–E Asia. 3 ssp, 1 in region: *malayorum* (Sum, Bor, S–SE Asia). Scarce in submontane forest, 1000–1800 m (Sum), <1200 m (Bor). Singly or pairs, often joining mixed feeding flocks. **ID** Tiny, short-tailed; olive-green above, crown greyer; broad black and white face stripes; whitish below with bold black spots. **M** rufous forehead with fine black bars. **Imm** duller plumage; paler bill. **Voc** (i) Very high-pitched "sis'sis'sit'tit'tit'tit'tit...", lasting 1.5–3 sec at 15 n/s; first few notes descending, then evenly pitched; (ii) loud, tinny, even-spaced, slow drumming, lasting 2–5 sec at 9 n/s, like a type-writer; (iii) call notes: sharp "tsit" and squeaky "sik-sik-sik".

Rufous Piculet *Sasia abnormis*

L 9 cm. Sundaic. 2 ssp: *abnormis* (GS, MPen); *magnirostris* (Nias). Fairly common in forest in dense undergrowth and bamboo, <1200 m. Singly or pairs, often joining mixed feeding flocks. **ID** Tiny, nearly tailless, green above; rufous underparts and face;

magnirostris longer and deeper bill. **M** yellow forehead. **Imm** dark olive grey. **Voc** (i) 2–15 high-pitched, slightly descending notes "kik-kik-kik...", at 6 n/s; (ii) loud, tinny, even-spaced drumming, lasting 1–2 sec at 10 n/s; (iii) most frequently heard a sharp "peet" or "PIP".

Grey-and-buff Woodpecker *Hemicircus concretus*

L 13–14 cm. Sundaic. 2 ssp: *concretus* (Jav); *sordidus* (Bor–Sum, MPen). Treatment as two species ('**Grey-and-buff**' *H. sordidus* and '**Lilliput Woodpecker**' *H. concretus*) possibly justified given discrete differences in head colouration. Scarce to fairly common in forest, <1500 m. Singly, pairs or small groups (<6) in canopy, rarely lower. **ID** Tiny, large-crested and thin-necked; short-tailed; boldly chequered black-and-buff above; rump plain buff; face, neck and underparts grey with buff barring on flanks. Ssp *sordidus* paler on upperparts, with whitish hindneck. **M** forehead to crest point red; in *sordidus* crest point grey. **F** crown and crest all grey. **Imm** rufous feather edges above; underparts more heavily barred with pale buff; crown rufous with narrow black tips; **M Imm** orange-red crest. **Voc** (i) Rapid thin chattering "kikikik...", lasting 1–2 sec, at 17 n/s, slightly rising at beginning; (ii) weak drums; (iii) explosive, high, downslurred "peew" or "peeyew", often followed by short rapid chattering; (iv) sharp "tsip". **SS** See Buff-rumped.

Buff-rumped Woodpecker *Meiglyptes tristis*

L 17–18 cm. Sundaic. 2 ssp: *tristis* (Jav); *grammithorax* (Bor–Sum, MPen). Sometimes treated as two species ('**Buff-rumped**' *M. grammithorax* and '**Zebra Woodpecker**' *M. tristis*) based on plumage differences, but vocal evidence lacking. Fairly common (Sum, Bor) in dipterocarp and peat-swamp forest, <1100 m. On Jav highly restricted, few recent records from lowland forest in E. Often in pairs, following mixed flocks, mostly in canopy. **ID** Small, short-tailed and short-crested; body black with dense narrow whitish barring above, and very narrow bars on head and crest; whitish buff rump, buff lores and eyering; underparts barred on flanks and thighs. Small red malar stripe absent in **F**. Ssp *grammithorax* has buff rather than white bars above; entire underparts barred. **Imm** duller, broader barring above; darker, less barred below. **Voc** (i) Rapid trill "ke'e'e'e'e'e'e'e'e'e'e'...", can rise or fall in first half but level-pitched during second half, lasting 1.5–2 sec at 17 n/s; (ii) loud, consistently pitched drumming lasting 1.5–2.5 sec at 13 n/s; (iii) single sharp "pit", also "pit-pit" and in loose series "pit-pit'it'it'it'it'it...", lasting <1 sec at 9 n/s; (iv) much longer "pee". **SS** Grey-and-buff fem is smaller with larger triangular crest, shorter tail and unbarred underparts and head. Buff-necked has pale neck patch, dark rump and no crest.

Buff-necked Woodpecker *Meiglyptes tukki*

L 21 cm. Sundaic. 5 ssp: *tukki* (Sum–N Bor and satellites, MPen): *batu* (Batu); *infuscatus* (Nias); *percnerpes* (S Bor); *pulonis* (Banggi). Fairly common in forest, <1000 m. Singly, pairs or small groups (<5); forages in mid and lower storeys. **ID** Dark brown with narrow buff barring except head; conspicuous buff neck patch. Red malar patch absent in **F**. Ssp *batu* blackish crown, more contrasting blackish breast patch; *infuscatus* shorter-winged, weak body barring, dark crown; *percnerpes* strongly buff-barred with brown body colour showing rusty not olive tones; *pulonis* longer-billed, less olive again and paler throat. **Imm** broader barring. **Voc** (i) Quite high-pitched trill, slightly rising "kit'tit'tit'tit...", lasting 2–4 sec at 14 n/s; (ii) surprisingly loud drumming, consistently rapid knocks lasting 1–2 sec at 18 n/s; (iii) high-pitched "tee tee tee tee, pee-pee-pee", and other quiet chattering while foraging. **SS** See Buff-rumped Woodpecker.

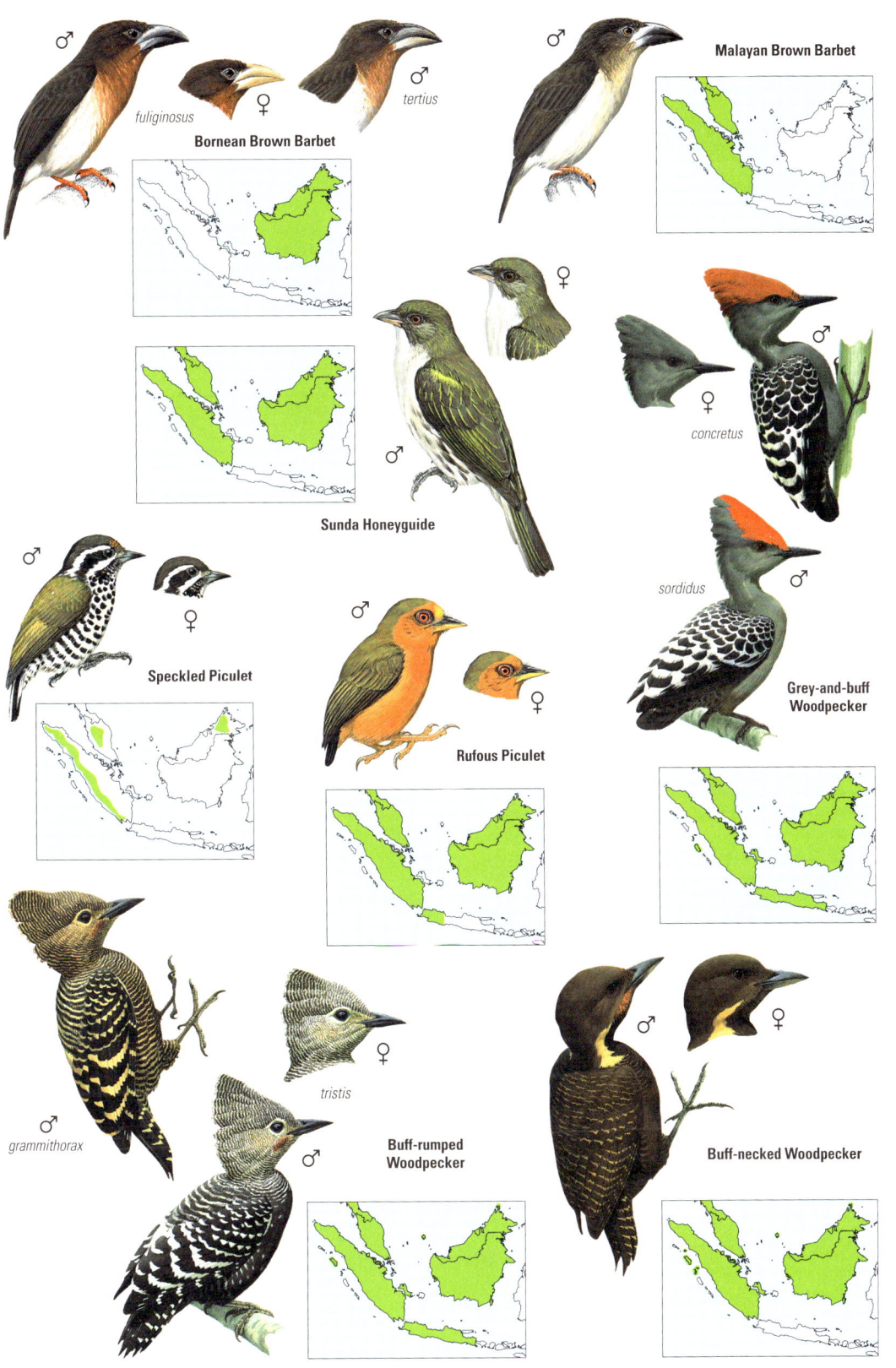

fuliginosus

♂ ♀

tertius ♂

Bornean Brown Barbet

♂ **Malayan Brown Barbet**

♀

♂

Sunda Honeyguide

♀

concretus ♂

♂

♀

sordidus ♂

Grey-and-buff Woodpecker

♂ ♀

Speckled Piculet

♂ ♀

Rufous Piculet

♂ ♀

grammithorax

tristis ♀

♂ **Buff-rumped Woodpecker**

♂ ♀ **Buff-necked Woodpecker**

Orange-backed Woodpecker *Chrysocolaptes validus*
L 30 cm. Sundaic. 2 ssp: *validus* (Jav); *xanthopygius* (Bor–Sum, MPen). Fairly common in forest, <2100 m. **ID M** blackish-brown upperparts with whitish to orange-buff stripe down back, darkest on rump and variably barred brown; red nape and crest; red underparts, narrowly yellow-edged on belly and flanks; brownish vent; flight feathers with broad rufous bands; long olive-yellow bill; *xanthopygius* usually less orange on rump/back without barring. **F** no red or yellow tones; blackish crown and crest; whitish back and rump, dull brownish below. **Imm** much as fem. **Voc** (i) Series of <10 nervous, squeaky notes "kit kit kit…", interspersed with rising double-note "kit-it"; (ii) soft drum, shortest of region's woodpeckers, lasting <0.5 sec; (iii) loud, fast, descending rattle, slightly fading in volume "pit'pit'pit…", lasting <2 sec at 10 n/s; (iv) squeaky "poot poot…" flight calls.

Greater Flameback *Chrysocolaptes guttacristatus*
L 32–34 cm. S–SE Asia. 4 ssp, 2 in region: *indomalayicus* (Sum, W Jav, MPen); *andrewsi* (Bor). Formerly united with Javan Flameback and 5–6 extralimital species (S Asia, Phil) into broadly-defined 'Greater Flameback' *C. lucidus*, but pronounced morphological differences dictate a break-up. On Jav only found west and north of Bogor, and north of Cirebon, where rare and local. Locally common on Sum, unusually highly localised with few records on Bor, in lowland forest, edge, possibly restricted to mangroves and swamp forest in region, <200 m. **ID** Olive-golden above with red rump; white head with red (**M**) or white-spotted black (**F**) crown and crest; black lores; black mask running to neck sides and black-looped malar stripe extending down neck; white centre of hindneck; black-scaled white underparts, denser on breast and extending onto upper mantle; pale eye. Ssp *andrewsi* larger, with distinctly browner markings below; flanks more barred. **Imm** more olive above, duller below. **Voc** (i) Sharp, monotonous, staccato, metallic "tit'tit'tit…", lasting <2 sec, at 9 n/s; often in flight, duetting; often slowing down once perched; (ii) loud and rapid drumming, weakening in volume in last third, like a bouncing ping-pong ball, lasting 2.5–3 sec at 21 n/s; (iii) single "kik" notes. **SS** See Common Flameback and Olive-backed Woodpecker. Smaller Javan (probably no overlap) has more yellow-green wings, duller rump, dark (not pale) eyes, and fem with yellow (not black) crown.

Javan Flameback *Chrysocolaptes strictus*　　**E**
L 28–30 cm. 2 ssp: *strictus* (C-E Jav, Bali); *kangeanensis* (Kangean). In W Jav found as far west as Mt Gede-Pangrango and south of Cirebon. Uncommon in open woodland, hill forest, in Jav locally to 2475 m, on Bali to 1280 m. **ID** Similar to Greater Flameback, but back and wings yellow-green, duller red rump, pale areas in face and breast distinctly buffish; dark brown eyes. Ssp *kangeanensis* smaller; redder rump; reduced black facial markings; narrower, browner markings below. **M** red crown and crest. **F** almost unmarked (or occasionally dark-barred) yellow crown and crest. **Voc** As Greater Flameback. **SS** See Common and Greater Flamebacks.

Olive-backed Woodpecker *Chloropicoides rafflesii*
L 25–26 cm. Sundaic. 2 ssp: *rafflesii* (Sum, Bangka, MPen); *dulitensis* (Bor). Scarce in primary and secondary forest, rarely mangroves, <1600 m. Singly or pairs in low and mid-level; inconspicuous unless calling. **ID** Olive-green upperparts; black hindneck; plain dull olive underparts; white head with two bold black stripes; *dulitensis* smaller. **M** red crown and pointed crest. **F** black crown and crest. **Imm** duller and greyer. **Voc** (i) Slow series of 6–30 loud, descending notes, often with last 1–2 notes detached, "chakchakchakchakchak, chak, chak", lasting 2–3 sec at 8 n/s, recalling a *Todiramphus* kingfisher; (ii) faster, more regular series of 10–15 notes, lasting 2–3 sec at 6 n/s; (iii) short series of 2–4 far-carrying "weer-weer-weer" at 1 n/s; (iv) longer series of slightly descending piping "wir'wir'wir…", <4 sec at 9 n/s; (v) squeaky "tiririt"; (vi) short, consistent and rapid drum, lasting ~0.5 sec at 10 n/0.5 s. **SS** Common and Greater Flamebacks have scaly black-and-white (not solid green) underparts, brighter upperparts and red rump.

Common Flameback *Dinopium javanense*
L 28–30 cm. S–SE Asia. 4 ssp, 4 in region: *javanense* (Sum–Jav, MPen); *raveni* (NE Bor, Eraban I); *borneonense* (most of Bor); *exsul* (Bali). Extralimital taxon *everetti* (Palawan) separated as monotypic Spot-throated Flameback based on plumage differences. Locally common in open secondary forest, mangroves, variety of plantations and gardens, <1000 m (Jav, Sum), <500 m (Bor). **ID** Shortish bill; golden-olive above with bright red rump and black upper tail; white head with black eyestripe extending to hindneck and dark single bold moustachial line to upper breast; buffish white underparts with narrow black fringes. Crown red (in **M**), black with white streaks (in **F**). Ssp *borneonense* smaller; *raveni* more buff and less black below, with more boldly spotted throat and crown streaks in **F** very narrow; *exsul* strongly barred below, and **F** with narrow orange to red nape band. **Imm** more blackish-brown breast spotted white; more obscurely barred on belly. **Voc** (i) Loud, striking rattle "ka'kik'kik'kik…", lasting <3.5 sec at 17 n/s, slightly tailing off at end; (ii) drums more softly than Greater; (iii) frantic "kowp-owp-owp-owp" in flight; "kow" or "kow-kow" when perched; (iv) hard, level-pitched "kik'kik'kik…", lasting <1 sec at 12 n/s. **SS** Greater and Javan Flamebacks have looped malar stripe (which can be very bleached in Javan), white (not black) centre of hindneck, and longer dagger-like bill. Greater has pale (not dark) eyes when Ad. Fem Javan is yellow-crowned (not black-crowned). See also Olive-backed Woodpecker.

Rufous Woodpecker *Micropternus brachyurus*
L 25 cm. S–SE–E Asia. 10 ssp, 3 in region: *brachyurus* (Jav); *badiosus* (Bor, Natuna); *badius* (Sum, MPen). Fairly common in lowland dipterocarp and swamp forest, wooded plantations, <1750 m. Often in pairs or small family groups, from ground to canopy. **ID** Uniformly rufous; black bill; black-barred upperparts, wings and tail; paler head with streaked throat; dark-barred flanks and belly. Small red patch below eye absent in **F**. Ssp *badius* more barred below, slightly shorter tail; *badiosus* longer-billed, black tail narrowly barred rufous, less barring above and almost unbarred below, scaly-patterned throat. **Imm** less barred. **Voc** (i) Series of 3–5 upslurred "kwee-kwee…" notes; (ii) distinctive drumming with rapid start, tapering off halfway, like a faltering motorbike, lasting 3–4 sec; (iii) slightly falling accelerating series of notes "tchit'chit'chit'chit…", lasting <1 sec at 17 n/s. **SS** Maroon Woodpecker has yellow (not black) bill, and is dark maroon-red, lacking brown tones and without significant dark barring. Also see Sumatran Woodpecker.

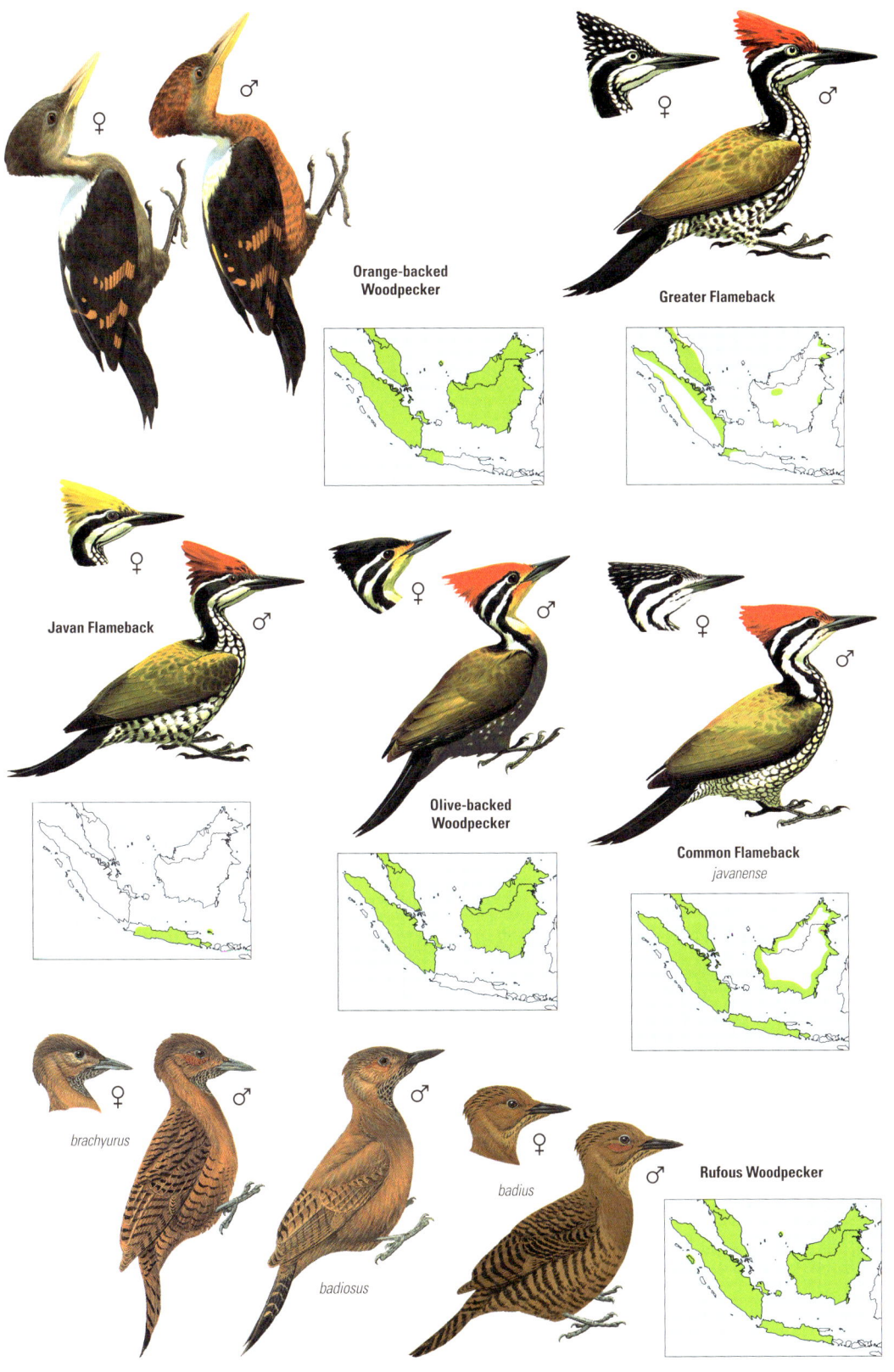

Orange-backed Woodpecker

Greater Flameback

Javan Flameback

Olive-backed Woodpecker

Common Flameback
javanense

brachyurus

badiosus

badius

Rufous Woodpecker

Banded Yellownape *Chrysophlegma miniaceum*

L 23–26 cm. Sundaic. 4 ssp, 3 in region: *miniaceum* (Jav); *malaccense* (Bor–Sum, S MPen); *niasense* (Nias). Uncommon in lowland forest, mangroves, wooded plantations, gardens, <1700 m. Singly or pairs in dense vegetation. **ID** Brownish-red head and upper breast (in **F** less red with buff-spotted cheeks); red crown and crest with yellow tip; rest of underparts buff with dark bars; olive-brown mantle with buff scaling; red wings; flight feathers brown edged red; rump yellow; uppertail black; grey bill; pale blue eyering; *malaccense* shorter-billed, breast less clearly barred; *niasense* smaller than previous, brighter overall, stronger red above, yellower below. **Imm** duller, more obscurely barred. **Voc** (i) Explosive, nasal, downslurred "keew", like squeaky toy, lasting 0.3 sec, repeated at 3–10 sec intervals; (ii) series of ~10 jumpy, nasal, excited, two-syllabic "keewik-keewik-keewik" notes, lasting <4 sec, often in duet. Drumming unrecorded. **SS** Crimson-winged Woodpecker and Checker-throated Yellownape are almost uniformly green above and below, lacking Banded's strong barring; Crimson-winged has yellow (not grey) bill; Checker-throated has green (not red) crown. **AN** Banded Woodpecker.

Checker-throated Yellownape *Chrysophlegma mentale*

L 26–28 cm. Sundaic. 2 ssp: *mentale* (Jav); *humii* (Sum, Bor, Bangka, MPen). Recent plumage-based treatment as two species ('**Javan Yellownape**' *C. mentale* and '**Checker-throated Yellownape**' *C. humii*) is possibly warranted given that characters are stable where ranges approach at Sunda Straits. Primary and secondary forest. Singly or pairs, often in mixed flocks at lower and mid-levels, <2100 m. **ID** Olive-green, with long yellow-tipped crest, chestnut collar, black tail, and red wings; mostly grey bill; *humii* smaller, paler and brighter above, proportionately longer-billed; chestnut collar extending less far to nape and crest. **M** black white-spotted throat and moustache, in *humii* with more extensive white mottling (moustache chestnut in **F**). **Imm** less red on wings; entirely chestnut below. **Voc** (i) 3–4 note call, slightly ascending, forceful "kik kee-kee-kee", lasting <2 sec, sometimes longer, 5–10 notes; (ii) drums in short bursts, lasting 1–1.5 sec at ~19 n/s, faster than Crimson-winged; (iii) single, upslurred "kyik". **SS** See Crimson-winged Woodpecker and Banded Yellownape. **AN** Checker-throated Woodpecker.

Greater Yellownape *Chrysophlegma flavinucha*

L 31–33 cm. S–SE–E Asia. 8 ssp, 2 in region: *korinchi* (S Sum); *mystacale* (N-C Sum). Scarce in hill and montane forest, secondary growth, 800–2000 m. Singly, pairs or small family parties; often joining feeding flocks containing laughingthrushes. **ID** Olive-green (paler on belly); yellow triangular hindneck, dull-rufous crown; black-and-rufous barred flight feathers. Moustache yellow in **M**, chestnut in **F**. Ssp *mystacale* paler green above; darker on belly; brighter-coloured wing barring. **Voc** (i) Single repeated "k'wee", or in a series as an accelerating "kwee-kwee-kwee-kwee-kwee-kwee-kwee-kwee-kwik-kwik-kwik-kwik-wik-wik-wik-wik"; (ii) drums infrequently with weak and rapid rolls; (iii) various slow "keep" or "chup-chup" calls; (iv) loud "kiyepp". **SS** Smaller-sized Lesser Yellownape has thin white moustachial (bordered by red in male), not Greater's wide solid yellow (male) or chestnut (fem) moustachial. Lesser Yellownape also has red lower crown (versus solid dull-rufous crown), faintly barred flanks (hard to see) and lacks wing-barring.

Crimson-winged Woodpecker *Picus puniceus*

L 25 cm. Sundaic. 3 ssp: *puniceus* (Jav); *observandus* (Bor–Sum, MPen); *soligae* (Nias). Likely a mimic of unrelated *Chrysophlegma* yellownapes. Fairly common in primary and secondary forest, wooded plantations, <900 m (Sum), <1700 m (Bor, Jav). Singly or pairs in canopy; joins mixed flocks. **ID** Olive-green; red wings; red crown with yellow crest; brownish throat, creamy barring on flanks and belly; black tail; mostly yellow bill, blue orbital skin. Red moustachial is absent in paler-bellied **F**. Ssp *observandus* smaller and paler; yellower rump, and olive-green throat; *soligae* paler still, yellower above and greyer below, red of crown extending further onto crest. **Imm** duller; speckled white head sides and underparts; red only on hindcrown, **M Imm** with reduced red moustache. **Voc** (i) "PEe-bee", sometimes extended to descending "PEe-hee-hee-hee", lasting <1 sec; (ii) drums weakly, <1 sec, see Checker-throated Yellownape; (iii) plaintive "pe-eew"; (iv) single squeaky-toy "keew", similar to Banded Yellownape but more strident and longer. **SS** Checker-throated lacks red on crown, has checkered (not solid) throat, grey (not yellow) bill, chestnut (not green) collar, and lacks the blue orbital skin. Also see Banded Yellownape.

Lesser Yellownape *Picus chlorolophus*

L 25–28 cm. S–SE–E Asia. 7–9 ssp, 1 in region: *vanheysti* (Sum), sometimes separated with extralimital *rodgeri* (MPen) as '**Sunda Yellownape**' *P. rodgeri* based on several morphological distinctions. Likely a mimic of unrelated *Chrysophlegma* yellownapes. Fairly common in submontane forest, often in mixed flocks, 800–1400 m. **ID** Green body (darker olive-green below and on head); fluffy yellow crest; narrow white moustachial; sparsely white-barred flanks; blackish tail. **M** red lower moustache and lower crown; **F** has red only on rear lower crown. **Voc** (i) Territorial call a single, loud, plaintive, slightly downslurred "peea" lasting 0.5 sec; (ii) loud, descending series of <10 "kwee" notes; (iii) short "chak". **SS** See Greater Yellownape.

Laced Woodpecker *Picus vittatus*

L 30–33 cm. SE Asia. Monotypic. Locally fairly common in open coastal forest, mangroves, bamboo, plantations, <200 m (Sum), <1000 m (Bali). Perches low, occasionally feeds on ground. **ID** Green above with yellower rump; greyish ear-coverts, black moustache; buff-yellow throat and breast; pale scaly-patterned belly. **M** red crown and nape (black on **F**). **Imm** diffusely marked below. **Voc** (i) Short, sharp "keep" or "kee-ip", singly or in short or long series; (ii) drumming in steady rolls, lasting 1–2 sec at 22 n/s, very like Checker-throated Yellownape; (iii) series of "wick, a-wick, awick" and variations.

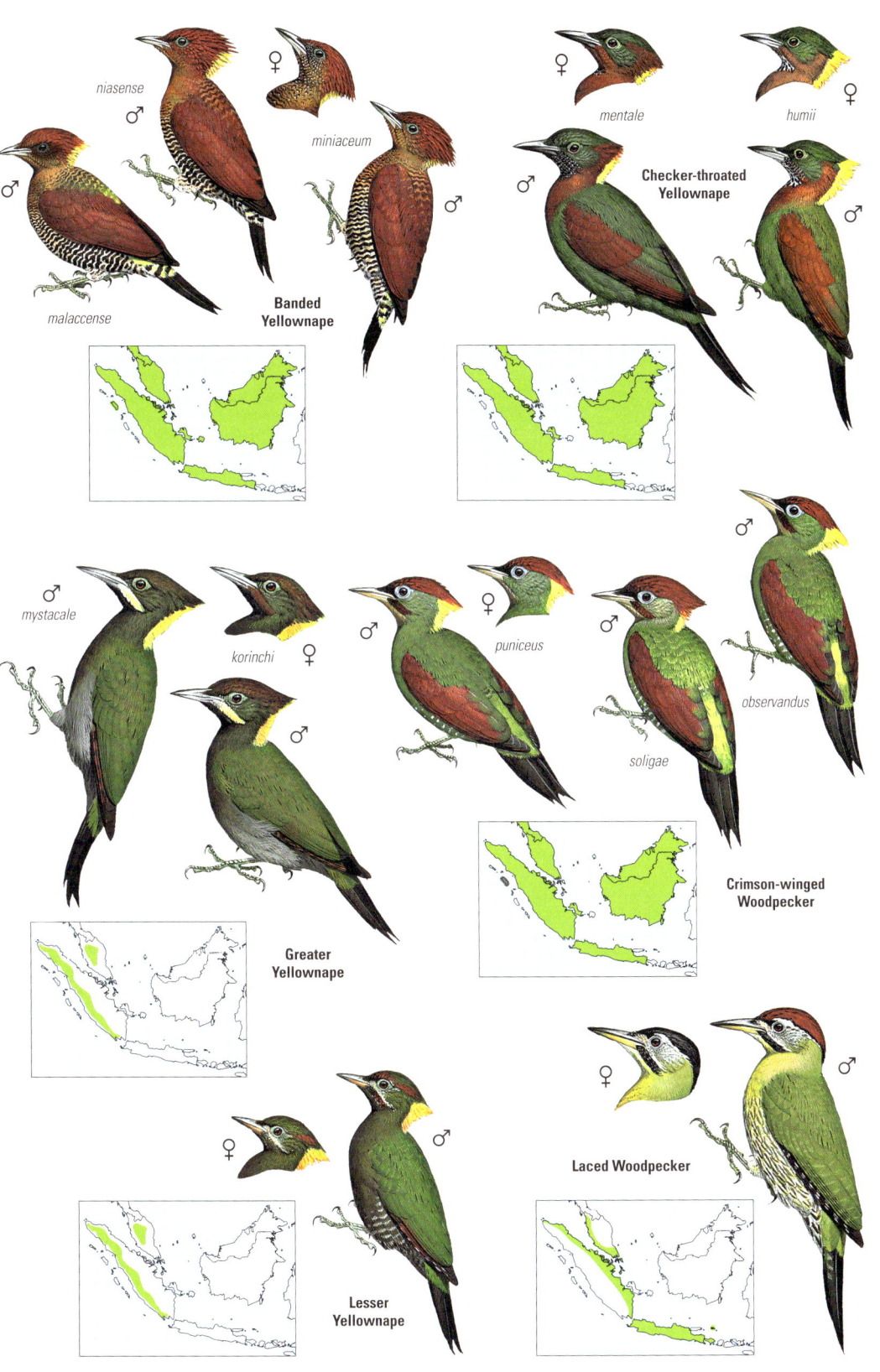

niasense

♂

♂

malaccense

♀

miniaceum

♂

Banded Yellownape

♀ *mentale*

humii ♀

♂

Checker-throated Yellownape

♂

♂ *mystacale*

korinchi ♀

♂

puniceus ♀

♂

observandus

soligae

Crimson-winged Woodpecker

Greater Yellownape

♀

♂

Lesser Yellownape

♀

♂

Laced Woodpecker

Sumatran Woodpecker *Picus dedemi* 🅔

L 26 cm. Monotypic. Often included in extralimital Grey-faced Woodpecker *P. canus* (Eurasia) but differs dramatically in plumage. Scarce in montane forest, 1000–2000 m. Little-known, with recent records from N-C Sum. **ID** Reddish upperparts with orange rump; grey cheeks and throat; black nape, moustache and tail; dusky-red breast; dusky-grey belly; finely white-barred black primaries; grey bill. **M** scarlet crown (black in **F**). **Imm** uniformly darker, less bright. **Voc** ~5 far-carrying, level to slightly descending, piercing notes, "kiew-kiew-kiew-kiew-kiew", lasting ~2 sec. Occasionally just single or double notes given. **SS** Maroon Woodpecker has yellow (not grey) bill. Rufous Woodpecker shorter-billed, warmer rufous (not as maroon-tinged) overall, with fine black barring over body. Both Maroon and Rufous have more uniform head, lacking Sumatran's grey face and black or red crown and nape.

Maroon Woodpecker *Blythipicus rubiginosus*

L 23 cm. Sundaic. Monotypic. Fairly common in lowland to upper montane forest, mangroves, plantations, <1800 m. Singly or pairs in lower and mid-storey. **ID M** purplish-brown above; olive-brown head; sides of neck and nape red; malar stripe spotted red; brown tail; underparts blackish-brown; bill pale yellow. **F** shorter bill; no red on head, but sometimes tinged red on nape. **Voc** (i) ~6 shrill descending "keek-eek-eek-eek-eek-eek", lasting 2 sec; (ii) nervously repeated, high-pitched "kik" or "kik-kik", also in wavering series; (iii) consistently spaced drum, lasting ~1 sec at 20 n/s, slightly rising in volume. **SS** See Rufous and Sumatran Woodpeckers.

Ashy Woodpecker *Dryocopus fulvus* 🅔

L 30 cm. 2 ssp: *fulvus* (N Sul, Lembeh, Manterawu, Togian); *wallacei* (C–S Sul). Fairly common in forest and disturbed habitat, coconut plantations, mangroves, <2200 m. Pairs or small groups (<5); on trunks and limbs in mid-storey and lower canopy. **ID** Dusky-grey upperparts; buff underparts; head and neck dark grey with fine white speckles. Bright red face and forecrown is absent in **F**. Ssp *wallacei* slightly paler plumage overall, **M** with facial red extending over crown and ear-coverts. **Imm M** red restricted to forecrown. **Voc** (i) Flat series of 6–8 rather weak "kik'kik'kik...", lasting <1.2 sec at 11 n/s, sometimes slowing after first 2 notes; (ii) slow drumming lasting 2–3 sec at 8 n/s; (iii) series of soft, short notes "twee-twee...".

Great Slaty Woodpecker *Dryocopus pulverulentus*

L 50 cm. S–SE Asia, Palawan. 2 ssp, 1 in region: *pulverulentus* (GS, MPen, Palawan). Uncommon (very rare and local Sum) in lowland dipterocarp, riverine and peat-swamp forest, <500 m. Pairs or groups (<6) in canopy; often holding wings out, manically calling on exposed canopy when in groups. **ID** Very large, long-necked and long-billed; grey overall (darker on wings and tail); buffish chin and throat; white-spotted head and neck. **M** red cheek patch (absent in **F**). **Imm** brownish with whiter chin and throat. **Voc** Noisy; (i) loud, whinnying "woi-kwoi-kwoi-kwoik", often in flight; (ii) upslurred "who-ICK"; (iii) single "dwot".

White-bellied Woodpecker *Dryocopus javensis*

L 40–48 cm. S–SE–E Asia, Phil. 15 ssp, 2 in region: *javensis* (GS, MPen); *parvus* (Simeulue). Complicated internal taxonomy: multiple ssp may merit elevation to species, possibly including '**Simeulue Woodpecker**' *D. parvus* on account of morphological and vocal differences. More research needed. Fairly common to scarce in lowland forest and mangroves, <1000 m. Regularly found on big bare snags and dead trucks. **ID** Very large, short-crested; head, up-perparts, breast and vent black; belly white; red crest (in **M** also red crown and malar stripe). Ssp *parvus* much smaller and very dark red on crown. **Imm** some white on rump. **Voc** Ssp *javensis*: (i) yelping and explosive "kyaw"; (ii) loud and accelerating drumming; (iii) rapid, staccato "kiaw-kiaw..." in flight and perched. Ssp *parvus*: (i) yelping "pee pee-yoo", different from *javensis*, thinner, less explosive; (ii) excited single, scratchy notes when in pairs; (iii) loud, consistent drum tailing off at end, lasting 1.5–2 sec at 13 n/s.

Sumatran Woodpecker

Maroon Woodpecker

fulvus

Ashy Woodpecker *wallacei*

javensis

parvus

Great Slaty Woodpecker

White-bellied Woodpecker

Sulawesi Pygmy-woodpecker *Picoides temminckii* [E]

L 13–14 cm. Monotypic. Fairly common in forest and edge, wooded cultivation, upper mid-storey and canopy, <2400 m. Forages on bare limbs and slender branches, sometimes joining mixed flocks. **ID** Very small; dusky-brown upperparts, white-barred back; dusky crown and cheeks; buffy-white underparts with dark streaks. **M** red hind-collar (absent in **F**). **Imm** browner, with barring and streaking less prominent. **Voc** Infrequently heard: (i) nasal, slightly descending trill, fading slightly towards the end; (ii) weak drumming lasting ~0.5 sec, sometimes in duet.

Sunda Pygmy-woodpecker *Picoides moluccensis*

L 13 cm. Sundaic, LS. 2 ssp: *moluccensis* (GS, MPen); *grandis* (Lombok–Alor). No longer includes Indian Pygmy-woodpecker *P. nanus* (S Asia). Scarce to fairly common in mangroves, beach forest, cultivation, edge, <1000 m (Sum, Bor), <1300 m (Jav), in LS extending into good forest habitat at <2000 m. **ID** Very small; dark brown above with white spots (becoming bands towards tail); dark brown cap; white face with dark brown auricular and broad black moustache; dirty white below with brown streaks. **M** red line at rear crown side (absent in **F**). Ssp *grandis* larger, longer-tailed, often washed yellow-buff with finer streaks below, less solid moustache, less barred uppertail, but broader pale wing spots. **Imm** browner, less contrasting. **Voc** (i) Whirring, thin, staccato "tr-trrrrr-it", lasting 1 sec; (ii) fairly loud, rapid, hollow drumming, lasting <1.5 sec at 26 n/s; (iii) short "pik". **SS** See Grey-capped Pygmy-woodpecker and Freckle-breasted Woodpecker.

Grey-capped Pygmy-woodpecker *Picoides canicapillus*

L 14–16 cm. S–SE–E–NE Asia. 11 ssp, 2 in region: *aurantiiventris* (Bor); *volzi* (Sum). Fairly common in forest, plantations; <1700 m but avoids coastal scrub, where replaced by Sunda. **ID** Small; black above with white-barred mantle, white-spotted outertail; dark grey forehead, crown and nape; white head sides with greyish-brown auricular and moustachial stripes; pale underparts streaked brown; belly buffish-orange. **M** with red spot at rear crown side (absent in **F**). Ssp *volzi* slightly larger with shorter bill, longer tail; less pronounced moustachial. **Imm** darker above; darker below with heavier streaking and often hint of barring. **Voc** (i) Shrill, short, squeaking rattle "click-r-r-r-rit", lasting <2 sec at 17 n/s; (ii) muted, very rapid, far-carrying drumming, lasting <1 sec at 29 n/s, ending like a bouncing ping-pong ball; (iii) repeated, sharp "kik"; (iv) "it-tit-erh-r-r-r-h", lasting <1.5 sec, almost *Calidris* sandpiper-like. **SS** More black-and-white than the dingy-looking, browner Sunda, with almost unmarked wings (barring mostly confined to back), and often with warmer-tinged belly. Also see Freckle-breasted Woodpecker.

Freckle-breasted Woodpecker *Dendrocopos analis*

L 18–19 cm. SE Asia. 3 ssp, 1 in region: *analis* (Jav, Bali), reported S Sum. No longer included in Fulvous-breasted Woodpecker *D. macei* (mostly S Asia) based on vocal and plumage traits. Open forest, mangroves, plantations, gardens, <2000 m. **ID** Black-and-white barred above; black nape; white head sides with black moustache; buffish below, faint red vent; barred flanks. **M** red crown (black in **F**). **Voc** (i) Short, quiet "pik" or rolling series "pipipipipipipipipip"; (ii) short, weak drumming, evenly spaced, gradually doubling in speed, tapering off slightly at end, lasting 2 sec at 10–18 n/s; (iii) loud "tik". **SS** Sunda and Grey-capped Pygmy-woodpeckers are much smaller, more streaked below, and lack red crown (in male), white face, and reddish vent.

ALCEDINIDAE
Kingfishers

34 species in region

A large family of small to medium-sized birds, typically with brightly coloured plumage, stocky bodies, short tail and wings and long dagger-like bills. Found in both wetlands and forest habitats, diving or pouncing to catch fish or ground-living prey, often sitting quietly for prolonged periods of time.

Green-backed Kingfisher *Actenoides monachus* [E]

L 31–32 cm. Monotypic. For taxonomy see Black-headed. Fairly common in primary and secondary forest, <1100 m. **ID** Red bill; deep-blue head, white throat; rufous underparts; olive-green upperparts with blue tinged tail. **F** rufous cheeks and supercilium (blue in **M**). **Imm** duller with horn bill. **Voc** Usually calls at dawn, sometimes at night: (i) strident whistle that increases in volume, "oooeeEE...", lasting ~2 sec, sometimes in duet; (ii) agitated call, almost chicken-like chuckles "ku-ku-ku...", "hak-hak-hak...". **SS** See Scaly Kingfisher.

Black-headed Kingfisher *Actenoides capucinus* [E]

L 33–34 cm. Monotypic. Separated from Green-backed Kingfisher based on pronounced size and plumage differences. Little-known, presumably fairly common in primary and secondary forest, <1300 m. **ID** Similar to Green-backed but head black (in **M**) or black with rufous face (in **F**), darker green upperparts and tail; bill almost twice as thick. **Imm** undescribed. **Voc** Usually calls just before dawn, sometimes at night: (i) strident whistle that increases in volume, "oooeeEE...", lasting ~2 sec, sometimes in duet; (ii) agitated call, almost chicken-like chuckles "ku-ku-ku...", "hak-hak-hak...".

Scaly Kingfisher *Actenoides princeps* [E]

L 24–25 cm. 4 ssp. Confused internal taxonomy with possibly between 2–4 species-level groups: '**Scaly-breasted Kingfisher**' *princeps* (NE Sul); '**Lore Lindu Kingfisher**' *erythrorhamphus* (C–NW–SW Sul); '**Regal Kingfisher**' *regalis* (SE Sul); '**Tumpu Kingfisher**' (undescribed taxon; E Sul). In Minahasa Peninsula, *erythrorhamphus* occurs E to the Matinan Mts, where it has the bill tinged dusky, indicating some intergradation with *princeps*. 'Regal' only known from two specimens (one fem, one near-adult male, from 2000 m in Mekongga Mts); 'Tumpu' only known from well-documented observation of single Ad male (from 2100 m on Mt Tumpu); even so, the two probably relate to distinct taxa because of plumage trait inconsistencies. More research needed before species is split. Uncommon in primary and secondary forest, 900–2100 m, rarely down to 250 m. **ID** Yellowish bill, deep-blue head (with buff loral spot in **M** or buff supercilium and moustachial stripe in **F**); buff collar, scalloped brown upperparts and finely-barred pale underparts (especially flanks). Ssp *erythrorhamphus* reddish bill, often buff on flanks and more intense buff tinge to collar; *regalis* considerably larger, has blue areas of head replaced with dull blue-green (most of head) and blackish (front of head), is even buffier on underparts (at least in **F**) with reduced barring, and lacks scaling on back; its bill colour is unknown. The undescribed 'Tumpu Kingfisher' displays odd combination of traits between *erythrorhamphus* and *regalis*, having the blue head, red bill and scaly back of the former while exhibiting unique solid-rufous, unbarred underparts. **Imm** duller, darker bill; more heavily barred. **Voc** (i) Long, drawn-out, quivering whistle "ssweeee...", lasting ~1.5 sec, sometimes given in duet; (ii) agitated calls include an excited "er-hoo, er-hoo, er-hoo...". **SS** 'Tumpu' form of present species superficially resembles Green-backed, but has buff loral spot (in male) or presumably buff moustachial and eyebrow (in fem), and scaled, brown (not solid olive) upperparts.

Sulawesi Pygmy-woodpecker
variant ♂ ♀

Sunda Pygmy-woodpecker
grandis ♂
moluccensis ♀ ♂

Grey-capped Pygmy-woodpecker
aurantiiventris ♂ ♀

Freckle-breasted Woodpecker
♂ ♀

Green-backed Kingfisher
♂ ♀

Scaly Kingfisher
princeps ♀ ♂
erythrorhamphus ♀ ♂
regalis ♀

Black-headed Kingfisher
♀ ♂

Rufous-collared Kingfisher *Actenoides concretus*
L 23–24 cm. Sundaic. 3 ssp, 2 in region: *concretus* (Sum, Bangka, Belitung, MPen); *borneanus* (Bor). Uncommon in primary and secondary lowland forest, <1200 m, rarely to 1700 m. **ID** Yellowish bill; blue crown; rufous collar; rufous breast (slightly paler in **F**); blue moustachial. **M** solid blue upperparts (darker in *borneanus*). **F** green upperparts with buff spots (more prominent in *borneanus*). **Imm** duller with blackish bill. **Voc** (i) Level series of upslurred notes "kwi-kwi-kwi..." at 8 n/10 s; (ii) descending series of harsh, hard, rolling "drrrwit-drrrwit-drrrwet-drrrwet...", at 1 n/s, with occasional cackling at end of sequence.

Common Paradise-kingfisher *Tanysiptera galatea*
L 33–43 cm. Aus. 15 ssp, 10 in region: *doris* (Morotai); *emiliae* (Rau); *browningi* (Halmahera); *margarethae* (Bacan); *brunhildae* (Doi); *sabrina* (Kayoa); *obiensis* (Obi and satellites); *acis* (Buru); *boanensis* (Boano); *nais* (Ambon, Seram, and satellites). Multiple species undoubtedly involved, with bioacoustic differences pointing to at least four species in region (see Voc). Fairly common in primary and secondary forest, <500 m, rarely to 800 m. **ID** (*acis*) Red bill; blue upperparts with brighter crown and wing-coverts; white underparts and rump; long blue tail tipped white; **F** slightly smaller. Ssp *obiensis* darker upperparts; *margarethae* as previous but more intensely blue-scaled rump; *brunhildae* as previous but white outertail; *browningi* as *margarethae* but with hint of cobalt supercilium and blue outertail; *doris* resembles *acis* but has white mantle; *emiliae* as *doris* but with white tail base; *sabrina* as *emiliae* but white mantle patch smaller; *nais* as *acis* but has white outertail and hint of pale-blue supercilium; *boanensis* as *nais* but paler crown. **Imm** brownish upperparts, scaled rufous breast and brown bill. **Voc** Much geographic variation, divided into multiple vocally distinct subspecies groups: In C Mol (*nais*, *boanensis*, *acis*) rapid, ascending but decelerating series of 30-40 tremulous nasal notes increasing in volume, lasting 3-4 s, at 10 n/s, preceded by downslurred introductory note at least in *nais* and *boanensis* but possibly not *acis*. Over most of N Mol (at least *browningi* and *margarethae*) similar but more rapid series (~13 n/s) at roughly constant speed, always preceded by distinct introductory note, *margarethae* possibly always higher-pitched (adjacent *brunhildae* and *sabrina* vocally unknown, but at least *sabrina* may be vocally divergent because of distinct plumage and island isolation). On Obi (*obiensis*) descending rattle, slightly decelerating and tailing off at end, lasting 1–3 sec, at 15 n/s, preceded by two nasal introductory notes. On Morotai (*doris*) series of 10-35 nasal notes, starting out with slow, long, introductory 'beeoo' followed by another 2-3 hesitant notes, rising and then levelling in pitch, continuously accelerating to a final flat trill of ~15 n/s, fading in the end, lasting 3-3.5 s in total (adjacent *emiliae* vocally unknown but probably similar).

Sulawesi Lilac Kingfisher *Cittura cyanotis* `E`
L 24 cm. 2 ssp: *cyanotis* (N Sul); *modesta* (C–SE Sul). Previously united with Sangihe Lilac under Lilac-cheeked Kingfisher *C. cyanotis* but differs considerably in plumage, genetic traits and vocalisations. Fairly common in primary and secondary forest, occasionally mixed plantations, <1000 m. **ID** Red bill; thin facial mask and wings deep-blue (in **M**) or black (in **F**); brown upperparts (slightly duller in **F**); rufous rump and tail; pale underparts with slight pink hue around face. Ssp *modesta* slightly rufous-tinged throat and face. **Imm** duller; grey bill. **Voc** Trogon-like descending "yop yap-yap-yap-ya", lasting 1.5 sec.

Sangihe Lilac Kingfisher *Cittura sanghirensis* `E`
L 23 cm. Monotypic. For taxonomy see Sulawesi Lilac. Scarce in primary and secondary forest, occasionally also mixed plantations; status on Siau unknown, no recent records. **ID Ad** similar to Sulawesi Lilac but smaller-bodied; longer tail, wings and bill; much broader mask wrapping around bill base; white-flecked supercilium; deep lilac face and breast band; brighter upperparts. **F** slightly duller, black mask and wings. **Imm** duller, grey bill. **Voc** (i) "Yap-yap-yap", slower and quieter than Sulawesi Lilac; (ii) plaintive, quivering, nasal wail; (iii) series of upslurred whistles.

Banded Kingfisher *Lacedo pulchella*
L 20 cm. SE Asia. 3 ssp, 2 in region: *pulchella* (Sum, Jav, MPen); treatment of *melanops* (Bangka, Bor) as monotypic species '**Bornean Banded Kingfisher**' (as opposed to '**Malayan Banded**' *L. pulchella*) may be warranted given discrete differences in male head pattern and genetic traits; more research required. Fairly common in primary and secondary forest, <1200 m, rarely to 1700 m. Usually in mid-canopy, sometimes canopy. Slowly raises crown feathers when alarmed. **ID** Red bill. **M** forehead, cheeks and collar rufous (black in *melanops*); upperparts and crown barred blue-black; underparts white with rufous wash on breast. **F** head and upperparts barred brown-and-black; underparts white with fine barring. **Imm** duller in both sexes; dark bill and heavily barred underparts; *melanops* M Imm has rufous, not black, cheeks. **Voc** Song: drawn-out, slow whistle, then <20 slow couplets: "wheeoo chi-wit chi-wit chi-wit...", lasting 10–20 sec at 1 n/s. Call: agitated sharp "wiak wiak".

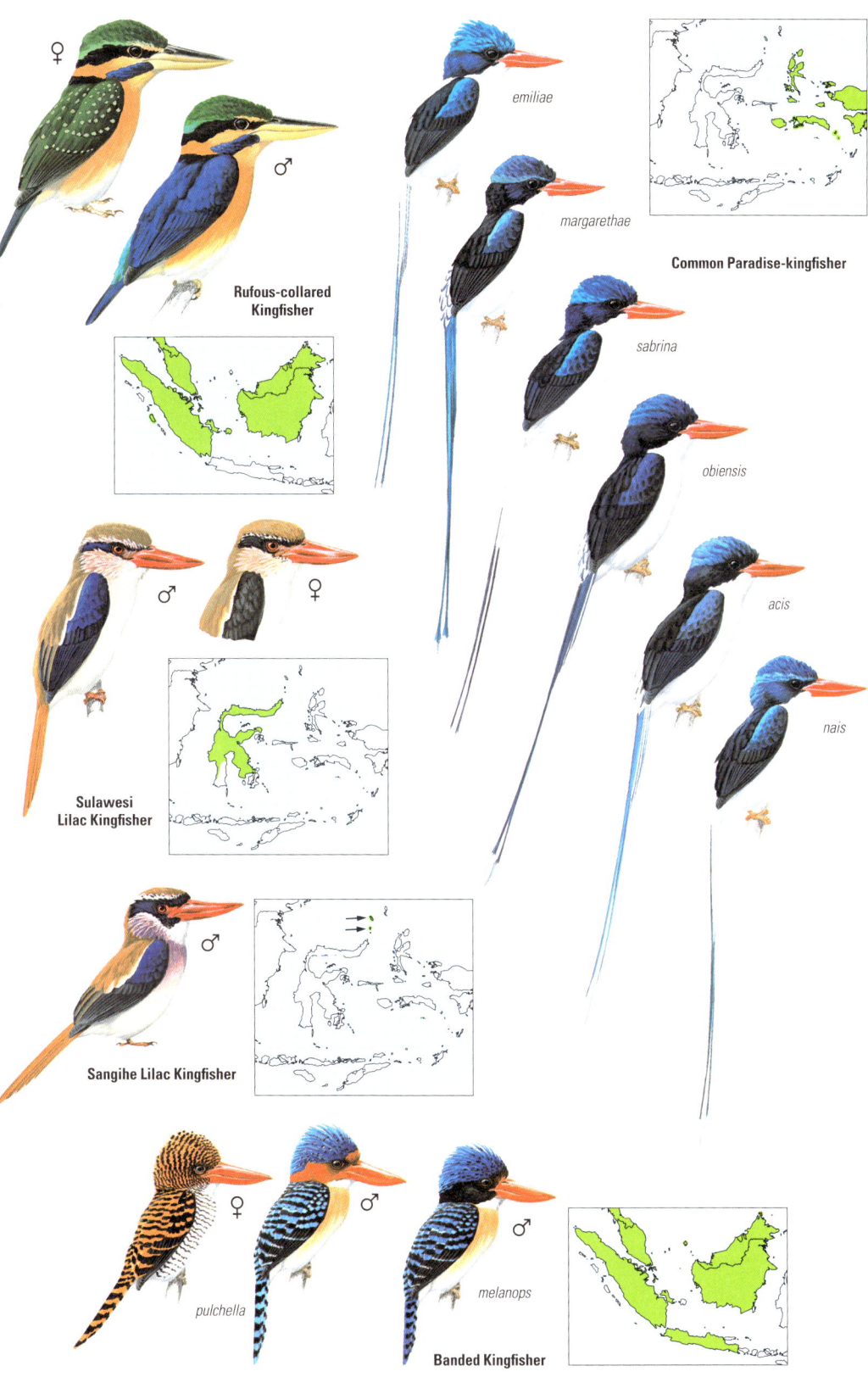

♀

♂

Rufous-collared Kingfisher

emiliae

margarethae

sabrina

obiensis

acis

nais

Common Paradise-kingfisher

♂   ♀

Sulawesi Lilac Kingfisher

♂

Sangihe Lilac Kingfisher

♀   ♂   ♂

pulchella   melanops

Banded Kingfisher

White-rumped Kingfisher *Caridonax fulgidus* E

L 30 cm. 2 ssp: *fulgidus* (Lombok, Sumbawa); *gracilirostris* (Flores, Besar). Fairly common in primary, secondary and heavily degraded forest, <1700 m, occasionally village scrub and plantations at forest edge. **ID Ad** strikingly patterned: large red bill and orbital skin, black head, purple-blue upperparts, white underparts and striking pale-blue rump. Ssp *gracilirostris* slightly longer wings and tail. **Imm** buffy underparts; yellowish bill. **Voc** Single loud "OWH" continually repeated every ~1 sec, predominantly at dawn and dusk. **AN** Glittering Kingfisher.

Stork-billed Kingfisher *Pelargopsis capensis*

L 35 cm. S–SE Asia, Phil. 13 ssp, 7 in region: *malaccensis* (Riau Is, Lingga, MPen); *cyanopteryx* (Sum, Bangka, Belitung); *simalurensis* (Simeulue, Babi); *sodalis* (Banyak, Nias, Batu, Mentawai); *innominata* (Bor); *javana* (Jav); *floresiana* (Bali–Flores). Fairly common in most habitats close to water, particularly mangroves, edge and water-ways through forest, <1200 m. **ID** Thick, long, red bill. **Ad** greyish-brown cap; rufous underparts and collar; mid-blue upperparts with brighter rump, slightly more turquoise on mantle. Ssp *cyanopteryx* more uniformly blue upperparts; *innominata* as previous but indistinct cap almost concolourous with collar; *javana* reportedly most similar to previous but upperparts greenish-blue, underparts deeper buff; *simalurensis* as *cyanopteryx* but slightly duller; *sodalis* as previous but slightly larger; *floresiana* larger still, with darkest sooty-brown cap. **Imm** scaled, dusky underparts. **Voc** Song: hollow whistled "ewee-ewee ewee-ewee", often in duet. Call: explosive cackling "kek-kek-ek-ek...", lasting 2–7 sec at 5 n/s.

Great-billed Kingfisher *Pelargopsis melanorhyncha* E

L 35 cm. 3 ssp: *melanorhyncha* (Sul and satellites); *dichrorhyncha* (Banggai); *eutreptorhyncha* (Sula). Species shows puzzling leapfrog pattern in which terminal ssp (*melanorhyncha* and *eutreptorhyncha*) look similar and are geographically bridged by different-looking *dichrorhyncha*; more research needed to examine potential internal species boundaries. Uncommon, locally fairly common, in most habitats close to water, particularly mangroves, coastal scrub, forest edge and water-ways through forest, <900 m. **ID Ad** similar shape and habits to Stork-billed Kingfisher but black bill, whitish underparts and head with dusky face, blackish upperparts with white rump. On Togian Is, some birds show variable amounts of red at hill base. Ssp *dichrorhyncha* larger, bill with variable amounts of red at base, covering much of lower mandible; *eutreptorhyncha* smaller than previous, with blacker bill. **Imm** scaled breast and hindneck. **Voc** As Stork-billed. **AN** Black-billed Kingfisher.

Ruddy Kingfisher *Halcyon coromanda*

L 25 cm. S–SE–NE Asia, Phil. 10 ssp, 7 in region: *coromanda* (breeds mainland S–SE Asia; winters to Sum, Jav); *major* (breeds NE China, Korea, Japan; winters Phil, Bor, Talaud); *bangsi* (breeds Ryukyu Is; winters Phil, Talaud, Sul); *minor* (resident GS, MPen); *rufa* (resident Sul, Sangihe, Talaud); *pelingensis* (resident Banggai); *sulana* (resident Sula). Internal taxonomy confused; more than one species may be involved. Uncommon; migrant forms can occur in variety of habitats; *minor* is mostly restricted to coastal growth, such as mangroves, swamp forest and Nipa palm; Wallacean resident forms occur in wide range of lowland and hill forest, <1300 m. Quite shy and secretive, seldom perches conspicuously. **ID** Red bill. **Ad** wholly lilac head and upperparts with silvery-blue rump; rufous underparts. Ssp *major* paler, more violaceous upperparts, rump reduced to narrow stripe, underparts buffier; *bangsi* darker overall, more violaceous; *minor* even darker overall, breast washed violet, large silvery rump; *rufa* as previous but not as dark, rump pale-blue; *pelingensis* as previous but rump silver; *sulana* as nominate but more violaceous. **Imm** darker and duller (including rump), lightly barred breast. **Voc** (i) Soft, assertive, tremulous "kyorrrrr..." lasting 0.4 sec, regularly repeated; (ii) soft, rolling "ka-rroow", regularly repeated; (iii) in alarm, loud, assertive "kakaka...". Migratory races may produce different vocalisations.

White-breasted Kingfisher *Halcyon smyrnensis*

L 27–28 cm. SW–S–SE–E Asia. 3 ssp, 1 in region: *fusca* (Sum, S–SE–E Asia). Colonizing W-C Jav, W Bor. Excludes Brown-breasted Kingfisher *H. gularis* (Phil) because of pronounced plumage differences. Fairly common in open country, coastal areas, ponds, plantations, gardens, <2000 m, rarely above. Often perches conspicuously, especially early morning when calling. **ID Ad** chestnut head and underparts with broad white throat and breast; upperparts bright blue with black and brown wing-coverts; red bill; strongly patterned wings conspicuous in flight. **Imm** duller with barred breast. **Voc** (i) Whinnying, slightly descending "kli'li'li'li...", lasting 0.5–2 sec at 12–15 n/s; (ii) 10–30 loud, alarming "kek-kek-kek..." at ~10 n/s. **SS** See Javan. **AN** Smyrna Kingfisher, White-throated Kingfisher.

Javan Kingfisher *Halcyon cyanoventris* E

L 27 cm. Monotypic. Uncommon in open country, scrubby hillsides, ponds, plantations, gardens, <1500 m, rarely above. **ID Ad** red bill; blackish head; rufous collar; purple body with bright blue outorwing and tail. Strongly patterned wings conspicuous in flight. **Imm** duller; whitish throat; dull bill. **Voc** (i) whinnying, slightly descending "kli'li'li'li...", lasting 0.5–2 sec at 12–15 n/s, often given in aerial display, similar to White-breasted; (ii) loud alarm call "kek-kek-...". **SS** White-breasted Kingfisher paler, with white (not dark) breast, and shows paler blue mantle in flight with large white wing patch.

Black-capped Kingfisher *Halcyon pileata*

L 28 cm. Breeds E Asia; winters S–SE Asia. Monotypic. Uncommon migrant in open country, scrub, ponds, plantations, forest edge, <1550 m. **ID Ad** black head; white collar and breast; peachy underparts; dark-blue upperparts with black shoulder; red bill. In flight shows conspicuous white outer primaries. **Imm** duller, buffier, with scaled underparts and buff loral spot. **Voc** Short, tremulous "krr", lasting 0.2 sec at <6 n/s, regularly repeated.

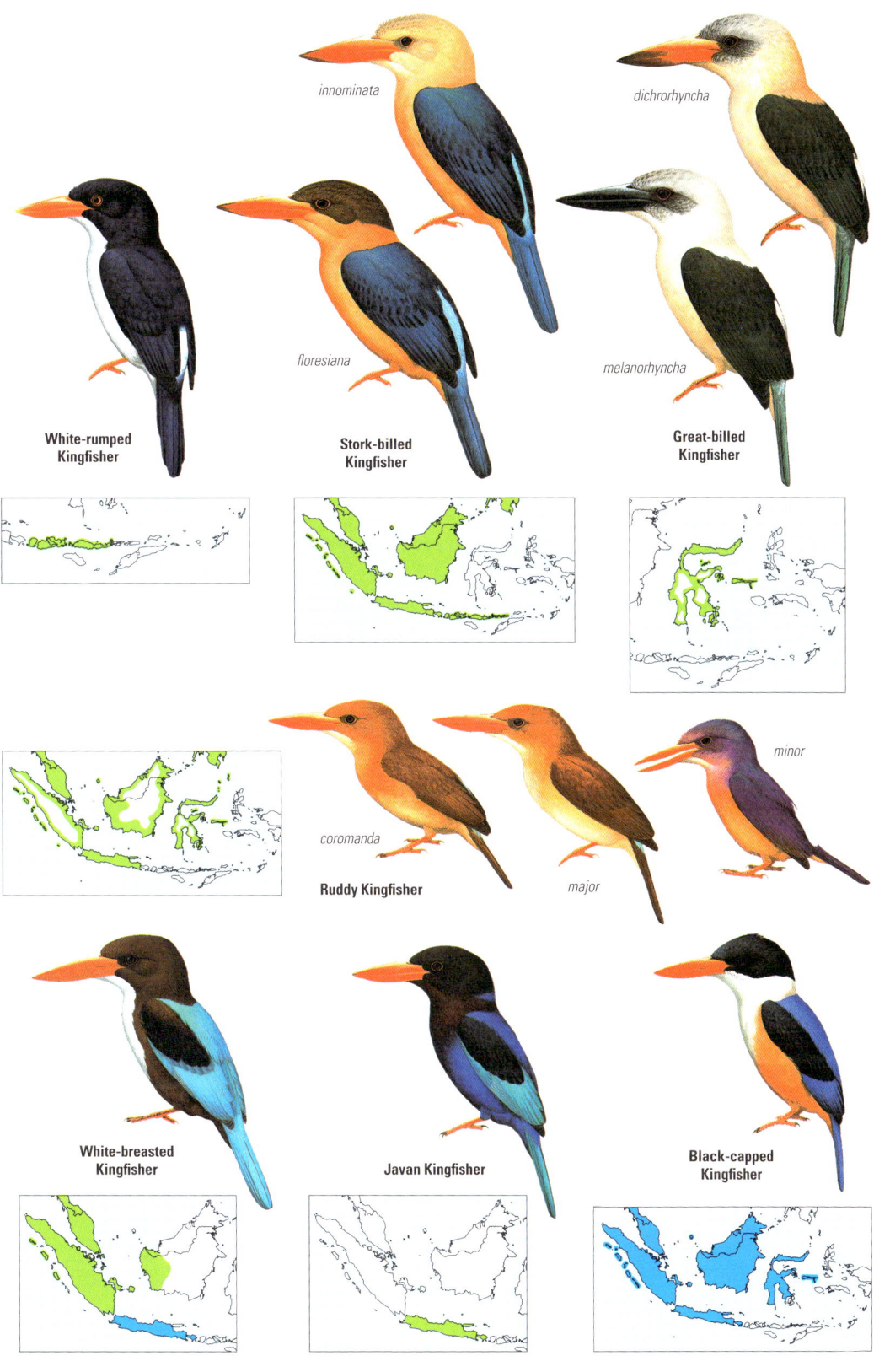

innominata

dichrorhyncha

White-rumped Kingfisher

floresiana

Stork-billed Kingfisher

melanorhyncha

Great-billed Kingfisher

coromanda

Ruddy Kingfisher

major

minor

White-breasted Kingfisher

Javan Kingfisher

Black-capped Kingfisher

Blue-and-white Kingfisher *Todiramphus diops* **E**

L 19 cm. Monotypic. Fairly common in secondary and degraded forest, edge, plantations and orchards, <700 m. **ID** Dark-blue head, wings and tail; paler blue mantle; white loral spot and underparts. In flight shows white patch at base of primaries. **M** white collar. **F** broad blue breast band and darker upperparts lacking white collar. **Imm** buff loral spot, collar and breast. **Voc** Quiet, rasping "tchew-tchew-tchew". **SS** Male told from larger, paler Collared Kingfisher by bluer (less turquoise) upperparts and crown, and by all-black bill (lacking pale spot at base). **AN** Moluccan Kingfisher.

Lazuli Kingfisher *Todiramphus lazuli* **E**

L 22 cm. Monotypic. Uncommon in primary and secondary forest, edge, plantations and orchards, <650 m. **ID M** dark-blue upperparts and head with pale blue mantle and belly; white loral spot and chin to breast. **F** pale-blue underparts extend to upper breast. **Imm** buff loral spot, scaled breast and collar. **Voc** (i) Loud, repeated "kee-kee-kee..." at 3 n/s, increasing and decreasing in tempo; (ii) 2-note upslurred "k-kee" at 2 n/s, often in duet.

Forest Kingfisher *Todiramphus macleayii*

L 20 cm. Aus. 3 ssp, 2 in region: *macleayii* (breeds N Aus; winters to Sermata, Aru); *incinctus* (breeds E Aus; winters to Kai, NG). Rare in forest, edge, mangroves, urban areas, open countryside. **ID M** similar to Blue-and-white Kingfisher but pale base to lower mandible, more contrast between crown and darker cheeks. **F** has dark-blue hindneck and lacks Blue-and-white's breast band. Both sexes show large white wing patch in flight. Ssp *incinctus* greenish mantle, smaller wing patch. **Imm** buffy loral spot, buff flanks and scaled breast; in flight shows white patch at base of primaries. **Voc** (i) Rolling, rapidly repeated, slightly descending "pep'pep'pep...", lasting 2–5 sec at 11 n/s; (ii) harder, higher-pitched, rolling call like a creaking door "k'k'k...", lasting <6 sec at 11 n/s. **SS** Male told from larger, paler Collared Kingfisher by darker-blue (less turquoise) wings and crown; white loral spot more square-shaped (does not point towards eye); conspicuous white patch at base of primaries.

Collared Kingfisher *Todiramphus chloris*

L 23–25 cm. Africa–Aus. ~50 ssp, 6 in region: *chloris* (Sul, LS, Mol, NG); *armstrongi* (NE Sum, mainland SE Asia); *laubmannianus* (Sum–Bor); *azelus* (Enggano), *palmeri* (Jav, Bali, Bawean, Kangean); *occipitalis* (breeds Nicobars; recently recorded in N Sum). Internal taxonomy in need of revision; recent molecular species delimitation work (using 20 out of 50 ssp) separated complex into 19 species, but test non-conservative and some of these divisions doubtful, while others very plausible. Some extralimital ssp shown to be possibly more closely related to Beach and Sacred Kingfishers. Within region, ssp *chloris* apparently deeply diverged genetically from forms in GS and mainland Asia; surprisingly deep genetic division apparent also between the rather similar *laubmannianus* and *armstrongi*. More research needed. See also Talaud Kingfisher for taxonomy. Common in wide variety of habitats: open country, coastal areas, ponds, plantations, gardens, but particularly mangroves, <1500 m, rarely above. **ID** Green-blue crown; black mask and nape-band; white loral spot;

greenish mantle; blue wings and tail; underparts and collar white. **M** wings and tail more intensely coloured; cap and mantle darker than **F**. Ssp *laubmannianus* larger-billed, dark-blue on upperparts; *palmeri* as previous but smaller-billed, paler blue on upperparts, with dark bluish-green mask and obsolete nape-band; *azelus* as *laubmannianus* but slightly smaller; *armstrongi* as *laubmannianus* but smaller, with more bluish-green mask and narrower or obsolete nape-band; distinct *occipitalis* large with buffy brow band that meets at nape; some birds on Simeulue show vestigial pale nape triangle and rudimentary pale brow, possibly indicating admixture from adjacent *occipitalis*. **Imm** generally duller, greener above; some buff on underparts and on loral spot. **Voc** (i) Loud, shrieking "KICK-kjew" continually repeated; (ii) loud "KEK-KEK-KEK...", rapidly repeated, often ending "jee-jaw"; often duets; (iii) quiet, agitated "chikpreeEW". **SS** See Blue-and-white, Forest, Sacred and Talaud Kingfishers.

Talaud Kingfisher *Todiramphus enigma* **E**

L 21 cm. Monotypic. Sometimes included as ssp of Collared Kingfisher, and its validity as a species is somewhat doubtful as specimen series show size and plumage overlap. More research needed. Fairly common in primary and secondary forest, particularly clearings. Replaced in coastal areas by Collared Kingfisher. **ID Ad** similar to Collared Kingfisher but 15% smaller with shorter tail and bill; slightly greener upperparts. **Imm** undescribed. **Voc** Similar to Collared but slightly faster, more shrill. **SS** Larger, bluer Collared is said to be restricted to coastal mangroves on Talaud. See also Sacred.

Beach Kingfisher *Todiramphus saurophagus*

L 30 cm. Aus. 3 ssp, 1 in region: *saurophagus* (N Mol, Seram, NG, Melanesia). See Collared Kingfisher for taxonomy. Uncommon in coastal areas: beaches, mangroves, rocky areas, occasionally found several hundred metres inland. Generally absent or rare where Collared Kingfisher occurs. **ID** Large. **Ad** white head and underparts; bright green-blue upperparts; dark line behind eye. **Imm** duller blue upperparts and buffish underparts. **Voc** (i) <15 loud, ringing "KIK-KIK-KIK..." at 4 n/s, very similar to Collared; (ii) loud, shrieking "CHEW-CHEW-CHEW..." at 4 n/s, softer start to note than Collared; (iii) loud, softer "ke-chew", lasting 0.5 sec, regularly repeated with other calls.

Sacred Kingfisher *Todiramphus sanctus*

L 22 cm. Aus. 4–5 ssp, 1 in region: *sanctus* (breeds Australia; winters to N). Fairly common in E, scarcer in GS, in open country, coastal areas, ponds, plantations, gardens, but particularly mangroves. **ID/SS Ad** similar to larger Collared and smaller Talaud Kingfishers but in most plumages separated by buffy loral spot, buff-washed collar and flanks, and greener upperparts. Beware of confusion with occasional buffy-looking Imm Collared, which usually have fine dark barring or scaling on flanks, neck or breast. **Imm** stronger buff-washed underparts with fine barring, mantle dull grey-green. **Voc** (i) Loud "KIK-KIK-KIK...", similar to Collared but slightly softer; (ii) whinnying "klilililililil", similar to White-breasted but slightly softer.

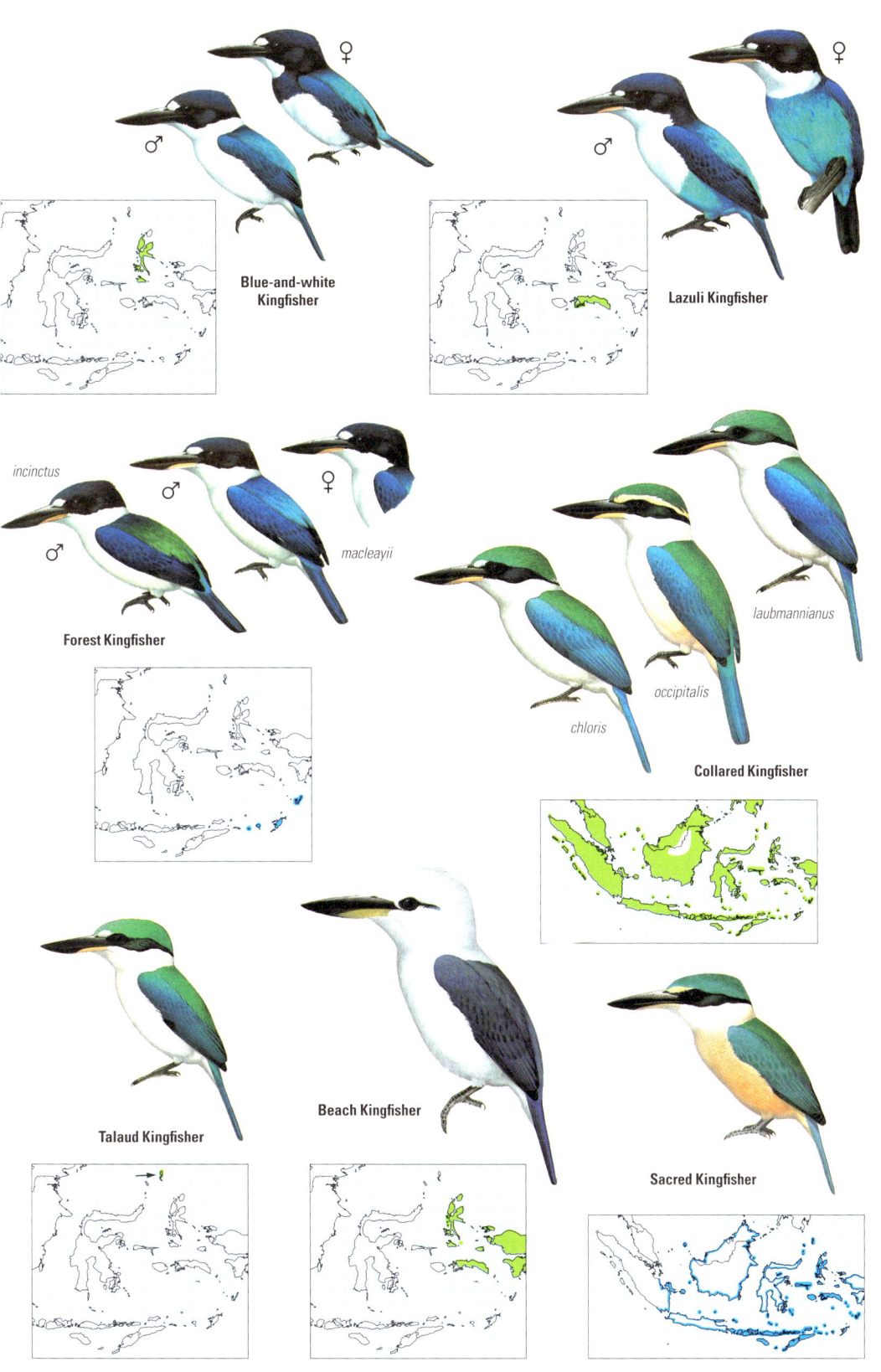

♀

Blue-and-white
Kingfisher

♂

♀

Lazuli Kingfisher

♂

incinctus

♂

macleayii

♀

Forest Kingfisher

laubmannianus

occipitalis

chloris

Collared Kingfisher

Talaud Kingfisher

Beach Kingfisher

Sacred Kingfisher

Sombre Kingfisher *Todiramphus funebris* [E]
L 30 cm. Monotypic. Uncommon in primary and secondary forest, rarely edge, plantations, <650 m. **ID M** black upperparts with green hue; white supercilium, underparts and collar; pale base to lower mandible. **F** blackish-brown upperparts. **Imm** duller with dirty wash to underparts. **Voc** (i) Descending series of <10 laugh-like "wer-wer-wer..." at 3 n/s; (ii) repeated, slow, loud "YOERR" notes; (iii) short series of loud, crackling "ker-ker-ker..." at 4 n/s.

Cinnamon-banded Kingfisher [E]
Todiramphus australasia
L 21 cm. 5 ssp: *australasia* (Lombok, Sumba, Wetar, Timor); *tringorum* (Romang); *dammerianus* (Damar, Babar); *interpositus* (Leti, Moa); *odites* (Tanimbar). Uncommon in primary and secondary forest, also edge, <700 m. **ID M** blue-green crown; rufous headband above deep-blue mask; rufous underparts and collar; green-blue upperparts; **F** slightly duller. Ssp *tringorum* extensive rufous forecrown, green hindcrown; *dammerianus* rufous extends to centre of crown; *interpositus* paler rufous overall, green crown small or absent; *odites* much paler overall, underparts and collar washed-out whitish, supercilium buff, upperparts paler, greener. **Imm** paler bill; barred underparts and buff-fringed upperparts. **Voc** (i) Rapid, slightly descending trill "kirirIririririririririririr", lasting 1.2 sec, regularly repeated, particularly at dusk; (ii) agitated call, often in duet, an excited loud "KE-REE", regularly repeated.

Black-backed Dwarf-kingfisher *Ceyx erithaca*
L 14 cm. Breeds S–SE Asia, winters to S. 2 ssp, 1 in region: *erithaca* (breeds mainland SE Asia, S Asia; winters MPen, Sum, perhaps also N Bor). Often united with Rufous-backed Dwarf-kingfisher into a larger '**Oriental Dwarf-kingfisher**' *C. erithaca* because of occasional hybridisation where ranges meet in MPen. However, incidence of co-occurrence often misinterpreted based on seasonal overlap, and ssp *motleyi* of Rufous-backed often misinterpreted as hybrid in the past. Uncommon migrant to forest, gardens, parks, <1300 m. **ID Ad** black spot on forehead; violaceous-orange head, rump and tail; blue-and-white on neck; blue-black upperparts and back. **Imm** duller, especially crown and mantle, with reduced, less shiny blue-black on mantle and coverts. **Voc** (i) Sharp, metallic whistle, "tit", given while perched; (ii) sharp, metallic, high-pitched "tst" either in flight or perched. **SS** See Rufous-backed Dwarf-kingfisher.

Rufous-backed Dwarf-kingfisher *Ceyx rufidorsa*
L 14 cm. Sundaic, Palawan. 5 ssp: *rufidorsa* (LS, MPen, Palawan, most of GS except NE Bor); *motleyi* (Sabah at least into E Kalimantan); *captus* (Nias); *jungei* (Simeulue); ssp. (Mentawai). Ssp *motleyi* widely confounded as a 'hybrid swarm' but is in fact a stable population with Black-backed-like plumage traits, possibly worthy of recognition as monotypic species '**Sabah Dwarf-kingfisher**' because of lack of known intergradation with *rufidorsa* in areas of contact. Geographically isolated ssp *captus* appears nearly identical in plumage to *motleyi*, very different from adjacent *rufidorsa* on Banyak Is, and may be worthy of species status ('**Nias Dwarf-kingfisher**'). Population on Mentawai also distinct in plumage but undescribed. See also Black-backed Dwarf-kingfisher for taxonomy. Uncommon in primary and secondary forest, <1300 m. Often heard or seen flying fast through forest, close to ground. **ID Ad** bright red bill; yellow underparts and lilac-rufous upperparts; blackish-purple outerwing. Ssp *jungei* larger; *motleyi* rufous back but otherwise similar to Black-backed; *captus* as previous but longer-billed and larger-sized, with less blue on head. Undescribed Mentawai population has distinct dusky-mottled upperwing. **Imm** duller overall; paler bill with dark markings. **Voc** As Black-backed. **SS** Black-backed resembles *motleyi* and *captus* but always has blue-black (not rufous) mantle.

Sulawesi Dwarf-kingfisher *Ceyx fallax* [E]
L 12–13 cm. 2 ssp: *fallax* (Sul); recent treatment of *sangirensis* (Sangihe; possibly extinct) as monotypic species '**Sangihe Dwarf-kingfisher**' requires further research; both known specimens reported to be from Sangihe but obtained in Manado. No sightings ever confirmed from Sangihe. Scarce in primary and secondary forest, <600 m, rarely <1000 m. **ID Ad** banded blue crown; broad rufous supercilium; lilac cheek; brown back with electric blue rump and tail. Ssp *sangirensis* larger-sized, with more extensive blue-speckled crown extending onto supercilium; turquoise rump and tail. **Imm** darker and duller; underparts more rufous; blackish bill. **Voc** (i) <5 very high-pitched, rapidly repeated, insect-like "ts-ts-ts-ts-tst", lasting 1 sec; (ii) downslurred, high-pitched "tsst", lasting 0.4 sec.

Variable Dwarf-kingfisher *Ceyx lepidus*
L 14 cm. Aus. 15 ssp, 4 in region: *lepidus* (C Mol except Buru); *cajeli* (Buru); *wallacii* (Sula); *uropygialis* (N Mol). Recent molecular work found extremely deep genetic divergence between most forms (albeit less between *cajeli* and *wallacii*) and recommended elevating each of the 15 ssp to species level (i.e. regionally '**Seram Dwarf**', '**Buru Dwarf**', '**Sula Dwarf**' and '**Halmahera Dwarf-kingfisher**', respectively). This treatment may be warranted but is here not followed because of limited plumage differences. Scarce in primary and secondary forest, overgrown plantations, <1500 m. Uncommon along forest streams even when dry, gullies and swampy areas but not water-dependent, perching quietly in understorey in any forest type. **ID Ad** red bill; orange loral spot; head and upperparts dark-blue finely spot-speckled; ultramarine back to tail; deep orange underparts; white throat. Ssp *uropygialis* darker overall, slender bill; *cajeli* has paler underparts and loral spot, darker head and upperparts contrast more with back; *wallacii* has paler spots on head and upperparts, back to tail brilliant cobalt-blue, undertail-coverts ultramarine-blue. **Imm** darker above, less blue; more orange bill with dusky base. **Voc** Single, high-pitched "tst", in flight and perched, similar to Black-backed. **SS** On Sula, Imm of larger, more water-dependent Blue-eared Kingfisher can share all-red bill but is paler (less blackish-blue) on head and wings and should always still show rufous facial suffusion.

Little Kingfisher *Ceyx pusillus*
L 11 cm. Aus. 9 ssp, 2 in region: *pusillus* (Kai, Aru, NG, Aus), *halmaherae* (N Mol, Seram). Scarce in variety of open, wet areas: estuaries, lagoons, mangroves, swamps and wooded creeks. **ID** Tiny. **Ad** marine-blue upperparts; pure white underparts; white loral spot. Ssp *halmaherae* paler blue. **Imm** greenish-washed upperparts; buffy loral spot; dusky underparts. **Voc** Typical high-pitched "tsee", regularly repeated.

Azure Kingfisher *Ceyx azureus*
L 18 cm. Aus. 7 ssp, 2 in region: *affinis* (Morotai, Halmahera, Bacan), *yamdenae* (Romang, Tanimbar). Scarce, in region largely tied to swamps, wooded creeks and forested pools. **ID M** marine-blue upperparts extend to side of breast and upper flanks; black bill with pale tip; white throat contrasts with deep rufous underparts; **F** slightly duller. Ssp *yamdenae* brighter with reddish-tipped bill. **Imm** duller and paler with larger pale bill tip. **Voc** Similar to Common but higher-pitched: (i) high-pitched, piping "zeep" in flight or perched; (ii) short, shrill "zeet-zit". **SS** Smaller resident Common Kingfisher (*hispidoides*) lacks Azure's pale bill tip (has various amounts of red on lower mandible instead) and has contrasting shiny-blue line down mid-back. Wintering Common (*bengalensis*) is additionally paler aquamarine overall with red (not blue) cheek.

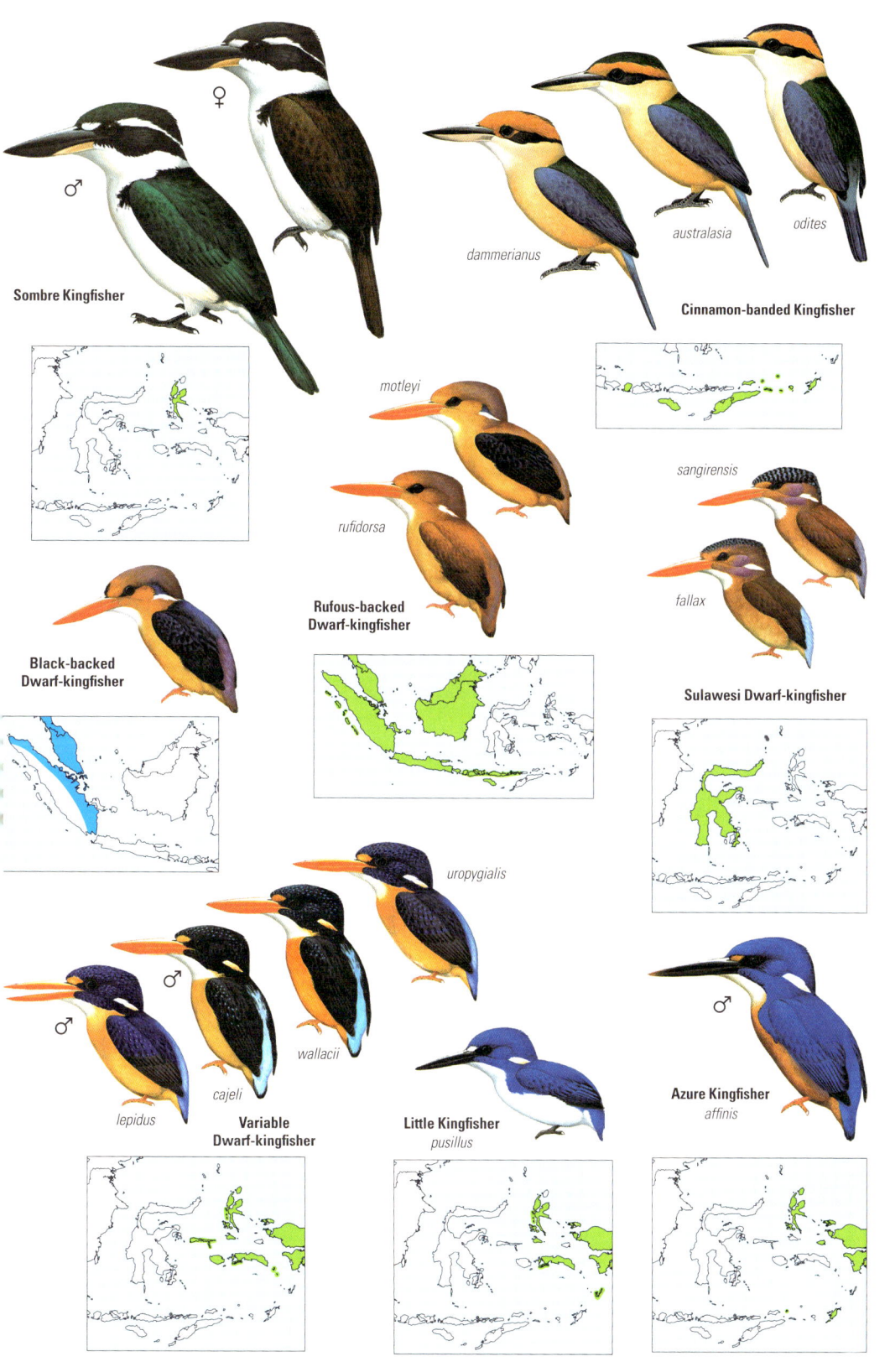

Sombre Kingfisher

♂

♀

dammerianus

australasia

odites

Cinnamon-banded Kingfisher

motleyi

rufidorsa

Rufous-backed Dwarf-kingfisher

sangirensis

fallax

Black-backed Dwarf-kingfisher

Sulawesi Dwarf-kingfisher

uropygialis

♂

♂

wallacii

cajeli

lepidus

Variable Dwarf-kingfisher

Little Kingfisher
pusillus

Azure Kingfisher
affinis

Cerulean Kingfisher *Alcedo coerulescens* **E**

L 13 cm. Monotypic. Common on streams, ponds, swamps, coastal areas, flooded paddyfields, <800 m. Appears to be spreading in response to increase in coastal shrimp ponds. **ID** Only small kingfisher in range lacking rufous in plumage. **M** two-toned appearance; cerulean upperparts and breast band, white underparts. **F** slightly greener upperparts with less distinct breast band. **Imm** greyer upperparts; indistinct breast band. **Voc** Similar to Common but noticeably higher-pitched "zeep" in flight or perched. **AN** Small Blue Kingfisher.

Blue-banded Kingfisher *Alcedo euryzona*

L 17 cm. Sundaic. 2 ssp: *euryzona* (Jav, few recent records from W+C); *peninsulae* (Sum, Bor, MPen). Treatment as separate species, '**Javan Blue-banded**' and '**Malayan Blue-banded Kingfisher**', respectively, may be warranted based on discrete plumage differences. Scarce, rare on Jav, on secluded slow-flowing streams and rivers in primary and tall secondary forest, locally <1500 m. **ID** Distinct blue breast band and white throat; silver-blue back and tail. **M** blackish bill; blackish-blue wings and head; white underparts. **F** reddish lower mandible; dusky-tinged wings and head; orange underparts. Ssp *peninsulae* **M** mottled breast band; **F** all orange below, lacks breast band. **Imm** duller, **M** shows rufous washed underparts. **Voc** Similar to Common but less shrill, harder, "zeep". **SS** Smaller Blue-eared Kingfisher lacks blue breast band of male Blue-banded, and has more intense and brighter blue (less dusky) wings and head than female Blue-banded.

Blue-eared Kingfisher *Alcedo meninting*

L 17 cm. S–SE Asia, W Phil. 6 ssp, 2 in region: *meninting* (Sum–Lombok, Sul, Banggai, Sula); *verreauxii* (Bor, Riau, Bangka, Belitung, Palawan, Sulu, MPen). Uncommon, locally fairly common in variety of wet habitats, generally near wooded areas, rarely plantations, <1000 m. **ID M** Ultramarine head and upperparts (darker in *verreauxii*) with contrasting, brilliant back and tail; white throat, white patch on neck-sides and broad rufous loral spot; underparts deep-orange; black bill with red at gape only; **F** lower orange ear-coverts and head-sides, variable amount of red on bill mostly limited to lower mandible. **Imm** as female but Imm M progressively blue on face starting with moustachial; bill initially all red, gradually becoming darker with age. **Voc** Similar to Common but noticeably higher-pitched, shorter, with more trills: (i) high-pitched, piping "zeep" in flight or perched; (ii) short, shrill "zrreet-zit". **SS** Migrant *bengalensis* Common Kingfisher is paler aquamarine overall with red (not blue) cheek, but beware Fem/Imm Blue-eared whose red facial markings are never separated from white throat by wide blue malar stripe as in Common (Imm M Blue-eared has much narrower blue moustachial well above malar area); Imm Blue-eared always shows much more extensive red on bill than Common of any age. Common's 'Hispid Kingfisher' races can be hard to ID, especially *hispidoides* which lacks the red cheek: although not as turquoise as migrant Common Kingfishers, 'Hispid Kingfishers' are still less ultramarine (more cobalt) than Blue-eared and show a much smaller loral spot. 'Hispid' bills are all-black (male) or only show a bit of red on underside of lower mandible (female) even at younger age, whereas Imm Blue-eared has extensive red bill becoming darker with age, but always retaining a bright red gape (even in Ad male bill which is otherwise all-black). See also Variable Dwarf and Blue-banded Kingfishers.

Common Kingfisher *Alcedo atthis*

L 16 cm. Palaearctic to Aus. 7 ssp, 3 in region: *bengalensis* (breeds S–SE–E–NE Asia; winters to GS, Sul, N Mol); the resident ssp *floresiana* (Bali–Wetar, Timor) and *hispidoides* (Sul, Mol, NG) look distinct and may be combined with extralimital *salomonensis* (Solomon Is.) into '**Hispid Kingfisher**' *A. hispidoides*, although genetic divergence is limited. Common migrant and resident in variety of open, wet areas: estuaries, ponds, lagoons, mangroves, rocky coastline, swamps and wooded creeks. **ID** Aquamarine head and upperparts (tinged green in **F**); rufous ear-coverts; pale rufous underparts; **M** black bill, **F** has limited red on lower mandible. Ssp *hispidoides* and *floresiana* have darker, more cobalt-blue upperparts in both sexes (though not quite ultramarine as in Blue-eared) and wholly blue ear-coverts (with a rufous patch of variable size in *floresiana*). **Imm** duller, greener, paler below with dusky markings. **Voc** (i) High-pitched, piping "zeep", perched or in flight; (ii) short, shrill "tist-zit" when perched. Often in duet. **SS** See Blue-eared and Azure Kingfishers.

MEROPIDAE
Bee-eaters
6 species in region

Elegant, brightly coloured birds occupying a variety of open country and forest habitat. Sally from open perches to catch airborne insects or to pick them from the ground or foliage. Open-country species are typically conspicuous, while forest species can be shy and unobtrusive. Nest in holes on sandy banks.

Red-bearded Bee-eater *Nyctyornis amictus*

L 27–31 cm. Sundaic. Monotypic. Uncommon in primary, secondary and degraded forest, <1500 m. Singly or pairs, in forest interior, at clearings and along forested roads. **ID** All-green; shaggy red beard; broad black undertail tip. **M** purplish-pink forecrown. **F** red forecrown, tipped pink. **Imm** mostly green head and breast, bluish lores, whiter and duller underparts. **Voc** (i) Variety of loud, gruff, descending chatter "kak-kak-kak-ka-kah..."; (ii) "chachacha..."; (iii) guttural croaking "aark, kwok", repeated.

Purple-bearded Bee-eater *Meropogon forsteni* **E**

L 25–26 cm. Monotypic. Uncommon in clearings, openings in primary and secondary forest, edge, <1850 m, usually above 1000 m. Singly or pairs, sitting quietly in mid-storey, becoming more conspicuous and vocal when breeding. Often nests on trackside embankments. **ID** Slender bill. **M** purple head and beard (reduced in **F**); green upperparts with chestnut-fringed outertail; russet underparts. **Imm** head and breast largely green with dark mottling; duller upperparts; lacks tail streamers. **Voc** (i) High-pitched, shrill "tsit", repeated occasionally; (ii) also a less often heard "tsit-wip".

Chestnut-headed Bee-eater *Merops leschenaulti*

L 20 cm. S–SE Asia. 3 ssp, 1 in region: *quinticolor* (S Sum, Jav, Bali). Uncommon in variety of open habitats: scrub, clearings, plantations. Gregarious; colonial breeder on sandy embankments. **ID Ad** green with rich chestnut crown and mantle; black face mask and gorget; strong yellow throat; no tail prongs. **Imm** greenish forecrown, paler overall. **Voc** (i) Bubbling "prruuip" and airy "chew-chew-chew"; (ii) sharp "clip" in alarm.

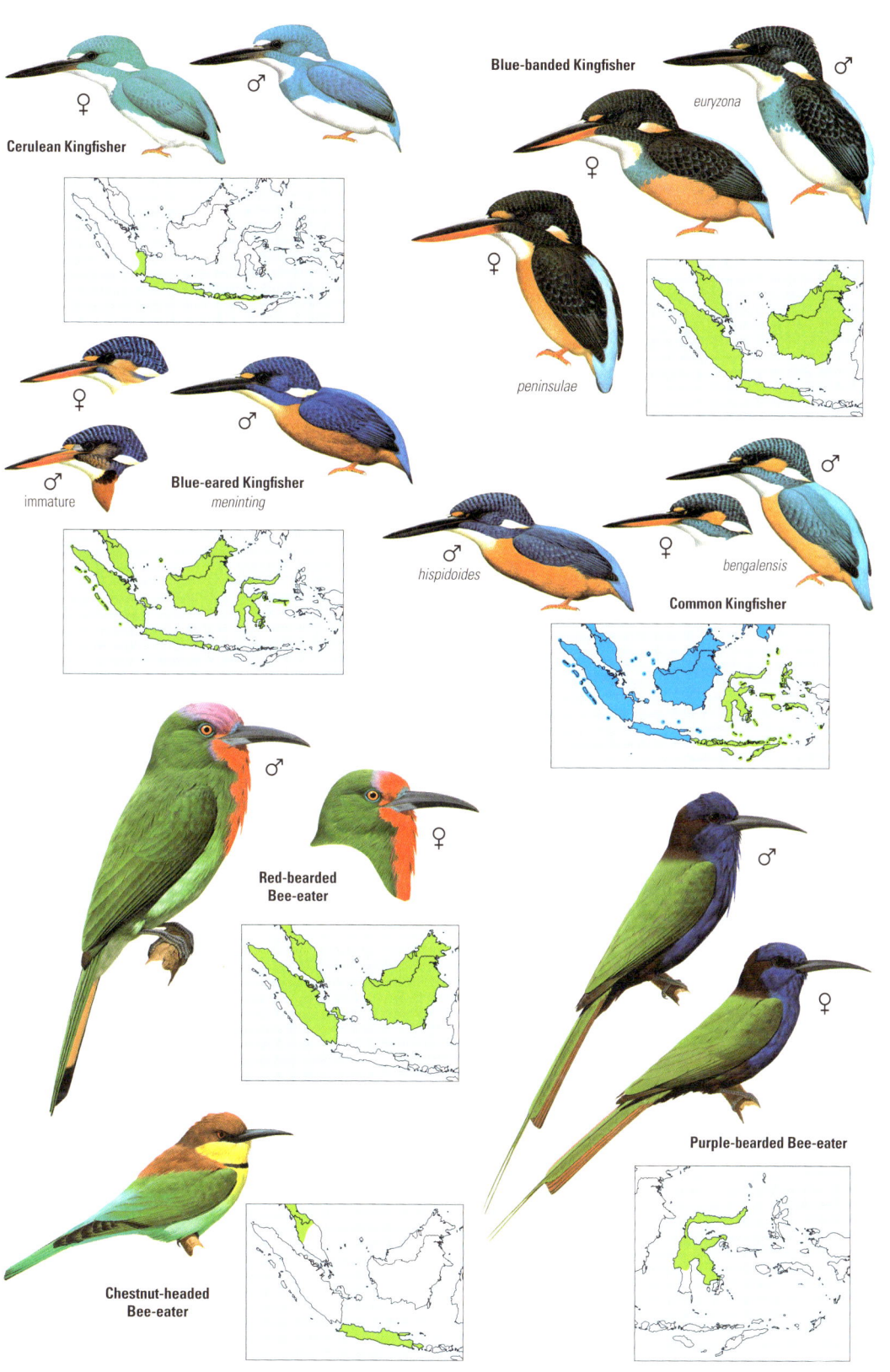

Cerulean Kingfisher

♀ ♂

Blue-banded Kingfisher

♂

euryzona

♀

♀

peninsulae

Blue-eared Kingfisher

♀

♂

immature *meninting*

hispidoides ♂ ♀ *bengalensis*

Common Kingfisher

**Red-bearded
Bee-eater**

♂

♀

♂

♀

Purple-bearded Bee-eater

**Chestnut-headed
Bee-eater**

Blue-tailed Bee-eater *Merops philippinus*

L 29 cm. S–SE–E Asia to Aus. Monotypic. Common in variety of habitats; open countryside, mangroves, forest clearings, plantations, urban areas. Gregarious, on migration forms large flocks (<100); breeds colonially on embankments and cliffs. **ID Ad** green overall; yellow throat, bordered reddish-orange; black mask; mid-blue rump and tail with protruding tail prongs; buff underwing. In flight shows all green outerwing on upperparts. **Imm** duller; washed-out throat and underparts; lacks tail prongs. **Voc** Liquid, slightly hoarse (i) "rillip, rillip..."; (ii) also "chip". **SS** See Rainbow and Blue-throated Bee-eaters.

Rainbow Bee-eater *Merops ornatus*

L 19–21 cm. Breeds Australia; winters to N, but year-round presence on some islands in LS. Monotypic. Common in open countryside, mangroves, forest clearings, plantations, becoming scarce W and N of Flores. Vagrant Sabah (Apr–Aug 2016, Aug 2020). **ID M** similar to Blue-tailed Bee-eater but has black gorget, rufous rear-crown and extensive yellow throat; tail black with blunt-ended streamers. In flight shows rufous outerwing on upperparts. **F** black gorget thinner with blue suffusion; tail streamers shorter and more clubbed. **Imm** lacks gorget and lacks tail streamers. **Voc** Similar to Blue-tailed but slightly harder, less melodious, "drrrt" and "prrrp". **SS** Larger-sized Blue-tailed lacks black gorget, has much less extensive yellow on throat, is greener (not warm-rufous) on rear crown, has blue (not black) tail with pointed (not blunt-ended) streamers, and all-green upperwings lacking rufous patch.

Blue-throated Bee-eater *Merops viridis*

L 21 cm. SE–E Asia. Monotypic. No longer includes Philippine Bee-eater *M. americanus* based on genetic and plumage differences. Fairly common in variety of habitats: primary forest, clearings, plantations, riversides. Gregarious; colonial breeder on sandy embankments. **ID Ad** green overall except chestnut crown and mantle, blue throat and rump; long tail prongs. **Imm** duller and lacking chestnut crown and mantle. **Voc** Liquid "terrip-terrip...", quieter, less hoarse than Blue-tailed Bee-eater. **SS** Imm Blue-tailed shows pale chestnut and yellow throat and is greener overall.

CORACIIDAE
Rollers
3 species in region

Distinctive, brightly-iridescent birds of open and wooded country with a hooked, raptorial beak. Often perching or posts conspicuously on exposed branches, feeding by pouncing on ground-living prey. Broad-winged with laboured flight and deep wingbeats.

Sulawesi Roller *Coracias temminckii* [E]

L 30–40 cm. Monotypic. Uncommon in variety of open and wooded habitats, sometimes in forest canopy, <1400 m. Often sits prominently on dead branches and wires, sallying for insects. **ID Ad** cobalt-blue crown and uppertail-coverts; deep-purple body with greyish-brown mantle. **Imm** duller crown and brownish-washed underparts. **Voc** Harsh, dry rattle, "RRWAHH", lasting 1 sec; sometimes double-note "RAH-RAWAH". **SS** Common Dollarbird has all-dark head without iridescent blue crown, red (not black) bill, more greenish (less brownish) body and pale primary patch in flight. **AN** Purple-winged Roller.

Common Dollarbird *Eurystomus orientalis*

L 27–32 cm. S–SE–E Asia to Aus. 10 ssp, 4 in region: *orientalis* (resident GS, SE Asia, Phil; winters to N Sul and N Mol with sporadic breeding records [Halmahera] probably referring to this form); *cyanocollis* (breeds S–E Asia; winters to GS); *oberholseri* (Simeulue); ssp *pacificus* (resident LS, Australia; winters to Wallacea and NG, with potential breeding records [S Sul, Sula] perhaps referring to this form) should perhaps be separated as '**Eastern Dollarbird**' *E. pacificus* (Australasia; 4 ssp) because it appears genetically more closely related to Azure Dollarbird. Fairly common in variety of open habitats, generally close to wooded areas, <1500 m. Perches conspicuously and high, often on dead snags, sallying for insects. Flight is leisurely on long wings. **ID** Bulky. **Ad** green-blue body with darker blackish-blue or brownish-blue head, blue throat and short red bill. In flight shows broad white patch at base of primaries. Ssp *cyanocollis* more purplish, longer wings with shorter tail; *oberholseri* brighter head, bluer plumage with shorter wings and longer tail; *pacificus* paler overall, grey-tinged upperparts. **Imm** blackish bill; duller upperparts; bluer underparts with less obvious wing patch. **Voc** Short, raspy "chak", lasting 0.1 sec, slowly repeated or in a faster series "chak-chak, chak...", often in flight. **SS** See Sulawesi Roller and Azure Dollarbird.

Azure Dollarbird *Eurystomus azureus* [E]

L 27–35 cm. Monotypic. For taxonomy see Common Dollarbird. Scarce and local in primary and tall secondary forest at edge and clearings, <600 m. Singly and pairs, often sitting on exposed perches. **ID Ad** similar to Common Dollarbird but uniform deep-blue body with striking red bill and feet. In flight shows white primary patch. **Imm** dull sooty-purple; indistinct wing patch; blackish-orange bare parts. **Voc** 1–8 mechanical, rasping laughs "EEK-EEK-EEK...", last notes sometimes tapering off. **SS** Smaller-sized and smaller-billed Common Dollarbird similar and often confused but has paler, less uniform, more contrasting plumage including greenish and brownish-black plumage parts. **AN** Purple Dollarbird.

UPUPIDAE
Hoopoes
1 species in region

Medium-sized bird of open country with distinctive crest and long, curved bill. Typically feed on the ground on insects. Distinctive call uttered frequently, often from high perches.

Hoopoe *Upupa epops* [V]

L 27–32 cm. Breeds across Old World; winters to Africa, S–SE Asia. 8 ssp, 1–2 presumed in region: *longirostris* (SE–E Asia); *saturata* (breeds NE–E Asia; winters to S). Recorded Sum (Sep 1912), N Sul (Sep 2011) and multiple records from N Bor. Open country, semi-desert, scrub and open woodland, <2500 m. Slow, undulating, floppy flight. Generally feeds on the ground, probing for insects, often holding its crest erect or fan-like, particularly after landing. **ID** Unique in region: long, narrow decurved bill; upper body cinnamon with long black-tipped crest (with tiny white subterminal band to tips in *saturata*); rest of upperparts broadly black-and-white barred (with white bars tending to be wider in *saturata*). **Voc** Soft, far-carrying "hoop-hoop-hoop", sometimes only 2 notes.

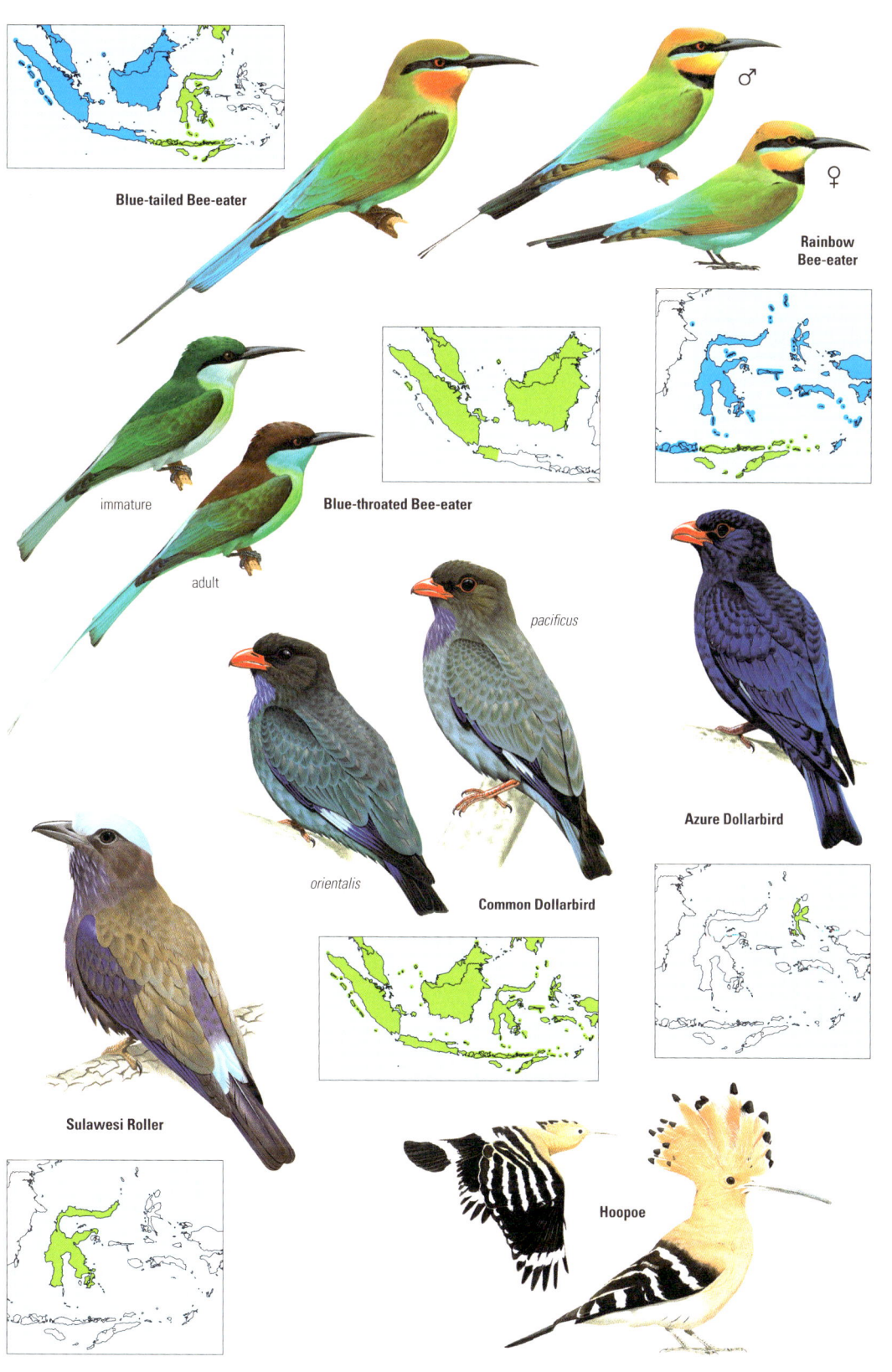

Blue-tailed Bee-eater

♂

♀

Rainbow Bee-eater

immature

Blue-throated Bee-eater

adult

pacificus

Azure Dollarbird

orientalis

Common Dollarbird

Sulawesi Roller

Hoopoe

FALCONIDAE
Falcons
9 species in region
Small to medium-sized predators. Strong fliers, typically with long pointed wings, feeding by diving on smaller vertebrates or insects. Found in various forest and open-country habitats.

Eurasian Kestrel *Falco tinnunculus* [V]
L 27–35 cm, **WS** 57–79 cm/2.2. Old World. 10 ssp, 1 in region: *interstinctus* (breeds E Asia; winters to SE Asia, Phil). No longer includes African Rock Kestrel *F. rupicolus*. Several winter records N Bor; also Nias (Nov 1895), Sum (Sep–Oct 2007). Open country; regularly perches on poles and wires. Often hovers. **ID** Black moustache. Underparts pale with dense dark streaks/spots. **M** chestnut mantle sparsely spotted black; grey head, rump and tail with black subterminal bar. **F/Imm** upperparts and tail rufous, heavily spotted black. **Voc** Fast series "kee-kee-kee...". **SS** Indonesian Kestrel has grey tail (unlike fem Eurasian), never has male Eurasian's grey head, and has darker buff underparts with thicker, blotchier spotting. Underparts streaking on Australian Kestrel much thinner and sparser.

Indonesian Kestrel *Falco moluccensis*
L 26–32 cm, **WS** 59–71 cm/2.2. 2 ssp: *moluccensis* (Mol); *microbalius* (Jav–Tanimbar, Sul). Nearly endemic, discovered in S Phil (2016). Fairly common in grassland, mangroves, edge, clearings. Often hovers, perches on dead trees. **ID** Chestnut above with dense spotting, greyish tail plain (in **M**) or barred (in **F**) with black subterminal band; buff underparts heavily spotted and mottled black. Ssp *microbalius* smaller with greyer cheeks. **Imm** more heavily barred. **Voc** Shrill "keek-keek-keek" and screaming "rrrrit-rrrrit-reeeet-..." in aerial display. **SS** See Eurasian and Australian Kestrels. **AN** Spotted Kestrel.

Australian Kestrel *Falco cenchroides*
L 28–35 cm, **WS** 66–78 cm/2.3. Aus. 2 ssp, 1 in region: *cenchroides* (breeds Aus; winters to NG; recorded Jav, LS, Mol). Rare, few recent records, open country, towns and airfields. Often hovers and perches conspicuously. **ID** Pale chestnut upperparts spotted black (**M** less heavily spotted with pale greyish head); whitish underparts finely streaked (more heavily in **F/Imm**); tail grey (in **M**) or chestnut with fine bars (in **F/Imm**) with black subterminal band. **Voc** Shrill, rapid "keekeekeekee"; wavering "keer, keer, keer". **SS** See Eurasian Kestrel. Indonesian Kestrel never has grey head or chestnut tail, and is more heavily spotted/mottled below and above. **AN** Nankeen Kestrel.

Oriental Hobby *Falco severus*
L 27–30 cm, **WS** 61–71 cm/2.5. S-SE Asia to Aus. Monotypic. On Bor two specimens (C Kal 1877; Mt Kinabalu ~1893). Uncommon and local in open and wooded habitats, often by cliffs, <1550 m. Swift and dashing flight; often crepuscular. **ID Ad** slaty grey above; black head-sides; rufous below (also underwing) with buffish-white throat and fore-collar. **Imm** darker and browner, with blackish spotting on underparts. **Voc** rapid series of sharp, high-pitched notes. **SS** See Eurasian Hobby. Oriental Hobby's underparts either solid (Ad)

or splotchy/spotted (Imm), but similar to sparsely-streaked, larger Australian Hobby during transition. The latter has more extensive white half-collar curving up behind cheek. Safest ID mark is yellow cere and orbital skin of Oriental (even in Imm), not blue as in Australian, and blacker forecrown of Oriental, lacking any paler grey or buff suffusion. The more massive Imm Peregrine ssp *ernesti* is similarly rufous on underparts as Imm Oriental Hobby, but lacks the narrow white half-collar curving up behind cheek and is densely streaked black up to lower throat, while Imm Oriental Hobby's markings are more spotted and do not extend upward beyond breast. In addition, at rest Peregrine's wing tips fall short of tail tip (not extending beyond tail as in Oriental Hobby).

Eurasian Hobby *Falco subbuteo* [V]
L 30–36 cm, **WS** 68–84 cm/2.5. Breeds Palaearctic; winters Africa. 2 ssp, 1 in region: *subbuteo* (most of range). Few records in W Jav (collected Feb 1927; 5 in Sep-Nov 2012), Layang-Layang (Sep 1998) and Timor (immature collected Jan 1896). Wooded and open areas, <2000 m. Very slender wings, looking like a giant swift. **ID/SS Ad** like small Peregrine, but unbarred uppertail, heavily streaked (not barred) breast and belly, reddish-rufous thighs and vent. Oriental and Australian Hobbies have entirely rufous underparts. **Imm** duller above with buffish feather fringes and buff head sides and vent.

Australian Hobby *Falco longipennis*
L 29–35 cm, **WS** 66–83 cm/2.3. Aus. 2 ssp: *hanieli* (LS); *longipennis* (Aus; winters to NG, LS and Mol). Rare in open woodland, grassland. Often chasing small birds, especially at dusk. **ID Ad** slate blue above; black helmet with short broad moustache; rufous below with streaked breast and blotched flanks. Ssp *hanieli* smaller and paler below, but can probably not be distinguished in the field. **Imm** rufous extending to face. **Voc** Shrill, high-pitched "kek kek kek" accelerating into rapid "kee-kee-kee-kee". **SS** See Oriental and Eurasian Hobbies.

Peregrine Falcon *Falco peregrinus*
L 38–48 cm, **WS** 79–114 cm/2.2. Cosmopolitan. ~17 ssp, 3 in region: *ernesti* (MPen, GS and Phil to Melanesia); *calidus* (breeds N Palaearctic; winters S to Africa and NG); *japonensis* (breeds NE Asia; winters S to Phil, Bor). Ssp *ernesti* uncommon, breeding in hilly areas, but also volcanic islands; migratory races uncommon, mainly coastal, but also inland, including cities. Broad based pointed wings, shortish tail, swift and powerful flight, sometimes soaring very high. **ID** Large. **Ad** dark, stocky falcon with pale throat and upper breast; no rufous on underparts. Ssp *japonensis* slaty-grey above, black moustachial stripe, underparts rusty white with dark bars on flanks, belly and undertail; *calidus* paler grey blue above, narrower moustache and large white cheek patch, whiter underparts; *ernesti* smaller, blackish above, solid black head sides without moustache and denser dark barring below. **Imm** duller, brownish above; underparts buffish-white (but rufous in *ernesti*) with dense dark streaks. **Voc** Series of 9–14 slightly upslurred plaintive nasal notes "way, way, way...", 1.4 n/s. **SS** Bat Hawk is entirely blackish or blotched white when imm, with crest, bigger head, smaller bill. Also see Eurasian Hobby. For imm *ernesti*, see Oriental Hobby.

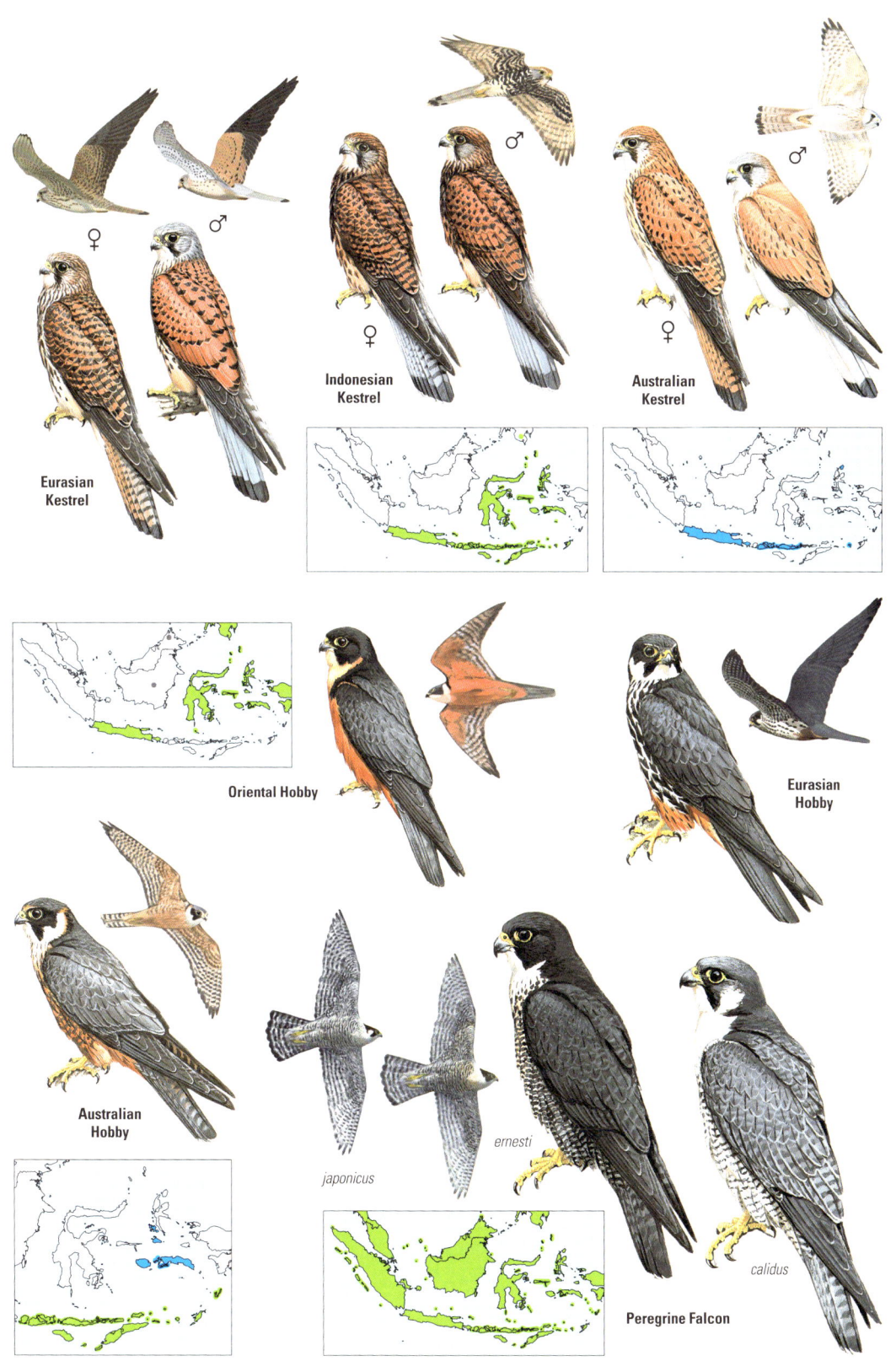

Eurasian Kestrel

Indonesian Kestrel

Australian Kestrel

Oriental Hobby

Eurasian Hobby

Australian Hobby

japonicus

ernesti

calidus

Peregrine Falcon

Black-thighed Falconet *Microhierax fringillarius*

L 14–16 cm, **WS** 27–32 cm/2.0. Sundaic. Monotypic. Fairly common in open woodland, edge, clearings, <1500 m. Perches on prominent bare snags singly or in family groups of <5. Sallies for large insects and small birds. Flight direct with rapid wingbeats. **ID** Tiny. **Ad** glossy black upperparts, thighs, flanks, and cheeks; white chin to breast and streak behind eye; white spots on wings and tail; rufous belly and vent. **Imm** rufous frontlet spot and eyestripe. **Voc** Single high-pitched "tew" in flight; fast, woodpecker-like "titititit".

White-fronted Falconet *Microhierax latifrons* **E**

L 14–16 cm, **WS** 28–31 cm/2.0. Monotypic. Uncommon in forest edge, clearings, <1200 m. Perches on prominent bare snags singly or in family groups of <5. Flight direct with rapid wingbeats. **ID** Tiny. Glossy black upperparts with white (**M**) or rufous (**F**) crown; white cheeks, breast and belly, the latter washed rufous; white spots on wings and tail; black thighs, flanks, vent and undertail. **Imm** lacks white tail spots. **Voc** as Black-thighed.

CACATUIDAE
Cockatoos

5 species in region

Distinctive, medium to large-sized parrots with characteristic white (or black) plumage. Largely arboreal in habit, they are typically found in forest or well-wooded habitat. Strong fliers with loud raucous calls, roosting communally. All species in region are severely threatened by over-trapping for the pet trade, with local extinctions through much of their range.

Tanimbar Cockatoo *Cacatua goffiniana* **E**

L 30–32 cm. Monotypic. Uncommon in forest, edge, partly-cleared areas and cultivation. Usually in pairs; roosts in small groups. **ID** All white; medium-sized crest with pinkish lores; underwing and tail yellowish. **M** brown eye. **F** reddish-brown eye. **Imm** dark grey eye. **Voc** Various loud screeches "WHA-WHA-WHA...", and "EYA-EYA-EYA...". **AN** Goffin's Corella.

Yellow-crested Cockatoo *Cacatua sulphurea* **E**

L 33 cm. 6 ssp: *sulphurea* (Sul and satellites); *abbotti* (Masakambing, extinct Masalembu); *occidentalis* (Nusa Penida, Lombok–Alor; presumed extinct on most islands); *parvula* (Timor, Rote, Semau); *djampeana* (Flores Sea Is); *paulandrewi* (Tukangbesi). See Orange-crested Cockatoo for taxonomy. Largely extinct throughout historical range: few remaining viable populations, often with single figure counts. Largest remaining strongholds on Komodo and East Timor but in decline. Forest, edge, partly cleared areas and cultivation, <1200 m. Usually in pairs or small groups. **ID M** all white with long, erectile yellow crest and diffused yellow cheeks, underwing and undertail; bluish eyering; black eye. Ssp *sulphurea* has largest bill and largest, richest lemon-yellow ear-covert patch. Ssp *abbotti* longest crest, wings and tail, mid-sized bill and small, brownish ear-covert patch; *occidentalis* large bill, short wings and tail, relatively small, pale ear-covert patch; *parvula* smallest bill and ear-covert patch (the latter very pale), longer tail; *djampeana* smaller bill and large, bright ear-covert patch; *paulandrewi* bill smaller than previous, and small ear-covert patch. **F** red-brown eye; smaller bill. **Imm** pale iris. **Voc** Harsh, loud "KEK-KEK-KEK...", and "WHAK-WHAK-WHAK...".

Orange-crested Cockatoo *Cacatua citrinocristata* **E**

L 33 cm. Monotypic. Previously considered conspecific with Yellow-crested Cockatoo. Now scarce in forest, edge, partly cleared areas and cultivation. Usually in pairs or small groups (< 20). **ID** All white with long, erectile orange crest and diffuse orange cheeks; under-side of wings and tail diffused yellow; larger bill, longer crest, longer wings and tail compared to *sulphurea* Yellow-crested. **M** black eye. **F** red-brown eye, smaller bill. **Imm** pale iris. **Voc** Harsh, loud "KEK-KEK-KEK...", and "WHAK-WHAK-WHAK...". **AN** Citron-crested Cockatoo.

Umbrella Cockatoo *Cacatua alba* **E**

L 46 cm. Monotypic. Fairly common in forest, edge, partly cleared areas and cultivation, <1000 m. Usually in pairs or small groups. **ID** All white with yellowish underside to wings and tail; broad erectile crest, spreading sideways, giving massive head impression. **M** black eye. **F** red-brown eye. **Imm** dark-grey eye. **Voc** Typical loud, noisy cockatoo calls but at a faster tempo "WHA-WHA-WHA...", and "EK-EK-EK...". **AN** White/Halmahera Cockatoo.

Salmon-crested Cockatoo *Cacatua moluccensis* **E**

L 50 cm. Monotypic. Uncommon in forest, edge, partly cleared areas and cultivation, <1400 m. Usually in pairs or small groups. **ID** White tinged salmon-pink; huge, 15 cm long salmon-pink erectile crest. **M** black eye. **F** dark-brown eye. **Imm** as male. **Voc** Loud, noisy piercing "EK-EK-EK...", curious "DUA-DUA-DUA...", and "WHA-WHA-WHA...". **AN** Moluccan Cockatoo.

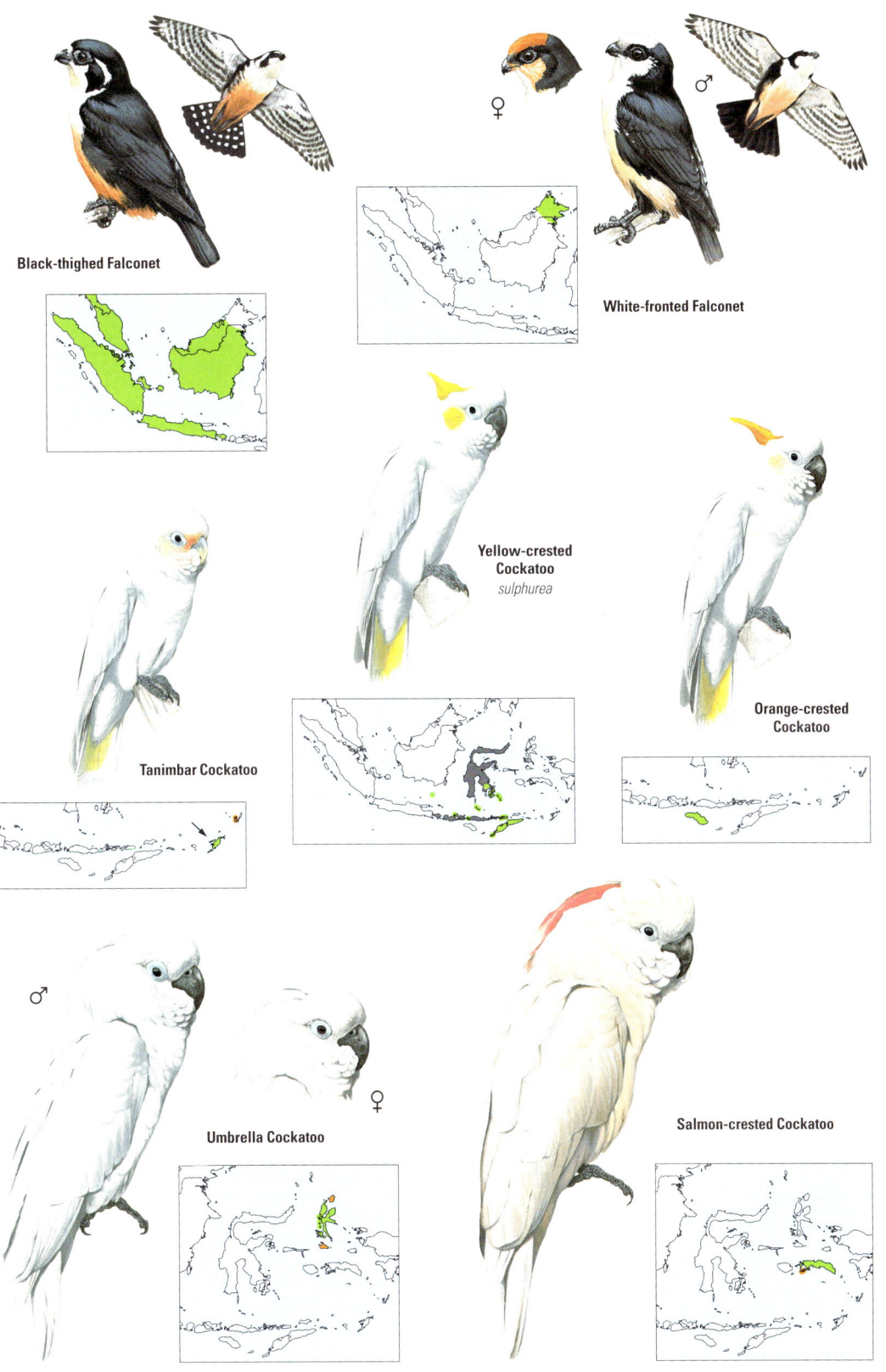

Black-thighed Falconet

♀

White-fronted Falconet

♂

Yellow-crested Cockatoo
sulphurea

Orange-crested Cockatoo

Tanimbar Cockatoo

♂ **Umbrella Cockatoo** ♀

Salmon-crested Cockatoo

PSITTACIDAE
Parrots
45 species in region

A large family of small to medium-sized birds. Most are arboreal in habit, being found in a variety of forest and wooded habitats. Strong, fast fliers, often with loud calls; many roost communally. Most are brightly coloured, some extremely so. Many have become highly threatened due to over-trapping for the pet trade, with local extinctions of many populations.

Red-and-blue Lory *Eos histrio* `E`
L 31 cm. 2 ssp: *histrio* (formerly Sangihe, Siau, Ruang; now extinct); *talautensis* (Talaud). The name *challengeri*, pertaining to possibly immature specimens of unknown origin, may apply to Talaud populations, thereby replacing *talautensis*. Uncommon to locally fairly common in forest and edge, visits plantations. Usually feeds in pairs or small flocks, roosting communally, formerly hundreds in single tree. **ID Ad** red body; orange bill; violet crown, lores to mantle stripe, mantle, breast band and thighs; black outerwing and black tips to wing-coverts (less black on *talautensis*). **Imm** can have different pattern of blue on crown. **Voc** Various harsh, loud screeches, mainly in flight "ek-ek-ek..."; rather quiet while feeding.

Violet-necked Lory *Eos riciniata* `E`
L 27 cm. Monotypic. Formerly considered conspecific with differently-coloured Scaled Lory. Fairly common in forest and edge; visits plantations and cultivation in search of food. Usually feeds in pairs or small flocks. Often observed flying high over forest in early morning. **ID Ad** bright red plumage; broad violet collar, extending to belly; dusky tail, blackish-purple outerwing and covert fringes. **Imm** similar to Ad. **Voc** Various high-pitched, piercing screeches, mainly in flight, include "eek-eek-eek...", "wee-wee...", "wir-wir-wir..."; rather quiet while feeding.

Scaled Lory *Eos squamata*
L 27 cm. West Papuan Is to Obi. 2 ssp, 1 in region: *obiensis* (Obi, Bisa). For taxonomy see Violet-necked Lory. Fairly common in forest and edge but visits plantations and cultivation in search of food. Usually feeds in pairs or small flocks. **ID Ad** red plumage; deep purple belly patch; dusky-purple tail, outerwing and scapulars. **Imm** similar to Ad. **Voc** Various high-pitched, piercing screeches, mainly in flight, include "eek-eek-eek...", "wee-wee-wee...", "wir-wir-wir..."; rather quiet while feeding.

Red Lory *Eos bornea* `E`
L 31 cm. 2 ssp: *bornea* (Ambon, Haruku, Saparua, Seram, Watubela, Tayandu, Kai); *cyanonotha* (Buru). Locally common in forested lowlands including mangroves and plantations, <1400 m (Seram) and <1800 m (Buru). Usually feeds in pairs or small flocks. **ID Ad** red plumage; blue restricted to outer-wing, undertail and orbital skin. Ssp *cyanonotha* slightly darker; grey orbital ring, dark tail, outerwing black with some violet on innerwing. **Imm** duller, less blue. **Voc** Various harsh, loud screeches, mainly in flight, including "ek-ek-ek...", "wir-wee...", "dwee-dwee-dwee..."; rather quiet while feeding. **SS** See Blue-eared Lory.

Blue-streaked Lory *Eos reticulata* `E`
L 31 cm. Monotypic. Probably also introduced to Kai. Fairly common, though scarce on Babar, and Damar (where likely introduced), in forest, edge, mangroves and plantations. Usually feeds in pairs or small flocks. **ID Ad** red plumage; broad blue stripe from eye to blue-streaked mantle; much of wings and tail blackish. **Imm** dusky underparts. **Voc** Various harsh, loud screeches, mainly in flight "ek-ek-ek...", "wir-wir-wir..."; rather quiet while feeding.

Blue-eared Lory *Eos semilarvata* `E`
L 24 cm. Monotypic. Fairly common in montane forest, >1600 m, scarce and nomadic to 1200 m when suitable trees are flowering. Usually feeds in pairs or small flocks. **ID Ad** red plumage; blue throat and ear-coverts; blue belly and thighs; black outerwing; dark reddish tail. **Imm** duller, much less blue. **Voc** Various high-pitched, piercing screeches, mainly in flight, including "eek-eek-eek...", "ee-err...", "wir-wir-wir..."; rather quiet while feeding. Call is higher-pitched and less harsh than Red Lory. **SS** Red Lory is larger, with red (not blue) belly and thighs, and with blue on head restricted to orbital skin. Note elevation.

Coconut Lorikeet *Trichoglossus haematodus*
L 30 cm. Aus. 9 ssp, 2 in region: *haematodus* (C Mol, NG); *nigrogularis* (Kai, NG). Formerly united into large umbrella species, '**Rainbow Lorikeet**' *T. haematodus*, together with the following three and additional Australian and Melanesian species. Present treatment follows the most widely-advocated modern taxonomy based on pronounced plumage differences, but genetic inquiry has revealed unexpectedly low divergences between species; more research needed. Still fairly common in forested lowlands, <1300 m. **ID Ad** dark-blue head; yellow nuchal collar; barred red breast; green upperparts. Ssp *nigrogularis* lighter blue head; paler breast with narrower barring; centre of belly blackish. **Imm** duller with brownish-black bill. **Voc** Screeching "EEK-EEK-EEK...".

Leaf Lorikeet *Trichoglossus weberi* `E`
L 25 cm. Monotypic. For taxonomy see Coconut, Sunset and Marigold Lorikeets. Increasingly scarce in submontane forest and edge, >600 m. **ID Ad** wholly green, paler so on breast and nuchal collar; forehead and lores with diffuse blue; red bill. In flight shows yellow underwing-coverts. **Imm** duller with brownish-black bill. **Voc** Thin, high-pitched "EEK-EEK-EEK...".

Marigold Lorikeet *Trichoglossus capistratus* `E`
L 28–30 cm. 3 ssp: *capistratus* (Timor, Atauro, Rote); *flavotectus* (Wetar, Romang); *fortis* (Sumba). For taxonomy see Coconut and Sunset Lorikeets. Ssp *flavotectus* may have signature of genetic admixture with Leaf Lorikeet and looks somewhat intermediate; more research needed. Increasingly scarce, with nominate *capistratus* now rare away from East Timor; in all types of wooded lowlands, <1000 m. **ID Ad** orange breast with red flecking; dark green head and belly; yellowish nuchal collar; green upperparts; red bill. Ssp *flavotectus* pale yellow breast, and paler green head and belly; *fortis* larger; yellow breast, darker green belly and head. All races show yellow underwing-coverts in flight. **Imm** duller with brownish-black bill. **Voc** Screeching "EEK-EEK-EEK...". **SS** See Iris Lorikeet.

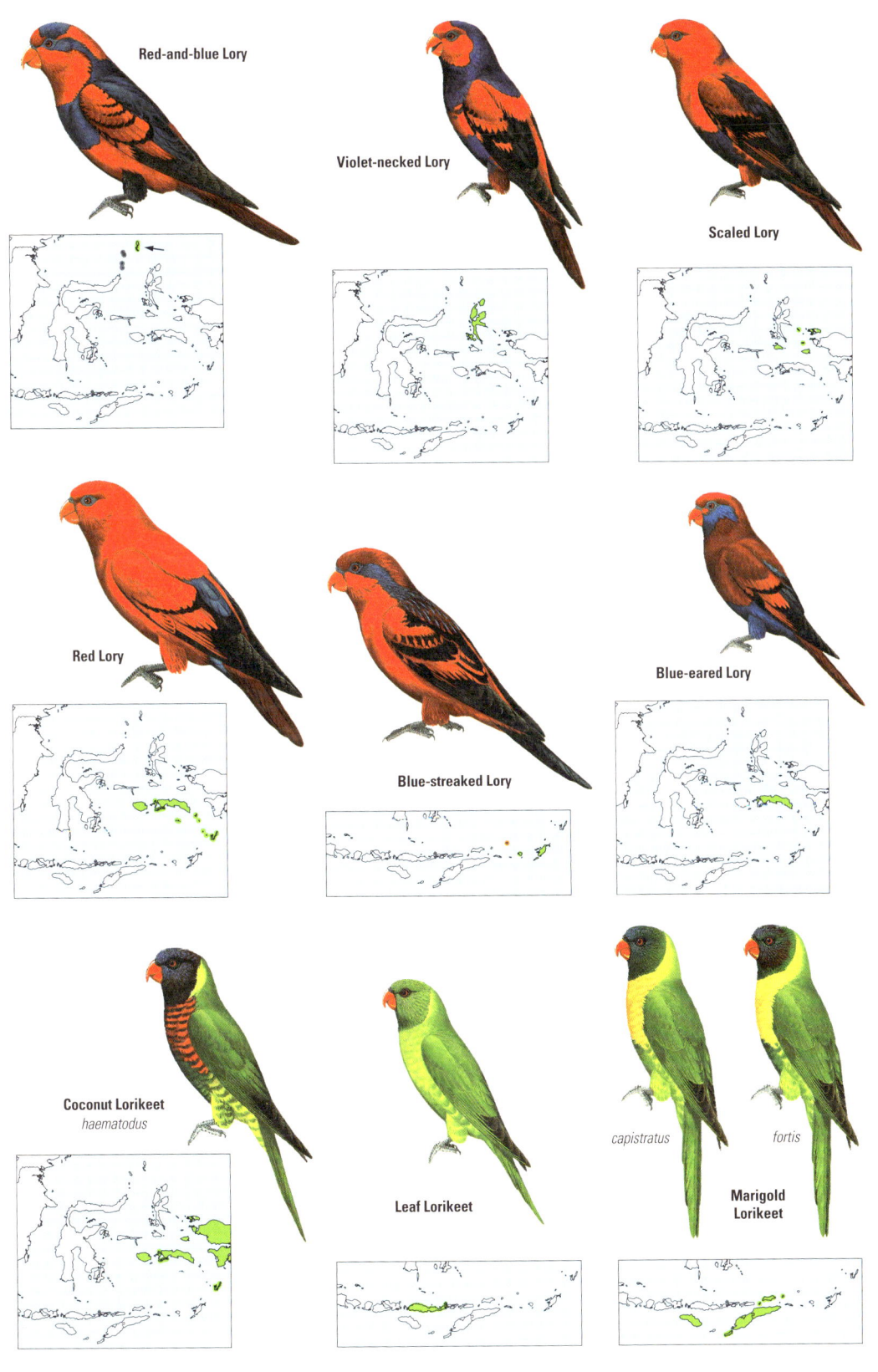

Red-and-blue Lory

Violet-necked Lory

Scaled Lory

Red Lory

Blue-streaked Lory

Blue-eared Lory

Coconut Lorikeet
haematodus

Leaf Lorikeet

capistratus

fortis

Marigold Lorikeet

Sunset Lorikeet *Trichoglossus forsteni* `E`

L 28–30 cm. 4 ssp: *forsteni* (Sumbawa); *mitchellii* (Lombok, Bali); *djampeanus* (Tanahjampea, now probably extinct); the isolated ssp *stresemanni* (Kalaotoa, likely extinct) occupies an unusual phylogenomic position close to Leaf and Marigold Lorikeets, despite its plumage resemblance with other Sunset subspecies, and likely represents an admixed population derived from western Sunset colonists and southern Leaf/Marigold colonists. For taxonomy also see Coconut Lorikeet. Formerly in many types of woodland, but now very rare, mostly in montane forest. No recent records of *djampeanus* or *stresemanni*. **ID Ad** brownish-black head with fine silvery-blue streaks; black belly; red breast and bill; green upperparts and thin yellow nuchal collar; in flight shows red and yellow underwing-coverts. Ssp *djampeanus* slightly larger, with purplish-black patch on upper mantle below nuchal collar rarely shown in other ssp; *mitchellii* smallest form, with fine olive-green streaks on head; *stresemanni* largest in size but otherwise overlapping in colour characters. **Imm** duller with brownish-black bill. **Voc** Screeching "EEK-EEK-EEK…".

Olive-headed Lorikeet *Trichoglossus euteles* `E`

L 25 cm. Monotypic. Abundant in montane eucalypt forest in E Timor, >700 m; now locally uncommon in W Timor, regularly disperses to lowlands. On other islands found commonly throughout lowlands. **ID Ad** olive-mustard head; broad green collar with yellowish underparts; darker green upperparts. **Imm** greener head. **Voc** Various high-pitched shrills, occasionally harsher "eek-eek-eek…". **SS** See Iris Lorikeet.

Ornate Lorikeet *Saudareos ornata* `E`

L 25 cm. Monotypic. Uncommon and increasingly local in all types of woodland, including plantations, <1500 m. Usually feeds in pairs or small flocks. **ID Ad** blue forecrown and ear-coverts, red face and postocular stripe; red breast barred blue; green upperparts. **Imm** brownish bill and yellowish belly. **Voc** Various high-pitched shrills and screeches, "wir-wee-wir…".

Sula Lorikeet *Saudareos flavoviridis* `E`

L 23 cm. Monotypic. For taxonomy see Meyer's Lorikeet. Uncommon to fairly common in forest and edge, often in flocks (~10–20), mostly in hilly areas around - 300–800 m, occasionally higher or lower in search of flowering trees. **ID Ad** dusky-brown face; yellowish crown; yellowish underparts scaled green; wholly green upperparts; red bill. **Imm** greener in colouration. **Voc** Probably similar to Meyer's Lorikeet.

Meyer's Lorikeet *Saudareos meyeri* `E`

L 21 cm. Monotypic. Formerly united with Sula Lorikeet into **'Yellow-and-green Lorikeet'** *S. flavoviridis* but plumages quite distinct and Meyer's shown to be genomically closer to Ornate Lorikeet. Fairly common in any wooded habitat and open country in search of flowering trees, 800–2400 m, occasionally disperses to lowlands. **ID Ad** differs from larger Sula Lorikeet in having more heavily scaled green underparts, dusky (not yellow) crown and yellow ear patch. **Imm** greener in colouration. **Voc** Higher pitched than Ornate Lorikeet but similar shrills and screeches, including different "wip-wip-wee-wir-ip…". **AN** Citrine Lorikeet.

Iris Lorikeet *Saudareos iris* `E`

L 20–22 cm. 2 ssp: *iris* (Timor); *wetterensis* (Wetar). Uncommon in all types of woodland, <1800 m, mainly 600–1200 m. Often in pairs or small groups (<30), flocks less than other lorikeet species, and generally less conspicuous. **ID M** red forecrown, violet crown and ear-coverts; yellowish nape and red bill; *wetterensis* larger with extensive red crown reaching rear. **F** shows green forecrown with some red. **Imm** like fem but less red, duller. **Voc** Harsher than Olive-headed, "ek-ek-ek…", "ee-ee-ee…", "twet-twet-twet…", lacking high-pitched shrills. **SS** In flight, similar to larger Olive-headed and Marigold Lorikeets but note noticeably shorter tail and shorter wings. Marigold has extensive yellow on underwing coverts, which are all green in Iris.

Chattering Lory *Lorius garrulus* `E`

L 30 cm. 3 ssp: *garrulus* (Halmahera); *morotaianus* (Morotai, Rau); *flavopalliatus* (Bacan, Obi, Kasiruta, Mandiole). Scarce in primary and secondary forest, more numerous in uplands. Usually in pairs; vocal but shy. **ID Ad** red body, green wings and thighs; tail dark green; can show yellowish spotting on mantle. Ssp *morotaianus* has small yellow mantle-patch; *flavopalliatus* with bold yellow mantle patch and brighter green wings. **Imm** shows brownish bill. **Voc** Wide variety of squeaks, shrills, whistles and harsh notes, "uw-wee…", "eew-ee-ee-wir-wee…", and piercing "uuw-wee-uuw-wee…".

Purple-naped Lory *Lorius domicella* `E`

L 28 cm. Monotypic. Rare in hill forest, 300–1300 m. Escapes occasionally seen on Ambon. Usually in pairs, inconspicuous, rarely flies above forest, prefers to keep to forest canopy where can be highly vocal. **ID Ad** red; black crown; purple nape; orange bill; narrow yellow breast band; purple thighs; green wings. **Imm** broader breast band and deeper violet nape. **Voc** Wide variety of squeaks, shrills, whistles and harsh notes: (i) distinctive, harsh screeches with quivering quality, "whir-weee-ww-ww-wee-wee…"; (ii) single high-pitched whistled "wir" and "whirr"; (iii) repeated, up-and-down, high-pitched whistle "werwewerwe", lasting 0.7 sec.

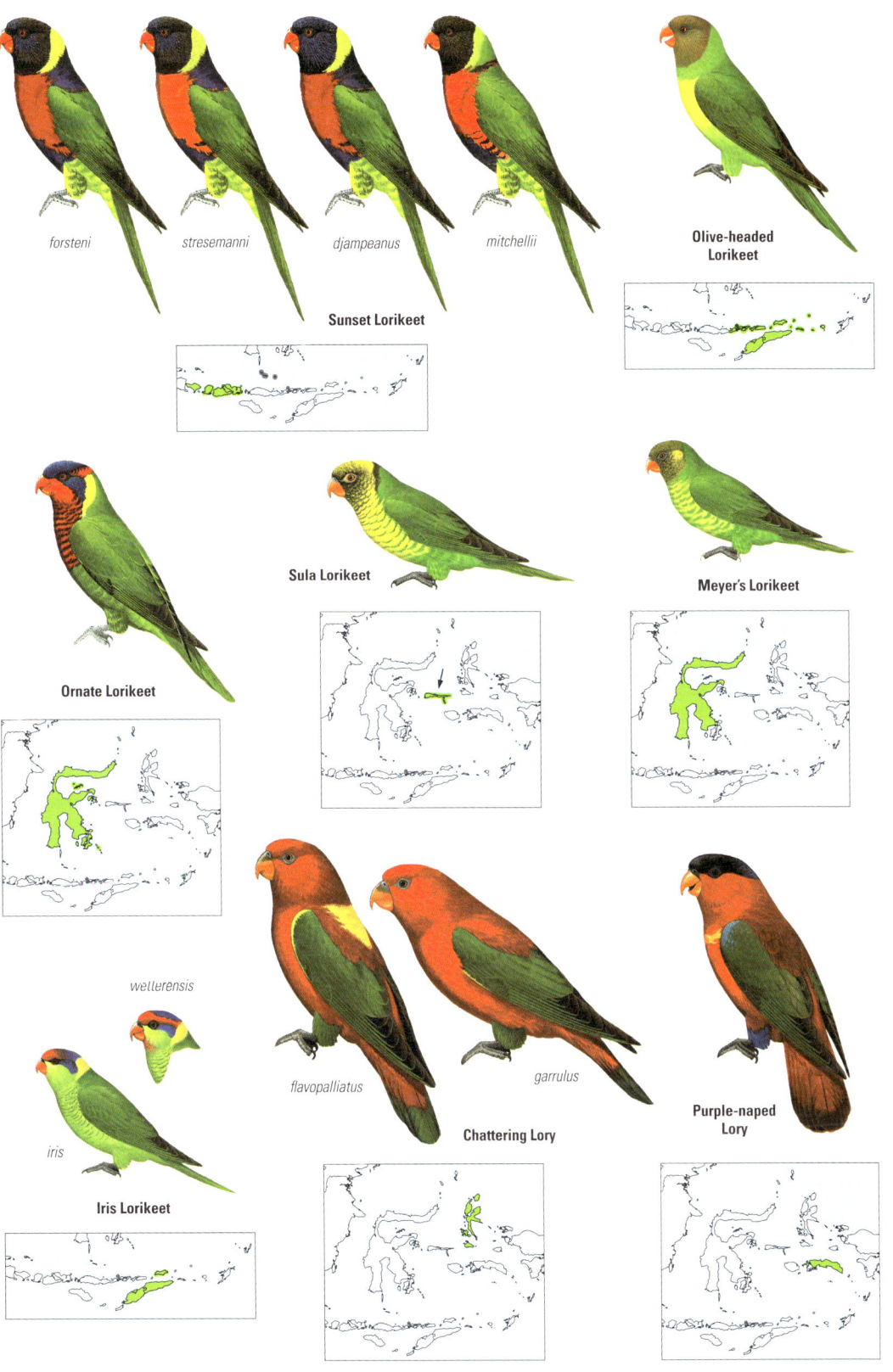

forsteni   *stresemanni*   *djampeanus*   *mitchellii*

Sunset Lorikeet

Olive-headed Lorikeet

Ornate Lorikeet

Sula Lorikeet

Meyer's Lorikeet

wellerensis

iris

Iris Lorikeet

flavopalliatus   *garrulus*

Chattering Lory

Purple-naped Lory

Buru Lorikeet *Charmosyna toxopei*

L 16 cm. Monotypic. Little known, reported 800–1400 m in submontane forest. Two recent records (Nov/Dec 2014) of birds at 1350 m, including feeding in flowering tree with Buru Honeyeaters. **ID M** all green with blue hue to crown; orange bare parts; yellow band across underside of secondaries and yellowish undertail. **F** stronger secondary band, less blue on crown. **Imm** darker and duller. **Voc** High-pitched, shrill, similar to Red-flanked Lorikeet. **AN** Blue-fronted Lorikeet.

Red-flanked Lorikeet *Hypocharmosyna placentis*

L 15–17 cm. Aus. 5 ssp, 2 in region: *placentis* (C–S Mol, NG); *intensior* (N Mol). Fairly common in all types of woodland, including mangroves, <1400 m. Usually found in pairs or small flocks (<15). **ID** Small, short-tailed with fast, rapid flight. **M** extensive red flanks; red chin and lores with blue ear-coverts; tail tipped red, lined yellow; bare parts red; blue rump is darker on larger *intensior*. **F** all green body with yellow streaking on ear-coverts. **Imm** all green. **Voc** High-pitched shrill calls and chatters similar to *Trichoglossus* lorikeets.

Yellow-capped Pygmy-parrot *Micropsitta keiensis*

L 9 cm. NG to Kai. 3 ssp, 1 in region: *keiensis* (Kai, Aru). Uncommon in woodland, even trees in villages, <250 m. Usually in small flocks (<20), creeping slowly along branches to feed; fast flight, like a hanging parrot. **ID** Tiny. **Ad** all green with dusky-brown face; blackish bare parts. **Imm** as Ad. **Voc** Very high-pitched "see-see-see…".

Red-breasted Pygmy-parrot *Micropsitta bruijnii*

L 8–9 cm. Aus. 5–6 ssp, 2–3 in region: *pileata* (Seram); *buruensis* (Buru); Obi (ssp.). Population on Obi likely an undescribed new form. Fairly common in all types of woodland, particularly hill forest, favouring canopy. Usually in flocks (<60), creeping slowly along branches to feed. **ID M** brightly coloured; red underparts (more orange in *buruensis*), reddish face (more orange in *buruensis*, creamy-white on Obi); brownish crown (duller and more extensive in *buruensis*; more whitish on Obi) surrounded by blue band (grey-brown on Obi); green upperparts and flanks. **F** underparts and face yellow; blue crown; rest of body green. **Imm** as fem but whitish face. **Voc** High-pitched, easily missed "see-see-see…". **SS** In flight, vocalisation, diminutive size and fast flight may imply Blue-faced Parrotfinch.

Blue-rumped Parrot *Psittinus cyanurus*

L 18 cm. Sundaic. 2 ssp: *cyanurus* (Bor, Sum, MPen); *pontius* (Mentawai). For taxonomy see Simeulue Parrot. Fairly common in forest, <700 m. Will stray to plantations in search of fruit in flocks (<30); often flying high, vocalising. **ID M** large blue head, red bill; mantle blackish; blue rump and greyish underparts; scalloped green upperparts with red shoulder patch; in flight shows red underwing-coverts, fast stiff wing-beats. Ssp *pontius* larger. **F** green body and dirty-brown head and bill. **Imm** greenish head and yellow fringes to wing-coverts. **Voc** Very different sounding from typical parrot-like vocalisations: (i) Distinctive, musical "chew-chew…"; (ii) melodious, tinkling "twet-tee-twee-tee…"; (iii) "duwe-dee…".

Simeulue Parrot *Psittinus abbotti*

L 24 cm. Monotypic. Often considered conspecific with Blue-rumped Parrot but differs considerably in size and plumage. Fairly common in primary and secondary forest, plantations. Often seen flying high over forest and open areas, calling in flocks (<10). **ID M** bright blue head; black nape; scalloped green upperparts; red shoulder-patch; bright green body. **F** all green plumage. **Imm** undescribed. **Voc** Similar to Blue-rumped but more strident, less musical.

Red-cheeked Parrot *Geoffroyus geoffroyi*

L 21–27 cm. Aus. 16 ssp, 7 in region: *geoffroyi* (Timor, Wetar); *cyanicollis* (N Mol); *obiensis* (Obi); *rhodops* (C Mol); *keyensis* (Kai); *floresianus* (Lombok–Flores, Sumba); *timorlaoensis* (Tanimbar). Substantial geographic variation in vocalisations (with much higher-pitched calls in south of region) indicates that division into several species may be warranted. Fairly common in all types of woodlands, <1400 m, regularly visits plantations. Singly, pairs or small flocks in canopy. **ID** Short, square-cut tail; large-headed appearance. **M** red face; violet crown; dark-red stain on median-coverts. Ssp *floresianus* has more extensive violet crown; *rhodops* is larger, darker overall; long blue collar on *cyanicollis* and *obiensis*, lower mantle brownish in latter; large *keyensis* and smaller *timorlaoensis* are yellowish with paler tail. **F** all green with dark-brown head, similar across ssp although *cyanicollis* and *obiensis* show blue collar. **Imm** greenish head, dull bill. **Voc** Harsh, loud, noisy monotonous; (i) "KEE-KEE-KEE…"; (ii) "EUW-EUW-EUW…"; (iii) "PEEP-PEEP-PEEP…".

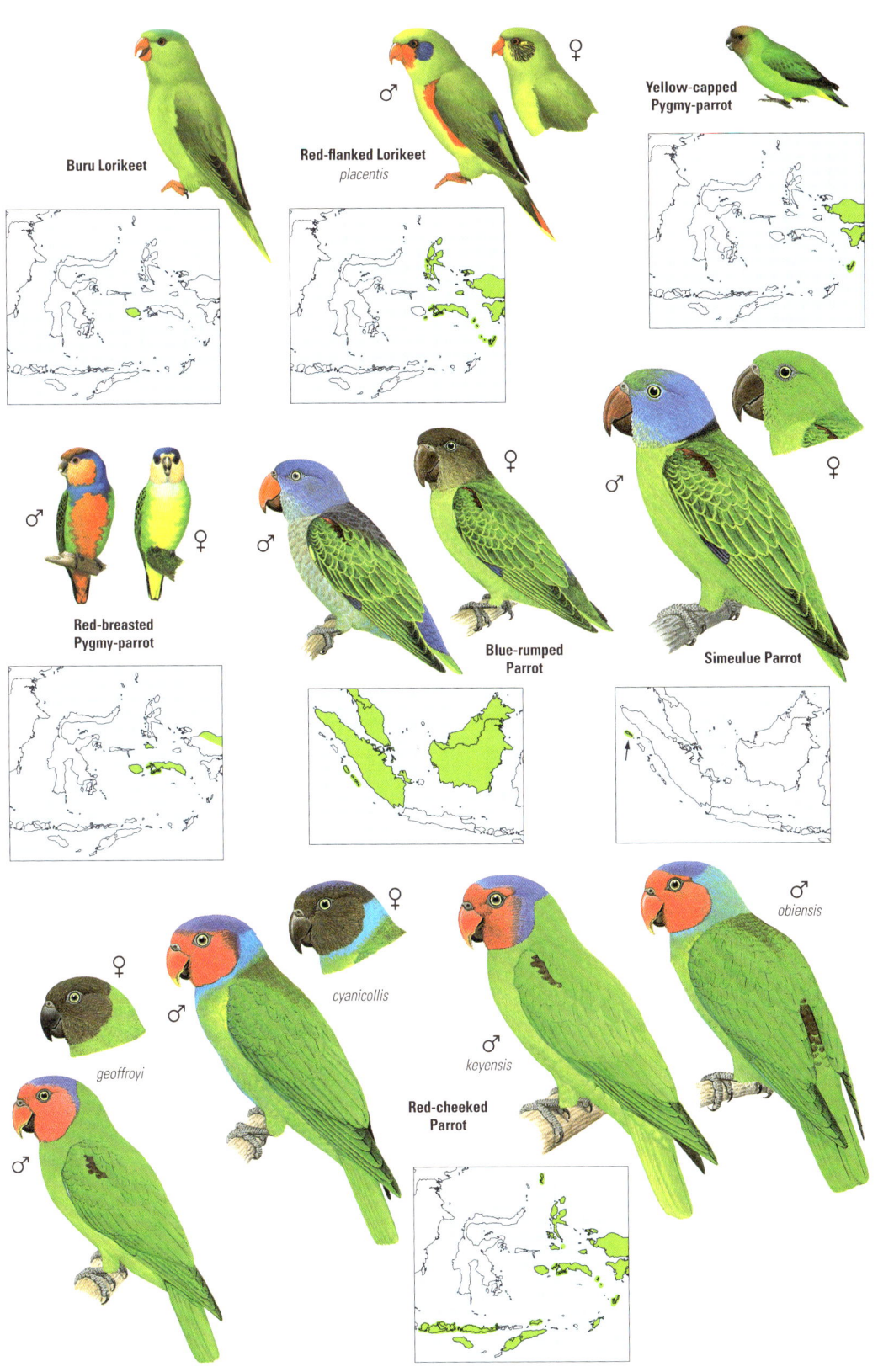

Buru Lorikeet

Red-flanked Lorikeet
placentis

♂ ♀

Yellow-capped Pygmy-parrot

Red-breasted Pygmy-parrot

♂ ♀

♂ ♀

Blue-rumped Parrot

♂ ♀

Simeulue Parrot

♀

cyanicollis

geoffroyi

♀

♂

♂

keyensis

♂

Red-cheeked Parrot

obiensis

♂

Minahasa Racquet-tail *Prioniturus flavicans* ▪E▪

L 37 cm. Monotypic. Uncommon in primary and secondary forest, edge, <1000 m. Pairs or small flocks (<5). **ID** Short-looking, square-tailed with spatules. **M** green; strong yellow wash to nape and mantle extending across breast; blue crown with red patch. **F** lacks crown markings and less yellow on body; shorter spatules. **Imm** lacks spatules. **Voc** Harsh and loud; (i) "WAA-WAA-WAA..."; (ii) "EWW-EWW-EWW..."; (iii) comical, stuttering "W-W-WHIR...", and other bizarre bubbling squeaks. **SS** Sulawesi Racquet-tail smaller, lacks yellow breast. Note vocalisations. **AN** Yellowish-breasted Racquet-tail.

Sulawesi Racquet-tail *Prioniturus platurus* ▪E▪

L 28 cm. 3 ssp: *platurus* (Sul and satellites); *talautensis* (Talaud); *sinerubris* (Sula; in Banggai probably this ssp). Fairly common in forested lowlands, <3000 m, occurring in more open areas than Minahasa Racquet-tail. Pairs or small flocks (<20), regularly flying high over canopy. **ID** Small, short-looking, square-tailed with spatules. **M** green; strong golden-orange wash on nape; greyish-green mantle and yellowish undertail-coverts; crown bluish-purple behind red crown spot. Ssp *sinerubris* lacks red crown spot and shows lilac wash on shoulder; *talautensis* less grey on mantle. **F** all green with no obvious markings. **Imm** lacks spatules. **Voc** Loud, high-pitched; (i) "wir-wir-wir..."; (ii) piercing "pip-pip-er-er...", similar to *Trichoglossus* lorikeets. **SS** See larger Minahasa Racquet-tail. **AN** Golden-mantled Racquet-tail.

Buru Racquet-tail *Prioniturus mada* ▪E▪

L 32 cm. Monotypic. Locally fairly common in primary and secondary forest, edge, can occur in plantations but prefers mid-altitude forest. Usually found in pairs or small flocks (<10). Highly vocal. **ID** Small, short-looking and square-tailed with short spatules. **M** green; purple crown to nape and shoulder patch. **F** uniformly dark green, with hint of purple on nape. **Imm** lacks spatules. **Voc** Loud, high-pitched screeches and musical whistles; (i) "beep-beep-beep..."; (ii) "huwep-huwep-huwep..."; (iii) "buup-ee-weep...".

Eclectus Parrot *Eclectus roratus*

L 35–42 cm. Aus. 9 ssp, 5 in region: *roratus* (C Mol); *vosmaeri* (N Mol); *cornelia* (Sumba); *riedeli* (Tanimbar); *polychloros* (Kai, NG). Substantial variation in plumage, particularly female, across taxa (especially *cornelia* and *riedeli* compared to other taxa) may warrant taxonomic overhaul. Uncommon in primary and secondary forest, occasionally straying away from forest, <1900 m. **ID** Large and plump with short tail; broad rounded wings in flight. **M** all green with red flanks and bluish leading edge of wing with darker blue primaries; red upper and black lower mandible. Ssp *cornelia* larger; *riedeli* smaller than nominate; *vosmaeri* shows yellowish-tinged head; *polychloros* with yellowish tail tip. **F** black bill; red body; purplish band across breast, underwing-coverts, mantle and upperwing (this band less purple, more blue, in *polychloros*). Ssp *vosmaeri* shows more contrast between head and purple breast band and has yellowish vent and undertail; *cornelia* entirely red except upperwing; *riedeli* also entirely red but much smaller with yellow undertail and vent. **Imm** similar to respective sexes but grey bill. **Voc** Similar to cockatoos but less harsh; (i) "UREK-UREK-UREK..."; (ii) "EK-EK-EK..."; (iii) single note "ERR"; (iv) curious "UW-R"; (v) shaky "DA-LILI-DA-LILI...".

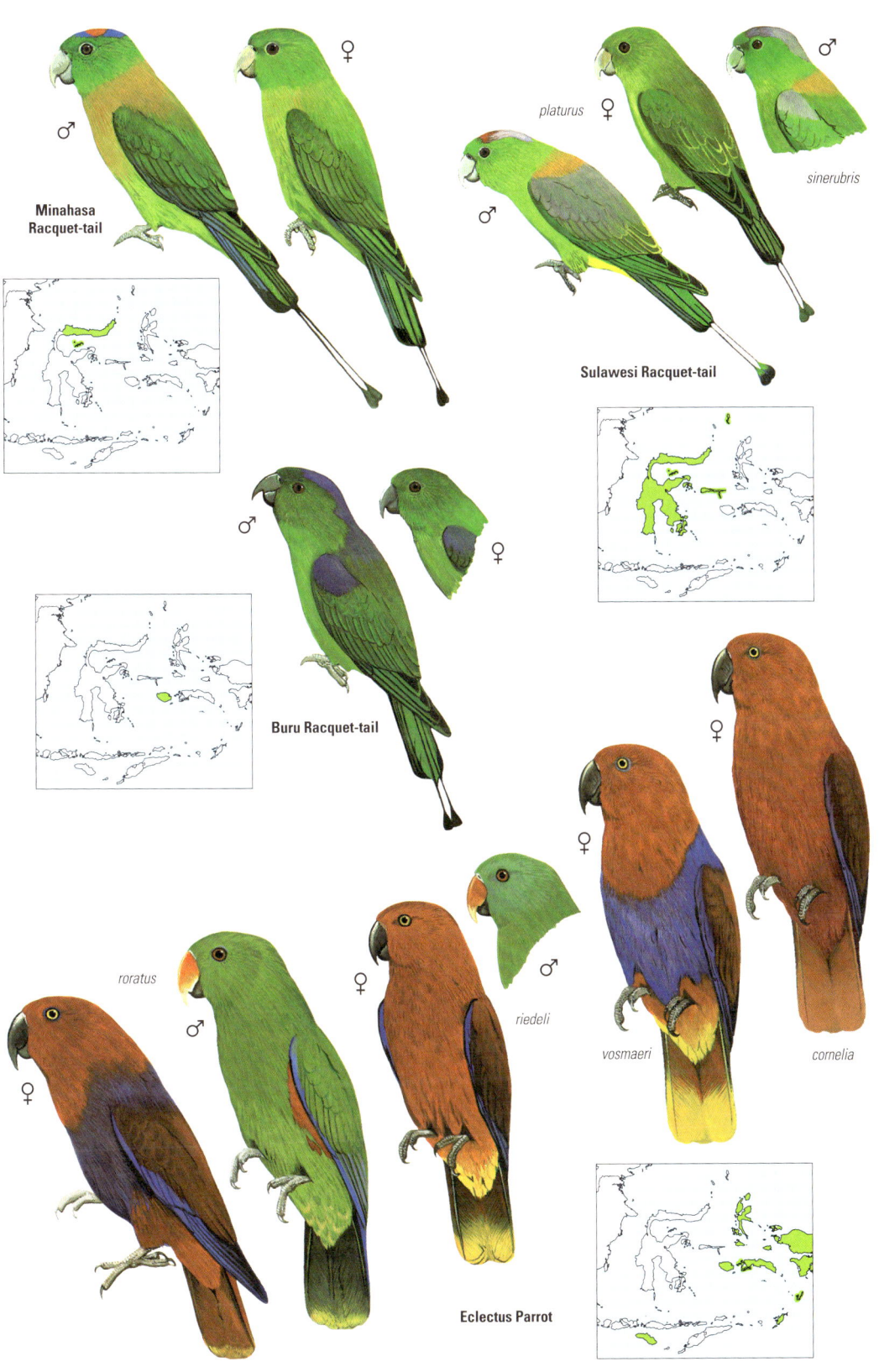

Minahasa Racquet-tail

♂

♀

platurus

♀

♂

sinerubris

Sulawesi Racquet-tail

♂

♀

Buru Racquet-tail

roratus

♂

♀

riedeli

♂

♀

vosmaeri

♀

cornelia

Eclectus Parrot

Great-billed Parrot *Tanygnathus megalorynchos*
L 33–43 cm. West Papuan Is to Wallacea. 5 ssp: *megalorynchos* (Talaud, Sangihe, Togian, Tukangbesi, Flores Sea Is., Banggai, Sula, N Mol, Flores, W Papuan Is); *affinis* (C Mol); *sumbensis* (Sumba); *hellmayri* (Timor, Rote, Semao); *subaffinis* (Tanimbar, Babar). Generally uncommon on small islands and coastal forests on larger islands but does wander to plantations, mangroves and orchards; *hellmayri* now rare and local, likely in E Timor only. In pairs or small flocks (<10, rarely <40). Often flies high over canopy at dawn and dusk. **ID** Massive. **Ad** distinctive stiff-winged flight with yellow underwing-coverts. Much individual/clinal variation in *megalorynchos* but always shows massive red bill, yellow fringing to dark coverts, and bluish rump. Ssp *affinis* shows bluish-tinged head, green scapulars; *subaffinis* similar but paler rump and bluish upperwing-coverts; *hellmayri* like *affinis* but yellowish-tinged head; *sumbensis* as nominate but darker overall. **Imm** lacks black on shoulder. **Voc** Various very loud, harsh screeches; (i) "EK-EK-EK...", "EYOR-EYOR-EYOR..."; (ii) softer, hollow "WEEP-PEE-PEE-WEEP...". **SS** See Blue-naped, Azure-rumped and Black-lored Parrots.

Black-lored Parrot *Tanygnathus gramineus* E
L 40 cm. Monotypic. Little known, scarce in montane forest, 600–1300 m. Evidence suggests it is largely but not wholly nocturnal, with birds flying noisily over forest canopy at after dusk and predawn, and found feeding noisily in canopy at night. **ID** Generally dull green overall; black lores bisect purplish upper cheeks and forecrown. **M** red bill. **F** pinkish-grey bill. **Imm** undescribed. **Voc** Highly vocal at dusk and just before dawn; (i) "WERK-WERK-WERK..."; (ii) slightly curious, desperate "WEER-WEER-WEER...", often delivered in couplets. **SS** Great-billed Parrot shows well-marked upperwing, yellow underwing-coverts, and has stiff, rigid wingbeats.

Blue-naped Parrot *Tanygnathus lucionensis*
L 31 cm. Phil and neighbouring islands. 5 ssp, 3 in region: *talautensis* (Talaud); *salvadorii* (islands off NE Bor, Phil; introduced Kota Kinabalu, Mantanani [Sabah]); *horrisonus* (Maratua). Uncommon in primary and secondary forest, occasionally orchards, plantations and mangroves in search of food, <1000 m. **ID Ad** greenish-yellow overall with yellow-fringed bluish wing-coverts; azure-blue nape and bluish head sides. Ssp *horrisonus* has greener head sides and no yellow tinge to back and underparts. Smaller *salvadorii* is less blue around wing-coverts. **Imm** duller with little blue on nape. **Voc** Various loud screeches, "WER-WER-WER...". **SS** Azure-rumped Parrot lacks yellow-fringed covert markings and blue nape. Larger Great-billed Parrot has yellow underwing-coverts and lacks blue on head.

Azure-rumped Parrot *Tanygnathus sumatranus* E
L 32 cm. 2 ssp: *sumatranus* (Sul region, Sula); *sangirensis* (Sangihe, Talaud). Now separated from Blue-backed Parrot *T. everetti* (Phil) based on plumage, eye colour and genetic divergence. Uncommon in primary and secondary forest, occasionally straying away from forest in search of food, <800 m. On Sula largely coastal, tolerating cultivation. Also active at night. **ID** Greyish-white iris. **M** wholly green with large red (in **M**) or horn-coloured (in **F/Imm**) bill and bluish shoulder; *sangirensis* longer wings and tail. **Voc** Various loud screeches including: (i) disyllabic "OO-WER, OO-WER..."; (ii) "WER-WER-WER...". **SS** See Blue-naped Parrot. Lacks extensive wing markings of larger Great-billed Parrot.

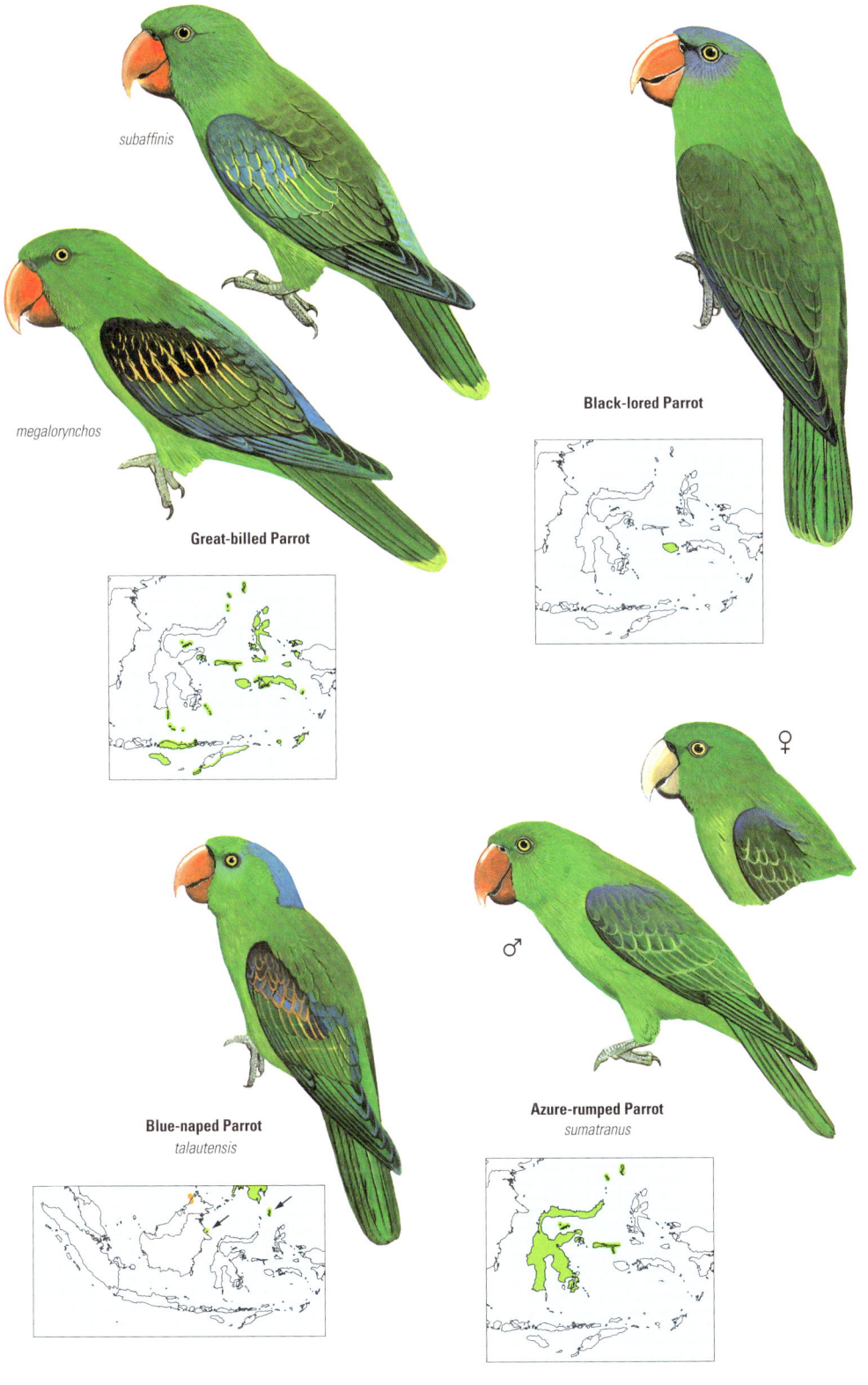

subaffinis

megalorynchos

Great-billed Parrot

Black-lored Parrot

Blue-naped Parrot
talautensis

Azure-rumped Parrot
sumatranus

♀

♂

Moluccan King Parrot *Alisterus amboinensis*
L 35 cm. West Papua to Wallacea. 6 ssp, 5 in region: *amboinensis* (Ambon, Seram); *buruensis* (Buru); *versicolor* (Peleng); *sulaensis* (Sula); *hypophonius* (Halmahera). Uncommon in primary and secondary forest, <1500 m. Rarely strays far from forest though regularly found feeding in banana plantations; singly or small flocks (<10). **ID** Slim, elongated with very long, thin tail and slow, languid flight usually below canopy. **Ad** red head and body; blackish-blue tail; deep-blue mantle, rump and underwing-coverts; green outerwing and upperwing-coverts; red upper and black lower mandible. Ssp *versicolor* smaller; *sulaensis* variable greenish on mantle; *buruensis* as latter, but grey bill; *hypophonius* wholly deep-blue wings. **Imm** greenish mantle, grey bill. **Voc** (i) Drawn-out piercing "SPEAR-SPEAR-SPEAR..."; (ii) harsh "WHAK-WHAK-WHAK..."; (iii) "TCHA-TCHA-TCHA...".

Jonquil Parrot *Aprosmictus jonquillaceus* **E**
L 35 cm. 2 ssp: *jonquillaceus* (Timor, Rote); *wetterensis* (Wetar). Fairly common, though rare in W Timor, in primary and secondary forest, savanna woodland, plantations and scrubby secondary growth, <2200 m; usually singly or small flocks (<10). **ID** Slim body, longish tail and wings. Pale green head and underparts with darker green upperparts and tail; orange bill; blue rump (absent in **F/Imm**); in **M** bend of wing blue with red and yellowish coverts. Ssp *wetterensis* smaller, with less yellow and red in wing. **Voc** Various squeaky, short, quiet notes including "WHIRR", "CH-CH-CHUP...", "WHAA-WHAA-WHAA...", and "DUIT-DUIT-DUIT...". **AN** Olive-shouldered Parrot.

Red-breasted Parakeet *Psittacula alexandri*
L 33–38 cm. S–SE Asia. 8 ssp, 6-7 in region: *alexandri* (Jav–Bali, S Bor); *cala* (Simeulue); *major* (Lasia, Babi); *perionca* (Nias); *kangeanensis* (Kangean); *dammermani* (Karimunjawa); *fasciata* (mainland S-SE Asia; probably this form introduced Jav–Bali). Locally common, but *perionca*, *alexandri*, *kangeanensis* and *dammermani* now very local and rare; open areas, parks, woodland, lightly forested lowlands and hills; occurs in closed-canopy forest only on small islands; suburban populations on Java and Bali often of escaped status and showing character traits of extralimital *fasciata*. Often found in large, noisy flocks (<50). Nests communally. **ID** Slim, longish-tailed with shortish wings; green overall with grey head; black lores and thick moustachial; pinkish breast (duller in **F**) and bluish uppertail; yellowish shoulder patch; bill red. Ssp *kangeanensis* paler head, yellower shoulder; *dammermani* larger. The three W Sum Is. ssp (*cala, major, perionca*) and extralimital *fasciata* have black lower mandible in **M** and all black bill in **F**. Ssp *fasciata*, larger *cala* and yet larger *major* have bluish tinge to head, darker pink breast (with distinct bluish tinge in *fasciata*); *perionca* and *major* have belly and vent brighter, less bluish-tinged than *cala*. **Imm** greenish head and underparts. **Voc** Various loud, shrill, piercing screeches in flight; (i) "EWHAA-EWHAA"; (ii) sharp "KAINK-KAINK-KAINK..."; (iii) when perched "DA-DA-DUW-DA-DA-DUW...", and A-AH, A-AH, A-AH...".

Long-tailed Parakeet *Psittacula longicauda*
L 31–47 cm. Sundaic to Andamans. 4 ssp, 2 in region: *longicauda* (Sum–Bor, MPen); *defontainei* (Natuna; possibly this ssp on Anambas). The two extralimital subspecies from Andamans and Nicobars are often excluded from this species. Also see Enggano Parakeet for taxonomy. Locally fairly common, nomadic across coastal areas, mangroves, swamp forest and plantations, <300 m. Often in large flocks (>1000 at roosts). Nests communally. **ID** Slim and long-tailed with contrasting yellow underwing-coverts in flight. **M** red upper and black lower mandible; yellowish-green underparts; dark green crown and inner wing; darker blue outerwing and tail; reddish face extending round nape with black lores and thick black moustachial; turquoise mantle and rump; dark-blue inner and green outer-tail; *defontainei* darker red face and yellowish crown. **F** brownish bill; dull orange-red face with bluish nape, dirty green moustachial; darker iris. **Imm** mainly green with indistinct facial pattern. **Voc** Loud, nasal screeches; (i) "WHAA-WHAA-WHAA..."; (ii) "CHEE-Yo, CHEE-Yo, CHEE-Yo..."; (iii) scolding "CHEET-CHEET-CHEET...".

Enggano Parakeet *Psittacula modesta* **E**
L 35–50 cm. Monotypic. Here considered a species distinct from Long-tailed Parakeet based on moderate differences in size, shape and colouration. Fairly common in all wooded habitats. Usually in flocks. **ID M** red face, black lores and moustachial, dark-green forecrown fading to rear; emerald-green underparts, pale green upperparts; dark green wing much longer than Long-tailed, while dark-green tail shorter. **F** black moustachial, reddish face, dark-red crown; paler green underparts with darker green upperparts and tail. **Imm** uniform green with indistinct facial pattern. **Voc** Loud, nasal screeches: (i) rapid, machine gun-like "CHER'TER'TER'TER"; (ii) upslurred "WHAA", regularly repeated.

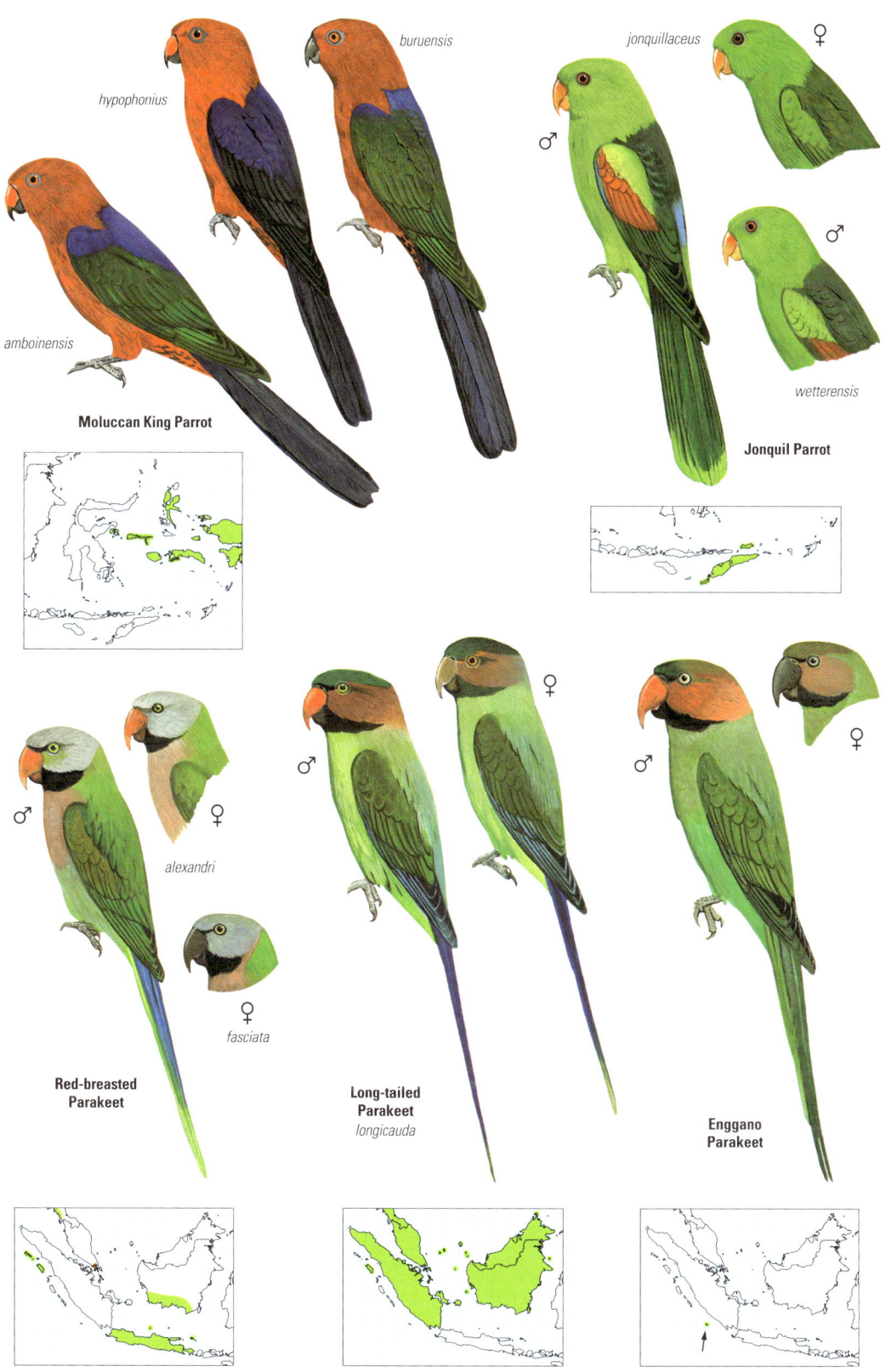

hypophonius

buruensis

jonquillaceus

♀

♂

amboinensis

♂

Moluccan King Parrot

wetterensis

Jonquil Parrot

♂

♀

alexandri

♀

fasciata

Red-breasted Parakeet

♂

♀

Long-tailed Parakeet
longicauda

♂

♀

Enggano Parakeet

Blue-crowned Hanging Parrot *Loriculus galgulus*

L 12 cm. Sundaic. Monotypic. Fairly common in primary and secondary forest, can occur in plantations, wooded gardens and cities, <1300 m. Escapees regularly recorded on Jav. Singly or pairs but groups together at flowering and fruiting trees. Usually seen zipping over canopy with a characteristic undulating flight, calling. **ID** Mostly green. **M** red throat patch; large red rump; golden mantle patch; yellowish undertail-coverts; blue crown spot. **F** lacks head markings; reduced golden mantle patch. **Imm** duller, with reduced red. **Voc** (i) High-pitched shrill "tsih" or "tsrri", regularly repeated; (ii) "tsi-tsi-tsit…", usually in flight.

Sulawesi Hanging Parrot *Loriculus stigmatus*　E

L 15 cm. 3 ssp: *stigmatus* (Sul); *croconotus* (Buton, Muna); *quadricolor* (Togian). Birds found on Manui may be morphologically distinct, further study required. Fairly common in primary and secondary forest, can occur in plantations and wooded gardens, <1600 m. Singly or pairs, groups together at flowering and fruiting trees. **ID** Green overall. **M** pale iris; red forecrown (reportedly orange in population on Manui); red throat and shoulder; large maroon rump; *croconotus* has paler green wings and tail and more intensely yellow (not yellowish green) upper back; *quadricolor* also has yellow back in addition to smaller throat spot and brighter, paler red rump than nominate. **F** lacks red crown; reduced throat patch; dark iris. **Imm** throat and shoulder yellowish. **Voc** High-pitched, shrill "zee-sip…", regularly repeated in flight. **SS** See Pygmy Hanging Parrot. **AN** Large Sulawesi Hanging Parrot.

Sula Hanging Parrot *Loriculus sclateri*　E

L 14 cm. 2 ssp: *sclateri* (Sula); *ruber* (Banggai). Common in primary and secondary forest, can occur in plantations and wooded gardens. Singly or pairs, flocks together at flowering and fruiting trees. **ID Ad** green overall, but throat, shoulder and rump red, and large golden mantle patch; pale iris. Ssp *ruber* has more consistently red (less yellow) mantle patch, paler red rump and a brownish-red forehead. **Imm** ill-defined markings. **Voc** High-pitched, shrill (i) "tsi-tsit…"; (ii) "zee-zee-zee…".

Moluccan Hanging Parrot *Loriculus amabilis*　E

L 11 cm. Monotypic. Fairly common in primary and secondary forest, can occur in plantations and wooded gardens. Singly or pairs, groups together at flowering and fruiting trees. **ID** Green overall. **M** rump, shoulder, throat and forecrown red; pale iris. **F** green crown and reduced throat patch; dark iris. **Imm** yellowish throat and shoulder. **Voc** High-pitched, shrill: (i) "tsi-tsit…"; (ii) "zee-zee-zee…".

Sangihe Hanging Parrot *Loriculus catamene*　E

L 12 cm. Monotypic. Uncommon in primary and secondary forest, can occur in plantations and wooded gardens. Singly or pairs, groups together at flowering and fruiting trees. **ID** Green overall. **M** red forecrown, throat, rump, vent and tail tips; pale iris. **F** green forecrown, less red on vent; dark iris. **Imm** undescribed. **Voc** (i) High-pitched, shrill "tsih" or "tsrri", regularly repeated; (ii) "tsi-tsi-tsit…", usually in flight.

Pygmy Hanging Parrot *Loriculus exilis*　E

L 10–11 cm. Monotypic. Uncommon in primary and secondary forest, can occur in plantations and wooded gardens, <1320 m. Singly or pairs, groups together at flowering and fruiting trees. **ID** Green overall. **M** pale iris; red throat and rump. **F** reduced throat patch; dark iris. **Imm** lacks throat patch; paler bill. **Voc** High-pitched "zee-zee-zee…", slightly higher pitched than Sulawesi Hanging Parrot. **SS** Larger, paler Sulawesi Hanging Parrot has black bill, darker rump and male shows red forecrown. **AN** Small Sulawesi Hanging Parrot.

Javan Hanging Parrot *Loriculus pusillus*　E

L 12 cm. Monotypic. Uncommon in primary and secondary forest, can occur in plantations and wooded gardens, <1800 m. Singly or pairs, groups together at flowering and fruiting trees. **ID** Green overall; orange bill. **M** large orange-yellow throat patch; red rump. **F** reduced throat patch. **Imm** undescribed. **Voc** (i) High-pitched, shrill "tsih" or "tsrri", regularly repeated; (ii) "tsi-tsi-tsit…", usually in flight. **AN** Yellow-throated Hanging Parrot.

Wallace's Hanging Parrot *Loriculus flosculus*　E

L 11–12 cm. Monotypic. Scarce and local in forested areas, can also be found in scrubby secondary growth, 200–1400 m. Singly or pairs, groups together at flowering and fruiting trees. Compared to other hanging parrots, seemingly much more difficult to encounter. **ID** Green overall; orange bill. **M** elongated red throat patch; nape tinged orange; red rump. **F** reduced throat patch **Imm** undescribed. **Voc** Higher-pitched than other *Loriculus*, more reminiscent of a *Dicaeum* flowerpecker, "sis-sis-sis…".

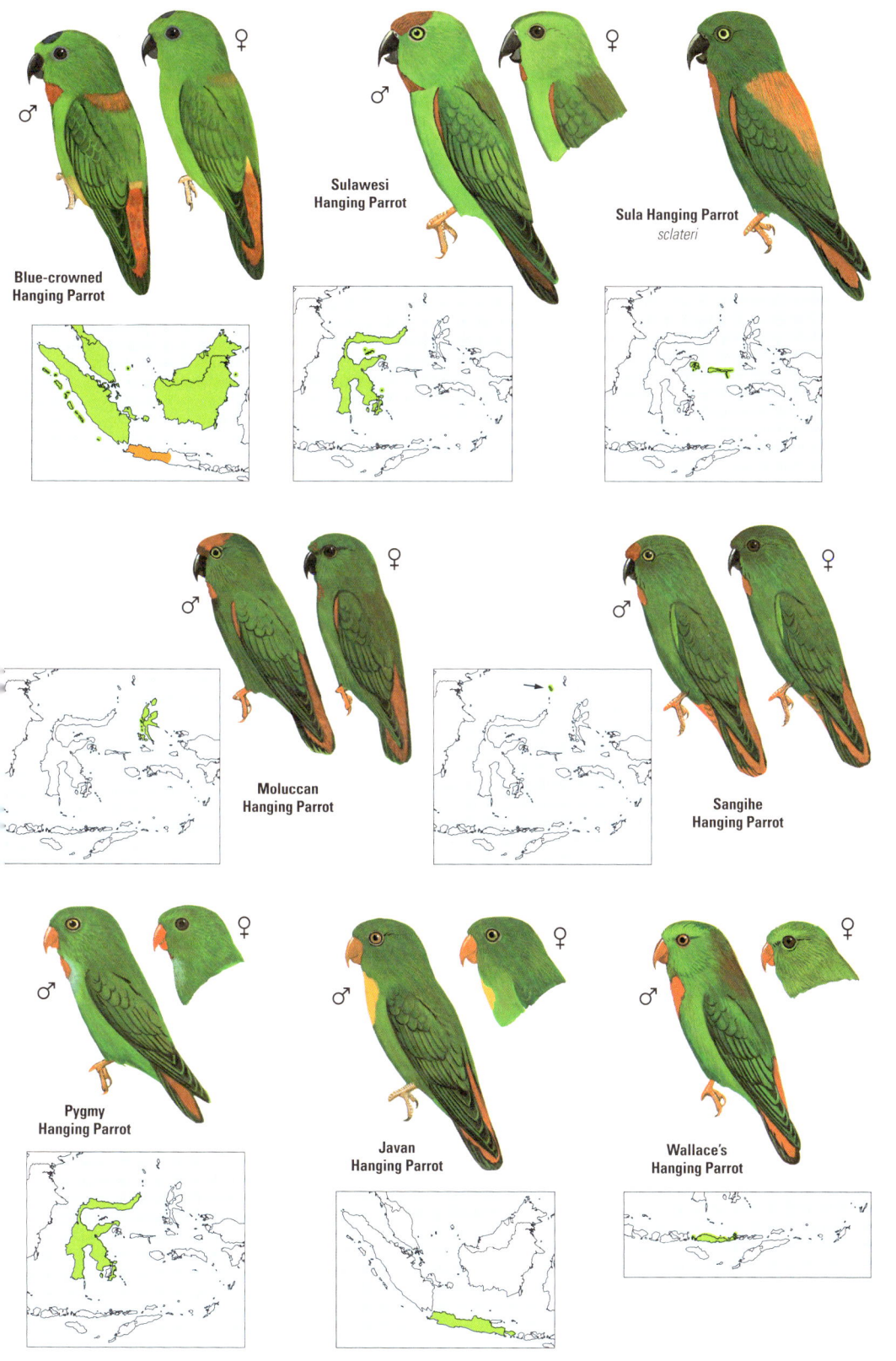

Blue-crowned Hanging Parrot

Sulawesi Hanging Parrot

Sula Hanging Parrot
sclateri

Moluccan Hanging Parrot

Sangihe Hanging Parrot

Pygmy Hanging Parrot

Javan Hanging Parrot

Wallace's Hanging Parrot

CALYPTOMENIDAE
Green Broadbills
3 species in region

Small to medium-sized, squat birds; wide bills and large-headed appearance with distinctive feather tuft on forehead. Bright-green in colour and generally found at mid- to upper storey of forest and edge where typically unobtrusive. All species build suspended purse-shaped nests.

Green Broadbill *Calyptomena viridis*
L 14–17 cm. Sundaic. 3 ssp, 2 in region: *gloriosa* (Bor, Sum, Nias, Batu, Lingga, Natuna); *siberu* (Mentawai). Uncommon to fairly common in forest, <1200 m, rarely to 1700 m. Singly, pairs, or groups (<5) around fruiting trees. **ID M** iridescent bright green; black spot on ear-coverts; black wing-tips and three black bars on wing-coverts; tiny bill; *siberu* larger, with some indistinct bluish feathering. **F** much duller, paler green, with no black markings. **Imm** paler, particularly on belly. **Voc** Song: quiet, bouncing trill "toi, toi-oi-oi-oi-oik", lasting 1.2 sec, increasing in tempo and pitch. In alarm can produce a loud, parrot-like "er-ya, er-ya, er-ya..." lasting 0.5 sec. Ssp *siberu* known to produce unique melodious monosyllabic whistle that is easily imitable. **SS** See Hose's and Whitehead's Broadbills.

Hose's Broadbill *Calyptomena hosii*   `E`
L 19–21 cm. Monotypic. Scarce in hill forest, usually 500–1200 m, rarely 200–1700 m. Unobtrusive; singly, pairs, or groups (<5) around fruiting trees. **ID M** iridescent bright green; electric blue underparts; black spots on wing-coverts; black spots on nape; black tail. **F** slightly duller, with paler blue underparts largely restricted to belly; no black spots on nape. **Imm** blue underparts barely visible; black spots on coverts not as pronounced. **Voc** (i) Soft cooing "hoo", regularly repeated; (ii) 2-note, drawn-out "hoow-wah", lasting 1.7 sec, last note upslurred, similar to Schneider's Pitta; (iii) <7 excited notes rising in tempo "ow-ow-ow-OWH". **SS** Smaller Green Broadbill lacks blue belly; covert-spots replaced by black bars. Larger Whitehead's Broadbill lacks blue on belly and has more black on upper breast and upperparts.

Whitehead's Broadbill *Calyptomena whiteheadi*   `E`
L 24–27 cm. Monotypic. Uncommon in montane forest, 900–1800 m, rarely 600–2000 m. Singly, pairs, or groups (<5) around fruiting trees. **ID M** iridescent bright green; black marks on forehead, ear-coverts, upper breast and tail; black streaking on flanks, belly, mantle and wing-coverts. **F** duller green; black restricted to tail, upper breast and back streaking. **Imm** duller green with black-streaked wing-coverts and black tail. **Voc** (i) Presumed song, rarely heard, a clear, loud 3-note "woc-woc-woc", lasting 1.6 sec; (ii) excited, loud "ke-chrrrr", lasting ~1–2 sec, "ke" is high and sudden, "chrrrr" can be soft and drawn-out; (iii) loud, staccato "kikikik..." lasting 1–2 sec, often given when flying off. **SS** Smaller Green Broadbill has no black on throat and underparts, and less black on upperparts. See also Hose's Broadbill.

EURYLAIMIDAE
Broadbills
6 species in region

Small to medium-sized, with stocky bodies, large heads and broad bills. Many species very colourful, but even so quite inconspicuous at mid- to upper storey of forest. Presence often betrayed by distinctive calls. All species build suspended purse-shaped nests.

Black-and-red Broadbill *Cymbirhynchus macrorhynchos*
L 20–24 cm. SE Asia. 3 ssp, 1 in region: *macrorhynchos* (Sum–Bor). Extralimital ssp *affinis* (SW Myanmar) sometimes separated as monotypic '**Arakan Broadbill**'. Uncommon, locally fairly common in forest and edge near water, particularly streams, <300 m, rarely to 900 m. Usually builds nest over water. Singly or pairs in the lower and mid-storey. **ID Ad** black head and upperparts with black breast band dividing red throat and underparts; broad white scapulars, conspicuous in flight. **Imm** upperparts and head more brownish; underparts more greyish-brown. **Voc** Song: <15 rasping, cicada-like notes, "krrk-krrk-krrk..." or "krek-krek-krek...", 2 n/s, usually slightly accelerating towards end. Call: sharp, metallic "pip".

Long-tailed Broadbill *Psarisomus dalhousiae*
L 23–26 cm. S–SE Asia. 5 ssp, 2 in region: *psittacinus* (Sum, MPen); *borneensis* (Bor). Uncommon to fairly common in submontane forest, 700–1500 m, rarely to 2500 m. Usually pairs or flocks (<20), often joining feeding flocks, favouring mid and upper canopy. **ID M** yellow head with black 'helmet' and cobalt-blue crown patch; green body and long, blue tail; in flight shows white wing patch; *borneensis* smaller with paler tail. **F** reduced blue crown patch. **Imm** duller green, head pattern washed green. **Voc** Song: <10 high-pitched, shrieking "pay-pay-pay...", ~2 n/s, first note loudest and highest, gradually tailing off, regularly repeated. Call: sharp, metallic "pik".

Silver-breasted Broadbill *Serilophus lunatus*
L 16–17 cm. SE Asia. 10 ssp, 1 in region: *intensus* (Sum). Uncommon in submontane forest, 800–2000 m. Usually pairs or small groups (<7), often joining feeding flocks. Generally quiet and unobtrusive, favouring mid-storey. **ID M** broad, black supercilium; silver-grey head and body with rich rufous back and black tail; striking black-and-blue flight feathers with white band across base. **F** narrow silver breast band. **Imm** darker with shorter tail. **Voc** High-pitched, metallic "PE–ooo", lasting 0.5 sec, second syllable much lower-pitched.

siberu *gloriosa*

Green Broadbill

Hose's Broadbill

Whitehead's Broadbill

Black-and-red Broadbill

Long-tailed Broadbill
psittacinus

Silver-breasted Broadbill

Banded Broadbill *Eurylaimus javanicus*
L 21–23 cm. SE Asia. 5 ssp, 3 in region: *brookei* (Bor, Natuna); *harterti* (Sum, Riau, Bangka, Belitung); ssp *javanicus* (Jav) sometimes separated as monotypic '**Javan Broadbill**' based on eye colour and slight plumage differences, though vocally undifferentiated. Fairly common in forest, <1500 m. Usually pairs, favouring canopy. **ID** Bulky-looking. **M** black forecrown and lores; purplish-red head and underparts with diffuse greyish breast band; upperparts black with broad yellow streaks; yellow rump and iris. Ssp *brookei* distinct breast band, darker underparts, greyish-purple head, blue iris; *harterti* additionally with black band above grey breast band. **F** reduced black on face and breast band. **Imm** yellowish-grey bill; underparts pale pinkish-yellow; pale brown upperparts with yellowish streaks. **Voc** Song: incredible, far-carrying song similar to Black-and-yellow's (also see that species); a single loud "wheeoo" followed by 8–100 very rapid, loud, frantic notes, "wir-wir-ir-ir-ir-ir-ir..." lasting 7–9 sec, eventually tailing off, at a rate of 10 n/s. Often in duet, with one bird starting slightly after the other. Call: (i) short "kwow"; (ii) single, loud "wheeoo".

Black-and-yellow Broadbill *Eurylaimus ochromalus*
L 13–15 cm. Sundaic. Monotypic. Fairly common in forest, <1300 m. Usually pairs, favouring canopy. **ID M** black head, upperparts and breast band (incomplete in **F**); white collar; pink underparts fading into yellow undertail-coverts; yellow back and wing markings. **Imm** brownish tinge to upperparts with reduced yellow markings; greyish underparts; lacks breast band, whitish supercilium. **Voc** Song: very similar to Banded; most important difference is that the introductory "wheeoo" is followed by notes at same pitch becoming successively shorter until eventually developing into a frantically paced series. In contrast, Banded's introductory note is followed by notes that are always at a lower pitch, and that are already extremely short and frantically-paced, not slowly building into a frantic pace. Black-and-yellow's series is often longer than Banded's, lasting 8–15 sec, continually rising and ending abruptly at a rate of 8 n/s. Call: short, squeaky "kwee".

Dusky Broadbill *Corydon sumatranus*
L 24–29 cm. SE Asia. 3 ssp, 2 in region: *sumatranus* (Sum, MPen); *brunnescens* (Bor, Natuna). Uncommon in forest, <800 m, rarely to 1800 m. Usually in small, noisy groups (<10), preferring mid–upper canopy. **ID** Bulky, big-headed with very broad, large, pink bill. **Ad** uniform dark-brown plumage with broad dirty-white bib. Rapid flight with broad white wing patch. Ssp *brunnescens* chocolate brown plumage with less-contrasting bib. **Imm** paler and browner, with indistinct paler bib. **Voc** Series of <10 upslurred, screaming, thin whistles "ky-ee, ky-ee, ky-ee...", and thin, piercing "pseeoo", often given in duet with several birds, sounding like a squeaky toy.

25 species in region
Small to medium-sized ground-dwelling forest species. Often extremely colourful and highly prized by birdwatchers, but shy and inconspicuous, foraging by hopping quietly on forest floor. Most species have distinctive, short calls, occasionally given from a low branch, and usually the best clue to their presence.

Schneider's Pitta *Hydrornis schneideri* **E**
L 20–23 cm. Monotypic. Uncommon in (sub-) montane forest, 900–2400 m. Predominantly terrestrial, occasionally perching <3 m off the ground when disturbed or calling. **ID M** rufous-buff face and underparts with a broad black eyestripe; thin black collar above deep blue mantle, wings and tail. **F** green-brown mantle and can show some black mottling around face. **Imm** mottled brown with greyish underparts and greenish mantle. **Voc** Song: 2-note, drawn-out "OOwww-wuup", lasting 1.4 sec. Call: sharp "keek". **SS** Larger, sympatric Giant Pitta lacks rufous on head.

Giant Pitta *Hydrornis caeruleus*
L 26 cm. Sundaic. 2 ssp: *caeruleus* (Sum, MPen); *hosei* (Bor). Scarce in forest, <600 m, rarely higher. Predominantly terrestrial, occasionally perching close to the ground when disturbed or calling. Shy. **ID** Large. **M** buffish or dirty-white body with black crown, black line through eye running to the nape; upperparts cobalt blue. **F** chocolate brown mantle and wings; ssp *hosei* more rufous head with black edgings reduced. **Imm** duller than fem. **Voc** Drawn-out, mournful "WUwaa", lasting 1 sec, repeated regularly, often after long pauses of several minutes. **SS** See Schneider's Pitta.

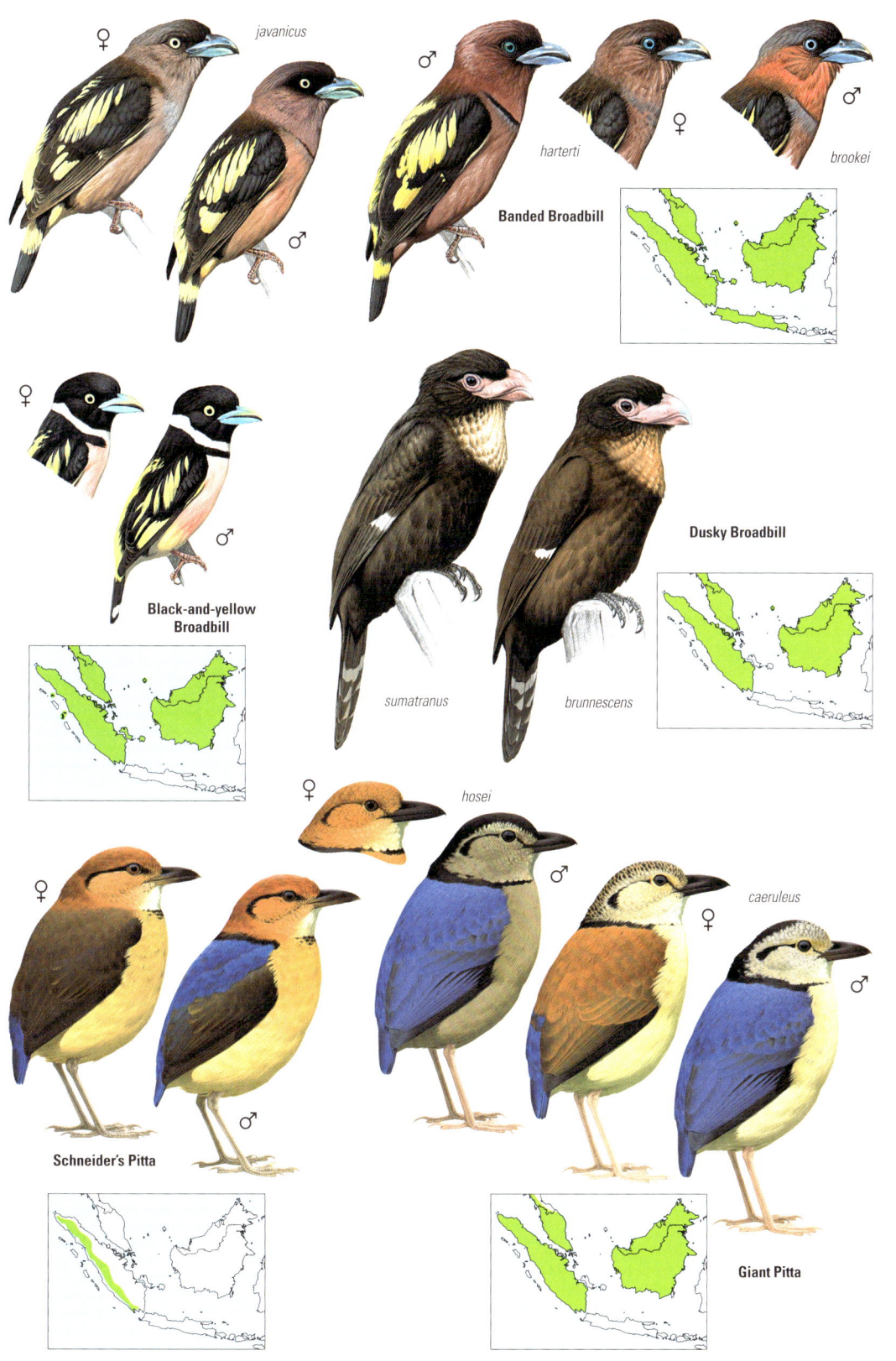

javanicus

♀

♂

♂

harterti

♀

brookei

♂

Banded Broadbill

♀

♂

**Black-and-yellow
Broadbill**

sumatranus

brunnescens

Dusky Broadbill

♀

hosei

♂

♀

caeruleus

♂

♀

♂

Schneider's Pitta

Giant Pitta

Javan Banded Pitta *Hydrornis guajanus* 🇪

L 21–24 cm. Monotypic. No longer includes Bornean and Malayan Banded as all three show discrete, non-clinal differences in plumage and vocalisations. Fairly common in forest, plantations, even scrub, <1200 m. Terrestrial, occasionally perching above ground when disturbed or calling. **ID M** black head with broad yellow supercilium, yellowish throat and broad blue collar; underparts yellow with bold black barring; mantle and inner wing brown with white wingbar and black flight feathers; tail blue. **F** duller with pale brown supercilium, brown crown and no blue collar. **Imm** duller than fem. **Voc** (i) Short, sharp "POUW", lasting 0.2 sec, regularly repeated; (ii) a rolling "krrr", lasting 0.4 sec.

Malayan Banded Pitta *Hydrornis irena*

L 21–24 cm. Sundaic. Monotypic. For taxonomy see Javan Banded Pitta. Locally fairly common in lowland forest, <600 m. Terrestrial, occasionally perching on low branches to call or when alarmed. **ID M** black crown and eyestripe separated by broad yellow supercilium turning bright orange-red at nape; white throat with black collar; underparts dark blue with orange-red on breast sides and heavy black barring; mantle and inner wing brown with white wingbar and black flight feathers; tail blue. **F** much duller overall with brown and black-barred breast. **Imm** face and wing pattern as Ad but duller; mottled breast. **Voc** (i) Short, sharp "POUW", lasting 0.3 sec, regularly repeated, fuller, mellower than Javan Banded; (ii) rolling "krrr", lasting 0.6 sec.

Bornean Banded Pitta *Hydrornis schwaneri* 🇪

L 21–24 cm. Monotypic. For taxonomy see Javan Banded Pitta. Uncommon in forest, <1100 m, mainly 300–800 m. Slope specialist. Terrestrial, occasionally perching on low branches to call or when alarmed. **ID M** black head with broad yellow supercilium and throat; underparts yellow with blue belly patch and heavy black barring; mantle and inner wing brown with white wingbar and black flight feathers; tail blue. **F** much duller overall. **Imm** face and wing pattern as Ad but duller; mottled breast. **Voc** (i) Short, sharp "POUW", as Malayan Banded but slightly shorter; (ii) rolling "krrr", lasting 0.3 sec higher-pitched than Malayan and Javan Banded.

Blue-headed Pitta *Hydrornis baudii* 🇪

L 16–18 cm. Monotypic. Uncommon in forest, <600 m. Terrestrial, occasionally perching above ground when disturbed or calling. **ID** Both sexes show reddish mantle and wing-coverts, white wingbars and blue tail. **M** bright blue crown; black mask and white throat; blue underparts becoming black on breast; white undertail-coverts. **F** buff-coloured head and underparts with reddish crown. **Imm** undescribed. **Voc** (i) "por-wee", with emphasis on the first note, quivering second note, lasting 0.7–1 sec; (ii) haunting "hu-wee", lasting 0.6 sec.

Blue-banded Pitta *Erythropitta arquata* 🇪

L 15 cm. Monotypic. Uncommon in forest. Hill slope specialist, 150–1500 m, primarily 300–900 m. Terrestrial, though often calls up to 15 m from ground. **ID Ad** orange head; red underparts and green upperparts with bright blue line behind eye, breast band and wing-coverts. **Imm** uniform brown with paler belly and reddish flanks. **Voc** Song: very similar to Garnet and Black-crowned but remains on level pitch, slightly dropping at end, making it sound plaintive, lasting 2–2.5 sec. Call: 3–4 hard knocking "tuck tuck tuck…" in alarm.

Garnet Pitta *Erythropitta granatina*

L 15–16 cm. Sundaic. 2 ssp: *granatina* (Bor, except NE); *coccinea* (Sum, MPen). No longer includes Black-crowned Pitta based on plumage differences with limited intergradation. Locally fairly common in forest, particularly swampy areas, <500 m. **ID Ad** mostly black head, forecrown and throat, with electric-blue postocular stripe; bright red mid to rear crown and belly; upperparts and breast blackish with purple gloss, bright blue upperwing-coverts. Ssp *coccinea* red crown extending to forecrown; indistinct red mottling on breast; brighter upperparts. **Imm** uniform plain brown, paler below; blue on wings and tail appearing with age. **Voc** Song: long, clear, upslurred whistle, gradually increasing in volume then ending abruptly; *granatina* lasting 3 sec; *coccinea* lasting ~1.5 sec. Call: 3–4 hard knocking "tuck tuck tuck…" in alarm.

Black-crowned Pitta *Erythropitta ussheri* 🇪

L 15–16 cm. Monotypic. See Garnet Pitta for taxonomy. Replaces Garnet approximately in Sabah. Fairly common in forest, particularly swampy areas, <500 m. **ID Ad** all black head with electric-blue postocular stripe, bright red mid to rear crown and belly; upperparts and breast blackish with purple gloss; bright blue upperwing-coverts. **Imm** uniform plain brown, paler below; orange bill base; blue on wings and tail appearing with age. **Voc** Song: long, clear, upslurred whistle, gradually increasing in volume then ending abruptly, as Garnet, but longer, lasting 3.5 sec, though sometimes shorter, 2 sec. Call: (i) 3–4 hard knocking "tuck tuck tuck…" in alarm; (ii) "por-wee", with emphasis on the first note, second note tailing off, lasting 0.8 sec, very similar to Blue-headed but quieter.

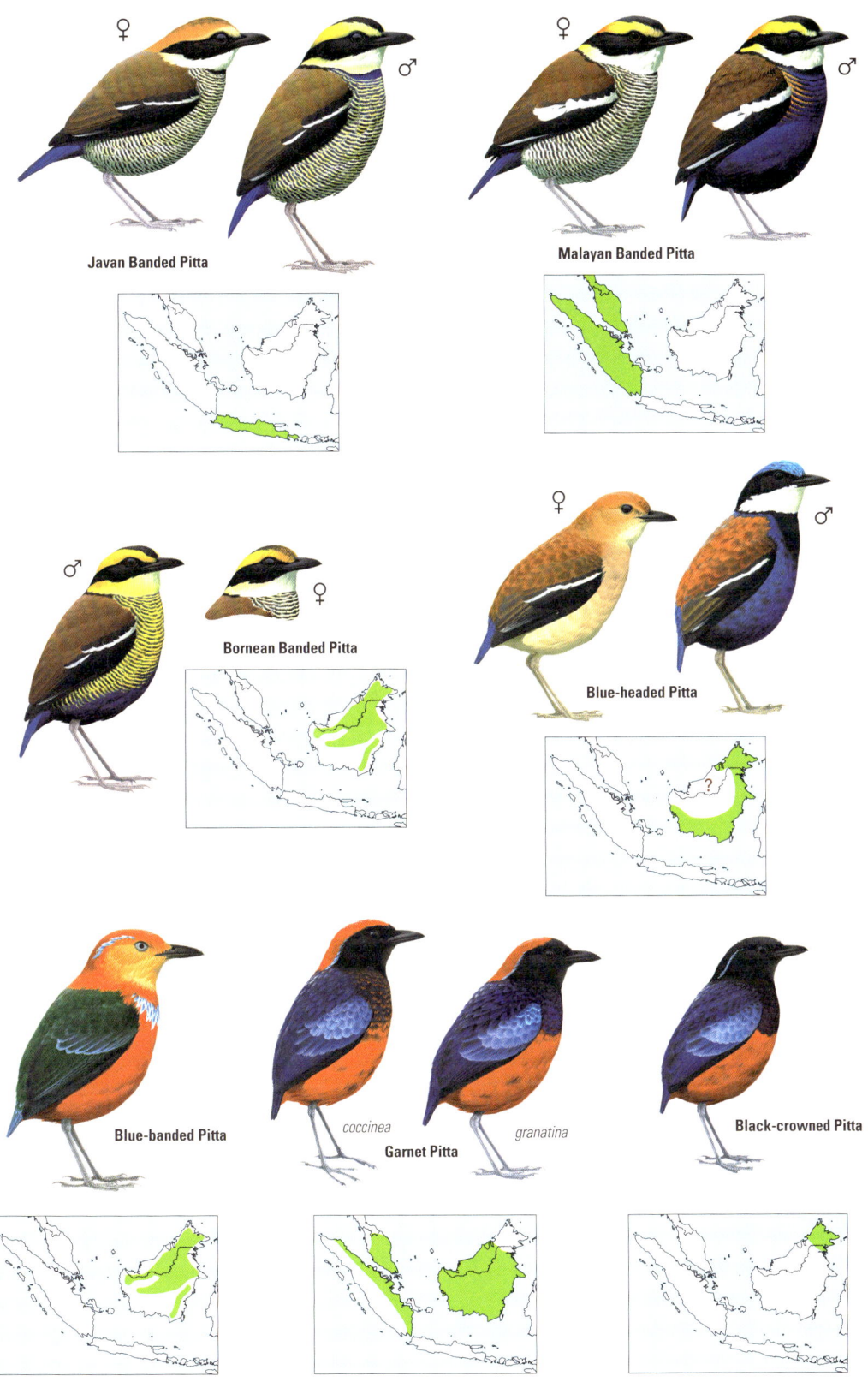

Javan Banded Pitta

Malayan Banded Pitta

Bornean Banded Pitta

Blue-headed Pitta

Blue-banded Pitta

coccinea
Garnet Pitta
granatina

Black-crowned Pitta

Graceful Pitta *Erythropitta venusta* **E**

L 18 cm. Monotypic. Uncommon in hill forest, 400–1400 m, most common 700–1100 m. Favours damp, dark gullies with thick understory. Terrestrial, rarely perching more than 2 m from ground. **ID Ad** black head, with electric-blue postocular stripe; upperparts and breast blackish-maroon, upperwing-coverts edged bright-blue; bright red belly. **Imm** uniform plain brown, paler below; orange bill base. **Voc** Song: single, clear whistle at a level pitch, lasting 1.7 sec, very similar to Blue-banded. Call: 3–4 hard knocking "tuck tuck tuck..." in alarm.

Philippine Pitta *Erythropitta erythrogaster*

L 15–18 cm. Phil, Talaud. 4-6 ssp, 1-2 in region: *inspeculata* (Talaud); undescribed ssp (Nanusa). Complex taxonomy. This and the following five species traditionally united into one umbrella species, '**Red-bellied Pitta**' *E. erythrogaster*, along with another 3-4 extralimital species from Australasia. 'Red-bellied Pitta' now variably divided into 13 species (8 of which in region) based on plumage scoring, or into 17 species (9 of which in region) based on coalescent species delimitation, including the elevation of ssp *inspeculata* to monotypic species status by both approaches. However, plumage variation across 'Red-bellied Pitta' is confusing and geographic variation in vocalisations remains ill-defined, while many mtDNA divergences are far below commonly-used species threshold. Present species accounts present 'middle-of-the-road' approach and divide regional 'Red-bellied Pitta' taxa into 6 species based on cohesion in plumage pattern, biogeography and widely-adopted mtDNA thresholds. More bioacoustic and genomic research urgently required. Undescribed population from Nanusa may merit description as subspecies or constitute outlier population of nominate ssp *erythrogaster* from Phil. Fairly common in forest, forest patches, often feeding along forest trails. **ID Ad** red belly; black head with chestnut-brown nape; upperparts all-blue; dark-blue breast band lacking black boundary. Undescribed Nanusa population shows green mantle, pale crown stripe, reddish nape. **Imm** dark crown; face and underparts dull buff; belly tinged reddish; chestnut nape; mantle dull green-brown; bluish wings and tail; pale bill base. **Voc** Song: long, drawn-out "wwaaaaaooop aaaaawwwwww", first note slightly quivering and rising, second mournful and slightly downslurred, notes of equal length, lasting 2 sec. Call: sharp, upslurred "whek".

Sula Pitta *Erythropitta dohertyi* **E**

L 15–18 cm. Monotypic. Traditionally united with other pittas into a larger umbrella species (see Philippine Pitta for taxonomy) but differs in mtDNA and exhibits substantial morphological distinctions. Uncommon in forest, usually <800 m. **ID Ad** entire head to upper breast black except chestnut crown; bluish-green mantle; blue wings; light-blue breast with broad black band below; red belly; pale eye. **Imm** undescribed. **Voc** (i) similar to Sulawesi Pitta, the two notes typically of equal length but variable, with second note particularly downslurred, lasting 2 sec in total; (ii) series of 5–8 notes, loud and strident, tapering off "whek-whek-whek-whek-wheeeer", lasting 5–9 sec.

Sulawesi Pitta *Erythropitta celebensis* **E**

L 15–18 cm. 3 ssp: *celebensis* (Sul, Togian), *caeruleitorques* (Sangihe), *palliceps* (Siau, Tahulandang). Traditionally united with other pittas into a larger umbrella species (see Philippine Pitta for taxonomy), but differs from all others in mtDNA and a set of minor plumage traits. Alternatively, all 3 Sulawesi Pitta ssp sometimes elevated to monotypic species status. However, plumage differences and mtDNA divergences minor, and consistent vocal differences remain undocumented. Uncommon, locally fairly common, in forest, usually <900 m, rarely to 2100 m. **ID Ad** red belly, green back and blue wings; bluish crown stripe; buff face with brownish-red nape and crown sides; azure-blue breast with broad black band above and below;

palliceps paler overall, crown with less blue, little or no black on breast; *caeruleitorques* like previous but top of head more uniformly brownish-red, brighter on nape. **Imm** dark crown; face and underparts dull buff; belly tinged reddish; chestnut nape; mantle dull green-brown; bluish wings and tail; pale bill base. **Voc** Song: *celebensis* long, drawn-out "wwaaaaaooop aaawwww", first note slightly quivering and rising, second note mournful, slightly downslurred, and shorter than first note, in total lasting 3.5 sec; *caeruleitorques* and *palliceps* similar but typically shorter at 2–2.5 sec.

North Moluccan Pitta *Erythropitta rufiventris* **E**

L 15–18 cm. 4 ssp: *rufiventris* (Morotai–Bacan), *cyanonota* (Ternate), *bernsteini* (Gebe), *obiensis* (Obi). Traditionally united with other pittas into a larger umbrella species (see Philippine Pitta for taxonomy), but differs from all others in mtDNA and a set of minor plumage traits. Uncommon, locally fairly common, in forest. Shy and elusive terrestrial dweller. **ID Ad** red belly; dull green upperparts; pale brown head, chestnut nape; extensive blue breast with thin black lower boundary; *cyanonota* upperparts dull blue, sometimes thin black line below breast; *bernsteini* like previous but paler blue overall; *obiensis* like nominate but paler blue throat. **Imm** dark crown; face and underparts dull buff; belly tinged reddish; chestnut nape; mantle dull green-brown; bluish wings and tail; pale bill base. **Voc** Song: long, drawn-out "wwaaaaaooop aaaaawwwwww", first note slightly quivering and rising, second note shorter, mournful and slightly downslurred, in total lasting 2.5–3 sec; typically lower-pitched than other 'Red-bellied' taxa.

South Moluccan Pitta *Erythropitta rubrinucha* **E**

L 15–18 cm. 2 ssp: *rubrinucha* (Buru), *piroensis* (Seram). Traditionally united with other pittas into a larger umbrella species (see Philippine Pitta for taxonomy), but differs from all others in mtDNA and pronounced plumage distinctions. Alternatively, *rubrinucha* and *piroensis* each sometimes elevated to monotypic species status. However, plumage differences and mtDNA divergences between the two are minor, and vocal differences remain undocumented. Uncommon, locally fairly common, in forest, predominantly >500 m, *piroensis* generally >1000 m. Shy and elusive terrestrial dweller. **ID Ad** red belly; deep chestnut head, red nape patch, pale blue crown stripe and ear-coverts; green upperparts; thin black bands above and below pale blue breast; *piroensis* darker green above, larger red nape patch. **Imm** dark crown; face and underparts dull buff; belly tinged reddish; chestnut nape; mantle dull green-brown; bluish wings and tail; pale bill base. **Voc** Song: *rubrinucha* long, drawn-out "wwaaaaaooop aaaaawwwwww", first note slightly quivering and rising, second mournful and slightly downslurred, notes of equal length, lasting 2.5 sec, regularly repeated; *piroensis* similar but slightly lower-pitched, first note rising less.

Papuan Pitta *Erythropitta macklotii*

L 15–18 cm. New Guinea to Aus. ~5 ssp, 1 in region; *macklotii* (Kai–Papua). Traditionally united with other pittas into a larger umbrella species (see Philippine Pitta for taxonomy). Alternatively, extralimital ssp *habenichti* (N Papua) is sometimes elevated to monotypic species status based on mtDNA, but lacks obvious vocal or plumage differences. Uncommon, locally fairly common, in forest, including heavily degraded patches. **ID Ad** red belly; blackish face; nape bright orange-rufous; ear-coverts and a stripe over eye tinged blue; green upperparts; blue breast with variable black lower breast band. **Imm** dark crown; face and underparts dull buff; belly tinged reddish; chestnut nape; mantle dull green-brown; bluish wings and tail; pale bill base. **Voc** Song: long, drawn-out "wwaaaaaooop aaaaawwwwww", first note slightly quivering and rising, second mournful and slightly downslurred, notes of equal length, lasting 2.5 sec; regularly repeated.

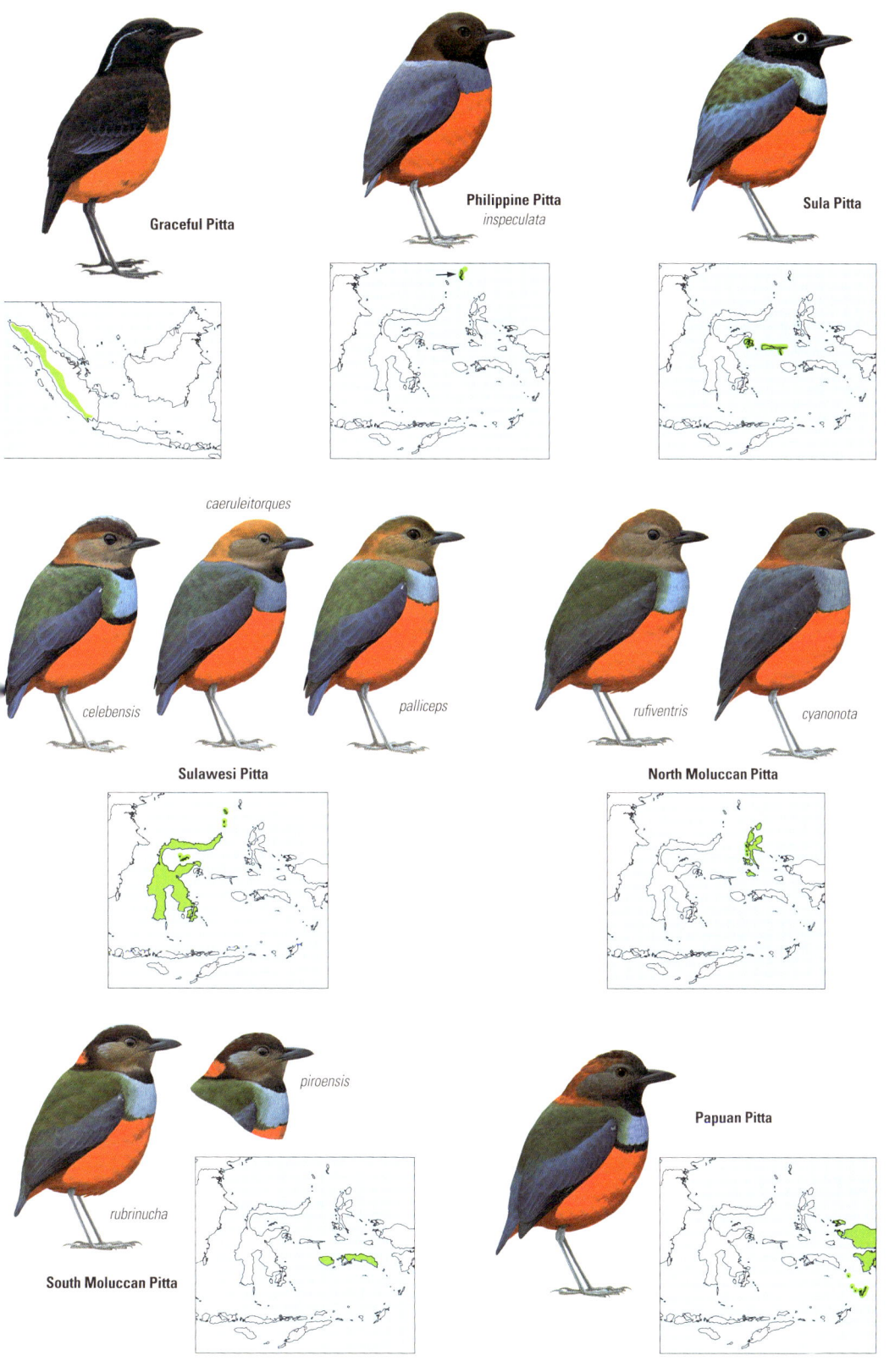

Graceful Pitta

Philippine Pitta
inspeculata

Sula Pitta

caeruleitorques

celebensis

palliceps

Sulawesi Pitta

rufiventris

cyanonota

North Moluccan Pitta

piroensis

rubrinucha

South Moluccan Pitta

Papuan Pitta

Blue-winged Pitta *Pitta moluccensis*

L 18–20 cm. Breeds mainland SE Asia; Sundaic winterer. Monotypic. Fairly common migrant in all types of woodland, including scrub, jungle, city parks and plantations, usually <500 m but recorded <1800 m. Terrestrial, but often perches up to 20 m when calling. **ID Ad** black head with broad, long, buff supercilium; white throat with black chin; green upperparts with blue rump and wing-coverts; black outerwing with large white wing patch; buff underparts with red vent and central belly-stripe. **Imm** duller overall; brownish head; dull green upperparts; lacks red vent. **Voc** Song: clear, whistled, double 2-note "WUHU-WUHU", lasting 1 sec (see Mangrove Pitta for similar vocalisation). Call: short, sharp "skyeew". **SS** Mangrove Pitta (note habitat and call) very similar but (i) has stronger and longer bill with flat (not arched) upper culmen and pronounced gonydeal angle, (ii) red on belly not extending to breast, (iii) white (not black) chin, (iv) duller darker-brown crown extending further back onto nape and down sides, almost reaching eyes; (v) thinner, less conspicuous black central crown stripe not reaching as far back onto hindcrown (whereas Blue-winged's thicker crown stripe almost meets black nape). Fairy Pitta has blue on wing restricted to lesser wing-coverts, paler underparts, smaller white wing patch, and crown distinctly tricoloured (with pale-buff supercilium, black central crown stripe and more rufous remainder of crown).

Mangrove Pitta *Pitta megarhyncha*

L 18–21 cm. SE Asia. Monotypic. Locally uncommon in mangroves and surrounding nipa palms. One specimen from Sarawak likely mislabeled. Feeds on ground amongst mangroves and surrounding vegetation at low tide. At high tide flies onto trees or moves to nearby dry vegetation. Has been found straying far outside mangroves into parks and scrub. **ID Ad** similar to Blue-winged Pitta but much longer, larger bill; buff-rufous crown; upperparts slightly duller. **Imm** duller; upperparts and crown largely blackish-green; dirty-buff underparts. **Voc** Song: loud, clear, whistled "WUHU-WHUU", lasting 0.8 sec, last note not disyllabic as in Blue-winged; shorter gap between notes. Call: short, sharp "skyeew". **SS** See Blue-winged Pitta.

Fairy Pitta *Pitta nympha*

L 19 cm. Breeds E Asia; winters Bor. Monotypic. Vagrant to Anambas (Oct 2019) and Java (3; Oct–Nov 2019). Rare, probably much overlooked, in all types of woodland including scrub and primary lowland forest, <1100 m. **ID Ad** similar to Blue-winged Pitta but smaller, crown sides buff-rufous, paler underparts and blue restricted to lesser wing-coverts; smaller white wing patch. **Imm** much duller; large white spots on wing-coverts; bill with orange tip. **Voc** Song: drawn-out, throaty, 2-note "wooHU-hu", lasting 1.2 sec. Call: sharp, explosive "kriaih" or "kahay-kahay". **SS** See Blue-winged Pitta.

Wallace's Elegant Pitta *Pitta concinna* 🄴

L 19 cm. Monotypic. Previously considered conspecific with Temminck's and Banda Elegant Pittas but split based on pronounced vocal and plumage differences. Resident in all types of woodland including scrub, plantations, <1500 m; less habitat-specific than other pittas. Largely terrestrial but can perch high up in canopy to call. **ID Ad** black head with rufous fore-supercilium turning white behind eye; dark, bright-green upperparts with turquoise-blue lesser-coverts and rump; white wing patch at base of black primaries; black tail tipped green; black triangle on throat extends to upper breast; extensive black belly patch turns red on vent. **Imm** duller; less blue on wings; pinkish belly patch; red bill base. **Voc** Song: throaty, loud, 2-note "wer-her", lasting 0.5 sec, first note more drawn-out than second. Call: sudden, hard "skew". **SS** Temminck's Elegant Pitta, which migrates through range of Wallace's, has black on throat not extending to upper breast, all-pale supercilium (no strong rufous anteriorly), and extensive red (less black) on lower belly. Also note strong vocal difference. **AN** Ornate Pitta.

Temminck's Elegant Pitta *Pitta elegans* 🄴

L 19 cm. 3 ssp: *elegans* (breeds Timor, Rote [Nov-Mar]; migrates through LS to Sul, Mol [Mar-Nov]), *virginalis* (Flores Sea Is), *maria* (Sumba). For taxonomy see Wallace's Elegant Pitta. Ssp *maria* exhibits important plumage distinctions but is vocally weakly differentiated; more research needed. All types of woodland including scrub, plantations, <1200 m, but *elegans* prefers coastal forest. Largely terrestrial but can perch high up in canopy to call. **ID Ad** black head with long, thin, pale-buff supercilium; black triangle on throat; black flight feathers with white wing patch at base of primaries; extensive red belly and vent patch with black upper belly. Ssp *virginalis* has broader, more rufous supercilium; less extensive black on throat appearing as prominent chin line; broader belly patch. Ssp *maria* wholly red belly patch; no white on wing. **Imm** duller overall; less blue on wings; pinkish belly patch; red bill base. **Voc** Song: *elegans* and *virginalis* throaty, loud 3-note "wer-doo-dew", lasting 0.7 sec; *maria* similar although perhaps marginally faster (especially first two notes). Call: sudden, hard "skew". **SS** See Wallace's Elegant Pitta. **AN** Elegant Pitta

Banda Elegant Pitta *Pitta vigorsii* 🄴

L 19 cm. Monotypic. For taxonomy see Wallace's Elegant Pitta. All types of woodland including scrub, plantations. May perform local movements, but more study required. Call activity highly seasonal; remains silent during other times. Largely terrestrial but can perch high up in canopy to call. **ID Ad** black head with long, thin, pale buff supercilium turning white to rear; white throat and chin; black flight feathers with white wing patch at base of primaries; extensive red belly patch with black upper belly; underparts slightly darker than other elegant pittas. **Imm** duller overall; less blue on wings; pinkish belly patch; red bill base. **Voc** Two song types (often given by same individual within short time): (1) loud, throaty two-note "werh werh", akin to Wallace's Elegant Pitta but with a much longer break, lasting 0.7 sec; and (2) three-note "werh werh werh" of the same quality, lasting 1.1 sec. Call: high-pitched, squeaky and long "skyeew". **AN** Banda Sea Pitta.

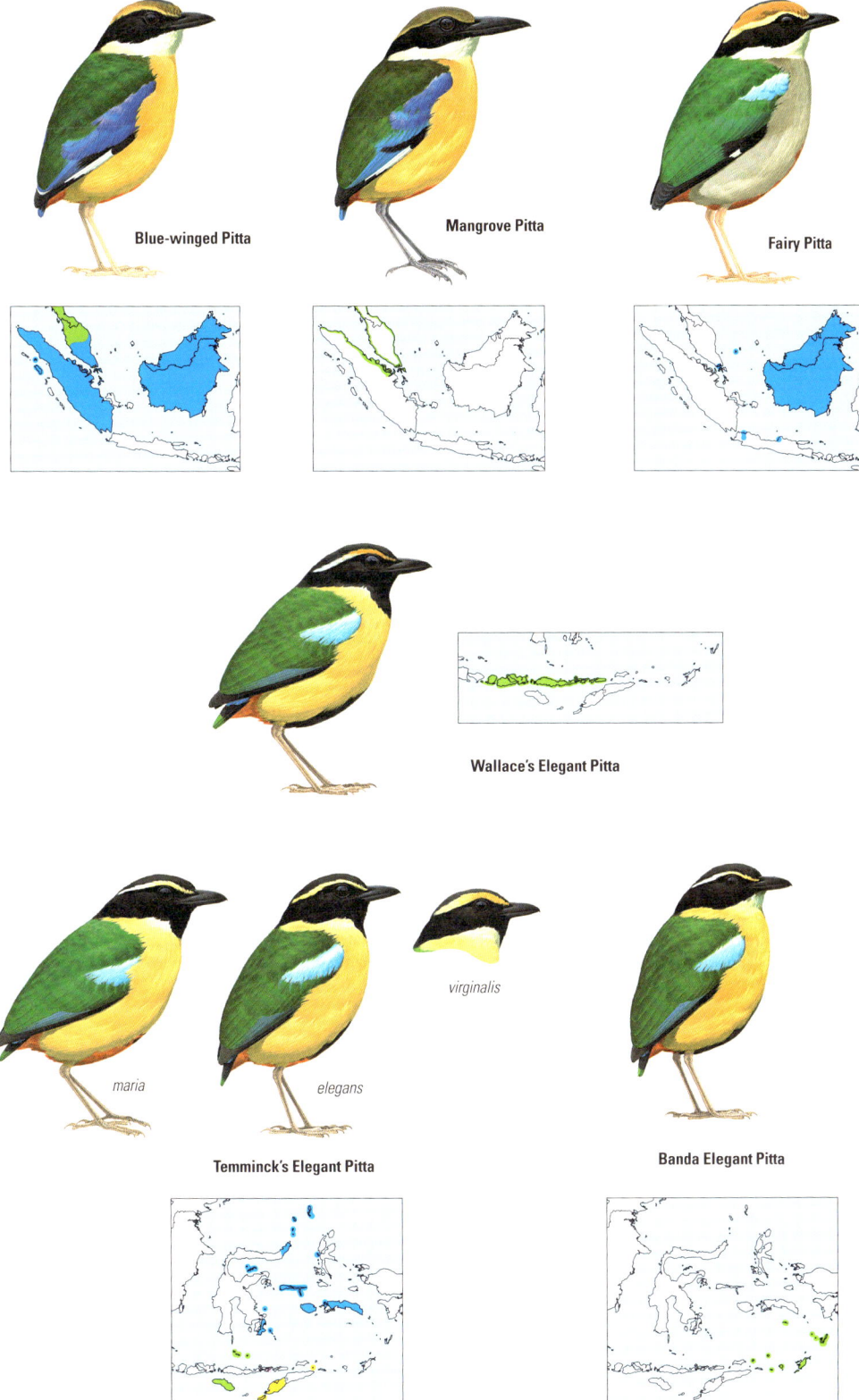

Blue-winged Pitta

Mangrove Pitta

Fairy Pitta

Wallace's Elegant Pitta

virginalis

maria

elegans

Temminck's Elegant Pitta

Banda Elegant Pitta

Ivory-breasted Pitta *Pitta maxima* E

L 24–27 cm. 2 ssp: *maxima* (Halmahera, Kasiruta, Bacan); ssp *morotaiensis* (Morotai) sometimes divided into monotypic species but plumage and vocal differences minor. Fairly common in primary, secondary and degraded forest, particularly on limestone, <500 m, on Morotai <800 m. Highly arboreal when vocalising, often calling from lower canopy, <20 m. **ID Ad** upperparts including head wholly black; azure-blue upperwing-coverts; white breast to lower flanks; undertail and belly red, tipped black; small white primary patch. Ssp *morotaiensis* darker blue upperwing-coverts and larger white primary patch. **Imm** buff on underparts. **Voc** (i) Loud, far-carrying, eerie "wok-whoou", lasting 1.5 sec, first note short and loud, second tailing off; *morotaiensis* has shorter second note, "wok-whou", lasting <1 sec. (ii) Single, hollow "whooou", lasting 1.5 sec.

Asian Hooded Pitta *Pitta sordida*

L 16–18 cm. S–SE Asia, Phil. 7 ssp, 4 in region: *cucullata* (breeds mainland S–SE Asia; winters to Sum, Jav), *bangkana* (Bangka, Belitung), *mulleri* (MPen, GS), *sanghirana* (Sangihe). Previously merged with Minahasa Hooded and extralimital Eastern Hooded Pitta *P. novaeguineae* (NG) into larger '**Hooded Pitta**' *P. sordida* umbrella species, but vocal, genomic and some plumage differences dictate the present division. Within Asian Hooded, ssp *sanghirana* and extralimital *sordida* (Phil) stand out in belly colour and are somewhat molecularly diverged, but extralimital *palawanensis* (Palawan) is the genomic bridge between them and remaining ssp. Migratory *cucullata* sometimes considered separate species based on strong ecological and plumage differences, but is virtually indistinguishable genomically and vocally from *mulleri*. Locally fairly common in lowland forest, particularly swamp forest, <600 m, even occurring in scrub and plantations on migration. Wintering *cucullata* may form loose flocks when migrating and is found from Sep–Apr. Perches <10 m to call. **ID Ad** (*cucullata*) black head; chocolate brown crown; green body (breast tinged blue); azure-blue rump and upperwing-coverts; red lower belly; small black patch on upper belly; large white primary patch. Ssp *mulleri* lacks blue breast tinge and has entirely black crown; *bangkana* intermediate between *mulleri* and *cucullata* with variable amounts of brown on crown; *sanghirana* like *mulleri* but darker overall, breast tinged blue, more black on belly. **Imm** duller overall; black-and-red belly undeveloped; buffy underparts. **Voc** Song: sharp couplet consisting of two well-separated whistles "whe whe", lasting 0.7 sec, sometimes given continuously. Call: sharp "skyew".

Minahasa Hooded Pitta *Pitta forsteni* E

L 17–18 cm. Monotypic. For taxonomy see Asian Hooded Pitta. Little-known in life, seemingly scarce and highly localised with few recent records. Favouring rattan and palm-dominated ravines in lowland forest. **ID Ad** like Asian Hooded Pitta ssp *sanghirana*, but larger, lacks white in primaries, has green tail, distinct turquoise tinge to nape, and extensive black belly. **Imm** undescribed. **Voc** Strident couplet like Asian Hooded but more high-pitched, notes delivered faster, less well-separated. **SS** When flushed, Temminck's Elegant Pitta shows conspicuous white wing patch.

MELIPHAGIDAE
Honeyeaters
35 species in region

Large, diverse family of small to medium-sized birds, most with long decurved bills. Typically arboreal, they are found in a variety of forest and wooded habitats where usually active and conspicuous. Some species are colourful, others are drab.

Lesser Myza *Myza celebensis* E

L 17 cm. 2 ssp: *celebensis* (N, C, SE Sul); *meridionalis* (SW Sul). Uncommon in montane forest, 900–2500 m. Forages in mid- to high storey. Singly, pairs or part of mixed flocks. Generally replaced by Greater Myza at higher elevations with some overlap. **ID Ad** uniformly olive-brown with dark blackish-brown streaking and scaling; bold whitish eyering; bill black; legs dark grey-brown. Ssp *meridionalis* smaller with greyer upperparts and finer streaking on underparts. **Imm** undescribed. **Voc** Song: excited whirring trill, increasing in tempo, "whir'r'r'r'r'r'…", lasting 0.5–1.5 sec at 10 n/s. Call: sharp, slightly rasping "kik". **SS** From larger Greater Myza by colder, less reddish underparts, presence of eyering and lack of ear patch. **AN** Dark-eared or Lesser Streaked Honeyeater.

Greater Myza *Myza sarasinorum* E

L 20 cm. 3 ssp: *sarasinorum* (N Sul); *chionogenys* (C Sul); *pholidota* (SE Sul). Fairly common in montane forest and heath, 1700–2800 m. Forages in mid- to high storey. Singly, pairs or part of mixed flocks. Generally replaces Lesser Myza at higher elevations with some overlap. **ID Ad** upperparts dark brown with blackish streaking; wings dark with reddish wash to edges; forehead, crown, lores and throat blackish with fine grey streaking, contrasting with prominent bare violet ear patch; underparts dark reddish brown with heavy streaking; bill and legs black. Ssp *chionogenys* has white ear patch; *pholidota* underparts greyer, with bolder blackish streaking. **Imm** undescribed. **Voc** Squeaky yelping "kip", regularly repeated at short intervals. **SS** See Lesser Myza. **AN** White-eared or Greater Streaked Honeyeater.

Scaly-crowned Honeyeater *Sugomel lombokium* E

L 14 cm. Monotypic. Not part of *Lichmera* honeyeaters with which formerly included, but more closely related to myzomelas. Common in montane forest to open flowering scrub, >1000 m, on Lombok >450 m. Singly or small groups, joins mixed flocks; active in mid- to lower storey. **ID Ad** olive-green upperparts, wings and tail; throat, face and forehead greyer with indistinct dark scaling on crown; underparts paler yellow-grey. **Imm** undescribed. **Voc** Poorly known; (i) constant, squeaky chattering; (ii) harsh, low-pitched "eeww". **SS** From Brown Honeyeater by lack of dark 'mask', yellower overall colour of underparts and lack of yellowish wing panel.

Brown Honeyeater *Lichmera indistincta*

L 15 cm. Aus. 5 ssp, 1 in region: ssp *limbata* (Bali–Timor), previously considered a monotypic species '**Indonesian Honeyeater**' but indistinct in plumage, vocalisations and genetics. Locally common in open forest, scrub, mangroves, villages and gardens, <2600 m. Singly or small groups; noisy and conspicuous in understorey to canopy. **ID M** grey head and upperparts with contrasting yellow panel on closed wing, yellow edging to tail, and dark grey-black mask; pale yellow patch behind eye not always visible; underparts pale grey, whiter on throat and tinged yellow on belly and flanks. **F** bright yellow throat. **Imm** lacks yellow face patch, has pale gape line. **Voc** Variety of loud, melodious notes with much variation. Song: typically repetitive series of 4–10 fast, upslurred "whit'whit'whit…" lasting ~1 sec, interspersed with call notes. Call: (i) sharp, loud "chit" or "chip"; (ii) buzzy, scratchy notes; (iii) loud, melodious "CHEWIT" or "CHEWIT-10IT". **SS** See Scaly-crowned Honeyeater.

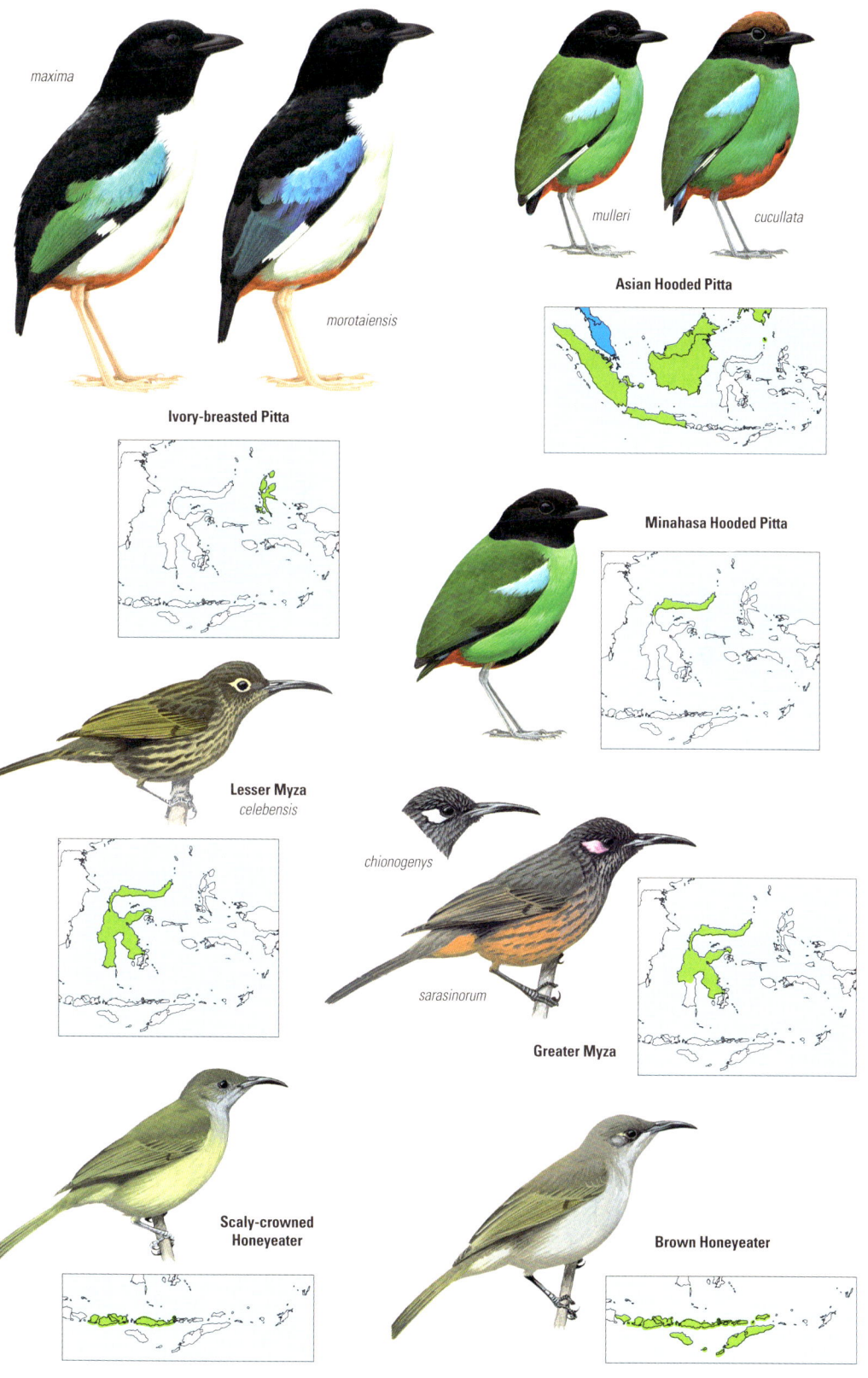

maxima

morotaiensis

Ivory-breasted Pitta

mulleri

cucullata

Asian Hooded Pitta

Minahasa Hooded Pitta

Lesser Myza
celebensis

chionogenys

sarasinorum

Greater Myza

Scaly-crowned Honeyeater

Brown Honeyeater

Olive Honeyeater *Lichmera argentauris*

L 13.5–15.5 cm. W Papuan Is, C–N Mol. Monotypic. Typical super-tramp from small wooded or scrubby islets, where can be noisy, conspicuous and abundant in mid-storey to undergrowth. Currently known in region only from Lusaolate (off N Seram), Kekek (off E Obi), and Damar (off S Halmahera) but presumably more widespread. Lusaolate, at least, appears to be inhabited seasonally. **ID Ad** olive-brown head and upperparts with contrasting yellow-edged flight and tail feathers; conspicuous pale yellow skin patch behind eye and variable pale silvery-blue feathering on ear-coverts; throat and rest of underparts pale grey with yellow wash and faint darker streaking. **Imm** pink facial patch. **Voc** Song: loud, stuttering, melodious "t't't'chit'chit'chit'chit'chit-whip", lasting 1 sec. Call: loud, melodious whiplash-like "whip'IT".

Buru Honeyeater *Lichmera deningeri* E

L 15–16 cm. Monotypic. Fairly common in montane forest, edge and scrub, >1000 m, most numerous >1500 m. Singly or pairs, often with mixed flocks. **ID Ad** upperparts olive-green tinged grey on head and back; wing and tail feathers edged yellow; sides of head, throat and breast grey, becoming yellower on belly; bill dark at tip becoming brighter yellow at base; thin yellow line extending from base of bill to base of yellowish orbital ring. **Imm** undescribed. **Voc** Song: 3–5 loud, monotonous "tchew-tchew-tchew", occasionally with disyllabic introductory "t'chit t'chit", lasting 1–2 sec. Call: very harsh, rasping screech "zzzzt", given singly or in bouts of 2–3 notes. **SS** See Buru Myzomela.

Seram Honeyeater *Lichmera monticola* E

L 15–17 cm. Monotypic. Fairly common in montane forest and heath, >1000 m, most numerous >1500 m. Singly or pairs, often with mixed flocks. **ID Ad** upperparts olive-green tinged grey on head and back; wing and tail feathers edged yellow; forehead and lores dark grey contrasting with pale yellow-white orbital ring, ear patch and thin line extending from base of bill to below eye; throat and breast streaked dark grey; underparts pale yellow-grey; bill dark at tip, yellow-buff at base. **Imm** undescribed. **Voc** Song: loud, melodious, ascending "twit-too twit-tit", lasting 1 sec. Call: mono- or disyllabic harsh, hissing "pisss", or "pisss-pisss". **SS** See Drab and Seram Myzomelas.

Banda Honeyeater *Lichmera squamata* E

L 15 cm. Monotypic. Common in wooded lowland habitat including forest, plantation, villages, scrub and mangroves. Singly or small groups; noisy and conspicuous in understorey to canopy. **ID Ad** head, upperparts and tail olive-brown with yellowish edging to flight feathers and tail and slightly paler yellow rump; dark mask around eye with small white spot often visible behind eye; pale whitish malar stripe; throat yellowish-white; breast and flanks grey, occasionally washed yellow-olive, with conspicuous dark scaling. **Imm** pale pinkish spot behind eye; may lack scaling on breast and flanks. **Voc** Wide variety of screeching and melodious whistling; (i) rapidly repeated, sharp and harsh whistling "tchit-tchit-tchit...", 6 n/s; (ii) squeaky, incessant "whit" or "witchit"; (iii) downslurred or upslurred whistled "chirrup"; (iv) loud descending trill of moderate pitch, "teu, tutututututututututututu-tu-lu", lasting 2–5 sec. **AN** Scaly-breasted Honeyeater, White-eared Honeyeater.

Yellow-eared Honeyeater *Lichmera flavicans* E

L 12–14 cm. Monotypic. Fairly common in monsoon and dry forest and edge, most numerous >1000 m. Singly, pairs or small groups (<12). **ID Ad** upperparts rich olive green; darker around lores and eye giving masked appearance, enhanced by grey-white submoustachial stripe and bright yellow-orange ear patch; underparts yellow, occasionally with grey wash, heavily streaked dark green. **Imm** grey underparts and lacks yellow-orange ear patch. **Voc** Song: bewildering variety of loud, melodious notes, often with staccato introductory notes, each series lasting 1–3 sec. Call: (i) short, soft nasal "bzz"; (ii) loud, melodious disyllabic "chip-chip". **SS** See Timor Meliphaga. **AN** Flame-eared Honeyeater.

Black-necklaced Honeyeater *Lichmera notabilis* E

L 13–15 cm. Monotypic. Common in eucalypt forest, less common in other forest types, edge. Singly, pairs or small groups (<10); usually around flowering trees. **ID Ad** olive-green upperparts boldly streaked black; forehead and crown blackish contrasting with blue-grey eyestripe and ear patch; bright white throat and upper breast, bordered black; underparts yellow, heavily streaked black; bill and legs black. **Imm** undescribed. **Voc** Song: 2-note, scratchy buzz "TZEE–TZEE".

Timor Meliphaga *Meliphaga reticulata* E

L 15 cm. Monotypic. Fairly common in forest, edge and lightly wooded areas, <1400 m. Singly, pairs or small groups; particularly around flowering trees. **ID Ad** upperparts olive-grey, with greener edging to wing feathers; underparts grey-white with bold brownish streaking becoming more diffuse to rear; head distinctly marked with bright yellow-orange ear patch and white submoustachial stripe thinly bordered black; bill black; legs dark grey. **Imm** undescribed. **Voc** (i) <15 continually repeated, loud, upslurred "wheep-wheep-wheep" notes at 4 n/s; (ii) slightly croaky, more level "week-week-week", repeated at uneven intervals. **SS** From Yellow-eared Honeyeater by white to grey-white (not yellow) throat and underparts. **AN** Streak-breasted Honeyeater.

White-streaked Honeyeater *Melitograis gilolensis* E

L 23 cm. Monotypic. Only distantly related to friarbirds, with which it was previously associated ("White-streaked/Halmahera Friarbird"). Uncommon in forest, edge, lightly wooded areas and mangroves. Singly, pairs or small groups; inconspicuous though not shy. **ID Ad** blackish-brown body, wings and tail; fine white streaking on underparts and back becoming more prominent on throat and head, and forming a distinctive tufty off-white crown; bare blue-black skin from lores around eye to nape; bill and legs blackish. **Imm** undescribed. **Voc** Song: reportedly a moderately high-pitched, unmusical note at 1 n/s. Call: harsh rasping note. **SS** See Halmahera Oriole. **AN** White-streaked Friarbird.

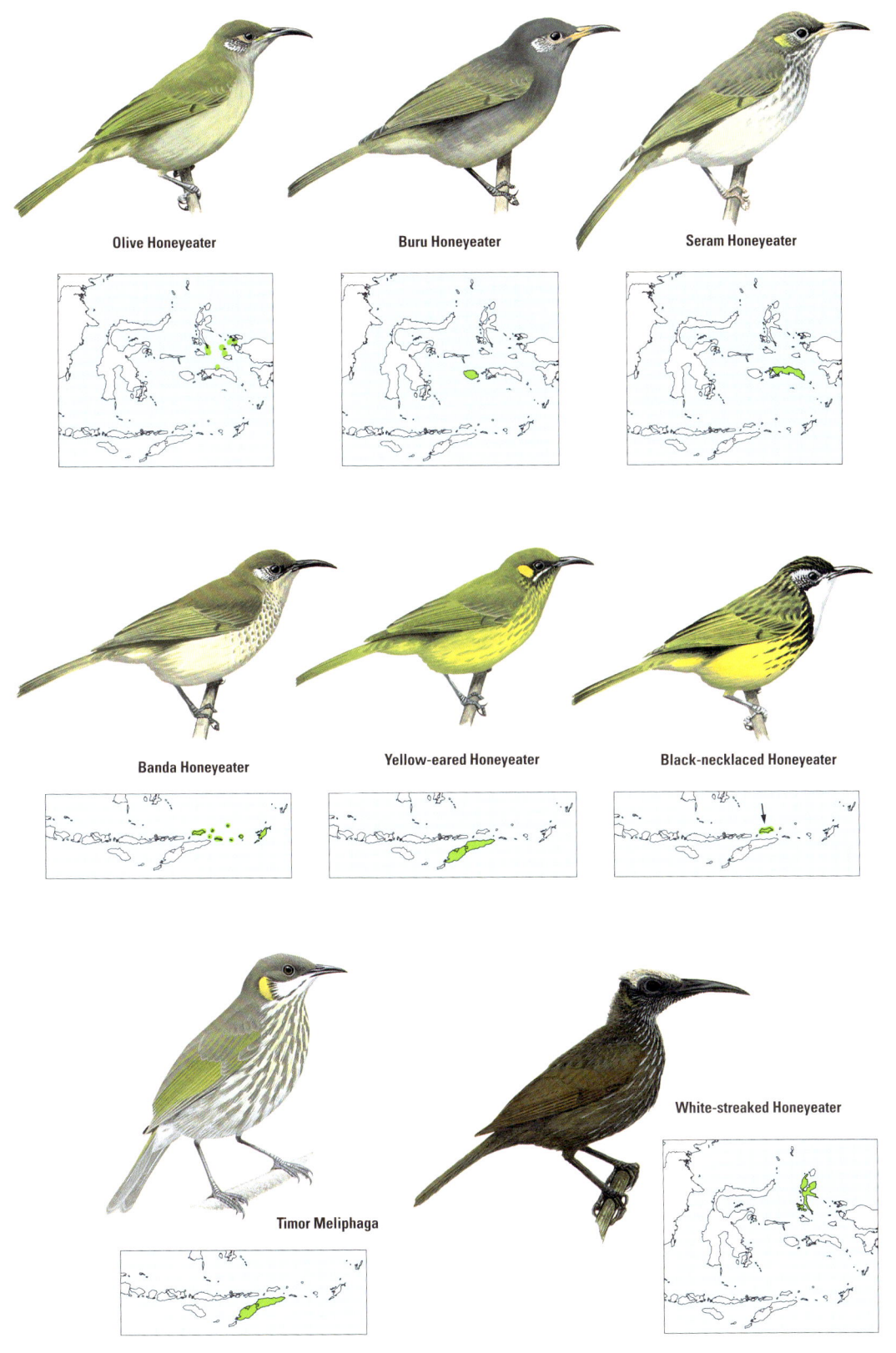

Olive Honeyeater

Buru Honeyeater

Seram Honeyeater

Banda Honeyeater

Yellow-eared Honeyeater

Black-necklaced Honeyeater

Timor Meliphaga

White-streaked Honeyeater

Drab Myzomela *Myzomela blasii* **E**
L 10–12 cm. Monotypic. Uncommon in forest and edge, 600–2200 m, rarely lower. Inconspicuous, often feeding in flowering treetops. **ID Ad** small and drab; upperparts dull olive-grey; underparts paler yellow-grey or grey; throat and upper breast whitish with conspicuous dark grey scaling; faint pale eyering; bill and legs black. **Imm** undescribed. **Voc** (i) Rapid, very high-pitched, thin "sis'sis'sis..." at 7 n/s, lasting <6 sec; (ii) constant mixed chatter, lower and higher notes with no obvious structure "pist-chit-chit-p'p'p't-pist-chit, pist-chit-chit...", >5 n/s. **SS** Larger Seram Honeyeater shows facial pattern and pale bill base. Told from fem Seram Myzomela by throat/breast scaling and lack of red-tinged head.

Sultan's Myzomela *Myzomela simplex* **E**
L 13–15 cm. 2 ssp: *simplex* (Halmahera, Ternate, Tidore, Kasiruta, Bacan); *mortyana* (Morotai). Formerly merged into larger Australo-Papuan '**Dusky Myzomela**' *M. obscura* along with Red-tinged Myzomela and two extralimital species. However, plumage differences relatively pronounced, and DNA research shows distant relationship within genus between some members, necessitating separation. Uncommon in forest and edge, more common at higher elevations. Singly or small groups, often associating with sunbirds and other species at fruiting trees. **ID Ad** generally dull drab-brown with variable pink wash on breast that is mostly indiscernible in the field; flight and tail feathers edged red (hard to see); bill and legs blackish. Ssp *mortyana* darker, with variable dull red (sometimes spots, sometimes indiscernible) on darker breast, contrasting with paler belly. **Imm** possibly with paler rump and paler edging to wing-coverts. **Voc** Song composed of tinkling repetitions of "tsit-tsut, tsit-tsut". Ssp *mortyana* additionally known to give song composed of 6 very thin, quiet simple notes "t't'tit-tit-too-tit", lasting 1.5 sec. Call: very quiet, thin, high "tih'". Songs are regularly repeated rapidly in longer series. **SS** Fem Black Sunbird has at least some yellow on underparts and a grey-versus-olive contrast on upperparts. See also Bacan Myzomela.

Red-tinged Myzomela *Myzomela rubrotincta* **E**
L 13–15 cm. Monotypic. For taxonomy see Sultan's Myzomela. Fairly common in forest and edge, more common at mid- to higher elevations. Singly or small groups, often associating with sunbirds and other species at fruiting trees. **ID Ad** similar to Sultan's Myzomela but darker brown, with strong red wash to wings, back and tail. **Imm** possibly with paler rump and paler edging to wing-coverts. **Voc** Song composed of 3 rising, thin, high-pitched notes "wit-see-sih'", lasting 0.4 sec, occasionally lower last note, regularly repeated rapidly in longer series. **SS** See Obi Myzomela.

Wetar Myzomela *Myzomela kuehni* **E**
L 11 cm. Monotypic. Fairly common in tropical and dry forest, edge, cashew plantations. Singly, pairs or small groups (<10); usually around flowering trees. **ID Ad** red head to upper breast contrasting with dull grey-brown nape, sides of neck, back and wings; rump and uppertail-coverts red; underparts greyish-white; blackish lores extending to form narrow black eyering; bill and legs blackish. **F** red hood not extending to breast. **Imm** undescribed. **Voc** Song: 20–25 rapid high-pitched twittering notes at 10 n/s. Call: hard, high-pitched, downslurred "tsieuw". **AN** Crimson-hooded Myzomela.

Alor Myzomela *Myzomela prawiradilagae* **E**
L 11 cm. Monotypic. Scarce in montane eucalypt forest of central and east Alor, >1000 m. Singly, pairs or small groups (<5); feeds in mid- and upper canopy. **ID M** bright crimson-red hood extending to lower throat; with black lores; mid-grey mantle and upper breast; paler and whiter belly; darker wings and tail; crimson rump. **F** similar but red hood less extensive with grey lower throat and nape. **Imm** olive-grey head and upperparts with red restricted to chin and forecrown. **Voc** Song: high-pitched series, with 2 introductory "sip-sip" notes followed by slightly higher-pitched and faster "tit'tit'tit..." at 9 n/s, lasting 1–2.5 sec. Call: high-pitched rising, then falling "tssip".

Sumba Myzomela *Myzomela dammermani* **E**
L 11 cm. Monotypic. Uncommon in forest and edge. Singly or pairs, joins mixed flocks; favouring canopy of flowering trees. **ID M** bright red hood and rump; back, wings, tail, breast and flanks black, becoming grey-white towards belly; black lores extend to narrow black eyering; bill and legs blackish. **F** grey-brown upperparts, slightly paler underparts with red wash to chin and narrowly on forecrown. Either sex can show yellow gape depending on breeding cycle. **Imm** undescribed. **Voc** Song: series of 3 different motifs, continuously alternating, from exposed perch; (i) thin, buzzy, undulating "tzeeepipizeep", lasting 0.6 sec; (ii) 3 thin, downslurred, slightly buzzy "tzip-tzip-zeep", lasting 0.5 sec; (iii) rapid, thin, rattled "ti'ti'ti'ti'tit..." at 12 n/0.5 s. Call: thin, sharp "swipt".

Rote Myzomela *Myzomela irianawidodoae* **E**
L 11 cm. Monotypic. Uncommon in montane, forest edge. Singly or pairs; favouring canopy. **ID M** as Sumba but narrower black breast band. **F** very similar to Sumba. **Voc** Variable repertoire. Most commonly heard song a series of hard, high-pitched, downslurred "zip" notes, lasting <1 sec, at 6 n/s. **Imm** undescribed.

Timor Myzomela *Myzomela vulnerata* **E**
L 10 cm. Monotypic. Uncommon in primary, secondary and montane forest and edge. Singly, pairs or mixed flocks. **ID M** head, breast and upperparts black apart from contrasting bright red crown, throat patch and rump; underparts grey-white. **F** black lacks gloss, faded to sooty-brown. **Imm** black parts are greyer. **Voc** Song: 8–12 rapid, very high-pitched, thin "sisisisisisis..." at 8 n/s. Call: metallic "sit", often in long series at 5 n/s. **AN** Black-chested, Black-breasted or Red-rumped Myzomela.

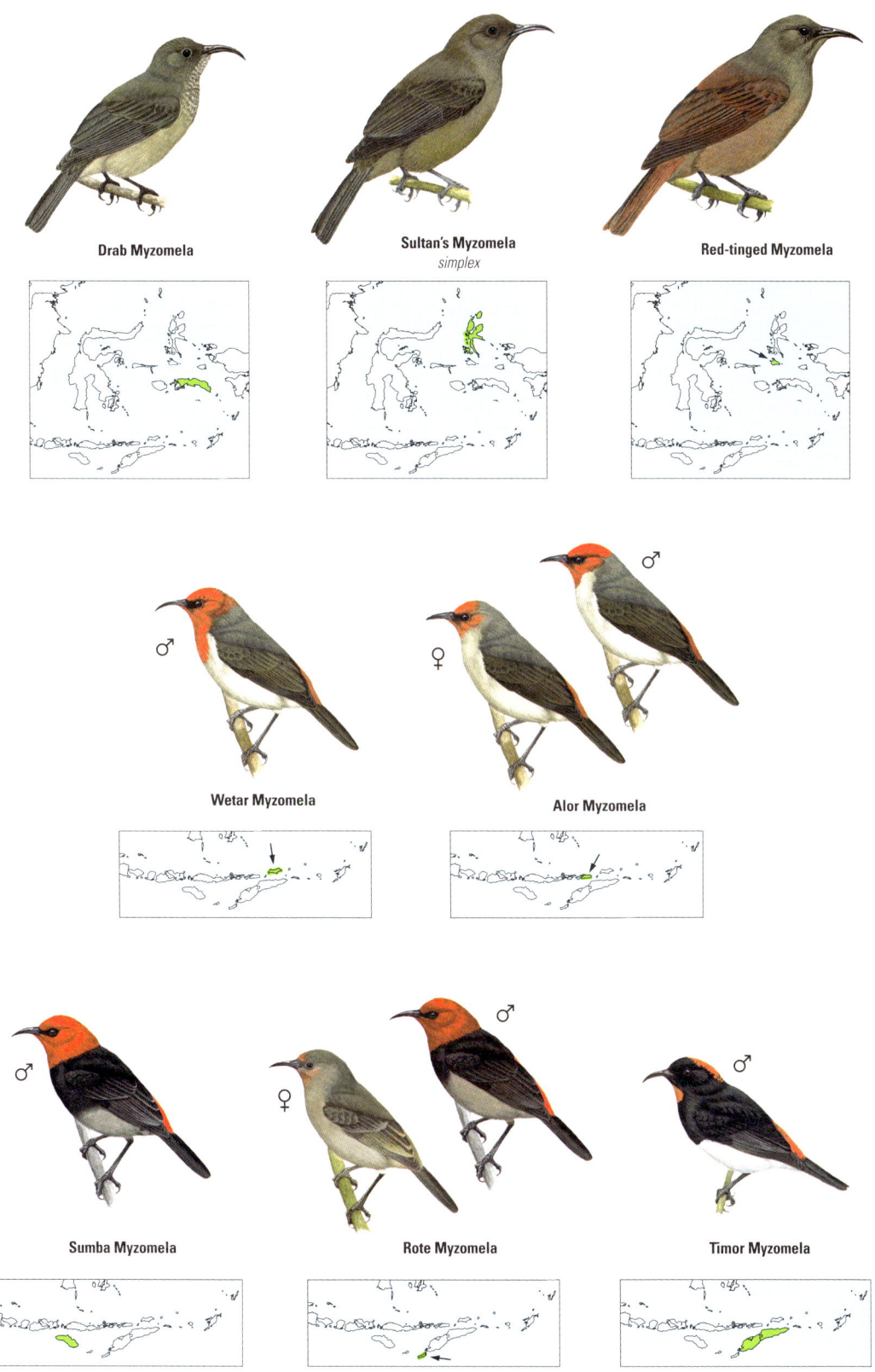

Drab Myzomela

Sultan's Myzomela
simplex

Red-tinged Myzomela

Wetar Myzomela

Alor Myzomela

Sumba Myzomela

Rote Myzomela

Timor Myzomela

Banda Myzomela *Myzomela boiei* [E]

L 9–12 cm. Monotypic. Has traditionally included Tanimbar Myzomela but exhibits strong vocal and some plumage differences. Uncommon in forest, edge, coconut groves, lightly wooded cultivation and mangrove. Singly, pairs or mixed flocks. **ID M** red head, back and uppertail-coverts contrasting with black wings and tail; red throat and upper breast bordered by thick black neck band; underparts grey-white with obscure streaking on breast and strong dusky streaks on vent. **F** similar to Tanimbar Myzomela. **Imm** undescribed. **Voc** Song: rapid high-pitched dissonant jumbly burst, very unlike Tanimbar Myzomela. Calls: variable "chip" notes, often alternating up and down; also di- or trisyllabic, thin, high-pitched "see-sit" or "s'see'sit".

Tanimbar Myzomela *Myzomela annabellae* [E]

L 9–12 cm. Monotypic. For taxonomy see Banda Myzomela. Uncommon in forest, edge, lightly wooded cultivation and mangrove. Singly, pairs or mixed flocks. **ID M** similar to Banda Myzomela but black breast band narrower; vent mostly pale-coloured, lacking strong dusky streaks; underparts variable from dull grey-white with grey streaking on flanks and lower breast (Tanimbar) to clean white with only slight grey tinge on flanks (Babar). **F** brown overall with paler brown head and underparts; variable red wash on head. **Imm** undescribed. **Voc** Song: melodious series of three level-pitched notes followed by pleasing trill "we-we-we-tr'r'r'r'r'r'r'r'r'r...", lasting 1 sec. Call: di- or trisyllabic, thin, high-pitched "see-sit" or "s'see'sit".

Sulawesi Myzomela *Myzomela chloroptera* [E]

L 9–12 cm. 3 ssp: *chloroptera* (SE–C –N Sul); *juga* (SW Sul; Selayar; Tanahjampea); ssp. (Peleng). The population on Peleng is poorly known in life and likely represents an undescribed subspecies. Often includes Bacan and Obi Myzomelas but consistent plumage and vocal differences comparable to those separating other species. Uncommon in forest, edge, gardens, >800 m, but to sea level on smaller islands. Singly, pairs, small groups or mixed flocks. **ID M** red head extending to belly and flanks; off-white to sooty-grey rear underparts, often becoming buff-yellow towards undertail-coverts; back and rump red; wings and tail black. Ssp *juga* slightly larger, with black of wings and tail replaced by dark brown. **F** dull brown above, with reddish rump and pale reddish throat to lower ear-coverts. **Imm** undescribed. **Voc** Song: (i) alternating series of high-pitched, rapid, upslurred elements with 2 introductory notes; first a series of <12 notes "pew-twit wip'wip'wip..." lasting <2 sec, followed by "too-wit tit'tit'tit..." lasting <1.5 sec, at 13 n/s; (ii) jumbled mix of ascending, thin, metallic notes "chee-tit-tit-toit", lasting 0.8 sec. Call: sharp disyllabic "treeu'tree", second note higher-pitched.

Bacan Myzomela *Myzomela batjanensis* [E]

L 9–10 cm. Monotypic. Obi Myzomela sometimes included here but differs substantially in plumage and voice. For taxonomy also see Sulawesi Myzomela. Little known; uncommon in forest, >900 m. Singly, pairs, small groups or mixed flocks. **ID M** red restricted to head and throat, extending slightly onto upper breast; underparts grey-white with some buff feathering; appears to show blackish 'tabs' (half collar) on sides of breast. **F** probably similar to fem Sulawesi Myzomela. **Imm** undescribed. **Voc** (i) 5-note high-pitched buzz, increasing slightly in tempo and pitch, "pisst-piss-piss-piss-pisst", lasting 1.8 sec; (ii) high-pitched, squeaky "pitchoo". **SS** Sultan's Myzomela identification requires care given that the smaller fem Bacan Myzomela is so poorly known: Sultan's should always be darker and more uniform overall than Bacan Myzomela, lacking a red throat that may be present in fem Bacan Myzomela.

Obi Myzomela *Myzomela* sp. [E]

L 9–10 cm. Undescribed monotypic species. For taxonomy see Sulawesi and Bacan Myzomelas. Little known; uncommon in forest, >350 m, more common at higher elevations. Singly, pairs, small groups or mixed flocks. **ID M** similar to Bacan Myzomela but red extending much further onto breast in centre, and greyer feathering on belly and flanks. **F** unknown, but probably similar to fem Sulawesi Myzomela. **Voc** Jumbled series of metallic thin "tit'twee-tet-tet", lasting 0.5 s. **SS** Red-tinged Myzomela much redder on back, tail and wings than fem Obi Myzomela.

Taliabu Myzomela *Myzomela wahe* [E]

L 9–10 cm. Monotypic. Common in montane forest and edge, mostly >800 m, but recorded almost to sea level. Singly or pairs; favouring flowering trees. **ID M** red head and mantle to uppertail-coverts; extensively red on underparts with dusky-black rear flanks and vent, black wings and tail. Red body colour may sometimes appear mottled black (especially on upper flanks and head) because of black feather margination. **F** undescribed in detail but generally similar to Sulawesi Myzomela. **Imm** undescribed. **Voc** Song: level series of thin, high-pitched "sip" notes increasing in volume, at 7 n/s, ending with jumble of lower-pitched, metallic notes "twee-twit-twee-too-wee", lasting 2–4 sec. Call: sharp, metallic high-pitched "tit".

Seram Myzomela *Myzomela elisabethae* [E]

L 9–11.5 cm. Monotypic. Often considered conspecific with Buru Myzomela as '**Wakolo Myzomela**' *M. wakoloensis* but consistent vocal and plumage differences comparable to those separating other species. Uncommon in (sub-) montane forest and edge, >1000 m, rarely lower. Singly, pairs or mixed flocks. **ID M** head and back bright red, contrasting with black tail, wings and scapulars; underparts red giving way to extensive black on upper and rear flanks, vent and central belly; lores black extending to form narrow black eyering; bill and legs blackish. **F** brown overall with paler brown head and underparts; variable red wash on head. **Imm** undescribed. **Voc** Song: jumbled series of metallic thin jingles "twee'ti'dee'dit'tee" lasting 1 sec; sometimes shorter "twee'ti'dee". Call: thin, rising "sip". **SS** Fem from Seram Honeyeater by small size, lack of breast streaks and plain facial pattern. See also Drab Myzomela.

Buru Myzomela *Myzomela wakoloensis* [E]

L 9–11.5 cm. Monotypic. For taxonomy see Seram Myzomela. Forest and edge, >900 m. Singly, pairs or mixed flocks. **ID M** similar to Seram but with all red underparts including undertail-coverts; may show small blackish belly patch; lesser and median-coverts tipped red forming double wingbar. **F** brown overall with paler brown head and underparts; variable red wash on head. **Imm** undescribed. **Voc** Song: upslurred, then descending, thin, high-pitched warble, "soooit-soo-soo", or flatter "tooo-to-to", lasting 0.6 sec. Call: upslurred, thin, metallic "teewit". **SS** Fem from larger Buru Honeyeater by all-dark bill (no pale base), lack of yellowish tones on underparts, lack of green on upperparts, and plain facial pattern with variable red wash. See also Madanga Pipit.

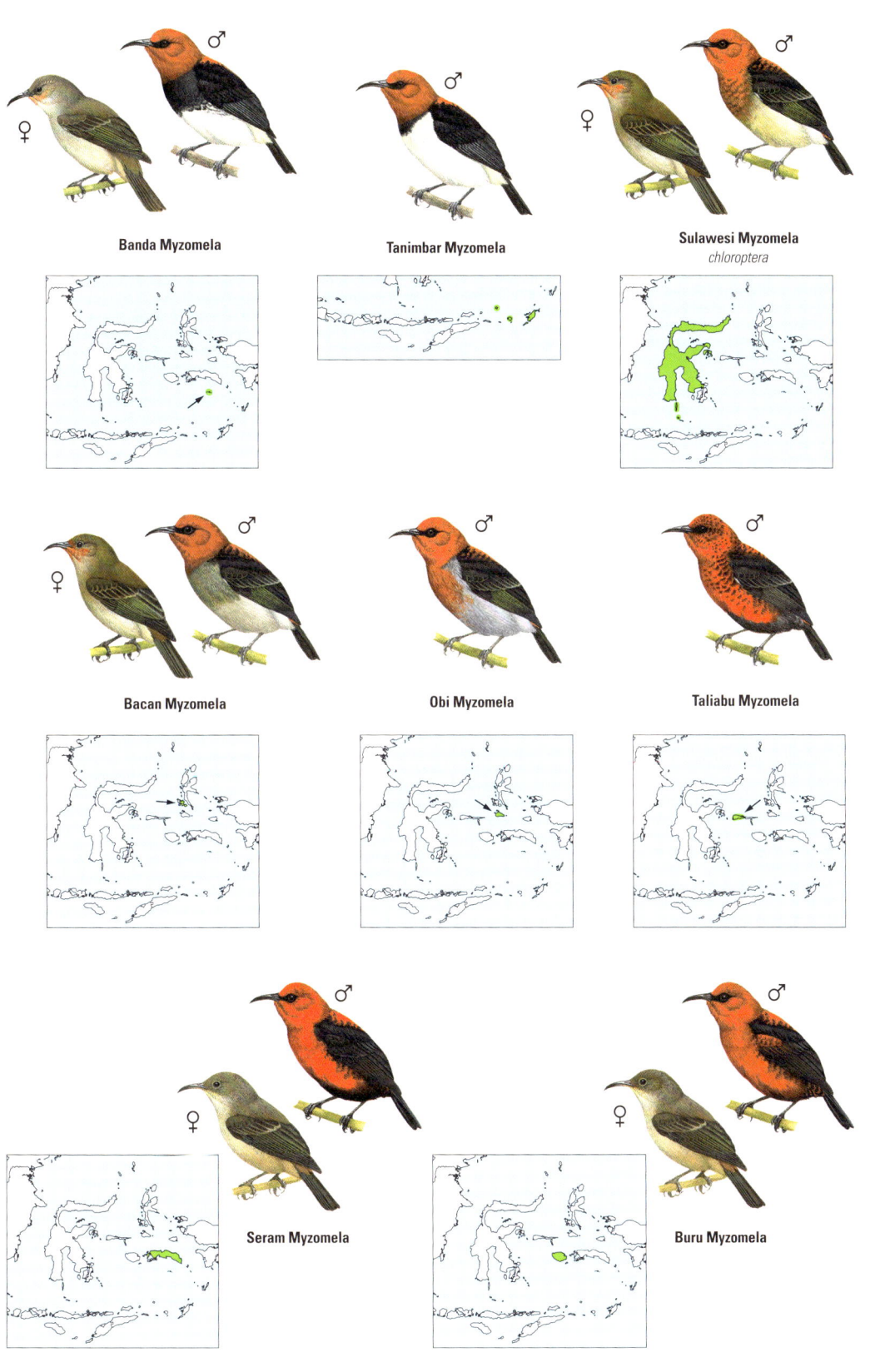

Banda Myzomela

Tanimbar Myzomela

Sulawesi Myzomela
chloroptera

Bacan Myzomela

Obi Myzomela

Taliabu Myzomela

Seram Myzomela

Buru Myzomela

Timor Friarbird *Philemon inornatus* **E**
L 24 cm. Monotypic. Fairly common in forest, edge, lightly wooded areas in villages. Singly, pairs or small groups; usually noisy and conspicuous but shy. **ID Ad** plain brownish-grey upperparts, wings and tail; side of neck, throat and underparts grey-white with diffuse streaking and scaling; crown and sides of head brownish grey, with slightly darker ear-coverts and sub-moustachial stripe; bare blue-black skin from lores to beneath eye; bill and legs black. **Imm** darker upperparts with yellowish panel on wings, yellow wash to underparts. **Voc** Song: in typical friarbird fashion, a noisy, extended duet; little introduction, raucous and monotonous, slower than other friarbird duets, "chip to-tee-too chip to-tee-too chip to-tee-too...", <1 min. Call: disyllabic, upslurred "chewit". **SS** Tenggara Friarbird is larger with more prominent facial mask and casqued bill.

Kisar Friarbird *Philemon kisserensis* **E**
L 25 cm. Monotypic. Sometimes considered conspecific with Little Friarbird *P. citreogularis* (Australia) based on plumage similarities and low genetic divergence. Detailed bioacoustic research required. Common in forest, edge, lightly wooded cultivation. Singly, pairs or small groups (<10); usually noisy and conspicuous, particularly around lontar palm. **ID Ad** plain brown upperparts; grey-white underparts and sides of neck, mottled brown; prominent bare blue-grey facial patch, bordered blackish to rear and around eye. **Imm** undescribed. **Voc** Song: in typical friarbird fashion, noisy, extended duet; complex, involving 3 elements, starting with rapid low trill lasting <3 sec, then series of nasal, coarse, croaking phrases "what-do-you-do what-do-you-do what-do-you-do...", finally a series of 20–30 rapid "kick-oo" notes. Call: quizzical, hollow, disyllabic "oo-WIP". **AN** Grey Friarbird.

Morotai Friarbird *Philemon fuscicapillus* **E**
L 30 cm. Monotypic. Fairly common in forest, edge. Singly or pairs; noisy and conspicuous. **ID Ad** dull, dark grey-brown upperparts, darkest on crown; paler underparts; whitish on throat, washed yellow from breast to belly; large bare pink skin patch from lores to around eye; legs black; bill black with small knob (casque) at base. **Imm** undescribed. **Voc** Song: in typical friarbird fashion, noisy, extended duet; starting quietly and slowly, building up to a loud raucous crescendo "cheewot oww cheewot oww cheewot oww, cheewot eeeoo cheewot eeeoo...", <1.5 min. Call: (i) sharp yelp "wuhk"; (ii) higher-pitched, upslurred whining "whiirrrt". **SS** See Halmahera Oriole. **AN** Dusky Friarbird.

Buru Friarbird *Philemon moluccensis* **E**
L 31–37 cm. Monotypic. See Tanimbar Friarbird for taxonomy. Fairly common in forest, edge, lightly wooded cultivation. Singly, pairs or small groups; usually noisy and conspicuous. **ID Ad** plain grey-brown upperparts; paler buffish underparts; throat and sides of neck tinged whitish; prominent bare black skin extending from lores to around eye; indistinct darker malar stripe and ear-coverts; bill and legs black to bluish-black. **Imm** yellowish wash to underparts and wings. **Voc** Song: in typical friarbird fashion, noisy, extended duet; "cheweeitweewoo, cheweeitweewoo..." or "chewoo, weewoot, chewoo, weewoot...", <1 min. Call: loud, far-carrying "hooWIT" or "hooWEOO". **SS** See Buru Oriole. **AN** Black-faced Friarbird.

Tanimbar Friarbird *Philemon plumigenis* **E**
L 31–37 cm. Monotypic. For many years erroneously merged with Buru Friarbird, a treatment that has little support. Common in forest, edge, lightly wooded cultivation. Singly or pairs; noisy and conspicuous but shy. **ID Ad** as Buru Friarbird, but underparts darker (similar to upperparts) and bill shows small knob (casque) at base. Bare facial skin blue below eye to upper ear-coverts, black on lores and above eye. **Imm** undescribed. **Voc** Song: in typical friarbird fashion, noisy, extended duet; upslurred, slightly stuttering, raucous "wit chew'it wit eeh chew'it wit eeh chew'it..." lasting <30 sec. Call: disyllabic, downslurred "to'wip". **SS** See Tanimbar Oriole.

Seram Friarbird *Philemon subcorniculatus* **E**
L 35 cm. Monotypic. Fairly common in forest, edge, lightly wooded cultivation and mangrove, <1100 m. Singly, pairs or small groups; usually conspicuous but shy. **ID Ad** olive-brown plumage strongly washed yellow on throat, breast, wings and tail; sides of neck and nape silvery-grey, contrasting with darker ear-coverts and often slightly raised crown feathers; prominent bare facial skin patch variable in colour from blue-black to yellow-brown; legs blue-black; bill black or blue-black with small knob (casque) at base. **Imm** yellowish-pink facial skin. **Voc** Loud, far-carrying disyllabic "PP'ROW". Characteristic sound of the island, starting pre-dawn, carries beyond sunset. Small groups sometimes very noisy, with counter-calling. **SS** See Seram Oriole.

Tenggara Friarbird *Philemon buceroides* **E**
L 32–36 cm. 2 ssp: *buceroides* (Sawu, Rote, Timor, Semau, Wetar); *neglectus* (Sumba, Lombok–Flores). Often includes ~8 extralimital ssp from Aus and NG, together forming an expanded '**Helmeted Friarbird**' *P. buceroides*, but morphological and vocal differences as well as a fairly deep genetic divergence suggest separation of regional taxa. Common in degraded forest, edge, lightly wooded cultivation, villages and mangrove, <1500 m. Singly, pairs or small groups; noisy and conspicuous. **ID Ad** Plain grey-brown upperparts, paler underparts; throat whitish with fine black streaks; prominent black or blue-black bare skin patch from lores to around eye, bordered below by black feathering on ear-coverts and malar stripe forming mask; rear of crown often raised to form indistinct tufty crest; smaller blackish patch usually visible on side of neck; bill black, with prominent casque; legs blue-black. Ssp *neglectus* slightly darker overall. **Imm** lacks prominent casque on bill, and may show some yellow feather edging on wings and underparts, and some mottled scaling on upperparts. **Voc** Song: in typical friarbird fashion, noisy, extended duet; (i) coarse, harsh, screeching "whirrt arhga whirrt arhga whirrt arhga..." lasting <3 min; (ii) less harsh, more musical, melodious "dowit'it too dowit'it too dowit'it too..." lasting <2 min. Call: (i) loud, metallic "chilink" with higher-pitched, stressed second syllable; (ii) harsh, grating "tchewIT" with higher pitched, metallic final syllable; (iii) scolding, whining "grrrk". **SS** See Timor Friarbird, and Timor and Wetar Orioles.

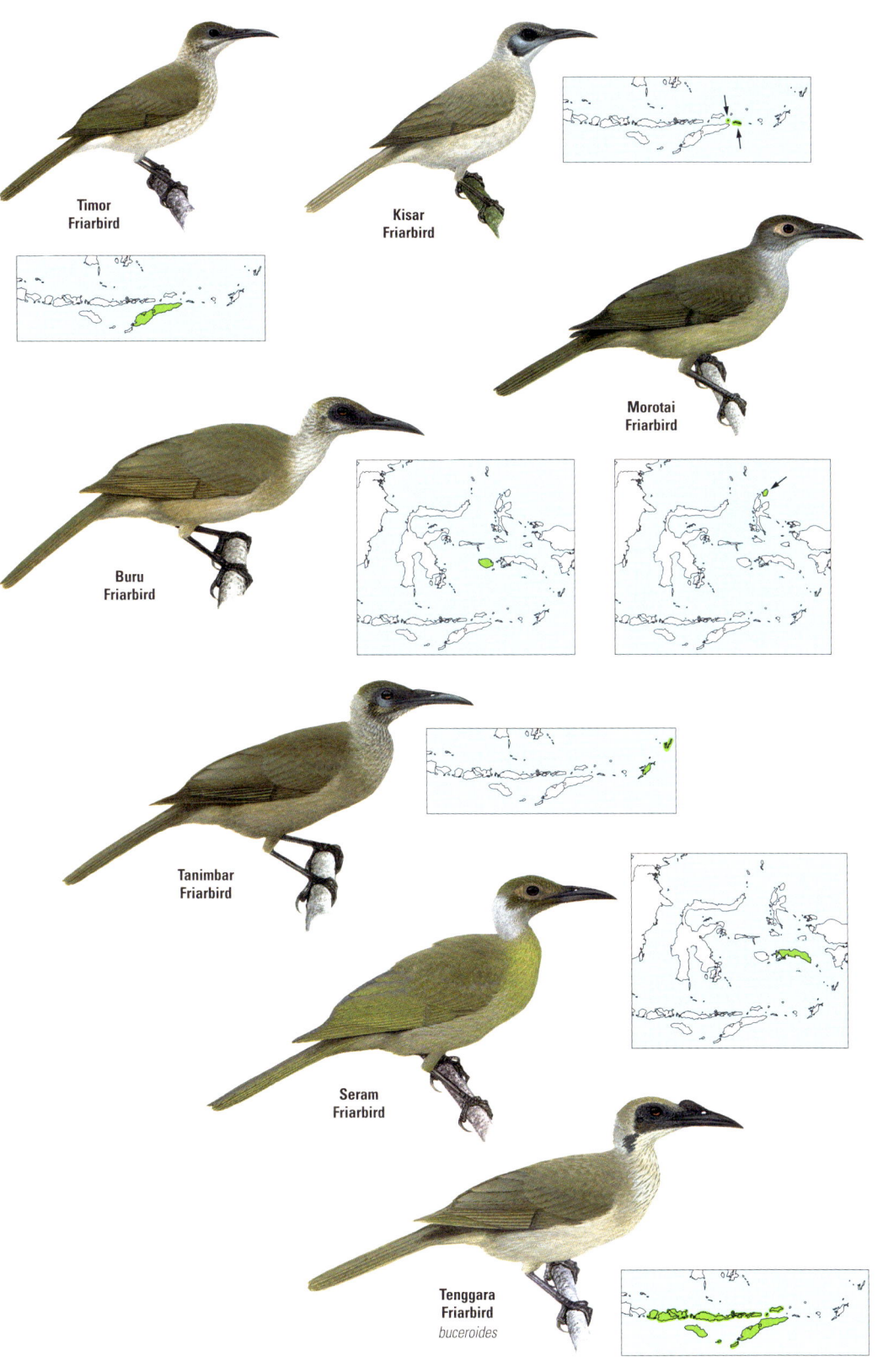

Timor Friarbird

Kisar Friarbird

Morotai Friarbird

Buru Friarbird

Tanimbar Friarbird

Seram Friarbird

Tenggara Friarbird
buceroides

PARDALOTIDAE
Pardalotes and Gerygones
3 species in region

Small, arboreal birds of Australo-Papuan descent. Occupy a variety of wooded habitats including mangrove and sparse woodland. Highly active and typically conspicuous, feeding at mid- to upper-storey; often calling continuously.

Banda Sea Gerygone *Gerygone dorsalis*   **E**
L 10 cm. 5 ssp: *dorsalis* (Tanimbar); *senex* (Kalaotoa, Madu); *fulvescens* (Romang, Leti, Moa, Kisar, Sermata, Babar); *kuehni* (Damar); *keyensis* (Kai, Tayandu). Fairly common in a variety of wooded habitats. Singly or pairs; forages in tangles. **ID Ad** grey head with indistinct pale supercilium in front of eye; dark-red iris; reddish-brown upperparts; white underparts with pale rufous flanks. Ssp *keyensis* slightly larger; *kuehni* darker upperparts and flanks, grey-brown crown; *fulvescens* as previous but slightly less reddish; *senex* as previous but perhaps darker, with whitish iris. **Imm** yellowish underparts. **Voc** Song: long series of 2–4 repetitive, descending, thin notes "soo-see-see-see-soo-see...". On Damar at least, sometimes more ascending series of notes. Call: squeaky, thin "wi'-wihrki". **AN** Rufous-sided Gerygone.

Golden-bellied Gerygone *Gerygone sulphurea*
L 10 cm. Sundaic, Phil, Wallacea. 5 ssp, 3 in region: *sulphurea* (GS, LS, MPen, Cochinchina); *muscicapa* (Enggano); *flaveola* (Sul, Selayar, Banggai). Extensive vocal variation may dictate break-up into three species: '**Sunda Gerygone**' *G. sulphurea* (including *muscicapa*), monotypic '**Sulawesi Gerygone**' *G. flaveola* and extralimital '**Philippine Gerygone**' *G. simplex* (Phil); more research needed. Fairly common in open habitats, mangroves, tree-lined urban areas, plantations, submontane forest, <2300 m. Singly or pairs; gleans foliage in mid- and upper canopy. **ID Ad** greyish-brown head, browner upperparts; pale lores and dark moustachial line; yellow underparts, paler belly; white tail-tips and black bill. Ssp *muscicapa* smaller, underparts more extensively and deeper yellow, paler head and neck; *flaveola* also brighter yellow underparts, indistinct tail tips. **Imm** narrow white eyering; paler underparts; pale bill base. **Voc** Song: <10 high-pitched, melancholy, musical, rising or falling whistles "zwee", "zrriii" and variants; Javan birds have descending wheezy phrase of 3–5 notes, regularly repeated; in Sulawesi (*flaveola*) thin wheezy trill, continuing to falling cadence, repeated many times, or an oft-repeated weakly whistled, sibilant, descending cadence of ~6 notes. Call: "chu-wee". **AN** Flyeater.

Timor Gerygone *Gerygone inornata*   **E**
L 10 cm. Monotypic. Fairly common in wooded habitats, mangroves, plantations, montane forest, <2500 m. Singly or pairs; gleans foliage in mid- and upper canopy, but also regularly comes near ground to feed. **ID Ad** grey head and upperparts; white underparts and tail tips; pale eye. **Imm** yellowish belly. **Voc** Song: (i) high-pitched, thin series of 6–15 descending notes, "peee-poo'poo'poo'poo, peee-poo'poo'poo..." at 4 n/s; (ii) thin, level-pitched trilling "pe'e'e'e'e'e'e'e... poo-poo pe'e'e'e'e'e'e..." lasting <10 min; (iii) quiet, well spaced introductory notes followed by a long descending series "pi'pi'pi..." at 8 n/s, lasting up to 12 sec. **AN** Plain Gerygone.

VIREONIDAE
Vireos and allies
4 species in region

Small, stout-billed forest birds. In Asia, the shrike-vireos are distinctively marked while Erpornis is more drab. Typically active and conspicuous in mid- to upper storey of forest, often with mixed flocks.

Pied Shrike-vireo *Pteruthius flaviscapis*   **E**
L 14 cm. Monotypic. Previously included Blyth's and several extra-limital taxa under a broadly-defined umbrella species, '**White-browed Shrike-vireo**' (or Shrike-babbler) *P. flaviscapis*, but differs substantially in plumage, voice and mtDNA. Fairly common in (sub-) montane forest, 1000–3000 m. Singly or pairs; favouring upper canopy. **ID** Robust, stout-billed appearance. **M** black head with broad white rear-supercilium; slate-grey upper mantle and rump; rest of upperparts black with yellow tertials tipped reddish; under-parts whitish. **F** grey head with broad white rear-supercilium; grey mantle; olive-green wings and tail; underparts buffish-white. **Imm M** slate-grey face, crown and mantle; olive-fringed coverts. **Imm F** grey-brown head and mantle; slate-grey ear-coverts. **Voc** Hard, loud singlet-doublet or singlet-triplet "ip chip-chip", or "ip chip-ch-chip", lasting 0.7 sec, regularly repeated. **AN** Pied Shrike-babbler.

Blyth's Shrike-vireo *Pteruthius aeralatus*
L 14 cm. S–SE–E Asia. 6 ssp, 2 in region: *cameranoi* (Sum, MPen); *robinsoni* (Bor). For taxonomy see Pied Shrike-vireo. Fairly common in (sub-) montane forest, 900–2700 m. Singly or pairs; favouring upper canopy. **ID** Robust, stout-billed appearance. **M** black head with broad white rear-supercilium, grey mantle and rump; rest of upperparts black with yellow tertials tipped reddish; throat pale grey grading to salmon-white belly; *robinsoni* more strongly pink-washed belly. **F** grey head with indistinct paler rear-supercilium; grey mantle; olive-green wings and tail; underparts buffish-white, peach-tinged belly. **Imm M** grey-olive crown; slate-grey face; brownish mantle; coverts edged buff. **Imm F** grey-brown head and mantle; slate-grey ear-coverts. **Voc** Hard, loud 4–6 notes, usually given in doublet-doublet or doublet-singlet-doublet, though some variation; "chip-chu chip-chu", "chip-ip chip-chip chip-chu", or "chip-chip chip chip-chu", and "chip-ip chip-ip chip-ip", lasting 1–1.5 sec. **AN** Blyth's Shrike-babbler.

Trilling Shrike-vireo *Pteruthius aenobarbus*   **E**
L 11 cm. Monotypic. Previously included extralimital Clicking Shrike-vireo *P. intermedius* (mainland SE Asia) under a broadly defined umbrella species, '**Chestnut-fronted Shrike-vireo**' (or Shrike-babbler) *P. aenobarbus*, but differs substantially in voice and mtDNA. Fairly common in (sub-) montane forest, 1000–3000 m. Singly or pairs, joins mixed flocks; favouring mid-canopy. **ID** Robust, stout-billed appearance. **M** chestnut throat, upper breast and forecrown; white eyering bordered by black postocular; white super-cilium; olive-green crown and upperparts with broad white wingbars and blackish outerwing; rest of head and underparts deep yellow. **F** duller overall, lacks strong yellow tones, with peach buff forehead; buff wingbars, whitish throat to belly. **Imm** undescribed. **Voc** Song monarch-like: (i) loud trill "too'too'too..." lasting 1–6 sec at 6 n/s; (ii) quiet "towit-towit-towit..." lasting 3 sec at 3 n/s. Call: characteristic, buzzy, sharply rising "tew-chi'-chi'". **AN** Trilling Shrike-babbler.

Erpornis *Erpornis zantholeuca*
L 11–13 cm. S–SE–E Asia. 5 ssp, 2 in region: *brunnescens* (Bor); *saani* (NW Sum; known from single specimen). Uncommon in primary, secondary and submontane forest, <1800 m. Singly or small groups (<5), joins mixed flocks; favouring mid-canopy. **ID Ad** short but conspicuous crest; yellowish-green upperparts; pale grey face and underparts; yellow vent. Ssp *saani* greener; less yellow upperparts; darker crown. **Imm** shorter crest. **Voc** Song: short, high-pitched, descending trill "si'i'i'i'i'l", at 6 n/s. Call: nasal, buzzing, tit-like "nhi" and "nher-nher-nher". **AN** White-bellied Erpornis.

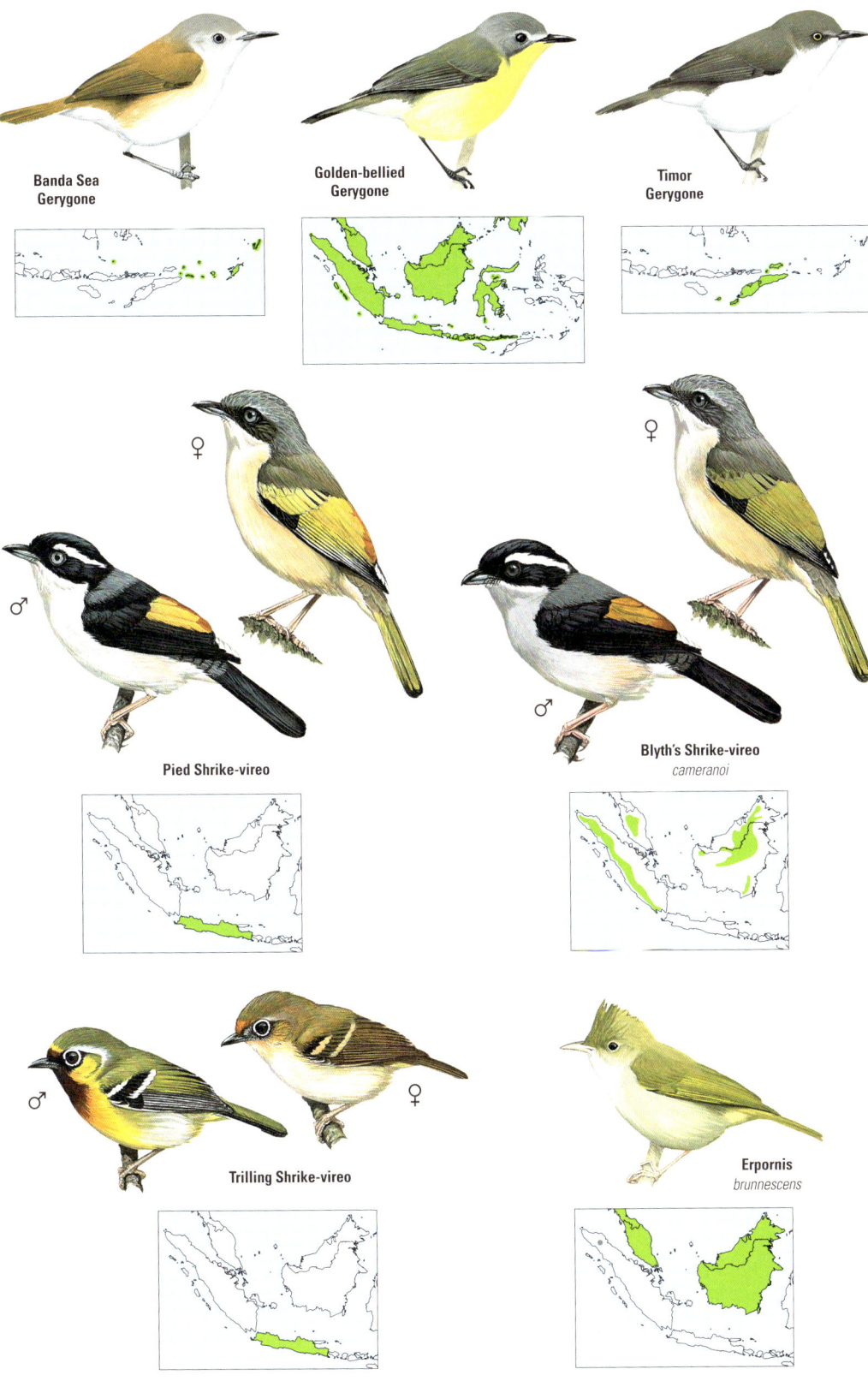

Banda Sea Gerygone

Golden-bellied Gerygone

Timor Gerygone

♀ ♂ **Pied Shrike-vireo**

♀ ♂ **Blyth's Shrike-vireo**
cameranoi

♂ ♀ **Trilling Shrike-vireo**

Erpornis
brunnescens

ORIOLIDAE
Orioles and Figbirds
17 species in region

Diverse family, many species highly colourful, others more drab. Several species mimic large honeyeaters both in appearance and vocalisations. Arboreal, found in a variety of forest and wooded habitats. Usually conspicuous and vocal.

Green Oriole *Oriolus flavocinctus*

L 25–30 cm. Aus. 6 ssp, 1 in region: *migrator* (Romang, Leti, Moa). Fairly common on Romang in secondary forest, edge. No records on Moa and Leti since 1902. Singly, pairs or as part of mixed flocks; usually in mid- to upper storey. **ID M** yellow-green head and body with blackish streaking on crown and mantle, and fainter dark streaking on underparts; dark lores; wings darker with feathering edged creamy-white forming distinctive wingbars; tail blackish brown with pale yellowish tip; iris and bill red-orange; legs grey. **F** duller and more heavily streaked. **Imm** yellow supercilium; heavily streaked underparts; bill black. **Voc** Song: 3–4 melodious, loud fluty notes, either descending "pop-chonk-chonk" or ascending "chonk-chonk-chit", lasting 0.6 sec. Call: harsh, upslurred, sneezing sound. **SS** See Olive-backed Oriole. **AN** Yellow Oriole.

Timor Oriole *Oriolus melanotis* E

L 25 cm. Monotypic. Formerly united with Wetar Oriole into more broadly defined species 'Olive-brown Oriole' *O. melanotis*, but separated by substantial genetic, plumage and vocal differences. Fairly common in forest, edge, mangrove, wooded cultivation. Singly or pairs; inconspicuous within mid- to upper storey. **ID M** crown and mantle dark olive-green; wings dark brown; tail brown with whitish terminal spots on underside; face dark grey-black; throat and breast grey, washed green; belly and undertail-coverts buff; iris and bill red; legs dark grey. **F** visual mimic of Tenggara Friarbird: upperparts pale brown, with dark streaks especially on crown; face and sides of neck black; narrow whitish supercilium; underparts buff-white, streaked brown on breast; bill blackish. **Imm** more heavily streaked. **Voc** 3–6 soft, liquid, descending whistles "p-pow-owh-woe", lasting <1 sec. Many slight variations. **SS** Fem from Tenggara Friarbird by smaller size, black on face formed by feathering (not bare skin), less pointed bill, lack of knob on bill. **AN** Olive-brown Oriole.

Wetar Oriole *Oriolus finschi* E

L 25 cm. Monotypic. For taxonomy see Timor Oriole. Fairly common in forest, edge, mangrove, wooded cultivation. Singly or pairs, often inconspicuous within mid- to upper storey. **ID Ad** resembles fem Timor Oriole, but greyer and darker; head pattern less distinct; chin and throat grey; underparts buff-white, streaked brown on breast; bill blackish. **Imm** more heavily streaked. **Voc** (i) Piercing whistled "twi'WIT", lasting 0.4 sec; (ii) 1–3 downslurred, then level, whistled "che'o'IT", lasting 0.5 sec, with slight variations. **SS** From Tenggara Friarbird by smaller size, black on face formed by feathering (not bare skin), less pointed bill, lack of knob on bill.

Tanimbar Oriole *Oriolus decipiens* E

L 23–32 cm. Monotypic. For taxonomy see Buru Oriole. Fairly common in forest, edge, mangrove, wooded cultivation. Singly or pairs; often inconspicuous within mid–upper storey. **ID Ad** uncanny visual mimic of Tanimbar Friarbird. Similar to Buru Oriole but darker and browner underparts and less distinct facial patch; greyish hindneck collar. **Imm** undescribed. **Voc** (i) 5–10 loud, fluty, rapid opening notes with down- then upslurred final 2 notes "p-p-p-peeew-er",

lasting 1–1.5 sec, main emphasis on penultimate downslurred note; (ii) tremulous, level-pitched, liquid whistle "w'w'w'w'w'w'whirr", lasting 2–3 sec. **SS** From Tanimbar Friarbird with difficulty by slightly smaller size, straighter, blunter bill, and dark colour on ear-coverts and face formed by greyish-brown feathering, not bluish bare skin.

Buru Oriole *Oriolus bouroensis* E

L 23–32 cm. Monotypic. Formerly united with Tanimbar Oriole into more broadly-defined 'Black-eared Oriole' *O. bouroensis*, but DNA reveals their rather distant relationship within Wallacean oriole radiation, corroborating plumage and vocal differences. Fairly common in forest, edge, mangrove, wooded cultivation, <1400 m. Singly or pairs; often inconspicuous within mid–upper storey. **ID Ad** uncanny visual mimic of Buru Friarbird. Upperparts brown; blackish-brown facial patch, bordered by pale supercilium, pale hindneck collar and pale, streaky chin and throat; rest of underparts whitish-buff; iris red; bill and legs black. **Imm** rufous edging to wing feathers. **Voc** 3 ascending, loud, fluty notes "p'po'eee", lasting 0.6 sec. **SS** From Buru Friarbird with difficulty by slightly smaller size, straighter bill and blackish-brown on face formed by feathering, not bare skin. **AN** Black-eared Oriole.

Seram Oriole *Oriolus forsteni* E

L 31 cm. Monotypic. Fairly common in forest and edge. Singly or pairs, occasionally with mixed flocks; often inconspicuous within lower to mid-storey. **ID Ad** uncanny visual mimic of Seram Friarbird. Uniformly dark olive-brown upperparts, wings and tail; crown paler, with dark streaks; sides of face darker grey-brown; small area of bare greyish skin around eye; distinctive pale grey nuchal collar; underparts yellowish-buff; bill and legs black. **Imm** undescribed. **Voc** Descending series of 5–6 loud, fluty, rapidly whistled "p'p'p'p'pow", lasting 0.6 sec. **SS** From Seram Friarbird with difficulty by shorter tail, less sharply pointed, straighter bill. Also note call. **AN** Grey-collared Oriole.

Halmahera Oriole *Oriolus phaeochromus* E

L 26 cm. Monotypic. Fairly common in forest, edge, mangrove, wooded cultivation. Singly or pairs, occasionally with mixed flocks; often inconspicuous within mid–upper storey. **ID Ad** uniformly dark brown, washed slightly greyish on head and breast; black bare parts. **Imm** undescribed. **Voc** Variety of 2–5 loud, fluty, liquid, whistled notes, including: (i) 3-note fluty, loud, liquid whistled "po-poo-awo", lasting 0.6 sec; (ii) 5 descending fluty whistled notes "k-k-kow poo awo" lasting 1 sec. **SS** Often described as being a visual mimic of Morotai Friarbird but quite unlike and does not share range. Superficially more similar to White-streaked Honeyeater in general size and colouration, but distinguished by lack of both pale crown and white streaks. **AN** Dusky-brown Oriole.

Olive-backed Oriole *Oriolus sagittatus* V

L 25–28 cm. Aus. 4 ssp. Single record from Luang (Nov 1902), probably migratory ssp *sagittatus* (E Aus). Forest edge, mangrove, parks. **ID M** head and mantle olive-green; wings grey-brown; tail grey-brown with white tips; throat greyish; rest of underparts creamy-white, heavily streaked black; bill orange-red; legs blue-grey. **F** greyer, with dark streaking on upperparts. **Imm** wings brown with paler cinnamon edging; iris and bill dark grey-brown. **Voc** Song: fast series of melodious, fluty, slightly descending notes "orry-orry-ole" or "or-ee-ee", lasting 0.6 sec. Call: harsh, sneezing "chee-et". **SS** From fem figbirds by larger red (not black) bill and lack of bare eye skin. From Green Oriole by whitish underparts.

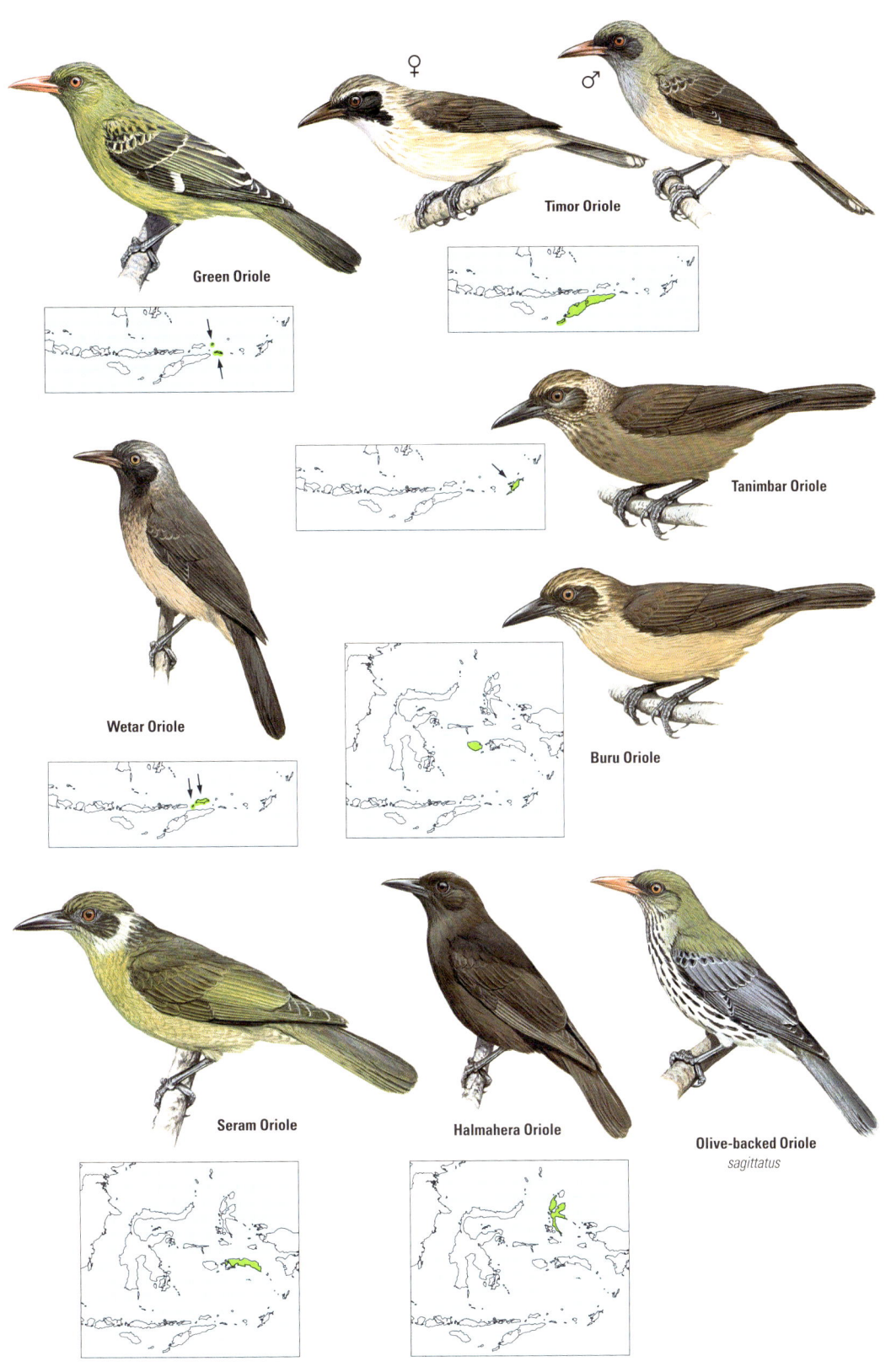

Green Oriole

Timor Oriole

♀

♂

Tanimbar Oriole

Wetar Oriole

Buru Oriole

Seram Oriole

Halmahera Oriole

Olive-backed Oriole
sagittatus

Black-naped Oriole *Oriolus chinensis*

L 23–28 cm. NE–E–S–SE Asia, Phil. 20 spp, 16 in region. Well-studied genetically: comprises nine deeply-diverged lineages, eight of which occur in region and can potentially be further elevated to species level pending bioacoustic confirmation: (1) '**Sunda Golden Oriole**' *O. maculatus*, including *maculatus* (Sum–Bali, MPen), *richmondi* (Siberut, Pagai), *sipora* (Sipora), *mundus* (Simeulue, Nias), *lamprochryseus* (Karimata, Masalembu) and *insularis* (Kangean); (2) '**Tenggara Golden Oriole**' *O. broderipi* (LS; monotypic); (3) '**Flores Sea Golden Oriole**' *O. boneratensis* (Flores Sea Is.; monotypic); (4) '**Celebes Sea Golden Oriole**' *O. formosus*, including *melanisticus* (Talaud), *sangirensis* (Sangihe) and *formosus* (Siau); (5) '**Sulawesi Golden Oriole**' *O. celebensis* (Sul; monotypic); (6) '**Sula Golden Oriole**' *O. frontalis*, including *frontalis* (Taliabu) and *stresemanni* (Peleng); (7) '**Philippine Golden Oriole**' *O. chinensis* (Phil), including *suluensis* (Sulu; presumably this ssp vagrant to Bor) and two extralimital ssp; and (8) '**Chinese Golden Oriole**' *O. diffusus* (breeds NE-E Asia, winters to S-SE Asia; single record Galang, Riau Is, Apr 2018). Generally fairly common, now scarce on Nias, Sum and Jav, in forest, edge and wooded cultivation, <1200 m. Singly, pairs or in mixed flocks in mid- to upper storey. **ID** (*maculatus*) Head and body entirely golden yellow (duller in **F**), greenish tinge to underparts; broad black band from lores to hindcrown; wings black with yellow median and secondary coverts, yellow tips to primary coverts, yellow edging to secondaries and tertials and white edging to primaries; tail black with yellow tip, broadest on outer feathers; bill pink; legs grey-blue. Larger *mundus* has more lemon mantle, lacks yellow primary covert spot; *richmondi* as *maculatus* but wings shorter, bill longer, secondaries and tertials less broadly edged yellow; *sipora* as previous but brighter on back, broader yellow wing edging; *lamprochryseus* larger than *maculatus*, upperparts more intensely golden-coloured, yellow tips to secondaries and tertials narrower and duller; *insularis* as *maculatus* but yellow crown extending to leave only narrow black hindcollar, yellow plumage tinged orange; *melanisticus* large heavy bill, entire crown and nape black, leaving only small area of yellow on forehead, broad yellow collar, mantle dark green mottled black, wings all black; smaller *sangirensis* as previous but mantle dark green-yellow; *formosus* as previous but slightly larger, with more yellow on forehead; *celebensis* smaller than *maculatus*, shorter bill, top of head variable but often entirely yellow so that black band becomes narrow and sometimes broken on nape, lacks yellow tipped primary coverts; *frontalis* as previous but crown and nape black, leaving only little yellow on forehead, wings entirely black; *stresemanni* as previous, but smaller and shorter-billed; *boneratensis* as *celebensis* but larger, with yellow on crown, mantle and underparts often orange, and yellow tipped primary coverts; *broderipi* as *frontalis* but deep orange-yellow overall, primary coverts with yellow tips, tertials tipped yellow; *suluensis* small yellow forehead patch, pale yellow mantle, entirely black wings, extensive yellow on outer tail; *diffusus* as *maculatus* but distinct large yellow tertial and secondary panel (**F** greener mantle and tail). **Imm** underparts yellow with thin black breast streaks, bill black; *diffusus* has white underparts with thick black streaks down to belly. **Voc** Much variation throughout range. Ssp *maculatus* produces a loud, fluty, clear whistle "doo-dlee-oo" or descending "too-o-lioo", lasting 0.8 sec with longer final note; call: rasping, nasal "kyehhr". Better studied variations include ssp *broderipi*: (i) rasping, harsh, cat-like miaowing "meee-aooww"; (ii) rapid, less melodious, descending whistled "what-to-do". Ssp *celebensis*: (i) "wot'to-tooow", lasting 0.4 sec; (ii) "whit-to-WOOO"; (iii) grating "grrrrk", lasting 1 sec. Ssp *formosus*: disyllabic, drawn-out, downslide whistle "ho'weeooo", lasting 0.8 sec, or slightly faster "ho'we'oo". Ssp *sangirensis*: (i) "t't'tooweeOO"; (ii) call "chierrk" like a trogon alarm call. Ssp *melanisticus*: emphasis more on first, upslurred syllable, "war'ho" or "ho'woo'wo". **SS** See Dark-throated Oriole.

Black-hooded Oriole *Oriolus xanthornus*

L 23–25 cm. S–SE Asia. 5 ssp, 2 in region: *xanthornus* (mainland S–SE Asia; wintering N Sum); *tanakae* (coastal NE Bor). Few recent records in region. Local and rare in forest, edge and wooded cultivation, <1000 m. Singly, pairs or in mixed flocks; mid- to upper storey. **ID** Glossy black head and breast; rest of body bright yellow (**F** duller); wings black with bright yellow marginal coverts and edging to primary, secondary and tertial coverts; primaries edged white and tipped yellow; tail yellow with broad black sub-terminal band across central feathers; bill pink. Ssp *tanakae* outer four (rather than outer three) tail feathers entirely yellow. **Imm** whitish eyering; forehead streaked yellow; throat whitish with dark streaks; bill blackish. **Voc** Extralimital data: (i) clear, fluty "h-HWEE'OOO" or "h-wo-CHEE–WOO", lasting 0.8 sec; (ii) loud, mellow "tcheeo".

Black Oriole *Oriolus hosii* E

L 22 cm. Monotypic. Locally fairly common in submontane forest, 900–1500 m. Singly, pairs or in mixed flocks; mid- to upper storey. **ID M** uniformly glossy black with chestnut vent; bill pink-red; legs grey-black. **F** belly and lower breast slaty grey. **Imm** grey bill; silvery-grey underparts and paler chestnut vent. **Voc** Wide repertoire of fluty, tuneful whistles, including (i) "toi-we-WHEEE", lasting 1 sec; (ii) high-pitched, thin metallic whistle "kit-tee-tee"; (iii) pure, undulating whistles "si-ho-WEE'E", lasting 0.5 sec; (iv) strained, grating opening note followed by pure upslurred final note "grrrr'oo WOOOEET", lasting 0.9 sec. **SS** From Black-and-crimson by chestnut vent and pink (not dark) bill. **AN** Bornean Oriole.

Black-and-crimson Oriole *Oriolus consanguineus*

L 21–24 cm. Sundaic. 3 ssp, 2 in region: *consanguineus* (Sum); *vulneratus* (Bor). Traditionally includes Javan Oriole but deep genetic divergence supported by vocal and – less so – plumage differences. Fairly common in montane forest and edge, 600–2400 m. Singly, pairs or in mixed flocks; mid- to upper storey. **ID M** glossy black except large, square crimson patch on belly and breast; almost entirely crimson primary coverts form large wing spot; bill and legs blue-grey. Ssp *vulneratus* smaller, with entirely crimson primary coverts; larger crimson breast patch. **F** sooty-grey underparts, no red belly patch; *vulneratus* similar to **M** but less extensive crimson breast patch, and primary coverts only tipped crimson. **Imm** belly patch greyish. **Voc** Song: (i) strained, piercing, cat-like, descending "keeeeu", lasting 0.5 sec; (ii) typical short, melodious, oriole whistle "chub-peeseoow". Call: short downslurred "chub". **SS** See Black Oriole.

Javan Oriole *Oriolus cruentus* E

L 21–24 cm. Monotypic. For taxonomy see Black-and-crimson. Rare, few recent records in montane forest, 800–1800 m. Singly, pairs or in mixed flocks; mid- to upper storey. **ID M** glossy black except crimson patch across belly (longer than it is broad), crimson tips to primary coverts form wing spot; bill and legs blue-grey. **F** belly patch more orange-red; lacking plumage gloss. **Imm** sooty-black; belly patch greyish-tinged. **Voc** Song: strained, cat-like, descending "keeeeu", lasting 0.5 sec, lower-pitched and harsher than Black-and-crimson. Call: short downslurred "chew", lower pitched than Black-and-crimson.

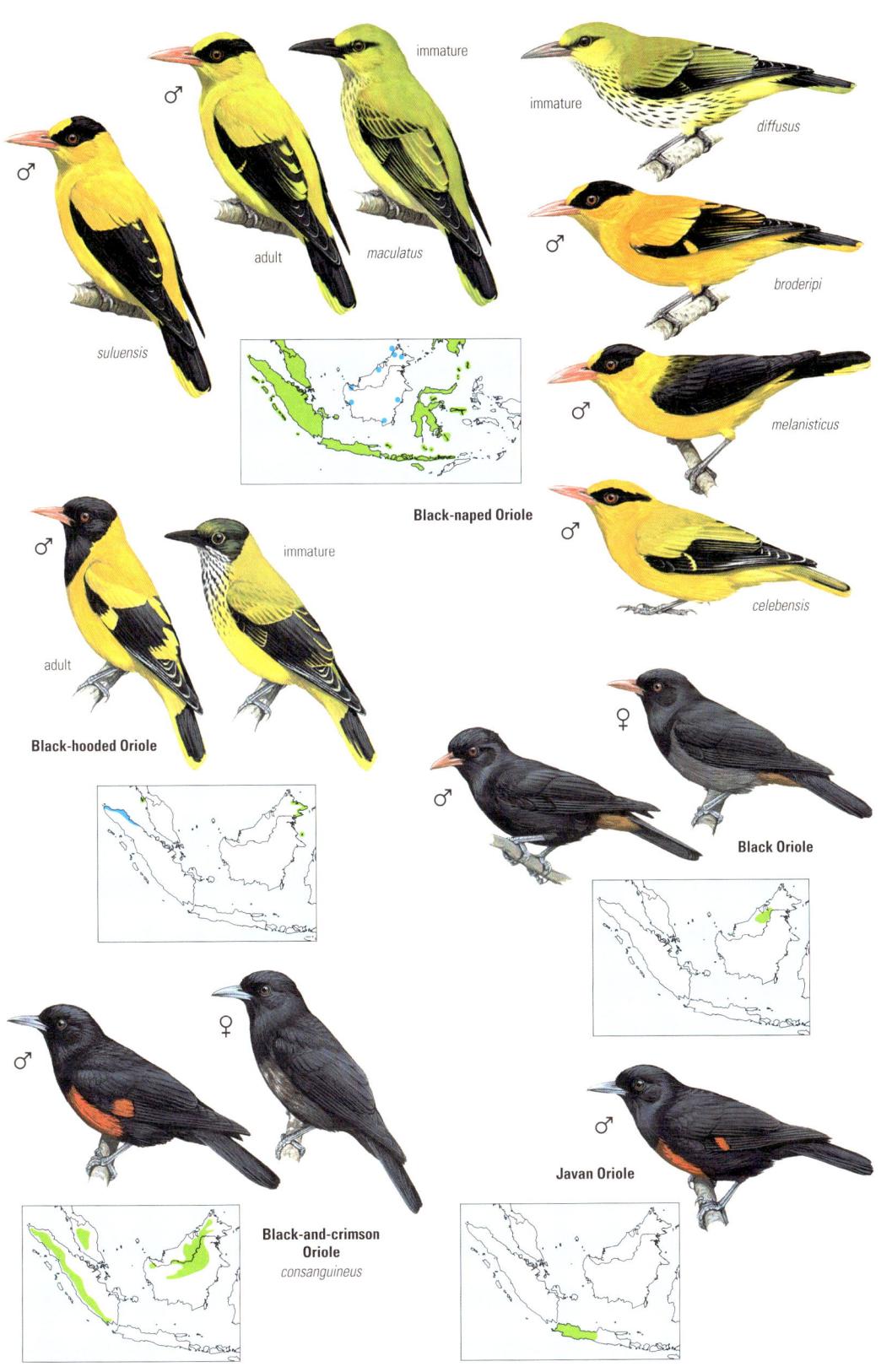

immature

diffusus

immature

maculatus

♂

♂

adult

suluensis

broderipi

♂

melanisticus

♂

Black-naped Oriole

celebensis

♂

immature

adult

Black-hooded Oriole

♀

♂

Black Oriole

♀

♂

Javan Oriole

♂

Black-and-crimson Oriole

consanguineus

Dark-throated Oriole *Oriolus xanthonotus*

L 17–19 cm. Sundaic, Palawan. 4 ssp, 3 in region: *xanthonotus* (Sum, S-W Bor, Jav, MPen); *consobrinus* (N-E Bor); *mentawi* (Mentawai). Ssp *consobrinus* and extralimital *persuasus* (Palawan) exhibit consistent differences in vocalisations and (especially female) plumage, and form a deep cryptic genomic lineage that may be more closely related to extralimital Philippine oriole species; may well warrant separation as independent species **'Ventriloquial Oriole**' *O. consobrinus*. Uncommon in forest, edge, <1200 m but commoner in lowlands. Singly, pairs or as part of mixed flocks; in mid- to upper storey. **ID M** wings, head and breast black; back, rump and vent yellow (greener in larger-sized *consobrinus*); tail black with yellow terminal spots on central tail feathers (larger spots in *consobrinus*); belly and flanks white with heavy black streaking; bill red-orange; legs blue-grey. **F** upperparts olive-green, slightly greyer on head, yellower on rump (but in *consobrinus* with strong contrast between dark grey-green crown and bright-olive back); usually shows narrow yellowish eyering; underparts grey-white with heavy black streaking; vent yellow. Ssp *mentawi* **F** described as having a darker crown with blackish feather centres, but may not be consistently separable. **Imm** throat whiter, with little streaking. **Voc** Song: ssp *xanthonotus* has wide repertoire of melodious, fluty motifs typical for the genus, mostly comprising 3-5 notes, such as sombre, pure, whistled "pi' pi'-ooo", or "pu'pu-weo-oo" lasting ~1 sec; *consobrinus* very different, ventriloquial 2-3 note "ho-ho whooo", similar to Bornean Black Magpie. Calls: all ssp give *Accipiter*-like, piping "kyew"; ssp *consobrinus* variable call repertoire, including (i) ventriloquial, drawn-out "hooooe", lasting over ~1 sec, similar to song component, (ii) single, creaking "eeaah", (iii) short, fluty but languid "heee", lasting ~1 sec, (iv) trumpeting "titichooowit" and variations; ssp *xanthonotus* gives 2-3 note calls reminiscent of short versions of its fluty song. **SS** Fem from Imm Black-naped Oriole by smaller size, redder bill, usually heavier streaking on underparts, eye ring (if present) and lack of any yellow feathering on throat or breast.

Australasian Figbird *Sphecotheres vieilloti*

L 27–30 cm. Aus. 5 ssp, 1 in region: ssp *cucullatus* (Kai), along with 2-3 Australo-Papuan taxa, sometimes separated from **'Green Figbird**' *S. vieilloti* (E Australasia) as **'Yellow Figbird**' *S. flaviventris* (N Australia, Kai) based on pronounced differences in colouration. However, sizeable hybrid zone between the two exists in Australia, and they lack deep vocal and DNA divergence. Fairly common in forest, edge, wooded cultivation. Singly or pairs, joins mixed flocks. Often calls from exposed tree tops. **ID M** head glossy-black with prominent reddish pink bare skin around eye; olive green back; blackish wings and tail; underparts bright yellow, becoming white towards undertail-coverts; bill black; legs grey-pink. **F** bare facial skin grey-pink; upperparts brown, streaked darker; underparts whitish buff, streaked brown. **Imm** less boldly marked. **Voc** Song: hesitant series of simple tuneless whistles ending in a downslurred "tu-tu-heer, tu-heer, tu-heer", containing much mimicry. Call: (i) short, sharp yelp "skluck"; (ii) loud "see-kew". **SS** See Olive-backed Oriole.

Timor Figbird *Sphecotheres viridis* E

L 26 cm. Monotypic. Common in forest, edge, wooded cultivation, <800 m. Singly, pairs or in groups around fruiting trees (<30). Often calls from exposed tree tops. **ID M** head glossy black with prominent reddish pink bare skin around eye; olive green back; blackish wings and tail; throat and breast olive-green, becoming yellower on lower breast and flanks and variably yellow or white on belly and undertail-

coverts; bill black; legs grey-black. **F** bare facial skin greyish pink; upperparts brown, streaked darker; underparts whitish buff, heavily streaked brown. **Imm** less boldly marked. **Voc** Song: quiet, constant chattering containing much mimicry (including parrots and king-fishers), lasting several minutes. Call: sharp, loud "kilk". **SS** See Olive-backed Oriole. **AN** Green Figbird.

Wetar Figbird *Sphecotheres hypoleucus* E

L 26 cm. Monotypic. Fairly common in forest, edge, wooded culti-vation. Singly, pairs or in groups around fruiting trees (<30). Often calls from exposed tree tops. **ID M** as Timor Figbird but underparts pure white. **F** as Timor Figbird. **Imm** less boldly marked. **Voc** Song: similar to Timor Figbird; quiet, constant chattering containing much mimicry (including parrots and kingfishers), lasting several minutes. Call: sharp, loud "whik".

PACHYCEPHALIDAE
Whistlers

18 species in region

Small stocky birds with large heads and stout bills. Range in plum-age from very drab to highly colourful. Arboreal in habit and found in a variety of forest, edge and wooded habitats. Most are highly vocal with distinctive, variable songs and calls.

Sangihe Whistler *Coracornis sanghirensis* E

L 17–19 cm. Monotypic. No longer misclassified as a shrike-thrush (*Colluricincla*). Rare and local in remnant patches of submontane forest, >550 m, likely less than 100 remaining. Usually pairs or small groups (<10); forages quietly in understorey. **ID Ad** greyish-brown head; browner upperparts; pale buffish-grey underparts, becoming more olive on belly; buff vent; pale horn bill base, dark tip. **Imm** un-described. **Voc** Song: primarily at dawn, or shortly after rain; repeti-tion of phrases, lasting 10 sec, typically comprising 4 distinct, rapidly uttered notes at 4 distinct pitches, each unit usually lower in pitch than the previous. Call: (i) short, sharp "wit" and "whik"; (ii) hard, thrush-like rolling "churr"; (iii) harsh, slightly wheezy "wweeaeh".

Maroon-backed Whistler *Coracornis raveni* E

L 15 cm. Monotypic. Uncommon in montane forest, 1400–2200 m. Unobtrusive and skulking, singly or pairs; in understorey. **ID M** overall very dark appearance: black head to lower breast and upper-parts except for dark-maroon mantle; olive-buff tinged belly. **F/Imm** dark rusty-brown upperparts; grey-tinged crown; dirty-buff under-parts with brighter buff vent. **Voc** Song: explosive, whiplash-like "swi'PIP", lasting 0.5 sec; can include quiet, winding introductory note.

Bare-throated Whistler *Pachycephala nudigula* E

L 19 cm. 2 ssp: *nudigula* (Flores); *ilsa* (Sumbawa). Locally common in montane forest, >1200 m, rarely lower. Singly, elusive when not sing-ing; forages in lower and mid-storey. **ID M** black hood; olive-green upperparts; brighter yellow underparts. When singing shows bright red bare skin on lower throat. Ssp *ilsa* brighter. **F** like M but grey head, whitish throat lacking bare skin. **Imm** yellowish throat. **Voc** Song: incredibly loud, powerful series of notes, containing much mimicry, each bout of monotonous notes changing pitch, at times reminiscent of a car alarm "WEE—WEE–WEE–WEE WEE–WEE–WEE..., HE'OO'HE– HE'OO'HE–HE'OO'HE..., WOO-WOO-WOO...". Often sings from exposed perch lasting several minutes to over an hour. **SS** See Tenggara Whistler.

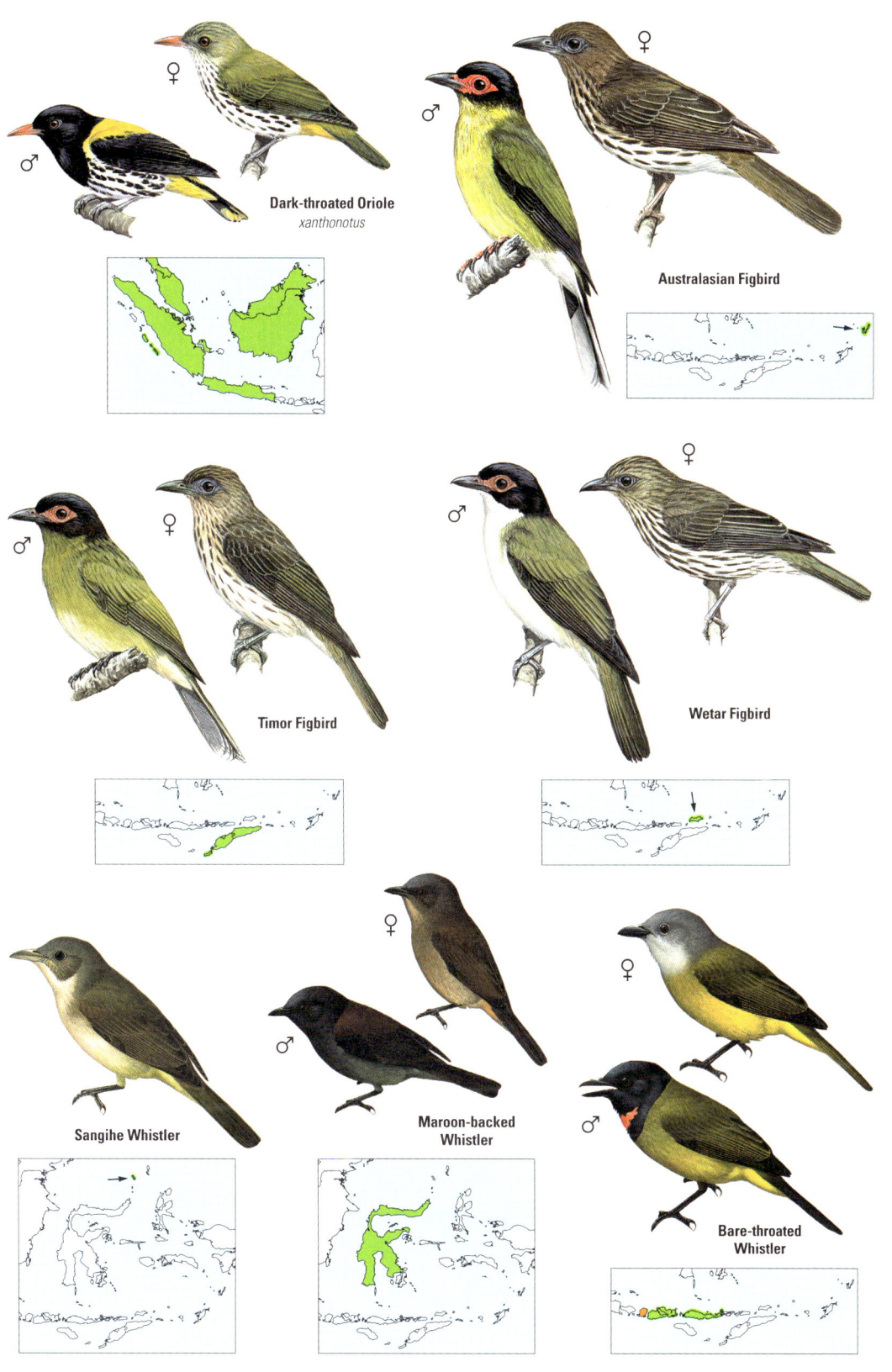

Dark-throated Oriole
xanthonotus

Australasian Figbird

Timor Figbird

Wetar Figbird

Sangihe Whistler

Maroon-backed Whistler

Bare-throated Whistler

Mangrove Whistler *Pachycephala cinerea*

L 17 cm. SE Asia to Palawan. 2 ssp, 1 in region: *cinerea* (GS–Lombok, Andamans, mainland SE Asia). Extralimital ssp *plateni* (Palawan) sometimes separated as '**Palawan Whistler**' based on plumage and song, leaving Mangrove Whistler monotypic. Locally fairly common in mangroves and adjacent vegetation; locally far inland, occurring to hills on Lombok, W Sum islands and other smaller islands. Singly; in mid-canopy. **ID Ad** drab-brown upperparts; grey-tinged head; white underparts with greyish breast; stout black bill. **Imm** rufous-tinged outerwing; paler bill. **Voc** Song: loud, liquid "whit-whit-whit-WHIPT", lasting ~1.5 sec, last note louder and explosive, often varying in pitch and structure even within individuals. Occasionally 2–3 extra notes at end, "WIT-PEW–CHEW". Call: short, high-pitched "eep". **SS** Compared to fem Tenggara Whistler, drabber and browner Mangrove lacks olive tones to upperparts, rump and tail, and has white (not bright-yellow) vent.

White-vented Whistler *Pachycephala homeyeri*

L 16–17 cm. Phil. 3 ssp, 1 in region: ssp *homeyeri* (Si Amil, Pandanan, Sipadan [off NE Bor]; Sulu) may be separable from the two extralimital ssp as monotypic '**Sulu Whistler**' based on plumage and song. Common in forest on islands where it occurs in region. **ID Ad** pale rufous-brown upperparts and wash across breast; underparts white; black bare parts. **Imm** darker rufous-edged wings and tail. **Voc** Song: loud, melodious notes "swee'OOP whit-whit'it", rather more bulbul-like. Call: emphatic "chonk, chonk-chonk".

Sulphur-bellied Whistler *Pachycephala sulfuriventer* E

L 14–15 cm. 2 ssp: *sulfuriventer* (N–C–E–SE Sul); *meridionalis* (SW Sul). Fairly common in (sub-) montane forest, 800–2500 m, rarely to lowlands. Forages mainly in mid-storey. **ID M** mid-brown head and upperparts; off-white throat and breast; pale yellowish belly, brighter yellow vent; black bill. Spp *meridionalis* paler below. **F** paler underparts. **Imm** greyish head; brighter upperparts. **Voc** Song: typically loud, liquid "whit-whit-whit-whit-WHIP", lasting ~1 sec, though variable, often additional explosive notes at end. Call: downslurred "see-choo". **SS** See Matinan Warbling-flycatcher.

Golden Whistler *Pachycephala pectoralis*

L 17–19 cm. Aus. ~12 ssp, 1 in region: *dammeriana* (Damar). Complex taxonomy. Previous treatments included 50–60 ssp in this species, incl. Tenggara, Babar, Selayar and Moluccan Whistlers, some ssp of Fawn-breasted Whistler and many extralimital forms, making this one of the most variable bird species on earth. Present taxonomic arrangement based on combination of mtDNA, bioacoustic and morphological insights, but further changes likely pending genomic data. Golden Whistler *P. pectoralis* as defined here mostly comprises Australasian forms, including those separated as Mangrove Golden Whistler *P. melanura* in previous treatments. The odd inclusion of regional *dammeriana* is based on strong mtDNA evidence although genome-wide analyses may re-align it with Tenggara Whistler as would be expected by geography. On Damar, uncommon in closed-canopy forest, not found in coastal degraded forest. Singly or pairs; in mid-canopy. **ID M** black head; white throat bordered black; deep yellow underparts and olive-green upperparts with primaries edged grey, rectrices broadly edged olive. **F** drab; grey crown, upperparts dull sandy-olive, slightly barred whitish throat with greyish band below, remainder of underparts bright buffy-yellow. **Imm** undescribed. **Voc** Ssp *dammeriana* utters short series of 3–8 notes "wit-wit-wit-Woot-Woot'DIR" at 3 n/s, whiplash-like ending. **SS** Fem Wallacean Whistler lacks yellowish or olive tones and has streaked breast.

Moluccan Whistler *Pachycephala macrorhyncha*

L 17–19 cm. W NG to Wallacea. 9 ssp, 8 in region: *macrorhyncha* (Seram, Ambon); *pelengensis* (Banggai); *clio* (Sula); *mentalis* (Morotai, Halmahera, Bacan); *tidorensis* (Ternate, Tidore); *obiensis* (Obi); *buruensis* (Buru); *fuscoflava* (Tanimbar). For taxonomy see Golden Whistler. Ssp *mentalis*, *tidorensis* and *obiensis* sometimes separated as '**Black-chinned Whistler**' *P. mentalis* even though all nine taxa exhibit similarly deep divergence in mtDNA, plumage and vocalisations (except *tidorensis* which closely resembles *mentalis*). Future treatment as seven young regional mostly-monotypic species ('**Seram**', '**Banggai**', '**Sula**', '**Halmahera**' including *mentalis* and *tidorensis*, '**Bupati's**', '**Buru**', and '**Tanimbar Whistler**', respectively) and one extralimital species likely warranted. Generally fairly common throughout in scrub, forest, edge. Singly or pairs; in mid-canopy. **ID M** head black; collar yellow; mantle brownish-olive; rump and tail black, wings dull black with olive to greyish edging; chin and throat white, black breast band, underparts golden-yellow. **F** upperparts dull-brown; crown olive-brown; wings blackish-brown with citrine to greyish feather edging; vent yellow; underparts whitish washed yellow becoming browner towards breast (with vaguely defined grey-tinged band); throat pale buff. Ssp *buruensis* **M** back dark greenish-olive, rump narrowly edged olive, breast band narrow near ear-coverts; **F** mantle dull brownish-olive faintly washed yellow, belly buff-brown, breast band greyer and more contrasting with paler throat and belly. Ssp *clio* small, **M** like previous but upperparts brighter and more yellow-tinged; **F** throat whitish with faint dark barring, underparts washed yellow. Ssp *pelengensis* small, **M** similar to previous; **F** as previous but upperparts more olive, underparts deeper yellow. Ssp *fuscoflava* very large, **M** collar narrow, chin and throat yellow; **F** underparts with buffy-rufous tinge, especially on breast. Ssp *mentalis* large, **M** chin black, throat extensively white, black breast patch (not meeting ear-coverts), olive-green upperparts; **F** crown grey, upperparts olive, throat and upper breast greyish-white, flanks olive, belly lemon. Ssp *tidorensis* as previous but slightly larger, **F** crown paler and olive areas yellower. Ssp *obiensis* as previous but **M** chin white, black breast patch more extensive, band-like; **F** crown and mantle brownish, buffier throat and band below, breast and flanks washed orange, belly bright yellow. **Imm** generally paler bill and rufous-edged primaries. **Voc** Highly variable, even within each taxon. Commonly heard song motifs include: ssp *pelengensis* (i) quite thin, sweet "wheet-wheet'choop-WIT'e'E", lasting 2.5 sec, last note higher-pitched, (ii) perhaps call, sweet "wit'chee"; *clio* reported sharp upslur followed by 2 evenly pitched whistles, then slightly explosive note, "whit tu tu tsit"; *mentalis* and *tidorensis* 5–10 loud, fluty "woop-woop-woop-WER-CHOP" at 2 n/s, last 2 notes explosive, "woop" can be replaced with "wee", last note downslurred, sometimes replaced with upslurred "WIT"; *obiensis* 7–10 loud "cheop-cheop-cheop-cheop-cheop-cheop-CHEOP", lasting 4–6 sec, increasing in volume and tempo; *buruensis* undescribed; *macrorhyncha* repetitive "wee'chop-wee'chop-wee'chop-WIT" at 2 n/s, single excited last note; *fuscoflava* series of 7–12 notes "chop-chop-chop-wit-chop-wee-WIT-CHOP" at 3 n/s, excited 5-note whiplash-like ending. Call: upslurred "whit". **SS** See Drab Whistler. On Tanimbar, fem Wallacean Whistler has white underparts (lacking buffy tinge) with dark shaft streaking (absent in Moluccan).

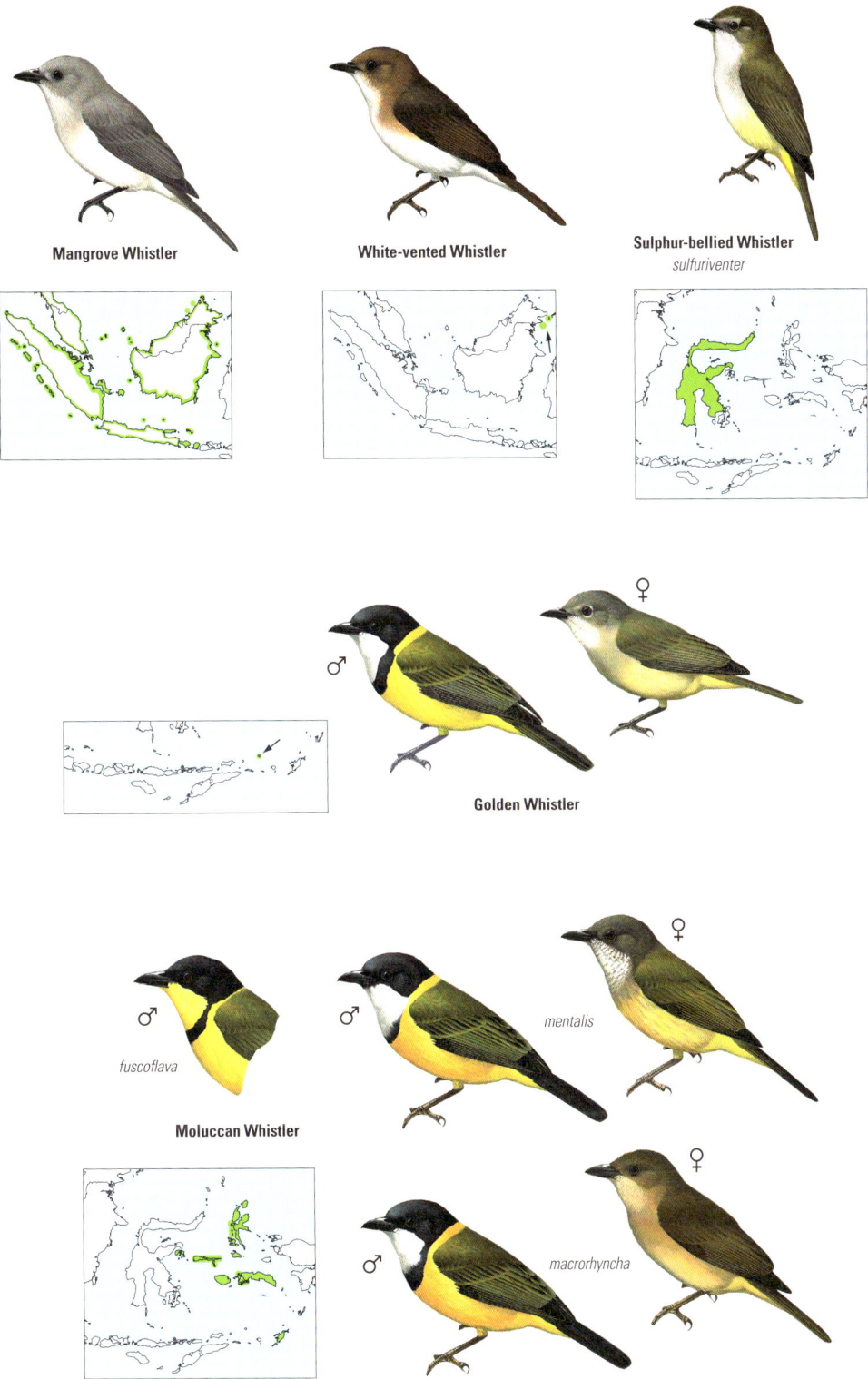

Mangrove Whistler

White-vented Whistler

Sulphur-bellied Whistler
sulfuriventer

Golden Whistler

♂
fuscoflava

Moluccan Whistler

♂
mentalis
♀

♂
macrorhyncha
♀

Tenggara Whistler *Pachycephala calliope* **E**

L 17–19 cm. 6 ssp: *calliope* (Timor, Semau); *arthuri* (Wetar); *javana* (E Jav, Bali); *fulvotincta* (Sumbawa–Alor); *fulviventris* (Sumba); *everetti* (Tanahjampea, Kalaotoa, Madu). See Golden, Babar, Selayar and Fawn-breasted Whistlers for taxonomy. Tenggara Whistler as here defined is conservatively circumscribed and unites multiple forms deeply divergent in mtDNA but similar in plumage and (occasionally) song. Future treatment of all ssp as young monotypic species may be warranted ('**Timor**' *P. calliope*, '**Wetar**' *P. arthuri*, '**Flores Sea**' *P. everetti*, '**Bali**' *P. javana*, '**Bima**' *P. fulvotincta*, '**Sumba Whistler**' *P. fulviventris*). On the other hand, genomic data may expose puzzlingly divergent mtDNA haplotype of *calliope* and *arthuri* as artefact, necessitating their merger with each other and possibly with other forms. Generally fairly common throughout in scrub, forest, edge; preference for higher elevation on Timor, Jav and Bali. Singly or pairs; in lower and mid-canopy. **ID M** black head; collar washed olive; white throat bordered black; pale yellow underparts; olive-green upperparts with primaries edged grey; rump and tail olive. **F** greyish crown; upperparts olive-brown; throat white with olive band below, underparts yellowish (brighter towards vent). Ssp *arthuri* longer-billed, **M** more yellowish upperparts, especially nape; **F** undescribed. Ssp *fulviventris* smaller; **M** yellow hindcollar, tail black, chin black, throat white (not reaching ear coverts), breast band narrow, breast and belly washed rufous; **F** similar to *calliope*. Ssp *javana* **M** resembles previous but white throat reaching ear coverts, tail tipped pale, underparts less intensely rufous; **F** whitish underparts, bright-yellow vent, olive upperparts, grey-brown crown. Ssp *fulvotincta* as previous but **M** only breast washed rufous, **F** drab sandy-brown crown and upperparts. Ssp *everetti* **M** like previous but broad breast band, underparts only slight rufous wash, back mottled black, wings black; **F** breast and belly more pinkish. **Imm** generally paler bill and rufous-edged primaries. **Voc** Highly variable, even within each taxon. Commonly heard song motifs: *calliope/arthuri* variable including (i) short series of "wih-wih-wih-WHIP-CHOO-CHU'IT" at 3 n/s, whiplash-like ending; (ii) excited, staccato mix of melodious, fluty notes lasting 1.5–2.5 s; (iii) short "wih-WHIT-soo-t't't'tih"; *javana* (i) short series of 4–8 loud, melodious "wee-wee-wee-CHOO-CHOO-CHOO" at 3 n/s; (ii) 3–7 melodious upslurred "wir-wir-wir" at 3 n/s, increasing in volume; (iii) 3–7 downslurred "wee'oo-wee'oo-wee'oo" at 2 n/s; *fulvotincta* (i) 4–9 equally spaced upslurred "WIT'hoo-WIT'hoo-WIT'hoo..." at 2 n/s, occasionally more forceful "w'WIT'choo-w'WIT'choo-w'WIT'choo..."; (ii) 4–9 equally spaced downslurred "CHOP-CHOP-CHOP" at 2 n/s; *fulviventris* (i) 4–9 equally-spaced downslurred "CHOP-CHOP-CHOP" at 2–3 n/s, sometimes increased to 10–20 notes at 6 n/s, or "chop-chop-chop-CHOP-CHOP-CHOP"; (ii) 3–8 evenly spaced disyllabic "s'chop-s'chop-s'chop..." at 3 n/s; (iii) 3–7 melodious upslurred "wir-wir-wir" at 3 n/s, increasing in volume; *everetti* (i) metallic "too WEE"; (ii) ~6 downslurred "tcho-tcho-tcho...doo" at 3 n/s, increasing in volume, lower final note. **SS** Fem Bare-throated has grey (not brown) crown, olive (not sandy-brown) upperparts and extensive yellow underparts (not restricted to vent). Also see Fawn-breasted and Mangrove Whistlers.

Selayar Whistler *Pachycephala teysmanni* **E**

L 16–17 cm. Monotypic. See Golden Whistler for taxonomy. Based on mtDNA, embedded within Tenggara Whistler (though deeply diverged from all its ssp) and possibly part of it; here separated based on highly distinct plumage. Fairly common in scrub, forest, edge. Singly or pairs; in lower and mid-canopy. **ID M** slate-grey head, olive-green upperparts, pure white throat, buff breast to yellowish belly; **F** buff lores and ear coverts; generally buffier in plumage. **Imm** brown-washed upperparts, streaked underparts. **Voc** Less variable than other species; (i) 2 flat metallic notes, second higher-pitched "wih-WEEE", lasting 1 s; (ii) short "wih-wih-WIH-WIH", 2 n/s; (iii) "wih-wih-CHOP", lasting 1.2 s, whiplash-like ending.

Babar Whistler *Pachycephala sharpei* **E**

L 17–19 cm. Monotypic. Puzzling, little-known species previously included in larger umbrella species (see Golden Whistler), and perhaps closely related to (or part of) Tenggara Whistler. Present treatment based on extremely divergent mtDNA and somewhat distinct female plumage, pending future genomic data. Local and uncommon in remaining areas of lush forest, not found in coastal degraded forest. **ID** Large bill. **M** black head, collar washed olive; olive-green upperparts; white throat; black breast band; underparts lemon-yellow. **F** upperparts brownish-olive; tail olive; throat white, narrow breast band grey-buff, breast and flanks tinged cinnamon; belly pale yellow. **Imm** undescribed. **Voc** Song: complex; (i) ~30 staccato, "tcho'tcho'tcho...", 9 n/s, rising with intensity, with final low "hoo" note; (ii) short series of "wih-wih-wih-wih-wih-WHIP", lasting 2.5 s, whiplash-like ending; (iii) single, repeated, flat "tweo", with a final flourish of complex notes, lasting 1 s. Call: flat, metallic "tcho". **SS** Fem Wallacean Whistler lacks yellow and olive in plumage and has streaked breast.

Fawn-breasted Whistler *Pachycephala orpheus* **E**

L 14–18 cm. 3 ssp: *orpheus* (Wetar, Timor, Rote); the two ssp *par* (Romang) and *compar* (Leti, Moa) were previously included as 'hen-colored' forms within an unrelated, broadly-defined umbrella species (see Golden Whistler). Present treatment under Fawn-breasted based on their close mtDNA affinity and shared colouration. Common in forest, tall scrub, <1600 m. Singly, pairs or family groups; usually in mid-storey, often in mixed flocks. **ID** In absence of Tenggara Whistler, populations on smaller islands, such as ssp *par*, ssp *compar* and *orpheus* on Rote, are bigger and more massive in dimensions. **M** grey-brown upperparts (greyer on crown and face, more olive on back); white throat contrasting with fawn-buff breast; paler belly and yellow vent; greenish-olive tail. **F** less contrasting crown. Ssp *par* both sexes olive-brown upperparts, crown slightly greyer, rump slightly rufous, throat white, underparts buff; *compar* lores and supercilium pale buff, belly paler and yellower. **Imm** faintly marked breast; paler bill. **Voc** Song: *orpheus* loud series of 8–15 "doo-doo-doo... DEE", rising in speed and volume, with abrupt final note; call a thin, soft "soo'wee". Ssp *par* undescribed. Ssp *compar* (i) series of 10–20 forceful "chop-chop-chop-oo'WIT" at 4 n/s, increasing in volume; (ii) drawn-out "whirrrl-W'WHIT" lasting 0.7s; (iii) call a thin, drawn-out "wir". **SS** Fem Tenggara Whistler is extremely similar in colouration, the two species possibly closely mimicking each other, but is more massive (>65% heavier), with an especially massive bill; Fawn-breasted looks diminutive where they co-occur. Also, Fawn-breasted often shows paler wing feather margination creating impression of pale wingbar, which always seems to be lacking in fem Tenggara. Fem Wallacean Whistler lacks yellowish or buff tones on underparts, has streaked breast and small bill.

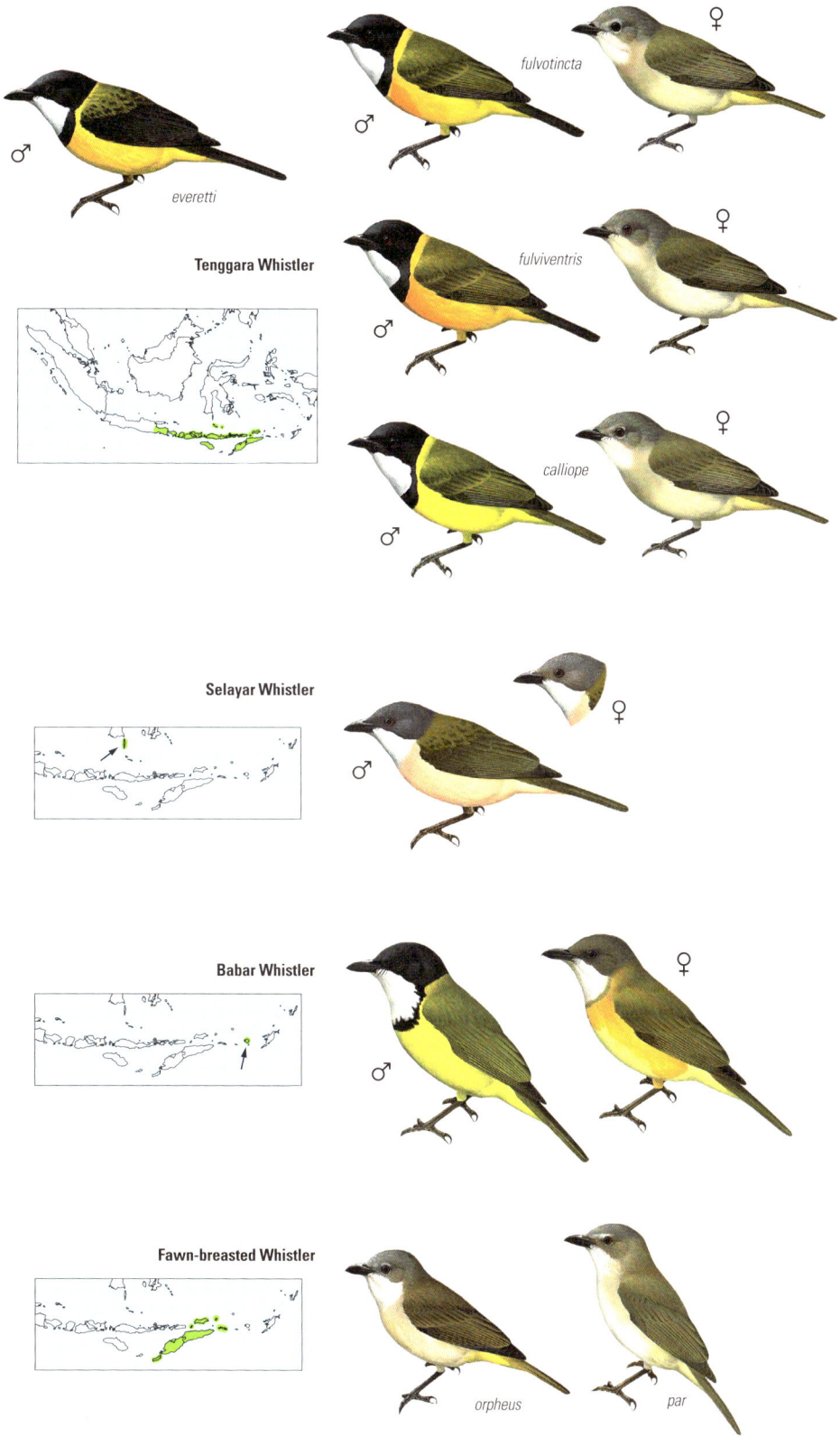

everetti

Tenggara Whistler

fulvotincta ♀

fulviventris ♀

calliope ♀

Selayar Whistler

♂ ♀

Babar Whistler

♂ ♀

Fawn-breasted Whistler

orpheus par

Island Whistler *Pachycephala phaionota*
L 16 cm. W Papuan Is to Moluccas. Monotypic. Uncommon in coastal vegetation. Typical 'supertramp' and small-island specialist, <500 m. **ID Ad** contrasting dark grey head with mid-brown upperparts; white throat contrasts with ochre-grey wash on breast and flanks, paler belly; black bill; pinkish legs. Birds on Nanusa (Talaud Is) appear to show browner, more extensive wash on underparts. **Imm** olive-brown head. **Voc** Song: loud "weet-chuw-weeee". Call: "chup" notes and more nasal notes. **SS** See Grey Whistler.

Obi Whistler *Pachycephala johni*   **E**
L 15 cm. Monotypic. See Drab Whistler for taxonomy. Common in all types of forest. **ID M** grey head; greyish-brown upperparts contrasting with rich rufous-cinnamon underparts. **F** similar but duller; dark streaking on breast. **Imm** undescribed. **Voc** Song: series of 3–10 varied, staccato, tuneful notes, lasting 0.5–2 sec.

Drab Whistler *Pachycephala griseonota*   **E**
L 15 cm. 5 ssp: *griseonota* (Seram); *kuehni* (Kai); *examinata* (Buru); *lineolata* (Sula, Peleng); *cinerascens* (N Mol). No longer includes Obi Whistler based on distinct colouration. Plumage variability among races makes further partitioning into species possible. More study required, particularly of complex vocalisations. Uncommon (e.g. Kai) to fairly common (e.g. Buru) in primary and degraded forest. Singly; favouring mid-canopy. **ID Ad** sooty-grey head; brownish-grey upperparts; off-white throat; buff-tinged underparts. Ssp *kuehni* uniform pale grey head and upperparts, white throat, brownish-grey breast, white belly; *examinata* darker grey upperparts, white throat and underparts with very pale buff tinge; *lineolata* paler grey upperparts, white underparts with light grey breast; *cinerascens* grey-brown head and upperparts, off-white throat, greyish breast with paler belly. **Imm** has dark breast streaking. **Voc** Song: *griseonota* series of 3–8 loud, explosive upslurred notes "che-che-che", lasting 1–1.5 sec at 2–4 n/s, gradually increasing in volume and occasionally speed; *kuehni* series of 3–8 upslurred notes "wit-wit-wit..." at 3 n/s, sometimes ending with short, fast melody; *examinata* (i) similar structure but 5–13 downslurred notes, "chup-chup-chup...che", lasting ~2 sec at 5 n/s, ending with single flatter note, (ii) series of 3–8 loud, explosive upslurred notes "che-che-che...WHIP", lasting 1–1.5 sec at 2–4 n/s, as *griseonota* but with explosive final note; *lineolata* 3–5 "woo-woo-woo" at 2 n/s; *cinerascens* series of 15–20 notes "wir-wir-wir..., WEH-WEH-WEH", lasting 1.5–2 sec, notes increasing in speed and volume until reaching crescendo. Call: (i) thin, downslurred, drawn-out "seeep"; (ii) drawn-out upslurred "weep". **SS** Fem Moluccan Whistler buffier-brown overall, with less grey upperparts and more yellowish-tinged underparts, lacking contrasting grey crown and breast band. See also Grey Whistler.

Wallacean Whistler *Pachycephala arctitorquis*   **E**
L 14 cm. 3 ssp: *arctitorquis* (Tanimbar); *kebirensis* (Romang, Damar, Moa, Babar); *tianduana* (Tayandu). Fairly common in variety of wooded habitats. Singly or pairs; favours understorey and lower canopy. **ID M** black hood; large white throat bordered black; silky-grey upperparts; white underparts. Ssp *tianduana* darker grey upperparts and tail; broader breast band; buffish flanks. **F** rufous-brown head, outerwing and tail, grey-brown mantle, underparts white with dark shaft-streaking; *kebirensis* greyer upperparts including crown; *tianduana* browner upperparts and paler, whiter underparts. **Imm** more rufous upperparts, paler bill. **Voc** Song: series of 4–15 upslurred "choo" notes, ending with higher-pitched, more explosive "WHEE" at 3 n/s, gradually increasing in volume; when excited increases tempo and speed; also drawn-out, rising "chooo-wit". Call: thin, fluty "seeup". **SS** See Moluccan, Golden, Fawn-breasted and Babar Whistlers.

Grey Whistler *Pachycephala simplex*
L 14–15. Australasia. 11 ssp, 1 in region: *rufipennis* (Kai). Uncommon in forest. Singly or pairs; in mid- and upper canopy. **ID Ad** dull grey-brown head and upperparts; whitish underparts with darker wash on breast; conspicuous pale supercilium in front of eye and darker lores. **Imm** chestnut wings. **Voc** Song: series of 5 unhurried notes, first 2 short and flat, last 3 powerful, down- and upslurred whistles "weh-weh-wip-WEEK-YOU", lasting <2.5 sec. Call: muted whistled notes. **SS** Island Whistler shows contrast between dark grey head and brown mantle (dull grey-brown in Grey); Island also lacks supercilium and has more contrasting pure white throat. Drab Whistler greyer overall, lacks supercilium and has paler lores.

Bornean Whistler *Pachycephala hypoxantha*   **E**
L 16 cm. 2 ssp: *hypoxantha* (Bor, except W); *sarawacensis* (Poi Range in W Bor). Common in (sub-) montane forest, 900–2600 m. Singly or pairs; usually in mid-storey, often in mixed flocks. **ID Ad** olive-green upperparts; bright yellow underparts with greenish tinge on upper flanks and breast; dark lores. Ssp *sarawacensis* lacks greenish breast. **Imm** greyish head; brighter upperparts. **Voc** Song: highly variable range of clear, explosive, fluty whistles; (i) series of 5–10 accelerating "choo-choo-choo..."; (ii) upslurred whiplash-like "wh'ip-WHIP". Call: fluty, short "sip".

VANGIDAE
Woodshrikes, Philentomas, Vangas and allies
5 species in region

A large, mostly African and Malagasy family of small- to medium-sized shrike-like forest birds. The flycatcher-shrikes and woodshrikes are usually conspicuous at mid- to upper storey, often as part of mixed flocks. The philentomas are shy and cryptic at lower to mid-storey. The family exhibits great variation in bill shape and foraging methods.

Bar-winged Flycatcher-shrike *Hemipus picatus*
L 14–15 cm. S–SE Asia. 4 ssp, 1 in region: *intermedius* (Bor, Sum, MPen). Fairly common in upper lowland to montane forest, edge and plantations, 500–2200 m, occasionally to sea level. Pairs or small groups (<8), joins mixed flocks. **ID M** black upperparts; whitish-buff underparts; long white wing patch. **F** brownish-tinged upperparts; paler underparts. **Imm** buff scaling on upperparts; buffish wing patch. **Voc** Song: minivet-like "jeep-jeep-te-ditit-jip". Call: short rapid thin shrill "swit't't'wit", lasting 0.3 sec; similar "sittit-wittit" and slight variations.

Black-winged Flycatcher-shrike *Hemipus hirundinaceus*
L 14–15 cm. Sundaic. Monotypic. Fairly common in forest, edge, <400 m on Sum and <1500 m on Jav–Bali. Pairs or small groups (<8), joins mixed flocks. **ID M** as Bar-winged Flycatcher-shrike but lacks white wing patch; paler, greyer underparts and longer-billed. **F** upperparts brown-tinged; paler underparts. **Imm** upperparts scaled buff; buffish wing-coverts. **Voc** Song: ringing "tsis-sis-sis-SIS–sis-SIS–sis-SIS–sis-SIS–sis-SIS–sis-SIS", lasting 3 sec, slightly slowing off towards end. Call: (i) 3–6 harsh, buzzy, descending notes "hee-tee-tee-teet", lasting ~0.7 sec; (ii) sharp, quick "tee-too".

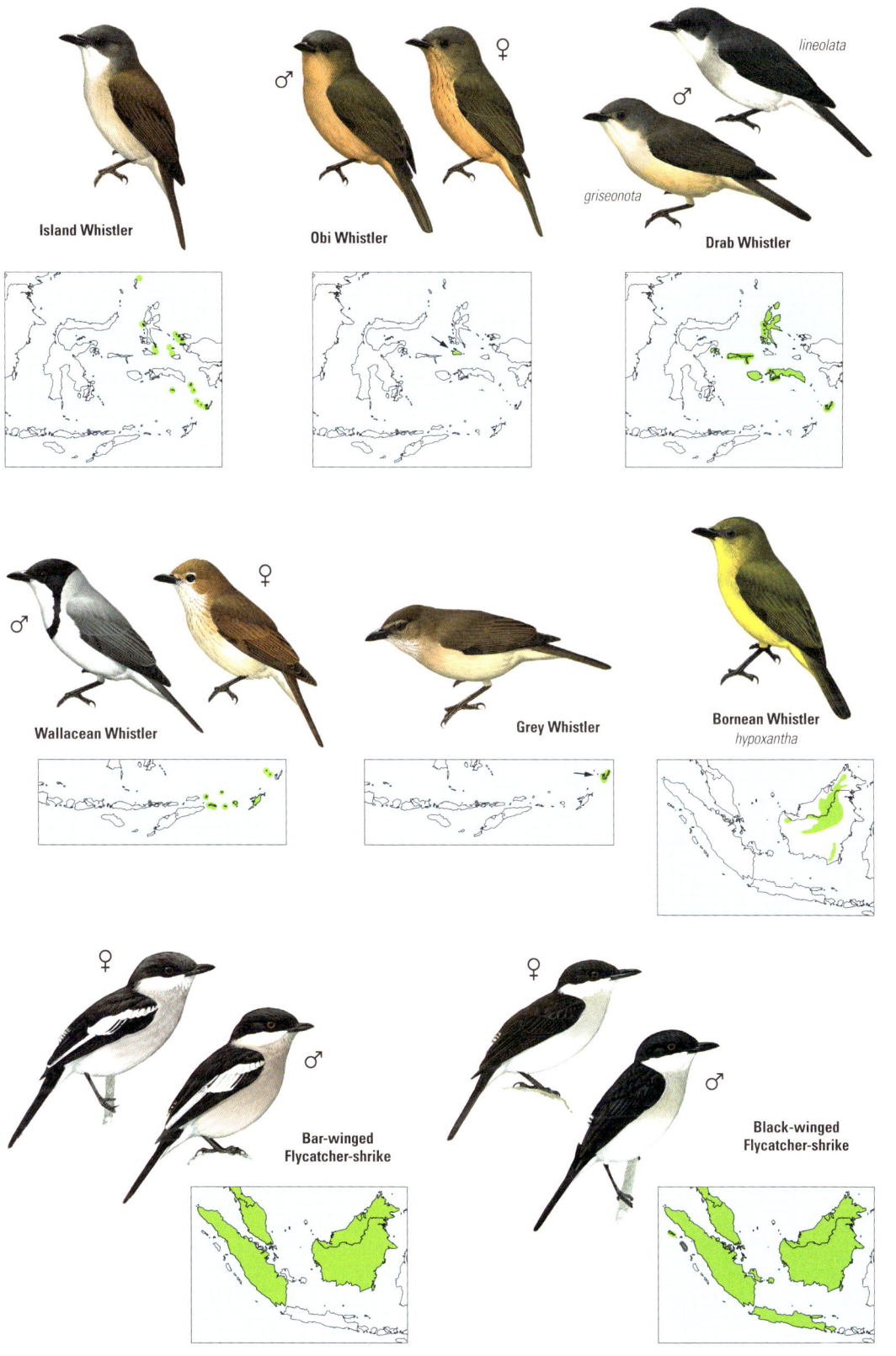

Island Whistler

Obi Whistler ♂ ♀

Drab Whistler *lineolata* ♂ *griseonota*

Wallacean Whistler ♂ ♀

Grey Whistler

Bornean Whistler *hypoxantha*

♀ **Bar-winged Flycatcher-shrike** ♂

♀ **Black-winged Flycatcher-shrike** ♂

Large Woodshrike *Tephrodornis virgatus*
L 19–23 cm. S–SE–E Asia. ~10 ssp, 3 in region: *virgatus* (S Sum, Jav); *fretensis* (N Sum, MPen); *frenatus* (Bor). Uncommon in forest, edge, <1500 m. Pairs or small groups (<10). **ID M** mid-grey crown and upperparts with white forecrown and rump; black tail; black mask; pale iris; soft whitish underparts. Ssp *fretensis* smaller, darker on mantle; *frenatus* larger white rump, less white on forehead, browner wings, rosier breast. **F** less contrasting facial pattern; no white on forecrown. **Imm** scaled, brownish upperparts, buff underparts. **Voc** Song: (i) loud, ringing "pip-pip-pip..." lasting 2–3 sec at 6 n/s on a level pitch; (ii) "pip-PIP-piw-pip-PIP-piw-..." or "pip-PIW-pip-PIW-..." lasting 2–3 sec at 4 n/s. Call: harsh, scolding "chree".

Rufous-winged Philentoma *Philentoma pyrhoptera*
L 16–17 cm. Sundaic. 2 ssp: *pyrhoptera* (Bor–Sum, MPen); *dubia* (Natuna). Fairly common in forest, <1200 m, rarely to 1600 m. Singly or pairs; prefers understorey, occasionally joins mixed flocks. **ID M** dull-blue head, breast and mantle, contrasting with chestnut greater-coverts, tertials, secondaries and tail; darker primaries; buff-white belly; red eye. **Blue morph** scarce: uniform dark dull-blue; white vent. Ssp *dubia* slightly smaller; less rufous rump and tail. **F** blue replaced by dark greyish-brown head and mantle, buff breast. **Imm** paler bill; dull chestnut wings and tail. **Voc** Song: clear disyllabic whistle "tit-eeeeeee" lasting 1.2 sec, first note higher-pitched (inaudible at distance), second note level or slightly rising. Call: harsh scolding notes. **SS** See Maroon-breasted.

Maroon-breasted Philentoma *Philentoma velata*
L 17–21 cm. Sundaic. 2 ssp: *velata* (Jav); *caesia* (Bor–Sum, MPen). Uncommon in primary, secondary and submontane forest, <1700 m. Singly or pairs, joins mixed flocks; inconspicuous in mid-canopy, sitting for prolonged periods. **ID M** slate-blue plumage with black face, forehead and throat; deep maroon breast (appears black in dull light); broad-based black bill; red eye. Ssp *caesia* more extensive black throat. **F** maroon and black replaced by dark slate-blue. **Imm** inadequately described, possibly as fem but with black eye. **Voc** Song: series of clear, sombre, bell-like "poo", gradually changing in pitch, often in tandem with forceful, bouncing squirrel-like "choot'ot, choot'ot" or swelling "chichiCHOWCHOW". Call: harsh, grating "churrt". **SS** Fem Maroon-breasted often confused with the rare blue morph of Rufous-winged. Extreme caution needed in identification: Rufous-winged is smaller, slightly slimmer-billed, often with a paler vent, and perhaps lighter-blue (more azure) overall with the throat and face at least as pale as the rest of the plumage (versus Maroon-breasted's more blackish face and throat).

1 species
Monotypic, enigmatic family endemic to Borneo. Large arboreal bird of the forest canopy. Robust with large hooked bill. Distinctive plumage and call. Often moving nomadically within suitable habitat.

Bristlehead *Pityriasis gymnocephala* 　　　　**E**
L 25 cm. Monotypic. Local and uncommon in forest incl. peatswamp, <600 m, recorded to 1200 m. Nomadic canopy-dweller in small flocks (<10), generally not mixing with other species, and rarely descending lower. **ID M** striking crimson head with yellow crown and black face patch; black bill very large, slightly hooked; body glossy black with short tail; crimson thighs; pink legs. In flight appears to show white wing patch due to base of primaries being finely feathered. **F** variable crimson streaking on flanks and upper breast. **Imm** lacks black face patch, yellow crown much reduced and heavy crimson streaking on underparts. **Voc** Variety of varied, unusual whistles mixed with screeches reminiscent of Black Hornbill: (i) whistled "pit-pit-PIOOO", often in duet, interspersed with unusual quieter wails and whining screams; (ii) harsh, low, scolding "kaw".

AEGITHINIDAE
Ioras
2 species in region
Small, active, arboreal birds, often forming part of mixed flocks. Brightly coloured and vocal; ioras are generally conspicuous in the mid- to upper storey.

Common Iora *Aegithina tiphia*
L 12–15 cm. S–SE Asia, Palawan. 11 ssp, 4 in region: *horizoptera* (Sum and satellites, MPen); *aequanimis* (Sabah, Palawan); *viridis* (Bor except Sabah); *scapularis* (Jav, Bali). Common in open woodland, edge, scrub, mangroves and parkland, <1000 m. Singly or small groups (<5). **ID M br** yellow face and underparts; tail, wings and crown mostly black with two white wingbars and white-fringed tertials; mantle green with variable amounts of black; white rump that puffs out in aerial display. Ssp *aequanimis* has yellow forehead and variably more black on mantle; *viridis* similar but smaller, green forehead; *scapularis* green tail, lacks non-breeding plumage. **M non-br** all ssp show green mantle and crown. **F** similar to male non-br but less bright, wings less contrasting. **Imm** duller; less distinct wingbars. **Voc** Song: noisy; range of strident, unmusical rasping, sometimes melodious whistling phrases including (i) glissading "did-dee-dweeo" or "did-dee-piyooo", lasting 1 sec; (ii) piercing, drawn-out, tuneless whistled "peeeeeee-yeo", lasting ~2 sec, first note level, last downslurred. Call: (i) dry, harsh rattle, often interspersed with song; (ii) excited "chit-chit-chit...". **SS** See Green Iora.

Green Iora *Aegithina viridissima*
L 12–15 cm. Sundaic. 2 ssp: *viridissima* (Bor–Sum, MPen); *thapsina* (Anambas). Fairly common in forest, usually in canopy, <850 m. **ID M** dark olive-green with yellow vent; broad yellow eyering; black wings with broad white wingbars and pale-fringed tertials; black tail. **F** paler olive-green with yellower underparts (esp. yellow in *thapsina*); median covert wingbar washed yellow; yellow eyering less distinct. **Imm** paler underparts, eye ring absent. **Voc** Song: high-pitched, buzzy "zer-zo-zer-zoooo", lasting 0.8 sec, or "zer-zo-zter-twee-zoooo", last note downslurred, lasting >1 sec. Often duets, with additional short, buzzy, scratchy notes. Call: repeated "zee-zee-zee..." at 5 n/s. **SS** Fem Green closely resembles male non-br/fem Common Iora but ghosts her partner's broad yellow eyering, has greener (not yellower) loral area and a median-covert wingbar with yellowish wash (always white in Common); best identified through accompanying males.

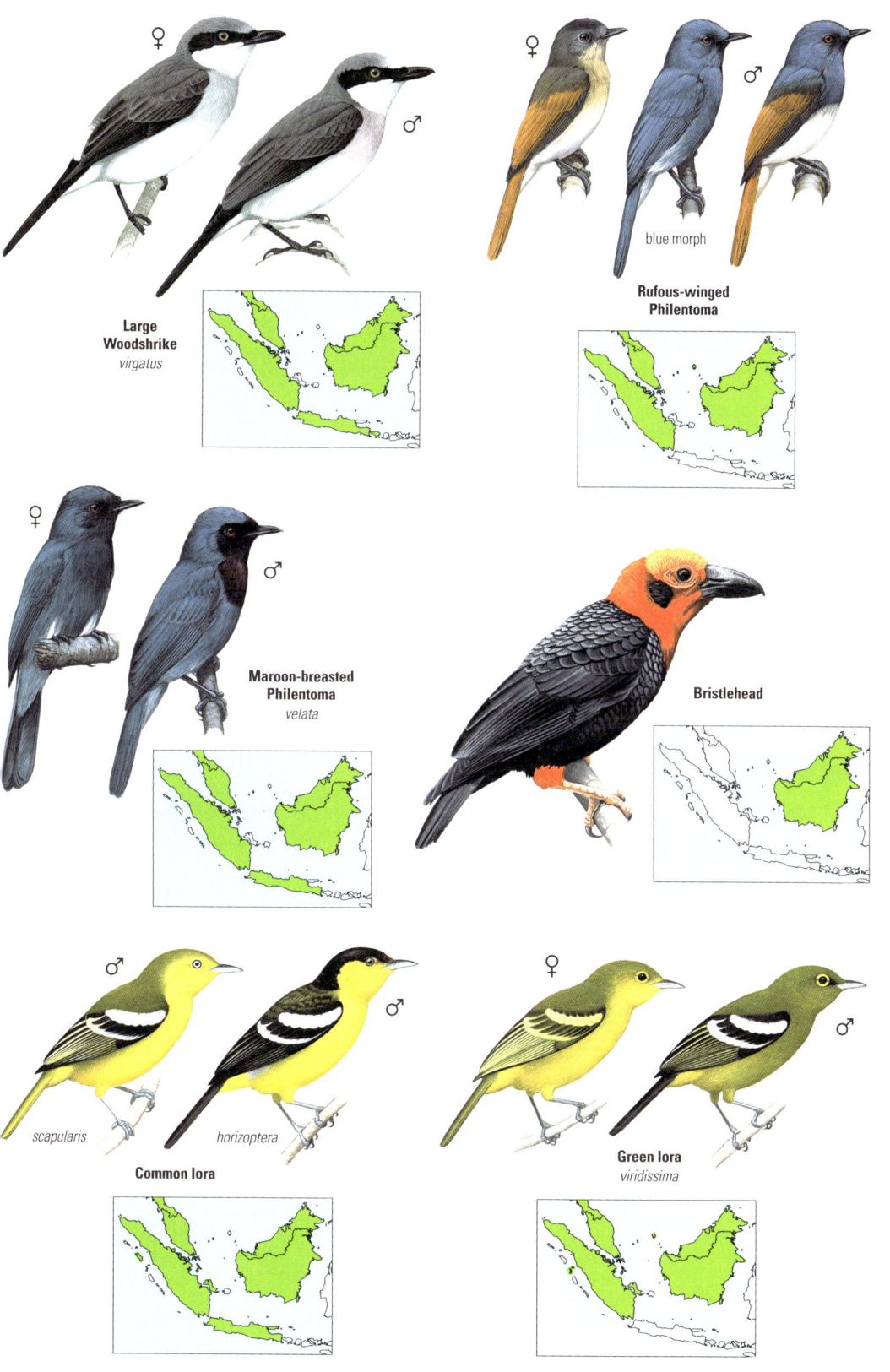

Large Woodshrike
virgatus

Rufous-winged Philentoma

blue morph

Maroon-breasted Philentoma
velata

Bristlehead

scapularis   *horizoptera*

Common Iora

Green Iora
viridissima

ARTAMIDAE
Woodswallows
3 species in region

Small, stocky aerial feeders with stout bills. Feed by sallying for insects from exposed perches in forest, edge and open country. Found singly, in pairs or small family groups. Generally very conspicuous.

White-breasted Woodswallow *Artamus leucorynchus*

L 18 cm. SE Asia to Aus. 9 ssp, 5 in region: *leucorynchus* (Bor–Phil, Natuna); *albiventer* (LS; Sul and satellites); *amydrus* (Sum–Bali, MPen); *leucopygialis* (Mol, NG, Aus); *musschenbroeki* (Babar, Tanimbar). Common in open habitats, cultivation, light woodland, edge, villages, and mangroves, <1800 m. Singly, pairs or small groups (<10). Soars and sallies above canopy; perches conspicuously for prolonged periods. **ID Ad** slate-grey head and upperparts with well demarcated pure white underparts and rump. In flight shows broad-based pointed wings with white underwing. Ssp *albiventer* slightly paler grey overall, longer bill, can show darker lores; *amydrus* as nominate but with paler hindneck and throat; *leucopygialis* indistinct, slightly paler crown and throat; *musschenbroeki* deeper-based bill, deeper grey mantle. **Imm** upperparts browner with pale fringing; mottled throat; underparts pale buff. **Voc** Song: quiet chattering and mimicry, seldom heard. Call: (i) sharp, repeated "cheep cheep cheep…"; (ii) rasping, slightly buzzy, upslurred "werk werk werk…" given in flight or perched. **SS** See Ivory-backed.

Ivory-backed Woodswallow *Artamus monachus* E

L 19–20 cm. Monotypic. Uncommon over forest, edge and clearings. Singly, pairs or small groups (<20). Soars and sallies above canopy; perches conspicuously for prolonged periods. **ID Ad** slate-grey head to upper breast, wings and tail; rest of body pure white; pale-blue eyering. **Imm** undescribed. **Voc** Chirpy "whirt whirt whirt…", lacking buzzy tone of White-breasted. **SS** White-breasted has slate-grey upperparts, prefers more open habitat.

Black-faced Woodswallow *Artamus cinereus*

L 18 cm. Aus. 5 ssp, 1 in region: *perspicillatus* (Rote–Sermata). Locally fairly common over savanna, scrub, cultivation, particularly along coast. Singly, pairs or small groups (<5). **ID Ad** uniformly grey-brown; thick black lores; black tail with white tip. In flight shows white underwing. **Imm** browner, with variable whitish streaks. **Voc** Song: quiet chattering and mimicry, seldom heard. Call: rasping, slightly buzzy, upslurred "werk werk werk…", extremely similar to White-breasted.

CAMPEPHAGIDAE
Cuckooshrikes and allies
35 species in region

A large and diverse family of small to medium-sized arboreal birds. Range in colour from the typically grey cuckooshrikes to the bright yellow-and-red minivets. Most species are canopy dwellers, but others can be found within sparsely wooded countryside and mangrove. Often part of mixed flocks and generally conspicuous.

Roving Cuckooshrike *Coracina sumatrensis*

L 24–32 cm. Sundaic, Palawan. 8 ssp, 7 in region: *sumatrensis* (Bor, Sum, Mentawai, Riau, MPen); *simalurensis* (Simeulue); *babiensis* (Babi); *kannegieteri* (Nias); *enganensis* (Enggano); *bungurensis* (Anambas, N Natuna); *vordermani* (Kangean). Usually united with Andaman Cuckooshrike *C. dobsoni* and six Philippine taxa into a more broadly defined umbrella species, '**Bar-bellied Cuckoo-shrike**' *C. striata*. However, morphological distinctions are pronounced, and limited mtDNA data indicate deep divisions even within Philippine taxa, prompting the current treatment. Uncommon in primary and mature secondary forest, <900 m, but common on many smaller islands, which it readily colonises. Singly, pairs or small family groups (<5); roaming across the upper canopy, coming lower in degraded vegetation. **ID M** pale slate-grey upperparts, head and breast; blackish outerwing and tail; white belly and rump with indistinct barring; pale iris. In flight underwing-coverts boldly barred. **F** more distinct barring on belly and rump. Ssp *kannegieteri* larger, with paler colouration in male, especially on wings and lores; *enganensis* as previous, but **M** with less distinct barring on rump and greyer belly and vent, **F** with barring almost entirely restricted to vent; *babiensis* **F** only shows limited, obscure barring on vent and axillaries, while **M** probably unbarred; smaller *simalurensis* only shows limited, obscure barring on underwing-coverts (probably in both sexes); *bungurensis* also larger than *sumatrensis*, with **F** showing more greyish-suffused back, rump and belly with less distinct barring; *vordermani* **M** barred vent, **F** unbarred whitish vent. **Imm** uniform scaled appearance, white fringes to outerwing; dark iris. **Voc** Squeaky, whiny, "kleeeup" or "pirririt", often given in flight. **SS** Smaller fem Lesser Cicadabird has more extensive barring on underparts, lacks barring on rump, has black (not pale) eyes and exhibits conspicuous white markings on undertail.

Javan Cuckooshrike *Coracina javensis* E

L 28 cm. Monotypic. Based on vocal and plumage traits, no longer considered conspecific with Malaysian Cuckooshrike *C. larutensis* or Large Cuckooshrike *C. macei*. Uncommon in open forest, clearings and savanna, occasionally hill forest, <1500 m. Singly or pairs; favours canopy around clearings. **ID M** mid-grey upperparts, head and breast; blackish lores and throat fading to ear-coverts; whitish belly. **F** slightly paler grey upperparts; less black on lores; variable light barring on underparts. **Imm** pale fringed upperparts and greyish underparts. **Voc** Loud, shrill "yieer'ik", lasting 0.5 sec. **SS** See Sunda Cuckooshrike and Lesser Cicadabird.

Sunda Cuckooshrike *Coracina larvata* E

L 26–27 cm. 3 ssp: *larvata* (Jav); *melanocephala* (Sum); *normani* (Bor). Fairly common in (sub-) montane forest, 800–2300 m. Singly or pairs, joins mixed flocks; favours canopy. **ID M** slate-grey plumage with black face, throat, outerwing and tail. Ssp *normani* slightly darker with more extensive black mask; *melanocephala* has entirely blackish head to upper breast. **F** reduced face mask; barred underwing-coverts. **Imm** whitish wing edges. **Voc** In all 3 ssp, whining, whistled "pit-teeoh", lasting 0.6 sec, first note usually rising, second drawn-out and descending. Occasionally followed by quiet, excited chattering. Often given in flight. **SS** See Lesser Cicadabird. Larger male Javan Cuckooshrike is much paler overall, especially on belly, and lacks pronounced facial mask.

Slaty Cuckooshrike *Coracina schistacea* E

L 31–32 cm. Monotypic. Uncommon in forest, scarcer in degraded forest. Singly or pairs. **ID M** dark slate-grey body with black head to upper breast and bill. **F** uniform dark slate-grey with blackish lores. **Imm** undescribed. **Voc** Nasal, scolding, descending "weeooit" lasting 0.4 sec, with slight trilling quality. **SS** Grey plumage of Common Cicadabird often confused with Slaty Cuckooshrike, but Cicadabirds are sleeker and smaller overall, thinner-billed with pale fringes to wing-coverts (unlike Slaty's more uniform wings and tail). Male Cicadabirds have black facial mask (unlike fem Slaty) but lack black on crown (unlike male Slaty). Compared to fem Slaty, larger imm Black-faced Cuckooshrike has unique white tail tip, more extensive black on face, white (not dark-grey) belly and usually shows at least slight barring on underparts.

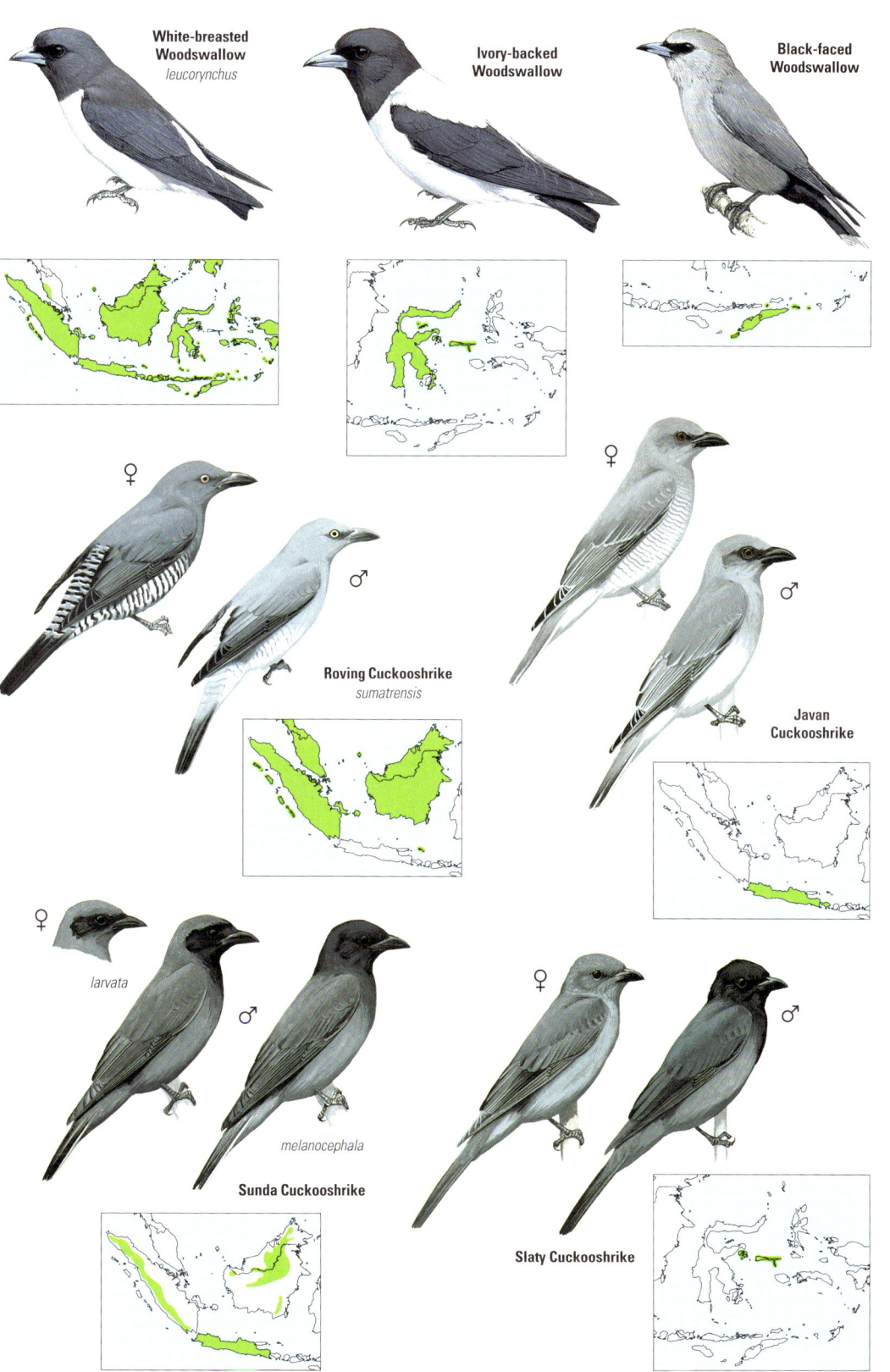

White-breasted Woodswallow
leucorynchus

Ivory-backed Woodswallow

Black-faced Woodswallow

♀ ♂ **Roving Cuckooshrike**
sumatrensis

♀ ♂ **Javan Cuckooshrike**

♀ *larvata* ♂
melanocephala
Sunda Cuckooshrike

♀ ♂ **Slaty Cuckooshrike**

White-rumped Cuckooshrike *Coracina leucopygia* `E`

L 29 cm. Monotypic. Fairly common in open habitats, including lightly wooded areas, scrub, mangroves, swamp forest, <1100 m. Can occur in small parties (<10). **ID M** mid-grey upperparts, head and breast; blackish lores, outerwing and tail; white underparts and rump; pale iris. **F** lacks blackish lores. **Imm** slightly paler grey, with indistinct barring on underparts. **Voc** (i) Series of weak, nasal chattering or squabbling notes, lasting 1–5 sec, often involving several individuals; (ii) single sharp "wheet". **SS** Fem Pied Cuckooshrike is darker grey and larger with dark iris. See also Cerulean Cuckooshrike.

Wallacean Cuckooshrike *Coracina personata* `E`

L 32 cm. 5 ssp: *personata* (Rote, Semau, Timor, Wetar, Romang, Leti, Moa, Sermata); *floris* (Sumbawa–Flores); *sumbensis* (Sumba); *unimoda* (Tanimbar); *pollens* (Kai). Much racial variation in plumage and voice. Each ssp may merit monotypic species treatment as **'Timor'**, **'Flores'**, **'Sumba'**, **'Tanimbar'** and **'Kai Cuckooshrike'**, respectively, but this treatment not followed here as plumage is roughly stepwise clinal from paler (W) to darker (E). Further study required. See also Alor Cuckooshrike for taxonomy. Uncommon, locally fairly common in a variety of forested habitats, including edge and scrub, <2200 m. Singly or pairs. **ID M** uniform slate-grey with black face and breast. Ssp *floris* paler-bodied, with paler grey underparts; *sumbensis* larger, paler overall, and whiter underparts; *unimoda* very dark slate-grey overall; *pollens* even darker, almost black. **F** similar but black on head reduced to lores and ear-coverts. **Imm** undescribed. **Voc** (i) Ssp *personata* variable, potential interisland variability, further study required; Wetar: upslurred whining "whiiirt", lasting 1 sec; Timor: rising, whiny "we'w'whiirt"; Romang: 3-note, higher-pitched "wi-te-tee"; (ii) *sumbensis* and *floris*: whining whistled "we'w'w'weeoh", lasting 0.7 sec, first upslurred, then drawn-out and descending. **SS** White-bellied Cuckooshrike is much paler overall and whiter-bellied (especially compared to Wallacean on Kai and Tanimbar) and has black restricted to lores (not extending over face). Black-faced Cuckooshrike has unique white tail tip and is much paler overall (especially on underparts) than eastern ssp of Wallacean; Black-faced resembles ssp *sumbensis* and *floris* in greyness, but has a more extensive black face mask. Also see Pale-shouldered and Tenggara Cicadabirds.

Alor Cuckooshrike *Coracina alfrediana* `E`

L 32 cm. Monotypic. Usually included with Wallacean Cuckooshrike, but this is the most distinct member of the complex in voice and colouration, disrupting the plumage cline (see under Wallacean); hence, here separated as monotypic species. Future molecular work may show that other members of the complex are genetically more distinct, requiring further divisions. Uncommon, locally fairly common in a variety of forested habitats. Singly or pairs. **ID M** wholly mid-grey including face, with darker ear-coverts ghosting a grey mask; whitish belly; darker tail and outerwing with conspicuous white edges. **F** similar but can show even paler belly. **Imm** undescribed. **Voc** Whining, whistled "pit't-teeoh", lasting 0.6 sec, first note rising, second note drawn-out and descending. **SS** Imm Black-faced has a unique white tail tip, and usually shows stronger black ear-coverts and some dark barring on belly. Also see male Tenggara Cicadabird.

Moluccan Cuckooshrike *Coracina atriceps* `E`

L 32–35 cm. 2 ssp: *atriceps* (Seram); *magnirostris* (N Mol). Uncommon in a variety of forested habitats, including edge and scrub, <1200 m. Singly or pairs. **ID M** black head and upper breast; pale grey upperparts; whitish underparts. Ssp *magnirostris* larger; slightly darker; black extending to lower breast and upper mantle. **F** variable blackish or slate-grey head. **Imm** undescribed. **Voc** Low harsh dry chatter "tr'tr'tr..." at 15 n/0.6 s. **SS** Stout-billed and Black-faced Cuckooshrikes lack Moluccan's black crown; Stout-billed is more uniformly grey, lacking white belly, and Black-faced shows unique white tail tip. See also Halmahera and Common Cicadabirds.

Black-faced Cuckooshrike *Coracina novaehollandiae*

L 32–35 cm. Aus. 3 ssp, 1 in region: *melanops* (breeds Australia, NG; winters to region). Seasonal, numbers vary annually during austral winter; scarce to fairly common in variety of open habitats including coastal scrub, cultivation and mangroves. Singly or small groups (<20). **ID Ad** silky-grey upperparts, crown and breast grading into whitish belly; black face and throat; mid-grey tail with white tail tips. **Imm** blackish lores to ear-coverts; slight barring on underparts. **Voc** Song: musical, rolling, purring "plee'e'e-urk", lasting <4 sec. Call: (i) short "pee'op", often given in flight; (ii) curious, quiet "weer'op". **SS** For separation from similarly sized cuckooshrikes, see Wallacean, Buru, Alor, Moluccan, Slaty, Stout-billed and White-bellied. Grey-plumaged cicadabirds are smaller, sleeker, thinner-billed, and virtually always show more contrasting pale fringes on wing feathers. Most cicadabirds have extensive white undertail markings not restricted to white tail tip, as in Black-faced. Those cicadabirds (e.g., Pale-shouldered, Common, Halmahera) with facial black masks as extensive as in ad or imm Black-faced Cuckooshrike are much darker overall, especially on belly and vent.

Buru Cuckooshrike *Coracina fortis* `E`

L 35 cm. Monotypic. Scarce and local, favouring hill forest, <1500 m, rarely to coastal forest. Singly or pairs, usually in forest canopy. **ID M** mid-grey with paler belly; blackish outerwing and tail; black lores becoming paler on face and throat. **F** less black lores, whiter belly. **Imm** undescribed. **Voc** Short, sharp "wheet", lasting 0.2 sec. **SS** Pale and male Common Cicadabirds much smaller, sleeker and thinner-billed with pale-fringed wing feathering and white markings on undertail; Pale also has less extensive black lores. Imm Black-faced Cuckooshrike has more extensive black on face, white tail tip, and usually shows at least slight barring on underparts.

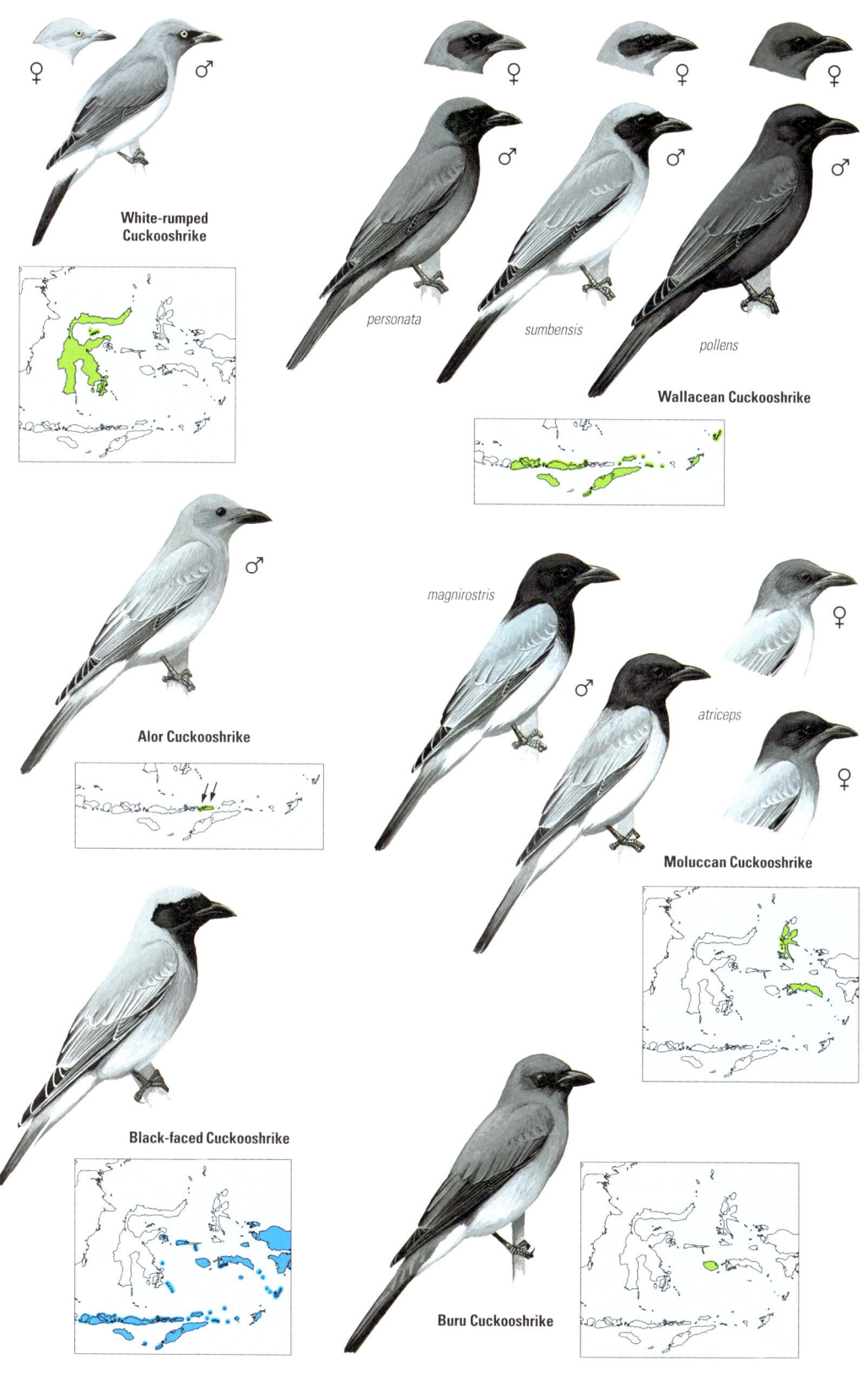

White-rumped Cuckooshrike

♀ ♂

personata

sumbensis

pollens

Wallacean Cuckooshrike

magnirostris

atriceps

Alor Cuckooshrike

Moluccan Cuckooshrike

Black-faced Cuckooshrike

Buru Cuckooshrike

White-bellied Cuckooshrike *Coracina papuensis*

L 22–29 cm. Aus. 13-14 ssp, 2 in region: *papuensis* (N Mol, NG; presumed this ssp migrant to Kisar, Sermata, Luang, Kai); *hypoleuca* (presumed this ssp migrant to Kai, Tanimbar). Limited DNA data hint that Australian and non-Australian ssp may not be each other's closest relatives, despite great vocal and plumage uniformity. If true, division into 2 species may be necessary: '**Papuan Cuckooshrike**' *C. papuensis* (Melanesia, NG into Indonesia; 8–9 ssp, incl. *papuensis* in region) and '**White-bellied Cuckooshrike**' *C. robusta* (Australia, migrates to LS; ~5 ssp; incl. *hypoleuca* in region). Fairly common in N Mol, scarce elsewhere in woodland, savanna, plantations and scrub, <800 m. **ID M** pale-grey head, upperparts and tail; white underparts with faint grey tinge to breast; black lores and outerwing. **F** slightly reduced duller blackish lores. Ssp *hypoleuca* (both sexes) larger; paler upperparts; white breast. **Imm** grey lores; slight brownish-grey mottling on upperparts. **Voc** (i) Squealing, squeaky "whee-eeyoo", lasting 0.4 sec, recalling a lorikeet; (ii) harsh scolding rattle, recalling alarm call of monarch. **SS** Greatest confusion potential on Obi with sleeker, thinner-billed Pale Cicadabird, which shows less extensive black lores, large white markings on undertail and distinct whitish wing fringes. Imm Black-faced Cuckooshrike has more extensive black on face, white tail tip, and usually shows at least slight barring on underparts. Larger Stout-billed lacks white on underparts and has much more massive bill. Male Common Cicadabird is sleeker, has thinner bill, pale-contrasting wing fringes and is much darker grey overall (incl. on underparts). Also see Halmahera Cicadabird and Wallacean Cuckooshrike.

Pied Cuckooshrike *Coracina bicolor* E

L 31 cm. Monotypic. Scarce and local in forest, rarely other wooded areas, <900 m. Singly or pairs. **ID M** contrasting black upperparts, tail and head; white underparts, throat and rump. **F** mid-grey mantle, head and breast; contrasting white belly and rump. **Imm** pale-fringed wings; brown-tinged head and breast. **Voc** Loud, ringing series of bouncing notes "tchew", "tchew-tchew...", given singly, as disyllabic or trisyllabic notes, often interspersed with rasping, harsh notes. **SS** See White-rumped Cuckooshrike.

Cerulean Cuckooshrike *Coracina temminckii* E

L 31 cm. 3 ssp: *temminckii* (N Sul), *rileyi* (C–SE Sul); *tonkeana* (E Sul). Locally fairly common in (sub-) montane forest. Singly or pairs. **ID Ad** uniform greyish-blue with black lores and throat; blue-white iris. Ssp *tonkaena* slightly bluer, with slightly paler underparts; *rileyi* slightly greyer. **Imm** slight barring on underparts. **Voc** (i) Drawn-out, very harsh, nasal, upslurred "sssssCHoot", lasting <1 sec, regularly repeated; (ii) single, drawn-out, high-pitched whistle lasting 0.8 sec. **SS** White-rumped also has pale iris but much paler belly and rump. Smaller, sleeker, thinner-billed male Common Cicadabird has black (not pale) iris and lacks blue overall plumage tone.

Stout-billed Cuckooshrike *Coracina caeruleogrisea*

L 33–37 cm. NG. 3 ssp, 1 in region: likely *strenua* (W NG). Recently discovered on Halmahera, known from submontane forest, >400m; presumably under-recorded resident. Usually found singly or pairs. **ID M** Blue-grey upperparts; mid-grey underparts; blackish outer-wing, tail and lores; rufous underwing-coverts. **F** lacks black lores. **Imm** duller; pale-fringed flight feathers. **Voc** Song: soft, rasping "chew'ch'ch'cheweer", lasting 1.5 sec, regularly repeated. Calls include short chirps, short soft rasps and harsh buzzy notes. **SS** Halmahera and male Common Cicadabirds are smaller, sleeker, have more extensive black mask, much smaller bill and are uniformly

darker (Common additionally with pale wing fringes). Imm Black-faced Cuckooshrike has white (not grey) belly, shows contrasting white tail tip, more extensive black on face, and usually exhibits at least slight barring on underparts. See also Moluccan and White-bellied Cuckooshrikes.

Pygmy Cicadabird *Celebesica abbotti* E

L 20 cm. Monotypic. Fairly common in montane forest, >1200 m. Joins mixed flocks, social. **ID M** strongly demarcated black face and throat; white underparts; bluish-grey upperparts and crown; black primaries; red iris. **F** face and throat bluish grey as upperparts. **Imm** undescribed. **Voc** Song: starts with 1–2 thin, barely audible "thip", followed by thin, high-pitched 4-note warble "twit-chew-choo'wee", lasting 1 sec. Call: thin, piercing "thip". **AN** Mountain Cicadabird.

Halmahera Cicadabird *Edolisoma parvulum* E

L 25 cm. Monotypic. Position unclear: often called 'Halmahera Cuckooshrike' and placed in *Coracina*, but vocal and morphological data suggest placement with cicadabirds. Uncommon in primary and tall secondary forest, <900 m, apparently more numerous in uplands. Singly or pairs. **ID Ad** dark slate-grey body and crown; black tail, outer wing, face and throat becoming greyer on breast. Individuals with face restricted to lores presumed **Imm**. **Voc** (i) Rapidly repeated series of 5–15 staccato, harsh chattering "chit'it'it'it...", 10 n/0.5 s; (ii) upslurred, surprised "chait"; (iii) quirky, upslurred "chwip". **SS** Often mistaken for similar male Common Cicadabird (ssp *grayi*), but has more extensive black throat and upper breast, and – unlike other cicadabirds – does not exhibit paler wing-covert fringing and white markings on undertail. Larger Moluccan Cuckooshrike shows white (not dark-grey) belly and black (not grey) crown. White-bellied Cuckooshrike is much paler overall (white on belly) and shows facial black only on lores (not extending to throat and ear-coverts). Also see Stout-billed and Black-faced Cuckooshrikes.

Pale-shouldered Cicadabird *Edolisoma dohertyi* E

L 20–24 cm. Monotypic. Forest, clearings and edge, <2000 m. Singly, pairs or small groups (<8), often joining mixed flocks; feeding in mid- to upper canopy. **ID M** silky-grey plumage with black face, throat, upper breast, tail and primaries; upperwing-coverts, tertials and secondaries broadly fringed grey-white. **F** underparts, throat and face white with thick grey barring. **Imm** undescribed. **Voc** Song: single low grating "grrrrrt", lasting 0.7 sec, regularly repeated. Call: upslurred, squeaky "whip". **SS** Wallacean Cuckooshrike much larger, thicker billed, with whiter belly, lacking contrasting pale wing panel. Also see Black-faced Cuckooshrike. **AN** Sumba Cicadabird.

Salvadori's Cicadabird *Edolisoma salvadorii* E

L 23–25 cm. 2 ssp: *salvadorii* (Sangihe, Siau), *talautense* (Talaud). Traditionally merged with ssp *morio* of Common Cicadabird (which see for taxonomy), but molecular data indicate distant relationship, instead closely linking Salvadori's with Palau *E. monacha* and perhaps Yap Cicadabirds *E. nesiote* from Micronesia. The latter two have very different plumages and are therefore here not included under Salvadori's despite shallow molecular divergence. Fairly common in variety of wooded habitats, including tall plantations. Singly, pairs or small groups (<5), often joining mixed flocks; feeding in mid- to upper canopy. **ID M** black face and throat; uniform pale bluish-grey with broad white-fringed wing coverts and tertials. Ssp *talautense* slightly smaller. **F** whitish ear-coverts and underparts with narrow black barring; *talautense* cinnamon-tinged underparts with narrower black barring. **Imm** undescribed. **Voc** undescribed.

papuensis

♂

hypoleuca ♀

White-bellied Cuckooshrike

♀ ♂

Pied Cuckooshrike

Cerulean Cuckooshrike

♀ ♂

Stout-billed Cuckooshrike

♀

♂

Pygmy Cicadabird

Halmahera Cicadabird

♀ ♂

Pale-shouldered Cicadabird

♀ ♂

Salvadori's Cicadabird
salvadorii

Common Cicadabird *Edolisoma tenuirostre*

L 23–27 cm. Aus. ~26 ssp, 8 in region: *amboinense* (Ambon, Seram); *sula* (Sula Is); *pelingi* (Banggai); *pererratum* (Tukangbesi); *grayi* (N Mol); *obiense* (Obi, Bisa); *morio* (Sul and satellites); *edithae* (SW Sul, known from one specimen near Maros). Complicated taxonomy (see also under Tenggara and Salvadori's Cicadabirds) because of confusing female plumage mosaicism. Traditionally ssp *sula* separated as monotypic species. More recently, complex has undergone multiple conflicting treatments by various authors. Present re-arrangement based on lack of deep mtDNA differentiation among all forms here merged, combined with inconclusive vocal variability (even within populations). Future vocal and genomic data likely to produce further re-arrangements. Uncommon and local in a variety of wooded habitats, <1500 m. Singly, pairs or small groups (<6); feeding in mid- to upper canopy. **ID M** slate-grey plumage with black face mask and throat, black median to greater coverts and outerwing with pale grey edges; black tail with large white markings on underside. Ssp *morio* entirely black underparts. **F** ssp *amboinense* paler grey upperparts, buff underparts with relatively sparse barring; *morio* buff underparts and face with heavy, narrow black barring; *sula* male-like uniform pale grey without barring, dusky lores; *grayi* olive-brown upperparts, rusty-buff underparts with stronger barring; *edithae* brown mantle, buffy underparts with barring; *pererratum* upperparts greyish-brown, underparts white with sparse, broken barring; *obiense* reddish olive-brown upperparts with grey cap, underparts unbarred rich cinnamon; *pelingi* as previous but with blue-grey cap and nape. **Imm** generally browner; scaled above; buffish underparts invariably barred. **Voc** Little-known in region and seemingly variable even within ssp. Song: level-pitched, mechanical, cicada-like "trzzzzz", lasting ~0.8 sec, slightly rising in volume, variable in quality and rhythm. Ssp *pelingi* also distinctive, disyllabic "chew-chew", lasting 0.5 sec; *sula* (i) upslurred, wheezy "whirrt", (ii) explosive, metallic "pik" notes, regularly repeated, (iii) downslurred, sharp "twirt"; *morio* rapidly repeated series of cicada-like buzzes "whirrrrrt", lasting 1 sec. Call: *morio* (i) nasal "kit", rapidly repeated; (ii) quiet nasal chatter, "chu'u'u'", regularly repeated; (iii) variety of quiet squeaks and chatter "chet, too-rit" or "chew-wit-wit-wit". **SS** Male Pale Cicadabird resembles male Common, but is much paler overall (e.g., whitish, not grey, belly) and has facial black colouration only on lores (not over most of face); Pale's wing-covert fringing much whiter (not grey), often forming distinct white wing panel. Larger, thicker-billed Moluccan Cuckooshrike shows white (not slate-grey) belly, has black head (not only face), and lacks pale wing-covert fringing and white undertail markings typical of cicadabirds. See also Slaty, Cerulean, Stout-billed, Buru, White-bellied and Black-faced Cuckooshrikes, as well as Halmahera Cicadabird.

Tenggara Cicadabird *Edolisoma dispar* E

L 22–25 cm. 4 ssp: *dispar* (Romang–Tanimbar–Kai–Banda), *timoriense* (Rote, Timor, Lembata–Atauro); *kalaotuae* (Kalaotoa); *emancipatum* (Tanahjampea). Traditionally, ssp *timoriense*, *kalaotuae* and *emancipatum* placed under Common Cicadabird (which also see for taxonomy). All three poorly known in life, but molecular data strongly contradict close relationship with Common and support present arrangement. Scarce and local in variety of wooded habitats, <1400 m. Only *dispar* seen with regularity. Singly

or pairs. **ID M** uniform glossy black plumage and bare parts, lacking any markings; *timoriense* considerably paler bluish-grey with black lores, outer tail and tail tips, black wings with narrow pale fringes; *kalaotuae* darker bluish-grey plumage with pale fringed wing feathers; *emancipatum* as previous but larger. **F** grey crown, dusky ear-coverts, mid-brown upperparts and tail, blackish outerwing, buffish underparts heavily barred; *timoriense* paler overall, underparts pale buff with narrow barring, grey head contrasting with buff mantle, broader fringed tertials; *kalaotuae* light grey upperparts, light buff underparts with sparse barring; *emancipatum* similar to previous but slate-grey upperparts. **Imm** undescribed. **Voc** Song: *dispar* 2 short introductory "grit" notes, followed by low, grating "grrrrit", lasting 2.5–3 sec in total. Call: *dispar* (i) single, quick "weck", (ii) upslurred, squeaky "whip"; *timoriense* (i) soft, explosive "twik", (ii) soft, squeaky, disyllabic "cheep-cheep". Other taxa undescribed. **SS** Bulkier and larger-billed Wallacean Cuckooshrike in range of *dispar* is dark slate-grey with black face (not all-black glossy body), and has broader wings in flight, which is regularly undulating (not fast and direct). Ssp *timoriense* told from larger, thicker-billed Wallacean and Alor Cuckooshrikes by pale fringed wing feathers, and at least from Wallacean by paler plumage and lack of extensive black face mask. See also Black-faced Cuckooshrike.

Pale Cicadabird *Edolisoma ceramense* E

L 24–25 cm. 2 ssp: *ceramense* (Buru, Boano, Seram); *hoogerwerfi* (Obi). Locally fairly common in a variety of wooded habitats. Singly, pairs or small groups (<5), often joining mixed flocks; feeding in mid- to upper canopy. **ID M** uniform mid-grey plumage; blackish lores and outerwing with whitish fringing; vent white. Ssp *hoogerwerfi* paler below but little-known. **F** much paler, with dark line through lores and behind eye. **Imm** undescribed. **Voc** Song: (i) at least on Seram harsh, rapid, dry rattle, "tr'r'r'r..." lasting 1 sec; (ii) at least on Buru dry rattle, but much slower and longer, lasting 1–7 sec at 12 n/s, increasing in volume. Call: repeated "chet". **SS** See Common Cicadabird, as well as Buru, Black-faced and White-bellied Cuckooshrikes.

Lesser Cicadabird *Lalage fimbriata*

L 19–21 cm. Sundaic. 5 ssp, 3 in region: *fimbriata* (Jav, Bali); *compta* (Simeulue, Siberut); *schierbrandi* (Sum, Bor). Uncommon in forest, <1000 m, rarely to 1500 m. Singly, pairs or small groups (<5), often joining mixed flocks; feeding in mid- to upper canopy. **ID M** slate-grey, slightly paler rump and vent with black wings; short-tailed with broad white tips to undertail feathers. Ssp *compta* smaller, slightly paler overall; *schierbrandi* smaller still, intermediate in plumage colour. **F** paler upperparts and crown; blackish lores; whitish underparts and face heavily barred dark grey. **Imm** brownish barring below, including slight barring on rump. **Voc** Song: sweet series in two types, both lasting 2 sec, regularly repeated; (i) song with descending last note "whi'-ti'-whi'-ti'-wheet-ti'-wheet-ti'-whee"; (ii) "tit-chit-chiw-chiw-chiw...". **SS** Sunda Cuckooshrike is larger, lacks white on undertail, has stronger bill and lacks contrast with darker wings. Javan Cuckooshrike even larger, bulkier and more thick-billed, with male showing white (not grey) belly, while fem is much less extensively barred below. See also Roving Cuckooshrike. **AN** Lesser Cuckooshrike.

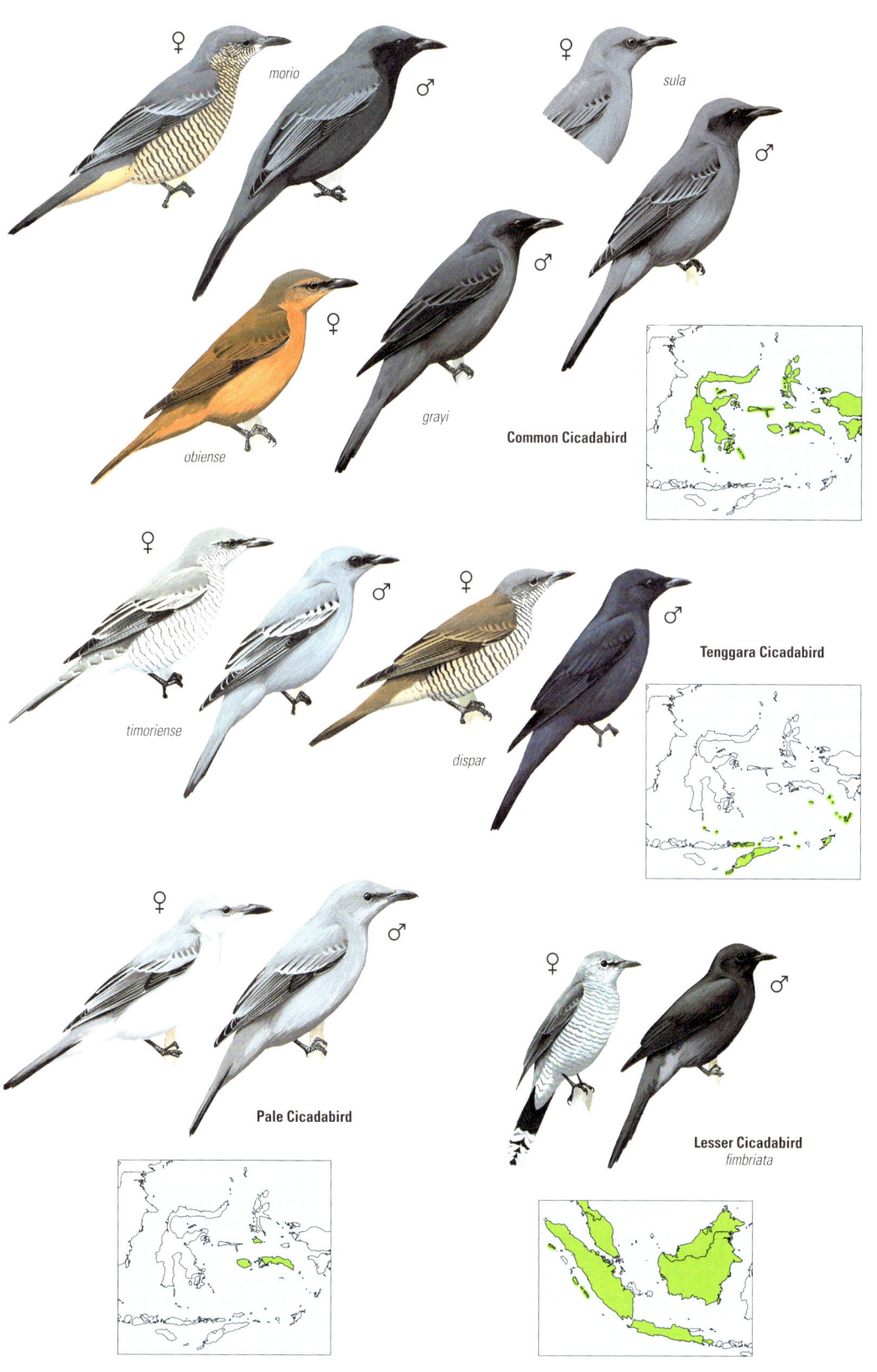

morio

sula

♀

♂

obiense

grayi

♀

♂

♂

Common Cicadabird

timoriense

dispar

♀

♂

♀

♂

Tenggara Cicadabird

Pale Cicadabird

♀

♂

Lesser Cicadabird
fimbriata

♀

♂

Pied Triller *Lalage nigra*

L 17–18 cm. Nicobars to Phil. 3 ssp, 2 in region: *nigra* (Bor–Phil); *striga* (Sum, Bangka, Belitung, Jav, Bali, MPen). Extremely deep mtDNA divergence between *nigra* and *striga* may necessitate separation into two species (monotypic '**Pied Triller**' *L. nigra* and '**Malayan Triller**' *L. striga* incl. extralimital *davisoni* [Nicobars]); present treatment as one species based on absence of apparent vocal or strong plumage differences; more research required. Co-occurs with Lesueur's in C–E Jav and Bali, likely hybridising extensively. Fairly common in mangroves, coastal scrub, open habitats, <1000 m. Singly or small groups (<5). **ID M** black upperparts with broad white covert bar, white-fringed tertials and broad white supercilium; white underparts; greyish rump. **F** upperparts greyer (in *striga* with slight brownish cast) with less contrasting light-grey rump; face and throat sometimes tinged or barred light grey; upper breast and rear supercilium can be buff-tinged. **Imm** buffish breast with black streaks; upperparts brownish-grey. **Voc** Song: slightly ascending, harsh, grating, loud rattle "che'che'che...", lasting 1–3 sec at 7 n/s, notes upslurred. Call: (i) whining "wheer"; (ii) short, sharp "wheck". **SS** See Lesueur's Triller.

Lesueur's Triller *Lalage sueurii* E

L 17–18 cm. Monotypic. Co-occurs with Pied in E Jav and Bali, likely hybridising extensively. Locally common in variety of lightly wooded habitats, clearings, mangroves, cultivation and coastal scrub, <2000 m. Often found in flocks (<40), feeding on ground. **ID M** similar to Pied Triller with variably broad white supercilium (sometimes nearly absent) and white-fringed coverts and tertials; greyish rump. **F** distinct dark clay tones to upperparts; white to buff fringes to wing feathers; pale greyish rump and supercilium; under-parts whitish with buff wash on breast. **Imm** scaled upperparts; underparts can show dark streaking. **Voc** Song: rapid staccato rattle "chew'chew'chew...", lasting 2–6 sec at 6 n/s, notes downslurred. Sounds much more melodious and reverberating than the equivalent songs of Pied and Sulawesi Trillers, which are harsher, more grating and mechanical. **SS** In C–E Jav and Bali sympatric and often con-fused with Pied Triller, with which it hybridizes, and which is often best told by voice. Male Pied always has broad supercilium and broad white fringes to tertials but some male Lesueur's also show these features, rendering only less white-marked male Lesueur's safe to identify. Fem Pied is often greyer overall but can sometimes approach Lesueur's dark clay colouration. Females best told by wing pattern: Pied always has white wing feather fringing, which is so dense on wing-coverts that it usually forms 1-2 uninterrupted white bars; Lesueur's wing feather fringing can be white or buff, and is usually not sufficiently dense on coverts to form uninterrupted bars, instead retaining the impression of a pale "fringing" pattern. Also see Sulawesi Triller. **AN** White-shouldered Triller.

Sulawesi Triller *Lalage leucopygialis* E

L 19 cm. Monotypic. Fairly common in edge, clearings, degraded forest, mangroves, plantations, <1000 m. Singly or in small parties (<10). **ID M** diagnostic large white rump, white underparts and supercilium; black upperparts with broad white fringes to coverts and tertials. **F** grey mantle; faint barring on breast and less white on wings. **Imm** buff-barred underparts; brownish tinge to upper-parts. **Voc** Song: rapid, mechanical, non-melodious chattering "chet'chet'chet..." lasting <2 sec at 9 n/s, slightly rising in pitch, notes level-pitched (compare Lesueur's more melodious series). Call: disyllabic chattering notes "chewek, chewek" of similar quality as song. **SS** Lesueur's Triller has greater plumage variability than often appreciated, and sometimes best told by voice. Male Lesueur's shows pale-grey (not white) rump, but harsh sunlight can make this difficult to judge. Some male Lesueur's have thinner supercilium and/or reduced white fringes to tertials, making identification of those straightforward. Fem Lesueur's has brownish-grey (not grey-and-black) upperparts. Lesueur's has a preference for more open, less wooded habitats, and is regularly found feeding on the ground, unlike Sulawesi. **AN** White-rumped Triller.

Varied Triller *Lalage leucomela*

L 17–19 cm. Aus. 15 ssp, 1 in region: *keyensis* (Kai). Complicated taxonomy; complex likely to be broken up into multiple species-level groups. More research needed. Fairly common in variety of wooded habitats, clearings and mangroves. Singly or small groups (<10). **ID M** black upperparts with white supercilium; mottled rump; white greater-coverts, and white fringed wing-feathers; underparts white with buff belly. **F** slate-grey upperparts; white-fringed wing-feathers and strongly barred underparts; narrow pale supercilium. **Imm** scaled upperparts and dusky streaks on underparts. **Voc** (i) 3-note "chew-it eeeeoow", lasting 0.7 sec, rising with descending final note; (ii) squeaky "chit"; (iii) scolding, harsh "airrrk", lasting 0.3 sec.

Tanimbar Triller *Lalage moesta* E

L 19 cm. Monotypic. Fairly common in a variety of wooded habitats, clearings and mangroves. Singly, pairs and small groups (<5). **ID Ad** black upperparts with white-fringed upperwing feathers; small white rump and white supercilium ending above eye; wholly white underparts. **Imm** undescribed. **Voc** (i) Loud, squeaky "chew'wit"; (ii) short "chit". **AN** White-browed Triller.

Rufous-bellied Triller *Lalage aurea* E

L 20 cm. Monotypic. Fairly common in variety of wooded habitats, clearings and mangroves, <450 m. Singly, pairs and small groups. **ID M** glossy black upperparts with narrow white supercilium, white-fringed wings and white ear-coverts and chin; underparts wholly rufous. **F** greyish crown and mantle. **Imm** lacks glossy upperparts, the latter mostly edged rusty. **Voc** Song: rapid series of piping, stac-cato notes "pip-pip'pip'pip..." lasting <2 sec at 8 n/s. Call: variety of soft squeaks and chattering.

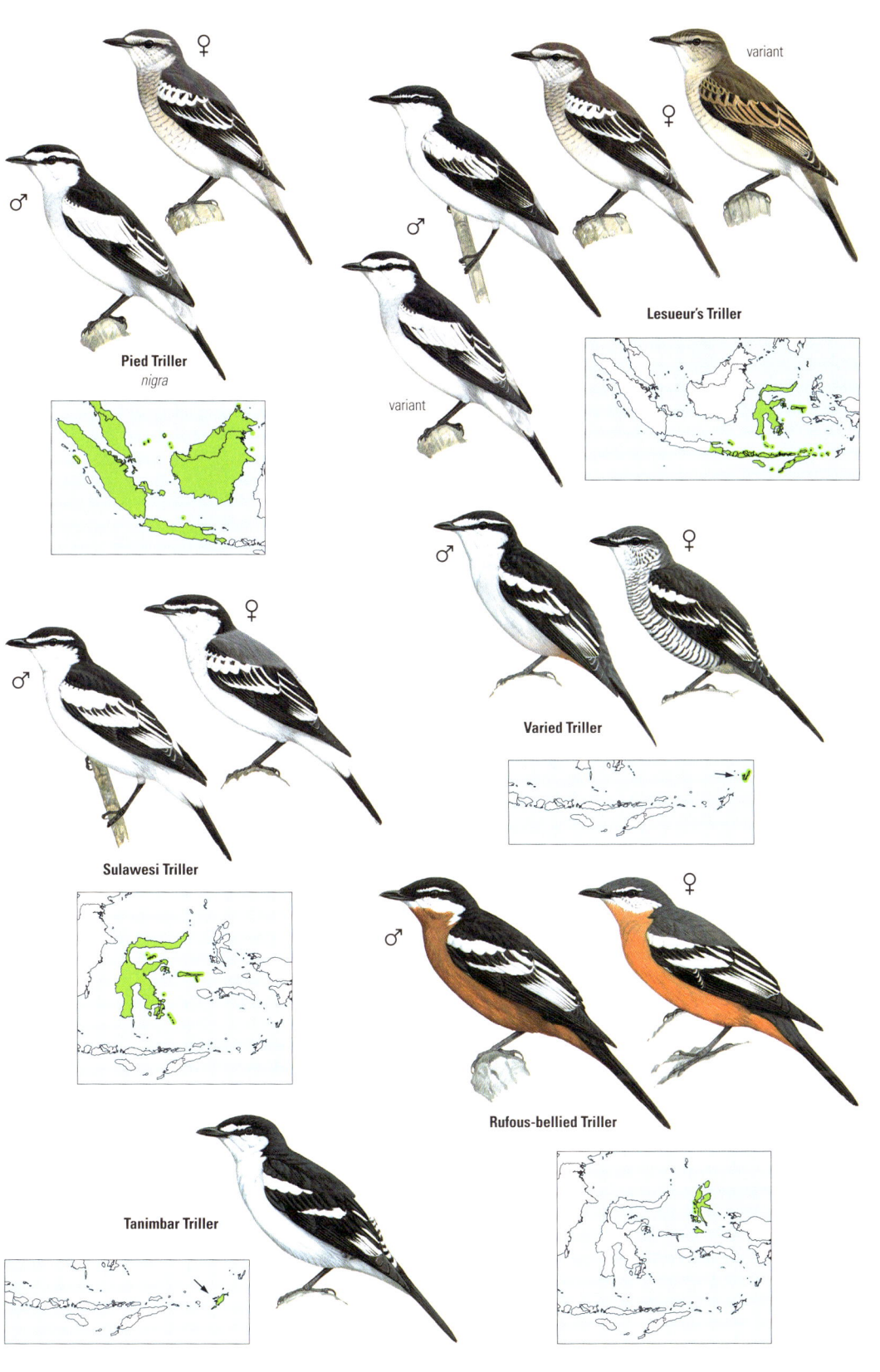

♀

♂

Pied Triller
nigra

variant

♀

♂

variant

Lesueur's Triller

♂ ♀

Varied Triller

♂ ♀

Sulawesi Triller

♂ ♀

Rufous-bellied Triller

Tanimbar Triller

Ashy Minivet *Pericrocotus divaricatus*

L 18–21 cm. Breeds NE–E Asia; winters S–SE Asia, Phil. Monotypic. No longer includes the morphologically distinct, extralimital Ryukyu Minivet *P. tegimae* (S Japan). Scarce migrant to open woodland, edge, tall plantations and city parks, <1300 m. Small to medium groups (<30), usually in canopy. **ID M** black crown, nape and eye-stripe with white forecrown, face and underparts; slate-grey upperparts with black outerwing and tail; in flight shows white outerwing bar. **F** face pattern less distinct, with grey crown and nape; black lores. **Imm** can show slight barring on underparts. **Voc** Metallic, jingling trill "tchoo-dee tchoo-dee-dee tchoo-dee-dee", often given in flight.

Scarlet Minivet *Pericrocotus flammeus*

L 17–22 cm. S–SE–E Asia, Phil. 19 ssp, 6 in region. Complicated internal taxonomy. Morphological and plumage analyses suggest separation into 4–5 species, but exact boundaries in SE Asia unclear. Ssp *exul* (Lombok) and *siebersi* (Jav–Bali) distinct in plumage and perhaps separable as '**Javan Minivet**' *P. exul*. Extralimital Philippine taxa may also warrant separate species status. When extralimital nominate ssp *flammeus* (W India, Sri Lanka) is divided as monotypic '**Orange Minivet**', the remaining regional ssp *xanthogaster* (Sum, MPen), *minythomelas* (Simeulue), *modiglianii* (Enggano) and *insulanus* (Bor) become part of '**Scarlet Minivet**' *P. speciosus* (Himalaya–SE-E Asia), but limited molecular work points to fairly deep divergences even within this latter species (i.e. between Bornean *insulanus* and Thai populations). More research needed. Fairly common in variety of forested habitats, <1500 m. Pairs or small groups. **ID** (*xanthogaster*) **M** black upperparts and head to upper breast; scarlet underparts, outertail and wing panel with diagnostic red spots on tertials and secondaries. Ssp *minythomelas* larger, more red in wing; *modiglianii* similar to previous but less red on tail; smaller *exul* has scarlet replaced by washed-out orange, lacks secondary patch; *siebersi* as previous but slightly deeper orange, including rump. **F** wing pattern as male, but grey mantle and crown, and yellow replacing scarlet/orange on body, including on face, throat and forecrown. Ssp *insulanus* darker upperparts, paler underparts; distinctions of *minythomelas* and *modiglianii* as in male but red replaced by yellow; *exul* and *siebersi* lack secondary patch and slightly paler, brighter yellow. **Imm** shows blotchy underparts; paler grey upperparts. **Voc** (i) Rapid, high-pitched, ringing, twittering "sweet-sweet-sweet..."; (ii) very rapid, excited, bouncing twitter "kapitit-kapitit-kapitit...". **SS** Male Scarlet identified from quite similar Grey-chinned and Sunda by presence of red tertial and secondary patches (Grey-chinned additionally has slightly paler blackish throat and upper breast, and a less extensive red wing patch not reaching as far onto wing-coverts); all three best told by accompanying females. Presence of tertial patch also helps identify from male Small Minivet, which is additionally smaller and greyer (less black) on mantle and crown and has a whitish (not orange) belly. See also Fiery Minivet.

Sunda Minivet *Pericrocotus miniatus* 🅴

L 19 cm. Monotypic. Fairly common in montane forest, including edge, 1200–2700 m. Usually in larger groups than other minivets (<50), regularly in mixed flocks, including with Grey-chinned Minivet. **ID M** similar to Scarlet Minivet but lacks tertial and secondary spots. **F** red mantle, face and supercilium. **Imm** duller; blotchy underparts. **Voc** Rapid, hard, shrill "t't'chee-t't'chee-t't'chee...", often several birds calling. **SS** Male Sunda best told from similar Grey-chinned by fully black (not extremely dark-grey) throat and upper breast, and more extensive red wing patch reaching further up onto wing-coverts; identification best confirmed by accompanying females. Also see Scarlet and Fiery.

Flores Minivet *Pericrocotus lansbergei* 🅴

L 16 cm. Monotypic. Fairly common in all types of forest and edge, <2000 m. Pairs or small groups (<10). **ID M** black upperparts and head; white belly; deep orange breast, wing panel and rump. **F** brownish-grey upperparts; wholly white underparts. **Imm** scaled upperparts. **Voc** Series of 5–10 high-pitched, thin, twittering notes "tee-tee-tee..." lasting 1–1.5 sec at 5 n/s. **AN** Little Minivet.

Grey-chinned Minivet *Pericrocotus solaris*

L 17–19 cm. Himalaya to SE–E Asia. 8 ssp, 2 in region: *montanus* (Sum, MPen); *cinereigula* (Bor). The two ssp in region sometimes raised to species level as '**Grey-throated Minivet**' *P. montanus*, but variation in throat colour is equally pronounced among extralimital ssp, and variation in mtDNA and bioacoustics seems limited. Fairly common in (sub-) montane forest, edge, 600–3000 m. Pairs or small groups (<10). **ID M** glossy blue-black upperparts; throat and upper breast slightly paler; underparts, rump and wing patch red. Ssp *cinereigula* slightly paler upperparts. **F** mid-grey upperparts; yellow replacing red, including onto throat; whitish chin. **Imm** slight scaling on upperparts, in **M** blotchy yellow-orange underparts. **Voc** High-pitched, short series of ringing notes "tee-t'tee'-t'tee", lasting 0.6 sec, regularly repeated. **SS** See similar Scarlet and Sunda Minivets. Male Grey-chinned from smaller Fiery by slightly paler blackish throat and upper breast, and less orange (more scarlet) overall colouration, but identification best confirmed by accompanying females.

Small Minivet *Pericrocotus cinnamomeus*

L 14–16 cm. S–SE Asia. 9 ssp, 1 in region: *saturatus* (Jav–Bali). Uncommon in open woods, coastal scrub, arid areas, <1300 m. Pairs or small groups (<10). **ID M** mid-grey upperparts; black face, throat, outerwing and tail; orange breast, rump and wing panel; whitish belly. **F** pale grey upperparts with orange rump and wing panel; blackish tail and whitish underparts. **Imm M** shows orange blotching on underparts. **Imm F** As Ad fem. **Voc** (i) Rapidly repeated, piercing, shrill, up-and-down "whir-ch'ch'chee", lasting 1 sec, often in duet; (ii) high-pitched, drawn-out "tsweeet", lasting 0.5 sec. **SS** See Scarlet.

Fiery Minivet *Pericrocotus igneus*

L 15–16 cm. Sundaic, Palawan. 2 ssp: *igneus* (Sum–Bor, MPen, Nias, Palawan); *trophis* (Simeulue). Locally fairly common in forest, rarely degraded areas and plantations, <1200 m. Pairs or small groups (<10) **ID M** black upperparts and head; red wing panel, rump and underparts, slightly paler towards belly, and usually with a strongly orange tinge (especially on wing). Ssp *trophis* larger. **F** grey upperparts; underparts to chin and forecrown yellow with orange tinge; orange-yellow wing panel and reddish rump. **Imm** shows blotchy underparts. **Voc** Much higher-pitched than Scarlet Minivet; trilling, repeated "tit tit" and "swee...", often calling in duet or in flight. **SS** Larger male Scarlet Minivet is generally more scarlet overall (less orange-tinged), while female Scarlet has yellow (not orange/reddish) rump, vent, undertail and wing panel. Both sexes of Scarlet show distinctive tertial and secondary patches absent in other minivets. Larger male Sunda is also more deeply scarlet, with a less orange overall tinge (especially on wing panel), and has a slightly more extensive wing panel. All male minivets best identified by reference to accompanying females. See also Grey-chinned.

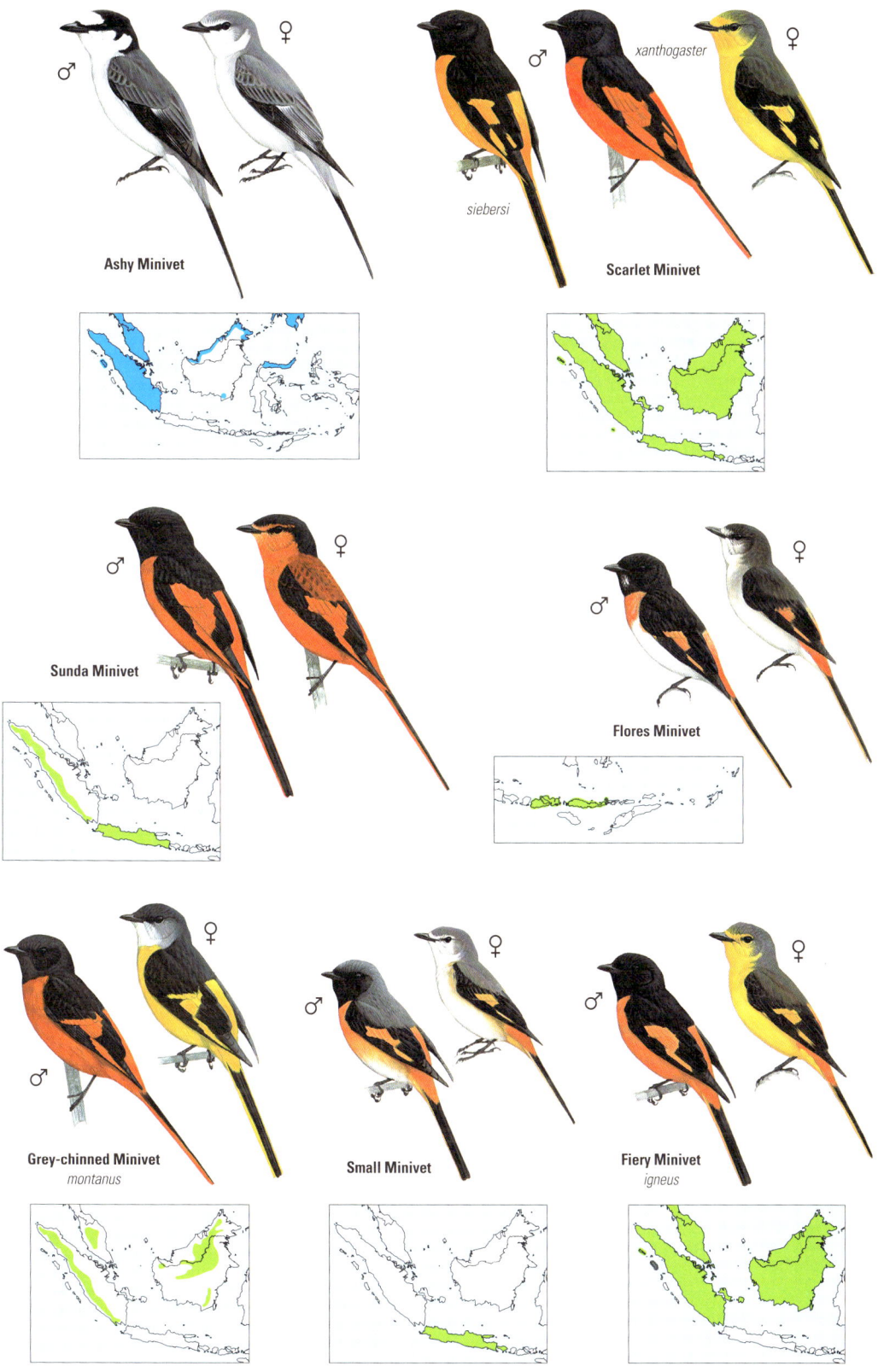

Ashy Minivet

Scarlet Minivet

siebersi

xanthogaster

Sunda Minivet

Flores Minivet

Grey-chinned Minivet
montanus

Small Minivet

Fiery Minivet
igneus

RHIPIDURIDAE
Fantails
23 species in region
Small forest and edge dwellers with distinctive long tails. Found in low to upper storey, feeding by gleaning and sallying for insects in flight. Usually quite conspicuous, with fanned tail angled up, and often found in mixed flocks.

Sulawesi Fantail *Rhipidura teysmanni* E
L 14 cm. 3 ssp: *teysmanni* (SW Sul); *toradja* (C–SE Sul); *coomansi* (N Sul). Traditionally merged with Taliabu Fantail, but differs genomically, vocally and in terms of subtle but consistent plumage traits. Fairly common in (sub-) montane forest, 800–2300 m, occasionally lower. Singly or pairs, in mixed flocks. **ID Ad** rufous forecrown, wings and tail, latter with black distal third; crown and mantle grey-brown; white throat with black necklace; breast mottled black; buff belly. Ssp *toradja* broader necklace, ash-grey breast; *coomansi* more sharply defined necklace. **Imm** undescribed. **Voc** Song: series of 4–7 descending, slightly accelerating, high-pitched notes "tsst tee-dee-deh-deh", lasting <2 sec. Call: thin, short "sip" or "seep"; (ii) irregular series "jib, jib-jib...".

Peleng Fantail *Rhipidura habibiei* E
L 14 cm. Monotypic. Fairly common in (sub-) montane forest, >800 m, occasionally lower. Singly or pairs, in mixed flocks. **ID Ad** similar to Sulawesi Fantail but has cleaner white throat, slightly warmer brown crown through upper back, less extensive grey mottling below black breast band, and more extensive black on tail. **Imm** undescribed. **Voc** Song: slow, deliberate series of 4–6 level metallic notes, initially rising in pitch, then descending, often decelerating towards end, "tchew tchee tchew..., too" lasting 2.4–3.1 sec, quite unlike the tinkling songs of similar species. Call: full-voiced, hard "cheep".

Taliabu Fantail *Rhipidura sulaensis* E
L 14 cm. Monotypic. See Sulawesi Fantail for taxonomy. Fairly common in (sub-) montane forest, >800 m. Singly or pairs, in mixed flocks. **ID Ad** similar to Peleng Fantail but shows widely buff-tipped tail, less distinct black scaling below breast patch and more whitish belly. **Imm** undescribed. **Voc** Song: fairly complex high-pitched tinkling, introduced by 3 ascending notes "tsew tsee tseep", and followed by 2–3 short glissading cadences climbing up and down the vocal scale. Call: comparatively low-pitched, drawn-out "chehp".

Tawny-backed Fantail *Rhipidura superflua* E
L 14 cm. Monotypic. Generally uncommon, more numerous in higher montane forest, >700 m. Singly or pairs, often in mixed flocks. **ID Ad** tawny crown and nape; rufous mantle and rump; blackish wings and tail with rufous tip; white throat, thin black necklace and buff underparts. **Imm** undescribed. **Voc** Song: series of 6–8 high-pitched descending "tsst-tis-tis-tis-tis-tis", lasting 2 sec.

Streak-breasted Fantail *Rhipidura dedemi* E
L 14 cm. Monotypic. Fairly common in (sub-) montane forest, 500–2300 m. Singly or pairs, often in mixed flocks. **ID Ad** brownish-black head with white marks above eye and behind ear-coverts; rufous upperparts and tail; white underparts with black breast streaking. **Imm** undescribed. **Voc** Song: series of 15–20 notes, slow start with single, squeaky notes leading to a crescendo of squeaks and descending whistles, "wip-two-wit-wit-two-whit-choo-whit-choo-whit-choo-whit..." lasting 4–5 sec.

Charming Fantail *Rhipidura opistherythra* E
L 17 cm. Monotypic. Uncommon in forest, favouring tangles. Surprisingly elusive, atypical of *Rhipidura*. **ID Ad** rather drab; upperparts and head greyish-brown with buff supraloral stripe; rufous wings, rump and long tail; white throat; buff underparts. **Imm** undescribed. **Voc** Song: simple 4-note "tyunk-whirr-tyunk-whirr", lasting 1.7 sec, first and third notes high-pitched, second and fourth descending and mournful. **AN** Long-tailed Fantail.

Supertramp Fantail *Rhipidura semicollaris* E
L 16–17 cm. W NG to Wallacea. 9–10 ssp, 9 in region: *semicollaris* (Flores–Wetar, Timor); *sumbensis* (Sumba, Savu); *celebensis* (Tanahjampea, Kalao); *mimosae* (Kalaotoa); *squamata* (Banda, Kekek, Lawin, W Papuan Is); *henrici* (Seram Laut, Tayandu, Kai, Aru); *elegantula* (Romang, Damar, Leti, Moa); *reichenowi* (Babar); *hamadryas* (Tanimbar). Usually subsumed under extralimital 'Arafura Fantail' *R. dryas* (N Aus); the latter's plumage closely resembles Supertramp Fantail's western taxa (especially *semicollaris*), but eastern taxa form leapfrog pattern, becoming successively more different as they approach *R. dryas*. Supertramp Fantail additionally has a more complex tinkling song than *R. dryas*. Common in variety of wooded habitats, including scrub and plantations. Fulfils the definition of a typical supertramp, readily colonising small islands that lack strong competitors. Singly or pairs; favouring the understorey, often feeding on ground. **ID Ad** forehead dull rufous; crown and mantle grey-brown; remainder of upperparts rufous; throat white; breast band black with moderate white scaling on lower edge; belly creamy white; flanks and vent light cinnamon; tail slate-grey, outer rectrices extensively tipped white. Ssp *sumbensis* larger, breast band broader with scalier margin; *celebensis* breast band without scaly edges; *mimosae* warmer brown on crown and nape, with narrower black breast band; very different *elegantula* has crown and back rufous, white forehead with rufous supraloral line, black facial mask; *reichenowi* as previous but forehead rufous; *hamadryas* more like nominate *semicollaris*, but lores and face duskier, ghosting the black mask of *elegantula*; *squamata* forehead and face black, white supraloral line, black breast band very broad and heavily scaled; *henrici* like previous, but edges of secondaries more cinnamon. **Imm** duller, less distinct markings. **Voc** Song: consistent throughout races, tinkling series of 6–10 ascending, then descending notes, with sharp, high-pitched introductory note "huit, se-se-se-tee-hee-het", lasting 1–1.5 sec. Call: (i) startled, upslurred "huit"; (ii) sharp, high-pitched "sirt"; (iii) short, sharp "tic".

Gilolo Fantail *Rhipidura torrida* E
L 16–18 cm. Monotypic. Often considered conspecific with extralimital Rufous Fantail *R. rufifrons* (Aus), and the two sometimes additionally merged with Supertramp Fantail and other, extralimital species, but here separated on basis of combination of plumage and vocal characters. Fairly common in (sub-) montane forest, >700 m. **ID Ad** rufous forecrown, rump and base of tail; greyish-brown crown, upperparts and tail, the latter with white tip; white throat and belly with black necklace and breast mottling. **Imm** undescribed. **Voc** Song: series of 5–15 thin, high-pitched, tinkling metallic notes, usually a descending "sit-sit-see-see-tee-tee-tew-tew-tew-to-to", lasting <5 sec. Call: flowerpecker-like high-pitched "sit", disyllabic "si'sit", or trisyllabic "si'si'sit".

Sulawesi Fantail

Peleng Fantail

Taliabu Fantail

Tawny-backed Fantail

Streak-breasted Fantail

Charming Fantail

elegantula

Gilolo Fantail

squamata

Supertramp Fantail

Trumpeting Fantail *Rhipidura diluta* **E**

L 17 cm. 2 ssp: *diluta* (Flores, Lembata); *sumbawensis* (Sumbawa). Fairly common in primary, secondary and montane forest, more numerous >1000 m. Singly or pairs, joins mixed flocks. **ID Ad** dark grey-brown upperparts, slightly darker crown and tail with paler outer retrices, rufous fringed remiges; white throat and buff underparts. Ssp *sumbawensis* slightly darker upperparts. **Imm** undescribed. **Voc** Song: amusing, toy trumpet-like "ch-che-che-cheE", lasting 0.6 sec. Call: (i) excited, rolling chatter; (ii) upslurred, squeaky "chit"; (iii) squeaky "pip". **AN** Brown-capped Fantail.

Cinnamon-tailed Fantail *Rhipidura fuscorufa* **E**

L 18 cm. Monotypic. Marked vocal differences on Babar suggest undescribed taxon. Fairly common in variety of woodland, including plantations and scrub around villages. Conspicuous, hover-gleaning and flycatching from exposed perches. **ID Ad** dark grey-brown head, upperparts and central rectrices; indistinct pale supercilium; rufous wing-coverts, secondaries and outertail; white throat and upper breast; rich-buff belly. **Imm** undescribed. **Voc** Song: (i) on Babar series of 7 ascending, staccato, cheery whistled "p'p'per-per-pee-pee-pee", lasting 3 sec; (ii) on Tanimbar repeated descending, then ascending "t't'tchew pu-pee, t't'tchew pu-pee", lasting 2.8 sec. Call: squeaky "yep".

Timor Fantail *Rhipidura rufiventris* **E**

L 16–18 cm. 2 ssp: *rufiventris* (Timor, Semau); *pallidiceps* (Wetar). Previously merged with Banda Sea, Rote, Buru, Seram, Obi, Kai Fantails and extralimital Australasian taxa into broadly defined umbrella species, '**Northern Fantail**' *R. rufiventris*, but pronounced vocal and plumage differences dictate break-up. Fairly common in variety of woodlands, including plantations and scrub around villages. Singly or pairs. **ID Ad** slate-grey upperparts, darker head; white fore-supercilium; pale tips to wing-coverts, brown remiges; white throat and breast with indistinct grey mottling; buff belly; rectrices extensively tipped white. Ssp *pallidiceps* head concolourous with more brown-tinged upperparts. **Imm** browner upperparts with extensively buff-fringed remiges. **Voc** Song: series of 7–10 alternately inflected and deflected, drawn-out, whistled stop-start notes "wir-wor-wir-wor-wir-wor..." lasting ~3 sec, fairly even in pitch. Call: *rufiventris* rasping, sucking-like "suct"; *pallidiceps* downslurred "chew".

Banda Sea Fantail *Rhipidura hoedti* **E**

L 16–18 cm. Monotypic. For taxonomy see Timor Fantail. Fairly common in variety of woodlands, including plantations and scrub around villages. Singly or pairs. **ID Ad** sooty-black head and upperparts; tiny white fleck above eye; broad white throat, white-flecked grey breast band, buff-washed belly; white outertail and distal third of central rectrices. **Imm** undescribed. **Voc** Song: (i) series of 4–5 descending, thin, melodious notes "see-tee-dee-dee-de" lasting 1 sec, occasionally repeated twice immediately in a single series; (ii) excited series of jumbled, buzzy and jingled notes in duet, "t't't'too-too-chew-t't'too-too-chew". Call: harsh, downslurred "t'cher-cher".

Rote Fantail *Rhipidura tenkatei* **E**

L 16–18 cm. Monotypic. For taxonomy see Timor Fantail. Fairly common in variety of woodlands, including plantations and scrub around villages. Singly or pairs. **ID Ad** slate-grey head, upperparts and breast with thick white breast streaking; white spot in front of eye; variable buffish belly; white outertail and distal third central rectrices. **Imm** undescribed. **Voc** Song: (i) 8–10 short, quiet, spaced-out notes "che-che-che-che-WEE–we-che-che", lasting 4.5–5 sec; (ii) excited series of jumbled, buzzy and jingled notes in duet, "che-che...", "wee-wir...", "dee-doo-dee...", lasting 4–7 sec. Call: single, repeated "che".

Buru Fantail *Rhipidura bouruensis* **E**

L 16–18 cm. Monotypic. For taxonomy see Timor Fantail. Common in variety of woodlands, including plantations and scrub. Singly or pairs, joins mixed flocks. **ID Ad** slate-grey head, upperparts and breast; white throat and dense breast streaking; rufous belly, all-black tail. **Imm** undescribed. **Voc** Song: 3–8 notes, first 2 rising, remainder even, occasionally with fourth note higher-pitched and last note descending "wee-wee-wiir-WEE–wiir-wir-wee", lasting 4–5 sec. Call: surprised, metallic "ch'a", sometimes given with a jumbled series of unstructured notes included "tee-tee-TWEE–tee-tee-TWEE".

Seram Fantail *Rhipidura cinerea* **E**

L 16–18 cm. Monotypic. For taxonomy see Timor Fantail. Uncommon and local in variety of woodlands, including plantations and scrub, <1200 m. Singly or pairs, joins mixed flocks. **ID Ad** slate-grey head, upperparts and breast; white belly; thin white supercilium; little white on rectrices. **Imm** undescribed. **Voc** Song: (i) 1-5 metallic introductory notes, followed by a series of high-low-high paired notes "ee'ee'oo'oo'ee'ee'oo'oo...", at 16 n/s, slowing to 8 n/s, lasting 2–5 s; (ii) gently rising, rapid stutter, like kettle coming to boil, followed by flat, higher pitched single whistle, lasting 1 s, "ho'o'o'o'o... PEE".

Obi Fantail *Rhipidura obiensis* **E**

L 16–18 cm. Monotypic. For taxonomy see Timor Fantail. Common in variety of woodlands, including plantations and scrub, <1210 m. Singly or pairs. **ID Ad** black head with thin white supercilium; slate-grey upperparts and breast band with relatively indistinct, sometimes absent, small white spotting; white throat and belly; broad, white fringes on tertials, and white edges and tips to central rectrices. **Imm** undescribed. **Voc** Song: (i) 6–8 high-pitched, mournful, drawn-out, whistled "wer-wir-wiir-wiir-wiir-do'd'do", lasting 3–4 sec, first note ascending to level middle notes with last note suddenly descending; (ii) rapid series of shrill, even-pitched notes "wit-de-de-de-dee-dee-dee..." lasting 2–2.5 sec. Call: (i) metallic "chink"; (ii) squeaky chattering.

Kai Fantail *Rhipidura assimilis* **E**

L 16–18 cm. 2 ssp: *assimilis* (Kai, Tayandu); *finitima* (Watubela). For taxonomy see Timor Fantail. Fairly common in woodlands, edge, regrowth. Singly or pairs, joins mixed flocks. **ID Ad** pale-grey crown with long, broad, white supercilium; upperparts and face grey-brown; breast band grey with smudgy white spots; belly tinged ochraceous; outertail broadly tipped whitish. Ssp *finitima* buff-tinged outertail tip. **Imm** undescribed. **Voc** Song: (i) continuous alternating metallic "tee-two-tee-two-tee-two" at 1 n/s; (ii) excited series of jumbled, buzzy and jingled notes in duet, "too-too-dee-BZZ-too-dee-tee-dee...", lasting <10 sec. Call: short, sharp, metallic "chit".

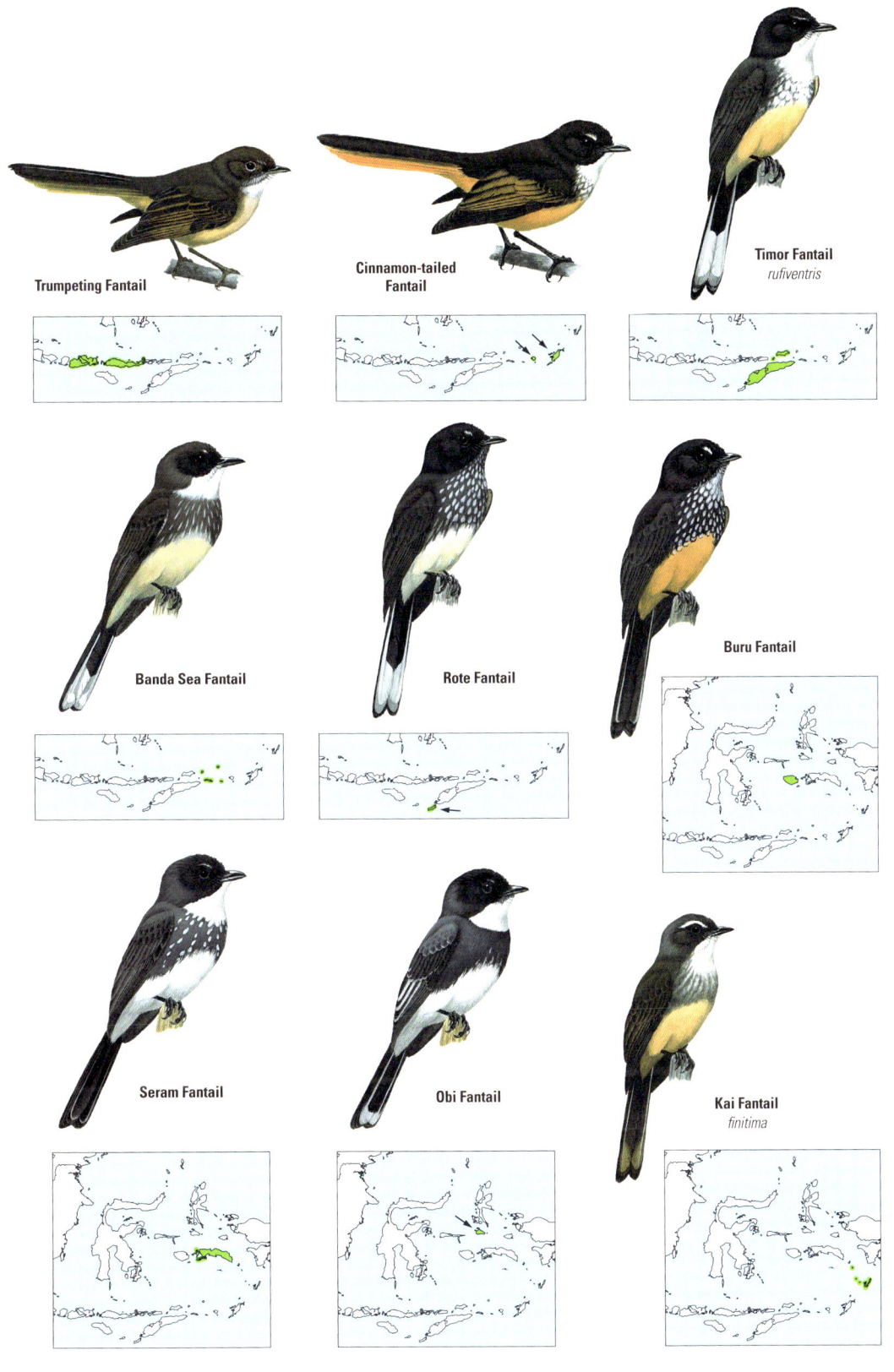

Trumpeting Fantail

Cinnamon-tailed Fantail

Timor Fantail
rufiventris

Banda Sea Fantail

Rote Fantail

Buru Fantail

Seram Fantail

Obi Fantail

Kai Fantail
finitima

Spotted Fantail *Rhipidura perlata*
L 17–18 cm. Sundaic. Monotypic. Uncommon in primary and tall secondary forest, <900 m, rarely to 1700 m. Usually pairs or in mixed flocks. **ID Ad** blackish-slate plumage with thin white supercilium; white belly; white spotting on throat and breast; white-tipped outer rectrices. **Imm** brown-tinged upperparts. **Voc** Song variable: (i) metallic, cheery series of descending notes "chil'ip-pe'chil'ip-chi'chi'cheet", lasting 1.5 sec; (ii) jingly, chirpy, drongo-like "chap-go-TREE–HEE". Call: sparrow-like "chip" or "chip-chew".

Rufous-tailed Fantail *Rhipidura phoenicura* `E`
L 17 cm. Monotypic. Fairly common in submontane and primary forest, >1000 m. Singly or pairs, joins mixed flocks. **ID Ad** sooty-brown head, upperparts and underparts with white throat and supercilium; bright rufous tail and rump; buffish flanks. **Imm** undescribed. **Voc** Song: squeaky, buzzy "he-tee-tee-oh-twee", lasting 1–2 sec, can be quite variable. Call: buzzing, harsh "chrut".

White-bellied Fantail *Rhipidura euryura* `E`
L 18 cm. Monotypic. Scarce and local in submontane forest, 900–1500 m, rarely to 2300 m. Usually pairs or mixed feeding flocks. **ID Ad** slate-grey plumage with broad white supercilium; white belly and white-tipped rectrices. **Imm** undescribed. **Voc** Song: jumbled series of 8–15 rich notes, ascending at first, then descending while accelerating "ho-wit-wit-twee-wee-chew-chew-wee-wit-wit", lasting 2–3 sec. Call: (i) short, quiet "cheet"; (ii) buzzy "tweer"; (iii) sharp, short "twit".

White-throated Fantail *Rhipidura albicollis*
L 18–20 cm. Himalaya to SE Asia. 9 ssp, 3 in region: *atrata* (Sum, MPen); *kinabalu* (N-E Bor); *sarawacensis* (W Bor). Common in (sub-)montane forest, sometimes plantations and open habitat, 900–2700 m. Usually pairs or in mixed flocks. **ID Ad** blackish-slate plumage with contrasting white supercilium and throat and white-tipped tail. Ssp *kinabalu* even blacker plumage; *sarawacensis* upperparts tinged brown, indistinct white mottling on underparts, white tail tips more extensive. **Imm** plumage tinged brown; supercilium and throat less distinct, buffish. **Voc** Song: series of 5–8 descending, cheery notes "tsu-sit-tsu-sit-sit-sit-tsu", lasting <2 sec. Call: squeaky, harsh "jick".

Sunda Pied Fantail *Rhipidura javanica*
L 18–20 cm. SE Asia. 2 ssp: *javanica* (Jav–Lombok); *longicauda* (Bor–Sum, mainland SE Asia). No longer includes extralimital Philippine Pied Fantail *R. nigritorquis* based on deep genetic divergence. Common in variety of open habitats, mangroves, scrub, gardens and degraded forest, <1500 m. Usually pairs or in mixed flocks, favouring understorey. **ID Ad** blackish-brown upperparts; thin white supercilium; white throat, broad black breast band; cream belly; white-tipped rectrices. Ssp *longicauda* has whiter belly, some black on chin and blacker upperparts. **Imm** paler brown upperparts; lacks breast band. **Voc** Song: series of 8–12 high-pitched, squeaky notes, introduced by "chit-chit-chit" followed by "chew-weet chew-weet chew-weet-chew", lasting 2–2.5 sec. Call: (i) variable squeaky chattering; (ii) squeaky, upslurred "chit"; (iii) harsh, grating "cheet".

Willie Fantail *Rhipidura leucophrys*
L 19–21 cm. Aus. 3 ssp, 1 in region: *melaleuca* (N–C Mol to Melanesia). Record from Sandakan, N Bor, of unknown origin, likely ship-assisted (Jul 2013). Common in variety of open habitats, scrub, waterways, villages, <1200 m. Conspicuous, singly or pairs; perching on wires, fences, and outposts. **ID Ad** black head, breast, upperparts and tail; narrow white supercilium and white underparts. **Imm** upperparts brownish-tinged. **Voc** Song: series of ~5 tuneful, melodious notes with abrupt end, "tee-too-tee-det'doer" lasting 1–1.5 sec. Often sings at night. Call: (i) harsh "churr"; (ii) metallic, hard "pik". **AN** Willie Wagtail.

LAMPROLIIDAE
Silktails
1 species in region
Newly elevated family of arboreal songbirds of odd composition, otherwise represented by 2-3 species in Papua and Oceania.

Cerulean Silktail *Eutrichomyias rowleyi* `E`
L 18 cm. Monotypic. Traditionally called Cerulean Paradise-flycatcher but now known to be unrelated to *Terpsiphone*. Rare (likely less than 50 remain) in forest, 400–700 m. Singly or pairs, joins mixed flocks; often foraging in mid- to upper storey near steep forested streams and gullies. **ID Ad** head and upperparts uniformly cerulean-blue; underparts whitish with pale blue wash, especially on breast; incomplete white eyering; blue-grey bare parts. **Imm** head washed grey-brown; underparts dull grey, lacking any blue. **Voc** (i) Loud, rasping "chew chew chew chew chew", with stress on last 3 notes; (ii) single "tuk"; (iii) loud, descending trill "chreechreechree...", lasting 5 sec; (iv) high, scratchy, fizzing "streeeeee"; (v) strident, sharp notes "shweek shweek"; (vi) wispy mixture of thin notes, lasting 5 sec. **AN** Cerulean Paradise-flycatcher.

DICRURIDAE
Drongos
26 species in region
Medium-sized birds of forest, edge and open country. Most species are predominantly black and glossy, with long, often deeply forked tails. Generally active and vocal, drongos are often a conspicuous inhabitant of the mid- to upper storey. Some species act as sentinels in mixed flocks, alarming other birds of incoming danger.

Black Drongo *Dicrurus macrocercus*
L 26–31 cm. S–SE–E Asia. 7 ssp, 2 in region: *javanus* (Jav, Bali); *cathoecus* (breeds SE–E Asia; winters to MPen; vagrant Bor, Riau Is). Now scarce in open country and cultivation, <1600 m. Singly or pairs; perches conspicuously on fences, cattle, and open structures low to ground. **ID Ad** sleek and elegant appearance: uniform black plumage, slightly glossed bluish, with long, deeply forked, floppy tail. Ssp *cathoecus* has dark, rather than pale, wing linings, small rictal spot, plumage glossed greenish. **Imm** large bare rictal spot; brown-tinged, less glossy plumage; vent tipped white; shorter tail. **Voc** Song: long series of constant, scratchy chatter with occasional unmelodious upslurred whistles. Call: (i) rasping "jeez"; (ii) metallic "pik", often in flight. **SS** Most often confused with Crow-billed, which may occur in similarly open landscapes on migration but rarely perches as openly: Crow-billed's massive beak is thicker, greater in depth than half the bird's head (from crown-tip to lower ear-coverts), whereas Black has thinner, attenuated beak less than half as "deep" as head height. Black's eye appears tiny, Crow-billed's eye is large and redder in good light. Adult Black has less overall gloss (especially matte on breast) and longer tail with deeper fork (tail fork is up to a third of entire tail length beyond wings), while Crow-billed's tail fork is always much shallower. Immatures dominate in migratory settings: imm Crow-billed is extensively spotted white on underparts (always restricted to vent in Black), while imm Black shows bare rictal spot (always absent in Crow-billed). In poor light, beware of less deeply-forked Ashy Drongo (especially on Jav–Bali where latter lacks white face patch): Ashy always has dark-grey (not black) overall plumage often contrasting with blackish lores. Only other confusion species are forest drongos unlikely to venture into open land inhabited by Black Drongo: forest drongos always have shorter tail much less deeply forked, iridescent breast spangles (absent in Black) and – sometimes – other tell-tale features (hackles, filaments, tail curls etc).

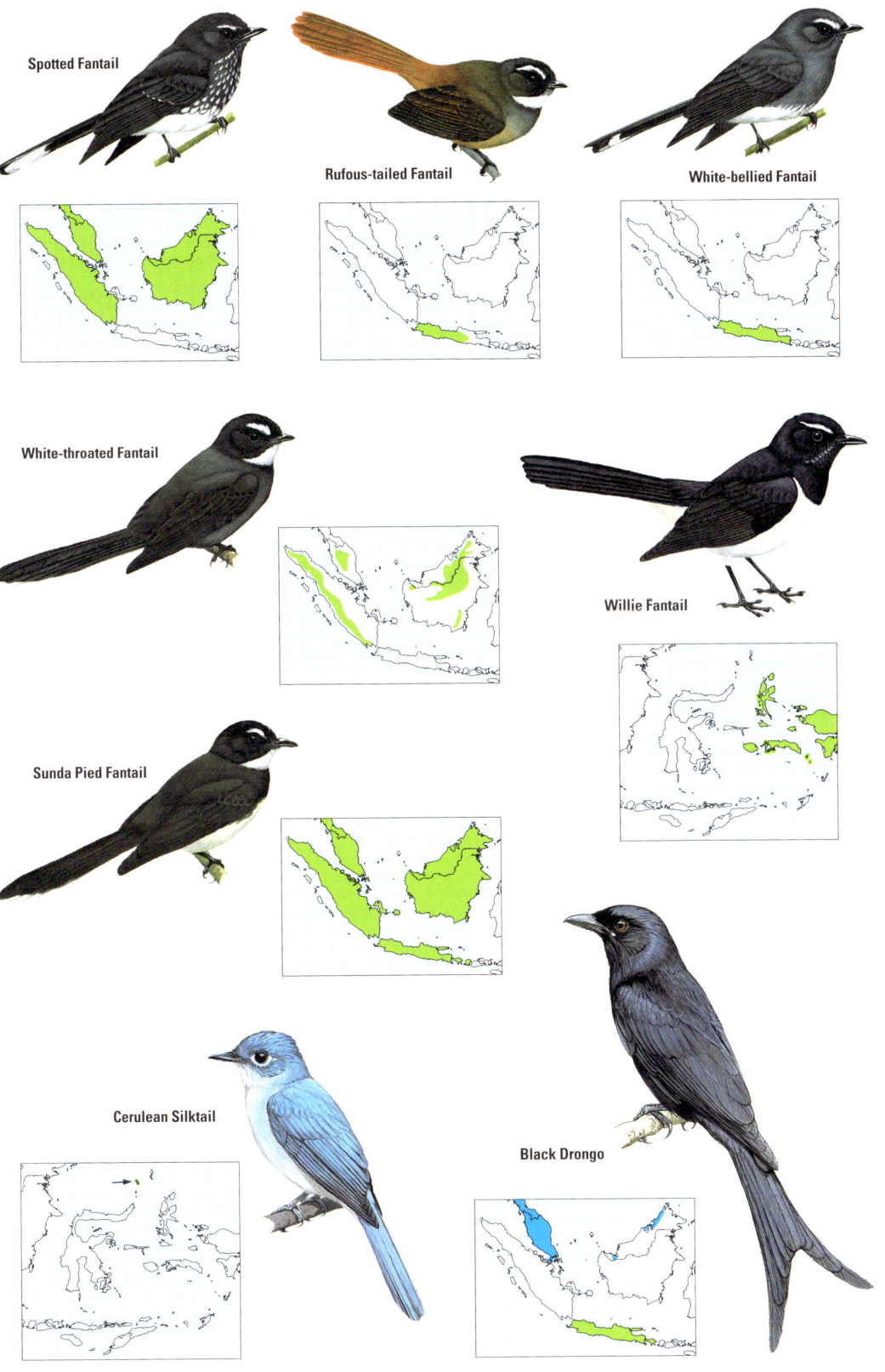

Spotted Fantail

Rufous-tailed Fantail

White-bellied Fantail

White-throated Fantail

Willie Fantail

Sunda Pied Fantail

Cerulean Silktail

Black Drongo

Bronzed Drongo *Dicrurus aeneus*
L 23–24 cm. S–SE–E Asia. 3 ssp, 1 in region: *malayensis* (Bor, Sum, MPen). Uncommon in forest, edge, bamboo regrowth, <1500 m. Singly, pairs or small groups (<10); perching conspicuously in mid-canopy, performing short sallies. **ID Ad** small bill; comparatively short, deeply forked tail with no upcurl; brilliant blue-green glossed crown and upperparts and well-defined breast spangles, contrasting strongly with matte black face. **Imm** lacking gloss with indistinct white spotting on underparts. **Voc** Wide and varied repertoire of simple, short notes mixed with scratching sounds: (i) rapid series of high-pitched notes rapidly descending "ki-ki-ki-kew-kew…" lasting <1.5 sec, regularly repeated, interspersed with various short simple whistled phrases; (ii) series of simple, single notes, alternately up- and downslurred, "chip", "t'wee" and "tchoo"; (iii) long series of constant chatter, usually given in pairs, lacking the harsh scolding quality of other drongos. **SS** See Crow-billed and Black Drongos. Larger-sized Bornean and Sumatran Spangled have much more powerful and more strongly arched/decurved beaks, long neck or breast hackles (or facial horns in Sumatran), and show strongly upcurled (not flat) tail tips. In good light, 'spangled drongos' lack Bronzed's strong contrast between iridescent crown and matte-black face, but exhibit unmistakeable contrast between turquoise-shining wing panel and black mantle. Beware of Greater Racket-tailed Drongos without tail extensions (because of moult or damage): Bronzed is smaller, thinner-billed, with much deeper and wider tail fork, and always lacks tufts on forehead.

Lesser Racket-tailed Drongo *Dicrurus remifer*
L 26 cm (<40 cm including tail). Himalaya to SE Asia. 4 ssp, 1 in region: *remifer* (Sum, Jav). Fairly common in montane forest, 600–2500 m. Singly or pairs, often joins mixed flocks. **ID** Distinct hammerhead shape with very small bill and long, straight forehead peaking in hindcrown. **Ad** slim body with wholly glossed upperparts and breast spangles; square-cut tail with very long bare outer shafts ending with long, thin pendant. **Imm** lacking gloss and no tail extensions. **Voc** Extremely varied and complex repertoire. Song: series consists of short, thin musical notes, thinner and higher-pitched than other drongos, usually alternating up- and down, lasting 2–5 sec. Call: constant, quiet chattering. **SS** Only drongo in region with square-cut tail and unique small-billed hammerhead shape. From Greater Racket-tailed additionally by lack of forehead tuft and thin rackets. See Sumatran Spangled Drongo. **AN** Lesser Racquet-tailed Drongo.

Crow-billed Drongo *Dicrurus annectens*
L 27–29 cm. Breeds Himalaya to SE Asia; winters to region. Monotypic. Uncommon in Sum, few confirmed records from coastal NW Bor, in coastal vegetation, parkland, all types of forest. Singly; perches in low and mid-storey in shade, making short sallies; at dawn sings from high tree perch even in winter quarters. **ID Ad** strong, slightly hooked, broad-based bill; broad shallow-forked tail, slightly raised tail tips; all-black plumage with lightly bluish-glossed upperparts, lacking neck hackles and showing only very faint breast spangles. **Imm** conspicuous white spotting on belly, often to breast. **Voc** Song: rising crescendo of bell-like notes and whistles. Calls: (i) downslurred, hawk-like "whiiir" and "whirrer"; (ii) harsh, short scolding. **SS** Compared to smaller Bronzed, Crow-billed has much more massive bill structure: Crow-billed's beak depth makes up more than half of head height (from crown-tip to lower ear-coverts), but much

less than half in Bronzed; Crow-billed's gape line almost reaches as far back as eye (in Bronzed falls far short of eye); bristles (when seen well) can reach half of bill length in Bronzed, much less in Crow-billed; Bronzed has much smaller black (not red) eye and shows brighter iridescent breast spangles that contrast sharply with matte face. Crow-billed lacks the facial filaments, hackles and horns of the three 'spangled drongos' (Sumatran, Javan and Bornean), which have much more iridescent spangles extending further up the breast to necksides; 'spangled drongos' also have a distinctly decurved or arched (not straight, hooked) beak, much more extremely upcurled outertail tips and a large and diagnostically turquoise-shining wing panel absent in Crow-billed. Beware of Greater Racket-tailed individuals that lack tail extensions (because of damage or moult): these are best told from Crow-billed by forehead tuft (though can be very vestigial on Borneo), glossier upperparts, and more iridescent breast spangles reaching onto necksides (faint and restricted to breast on Crow-billed); unless tail too damaged, its shape can be helpful: Crow-billed more deeply and widely forked with sharp inverted V, whereas Greater Racket-tailed shows a more linear tail fork. Imm Crow-billed told from all species by unique white belly spotting. Also see Ashy and Black Drongos.

Greater Racket-tailed Drongo *Dicrurus paradiseus*
L 30 cm (<65 cm including tail). S–SE Asia. 13 ssp, 5 in region: *platurus* (Sum, Bangka, Simeulue, Nias, MPen); *microlophus* (Anambas, Natuna, Tioman Is); *formosus* (Jav–Bali); *brachyphorus* (Bor); *banguey* (Balambangan, Banggi). Much variation throughout range, further study required. Fairly common in forest, <1000 m. Singly or pairs, joins mixed flocks. Raucous, usually the first song in dawn chorus, often from conspicuous high perch. **ID Ad** tufted forecrest; long, forked, pointed tail with long, bare outer shafts and broad pendants (often absent); upperparts including crown, mantle and wings heavily glossed purple-blue; bright red eye. Ssp *microlophus* variably smaller with shorter bushy tuft; *formosus* much smaller with small but distinct forehead tuft, much longer tail streamers; *brachyphorus* smallest of all races, only shows vestigial tuft, dark-reddish to blackish eye, often has abnormal tail streamers, one can be absent, or of different lengths; *banguey* as previous but longer wings. **Imm** shorter tuft; less contrasting glossy upperparts; white-fringed undertail-coverts; lacks tail streamers; dark eye. **Voc** Broad variation, individually and possibly racially. Usually the first bird to begin dawn chorus. Song: most often heard is a repeated series of loud, melodious bell-like single notes, much individual variation but actual series monotonous, not so varied, includes "choot-choot-choot…", "kit-kit-kit…", "too-too-too…", and "too'it-too'it-too'it…", mixed with all kinds of odd, barely transcribable loud whistles including much mimicry. Call: (i) 2-note, tuneless "too-too", often slightly trilled; (ii) harsh scolding notes, regularly repeated, often with variety of single whistled notes. **SS** See Bronzed, Ashy, Black, Crow-billed and Lesser Racket-tailed Drongos. The three 'spangled drongos' in range (Sumatran, Bornean, Javan) can be told from Greater Racket-tailed individuals without tail extensions by distinctly upcurled outertail tips, decurved or arched (not straight) beak and much more shiny plumage with more strongly iridescent underparts spangles and large, distinct turquoise wing panel. 'Spangled drongos' lack forehead tuft of Greater Racket-tailed but have long bristles extending over crown (Javan, Bornean) or 'feather horns' (Sumatran) instead, and Javan has white (not dark) eyes. **AN** Greater Racquet-tailed Drongo.

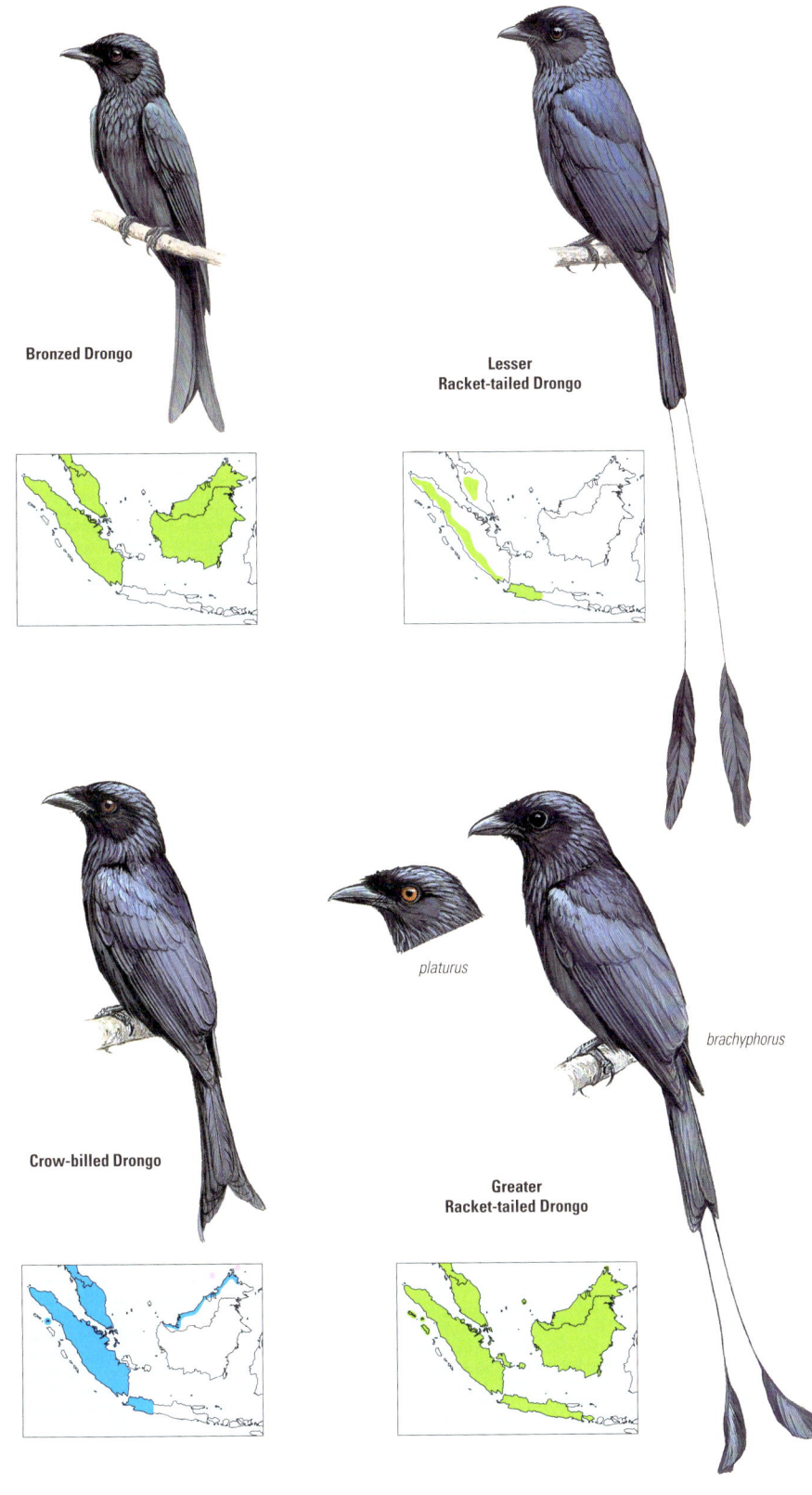

Bronzed Drongo

Lesser Racket-tailed Drongo

platurus

brachyphorus

Crow-billed Drongo

Greater Racket-tailed Drongo

Ashy Drongo *Dicrurus leucophaeus*

L 25–29 cm. S–SE–E Asia, Palawan. 16 ssp, 7 in region: *leuco-phaeus* (Jav–Lombok); *stigmatops* (Bor); *phaedrus* (C–S Sum); *batakensis* (N Sum); *periophthalmicus* (Sipora, Pagai); *siberu* (Siberut); *celaenus* (Simeulue). Complex may contain multiple species-level taxa but defies easy separation because of checker-board pattern of plumage variation across range. Detailed research required. Fairly common in forest, edge, clearings; >600 m, but down to sea level on small islands and Jav. Singly, pairs or family groups; perching conspicuously in mid- and upper storey, performing short sallies. **ID Ad** uniform ashy-grey with darker lores and chin; thin, long tail with deep fork lacking upcurl. Ssp *stigmatops* shorter tail, slightly paler plumage, with whitish lores extending around eye forming small facial patch; *phaedrus* as previous but smaller facial patch, mainly in front and below eye; *batakensis* shorter tail still, less white on face than previous with slightly darker plumage; *celaenus* as nominate but slightly darker with deeper tail fork; *periophthalmicus* huge white face patch, pale-grey plumage; *siberu* as previous but slightly darker with face patch not as extensive. **Imm** brown-tinged plumage, pale fringing on belly; brown eye. **Voc** Great vocal variation across subspecies. Common calls include: *stigmatops* long rapid, occasionally undulating trill lasting <10 sec at <13 n/s; *phaedrus* mix of thin, slightly up- or downslurred notes with occasional light, scolding, scratchy notes; *batakensis* jumbled series of 3–4 different, predominantly upslurred notes lasting <10 sec; *periophthalmicus/siberu* (i) various rapid trills, lasting <3 sec at 14 n/s, (ii) unstructured series of jumbled notes lasting <3 sec, regularly repeated, (iii) repeated metallic "toot-toot-toot..." at 4 n/s; *celaenus* (i) croaking, staccato phrase, starting with 3 repeated rising trill notes, "b'r'r't-b'r'r'rt-b'r'r'r't...", followed by 4–6 alternating high-low clicking notes, "t'e'e'e-t'o'o'o- t'e'e'e-t'o'o'o...", lasting <10 sec, (ii) long canary-like trill, (iii) rapidly repeated disyllabic "tr'rt-tr'rt-tr'rt...". **SS** With poor views, beware of black-coloured forest-inhabiting drongo species: Ashy lacks shiny spangles, tail upcurls, hackles, filaments etc., and blackish lores should contrast with paler grey head even in sub-optimal light. See also Black Drongo.

Bornean Spangled Drongo *Dicrurus borneensis* [E]

L 26 cm. Monotypic. Traditionally united with Javan, Sulu, White-eyed, Sula and Obi Spangled Drongos as well as extralimital forms into broadly-defined umbrella species, '**Hair-crested Drongo**' *D. hottentottus* (S–SE–E Asia, Phil); however, this complex encompasses an unusually diverse range of morphological and vocal variation, with some members probably not directly related to others. The current division of Hair-crested is based on present understanding of morphological, vocal and limited mtDNA data; genomic data required. Uncommon in (sub-) montane forest, >800 m. Singly or pairs, joins mixed flocks containing laughingthrushes and Bornean Green Magpie in forest interior. **ID Ad** robust, compact appearance with short, slightly decurved but broad bill and quite short, broad tail with very shallow fork but strongly upcurled tail-tips; well-defined glossy breast spangles and long glossy neck hackles; long bristles sometimes extend over crown; green-blue glossed wings contrasting with dull mantle. **Imm** lacks hackles and spangles; no gloss in plumage. **Voc** (i) High-pitched whistles, rising then falling, "tswee'it wee-wee, tswee'it wee wee", lasting 2.5 sec, regularly repeated, copied from Bornean Green Magpie, sometimes only opening note "twsee'it" given; (ii) drawn-out soft rattle on a sliding scale at two speeds, lasting 1.5 sec; (iii) bouncing, tuneful "chock-chock-chock...", often in duet, with short high trills and musical chatter; (iv) quiet, tuneful chattering using variety of single notes. **SS** See Bronzed, Crow-billed, Greater Racket-tailed and Black Drongos.

Javan Spangled Drongo *Dicrurus jentincki* [E]

L 27–29 cm. 3 ssp: *jentincki* (C Jav–Bali, Kangean, Masalembu Besar); *faberi* (Panaitan); *termeuleni* (Seribu, Jakarta Bay). For taxonomy see Bornean Spangled Drongo. Fairly common to uncommon in woodland, plantation (teak), secondary forest, edge on mainland Jav–Bali, <500 m; primary forest on small islands. Singly or pairs. **ID Ad** creamy-white eye; long, slightly decurved bill; quite long tail, shallow fork with strongly upcurled tail tips; very long glossy neck hackles and prominent breast spangles; greenish-glossed wings; very long rictal bristles extending over crown. Ssp *termeuleni* noticeably smaller; *faberi* bluish-glossed head and neck hackles, deeper black plumage, intermediate in size between other two races, with shorter tail. **Imm** lacks hackles and spangles; no gloss in plumage. **Voc** (i) Short series of alternating musical notes, with long final note, "chip-chop-chip-chop-chip-wheeeez", lasting <2 sec; (ii) rapid series of short, musical notes, lasting <1 sec; (iii) variety of loud, musical clicks, chirps and bell-like notes. **SS** See Black, Ashy, Greater Racket-tailed and Crow-billed Drongos.

Sumatran Spangled Drongo *Dicrurus sumatranus* [E]

L 29 cm. Monotypic. For taxonomy see Mentawai Spangled Drongo. Fairly common in submontane forest, 700–1600 m. Singly or pairs, joins mixed flocks; rarely perches conspicuously, favouring forest interior. **ID Ad** stocky and broad; relatively short tail with small notch and short but distinct outertail up-curl; head has 'horns' peaking slightly above crown and short, slightly arching bill; deep-blue glossed breast shackles and crown; large turquoise wing panel. **Imm** undescribed. **Voc** Wide repertoire: (i) series of 3–9 downslurred notes "choo-choo-tit-tit-choo-choo-choo", lasting <1.5 sec, middle notes higher, gradually descending in pitch, much variation to the phrase, including in duet with partner producing short ringing "to'to'to'to'to'to" simultaneously; (ii) downslurred, metallic "choo-choo", lasting 0.4 sec; (iii) most regularly heard call a thin, metallic "tooeee", lasting 0.5 sec. **SS** Lesser Racket-tailed individuals which lack tail extensions can be told by their distinct hammerhead shape with a tiny beak (lacking Sumatran Spangled's horns), by their their square-cut tail without an outertail up-curl, slimmer build, lack of iridescent spangles/hackles on underparts, and generally glossy upperparts, lacking Sumatran Spangled's strong contrast with a shiny turquoise wing panel and matte mantle. See also Bronzed, Greater-Racket-tailed, Crow-billed and Black Drongos. **AN** Sumatran Drongo.

Mentawai Spangled Drongo *Dicrurus viridinitens* [E]

L 28 cm. Monotypic. Previously considered conspecific with Suma-tran Spangled Drongo, but vocal and morphological differences are pronounced, and mtDNA confirms placement closer to extralimital members of the '**Hair-crested Drongo**' *D. hottentottus* complex (see Bornean Spangled for taxonomy). Common in forest, edge and heavily degraded habitat. Singly or pairs, joins mixed flocks. **ID Ad** well-proportioned with longish, slender, decurved bill; green-glossed breast shackles and crown; quite long greenish nape hackles; big turquoise wing panel; tail slightly notched with upcurled outertail tips. **Imm** undescribed. **Voc** Varied repertoire: (i) ~6 notes of similar, pure, penetrating quality, all downslurred except for final note "chew-tew-tew-chew-chew-eee", lasting 1.5 sec, occasionally last note replaced by short scolding note, often in duet with clicks and rattles made by partner resulting in a cacophony of noise; (ii) varia-ble motif of 2 hard whistled notes followed by harder, downslurred series "chip-hoo-chek-chek-chek", lasting 1.5 sec; (iii) 4 penetrating tuneless notes "hoop-tee-tee-hoo", lasting 1 sec; (iv) 3 short, ascending, then descending, pure whistles followed by drawn-out, descending, scratchy "tet-tit-to-grrrrrrit", lasting 2 sec.

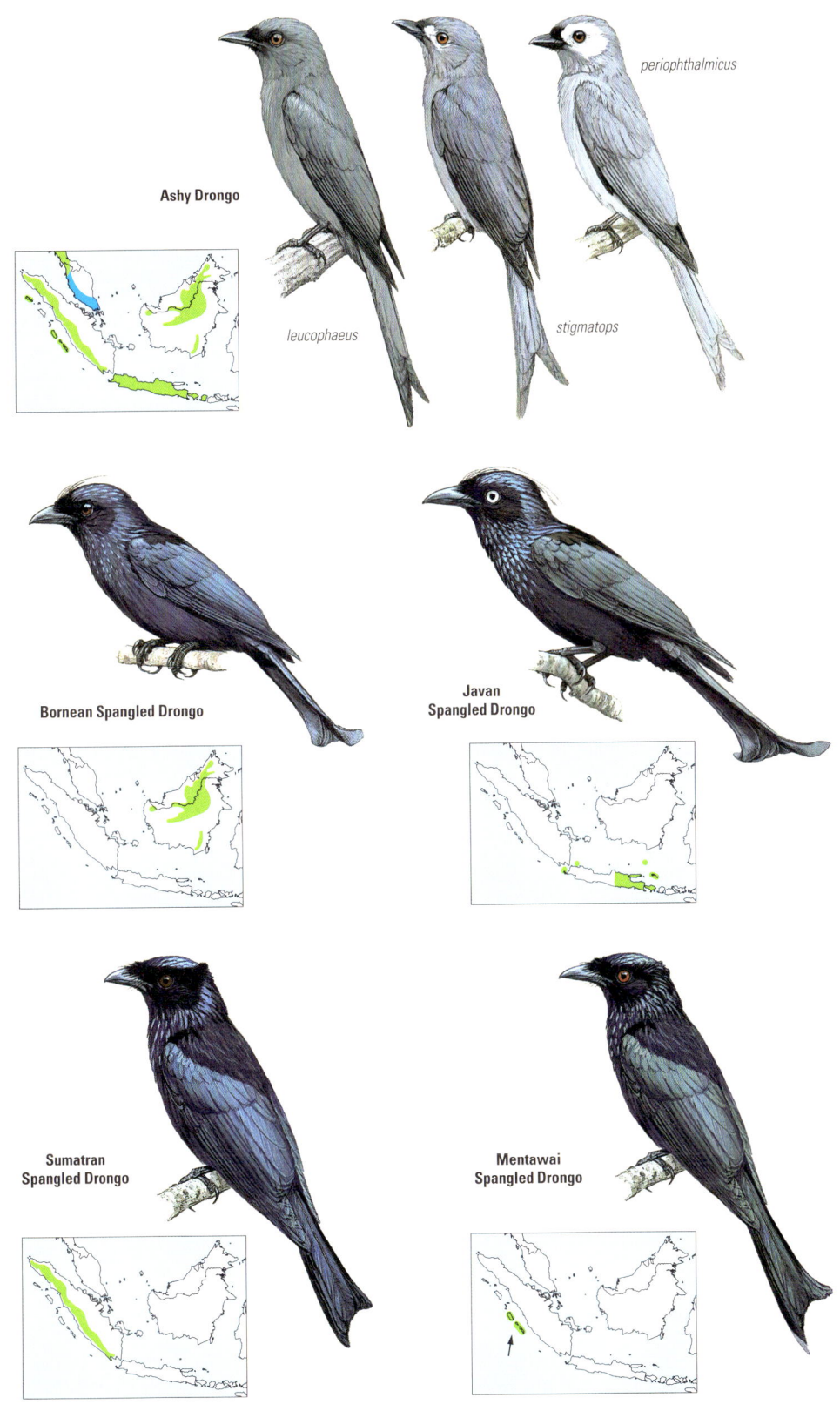

Ashy Drongo

leucophaeus

stigmatops

periophthalmicus

Bornean Spangled Drongo

Javan Spangled Drongo

Sumatran Spangled Drongo

Mentawai Spangled Drongo

Sulu Spangled Drongo *Dicrurus suluensis*

L 28 cm. Sulu. Monotypic. For taxonomy see Bornean Spangled Drongo. Reaches into region only on Maratua, where mixture of pale-eyed and red-eyed birds occur which may constitute admixed population. Fairly common in forest, edge. Singly or pairs, joins mixed flocks. **ID Ad** pale or red iris; glossy neck hackles, breast spangles and frontal filaments; tail deeply forked with slightly upcurled tail tips. **Imm** undescribed. **Voc** Undescribed on Maratua.

White-eyed Spangled Drongo *Dicrurus leucops*   E

L 29–32 cm. 3 ssp: *leucops* (Sul and satellites; perhaps Matasiri); *banggaiensis* (Peleng); ssp. (Siau, Sangihe). Ssp *banggaiensis* perhaps unstable hybrid swarm between this species and Sula Spangled Drongo, with most individuals in W lowlands similar to White-eyed and most montane birds similar to Sula Spangled. Birds on Matasiri (Java Sea) require further study, given odd geographical position, possibly part of Javan Spangled Drongo. Birds on Siau and Sangihe belong to undescribed taxon currently subsumed with *leucops*, but have red, not white, iris and potentially unique vocalisations; further study required. Also see Bornean Spangled for taxonomy. Fairly common in forest, edge, <1500 m. Singly or pairs, joins mixed flocks. **ID Ad** striking white eye (red on Siau and Sangihe). Very green glossed upperparts with long neck hackles and prominent breast spangles; long, broad tail with shallow fork and deeply upcurled tail tips; large bill with well-arched culmen. Ssp *banggaiensis* shows dark eyes in most highland individuals, pale eyes in the W lowlands and intermediate eye colour in many individuals in between. **Imm** shorter hackles; less glossed plumage; white-tipped belly. **Voc** (i) Upslurred, high-pitched "chee-it chee-it chee-it", often accompanied by short scolding notes; (ii) 2–4 soft, popping notes "pop-pop-pop", followed by hard, rapid double rattle "trrt trrrrrt", lasting <2 sec; (iii) 1–4 short, sharp scolding "whek"; (iv) short, scolding "whek" note followed by higher-pitched, downslurred "chee-chee", lasting 0.8 sec. Vocalisations of populations on Siau and Sangihe as well as ssp *banggaiensis* poorly known, possibly distinct. **SS** See Sulawesi Spangled.

Sulawesi Spangled Drongo *Dicrurus montanus*   E

L 25 cm. Monotypic. Fairly common in montane forest, edge, 500–1800 m. **ID Ad** thin bill; small body; long, slim tail with very deep fork and pointed outer tail tips; small, dull-glossed breast spangles and short neck hackles; upperparts weakly glossed; brown or dark red eye. **Imm** undescribed. **Voc** (i) Series of 4 penetrating, thin whistles, first upslurred followed by downslurred notes "tsoowee-chee-oo-ee", lasting 1.5 sec; (ii) loud, slightly ascending, hawk-like "keh-keh-keh...", lasting <1 sec at 5 n/s; (iii) penetrating "chew-chew" followed by hard, grating rattle "greeeeet", lasting 1.5 sec; (iv) variable, repeated, downslurred whistle, raptor-like "whir", fuller "choo", trisyllabic "t't'choo" and "h'tchew". **SS** From larger White-eyed Spangled Drongo by dark (not white) eye, smaller and thinner bill, more deeply forked tail lacking strong up-curls, shorter hackles. **AN** Sulawesi Drongo.

Sula Spangled Drongo *Dicrurus pectoralis*   E

L 28 cm. Monotypic. For taxonomy see Bornean and White-eyed Spangled Drongos. Fairly common in forest, edge. Singly or pairs, joins mixed flocks. **ID Ad** very long and broad glossy neck hackles and prominent breast spangles; tail relatively short with minimal fork and slightly upcurled tail tips; long wings; brilliant metallic bluish-green wings, crown and rump. **Imm** undescribed. **Voc** (i) Quick, upslurred note followed by short rattle and downslurred, mournful note "whip-trrrt-torhoo", lasting 2 sec; (ii) repeated downslurred "choo", "chip" or "chop", often doubled up or with third, higher-pitched note; (iii) typical drongo-like short, grated scolding note.

Obi Spangled Drongo *Dicrurus guillemardi*   E

L 32 cm. Monotypic. For taxonomy see Bornean Spangled Drongo. Fairly common in forest, edge. Singly or pairs, joins mixed flocks; fairly conspicuous, often perching on open branches. **ID Ad** long, broad, shallow-forked tail; broadest tail of all regional drongos; moderate breast spangles; long, broad, well-glossed neck hackles; very long wings reaching over halfway down tail's extension; brown eye. **Imm** undescribed. **Voc** Song: 2 introductory metallic tuneless whistles, first note higher, "tee-hoo", followed by series of 2–10 hard, downward notes "chok-chok-chok..." at 7 n/s. Call: (i) soft, short clicking; (ii) soft, curious "toop"; (iii) harsh, grated scolding in alarm.

Flores Spangled Drongo *Dicrurus bimaensis*   E

L 27–28 cm. Monotypic. Traditionally united with Sumba, Lombok, Timor, Tanimbar and Kai Spangled Drongos into more broadly-defined umbrella species, '**Wallacean Drongo**' *D. densus*. However, pronounced vocal and plumage differences dictate break-up into monotypic species. Fairly common in woodland and edge. Singly, pairs or small groups (<10); often perching prominently. **ID Ad** appears quite compact and broad-shouldered; crown, neck hackles, breast shackles and mantle glossed green-purple; wings and tail glossed green; tail quite short with shallow fork and upcurled tail tips. **Imm** white speckled belly; lacks gloss, particularly on head; hackles absent. **Voc** Song: buzzy, liquid phrase "CHopseejopseee'zee", lasting 1.5 sec. Call: 2-note metallic "chit-chit", or 3-note "weer-chi-chit" regularly repeated in quick succession when excited.

Sumba Spangled Drongo *Dicrurus sumbae*   E

L 28 cm. Monotypic. For taxonomy see Flores Spangled Drongo. Fairly common in woodland and edge. Singly, pairs or small groups (<10); often perching prominently. **ID Ad** similar to Flores Spangled but deeper tail fork, longer neck hackles and even glossier upperparts; bill shorter, less arched. **Imm** white speckled belly; lacks gloss, particularly on head; hackles absent. **Voc** Song: series of liquid, fluid notes, "WHEET'jewit'it'jewit" lasting <2 sec. Call: liquid, grating "gar-reeeoo".

Lombok Spangled Drongo *Dicrurus vicinus*   E

L 29 cm. Monotypic. For taxonomy see Flores Spangled Drongo. Fairly common in forest, woodland and edge. Singly, pairs or small groups (<10); often perching prominently. **ID Ad** very similar to Flores Spangled but slightly longer-tailed with deeper fork, less upcurled tail tip; mantle not as glossed. **Imm** undescribed. **Voc** Song: hesitant, scratchy introductory notes "chew-it-chew-it" followed by accelerating chirpy, descending notes "TOO-wit-too-wit-to-whirrrt", lasting 3–4 sec. Call: (i) 2-note, metallic, tuneless "tee-do"; (ii) harsh, scolding "check".

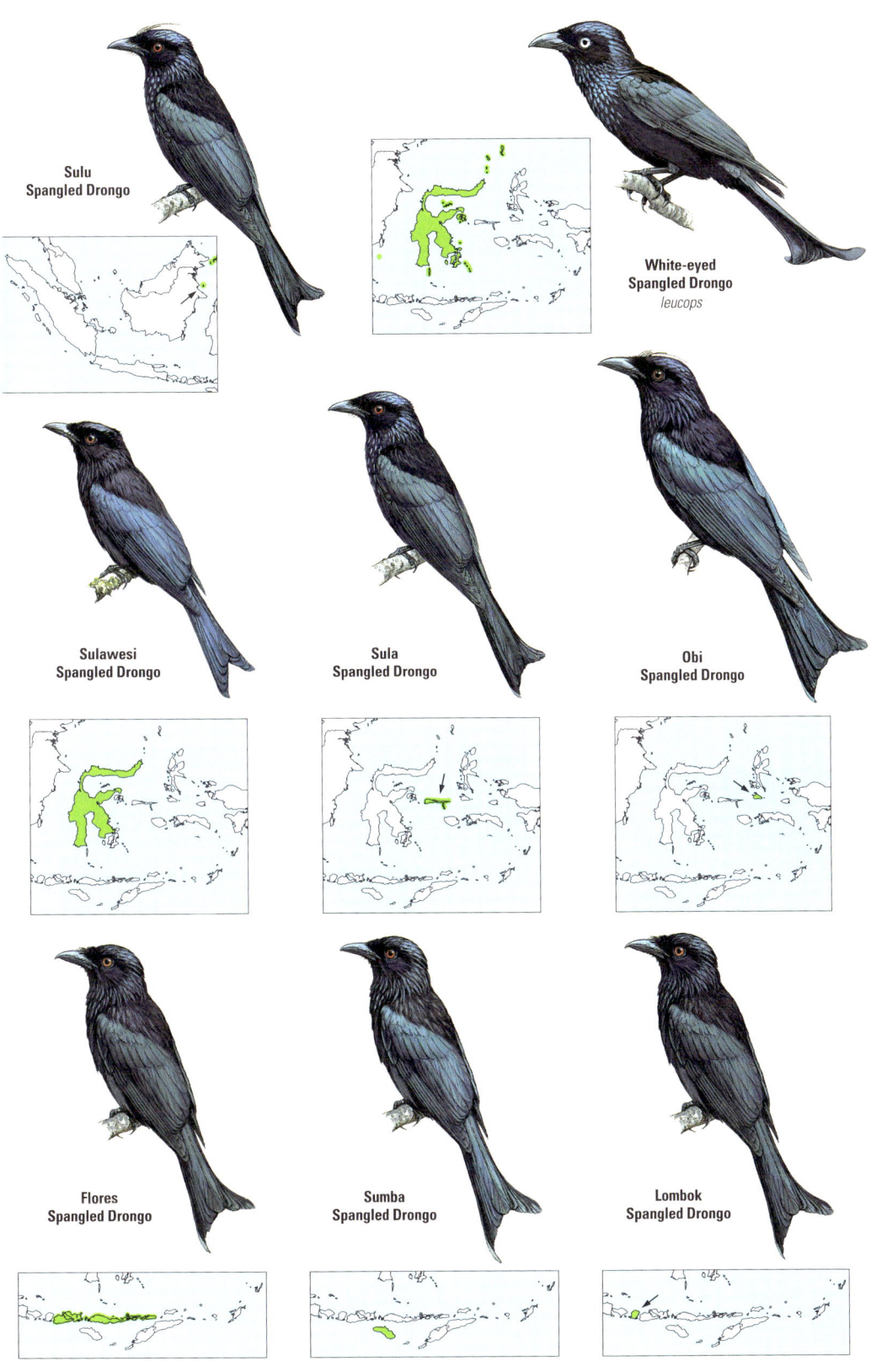

**Sulu
Spangled Drongo**

**White-eyed
Spangled Drongo**
leucops

**Sulawesi
Spangled Drongo**

**Sula
Spangled Drongo**

**Obi
Spangled Drongo**

**Flores
Spangled Drongo**

**Sumba
Spangled Drongo**

**Lombok
Spangled Drongo**

Timor Spangled Drongo *Dicrurus densus* E

L 31–33 cm. Monotypic. For taxonomy see Flores Spangled Drongo. Uncommon in forested areas, woodland, edge. Singly, pairs or rarely small groups (<6); usually in canopy, much warier than other drongos. **ID Ad** large, broad bill; long-bodied; long, deeply forked tail; lightly glossed purple-green wings and long neck hackles. **Imm** undescribed. **Voc** Song: series of harsh, abrasive notes interspersed with the occasional whining upslurred whistle, lasting <3 sec, regularly repeated; lacks melodious or fluty notes. Call: regularly repeated tuneless upslurred whistled note "wheeet".

Tanimbar Spangled Drongo *Dicrurus kuehni* E

L 28–29 cm. Monotypic. For taxonomy see Flores Spangled Drongo. Scarce in forest interior, very rarely perches in open. Singly or pairs, unobtrusive; not known to follow mixed flocks. **ID Ad** highly arched, massive bill; green-glossed wings, purple-glossed rear crown and small breast shackles; tail quite short with shallow fork. **Imm** undescribed. **Voc** Song: single, drawn-out "chchchop", lasting 0.5 sec. Call: short, sharp, metallic "chip".

Kai Spangled Drongo *Dicrurus megalornis* E

L 38 cm. Monotypic. For taxonomy see Flores Spangled Drongo. Fairly common in forest (including degraded), edge. Singly or pairs. **ID Ad** elongated body and tail with shallow fork and slightly upcurled tail tip; purple-green glossed crown, mantle, wings and particularly breast shackles; neck hackles indistinct; bill small and slender. **Imm** dusky-black, lacking gloss; belly tipped white. **Voc** Highly variable, main calls include: (i) metallic opening note, followed by lower-pitched fluty note, ending with short rattle "chit-woo-trrrt", lasting 1.3 sec, occasionally last 2 notes repeated in sequence; (ii) 4–7 metallic, knocking "trit'trit'trit'trit" at 1 n/0.1 s; (iii) 3-note "tit-ssrrrrt-tirit", lasting 1 sec, first note quiet, followed by rattled second and upslurred third notes; (iv) rolling, rattled, long note followed by downslurred, fluty second note "trrrrrt-chew", lasting 0.8 sec, regularly repeated in rapid succession.

Seram Spangled Drongo *Dicrurus amboinensis* E

L 27 cm. Monotypic. Traditionally united with Buru, Halmahera, Bacan and Morotai Spangled Drongos as well as extralimital forms into broadly-defined umbrella species, '**Spangled Drongo**' *D. bracteatus* (Aus); however, this complex encompasses an unusually diverse range of morphological and vocal variation, with some members probably not directly related to others. The current division of Spangled is based on present understanding of morphological, vocal and limited mtDNA data; genomic data required. Fairly common in forest, edge. Singly or pairs, joins mixed flocks. **ID Ad** dull-glossy upperparts; neck hackles relatively indistinct; glossed but tiny breast spangles; slim tail deeply forked with no terminal upcurl; bill long but thin. **Imm** dusky-black lacking gloss; belly tipped white. **Voc** Highly variable, many different high-pitched thin, shrill calls and clicking: (i) slow, downslurred grating followed by high-pitched shrill call, tailing off "grrrrrrrrt s'r'r'r'r'r'r'r'r'trit", lasting ~2 sec; (ii) pronounced upslurred, thin, comical whistle followed by high-pitched quiet trill "whirrrrrrr swirrrri'eee", lasting ~1.7 sec; (iii) rapid series of upslurred "chewee-chewee-chewee" notes, lasting <6 sec, followed by duet, one bird with low-pitched "oohwee-ohh-wee", second bird with rapid, machine-gun like trill, lasting <5 sec; (iv) simple, short "pip" accompanied by "peeyew" notes.

Buru Spangled Drongo *Dicrurus buruensis* E

L 30–32 cm. Monotypic. For taxonomy see Seram Spangled Drongo. Fairly common in forest, edge. Singly or pairs, joins mixed flocks. **ID Ad** upperparts more glossed than Seram Spangled with distinct, medium-length neck hackles and distinct breast spangles; very long tail with deep fork, little terminal upcurl; short wings only reach base of tail. **Imm** dusky-black lacking gloss; belly tipped white. **Voc** (i) Quivering, cicada-like rapid trill, increasing in volume and pitch "z'z'z'z'z'z'z'z'z CHEW", lasting 2 sec; (ii) series of 4–10 rapidly repeated "chit-chew-chew chit-chew-chew chit-chew-chew", each motif lasting 0.6 sec; (iii) downslurred, intense, rapid trill followed by penetrating, tuneless pure whistle "zrrrrrrrrrrt-fwhiiiiiiiiiit", lasting 2.5 sec.

Halmahera Spangled Drongo *Dicrurus atrocaeruleus* E

L 32 cm. Monotypic. Name *atrocaeruleus*, described from mixed series of syntypes from Bacan and Halmahera, to be fixed to Halmahera, with Bacan population here separated as monotypic species on account of pronounced vocal differences. For taxonomy also see Seram Spangled Drongo. Fairly common in forest, edge. Singly or pairs, joins mixed flocks. **ID Ad** long-winged; long tail with moderate fork, slightly upcurled tail tips; long, strong rictal bristles; large, glossy breast spangles. **Imm** dusky-black lacking gloss; belly tipped white. **Voc** (i) Tremulous, grating, trisyllabic note followed by upslurred whistle "wheeeiir-oooear", lasting 1.2 sec, repeated without pause for <10 sec; (ii) alternating higher and lower-pitched jumpy whistled notes "eeee-hoo-eeee-hoo-eeee-hoo", lasting 1.3 sec, with slight variations on similar theme; (iii) downslurred, slightly grating, drawn-out whistle "whiiiir", lasting 0.8 sec; (iv) 2 quiet introductory notes followed by high-pitched downslurred whistle, ending with low-pitched disyllabic whistle "hoo-hoo-SEEW–TODOO", lasting 1.5 sec.

Bacan Spangled Drongo *Dicrurus* sp. E

L 33 cm. Monotypic. Previously subsumed under Halmahera Spangled Drongo but vocally distinct, awaiting formal description. See Halmahera and Seram Spangled Drongos for taxonomy. Fairly common in forest, edge. Singly or pairs, joins mixed flocks. **ID** On current knowledge separable from Halmahera Spangled by longer, slightly more deeply forked tail, smaller bill (with some overlap) and glossier mantle. **Voc** (i) Harsh introductory rattle lasting 0.5 sec, followed by tremulous downslurred note, then 2 penetrating downslurred whistles, ending with tremulous higher-pitched note, "trrrrt t'cheeew too too weeezoh", phrase lasting 2.5 sec, often repeated without pause; (ii) quiet, drawn-out whine followed by a melodious 2-note, oriole-like "ah-hoo", lasting ~2 sec; (iii) 2-note, metallic "whit-whit", like metal-on-metal, regularly repeated; (iv) penetrating, pure, tuneless whistle "fwheeee", lasting 1 sec; (v) short, harsh bark lacking scolding quality of other drongo species.

Morotai Spangled Drongo *Dicrurus morotensis* E

L 30 cm. Monotypic. For taxonomy see Seram Spangled Drongo. Fairly common in forest, edge. Singly or pairs, joins mixed flocks. **ID Ad** from Halmahera Spangled Drongo by smaller bill, much shorter tail with deeper fork, marginally upcurled tail tip, short breast spangles. **Imm** dusky-black lacking gloss; belly tipped white. **Voc** Highly variable, with a variety of short whistled notes. Main call types as follows: (i) high-pitched level trill, lasting <1.5 sec, reminiscent of typical sparrowhawk call; (ii) high-pitched first note followed by bubbling rattle "eeee-wewewe eeee-wewewe-eeee-wewewe...", lasting <20 sec; (iii) raptor-like "whiiir", lasting 0.5 sec; (iv) metallic, tuneless, rising "boy-ink, boy-ink", often interspersed with high-pitched tuneless whistle "eeee"; (v) fluty, whistled, low-pitched "woorhoot-hoo-whoot", lasting 1 sec.

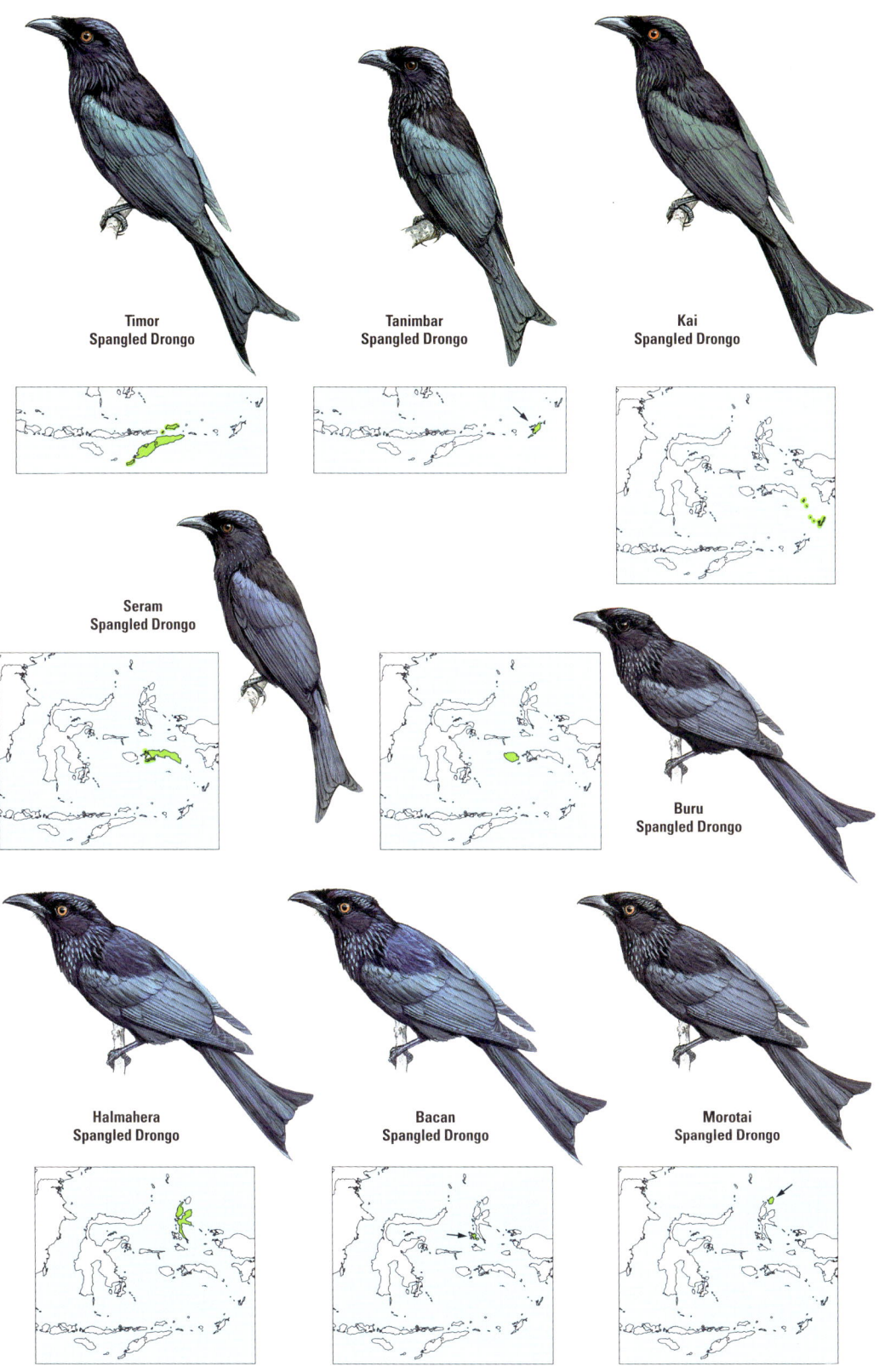

Timor Spangled Drongo

Tanimbar Spangled Drongo

Kai Spangled Drongo

Seram Spangled Drongo

Buru Spangled Drongo

Halmahera Spangled Drongo

Bacan Spangled Drongo

Morotai Spangled Drongo

PARADISAEIDAE
Birds-of-paradise
3 species in region

Includes some of the most ornately plumaged birds on earth. Many species congregate at lekking trees. Predominantly Papuan in origin, only few species occur in region: the flamboyant Wallace's Standardwing and the plainer paradise-crows. Inhabit forest and edge where generally conspicuous and vocal.

Halmahera Paradise-crow *Lycocorax pyrrhopterus* `E`

L 40–44 cm. 2 ssp: *pyrrhopterus* (Halmahera, Bacan, Kasiruta); ssp *morotensis* (Morotai, Rau) differs vocally and – less so – in plumage, and may be separable as monotypic '**Morotai Paradise-crow**'. See also Obi Paradise-crow for taxonomy. Fairly common in forest, edge. Singly, pairs or small groups (<5); feeds in mid- and upper canopy, shy. Not known to lek. **ID** Superficially resembles a *Corvus* crow but head appears small with pointed, deep-based, black bill and broad, rounded tail. **Ad** blackish-brown plumage lacking gloss; strongly rufous-brown wings; small bare skin patch behind eye; white base to primaries only visible in flight. Ssp *morotensis* larger, plumage slightly browner overall with more white on primaries. **Imm** uniformly browner; lacks gloss. **Voc** Often in duet. Ssp *pyrrhopterus* (i) mechanical, tuneless, flat "grrrrk"; (ii) slightly upslurred, thin dry bark "ekk". Ssp *morotensis* (i) loud, far-carrying, hollow "hoook"; (ii) bark as *pyrrhopterus* but flatter, lower-pitched; (iii) frog-like, mechanical "herk", slightly upslurred.

Obi Paradise-crow *Lycocorax obiensis* `E`

L 41–43 cm. Monotypic. Previously included with Halmahera Paradise-crow but separated here based on pronounced vocal and plumage differences. Fairly common in forest, edge, plantations. Singly, pairs or small groups (<5); feeds in mid- and upper canopy. Not known to lek. **ID Ad** similar to Halmahera Paradise-crow but darker and glossy with green-blue tinge; slightly contrasting blue-black crown and tail; only trace of white at base of primaries. **Imm** uniformly browner; lacks gloss. **Voc** (i) Disyllabic, loud trumpet "OO'lip"; (ii) 1–5 loud, croaking "wick" or "wuhk"; (iii) curious, low-pitched, grated growling.

Wallace's Standardwing *Semioptera wallacii* `E`

L 25–30 cm. 2 ssp: *wallacii* (Bacan, Kasiruta); *halmaherae* (Halmahera). Uncommon in closed-canopy forest. Polygynous; promiscuous Ad males lek in groups (3–40) on traditional display perches, primarily in early morning. Display involves limb-hopping with static postures and flight displays with movements of wings, pectoral shield and wing-standards. Away from lek birds feed quietly in mid and upper storey, usually solitary, but can join mixed flocks. **ID** Flat-crowned, broad bodied, short-tailed appearance with short, very broad wings; conspicuous tuft on upper mandible; longish, decurved bill; bright orange legs. **M** iridescent green breast shield; two long white plumes from bend in wing; crown iridescent grey with violet sheen. Ssp *halmaherae* pinkish coppery-purple iridescent crown and nape; slightly longer tail. **F** smaller; uniformly greyish-brown, lacking plumes and breast-shield. **Imm** undescribed. **Voc** At leks very noisy and loud. Song: (i) competing males' advertisement calls include 6–7 upslurred, loud, clear, strident, throaty "wark" notes, followed by repeated clearer "wow-wow-wow..."; (ii) quieter musical chatter and twittering in display. Call: series of loud, upslurred, nasal "wark" notes. **AN** Standardwing Bird-of-paradise.

MONARCHIDAE
Monarchs
22 species in region

A diverse family of small to medium-sized forest birds. Most feed by flycatching and gleaning insects in mid- to upper storey. Typically active, vocal, and frequently part of mixed flocks. Most species are conspicuous, while others are more shy.

Pale-blue Monarch *Hypothymis puella* `E`

L 15–16 cm. 2 ssp: *puella* (Sul and satellites); *blasii* (Banggai, Sula). Sometimes included with Black-naped Monarch but distinct in plumage, voice and DNA. Common in forest, edge, secondary growth and scrub, <1500 m. Singly, pairs or part of mixed flocks; active and conspicuous in lower to upper storey. **ID M** generally as Black-naped but lacks black nuchal tuft, breast band obscure or absent, underparts including belly pale-blue; *blasii* deeper blue. **F** duller. **Imm** slightly duller blue. **Voc** Varied song repertoire: (i) rapid series of 9–15 whistles, beginning faint, rapidly increasing in volume "s-si'-si'-si'-si'-see..." at 7 n/s; (ii) loud, rapid, bubbling series of upslurred syllables "whiwhiwhi..." at 7 n/s; (iii) level series of 4–8 upslurred, piercing whistles "whey-whey-whey..." at 4 n/s. Call: buzzy, whistling "szweey, szweey".

Black-naped Monarch *Hypothymis azurea*

L 15–17 cm. S–SE–E Asia, Phil. 24 ssp, 13 in region: *prophata* (MPen, Sum, Bor); *javana* (Jav, Bali); *penidae* (Nusa Penida); *symmixta* (W–C LS); *opisthocyanea* (Anambas); *gigantoptera* (Natuna); *karimatensis* (Karimata); *aeria* (Maratua); *richmondi* (Enggano); *leucophila* (Mentawai); *amelis* (Nias); *consobrina* (Simeulue); *abbotti* (Babi). Ssp *aeria* often proposed for elevation to monotypic species, but genetically indistinct from *prophata*. W Sumatran Is taxa (*consobrina, richmondi, leucophila, amelis* and *abbotti*) form a monophyletic group and have additional unique call types, potentially warranting species-level treatment as '**Barusan Monarch**' *H. consobrina*. The outsized *abbotti* has been proposed for monotypic species status but is embedded within 'Barusan Monarch'. Fairly common in forest, edge, secondary growth and scrub, <1500 m. Singly or pairs, joins mixed flocks; active and conspicuous in under to upper storey. **ID M** head, back, tail and breast azure-blue; wings greyer; belly and flanks white; small black nuchal tuft; black feathering at base of bill; narrow black band across upper breast; grey-blue bare parts. **F/Imm** duller, with blue restricted mainly to head; upperparts brownish-grey; lack black breast band and nuchal tuft. Ssp *gigantoptera* larger; *opisthocyanea* as previous but **M** purplish tinge to plumage, blue wash to flanks and vent; *karimatensis* **M** lacks black breast band, **F** tail washed blue; *javana* as *prophata* but **M** less intensively blue, **F** underparts bluer, upperparts greyer, washed with blue; *symmixta* as previous but **M** brighter blue; *penidae* as previous but **F** slightly brighter blue head; *aeria* as *prophata* but lacks black nuchal patch; *leucophila* **M** more extensive white abdomen, **F** upperparts more rufous with brownish wash to breast; *amelis* as previous but **M** overall more purplish-blue (incl. bluish wash to greyish belly); *richmondi* **M** violaceous tint to plumage, **F** upperparts more rufous, with throat and crown brighter blue; *consobrina* **M** belly and vent washed blue; *abbotti* largest race, **M** uniformly dull violet-blue, lacks black nape and breast band, **F** dull brown washed with blue, especially on head and breast. **Voc** Song: 3–10 monotonous, clear ringing "wee-wee-wee..." at 5–7 n/s. Call: (i) loud series of ≥3 clear, buzzy "wheet-wheet-wheet" or "treet-treet-treet"; (ii) shorter, harsher "shweb-shweb" or "chew-wit'". 'Barusan Monarch' group additionally utters a distinct, grasshopper-warbler-like trill consisting of 3–10 monotonous, high-pitched, rapidly-rattled, metallic notes "tit'tit'tit..." at 10 n/s, regularly repeated, and also a song consisting of 4–10 clear ringing "whit-whit-whit..." at 4 n/s. At least *abbotti* rocks slowly from side to side in display in upright posture and gives harsh, scolding, upslurred "whet" or "whet-whet" as call note.

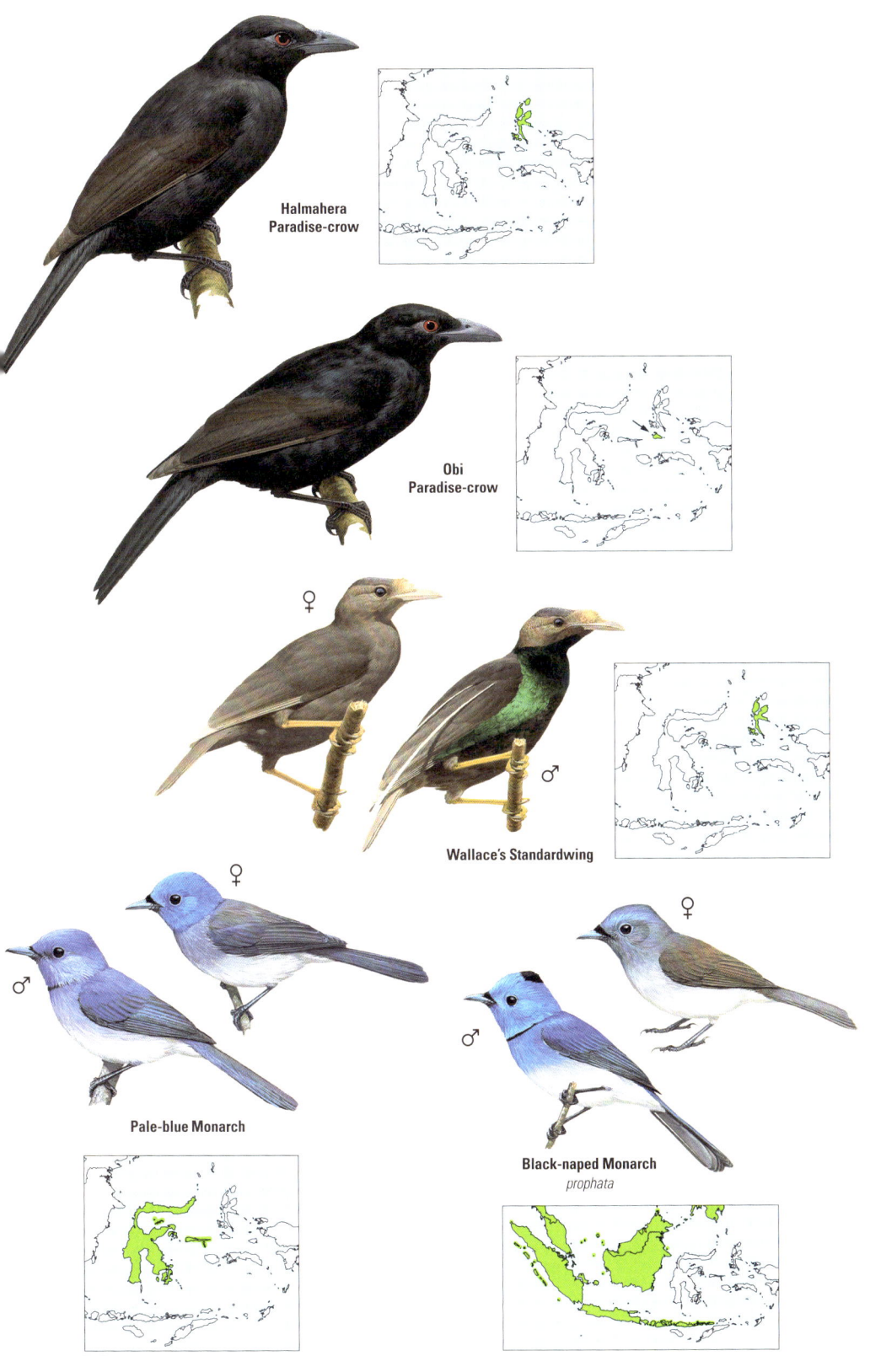

**Halmahera
Paradise-crow**

**Obi
Paradise-crow**

♀

♂

Wallace's Standardwing

♂

♀

Pale-blue Monarch

♀

♂

Black-naped Monarch
prophata

Blyth's Paradise-flycatcher *Terpsiphone affinis*

L 20–30 cm. S-SE Asia. 8 ssp, 5 in region: *affinis* (Sum, Riau, Bangka, Belitung, Jav, MPen); *indochinensis* (mainland SE Asia except MPen where only a migrant, but likely regularly winters on Sum); *borneensis* (Bor); *procera* (Simeulue); *insularis* (Nias). Traditionally united with Amur, Tenggara and extralimital Indian Paradise-flycatcher *T. paradisi* to form more broadly-defined umbrella species, '**Asian Paradise-flycatcher**' *T. paradisi*. All four split based on consistent genetic, morphological and vocal differences. Ssp *insularis* exhibits important plumage distinctions, but close genetic relationship with different-looking *procera* suggests more research is needed before splitting complex further. Fairly common in forest, edge; on migration also scrubland, cultivation, parks; <1300 m. Singly or pairs, often joins mixed flocks; conspicuous in under to upper storey. **ID** Blue-grey bare parts; blue eyering (more distinct in **M**). Dichromatic. **M red morph** black head with distinct glossy crest; rich chestnut upperparts and tail with elongated central tail feathers; throat and breast dark-grey delimited from white belly by blurry boundary. **M white morph** head black but rest of body entirely white apart from black primaries. **F** as male red morph but duller with shorter crest, lacks elongated central tail feathers. Ssp *indochinensis* is more rufous (less chestnut) on upperparts and has paler grey throat (contrasting with black crown), more gradually turning into white belly; *borneensis* as nominate but **M** white morph predominates, **F** buff belly. In *procera* **M** white morph predominates and lacks any black in scapulars, **F** duller-brown than nominate. Ssp *insularis* red morph predominates; wholly greyish head and underparts down to vent, with no black and no gloss apparent in plumage. **Imm** breast feathers show indistinct mottling; pale bill base to entire bill. **Voc** Song: monotonous, ringing, whistled "wu-wu-wu..." lasting <5 sec at 7 n/s, lower-pitched than Black-naped Monarch. Call: (i) short, abrupt, very harsh, upslurred "skreek"; (ii) rasping "whee whe-whoo"; (iii) nasal "che'" or "chechwe'". **SS** See Japanese and Amur Paradise-flycatchers. **AN** Oriental Paradise-flycatcher.

Tenggara Paradise-flycatcher *Terpsiphone floris*　🄴

L 20–25 cm. 2 ssp: *floris* (Sumbawa–Alor); *sumbaensis* (Sumba). For taxonomy see Blyth's Paradise-flycatcher. Scarce to fairly common in forest, edge; <1300 m. Singly or pairs, often joins mixed flocks; conspicuous in under to upper storey. **ID M** generally as Blyth's but lacks red morph; broader, longer crest; unmarked, clean white mantle; more extensive white on outerwing (black largely limited to primaries) and retrices; narrower eye-ring; broader central tail feathers. **F** as Blyth's but darker, with rich buff belly; *sumbaensis* with buff extending to upper breast. **Imm** undescribed. **Voc** Similar to Blyth's, but song notes delivered as couplets, "wu-wu, wu-wu, wu-wu...", at 0.5 sec per couplet.

Amur Paradise-flycatcher *Terpsiphone incei*

L 20–25 cm. Breeds NE–E Asia; winters to Jav. Monotypic. Known to hybridise with Japanese Paradise-flycatcher. See also Blyth's for taxonomy. Scarce in forest, edge; on migration also scrubland, cultivation, parks; <1000 m. Usually singly, often with mixed flocks; tends to keep to mid- to upper storey in wintering grounds. **ID/SS M** predominantly red morph. **M white morph** told from Blyth's by more extensively broad white (less black) primary edges, and cleaner, whiter mantle and wing coverts, broader crest, slightly broader eyering, internal gape lime-green (not orange-yellow). **F/red morph/Imm** have deep chestnut upperparts similar to many Blyth's (especially ssp *affinis*) but sometimes with deep violet or maroon tinge on mantle which is diagnostic when present; black of throat demarcated from paler grey breast by sharp dividing line (less clean in Imm), different from more gradual colour transition in Blyth's; also – on average – has more black edging on wing, with primary coverts usually black (rufous/chestnut in Blyth's). See also Japanese for comparison. **Imm** with pale bill or bill base; probably more mottled on breast. **Voc** Song unlikely to be heard in region: short bouts of monotonously repeated, ringing "tit-tit-wu tit-tit-wu tit-tit-wu..." or "wu-wu-wu-wu...", slightly slower than Blyth's. Call: as Blyth's. **AN** Chinese Paradise-flycatcher.

Japanese Paradise-flycatcher *Terpsiphone atrocaudata*

L 20–25 cm. Breeds E Asia; winters SE Asia, Phil. 2 ssp, 1 in region: *atrocaudata* (breeds E Asia; winters S to Sum, Jav; single record from Sabah, Jan 1992). As here circumscribed, no longer includes extralimital Lanyu Paradise-flycatcher *T. periophthalmica* (N Phil, S Taiwan) based on genetic, morphological and vocal data. Rare in forest, edge, <1600m. Singly or pairs, joins mixed flocks; often in mid-storey but winterers frequently follow flocks in high canopy, making them difficult to detect. **ID M** velvety black with purple gloss to wings and back; belly and vent white; bright-blue bill and eyering; legs grey-blue. **F/Imm** black head, dark grey throat and breast, chestnut upperparts (with maroon or purplish tinge in **Ad F** but duller rufous-brown in **Imm**), white belly. **Imm** has pale bill base or entire bill. **Voc** Song unlikely to be heard in region: cheery whistled "chooky-hee-hoshy hoy hoy hoy...". Call: as Blyth's. **SS** Fem/imm must be separated from Amur and various races of Blyth's with extreme care: of all three species, Japanese has the greatest amount of black edging in wing, with black primary coverts (rufous/chestnut in Blyth's). Blyth's *indochinensis* usually has more rufous upperparts (less chestnut than ad fem Japanese, but brighter than imm Japanese) and has paler mid-grey throat slowly grading into white belly (no narrow boundary between dark-grey breast and white belly). Blyth's *affinis* and *borneensis* have a similar narrow boundary (perhaps a bit blurrier than Japanese) between white belly and dark breast. Amur has a sharp demarcation between black throat and pale-grey breast (not all-dark throat and breast), but beware of tricky imm individuals of both species, in which these patterns can be less well-defined.

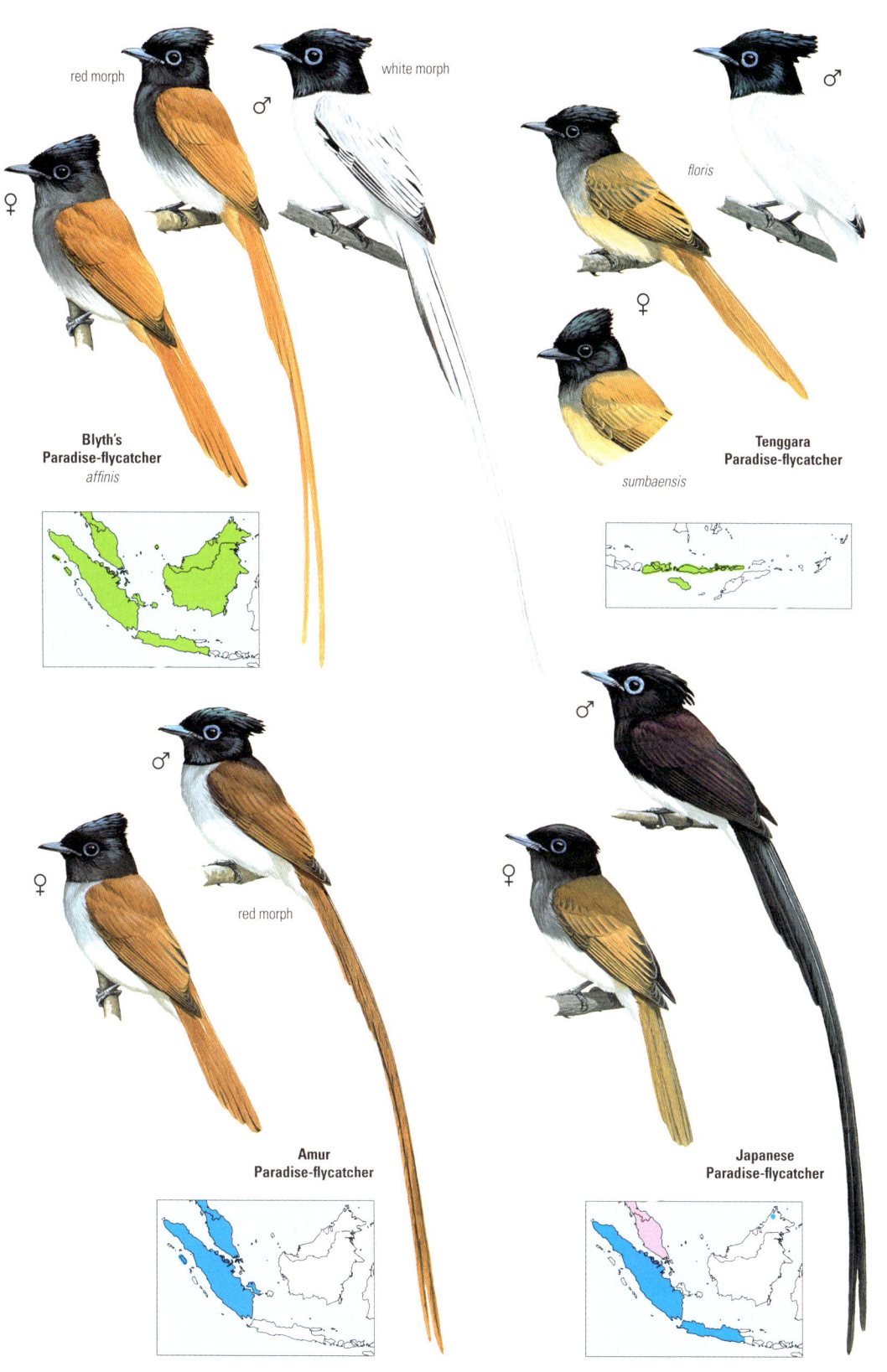

red morph

♀

♂

white morph

Blyth's Paradise-flycatcher
affinis

floris

♀

sumbaensis

Tenggara Paradise-flycatcher

♂

♀

red morph

Amur Paradise-flycatcher

♂

♀

Japanese Paradise-flycatcher

Southern Rufous Paradise-flycatcher
Terpsiphone cinnamomea
L 20–30 cm. Phil. 2 ssp, 1 in region: *talautensis* (Talaud). No longer includes Northern Rufous Paradise-flycatcher *T. unirufa* (N Phil) based on pronounced genetic and plumage differences. Common in forest, edge, scrub and cultivation. Usually in pairs, conspicuous in under to upper storey. **ID M** entirely rufous-orange with variable elongated central tail feathers and blue eye-ring; blue-grey bare parts. **F** whitish belly; lacks elongated tail. **Imm** as Ad. **Voc** Song: upslurred, ringing "whik-whik-whik...", lasting <12 sec at 3 n/s. Call: (i) hollow, upslurred whistle "hwhip"; (ii) harsh, raspy "tre-chee".

Moluccan Monarch *Myiagra galeata* E
L 14 cm. 3 ssp: *galeata* (N Mol); *buruensis* (Buru); *goramensis* (Ambon, Seram, Haruku, Boano, Kai). Common in forest, edge, coastal scrub and coconut, <950 m. Singly or pairs, joins mixed flocks; forages in mid- to upper storey. **ID M** dark slate-grey upperparts becoming blackish on forehead and face; white underparts and throat; bill and legs dark-grey. Ssp *buruensis* upperparts and head uniformly slate grey; *goramensis* back with greenish gloss, paler than head. **F/Imm** upperparts browner; rufous wash on throat and breast. **Voc** Song: (i) loud series of monotonous single whistles, "teu-teu-teu..." lasting <5 sec at 8 n/s, occasionally delivered more slowly at 2 n/s; (ii) series of medium-pitched notes "wik-wik-wik..." at 6 n/s. Call: cicada-like, rasping, metallic buzz "skwech", regularly repeated. **AN** Moluccan Flycatcher.

Broad-billed Monarch *Myiagra ruficollis*
L 15 cm. Aus. 3 ssp, 2 in region: *ruficollis* (Sumba, Flores Sea islands, Rote–Damar); *fulviventris* (Tanimbar). Common in forest, edge, thickets and mangrove, <1400 m. Singly or pairs, joins mixed flocks; forages in under to mid-storey. **ID M** glossy dark blue-grey head and upperparts; throat and breast orange, rest of underparts white; bill and legs blue-black. **F** paler, less glossy. Ssp *fulviventris* crown greyer; flanks and vent have orange wash. **Imm** buff margins to flight feathers. **Voc** Song: (i) <10 disyllabic, down- then upslurred "ch'wik-ch'wik-ch'wik..." at 2 n/s; (ii) <10 downslurred whistled "chew-chew-chew..." or "wheet-wheet-wheet..." at 3 n/s. Can produce other monotonous ringing whistled notes of similar quality. Call: (i) harsh, raspy, dry "zzzt"; (ii) short, "chip-chip-chip". **AN** Broad-billed Flycatcher.

Shining Monarch *Myiagra alecto*
L 17–19 cm. Aus. 8 ssp, 2 in region: *alecto* (N Mol); *longirostris* (Tanimbar). Limited plumage differentiation but deep mtDNA divergence among races. Genomic data and detailed bioacoustic analysis of varied vocal repertoire required. If mtNDA divergences are corroborated, ssp *alecto* may be separable as monotypic '**Moluccan Shining Monarch**', leaving *longirostris* as part of '**Sahul Shining Monarch**' *M. rufolateralis* (~5 ssp; NG, Tanimbar and Australia), with an additional extralimital '**Bismarck Shining Monarch**' *M. chalybeocephalus* (~2 ssp; Melanesia). Relatively common in lowland forest, swamp, mangrove, <1000 m. Singly, pairs or part of mixed flocks; forages low to on ground, flicking wings and tail constantly. **ID M** entirely glossy blue-black with slight crest, blue bill and grey-black legs; *longirostris* longer-billed. **F** glossy blue-black cap, rest of upperparts rufous-brown; throat and underparts white; *longirostris* **F** resembles Imm. **Imm** flanks, belly and vent washed rusty-orange. **Voc** Song: (i) tremulous, level-pitched whistle "to'o'o'o...", lasting 3–10 sec; (ii) frog-like "wick", followed by a quiet, nasal buzz "bzzzzz", lasting 1.5 sec. Call: harsh, rasping buzz "shhhhht". **AN** Shining Flycatcher.

Island Monarch *Monarcha cinerascens*
L 16–18 cm. Aus. 11 ssp, 2 in region: *cinerascens* (Mol, LS); *commutatus* (Sul, Sangihe, Siau, Talaud and satellites). Deep mtDNA divergence between some extralimital races (e.g. those on Bismarck Is) hints at possible existence of multiple species; more research needed. Typical 'supertramp' species: common on small islands that lack competitors; on some large islands seasonally common (e.g. Timor) or scarce (e.g. Halmahera) monsoon visitor. Forest, edge, coastal scrub and coconut plantations, <200 m. Singly or pairs, joins mixed flocks; under to upper storey. **ID Ad M** uniformly blue-grey apart from rufous-orange belly and flanks; blue-grey bare parts. **F** paler orange belly and flanks. Ssp *commutatus* reportedly darker grey overall with lighter rufous-orange belly and flanks. **Imm** brownish edging to wing feathers, mantle and tail; yellow base to bill. **Voc** Song: trisyllabic up- then downslurred whistles "s'see'yoo", lasting 0.5 sec. Call: (i) harsh scolding chatter; (ii) short jingling and squeaky twittering notes.

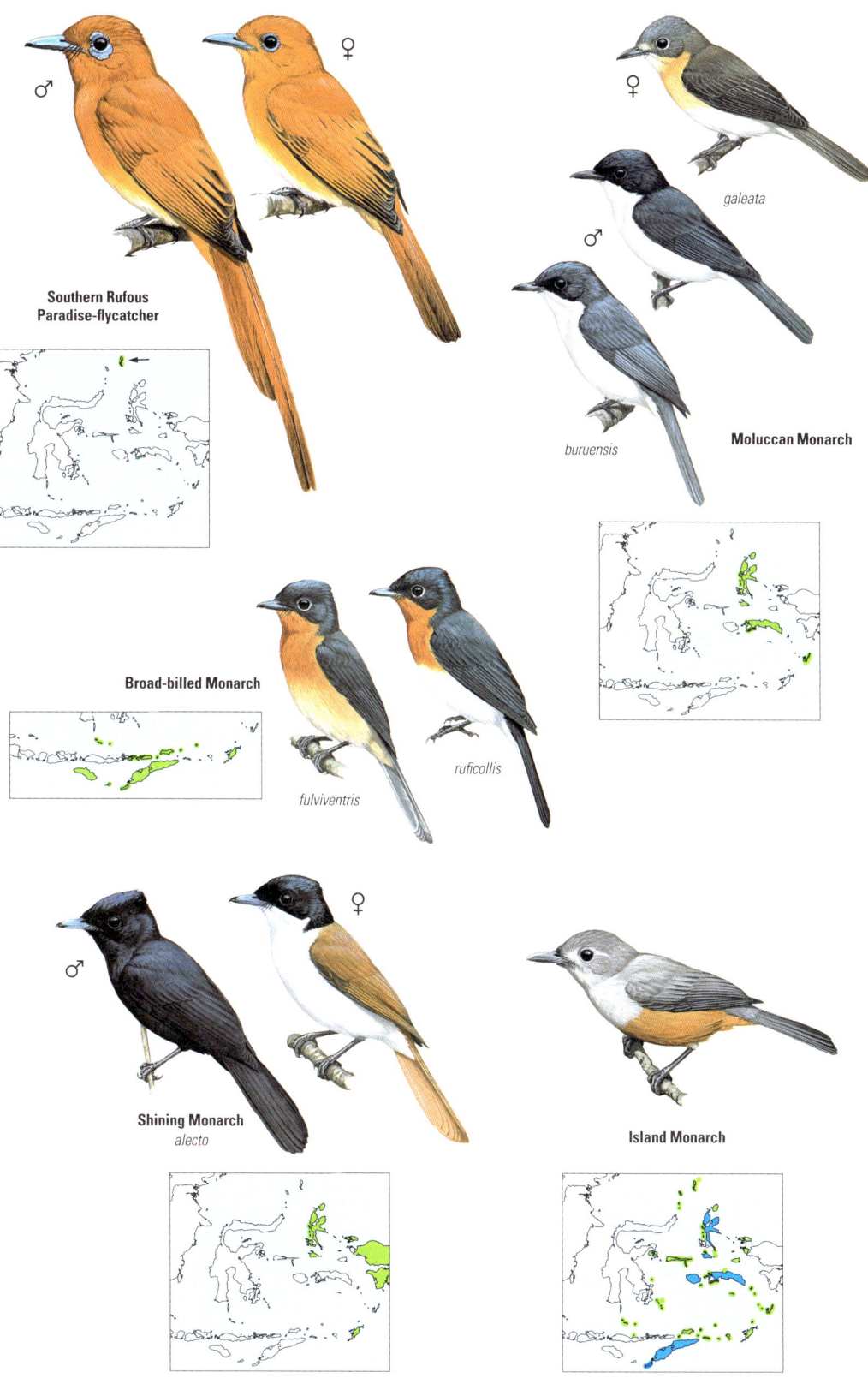

**Southern Rufous
Paradise-flycatcher**

galeata

buruensis

Moluccan Monarch

Broad-billed Monarch

fulviventris

ruficollis

Shining Monarch
alecto

Island Monarch

Tanahjampea Monarch *Symposiachrus everetti* `E`

L 14 cm. Monotypic. Fairly common in forest, uncommon in edge, scrub and mangrove on Tanahjampea. Singly or pairs, joins mixed flocks. **ID Ad** black head and upperparts; white rump and underparts; central tail feathers black, outer tail feathers progressively more white to tip; bill blue-grey; legs blackish. **Imm** upperparts paler grey-brown, rump buff; breast bright buff. **Voc** Song: drawn-out, slightly down- then upslurred, tuneless whistle "tooweee", lasting 0.7 sec, easily imitated. Call: (i) typical scratchy buzz "tzzpt, tzzpt"; (ii) upslurred, tuneless whistle "wheet wheet"; (iii) constant, bouncing chattering. **AN** White-tipped Monarch.

Boano Monarch *Symposiachrus boanensis* `E`

L 16 cm. Monotypic. Fairly common in limestone forest and edge on Boano. Singly or pairs, joins mixed flocks; usually understorey. **ID Ad** black head, throat and upperparts with slight bluish gloss to crown and mantle; variable white spots or bar on forehead; tail black with distal half of outer feathers white; underparts white; blue-grey bare parts. **Imm** upperparts slate-grey; underparts white with buff wash. **Voc** Song: series of 1–5 phrases; high opening note followed by prolonged soft, buzzing trill, "t'jeeeew-t'jeeeew-t'j'eeeew...", lasting 2–2.5 sec, regularly repeated. Call: rasping "shrrwee, shrrwee", repeated continuously, also a subdued rasping trill. **AN** Black-chinned Monarch.

Kai Monarch *Symposiachrus leucurus* `E`

L 15–16 cm. Monotypic. Fairly common in forest and edge. Singly or pairs, joins mixed flocks; usually under to mid-storey. **ID Ad** head and upperparts black; underparts white; central tail feathers black, outer tail feathers white. **Imm** upperparts slate-grey; underparts white with buff wash; buff-orange face resembling Australian Spectacled Monarch but note tail pattern. **Voc** Song: monosyllabic or disyllabic tuneless whistle, first syllable drawn-out and level-pitched, second sharp and inflected "whrrrr'swip", lasting 0.8 sec. Call: (i) tremulous, rapid chatter; (i) rasping, buzzy notes typical of genus. **AN** White-tailed Monarch.

Moluccan Spectacled Monarch
Symposiachrus bimaculatus `E`

L 14–16 cm. 3 ssp: *bimaculatus* (Morotai, Halmahera, Bacan); *diadematus* (Bisa, Obi); *nigrimentum* (Seram, Ambon, Gorong, Watubela). Traditionally subsumed under Australian Spectacled Monarch, but plumage distinct, and genomic evidence indicates closer relationship to other monarch species. Fairly common in forest, edge, <1400 m. Singly or pairs, joins mixed flocks; usually lower to mid-storey. **ID M** as Australian Spectacled but with darker wings, orange less extensive on underparts, largely restricted to neck and upper breast, white undertail restricted to distal third; **F** paler orange extends to lower breast. Ssp *diadematus* **M** has small white patch at front of crown with all-white underparts lacking orange; **F** has orange forecrown spot, black face markings less extensive, pale orange neck and breast. Ssp *nigrimentum* **M** black face markings less extensive, reaching from ear-coverts to chin, while there is more extensive orange from neck to throat and upper breast; **F** facial black replaced by dark grey restricted to ear-coverts and chin, with extensive orange throat and upper breast. **Imm** black of head replaced by grey, darkest on ear-coverts. **Voc** Song *bimaculatus*: (i) series of forced, tremulous, flat whistles, sometimes with hard introductory doublet "(chit-chit-)tzzzzzz, (chit-chit-)tzzzzzz, (chit-chit-)tzzzzzz...", each note lasting 1.5 s; (ii) more excited, faster "wip-wip-werrrt, wip-wip-werrrt, wip-wip-werrrt...", each note lasting 0.7 s. Song *nigrimentum*: extended, gradually ascending, pure whistle "weeeer", lasting 1.5 s. Song *diadematus* undescribed. Call: (i) short, dry rattle; (ii) quiet, sneaky chatter.

Australian Spectacled Monarch
Symposiachrus trivirgatus

L 14–16 cm. Aus. 5 ssp, 1 in region: *trivirgatus* (Sumba–Timor, Flores–Damar). See Moluccan Spectacled Monarch for taxonomy. Fairly common in forest, edge and mangrove, <1200 m. Singly or pairs, joins mixed flocks; usually lower to mid-storey. **ID M** black face mask, forehead and throat; crown, nape and upperparts grey; tail black with white on distal two thirds of outer feathers; rufous-orange throat and breast; white belly; bill blue-grey, legs grey-black. **F** black of head replaced by grey, darkest on ear-coverts; whitish crescent through lores; paler orange breast, extending down flanks. **Imm** paler orange below; face pattern less distinct. **Voc** Song: (i) ringing, initially slightly inflected, pure whistle "whirrrr", lasting 0.8 sec; (ii) series of clear, melodious, level whistles, each introduced by descending doublet, "wip-pip-weeee, wip-pip-weeee, wip-pip-weeee...". Call: (i) short, dry rattle; (ii) quiet, sneaky chatter. **SS** Imm Flores Monarch never as extensively rufous or orange on breast, throat and face.

Flores Monarch *Symposiachrus sacerdotum* `E`

L 15 cm. Monotypic. Very locally fairly common, few known sites, submontane forest, 350–1000 m. Singly or pairs, joins mixed flocks; usually lower to mid-storey. **ID Ad** black face mask, forehead and throat; crown, nape and upperparts grey; tail black with white outer feathers; underparts white; bill and legs grey. **Imm** variable peach wash on breast. **Voc** Song: 1–5 upslurred, piercing, ringing whistles with quiet 2-note introductory motif "w'w'wheeee", lasting 1 sec. Call: rasping, scratchy and buzzy chattering, "sjer-sjer-jer-jer-jer", or more nasal "shr-shr-shr", typical of genus.

Buru Monarch *Symposiachrus loricatus* `E`

L 18 cm. Monotypic. Fairly common in forest and edge, <400 m, rarely to 1200 m. Singly or pairs, joins mixed flocks; usually understorey. **ID Ad** black head, throat and upperparts with bluish gloss to crown and mantle; white outertail tipped black; underparts white; blue-grey bare parts. **Imm** upperparts and throat brown; underparts pale reddish-brown. **Voc** Song: 1–3 level, tuneless whistles "teeeeow", lasting 1.5 sec, each note progressively higher, occasionally extended to "tee't'teeeeeow", lasting 2.5 sec. Call: rasping, scratchy and buzzy chattering, typical of genus. **AN** Black-tipped Monarch.

Banda Sea Monarch *Symposiachrus mundus* `E`

L 16 cm. Monotypic. Fairly common in forest, edge. Singly or pairs, joins mixed flocks; usually lower to mid-storey. **ID Ad** black face mask, forehead and throat; crown, nape and upperparts grey; central tail feathers black, outer tail feathers progressively more white; underparts white; long dagger-like bill; legs grey. **Imm** grey-brown upperparts; whitish face and forecrown; underparts cinnamon-brown. **Voc** Song: 1–10 shrieking, quavering, upslurred whistles "shrrrrrrrk", lasting 1 sec, rapidly repeated. Call: rasping, scratchy and buzzy chattering, typical of genus. **AN** Black-bibbed Monarch.

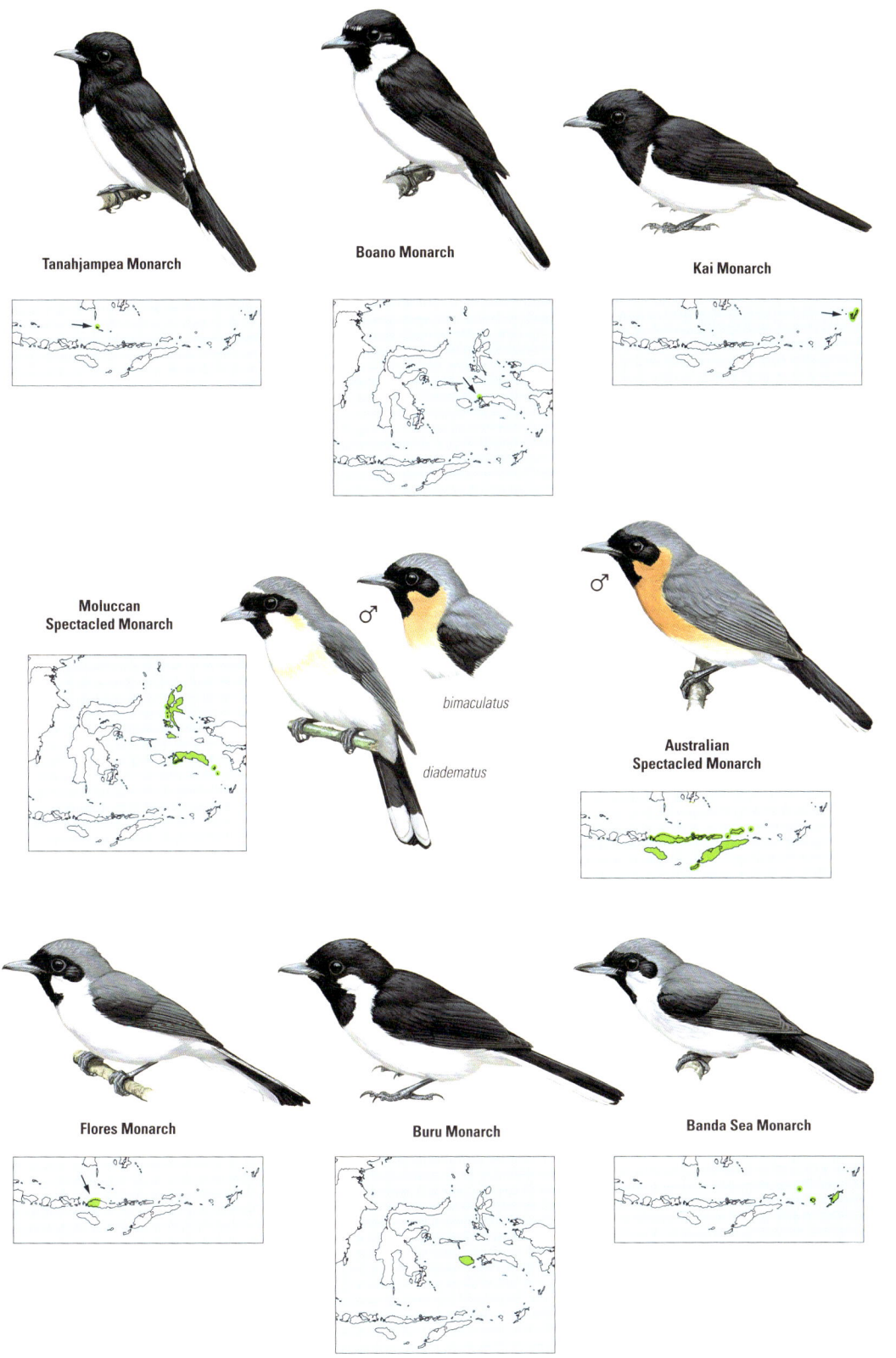

Tanahjampea Monarch

Boano Monarch

Kai Monarch

Moluccan Spectacled Monarch

bimaculatus

diadematus

♂

Australian Spectacled Monarch

Flores Monarch

Buru Monarch

Banda Sea Monarch

White-naped Monarch *Carterornis pileatus* [E]

L 14–15 cm. 2 ssp: *pileatus* (Halmahera); *buruensis* (Buru). Despite limited plumage and vocal differences, mtDNA divergence between the two races is fairly deep, possibly warranting their separation into two species ('**Halmahera Pied Monarch**' and '**Buru Pied Monarch**', respectively); more genomic and bioacoustic research desired. Also see Tanimbar Monarch for taxonomy. Uncommon in forest, edge, <450 m (Halmahera), <1200 m (Buru). Singly or pairs, joins mixed flocks; usually in mid- to upper storey. **ID** Bill and legs blue-grey. **M** distinctive black-and-white head pattern; upperparts black with conspicuous white wing panel, white scapulars (less so in *buruensis*), rump and outertail feathers; centre of throat white bordered by black gular bib; underparts white. **F** duller, with less distinct gular bib. **Imm** upperparts browner; throat and breast ochre-brown. **Voc** Song: metallic, bouncing "tzoo'it-tzoo'it", often interspersed with call. Call: (i) buzzy, short "tzit"; (ii) tuneless, flat whistle, downslurred "tchoo".

Tanimbar Monarch *Carterornis castus* [E]

L 14–15 cm. Monotypic. Formerly included with White-naped Monarch but differs vocally and – less so – in plumage. Fairly common in forest. Singly or pairs, joins mixed flocks; usually in mid- to upper storey. **ID M** as White-naped Monarch, but all-black throat with white mottling/spotting. **F** peach-washed breast. **Imm** undescribed. **Voc** Song: pure, downslurred whistle "pseeoo", lasting 0.5 sec, or "pseeoo t't'teeooo", lasting 1.7 sec, second note with tremulous beginning. Call: (i) scolding, raspy "bzzt"; (ii) pure, whistled "whit-whit-tchew"; (iii) squeaky chattering. **AN** Loetoe Monarch.

Magpie-lark *Grallina cyanoleuca*

L 25–30 cm. Aus. 2 ssp, 1 in region: *neglecta* (E Timor, N Aus, S NG). Specimens from Kur (Jul 1899), Luang (Nov 1905); sight record Tanimbar (Aug 2011). Open habitats: cultivation, grassland, roadside vegetation, waterside, <1000 m. Considered resident E Timor until 1970s. Singly or pairs; terrestrial forager, perches in trees. **ID** Yellow iris and bill; pied plumage. **M** black upperparts and hood with broad white supercilium and face patch; white underparts; pied wings and tail. **F** white forehead, lores and throat. **Imm** black forehead; white throat; dark eye. **Voc** (i) Strident, emphatic, scratchy "peE peE peE...", short series regularly repeated, upslurred or downslurred notes; (ii) repeated scratches, often interspersed with previous; (iii) liquid, mellow "chop chop chop...".

LANIIDAE
Shrikes
5 species in region

Small to medium-sized birds, mostly of open country and forest edge. Large heads and stout hooked bills. Feed by pouncing on prey from exposed perches. Generally conspicuous, at least when hunting, except for the unusual Jay Shrike, an elusive forest dweller.

Tiger Shrike *Lanius tigrinus*

L 17–18 cm. Breeds NE–E Asia; winters SE-E Asia. Monotypic. Uncommon to scarce in secondary forest, edge, cultivated and open habitats, <1500 m. Often skulks in low vegetation, occasionally conspicuous hunting from exposed perches. Can be quite vocal in winter quarters. Singly or pairs. **M** crown and nape grey contrasting with black facial mask; back, wings and tail rich chestnut brown with blackish barring on mantle and rump; underparts white, often with faint blackish barring on flanks. **F** duller, often shows whitish lores and supercilium; underparts white, usually with extensive barring on flanks and belly. **Imm** facial mask indistinct; crown, sides of head and nape grey-brown with blackish barring; underparts washed buff, usually heavily scaled or barred; pale bill with black tip. **Voc** Call: harsh, grating, rapid "khek-khek-khek-khek-...". **SS** Imm from imm Brown Shrike by heavier overall barring, particularly on mantle, rear flanks and rump, lack of prominent facial mask and larger bill.

Brown Shrike *Lanius cristatus*

L 17–20 cm. Breeds N–NE–E, Asia; winters S–SE-E Asia, Phil. 4 ssp: *cristatus* (breeds N–NE Asia; winters S to GS, S Asia); *confusus* (breeds NE Asia; winters S to GS); *lucionensis* (breeds E Asia; winters S to GS, LS, Sul, Mol); *superciliosus* (breeds E Asia; winters S to Jav–Sumbawa). All ssp widely intergrade, making subspecific identification of many individuals difficult. Uncommon in forest edge, village edge, cultivated and open habitats, usually in lowlands. Ssp *superciliosus* now very rare, having suffered catastrophic decline of over 90%, presumably due to trapping pressure on wintering grounds, historically common on Jav, but few recent records. Solitary, hunts from low or exposed perches, such as wires. Often territorial and highly vocal while wintering. **ID Ad M** prominent black facial mask; white supercilium extends over bill to join on forehead; crown, nape, mantle, rump and tail uniform russet-brown; wings darker with paler buff-white edging; underparts white washed rufous-buff except on throat; bill black (**br**) or grey with black tip (**non-br**); legs black. **F** generally duller with less distinct mask and can show variable amounts of barring on buffier flanks. Ssp *confusus* very similar, with many intergrades, but upperparts paler with broader white patch on forehead, while crown and nape still brownish. Ssp *lucionensis* crown grey (not brown-tinged) grading into dull-brown mantle, with less contrasting supercilium; underparts can be distinctly orange-buff. Ssp *superciliosus* upperparts bright rufous with distinct reddish tinge, particularly on crown and tail, contrasting sharply with gleaming white forehead and broad supercilium; underparts vary from snow white when breeding to strong buff; **F** warm brown mantle contrasting with reddish crown and tail, and pale buff flanks. **Imm** facial mask dark brown; upper- and underparts lightly barred, with retention of barred underparts into first winter. **Voc** Call: harsh, grating "khekh-khekh-khekh-khekh-...", very similar to Tiger Shrike. **SS** See Tiger Shrike.

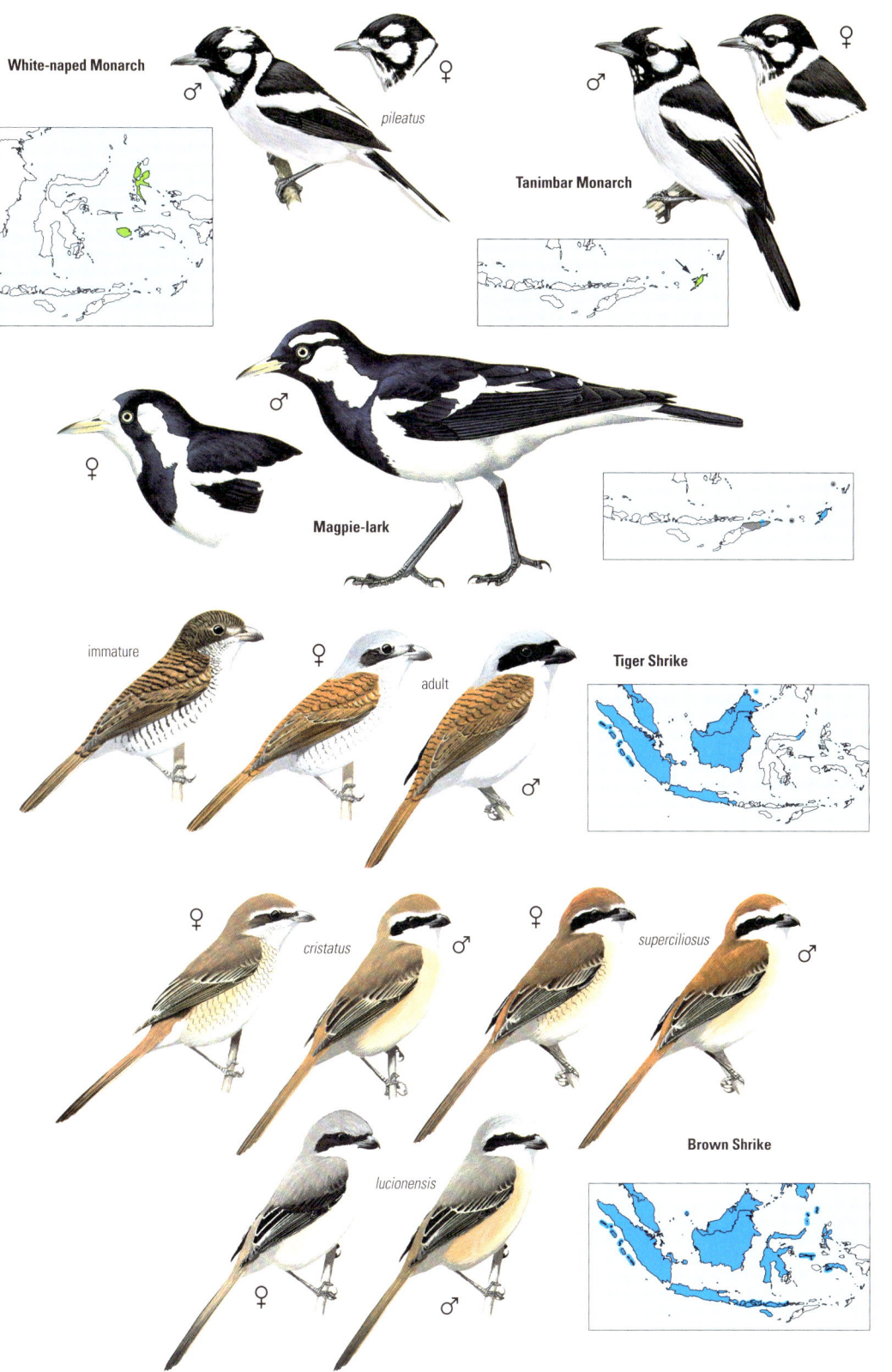

White-naped Monarch

♂

pileatus

♀

Tanimbar Monarch

♂

♀

Magpie-lark

♀

♂

immature

♀

adult

♂

Tiger Shrike

♀

cristatus

♂

♀

superciliosus

♂

lucionensis

Brown Shrike

♀

♂

Long-tailed Shrike *Lanius schach*

L 20–25 cm. C–S–SE–E Asia to Aus. 9 ssp, 1-2 in region: *bentet* (MPen, GS–LS, introduced Salibabu); birds currently expanding through N Bor may partly be derived from Phil ssp *suluensis* (Sulu) or *nasutus* (main Phil) based on plumage, but much individual variation suggests largely admixed population. Fairly common, now scarce on Jav, in edge, cultivated and open habitats, <1600 m. Singly or pairs; conspicuous, hunting from exposed perches. **ID Ad** prominent black facial mask extending broadly across forehead; crown and nape variable, usually form grey contrast but can extend into a fully black cap; mantle and rump generally grey, with variable rufous wash; wings black with whitish edging to tertials and variable white patch at base of primaries (sometimes absent); tail long, black, tipped white; underparts white with rufous-buff wash to flanks; bill and legs blackish. Ssp *suluensis* and *nasutus* have black crown, grey mantle (almost whitish-grey in *suluensis*) and paler rufous lower back, but birds in N Bor are largely intermediate between *bentet* and Phil races. **Imm** duller and browner with less prominent facial mask and variable narrow barring on upper- and underparts. **Voc** Song: reminiscent of an *Acrocephalus* warbler; long warbling, scratchy repertoire consisting of harsh, unmusical notes lasting <5 min, including much mimicry. Call: (i) scratchy "towet"; (ii) harsh, loud "keek-keek-keek…", regularly repeated.

Great Grey Shrike *Lanius excubitor*   V

L 24–25 cm. W Palaearctic to C–S Asia. ~7 ssp, 1 in region: *pallidirostris* (C Asia). Confused taxonomy. Ssp *pallidirostris* sometimes merged with *lahtora* (India) to form 'Steppe Grey Shrike' *L. lahtora*, which – in turn – is often merged with others into 'Southern Grey Shrike' *L. meridionalis* (SW Palaearctic to C–S Asia). Current arrangement, which excludes most W races of 'Southern Grey Shrike', merges *pallidirostris* and *lahtora* with multiple N Palaearctic taxa into Great Grey Shrike based on similar mtDNA, but genome-wide data may well refute this treatment and re-align *pallidirostris* with Southern Grey Shrike. Single record in Brunei (Oct 1990). Open country including cultivation. Hunts from low perches. **ID** Large; black, white and grey (lacking any brown or rufous tones). **Ad** black mask bordered by white supercilium, lores and forehead; crown, nape and mantle pale grey; wings black with white primary patch and broad white tips to tertials; tail black with white outer feather edging; underparts white; bill and legs black. **Imm** duller and paler; underparts washed grey, occasionally with fine barring. **Voc** Harsh, repeated double note "kwirick". **SS** Specialist literature must be consulted for identification of any vagrant 'grey shrikes'.

Jay Shrike *Platylophus galericulatus*

L 31–33 cm. Sundaic. 4 ssp, 3 in region: *galericulatus* (Jav); *coronatus* (Sum; Bor except N); *lemprieri* (N Bor). Often erroneously classified as a jay ('Crested Jay'). Uncommon, now rare on Jav, in forest, <1300 m on Sum and Jav, <1800 m on Bor. Singly or pairs; shy in forest interior. **ID Ad** uniform black with white patch on neck side and eye crescents; unusually long, forward-pointing crest always raised. Ssp *coronatus* chocolate-brown in plumage, with slightly shorter and more rounded crest; *lemprieri* as previous but slightly paler. **Imm** pale barring and shaft streaks on underparts; rufous upperparts. **Voc** (i) Machine-gun-like loud, startling, rapid rattle "TIT'IT'IT'IT…" lasting <1 sec at 11 n/s; (ii) odd, fluty whistle "pSSS hee-woo" lasting 0.6 sec. **AN** Crested Jay, Crested Shrikejay.

CORVIDAE
Crows, Jays, Treepies and Magpies
18 species in region (1 introduced)

A large and diverse family ranging from typical crows to ornately-plumaged green magpies and treepies. Most species are inhabitants of forest, while others occupy open country and farmland. Generally conspicuous and characterised by great vocal prowess and intelligence. A few species within the family, such as green magpies, are heavily hunted for the pet trade.

Bornean Treepie *Dendrocitta cinerascens*   E

L 40 cm. Monotypic. Fairly common in (sub-) montane forest, edge, 300–2600 m. Singly, pairs or small groups. **ID Ad** long, slim body with very long, thin tail; silky grey crown, upperparts and tail with black terminal band and outertail; black wings with small white patch; dark buff face and breast; brighter belly. **Imm** buff-fringed feathers, less contrasting plumage. **Voc** Variety of loud, grating and bell-like liquid notes including: (i) bell-like, throaty "choing"; (ii) harsh, grating "krek-krek-krek…"; (iii) harsh, grating "graah", regularly repeated and often mixed with other calls; (iv) liquid, loud "be-clunk-eeer", lasting 1 sec; (v) bell-like "kil-awk".

Sumatran Treepie *Dendrocitta occipitalis*   E

L 40 cm. Monotypic. Fairly common in (sub-) montane forest, edge, 400–2300 m. Singly, pairs or small groups. **ID Ad** similar to Bornean Treepie but dark brown head and crown, darker orange-buff underparts and mantle. **Imm** buff-fringed feathers and sooty-black head. **Voc** Variety of odd, bell-like, loud notes including: (i) hollow, bell-like note followed by grating louder note "pop-PRRRT", lasting 0.6 sec; (ii) loud, downslurred "Eee-huh"; (iii) curious, odd "breeet-oop"; (iv) grating "krek-krek-krek…", regularly repeated.

Racket-tailed Treepie *Crypsirina temia*

L 31–33 cm. SE Asia. Monotypic. Scarce in open, arid habitat: scrub, bamboo, edge, plantations, <900 m. On Bor only known from two specimens collected in 1852 near Banjarmasin, current status unknown; recent records from Balikpapan (E Kalimantan) likely to involve escapes from trade due to proximity to trading port. Singly, pairs or small groups. **ID** Slim. **Ad** all glossy-black plumage with long, straight spatulate tail; pale blue iris. **Imm** brownish-tinged plumage; narrower tipped tail; dark iris. **Voc** Variety of curious, odd clicks, croaks and rattles including: (i) fluty, yelping "whAP"; (ii) 2–6 rasping "churg-churg-churg…" at 4 n/s; (iii) curious, quirky "choonk" and "zer'oop", (iv) dry, rattled creak "krrrr'rook", lasting <1 sec, regularly repeated. **SS** Note superficial resemblance with drongo species, but much longer tail with rounded tail tips. **AN** Racquet-tailed Treepie.

nasutus

bentet

Long-tailed Shrike

Great Grey Shrike

galericulatus

coronatus

Jay Shrike

Bornean Treepie

Sumatran Treepie

Racket-tailed Treepie

Malayan Black Magpie *Platysmurus leucopterus*

L 39 cm. Sundaic. Monotypic. No longer includes Bornean Black Magpie because of pronounced vocal and plumage differences. Uncommon in forest, edge, occasionally plantations, <800 m. Usually pairs or small groups (<6), favouring mid- and upper canopy. **ID Ad** all-black with white wing band; long, broad tail (especially in flight); short, tufted forecrest; red iris. **Imm** brownish-tinged plumage; dark iris. **Voc** Variety of peculiar metallic, hollow whistles and cackles including: (i) metallic, xylophone-like "tok-tok", "tek-tek" and "klink-klink"; (ii) hoarse "graaah"; (iii) cowbell-like "klong-klong"; (iv) goat-like "e-e-e-e" often in combination with other calls; (v) wings producing a low throbbing "boobooboo…" in flight.

Bornean Black Magpie *Platysmurus aterrimus* `E`

L 41 cm. Monotypic. For taxonomy see Malayan Black Magpie. Uncommon in forest, edge, occasionally plantations, <300 m. Usually pairs or small groups (<6). **ID Ad** as Malayan Black Magpie but wholly black with longer, broader crest. **Imm** brownish-tinged plumage; shorter crest. **Voc** Wide repertoire, some mimicry: (i) monotonous, mellow whistle "whooo", lasting 0.6 sec, similar to a bamboo flute, regularly repeated; (ii) <5 monotonous, mellow whistles, "whoo ho'ho'ho'ho", at 3 n/s, series either descending or ascending; (iii) hoarse, grating "kek'ke'ke'kekek", at 5–15 n/s, slowing at end; (iv) wings producing a low throbbing "boobooboo…" in flight.

Common Green Magpie *Cissa chinensis*

L 37–39 cm. Himalaya–SE Asia. 4-5 ssp, 1 in region: *minor* (Bor, Sum). Hill and montane forest, edge; uncommon on Sum, 600–2100 m, mainly 800–1400 m, much scarcer on Bor. Usually pairs, often joining mixed flocks. **ID Ad** bright green plumage; yellowish forecrown; striking black mask; dark-red iris; red bare parts and eyering; chestnut wings with black-and-white pattern on tertials and undertail. **Imm** duller green underparts; duller bare parts. **Voc** Wide and varied repertoire including: (i) continually repeated, loud piping "tsweek-week-week-week" at 2–4 n/s; (ii) piping "wik, wik-wik", regularly repeated, often mixed with previous; (iii) rasping "shwooh"; (iv) short, sharp, upslurred whistle "soowee". **SS** See Bornean Green Magpie.

Javan Green Magpie *Cissa thalassina* `E`

L 31 cm. Monotypic. Previously merged with Bornean Green Magpie to form '**Short-tailed Green Magpie**' *C. thalassina* but vocal and plumage differences dictate break-up. Now very rare in (sub-) montane forest, edge, 500–2000 m, few records since 1990 and heading towards extinction in the wild. Usually pairs, joining mixed parties in the mid-storey. **ID Ad** bright green plumage; striking black mask; red bare parts and eyering; chestnut wings; white tertials; unpatterned green undertail; dark-red iris. **Imm** duller green underparts; duller bare parts. **Voc** Wide repertoire, often mixing different vocal types: (i) high, metallic "tink" in bouts of 1–5; (ii) 2–4 note metallic, nasal "ekek ge-LING"; (iii) whistled, painful "whirr"; (iv) whistled "whirr-eh", similar to previous but second syllable deflected.

Bornean Green Magpie *Cissa jefferyi* `E`

L 33 cm. Monotypic. See Javan Green Magpie for taxonomy. Fairly common in montane forest, 1400–2800 m, recorded to 300 m, replaced by Common Green Magpie at lower elevations and forest edge. Usually pairs, but regularly joins mixed flocks with laughing-thrushes, Bornean Spangled Drongo and Bare-headed Scimitar Babbler; mid-storey. **ID Ad** as Javan Green Magpie but has white eye, black-and-white marked undertail, longer tail and legs, and shorter bill. **Imm** duller green underparts; duller bare parts. **Voc** Wide repertoire, often mixing vocal types, much more melodious and varied than Javan: (i) series of 5–10 high-pitched chirping "sur-swee, swee-swee, deh-deh-deh", continually rising and falling in pitch, drongo-like; (ii) high-pitched whistles, rising then falling, "twsee'it wee-wee, twsee'it wee wee", regularly repeated; (iii) remarkable 5-note melody with 3 mellow, even whistles followed by a short quivering mechanical note, finishing with an oriole-like penetrative downslurred whistle "wer-wer-wer eek sweeeoo", lasting 3 sec, occasionally adding whistles and clicking notes; (iv) single, short "psst"; (v) piping, whistled "tssweet-wit-wit-woo-weep", lasting 2.5 sec. **SS** Common Green is larger, with black-and-white (not white) pattern on tertials, dark-red (not white) iris, more yellowish forecrown and longer tail.

Long-billed Crow *Corvus validus* `E`

L 46–53 cm. Monotypic. Primary, secondary and heavily degraded forest, edge, strays into plantations, <1200 m. Gregarious in canopy, often calling from bare perches, rarely comes lower. **ID Ad** long, slender body and wings; long legs; relatively short tail and long, slightly curved bill; glossy purple-black plumage; conspicuous pale-blue iris. **Imm** dark iris; non-glossy plumage. **Voc** Short, dry, upward croak, "cruk cruk cruk", regularly repeated.

Torresian Crow *Corvus orru*

L 48–53 cm. Aus. 3 ssp, 2 in region: *orru* (N Mol, NG); *latirostris* (Babar, Tanimbar). Lack of vocal differentiation argues against previously proposed species separation of *latirostris*. Now scarce in degraded, open and coastal habitat, <150 m. Singly or pairs, rarely congregating. **ID Ad** all-black plumage; stout bill; white iris. In flight appears quite compact, short-tailed and blunt-winged. Ssp *latirostris* larger bill; iris can be pale-blue. **Imm** brown iris. **Voc** Series of harsh, gargled notes "uk", lasting 0.2 sec, sometimes last note(s) drawn-out. Also various gurgling calls like "k-k-k-k-k-waaaah".

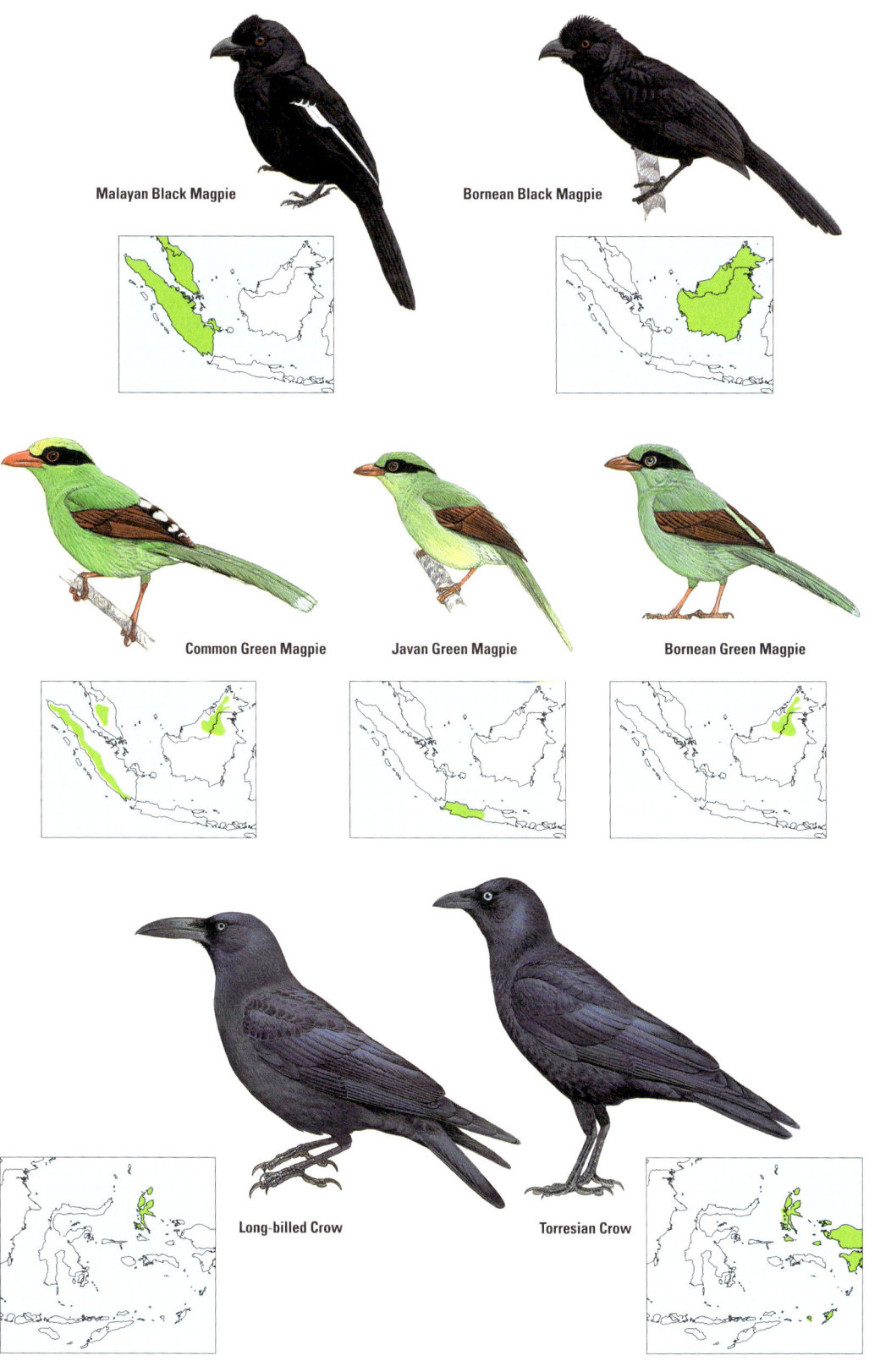

Malayan Black Magpie

Bornean Black Magpie

Common Green Magpie

Javan Green Magpie

Bornean Green Magpie

Long-billed Crow

Torresian Crow

House Crow *Corvus splendens* **I**

L 40–43 cm. S Asia (native range). 2–3 ssp, 1 in region: *splendens* (India; probably forms main stock of introduced birds in the region). Ship-assisted colonist, found in ports, urban areas. Currently known at least from Kota Kinabalu, Medan, Batam and Krakatau, but possibly spreading. **ID Ad** all blackish plumage with broad dull greyish collar, mantle, neck and breast; neatly proportioned slender bill; steep forehead. **Imm** duller; browner head. **Voc** Loud, flat, hoarse, somewhat high-pitched "kaah", regularly repeated. **SS** Beware of poor light and reflectance which may suggest similar pale contrast in other crows.

Large-billed Crow *Corvus macrorhynchos*

L 47–50 cm. S-SE-E-NE Asia. ~11 ssp, 1 in region: *macrorhynchos* (MPen, GS, LS). No longer includes vocally and genetically distinct monotypic '**Philippine Jungle Crow**' *C. philippinus* (Phil). Taxonomy of complex confused; often divided into 3-5 species, including split of ssp *macrorhynchos* in region as monotypic '**Southern Jungle Crow**', but vocal, morphological and genetic evidence so far fragmentary, partly incongruent and insufficient. Status on Bor not well known: individual photographed in Sandakan, Sabah likely ship-assisted (Apr 2007), with specimens apparently from S Kalimantan and Labuan, some of which may refer to extralimital ssp. Throughout main range, fairly common in open habitat, edge, villages, mangroves, <1500 m. Gregarious and pairs. **ID Ad** bulky, with long, broad wings, a slightly graduated tail and steep forehead; long, dagger-like bill with arching culmen; wholly glossy black plumage tinged purple. **Imm** matte plumage; lacks throat hackles. **Voc** Loud, throaty, usually drawn-out "KHARRR", often repeated, typically lower-pitched than similar call of House Crow. In areas of overlap with Sunda Crow, Large-billed's individual notes are usually more drawn-out, have a hoarser and less croaking quality and are less often combined into a rapid series. **SS** Often mistaken for the smaller Sunda Crow (see Voc for challenging call ID): Sunda has shorter, square-cut (not graduated) tail not extending beyond wings when perched. Sunda's bare skin behind eye often concealed but diagnostic when seen. With close facial views, the two large bristle patches on either side of upper bill base are disconnected in Sunda, but are linked via smaller bristles in Large-billed. Sunda routinely flies with unusually rapid, shallow wingbeats, Large-billed only occasionally displays this behaviour. Also see House and Flores Crows.

Seram Crow *Corvus violaceus* **E**

L 34–36 cm. Monotypic. For taxonomy see Sunda Crow. Uncommon in forest, edge, bordering plantations; <1800 m. Singly, pairs or small groups (<5); favours canopy. **ID Ad** appears diminutive and shorter-necked in comparison with larger Sunda Crow, culmen more decurved, bill considerably shorter; triangular (not linear) rictal bristles patch; tail extends beyond wing tips. Plumage matte black with mauve sheen; shorter tail, wings and bill than Sulawesi Crow. **Imm** mauve sheen absent. **Voc** (i) 1–3 simple nasal, slightly metallic barks; (ii) somewhat trumpeting "erk". **AN** Violaceous/Violet Crow.

Sunda Crow *Corvus enca*

L 43–47 cm. Sundaic. 2 ssp: *enca* (Jav–Bali); *compilator* (Bor–Sum, W Sum Is, MPen). Traditionally includes Seram and Sulawesi Crows and extralimital Philippine taxa to form more broadly-defined umbrella species '**Slender-billed Crow**' *C. enca*. However, deep mtDNA divergences and vocal differences dictate break-up. Fairly common to uncommon in forest, edge, clearings, certain plantations. Singly, pairs or small groups (<10); quite wary. Often flies with unusually rapid, shallow wingbeats, sometimes while giving call series. **ID Ad** fairly slim build with medium-length tail not extending beyond tip of wings; inconspicuous throat hackles; forecrown slightly peaked; triangular patch of bare black skin behind eye (often concealed); all-black plumage lightly glossed purple-violet; straight culmen except for gentle downward distal curve; narrow, linear rictal bristles patch; black iris. In flight square-cut tail, wings appear broad and blunt. Ssp *compilator* slightly larger; glossier plumage. **Imm** less glossy plumage; grey iris. **Voc** (i) Loud, hoarse "akh-akh-akh" or "kah kah kah-ah-ah-ah", with shorter notes of a more croaking quality, usually repeated in faster series than Large-billed Crow; (ii) call can be interspersed with peculiar resonant twanging notes. When taking to air, vibrating wingbeats can produce sound. **SS** See Large-billed Crow.

Sulawesi Crow *Corvus celebensis* **E**

L 40–43 cm. 2 ssp: *celebensis* (Sul and satellites); *mangoli* (Sula). For taxonomy see Sunda Crow. Fairly common in forest, edge, bordering plantations, mangroves, <1600 m. Singly, pairs or small groups (<5); favours canopy. **ID Ad** similar to larger Sunda Crow but mauve sheen; slightly shorter bill; larger rictal bristles patch and tail extending just beyond wing tips. Ssp *mangoli* smaller overall with longer bill and duller plumage. **Imm** mauve sheen absent. **Voc** 1–10 throaty, screeching "arrrh" or slightly sharper "errrhk". **SS** See Banggai Crow.

Banggai Crow *Corvus unicolor* **E**

L 40 cm. Monotypic. Scarce in montane forest, edge, >800 m, rarely down to 300 m. Shy canopy dweller, rarely perches conspicuously; pairs or small groups (<5). When calling pumps tail downwards, holding body horizontally, throwing head back-and-forth. **ID** Short, thick-necked appearance with short tail; wings reach tail tip. **Ad** all-black plumage lightly glossed purple; pale-blue iris; bill is thick and short. In flight appears broad-winged, short-tailed, makes whooshing sound with wings. **Imm** undescribed. **Voc** Song: metallic, jerky-like "worh whir whir", and "whir-whir-wah-whir", lasting 1–2 sec, occasionally followed by ascending, curious, whining 3-note "whoo-way-wee". Call: short, sharp "whirrk". **SS** Lowland-inhabiting Sulawesi Crow has dark (not pale) iris, much longer, narrower bill and calls very differently.

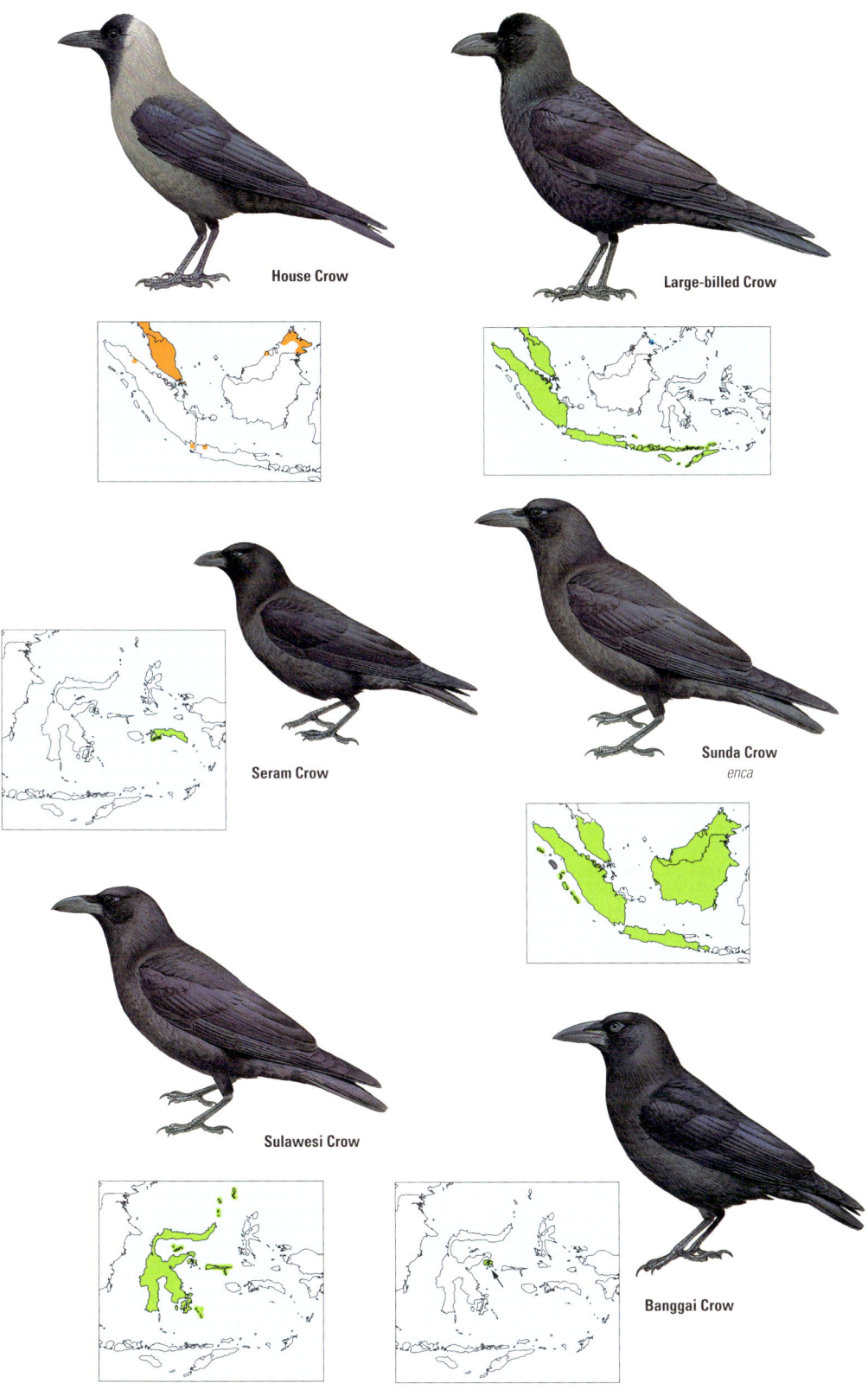

House Crow

Large-billed Crow

Seram Crow

Sunda Crow
enca

Sulawesi Crow

Banggai Crow

Piping Crow *Corvus typicus* E

L 35–40 cm. Monotypic. Uncommon in forest, edge, 600–1800 m, scarcer above and below. Shy canopy dweller, rarely perches conspicuously except when calling; pairs or small groups (<5). **ID** Pied appearance with short, square-cut tail; white wraps around nape, neck and underparts; black plumage with bluish gloss; bill relatively small. **F** has more diffuse demarcation between throat and breast. **Imm** white sullied with greyish-brown. **Voc** Variety of piping whistles and nasal calls, including: (i) high-pitched whistled "sooo-weee", lasting 0.8 sec, often followed by a short, rattled croak; (ii) loud, metallic "whack whack, whir-whir..."; (iii) ascending, jerky "whit-whit-whir", lasting 1 sec, or "whit-whir-whir-whir"; (iv) eagle-like, ascending, whistled "whoor'it", lasting 0.5 sec.

Flores Crow *Corvus florensis* E

L 40 cm. Monotypic. Uncommon in forest, rarely edge, <1000 m. Shy, rarely perches conspicuously, preferring forest interior. Pairs or small groups (<5). When calling pumps tail downwards, holding body horizontally, throwing head back-and-forth. Sometimes observed moving through canopy at night during spot-lighting. **ID Ad** all-black plumage, appearing compact with stout bill; short wings extending half way down long, thin, square tail; small bare postocular patch. In flight appears broad-winged with narrow tail, producing whooshing sound with wings. **Imm** undescribed. **Voc** Voice has distinct, baby-like, wailing quality. Calls include (i) high-pitched, startling, downward "kwaa", sometimes repeated, often followed by peculiar gurgling noise; (ii) peculiar "pooh", similar to human loudly blowing air. **SS** Large-billed Crow is larger, more conspicuous, has different call, lacks bare postocular patch, has longer wings, more graduated (less square-cut) tail and steeper forehead.

EUPETIDAE
Rail-babbler
1 species in region

Monotypic, unique. Medium-sized, long-necked and long-tailed inhabitant of dense forest. Terrestrial, shy and secretive, its presence typically revealed by its distinctive whistling call.

Rail-babbler *Eupetes macrocerus*

L 28–30 cm. Sundaic. 2 ssp: *macrocerus* (Sum, Natuna, MPen); *borneensis* (Bor). Uncommon and local in primary, secondary forest, <1300 m. Singly or pairs; terrestrial, walks on forest floor, reluctant to fly. **ID Ad** long, slender body with long, graduated tail. Uniform reddish-brown becoming more reddish towards front including red throat; conspicuous broad white supercilium bordered below by thick black line from bill to collar; bright buff forecrown. When calling produces cobalt-blue gular sacs. Ssp *borneensis* has more rufous underparts and redder upperparts, particularly tail. **Imm** duller plumage with grey forehead and white throat. **Voc** Song: level-pitched, clear, pure mournful whistle slowly rising in volume, lasting 1.7–3 sec; usually higher-pitched than similar Blue-banded, Black-crowned and Garnet Pittas. Call: continual soft clucking when agitated, discernible only at close range.

PETROICIDAE
Flyrobins
1 species in region

Small flycatcher-like birds of forest and wooded habitats. Predominantly Australo-Papuan. Sally for prey from exposed perches within mid- to upper storey. Generally active and conspicuous.

Tanimbar Flyrobin *Microeca hemixantha* E

L 12 cm. Monotypic. Sometimes included in extralimital Lemon-bellied Flyrobin *M. flavigaster* (Aus) but plumage distinct. Fairly common in variety of wooded habitats, clearings, plantations. Singly or pairs; sallies for prey in mid-canopy. **ID** Stubby bill, short tail and plump appearance. **Ad** olive-green upperparts; bright yellow underparts; indistinct supercilium. **Imm** undescribed. **Voc** Song: (i) thin, high-pitched 3- to 4-note "o'oo-tit-tit" lasting 0.5 sec; very similar to Yellow-bellied Warbler; (ii) pleasant, loud warbled notes, lasting 2-2.5 sec. Call: short, high-pitched "see". **AN** Golden-bellied Flyrobin.

STENOSTIRIDAE
Canary-flycatchers and allies
2 species in region

Small birds of forest and edge with flycatcher resemblance. Generally conspicuous, sallying from exposed perches in mid- to upper storey and often joining mixed flocks.

Grey-headed Canary-flycatcher *Culicicapa ceylonensis*

L 12–13 cm. S–SE–E Asia. 5 ssp, 3 in region: *antioxantha* (GS, MPen); *sejuncta* (Flores, Lembata); *connectens* (Sumba). Common in forest, woodland, edge, plantations, <3000 m. Singly or pairs, joins mixed flocks; conspicuous, sitting on open branches inside forest, tame. **ID Ad** plain-grey head with narrow white eyering and slight crest; slightly paler throat and breast, bright yellow underparts; olive-green upperparts. Ssp *sejuncta* lacks crest, paler face and throat, yellow extends higher up breast; *connectens* as previous but greyer face. **Imm** yellow-tipped coverts; duller underparts; brownish-grey head. **Voc** Song: loud, squeaky, high-pitched 4–5 note sequence, "tit-titoo-whee" or "chik which ee-whitchee" or "twoi-toi-teeh-deeh", lasting 0.8 sec. Call: sharp metallic trill and twittering.

Citrine Canary-flycatcher *Culicicapa helianthea*

L 11–12 cm. Phil, Wallacea. 5 ssp, 1 in region: *helianthea* (Sul–Sula, Selayar). Fairly common in forest, woodland, edge, plantations, <3000 m. Singly or pairs, joins mixed flocks; conspicuous, sitting on open branches inside forest, tame. **ID Ad** olive-yellow head and upperparts; bright yellow underparts, rump and narrow eyering. **Imm** undescribed. **Voc** Song: loud, squeaky, high-pitched 5-note sequence "tsoo-sit-choo-sit-sit", lasting ~1 sec. Call: long, nasal trill.

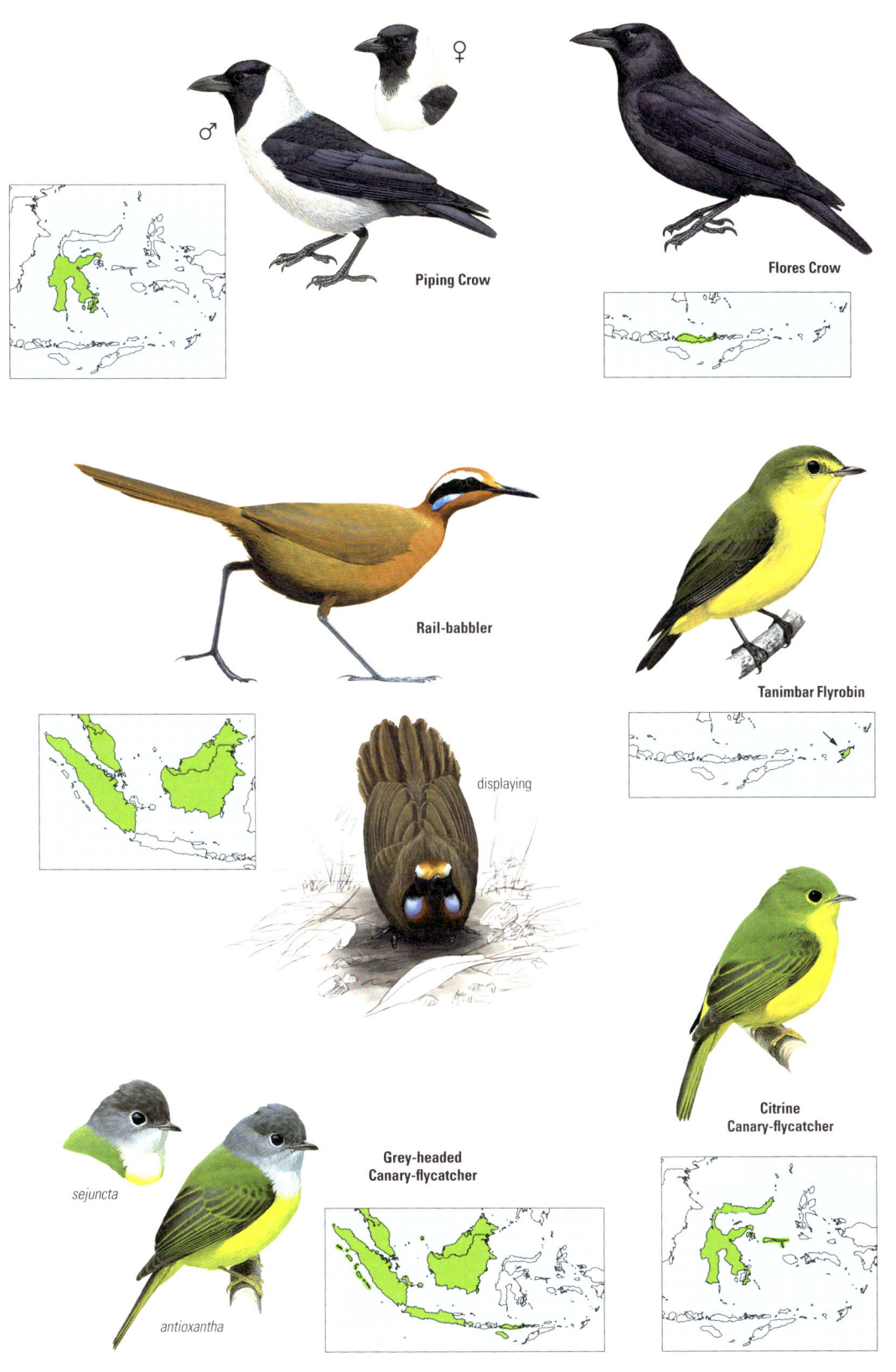

Piping Crow

♂ ♀

Flores Crow

Rail-babbler

displaying

Tanimbar Flyrobin

Citrine Canary-flycatcher

sejuncta

antioxantha

Grey-headed Canary-flycatcher

Small robust birds with stout bills. Typically active, feeding by gleaning insects from foliage in mid- to upper storey. Inhabit a wide range of wooded habitats where often join mixed flocks.

Cinereous Tit *Parus cinereus*

L 12 cm. S–SE Asia. ~12 ssp, 3 in region: *cinereus* (Jav–LS); *ambiguus* (Sum, MPen); *sarawacensis* (coastal Bor; few recent records). Formerly considered part of a more broadly-defined umbrella species, '**Great Tit**' *P. major* (Eurasia), but genetic and plumage differences have led to division into 3–4 species. Fairly common in wooded habitats, mangroves, montane forest. Singly or pairs, mid-canopy. **ID M** head black with large white cheek and sometimes tiny white nuchal patch; upperparts grey with white wingbar; tail black with white outertail; underparts whitish with black ventral stripe. **F** duller; thinner ventral stripe. Ssp *ambiguus* upperparts slightly paler, buff-tinged underparts, reduced white in tail; *sarawacensis* slightly darker overall, nuchal patch always absent, broader ventral stripe, white reduced to outermost tail feather. **Imm** yellowish cheek patch and underparts. **Voc** Pronounced individual song variability: (i) soft, buzzing "chezz-chezz-chezz..."; (ii) 2–4 whistled notes "pit-chit-chew pit-chit-chew...", "wit-wit-wit chirr...", "spit-tooi spit tooi". Call: churring, scratchy "chich-ich-ich-ich".

Small, predominantly terrestrial birds of open country. Cryptic colouration often renders their detection difficult as they forage, while generally conspicuous when singing from exposed perches or in flight.

Australasian Bushlark *Mirafra javanica*

L 13–15 cm. SE Asia to Aus. 16 ssp, 3 in region: *javanica* (S Bor, Jav, Bali, Lombok); *parva* (Sumbawa–Flores, Sumba); *timorensis* (Sawu, Timor). Previously common, now increasingly local because of poaching, no recent records from Jav. Dry grassland, rarer in cultivated fields. Singly, pairs or groups (<10). **ID Ad** broad buff supercilium; greyish-brown upperparts with heavy mottling and rufous primaries; ochraceous underparts with finely streaked upper breast; stout bill. In flight shows rufous primaries and short tail with white outer feathers. Ssp *timorensis* smaller, with less heavy bill and slightly paler ochraceous underparts; *parva* paler and more greyish overall. **Imm** paler; upperpart streaks less well-defined; diffuse breast streaking. **Voc** Song from perch or in hovering flight: long series of sweet, rich notes, containing chips, whistles, metallic and rattling notes with much mimicry (e.g. of chats, shorebirds and raptors). Call: harsh "zip", or "zip-zip-zip". **SS** See Eurasian Skylark.

Eurasian Skylark *Alauda arvensis* **V**

L 16–19 cm. Palaearctic. 12–13 ssp, unknown ssp in region, presumed *pekinensis* or *intermedia* (both breed NE Asia; winter S to E Asia). Recorded N Bor (Nov–Dec 1950, Feb 1966, Nov 2018). Grassland and open cultivation. Forages on ground. **ID Ad** upperparts grey-buff, streaked black-brown; small erectile crest; whitish supercilium and eyering; wings dark brown, edged rufous-buff; prominent white trailing edge to secondaries visible in flight; tail blackish brown with buff-white outer edges; underparts buff or almost white, generally more rufous on breast, black streaks extending from breast onto flanks; bill pink-grey; legs brownish. **Imm** crown and mantle blackish with broad buff-white feather fringes. **Voc** Call: typically given at take-off, rich, rolling "chirrup". **SS** From Australasian Bush-

lark by larger size, thinner bill, much less conspicuous rufous edging to flight feathers, erectile crest (absent in Bushlark), and heavier streaking on underparts. **Oriental Skylark** *A. gulgula* (C–S–SE–E Asia, Phil) possible vagrant to region, extremely similar and must be separated from Eurasian with care: Oriental has more open facial expression with larger eye and broader white superciliary just behind eye, but conclusive ID should rely on Oriental's shorter primary projection and buff (not white) outertail and trailing edge to wings.

Small aerial feeders. Most common in open country, often in large flocks. Typically construct mud nests on cliffs or buildings and roost communally.

Sand Martin *Riparia riparia*

L 12 cm. Breeds Holarctic; winters to tropics. 4 ssp, 1 in region: *ijimae* (breeds NE–E Asia; winters to S). Recorded in W–N Bor (annually) and Talaud (Nov 2011). Open country, often near water. Singly, pairs or flocks. **ID Ad** chocolate-brown head and upperparts; dark brown breast band contrasting with white throat and underparts. In flight, brown underwing and forked tail. **Imm** buff edging on upperparts. **Voc** Call: dry, scratchy "chrr". **SS** Extralimital **Pale Martin** *R. diluta* (breeds C–S–E Asia; winters to S; 4 ssp) ssp *fohkienensis* (breeds E China) possible vagrant though field ID on current knowledge not possible: Pale Martin paler overall with fainter breast band and shallower tail fork, but seemingly much overlap.

Barn Swallow *Hirundo rustica*

L 18 cm. Breeds Holarctic; winters to tropics. 8 ssp, ~4 in region: *gutturalis* (breeds E Asia; winters to Australia); the three ssp *mandschurica* (breeds NE Asia; winters to SE Asia), *tytleri* (breeds N Asia; winters to S–SE Asia) and *saturata* (breeds NE Asia; winters to SE Asia) may occur but plumage clinality and seasonality render ID difficult. Common in open country, often near water. Small to large flocks. **ID Ad** upperparts glossy dark-blue, wings and tail blacker; tail shows white patches on inner webs, visible when fanned; outer tail feathers elongated (shorter in **F**); forehead and throat rufous; dark blue breast band; underparts creamy white in *gutturalis*, more ochre in *mandschurica*, deep rusty-ochre in *saturata*, and more chestnut in *tytleri*, but differences possibly only apparent in autumn, disappearing with winter moult into fresh, white feathers which start to turn reddish only in breeding quarters. **Imm** duller; paler throat and forehead; shorter tail. **Voc** Call: sharp "witt-witt". **SS** See Pacific Swallow.

Pacific Swallow *Hirundo javanica*

L 13 cm. SE–E Asia to Aus. 6 ssp, 1 in region: *javanica* (SE Asia–Phil). No longer includes monotypic Tahiti Swallow *H. tahitica* (Polynesia) and Hill Swallow *H. domicola* (S Asia) based on ecological and plumage differences. Common in open country and cultivation, often near water or human settlements, particularly along coast, <1500 m. Singly, pairs or small flocks. **ID Ad** crown and upperparts dark glossy purple-blue; wings and tail blacker; tail shows large white patches on inner webs, visible on fanned tail; outer tail feathers slightly elongated; forehead, throat and breast rufous-chestnut; rest of underparts dull grey-white with faint darker streaking; vent blackish with broad white edging. In flight compact body, short tail, dark underwing. **Imm** duller; paler throat and forehead; shorter tail. **Voc** Song: twittering "twsit-twsit-twsit..."; sometimes rather melodious and varied when perched. Call: sharp, high "tseep". **SS** From Barn Swallow by darker, dirtier underwings, belly and vent, lack of blue breast band and consistent lack of long tail streamers.

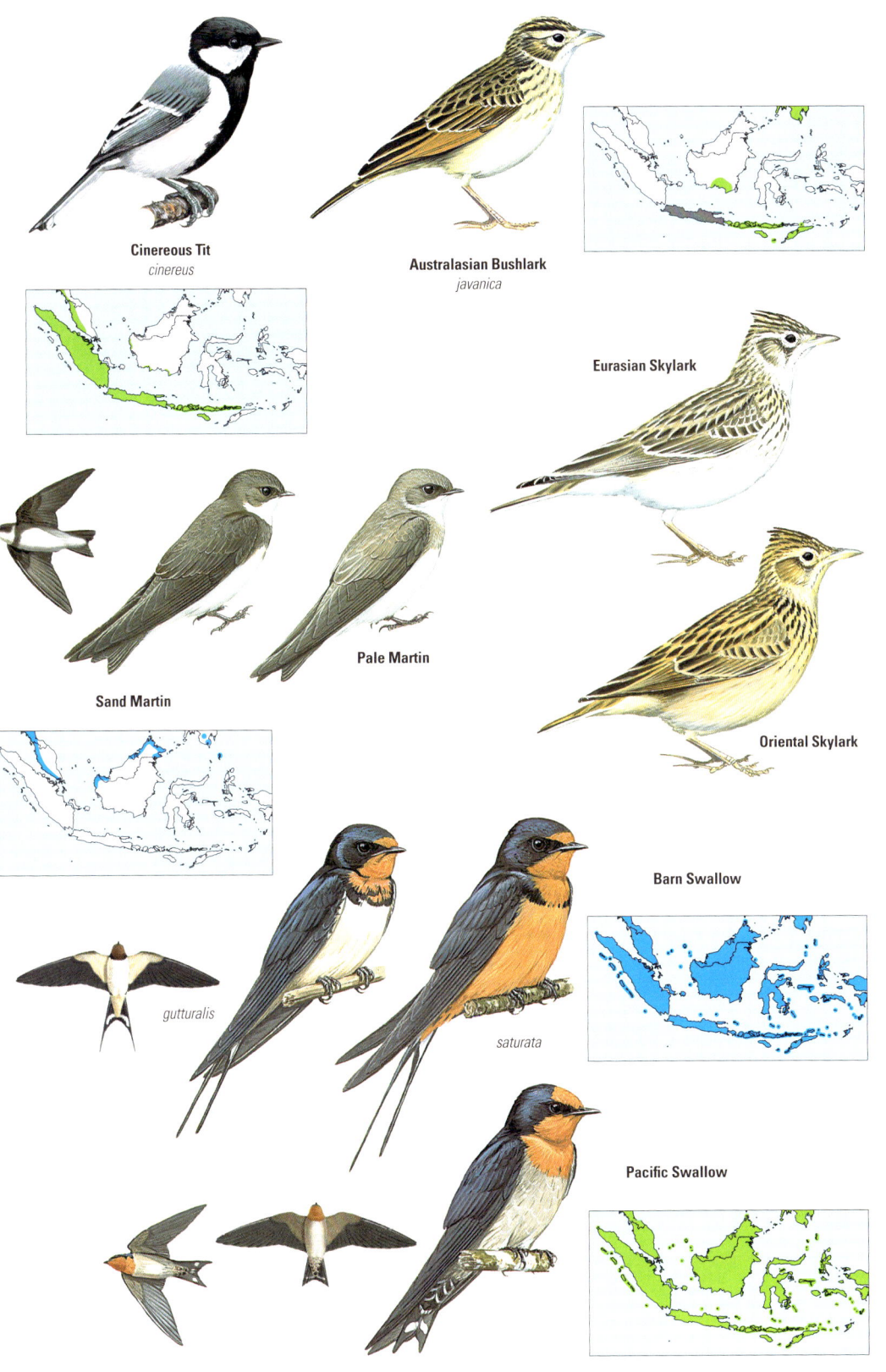

Cinereous Tit
cinereus

Australasian Bushlark
javanica

Eurasian Skylark

Pale Martin

Sand Martin

Oriental Skylark

gutturalis

Barn Swallow

saturata

Pacific Swallow

Daurian Swallow *Cecropis daurica*

L 16–19 cm. Breeds C–S–SE–E–NE Asia, Phil; winters S to Australia. 8 ssp, 2–3 in region: *japonica* (breeds NE–E Asia; winters SE Asia to Australia); *striolata* (resident Jav–LS, Phil, Taiwan); possibly also *daurica* (breeds C–E Asia; winters S–SE Asia) on migration. Confusing taxonomy. Present treatment very different from previous works, with Daurian Swallow a combination of taxa previously classified as Striated *C. striolata* and Red-rumped Swallow *C. daurica*. Ssp *striolata* and three ssp from northern mainland SE Asia usually divided as '**Striated Swallow**' *C. striolata*, but such separation almost certainly unjustified because of continuous range and plumage clinality with E Asian breeders *daurica* and *japonica*. As here defined, Daurian Swallow excludes four ssp from tropical Africa which form at least two independent species, and excludes monotypic Red-rumped Swallow *C. rufula* (W Palaearctic), in both cases based on plumage and mtDNA. Also excludes two adjacent taxa, monotypic Rufous-bellied Swallow *C. badia* (MPen) and monotypic Sri Lankan Swallow *C. hyperythra* (Sri Lanka) based on strong plumage differences (and despite signs of limited admixture). Locally fairly common in open country and cultivation, often near water or around human settlements, <1500 m. Difficulties with ssp identification complicate efforts to separate local from migrant records in Jav–LS. Singly or small flocks. **ID** (*striolata*) **Ad** crown and back glossy dark-blue; sides of neck rufous but lacking well-defined pale or rufous hindcollar; rump rufous-chestnut; wings and tail blue-black; outertail feathers elongated (longer in **M**); throat, ear-coverts and underparts white with heavy black streaking; vent blackish. Ssp *japonica* smaller, with variable narrow pale hindcollar and slightly finer streaking on underparts; *daurica* equally small, usually with a less distinct or missing hindcollar and even finer streaking on underparts. **Imm** duller and browner; shorter tail. **Voc** Song: soft twittering and rippling "purr" notes, often in flight. Call: high, short "chwit" or "weet".

Fairy Martin *Petrochelidon ariel*　　　　　　　**V**

L 11 cm. Australia. Monotypic. Recorded in Sumba, E Timor and Babar (May–Nov). Open country and cultivation, often near water or around human settlements. Singly or small flocks. **ID Ad** rufous crown and nape; mantle dark glossy-blue, with some paler streaking; wings and tail blackish-brown; tail slightly forked; ear coverts, throat and underparts dull-white with fine rufous streaking on throat and breast. **Imm** duller and browner with buffy feather edging. **Voc** Song: series of bubbly squeaks. Call: sharp, rolling "chrrr" or "prrrt-prrrt". **SS** Tree Martin has glossy blue (not rufous) crown and nape.

Tree Martin *Petrochelidon nigricans*

L 13 cm. Aus. 3 ssp, 2–3 in region: *timoriensis* (Timor, Sumba, Alor); migrant race either *nigricans* (breeds Tasmania) or *neglecta* (breeds mainland Australia), both wintering to N. Fairly common in open country and cultivation, often near water, trees or around human settlements. Singly or small flocks (<10). **ID** (*nigricans*) **Ad** glossy blue crown and back; wings and tail blackish; tail slightly forked; rump dull-white with some streaking; forehead with small rufous patch; ear coverts, side of neck, throat and underparts dull grey-white with faint dark streaks, tinged rufous on breast, flanks and undertail-coverts. In flight shows dark underwing and tail. Ssp *neglecta* smaller with less rufous tinge; *timoriensis* as previous but has darker streaks on throat. **Imm** duller and browner with pale edging. **Voc** Song: short series of twittering containing liquid notes. Call: (i) sharp "chit"; (ii) squeaky "tsweet". **SS** See Fairy Martin.

Asian House Martin *Delichon dasypus*

L 13 cm. Breeds Himalaya to NE–E Asia; winters to S–SE Asia, Phil. 3 ssp, 1 in region: *dasypus* (breeds NE–E Asia; winters S to Phil, GS). Deep mtDNA divergence between Japanese and mainland populations of ssp *dasypus* hints at potential cryptic diversity; provenance of local visitors not known. Scarce from Oct–Mar (probably more regular but overlooked). Feeds in high-flying flocks; joins mixed flocks with Pacific Swift. **ID Ad** glossy blue-black crown, face and upperparts with contrasting white rump and underparts. In flight appears compact with dark forked tail and black underwing-coverts. **Imm** duller; buffish wash to underparts. **Voc** Call: dry, rattled "pirit". **SS** Contrasting, pied, compact appearance and short but well-forked tail separate from other swallows.

PYCNONOTIDAE
Bulbuls
43 species in region

Diverse family of small to medium-sized arboreal birds. Generally inhabit forest and edge, gleaning invertebrate prey or consuming fruit in low to high storey. Most species are relatively conspicuous despite typically dull colouration.

Sooty-headed Bulbul *Pycnonotus aurigaster*

L 19–21 cm. SE–E Asia. 9 ssp, 1 in region: *aurigaster* (Jav, Bali; widely introduced elsewhere in region). Fairly common in variety of open habitats including villages, cultivation and scrub, <1800 m. Usually in small groups (<10). **ID Ad** black cap, face and chin; white cheek; pale grey underparts; brownish-grey upperparts with conspicuous whitish rump and yellow vent. **Imm** browner face and crown; duller vent. **Voc** Song: cheerful series of shrill, chatty notes "whi'-wi'-wiwi'-wiwi'…" and "whi'-hi'-oo-ih-ih-wiwi'…" lasting 2–10 sec. Call: (i) shrill, downslurred "pee"; (ii) single downslurred, warbled "b'brrp".

Sunda Yellow-vented Bulbul *Pycnonotus analis*

L 19–21 cm. SE Asia. 3 ssp, 2 in region: *analis* (Sum–Sumbawa, Bangka, Belitung, Riau Is, Kangean, MPen; widely introduced elsewhere in region); *gourdini* (Bor, Karimunjawa, Maratua). Here separated from Philippine Yellow-vented Bulbul *P. goiavier* (Phil) based on different, more complex dawn song and deep mtDNA divergence. Common in open habitat: parks, villages, scrub, oil palm plantations, occasionally forest clearings, <1900 m. Usually in small groups (<20). **ID Ad** white supercilium, face, throat and underparts; black lores and bill; dark brown crown; mid-brown upperparts; yellowish vent. Ssp *gourdini* off-white supercilium; duskier breast and flanks. **Imm** weaker and paler facial pattern. **Voc** Song: continuous, warbled "tudd'liu-tudd'liu-tudd'liu…" or more complex variations thereof, lasting 5 sec–1 min. Call: soft, warbled "chic-chic-chic…". **SS** See Pale-faced Bulbul.

Pale-faced Bulbul *Pycnonotus leucops*　　　　　**E**

L 18–19 cm. Monotypic. Previously included with extralimital Flavescent Bulbul *P. flavescens* (mainland SE Asia) but distinct in plumage and more closely related to Orange-spotted and Aceh Bulbuls on mtDNA evidence. Fairly common in montane forest, particularly around small clearings, 900–3500 m, primarily >1400 m. Usually pairs or small groups (<5). **ID Ad** white face and underparts with yellow vent; upperparts olive-brown, more olive on outerwing; crown fringed grey. **Imm** duller vent; lacks olive in wing; paler nape. **Voc** Song: bubbly, emphatic, rolling "kw't kw't tu-weety-weety…", continuously repeated, often in duet. Call: metallic "tink". **SS** Sunda Yellow-vented Bulbul has black lores and darker upperparts.

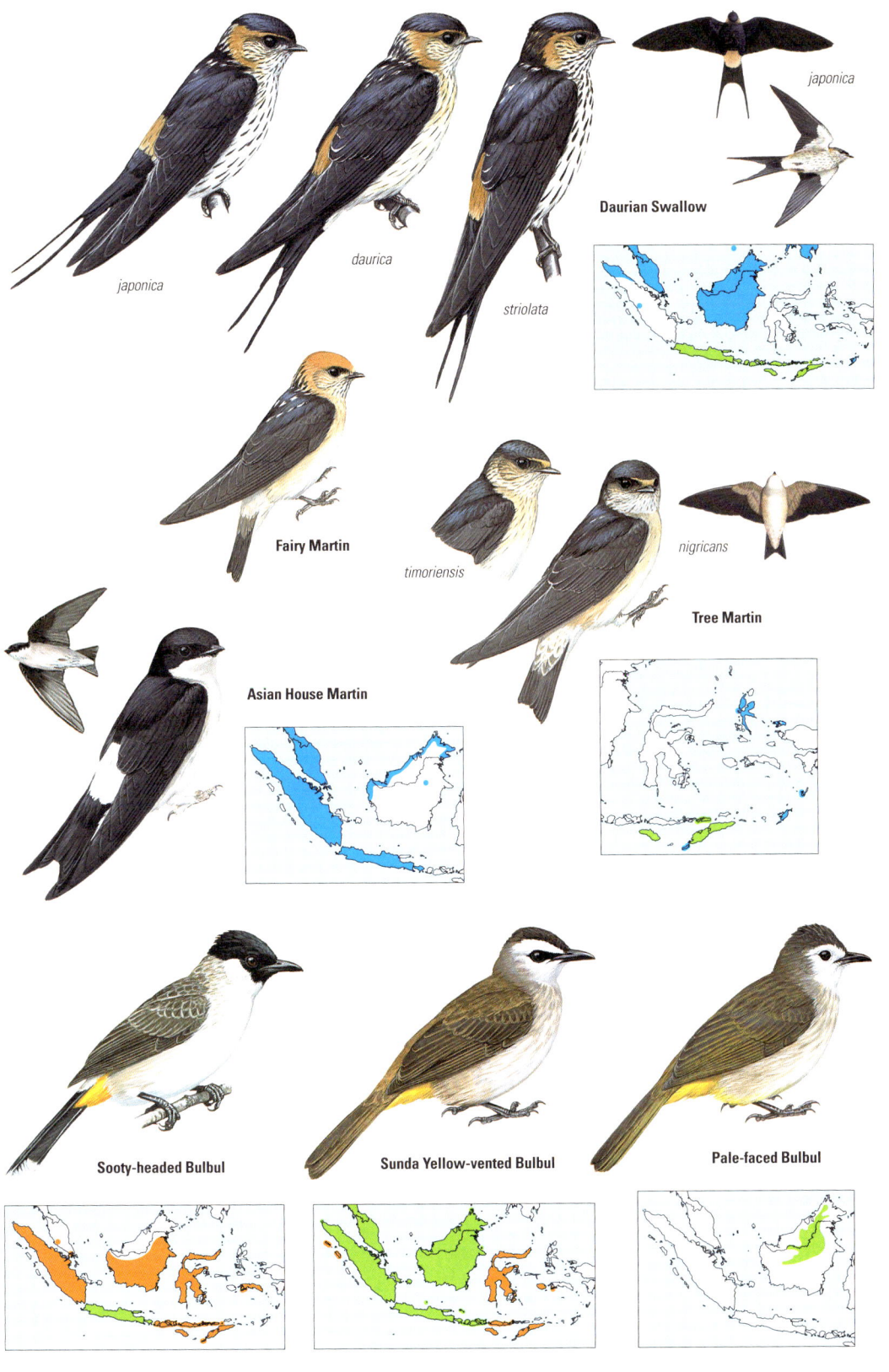

japonica

daurica

striolata

japonica

Daurian Swallow

Fairy Martin

timoriensis

nigricans

Tree Martin

Asian House Martin

Sooty-headed Bulbul

Sunda Yellow-vented Bulbul

Pale-faced Bulbul

Orange-spotted Bulbul *Pycnonotus bimaculatus* **E**

L 20 cm. 2 ssp: *bimaculatus* (C–S Sum, W–C Jav); *tenggerensis* (E Jav, Bali). See Aceh Bulbul for taxonomy. Locally fairly common in (sub-) montane forest, 800–3000 m. Introduced (probably ssp *tenggerensis*) on Mt Rinjani (Lombok), where common at higher elevations. Pairs and small groups (<5), favouring fern-dominated clearings. **ID Ad** dark brown-grey head, upperparts and breast; yellowish ear-coverts, orange spot above eye and orange supraloral tuft; mottled lower breast with white belly and yellow vent; outer-wing and tail olive. Ssp *tenggerensis* indistinct ear-covert patch; less olive wings. **Imm** duller; head pattern less distinct. **Voc** Song: series of 8–15 staccato, cheery, rapid notes "wir-weet-weet-wir-weet-wer-wee..." lasting 1–2 sec. Call: sharp "chik".

Aceh Bulbul *Pycnonotus snouckaerti* **E**

L 21 cm. Monotypic. Previously included with Orange-spotted Bulbul but pronounced morphological differences warrant species status. Rare and local in (sub-) montane forest, >800 m. Pairs and small groups (<5), favouring fern-dominated clearings. **ID Ad** sizeable orange supraloral tuft, larger than in Orange-spotted. Uniform dark brownish-grey with underparts and crown fringed grey; olive wings and outertail; yellow vent; slightly longer tail than Orange-spotted. **Imm** undescribed. **Voc** Song: series of ~10 ascending notes, first notes trilling "prrrt", followed by sharp, metallic "pip" notes, lasting ~3 sec. Call: harsh "chek".

Straw-headed Bulbul *Pycnonotus zeylanicus*

L 28–29 cm. Sundaic. Monotypic. Now rare and very local due to trapping: extinct in most of former range, in region possibly only found on Bor now. Favours forested banks along rivers and streams, <500 m, rarely to 1800 m. Usually in vocal, territorial pairs. **ID Ad** large and uniquely patterned; golden-orange head with black eye-stripe and broad black moustachial; white throat; brownish mantle and breast streaked white; olive wings and tail; buffish belly. **Imm** face pattern faded buffish. **Voc** Song: mix of loud, explosive and fruity "wit-wooty-woo-wooty-woo...", lasting 3–6 sec. Call: short, quiet "brrrrt".

Ruby-throated Bulbul *Pycnonotus dispar* **E**

L 17–20 cm. Monotypic. Distinct plumage and iris colour on Sum require further study. Now scarce and local in forest, clearings; largely trapped out of more open habitats, particularly on Jav, <1100 m. Usually pairs or small groups (<5). **ID** (Jav–Bali) **Ad** black head with steep crown; red throat; underparts yellow; darker olive upperparts and blackish tail; pale iris. Sum birds have red iris and red throat bleeding into breast. **Imm** yellow throat. **Voc** Song: 3–8 variable, cheery "wee-wit-it-weet" notes, first 2 notes downslurred, remaining notes inflected, sharper than Bornean Bulbul. Call: metallic "chick".

Bornean Bulbul *Pycnonotus montis* **E**

L 17–18 cm. Monotypic. Fairly common in submontane forest, edge and clearings, 600–1600 m. Usually pairs or small groups (<10). **ID Ad** black head with elongated crest; yellow-olive body with paler yellow throat. **Imm** slightly duller; shorter crest. **Voc** Song: 3–5 cheery "wee-wit-it-weet" notes, first note downslurred followed by inflected notes. Call: rising "yip-yip".

Scaly-breasted Bulbul *Pycnonotus squamatus*

L 14–16 cm. Sundaic. 3 ssp: *squamatus* (Jav); *borneensis* (Bor); *webberi* (Sum, MPen). Locally uncommon and nomadic in forest, edge, <1400 m. Singly, pairs or small groups (<6). **ID Ad** black head; white throat; white-scaled black breast and flanks; olive upperparts; yellow vent; black tail tipped white. Ssp *webberi* darker olive upperparts, greyer flanks, larger white tail tips; *borneensis* not as bright, greener mantle and more white on undertail. **Imm** smudgy breast pattern; less bright vent. **Voc** Song: short "wit", followed by a short, rattled "prrrt". Call: higher-pitched "wit" or "wit-wit".

Grey-bellied Bulbul *Pycnonotus cyaniventris*

L 16–17 cm. Sundaic. 2 ssp: *cyaniventris* (Sum, MPen); *paroticalis* (Bor). Locally uncommon and nomadic in forest, edge, <1400 m. Singly, pairs or small groups (<6). **ID Ad** grey head and underparts; bright olive upperparts and uppertail with yellow vent; *paroticalis* larger; brighter golden-yellow margins on wing-coverts; paler, more conspicuous supercilium and darker head. **Imm** undescribed. **Voc** Song: level-pitched, quick "wi'wi'wi'wit". Call: (i) nervous "dupdupdup..."; (ii) thin, plaintive "we-we-we-we"; (iii) squeaky "pee-pee-pee-pee".

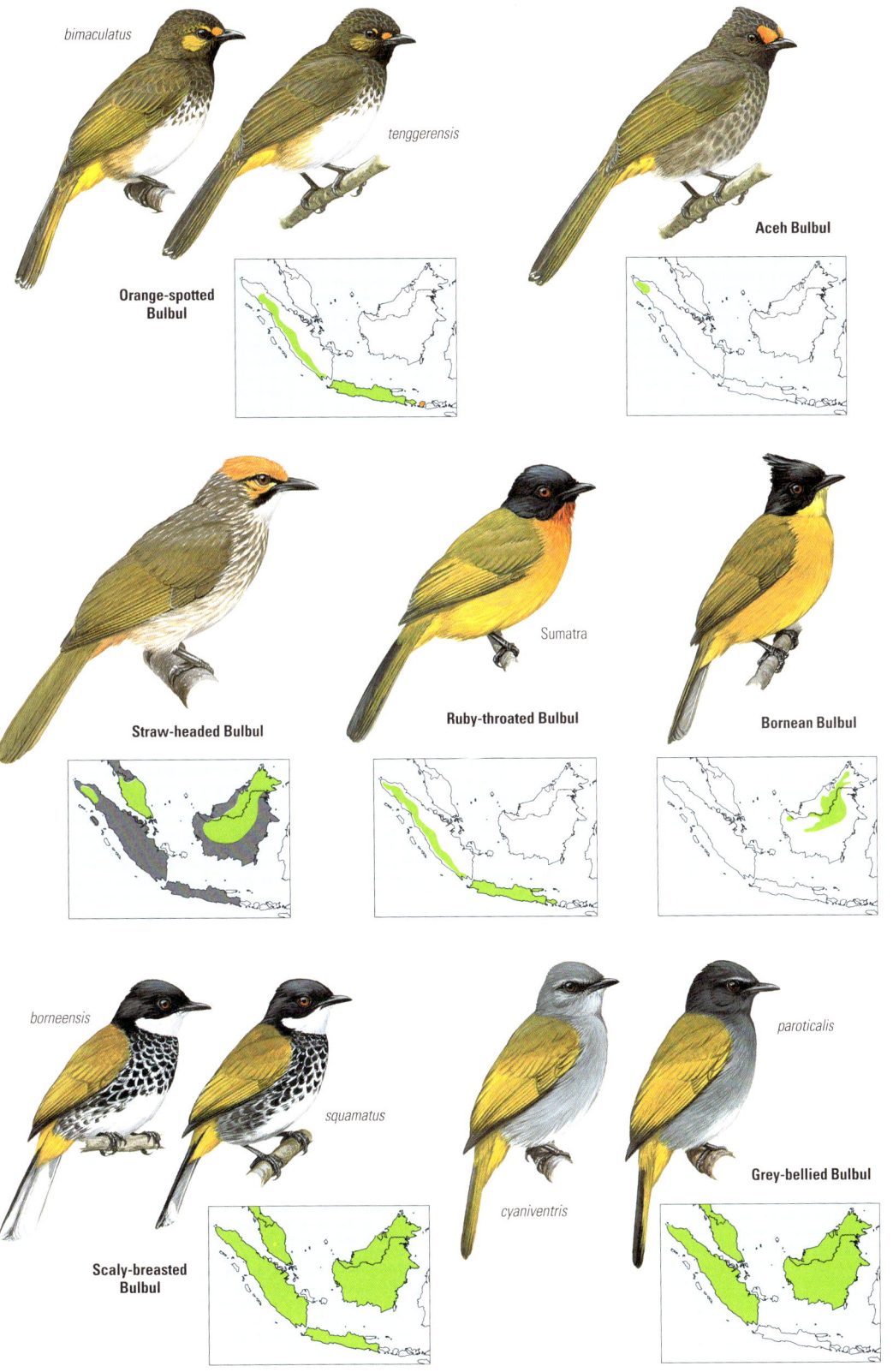

bimaculatus

tenggerensis

Orange-spotted Bulbul

Aceh Bulbul

Straw-headed Bulbul

Ruby-throated Bulbul

Sumatra

Bornean Bulbul

borneensis

squamatus

Scaly-breasted Bulbul

cyaniventris

paroticalis

Grey-bellied Bulbul

Olive-winged Bulbul *Pycnonotus plumosus*

L 20–21 cm. Sundaic. 3 ssp: *plumosus* (E Sum, Riau Is, Bangka, Belitung, MPen, Jav–Bali, Bawean, Anambas); *hachisukae* (N Bor Is, Cagayan Sulu); *hutzi* (Bor). No longer includes extralimital Ashy-fronted Bulbul *P. cinereifrons* (Palawan). See also Barusan Bulbul for taxonomy. Fairly common in secondary and degraded forest, edge, scrub, riverside vegetation, plantations, <1300 m. Pairs or small groups (<10). **ID Ad** dull greyish head turning olive on wings, lower back and tail; whitish streaks on ear-coverts; whitish throat; olive-brown breast, flanks and vent (the latter with buff tinge) becoming whitish on belly; dark red iris. Ssp *hutzi* tail and wings less olive, vent lacks buff tinge; *hachisukae* larger than previous. **Juv/Imm** duller overall; less olive; iris blackish, becoming redder with age. **Voc** Song: 3–5 uprising "whip-wit-witty-witit", lasting <1 sec, or a longer series of 10-15 notes lasting 2 sec, sometimes given slowly. Call: harsh, trilled "brrt" and throaty "whip-whip". **SS** In W Sum, see Barusan Bulbul. From other dull *Pycnonotus* and *Iole* bulbuls by more olive wings (often only visible as indistinct olive feather margins), whitish streaks on ear-coverts and avoidance of good forest interior. Olive-winged's dark-red eye lacks an eye-ring and is darker than in most similar species (except Cream-vented on Bor), but beware of dark-eyed juv bulbuls of other species (told by fleshy gapes). See Charlotte's and Buff-vented for additional differences.

Barusan Bulbul *Pycnonotus porphyreus* E

L 20 cm. Monotypic. Traditionally included with Olive-winged Bulbul but genomic data, plumage, eye colour and vocalisations support species recognition. Areas of overlap between Barusan and Olive-winged in W Sum unknown, requiring research. Singly or pairs, in woodland, forest, edge. **ID Ad** Similar to Olive-winged but darker, greyer head with dark mottling on crown and nape, contrasting more sharply with olive mantle and wings; white ear-covert stripes more conspicuous; ochre to pale-orange eye. **Juv/Imm** undescribed, but eye colour probably much darker. **Voc** Song: 1-2 well-spaced low introductory notes, followed by short burst of ~5–7 mixed, fruity, slightly scratchy, deflected notes, "wip–wit–wit-wip-wit-wip-wip", lasting 2 s. Call: scratchy "wip". **SS** In areas of potential contact with Olive-winged Bulbul in W Sum, see ID section for separation. From other dull *Pycnonotus* and *Iole* bulbuls by more olive wings, greyer (less brownish) crown, and presence of whitish streaks on ear-coverts. Barusan's eye is warmer-colored (less pale-greyish) than in Cream-vented and Buff-vented, and much paler than in Asian Red-eyed and Spectacled. See Buff-vented for additional differences.

Cream-vented Bulbul *Pycnonotus simplex*

L 18 cm. Sundaic. 5 ssp: *simplex* (Sum, MPen, Riau Is, Batu, Nias); *halizonus* (Anambas, N Natuna), *prillwitzi* (Jav); *perplexus* (NE Bor, Balambangan); *oblitus* (rest of Bor, S Natuna, Belitung, Bangka). Genomic data indicate deep divergence between red-eyed Bornean (*perplexus, oblitus*) and white-eyed western Sundaic (*simplex, halizonus*) taxa, suggesting lack of gene flow via most recent Pleistocene land bridge; however, affinity of orange-eyed Javan ssp *prillwitzi* remains unknown. Future division into 2-3 species highly likely. See also Cream-eyed Bulbul for taxonomy. Common in forest, edge, <1300 m. Singly, pairs or small groups (<6). **ID Ad** dark-brown upperparts; off-white underparts (with more yellow or buff tinge in *prillwitzi*), belly slightly paler than breast; iris white in *simplex* and the heavier-billed *halizonus*, scarlet-red in *perplexus* and the heavier-billed *oblitus*, and paler orange in *prillwitzi*. **Juv/Imm** warmer upperparts; iris blackish, gradually attaining paler colouration (according to ssp) with age. **Voc** Song: monotonous, up-and-downslurred, 2-note "PEE–quick"; sometimes interspersed

with a "whi'-whi'-whi'..." warble, lasting 1–2 sec. Call: (i) quiet, long, trilling "prrrt"; (ii) mewing, descending "weh-weh-weh". **SS** Bornean ssp *perplexus* and *oblitus* separable from similar Asian Red-eyed Bulbul with difficulty and experience: Red-eyed's adult eye colour is best described as dark-orange on a large eye disc, whereas Bornean Cream-vented's is dark scarlet-red on a much smaller-looking eye disc. Cream-vented is sleeker and less dumpy, has colder cast to brown upperparts, contrasting distinctly with off-white underparts (incl. whitish lower flanks), whereas Red-eyed has more brownish suffusion on flanks, reducing body contrast. Red-eyed's beak is proportionately thicker, with beak depth (at bill base) easily as long as the distance from eye to gape, whereas Cream-vented's beak depth is never as long as distance from eye to gape. See also Cream-eyed, Olive-winged, Barusan, Buff-vented, Charlotte's and Spectacled Bulbuls.

Cream-eyed Bulbul *Pycnonotus pseudosimplex* E

L ~16 cm. Monotypic. Little-known cryptic species, in the past erroneously interpreted as eye colour morph of Cream-vented Bulbul. Sound recordings from N Sum indicate species likely to occur there too, further investigation required. Scarce in forest, edge, <1000 m. Singly or pairs. **ID** Slim; striking creamy-whitish eye; olive-brown upperparts and head; whitish underparts show variable brownish suffusion on flanks and breast, often leaving belly and throat to gleam with creamy-yellowish tinge. **Juv/Imm** dark iris. **Voc** Song: series of excited, nasal "tchew–it" or "tchew–it–chew", either in short, rapid series of 1–5 notes, or single notes drawn out over >10 s. Call: short, rapid trill "prrrt", lower-pitched than Cream-vented. **SS** Ad Cream-vented and Asian Red-eyed Bulbuls have red (not pale creamy) eyes. Also appears to have slightly longer, more pointed bill than Cream-vented. Charlotte's Bulbul's eye colour has greyish tinge (see that species for additional differences). Also see Spectacled and Olive-winged Bulbuls.

Asian Red-eyed Bulbul *Pycnonotus brunneus*

L 19 cm. Sundaic. 2 ssp: *brunneus* (Sum–Bor, MPen, Nias); *zapolius* (Anambas). Common in forest, edge, <1000 m. Singly, pairs or small groups (<15). **ID Ad** nondescript; uniform dark-brown, paler underparts; dark-orange to pale-red iris. Ssp *zapolius* slightly darker, more greenish-tinged upperparts. **Juv/Imm** dark iris becoming paler with age; warmer upperparts. **Voc** Song: series of sharp, inflected "prree-prree-prree...". Call: short, twittering "whit-it, whit-it...". **SS** See other drab *Pycnonotus* species (Cream-vented, Cream-eyed, Spectacled, Barusan, Olive-winged). Drab *Iole* species have pale grey (not red) eyes, but see those species for further ID characters.

Spectacled Bulbul *Pycnonotus erythropthalmos*

L 16–18 cm. Sundaic. 2 ssp: *erythropthalmos* (Sum, MPen, Nias, Bangka, Belitung); *salvadorii* (Bor). Fairly common in forest, edge, <1100 m. Singly, pairs or small groups (<6). **ID Ad** olive-brown upperparts, pale-grey face to underparts becoming white on belly; small, rounded head and small bill; scarlet-red iris with diagnostic yellow eyering. Ssp *salvadorii* has darker rear flanks and belly. **Juv/Imm** yellow-tinged underparts; no eyering; dark iris. **Voc** Song: distinct high-pitched series of 3–5 rising, warbled, cheery notes "wip-wip- wi'i'i'i...", occasionally a longer series of notes "wip-wip-wip-dee-dee...". Call: single, short "chip". **SS** Differs from other nondescript *Pycnonotus* bulbuls by smaller size, dark-red eye in combination with yellow eyering (sometimes hard to see), smaller and more rounded head, and smaller bill. With practice, Spectacled's unique body contrast between olive-brown upperparts versus grey underparts gives it away at first glance in good light. Also see Buff-vented and Charlotte's Bulbuls.

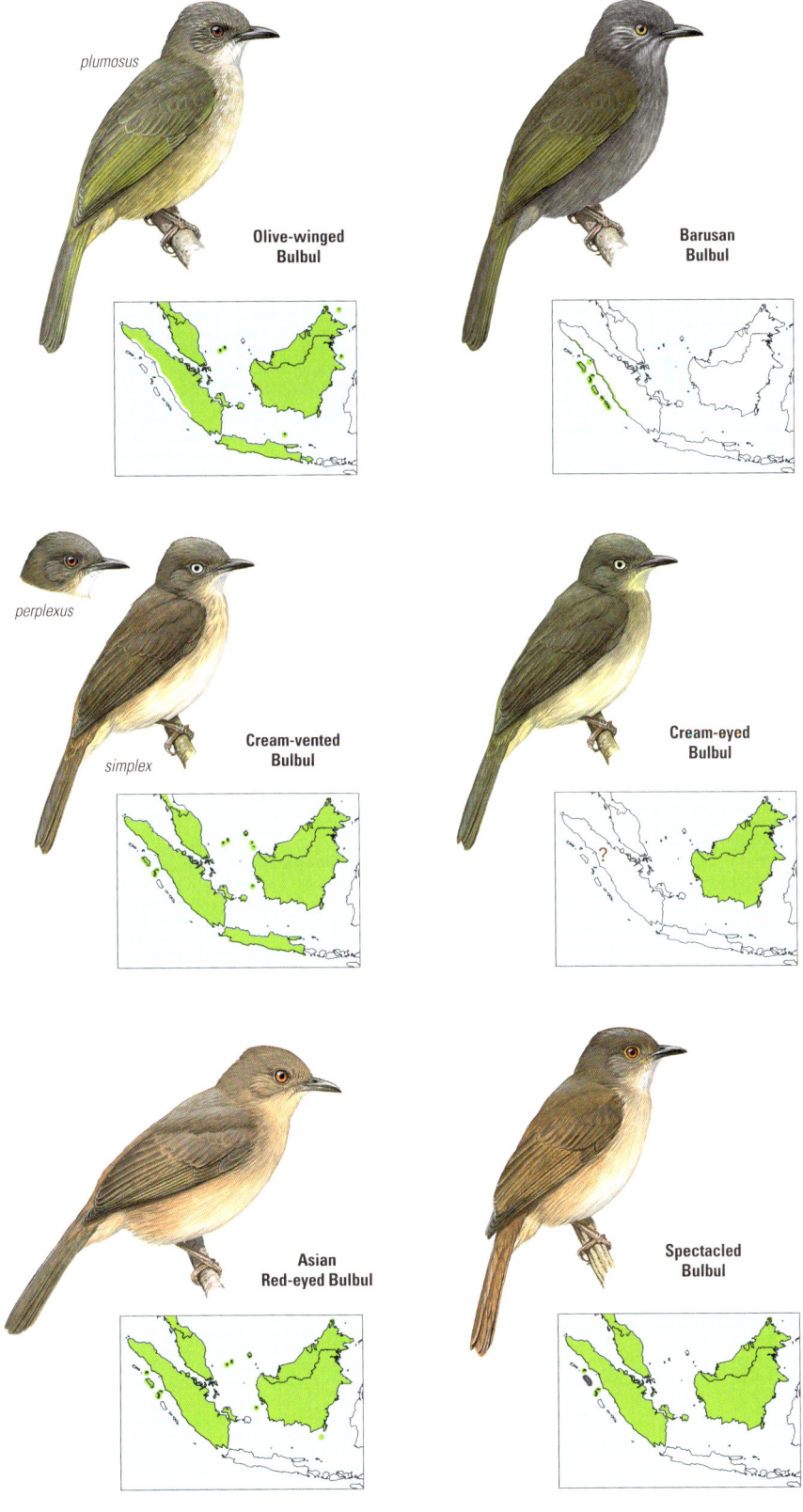

plumosus

Olive-winged Bulbul

Barusan Bulbul

perplexus

simplex

Cream-vented Bulbul

Cream-eyed Bulbul

Asian Red-eyed Bulbul

Spectacled Bulbul

Yellow-bellied Bulbul *Alophoixus phaeocephalus*

L 20–21 cm. Sundaic. 4 ssp: *phaeocephalus* (Sum, Bangka, Belitung, Riau Is, Lingga, Natuna, Mentawai, MPen); *diardi* (W Bor); *connectens* (NE Bor); *sulphuratus* (C–E–S Bor). Confusing taxonomy. Complicated mosaic of plumage traits across range, and deep mtDNA divergence at least between nominate versus the three Bor ssp, suggesting possible separation into **'Malayan Yellow-bellied Bulbul'** *A. phaeocephalus* and **'Bornean Yellow-bellied Bulbul'** *A. sulphuratus* (including *diardi* and *connectens*); more research into vocal and genomic differences required. Fairly common in forest, <1000 m. Singly or pairs, joins mixed flocks; always in understorey. **ID Ad** bluish-grey head; whitish lores and throat; olive-green mantle; rusty wings and tail; bright lemon-yellow underparts with dark-green upper flanks; dark-red iris; greyish-horn bill. Ssp *connectens* as previous but green upper flanks more extensive, and greyish upper breast forming diffuse breast band, deeper yellow belly; *diardi* as previous, but with yellow-tipped tail; *sulphuratus* as previous but breast less grey, more white. **Juv/Imm** darker iris. **Voc** (i) Raspy, buzzing, repeated "kwee kwee kwee…", often only in doublets; (ii) rasping, repeated "chew'it" and "chew'it-chew".

Grey-cheeked Bulbul *Alophoixus tephrogenys*

L 19–21 cm. Sundaic. 2 ssp: *tephrogenys* (MPen, Sum); *gutturalis* (Bor). Taxonomy confused. MtDNA indicates three deep lineages potentially recognizable at the species level: nominate *tephrogenys* and two on Bor (one in Sabah and one in remainder of Bor), but only one name (*gutturalis*) exists for Bor populations. Pronounced plumage differences between nominate and Bor ssp support split, but less is known about plumage distinctions within Bor, and varied song repertoire complicates vocal analysis. Genomic and detailed bioacoustic inquiry required. For taxonomy also see Melodious Bulbul. Formerly fairly common in forest, but becoming rarer due to poaching; <1000 m. Singly or pairs, joins mixed flocks. **ID Ad** rufous erectile crown; pale-grey cheeks; olive mantle; rusty-tinged wings and tail; olive-grey breast; yellow belly and vent; dark-red iris; greyish-horn bill. Ssp *gutturalis* (in Sabah) browner (less olive) upperparts, darker brown crown, darker olive-brown breast, belly more olive, lacking bright yellow tones, becoming buff on vent; elsewhere on Bor underparts are possibly even more brownish-tinged (less olive), with a deeply buff vent. **Imm** lacks crested appearance; more uniform face and upperparts. **Voc** Song: series of variable, thrush-like, rolling notes interspersed with some mimicry, with a typical upslurred note (or double notes) "whit'chooee" at the end; in *gutturalis* notes are less strident, more pure and melodious on average. Call: (1) rolling "brrrrrt"; (2) extended series of "chik-chik-chik-chik-chik-…". **SS** Ochraceous and Penan Bulbuls (ssp *ruficrissus* and *fowleri*) from higher elevations have larger, more erect crests; much browner overall body colouration lacking yellow and olive tones; larger, more conspicuous, white, puffy throat; and lack contrast between grey cheek and brown crown. Penan Bulbul ssp *ruficrissus* and *fowleri* in particular are more massive in size and much darker, more chestnut-brown overall (especially on wings, lower belly and vent). At lower hilly elevations in Meratus Mts (SE Kalimantan), Grey-cheeked co-occurs with extremely similar Penan Bulbul ssp *meratusensis*, which has a more greyish-olive (not brown) crown, more olive (less brownish) upperparts, a deeper buff/cinnamon vent, and brighter yellow (versus olive) underparts.

Ochraceous Bulbul *Alophoixus ochraceus*

L 19–21 cm. Sundaic. 4 ssp, 1 in region: *sumatranus* (Sum). Traditionally includes Penan Bulbul and extralimital taxa from Cambodia and S Vietnam, but none of those appear to be genetically most closely related to Ochraceous. Fairly common in (sub-) montane forest, edge, <2600 m, mainly 500–1700 m. Singly or pairs, joins mixed flocks. **ID Ad** bulky, large-billed with pronounced crest usually held erect; rich brown plumage with rufous-tinged crown, tail and wings; conspicuous white throat often puffed out; underparts solid ochre-brown, darker on vent; dark-red iris. **Imm** more rufous on wings and tail; duller iris; smaller crest. **Voc** Song: repeated series of rapid, evenly-spaced "chik'it-chik'it-chik'it…" notes interspersed with higher-pitched, more musical "tew-tew-tew…" or "tee-tee-tee…", often in duet. Call: raucous, coarse "chrrt chrrt-chrrt…" or "chik-chik-chik…", often in duet. **SS** See Grey-cheeked Bulbul.

Penan Bulbul *Alophoixus ruficrissus*   `E`

L 20–22 cm. 3 ssp: *ruficrissus* (NE Bor); *fowleri* (NW Bor); *meratusensis* (Meratus Mts, SE Kalimantan). Ssp *meratusensis* is deeply diverged in mtDNA and has plumage more reminiscent of Grey-cheeked Bulbul; likely to deserve status as monotypic species **'Meratus Bulbul'**. For taxonomy also see Ochraceous Bulbul. Fairly common in (sub-) montane forest, edge, <2600 m, mainly 500–1700 m. Singly or pairs, joins mixed flocks. **ID Ad** similar to Ochraceous Bulbul but darker, rather more uniform: richer, reddish-tinged upperparts and crown; darker, more greyish-brown underparts with deep rufous vent; diffuse greyish face; dark-red iris. Ssp *fowleri* greyish crest; less rufous plumage. Smaller ssp *meratusensis* distinct, with crown more greyish-olive, sporting smaller crest; breast olive-yellow becoming pure yellow on belly; upperparts olive-tinged; cinnamon vent. **Imm** more rufous on wings and tail; duller iris; smaller crest. **Voc** Song: repeated series of rapid, hard, evenly-spaced notes "ch'chit-choo-choo-choo…" lasting 1–3 sec, with a harsh, rattled opening note, interspersed with call, often in duet. Call: raucous, coarse "brrrt-brrrt-brrrt…" often in duet. Vocalisations of *meratusensis* undescribed. **SS** See Grey-cheeked Bulbul.

Melodious Bulbul *Alophoixus bres*   `E`

L 19–22 cm. Monotypic. Traditionally included Grey-cheeked and extralimital Palawan Bulbul *A. frater* (Palawan) as part of larger umbrella species **'Grey-cheeked Bulbul'** *A. bres*, but all three are deeply diverged genetically and exhibit pronounced vocal and plumage differentiation. Locally still fairly common in primary, secondary and submontane forest, but decreasing because of poaching; <1500 m. Singly or pairs, joins mixed flocks. **ID Ad** rufous erectile crown; brownish cheeks; olive-brown mantle; rusty-tinged wings and tail; pure white throat often puffed out, contrasting with yellow underparts; dark-red iris. **Imm** duller underparts; face pattern more uniform. **Voc** Song: series of mixed, squeaky notes interspersed with typical "kwrresh" call note and staccato series "jogjogjog…". Call: harsh rattle "kwrresh". **AN** Brown-cheeked Bulbul.

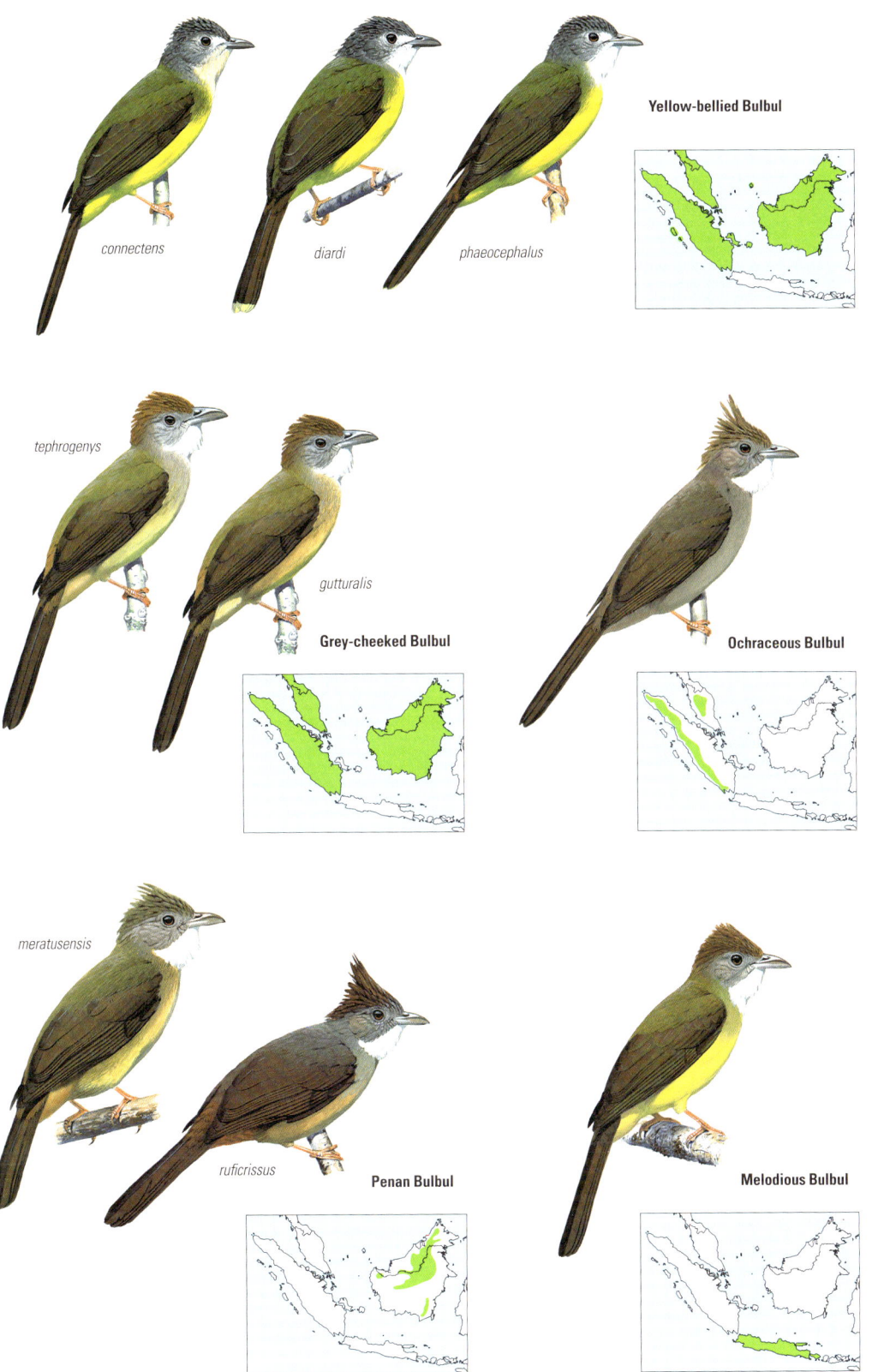

connectens

diardi

phaeocephalus

Yellow-bellied Bulbul

tephrogenys

gutturalis

Grey-cheeked Bulbul

Ochraceous Bulbul

meratusensis

ruficrissus

Penan Bulbul

Melodious Bulbul

Black-headed Bulbul *Microtarsus melanocephalos*

L 16–18 cm. SE Asia, Palawan. 4 ssp: *melanocephalos* (GS, Nias, Mentawai, Palawan, mainland SE Asia); *hyperemnus* (Simeulue); *baweanus* (Bawean); *hodiernus* (Maratua). This species encompasses great plumage polymorphism and deep mtDNA divergence in the absence of pronounced genome-wide differentiation, indicating it may be the product of an ancient species merger. Birds described as '**Blue-wattled Bulbul**' *M. nieuwenhuisii* (rare in Sum–Bor) are almost certainly a rare morph of Black-headed or – less likely – a hybrid between Black-headed and other species. Ssp *hodiernus*, for which genome-wide data appear absent, may deserve recognition as monotypic species '**Maratua Bulbul**' because of moderately deep mtDNA divergence and lack of widespread yellow morph. Fairly common in forest, edge and clearings, <800 m, rarely to 1600 m. Usually pairs or small groups (<10) in canopy, but small-island populations can be abundant and occupy wider ecological conditions. **ID Ad** glossy black head; bright yellowish-green body; broad black subterminal tail band and primaries; blue iris. A rare **grey morph** occurs (almost absent in *melanocephalos*) with yellow being replaced partly, sometimes entirely, by silky-grey. Ssp *nieuwenhuisii* **morph** has a distinctive blue eyering and is greenish-olive overall (brighter yellow on belly) with darker, smudgy, poorly-delimited grey-brown head, throat and subterminal tail band (contrasting with bright yellow tips). Ssp *hyperemnus* has stouter body and thicker bill; *baweanus* larger, with grey morph predominating; *hodiernus* also larger, lacks 'normal' yellow morph, resembles grey morph but much darker overall. **Imm** duller overall, head dull dark-green. **Voc** Song: 5–15 staccato notes "dit-dit-doo-doo-dit-doo-chew-chew...", lasting 1–3 sec. Call: (i) single, hard "chew", occasionally doubled; (ii) glissading "chirrup". Ssp *hodiernus* song: slower, more deliberate, lower-pitched. Call: louder, longer and lower-pitched down-slurred "chew".

Black-and-white Bulbul *Microtarsus melanoleucos*

L 16–18 cm. Sundaic. Monotypic. Nomadic, generally scarce in forest, particularly around fruiting trees, <1500 m, recorded to 3050 m. Singly; unobtrusive. **ID M** all-black except conspicuous white upperwing coverts. **F** brownish-tinged; less white on upperwing-coverts. **Imm** confusing: ashy-brown, lacking white upperwing-coverts; belly pale grey; best identified with accompanying Ad. **Voc** Song: simple, tuneless, metallic "pet-it", regularly repeated. Call: reported "cherlee".

Puff-backed Bulbul *Microtarsus eutilotus*

L 20–22 cm. Sundaic. Monotypic. Uncommon in forest, <1300 m. Singly or pairs; often in canopy, hence widely overlooked. **ID Ad** rich-brown upperparts and tail contrasting with greyish-washed underparts; short crest; brownish-grey head with paler ear-coverts; red iris; strong black bill; white-tipped outertail. **Imm** less cleanly white-tipped outertail. **Voc** Song: short series of 3–8 high-pitched, descending, cheerful warbled notes "tchoo-oowee-eewoo-ewee...", lasting 1 sec. Call: hollow, short "ho". **SS** Distinctive when crest is seen. When crest is not visible, relatively large body size combined with unique contrast between rich-brown back and more greyish head and breast rule out all other drab bulbuls.

Hook-billed Bulbul *Setornis criniger* **E**

L 20 cm. Monotypic. Very local, uncommon in peat-swamp and kerangas forest, very rarely strays to dipterocarp forest, <500 m, very locally to 1000 m. Singly, pairs or small groups (<6). **ID Ad** rufous-brown crown and upperparts; creamy-white underparts; distinctive face pattern: white supercilium wide on lores and narrowing behind eye, thin black eyestripe and malar stripe; pale grey face and throat; tail conspicuously tipped white; large grey-blue bill conspicuously hooked. **Imm** undescribed. **Voc** Loud series of scolding rattled notes "btrt" or "trt", often in duet, occasionally given singly.

Finsch's Bulbul *Iole finschii*

L 17 cm. Sundaic. Monotypic. Locally uncommon in forest, more numerous in alluvial forest, <900 m. Singly or pairs; unobtrusive. **ID Ad** brownish-olive upperparts; subdued greenish-olive breast with lemon-yellow belly and puffed-out throat triangle; short, pinkish-grey bill; orange-brown eyes. **Juv/Imm** paler bill, darker eyes. **Voc** Song: rarely heard, squeaky "chew'twe'twe'twe". Call: nasal, upslurred "skweet". **SS** Finsch's has brighter yellow underparts than other "drab bulbuls", especially the vocally similar but paler-eyed Buff-vented and Charlotte's Bulbuls. Even drab Finsch's individuals always have a lemon tone to their puffed-up throat, compared to conventional white or buff throats on other drab bulbuls.

Charlotte's Bulbul *Iole charlottae* **E**

L 20–21 cm. Monotypic. Unnamed Sabah population exhibits unusual mtDNA divergence from birds elsewhere on Bor and may constitute cryptic species; more research required. For taxonomy also see Buff-vented Bulbul. Fairly common in forest, <1100 m. Singly, pairs or small groups (<10). **ID Ad** rather nondescript: rich-brown sloping flat crown appearing slightly streaked with narrow, black supercilium and pale-greyish iris; brown upperparts and tail (the latter possibly more rufous in populations outside Sabah); creamy-whitish underparts; pinkish-horn bill and legs. **Imm** paler bare parts; darker iris. **Voc** (i) Simple "er-whit", first note upslurred followed by loud, flat, sharp, metallic second note; (ii) flatter, harsher series of fast "er-whirt-whirt-whirt..."; (iii) single, upslurred "whirt". **SS** Superficially similar drab *Pycnonotus* bulbuls have more compact shape, lacking flat sloping crown, have a shorter, thicker, often blacker bill that looks stout and straight (not appearing slightly decurved as in Charlotte's), lack black supercilium and fine crown streaks, and mostly have less rich-brown upperparts and crown. Charlotte's greyish-white eye much paler than dark eyes of Bornean ssp of Cream-vented and other drab bulbuls. Also see Cream-eyed, Olive-winged, Asian Red-eyed and Spectacled for additional differences, and see Finsch's Bulbul.

Buff-vented Bulbul *Iole crypta*

L 20–21 cm. Sundaic. Monotypic. Traditionally includes Charlotte's Bulbul but the two exhibit vocal and deep mtDNA differentiation. Fairly common in forest, <1100 m. Singly, pairs or small groups (<10). **ID Ad** similar to Charlotte's Bulbul but slightly paler ear-coverts; on average duller white, less creamy underparts. **Juv/Imm** duller; paler bare parts; darker iris. **Voc** Similar to Charlotte's but notes typically exhibit greater bandwidth, making them sound more nasal and fractionally higher-pitched. **SS** Superficially similar drab *Pycnonotus* bulbuls have more compact shape, lacking flat sloping crown, have a shorter, thicker, often blacker bill that looks stout and straight (not appearing slightly decurved as in Buff-vented), lack black supercilium and fine crown streaks, and mostly have less rich-brown upperparts and crown. Buff-vented's eye more greyish-tinged, less strikingly white than the big eye-disc of co-occurring Cream-vented. Also see Barusan, Olive-winged, Asian Red-eyed and Spectacled for additional differences, and see Finsch's Bulbul.

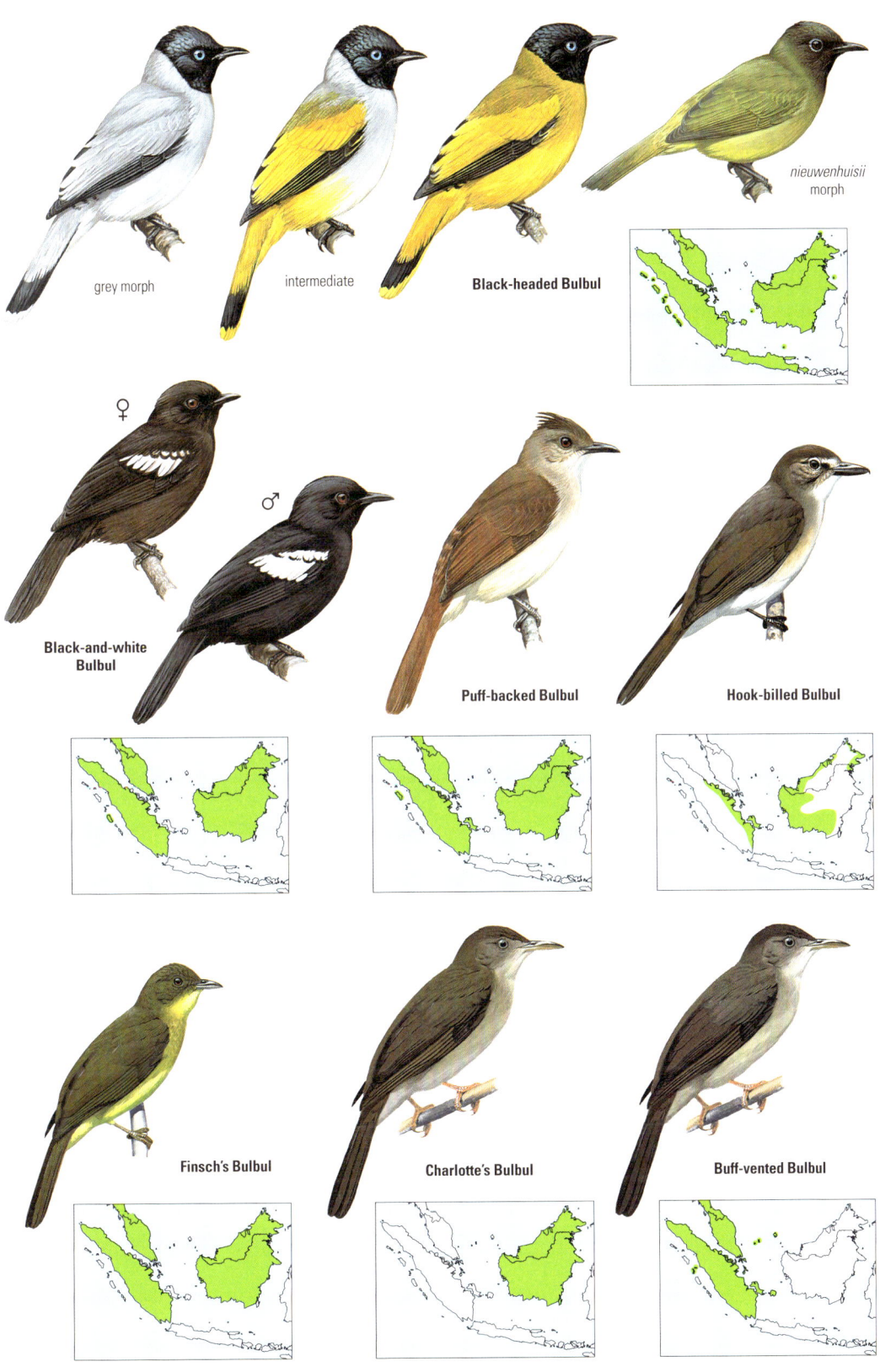

grey morph

intermediate

Black-headed Bulbul

nieuwenhuisii morph

♀

♂

Black-and-white Bulbul

Puff-backed Bulbul

Hook-billed Bulbul

Finsch's Bulbul

Charlotte's Bulbul

Buff-vented Bulbul

Hairy-backed Bulbul *Tricholestes criniger*

L 16–17 cm. Sundaic. 3 ssp: *criniger* (E Sum, MPen, Natuna, Lingga); *sericeus* (W Sum, Batu); *viridis* (Bor). Taxonomy confused: populations from Sabah are deeply diverged in mtDNA and have distinct bill colour, possibly requiring elevation to monotypic species '**Pink-billed Bulbul**' if confirmed by vocal and genome-wide data. However, type locality and specimen for Bor ssp *viridis* probably lost, necessitating nomenclatural resolution. Fairly common in forest, <1000 m. Often in small groups (<10), gleaning foliage more akin to a babbler. Very inquisitive. **ID Ad** big dark button-eye accentuated by extensive yellow on lores and peri-orbital area; yellowish underparts with olive mottling on breast; olive-brown crown and upperparts. Ssp *sericeus* larger with duller vent; *viridis* reported to have marginally brighter upperparts, rear ear-coverts slightly paler. Bill pink in Sabah, dark horn-grey in rest of species range. **Juv/Imm** greyish iris; paler legs. Imm like adult but often much less yellow on underparts, more extensively mottled. **Voc** Song: mix of jumbled, unstructured chatters and warbles, interspersed with a repetitive quavering "whirrh". Call: (i) single, repeated quavering "whirrh"; (ii) single, high-pitched, whistled "wheee". **SS** Less brightly yellow Imm can be confusing and non-descript: watch out for big button-eye contrasting against yellow lores.

Cream-striped Bulbul *Alcurus leucogrammicus* `E`

L 17–18 cm. Monotypic. Fairly common in forest, edge and clearings, 700–1500 m, rarely to 1900 m. Usually in small groups (<10) around fruiting trees. **ID Ad** greyish-brown upperparts, head and breast, the latter two heavily streaked white and contrasting with white throat triangle; olive-tinged wings; orange iris; crown is peaked with modest crest. **Imm** undescribed. **Voc** Song: duet involving one bird producing squeaky "whit-wi'i'ee...", as additional bird(s) may produce a jumble of scratchy coarse notes, eventually building up to a crescendo, swiftly repeated. Call: upslurred "whit" or 3-note "whit-cheh-cheh", latter notes scratchy and quieter. **SS** Larger-sized Sumatran and Streaked Bulbuls have dark-red or dark-orange (not pale orange) iris, lack strongly contrasting white throat triangle, lack strong white facial streaking, have a distinctly longer bill, and lack a pointed crest (although Sumatran may have shaggy crown when excited).

Spot-necked Bulbul *Alcurus tympanistrigus* `E`

L 16 cm. Monotypic. Fairly common in forest, edge and clearings, 500–1400 m, rarely 300–1900 m. Usually pairs or small groups (<10) around fruiting trees. **ID Ad** yellow crescent-like rear ear-covert patch; olive-brown upperparts and crown; brownish underparts streaked white, vent yellow; bare black skin patch around eye confers small-headed appearance. **Imm** undescribed. **Voc** Song: disyllabic "tdip-diew", first note higher. Call: repeated, emphatic "jret-jret-jtry".

Cinereous Bulbul *Hemixos cinereus*

L 21 cm. Sundaic. 2 ssp: *cinereus* (Sum, MPen); ssp *connectens* (Bor) is sometimes separated into monotypic species '**Green-winged Bulbul**' because of colouration differences. Fairly common in submontane forest, usually 500–1500 m, eruptions can reach lowlands and 2000 m. Singly, pairs or small groups (<10), joins mixed flocks. **ID Ad** diagnostic black facial patch; greyish-brown upperparts and crown with elongated crown feathers pale-tipped, often raised; pure white, shaggy throat contrasting with pale grey breast and white belly. Ssp *connectens* less distinctly black on face; upperwing and tail bright olive-yellow, with yellowish vent. **Imm** less distinct face pattern; paler bare parts. **Voc** Song: monotonous, simple "brrt ditdeet dit-deet..." regularly repeated, can last >2 min. Call: (i) whining "whear"; (ii) sharp "chyap"; (iii) double "wheesh-wheesh".

Streaked Bulbul *Ixos malaccensis*

L 23 cm. Sundaic. Monotypic. Fairly common in forest, <1200 m. Singly, pairs or small groups (<10). **ID Ad** elongated appearance featuring long, thick, greyish-horn, dagger-like bill with pinkish lower mandible base; olive upperparts; greyish throat and breast with coarse and blotchy white streaks; white belly; dark-orange iris. **Imm** breast less distinctly marked; upperparts less olive, more brownish; bill more pinkish-horn. **Voc** Song: thin, high-pitched, squeaky, descending notes "cheew-cheew-cheew", occasionally with additional, more varied notes, especially its typical call note. Call: loud, harsh, rattled "chrreet", often given in flight. **SS** See Sumatran and Cream-striped Bulbuls.

Javan Bulbul *Ixos virescens* `E`

L 20 cm. Monotypic. Traditionally included Sumatran Bulbul as part of larger '**Sunda Bulbul**' *I. virescens*, but pronounced plumage and vocal differences dictate break-up. Uncommon in (sub-) montane forest, 800–3000 m. Singly, pairs or small groups (<10), joins mixed flocks. **ID Ad** steep grey crown; olive-green upperparts; white throat contrasting with dark-olive breast with bold white streaks fading towards lower belly. **Imm** duller. **Voc** Song: endless series of "twink" and thinner notes at different frequencies at 2 n/s. Call: cheery single "twink", regularly repeated at short intervals.

Sumatran Bulbul *Ixos sumatranus* `E`

L 20 cm. Monotypic. For taxonomy see Javan Bulbul. Uncommon in (sub-) montane forest, 850–2500 m. Singly, pairs or small groups (<10), joins mixed flocks. **ID Ad** bronzed olive-brown upperparts and shaggy crest with steep forehead; throat, face and breast slightly paler than upperparts, with white shaft streaks extending to white belly; dark-red iris; blackish-horn bill. **Imm** duller; less distinct streaking. **Voc** Song undescribed. Call: short, sharp, high-pitched "swit", sometimes doubled-up, "swit-it". **SS** Streaked Bulbul has more greenish-olive (less brown) upperparts; has paler, greyish throat and breast with blotchy white streaks (not dark olive-brown throat and breast with fine white streaks); has more orange (less dark-red) eye colour; and has pinkish base to lower mandible on a paler grey bill (not all-blackish bill). See also Cream-striped Bulbul.

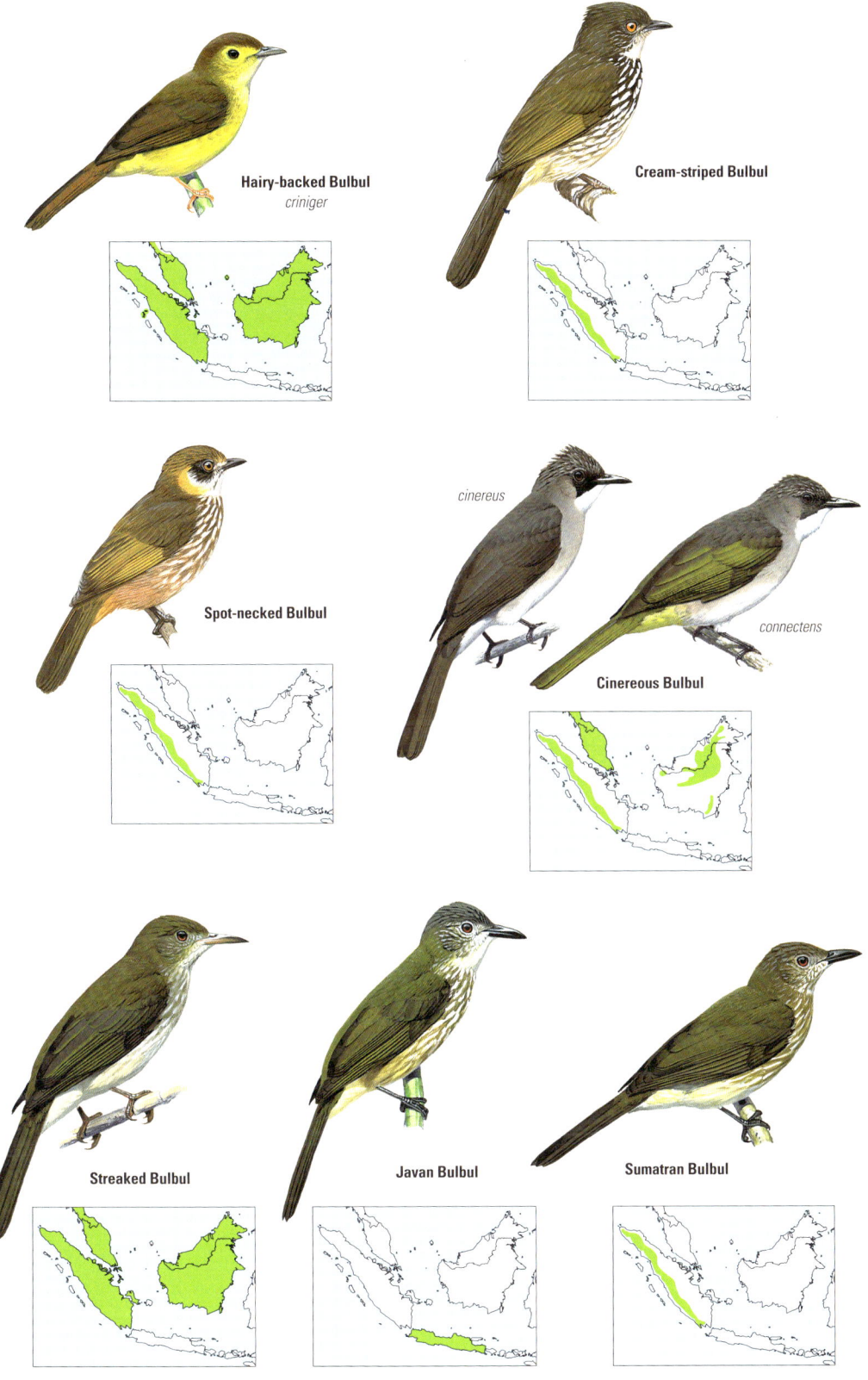

Hairy-backed Bulbul
criniger

Cream-striped Bulbul

Spot-necked Bulbul

cinereus

connectens

Cinereous Bulbul

Streaked Bulbul

Javan Bulbul

Sumatran Bulbul

Seram Golden Bulbul *Hypsipetes affinis* E

L 23 cm. 2 ssp: *affinis* (Seram); *flavicaudus* (Ambon). All eight *Hypsipetes* golden bulbuls traditionally merged into one broadly-defined umbrella species, '**Golden Bulbul**' *H. affinis*, but large range of morphological and bioacoustic differences argues against such a treatment. Ssp *flavicaudus* is vocally distinct, perhaps warranting monotypic species status as '**Ambon Golden Bulbul**'; more research required. Fairly common in primary, secondary and degraded forest, mixed plantations. Usually pairs or small groups (<10). **ID Ad** olive-green upperparts and uppertail with bright yellow distal third; paler, more yellowish underparts; bright yellow throat, undertail and vent; small yellow loral spot; yellow-tipped rump feathers. Ssp *flavicaudus* with slightly more yellow, less olive on tail. **Imm** undescribed. **Voc** Song: ssp *affinis* utters series of 5–10 drawn-out, scratchy, flat whistles, each slightly longer than previous, with final 2 notes slower, throatier "WE–WEE–WEE–WEEE–WEEE–WUU-WUU", lasting 3–5 sec. Song of *flavicaudus* comprises ~12 whistles, fairly flat "we-wo-we-we-we-wo-we-wo-we-we-wo-woo", lasting <4 s. Call: buzzy, inflected, whistled "bzzt".

Buru Golden Bulbul *Hypsipetes mysticalis* E

L 21 cm. Monotypic. For taxonomy see Seram Golden Bulbul. Fairly common in primary, secondary and degraded forest, mixed plantations. Usually pairs or small groups (<10). **ID Ad** uniform olive-green with distinct yellow lores, upper eye margin, chin and vent; comparatively short tail. **Imm** undescribed. **Voc** Song: long and drawn-out, initially a series of "chet" notes, followed by a long series of glissading notes "pip up-pip up WEE–WEE–WEE–pwee-pwee-pwee-wir-WEE–WEE...", lasting 5–15 sec, often in duet. Call: drawn-out, deflected "teeeew".

Togian Golden Bulbul *Hypsipetes aureus* E

L 21–22 cm. Monotypic. See Seram Golden Bulbul for taxonomy. Fairly common in primary, secondary and degraded forest, mixed plantations. Usually pairs or small groups (<10). **ID Ad** dark olive-green head and upperparts; golden-yellow throat and underparts, slightly paler lores; narrow yellow tail fringe; brownish-red iris. **Imm** duller; paler iris. **Voc** Song: rapid series of sharp notes followed by loud jumble of short whistes "didlyDOOdidlyDOOdidlyDOOdoodododo...", accelerating and tailing off in latter half. Call: short, sharp "charp".

Sangihe Golden Bulbul *Hypsipetes platenae* E

L 21–22 cm. Monotypic. For taxonomy see Seram Golden Bulbul. Very rare in remnant native forest, >900 m. Usually pairs or small groups (<5). **ID Ad** uniform olive-green; vivid-yellow lores extending to eyering; yellow ear-coverts, throat and vent; dark-red iris. **Imm** duller; paler iris. **Voc** Song: 4 nasal, rich, inflected notes followed by several high-pitched, quirky whistles "kwee-kwee-kwee-kwee-DEEP-pDEEP-pDEEP...", lasting 3–5 sec, often in duet. Call: inflected, warbled "bwit".

Halmahera Golden Bulbul *Hypsipetes chloris* E

L 20 cm. Monotypic. For taxonomy see Seram Golden Bulbul. Fairly common in primary, secondary and degraded forest, mixed plantations. Usually pairs or small groups (<10). **ID Ad** uniform olive-green; slightly paler underparts and paler, yellower throat; dusky lores; dark-red iris. **Imm** duller; paler iris. **Voc** Song: series of 8–15 drawn-out, high-pitched, descending whistles "WE–WEE–WEEE–WEEE–WEEEEW..." lasting 0.5 sec. Call: thin, quiet "see".

Obi Golden Bulbul *Hypsipetes lucasi* E

L 21 cm. Monotypic. For taxonomy see Seram Golden Bulbul. Fairly common in primary, secondary and degraded forest, mixed plantations. Usually pairs or small groups (<10). **ID Ad** pale olive-green upperparts; bright yellow underparts and loral spot; blackish chip at gape. **Imm** undescribed. **Voc** (i) 3–4 flat, nasal "too-too-too..." notes; (ii) descending, then rising, high-pitched "TSEEooooeeee" note, lasting 0.7 sec; (iii) thin, high-pitched, sharp "zoo-WIT", regularly repeated.

Sula Golden Bulbul *Hypsipetes longirostris* E

L 23–24 cm. Monotypic. For taxonomy see Seram Golden Bulbul. Fairly common in primary, secondary and degraded forest, mixed plantations. Usually pairs or small groups (<10). **ID Ad** olive-green head, upperparts and tail; olive-yellow underparts and tertials; yellow-fringed rectrices; large, long bill and long tail. **Imm** undescribed. **Voc** Song: rapid series of accelerating "charrr" notes, often in bouts of different frequencies, "charrr charrr churrr churrr churrr...", followed by loud jumble of short whistes "didlyDOOdidlyDOOdidly-DOO...". Call: (i) rolling, throaty "charrr"; (ii) alarm call a loud, high-pitched, nasal, piercing "week", variably rising, descending or both, often repeated in quick succession.

Banggai Golden Bulbul *Hypsipetes harterti* E

L 23–24 cm. Monotypic. For taxonomy see Seram Golden Bulbul. Fairly common in primary, secondary and degraded forest, mixed plantations. Usually pairs or small groups (<10). **ID Ad** similar to Sula Golden but darker olive breast contrasting with clear yellow throat, slightly darker upperparts; undertail broadly tipped yellow. **Imm** undescribed. **Voc** Song variable, includes: (i) introductory "chupp" notes followed by abrupt, melodious "chrrreeyoo" or "chreewee"; (ii) melodious, throaty "che-chrrreeyee-doo" with last note lower-pitched. Call: (i) melodious "chrreewee", same motif as used in many songs; (ii) unmelodious churring noises.

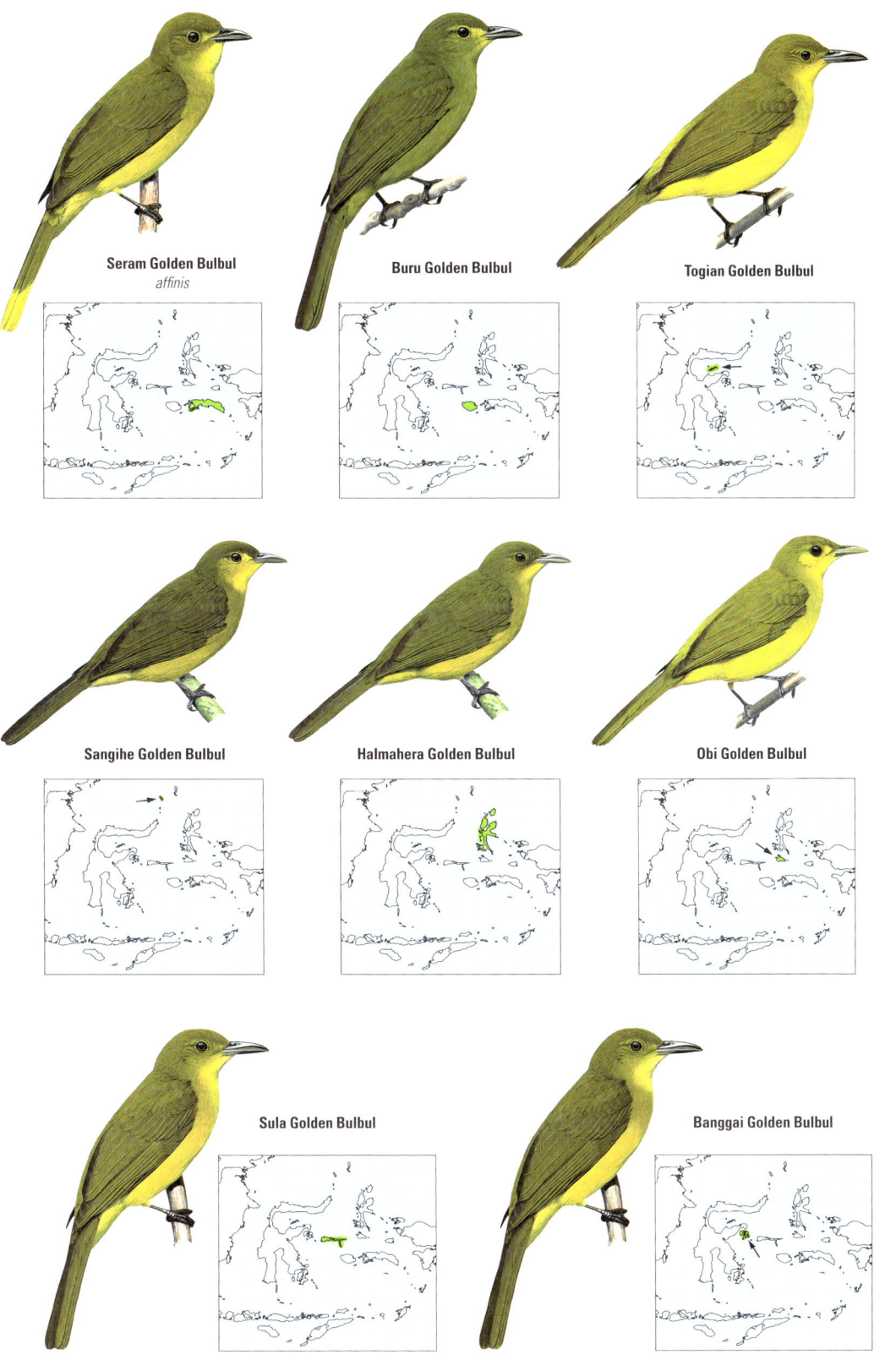

Seram Golden Bulbul
affinis

Buru Golden Bulbul

Togian Golden Bulbul

Sangihe Golden Bulbul

Halmahera Golden Bulbul

Obi Golden Bulbul

Sula Golden Bulbul

Banggai Golden Bulbul

TIMALIIDAE
Tit Babblers, Scimitar Babblers and allies
22 species in region

Diverse family of small to medium-sized birds from forest and edge. Often forage for invertebrates in the low to upper storey, frequently as part of mixed flocks. Many family members are dead-leaf specialists dependent on thick viny tangles with dead leaf clusters. Numerous species exhibit distinct duetting behaviour.

Chestnut-capped Babbler *Timalia pileata*
L 16–17 cm. S–SE–E Asia. 6 ssp, 1 in region: *pileata* (Jav–Bali). Due to poaching, now rare in rank grassland, marsh, cultivation, reed-beds, <1400 m. Pairs or small groups (<10), elusive in dense vegetation, rarely sits out. **ID Ad** striking head pattern: thick black lores and eyestripe, white face and forecrown with chestnut crown and grey nape; thick black bill; mid-brown upperparts; lightly streaked white breast; buff belly. **Imm** duller; head pattern less distinct; warmer brown upperparts; lacks breast streaking. **Voc** (i) Soft, husky notes followed by higher, stuttering notes "wer-wer-wer-witch-it-it'it'it", lasting 1.5 sec; (ii) loud, melodious, upslurred disyllabic "too'wit-too'wit". Call: excited, repeated "pik-pik-pik".

Pin-striped Tit Babbler *Mixornis gularis*
L 11–12 cm. S–SE Asia, Palawan. 13 ssp, 1 in region: *gularis* (Sum, MPen). Traditionally included Bold-striped as part of larger umbrella species, '**Striped Tit Babbler**' *M. gularis*, but modern taxonomic treatments separate them based on vocalisations, genomic divergence and plumage. Some extralimital ssp of Pin-striped exhibit additional unusual vocal, mtDNA and apparently genome-wide differentiation; more research required. See Bold-striped for additional taxonomic information. Common in secondary and degraded forest, peat-swamp, edge, scrub and plantations with understorey, <1500 m. Usually pairs or small groups (<5), forages in understorey. **ID Ad** rufous crown, wings and tail; olive mantle; yellowish face and underparts with brighter supercilium; narrow blackish throat streaking; blue loral skin. **Imm** more uniform, duller overall with indistinct throat streaking. **Voc** Song: series of <40 barbet-like continuous knocking "chonk-chonk-chonk..." at 3 n/s. Call: (i) harsh "chrrrt-chrr", or "chrrrt-chrr-chrr"; (ii) longer, harsher, rolling "tititit-chrreeoo" or "chrreeoo".

Bold-striped Tit Babbler *Mixornis bornensis*
L 11–12 cm. Sundaic, Cagayan Sulu (Phil). 9 ssp, 8 in region: *bornensis* (Bor except NE, Bangka, Belitung); *zopherus* (Anambas); *everetti* (Bunguran in N Natuna); *zaperissus* (other islands in N Natuna); *argenteus* (Banggi, Malawali); *montanus* (NE Bor); *javanicus* (W–C Jav); isolated ssp *prillwitzi* (Kangean) traditionally included with Javan Tit Babbler and sometimes separated as monotypic species '**Kangean Tit Babbler**' but vocal data suggest affinity with Bold-striped; more research needed. Bioacoustic and plumage data indicate some trait admixture from Pin-striped Tit Babbler into Bold-striped ssp *everetti* on Natuna, suggesting that Bold-striped races on small islands between Borneo and mainland may have experienced genetic introgression via land bridges during recent global cooling cycles. For taxonomy also see Pin-striped. Common in secondary and degraded forest, peat-swamp, edge, scrub and plantations with understorey, <1500 m. Usually pairs or small groups (<5), forages in understorey. **ID Ad** grey face, chestnut crown and upperparts, underparts creamy-white with thick blackish streaking, piercingly pale iris; *javanicus* as previous but paler overall with lighter streaking, grey-buff face; *montanus* as *bornensis* but greyish tinge to crown and mantle; *argenteus* as previous but even greyer crown and less streaking; *everetti* looks intermediate between *bornensis* and Pin-striped *gularis* with chestnut crown becoming less reddish on back, lime-yellow throat and breast turning white on belly, and intermediate breast streaking not pin-like, yet also not bold either; *zaperissus* as previous but with narrower streaking and paler above; *zopherus* similar to previous but paler overall, more heavily streaked underparts; *prillwitzi* greyish-brown head and no underparts streaking. **Imm** more uniform, duller overall, unstreaked and with buffish underparts. **Voc** Song: often duets unlike Pin-striped, uttering 3–6 undulating, melodious, knocking notes "oo'choot-oo'choot-oo'choot", at 3 n/s, or 3–8 barbet-like melodious, knocking notes "chock-chock-chock...". Call: (i) harsh "chrrrt-chrr", or "chrrrt-chrr-chrr"; (ii) longer, harsher, rolling "tititit-chrreeoo" or "chrreeoo". **SS** See Javan Tit Babbler and Chestnut-rumped Babbler.

Javan Tit Babbler *Mixornis flavicollis*　🟩E
L 13–14 cm. Monotypic. See Bold-striped Tit Babbler for taxonomy. Uncommon in variety of woodland, edge, <1000 m. Usually pairs or small groups (<5), forages in understorey. **ID Ad** pale grey face; bright cinnamon-buff throat and breast with vestigial, indistinct streaking; belly whitish; crown and upperparts olive-rufous; pale iris. **Imm** undescribed. **Voc** Song: similar to Pin-striped but lower in pitch, monotonous series of 4–30 even bell-like notes "choot-choot-choot..." at 4 n/s, repeated after short pauses. Call: (i) husky, harsh "chukut"; (ii) rasping "chrrrt", "chot'rt" or "chrrr'rrp". **SS** Sympatric Bold-striped Tit Babbler ssp *javanicus* has distinct blackish breast streaking on more uniform creamy-white underparts, whereas Javan has strong contrast between white belly and buff-cinnamon breast with hardly visible streaking. **AN** Grey-cheeked Tit Babbler.

Fluffy-backed Tit Babbler *Macronus ptilosus*
L 16–17 cm. Sundaic. 2 ssp: *ptilosus* (Sum, Batu, MPen); *trichorrhos* (Bor, Bangka, Belitung). Fairly common in forest, peat-swamp, edge, <1000 m. Usually pairs or small groups (<5), forages in understorey. **ID Ad** rufous crown; broad black throat; blue orbital and loral skin; dark rufous-brown body; elongated lower back plumes difficult to perceive in the field. Ssp *trichorrhos* is paler, particularly on face and breast. **Imm** duller; paler orbital skin. **Voc** Song: repeated series of 2–5 hollow, rather low-pitched "puh puh-puh-puh..." lasting ~1.5 sec. Call: low, husky, rasping scratches and frog-like croaking "aahkhh-eahh-ehh", often in duet with song.

Golden Babbler *Cyanoderma chrysaeum*
L 10–12 cm. Himalaya to SE Asia. 6 ssp, 1 in region: *frigidum* (Sum). Fairly common in (sub-) montane forest; >600 m. Usually pairs or small groups in understorey (<10). **ID Ad** bright yellow black-streaked crown; blackish lores; green-olive face, nape and flanks; yellow underparts; darker olive upperparts. **Imm** much duller; less streaking on olive crown; washed-out face; whitish belly. **Voc** Song very similar to Rufous-fronted Babbler but tends to give clearer notes and longer pause between introductory note and subsequent ones. Call: descending, soft rattle "trrrrr".

Rufous-fronted Babbler *Cyanoderma rufifrons*
L 12 cm. S–SE Asia. 9 ssp, 2 in region: *poliogaster* (Sum, N–C Bor, MPen); *sarawacense* (W Bor). Deep mtDNA differentiation of extralimital ssp in northwest of range may necessitate taxonomic split in the future. More research into bioacoustics, genomics and morphology required. Scarce in forest, particularly hill forest, <1500 m. Singly or pairs; usually in mid-storey and canopy (hence widely overlooked). **ID Ad** rufous crown; grey-tinged supercilium; olive-grey face; buff-tinged breast with thin but distinct throat streaking; whitish belly; olive-brown upperparts. Ssp *sarawacense* brighter crown; slightly greyer face. **Imm** paler crown; rufous-tinged wings; paler underparts. **Voc** Song: repeated series of 5–10 piping whistles "tuh tuh-tuh-tuh...", lasting 1–1.5 sec. Call: (i) quirky rolling "wirrrree"; (ii) soft "wit".

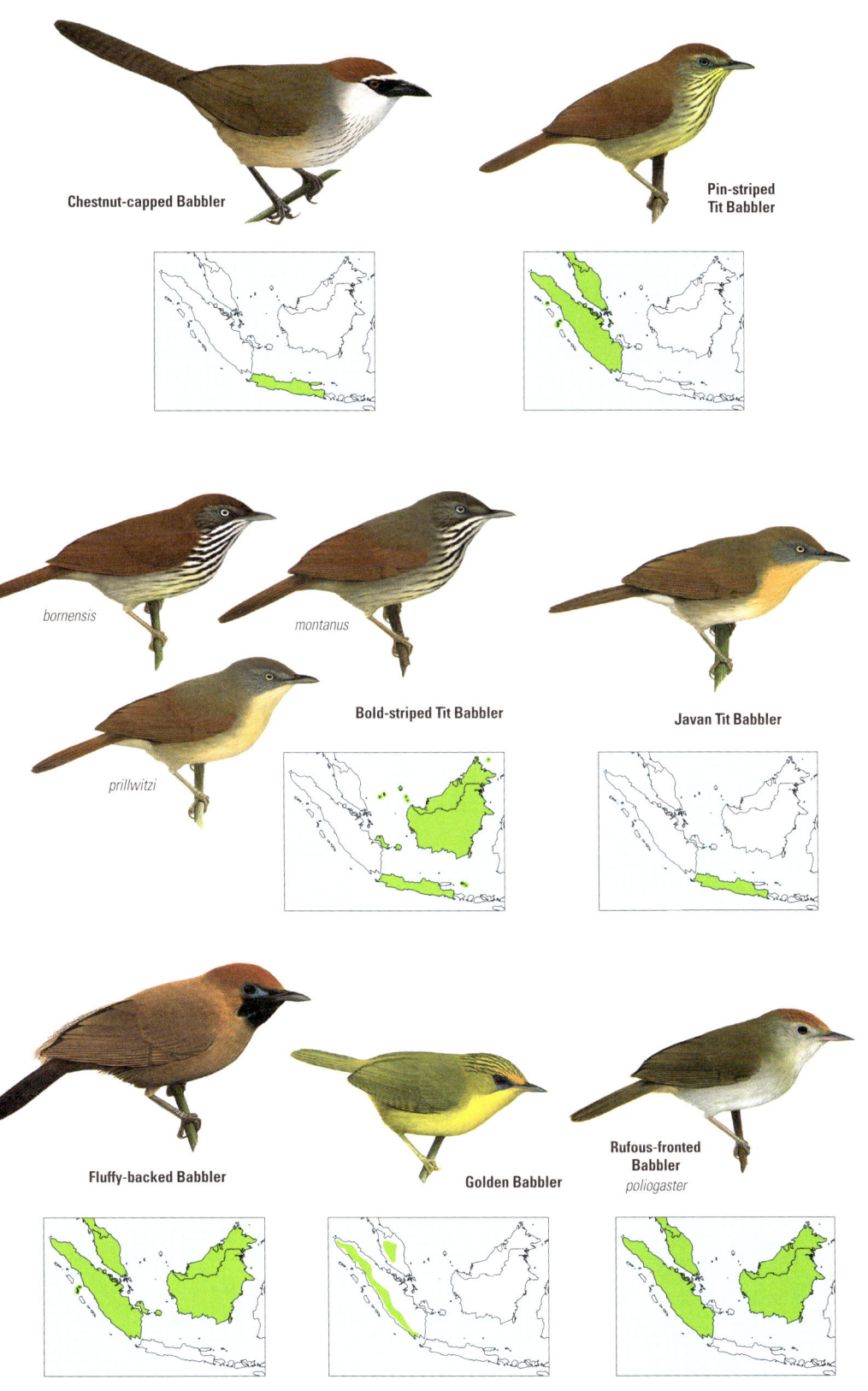

Chestnut-capped Babbler

Pin-striped Tit Babbler

bornensis

montanus

prillwitzi

Bold-striped Tit Babbler

Javan Tit Babbler

Fluffy-backed Babbler

Golden Babbler

Rufous-fronted Babbler
poliogaster

Chestnut-winged Babbler *Cyanoderma erythropterum*
L 12–13 cm. Sundaic. 3 ssp: *erythropterum* (Natuna, MPen); *pyrrhophaeum* (Sum, Batu, Bangka, Belitung); *fulviventre* (Banyak). Natuna population has seemingly distinct plumage; currently merged with nominate but may be separate ssp. For taxonomy also see Bicoloured Babbler. Fairly common in forest, <1200 m. Singly or pairs; in understorey. Mainly forages in dead leaves. **ID Ad** blue orbital skin; ash-grey face and breast; buffish belly; rufous crown and upperparts. Unnamed population on Natuna appears paler on underparts, especially belly and flanks. Ssp *pyrrhophaeum* darker greyish breast; *fulviventre* even darker grey face and breast, grey-tinged belly. **Imm** less rufous upperparts; paler underparts. **Voc** Song: repeated series of 7–13 hollow, piping notes "uh-huh-huh-huh…" at ~10 n/s, sometimes accompanied by low "chrrr" and squeaky "tew-tew" from mate. Call: low, harsh, scolding "trrrt" and when agitated various odd croaks and squeaks.

Bicoloured Babbler *Cyanoderma bicolor* `E`
L 12–13 cm. 2 ssp: *bicolor* (N Bor); *rufum* (S Bor). Traditionally included with Chestnut-winged Babbler, but genomic signature indicates lack of gene flow during times of land connection, accompanied by pronounced differences in plumage and voice. Fairly common in forest, <1200 m. Singly or pairs; in understorey. Mainly forages in dead leaves. **ID Ad** blue orbital skin; dark grey head to lower breast; rich buff belly; rich chestnut upperparts. Ssp *rufum* richer upperparts. **Imm** less rich upperparts; paler underparts. **Voc** Song: introductory note separated from main series of 7–13 hollow, piping notes "puh uh-huh-huh-huh…", at ~10 n/s, sometimes accompanied by low "chrrr" and squeaky "tew-tew" from mate. Call: low, harsh, scolding "trrrt" and when agitated various odd croaks and squeaks. **AN** Grey-hooded Babbler.

Crescent-chested Babbler
Cyanoderma melanothorax `E`
L 13 cm. 3 ssp: *melanothorax* (W–C Jav); *intermedium* (E Jav); *baliense* (Bali). Fairly common in forest, more tolerant of disturbed forest than other *Cyanoderma* babblers. Singly or pairs; in understorey, <2000 m. **ID Ad** pale grey face; thin black malar stripe and distinctive black crescent separating white throat from pale-grey breast; crown and upperparts rufous with brighter wings; buffish belly. Ssp *intermedium* sometimes more buff on breast; *baliense* buff breast and buff-tinged throat, longer bill. **Imm** undescribed. **Voc** Song: fast, rolling series of 7–25 slightly descending piping notes "pr-r-r-r…" at 10–20 n/s. Call: soft low churring "tchrr".

Javan Scimitar Babbler *Pomatorhinus montanus* `E`
L 21 cm. 2 ssp: *montanus* (W–C Jav); *ottolanderi* (E Jav, Bali). See Sunda Scimitar for taxonomy. Introduced population now common on Mt Rinjani (Lombok). Uncommon, locally now rare, in montane forest, 1000–2200 m. Usually in noisy, small groups (<10) in mid-storey. **ID Ad** sooty-black head with thin white supercilium; long decurved yellow bill; white underparts; dull rufous upperparts and flanks with darker long tail. Ssp *ottolanderi* has supercilium only behind eye. **Imm** rufous-washed face; reduced flanks; paler rufous upperparts. **Voc** Song variable: (i) excited, ascending 3-note "wuh-wuh-wee", third note throaty; (ii) repeated, excited, upslurred "wu-pu wu-pu wu-pu…", often in duet with mate producing third note, a higher, throaty "wee"; (iii) 5–10 fast, repeated, hollow "wu-hu-hu-hu…", often in duet with previous songs. Call: harsh "whit-it-it-it…" and "whip".

Sunda Scimitar Babbler *Pomatorhinus bornensis*
L 19 cm. Sundaic. 2 ssp: *bornensis* (Bor, Bangka); *occidentalis* (Sum, MPen). Traditionally included with Javan Scimitar to form '**Chestnut-backed Scimitar Babbler**' *P. montanus*, but separated based on colouration, vocalisations and habits. Uncommon in forest, <1200 m, rarely to 1800 m. Singly or pairs; in mid-storey. **ID Ad** similar to Javan Scimitar Babbler but shorter, pale horn-coloured bill; broader supercilium; glossy black crown; brighter rufous mantle; shorter rufous tail; and reduced rufous on flanks. Ssp *occidentalis* paler tail and wings; darker crown. **Imm** rufous-washed face; reduced flanks; paler rufous upperparts. **Voc** Song: 2–3 clear, harsh, hollow whistled notes "woi-whu-whu" varying greatly in delivery, usually level or descending, typically preceded by a rapid short series of similar notes.

Black Scimitar Babbler *Melanocichla lugubris*
L 25–27 cm. Sundaic. Monotypic. Traditionally merged with Bare-headed Scimitar Babbler but pronounced morphological and vocal differences support separation. In the past, the two were erroneously placed within laughingthrushes ("Black Laughingthrush"), but genetic evidence indicates placement with scimitar babblers. Now scarce and local in submontane forest, 500–1600 m. Usually in groups (<20), joins mixed flocks. **ID Ad** blackish with pale blue bare skin behind eye; reddish bill; blue gular pouch inflates when singing. **Imm** more brownish-tinged, particularly on wings. **Voc** Usually duets in an amazing sequence: starting with <80 loud, odd "okh-okh-okh…" at 8 n/s, then <20 loud, hollow "huup-huup-huup…" at 4 n/s, interspersed with curious "awk" notes. During song birds inflate their gular pouch and raise back feathers. **AN** Black Laughingthrush.

Bare-headed Scimitar Babbler *Melanocichla calva* `E`
L 25–26 cm. Monotypic. See Black Scimitar Babbler for taxonomy. Scarce and local in (sub-) montane forest, 800–1900 m. Usually pairs or small groups (<6), often foraging with Sunda Laughingthrushes, favouring mid- and upper canopy. **ID Ad** bare yellowish-brown skin on crown and lores to just below eye; red bill; blue gular pouch inflates when singing; rest of plumage sooty black with brownish tinge. **Imm** crown has sparse blackish feathering. **Voc** Usually duets in an amazing sequence: starting with <10 loud, odd, repeated "yow-yow-yow…", then <20 loud, hollow "ooh-ooh-ooh…" at 2 n/s, with duetting partner (presumed fem) uttering a curious, higher-pitched "how-how-how…". During song, birds inflate their gular pouch and raise back feathers. **AN** Bare-headed Laughingthrush.

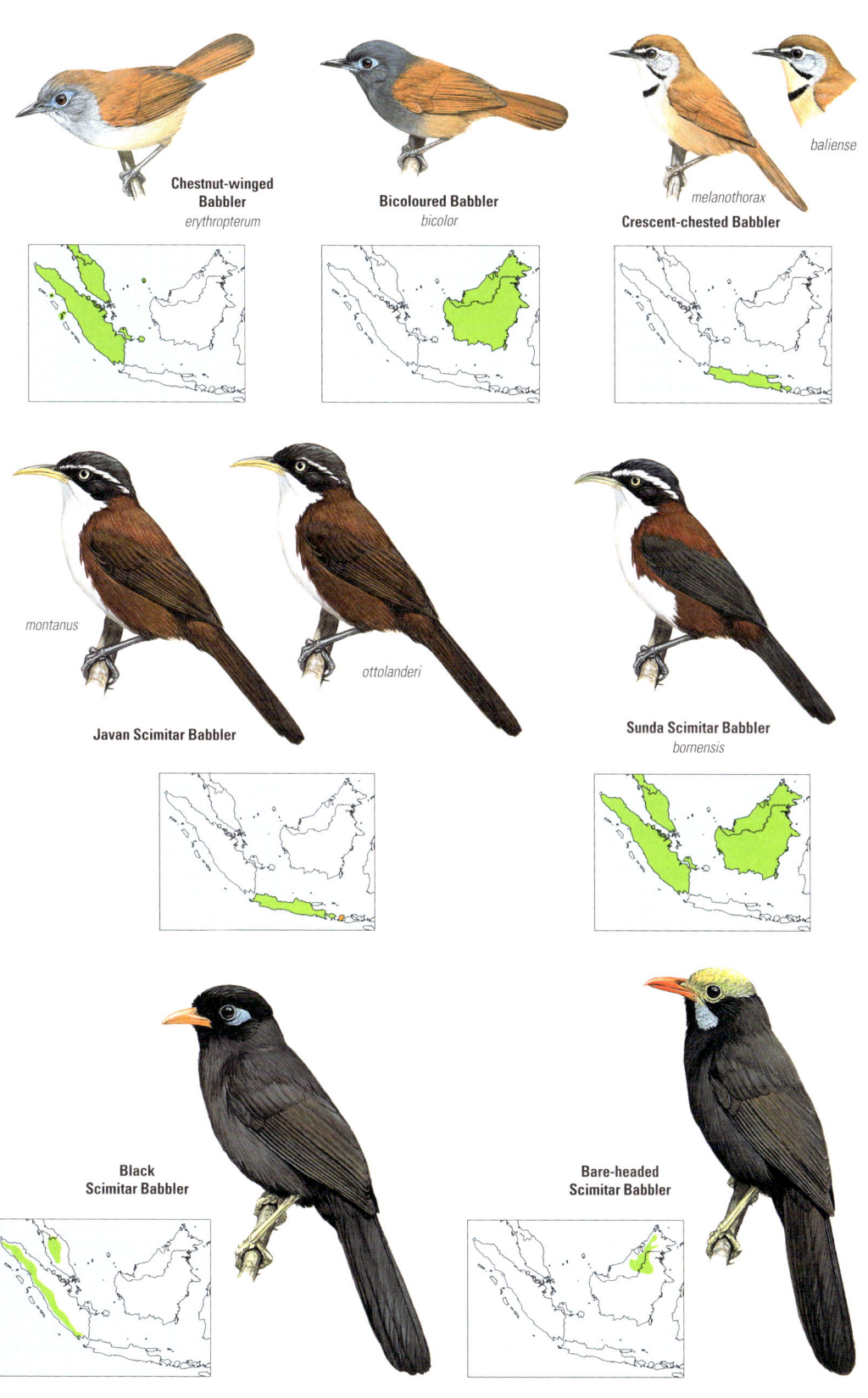

Chestnut-winged Babbler
erythropterum

Bicoloured Babbler
bicolor

baliense

melanothorax

Crescent-chested Babbler

montanus

ottolanderi

Javan Scimitar Babbler

Sunda Scimitar Babbler
bornensis

Black Scimitar Babbler

Bare-headed Scimitar Babbler

White-bibbed Babbler *Stachyris thoracica* [E]
L 18 cm. 2 ssp: *thoracica* (W Jav); *orientalis* (C–E Jav). The two ssp may be separable into monotypic species, '**Western**' and '**Eastern White-bibbed Babbler**', respectively, because of minor plumage differences; more research needed in potential contact zone. Uncommon in submontane forest, 600–1600 m. Forages in small groups (<20) in understorey. **ID Ad** striking head pattern: black face and throat, blue orbital skin; broad white breast band and chestnut crown and body; chunky bill. Ssp *orientalis* has blackish crown. **Imm** undescribed. **Voc** (i) Single, deflected whistle "wrrruu", lasting 0.8 sec; (ii) chattering interspersed with short and long rattles "chit-chit-chit…" and "u-wrrrrr", multiple birds typically calling together.

White-necked Babbler *Stachyris leucotis*
L 14–15 cm. Sundaic. 3 ssp, 2 in region: *sumatrensis* (Sum); *obscurata* (Bor). Undescribed Sabah population distinctly differs from all other populations in mtDNA and main song; may constitute cryptic undescribed species ('**Fluting Babbler**'). Scarce in forest, <1000 m. Singly or pairs; favours thickets on slopes. **ID Ad** striking head pattern: dark-grey crown; black throat triangle; grey face bordered by broad white supercilium and white auricular spots; buffish loral patch; strong black bill with blue lower mandible; rufous belly and upperparts with coverts tipped paler; grey breast. Ssp *obscurata* duller crown; darker grey ear-coverts; more olive-brown lower belly. **Imm** white replaced by pale buff; brown-grey face and underparts; throat blackish-brown. **Voc** In most of range song is a 4-note "oo-oo-wee-oo", "oo-we-oo-we" or "wee-oo-wee-oo", with alternating high and low-pitched notes, lasting 1 sec, or variations thereof; Sabah population: fluting, melodious but simple "wirr-dee-dew-wuu", lasting 1 sec (second note highest then dropping). Call: high-pitched "weew" followed by rattled "wrrree" (presumably given by mate); when agitated introductory "weew" can be followed by quick, thrush-like "chwee-chew chwee-chew".

Spot-necked Babbler *Stachyris strialata*
L 15–16 cm. SE Asia. 7 ssp, 2 in region: *strialata* (C–S Sum); *umbrosa* (N Sum). Uncommon in (sub-) montane forest, 400–2200 m. Singly or pairs; often feeds with Grey-throated Babblers in understorey. **ID Ad** white-flecked supercilium and necksides; grey face; white throat; upperparts and crown rich dark-brown; underparts bright rufous. Ssp *umbrosa* more rufous upperparts; more blackish on crown. **Imm** colder underparts. **Voc** Song: (i) high-pitched 3-note whistle "tuh-tih-tuh", lasting 1 sec; (ii) rarely heard complex warbled melody with much mimicry. Call: (i) dry rattle "tititit…" lasting up to 1 sec; (ii) scolding "tchrrrt…". **SS** Grey-throated lacks Spot-necked's distinctive white 'pearls' on necksides and has drabber cinnamon (not as rich-rufous) underparts. Spot-necked has white throat (dark-grey in Grey-throated, but beware large bordering white malar patches).

Grey-headed Babbler *Stachyris poliocephala*
L 13–14 cm. Sundaic. Monotypic. Uncommon in forest, <1200 m. Often in small groups (<10) in understorey. **ID Ad** grey head with whitish-streaked forecrown and throat; pale iris; strong black bill with blue lower mandible; dark rufous upperparts; slightly paler underparts. **Imm** head pattern less distinct; plumage less rich. **Voc** Variable; (i) clear, 3–6 note, cheery, undulated "choo-chee-cheewee" and "chit-tiwit-we-wee", and variations; (ii) descending 3–5 note "djid-djid-djid-doo".

Grey-throated Babbler *Stachyris nigriceps*
L 12–15 cm. Himalaya to SE Asia. 13 ssp, 4 in region: *larvata* (Sum, l ngga); *natunensis* (Natuna); *hartleyi* (W Bor; presumably this ssp in S Bor); *borneensis* (N Bor). Genome-wide DNA indicates four deep lineages within complex with limited gene flow even during recent periods of land connection, likely warranting species status as: '**Himalayan Montane Babbler**' *S. nigriceps* (Himalaya to W Myanmar), '**Indochinese Montane Babbler**' *S. yunnanensis* (E Myanmar to Indochina), and two in region, (1) **Malayan Montane Babbler**' *S. larvata* (including *natunensis* plus extralimital *tionis* [Tioman Is], *davisoni* [S–C MPen] and *dipora* [N MPen]) and (2) '**Bornean Montane Babbler**' *S. borneensis* (including *hartleyi*). Bioacoustic confirmation of these splits desirable. Common in (sub-) montane forest, 600–2300 m, occasionally to lowlands (especially on Natuna). Usually in small groups in understorey (<20). **ID Ad** greyish-black crown with white streaking; greyish throat and lores with short white supercilium and malar patches; yellow iris; cinnamon-brown underparts; brown upperparts. Ssp *natunensis* has darker throat, greyer forecrown and more olive-tinged upperparts; *hartleyi* crown streaking reduced, grey throat bordered below by diffuse grey breast flecking, duller upperparts; *borneensis* like previous but lacks breast flecking, has darker crown. **Imm** paler below; reduced facial markings. **Voc** Song: series of 12–20 high-pitched quivering notes "tit-sit-su'u'u'u'u'e'e'e'e'…", 10 n/s, introductory 1-2 notes longer, can be descending or slightly ascending. Call: scolding, slightly rolling "chrrt". **SS** See Spot-necked Babbler.

Chestnut-rumped Babbler *Stachyris maculata*
L 17–18 cm. Sundaic. 3 ssp: *maculata* (Sum–Bor, MPen); *banjakensis* (Banyak); *hypopyrrha* (Batu). Fairly common in forest, <800 m. Usually in small groups (<5) in mid-storey. **ID** Large with long, dagger-like bill. **Ad** grey face; blue orbital skin; pale-orange to yellow iris; black throat with distinct scallop-like black streaks on whitish underparts; greyish-brown to dark-brown upperparts, vent and crown (the latter with some black streaking); rufous rump and uppertail. Ssp *banjakensis* larger with greyer crown and mantle; *hypopyrrha* darker above, with rusty lower belly. **Imm** brighter upperparts; less extensive black throat with smaller breast streaks; buffish flanks; darker orange eyes. **Voc** Song: highly varied, often with multiple birds calling simultaneously; usually starting with a rapid series of <20 "tr-r-r-r…" notes followed by slower, loud "woop-woop-woop…" and "woohoop-woohoop…" and occasional harsh scratchy notes. Call: (i) harsh scratchy notes; (ii) a soft, curious, repeated "yep…". **SS** Frequently confused with the vocally different Bold-striped Tit Babbler from more degraded habitat or edge: Chestnut-rumped has longer, more dagger-like bill, a fully black throat (not a white throat with black streaking up to chin), brown (not white) vent, and has sizeable inflated gular pouches when singing.

Javan Babbler *Stachyris grammiceps* [E]
L 12 cm. Monotypic. Uncommon and local in forest, <1500 m. Usually in small groups (<30) or mixed flocks. **ID Ad** white-flecked blackish forecrown; mid-grey head and flanks; pure white underparts and throat; rufous upperparts. **Voc** Song: long, fast, rattling trill "trrrrreeee…" at 40 n/2 s. Call: (i) quiet, harsh "chrr"; (ii) a soft "tik". **AN** White-breasted Babbler.

Black-throated Babbler *Stachyris nigricollis*
L 15–16 cm. Sundaic. Monotypic. Uncommon in forest, <1400 m. Singly or pairs; favouring thickets in understorey. **ID Ad** striking head pattern: broad black throat, face, forehead and upper breast with white patch below eye, short white supercilium behind eye and white forecrown streaking. White scaly crescent delimits upper breast from grey belly; strong black bill with blue lower mandible; rufous upperparts and vent. **Imm** head pattern reduced to dull blackish-brown with whitish face patch and supercilium; underparts brownish-grey. **Voc** Song: repeated series of 10–25 hollow piping "puh-puh-puh…" at ~12 n/3 s, sometimes preceded by a softer downslurred note. Call: (i) harsh rattle "tchrrr" and "tchrr-rt"; (ii) harsh, scolding "tchoo".

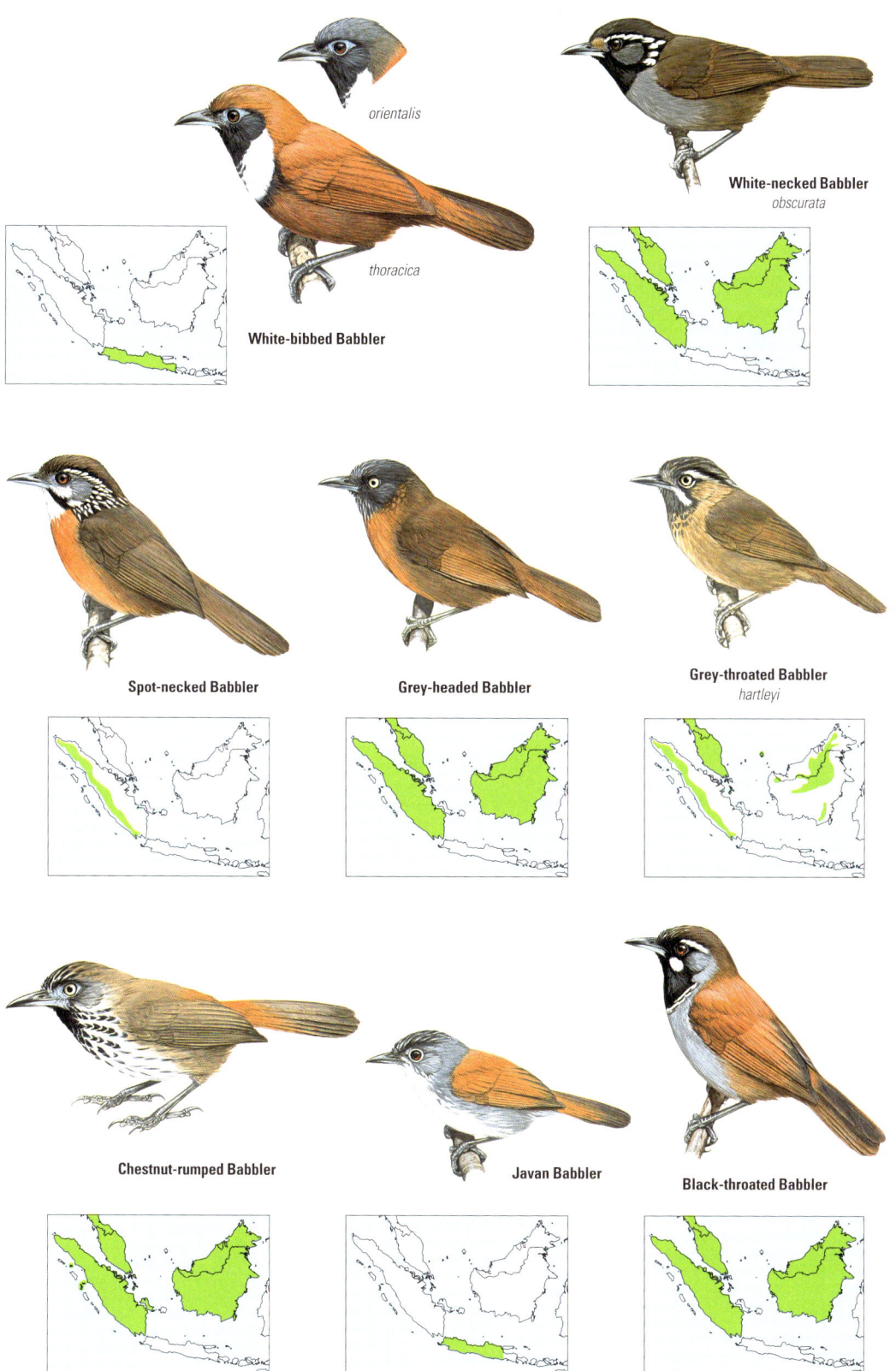

orientalis

thoracica

White-bibbed Babbler

White-necked Babbler
obscurata

Spot-necked Babbler

Grey-headed Babbler

Grey-throated Babbler
hartleyi

Chestnut-rumped Babbler

Javan Babbler

Black-throated Babbler

Large family of small forest dwelling birds. This is one of the dominant families inhabiting undisturbed Sundaic rainforests. Generally cryptic in colouration, many species are shy, preferring to skulk in low vegetation or feed on the ground; others are more conspicuous, feeding actively in the mid- to upper storey.

Moustached Babbler *Malacopteron magnirostre*

L 18 cm. Sundaic. 2 ssp: *magnirostre* (Sum, Anambas, Lingga, MPen); *cinereocapilla* (Bor). Ssp *cinereocapilla* exhibits considerable vocal and plumage differences from *magnirostre*, likely warranting division into two monotypic species, '**Malayan**' and '**Bornean Moustached Babbler**', respectively. Indications of deep mtDNA divergence between populations in Sabah and the remainder of Bor require bioacoustic confirmation. Locally fairly common in forest, particularly on slopes, <1200 m. Singly or small groups (<5); in midstorey. **ID Ad** olive-brown crown and upperparts; greyish face, dark moustachial stripe, white throat; whitish underparts with grey-tinged breast; tail rufous-tinged; thick bluish-horn bill. Ssp *cinereocapilla* darker crown; darker greyish breast suffusion. **Imm** indistinct moustachial stripe; yellow lower mandible base. **Voc** *magnirostre* main song consists of 3–6 well-spaced, clear, descending, melodious notes "tee-tew-too-tuw..." lasting ~3 sec, most often prompted in duet by partner giving a short clear "chick" or bisyllabic "chirrick". In *cinereocapilla*, main song is instead prompted by harsher "chyurr" note, and often starts out with a couplet of even pitch, "tee-tee-tew-tew-too...". Song variant of *cinereocapilla* can include a lot more sequential descending notes at faster delivery, "teedidi'-tewtewtew-too-tooo". Call: both ssp frequently utter the introductory note that sometimes prompts the main song ("chyurr" in *cinereocapilla*; "chick" or "chirrik" in *magnirostre*); ssp *magnirostre* additionally gives a high-pitched "chirr". **SS** Mourning, Glissando and Leaflitter Babblers are more terrestrial, have much shorter tail and extensive warm-buff (not greyish) wash on flanks and breast. Moustached told from Sooty-capped and comparable drab babblers by moustachial stripe and thicker, more hooked bill. Beware younger Moustached individuals on which moustachial stripe can be almost non-existent, but which still show discrete divide between grey face and white throat (more washed out in Sooty-capped). Sooty-capped's pale spectacles and lores are distinctive when seen (Moustached has more uniform grey face). Moustached Babbler's colouration superficially similar to Grey-chested Jungle-Flycatcher, which has thinner and blacker bill, richer brown face and crown, and much different habits and posture.

Rufous-crowned Babbler *Malacopteron magnum*

L 18–19 cm. Sundaic. 2 ssp: *magnum* (Bor except NE, Sum, Natuna, MPen); *saba* (NE Bor). More research required into potential geographic variation in song. Fairly common in forest, <1200 m. Singly or small groups (<10); in mid- to upper storey. **ID Ad** rufous crown; black rear crown; olive-brown upperparts with rufous-tinged tail; whitish underparts; greyish face with greyish breast streaks; thick, strongly hooked, bluish-horn bill; bluish-horn legs. Ssp *saba* rufous crown more extensive, less black. **Imm** with yellow lower mandible. **Voc** More varied than other *Malacopteron* babblers. Song: series of 5–15 level notes with occasional forceful, upslurred and slower, mournful notes "ch-chu-chu-chu-chuwee-tu-tu-too...". Can be rendered in ascending or descending series or combination thereof. Frequent variant includes initial ascending sequence followed by long descending sequence. Call: surprised "chut", often given while another bird sings. **SS** Identified from the smaller Scaly-crowned Babbler by more massive and strongly-hooked bill that is more uniformly bluish-horn (not dark with pink base), bluish-horn (not pinkish) legs, coarse greyish breast streaks (absent on Scaly-crowned's pure white breast) and – with good views – lack of Scaly-crowned's intricate black scales on rufous crown.

Scaly-crowned Babbler *Malacopteron cinereum*

L 14–16 cm. Sundaic. 3 ssp: *cinereum* (Bor, Sum, Batu, Bangka, Lingga, Natuna, MPen); *niasense* (Nias); *rufifrons* (Jav). Extralimital taxon *indochinense* (Indochina) differs markedly in vocalisations, plumage and mtDNA and is here separated as monotypic '**Indochinese Babbler**'. Javan ssp *rufifrons* sometimes thought to be more closely allied with *indochinense* because of similar crown colouration, but here retained with Scaly-crowned based on bioacoustics. Fairly common in forest, <1200 m. Singly or small groups (<10); in midstorey. **ID Ad** rufous crown tipped black, blackish rear crown, greyish face; whitish underparts with buff-tinged upper flanks; olive-brown upperparts; rufous-tinged tail; dark-horn bill with pink base to lower mandible; pinkish-horn legs. Ssp *niasense* slightly darker and larger, with bigger and more strongly hooked bill; *rufifrons* rufous extends to rear crown. **Imm** as Ad. **Voc** Song: ascending series of 3–8 level "too-too-twee-tee" notes, often prompted and/or followed by mate's sharp, trilling series of "chit" notes. Call: (i) sharp, high "chit", often in a rapid series of <20 notes, frequently given in duet with main song; (ii) rattled "chit-chit-chit..."; (iii) sharp "CHIT-chew". **SS** See Rufous-crowned.

Grey-breasted Babbler *Malacopteron albogulare*

L 14–16 cm. Sundaic. 2 ssp: *albogulare* (Sum, Lingga, Batu, MPen); *moultoni* (Bor). Very local, favouring peat-swamp and kerangas forest, also other forest on poor soils, <200 m, very locally to 900 m. Singly or pairs; in understorey, often clinging onto vines. **ID Ad** striking head pattern: white supercilium and throat, grey head and breast band; mid-brown upperparts and short tail; whitish underparts, buffish flanks. Ssp *moultoni* paler buff flanks, perhaps locally with yellow lores. **Imm** undescribed. **Voc** Song, mainly at dawn: long variable series of poorly structured, subdued notes "whu'-whi', whu'-whu'-whu..., whi'-whi'-whu'-u', de'-de'-de'-du'-de'...". Call: short rattle followed by a stretched, ascending chick-like "errr" note.

Sooty-capped Babbler *Malacopteron affine*

L 15–17 cm. Sundaic. 2 ssp: *affine* (Sum, Banyak, Bangka, MPen); *phoeniceum* (Bor). Research into potential geographic variation in the variable song of this species needed. Common in forest, <700 m. Singly or small groups (<10); in midstorey. **ID Ad** rather nondescript; dusky crown; greyish face with paler whitish lores and spectacles; greyish suffusion on breast; whitish underparts; olive-brown upperparts with rufous tail; slender bluish-horn bill, thick bluish legs. Ssp *phoeniceum* has browner crown. **Imm** crown olive-grey as mantle; rufous-tinged wings; yellow lower mandible. **Voc** Song: often in duet, distinctive series of level whistles, lacking direction and sounding like an improvised tune whistled by a person, at 6 n/3 s, often with partner responding with a single sharp "pwit" or an aggressive series of "pwit" notes when agitated; in some areas constitutes the dominant sound of the morning chorus. Call: short, sharp "pi'weeut". **SS** From other *Malacopteron* babblers by indistinct crown colour, but see Moustached. Also see Bornean Swamp Babbler, Abbott's and Horsfield's Babblers and Sunda Fulvetta.

cinereocapilla

magnirostre

Moustached Babbler

Rufous-crowned Babbler

Scaly-crowned Babbler
cinereum

Grey-breasted Babbler

Sooty-capped Babbler
affine

Büttikofer's Babbler *Pellorneum buettikoferi* E

L 15 cm. Monotypic. Further research into geographic variation in song required. Locally uncommon in C–S Sum, locally common in Aceh in edge, scrub and forested clearings with dense understorey, <1100 m. Singly or pairs; skulking in undergrowth. **ID Ad** rather nondescript; diffuse pale grey facial colouration with indistinct streaking; olive-brown crown, flanks and upperparts; whitish underparts; short tail; pink bill and legs. **Imm** similar but underparts more buff. **Voc** Song: in C–N Sum a loud and clear 2-note "pwi'-yew", lasting 0.4 sec, second note downslurred; in S of range a 2 or 3-note "(pi-)too-twee", lasting 0.8 sec, sometimes followed by a series of ~5 descending cheery notes "tzip-wir-wir-wir-wir", often in duet. Call: harsh, scolding, rolling "chrrr". **SS** Horsfield's and Abbott's Babblers have thicker, more greyish-horn (not pink) bill and legs; more distinct grey supercilium. See also Malayan Swamp Babbler and Sunda Fulvetta. Similarly drab *Malacopteron* babblers are higher up in foliage, have greyer and thicker bills and longer, more rufous-contrasting tails (see Moustached for additional marks). **AN** Sumatran Babbler.

Temminck's Babbler *Pellorneum pyrrogenys* E

L 15 cm. 4 ssp: *pyrrogenys* (Jav); *canicapillus* (Sabah); *longstaffi* (C–E Sarawak to S–E Kalimantan); *erythrote* (W Sarawak and adjacent Kalimantan). Population on Meratus Mts (S Kalimantan) unassigned to ssp. Locally fairly common in submontane forest, edge, 500–1500 m. Singly or pairs; skulking in undergrowth. **ID Ad** greyish crown with pale shaft streaks; brownish-grey face with indistinct streaks; variable extent of rich buff ear-coverts to flanks; white throat and underparts; upperparts rufous-brown; blackish bill; pinkish legs. Ssp *erythrote* paler upperparts, richer buff extending across breast; *longstaffi* like previous but more blackish crown and more rufous-buff flanks and belly; *canicapillus* like previous but less extensive breast band and blackish-grey crown. **Imm** undescribed. **Voc** Song: 4, rarely 6-note, "wi'-chew wi'-chew", lasting 0.7–1 sec, slightly faster in Bornean races; mate occasionally duets with a high-pitched, repeated "tip-tit'tit'tit-zuu". Call: (i) rolling, high rattle "trreee"; (ii) warning call (at least on Jav) a liquid, sharp "plikt", often doubled or tripled in quick succession. **SS** No other babbler in range combines such rich and warm upperparts and flanks with a cold-grey to blackish crown except for the larger, more terrestrial Javan and Bornean Black-capped Babblers, which always exhibit a well-defined fully black crown (not poorly defined greyish-black) and a long, distinct, pale supercilium (absent in Temminck's)

Malayan Swamp Babbler *Pellorneum rostratum*

L 15 cm. Sundaic. Monotypic. Traditionally merged with Bornean Swamp Babbler and then called '**White-chested Babbler**' *P. rostratum*, but now divided because vocal differences and genomic data indicate a lack of gene flow during recent epochs of land connection. Fairly common in riverine forest, wooded habitat along waterways and flooded areas, <300 m. Singly or pairs; forages on ground and on tangles along water's edge. **ID Ad** quite long, slender, dark greyish-horn bill; long, pinkish-horn legs; cold brown crown and mantle; warmer, rufescent wings and tail; slightly paler brown face, usually with warm buff lores and spectacles; clean white underparts; breast sides washed light grey. **Imm** lacks bright tones, yellow lower mandible. **Voc** Song: repeated clear whistled "wee-chew-tew-twee" or variations thereof (3-4 syllabled), virtually always introduced by mate's prompting call, a deep, harsh "churr", as part of a duet. Call: (i) harsh rattles; (ii) deliberate "hew-hew-hew". **SS** Büttikofer's has pink (not grey) bill; Abbott's and Horsfield's Babblers have much thicker bill. All three (Büttikofer's, Abbott's and Horsfield's) differ from Malayan Swamp in their grey supercilium or other facial features (versus warm-brown face) and their brown (not greyish) breast sides / flanks. Also see Ferruginous and Moustached.

Bornean Swamp Babbler *Pellorneum macropterum* E

L 15 cm. Monotypic. For taxonomy see Malayan Swamp Babbler. Fairly common in riverine forest, wooded habitat along waterways and flooded areas, <300 m. Singly or pairs; forages on ground and on tangles along water's edge. **ID Ad** similar to Malayan Swamp Babbler but mantle and rump slightly more olive-tinged. **Imm** as Malayan Swamp. **Voc** Song: repeated clear whistled "wee-tew-twee" or variations thereof (3-4 syllabled), but not known to be given as a response to partner's prompting call in a duet. Call: (i) harsh rattles; (ii) deliberate "hew-hew-hew". **SS** Abbott's and Horsfield's Babblers have much thicker bill, exhibit grey supercilium (versus warm-brown face) and have rich-brown (not greyish) breast sides / flanks. Sooty-capped Babbler from further up the canopy has thicker bill, more contrastingly rufous tail and pale-grey or whitish (not warm-buff) spectacles and lores. Also see Ferruginous and Moustached.

Sulawesi Babbler *Pellorneum celebense* E

L 15 cm. 4 ssp: *celebense* (N Sul); *togianense* (Togian); *rufofuscum* (C–SE Sul, Buton); *finschi* (SW Sul). Pronounced morphological and vocal differentiation may indicate presence of multiple species. Common in primary, secondary and submontane forest, edge, thickets, <1900 m. Singly or pairs; in understorey. **ID Ad** mid-brown upperparts; slightly paler, greyish face; greyish-buff flanks and vent; whitish underparts. Ssp *togianense* clearer white underparts with brighter buff flanks and vent; *rufofuscum* ochre-washed throat and breast; *finschi* more cold olive-grey on upperparts and buff-ochre on underparts with white throat. **Imm** similar to Ad. **Voc** Song: series of 3–8 loud, fluty ascending notes "duwee-wu-wu-way..." lasting ~1 sec, occasionally in duet with mate producing slightly descending "kew-kew-kew...". Call: (i) agitated chattering; (ii) forceful, high-pitched "pist-pist-pist...".

Ferruginous Babbler *Pellorneum bicolor*

L 16–18 cm. Sundaic. Monotypic. Fairly common in forest, <950 m. Singly or pairs; in lower to mid-storey. **ID Ad** bright rufescent upperparts, even brighter crown and tail; clean buffish-white underparts; bright buff upper flanks. **Imm** even brighter above. **Voc** Song: (i) repeated, clear, easily impersonated "oo-wit", second note upslurred, not unlike some dialects of Malayan Black-capped Babbler; (ii) when agitated also produces a series of <30 "wit" notes, sometimes accelerating, descending then levelling. Call: series of rasping notes, interspersed with curious "wir-wir-wir...". **SS** Closest in plumage to Malayan and Bornean Swamp Babblers, but far more rufescent on upperparts (especially crown) than them and any other comparable *Pellorneum* babblers.

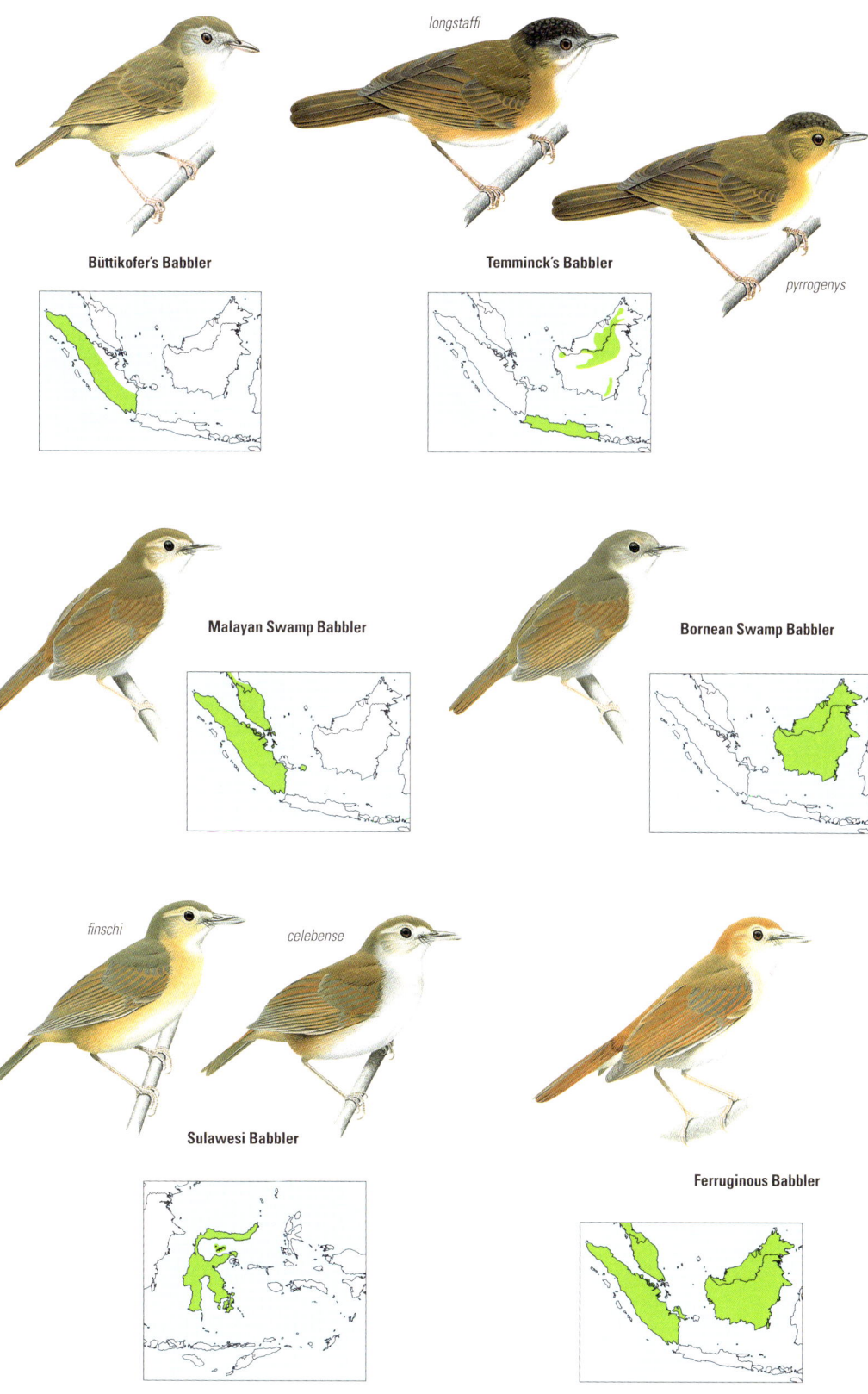

Büttikofer's Babbler

longstaffi

Temminck's Babbler

pyrrogenys

Malayan Swamp Babbler

Bornean Swamp Babbler

finschi

celebense

Sulawesi Babbler

Ferruginous Babbler

Mourning Babbler *Pellorneum malaccense*

L 14 cm. Sundaic. Monotypic. Traditionally merged with Leaflitter and Glissando Babblers into larger species, '**Short-tailed Babbler**' *P. malaccense*, but pronounced vocal and genome-wide differences indicate lack of gene flow despite range contact. Fairly common in forest, old plantations, <1000 m. Singly or pairs; largely terrestrial, feeding in leaf-litter. **ID** Appears long-legged, with short tail and thin, greyish-horn bill. **Ad** rufous crown and upperparts with contrasting grey face, black moustachial line and clean white throat; buff-washed flanks and breast grading into white belly; pink legs. **Imm** buff throat and brown-grey face. **Voc** Song: introduced by 3-20 agitated downslurred notes, "tchew-tchew-tchew-...", followed by a descending decelerating series of 5–10 mournful whistles "weew-weeew-weeeew...", each note becoming gradually longer, lasting 5–8 sec. Call: (i) aggressive, scratchy "trrt-trrt-trrt..."; (ii) upslurred "peyew-peyew-peyew...", often mixed with scratchy call. **SS** See Moustached.

Glissando Babbler *Pellorneum saturatum*

L 14 cm. Monotypic. A truly cryptic species, long overlooked. For taxonomy see Mourning Babbler. On current knowledge, known as far east as the lower Baram River, Mount Mulu (Sarawak), and Barito River (S–C Kalimantan), but exact dividing line with Leaflitter Babbler not fully understood. Fairly common in forest, old plantations, <1000 m. Singly or pairs; largely terrestrial, feeding in leaf-litter. **ID** Appears long-legged, with short tail and thin, greyish-horn bill. **Ad** as Mourning but with slightly darker, more rufescent crown; darker ear-coverts and moustachial stripe; more olive (less chestnut) upperparts; more intensively buffy-orange flanks and breast. **Imm** buff throat and brown-grey face. **Voc** Song: introduced by decelerating but loudening series of 5–15 downslurred "tch-tch-tchew-tchew-tchew-tcheew-tcheeew...", followed by a long descending glissando of 20–30 rapidly whistled "pi'pi'pi'pi'pip-pee-pee-pee...", gradually levelling off with progressively longer notes, lasting 3–5 sec. Call: (i) aggressive, rapid chattering "trrt-trrt-trrt..."; (ii) downslurred "tchoo-tchoo-tchoo...", at 3 n/sec. **SS** See Moustached.

Leaflitter Babbler *Pellorneum poliogene*

L 14 cm. Monotypic. For taxonomy and range, see Mourning and Glissando Babblers. Known to occur east of the Baram drainage (e. g. Brunei) and Barito River (S Kal), but situation in heart of Borneo unresolved. Fairly common in forest, old plantations, <1000 m. Singly or pairs; largely terrestrial, feeding in leaf-litter. **ID** Appears long-legged, with short tail and thin, greyish-horn bill. **Ad** Very similar to Glissando Babbler but perhaps more apricot-coloured flanks and breast; more rufous tail. **Imm** buff throat and brown-grey face. **Voc** Song: similar to introductory notes of Mourning and Glissando Babblers, series of 5-20 downslurred "tch-tch-thew-tchew-tchew-tcheew-tcheeew...", at 2 n/sec, though lacking the subsequent mournful descending main song. Occasionally first 1–3 notes lower-pitched. Call: (i) aggressive, rapid chattering "trrt-trrt-trrt..."; (ii) as song, series of downslurred "tchoo-tchoo-tchoo..., randomly changing in pitch and pace, but continuing up to 80 n. **SS** See Moustached.

Javan Black-capped Babbler
Pellorneum capistratum

L 16–17 cm. Monotypic. Traditionally merged with Malayan and Bornean Black-capped Babblers into umbrella species, '**Black-capped Babbler**' *P. capistratum*. However, all three exhibit pronounced vocal, plumage and genome-wide differences incompatible with gene flow during recent land connections. Uncommon in forest, wooded areas, <1000 m. Singly or pairs; often found walking on ground. **ID Ad** uniformly rufous (upperparts more olive-tinged) with contrasting black cap, small white throat, olive-greyish face and bright rufous supercilium becoming white on rear crown. **Imm** dark brown crown; less contrasting, rufous throat. **Voc** Song: melodious multi-syllabic "WEE–deoo", or "we DEE–doo" or variations, sometimes followed by 1–2 short rasping notes. **SS** See Temminck's Babbler. **AN** Rufous-browed Babbler.

Malayan Black-capped Babbler
Pellorneum nigrocapitatum

L 16–17 cm. Sundaic. Monotypic. For taxonomy see Javan Black-capped Babbler. Extralimital populations (MPen) have complex dialectal song variability seemingly incongruent with genomic data; more research required. Fairly common in forest, wooded areas, <1400 m. Singly or pairs; often found walking on ground. **ID Ad** Similar to Javan Black-capped but darker overall, less bright rufous, with pale-grey supercilium, mid-grey ear-coverts and broad white throat. **Imm** dark brown crown; less contrasting, rufous throat. **Voc** Song: repeated, high-pitched, piercing, descending "PEEUW", lasting 0.5 sec. Extralimital populations in MPen also give a rising variant, "TOOWEET".

Bornean Black-capped Babbler
Pellorneum capistratoides

L 16–17 cm. 2 ssp: *capistratoides* (W–C–S Bor); *morrelli* (NE Bor, Banggi). Deep mtDNA divergence between the two subspecies seems artefactual, not reflected in genome-wide data and bioacoustics. For taxonomy also see Javan Black-capped Babbler. Fairly common in forest, wooded areas, <1400 m. Singly or pairs; often found walking on ground. **ID Ad** as Malayan Black-capped but thinner and whiter supercilium, blackish ear-coverts, even darker plumage. Ssp *morrelli* slightly paler plumage, blackish-grey ear-coverts. **Imm** dark brown crown; less contrasting, rufous throat. **Voc** Song: variable, high-pitched, piercing, descending then rising "TEEEUWEE", sometimes with first part separated as independent note "tee weet" or "tee doo" or "choowee". **SS** See Temminck's Babbler.

Black-browed Babbler *Malacocincla perspicillata*
Monotypic. Only known from single specimen, collected in S Bor between 1843 and 1848 by Schwaner, until recently rediscovered in rugged karst slope habitat in lowland S Kalimantan. Continues to be poorly known in life. **ID** Distinctive, unique appearance with strong, large bill, short tarsus and wings, and short tail. **Ad** conspicuous black supercilium, white lores, pale grey face; dark brown crown and upperparts; grey breast thinly streaked white; rufous-brown belly. **Imm** undescribed. **Voc** Undescribed.

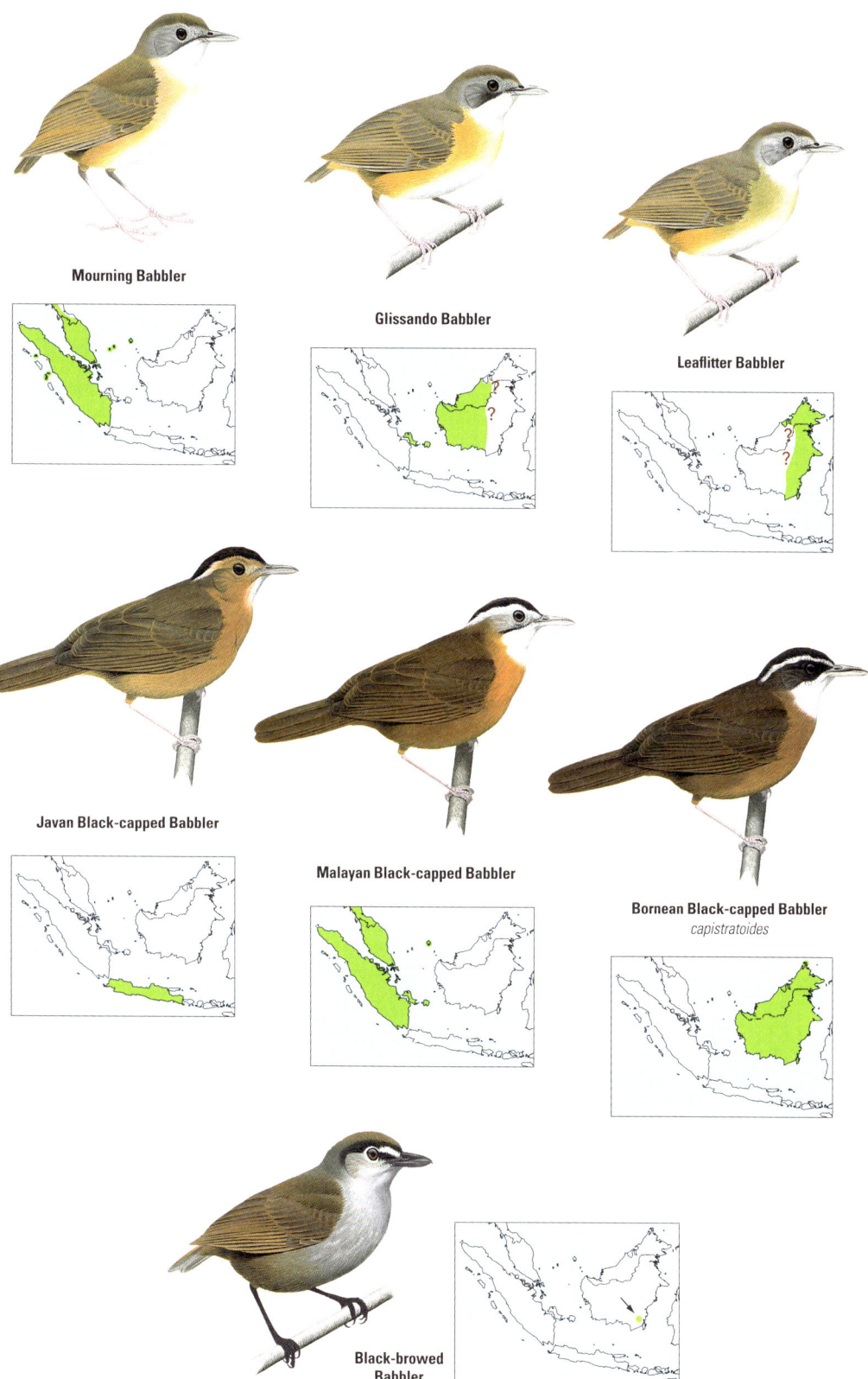

Mourning Babbler

Glissando Babbler

Leaflitter Babbler

Javan Black-capped Babbler

Malayan Black-capped Babbler

Bornean Black-capped Babbler
capistratoides

**Black-browed
Babbler**

Abbott's Babbler *Malacocincla abbotti*

L 15–17 cm. S–SE Asia. 8 ssp, 3 in region: *olivacea* (Sum, MPen); *concreta* (Bor, Belitung); *baweana* (Bawean). Fairly common on Sum, rare and local on Bor in secondary forest, edge, thickets and mangrove, <1100 m. Singly, pairs or small groups (<5); in understorey. **ID** Short-tailed with thick bluish-horn bill. **Ad** ill-defined, chunky, grey supercilium, often with greyish obfuscation around eye; buff ear-coverts; buff-brown crown and upperparts; rufous-buff flanks and vent; pale grey breast; rufescent tail; thick pink legs. Ssp *concreta* more restricted rufous-buff flanks and vent, paler breast; *baweana* paler overall with less rufescent tail. **Imm** darker crown and upperparts; yellowish lower mandible. **Voc** Song: 3–5 loud, slightly variable, cheerful notes (tendentially more notes in *concreta* than in *olivacea*), "chew-woo-wee" or "whyew-woo-yoo-weeuw". Call: short, harsh, rasping "cheeo". **SS** Horsfield's Babbler from interior of good forest is very similar (especially brown-crowned ssp *barussana* [Sum] and *harterti* [NE Bor]), but usually has less well-defined grey supercilium, with greyish obfuscation often reaching onto ear-coverts and below eye, whereas Abbott's has lighter-grey supercilium contrasting against buff ear-coverts. Horsfield's has shorter, blunter, less dagger-shaped bill: as measured from base of upper bill ridge, distance to eye roughly equals distance to bill tip in Horsfield's, whereas upper bill ridge length in Abbott's noticeably exceeds distance to eye. Horsfield's is also more vividly rufous (less buff-brown or earthen-brown) above, has more vividly ochre-coloured flanks and a slightly shorter tail. Without practice, identification from Horsfield's should preferably rest on vocal evidence. Drab *Malacopteron* babblers from higher strata are much longer-tailed, lack the warm rufous flanks and differ in facial features. See also Malayan and Bornean Swamp Babblers, Büttikofer's and White-chested Babblers.

Horsfield's Babbler *Malacocincla sepiaria*

L 15–16 cm. Sundaic. 5 ssp, 4 in region: *sepiaria* (Jav, Bali); *barussana* (Sum); *harterti* (NE Bor); *rufiventris* (rest of Bor). Taxonomy confused: 2–3 species almost certainly involved because of pronounced differences in plumage, song and duetting behaviour. If split, Bornean races would form '**Salvadori's Babbler**' *M. rufiventris* (including *harterti*) and nominate *sepiaria* would become monotypic '**Horsfield's Babbler**', leaving the remaining two ssp as '**Hartert's Babbler**' *M. tardinata* (MPen–Sum, including *barussana*). Fairly common in primary, secondary and degraded forest, <1400 m, locally <1700 m. Singly, pairs or small groups (<6); favours darker understorey, occasionally clambering higher. **ID** Dumpy, short-tailed with thick bluish-horn bill and short tarsus. **Ad** rather dull; crown and ear-coverts variably greyish to brownish, but always shows short grey supercilium and paler lores; buff to rufous-brown upperparts; pale grey throat and breast gradually becoming ochre-buff on flanks and lower belly; pinkish-horn legs. Ssp *barussana* darker overall, richer brown upperparts, always exhibits brownish crown and ear-coverts; *rufiventris* slate-grey crown contrasting with rufous brown upperparts, paler grey supercilium, darker lores, breast with indistinct grey streaking, contrasting with extensive bright ochre-buff flanks and lower belly; *harterti* as previous but crown and nape brown, underparts less bright, and less distinct upper breast streaking. **Imm** more rufous upperparts; yellowish lower mandible. **Voc** Song geographically variable: *sepiaria* most often gives loud, fluty, 2-4 syllabic "chip whooeet", "chwee poowit (chup-chwee)" or variations, often with duetting partner's simultaneous accompanying "chip, chip chip..." series; Bornean races most often give a unique, characteristic, constantly repeated "chip-whoeet, chip-whoeet, chip-whoeet...", similar to main theme in *sepiaria*, second note distinctly rising and sometimes given on its own; *barussana* utters full-throated single notes, e.g., descending "CHEEUW", slightly ascending "TWEY" or variations, sometimes combined into multi-

syllabic motifs, with duetting partner occasionally responding with harsh "chip" or burry "bweew". Call: (i) short, grating "chrrr", often given in quick succession; (ii) 2-note call including rattling chur of variable length, "witch-churrrrrt"; (iii) harsh "wit, wit-chr-chr-chr..."; (iv) short, quiet, quivering "brrrt". **SS** See Abbott's Babbler, Malayan and Bornean Swamp, and Büttikofer's Babblers. Drab *Malacopteron* babblers (e.g., Sooty-capped) from higher strata are much longer-tailed, lack the warm rufous flanks and differ in facial features.

Mountain Wren Babbler *Malacocincla crassa*   E

L 14 cm. Monotypic. Fairly common in montane forest, 900–2900 m. Usually pairs or small groups (<10), forages in leaf-litter. **ID Ad** broad, pale-grey supercilium; white throat; dark-brown crown and upperparts with bright buff shaft streaks; underparts bright-buff with paler streaking; short, stubby bill and legs greyish-horn. **Imm** similar to Ad. **Voc** Song: (i) loud, repeated, melodious, descending 3-note "he-he-heu", lasting 1 sec; (ii) cheery duet, one bird giving 3–5 descending "hu-hu-hu-hu" notes, while the other gives a thinner descending "he-he-he-hoo". Call: (i) quick, repeated "whit"; (ii) short, scolding "chrrt". **SS** Eye-browed Wren Babbler superficially similar, but much smaller, with thinner and longer bill, pinkish (not greyish) legs, distinct whitish covert spots (absent in Mountain), narrower and whiter supercilium and more secretive, solitary behaviour.

Sumatran Rimator *Rimator albostriatus*   E

L 13 cm. Monotypic. Uncommon in montane forest, 1200–2800 m. Singly or pairs; forages in leaf-litter and tangles. **ID** Very long, decurved bill. **Ad** white throat; black malar stripe; dark grey-brown plumage with long, whitish shaft streaks on underparts and mantle. **Imm** undescribed. **Voc** Song: short, sharp, metallic whistled "poo" lasting 0.5 sec, repeated every 3–6 sec, when excited interspersed with fast, quickly repeated "whipoo-wip whipoo-wip whipoo-wip...". Call: rolling "trrrp". **AN** Sumatran Wren/Ground Babbler.

Eye-browed Wren Babbler *Napothera epilepidota*

L 10–11 cm. SE–E Asia. 13 ssp, 4 in region: *epilepidota* (Jav); *exsul* (Bor); *diluta* (Sum, >1200 m); *lucilleae* (Sum, 900–1200 m). Extremely deep mtDNA divergences may suggest division into as many as 6 species, but genomic and bioacoustic confirmation required. In region, the mtDNA group comprising ssp *epilepidota* and *diluta* has diagnostic level-pitched vocalisation and darker plumage and may qualify as independent species, '**Sunda Wren Babbler**' *N. epilepidota*, while ssp *exsul* forms separate mtDNA cluster possibly qualifying as monotypic species '**Whitehead's Wren Babbler**'. Ssp *lucilleae* replaces *diluta* at lower elevations and differs in vocalisations: for now perhaps best placed with all extralimital ssp into umbrella species, '**Austen's Wren Babbler**' *N. roberti*, until further divided. Fairly common in (sub-) montane forest, >900 m. Scarce in Bor, 200–1700 m. Singly or pairs; forages in leaf-litter and tangles. **ID** Small and short-tailed. **Ad** long, narrow white supercilium; broad blackish eyestripe and crown; whitish throat; upperparts dark brown with paler, bright streaks; distinct pale tips to wing coverts; underparts dark-brown with pale streaks. Ssp *diluta* greyer face, fine spotting on moustachial area and rear ear-coverts. Ssp *exsul* browner crown; much paler brown to rufous overall; buff throat; more uniform, scalloped (not striped) underparts; *lucilleae* paler underparts than previous. **Imm** more uniform and slightly darker overall. **Voc** Song: *epilepidota* and *diluta* single, thin whistle, "peeeee", flat or with slight, almost inaudible initial descent in pitch, lasting 0.7–0.9 sec; *exsul* and *lucilleae* slightly higher pitched, mournful, descending thin "peeooo", lasting 0.8–1.2 sec. Song of all taxa occasionally interspersed with an excited, repeated "chi'ka-chi'ka-chi'ka...". Call: (i) short, sharp "chut"; (ii) rolling "chrrt". **SS** See Mountain Wren Babbler.

Abbott's Babbler

sepiaria

Horsfield's Babbler

rufiventris

Mountain Wren Babbler

Sumatran Rimator

lucilleae

epilepidota

Eye-browed Wren Babbler

Striped Wren Babbler *Kenopia striata*

L 14–15 cm. Sundaic. Monotypic. Uncommon and local in forest, particularly swampy areas, <600 m, recorded to 1200 m. Singly or pairs; in understorey. **ID Ad** white face and underparts; buff-yellow supraloral spot; bold white streaking on black crown and brown upperparts; buffish rear flanks. **Imm** streaking less distinct; crown and flanks browner; paler head. **Voc** High-pitched, metallic, whistled "didi'-deeee", lasting 1 sec. Introductory notes only audible at closer range.

Bornean Ground Babbler *Ptilocichla leucogrammica* E

L 15–16 cm. Monotypic. Uncommon and local in forest, favouring dry gullies and slopes, <800 m. Singly, pairs or small groups (<5); forages in leaf-litter. **ID Ad** rather oddly shaped: chunky-bodied, thin-necked and short-tailed, with longish, thick bill and long legs; crown and upperparts chestnut-brown; grey face with paler supercilium; white throat; black underparts with broad white streaking. **Imm** upperparts less bright; lightly streaked crown. **Voc** (i) 2 mournful, pure, high-pitched whistles "doo-dee", lasting 1.3 sec, rarely a "dee-doo"; (ii) occasionally duets with mate giving an even series of ~50 notes "prr-prr-prr..." lasting ~3.5 sec.

Marbled Wren Babbler *Turdinus marmoratus*

L 21 cm. Sundaic. 2 ssp, 1 in region: *marmoratus* (Sum). Uncommon in submontane forest, favouring damp gullies, 800–2000 m. Usually in pairs, forages in leaf-litter, shy. **ID** Dumpy. **Ad** rufous ear-coverts; white lores and throat; black underparts scaled white; blackish-scaled brown crown and upperparts; longish tail. Shows either pink or blue skin behind eye, possibly sex-specific. **Imm** rufous streaks on head and upperparts. **Voc** Song: (i) clear 2-note whistle "poooo-cheee..." lasting 1.3 sec, first note is flat and even, second is buzzy, slightly higher-pitched and downslurred; (ii) in duet or in excitement on its own, can produce a long series of fast, repeated, alarm-like "pewit-pewit-pewit..." notes.

Large Wren Babbler *Turdinus macrodactylus*

L 19 cm. Sundaic. 3 ssp, 2 in region: *beauforti* (Sum); *lepidopleura* (Jav). Recently discovered in C Kalimantan, ssp unknown. Uncommon and local in primary and mature secondary forest, favouring rattan thickets, <700 m on Sum, <1100 m on Jav. Singly or pairs; foraging in leaf-litter, shy. **ID Ad** black ear-coverts and lores; blue orbital skin; conspicuous white throat delimited by dark breast band; pale greyish-buff underparts with white streaks; dark brown upperparts and crown scaled black. Ssp *lepidopleura* darker upper- and underparts; lacks dark breast band. **Imm** plainer, paler upperparts and buffier underparts with whitish belly. **Voc** Song variable: (i) most often 3–5 loud, clear, whistled notes "choo-pwee-wooo", lasting 1.5–2 sec, first note flat, second upslurred, third buzzy and downslurred; (ii) 3–5 clear, even notes, followed by long, upslurred note "dwee-wee-wee-wuuh"; (iii) longer series of 5–8 clear, loud, slightly descending notes "wee-tut-tut-tut..."; (iv) similar to Marbled Wren Babbler, 2-note "pooy-cheee", but first note upslurred. Call: (i) mournful, drawn-out "pooee" lasting 1.5 sec, similar to Giant Pitta; (ii) buzzy, scolding "weeuh".

Black-throated Wren Babbler *Turdinus atrigularis* E

L 18 cm. Monotypic. Uncommon and local in forest, <1200 m. Usually pairs or small groups (<5), forages in leaf-litter, shy. **ID Ad** whitish belly; buff flanks; ear-coverts, throat and upper breast black, with black scaling extending onto flanks and lower breast; blue skin behind eye and lateral gular pouch (inflated when singing); brown upperparts with some scaling (especially on mantle); longish bill and tail. **Imm** scaly underparts up to throat; more rufous, streaky upperparts. **Voc** Song variable, strikingly loud: (i) 6–10 short then long, powerful, plaintive, descending whistles "wu-wu-wu-wu-woo-woo-wooh"; (ii) 4–6 loud, clear, mournful notes, first note upslurred, "wuuah-oowa-whu-whu"; (iii) in duet, a loud, clear "peuw-peuw-peuw..." at 2 n/s, up to 1 min, with mate giving a "we-ah we-ah we-ah...". Call: quiet, rasping "krah".

Rusty-breasted Wren Babbler *Turdinus rufipectus* E

L 18–19 cm. Monotypic. Fairly common in montane forest, 900–2600 m. Pairs or small groups (<6), forages in leaf-litter. Quite bold and conspicuous, not as shy as other *Turdinus* wren babblers. **ID M** rufous overall with obscure blackish scaling and some paler shaft streaks; bluish orbital skin; greyish-tinged face; whitish throat. **F** lacks blue orbital skin; breast paler, brighter rufous. **Imm** undescribed. **Voc** Song: loud and piping, starting with an introductory "pu-pu-pu-pu-poooo", lasting 1–1.5 sec, followed by a long series of quickly repeated "hu-wip-pi' hu-wip-pi' hu-wip-pi'..." often transcribed as "hot wet tea, hot wet tea...", lasting <1 min, often in duet.

2 species in region

Small forest birds of the canopy with indistinct markings. Often in small noisy groups or the main component in mixed flocks.

Sunda Fulvetta *Alcippe brunneicauda*

L 14–15 cm. Sundaic. 2 ssp: *brunneicauda* (MPen, Sum, Batu); *eriphaea* (Bor, Natuna). Ssp *eriphaea* differs significantly in voice and is likely a monotypic species, '**Bornean Fulvetta**'. Fairly common in forest, <1200 m. Usually in small flocks (<20), favours mid- to upper canopy. **ID Ad** plain greyish head with brownish-tinged crown, sometimes with rudimentary dark supercilium; brown mantle; rufous-brown wings and tail; dirty white to buff underparts; olive-horn to greyish bill slightly decurved; pinkish-horn legs. Ssp *eriphaea* on current knowledge only identifiable through voice, although plumage differences doubtless exist. **Imm** paler brown upperparts; brownish head; yellowish bill. **Voc** Song: (i) *eriphaea* characteristic high-pitched undulating 6–10 note "hee-hew-hoo-hew-hoo-hee-hoo", usually first 3 notes descending, fourth higher, fifth lower-pitched again, sixth highest and final note lowest, lasting 2 sec; another version with the last 4 notes descending; (ii) *brunneicauda* 6–10 slow, high-pitched, descending notes "tee-tee-tip-tep-tew-tew-tooo", lasting 2 sec. Call: (i) buzzy "zeechu" and burring "zree-ZREE–zree"; (ii) stressed "whit". **SS** In its canopy haunts, beware of Sooty-capped Babbler (especially *phoeniceum* from Bor), which has thicker bluish (less pinkish) legs, straighter and darker bluish-horn (less olive) bill, and more uniformly brown upperparts and crown with pale spectacles (versus a bland grey head in Fulvetta). Other bland *Malacopteron* babblers share same differences in leg and bill colour/structure while sporting distinct facial and crown features. Similar Büttikofer's Babbler from understorey has longer, straighter pink (not olive-grey) bill. Various other drab understorey babblers superficially resemble Fulvetta but are browner-headed, lacking drab grey face. **AN** Brown Fulvetta.

Javan Fulvetta *Alcippe pyrrhoptera* F

L 14–15 cm. Monotypic. Common in (sub-) montane forest, 900–2400 m. Usually in small flocks (<20), including mixed flocks, favours mid-canopy. **ID Ad** plain-looking: mid-brown mantle, slightly darker crown with blackish lateral crown stripes (sometimes faint), paler face, rufous wings and tail, buffish to creamy-white underparts. **Imm** more rufescent overall, yellowish bill, lacks dark crown stripes. **Voc** Song: melodious, high-pitched, variable notes, including "tit-tit-chit-chit-chew" and "whir-dah-dee-deeo". Call: (i) buzzy rattles "whirzee"; (ii) sharp "zechip".

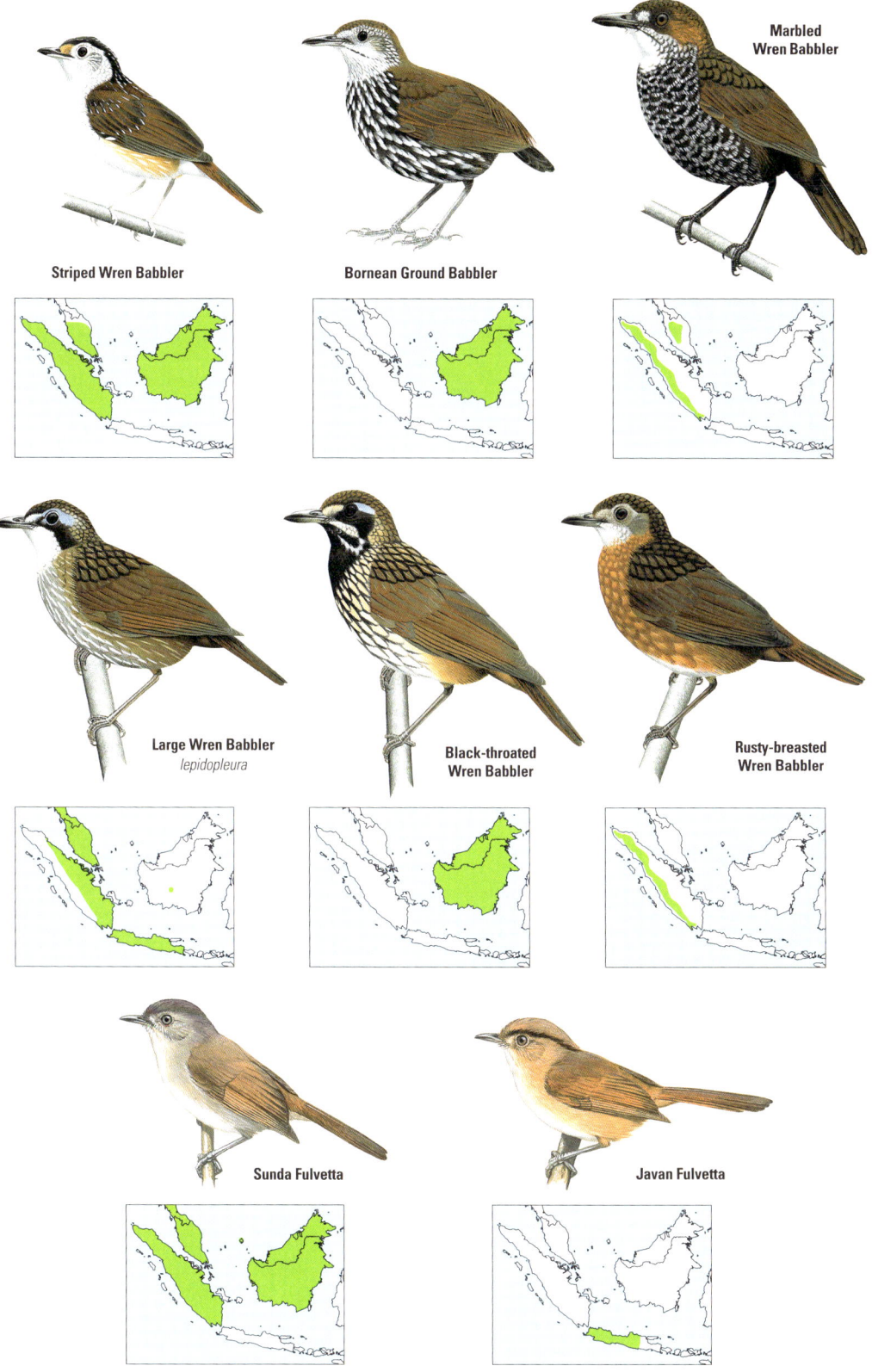

Striped Wren Babbler

Bornean Ground Babbler

Marbled Wren Babbler

Large Wren Babbler
lepidopleura

Black-throated Wren Babbler

Rusty-breasted Wren Babbler

Sunda Fulvetta

Javan Fulvetta

LEIOTHRICHIDAE
Laughingthrushes and allies
8 species in region

Small to medium-sized forest birds, many with distinctly marked plumage. Found in low to upper storey, often in small noisy groups or mixed flocks. Several species heavily trapped for the pet trade and becoming increasingly rare and endangered.

Sumatran Laughingthrush *Garrulax bicolor* **E**

L 24–28 cm. Monotypic. Now rare and localised, locally extinct, in submontane forest, 750–2000 m. Usually in small groups (<10), very shy. **ID Ad** pure white head and breast with black tufts at bill base and black 'goggles'; rest of body sooty black-brown. **Imm** paler underparts. **Voc** Multiple birds usually performing a cacophony of sudden loud outbursts of extended cackling laughter and rattles, including repeated "weer-wir-he-he wir-he-he, wir-he-he...", rattling "wrrrr'ou" and various short notes and yelps.

Sunda Laughingthrush *Garrulax palliatus* **E**

L 24–25 cm. 2 ssp: *palliatus* (Sum); *schistochlamys* (Bor). Locally fairly common, but now rare and locally extinct in Sum, in (sub-) montane forest, 800–2200 m, rarely to 300 m. Usually in groups (<20), often mixed with other laughingthrushes. **ID Ad** slate grey head, mantle and breast contrasting sharply with chestnut-brown wings, tail and belly; pale blue orbital skin. Ssp *schistochlamys* slightly paler face; darker upperparts; richer belly. **Imm** duller, more brownish-tinged mantle. **Voc** Song: flock starts gently with "yeeoo, yeeoo", speeding up into raucous, bubbling, tumbling chaos of chattering, easing into either "wikachwakachwikadiwik...", or 5–30 quickly repeated "wikoo" notes, or flowing "wipiwuwipiwipiwu...". Grating, rattling, churring sounds also given. Call: soft, yelping "yo, yo, yo...", "jeeuw, jeeuw, jeeuw...", "yuk, yuk, yuk...", "jip, jip, jip...".

Rufous-fronted Laughingthrush *Garrulax rufifrons* **E**

L 27 cm. 2 ssp: *rufifrons* (W Jav), *slamatensis* (Mt Slamet). Increasingly rare and local in montane forest, 900–2500 m. Usually in small groups (<8), often foraging with Javan Scimitar Babblers, shy. **ID Ad** reddish-rufous forehead and lores; yellow iris; greyish mid-brown head and underparts; olive-tinged mantle; rufous-tinged wings and tail. Ssp *slamatensis* rufous breast to chin; slightly darker overall. **Imm** undescribed. **Voc** Song: multiple birds usually producing a cacophony of 10–30 agitated whinnying notes, "he-he-he-tu-tu-tu-tu..." at 7 n/s, starting at slow even pitch before descending at a faster rate. Call: loud, sharp, woodpecker-like yelp "pee". **AN** Javan Laughingthrush.

Spectacled Laughingthrush *Garrulax mitratus* **E**

L 22–24 cm. Sundaic. 2 ssp, 1 in region: *mitratus* (Sum). Formerly included the closely-related Chestnut-hooded Laughingthrush but now usually considered separate species based on moderate morphological and vocal differences. Increasingly uncommon in (sub-) montane forest, 500–3200 m. Usually in groups (<30), often forages with Sunda Laughingthrushes. **ID Ad** chestnut crown with white flecks on forecrown; broad white eyering; black lores; largely mid-grey plumage with chestnut vent, darker tail tip and white primary flashes; orange bare parts. **Imm** duller, more brownish-tinged plumage. **Voc** Song: series of 3–5 cheery, melodious "we woo-we-woo", lasting <2 sec. Call: (i) thin, melodious notes "we-jujujuju..."; (ii) rapid, harsh, cackling "wekakakaka..."; (iii) low, harsh scolding. **AN** Chestnut-capped Laughingthrush.

Chestnut-hooded Laughingthrush *Garrulax treacheri* **E**

L 22–24 cm. 4 ssp: *treacheri* (Sabah); *damnatus* (E Sarawak, NE Kalimantan); *griswoldi* (Mt Batu Tibang in C Bor; this ssp in W Sarawak?), undescribed ssp (Meratus Mts, SE Kalimantan). The undescribed form from Meratus Mts is highly distinct in plumage and may warrant recognition as monotypic species '**Meratus Laughingthrush**'. For taxonomy also see Spectacled Laughingthrush. Common in (sub-) montane forest, 600–3300 m, recorded down to 200 m. Usually in groups (<30), often forages with Sunda Laughingthrushes and Bornean Treepies. **ID Ad** chestnut hood with grey flecks on forecrown; bold bare yellow eye crescent; slaty-grey plumage with prominent white wing patch; buff-streaked breast; rufous vent; dark-tipped tail. Ssp *damnatus* breast less streaked and more greyish; *griswoldi* richer vent; undescribed ssp from Meratus peachy-buff underparts down to upper belly, paler grey upperparts and white flecks below eye. **Imm** duller; less distinct crown. **Voc** Song: charming, whistled "choo-woo chwi'-wi'-wi'-weee-weoo-we..." at 3 n/s, lasting <10 sec. Call: (i) harsh, low, hoarse scolding; (ii) stuttering harsh notes "we'e'e'er-eoo".

Long-tailed Sibia *Heterophasia picaoides*

L 28–34 cm. Himalaya to SE Asia. 4 ssp, 1 in region: *simillima* (Sum). Fairly common in (sub-) montane forest, 500–3000 m. Usually in small groups (<10) in mid- and upper canopy. **ID Ad** sleek, all grey, belly slightly paler; very long white-tipped tail; conspicuous white wing patch. **Imm** brownish-tinged plumage, particularly on head; paler belly; shorter, blunter tail. **Voc** Song: series of 4–8 high-pitched, thin, metallic "tsit-tsit-tsit..." at 5 n/s, slightly descending. Call: (i) thin, high "sic"; (ii) dry, level-pitched, scolding rattles "chrrrrt", often several birds calling together, particularly vocal in flight.

Silver-eared Mesia *Leiothrix argentauris*

L 15–17 cm. Himalaya to SE Asia. 7 ssp, 2 in region: *laurinae* (C–S Sum); *rookmakeri* (N Sum). The two regional ssp are morphologically distinct from all extralimital subspecies and have been proposed for independent species status as '**Sumatran Mesia**' *L. laurinae*. Now rare because of trapping and locally extinct, especially ssp *laurinae*, in all but a few remaining remote areas in (sub-) montane forest, 600–2100 m. Usually in groups (<10) accompanying mixed flocks. **ID Ad** bright and neatly-marked (less neat in **F**): glistening silver ear-coverts; black crown and rest of face; small orange-red fore-crown spot; red rump, throat, breast and nuchal collar; pale greenish-grey belly; grey mantle with orange and yellow wing patches; black tail with yellow outertail; yellow iris; yellow bill and legs. Ssp *rookmakeri* greener overall (especially on mantle); more contrasting nuchal collar; black iris. **Imm** less contrasting head pattern; body colours less bright. **Voc** Song: loud, clearly-spaced "tiweet, tuweet-tureet-tuwiu"; last note typically downslurred (often upslurred in extralimital ssp). Call: harsh chattering, singly and in groups.

Javan Crocias *Laniellus albonotatus* **E**

L 20 cm. Monotypic. Uncommon in (sub-) montane forest, 900–2400 m. Usually in small groups (<10) in mid- and upper canopy joining mixed flocks. **ID** Slim, with long rounded tail. **Ad** contrasting blackish-grey head with creamy-white underparts and throat (latter with yellow tinge); white streaks on mid-brown mantle, flanks and rump; black tail tipped white. **Imm** undescribed. **Voc** Song: agitated, continuous, rapid series of rolling "jhrew" or "jhrew'it" notes, often slightly rising in pitch, lasting 5–30 sec at 4 n/s; often 2–6 birds in duet while perched side-by-side. **AN** Spotted Crocias.

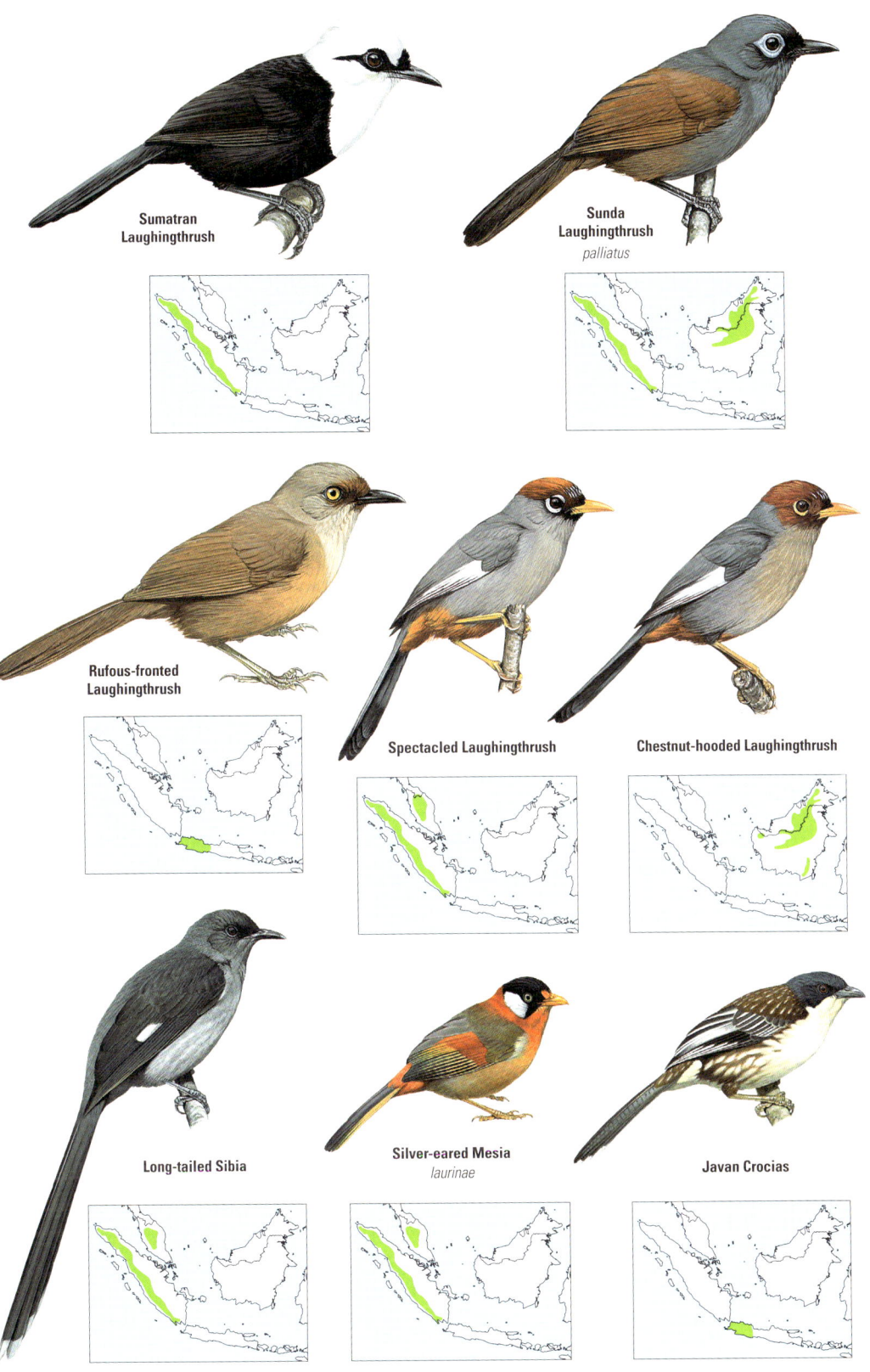

Sumatran Laughingthrush

Sunda Laughingthrush
palliatus

Rufous-fronted Laughingthrush

Spectacled Laughingthrush

Chestnut-hooded Laughingthrush

Long-tailed Sibia

Silver-eared Mesia
laurinae

Javan Crocias

ZOSTEROPIDAE
White-eyes and allies
40 species in region

Small warbler-like arboreal birds of forest, edge and a variety of wooded habitats. Typically active, vocal and conspicuous, often in small or mixed species flocks. Famously labelled a 'great speciator', the family is renowned for its propensity to colonise small islands and has brought forth a high diversity of 'supertramps' and small-island endemics.

Chestnut-crested Yuhina *Staphida everetti*   E
L 14–15 cm. Monotypic. Common in (sub-) montane forest, 900–2800 m. Usually pairs or flocks (<40), favouring canopy. **ID Ad** crested chestnut head; grey upperparts; black tail with broad white tips; white underparts. **Imm** similar to Ad. **Voc** (i) Continual chattering and churring, "tchut", "tchit" and "twee", with occasional high-pitched notes, often multiple birds calling together; (ii) in flight, flocks give an excited, repeated "twit" and "twee".

Eyebrowed Heleia *Apalopteron superciliare*   E
L 13 cm. 2 ssp: *superciliare* (Flores); *hartertianum* (Sumbawa). Common in primary montane forest, >1000 m. Forms small to larger groups, sometimes in mixed flocks, in mid-storey. **ID Ad** dull olive-green upperparts; greyish-olive sides of head; pale creamy-yellow lores and supercilium; dull yellowish-green underparts, mostly yellow on throat and centrally. Ssp *hartertianum* with brighter yellow eyebrow becoming golden-yellow towards forehead. **Imm** undescribed. **Voc** Song: rapid, slightly melancholy series of fairly high-pitched, bubbling, sometimes almost trilled, warbled notes interspersed with occasional brief "tchee-tchee", lasting 6–17 sec. Call: ringing "peu-peu". **AN** Yellow-browed/Cream-browed White-eye/Dark-eye.

Crested Heleia *Apalopteron dohertyi*   E
L 12 cm. 2 ssp: *dohertyi* (Sumbawa, Satonda); *subcristatum* (Flores). Locally common in primary hill and lower montane forest, scarcer in wooded cultivation and scrub, 200–1400 m. Singly, pairs or groups (<8), joins mixed flocks with Thick-billed Heleias in understorey. **ID Ad** blackish chestnut-brown crown with elongated, white-spotted feathers; rudimentary white eyering; black lores and sides of forehead; short lemon supercilium behind eye; olive ear-coverts; greyish-olive upperparts; sulphur-yellow underparts, paler on throat. Ssp *subcristatum* shorter crest; paler crown sharply spotted only on forecrown; less conspicuous supercilium; more yellow ear coverts. **Imm** undescribed. **Voc** Song: moderately rapid musical warble of ~14 clear, sweet whistles interspersed with high-pitched notes, lasting 5 sec. Call: soft "tsip-tsip". **AN** Crested White-eye/Dark-eye.

Wallace's Heleia *Apalopteron wallacei*   E
L 12 cm. Monotypic. In the past erroneously considered a *Zosterops* white-eye under the name 'Yellow-spectacled White-eye'. Common in coastal savanna, forest, <1050 m. Singly, pairs or groups (<15), joins mixed flocks. **ID Ad** olive-yellow head with orange forehead; olive-green upperparts; throat, breast and vent yellow; belly pale-grey with white central stripe; black iris. **Imm** pale brown iris. **Voc** Song: sweet, warbled, descending series of 10–14 jumbled notes, often preceded by 1–2 indistinct, short, insect-like notes, lasting 3–4 sec. Call: (i) plaintive "cheuw"; (ii) churring notes when agitated; (iii) dreary whistled notes. **SS** Warbling and Ashy-bellied White-eyes have distinct white eyering (absent in Wallace's Heleia). Lemon-bellied and Flores White-eyes additionally have yellow (not grey) underparts. **AN** Yellow-spectacled White-eye.

Thick-billed Heleia *Apalopteron crassirostre*   E
L 14 cm. Monotypic. Uncommon in semi-evergreen and monsoon forest, edge and *Eupatorium* scrub. Singly, pairs or groups (<6); joins mixed flocks; in under- and lower mid-storey. **ID Ad** creamy-white forehead grading into olive-brown nape and upperparts; black scaling on mid-crown; blackish face mask; underparts creamy-white; pale iris. **Imm** uniformly creamy-buff forehead and crown. **Voc** Song: (i) series of mellow melancholy whistles interspersed with single trilled notes, each phrase starting hesitantly, often working up to a descending trill ending with a "cheep"; (ii) rapid series of variable, mellow, mostly descending trills, often with abrupt changes in pitch. Call: quiet, deep, unobtrusive "chup, chup, chup…". **AN** Thick-billed/Flores White-eye/Dark-eye.

Timor Heleia *Apalopteron muelleri*   E
L 14 cm. Monotypic. Local, uncommon in monsoon and dry forest, occasionally montane forest. Pairs or tight groups (<6); joins mixed flocks in mid-storey and canopy. **ID Ad** yellow face and throat with black lores; deep-olive upperparts and crown, the latter black-spotted; pale whitish-yellow underparts with dark spots on breast. **Imm** duller, almost no spots on crown and breast. **Voc** Song: unmusical rattle of 10–20 very rapid mechanical notes, initially rising then falling, lasting 3–4 sec. Call: harsh but weak grating notes. **AN** Spot-breasted White-eye/Dark-eye.

Sulawesi Heleia *Apalopteron squamiceps*   E
L 12 cm. 6 ssp: *squamiceps* (SW Sul); *heinrichi* (NW Sul); *stresemanni* (NE Sul); *striaticeps* (NC Sul); *stachyrinum* (SC Sul); *analogum* (SE Sul). Common in montane forest, edge and secondary growth, 1000–2500 m. Pairs or small groups; follows mixed flocks, favours canopy. **ID Ad** blackish-brown crown and auriculars mottled with white shaft streaks and feather tips; dark olive-green upperparts; whitish throat feathers with broad dark fringes; dirty-yellow breast; yellow rest of underparts with olive-green flanks. Ssp *heinrichi* greyish-sepia crown with broad grey edges and inconspicuous white shaft streaks, white throat feathers with very narrow black fringes; *striaticeps* uniform buffy-white throat, black crown feathers have narrower white shaft streaks and grey (not white) edges, brighter yellow underparts; *stresemanni* with broader and longer contrasting shaft streaks, more bright-yellow on underparts than any other ssp, white throat without black fringes; *stachyrinum* as *striaticeps* but larger with paler and greyer flanks, paler ear-coverts, crown streaked with broader white shaft streaks and even less white on feather tips; *analogum* the smallest race with white throat lacking black edges to feathers, crown with broad silvery-grey edges and contrasting shaft streaks. **Imm** crown tinged greenish; slightly paler yellow underparts. **Voc** Song: warbled melancholy series of loud, clear, sibilant, high-pitched notes lasting 4–5 sec, typically repeated at intervals of 5–9 sec. Calls: (i) harsh chirruping trill; (ii) a more mellow "dididdid" slightly dropping in pitch. **AN** Streak-headed White-eye/Dark-eye.

Chestnut-crested Yuhina

Eyebrowed Heleia

Thick-billed Heleia

Wallace's Heleia

Crested Heleia

stachyrinum

squamiceps

Sulawesi Heleia

Timor Heleia

Javan Heleia *Apalopteron javanicum* E

L 12 cm. 3 ssp: *javanicum* (C Jav); *frontale* (W Jav); *elongatum* (E Jav–Bali). Shows peculiar leapfrog pattern in which two terminal taxa (*frontale*, *elongatum*) resemble each other but are separated by dissimilar form (*javanicum*), indicating potential for separation into more than one species. More research required. Common in forest, dense secondary growth, farmland, >900 m. Pairs, small groups; follows mixed flocks, mostly in canopy. **ID Ad** dark olive-grey head with forehead, lores, eyering and supercilium creamy-white; olive-green upperparts; pale-grey throat; darker grey breast grading into yellow belly. Ssp *frontale* lacks creamy-white facial pattern, but has broad black lores and variable buff suffusion around forehead; *elongatum* as previous but slightly larger bill (most pronounced on Bali). **Imm** greenish tinge to grey crown. **Voc** Song: series of 5–18 melodious down- or upslurred whistles, lasting 1.5–3.5 sec. Call: (i) repetitive, loud, high-pitched, long-drawn, downslurred "cheep"; (ii) rather throaty "turrr", "teerrr" or "chreeet- chreet-chreet...". **AN** Javan Grey-throated White-eye/Dark-eye.

Grey-hooded Heleia *Apalopteron pinaiae* E

L 14 cm. Monotypic. Of uncertain affinity, and perhaps not closely related to other members of this genus. Locally fairly common in montane forest, more common at higher altitudes, >1100 m. Pairs or small groups (<10), joins mixed flocks in canopy. **ID Ad** grey head and breast; dirty white forehead; strong white eyering; dark-olive upperparts; whitish belly; bright yellow vent. **Imm** undescribed. **Voc** Mellow rattles "chow-trrit" and "chow-tritritritritritrit". **AN** Grey-hooded White-eye/Dark-eye, Binaia Heleia.

Pygmy Heleia *Apalopteron squamifrons* E

L 9–9.5 cm. Monotypic. Locally fairly common but inconspicuous; hill and montane moss forest, secondary growth, 550–1000 m, occasionally up to 2150 m and down to 50 m. Flocks (2–50) associating with other species when feeding on berries in crowns of tall trees and mid-storey along edge. **ID** Diminutive. **Ad** olive brown upperparts and crown; pale-mottled forehead; thin white eyering; yellowish-white underparts; pale iris. **Imm** undescribed. **Voc** Song: cheerful warble, starting with a high-pitched, long, descending trill, lasting 5 sec. Calls: (i) rapid 3-note "chichichit", slightly or sharply dropping in pitch; (ii) high-pitched trill; (iii) high-pitched, thin "tsee"; (iv) plaintive "tsew". **SS** Often feeds side-by-side with similarly tiny flowerpeckers, which can be hard to distinguish with distant views. Most flowerpeckers lack pale iris and mottled forehead. **AN** Pygmy White-eye/Dark-eye, Pygmy Ibon.

Bicoloured White-eye *Tephrozosterops stalkeri* E

L 12–13 cm. Monotypic. Traditionally thought to be member of heleia group ('Bicoloured Heleia'), but more closely related to *Zosterops* white-eyes. Uncommon in edge, scrub and overgrown cultivation, 500–1200 m. Joins mixed flocks, especially with Seram or Warbling White-eyes. **ID Ad** rusty-brown upperparts; white underparts washed brown on flanks and thighs; yellow-washed vent. **Imm** undescribed **Voc** High-pitched twittering when feeding. **AN** Rufescent White-eye/Dark-eye.

Mountain Black-eye *Zosterops emiliae* E

L 11–12 cm. 4 ssp: *emiliae* (Mt Kinabalu area); *trinitae* (Mt Trus Madi [Sabah]); *moultoni* (Sarawak and Kalimantan mts); *fusciceps* (Paya Maga Mts at Sabah/Sarawak border). Genomic data refute previous mtDNA results suggesting deep divergence between the two eastern and western ssp. Montane mossy and stunted forest, >1600 m, rarely to 1200 m. Pairs or small flocks (<6) in tree tops and lower canopy. **ID Ad** dark olive-green upperparts and crown with blackish cast; small black face mask fringed yellow; underparts dark-green, paler and more yellowish on central belly; bill orange, blackish at nostrils. Ssp *trinitae* paler green to yellowish underparts; *moultoni* smaller, shorter-tailed, with facial areas, foreneck and underparts much yellower; *fusciceps* darker sepia-coloured crown and forehead. **Imm** dull orange to blackish bill; brighter yellow overall. **Voc** Song *emiliae*: (i) melodious "werwit-kukew toweeo", or "wit-a-wit, wit-wit wheer"; (ii) melodious "tititweeio" with pronounced rise and elongation at the end. Call (*emiliae* and *moultoni*): twittering "eewee-oo" or "ee-wew". Ssp *emiliae* also gives stuttering "gujugu-jug" and jangling call in flight.

Warbling White-eye *Zosterops japonicus*

L 11.5–12 cm. GS, Wallacea, Phil, E Asia. 18 ssp, 4 in region: *montanus* (C Sum); *difficilis* (S Sum); *neglectus* (E-C Jav–Timor, Sul, Taliabu, Buru); *obstinatus* (Ternate, Tidore, Bacan, Obi, Seram). This species is a newly-defined composite of former '**Mountain**' *Z. montanus* (Indo Archipelago, Phil), '**Lowland**' *Z. meyeni* (N Phil) and parts of '**Japanese White-eye**' *Z. japonicus* (E Asia) following a taxonomic revision based on genetics. In region, Warbling White-eye is a mountain-top specialist although it ranges to lowlands at higher latitudes. Apart from saturation of yellow pigmentation on underparts, species is uniform in morphology and call across vast distances, indicating great eruptive potential and dispersal capability despite fragmented montane distribution. Fairly common in montane and moss forest, pine and *Casuarina* forest, scrub, bushes on barren mountain tops, >1000 m, but >700 m on smaller islands. In noisy, fast-moving flocks of ≥5, joins mixed flocks, e.g. with Sangkar White-eye on Jav and Bali. **ID Ad** intense yellow supraloral grading into olive-green crown and upperparts, with yellower rump; white eyering broken at front by indistinct, dusky loral stripe; distinct pale-grey iris visible with good views; yellow throat and upper breast usually 'bleed' into faint yellow median belly line running across greyish-white underparts sometimes all the way to yellow vent. Ssp *neglectus* usually has fainter or absent yellow belly line, whereas underparts almost all-yellow in ssp *difficilis*, and entirely yellow in ssp *obstinatus*. **Imm** duller, with more greenish throat; forehead less contrasting with crown. **Voc** Song: (i) melodious *Phylloscopus*-like warble; (ii) low-pitched but melodious song on 3 notes (Sum). Call characteristic and almost identical across range: high-pitched, metallic, 'elastic', descending "tsew" or "ts-tsew". **SS** Warbling White-eye shows strong character displacement, exhibiting all-yellow plumage on islands where some competitors are grey/white-bellied (e.g., Seram; Bacan; Obi) and vice versa (e.g., Buru; LS [Lemon-bellied, Flores White-eye] and Sul [Lemon-bellied]). This displacement also occurs where all-yellow Sangkar (ssp *melanurus*) meets grey-bellied Warbling (ssp *neglectus*) in E-C Jav–Bali and where grey-bellied Sangkar (ssp *buxtoni*) meets all-yellow Warbling (ssp *difficilis*) in S Sum. In C Sum, grey-bellied Warbling (ssp *montanus*) best told from Sangkar (ssp *buxtoni*) and Swinhoe's (both usually at lower elevations) by paler grey (not dark-brown) iris and by less distinct dusky or black loral patch with a less pronounced break in eyering. Sangkar ssp *buxtoni* on Sum additionally has darker grey underparts with yellow median stripe cut off at breast (versus Warbling's yellow throat bleeding into a faint continuous mid-belly line which is sometimes absent). Swinhoe's additionally differs from Warbling by longer, stronger bill and much thicker lower portion of eyering (easily as wide as eye's diameter in Swinhoe's versus only roughly half the eye's diameter in Warbling). Also see Black-crowned, Black-capped, Ashy-bellied and Kendari White-eyes and Wallace's Heleia.

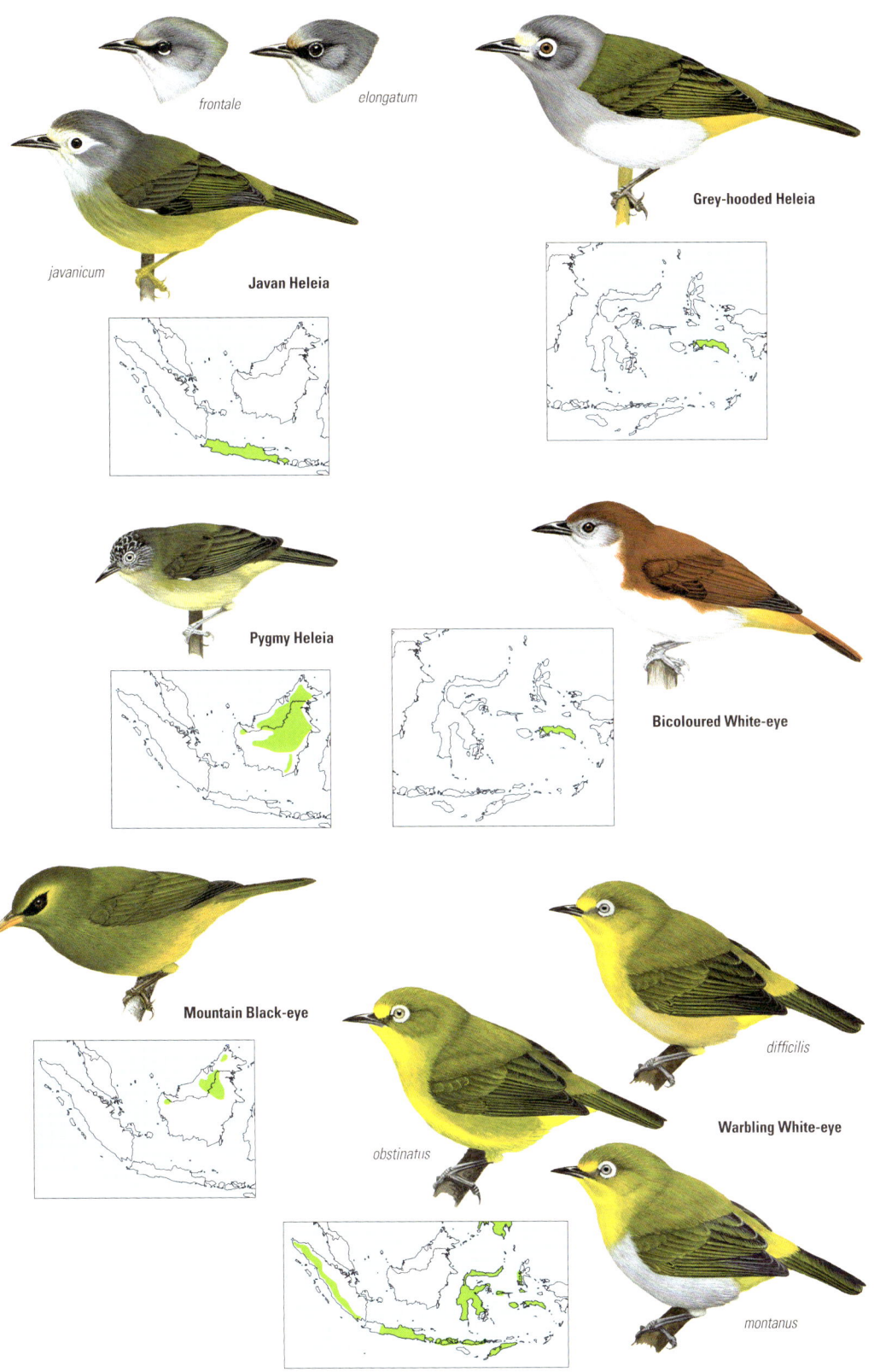

frontale

elongatum

javanicum

Javan Heleia

Grey-hooded Heleia

Pygmy Heleia

Bicoloured White-eye

Mountain Black-eye

difficilis

Warbling White-eye

obstinatus

montanus

Sangkar White-eye *Zosterops melanurus* E

L 10–11 cm. 3 ssp: *melanurus* (E-C Jav into eastern W Jav, Bali); *buxtoni* (W Jav); *sumatranus* (Sum mts). This species – along with Flores White-eye, parts of Swinhoe's White-eye and extralimital Indian White-eye *Z. palpebrosus* (S Asia, northern SE Asia) – was formerly classified into a large unnatural composite ('**Oriental White-eye**' *Z. palpebrosus*) before taxonomic revision. Genomic evidence suggests rare hybridization between ssp *sumatranus* and Swinhoe's. Widespread intergradation between ssp *buxtoni* and *melanurus* around Bogor (W Jav). On Sum common in forest, ~800-1600 m. On Jav–Bali becoming scarce, only locally common, in various forest and woodland types, <1600 m. Noisy groups (3–30, sometimes 100+); joins mixed flocks, upper canopy. **ID Ad** narrow yellow supraloral contrasting against olive-green crown and upperparts; white eyering broken at front by thick black loral stripe, which also extends to below eyering ("eyeliner"); yellow underparts, brighter on throat and vent; iris dark-brown; bill and legs bluish-horn. Ssp *buxtoni* smaller with yellow throat, upper breast and vent; belly pale greyish-white with yellow median stripe not connected to yellow throat. Ssp *sumatranus* as previous but yellow supraloral smaller or absent; darker grey underparts. **Imm** duller. **Voc** Song: long series of simple high-pitched notes between 3–8 kHz. Call: (i) repeated "cheer" of day-old feral chick, 4-8 kHz; (ii) distinctive nasal, gradually downslurred, guttural "djeeeeer". **SS** See Lemon-bellied, Javan, Warbling, Swinhoe's and Black-capped White-eyes.

Swinhoe's White-eye *Zosterops simplex*

L 11–12 cm. E Asia, Sundaic. 5 ssp, 2 in region: *erwini* (lowland Sum, Riau, Natuna, Bangka, coastal W-N Bor, MPen), *salvadorii* (Enggano, Mega). This species is a newly-defined composite consisting of ssp formerly comprising parts of '**Japanese**' *Z. japonicus* (E Asia) and '**Oriental White-eye**' *Z. palpebrosus* (S-SE Asia); see Warbling and Sangkar White-eyes for more taxonomic details. Ssp *salvadorii* previously considered monotypic '**Enggano White-eye**' but shown to be genetically embedded within Swinhoe's. Ssp *erwini* previously called *auriventer*, but that name has been shown to apply to Hume's White-eye. Swinhoe's escapees have been photographed in coastal Java. Fairly common in secondary growth, woodland, shrub and mangrove. Small restless flocks (<40). **ID Ad** broad white eye-ring widely broken at front by distinct black loral stripe that often extends below eyering ("eyeliner"); olive-green head and upperparts, yellower on rump, often contrasting with distinct yellow supraloral; greyish white underparts with variably weak yellow median stripe often interrupted at both ends; iris dark-brown; legs and bill bluish-horn. Ssp *salvadorii* darker olive upperparts, particularly head; less distinct yellow median stripe. **Imm** greener overall; underparts duller. **Voc** Song: ssp *erwini* only known to produce series of call-like notes. Call: (i) downslurred, sharp, slightly buzzy "tzeep", 3-6 kHz; (ii) hard, slightly ascending rattle "p'r'r'r't't", lasting <0.5 s. **SS** Sangkar usually occurs at higher elevations on Sum but is similar (also beware of Swinhoe's escapees in Javan range of Sangkar); main differences are (1) Swinhoe's wider eyering (often roughly same width as eye's diameter along lower eyering portion, versus only roughly half as wide as eye's diameter in Sangkar), (2) Swinhoe's more distinct yellow supraloral (small in Sangkar on Sum), (3) Swinhoe's larger and more pointed bill (versus blunter in Sangkar), (4) Swinhoe's paler grey underparts with fainter yellow median stripe often interrupted, whereas Sangkar on Sum has darker grey breast band and flanks separated by clearer, more extensive yellow median stripe. Also see Warbling, Black-capped and Hume's.

Everett's White-eye *Zosterops everetti*

L 11–11.5 cm. Phil. 6 ssp, 1 in region: *babelo* (Talaud). For taxonomy see Hume's White-eye. Fairly common in forest. Only white-eye on island. **ID Ad** white eyering broken at front; indistinct dusky loral

line; olive-green upperparts; throat to upper breast yellow, connected to yellow vent via broad yellow median stripe (often interrupted at breast); pure grey remainder of underparts, darker grey on flanks; bluish-horn iris and legs. **Imm** undescribed. **Voc** Song *babelo* undescribed. Extralimital ssp: rapid series of downslurred twittering notes, 2-3 s. Call: repeated, high-pitched, buzzy, downslurred "tzeep".

Hume's White-eye *Zosterops auriventer*

L 12 cm. SE Asia. 4 ssp, 2 in region: *medius* (Bor); *tahanensis* (MPen, Lingga). Previously included with Everett's White-eye, but now separated based on morphological and genomic evidence. Also see Swinhoe's White-eye for taxonomy. Locally fairly common in hill forest, edge and cultivation, 200–1700 m. **ID Ad** olive-green crown and upperparts; extensive black loral area interrupting white eye ring at front; yellow throat and upper breast; yellow vent extending into broad yellow median belly stripe not connected to throat; remainder of underparts mid-grey, darker on flanks, creating grey-vested appearance; dark-red iris; bluish-horn legs and bill. Ssp *tahanensis* larger. **Imm** less contrasting underparts; greener upperparts. **Voc** Song: clear, pleasant, sweet but rather weak series of twittering notes, thinner and higher-pitched than those of Sangkar. Call: (i) "tsee-tsee" or metallic "spreet" or "peet" while perched and in flight; (ii) high-pitched buzzing "dzee"; (iii) more musical, inflected "dzee-ap", mainly in flight. **SS** Swinhoe's White-eye overlaps at lower elevations; Hume's best told by (1) darker 'grey-vested' appearance with wide and distinct yellow median belly wedge (versus Swinhoe's whiter underparts with narrower yellow median-belly line often interrupted towards vent), (2) lack of contrasting yellow supraloral stripe on olive crown (present in Swinhoe's), (3) on average less bright, greener upperparts (especially rump) than Swinhoe's, (4) shorter, blunter bill, (5) narrower eye-ring (lower portion's width roughly 50-70% of eye's diameter, versus roughly equal width to eye's diameter in Swinhoe's). See also Black-capped White-eye.

Black-capped White-eye *Zosterops atricapilla* E

L 9.5–10 cm. 3 ssp: *atricapilla* (C–S Sum); *viridicatus* (N Sum); *clarus* (Bor). Preliminary genomic evidence indicates that Sum and Bor ssp may not be each other's closest relatives, leading to possible separation into '**Lumut White-eye**' *Z. atricapilla* (incl. ssp *viridicatus*) and monotypic '**Orchid White-eye**' *Z. clarus*. Common in (sub-)montane forest, 700–3000 m (Sum), 900–2100 m (Bor). In groups (4–20), joins mixed flocks in lower and mid-storey. **ID Ad** black forecrown and lores; thick white eyering broken at front; upperparts olive-green, rump yellower; throat and vent greenish-yellow; remainder of underparts mid-grey with yellow median belly stripe interrupted on breast; dark iris; legs grey or pink (probably age-related). Ssp *viridicatus* slightly greener, less yellow, especially throat and rump. Ssp *clarus* distinct pale-grey iris. **Imm** duller; pink legs probably imm trait. **Voc** Song: loud ringing warble of slightly trembling quality, sharply changing in pitch, often ending with ascending, 'questioning' motif, lasting <3 sec. Call: (i) loud trembling contact call; (ii) metallic "tsee-tsee-tsee...". **SS** Warbling, Swinhoe's, Hume's and Sangkar White-eyes easily told by olive (not black) forecrown.

Meratus White-eye *Zosterops* sp. E

Undescribed species from Meratus Mts, SE Kalimantan. Common in montane forest mostly >1200 m. In groups (4–20); joins mixed flocks. **ID Ad** white eyering narrowly broken at front; indistinct black loral line connecting to lower eyering; narrow bright yellow supraloral; dull olive-green overall with slightly brighter-yellow throat, vent and median belly; pinkish-horn lower mandible, slightly darker upper mandible. **Imm** undescribed. **Voc** Song: warbling series of short high-pitched notes ending with faster, lower notes, lasting 1–3 sec. Call: high-pitched, buzzy "zip". **SS** See Javan White-eye.

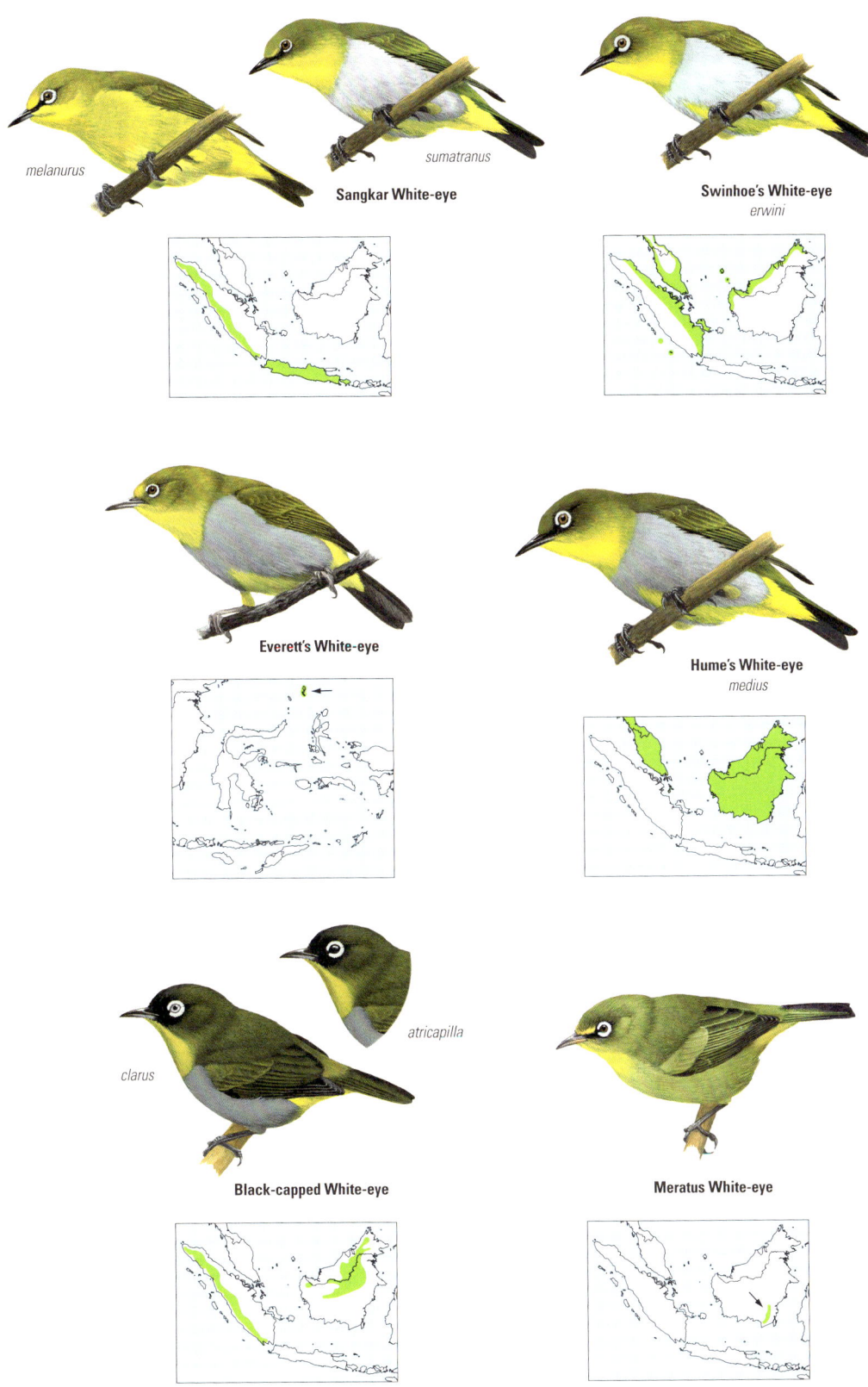

melanurus

sumatranus

Sangkar White-eye

Swinhoe's White-eye
erwini

Everett's White-eye

Hume's White-eye
medius

clarus

atricapilla

Black-capped White-eye

Meratus White-eye

Lemon-bellied White-eye *Zosterops chloris*

L 11–12 cm. Indonesian Archipelago to Aru. 5 ssp: *chloris* (Kai, Banda, Aru and small Mol islands N to Nanusa [off Talaud] and Raja Ampat); *mentoris* (N-C-E-SE Sul); *intermedius* (SW Sul, Selayar–Kalaotoa); *sumbavensis* (Lombok–Pantar; small Java Sea islands from Karimunjawa to islands off Bali and S Kalimantan), *maxi* (small islands N of Banten and W Jav). Preliminary genomic results indicate this is a chimeric species containing two unrelated lineages that may require division into an eastern monotypic **'Banda White-eye'** *Z. chloris* (more closely related to Ashy-bellied) and a western **'Sombre White-eye'** *Z. intermedius* (containing all four other ssp). Typical supertramp: adept at colonising small islands. Common in wide variety of forested and cultivated habitats, even including shrub in coconut groves, mangroves and small islands with dense human population, <1000 m (NC Sul), <1200 m (Flores), <1660 m (Lombok) and <1800 m (S Sul). Small restless flocks (<40) at all levels of vegetation; local seasonal movements occur. **ID** [*sumbavensis*] **Ad** subdued olive upperparts and olive-yellow underparts, more washed-out on flanks, but on average becoming brighter eastwards towards Flores; distinct wide unbroken white eyering; thick black loral stripe diagnostically continues below eyering ("eye-liner"); smallish yellow supraloral patch contrasts against olive crown; bill colour variable from all pinkish-horn to dark-horn (probably age-related). Ssp *maxi* with pale eyes, greener upperparts and apparently always pink bill. Ssp *intermedius* as *sumbavensis* but yellower underparts, narrow break in anterior part of eyering. Ssp *mentoris* in N-C Sul as previous but has eyering more distinctly broken, with thick black loral stripe extending into broken eyering portion, much less eye-liner along lower ring; yellow supraloral patch often wider than in other ssp; populations in SE Sul approach ssp *intermedius* in many respects (more black eye-liner below ring, mostly small supra-loral patch). Ssp *chloris* has narrower eyering, broken in front by black loral stripe but with minimal black eye-liner below ring (black lores faint in Nanusa [Talaud]); lacks contrasting yellow supra-loral patch; wings and greyish-horn bill longer than in other ssp. **Imm** greener; underparts duller. **Voc** Song: jumbled mixture of rapid high-pitched musical "see-sawing" and more sibilant "sit-sit" notes, given in short bursts of 1.5–4 sec, a longer version starting softly. Subspecific song analysis required. Call: (i) plaintive "chew"; (ii) loud sparrow-like "shilp". **SS** Flores White-eye is much brighter yellow (less lemon) overall, especially on rump, with minimal contrast between upper- and underparts, and lacking strongly contrasting supra-loral patch. All-yellow Sangkar White-eye ssp *melanurus* from mainland of Jav–Bali (not offshore islands) should only overlap in escapee situations: more saturated yellow overall (less olive), especially on underparts; Sangkar's eyering is usually narrower and is broken at the front (unbroken in adjacent ssp of Lemon-bellied); Sangkar always has bluish-horn bill (often pink in adjacent populations of Lemon-bellied). See also Javan White-eye, Warbling White-eye and Wallace's Heleia.

Wakatobi White-eye *Zosterops flavissimus* **F**

L 11–12 cm. Monotypic. Common in forest, woodland and cultivation. Small restless flocks (<40) at all levels of vegetation, often mixing with Wangi Wangi White-eye. **ID Ad** bright yellow overall, especially on rump and underparts, only slightly more olive on upperparts; variably orange-tinged forehead; broad white eyering slightly broken at front; faint black loral stripe connects to below eyering, pinkish-horn bill; dark pinkish-horn legs. **Imm** greener; underparts duller. **Voc** Song: short series of cheery, complex, downslurred notes, lasting 3 s. Call: (i) plaintive "chew"; (ii) downslurred "tseep".

Javan White-eye *Zosterops flavus* **E**

L 9.5 cm. Monotypic. Surprisingly distinct genomically, with closest relatives in India and Africa. Now local and rare in mangroves and adjacent dry edge and shrubby areas; status in Kalimantan not well-known. Arboreal feeder in tight flocks (4–50). **ID Ad** broad yellow forehead grading into yellowish olive remainder of upperparts; brighter rump; yellow underparts; narrow white eyering usually slightly broken at front; indistinct black loral line sometimes connecting to lower eyering; bluish-horn bill. **Imm** even narrower eyering. **Voc** Song: hurried series of 6–12 call notes at different frequencies. Call: (i) contact note "treeew" and short "trip"; (ii) alarm call "wiwi-wiwit". **SS** Most likely to be confused with more generalist Sangkar ssp *melanurus* in large parts of Jav (except far W): Javan has broad yellow forehead grading into more olive nape whereas Sangkar *melanurus* has narrow yellow supraloral contrasting with more olive crown; Javan's narrow, indistinct loral stripe connects to lower eyering (not to centre of eyering). Lemon-bellied White-eye (from small offshore islands but not mainland of Jav/Bor) is duller olive-tinged overall (especially underparts), has contrasting yellow supraloral akin to Sangkar and much thicker black lores, and has eyering width almost equal to eye's diameter (less than half the eye's diameter in Javan). Lemon-bellied ssp *maxi* and *sumbavensis* (most adjacent to Javan's range) always have unbroken eyering, with black lores extending into unique eye-liner band along lower eyering (absent in Javan), and mostly have pinkish (not bluish-horn) bill; *maxi* has pale (not dark) iris; however, other Lemon-bellied ssp may be found in Javan's range as escapees. Meratus White-eye from higher elevations in SE Kalimantan is much darker olive-green overall (especially on forecrown and underparts) and has pinkish (not bluish-horn) bill.

Flores White-eye *Zosterops unicus* **E**

L 11–12 cm. Monotypic. Despite plumage differences, closely related to Ashy-bellied White-eye and sometimes merged based on mtDNA, but genome-wide data suggest status as distinct species. For taxonomy also see Sangkar White-eye. Common in forest, secondary growth and woodland. Small flocks (<40) at all levels of vegetation. **ID Ad** bright yellow overall, hardly any darker olive on upperparts than on underparts, with very yellow rump; well-defined, thin black loral stripe connecting to below thick, white, unbroken eyering; dark-brown iris; bluish-horn legs and bill. **Imm** duller. **Voc** Song: jumbled, pleasant twittering of mainly downslurred notes, 2-4 s, at 3-8 kHz. **SS** See Wallace's Heleia and Lemon-bellied White-eye.

Ashy-bellied White-eye *Zosterops citrinella* **E**

L 10–11 cm. 2 ssp: *citrinella* (Sumba, Sawu, Timor, Rote, Lembata–Alor); *griseiventris* (Leti–Tanimbar, Wetar–Damar). Previously thought to extend to Torres Strait and Queensland, but genomic data indicate Australian populations (ssp *albiventris*) are not closely related to this species. For taxonomy also see Flores and Lemon-bellied White-eyes. Common in scrub, forest, mangroves, often on small islands, <1400 m. Singly, pairs or flocks (<30); at all levels of vegetation. **ID Ad** yellow supraloral contrasting with olive-yellow crown and upperparts, but rump brighter yellow; white eyering broken at front by thick black loral stripe; yellow throat, upper breast and vent; greyish-white rest of underparts, sometimes faintly ghosting yellow median stripe; dark-brown iris; bluish-horn legs and bill. Ssp *griseiventris* slightly heavier and larger bill; darker greyish cast to underparts; duller olive upperparts with little yellow rump contrast. **Imm** paler. **Voc** Song: warble of 10–16 rather sweet, moderately high-pitched, up- and downslurred, twittering notes containing trills, rapidly repeated, ranging between 2-6 kHz, lasting 0.8–3.5 sec. Call: trembling, buzzy, downslurred "tzee" at 3-5 kHz. **SS** Warbling White-eye (at higher elevations) very similar but has mid-grey (not dark) iris and usually less extensive and more dusky (less black) loral stripe. See also Wallace's Heleia.

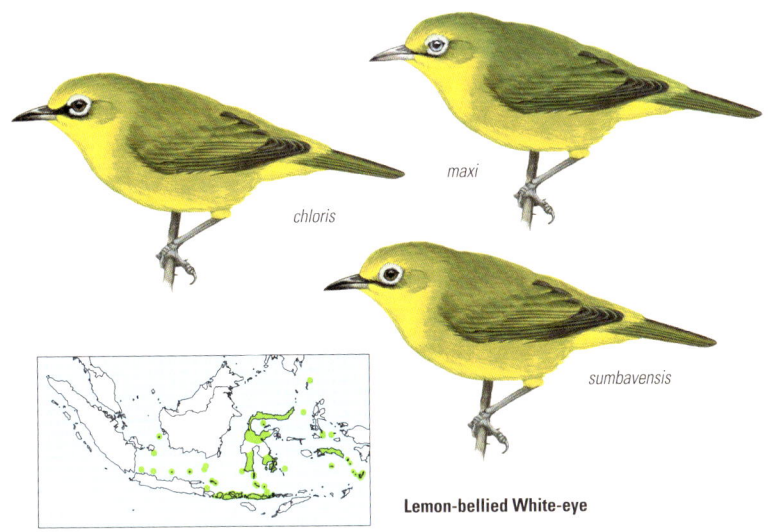

chloris

maxi

sumbavensis

Lemon-bellied White-eye

Wakatobi White-eye

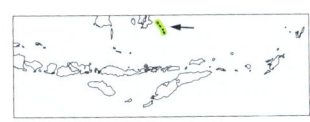

Javan White-eye

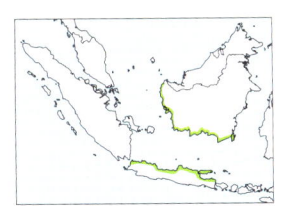

Flores White-eye

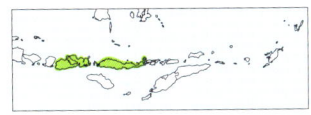

Ashy-bellied White-eye

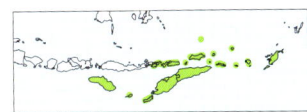

Black-crowned White-eye *Zosterops atrifrons* `E`

L 11–12 cm. 5 ssp: *atrifrons* (N Sul); *surdus* (C Sul); *subatrifrons* (Banggai); *sulaensis* (Sula); undescribed ssp (L Matano, EC Sul). Taxonomy confused. Previously included Seram and Sangihe White-eyes and multiple extralimital species from Melanesia, but each of those shown to differ sufficiently in morphology and/or genomics . Ssp *sulaensis* differs considerably in morphology and often proposed as separate species, but colouration of *subatrifrons* and the undescribed form from L Matano is somewhat intermediate between *sulaensis* and *surdus*/*atrifrons*. Vocally, *sulaensis* and *subatrifrons* differ from each other and from other taxa, perhaps warranting separation as monotypic '**Sula**' and '**Banggai White-eye**', respectively. Whole complex best considered single species pending more in-depth research. Fairly common in forest, cultivated highlands, <1500 m. **ID Ad** white eyering broken at front; black forecrown and lores; olive-green crown, upperparts and tail (yellower on rump); throat and vent dull lemon-yellow; breast and belly greyish white; bluish-horn bill; dark iris. Ssp *surdus* larger, duller overall, narrower eyering often broken both at front and at back, more extensive black forecrown often narrowly enveloping eyering from below and even from the back; undescribed ssp (L Matano) has more distinct and contrasting yellowish rump, throat and vent, white rest of underparts, longish tail; *subatrifrons* as previous but larger with wider eyering broken at front; *sulaensis* as previous but even wider eyering, darker head colouration. **Imm** undescribed. **Voc** Song: *atrifrons*/*surdus* distinctive, sweet, high-pitched, metallic, tinkling, stereotyped jumble of 1.8–2.2 sec; *subatrifrons* melodious jumble with drawn-out notes, much less metallic or high-pitched than *surdus* although contains strident high-pitched "tzeee" notes; *sulaensis* utters a stereotypical melodious oft-repeated 7–9 note motif "cheep chew-you-witt-witt-djew-djwee-wee-widdle", lacking any strident or metallic notes. Call: (i) noisy twittering chirrups; (ii) excited twittering (within flocks) consisting of repeated brief high-pitched rising double notes; (iii) high-pitched "ttttttt" trill, wheezy "zzzzzz", and "zi-zi-zi-zi..." calls; (iv) weak, plaintive, high-pitched, single "peee" or "teew" within flocks. **SS** Kendari White-eye (should not overlap) and Warbling White-eye have olive or yellow (not black) forecrown, Warbling with mid-grey (not dark) iris.

Sangihe White-eye *Zosterops nehrkorni* `E`

L 10.5–12 cm. Monotypic. For taxonomy see Black-crowned White-eye. Extremely rare, mostly in primary stunted ridgetop forest, 750–920 m. Since collected in 1886, only confirmed records between 1996–1999. Only white-eye on island. **ID Ad** black forecrown contrasting with bright golden-olive rear crown; yellowish olive-green upperparts; white eyering; throat and vent yellow; rest of underparts white, greyer on flanks; orange-flesh bare parts. **Imm** undescribed. **Voc** Song: as Black crowned *atrifrons*, but thinner, even more tinkling and less jumbly, first notes more constant in frequency, terminal section descending strongly. Call: thinner and higher-pitched than Black-crowned, e.g. 3 high-pitched "sweet..., sweet..., sweet", lasting 2 sec, sharper and higher pitched than those of some *Dicaeum* flowerpeckers.

Togian White-eye *Zosterops somadikartai* `E`

L 11 cm. Monotypic. Low bushes near mangroves, gardens, secondary scrub, up to 100 m. Pairs or groups (<5). **ID Ad** slaty-grey eyering; olive crown and upperparts with black forecrown; throat and vent sulphur-yellow; whitish underparts (greyer on breast). **Imm** undescribed. **Voc** Song: sweet jumble, similar to that of Black-crowned White-eye ssp *surdus*. Call: twittering "chirrups"

Black-ringed White-eye *Zosterops anomalus* `E`

L 12 cm. Monotypic. Locally common in scrubby hills, disturbed and intact forest, edge, bushes, village gardens, <1400 m. Singly, pairs or groups (<15), joins mixed flocks; in canopy and understory. **ID Ad** yellow forehead, throat, upper breast and vent; rest of underparts pale grey to whitish; black lores and eyering; olive-green upperparts. **Imm** undescribed. **Voc** Song: (i) muted series of slightly musical, teetering, chattering notes, typically ending with "dididid-wit", lasting 1–2 sec, repeated 2–3 times; (ii) several trilling notes with a melodious prelude, e.g. "chewchicheruit, chewticheroo-ee-oo rrrr". Call: peculiar quivering whistle, like a soft version of a police whistle.

Kendari White-eye *Zosterops consobrinorum* `E`

L 12 cm. Monotypic. Birds from islands off SE Sul may be subspecifically distinct. Fairly common in edge, gardens, woodland plots, <1400 m. Pairs or family parties, joins mixed flocks. **ID Ad** olive-green upperparts and crown, with yellow supraloral either inconspicuous or absent; white eyering broken at front by dusky loral stripe; yellow throat and vent; white rest of underparts; dark bluish-horn bill; dark iris. Birds on (at least) Kabaena larger. **Imm** undescribed. **Voc** Song: loud, pleasing, descending warble, lacking the trilling notes of Black-ringed White-eye, lasting 1.5–3 sec. Call: (i) ringing, downslurred "cheep", often in short, repeated bursts; (ii) high-pitched, disyllabic "zip-zip". **SS** Warbling White-eye from higher elevations has pale grey (not dark) iris surrounded by narrower white eyering, usually has yellow forehead contrasting with more olive rest of crown (little contrast in Kendari), often has faint yellow mid-belly line (absent in Kendari) and – at least on Sul – has yellow (not white) 'trousers' (=thighs) though sometimes difficult to discern. See also Black-crowned White-eye. **AN** Pale-bellied / Sulawesi White-eye.

Wangi-wangi White-eye *Zosterops* sp. `E`

L 13 cm. Unnamed species awaiting description. Locally common, found only in taller forest and in cultivation with tall trees on Wangi-wangi. Associates with Wakatobi White-eye. **ID Ad** olive green upperparts; broad white eyering narrowly interrupted at front; yellow throat and lores; white breast and belly; large orange bill; greyish legs with pale toes. **Imm** undescribed. **Voc** Song: pleasant warble of alternating high- and relatively low-pitched notes at 2.5–6.5 kHz, lasting 1–1.5 sec. Call: loud, rather low-pitched "chewp".

Kai Besar White-eye *Zosterops grayi* `E`

L 13 cm. Monotypic. Fairly common in forest, open woodland and gardens. Singly, pairs, or groups (<10). **ID Ad** bright yellow-olive upperparts and crown; distinct wide yellow supraloral; broad white eyering broken at front by thick black loral stripe; throat, upper breast, 'trousers' (=thighs), narrow mid-belly line and vent lemon-chrome. **Imm** undescribed. **Voc** Song: series of strident, squeaky, chattering notes punctuated by 3 short, sharp, high-pitched notes repeated in quick succession, lasting 7 sec. Call: (i) unmusical, squeaky double note of bubbling quality, (ii) "pipip" and "trrr" **AN** Pearl-bellied White-eye.

Kai Kecil White-eye *Zosterops uropygialis* `E`

L 12.5 cm. Monotypic. Uncommon in forest and cleared land with scattered trees. Pairs or groups (<10) in canopy. **ID Ad** fuscous cap; bright yellow-olive upperparts; underparts entirely bright yellow; dark-blue eyering barely contrasting. **Imm** undescribed. **Voc** Song undescribed. Call: (i) brief bubbling notes reminiscent of Kai Besar White-eye; (ii) variable squeaky nasal chatters and harsh raspy squeaks; (iii) loud, mellow, nasal "chow". **AN** Golden-bellied White-eye.

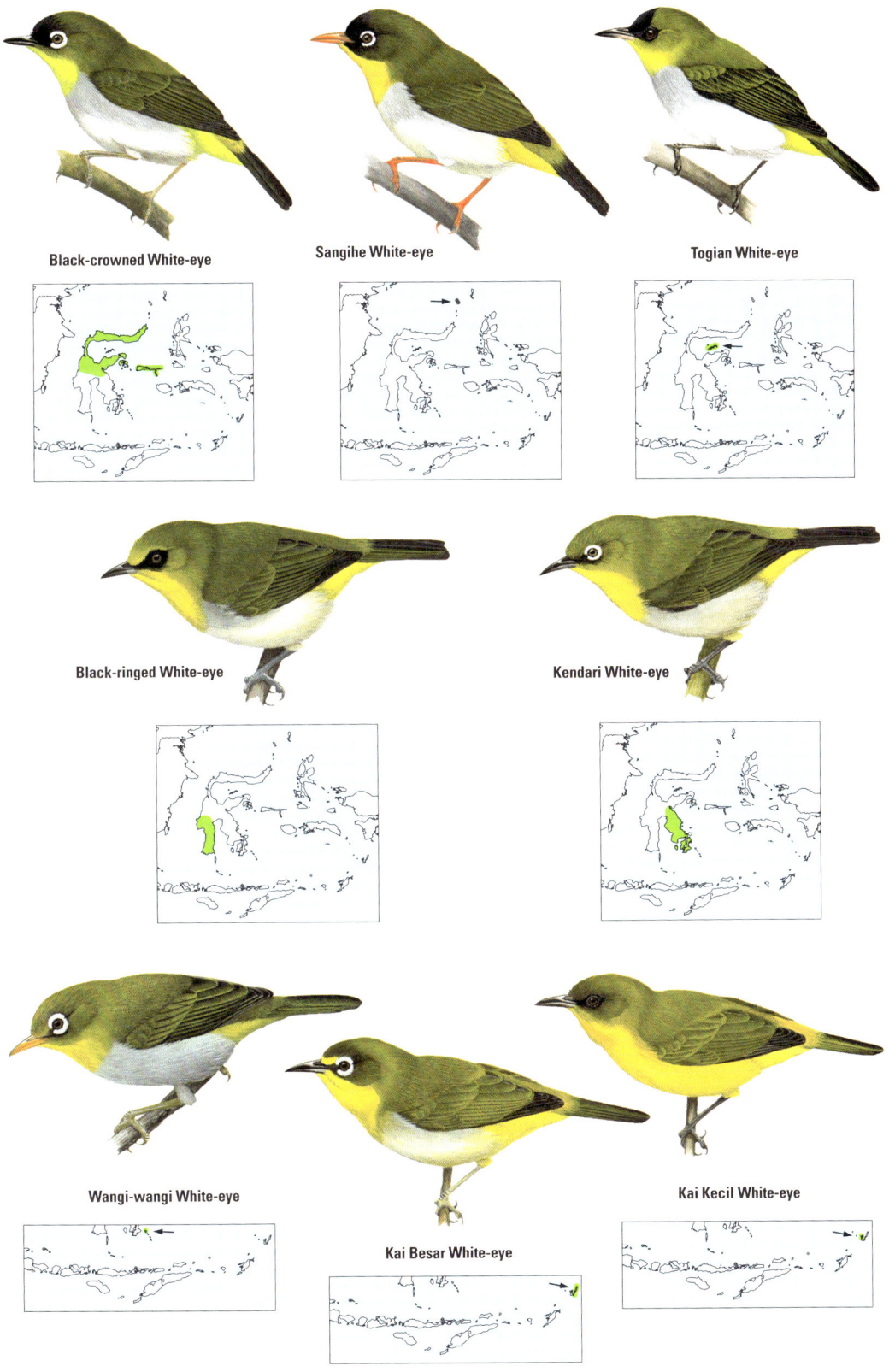

Black-crowned White-eye

Sangihe White-eye

Togian White-eye

Black-ringed White-eye

Kendari White-eye

Wangi-wangi White-eye

Kai Besar White-eye

Kai Kecil White-eye

Seram White-eye *Zosterops stalkeri* `E`

L 11 cm. Monotypic. For taxonomy see Black-crowned White-eye. Fairly common in secondary forest and woodland, 100–1200 m. Not very gregarious, sometimes in small groups, joins mixed flocks. **ID Ad** white eyering broken at front; black crown, lores and ear-coverts grading into bronzy olive upperparts with bronzy-yellow rump and throat, whitish underparts, yellow vent. **Imm** undescribed. **Voc** Song: (i) series of rapidly repeated, sweet tinkling notes terminating with multiple ringing notes; (ii) fairly rapid series of slightly rolling, short "swee" notes unlike sibling species. Call: in flock, typical white-eye call notes. **SS** Ambon White-eye overlaps only exceptionally and has olive-green (not black) crown and face. Also see Warbling White-eye.

Buru White-eye *Zosterops buruensis* `E`

L 11.5–12 cm. Monotypic. Common in forest, farmland. Joins mixed flocks in dense (sub-) canopy. **ID Ad** olive upperparts; wide white eyering broken in front by thick black loral markings extending to below eye like teardrops; pale lemon-yellow throat and underparts, often whitish on centre of breast; dark iris. **Imm** undescribed. **Voc** Song: series of 15–20 high-pitched, rapid "chew" notes, lasting 3–4 sec. Call: (i) quiet, quickly repeated "tsu-tsu-tsu..." during foraging; (ii) "chewit, chewit, chewit...". **SS** See Warbling White-eye.

Ambon White-eye *Zosterops kuehni* `E`

L 12 cm. Monotypic. Fairly common but local. Single specimen and sighting from N coast Seram indicates potential occasional dispersal to neighbouring islands. Lowland forest, scrub and gardens, <500 m. Pairs or small groups (<6). **ID Ad** olive-green upperparts and crown; no yellow supraloral but extensive blackish loral area often extending to forecrown and below eye; thick white eyering widely broken at front; throat and vent yellow; remainder of underparts greyish-white. **Imm** undescribed. **Voc** Song: musical, medium to high-pitched, rapid warble lasting 1.5 sec. Call: sibilant, single, downslurred, plaintive "teew". **SS** See Seram White-eye.

Bacan White-eye *Zosterops atriceps* `E`

L 12 cm. Monotypic. Previously included Halmahera, Morotai and Obi White-eyes to form more broadly-defined umbrella species, '**Cream-throated White-eye**' *Z. atriceps*. Current separation of these forms based on combination of voice and morphology. Uncommon in forest, edge and cultivation, <700 m. Singly, pairs or small groups (<6); in lower to upper storey. **ID Ad** blackish forehead and lores; white eyering; olive-green upperparts, crown and ear-coverts separated by large grey nape patch; white throat to belly, slightly greyer on breast; yellow vent; bill blackish with yellow-orange base of lower mandible. **Imm** undescribed. **Voc** Song: short series of undulating, sweet musical notes peaking in middle, "too-wit-too-wit-wit-too-wit", lasting ~1 sec. Call: (i) wheezy, mid-pitched "wee-wee-wee..."; (ii) soft, repeated "tip". **SS** See Warbling White-eye.

Halmahera White-eye *Zosterops fuscifrons* `E`

L 11 cm. Monotypic. For taxonomy see Bacan White-eye. Fairly common in forest and edge. Singly, pairs or small groups (<10); in lower to upper storey. **ID Ad** blackish forehead and lores; olive-green crown and upperparts; pale-grey eyering; pale-grey underparts; yellow vent; black bill with yellow base to lower mandible. **Imm** undescribed. **Voc** Song: rather thin, high-pitched series of sweet, musical whistles alternating rapidly up and down, each phrase ending with 1–2 upslurred, whistled disyllabic "tu-it" notes, lasting ~1.5 sec, phrases repeated at 4–5 sec intervals; (ii) louder, harder version of song without concluding double note. Call: rather soft "pip".

Morotai White-eye *Zosterops dehaani* `E`

L 12 cm. Monotypic. For taxonomy see Bacan White-eye. Uncommon in forest and edge, commoner towards higher elevations. **ID Ad** black head with wide, contrasting white eyering and lores; nape and mantle grey; olive-green wings, rump and tail; white throat and underparts; heavy, black bill. **Imm** undescribed. **Voc** Song: high-pitched twittering notes, "ti'ti'tit'twititwititwititit..." lasting ~2 sec. Call: series of "twit" notes lasting <1.5 sec.

Obi White-eye *Zosterops* sp. `E`

Unnamed species awaiting description. For taxonomy see Bacan White-eye. Uncommon in forest, edge and cultivation, >380 m. Singly, pairs or small groups; from lower to upper storey. **ID Ad** similar to Halmahera White-eye but possibly less black on forecrown, whiter and narrower eyering broken at front, slightly darker grey underparts, particularly throat, and more extensive and paler lemon-yellow lower mandible base. **Imm** undescribed. **Voc** Song: long, winding series of sweet musical notes, predominantly downslurred "tew-wit-tew-tew-tew-wit-tew-tew-wit..." lasting 4–10 sec. Call: hard "peep-peep-peep...". **SS** See Warbling White-eye.

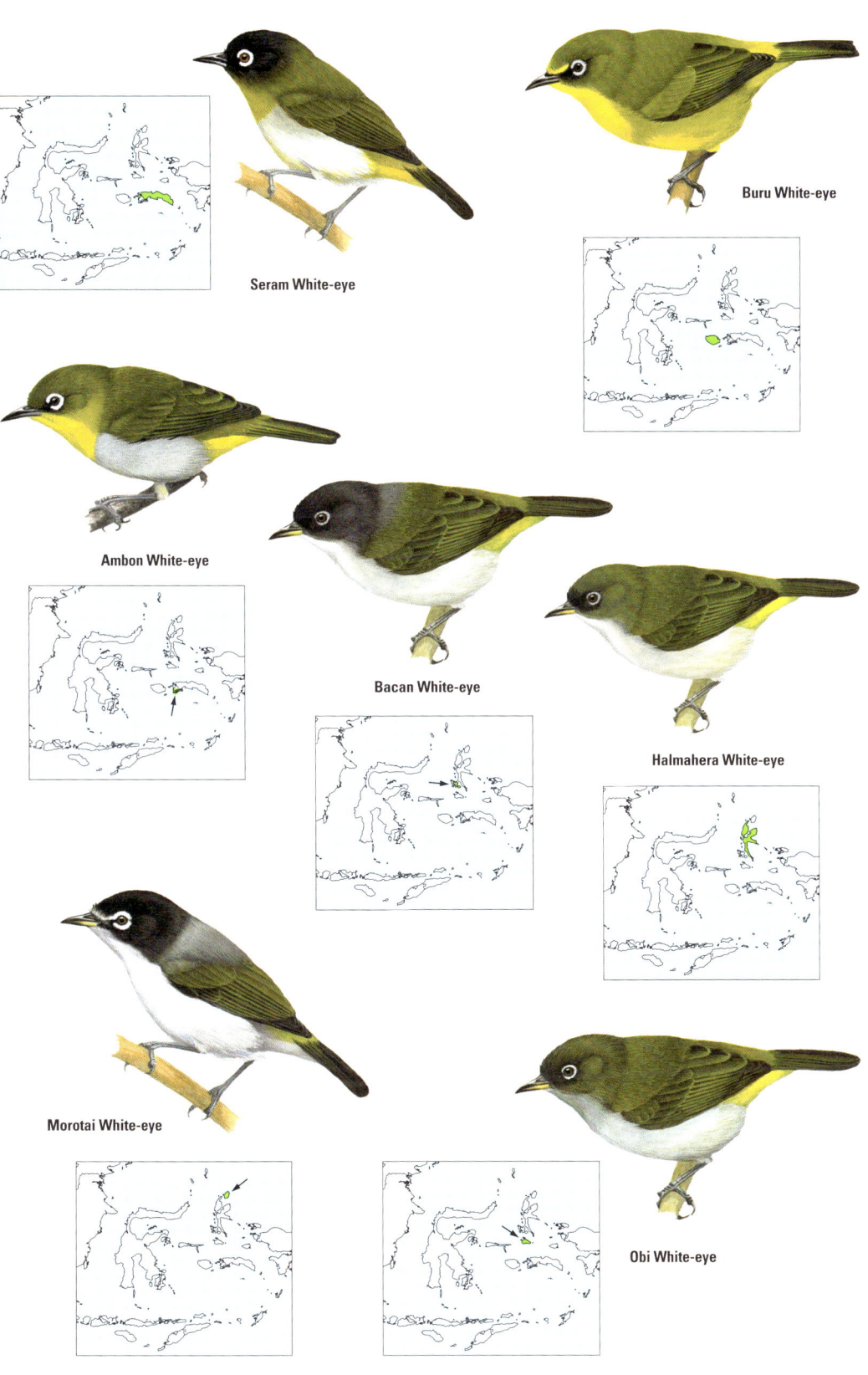

Seram White-eye

Buru White-eye

Ambon White-eye

Bacan White-eye

Halmahera White-eye

Morotai White-eye

Obi White-eye

23 species in region

Small active birds of forest and edge, typically feed in the mid- to upper storey, occasionally as part of mixed flocks. Both migrants and residents occur. The family is a source of great cryptic diversity, with many forms only recently recognised at the species level.

Yellow-browed Warbler *Phylloscopus inornatus*

L 10–11 cm. Breeds N–NE Asia; winters S–SE–E Asia. Monotypic. Favours canopy in forest, edge; usually picked up on characteristic call first. **ID Ad** broad, long whitish supercilium and double wingbars, with conspicuous pale tertial tips; plain olive-green crown, upperparts and tail; greyish-white underparts; orange legs; short, dark bill with orange base to lower mandible. **Imm** slightly weaker greater covert wingbar. **Voc** Call: frequently given rising whistle "soo-weet", easily imitated. **SS** Eastern Crowned, Two-barred, Arctic, Kamchatka and Japanese Leaf Warblers are larger, with larger bills, and lack Yellow-browed's distinct pale tertial tips. No other *Phylloscopus* in region has such wide wingbars accentuated by black trailing bar.

Two-barred Warbler *Phylloscopus plumbeitarsus* [V]

L 12 cm. Breeds N-NE Asia, winters to SE Asia. Monotypic. Vagrant to Tiga, off Sabah (Oct 2011), and N Sumatra at 1600 m (Dec 2015). All types of woodland, edge, and coastal areas on migration. Singly, or joining mixed species flocks. **ID/SS** Very similar to larger Arctic Warbler (refer to that account for similar species), with subtle differences: (1) Two-barred's supercilium generally broader, more even, especially above and behind eye, whereas Arctic's supercilium typically shorter and tapering off behind eye; (2) Arctic often has dark tip to lower mandible (versus all-orange in Two-barred); (3) Arctic has longer primary projection; (4) Two-barred's double wingbar generally more distinct but can be indistinct when worn by spring, whereas Arctic's greater covert wing bar often appears broken; (5) Arctic's ear-coverts can appear more mottled; (6) Two-barred has – on average – darker legs; (7) Arctic appears flatter-crowned, less rounded. **Voc** Song, unlikely to be heard in region: rapid series of whistles, warbles and chatters. Call: dry, flat di- to trisyllabic "tissheep", or "chi-ree-wee".

Arctic Warbler *Phylloscopus borealis*

L 13 cm. Breeds N Palaearctic–Alaska; winters SE–E Asia, Phil. Monotypic. Traditionally included Japanese and Kamchatka Leaf Warblers but all three differ bioacoustically and genetically. Common in coastal areas on migration, wintering in forest, <1500 m. Singly or small groups (<10), often with mixed flocks; favouring canopy. **ID Ad** crown and upperparts greyish olive-green with one (sometimes a faint second) white wingbar; whitish underparts to throat with greyish wash to flanks; long yellowish-white supercilium; dark olive-dusky eyestripe; dark bill with orange base of lower mandible; yellowish to flesh-coloured legs. **Imm** duller; greyish-cream underparts. **Voc** Song frequently given in region: harsh, fast, rattling "zezeze...", lasting 2.5–4 sec, gradually increasing in strength, often fading slightly at end; frequently interspersed with call notes between strophes. Call: high-pitched "dzrit", sometimes doubled-up to "dze-zet". **SS** See very similar migratory Two-barred, Japanese and Kamchatka, Eastern Crowned, Willow, Dusky and Yellow-browed Warblers. Most resident montane leaf warblers have some yellow on underparts and/or exhibit central crown stripes.

Japanese Leaf Warbler *Phylloscopus xanthodryas*

L 13 cm. Breeds Japan; winters to Phil and Indonesia. Monotypic. For taxonomy see Arctic Warbler. Incompletely known due to identification difficulties from Arctic: presumed scarce in coastal habitat and forest, though further study required to map exact wintering range; existing specimens from Sarawak and Sabah suggest main wintering area is in Bor. Single specimen from Jav (1925). Favours canopy, presence usually betrayed by call. **ID/SS** As Arctic and Kamchatka Leaf (refer to those accounts for similar species), though sometimes shows yellower ear-coverts, yellow-tinged throat, flanks and vent, brighter-green upperparts with broader wingbar, and broader bill base. Field identification from Arctic and Kamchatka Leaf only reliable when vocalising. **Voc** Song: similar to Kamchatka Leaf but lower-pitched, with different rhythm, "tree'diret-tree'diret-tree'diret ...", alternating between a long higher-pitched note and a descending or level couplet, lasting 1.5–2 sec; often interspersed with call notes between strophes. Call: lower-pitched, drier and less sharp and rasping than Arctic and Kamchatka, "brrt" or doubled "brr-brrrt" or tripled "brr-brr-brr".

Kamchatka Leaf Warbler *Phylloscopus examinandus*

L 13 cm. Breeds NE Asia; winters to Phil and Indonesia. Monotypic. For taxonomy see Arctic Warbler. On current knowledge fairly common winterer in woodland and coastal scrub in eastern half of region, especially common from late Oct in LS. **ID/SS** As Arctic and Japanese Leaf (refer to those accounts for similar species) but sometimes shows yellow wash on lower ear-coverts, central breast and vent, possibly less bright than in Japanese; also has a longer second primary (outermost visible primary) and heavier bill. Field identification from Arctic and Japanese Leaf only reliable when vocalising. **Voc** Song: harsh, ringing, fast, series of notes with a regular pulsating rhythm "t'treet't'treet't'treet...", alternating between 1–2 short notes and one longer note (either higher-pitched or lower-pitched than preceding notes), lasting 2–2.5 sec, gradually increasing in strength; often interspersed with call notes between strophes. Call: dry, crackling "trrrt", sometimes doubled "trr-trrt", higher-pitched and more strident than call of Japanese Leaf, although usually lower-pitched, longer and harder than similar call of Arctic, and only separable with practice unless sonograms are inspected.

Eastern Crowned Warbler *Phylloscopus coronatus*

L 11–12 cm. Breeds NE–E Asia; winters SE Asia. Monotypic. Fairly common in forest, woodland, on passage also in coastal scrub, <2000 m. Joins mixed flocks, often found in groups (<15) favouring mid- to upper canopy. **ID Ad** similar to Arctic but darker, greyer crown contrasting with brighter olive back; conspicuous pale central crown stripe (not extending to forehead); more conspicuous single wingbar; brighter orange legs; wholly orange lower mandible; lemon flush on vent (often faint). **Imm** ill-defined crown stripe; less bright overall. **Voc** Song, often heard in region before departure: series of rising, clear notes, "pitchoo-pitch-wee" or slightly longer "toweeoo toweeoo toweeoo tsoo-eet, tsoo-eet-tzaah", ending on harsh, buzzy note. Call, rarely heard: (i) soft "pit pit"; (ii) harsh, nasal "zweet". **SS** The similar 'Arctic trio' (Arctic, Japanese and Kamchatka Leaf Warblers) as well as Two-barred Warbler differ in (1) lacking central crown stripe, (2) lacking lemon vent, (3) lacking contrast between brighter-olive upperparts and darker, greyer crown, (4) exhibiting a smaller bill (in 'Arctic trio' additionally not as bright on lower mandible). See also Yellow-browed Warbler.

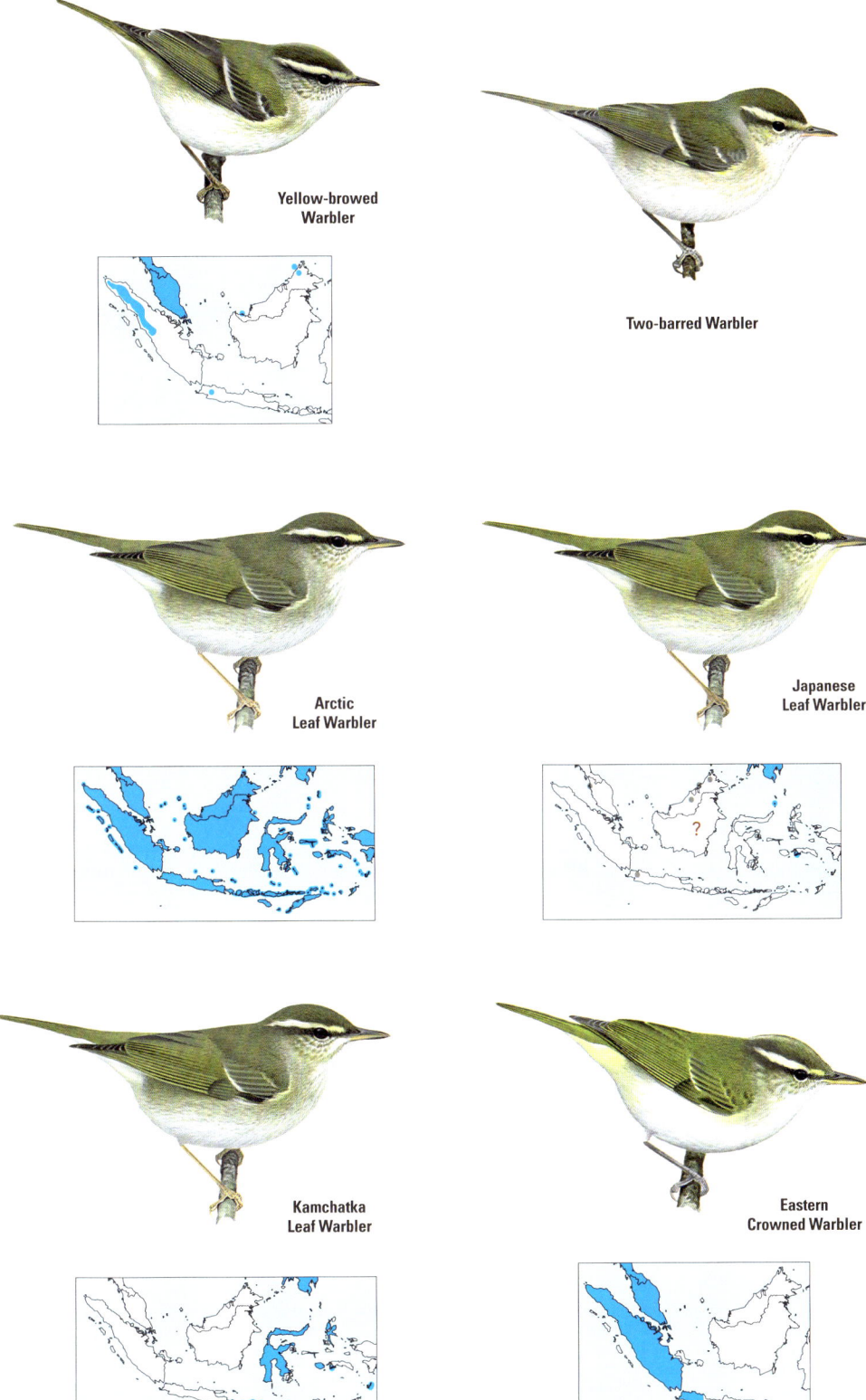

Yellow-browed
Warbler

Two-barred Warbler

Arctic
Leaf Warbler

Japanese
Leaf Warbler

Kamchatka
Leaf Warbler

Eastern
Crowned Warbler

Dusky Warbler *Phylloscopus fuscatus* V

L 11–12 cm. Breeds N-NE Asia, winters S-SE-E Asia. 2ssp, 1 in region: *fuscatus* (most of range). Single record Mantanani, Sabah (Nov 2019). Skulks in low vegetation: weeds and scrub in open habitat, often in wet areas, where presence usually betrayed by call. **ID Ad** plain-looking, dark olive-brown upperparts; dusky-brown flanks becoming more paler on mid-belly, lacking any bright tones; long, relatively broad, whitish supercilium, narrower before eye, broadening slightly behind eye; legs orange-horn; dark bill pale at base. **Voc** Call: dry, harsh, clicking "teck", regularly repeated. **SS** Willow Warbler has less distinct facial features (i.e., thinner, yellow-hued supercilium and less distinct lores); more uniformly whitish underparts (lacking brownish flanks); brighter, olive-green (not olive-brown) upperparts, with longer primary projection. 'Arctic trio' variants which lack wing bars are much more greenish-olive overall, lacking strong brown tones on upperparts and flanks. Dusky differs from all *Phylloscopus* species in region by more skulking behaviour in undergrowth (versus canopy feeding in other species).

Willow Warbler *Phylloscopus trochilus* V

L 11–12 cm. Breeds Palaearctic; winters Africa. 3 ssp, 1 in region: *yakutensis* (breeds E Siberia; winters Africa). Single record, Mantanani off Sabah (Oct 2015). On passage occurs in any vegetated areas. **ID Ad** rather featureless with narrow yellowish-hued supercilium. Upperparts subdued olive-yellow with paler, whiter underparts (can show indistinct grey breast streaking); long primary projection; dark bill with pale orange base to lower mandible; orange legs. **Imm** yellow-tinged supercilium and underparts. **Voc** Call: soft disyllabic "hewit". **SS** 'Arctic trio' occasionally lack wingbars but, like other leaf warblers in region, always show brighter, more olive-green upperparts contrasting strongly with whiter flanks, a much longer, broader supercilium and paler lower mandible. Can be confused with reed-warblers but separated by smaller bill, shorter, notched tail and longer primary projection. See also Dusky Warbler.

Mountain Leaf Warbler *Phylloscopus trivirgatus*

L 10–11 cm. Sundaic, LS. 4 ssp, 3 in region: *trivirgatus* (Sum–Sumbawa); *kinabaluensis* (Mt Kinabalu [N Bor]); *sarawacensis* (rest of Bor). Previously included seven Philippine taxa now known to differ in mtDNA and vocalisations, and constituting multiple independent species. Some populations of present species may be deeply diverged, more studies necessary. Common in montane forest, >800 m (on Lombok and Sumbawa >450 m). Singly, pairs or small groups in mixed flocks. **ID Ad** black crown with thick yellow central crown stripe and supercilium; upperparts yellow-green with bright-yellow underparts. Ssp *sarawacensis* brighter yellow underparts; *kinabaluensis* lacking yellow pigmentation with dull greyish underparts and grey-green upperparts. **Imm** less yellow, with less distinct duller crown. **Voc** Song: melodious, rapid, long, jumbled warble "tseewichiwichiwichit…" lasting <2 sec; often several birds singing simultaneously. Call: high-pitched, ~4–syllabled "tisiviswet", last note often lower.

Timor Leaf Warbler *Phylloscopus presbytes* E

L 11 cm. Monotypic. Morphological and vocal differentiation of some populations requires more research. See also Flores Leaf Warbler for taxonomy. Fairly common in montane forest, progressively scarcer to sea level. **ID Ad** distinct broad whitish supercilium and indistinct central crown stripe; head and upperparts dull greenish-brown; lemon-tinged underparts, white throat; bill blackish. Birds in lowlands appear slightly brighter, yellower, particularly on face and underparts. **Imm** browner; lacking crown stripe. **Voc** Song: melodious, high-pitched, short warble with emphasis on final, highest-pitched note "swit'wee'swit'SWEE", lasting 1.2 sec. Call: rapid, ascending "swetweewee". **SS** Beware of the 'Arctic trio'.

Flores Leaf Warbler *Phylloscopus floresianus* E

L 10 cm. Monotypic. Previously included with Timor Leaf Warbler but differs in plumage and voice. Common in montane forest and edge, >1000 m. Singly, pairs or small groups (<5). **ID Ad** olive-greyish crown and face with broad whitish supercilium and chin; upperparts olive-green with indistinct, sometimes absent, pale wingbar; underparts bright lemon-yellow. **Imm** undescribed. **Voc** Song: high-pitched warble with downslurred final note "sooee'woo'wee'woot", lasting <1 sec; first notes show slight variation. Call: high-pitched, rapid "soo'we'woot". **SS** Beware of the 'Arctic trio'.

Rote Leaf Warbler *Phylloscopus rotiensis* E

L 10 cm. Monotypic. Fairly common in woodland, dense and tall scrub. Singly or pairs; favouring canopy. **ID Ad** similar to Timor Leaf Warbler but has much longer, slightly decurved, pinkish bill unlike other leaf warblers; broader supercilium; paler olive upperparts; extensive lemon underparts to throat and ear-coverts; single indistinct wingbar. **Imm** undescribed. **Voc** Song: (i) ascending warble of notes "swoo'wer'wee…" lasting 1.3–1.8 sec; (ii) more level-pitched "swoo'wee'woo'we'we'whit", lasting 1.3–1.8 sec, thinner and more complex than Timor Leaf. Call: penetrating "t't'cheewit".

Lompobattang Leaf Warbler E
Phylloscopus sarasinorum

L 11 cm. Monotypic. For taxonomy see Sulawesi Leaf Warbler. Fairly common in (sub-) montane forest, edge, >600 m. Singly or pairs, joins mixed flocks. **ID Ad** brownish-olive upperparts with broad, pale yellowish central crown stripe and supercilium, dark eye stripe; pale yellow throat and breast; whiter belly; single, pale yellow wingbar; white outertail (2 outermost rectrices); orange lower mandible on otherwise dark bill. **Imm** undescribed. **Voc** Song: series of mid- and higher-pitched, repetitive, warbled notes. Generally lower-pitched, shorter strophes and lacking squeaky notes of Sulawesi Leaf.

Sulawesi Leaf Warbler *Phylloscopus nesophilus* E

L 11 cm. Monotypic. Previously merged with Lompobattang Leaf Warbler, but exhibits extensive genetic, vocal and plumage differences. Fairly common in (sub-) montane forest, edge, >600 m. Singly or pairs, joins mixed flocks. **ID Ad** vaguely similar to Lompobattang but lacks central crown stripe; darker brown above; more extensive yellow on underparts; darker lower mandible; no wingbar; lacks white in tail. **Imm** undescribed. **Voc** Song: highly variable series of repetitive, rapid notes, typical *Phylloscopus*-like warble, lasting <3 sec, typically "chewit'chewit'chewit…", either level or ascending. Call: thin, rapid "siptisissywoo". **SS** Beware of the 'Arctic trio' (Arctic, Japanese and Kamchatka Leaf Warblers; see under Arctic).

Selayar Leaf Warbler *Phylloscopus* sp. E

Undescribed species known only from Selayar, awaiting formal description. Fairly common in remnant native forest and mixed bamboo scrub, >200m. Singly or pairs. **ID Ad** broad, whitish supercilium and central crown stripe; olive-green upperparts; plain ear-coverts; clean white underparts; black legs; dark bill appears large. **Imm** undescribed. **Voc** Song: alternating series of repeated notes; for example, 3–5 pleasant notes followed by a short series of trilled notes, or a repetition of simple rattled notes; lasts 0.8–2 s. Lacks complexity of both Sulawesi and Lompobattang. **SS** Told from migrant 'Arctic trio' by central crown-stripe, more distinct wing bars, dark lower mandible and darker legs.

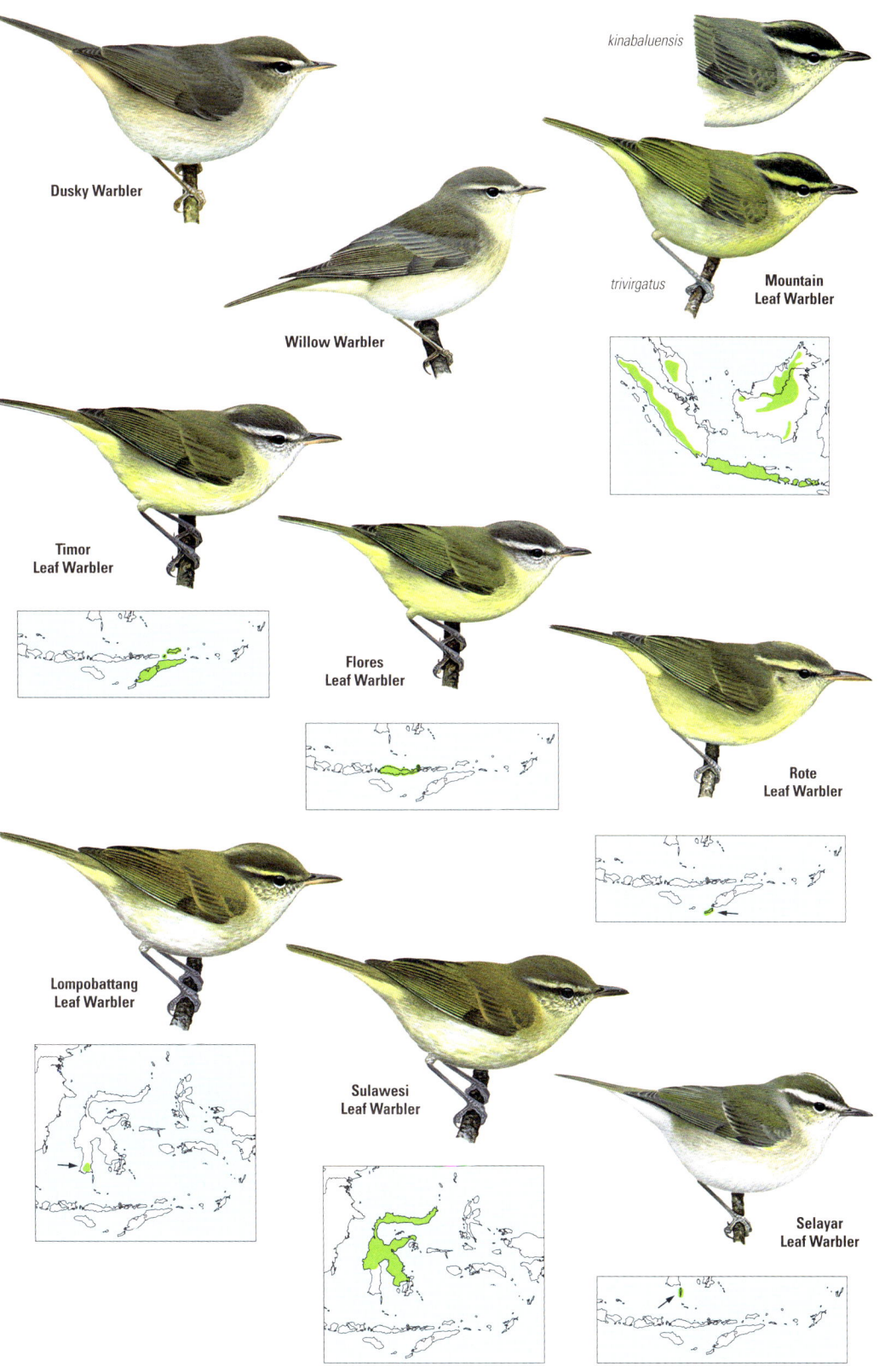

Dusky Warbler

Willow Warbler

kinabaluensis

trivirgatus

Mountain Leaf Warbler

Timor Leaf Warbler

Flores Leaf Warbler

Rote Leaf Warbler

Lompobattang Leaf Warbler

Sulawesi Leaf Warbler

Selayar Leaf Warbler

Kai Leaf Warbler *Phylloscopus avicola* `E`

L 10–11 cm. Monotypic. Previously merged with Seram, Buru and North Moluccan Leaf Warblers as well as ~13 other taxa from NG and Melanesia into a more broadly-defined umbrella species, '**Island Leaf Warbler**' *S. poliocephalus*. However, the range of morphological and vocal diversity encompassed by such an arrangement considerably exceeds phenotypic diversity in most other leaf warbler species. Uncommon in closed-canopy forest on Kai Besar, >350 m. Singly or pairs; favouring canopy. **ID Ad** dark grey crown with dull paler central stripe and supercilium; brownish-olive upperparts; white underparts slightly streaked. **Imm** undescribed. **Voc** Song: medium-pitched, short, usually ascending series of notes "tsootsweesootweesweey", lasting 1–2 sec, continuously repeated every 0.5–1 sec. Call: descending "wir'chew'ee". **SS** Beware of the 'Arctic trio'.

Seram Leaf Warbler *Phylloscopus ceramensis* `E`

L 10–11 cm. Monotypic. For taxonomy see Kai Leaf Warbler. Common in montane forest, >900 m. Singly or pairs, joins mixed flocks. **ID Ad** dark grey crown and eye stripe with paler central crown stripe; white supercilium; distinct lemon-whitish double wingbar; whitish throat and bright yellow underparts with olive flanks. **Imm** olive-green crown, indistinct crown stripe; yellowish throat. **Voc** Song: (i) medium-pitched series of highly repetitive notes, ascending "t't't'tsee'tsee'tsee'see'see'seey..."; (ii) level "chewit'chewit'chewit..." lasting 1–2 sec, repeated every 2–8 sec; both vocalisations often with thin introductory notes. Call: thin, downslurred "tcheweeoot".

Buru Leaf Warbler *Phylloscopus everetti* `E`

L 10–11 cm. Monotypic. For taxonomy see Kai Leaf Warbler. Common in montane forest, >800 m. Singly or pairs, joins mixed flocks. **ID Ad** mid-grey crown with whitish supercilium; pale grey face; whitish throat extending to upper breast with lemon-yellow remainder of underparts; distinct whitish wingbar. **Imm** olive-green crown; yellowish throat. **Voc** Song: long, high-pitched, drawn-out warble with little structure, usually ascending "tsoo'we'tsoo'wee'see'wee e'see'wee...", lasting 1.3–3 sec, repeated every 2–8 sec. Call: thin, quiet "sip" or "tzip". **SS** Beware of the 'Arctic trio'.

North Moluccan Leaf Warbler `E`
Phylloscopus waterstradti

L 10–11 cm. 2 ssp: *waterstradti* (Bacan, Obi); *henrietta* (Ternate, Halmahera, Morotai). Ssp *henrietta* displays some morphological and vocal distinctions and may merit monotypic species treatment as '**Halmahera Leaf Warbler**', leaving *waterstradti* as monotypic '**Bacan Leaf Warbler**'. Population on Obi provisionally included with *waterstradti* but possible differences in bioacoustics and plumage may warrant status as undescribed subspecies or species ('**Obi Leaf Warbler**'). For taxonomy also see Kai Leaf Warbler. Fairly common in forest, >360 m, becoming more common with increasing elevation. Singly or pairs, joins mixed flocks. **ID Ad** mid-grey crown; paler face with long, white supercilium and dark eye stripe; olive-green upperparts (less bright on *henrietta*) with 1–2 wingbars (indistinct on *henrietta*); lemon-yellow underparts extend to paler whitish throat; steel-grey bill and legs. **Imm** undescribed. **Voc** Song: *henrietta* alternate low- and high-pitched, rapid, repetitive rattled notes "chit'chit'chit..." at 4–6 n/s, followed by more rapid, higher-pitched "si'si'si...'", at 6–8 n/s, lasting <1 sec; series can show slight variation and contain quieter introductory notes. In *waterstradti* notes on average less repetitive, more warbling and faster, with shorter gaps between motifs. Call: *henrietta* thin, descending "chewit-chewit". **SS** Beware of the 'Arctic trio'.

Peleng Leaf Warbler *Phylloscopus suaramerdu* `E`

L 10 cm. Monotypic. Fairly common in montane forest, edge, >700 m. Singly or pairs, joins mixed flocks. **ID Ad** brownish-grey upperparts, crown slightly darker with thin white supercilium and mottled grey face; white throat; olive-mottled yellow underparts; lacks crown stripes and wingbars. **Imm** undescribed. **Voc** Song: short, melodious series of low-pitched introductory notes, followed by simple, medium-pitched phrase "weep'wid'dee'SIP'DEE'DEE" and more level "whip'dee'whip'dee...", lasting 1–1.3 sec, repeated at regular intervals. **SS** Beware of the 'Arctic trio'.

Taliabu Leaf Warbler *Phylloscopus emilsalimi* `E`

L 10 cm. Monotypic. Fairly common in montane forest, edge, >450 m. Singly or pairs, joins mixed flocks. **ID Ad** dull olive upperparts with narrow yellowish supercilium, mottled yellowish face; strongly yellow-steaked underparts; lacks crown stripes and wingbars. **Imm** undescribed. **Voc** Song: extremely varied, including mixed series of 3–6 repetitive notes "tooit-tooit-tooit", lasting 1–2 sec, and ascending jumble of high-pitched notes "sooit'titit'see-it'si'eeoo..." lasting 2–3 sec. **SS** Beware of the 'Arctic trio'.

Sunda Warbler *Phylloscopus grammiceps*

L 10 cm. Sundaic, Palawan, LS. 8 ssp, 6 in region: *grammiceps* (Jav–Bali); *sumatrensis* (C–S Sum); *barisanus* (N Sum); *montis* (Bor); *floris* (Flores, Alor); *paulinae* (Timor). Yellow-breasted races *barisanus*, *montis*, *floris*, *paulinae* and two extralimital ssp have traditionally been separated as '**Yellow-breasted Warbler**' *S. montis* because of dramatically different colour of underparts, but their geographic checkerboard distribution suggests an unnatural arrangement. Conversely, ssp *grammiceps* and *sumatrensis* sometimes separated into two monotypic species, '**Javan**' and '**Sumatran Warbler**', respectively, because of rump colouration and call note. All taxa are virtually identical in mtDNA and territorial song, and underparts colour in leaf warblers is often defined by relatively small genetic changes (see also Mountain Leaf). Provisional treatment as single species here preferred pending genomic evidence. Fairly common in montane forest, 1000–2600 m. Singly or pairs, joins mixed flocks. **ID Ad** rufous head; black lateral crown stripes; white eyering; green mantle and wings; white underparts and rump; yellow wingbars. Ssp *sumatrensis* grey rump; *montis* white or grey on underparts and rump replaced by yellow; *barisanus* as previous but rufous extends to breast sides; *floris* as *montis* but lacks yellow rump, crown stripes reduced; *paulinae* as previous but crown stripes barely discernible, paler upperparts. **Imm** greyish crown, rufous face less bright; yellow-bellied races possibly with weaker crown stripes and paler overall. **Voc** Song: high-pitched series (with slight variations) of delicate, piercing notes "we si'si'si'si'see", lasting ~1 sec. Call: short, sharp, buzzy, downslurred "chiirt"; *sumatrensis* short, sharp "psitt". **SS** See Chestnut-crowned Warbler.

Chestnut-crowned Warbler *Phylloscopus castaniceps*

L 9 cm. Himalaya to SE–E Asia. 9 ssp, 1 in region: *muelleri* (Sum). Fairly common in submontane forest, 800–1400 m. Singly or pairs, joins mixed flocks. **ID Ad** rufous crown with black lateral crown stripes; yellow rump, flanks, belly and wingbars; grey breast and mantle; green wings and tail; white eyering. **Imm** dull brown crown; plumage less bright. **Voc** Song: as Sunda, high-pitched series of delicate, piercing notes "we si'si'si'si'see", lasting ~1 sec. Call: short, sharp, buzzy downslurred "chiirt". **SS** Sunda Warbler (typically from higher elevations) has chestnut (not grey) face and either wholly white (*sumatrensis*) or yellow (*barisanus*) underparts versus white belly with yellow flanks in Chestnut-crowned.

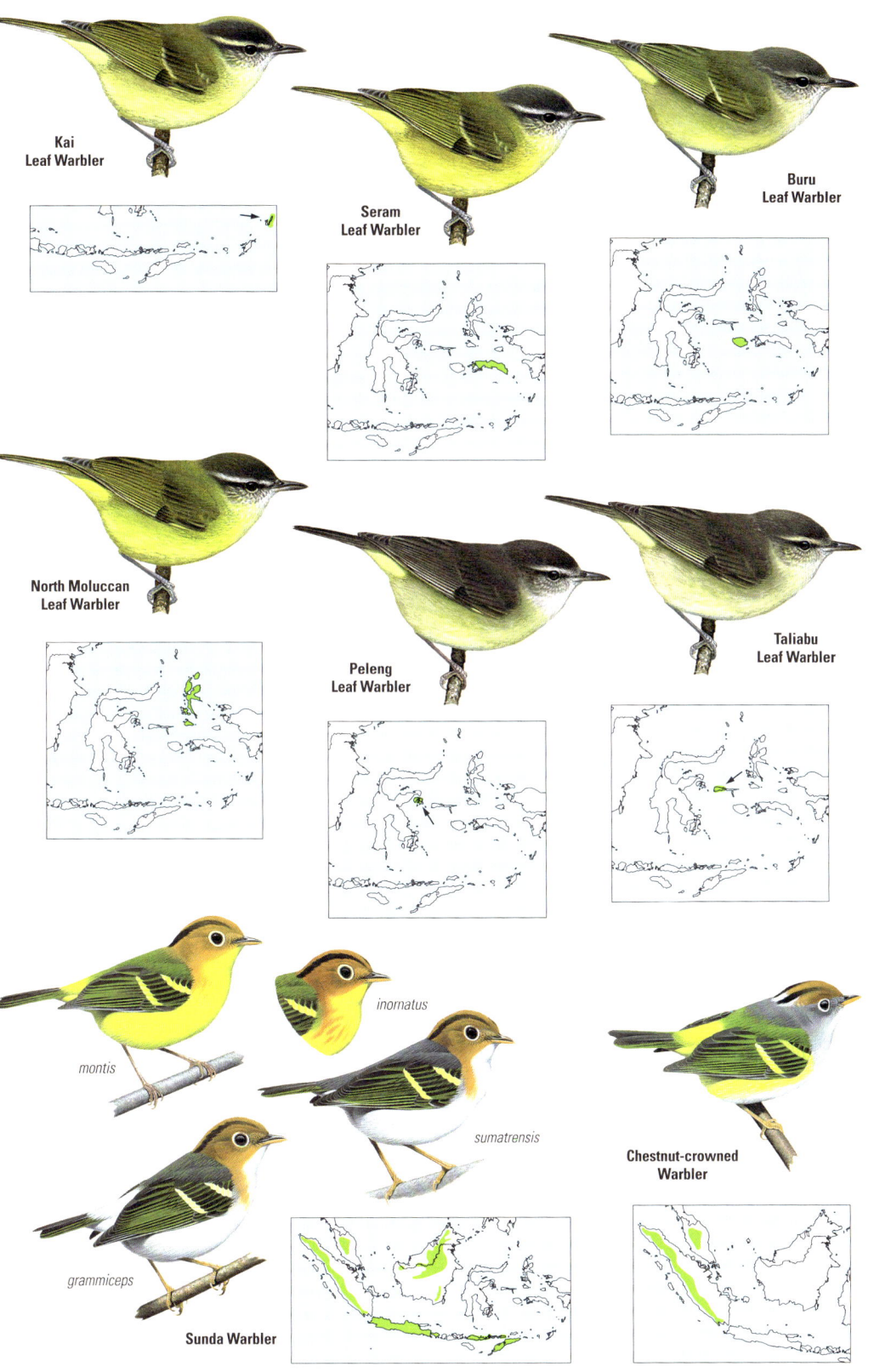

**Kai
Leaf Warbler**

**Seram
Leaf Warbler**

**Buru
Leaf Warbler**

**North Moluccan
Leaf Warbler**

**Peleng
Leaf Warbler**

**Taliabu
Leaf Warbler**

montis

inornatus

sumatrensis

grammiceps

Sunda Warbler

**Chestnut-crowned
Warbler**

AEGITHALIDAE
Bushtits
1 species in region

Small active tit-like birds of the forest canopy. Primarily Himalayan and Palaearctic in origin, only one species found in region. Usually in small groups, occasionally with mixed flocks. Feeds by gleaning for invertebrates among foliage.

Pygmy Bushtit *Aegithalos exilis* 🟩E

L 9 cm. Monotypic. Fairly common in (sub-) montane forest, edge, plantations, >800 m. Usually in small groups (<20), forages in mid-canopy. **ID** Tiny, long-tailed and rather nondescript with conical bill. **Ad** dull mid-brown upperparts, browner on wings; cream-white underparts with grey mottling on breast; pale iris; orange legs. **Imm** similar to Ad. **Voc** Continuous, high-pitched "tsi'-tsi'-tsi'..." and "trrrt" notes, particularly while foraging, reminiscent of extralimital bushtits but slightly softer.

CETTIIDAE
Bush Warblers
9 species in region

Small to very small warblers of forest, edge and shrubby habitats. Most species cryptic in colouration, shy and skulking, preferring to forage on or near the ground within dense vegetation. Presence often revealed by distinctive melodious, whistling or chippy vocalisations.

Timor Stubtail *Urosphena subulata* 🟩E

L 9 cm. 2 ssp: *subulata* (Timor); *advena* (Babar). Racial identity unknown on Rote, Alor, Atauro and Wetar, with possibly undescribed taxa involved. Fairly common ground-dweller, preferring tangles and bamboo thickets; shuffles along forest floor; can perch 1–3 m off the ground to sing. Singly or pairs. **ID** Tailless, strong-legged appearance. **Ad** mid-brown upperparts; broad, bold, buff supercilium; whitish underparts; long, pink legs and feet. Ssp *advena* slightly warmer, rusty upperparts; blacker upper mandible; longer wing. **Imm** warmer upperparts; less contrasting supercilium and duller underparts. **Voc** Song: rising, thin, high-pitched, barely-audible whistle "tzee", lasting 1.2 sec. On Alor, Atauro and Babar at least, whistle can last to 1.6 sec. Call: short, thin "tik".

Bornean Stubtail *Urosphena whiteheadi* 🟩E

L 9 cm. Monotypic. Fairly common in montane forest, typically 1100–2600 m, recorded to 500–3150 m. Solitary ground-dweller, preferring tangles and dense undergrowth; shuffles along forest floor, perching 1–2 m off the ground to sing. **ID** Tailless, strong-legged appearance. **Ad** chocolate-brown upperparts; long, bold supercilium varies from white to deep buff; dusky-grey belly; whitish throat and breast. **Imm** undescribed. **Voc** Song: 2 thin, incredibly high-pitched introductory notes, audible only at close range, followed by an equally thin and high-pitched longer note "tzi'tzi' tzee", lasting <1 sec, barely audible to the human ear. Meratus Mts birds lack introductory notes. Call: thin, slightly lower-pitched "piririt", lasting 0.2 sec.

Javan Tesia *Tesia superciliaris* 🟩E

L 9 cm. Monotypic. Common in montane forest, >1000 m. Feeds on or close to ground in dense undergrowth and thickets. **ID** Round, long-legged, tailless appearance. **Ad** sooty-black crown and eye-stripe; grey underparts; broad supercilium; dull olive-green upperparts. **Imm** undescribed. **Voc** Song: series of loud, explosive notes increasing in volume and speed, starting with 2–3 quiet introductory notes "hueet-hueet tseeooweechee-cheeoeeet", lasting ~2 sec. Call: (i) sharp, metallic "chip"; (ii) short, deflated, rattled "trrrt".

Russet-capped Tesia *Tesia everetti* 🟩E

L 9 cm. 2 ssp: *everetti* (Flores, Adonara); *sumbawana* (Sumbawa). Common in primary and degraded forest with lush undergrowth, scrub, mainly >500 m. Feeds on or close to ground in dense undergrowth and thickets. **ID** Round, long-legged, tailless appearance. **Ad** rich russet-brown crown, paler orange-brown face and ill-defined supercilium; dull grey-brown upperparts; mid-grey underparts. Ssp *sumbawana* crown duller; ear-coverts greyer; tarsus more reddish-brown. **Imm** undescribed. **Voc** Song: similar to Javan Tesia but shorter, faster tempo, "sip-sip chwee-cheeeeweee-cheeweeree", lasting 1 sec. Call: hard, sharp "chip".

Yellow-bellied Warbler *Abroscopus superciliaris*

L 9 cm. Himalaya to SE Asia. 10 ssp, 3 in region: *schwaneri* (Bor); *papilio* (Sum); *vordermani* (Jav). Often erroneously considered a close relative of leaf warblers, but forms part of the bush warbler group. Taxonomic situation in Bor confused: unnamed population from Sabah ('**Sabah Bamboo Warbler**') is unusually distinct in vocalisations from the rest of the range. Further bioacoustic and genetic research required. Fairly common in bamboo-dominated forest understorey, secondary regrowth, mainly 500–1500 m. Singly, pairs or groups (<5), joins mixed flocks. **ID Ad** crown dark brownish-grey with strong white supercilium; greenish-olive upperparts; white throat and upper breast well demarcated from yellow belly. Ssp *papilio* more intensely olive-green nape and mantle, paler yellow underparts; *vordermani* as previous but head tinged buff. **Imm** paler below; less contrasting head pattern. **Voc** Song: 3–4 (in *schwaneri* often more) pleasant, thin, ascending "dip-dee-di'di'", lasting ~1 sec, second note sometimes lower-pitched. Unnamed Sabah population distinct with a series of 5–8 notes briefly rising then descending "di'-dee-di'-di'-dew-dew", lasting ~1.2 sec. Call: continuous chatter and upslurred trills when excited. **AN** Bamboo Bush Warbler.

Tanimbar Bush Warbler *Horornis carolinae* 🟩E

L 11–13 cm. Monotypic. Uncommon in forest. Unusually arboreal, often found >5 m in mid-storey as well as undergrowth. **ID Ad** rufous crown; long buff supercilium; mid-brown upperparts and flanks; whitish underparts; horn-coloured bare parts. **F** smaller. **Imm** undescribed. **Voc** Song: long, drawn-out, level-pitched whistle followed by sudden, louder-ending note, "toooooo'CHURP", lasting 1.5 sec. Call: short, quiet "chuck".

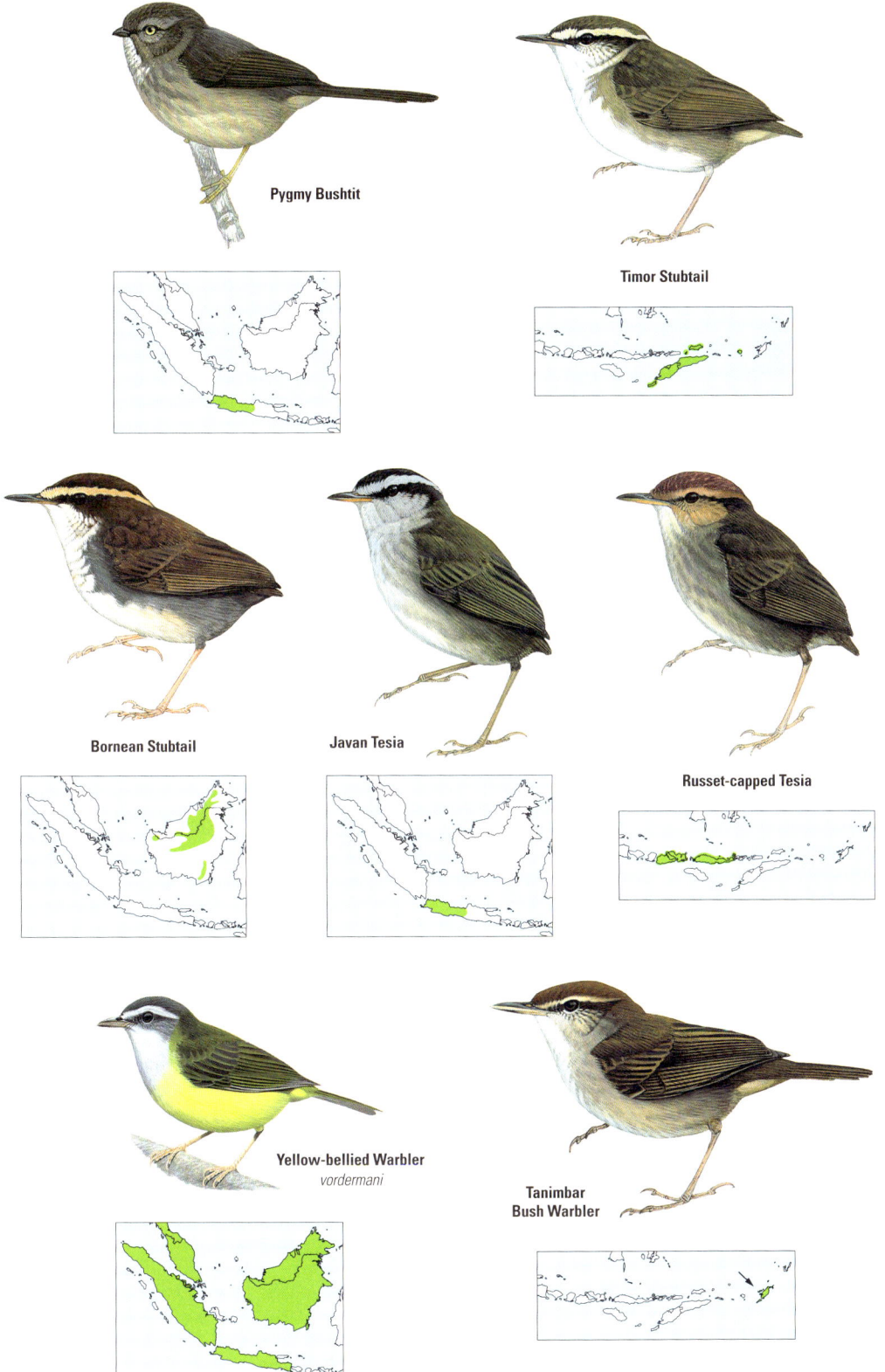

Pygmy Bushtit

Timor Stubtail

Bornean Stubtail

Javan Tesia

Russet-capped Tesia

Yellow-bellied Warbler
vordermani

**Tanimbar
Bush Warbler**

Sunda Bush Warbler *Horornis vulcanius*

L 12–13 cm. SE–E Asia, Palawan. 10 ssp, 7 in region: *vulcanius* (Jav–Sumbawa); *oreophilus* (Mt Kinabalu [N Bor]); *banksi* (rest of Bor); *sepiarius* (N Sum); *flaviventris* (C–S Sum); *everetti* (Timor, Wetar); *kolichisi* (Alor). Based on near-identical song and mtDNA, species as here defined includes two mainland SE–E Asian ssp (*oblitus*, *intricatus*) usually attributed to extralimital Aberrant Bush Warbler *H. flavolivaceus* (Himalaya). Common in undergrowth of montane forest, thickets bordering edge, >1400 m, on Alor >600 m, also occurs in lowlands on Timor and Wetar. Singly or pairs; tame. **ID Ad** plain-brown upperparts; long and narrow buff supercilium; well-defined dark eye stripe; slightly mottled ear-coverts; pale-buff underparts. Ssp *flaviventris* slightly darker upperparts, less contrasting face pattern, darker and greyer underparts; *sepiarius* slightly duller than previous; *oreophilus* darker chestnut-brown upperparts, whitish supercilium, dusky-grey throat, grey-brown underparts; *banksi* marginally darker than previous; *everetti* slightly smaller, slightly paler upperparts, much paler whitish underparts and distinct, white supercilium; *kolichisi* as previous but greyish crown, greyish-brown upperparts and darker eye stripe. **Imm** ill-defined yellowish supercilium; yellow-tinged underparts. **Voc** Song: slurred phrase of short ascending notes followed by a long, drawn-out downward note that rises and falls at the end "wit-a-cheeeee'HEow", lasting 1.2–1.5 sec. Pronounced individual variation but on average *vulcanius* lowest pitched, *oreophilus*/*banksi* more ascending final note, *sepiarius*/*flaviventris* longer upslurred final note, *everetti* flatter, *kolichisi* highest-pitched. Call: short, dry, rattling "trr trr". **SS** Some leaf and reed warblers show superficial plumage similarities, but montane undergrowth lifestyle instantly separates this species. See Friendly Grasshopper Warbler.

Manchurian Bush Warbler *Horornis canturians* 🟦V

L 15–18 cm. Breeds NE-E Asia; winters SE–E Asia, Phil. 2 ssp, 1 in region: *borealis* (breeds NE Asia, winters Taiwan, Phil). Confused taxonomy: mtDNA places nominate ssp *canturians* (E Asia) within extra-limital Japanese Bush Warbler *H. diphone* (NE–E Asia) but vocal evidence supports traditional conspecific treatment of *canturians* and *borealis*; genomic enquiry urgently required. Single record coastal Sabah (Mar 2015). Skulks in thick rank vegetation, occasionally feeding higher in tree canopy. Presence usually betrayed by loud song. **ID Ad** cinnamon-rufous crown with broad, pale supercilium; warm-brown upperparts; paler buff underparts. **F** noticeably smaller. **Imm** yellowish wash on underparts; cinnamon-tinged wings and tail. **Voc** Song: quiet introductory notes gradually increasing in volume and tempo with loud ending; short, liquid "lu-lu-lu-lu-lu-WIK-LU-EE" lasting <1 sec; regularly heard on migration and wintering grounds. Call: short, dry, rattling "trrrr". **SS** Can be confused with reed warblers or migratory leaf warblers that lack a wingbar but separated by combination of stout bill and body, long rounded tail and contrasting rufous crown. **AN** Korean Bush Warbler.

Mountain Leaftoiler *Phyllergates cucullatus*

L 10–12 cm. SE Asia, Phil. 17 ssp, 12 in region: *cucullatus* (Sum–Bali); *cinereicollis* (Bor); *everetti* (Flores); *riedeli* (N Sul); *stentor* (C–SE Sul); *meisei* (SC Sul); *hedymeles* (SW Sul); *dumasi* (Buru, Seram); *batjanensis* (Bacan); *sulanus* (Taliabu); *relictus* (Peleng); undescribed ssp (Obi). Formerly thought to be a tailorbird ('Mountain Tailorbird' *Orthotomus cucullatus*), but now known to be a bush warbler. Eastern ssp look distinct but vocal variation not clear-cut and mtDNA divergences are small: genomic and bioacoustic study needed. Fairly common in (sub-) montane forest, 500–3000 m. Singly or pairs, joins mixed flocks in understorey. **ID** Delicate appearance with long, thin bill. **Ad** rufous forecrown; indistinct whitish supercilium; blackish eye stripe; grey head with paler-grey throat and breast; yellow belly; olive upperparts. Ssp *cinereicollis* brighter ashy neck sides; *everetti* green-tinged rear crown, paler belly, duskier throat and breast; *dumasi* pale-rufous crown, indistinct buff supercilium, brownish-olive upperparts and face, whitish breast, dull yellow underparts; *batjanensis* similar to previous but underparts more olive-yellow; *sulanus* lacks supercilium, has rufous-tinged throat and breast, warmer bronze-olive upperparts, flanks tinged rufous; *relictus* as previous but darker crown, less warm upperparts, largely lacking rufous-tinged throat and underparts, flanks washed cold-olive; *riedeli* rufous crown, dusky-brown face, bright-green upperparts, whitish underparts with yellow flanks; *stentor* as previous but duller brownish upperparts and darker flanks; *meisei* as previous but rufous ear-coverts, paler crown, flanks even less bright, greyish upperparts; *hedymeles* as previous but lighter crown, darker washed-out flanks; Obi population poorly documented . **Imm** grey forecrown; yellowish breast and throat. **Voc** Song exhibits great geographic and individual variability, but is generally a repetition of melodious high-pitched series of tinkling notes ending with a longer, level note; *cucullatus* sweet, quavering, very thin and high-pitched series of short notes followed by a long, level final note at a different pitch for each repeated strophe, roughly like "tit-tit-TIT-tyOOO, wih-wih-wih-WHIRRRR, tit-tit-TIT-tyEEE..." at 4 n/s; *hedymeles* sweet, quavering, very thin and high-pitched "tit-twee", lasting 1 sec, regularly repeated, occasionally including downslurred "whih-wir; *riedeli* and *stentor* thin, high-pitched "tit-tut-TIT-TEE, tit-TEE–whir", regularly repeated at a faster rate than *cucullatus* at 4 n/0.7 s, downslurred notes irregular and often just a single "wi'wirru"; *dumasi* consistent thin, high-pitched series of 6–10 notes "twit-dee-do-di'-twe-tit-tee-tee-teee-tee", opening with 1–4 downslurred notes, then rising, at 10 n/1.5 s. Call geographically variable, including: (i) *cucullatus*/*cinereicollis*/*dumasi* harsh, scolding, although thin "trrit" (slightly longer and higher-pitched in *dumasi* than in GS races); (ii) *cucullatus*/*cinereicollis* rapid, dry, random series of thin, high-pitched notes, often leading to song; (iii) (Sul races) very high-pitched, thin "zipt"; (iv) (Sul races) squeaky, trilled "trrrr". **AN** Mountain Tailorbird.

PNOEPYGIDAE
Cupwings
1 species in region

Very small, long-legged, nearly tailless birds of dense forest undergrowth where they forage on the ground and in low vegetation. Cryptic in colouration, shy and skulking, their presence is often revealed by distinctive vocalisations.

Pygmy Cupwing *Pnoepyga pusilla*

L 8–9 cm. Himalaya to SE–E Asia. 7 ssp, 4 in region: *lepida* (Sum), *rufa* (Jav), *everetti* (Flores), *timorensis* (Timor). Fairly common in montane forest, 900–3000 m (>1500 m on Timor). Forages on ground in dense thickets, usually solitary. **ID** Small, tailless. **Ad** head and upperparts dark-brown with small buff spots on wings; face rusty-tinged; dark underparts have thick whitish scaling. Ssp *rufa* less rusty, darker face, even paler scaling; *everetti* darker overall, lacks buff tinge to plumage; *timorensis* greyer, particularly face and mantle, underparts scaling weak, except for rear flanks, longer bill. **Imm** plainer upperparts; lacks scaling; more greyish underparts. **Voc** Song: (i) a repeated, high-pitched "teet, toot, teet" or "teet, toot, toot", lasting 2.8 sec, occasionally 4 notes, interspersed with short "trrr"; in E Jav and Flores 2-note version predominant, in Timor 3–5 notes; (ii) series of 15–20 rising, then dropping "tsi-sisisi..." lasting ~4 sec, like an old kettle beginning to boil. Call: sharp, loud "chit".

oreophilus

everetti

vulcanius

Sunda Bush Warbler

Manchurian Bush Warbler

riedeli

cucullatus

dumasi

Mountain Leaftoiler

Pygmy Cupwing

lepida

timorensis

ACROCEPHALIDAE
Reed Warblers
3 species in region

Small to mid-sized slender warblers typical of open wetland habitats, particularly reedbeds and waterside scrub. Generally drab in appearance and skulking in behaviour, their presence is most often revealed by their loud scratchy calls and complex, repetitive songs.

Oriental Reed Warbler *Acrocephalus orientalis*
L 19 cm. Breeds NE–E Asia; winters SE Asia, Phil. Monotypic. Fairly common in reedbeds, waterside scrub and tall grasses. Generally feeds higher and in the open more than other reed warblers. **ID** Bulky, thick-set appearance, with large bill. **Ad** olive-brown upperparts with distinct long, greyish-white supercilium extending behind eye; pale buff belly; pale greyish-white throat with indistinct darker streaks; pale tail tip. **Imm** pale fringes to flight feathers; slightly paler overall. **Voc** Song: loud, raucous, scratchy series of continuous notes, lacking rich, sweet notes, "ka-ka-rik-rik-rik-rik-rik-goork-goork-goork-kawa-kawa-kawa-eek-eek-eek...", occasionally heard in region. Call: (i) hard, grating "krrk"; (ii) squeaky "kwak"; (iii) hard, tapping "trik". **SS** Australasian Reed Warbler extremely similar but has thinner bill, supercilium only in front of eye, shorter primary projection, an unmarked breast, and lacks white tail tips; without practice identification should also be based on voice. Also see Black-browed Reed Warbler.

Australasian Reed Warbler *Acrocephalus australis*
L 14–16 cm. Aus, Phil. 8 ssp, 4 in region: *siebersi* (W Jav); *lentecaptus* (C Jav–Sumbawa, Bor); *sumbae* (Buru, Sumba, Timor, NG, Melanesia); *celebensis* (Sul). Taxa in region and Philippine *harterti* often considered part of extralimital Clamorous Reed Warbler *A. stentoreus* (W Palaearctic, S-SE-E Asia); current treatment based on plumage and vocal evidence. Locally fairly common in *Phragmites, Juncus* and sedges, usually surrounding water bodies and marshes, <1100 m. Presence usually betrayed by far-carrying song, otherwise elusive, feeding low down in dense vegetation. **ID** Slim, elongated appearance. **Ad** Unstreaked and fairly nondescript with long, slender bill and long, rounded tail; indistinct, pale buff supercilium in front of eye; flat crown raised when singing; mid grey-brown upperparts with buff belly and whitish throat. Ssp *lentecaptus* warmer, more extensive buff underparts, supercilium more conspicuous; *sumbae* smaller overall, indistinct supercilium; *celebensis* as previous but on average warmer belly and longer bill. **Imm** yellowish tone to underparts and rump. **Voc** Song: far-carrying, loud, melodious warble, variously alternating between rich sweet notes and guttural, hard notes; starts with single, short opening notes followed by 1–4 sequences, each of which can be very different: "chit-chit-chit WHICHEE–WHICHEE–WHICHEE CHEEWIP-CHEEWIP-CHEEWIP WHEEHER-WHEEHER-WHEEHER CHOOTCHEE–CHOOTCHEE–CHOOTCHEE", lasting <10 sec, repeated continuously in early morning. Call: (i) hard "tek", like two stones tapping; (ii) short, scolding, dry rattle. **SS** See Oriental and Black-browed Reed Warblers.

Black-browed Reed Warbler *Acrocephalus bistrigiceps*
L 14 cm. Breeds NE–E Asia; winters to SE Asia. Monotypic. Uncommon in reedbeds, waterside scrub and tall grasses. **ID Ad** unstreaked, grey-brown upperparts; diagnostic square-ended broad supercilium bordered above by blackish stripe; pale lores; creamy-white underparts and warmer flanks. **Imm** warmer upperparts and flanks. **Voc** Song: rapid mix of simple notes and phrases, various "chirps" and "churrs" with whistles, quite high-pitched, continuously repeated; rarely heard in region. Call: (i) soft, rich "tack"; (ii) soft, rolling "churr". **SS** Larger Australasian Reed Warbler has thinner bill, much less conspicuous supercilium only in front of eye. Oriental Reed Warbler much larger, bigger-billed, lacks black stripe above supercilium; plumage more olive-toned.

LOCUSTELLIDAE
Grasshopper Warblers
14 species in region

A diverse family that ranges from small and medium-sized warblers to the enigmatic, unique Malia of Sulawesi. Most species are shy and secretive, skulking in low vegetation and even walking on the ground; however, the larger species may be more conspicuous. Presence is usually revealed by distinctive vocalisations, often more insect than bird-like.

Malia *Malia grata*　　E
L 28 cm. 3 ssp: *grata* (SW Sul); *stresemanni* (C–SE Sul); *recondita* (N Sul). For a long time taxonomically enigmatic, this bird is now known to be part of the grasshopper warbler family. Fairly common in (sub-) montane forest, 900–2400 m. Pairs or small groups (<10), leader of mixed flocks, foliage-gleaning from lower to upper storey, often feeding on mossy trunks. **ID** Slim, elongated appearance. **Ad** olive-yellow head and breast with darker olive-green upperparts; black iris; pale pink bare parts. Ssp *recondita* wings and tail deeper green-tinged, smaller bill with duller lower mandible; *stresemanni* wings and tail rufous-tinged. **Imm** undescribed. **Voc** Song: loud, penetrating, fluty "cheew-chwee-choo-choo..." followed by hoarse cackles and noisy chatter. Call, usually in groups: one bird begins with quiet, scolding chatter for <5 sec before several birds join in with loud, hoarse cackles and chatter, interspersed with penetrating fluty "tyoo" or "t'tyoo-too tyoo-too".

Timor Thicketbird *Cincloramphus bivittatus*　　E
L 17–19 cm. Monotypic. Fairly common in W Timor but local in E, in dense thickets and scrub inside monsoon forest, occasionally shade coffee, <1100 m. Singly or pairs; mainly terrestrial but can sing from low canopy. Presence usually betrayed by vocalisations. **ID Ad** very long and broad bright-buff supercilium; thick rufous eye stripe and crown; buff face and underparts; olive-grey upperparts with broad, longish tail; black bill; flesh-coloured legs. **Imm** less distinct face pattern; lacking bright, rich tones; paler underparts. **Voc** Song: ventriloqual, loud, penetrating, staccato "zi-ka-cheet" or slightly shorter "tswit-chit", lasting 0.3 sec. Call: downslurred, hard, dry rattle lasting <1.5 sec. **AN** Buff-banded Thicket-warbler/Bushbird.

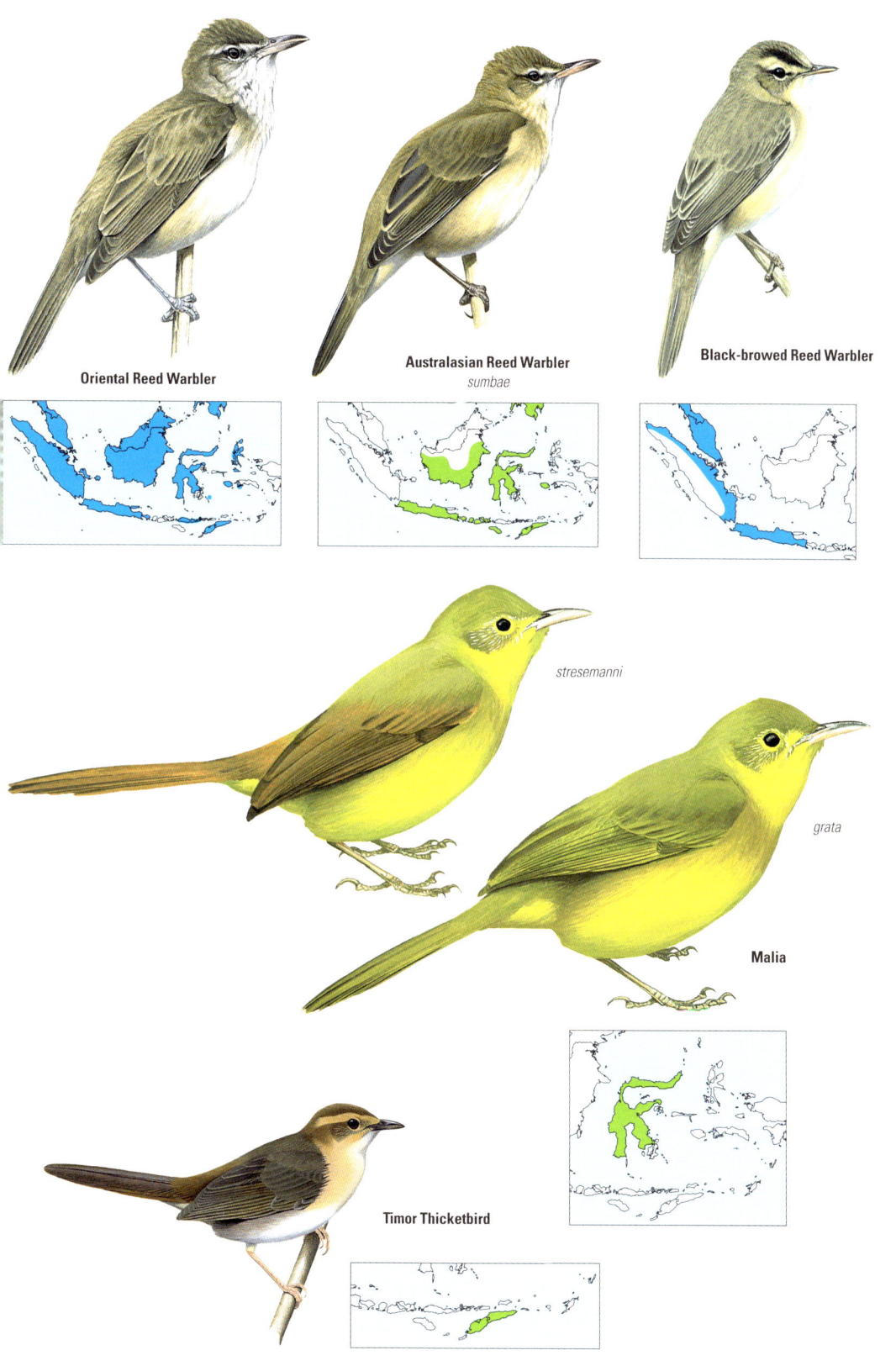

Oriental Reed Warbler

Australasian Reed Warbler
sumbae

Black-browed Reed Warbler

stresemanni

grata

Malia

Timor Thicketbird

Tawny Grassbird *Cincloramphus timoriensis*

L 18–21 cm. Aus, Phil. 10 ssp, ~4 in region: *timoriensis* (Timor, Wetar; populations on Romang and Tanimbar probably belong here); *celebensis* (Sul); *amboinensis* (Ambon); *inquirendus* (Sumba). Confused taxonomy with complex bioacoustic variation; deep mtDNA divergences among extralimital ssp, some of which may be more closely related to extralimital Papuan Grassbird *C. macrurus* (NG), suggesting that the complex may consist of as many as ~5 species. Fairly common locally in grassland, wet sedge plains, grasses in recently deforested areas, scrub. Singly or pairs; elusive, presence usually betrayed by vocalisations, though in wet season can perch prominently and perform song flight. **ID Ad** short whitish supercilium contrasting with lightly streaked, rufous crown; plain face; rufous mantle boldly streaked black, tertials with wide black centres and rich buff edges; streaked rump; long, graduated rufous tail with darker shafts; horn bill; fleshy-pink legs. Ssp *amboinensis* slightly smaller, crown and rump unstreaked; *inquirendus* well-defined breast and crown spotting; *celebensis* larger, brighter overall with rufous-cinnamon crown, indistinct mantle streaking; unstreaked underparts; flanks greyer. **Voc** Song, primarily in wet season: at least Timor and Tanimbars similar to Australia, descending series of <30 twittering notes "ch'ch'ch'zt'zt'zt..." lasting <1.5 sec; often given as song flight. Call: (i) scratchy "which"; (ii) *Acrocephalus*-like low "chuck"; (iii) on Timor and Sumba, at least, also disyllabic, loud "whit'chit". Ssp *celebensis* song: upslurred, melodious, loud "whit'chit", with buzzy second note.

Striated Grassbird *Megalurus palustris*

L 22–28 cm. S–SE Asia, Phil. 3 ssp, 2 in region: *palustris* (Jav, Bali); *forbesi* (NE Bor, Phil). Extralimital ssp *toklao* (mainland SE-S Asia) deeply diverged from *forbesi* in mtDNA, suggesting possible separation as monotypic '**Toklao Grassbird**' pending genomic and bioacoustic analysis. Fairly common (now uncommon on Jav) in marshland, wet grassland, stands of tall grass along edge of cultivation, tea plantations, <2000 m. Singly or pairs; often perching conspicuously on top of grasses, posts or wires. **ID** Long, graduated, pointed tail. **Ad** broad whitish supercilium; bland face with lightly streaked rufous crown; buff upperparts with thick black mantle streaking, dark centres to wing feathers; whitish throat to buff belly and flanks. **F** smaller. Ssp *forbesi* greyer nape; upperparts less bright with less streaking. **Imm** supercilium and underparts washed yellow; paler bill. **Voc** Song, from perch or in parachuting display flight: loud, rich, warbling "chot-chot-chot which-oo-queeee-chot-trrrrt-kwit-kwit-kwit-cheee-chwot", lasting 1.5–3 sec, often drops latter half of notes. Call: (i) explosive "pwit"; (ii) harsh "chat".

Lanceolated Warbler *Locustella lanceolata*

L 12 cm. Breeds Palaearctic; winters to SE Asia, Phil. 2 ssp, ~1 in region: *lanceolata* (probably only this ssp in region: breeds most of range; winters to GS). Scarce, few records in damp grasslands, paddies, marshes, predominantly coastal. Creeps through grasses and tangles; usually presence betrayed only when calling. **ID Ad** olive-brown upperparts with black-streaked crown, mantle and rump; dark-centred tertials and coverts; pale lores and supercilium tapering behind eye; whitish underparts buffier on flanks, with black streaks on breast, flanks and vent. **Imm** indistinct supercilium; underparts streaking diffuse. **Voc** Song unlikely to be heard in region: rapid delivery of disyllabic notes "tz'ze", at 15 n/s. Call: hard, explosive "tchk", regularly repeated. **SS** Pallas's and Middendorff's Grasshopper Warblers paler, more buff or rufous-toned on upperparts with broader, whiter supercilium and lack of underparts streaking.

Gray's Grasshopper Warbler *Locustella fasciolata*

L 16–17 cm. Breeds C–N–NE Asia; winters to NG, Phil and Wallacea. Monotypic. Fairly common in dense undergrowth: scrub, edge, grassland, marshes. Largely terrestrial, creeps through undergrowth; presence usually betrayed by its call. **ID Ad** large, drab and nondescript: large, strong, grey bill (more pinkish-horn on lower mandible) and pink legs; rich-brown upperparts; long, rounded tail; dull-grey underparts with paler throat and thin grey supercilium. **Imm** yellowish underparts; olive-tinged ear-coverts and less conspicuous supercilium. **Voc** Song: loud, explosive and fluid series of notes "chut-chit-chut-chit-chut-cheterrrrrreeet", lasting 3–4 sec, often heard in region. Call: rapidly repeated, rolling, harsh, usually disyllabic, "trk-trk". **SS** Note **Sakhalin Grasshopper Warbler** *L. amnicola* (monotypic; breeds Sakhalin, Kuril Is, Hokkaido) likely to winter in region alongside Gray's but as yet no confirmed records away from breeding range. Possibly visually inseparable from Gray's after post-breeding moult. Imm reportedly lacks Gray's olive-yellow tones on underparts, throat and supercilium in autumn, possibly due to later post-juvenile moult before plumage wears. Song is similar but significantly slower, less hurried, "chut chitt, chut chitt chet churut", lacking the loud gurgling warble at the end. Also see Middendorff's.

Pallas's Grasshopper Warbler *Locustella certhiola*

L 12–14 cm. Breeds C–N–NE Asia; winters to S–SE Asia. 4 ssp, 1 in region: *certhiola* (breeds N–NE Asia; winters to SE Asia). For taxonomy see Middendorff's. Locally fairly common in damp grasslands, marshes. Creeps through grasses and tangles; presence usually betrayed only when calling or flushed, when will fly directly away, close to ground. **ID Ad** dark rufescent upperparts with black-centred crown, mantle and rump feathers giving densely streaked appearance; conspicuous supercilium flaring behind eye; unstreaked whitish underparts with variable buffish flanks. When flushed, often shows pale tail tips with rusty-rumped appearance. **Imm** yellowish underparts with slight spotting on lower throat. **Voc** Vocal on wintering grounds, often heard singing at dusk. Song: starts with 2–3 quiet, harsh "shrip" notes followed by variable, scratchy, *Acrocephalus*-like series of harsh, inflected notes "chit-chrit-werwerwer-tatatatata-cherwee-cherwee-cherwee-checheche", lasting <4 sec. Call: (i) hard, metallic "pwit"; (ii) quiet, tinkling "rit-tititit". **SS** See Middendorff's and Lanceolated.

Middendorff's Grasshopper Warbler *Locustella ochotensis*

L 14–15 cm. Breeds NE Asia; mainly winters Phil. Monotypic. Hybridises with Pallas's; presumed hybrid specimen SE Sul. Scarce in damp grasslands, marshes. Creeps through grasses and tangles, presence usually betrayed only when calling. **ID Ad** rufescent upperparts, rump and crown, with indistinct black mottling and contrasting greyish nape; greyish-white supercilium, less distinct than Pallas's; greyish-white underparts. In flight can show pale tail tips with distinctly rusty rump. **Imm** yellowish underparts with slight spotting on lower throat. **Voc** Song: similar to Pallas's but more strident with more distinct individual sequences, "chrit-chrit-chut-witwit- cherwee-cherwee-wootwootwoot-werwerwer". Call: quiet, hard "chrit" or "kit", slightly harder than Pallas's. **SS** Pallas's often warmer rufescent above with distinct crown and mantle streaking, lacking contrasting grey nape; beware of possible hybrids which can approach Middendorff's duller and more weakly mottled appearance. Gray's is much larger overall, bigger-billed, with darker, greyer underparts, lacking any mottling on mantle. Also see Lanceolated.

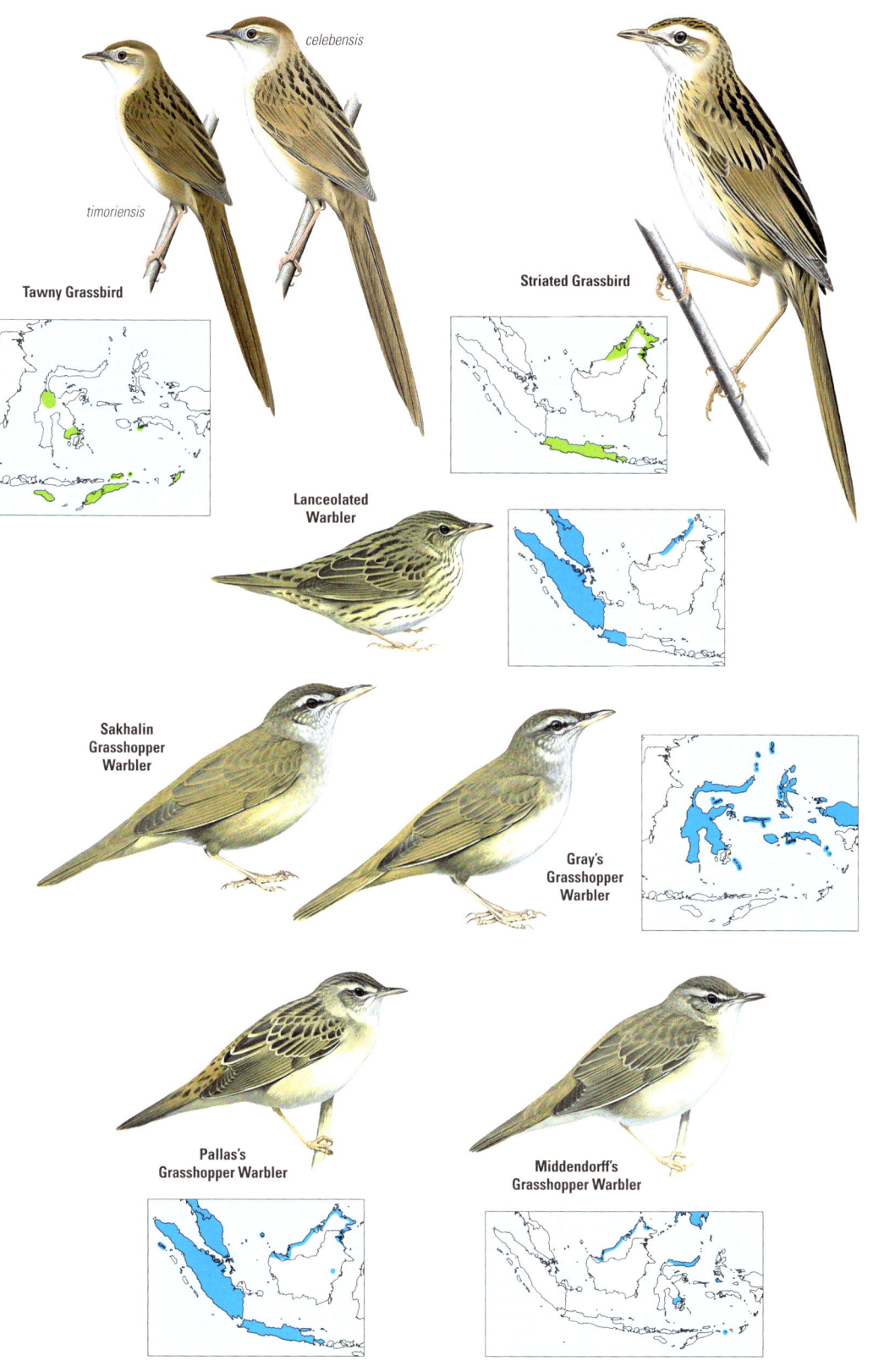

celebensis

timoriensis

Tawny Grassbird

Striated Grassbird

Lanceolated Warbler

Sakhalin Grasshopper Warbler

Gray's Grasshopper Warbler

Pallas's Grasshopper Warbler

Middendorff's Grasshopper Warbler

Friendly Grasshopper Warbler *Locustella accentor* [E]

L 15 cm. Monotypic. Fairly common in scrub and ground vegetation of stunted forest and heath, 1800–3800 m, most numerous 2300–2900 m. Largely terrestrial, creeping mouse-like along forest floor and in dense undergrowth, but can sing from exposed perch close to ground. **ID Ad** dark, rich rufous-brown plumage with black speckles; white throat and grey breast; grey-tinged ear-coverts and hint of supercilium. **Imm** generally drabber; less distinct throat markings. **Voc** Song: far-carrying, high-pitched, repetitive, rasping, buzzy "trp-teeerrrzz trp-teeerrrzz trp-teeerrrzz...", lasting a few sec to <5 min. Shows slight variation, including weaker "tit-tit-teeee". Call: subdued "chit". **SS** Smaller, daintier Sunda Bush Warbler has pronounced supercilium, lacks throat markings, and sings very differently.

Sunda Grasshopper Warbler *Locustella montis* [E]

L 13–15 cm. 2 ssp: *montis* (Jav, Bali); *timorensis* (Timor, Alor). Confused taxonomy: ssp *timorensis* sometimes separated as monotypic 'Timor Grasshopper Warbler' (with *L. montis* becoming '**Javan Grasshopper Warbler**') based on purported vocal differences, but most of them do not hold up when full individual variation is taken into account. Ssp *timorensis* and *montis* are almost undifferentiated in mtDNA, indicating evolutionarily recent colonisation of Timor and Alor. Sunda Grasshopper Warbler is similar in song, DNA and plumage to a variety of extralimital grasshopper warblers (e.g. Russet *L. mandelli* [mainland SE–E Asia]; Sichuan *L. chengi* [E Asia]; Benguet *L. seebohmi* [Phil]), all of which are sometimes merged as '**Russet Grasshopper Warbler**' *L. mandelli*; genomic inquiry needed. Very locally fairly common, though not recorded from W Timor since collection in 1932, in tall grasses and forest undergrowth, 800–2500 m. Largely terrestrial, creeping mouse-like along forest floor and in dense undergrowth. **ID Ad** chestnut-brown upperparts; long, graduated tail; grey face and flanks; whitish throat with well-defined black spotting on lower throat and breast; weakly-defined grey supercilium. Ssp *timorensis* smaller, uniformly paler; longer indistinct supercilium, breast spotting reduced; rufous-brown rear flanks and lower belly. **Imm** yellow-washed underparts; pale lower mandible and legs. **Voc** Song: *montis* simple, repetitive rasping "zeeurt-zeeurt-zeeurt..." at 2 n/s (3–5 kHz), lasting up to several minutes; *timorensis* similar but often with faster delivery and shorter notes; Alor birds higher-pitched (4–6 kHz) "dzrrrp-dzrrrp-dzrrrp..." at 2.5 n/s although birds elsewhere also known to approach this pitch. Call: hard, rapidly repeated "tuk".

Sulawesi Grasshopper Warbler *Locustella castanea* [E]

L 14–15 cm. 2 ssp: *castanea* (Sul, except SW); *everetti* (SW Sul). Pronounced geographic variation in song requires genomic, bioacoustic and morphological investigation as multiple young species likely involved. Previously included Buru and Seram Grasshopper Warblers to form more broadly-defined '**Chestnut-backed Grasshopper Warbler**' *L. castanea*, but all three are distinct vocally and genetically. Scarce in undergrowth of montane forest, >950 m. Largely terrestrial, creeping mouse-like along forest floor and in dense undergrowth. **ID Ad** chestnut-brown crown,

upperparts and belly; dark-grey breast; whitish throat and face with paler, distinct supercilium; black bill. Ssp *everetti* similar, with no currently known fixed plumage differences, but vocally distinct and hence valid. **Imm** undescribed. **Voc** Has two song types (perhaps sex-specific as occasionally given in duet), both of which strongly vary across range. (1) 'Piercing song' consists of 1-3 high-pitched, level, piercing notes preceded by 1-2 brief (sometimes inaudible) introductory notes: in C Sul 2-3 main notes "tzp tzreee-tzreee-tzreee"; in N Sul 3 notes in quick succession (sometimes sounding like single note) "tzp tzreesreesree"; in SW Sul (*everetti*) 2 shorter notes "tsp tzreet tzreet"; in SE Sul only one main note preceded by two introductory notes "tzp tzp tzreeeeer". (2) 'Wavy song' (apparently absent in SW and N Sul) consists of one high-pitched, piercing but wavy note, wavering up and down multiple times, in C Sul "tseeooeeooeeoo", in SE Sul less high-pitched, more creaking "tsewtsewtseewee". In N Sul known to respond to playback with twanging sound followed by piercing trill "tch-twang-tch-twang-tzreee". Can also produce a descending series of high-pitched, buzzy notes. Call: short, sharp "spit", often interspersed with song motifs.

Buru Grasshopper Warbler *Locustella disturbans* [E]

L 14–15 cm. Monotypic. For taxonomy see Sulawesi Grasshopper Warbler. Uncommon in undergrowth of montane forest, >750 m. Largely terrestrial, creeping mouse-like along forest floor and in dense undergrowth. **ID Ad** similar to Sulawesi Grasshopper but lacks rufous tones in plumage. Distinct white supercilium; unmarked white throat and breast edged grey on upper belly. **Imm** darker underparts, lacks supercilium and shorter tail. **Voc** Song: high-pitched, repeated, grating "tsu'tzeet tsu'tzeet tsu'tzeet..." lasting 0.7 sec at 8 n/10 s. Call: undescribed.

Seram Grasshopper Warbler *Locustella musculus* [E]

L 14–15 cm. Monotypic. For taxonomy see Sulawesi Grasshopper Warbler. Uncommon in undergrowth of montane forest, >850 m. Largely terrestrial, creeping mouse-like along forest floor and in dense undergrowth. **ID Ad** similar to Sulawesi Grasshopper but darker overall, sooty-brown upperparts, darker grey face and inconspicuous grey supercilium. **Imm** undescribed. **Voc** Song: unusual frog-like, croaking "creek-grrg-creek", less high-pitched and piercing than other grasshopper warblers, lasting 0.6 sec at 5 n/10 s. Call: short, sharp "ZIP".

Taliabu Grasshopper Warbler *Locustella portenta* [E]

L 14 cm. Monotypic. Scarce in undergrowth of montane forest, >1000 m, now very restricted because of habitat destruction. Largely terrestrial, creeping mouse-like along forest floor and in dense undergrowth. **ID** Similar to Sulawesi Grasshopper Warbler but more distinct breast spotting, mantle to rump colder brown, wings and tail much darker blackish-brown, head browner, and underparts entirely dull warm-brown. **Voc** Song: high-pitched, grating notes "tit'tzeeeet tit'tzeeeet tit'tzeeeet...." lasting 1 sec at 5 n/10 s. Calls: (i) buzzy "chew'tzzt'tzzt", lasting 1 sec, first note downslurred, regularly repeated at intervals; (ii) wheezy "wheer-wheer-wheer-wheer...".

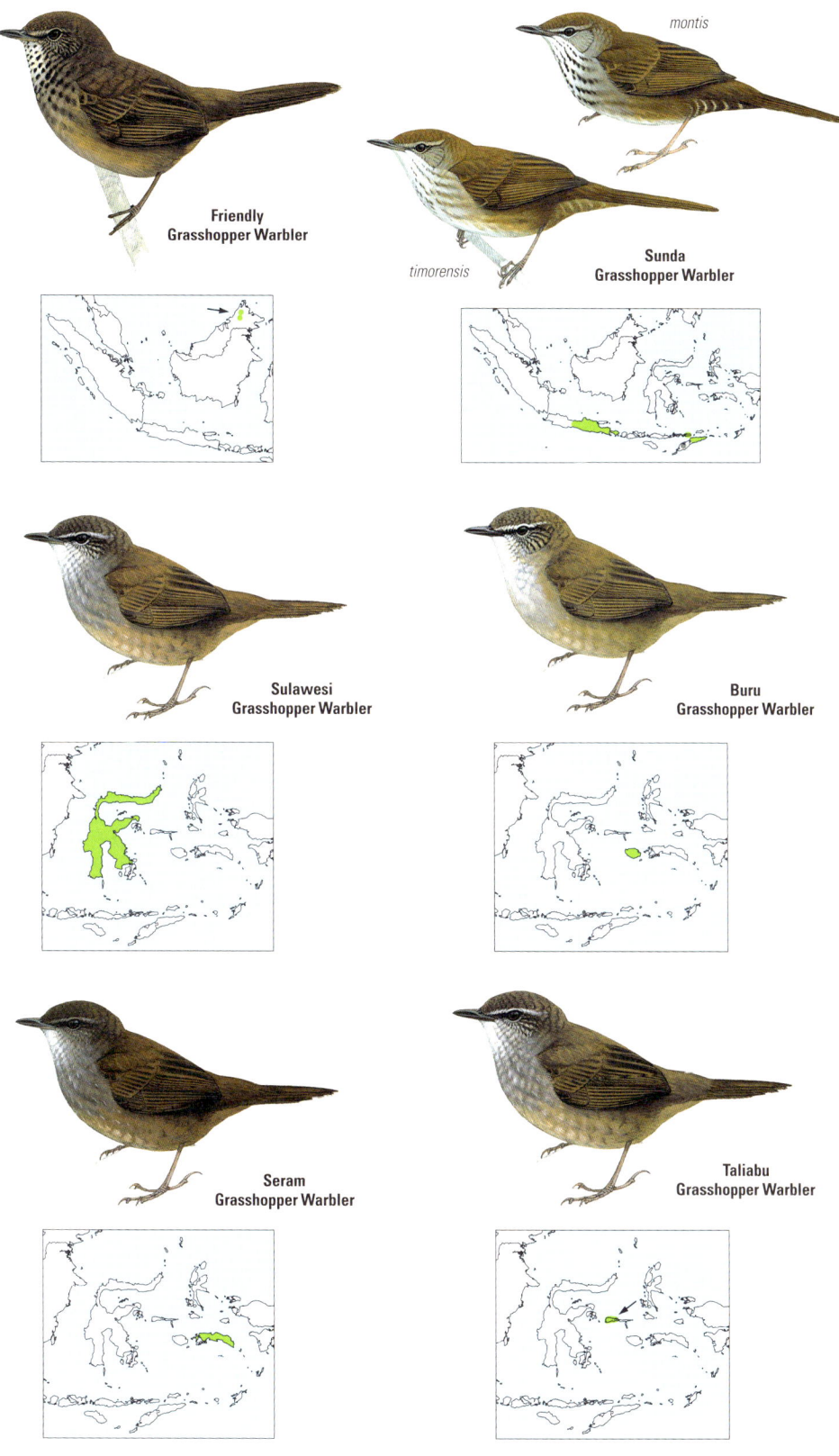

Friendly Grasshopper Warbler

montis

timorensis

Sunda Grasshopper Warbler

Sulawesi Grasshopper Warbler

Buru Grasshopper Warbler

Seram Grasshopper Warbler

Taliabu Grasshopper Warbler

CISTICOLIDAE
Tailorbirds, Prinias and Cisticolas
12 species in region
Small warblers, some of forest and edge, while others are found in open grasslands and even urban gardens. Usually active, foraging in low vegetation. Typically very vocal, some species are conspicuous, while others shy and skulking.

Common Tailorbird *Orthotomus sutorius*
L 10–14 cm. S–SE–E Asia. 9 ssp, 2 in region: *edela* (Jav); *maculicollis* (southern mainland SE Asia; Riau Is). Common in scrub, degraded forest and plantations around villages, parks, gardens, even cities. Avoids dense forest, <1500 m. Singly or pairs. **ID M** rufous forecrown; whitish supercilium; greenish upperparts; pale-grey underparts with darker flanks; long bill and tail. **F** shorter tail; less distinct forecrown fading to mid-crown. Ssp *maculicollis* with fine grey streaks on sides of head and neck (less distinct in **F**). **Imm** duller; forecrown greenish. **Voc** Song: repeated, chirping "chee-yup, chee-yup, chee-yup..." at 2.5 n/s. Call: sharp, thin "pip-pip-pip..." or "cheep-cheep-cheep..." at 4 n/s. **SS** On Riau Is separated with difficulty from fem Dark-necked, which lacks Common's faint white supercilium and has diagnostic yellow (not white) vent.

Dark-necked Tailorbird *Orthotomus atrogularis*
L 11–12 cm. SE Asia. 3 ssp, 2 in region: *atrogularis* (Sum, most of Bor, Anambas, Natuna, MPen); *humphreysi* (NE Bor). Common in forest canopy, most conspicuous at clearings and edge, <1000 m. Usually pairs, more arboreal than other tailorbirds. **ID M** rufous crown; greyish face; underparts whitish-grey; blackish upper breast with streaks to throat and breast; yellow vent; dark olive-green upperparts and tail. Ssp *humphreysi* black breast more extensive; yellow on vent extends to lower belly. **F** duller rufous crown and duller vent; lacks black breast patch but instead has dusky breast markings. **Imm** duller overall; crown greenish; lacking black and grey on underparts. **Voc** Song variable, with repeated rolling motifs, such as high-pitched, buzzy, shivery "pirra", lasting 0.5 sec, regularly repeated 10–20 times, or emphatic, rolling "chweEP-chweEP-chweEP..." at 1.5 n/s; often duetted with a scratchy, repeated "tittruit". Call: (i) short "tew"; (ii) staccato "kre'e'e'e'e'e". **SS** See Common.

Ashy Tailorbird *Orthotomus ruficeps*
L 11–12 cm. Sundaic. 8 ssp, 6 in region: *ruficeps* (Jav); *cineraceus* (Sum, Bangka, Belitung, Nias, MPen); *concinnus* (Mentawai); *borneoensis* (Bor); *baweanus* (Bawean); *palliolatus* (Kangean, Karimunjawa). Common in mangroves and other lowland habitats close to water, on Bor also found in lowland and hill forest, <1100 m. **ID M** rufous face; grey body with paler belly. **F** paler face; whitish throat; paler underparts. Ssp *cineraceus* has darker head; *concinnus* paler grey overall, face brighter; *borneoensis* even darker head; *baweanus* longer wings and tail; *palliolatus* paler chestnut head. **Imm** grey face; olive-grey upperparts. **Voc** Song variable, but most common motifs include: (i) repetitive "chip-WEE–chip, chip-WEE–chip, chip-WEE–chip...", stress on second note; (ii) repetitive "chu-EEP", stress on second note, sometimes quavering. Songs often duetted with call notes. Call: (i) hard trill, "prrrrt"; (ii) single "chuk"; (iii) nasal "checheche...". **SS** See Olive-backed Tailorbird.

Olive-backed Tailorbird *Orthotomus sepium* E
L 12 cm. 2 ssp: *sepium* (Jav–Lombok); *sundaicus* (Panaitan). Population recently discovered in and around Waingapu (Sumba) presumed escapees. Was fairly common, now becoming increasingly uncommon in scrub, thickets, cultivation, edge, degraded forest, mangroves, <1900 m. **ID M** rufous face; olive-grey upperparts and breast; whitish belly. **F** less extensive rufous face; whitish throat; paler underparts. Ssp *sundaicus* larger overall; longer tail and wings; upperparts duller; underparts paler. **Imm** olive-grey face; more olive upperparts; yellowish belly. **Voc** Song: repetitive "chu-EEP", difficult to differentiate from Ashy Tailorbird. Song often duetted with call notes. Call: (1) hard trill, "prrrrt"; (2) hard, squeaky "chu-chu-chu...". **SS** Ashy Tailorbird is darker, greyer, lacking any olive tones, with a more contrasting orange face. On Java, Ashy is restricted to mangrove and coastal habitat. **AN** Javan Tailorbird.

Rufous-tailed Tailorbird *Orthotomus sericeus*
L 12 cm. Sundaic, Palawan, Sulu. 3 ssp: *sericeus* (Bor, Palawan, Sulu); *hesperius* (Sum, Belitung, MPen); *rubicundulus* (Natuna). Fairly common in secondary and swampy forest, edge, clearings, locally mangroves and scrub, even on small offshore islands. **ID Ad** rufous crown and tail; mid-grey upperparts and whitish underparts. Ssp *hesperius* smaller, darker, with less grey upperparts; *rubicundulus* larger bill. **Imm** rufous only on forecrown; olive-grey nape and upperparts; yellowish underparts; dull rufous tail. **Voc** Song: rolling "do-dee do-dee do-dee..." rapidly repeated; slight variations include "chik-wir chik-wir chik-wir...", "dwuee-wir dwuee-wir dwuee-wir...", "pu-cher pu-cher pu-cher...", generally lower-pitched than Ashy Tailorbird. Call: wheezy, soft "tzee-tzee-tzee...".

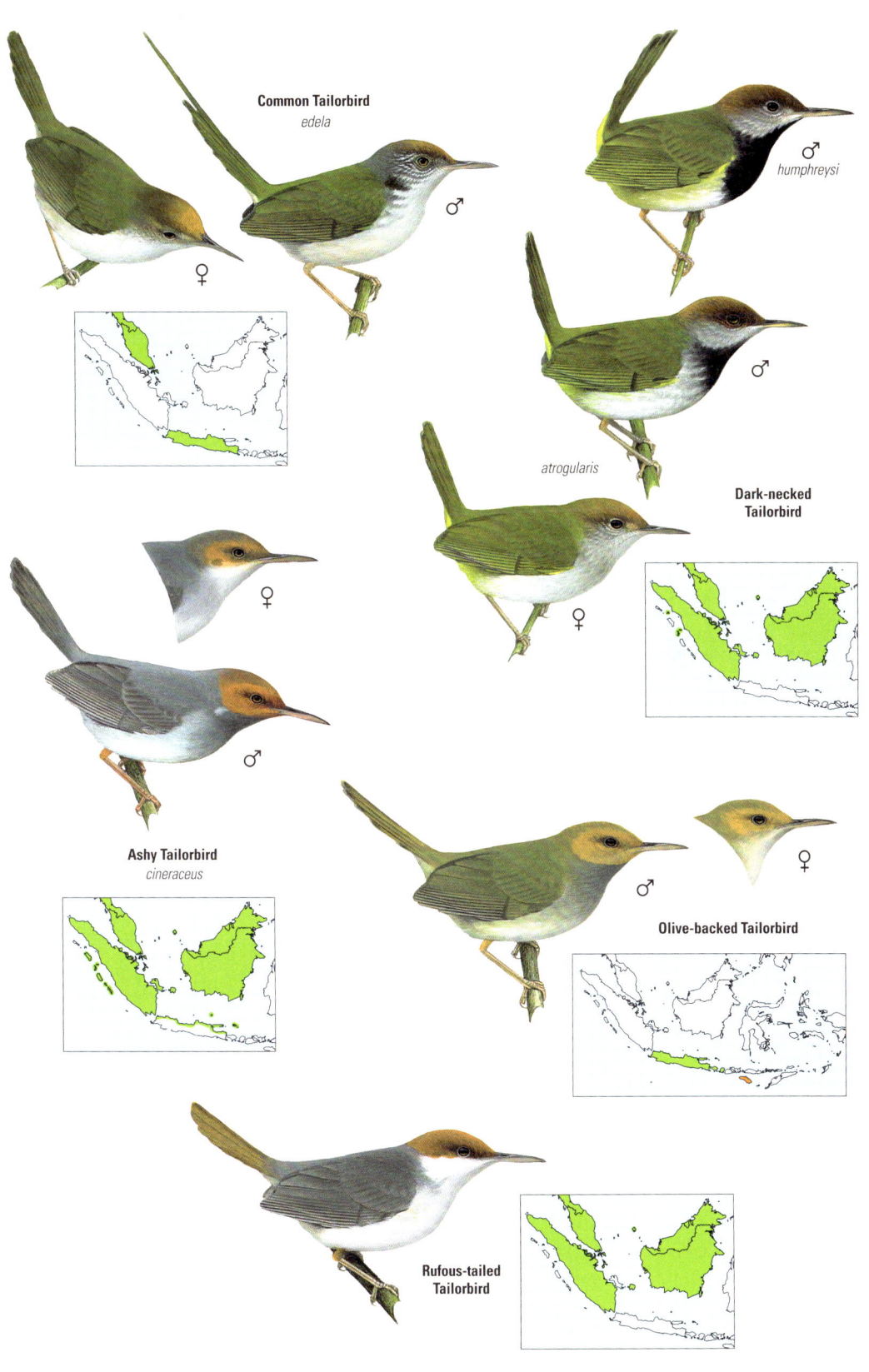

Common Tailorbird
edela

♀

♂

humphreysi

♂

atrogularis

♂

Dark-necked Tailorbird

♀

♀

Ashy Tailorbird
cineraceus

♂

♂

♀

Olive-backed Tailorbird

Rufous-tailed Tailorbird

Deignan's Prinia *Prinia polychroa*

L 16 cm. SE Asia. 2 ssp, 1 in region: *polychroa* (Jav). Previously considered conspecific with extralimital Burmese Prinia *P. cooki* (Myanmar) and Annam Prinia *P. rocki* (Indochina) to form larger umbrella species '**Brown Prinia**' *P. polychroa* but now separated based on vocal and genetic evidence. Local and uncommon in dry grassland mixed with scrub, tea plantations, <1500 m. **ID Ad** greyish-brown upperparts, crown and long tail, faintly mottled on mantle and with distinct pale streaks on crown; whitish supercilium in front of eye; dusky lores; pale, buffish underparts; pink legs; pale red iris; blackish bill. **Imm** less streaking, more buffish underparts. **Voc** Song: monotonous, "ts'weep ts'weep ts'weep..." at 2 n/s lasting 2–30 sec, more powerful than Plain Prinia. Call: downslurred, rising at end, "chwee", similar to Olive-backed Sunbird; often interspersed with song. **SS** Plain Prinia lacks streaking on crown, has wider supercilium spilling onto lores (Deignan's lores more extensively dark), generally whiter underparts and mostly pink (not blackish) bill.

Hill Prinia *Prinia superciliaris*

L 16–20 cm. SE-E Asia. 5 ssp, 1 in region: *dysancrita* (Sum). Formerly called *P. atrogularis* when including additional taxa from E Himalayan region, but now reduced to five SE-E Asian ssp because of morphological and vocal differences. Further genetic and bioacoustic research required to determine whether there are additional species boundaries within Hill Prinia as here delimited. Fairly common in scrub, clearings, cultivated and grassy areas, 800–2200 m, locally to lowlands in N Sum. **ID Ad** grey head; variably conspicuous white supercilium (much reduced in **F**); dull brown upperparts and long tail; white underparts with faint black streaking on neck sides; buff flanks and lower belly; milky-grey iris; dark pinkish-horn bill; pink legs. **Imm** less distinct streaking on neck sides; brown-tinged head; shorter tail. **Voc** Song: repeated, loud, clear "tew tew tew..." at variable speed depending on excitement, often in duet with second bird slightly higher-pitched. Call: repeated "teek teek teek...". **SS** Much smaller Yellow-bellied Prinia (usually found in damper vegetation) has supercilium only in front of eye, lacks streaking on neck sides, has redder (not milky-grey) iris, blacker bill and has yellower (less buff) belly (although some Yellow-bellied can appear buff).

Bar-winged Prinia *Prinia familiaris*　**E**

L 13 cm. Monotypic. Previously common, now local and increasingly uncommon on Jav–Bali, but still locally common on Sum. Inhabits variety of open scrubby habitats including gardens, mangroves, plantations and clearings, <1500 m. Often feeds on ground. Pairs or small groups (<15). **ID Ad** distinctive double white wingbar and tail tips; olive-brown upperparts; grey head; red iris; white throat and breast to yellowish belly; greyish-horn bill. **Imm** more pink bill base; wingbars less distinct. **Voc** Highly variable, producing a broad range of squeaky, high-pitched, sharp and excited calls, usually in duet and mixing the notes. Notes include: (i) sharp "chip"; (ii) sharp, repeated "tuwee tuwee tuwee..."; (iii) squeaky, high-pitched "chee-chee-chee..."; (iv) rolling, upslurred "ch-ch-chee-cheeep".

Yellow-bellied Prinia *Prinia flaviventris*

L 12–14 cm. S–SE–E Asia. 7 ssp, 3 in region: *rattlesi* (Sum, Jav, southern mainland SE Asia); *halistona* (Nias); *latrunculus* (Bor). Substantial geographic variability in song and plumage suggests separation into multiple species pending genomic analysis, in which case the three taxa in region would form '**Raffles's Prinia**' *P. rafflesi*. Similar ssp *halistona* and *latrunculus* form leapfrog pattern, interrupted by different-looking ssp *rafflesi*. Common in

damp, vegetated areas, particularly tall grasses and marshes, but also gardens; uncommon on Jav. **ID Ad** grey head with short white supercilium in front of eye, white throat and breast; olive upperparts; bright yellow belly; iris red; bill black. Ssp *latrunculus* lacks yellow belly but has buff tinge to breast and upper belly, more grey-tinged upperparts; *halistona* as previous but larger. **Imm** dull yellowish underparts, face and supercilium. **Voc** Song: series of sharply descending, repetitive, chucking "wit-wit-weety-weety-wit", lasting 0.7 sec, sounding like a rattle, regularly repeated. Call: nasal mewing "cheet". **SS** See Hill Prinia.

Plain Prinia *Prinia inornata*

L 11 cm. S–SE–E Asia. 10 ssp, 1 in region: *blythi* (Jav). May comprise multiple species-level taxa; genomic and bioacoustic inquiry needed. Fairly common in thickets, marshes, grassland, scrubby areas and sometimes gardens, <1500 m. **ID Ad** unstreaked, grey-brown upperparts with distinct broad white supercilium; white underparts (seasonally buffy flanks); bright pink legs; pink bill (except dark tip); yellowish iris with narrow red eyering (mostly visible during breeding). **Imm** buffish belly; less distinct supercilium; darker eye. **Voc** Song: monotonous, rapidly repeated "jit-jit-jit..." at 4 n/s. Call: (i) monotonous hard "tee-tee-tee..." at 5–7 n/s; (ii) single, soft "berp". **SS** See Deignan's Prinia.

Zitting Cisticola *Cisticola juncidis*

L 10 cm. Old World. 18 ssp, 3 in region: *malaya* (Sum and satellites, W Jav, mainland SE Asia, Nicobars); *fuscicapilla* (Kangean, Bawean, E Jav–LS); *constans* (Sul and satellites). Considerable vocal variation across range may warrant separation into at least three species: the regional taxa belong to a vocally distinct group of ~8 ssp from Aus to SE–E Asia ('**Double Zitting Cisticola**' *C. tinnabulans*) that differ considerably from taxa further north (monotypic '**Japanese Zitting Cisticola**' *C. brunniceps* [E Asia]) and further west ('**Western Zitting Cisticola**' *C. juncidis* [S Asia, W Palaearctic, Africa]). Fairly common mainly in wet tall grasses, paddyfields and marshes. **ID Ad br** buff-brown upperparts and crown with bold blackish streaking; broad white supercilium; buff flanks; white-and-black tipped tail. Ssp *fuscicapilla* less pronounced streaking. **Ad non-br** shorter tail and less bold streaking. Ssp *constans* lacks non-br plumage. **Imm** yellowish underparts. **Voc** Song: (i) characteristic disyllabic "double zitting" "tsit-tsip", 1 n/s, repeated while performing undulating, slowly rising aerial display; (ii) faster, monotonous, hard, high-pitched "plick", 6 n/s, given irregularly in flight or perched. Call: soft "chip". **SS** See Golden-headed Cisticola.

Golden-headed Cisticola *Cisticola exilis*

L 9 cm. S–SE–E Asia to Aus. 12 ssp, 2 in region: *lineocapilla* (GS, LS, NW Aus); *rusticus* (Sul–C Mol). Locally fairly common in grassland, bracken scrub and fields, generally in drier areas than Zitting Cisticola. **ID M br** unstreaked golden-rufous crown, nape and rump; black-streaked mantle and short tail; extensive rich buff flanks; whitish underparts. Ssp *rusticus* buff flanks more extensive including across belly. **M non-br/F** crown and rump dark-streaked (though nape still unstreaked buff); buff supercilium; longer tail. **Imm** yellowish underparts; diffusely streaked upperparts. **Voc** Song: comical buzzy nasal mew "bzzee", lasting 0.6 sec, usually followed by 1–2 explosive "prruk" notes; often given in a weak circular aerial display. Call: soft rattles and nasal bleats. **SS** From Zitting Cisticola in non-breeding plumage by buffish (not white) supercilium, contrastingly unstreaked buff nape, more extensive, richer buff flanks, and less white on tail tip.

Deignan's Prinia

Hill Prinia

latrunculus

Bar-winged Prinia

Yellow-bellied Prinia

rafflesi

Plain Prinia

Zitting Cisticola
malaya

♀ / ♂ non-breeding

Golden-headed Cisticola

♂ breeding

HYLOCITREIDAE
Hylocitrea
1 species in region

Monotypic family. Small, whistler-like frugivore of Sulawesi's montane forests. Drab in appearance and shy and unobtrusive in habits. Typically forages quietly within low- to mid-storey.

Hylocitrea *Hylocitrea bonensis* `E`

L 14–15 cm. 2 ssp: *bonensis* (Sul, except SW); *bonthaina* (SW Sul). The two sometimes divided into monotypic species, '**Southern**' *H. bonthaina* and '**Northern Hylocitrea**' *H. bonensis* based on plumage; vocal and genomic analysis required. Uncommon in montane forest, >1200 m. Singly or pairs; unobtrusive in mid-canopy. **ID M** dusky-olive head and upperparts; dull grey collar and breast; olive-yellow flanks, belly, and rump; cinnamon vent. **F** cinnamon-buff throat, can show streaking. Ssp *bonthaina* brighter olive-yellow face; paler underparts; brighter flanks; grey extending down mantle; **F** with whiter throat streaking. **Imm** head and neck olive-brown; upperparts olive; underparts striped buff. **Voc** Song: (i) high-pitched, flowerpecker-like series of 5–30 thin piercing notes, first note slightly longer "seee-sioo-sioo-sioo-sioo", 3 n/s; (ii) series of wavy, squeaky notes, reminiscent of a *Phylloscopus* song but much higher-pitched (8–11khz), lasting <7 s. Call: (i) sharp "tssk"; (ii) piercing, thin "tzip", can be repeated in quick succession.

SITTIDAE
Nuthatches
2 species in region

Small forest birds with distinctive blue colouration. Characteristically feed by clinging to branches and tree trunks and foraging for invertebrates within the bark. Often found in small groups or as part of mixed flocks where typically conspicuous.

Velvet-fronted Nuthatch *Sitta frontalis*

L 12 cm. S–SE–E Asia, Palawan. 5 ssp, 3 in region: *velata* (Jav); *saturatior* (Sum, Lingga, Simeulue, Bangka, MPen); *corallipes* (Bor, Maratua). Fairly common in forest, <2200 m. Singly or pairs; in mid- and upper canopy, gleans bark of trunks and branches, joins mixed flocks. **ID M** red bill, eyering and legs; upperparts violet-blue; black forehead and post-ocular line; whitish throat and pale lavender underparts. **F** lacks post-ocular line; buff-tinged underparts. Ssp *saturatior* darker, more lilac overall; *corallipes* as previous but orange-red feet. **Imm** grey bill; duller upperparts; buff underparts. **Voc** Song: rapid series of high-pitched, far-carrying "tsit" notes, "tsruk-tsruk-tsit-tsit-tsit..." at 7 n/s, often in duet. Call: quiet "chweet-chweet".

Blue Nuthatch *Sitta azurea*

L 13 cm. Sundaic. 3 ssp: *azurea* (C–E Jav); *nigriventer* (W Jav); *expectata* (Sum, MPen). Fairly common in (sub-) montane forest, 900–2800 m. Usually in pairs or small groups (<10), joins mixed flocks. **ID Ad** grey bill; dark blue-tinged head, mantle and belly; cobalt blue tail; broad pale eyering; silver and black wing linings; white throat to lower breast. Ssp *nigriventer* often has buff-washed breast; *expectata* as previous but much darker upperparts and belly with faint purple tinge. **Imm** brown-tinged head; less bright plumage. **Voc** Variety of quiet, thin calls: (i) squeaky "zhe"; (ii) mellow "tup"; (iii) abrupt "whit"; (iv) short, rapid, thin trill.

STURNIDAE
Starlings and Mynas
27 species in region (1 introduced)

Small to medium-sized arboreal birds, ranging in plumage from drab to colourful. Usually active, vocal and gregarious, foraging in groups and nesting communally. Inhabit a range of habitats from forest to dry open country and towns. Several species heavily trapped for the pet trade and becoming endangered.

Metallic Starling *Aplonis metallica*

L 25 cm. Aus. 5 ssp, 2 in region: *metallica* (Sula–Mol, NG, Aus); ssp *circumscripta* (Tanimbar, Damar) sometimes split as monotypic '**Purple-chinned Starling**' based on plumage. Locally common but scarce on Tanimbar, no recent records from Damar. Inhabits forest, edge. Forms large flocks and noisy breeding colonies, with large, hanging nests (<500); mid- to upper canopy. **ID Ad** sleek, longish, graduated tail; black plumage glossed green on nape and underparts, glossed purple on crown, mantle and tail; matte black lores and conspicuous red eye. Ssp *circumscripta* has purple chin patch with inverted U-shape; narrower green nape; longer tail and shorter wings. **Imm** white underparts with pale grey breast and throat and flank streaking; glossy grey-brown head and upperparts. **Voc** Song: long series of high-pitched, disjointed, scratchy notes. Call: (i) forceful, nasal, downslurred notes, "tchew" and "chrrr"; (ii) short, sharp "chrt". **SS** See Moluccan and Tanimbar Starlings. **AN** Shining Starling.

Tanimbar Starling *Aplonis crassa* `E`

L 20 cm. Monotypic. Uncommon in forest, edge. Singly, pairs or small groups (<20, rarely larger); canopy forager and cavity nester. **ID Ad** compact, sturdy bill and short, square-cut tail; uniform sooty-black plumage with slightly glossed bluish-green upperparts; black eye. **Imm** uniform brownish-grey overall with pronounced breast streaking; black lores; tail noticeably rufous. **Voc** (i) Medium-pitched, rising trill "brrrr"; (ii) high-pitched "bee-wit", lasting 0.3 sec, lorikeet-like. **SS** Metallic Starling has red (not black) eye in all ages, longer and graduated tail, and glossier appearance; Imm Metallic has much whiter, less streaked underparts and paler throat.

Moluccan Starling *Aplonis mysolensis*

L 20 cm. Wallacea, W Papuan Is. Monotypic. Locally fairly common in woodland, edge, cultivation, occasionally around settlements, <1000 m. Nests colonially in cavities in decaying limbs and trunks, often in large groups (<200). **ID Ad** sleek, with long, strongly graduated tail; black plumage lightly glossed greenish-purple; lanceolated neck and throat feathers; black eye. **Imm** shorter-tailed; less glossy upperparts; white-fringed underpart feathers create heavily streaked appearance. **Voc** Song: series of 3–10 up-and-down short nasal ringing notes, "twee-bree-twee-bree...", at 3 n/s. Call: (i) upslurred, whiny "whirrp"; (ii) squeaky toy-like "whir'it", sometimes rapidly repeated; (iii) high-pitched, thin "tsit". **SS** Metallic Starling has red (not black) eye in all age groups, and a much more iridescent plumage; Imm Metallic has much whiter, less streaked underparts and paler throat.

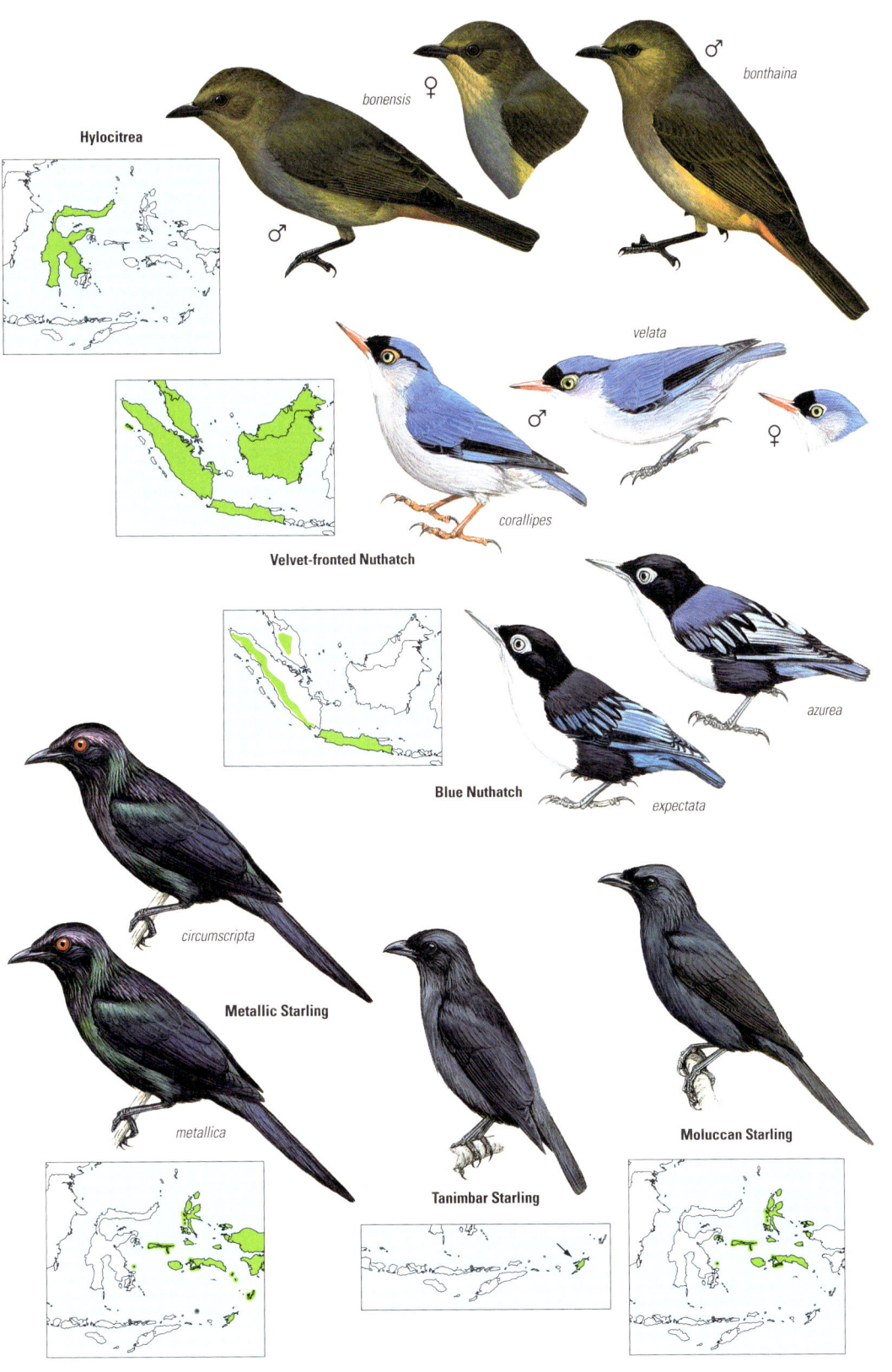

Hylocitrea

bonensis ♀

bonthaina ♂

♂

Velvet-fronted Nuthatch

velata

♂

corallipes

♀

Blue Nuthatch

azurea

expectata

circumscripta

Metallic Starling

metallica

Tanimbar Starling

Moluccan Starling

Asian Glossy Starling *Aplonis panayensis*

L 20 cm. SE Asia, Phil. 14 ssp, 12 in region: *panayensis* (N Sul, Phil); *sanghirensis* (Talaud, Sangihe, Siau and satellites); *strigata* (Sum–W Bor, Jav, MPen); *albiris* (Nicobars; vagrant N Sum); *eustathis* (E Bor); *alipodis* (Maratua); *altirostris* (Simeulue, Banyak, Nias); *nesodramus* (Babi); *pachistorhina* (Batu, Mentawai); *enganensis* (Enggano); *heterochlora* (Anambas, Natuna); *gusti* (Bali). Common (now uncommon on Jav) in degraded forest, mangroves, cultivation, settlements, <800 m; mostly canopy, but even on city buildings. Flocks in large numbers (roosts of ~10,000), nesting in decaying trees. **ID Ad** compact with square-cut tail; glossy black-green plumage with matte black lores and conspicuous red eye. Ssp *sanghirensis* bigger bill, slight crest on forecrown; *strigata* smaller, upperparts glossed bluish; *albiris* as previous but duller, larger, with white iris; *eustathis* smaller than *strigata*; *altirostris* as *strigata* but heavier bill, bronze-tinged plumage; *nesodramus* as previous but pale cream iris; *pachistorhina* as *altirostris* but larger, with even heavier bill, green gloss, less lanceolated neck feathers; *enganensis* as *strigata* but larger, longer-winged, stronger-billed, and overall more greyish plumage tone; *heterochlora* larger than *strigata*, gloss more bronzy green; *gusti* small with short, weak bill, dorsal gloss intense blue, head feathers less elongated and lanceolated; *alipodis* as nominate but duller overall, larger. **Imm** dark brown above with some gloss on wings; whitish below with heavy dark streaks; paler iris; gloss develops progressively; on W Sumatran ls (at least in *altirostris*, probably also *pachistorhina* and *enganensis*) imm has pale feather fringes creating peculiarly scaled upperparts appearance unknown from the larger islands. **Voc** Song: continual jumble of unstructured, short, scratchy, melodious twittering lasting >1 min. Call: (i) shrill "tseu"; (ii) descending "tseeeer". Roosting flocks very noisy. Larger and bulkier ssp on small islands (at least in W Sum islands) have louder and more variable vocalisations, including various raucous calls and bell-like notes. **SS** See Short-tailed Starling.

Short-tailed Starling *Aplonis minor*

L 18 cm. Phil, Wallacea, GS. Monotypic. Fairly common in forest, edge, avoids urban areas, <2000 m. On Jav–Bali where co-occurs with Asian Glossy, restricted to forest at >800 m. Singly, pairs or small flocks (<50), forages mainly in canopy. **ID Ad** small, compact with short tail; uniformly black plumage; head, breast and nape glossed purple, underparts and mantle glossed green; red eye. **Imm** grey-brown upperparts; dark streaking on white underparts; red eye. **Voc** Song: jumble of unstructured, short, scratchy twittering, lasting 1–5 min; higher-pitched, less melodious than Asian Glossy Starling. Call: clear metallic "tsip", often in flight. **SS** Asian Glossy Starling has longer tail, longer bill. Asian Glossy is strongly green-glossed on head and green- (Sul) or blue- (Jav–Bali) glossed on upperparts, while Short-tailed exhibits purple gloss on head, throat and nape, with the rest of body green-glossed. Beware of incidence of light, which can make Short-tailed appear greenish on head at some angles.

Grosbeak Myna *Scissirostrum dubium* **E**

L 20 cm. Monotypic. Fairly common in degraded forest, edge, occasionally plantations, rarely primary forest, <1300 m. Breeds in large colonies utilising dead trunks. **ID Ad** compact with short wings and massive yellow bill; slate grey-blue plumage; rump and rear flanks streaked waxy-red. **Imm** brown-tinged plumage; orange-streaked rump; paler bill. **Voc** Very vocal at colonies, hundreds calling at once: liquid, high, shrill "chiroop". **AN** Finch-billed Starling/Myna.

Flame-browed Myna *Enodes erythrophris* **E**

L 27 cm. 3 ssp: *erythrophris* (N Sul); *centralis* (E–SE Sul); *leptorhynchus* (C Sul). Fairly common in forest, rarely edge, primarily 800–1800 m. Singly, pairs, occasionally small groups (<20); preferring canopy, coming lower to feed on fruit. **ID Ad** strikingly plumaged; elegant shape with long graduated tail. Slate grey-blue body; broad red supercilium; sooty ear-coverts; olive-yellow wings and tail; bright yellow rump and vent. Ssp *leptorhynchus* ridged bill; *centralis* as previous but yellow supercilium and longer bill. **Imm** brown-tinged plumage; yellowish supercilium. **Voc** Thin, high-pitched "zeek" and "zik-zik", regularly repeated, flowerpecker-like. **AN** Fiery-browed Starling/Myna.

Common Hill Myna *Gracula religiosa*

L 27–35 cm. S–SE Asia, Palawan. 9 ssp, 5 in region: *religiosa* (GS, MPen); *batuensis* (Mentawai, Batu); *enganensis* (Enggano); *robusta* (Nias, Babi, Banyak, Simuk); *miotera* (Simeulue). No longer includes Southern Hill Myna *G. indica* (S India, Sri Lanka) and Tenggara Hill Myna because of pronounced morphological and vocal differences. Internal taxonomy confused: ssp *robusta* and *enganensis* often separated as '**Nias**' and '**Enggano Hill Myna**', respectively, based on morphological evidence, but genomic and morphological study showed that *miotera* is at least as distinct. Comprehensive genomic study including many taxa required. Formerly common, but rare now over much of range due to trapping. Ssp *batuensis*, *enganensis* and *robusta* decreasing fast; *miotera* (nearly?) extinct. Forest, edge, clearings, <1300 m. Singly, pairs or small groups (<10); canopy dweller. **ID Ad** black plumage glossed purple; heavy orange bill; yellow wattles on nape and ear-coverts linked by narrow connector. In flight appears barrel-chested, short-tailed with broad wings and fast wingbeats, conspicuous white primary patch. Ssp *batuensis* larger, lacking connector between nape an ear wattle; *robusta* as previous but larger still, with stronger bill, larger yellow crown wattles and larger white wing patch; *miotera* almost as large as *robusta*, also with larger wing patch, but has partial connector between nape and ear wattle; *enganensis* smaller than nominate, more slender bill and proportionally larger white wing patch. **Imm** less glossy; smaller wattles. **Voc** Variety of loud fluty, melodious notes and cackles. Most common calls include: (i) dramatic, loud 'falling bombshell' whistle "FYEEuw"; (ii) flat, tuneless "eeeoooo" whistle; (iii) disyllabic, tremulous, upslurred bell-like "brrtit't't-brrtit't't". Racial variation difficult to characterise because of great repertoire, but *enganensis* reported to utter: (i) 2-note, loud "WIT-CHOO"; (ii) scratchy, metallic "cheeet"; (iii) and various whistles similar to but reportedly fuller and shorter than *religiosa*.

Tenggara Hill Myna *Gracula venerata* **E**

L 28 cm. Monotypic. For taxonomy see Common Hill Myna. Now rare and highly localised throughout its range due to trapping, widely extinct locally. Forest, edge, clearings, <1300 m. Singly, pairs or small groups (<10); canopy dweller. **ID Ad** slightly smaller than nominate Common Hill Myna; plumage glossed green not purple except for black breast band; wattles more extensive behind eye, extending to crown. **Imm** less glossy; smaller wattles. **Voc** Variety of loud fluty, melodious notes and cackles. Most common calls include: (i) nasal, downslurred whistle "neeeoh" or "meoh", lasting 1 sec, lacking the fluty quality of Common Hill; (ii) whining, creaking "whirrrt"; (iii) slightly downslurred, thin whistle "seeeoor".

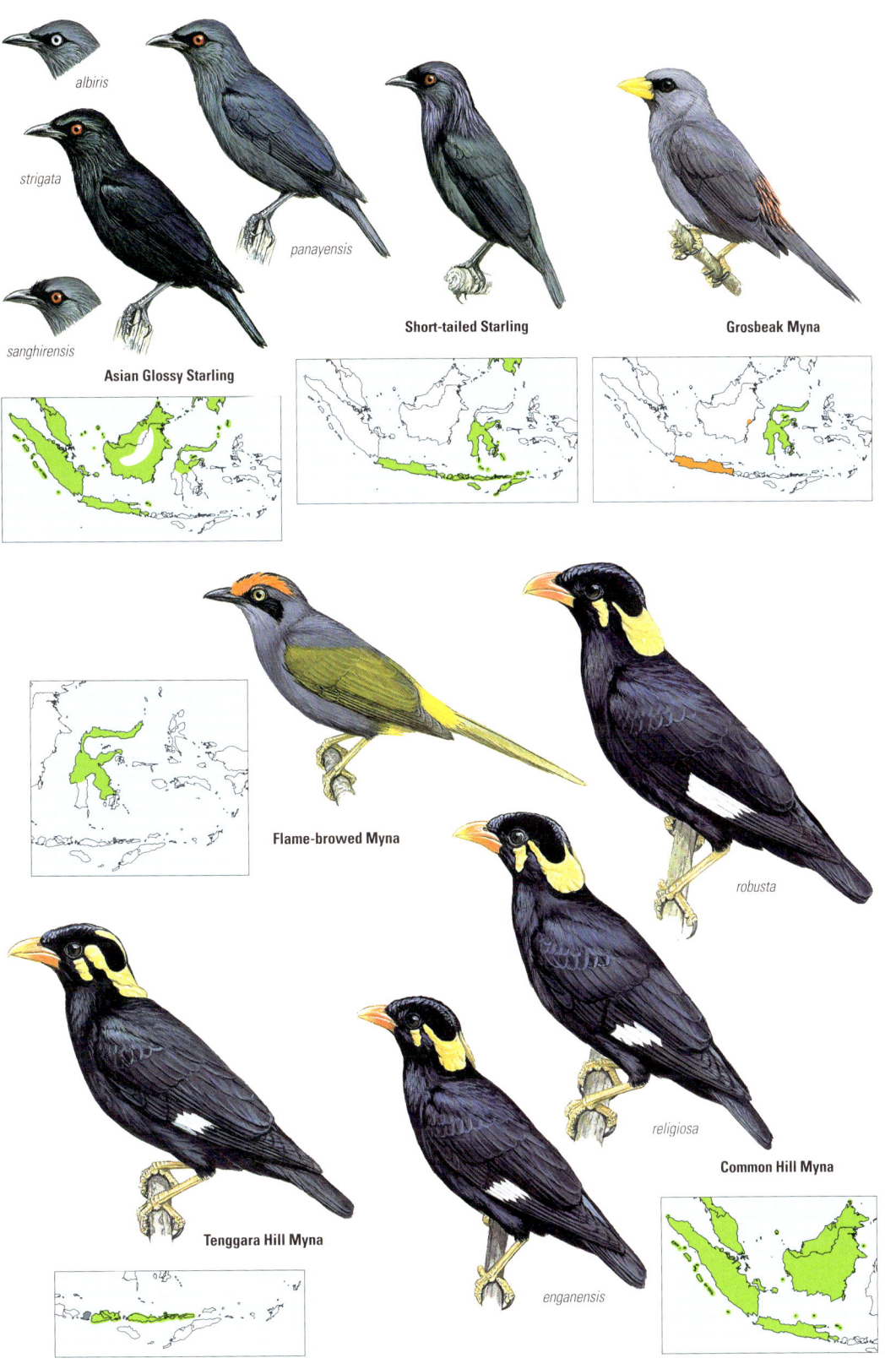

albiris

strigata

sanghirensis

panayensis

Asian Glossy Starling

Short-tailed Starling

Grosbeak Myna

Flame-browed Myna

robusta

religiosa

Common Hill Myna

Tenggara Hill Myna

enganensis

White-necked Myna *Streptocitta albicollis* `E`
L 50 cm (tail 25–30 cm). 2 ssp: *albicollis* (S–SE Sul, Muna, Buton); *torquata* (C–E–N Sul). The two ssp sometimes separated into two monotypic species, '**Northern**' *S. torquata* and '**Southern White-necked Myna**' *S. albicollis*, respectively, because of morphological traits. Uncommon in forest, edge, <1500 m. Pairs or small groups (<10), usually in upper canopy, often on bare snags. **ID Ad** long, slim body with very long, elongated tail; uniform black plumage glossed greenish; pure white mantle, collar and breast; yellow-tipped black bill. Ssp *torquata* has longer all-black bill; less extensive white breast; plumage glossed bluish; slightly shorter tail; strongly arched feathers across crown look less flat than on nominate. **Imm** lacks glossy plumage; shorter, dark bill. **Voc** (i) High-pitched, 2-note, metallic "tee-tee" lasting 0.8 sec, drongo-like quality; (ii) sliding, descending "seeeut" lasting 0.4 sec; (iii) harsh, nasal, rasping "wheeet" lasting 0.5 sec; (iv) quirky, squeaky, toy-like "choop-choop" lasting 0.5 sec.

Bare-eyed Myna *Streptocitta albertinae* `E`
L 45 cm (tail 25 cm). Monotypic. Scarce coastal plains inhabitant of remaining degraded forest and patches of tall trees amidst cultivation, <250 m. Pairs or small groups (<5), usually in upper canopy. **ID Ad M** long, slim body with very long, elongated tail; uniform glossy-black plumage; pure white crown, mantle, collar and underparts; bare facial skin; white eye; yellow bill and legs. **F** dark eye. **Imm** mottled crown. **Voc** Resembles sound made by a squeaky gate, in descending series typically of 5 notes.

Short-crested Myna *Basilornis celebensis* `E`
L 25 cm. Monotypic. Uncommon in primary forest, scarcer in degraded habitat, absent from plantations, <1600 m. Pairs or small groups (<20), in upper canopy, occasionally bare snags. **ID** Raised, rigid crest. **M** Uniform black plumage glossed purple on crest and upperparts, green on underparts; two white patches on ear-coverts down to breast sides. **F** shorter crest. **Imm** lacks iridescence; brownish plumage, paler underparts. **Voc** (i) High-pitched, drawn-out, descending "seeeoo" lasting 0.2 sec, regularly repeated, sometimes with ascending "sowee"; (ii) descending "tchoo" and "sip". **AN** Sulawesi (Crested) Myna.

Helmeted Myna *Basilornis galeatus* `E`
L 25 cm. Monotypic. Uncommon in forest, edge and clearings. Pairs or small groups (<20), usually in upper canopy, occasionally bare snags. **ID** As Short-crested Myna but crest much larger; bulging forecrown. **Voc** (i) Single or disyllabic, thin, deflected "seeow-seeow"; (ii) high-pitched, thin, short "chip".

Long-crested Myna *Basilornis corythaix* `E`
L 25 cm. Monotypic. Uncommon in forest, edge, <1500 m. Pairs or small groups (<5), usually in upper canopy, occasionally bare snags. **ID Ad** elongated plumes forming tall, rigid crest; uniformly iridescent black with two white patches on ear-coverts and neck sides; pale-blue bare orbital ring. **Imm** undescribed. **Voc** (i) Full, descending, whistled "tseeeow" and "tcheeow", lasting 0.4–6 sec; (ii) high-pitched, level "twit"; (iii) short, mechanical "zzit".

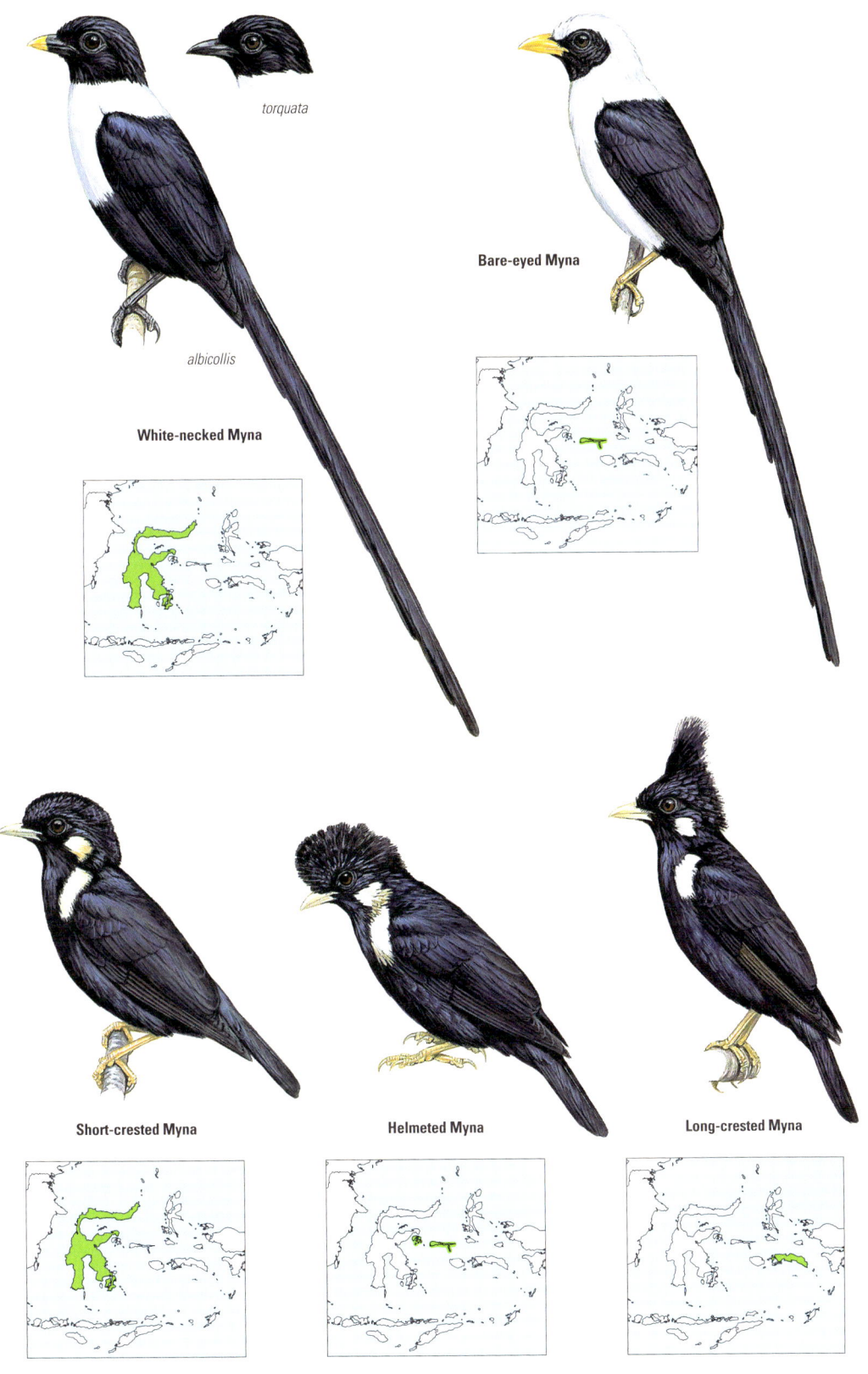

torquata

albicollis

White-necked Myna

Bare-eyed Myna

Short-crested Myna

Helmeted Myna

Long-crested Myna

Common Myna *Acridotheres tristis*

L 25 cm. C–S–SE Asia. 2 ssp, 1 in region: *tristis* (most of range). Multiple records across GS since 1975 are escaped cagebirds or ship-assisted. Now established on Riau Is from invasive population on Singapore. Open country, plantations, cultivation and cities. Largely terrestrial, feeding in pairs or flocks, often with other myna species. **ID Ad** brown body with black hood and tail; prominent yellow bill, legs and facial skin; white vent. In flight shows large white patch on primaries extending to underwing coverts. **Imm** paler grey-brown hood; less prominent, dirty-yellow bare parts. **Voc** Song: mixture of repetitive, forceful, musical notes and whistles, generally longer, more melodious phrases than Javan Myna. Call: (i) tremulous, melodious "kwerrh"; (ii) scolding "chake chake". **SS** Javan Myna has wholly black body, lacks yellow facial skin and has black underwing coverts.

Crested Myna *Acridotheres cristatellus* `I`

L 25 cm. SE–E Asia. 3 ssp, presumed *brevipennis* (SE Asia) in region. Introduced locally around cities and plantations. Largely terrestrial, feeding in pairs or flocks (<50), roosting communally. **ID Ad** uniform black plumage with prominent frontal crest; pale-mottled vent; large white base to primaries; white tips to outertail; ivory bill; orange legs and eye. **Imm** brownish-grey plumage; pale yellow bill and eye; smaller wing patch. **Voc** Song: repetitive series of tuneless, downslurred notes, lasting <2 sec, regularly repeated, often in duet. Call: short, sharp, downslurred "zeet". **SS** Javan and Makassar Mynas have paler ashy plumage (Makassar especially on belly), less pronounced frontal crest, white (not mostly dark) vent, and a brighter yellow bill. Javan also has yellow (not orange) eye.

Javan Myna *Acridotheres javanicus* `E`

L 21 cm. Monotypic. Formerly common, now local and uncommon in native range, but introduced widely across MPen and archipelago, where locally abundant. Open country, plantations, cultivation and cities. Largely terrestrial, feeding in pairs or flocks (<100), roosting communally. **ID Ad** dark ashy plumage with black head and short frontal crest; contrasting bright-yellow bill, legs and eye; white vent, tail tips and base to primaries. **Imm** paler grey-brown plumage, lacking frontal crest; duller bare parts. **Voc** Song: mixture of quiet chattering with series of repetitive, forceful, musical notes and whistles; lacks buzzy or grating notes. Call: variety of melodious, forceful notes and whistles. **SS** See Common, Crested and Makassar Mynas.

Makassar Myna *Acridotheres cinereus* `E`

L 25 cm. Monotypic. Scarce and local in edge, open country and cultivation, away from urban areas. Largely terrestrial, feeding in pairs or flocks (<20). **ID Ad** short frontal crest; silky pale grey body; glossy black head, wings and tail; white tail tips, vent and wing patch; dark orange iris and legs; yellow bill with blackish base to lower mandible. **Imm** pale brown head; brown-tinged body. **Voc** Undescribed. **SS** From Javan Myna by paler grey body (especially belly), more heavily contrasting with blackish head and wings; dark-orange (not yellow) eyes; and blackish bill base (all-yellow in Javan). Also see Crested Myna. **AN** Pale-bellied Myna.

Black-winged Myna *Acridotheres melanopterus* `E`

L 23 cm. 3 ssp: *melanopterus* (W–C Jav); *tricolor* (E Jav); *tertius* (Bali). Increased melanism in eastern ssp shown to have originated from genetic introgression of Javan Myna DNA through hybridisation in the past. Now local and very rare; ssp *melanopterus* probably extinct in the wild. In savanna, coastal habitat and monsoon woodland, <2400 m. Singly, pairs or small flocks (<20); more arboreal than other *Acridotheres* mynas. **ID Ad** striking white plumage; black outerwing and tail with white tips; yellow bare parts and facial skin. Ssp *tricolor* black wing-coverts and grey mantle; *tertius* as previous but more black on upperwing and grey extending to rump. **Imm** tinged buff overall; pink facial skin and legs. **Voc** Song: continual quiet chattering interspersed with long, grating, upslurred buzz every few seconds. Call: upslurred grating buzzy note, slightly drawn-out. **SS** See Bali Starling.

Bali Starling *Leucopsar rothschildi* `E`

L 25 cm. Monotypic. Highly prized in the trade: repeatedly going extinct and getting reintroduced into the wild on Bali where local and rare; also introduced on Nusa Penida and Lembongan but rare due to continued trapping. Found in coastal monsoon forest. Largely arboreal, in pairs or small groups (<10). **ID** Striking silky-white plumage with hackled crown, erectile crest and blue facial skin; black restricted to primaries and terminal tail band; grey legs; pale yellow bill. **Imm** yellowish-tinged plumage; shorter hackles and crest. **Voc** Song: complex jumble of notes, chattering and grating, typically consisting of limited repertoire of short motifs, particularly an upslurred "whir-chit" call, repeated regularly. Call: 2-note "whir-chit", first note upslurred whistle, second grating, along with other short grating notes and whistles. **SS** Black-winged Myna has yellow (not blue) facial skin, lacks crest, has all-black tail (not only terminal band) and more extensively black wings.

Javan Pied Starling *Gracupica jalla* `E`

L 22 cm. Monotypic. Formerly united with Thai Pied Starling *G. floweri* (SE Asia) and Indian Pied Starling *G. contra* (S-SE Asia) into larger umbrella species, '**Asian Pied Starling**' *G. contra*, but genomic and morphological data suggest separation. Poaching and pesticide use have driven it to extinction in the wild as no recent sightings of wild birds, all likely escapees. Formerly in lowland savanna, cultivation, open areas. Largely terrestrial, in pairs or small groups (<10). **ID Ad** pied plumage: black head, breast and upperparts (but browner mantle) with white cheeks, underparts, scapulars and rump; red facial skin extending to above ear-coverts; pink legs; ivory bill; lemon-yellow eyes. Individuals from captivity often have abnormally long bill. **Imm** greyish underparts and face, lacking facial skin; mottled black throat. **Voc** Song: prolonged series of phrases with shrill "churr" notes, croaking and buzzing notes; more melodious than Javan Myna; incorporates some mimicry. Call: (i) loud "staar-staar"; (ii) shrill "shree-shree". **SS** Beware of escaped extralimital Thai Pied Starlings *G. floweri* that are frequently kept and hybridised with Javan Pied: Thai's mantle is black (not brown), with extensive reddish bill base, less extensive facial skin and white (not black) forehead.

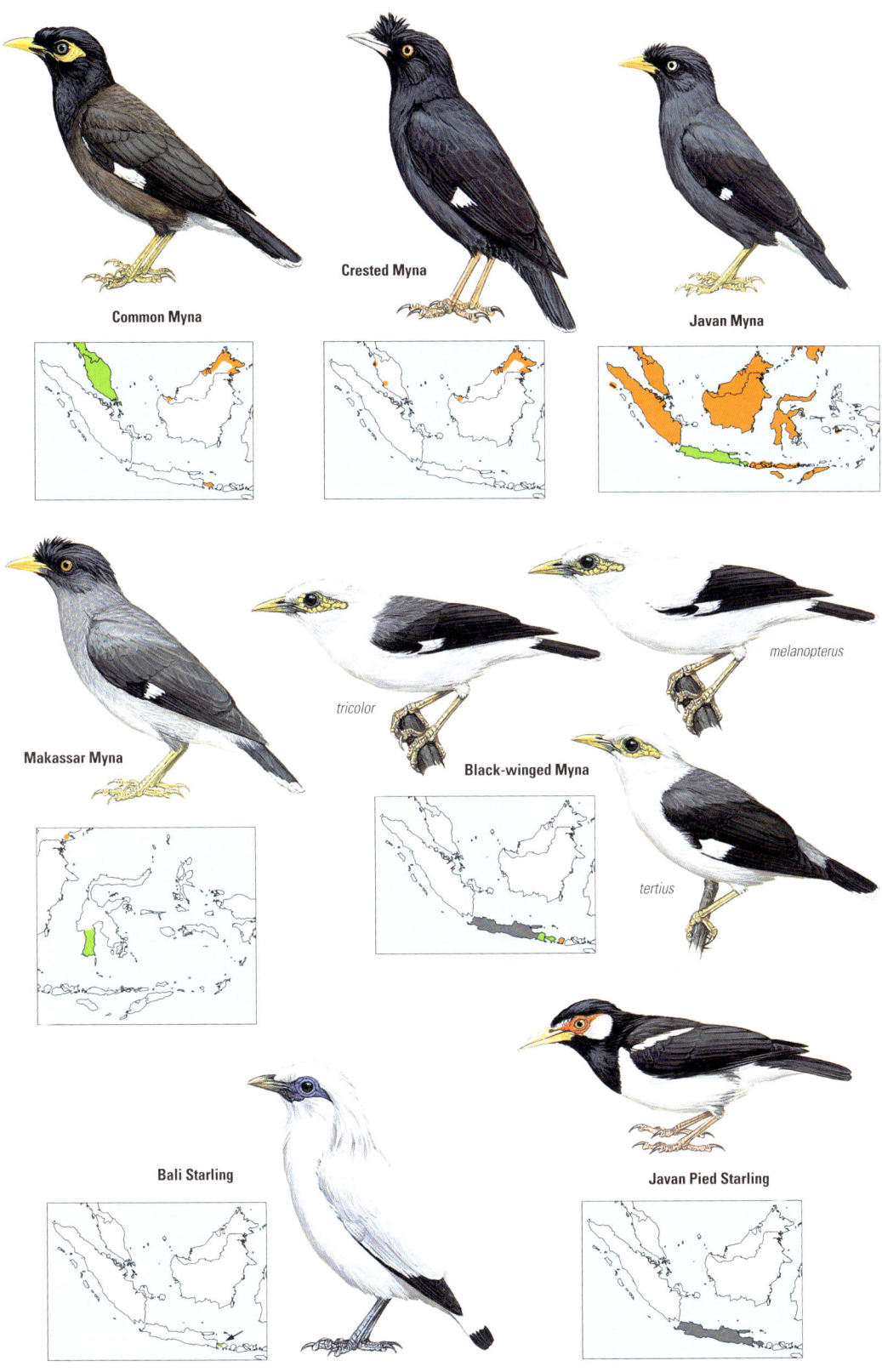

Common Myna

Crested Myna

Javan Myna

Makassar Myna

tricolor

melanopterus

Black-winged Myna

tertius

Bali Starling

Javan Pied Starling

Red-billed Starling *Spodiopsar sericeus*

L 22 cm. E Asia. Monotypic. Vagrant to Sabah (Dec 2011). Open country: cultivation, coastal and urban areas. **ID M** white hood; silky-grey body with paler vent and rump; black tail and wings with white panel at base of primaries (distinct in flight); red bill and orange legs. **F/Imm** greyish-brown head, contrasting less with grey-brown mantle; orange-red bill extensively tipped black. **Voc** Call: chattering "jree-eep". **SS** Chestnut-cheeked and Daurian Starlings have dark-grey (not red or orange) bill and legs with white median-coverts (absent in Red-billed).

White-shouldered Starling *Sturnia sinensis*

L 17 cm. Breeds E Asia; winters to SE Asia. Monotypic. Vagrant to N Bor: Sarawak (Oct 1962, Nov 2020), Brunei (Nov 1988), Sabah (Nov 2015). Agricultural areas with scattered trees, often perching on wires. **ID Ad** silky-grey plumage with gleaming white scapulars and wing-coverts, contrasting with black outerwing; white rump; black tail tipped white; white eye; grey-blue bill. **Imm** brownish-grey head; dirty-grey plumage; grey scapulars; when perched white coverts less distinct. **Voc** Call: soft "preep". **SS** From other vagrant starlings by conspicuous white wing-coverts, especially in flight, contrasting with black outerwing; all plumages have white eye and grey-blue bill.

Daurian Starling *Agropsar sturninus*

L 17 cm. Breeds NE Asia; winters S to Sum–Bali. Monotypic. Vagrant to Borneo: Sarawak (1892), Sabah (Sep–Oct 2007), Brunei (Sep 2013). Uncommon in woodland, lowland parks, tree-lined urban areas, coastal vegetation and fallow land. Arboreal, in flocks (<500), roosting communally, often with Asian Glossy Starling. **ID M** pale grey head and underparts; purple mantle; dark-green upperwing with faint white greater covert bar and strong white scapular line. In flight shows white rump, white scapular and covert lines and pointed wings. **F** head and underparts tinged buff; mantle and wings less bright, brownish, lacking gloss. **Imm** browner above. **Voc** Song unlikely to be heard in region: variety of whistles, mimicry, trills and chatters. Call: melodious "cheer'erop" and shorter "erop". **SS** See Red-billed and Chestnut-cheeked Starlings. **AN** Purple-backed Starling.

Chestnut-cheeked Starling *Agropsar philippensis*

L 17 cm. Breeds Japan; winters S to Phil and N–E Bor, rarely disperses further W, S and E. Monotypic. Scarce in woodland, lowland parks, tree-lined urban areas, coastal vegetation and fallow land. Arboreal, in flocks (<200), roosting communally. **ID M** similar to Daurian Starling but chestnut face patch, darker grey flanks; glossed purple mantle and green wings with white restricted to median-coverts and base of outer secondaries. **F/Imm** extremely similar to Daurian but white restricted to median-coverts. **Voc** Song unlikely to be heard in region: babbling interspersed with harsher, louder notes, incorporating much mimicry. Call: excited "air" and in flight melodious "chorerochoo". **SS** In flight lack of white scapular line separates it from Daurian Starling. Fem and juv very similar to Daurian but note lack of long white scapular line, with white restricted to median coverts instead. Daurian can show white distal tips to greater coverts (and tertials), which Chestnut-cheeked does not. Chestnut-cheeked's face can appear slightly darker, contrasting with paler underparts, especially in early spring. Also see Red-billed Starling.

Rosy Starling *Pastor roseus*

L 21 cm. Breeds C Palaearctic; winters S Asia. Monotypic. Highly nomadic and dispersive, with presumed vagrants recorded in Sabah (Dec 1999, Oct 2011, Oct 2012) and Yogyakarta (Oct 2013), while presumed escapees recorded elsewhere on Jav and Bali. Open arid areas, cultivation, coastal scrub and around settlements in flocks with Asian Glossy, Daurian and Chestnut-cheeked Starlings. **ID Ad br** black hood, wings and tail with contrasting pink upperparts and underparts; pink legs and bill. **Ad non-br** much duller; greyish-pink underparts, darker upperparts; dark greyish legs; yellow bill. **Imm** sandy grey-brown with paler underparts and darker wings; pink legs; yellow bill. **Voc** Call: short, rasping "kyururi" or "chit".

Eurasian Starling *Sturnus vulgaris*

L 21 cm. W–C Palaearctic. 13 ssp: vagrants in region of unknown affinity, presumed *porphyronotus* (breeds C Asia; winters to S Asia) or *poltaratskyi* (breeds C Siberia, C Asia; winters to S). Vagrant to Sabah (Oct 2007, Dec 2011). Open country: cultivation, coastal and urban areas. Forages terrestrially and arboreally, associating with other starlings and mynas. **ID Ad br** black plumage; heavy white and buff arrow markings over body, smaller speckles on head; yellow bill; pink legs; black eye. Ssp *poltaratskyi* glossed purple on head, greenish-purple on wings, and bluer on underparts; *porphyronotus* glossed greenish on head, reddish-purple on upperparts and bronzy-purple on underparts. **Ad non-br** less glossy overall with more extensive pale markings over body; black bill. **Imm** dusky-brown overall, paler on underparts with light mottling and streaking; black eye. **Voc** Call: (i) soft "proorrp"; (ii) short, metallic "chip".

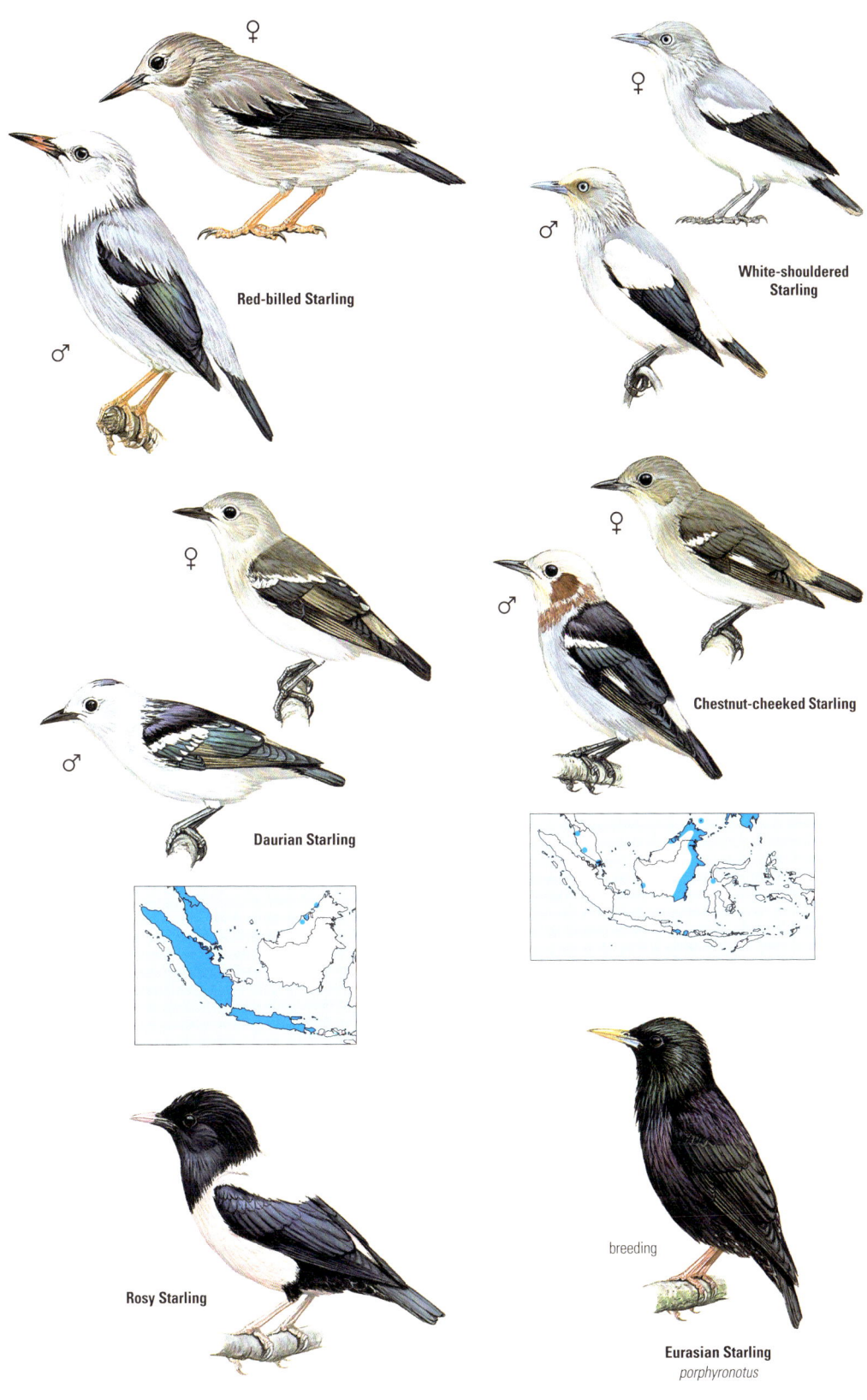

♀

♂

Red-billed Starling

♀

♂

White-shouldered
Starling

♀

♂

Daurian Starling

♂

♀

Chestnut-cheeked Starling

Rosy Starling

breeding

Eurasian Starling
porphyronotus

24 species in region

A diverse family of medium-sized birds, generally of forest and edge. Many species are shy, skulking ground feeders, while others are almost entirely arboreal, feeding in the mid- to upper storey. Some species are trapped for the pet trade and becoming scarce.

Geomalia *Zoothera heinrichi*   **E**

L 28–30 cm. Monotypic. For a long time a taxonomic enigma, this unique species is now known to be embedded within *Zoothera* thrushes. Uncommon and local in montane forest, 1400–3500 m. Singly or pairs; inconspicuous, shy and much overlooked. Terrestrial with weak flight, hops with horizontal posture on ground like babbler, pausing with upright posture as a thrush. Often on forest tracks. **ID Ad** medium-sized with long, graduated tail and short wings; slaty-grey upperparts; dusky malar; broad rusty edges to secondaries; paler rufous-brown underparts and head (the latter tinged grey); black bill; dark-pinkish legs; dark eye. **Imm** thrush-like dark-mottled on breast. **Voc** Thin, slightly dry, high-pitched whistle lasting ~1 sec, repeated at 0.5 sec intervals, given insistently but intermittently. **SS** Sulawesi and Island Thrushes are smaller with orange-yellow bill, legs and eye ring.

Everett's Thrush *Zoothera everetti*   **E**

L 19–20 cm. Monotypic. Scarce in montane moss forest (not recorded in Kalimantan), 1200–2200 m. Shy, inconspicuous bird of the forest floor, occasionally found feeding on grassy verges along montane forest tracks. Singly or pairs. **ID Ad** deep olive brown upperparts; paler area on face and throat variable in extent; dark malar streak; orange-chestnut breast; white belly; pale-orange vent and undertail. **Imm** pale-speckled wing-coverts; brown scales below. **Voc** Song: long series of various short "cheep" notes and longer, downslurred, whistled "tseeew" notes at 1–2 sec intervals. Call: (i) downslurred, rather mournful "tseeew"; (ii) sharp "tsak!".

Sunda Thrush *Zoothera andromedae*

L 23–25 cm. GS, LS, Phil. Monotypic. No genetic or morphological differentiation evident across its vast range. Uncommon to rare in hill and montane forest, 350–2000 m (sea level on smaller islands). Singly; very shy skulker within dense herbs on forest floor; around dawn and dusk can be found along forest trails. **ID Ad** dark grey upperparts and crown with vague dark scaling on mantle; vague whitish pattern on face; paler blue-grey throat and breast; white belly; broad black scaling on flanks; long, thin dark bill; short legs. **Imm** dark mottled brown upperparts with buff streaks on wing, mantle and crown; buffy white underparts, darker on breast, heavily scaled black. **Voc** Possible song: series of downslurred, not rattling, "tseeew" notes alternating with similar but upslurred notes. Call: high-piched, thin, long-drawn, slightly downslurred, rattling "tsrsrsree".

White's Thrush *Zoothera aurea*   **V**

L 30 cm. Breeds C–E Palaearctic; winters S to SE–E Asia, Phil. 2-3 ssp, vagrants in region presumably *aurea* (most of range). For taxonomy see Horsfield's Thrush. Few records from offshore islets and Mt Kinabalu, N Bor. Quiet ground feeder in undergrowth and low vegetation, may venture out on forest trails. **ID Ad** pale yellow-olive upperparts mottled heavily with black crescents; buff-white underparts with black crescents; black-and-white underwing. **Imm** undescribed. **Voc** Song unlikely to be heard in region: slow, variable, mechanical series of thin, level, melancholy, long-drawn whistles, each lasting ~1.5 sec, delivered several seconds apart, gaining volume before dying away, giving an echoing effect. Call: faint "horr-horr". **SS** Horsfield's Thrush probably never overlaps: it is smaller than White's, has shorter wings and tail, longer legs and bill, and – on average – rustier (less olive) wing feathers, but these differences are very subtle.

Horsfield's Thrush *Zoothera horsfieldi*   **E**

L 28 cm. Monotypic. Often lumped with Scaly Thrush *Z. dauma* (Himalaya to SE Asia), White's Thrush and other extralimital forms, but combination of vocal, plumage and morphometric traits argues for their separation. Scarce in montane forest, 920–2800 m. Quiet ground feeder in undergrowth and low vegetation, may venture out on forest trails; often gives itself away by loud wing rustle. **ID Ad** deep olive golden-brown upperparts; white underparts with black crescents. **Imm** buffier above; more spotted than scaled below. **Voc** Pre-dawn song for brief period in concert with neighbours, series of slow, melancholy down- and/or upslurred short whistles at slightly different frequencies. Call: quiet, plaintive, thin "srreeeet" lasting 0.5 sec. **SS** See White's Thrush and White-throated Rock-thrush.

Fawn-breasted Thrush *Zoothera machiki*   **E**

L 21–22 cm. Monotypic. Locally common in forest. Solitary; skulking in dense scrub, favouring recently burnt areas, even road verges. **ID Ad** pale olive-brown upperparts; rusty rump; two white wingbars; buffy throat and breast; whitish belly with dark scaling; outertail feathers with white tips. **Imm** undescribed. **Voc** Song: series of plain, high-pitched, thin whistled or piping notes with stress on first part, then fading away. Call: thin high "tsee", longer than Slaty-backed.

Slaty-backed Thrush *Geokichla schistacea*   **E**

L 16–17 cm. Monotypic. Fairly common in forest. Generally more arboreal than other thrushes; sings in canopy. **ID M** grey upperparts with black forehead and tail; white eyebrow, ear-coverts, wingbars and tips to outer rectrices; black throat and breast; remaining underparts white with black drops on upper belly. **F** less black on crown and fewer spots on belly. **Imm** undescribed. **Voc** Song: (i) series of phrases with variable intervals, each a variable melody of ~8 clear, sweet whistled notes of 3–4 sec, first note drawn-out and upslurred, followed by short notes that alternate up and down the scale; (ii) 3–4 clear whistles preceded or concluded by 4–6 quick notes. Call: (i) long, penetrating, upslurred, high-pitched whistle; (ii) sharp "tsit".

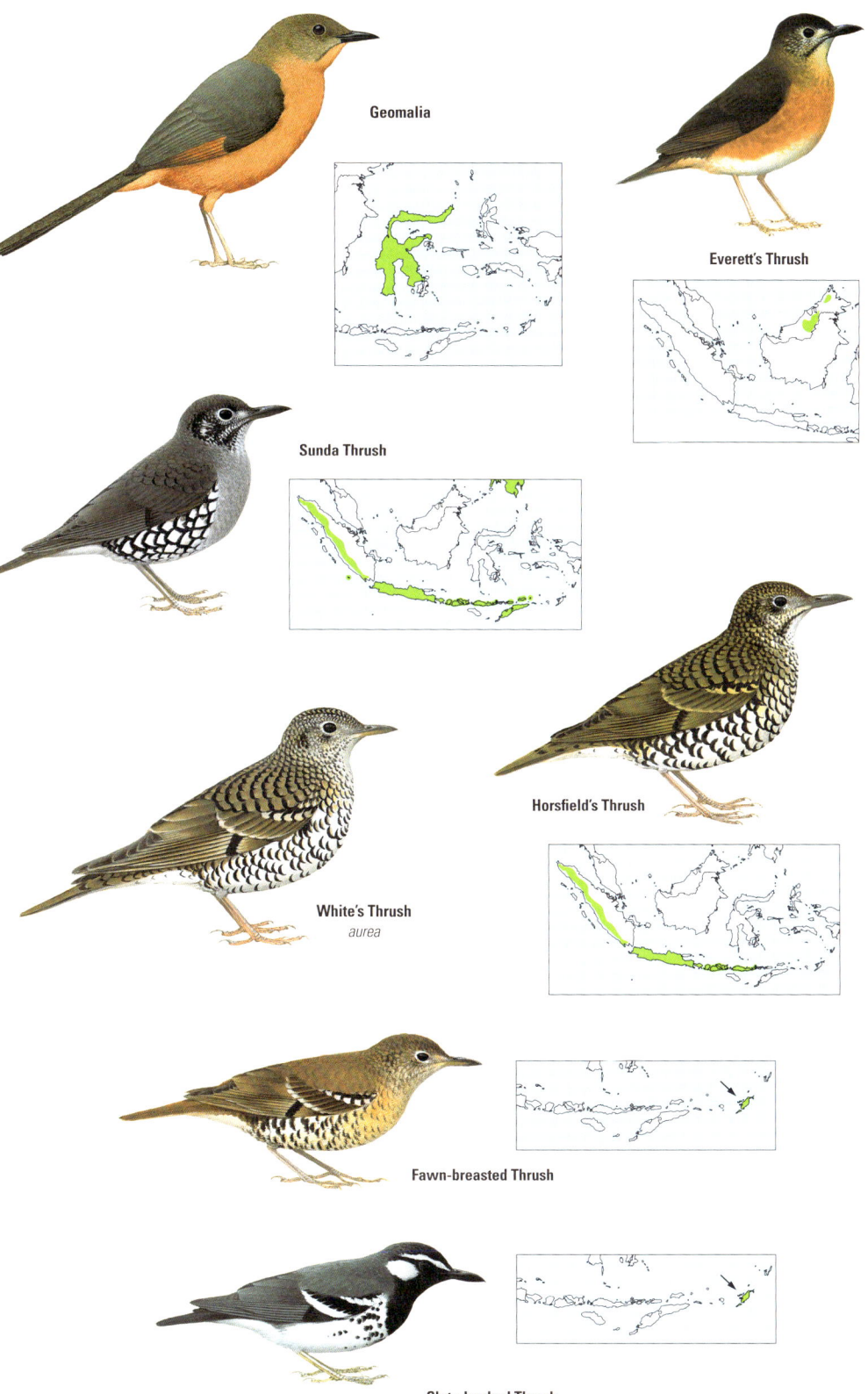

Geomalia

Everett's Thrush

Sunda Thrush

Horsfield's Thrush

White's Thrush
aurea

Fawn-breasted Thrush

Slaty-backed Thrush

Orange-banded Thrush *Geokichla peronii* `E`

L 19–21 cm. 2 ssp: *peronii* (Rote, W Timor); *audacis* (E Timor, Wetar–Babar). Recently recorded W–E Flores, but presumed escapees. Fairly common in all types of woodland, <1800 m. Singly or pairs, sometimes gathering in fruiting trees; feeding on ground, mid-storey or low tree tops. **ID Ad** orange-brown upperparts, more rufous on rump; black-and-white face; two broad white-on-black wingbars; orange-rufous breast and flanks; white throat and belly. Ssp *audacis* shorter wings; darker, more chestnut chest and sides of body; more uniform and much deeper chestnut-rufous upperparts. **Imm** pale-streaked above; rusty wing spots; black-and-buff mottled breast band; black-spotted rusty flanks. **Voc** Song: series of varied phrases, sometimes repeated a few times, consisting of 3–4 loud, ringing, upslurred whistles followed by a variable set of shorter staccato, chattering or thin, high-pitched notes. Call: thin, high-pitched, upslurred "tseeey".

Chestnut-backed Thrush *Geokichla dohertyi* `E`

L 16–18 cm. Monotypic. Uncommon to fairly common in forest, >400 m, lowlands on Sumba. Singly, occasionally in small groups in fruiting trees; sings from substage perch, largely foraging on ground. **ID Ad** black crown and nape; white face with black ear patch and malar stripe; chestnut back and paler chestnut rump; white wing-bars; black breast; white belly and vent with black spots on upper belly. **Imm** darker above with chestnut spots; buffy wingbars; buffy underparts with black spots on sides. **Voc** Song: series of warbles separated by ~1 sec, each consisting of 3–7 clear sweet, mellow whistles with more complex interwoven phrases. Call: (i) scratchy note; (ii) flat or downslurred high-pitched whistles; (iii) very high squeaky whistle. **SS** See Chestnut-capped Thrush.

Chestnut-capped Thrush *Geokichla interpres* `E`

L 16–18 cm. Sundaic, Sulu, LS. Monotypic. For taxonomy see Enggano Thrush. Uncommon and elusive in GS in forest, but few recent records from Jav; in LS formerly common but now local and uncommon because of trapping, <1000 m. Generally terrestrial but sometimes found in fruiting trees, shy. **ID Ad** chestnut crown and nape; dark slaty-grey upperparts; conspicuous white shoulder and wingbar; black face, throat and breast; white lores and ear patch; white belly with black spots on mid- and upper belly. **Imm** crown and back slaty black, mottled rufous; throat and breast buffy-rufous with black spots; buffy wingbars. **Voc** Song: series of rich notes and phrases consisting of short, rising, fluting whistles interspersed with "chirrup" and occasional harsh notes lasting 1.5–2 sec, repeated at intervals of 6–10 sec. For similar song, see Orang-headed Thrush. Call: (i) harsh loud "tac (-tac)"; (ii) thin, high "tse-e-e-it"; (iii) harsh ringing "turrrr-turrrr". **SS** Chestnut-backed Thrush has chestnut (not grey) back, black (not chestnut) crown and nape, and more white in face.

Enggano Thrush *Geokichla leucolaema* `E`

L 16–19 cm. Monotypic. No longer included in Chestnut-capped Thrush because of considerable plumage differences. Fairly common in forest and edge. Generally terrestrial, but sometimes found in fruiting trees. **ID Ad** rufous-brown crown and nape; lores, sides of head and neck black; white throat; olive-brown mantle to rump; black spots on flanks and lower breast forming a breast band; white belly and vent. **Imm** more chestnut above with pale streaks; rusty-buff wingbars; rusty-buff underparts with rusty and black spots forming breast band; white centre of belly. **Voc** Song: continuous subsong-like series of very thin short whistles, chirrups and ringing notes, some resembling juv begging call. Call: thin "tseet" or "srreeet(-srreeet)".

Red-backed Thrush *Geokichla erythronota* `E`

L 20 cm. 2 ssp: *erythronota* (Sul, Buton); *kabaena* (Kabaena). For taxonomy see Red-and-black Thrush. Uncommon in forest, <1000 m. Singly or pairs; secretive and shy, forages on ground in shady parts of forest. **ID M** chestnut upperparts; black wings with two white bars; black throat and breast; white belly with bold black scales on flanks and upper belly, separated from breast by broad white bar. Ssp *kabaena* slightly larger with black on crown to upper mantle. **F** paler above; less clearly marked on flanks. **Imm** orange-buff streaked crown and mantle; buff-white throat and malar stripe. **Voc** Song: rarely heard, a liquid, typically thrush-like series of notes. Call: (i) very thin and high-pitched upslurred whistle, preceded by 2–3 notes in descending scale; (ii) harsh "chak-chak-chak...".

Red-and-black Thrush *Geokichla mendeni* `E`

L 20 cm. Monotypic, though Taliabu population may be undescribed ssp. No longer considered conspecific with Red-backed Thrush based on striking plumage differences. Fairly common on Peleng to 1000 m, but rare and probably restricted to lowlands on Taliabu where only one recent record (Mar 2017); inhabits primary and logged forest, including smaller patches. **ID Ad** entirely bright cinnamon-rufous rear crown to rump; black face with narrow white patch above eye and white ear patch; entirely black wings, underparts and tail. On Taliabu reported to lack white patch above the eye, possibly more chestnut upperparts, but no specimen or photo exists. **Imm** undescribed. **Voc** Song: typically thrush-like, short relaxed phrases consisting of fluting, thin and burring notes of different length, often with emphasis on first or second note. Call: thin, high-pitched, upslurred "tseee".

Buru Thrush *Geokichla dumasi* `E`

L 17 cm. Monotypic. No longer considered conspecific with Seram Thrush based on plumage differences and mtDNA. Uncommon in submontane forest, >700 m. Generally terrestrial, shy, favouring damp, dark gullies. **ID Ad** warm brown upperparts; conspicuous white eyering; black throat and breast; two white spotted lines on black wings; white belly and vent; olive underwing-coverts. **Imm** undescribed. **Voc** Song: typically thrush-like, short, relaxed phrases of thin, short whistles and short scratchy notes. Call: a very high-pitched (up to 10 kHz) up- or downslurred note "seeeeeeeeet" lasting 2 sec.

Seram Thrush *Geokichla joiceyi* `E`

L 17 cm. Monotypic. For taxonomy see Buru Thrush. Scarce and little-known in submontane forest, >700 m. Generally terrestrial, shy. **ID Ad** as Buru Thrush, but slaty-black lower back, underwing-coverts and vent, the latter tipped white; one wingbar; lacks eyering. **Imm** undescribed. **Voc** Song: undescribed. Call: (i) very thin "tsee-eep", up- or downslurred; (ii) high-pitched, upslurred "tsree-tsree", lasting 3 s.

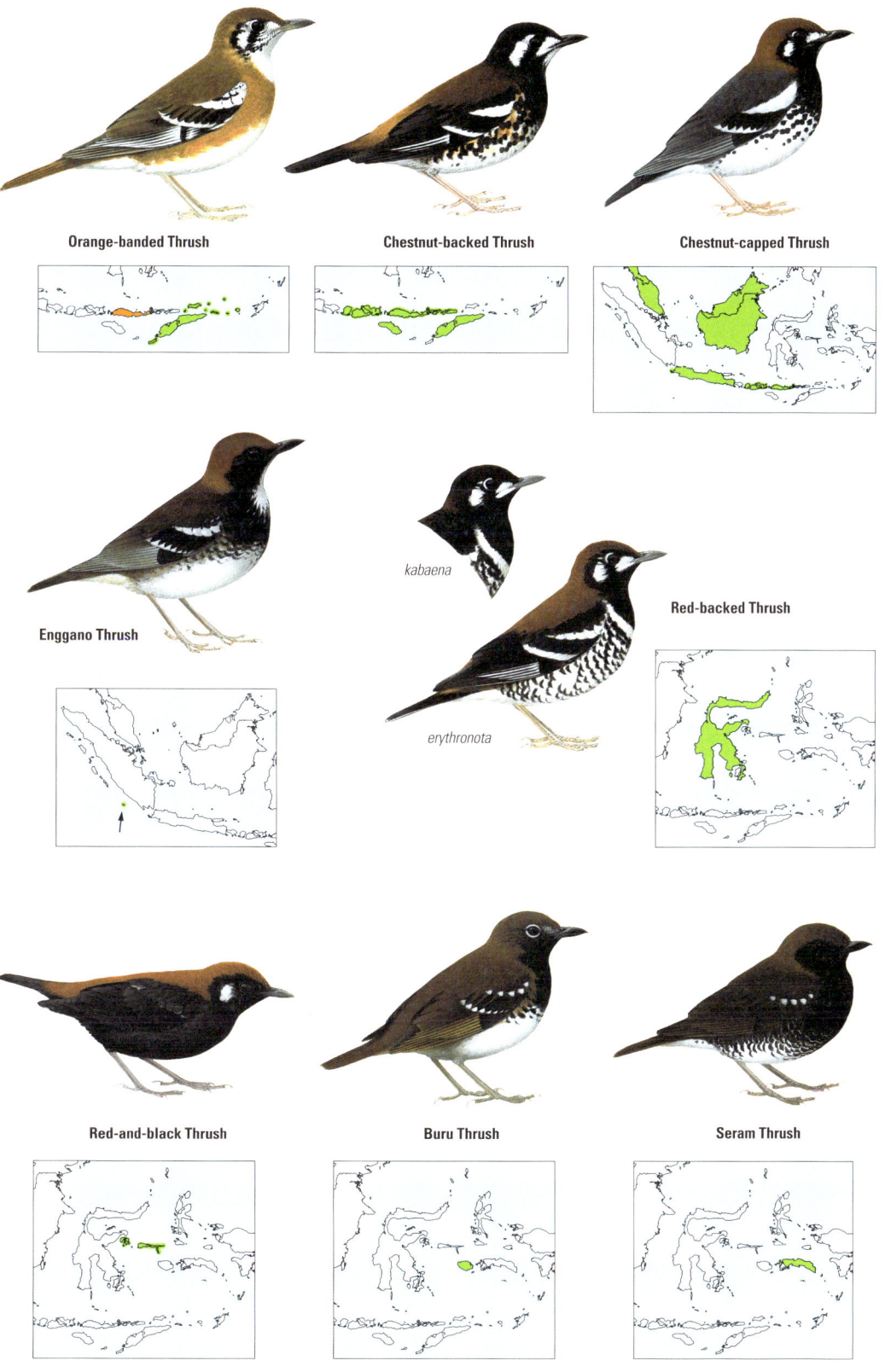

Orange-banded Thrush

Chestnut-backed Thrush

Chestnut-capped Thrush

Enggano Thrush

kabaena

erythronota

Red-backed Thrush

Red-and-black Thrush

Buru Thrush

Seram Thrush

Orange-headed Thrush *Geokichla citrina*

L 20–23 cm. S–SE–E Asia. 11 ssp, 3–4 in region: *aurata* (Bor); *rubecula* (Jav–Bali); *gibsonhilli* (breeds mainland SE Asia; winters MPen, expected vagrant Sum); *innotata* (breeds mainland SE Asia; winters MPen, vagrant Sum). Now local and widely extinct Jav-Bali; uncommon on Bor; migratory records from N Sum (1918, Feb 2020), Lampung, Sum (1979), W Kalimantan (Dec 1986), though probably overlooked as regular winter visitor. Feeds in leaf litter in forest understorey, but on migration in any wooded habitat, <1600 m (Jav), 900–1800 m (Bor). **ID** Ssp *aurata* and *rubecula* sexually monomorphic. **Ad** *aurata* dull orange head, breast and belly; white wing stripe; grey mantle, wings and tail; white to yellow-washed lower belly and vent. Ssp *rubecula* richer and darker orange, with clear-cut white lower belly to vent. Ssp *innotata* **M** paler orange, lacks white wingbar; *gibsonhilli* as previous but with vestigial or well-marked white wingbar; **F** *innotata/gibsonhilli* have brown olive-grey mantle. **Imm** dark orange-brown upperparts with buff flecking; dark facial bars; dull brown underparts with buff-orange flecking and spotting. **Voc** Song: loud, rich, melodious, varied series of short phrases involving slurred notes and trills, with some mimicry. Similar song phrases of Chestnut-capped Thrush are shorter, less varied. Call: (i) thin "tzzeet", often preceding song; (ii) subdued "tjuck"; (iii) shrill screeching "kreeee" or "teer-teer-teer...".

Siberian Thrush *Geokichla sibirica*

L 20–23 cm. Breeds E Palaearctic; winters SE Asia. 2 ssp: *sibirica* (breeds most of range; winters Jav, migrates through Sum; vagrant to Bor); *davisoni* (breeds Japan, Sakhalin; winters to Sum). Male plumage differences between taxa seem discrete; research required to verify if *davisoni* merits species rank as '**Nippon Thrush**'. No-madic, fairly common in forest, particularly >900 m. Flocks in fruiting trees, shy. **ID M** entirely slaty bluish black; long white eyebrow, narrow white belly stripe and white-tipped vent feathers. Ssp *davisoni* slightly larger; longer wings and tail; darker overall; lacks white on belly and undertail apart from vestigial pale tips on vent. **F** dark brown above; white or buff eyebrow; white throat and brown underparts spotted pale buff. Ssp *davisoni* fully scalloped to vent; no white mid-belly wedge. **Imm M** white submoustachial and throat; pale-buff spotted greater coverts; white-spotted underparts. **Imm F** stronger wing spots; weaker face markings; stronger markings on underparts. **Voc** Call: (i) quiet "tsit" or "tsip"; (ii) stronger "seep" or "tseee" when flushed and on migration; (iii) soft, dry, rattling "chrssSS". **SS** See Japanese Thrush.

Eyebrowed Thrush *Turdus obscurus*

L 21–23 cm. Breeds C–E Palaearctic; winters to SE–E Asia, Phil. Monotypic. Locally fairly common in forest, especially in hills; coastal areas on migration. Feeds in leaf litter but can congregate in fruiting trees. Forms large flocks, flying high over canopy (<300). **ID M** grey hood; white supercilium, chin and moustachial; brown upperparts; orange-brown flanks and breast; white belly and vent. **F** olive-brown head; more white on throat. **Imm** diffuse buff-spotted and dark-and-pale streaked head markings; pale-orange underparts with dark spots. **Voc** Chuckling subsong from flocks before spring departure. Call: (i) thin "zip-zip" or "dzit" when taking flight; (ii) chuckling "dack-dack" or "gigigig"; (iii) thin, drawn-out "zeeee" or "tsee"; (iv) crackling rattle "turrr".

Japanese Thrush *Turdus cardis*   **V**

L 21–22 cm. Breeds NE–E Asia; winters to SE–E Asia. Monotypic. Single record, Mt Kinabalu, Sabah (Mar 2006). Predominantly terrestrial in forest, edge. **ID M** black upperparts, head, breast and thighs; white belly and undertail with black spots on upper belly and flanks;

yellow bill and legs. **F** dusky-brown upperparts with rump and tail washed grey; white underparts with black spots; orange flanks and breast sides; darker yellowish-horn bill. **Imm** upperparts with pale and dark spots; buff underparts with brown spots, whiter on vent. **Voc** Call: (i) thin "tsweee" or "tsuuu"; (ii) hollow "chuk".

Island Thrush *Turdus poliocephalus*

L 17–25 cm. SE Asia to Aus. ~50 ssp, 13 in region: *loeseri* (N Sum); *indrapurae* (SC Sum); *fumidus* (W Jav); *javanicus* (C Jav); *stresemanni* (Mt Lawu in EC Jav); *whiteheadi* (E Jav); *seebohmi* (N Bor); *hygroscopus* (SC–E Sul); *celebensis* (SW Sul); *schlegelii* (W Timor); *sterlingi* (E Timor); *deningeri* (Seram); *sukahujan* (Taliabu). Doubtless comprises multiple species-level taxa. In region, GS populations ('**Greater Sundaic Island Thrush**' *T. [poliocephalus] javanicus*) are linked via rough, stepwise cline from all-dark birds in N Sum (*loeseri*) across those with reddish bellies in S Sum and W Jav (*indrapurae*, *fumidus*) back to less red on belly in C–EC Jav (*javanicus*, *stresemanni*) and back again to fully reddish belly in E Jav and N Bor (*whiteheadi*, *seebohmi*). Ssp in Sul (*hygroscopus*, *celebensis*, '**Sulawesi Island Thrush**' *T. [poliocephalus] celebensis*) and Timor (*schlegelii*, *sterlingi*; '**Timor Island Thrush**' *T. [poliocephalus] schlegelii*) resemble red-bellied forms from GS, but *deningeri* from Seram and *sukahujan* from Taliabu are distinct compared to adjacent taxa and may merit monotypic species treatment as '**Binaya Island Thrush**' and '**Taliabu Island Thrush**', respectively. Genomic evidence required. Fairly common in montane stunted forest and heath near tree line, generally >1800 m though descends to ~1200 m on smaller islands (e.g. Taliabu) and in W Timor; reportedly even lower in E Sul. Singly, pairs or groups (<15); favours understorey. **ID** Orange-yellow bill and legs. **F** duller than **M**. Ssp *loeseri* entirely black or very dark-brown; *indrapurae* dark earthen-brown upperparts with paler, more creamy-brown hood, rufous belly and flanks, dark-brown lower belly and pale-streaked vent; *fumidus* as previous but dark bronzy-grey olive-washed mantle, black cap, white lower mid-belly, and white-streaked brown vent; *javanicus* dull dark-brown upperparts, slightly paler brown head and underparts, face to throat pale buff-brown, centre of belly to vent orange (sometimes interspersed with grey-brown), vague white vent streaks; *stresemanni* as previous but larger, warmer brown overall, no rusty colour on belly in adults (although Imm shows light dull-rusty on belly); *whiteheadi* brown upperparts, grey-brown head, chestnut belly white in centre, white-streaked vent; *seebohmi* sooty black-brown hood and upperparts, rich chestnut breast and belly, white lower mid-belly, black flanks and thighs, black vent with buff-washed white streaks; *celebensis* greyish olive-brown upperparts with dusky-olive hood, chestnut breast, belly and flanks, mid-belly to vent white, vent streaked brown; *hygroscopus* as previous but larger, with paler (less olive-brown) hood more contrasting with darker olive-grey upper back, darker underparts, deeper rusty belly, black tail and flight feathers without olive wash, less or no white streaks on vent; an unnamed form reported from L Matano (E Sul) may resemble *hygroscopus*, more research needed; *schlegelii* as *fumidus* greyish olive-brown upperparts with grey-brown hood and rufous belly and vent; *sterlingi* as previous but sides of head, throat and upper breast sootier grey, belly deeper chestnut-brown; *deningeri* black with indistinctly separated white hood; *sukahujan* uniformly dark head and body, no reddish tones on underparts. **Imm** browner overall; buff spotting and streaks on upperparts; two wingbars; mottled dark-and-buff underparts. **Voc** Song rarely heard: pre-dawn song on Jav composed of strophes of varied "cheee", "chew" and pleasant rolling notes lasting several seconds. Call: (i) clucking "chak-chak"; (ii) high-pitched "seeee" or "sreeee". **SS** See Sulawesi Thrush and Geomalia.

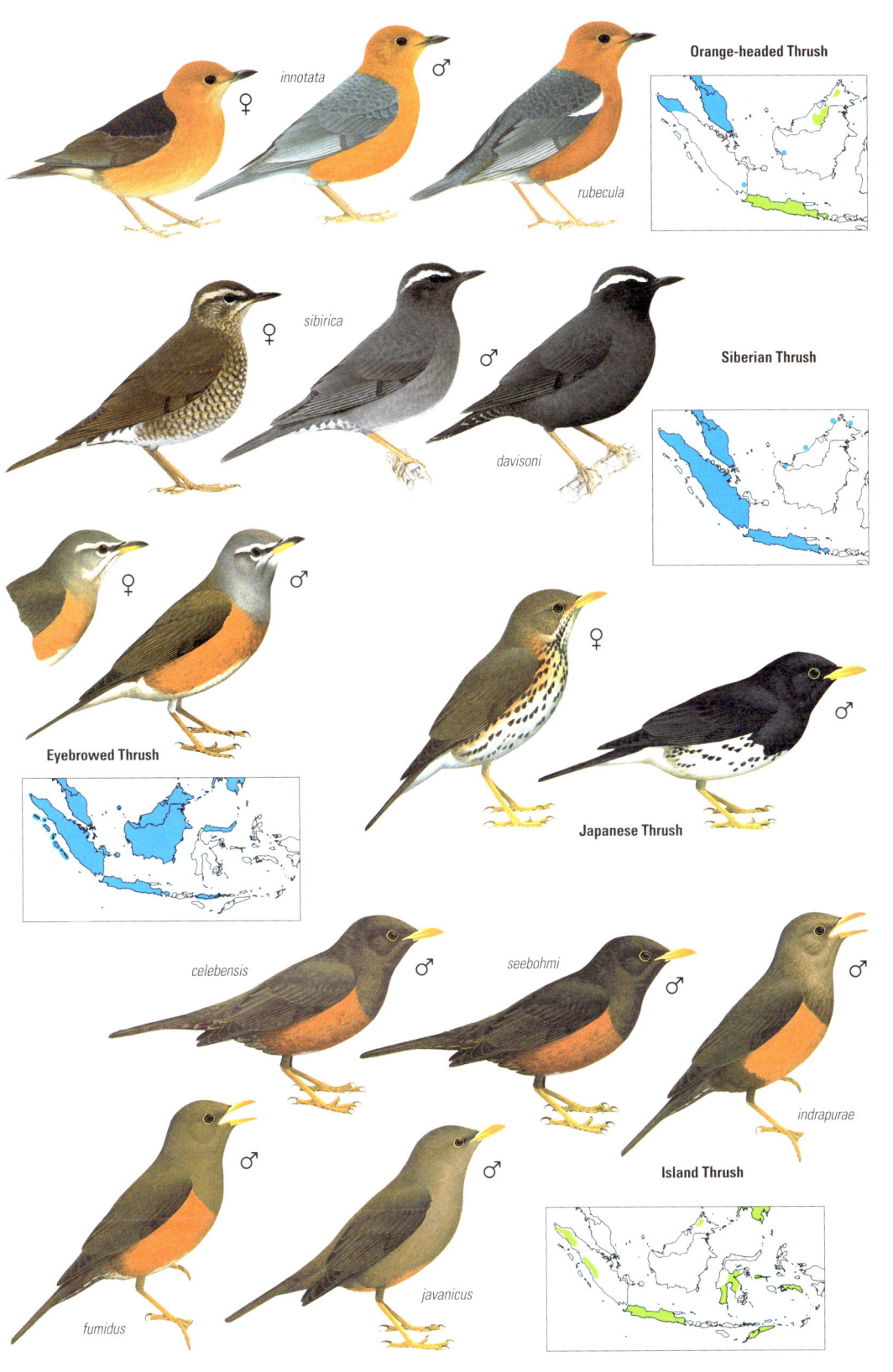

innotata ♀

rubecula ♂

Orange-headed Thrush

sibirica ♀

♂

davisoni

Siberian Thrush

♀

♂

Eyebrowed Thrush

♀

♂

Japanese Thrush

celebensis ♂

seebohmi ♂

♂

indrapurae

Island Thrush

fumidus ♂

javanicus ♂

Sulawesi Thrush *Turdus turdoides* E

L 20–25 cm. 4 ssp: *turdoides* (SW Sul); *abditivus* (C–E Sul); *heinrichi* (SE Sul); *tenebrosus* (Mt Latimojong, S Sul). Uncommon and local in montane forest, 1100–2400 m. Singly or pairs; often associates with groups of Malia, feeding in understorey, babbler-like. **ID Ad** dull olive-brown upperparts and cap; broad black loral and superciliary line engulfing eye; browner wings and tail; paler olive grey-brown underparts turning whitish on vent; orange bill and legs; pale-orange eyering. Ssp *abditivus* richer brown above, less broad supercilium and less black on lores and face; *heinrichi* and *tenebrosus* as previous but perhaps colder overall (especially on ear-coverts and throat in *tenebrosus*). **Imm** scaled underparts. **Voc** Song: thrush-like series of rich, sweet, melodious notes in short strophes, continually repeated. Call: 2 low, croaking notes, followed by 2-4 higher, more strident notes "uh-uh-wid'it-wid'it-wid'it", lasting 1 s. **SS** Island Thrush lacks contrasting black facial colouration. See also Geomalia.

Fruit-hunter *Chlamydochaera jefferyi* E

L 23 cm. Monotypic. A former taxonomic enigma, now known to be closely related to cochoas. Nomadic, locally uncommon in (sub-)montane forest, 700–3200 m. Singly, pairs or small groups (<6); favouring fruiting trees, primarily canopy dweller, unobtrusive. **ID M** crown and upperparts grey; forehead, cheeks and throat pale-buff; thick black superciliary stripe; black breast patch, wings and subterminal tail bar, the latter tipped white. **F** grey replaced by brown on upperparts and buff-brown on underparts. **Imm** crown and underparts scaled black. **Voc** Song: continual quiet, squeaky twittering. Call: (i) contact and flight call: quiet, flat or rising "seeeep", repeated at intervals of 7–10 sec; (ii) harsh, rapid, rolling "crraak-crrrak-(crrakcrrak)"; (iii) barely audible high-pitched whistle at nest by male.

Javan Cochoa *Cochoa azurea* E

L 23 cm. Monotypic. Nomadic and uncommon in montane forest, 900–3000 m. Singly or pairs, can gather in small groups (<5) at fruiting trees. **ID M** shiny dark-blue upperparts; paler glossy-blue crown and edges to wing feathers; deep purplish-blue underparts. **F** darker brown underparts contrasting more with bluer crown, edges of flight feathers and tail. **Imm** buff-brown spotted breast. **Voc** Song: monotonous whistle "fweeeet" at 2.2–2.8 kHz repeated at short intervals, lasting 1.8–2 sec. Call: (i) very high-pitched, thin "tseet"; (ii) tremulous "srrreet"; (iii) scolding "chet-chet-chet..." in alarm. **SS** Javan Whistling-thrush is larger, heavier, lacks contrast with crown, and lowers and fans its tail.

Sumatran Cochoa *Cochoa beccarii* E

L 28 cm. Monotypic. Nomadic, scarce and local in montane forest, 1600–2300 m, rarely to 1000 m. Singly or pairs, can gather in small groups (<5) at fruiting trees. **ID M** velvety black face and body with powder-blue crown; large electric-blue wing patch (coverts, tertials, base to secondaries) and blue tail with darker terminal band; brown eyes with red orbital ring. **F** ginger-buff speckling on face and breast. **Imm** buff-brown spotted breast; dark-blue mantle. **Voc** Song: as Javan Cochoa but lower-pitched mournful whistle, lasting 1.5 sec. Call: thin, quiet "sip".

MUSCICAPIDAE
Chats and Flycatchers
93 species in region

An extremely large and diverse family of small- to medium-sized elegantly-built insectivores. Many species exhibit distinct, brightly coloured plumage and beautiful songs while others are drab and vocally inconspicuous. Inhabit a range of habitats from forest to open country. Many forage by sallying for insects from exposed perches, while others are largely terrestrial.

Oriental Magpie-robin *Copsychus saularis*

L 19–21 cm. S–SE–E Asia. 11 ssp, 8 in region: *musicus* (MPen, Sum, Belitung, Bangka, W Jav, W–C Kalimantan, Sarawak); *zacnecus* (Simeulue); *nesiarchus* (Nias); *masculus* (Batu); *pagiensis* (Mentawai); *amoenus* (E Jav–Bali); *adamsi* (Brunei–Sabah, Banggi); *pluto* (Maratua, E–S Kalimantan). No longer includes Philippine Magpie-robin *C. mindanensis*, which has been shown to be more closely related to other members of the genus. All-black ssp *amoenus*, *pluto* and *adamsi* look substantially different from adjacent pied ssp *musicus*, from which they are separated by relatively narrow hybrid zones (Brunei, Kelabit Highlands through Kalimantan, C Jav), but genomic evidence indicates limited differentiation. Locally fairly common, now very rare on Jav and most parts of Sum, Bali and Kal where heavily trapped; urban and rural areas, cultivation, riverside scrub, disturbed forest, <1000 m, locally to 1900 m. Confident, though locally shy; feeds mostly on ground. **ID M** glossy blue-black upperparts, head and breast; white belly; buff tinge around vent; white bands along wing; long elongated tail, three outer pairs of tail feathers white with black bases, remaining uppertail black. **F** black replaced by grey except on wings; glossy dorsally. Ssp *zacnecus* **M** buff-tinged flanks and crissum, **F** darker than *musicus* with flanks and crissum more conspicuously ochraceous-buff. Ssp *nesiarchus* as previous but with more white on terminal portion of fourth rectrix, no buff on crissum; *masculus* larger, **F** darker, more glossy blue-black above, more dark-grey on throat and breast; *pagiensis* also large, glossy black parts more greenish. Ssp *amoenus* **M** black belly with white vent, **F** all grey below. Ssp *pluto* **M** as previous but larger, tail completely black; *adamsi* as previous but two outer pairs of rectrices white, next pair white with black bases. **Imm** dark brown-grey with black mottling above; white wing bands and belly to vent; rufous wing edging; face, breast and flanks mottled dark on buff. **Voc** Song: beautiful repetitive musical sequence, often strophes of <8 upslurred and downslurred notes. Call: (ii) upslurred "swee-ee-eet", often in combination with a harsh "chchr-r-t"; (ii) "zeee tet-tet". **SS** Pied Bushchat superficially resembles black-bellied races, but smaller with white rump, much shorter all-black tail, and different behaviour (vertical perching, no tail cocking).

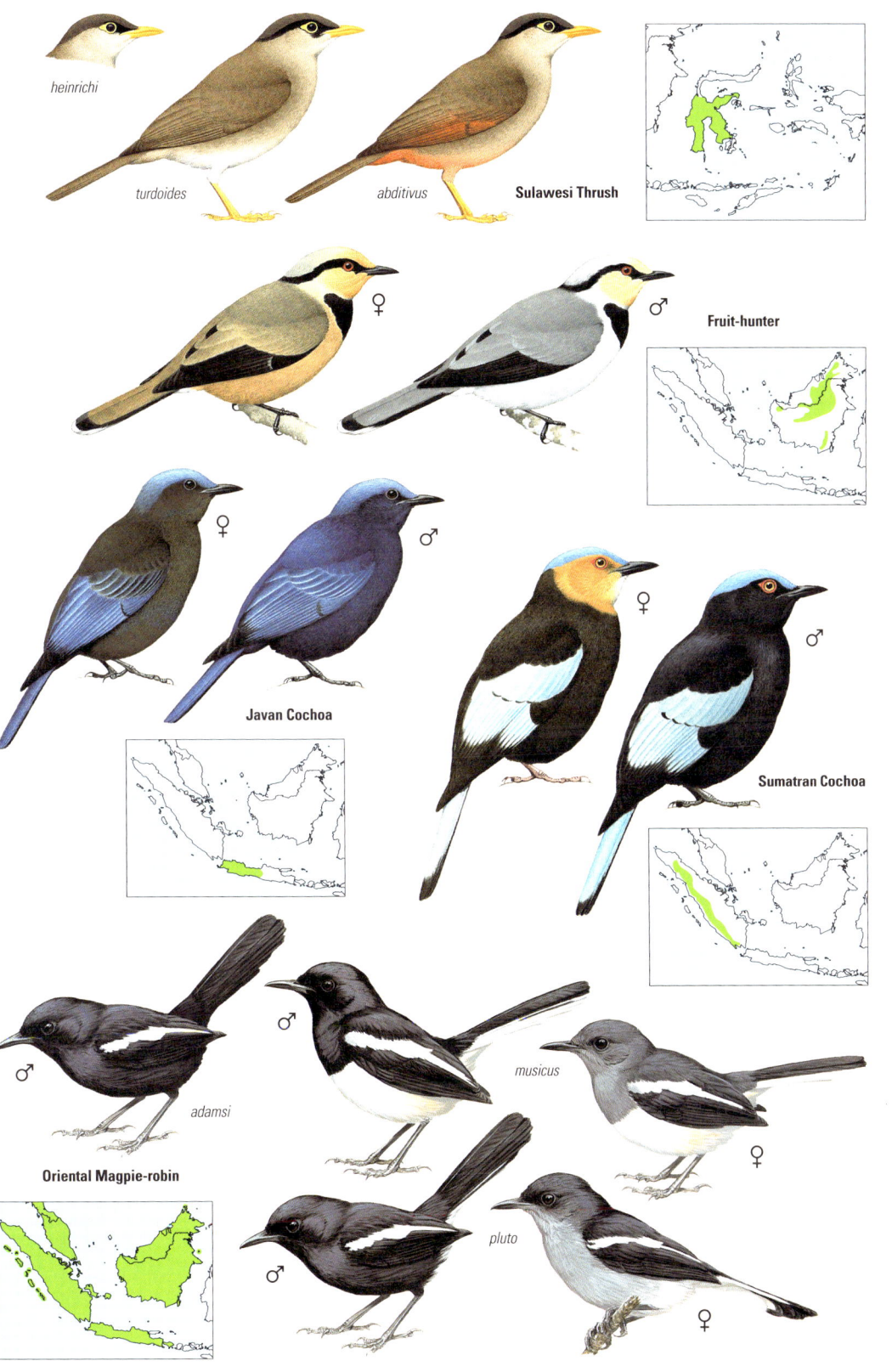

heinrichi

turdoides

abditivus

Sulawesi Thrush

♀ ♂ **Fruit-hunter**

♀ ♂ **Javan Cochoa**

♀ ♂ **Sumatran Cochoa**

♂ adamsi

♂ musicus

♀

Oriental Magpie-robin

♂ pluto

♀

Rufous-tailed Shama *Copsychus pyrropygus*

L 20–22 cm. Sundaic. Monotypic. Local, uncommon in shady forest understorey, <1100 m. Singly or pairs; secretive at low density, skulks in understorey. Cocks and fans tail, can sing from mid-canopy. **ID Ad M** blue-grey head to back and upper breast; bright rufous rump and basal two thirds of tail; white spot in front of eye; pale-rufous remaining underparts with white mid-belly. **F** grey-brown upperparts; buffy-rufous underparts with white belly. **Imm** rich buff-streaked above; dark-streaked on throat and breast. **Voc** Song: long series of slow, mournful, downslurred or upslurred, often glissading whistles of 1–4 syllables, several on equal pitch before shifting to another, rendered seemingly haphazardly. Call: scolding drawn-out "tchurr".

White-crowned Shama *Copsychus stricklandii*　E

L 25 cm. Monotypic. Porous species boundary with White-rumped Shama: presence of some hybridisation along their contact zone has prompted their merger into a single, more broadly defined species (expanded '**White-rumped Shama**' *C. malabaricus*). The two are nevertheless fairly deeply diverged genomically, suggesting that hybridisation is limited and justifying separation. The disjunct ranges of White-crowned Shama and its closely related sister species Maratua Shama (separated by populations of White-rumped Shama) suggest that White-rumped may slowly be replacing White-crowned across its range. For taxonomy also see Maratua Shama. Widespread and common but becoming uncommon with increasing poaching, in lowland and hill forest including logged forest, old rubber, <1220 m. Behaviour as White-rumped Shama. **ID Ad** as ssp *suavis* of White-rumped Shama but with white crown to nape, usually with some black spots. **F** smaller; less glossy-black. **Imm** head streaked buff; body mottled buff. **Voc** Extremely variable but generally similar to White-rumped Shama. **SS** See White-rumped Shama.

Maratua Shama *Copsychus barbouri*　E

L 25 cm. Monotypic. Usually included with White-crowned Shama (or sometimes both merged with White-rumped) but here separated based on discrete plumage differences of potential reproductive importance, a fairly deep mtDNA divergence, and its disjunction from White-crowned by intervening populations of White-rumped Shama; more research required to corroborate this treatment. For taxonomy, also see White-crowned Shama. Habits and habitat very similar to White-crowned Shama, but now probably extinct in the wild because of excessive trapping. **ID Ad** similar to White-crowned Shama but larger; longer tarsus and bigger feet; all-black tail; often exhibits whitish lower border of black breast. **Imm** undescribed. **Voc** Song: Similar to White-rumped, but perhaps slightly louder, with shorter, mostly rising phrases. Call: as White-rumped Shama.

Barusan Shama *Copsychus melanurus*　E

L 21–24 cm. ~4 ssp: *melanurus* (Nias; unnamed population on Mentawai usually included here); *hypolizus* (Simeulue); *opisthochrus* (Lasia, Babi); *mirabilis* (Panaitan). Usually included with White-rumped Shama, but plumage differs considerably. Genomic data demonstrate all sampled Barusan populations form one monophyletic group to the exclusion of White-rumped ssp *tricolor*, despite large geographic distances between islands. Restricted to deep-sea islands W and S of Sum; extinct neighbouring populations on shelf islands (Batu, Banyak) unlikely to form part of present species, as they had a conventional White-rumped Shama plumage. Population on Bangkaru (almost extinct) may constitute hybrid population with intermediate tail colouration. Habits and habitat very similar to White-rumped Shama. Now largely extinct in the wild, with the only likely surviving population on Siberut facing imminent extinction. **ID** Limited sexual dimorphism. **Ad** generally similar to shorter-tailed individuals of White-rumped Shama, but all-black tail; underparts darker rufous. Ssp *hypolizus* distinctly smaller than *melanurus*; *opisthochrus* is the largest race and has distinct paler belly; *mirabilis* smaller bill, longer wings and tail, undertail may have small white tips on the smaller quills. **Imm** as White-rumped Imm but lacking white outer tail feathers. **Voc** Captive individuals utter White-rumped Shama-like songs, but perhaps with fewer tremulous notes; more research required.

White-rumped Shama *Copsychus malabaricus*

L 21–28 cm. S–SE Asia. 8 ssp, 4 in region: *tricolor* (MPen, W Jav, Sum, Bangka, Belitung, Anambas, Natuna); *omissus* (E-C Jav); *nigricauda* (Kangean); *suavis* (Bor except NE). No longer includes Andaman Shama *C. albiventris* because of strong plumage differences. More taxonomic research required into ssp *nigricauda* ('**Kangean Shama**') – now likely extinct – which exhibits strong plumage differences. More taxonomic attention also needed for ssp *omissus* (traded as '**Larwo Shama**') – nearly extinct in the wild – which consistently differs in a suite of morphological characters and exhibits deep mtDNA differentiation. For taxonomy also see Barusan, White-crowned and Maratua Shamas. Formerly widespread and common in lowland and hill forest, riverside vegetation, plantations etc., but now extinct from most of the range in the region through excessive trapping for the bird trade. Occurs <800 m (Jav), <1200 m (Sum), <1750 m (Bor). Forages on the ground and in low vegetation. **ID M** glossy purplish upperparts, head, throat and upper breast; rump white; wings and tail duller black, strongly gradated; four outer pairs of rectrices white-tipped, broader towards outermost pair; belly deep rufous; thigh feathers buff-rufous. **F** less glossy, greyer overall, with much shorter tail. Ssp *suavis* **M** larger with shorter tail, three outer pairs of rectrices almost wholly white, **F** dusky above, paler belly and slightly less glossy on breast. Ssp *omissus* has reduced sexual dimorphism, is smaller, shorter-tailed, has a more extensive black breast, white thighs and often a white patch separating black breast from paler orange belly; male *omissus* characteristically raise their shorter crown feathers to a roundish crest during singing. Ssp *nigricauda* **M** unique, largely black tail with only few white tips on outer pair reminiscent of Barusan Shama, but white vent and rufous-orange belly more similar to adjacent *omissus*, **F** shorter-tailed. **Imm** head streaked buff; body mottled buff. **Voc** Song: series of powerful, rich, fluty and burring melodious phrases, very thrush-like and musical, incorporating much mimicry, especially in first introductory notes to each phrase. Call: harsh, scolding "chak", "krr-krr" and bill-snapping. **SS** White-crowned Shama has white crown, but intergradation occurs where both meet.

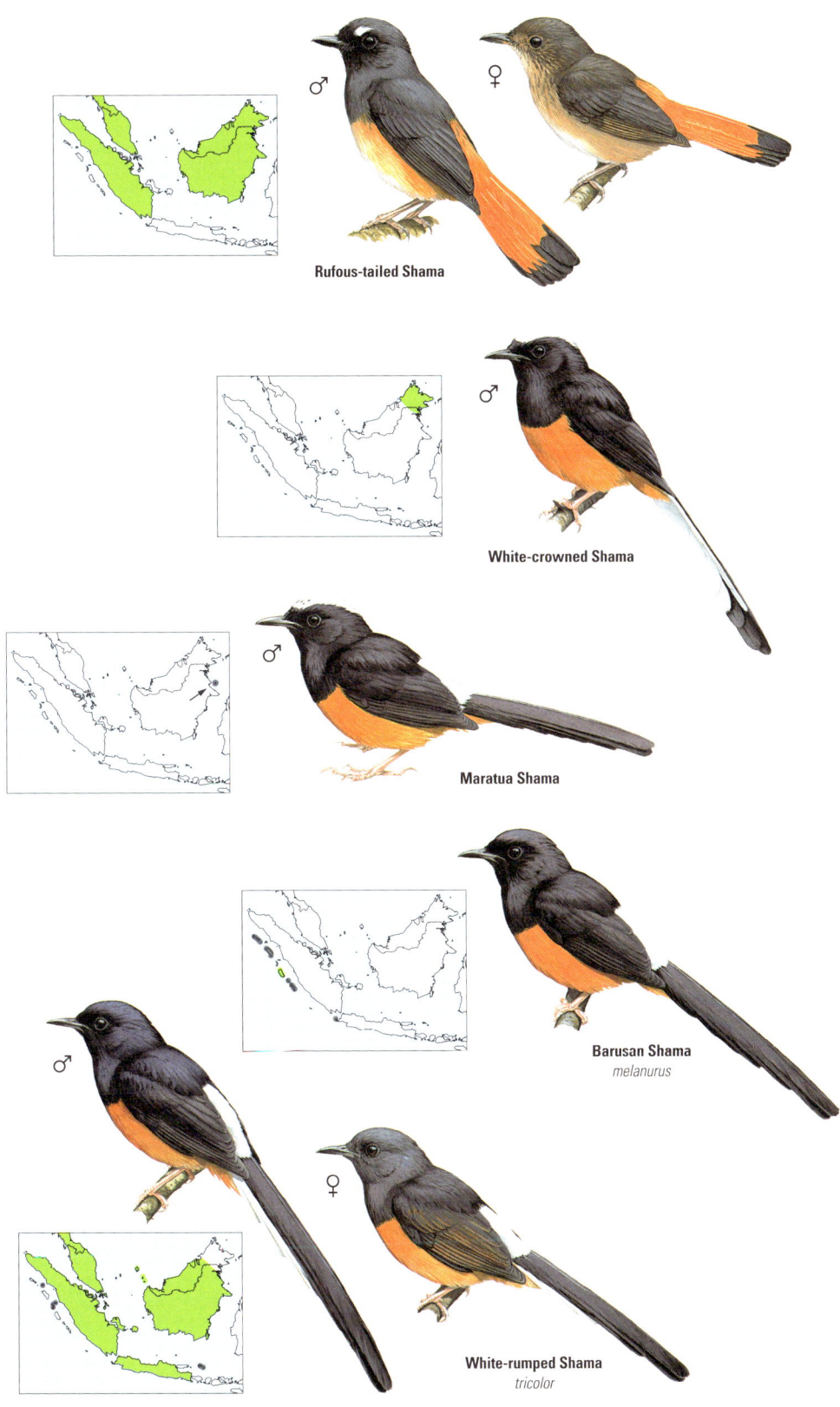

Rufous-tailed Shama ♂ ♀

White-crowned Shama ♂

Maratua Shama ♂

Barusan Shama
melanurus

White-rumped Shama ♂ ♀
tricolor

Ferruginous Flycatcher *Muscicapa ferruginea*

L 12–13 cm. Breeds Himalaya to E Asia; winters to SE Asia, Phil. Monotypic. Generally scarce winter visitor in hill forest, 500–1600 m. Singly; in lower and mid-levels of forest, often in small clearings and glades. **ID Ad** dark rusty-brown upperparts with slaty-grey head; white throat and neck sides; rump, tail and underparts rufescent; white mid-belly. **Imm** black crown with bold buff streaks; black mantle to upper rump buff-spotted; black-streaked breast. **Voc** Song unlikely to be heard in region: (i) several harsh and shrill notes; (ii) refrain of 3 notes. Call: short, sharp, high-pitched "tssit-tssit" and "tssit-tssit-tssit". **SS** Only flycatcher within its wintering range with uniform grey head and strongly rufescent underparts.

Asian Brown Flycatcher *Muscicapa dauurica*

L 12–14 cm. Breeds E Palaearctic; winters S–SE Asia, Phil. Monotypic. Species as here defined is an exclusively boreal breeder, does not include resident taxa from S–SE Asia (i.e., Brown-streaked and Umber Flycatchers) for which DNA data indicate a potentially distant relationship within subgenus. Common winter visitor to forest, woodlands, scrub, cultivation, edge, <1600 m. Singly; arboreal in mid-storey, hunting from prominent perch. Vocal and territorial in winter quarters. **ID** Grey-brown above; pale lores and eye ring; white underparts with breast sides often more or less faintly streaked or smudged greyish-brown; blackish bill with pronounced orange base to lower mandible. **Imm** pale spots on upperparts. **Voc** Song unlikely to be heard in region: short varied trills interspersed with whistled phrases, slurred notes, squawks and twitters. Call: (i) thin, piercing, rapid "tse-tit-tit-tit-tit", or "sit-it-it", or dry rattle "chititititit"; (ii) short "tze", or "tsee" or "neep" and low churr; (iii) soft and plaintive "tsr, tsr", slightly finer and higher-pitched than Grey-streaked Flycatcher. **SS** Dark-sided Flycatcher has shorter, thinner, often all-black bill (versus extensive orange base in Asian Brown), breast with prominent grey-brown smudging (*cacabata*) and/or apparent streaking (*sibirica*) (versus faint or no streaks on Asian Brown); Dark-sided also has longer vent with usually some dark feather tips (versus shorter, all-white vent) and characteristically rounded, dome-shaped head (less flat than Asian Brown). Fem Little Pied Flycatcher has greyer head and back, all-black bill (without orange base), a contrasting russet-brown rump and tail, and lacks prominent underparts markings and eyering. Sulawesi Streaked Flycatcher is much more heavily streaked below, with a less wide bill, less orange to lower mandible base, shorter wings, a shorter vent, and mostly lacking a white eye ring and loral area. Also see Taiga, Sumba Brown, Grey-streaked, Brown-streaked and Umber Flycatchers.

Brown-streaked Flycatcher *Muscicapa poonensis*

L 12 cm. Breeds mainland S-SE Asia; winters S to Sum. 3 ssp; probably only 2 in region: *williamsoni* (breeds N MPen; winters to S); *siamensis* (breeds mainland SE Asia; winters to S). Historical records from Bor require investigation, likely confined to Sum as a winter migrant. Has been suggested to include Umber Flycatcher, but the two show morphological differences comparable to those between other *Muscicapa* flycatcher species and are genetically not close. For taxonomy see also Asian Brown Flycatcher. Uncommon visitor and migrant in lowland forest, woodland, cultivation, parks. Migrants can arrive late July, up to a month earlier than Asian Brown Flycatcher. **ID Ad** as Asian Brown, but browner upperparts with warm-buff tinge on rump; breast and flanks buff-brown, broadly streaked brown; lower mandible extensively yellowish-orange with dark tip. Ssp *siamensis* has even more orange-yellow on

lower mandible. **Imm** rump tinged rufous; wing-coverts and tail heavily tipped creamy-buff. **Voc** Full song not described, but soft sustained subsong is recorded. Call: chitter call, slightly shriller, less dry-sounding than Asian Brown. **SS** Asian Brown very similar, especially if it shows breast streaking: Brown-streaked differs in (1) its greater extent of yellow-orange on lower mandible; (2) often lacks large pale loral spot; (3) typically has less conspicuous eye ring; (4) shows some throat markings (versus whitish and unmarked in Asian Brown); (5) has streaking extending below mid-breast and mid-flanks (in Asian Brown does not extend that far down); (6) upperparts warmer brown (never grey-tinged), especially rump and tail; (7) tertials fringed buff (versus white in Asian Brown); (8) tail tipped white (buff in Imm) versus usually all-dark in Asian Brown. Umber Flycatcher is smaller and darker, on average with warmer tinge to back (although this varies with wear); shows almost no eyering; has underparts extensively washed down to belly (versus more distinct streaks in Brown-streaked); has shorter primary projection and longer tail; has shorter vent; and exhibits shorter bill with less orange-yellow to lower mandible. Dark-sided Flycatcher has shorter, less wide bill with much less orange-yellow on lower mandible; lacks warm-brown tones on plumage; typically has more dome-shaped head; and has longer vent with usually some dark feather tips (versus shorter, all-white vent); especially Dark-sided ssp *cacabata* has more diffuse breast streaks becoming smudgy on flanks (not clear streaks). Grey-streaked Flycatcher, unrecorded from Sum, would be identified by lack of warm tones in plumage, longer vent, much darker, stronger underparts streaking, longer wings (reaching almost to within tail tip), and a narrower bill that has much less orange-yellow on lower mandible.

Umber Flycatcher *Muscicapa umbrosa*

L 12 cm. Sundaic. Monotypic. Taxonomically cryptic and long overlooked. Birds found breeding in central MPen match the plumage features of *umbrosa* and are here treated as part of it. For taxonomy also see Brown-streaked and Asian Brown Flycatchers. Rare in lowland dipterocarp forest, <230 m. **ID** Nondescript, 'plain' face, lacking pale eyering and lores. **Ad** rich dark rufous-brown upperparts (duller brown later in the year when worn), darker on wings and tail; warm rufous-brown on rump; very diffuse breast and flank streaking 'washing' into throat and belly; tail unusually long, primaries project just beyond base of tail; bill black with orange base to lower mandible. **Imm** very dark brown upperparts with bold rufous spots, finer on crown; darker brown breast markings; rufous-buff wingbar; rufous-fringed primaries; dark-brown tail with broad rufous-brown terminal fringe. **Voc** Song undescribed. Call: thin "tzit". **SS** No overlapping *Muscicapa* flycatchers have combination of such a long tail and short wings; none show such a plain face lacking eyering and other facial markings (moustachial, loral). In addition, Grey-streaked Flycatcher has much stronger and darker underparts markings, lacks warm plumage tones, has longer vent, and has less extensive orange-yellow colour to lower mandible. Dark-sided Flycatcher has shorter, narrower bill with much less orange-yellow on lower mandible, longer vent with usually some black feather tips (versus shorter all-white vent), lacks warm plumage tones, and has prominent grey-brown smudging (*cacabata*) or apparent streaking (*sibirica*) concentrating on the flanks versus uniform brownish streaky wash across whole underparts. Asian Brown also lacks warm plumage tones, has a longer vent, and lacks distinct streaking on underparts (at most faint greyish streaks on flanks). Also see Brown-streaked Flycatcher.

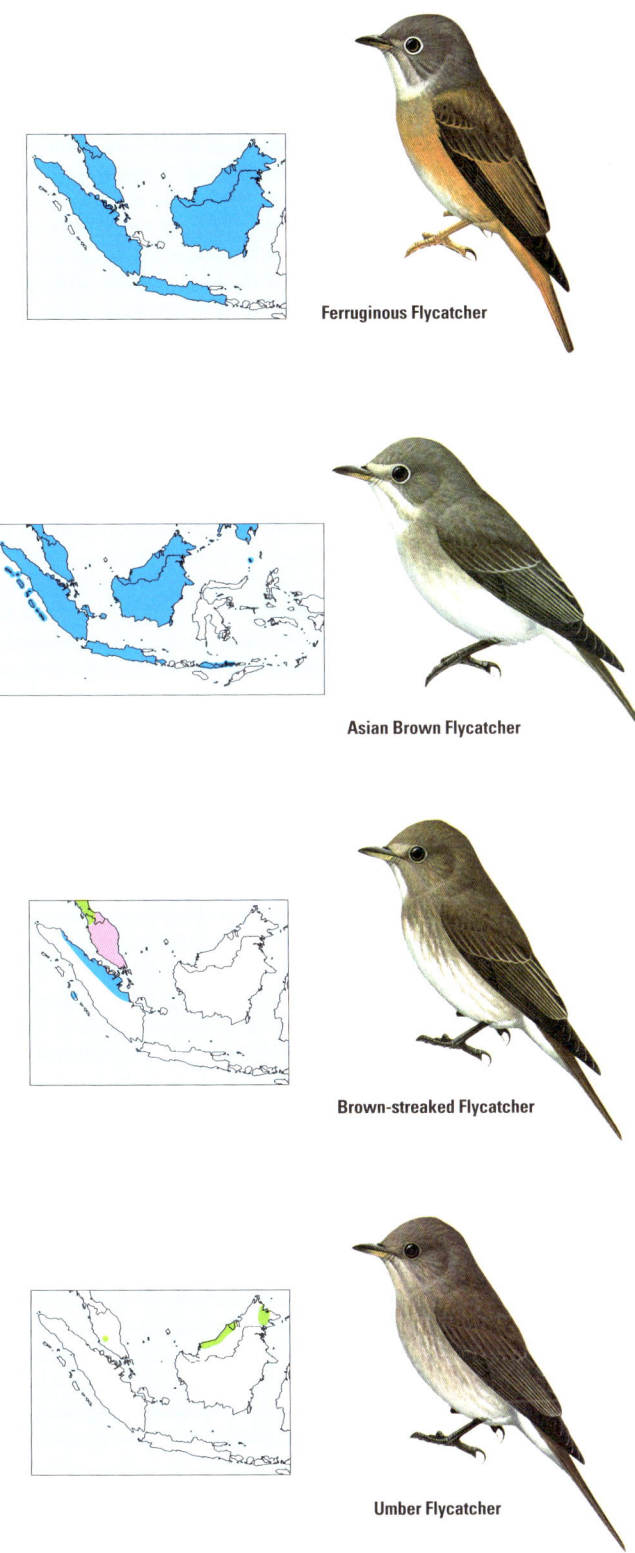

Ferruginous Flycatcher

Asian Brown Flycatcher

Brown-streaked Flycatcher

Umber Flycatcher

Sumba Brown Flycatcher *Muscicapa segregata* 🅔

L 13 cm. Monotypic. Uncommon in forest remnants, edge. Singly or pairs; mid to upper-levels of trees, inconspicuous. **ID Ad** brown upperparts; white lores and indistinct eyering; pale greyish-white underparts, slightly greyer breast; bright orange base to lower mandible. **Imm** pale spots on upperparts. **Voc** Song: jumbled series of rapid, high-pitched, whistled motifs, including harsher notes, usually terminating with a trill. Call: high-pitched, downslurred, thin, repeated whistle. **SS** Asian Brown Flycatcher has distinct eyering, slightly less orange-yellow on lower mandible, a longer vent, colder, greyer upperparts and usually shows stronger greyish flammulation on breast (sometimes even streaking) contrasting against a whiter throat. Sumba Flycatcher favours forest interior, has more silvery-white underparts, richer chestnut upperparts lacking pale tertial fringes, and exhibits an all-black bill (lacking orange lower mandible base). Sumba Warbling-flycatcher is larger overall with dingier grey underparts and face, richer chestnut wings and tail, larger all-black bill (lacking bright lower mandible base).

Sulawesi Brown Flycatcher *Muscicapa sodhii* 🅔

L 12 cm. Monotypic. Local and uncommon in forest, <1900 m. Singly or pairs, joins mixed flocks; mid- to upper canopy. **ID Ad** dull grey-brown upperparts; head plain-faced without eyering or marked lores; often shows two white wingbars; off-white underparts, throat and breast with strong dusky streaking; short primary projection to base of tail. **Imm** white scaling on head and mantle, broad buff tips to greater coverts and scapulars. **Voc** Song: similar to those of some of its congeners, but differs in being higher-pitched and within a narrower bandwidth (~6–10 kHz); consists of thin, high-pitched whistles, chirps, twitters, glissandos, buzzy notes and trills in strophes that last from less than a second to several seconds. **SS** See Grey-streaked, Dark-sided and Asian Brown Flycatchers. **AN** Sulawesi Streaked Flycatcher.

Grey-streaked Flycatcher *Muscicapa griseisticta*

L 13–14 cm. Breeds NE Asia; winters to Indonesia, Phil and NG. Monotypic. Fairly common in edge and clearings, open areas with emergent trees and dead snags, <2000 m. Singly; quiet on perches from understorey to canopy. **ID Ad** very long-winged with heavily streaked underparts. Brown-grey upperparts; white loral line and long moustachial streak; narrow white eye ring; underparts white with large blackish pencil-like streaks on breast and flanks; vent always white; mid-sized blackish bill with limited orange base to lower mandible. **Imm** upperparts duller brown with pale streaks and spots; wing-coverts spotted white; whitish underparts with grey spots or streaks, denser on breast and flanks. **Voc** Song unlikely to be heard in region: fairly quiet, twittering phrases incorporating a variety of whistling notes. Call: (i) sweet upslurred trill of 1 sec; (ii) loud and melodious "chipee tee-tee"; (iii) metallic "zt-zt-zt..."; (iv) soft and plaintive "tsr, tsr". **SS** Dark-sided Flycatcher (ssp *sibirica* most similar) has smaller bill, dark centres to some vent feathers, less strongly streaked underparts, usually less well-defined moustachial, more prominent eye ring (especially behind eye), and a rather domed head, looking 'cute'. Asian Brown is much less strongly streaked on underparts, has wider bill with more orange to lower mandible base, a shorter primary projection (versus wing tips almost within reach of tail tips in Grey-streaked), and a shorter vent. Sulawesi Brown Flycatcher differs in (1) its conspicuously shorter vent, (2) much shorter and more rounded wings (with wing tip just

barely beyond tail base, versus wing tip almost within reach of tail tip in Grey-streaked), (3) weaker head pattern with almost no visible eyering and less white on lores, (4) bill longer and more strongly hooked but relatively less broad, (5) dark-spotted (not mostly white) chin and throat, and (6) the lack of a pale moustachial stripe (present in Grey-streaked). Also see Brown-streaked and Umber Flycatchers. Juveniles and immatures of resident flycatchers are mottled, not streaked.

Dark-sided Flycatcher *Muscicapa sibirica*

L 13–14 cm. Breeds E Palaearctic, Himalaya to E Asia; winters SE–E Asia. 2 ssp: *sibirica* (breeds E Palaearctic; winters to GS); *cacabata* (breeds Himalaya to E Asia; winters to Sum–Jav). Scarce to locally common (Bor), rare (Jav) winter visitor; density of each ssp poorly understood in MPen–Sum–Jav, where both occur, due to ID difficulties in the field. Inhabits forest, on migration also scrub, gardens, <1500 m. Singly or pairs; on prominent perches, generally higher in canopy than Asian Brown (hence more overlooked), but after rain also closer to ground. **ID Ad** dark ash-grey upperparts; incomplete white eyering (especially prominent behind eye); diffuse white moustachial stripe; pale buff wingbar (in fresh plumage); white throat and half-collar; white underparts with smudgy grey-brown streaks on breast and flanks; long vent usually shows some dark streaks; small, broad-based, usually all-black bill (can have orange base to lower mandible). Ssp *cacabata* identifiable in the hand (without overlap) based on even smaller and less wide bill and much shorter wing and tail with a slightly less long vent; however, plumage differences subtle and sometimes overlap: ssp *cacabata* on average even darker grey above; flank and breast pattern often no longer discernible as individual streaks but a grey smudge, with less white on throat and usually missing half-collar; more prominently grey tips on vent. **Imm** darker; pale buff-streaked and spotted upperparts; whitish underparts with black markings on breast; buffish lower belly. **Voc** Song unlikely to be heard in region: similar but softer than Asian Brown Flycatcher. Call: (i) series of short metallic tinkling notes, "zt-zt-zt...", similar to Asian Brown and Grey-streaked Flycatchers; (ii) short trill; (iii) high, thin, downslurred "tseee"; (iv) soft "churr". **SS** See Asian Brown, Brown-streaked, Umber and Grey-streaked Flycatchers. Sulawesi Brown Flycatcher can be told from potential vagrant Dark-sided ssp *sibirica* by (1) longer, deeper bill, (2) virtual lack of eye ring, (3) clearer streaking across whole breast (not tending towards flanks), (4) shorter wings, (5) much shorter vent lacking any dark feather tips, and (6) shorter, less notched tail.

Rufous-browed Flycatcher *Anthipes solitaris*

L 12–13 cm. SE Asia. 3 ssp, 1 in region: *solitaris* (Sum). Locally common in (sub-) montane forest, 900–2400 m. Singly or pairs; in understorey, dense undergrowth, edge, and on the ground in forest trails; tame and approachable though inconspicuous unless singing. **ID Ad** Rich ochre-brown upperparts, more rufous on wings and tail; bright rufous lores and spectacles; chin and throat gorget pure white, finely bordered black; warm buff-brown on breast and flanks; whitish mid-belly to vent. **Imm** without white on chin and throat; heavily streaked buffish body; indistinct wingbar. **Voc** Song: slow, thin, high-pitched, tremulous warble, commonly rendered as a descending "three blind mice", but more often a longer series. Call: (i) thin, high-pitched "tseep"; (ii) sharp "tchik" or "tek" and repeated "tik-tik"; (iii) harsh churring alarm call.

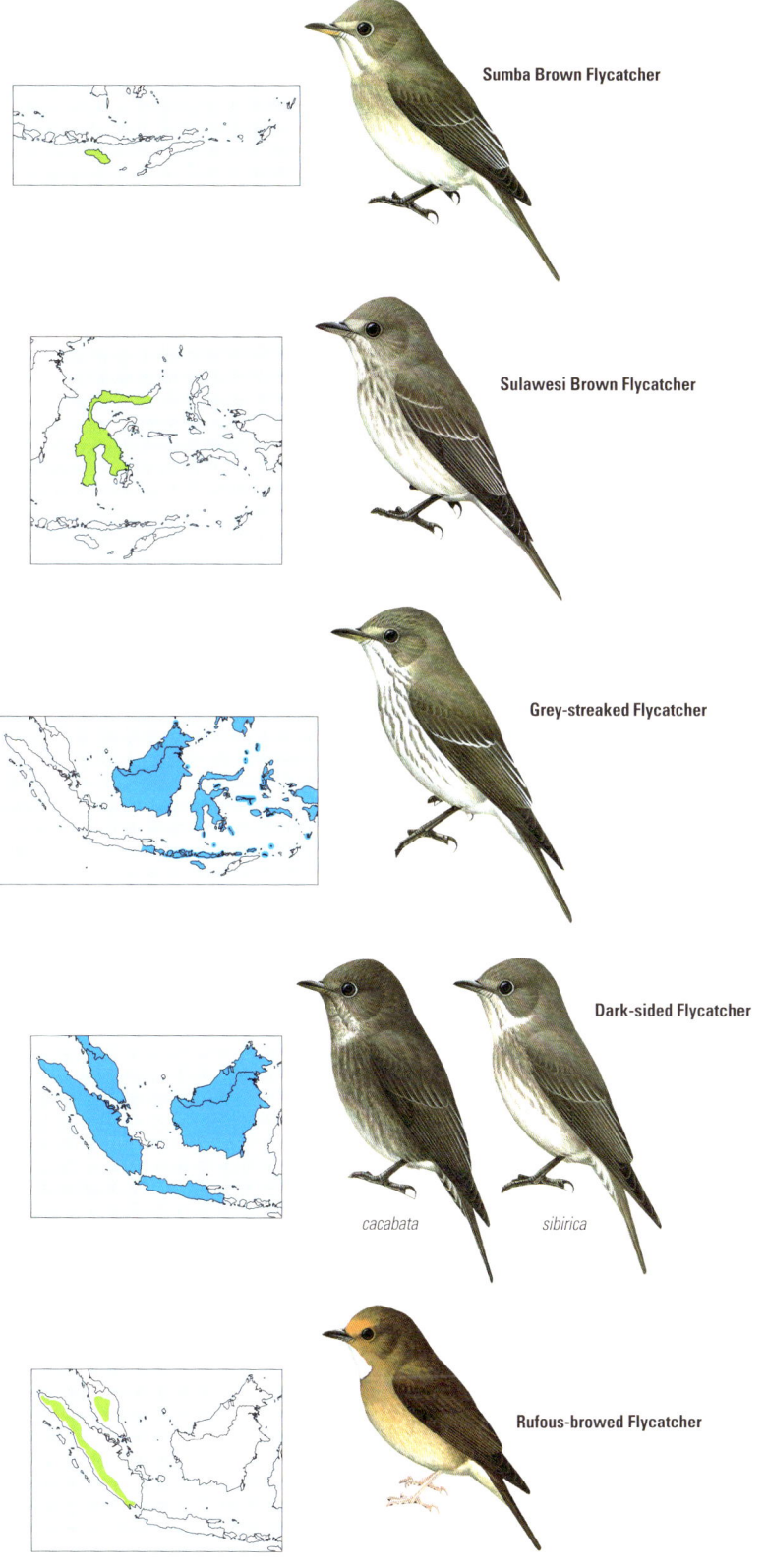

Sumba Brown Flycatcher

Sulawesi Brown Flycatcher

Grey-streaked Flycatcher

Dark-sided Flycatcher

cacabata

sibirica

Rufous-browed Flycatcher

Fulvous-chested Jungle-flycatcher *Cyornis olivaceus*

L 14–15 cm. Sundaic. 2 ssp: *olivaceus* (GS, MPen); *perolivaceus* (Banggi, Balambangan). Scarce (locally common in Sum) in lowland and hill forest, peatswamp forest, rubber plantations and edge, <1300 m, although on Bor preference for coastal habitat. Singly or pairs; in lower and mid-canopy. **ID Ad** olive-brown upperparts with warm-brown rump and tail contrasting with greyish-brown face; pale lores and indistinct eyering; white underparts with broad tawny-buff breast band; all-dark bill; pink legs. Ssp *perolivaceus* not well-marked, but tail perhaps less rufous. **Imm** warmer brown upperparts with buff and dark-brown speckles; buff and brown mottled breast and flanks. **Voc** Song: (i) rapid series of up to 9 short phrases at alternating pitch, consisting of musical notes, drawn-out churrs and scratchy and ticking notes; (ii) thin "sissit" followed by short series of high-pitched sweet phrases running down scale. Call: (i) low "tchuk-tchuk"; (ii) drawn-out "churr" or "trrt"; (iii) harsh "tac". **SS** See Brown-chested Jungle-flycatcher. Grey-chested Jungle-flycatcher differs in (1) its darker upperparts, (2) usually showing a grey (not tawny-buff) breast band (although this can look brownish in Fem), (3) brown (not greyish) face, (4) more contrasting pale loral spot (often absent in Fulvous-chested), and (5) a sharper moustachial divide between ear-coverts and white throat. Crocker Jungle-flycatcher from higher elevations has indistinct greyish breast nearly concolourous with throat (not a clearly defined tawny breast band contrasting against white throat) and a brown (not grey) face lacking contrast with rest of upperparts. Fem Bornean Jungle-flycatcher has brighter tail, more extensive brighter rufous breast (not really forming a distinct band) and much warmer brown upperparts. Javan Jungle female more solid orange on breast (lacking breast band impression), with much greyer head and mantle and conspicuous pale spectacles (absent in Fulvous-chested). Various other females of blue jungle-flycatchers (e.g. Pale Blue) also lack the distinct breast band impression.

Grey-chested Jungle-flycatcher *Cyornis umbratilis*

L 15 cm. Sundaic. Monotypic. Fairly common in lowland and hill forest, also peatswamp, kerangas, <1000 m, locally to 1200 m. Singly or pairs; inconspicuous in undergrowth and lower to mid-canopy. **ID M** dark olive-brown above, brighter on rump; lores pale-grey to whitish; often has dark malar streak or at least sharp divide between ear-coverts and white throat; white underparts with broad grey breast band, tinged brown on sides. **F** olive-brown tinged breast; shorter tail. **Imm** slightly paler upperparts with pale tips; mottled breast band. **Voc** Song: (i) thin, lilting or tinkling cadence, "tee, tit-tit-tut-tit-tut" or "see tit-tut-tit tlooeeu", often rather slurred and given with thin introductory "tee" or sharper "zeet"; (ii) series of 3 notes followed by a trill. Call: (i) scolding "chrrr-chrrr-chrrr..." alarm call; (ii) low clicking "tchk-tchk"; (iii) "trrrt it it it" with simultaneous tail flicking. **SS** See Fulvous-chested and Brown-chested Jungle-flycatchers. Crocker Jungle-flycatcher lacks pale loral spot and has more uniformly pale-grey throat and breast (not distinct grey breast band contrasting against white throat). Also see Moustached Babbler.

Brown-chested Jungle-flycatcher *Cyornis brunneatus*

L 15 cm. Breeds SE China; winters MPen, Sum, Jav. Monotypic. An atypical, migratory, vocally unique jungle-flycatcher. No longer includes Nicobar Jungle-flycatcher *C. nicobaricus* (Nicobars) based on strong vocal differences. Scarce to rare winter visitor. Singly; sometimes joining mixed flocks, in lower canopy and bushes, also on ground. **ID** Plump, with large, slightly hooked, shrike-like bicoloured bill, prominent yellow gape line. **Ad** Plain brown above; prominent pale eyering and supra-loral line; rufous-brown tail; white underparts with pale-brown flammulations on breast sometimes forming band; pale pink legs. **Imm** pale scaling on upperparts; dark-tipped lower mandible; breast band less prominent. **Voc** Song unlikely to be heard

in region: unlike many other jungle-flycatchers a loud, melodious, trumpeting couplet followed by 3–5 even-pitched notes at higher frequency and often preceded by a high-pitched, barely audible note, "pseet, toot-toot titidirit". Call: harsh "churr". **SS** Best told from Grey-chested, Fulvous-chested and various other drab flycatchers by shrike-like bicoloured bill (less massive and all-black in the others). Grey-chested additionally has a grey (not brown) breast band.

Crocker Jungle-flycatcher *Cyornis ruficrissa*   **E**

L 14–15 cm. 2 ssp: *ruficrissa* (Mt Kinabalu); *isola* (Bor except Mt Kinabalu). Previously merged with Philippine Jungle-flycatcher *C. ruficauda* (S Phil) and Sulu Jungle-flycatcher *C. ocularis* (Sulu) into '**Rufous-tailed Jungle-flycatcher**' *C. ruficauda*, but differs in vocalisations and colouration. Little-known, scarce in submontane forest, 800–2000 m. Singly, occasionally in mixed flocks; understorey and edge, keeping low to ground. **ID Ad** Plain olive-brown face; upperparts olive-brown with rufous tint on rump and outer webs of tertiaries and primaries; bright rufous tail; pale grey wash on throat and breast; whitish belly and vent. Ssp *isola* uniformly pale silky-grey throat, breast and belly with indistinct olive-brown flanks; duller tail. **Voc** Song: jumbled series of high-pitched, thin notes (thinner than other *Cyornis* in range) with seemingly little structure, interspersed with short, thin rattled notes. Call: very high-pitched, thin "sip". **SS** See Grey-chested and Fulvous-chested Jungle-flycatchers. Fem Bornean Jungle-flycatcher has brighter tail, rufous (not greyish) breast. Female Pale Blue Jungle-flycatcher has more distinct pale eye ring (especially under eye) and a more buff-grey tinge to throat/breast (not pure grey or silvery as in Crocker). Female Blue-and-white and Zappey's Flycatchers differ from Crocker structurally and in habits but have similar colouration: these two perhaps best told from Crocker by their thicker, shorter bill and brownish flammulations on breast (not greyish or silvery tinge).

Javan Jungle-flycatcher *Cyornis banyumas*   **E**

L 15 cm. 3 ssp: *banyumas* (C–E Jav); *mardii* (Panaitan); *ligus* (W Jav). Often merged with Dayak Jungle-flycatcher and extralimital taxa into a more broadly-defined umbrella species, '**Hill Jungle-flycatcher**' (or Hill Blue-flycatcher) *C. banyumas*. However, vocal, plumage and genetic evidence indicate the need for separation. Now rare (due to excessive trapping) in forest, wooded ravines and particularly bamboo thickets, <1300 m. Singly or pairs; in undergrowth and shaded lower storey. **ID M** bright pale-blue upperparts; black face; lighter iridescent blue supercilium and frontlet on forehead; orange underparts, slightly paler on belly and vent. Ssp *mardii* similar to nominate but separated geographically by intervening *ligus*; *ligus* even brighter forehead and whitish lower belly. **F** slaty-brown upperparts with warmer rump and tail; underparts as male with paler throat and belly; distinct whitish spectacles (lores and eye ring). **Imm** dark-brown upperparts with buff spots; throat and breast deep buff, dark-barred and scaled, becoming white and mottled on belly and vent. **Voc** Song: melodious cadence of warbling, thin notes that usually begins with short and thin "tsit" notes, similar to Indochinese Jungle-flycatcher but faster, more varied and with longer phrases. Call: (i) soft "tac"; (ii) harsh "chek-chek" in alarm; (ii) scolding "trrrt-trrt-trrt". **SS** Male Mangrove Jungle-flycatcher (from more coastal habitats) has darker upperparts, less iridescence on forehead and a narrow dark-blue to black chin (orange on Javan). Fem Javan is brighter orange on breast than many other drab or fem jungle-flycatchers; most closely resembles smaller, shorter-billed fem Rufous-chested and Mugimaki Flycatchers which are less slaty-tinged (browner) on upperparts, lack well-defined pale spectacles and often show 1-2 pale wingbars. See also Fulvous-chested Jungle-flycatcher.

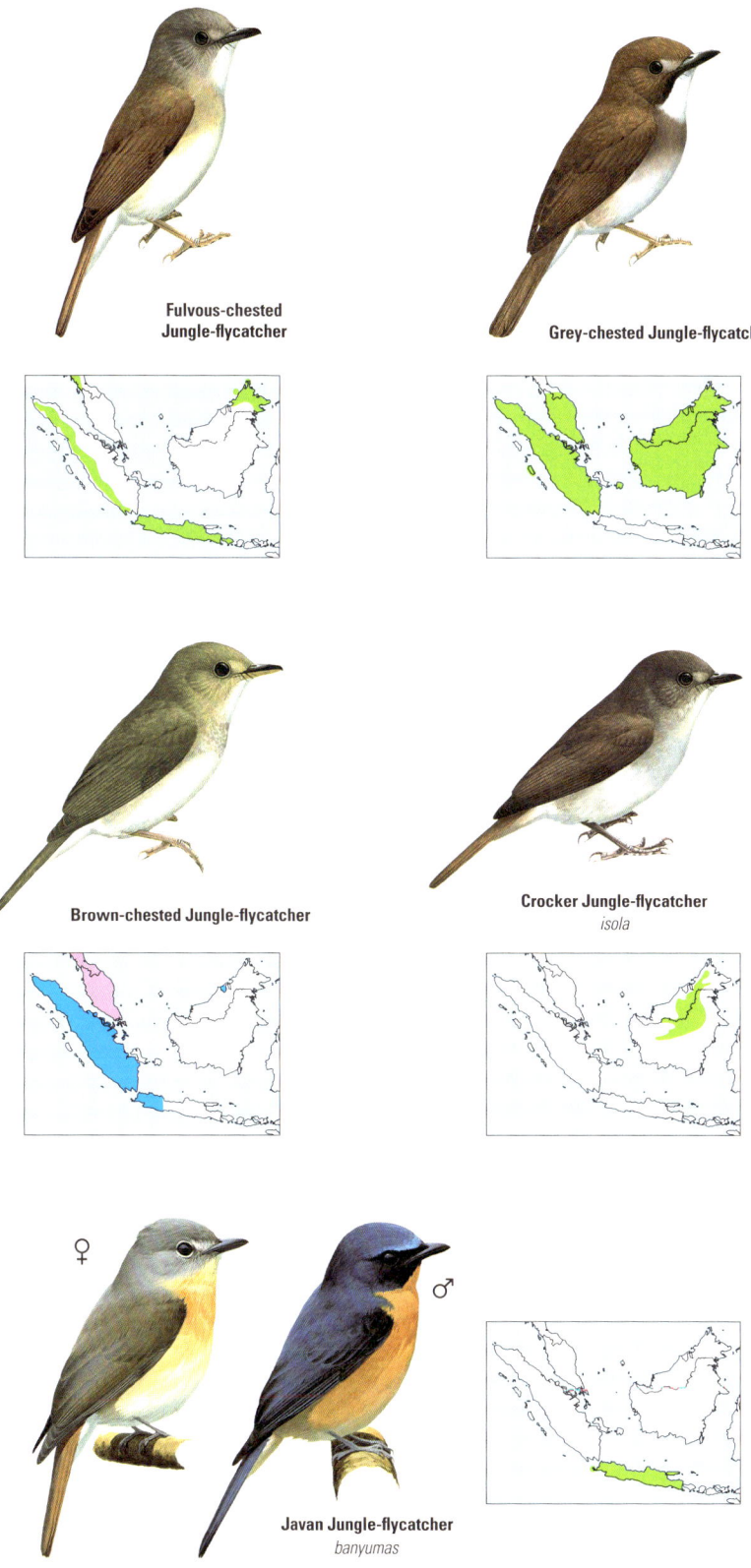

**Fulvous-chested
Jungle-flycatcher**

Grey-chested Jungle-flycatcher

Brown-chested Jungle-flycatcher

Crocker Jungle-flycatcher
isola

♀ ♂

Javan Jungle-flycatcher
banyumas

Dayak Jungle-flycatcher *Cyornis montanus* E

L 14 cm. Monotypic. For taxonomy see Javan Jungle-flycatcher. Local, uncommon in hill forest, 400–1400 m. Singly or pairs; in undergrowth and shaded lower storey. **ID M** similar to Javan Jungle-flycatcher but shorter-tailed, darker upperparts, less distinct supercilium, and brighter blue rump. **F** brown upperparts, slightly colder-brown head; deep orange underparts including throat and vent; slightly white-spectacled appearance (ghosting fem Javan's face pattern). **Imm** undescribed. **Voc** Song: series of alternating strophes, several high-pitched ascending notes followed by multiple descending notes, each lasting 1–2 sec; often preceded or followed by contact call. Call: (i) harsh "chek-chek"; (ii) flowerpecker-like "si'si'sit"; (iii) short, scolding trill. **SS** Male Bornean Jungle-flycatcher is brighter, more brilliant blue on upperparts (especially crown), whitish (not orange) on belly; fem Bornean has browner (less cold) head that makes a less spectacled impression, is more white on belly, and has brighter, longer rufous tail. Sunda Jungle-flycatcher has a larger, wider bill and longer tail, the male with blackish (not orange) chin and paler belly; fem Sunda unique with bluish tail. See also Meratus, Mangrove and Malaysian Jungle-flycatchers.

Meratus Jungle-flycatcher *Cyornis* sp. E

Undescribed species known only from Meratus Mts, SE Kalimantan. Monotypic. Relative of Dayak Jungle-flycatcher but exhibits deep mtDNA divergence and plumage differences. Fairly common in hill forest, 900–1300 m. Singly or pairs; in undergrowth and shaded lower and mid-storey. **ID** Large. **M** Deep-blue head and upperparts; slightly brighter, glossier forehead; pale orange throat, breast and flanks with white belly; pink legs. **F** greyish-brown head with pale narrow spectacles; grey-brown upperparts; orange breast with slightly paler orange throat, white belly. **Imm** undescribed. **Voc** Song: series of 3–7 glissading, prolonged, deliberate notes, occasionally with high-pitched final note, lasting 1–2 sec, regularly repeated. Call: (i) low-pitched, hollow "teow"; (ii) high-pitched "sit-sit". **SS** Male Bornean Jungle-flycatcher is brighter, more brilliant blue on upperparts, with distinct iridescence on head and rump; fem Bornean has a brighter rufous tail and a warmer-brown head lacking spectacled appearance. Sunda Jungle-flycatcher has a larger bill, male with blackish (not orange) chin; fem Sunda has unique bluish tail, browner head and lacks spectacles. Smaller, shorter-tailed Dayak Jungle-flycatcher has deeper orange underparts reaching vent in both sexes (versus white belly and vent in Meratus). Male Mangrove Jungle-flycatcher (from more coastal habitat) has black (not orange) chin and shows some orange on vent. Much smaller, shorter-billed female Mugimaki and Rufous-chested Flycatchers usually show 1-2 pale wingbars (absent in Meratus, but especially strong in Mugimaki), with Rufous-chested's upperparts warmer brown and orange restricted to breast (not extending down flanks). Also see Malaysian Jungle-flycatcher.

Sunda Jungle-flycatcher *Cyornis caerulatus* E

L 14 cm. 3 ssp: *albiventer* (Sum); *rufifrons* (W Bor); *caerulatus* (N–E–S Bor). Uncommon in lowland mixed dipterocarp forest, avoiding riverine habitat where Malaysian Jungle-flycatcher takes over, <500 m. Usually in pairs, sallying from low perches. **ID** Sturdy and wide bill. **M** deep-blue upperparts with black face and chin and brighter blue forehead, lower back and rump; buff throat; orange breast fading on belly towards white vent. **F** brown upperparts; blue lower back to tail; buff underparts with more orange breast; whitish belly to vent. Ssp *rufirons* **M** deeper orange-rufous underparts, **F** bluer scapulars and wing-coverts. Ssp *albiventer* as nominate but **M** whiter on lower belly, **F** lower belly to vent tinged buff, and upperparts tinged more blue. **Imm** undescribed. **Voc** Song: 2–3 phrases of thin metallic, rising-and-falling, mournful notes, "se-se-teeuuuw", resembling Grey-chested Jungle-flycatcher but lower-pitched and without introductory "zeet". **SS** Female's blue tail in combination with brown crown and back is unique in region. Male Mangrove Jungle-flycatcher extremely similar, but – in the region – always shows some buff/orange on vent (white in Sunda); also Mangrove is less iridescent on upperparts, less sturdy-billed and has a slightly less pronounced black chin. Male Bornean Jungle-flycatcher has brighter blue upperparts with some iridescence from crown through rump, and has orange (not black) chin. Male Indochinese Jungle-flycatcher doubtfully overlaps in N Sum, lacks Sunda's sturdy bill and black chin, and has whiter belly with straight dividing line to orange breast. See also Meratus, Dayak and Malaysian Jungle-flycatchers. **AN** Large-billed Blue-flycatcher.

Malaysian Jungle-flycatcher *Cyornis turcosus*

L 13–14 cm. Sundaic. 2 ssp: *rupatensis* (Sum, W Bor, MPen); *turcosus* (E Bor). Fairly common, especially in riverine habitat in lowland forest, bamboo, abandoned plantations, <500 m, locally to 1000 m. **ID M** deep bright-blue upperparts and throat; shining blue rump; pale-orange breast; white belly. Ssp *rupatensis* deeper coloured, more orange-rufous breast and flanks. **F** paler blue above; whitish-buff throat; more intense buff upper breast, rest of underparts white. **Imm** sooty brown upperparts with dense orange-buff spots, barred or scaled dark-brown; buff chin to breast. **Voc** Song: soft, weak, variable series of 5–6 whistled melodious phrases "diddle diddle dee diddle dee". Call: (i) hard "tk-tk-tk…"; (ii) harsh grating "chrrk". **SS** Male told from all overlapping blue jungle-flycatchers by combination of blue throat and orange breast. Fem recalls males of other species and should be identified with care: her throat and breast are less bright, with paler throat contrasting with deeper-buff breast (versus bright-orange throat and breast in Dayak, Indochinese, Meratus and Mangrove, or versus black chin and much sturdier-billed appearance in Sunda, or versus deeper orange breast and brighter, more electric-blue upperparts in Bornean).

Bornean Jungle-flycatcher *Cyornis superbus* E

L 15 cm. Monotypic. Uncommon in lowland and hill forest, <1600 m, chiefly 200–600 m. Singly or pairs; inconspicuous in lower, sometimes mid-level. **ID M** deep-blue upperparts with more shining electric blue on forehead to nape and lower back to rump; black face; deep-orange underparts, paler on throat and becoming white on lower belly. **F** warm-brown upperparts; bright-rufous rump to tail; orange-buff throat becoming darker on breast and paler to vent. **Imm** undescribed. **Voc** Song: thin, tinkling, high-pitched, quick phrase of 5 notes "wee-TIT-wee-tit-wee", second note highest, fourth lowest, interspersed with 3-note "wee-TIT-wee" phrases. Call: harsh "chrrt chrrt". **SS** See Malaysian, Sunda, Fulvous-chested, Crocker, Meratus and Dayak Jungle-flycatchers. Male Mangrove (usually from more coastal areas) differs in having less electric-blue upperparts and a narrow black chin.

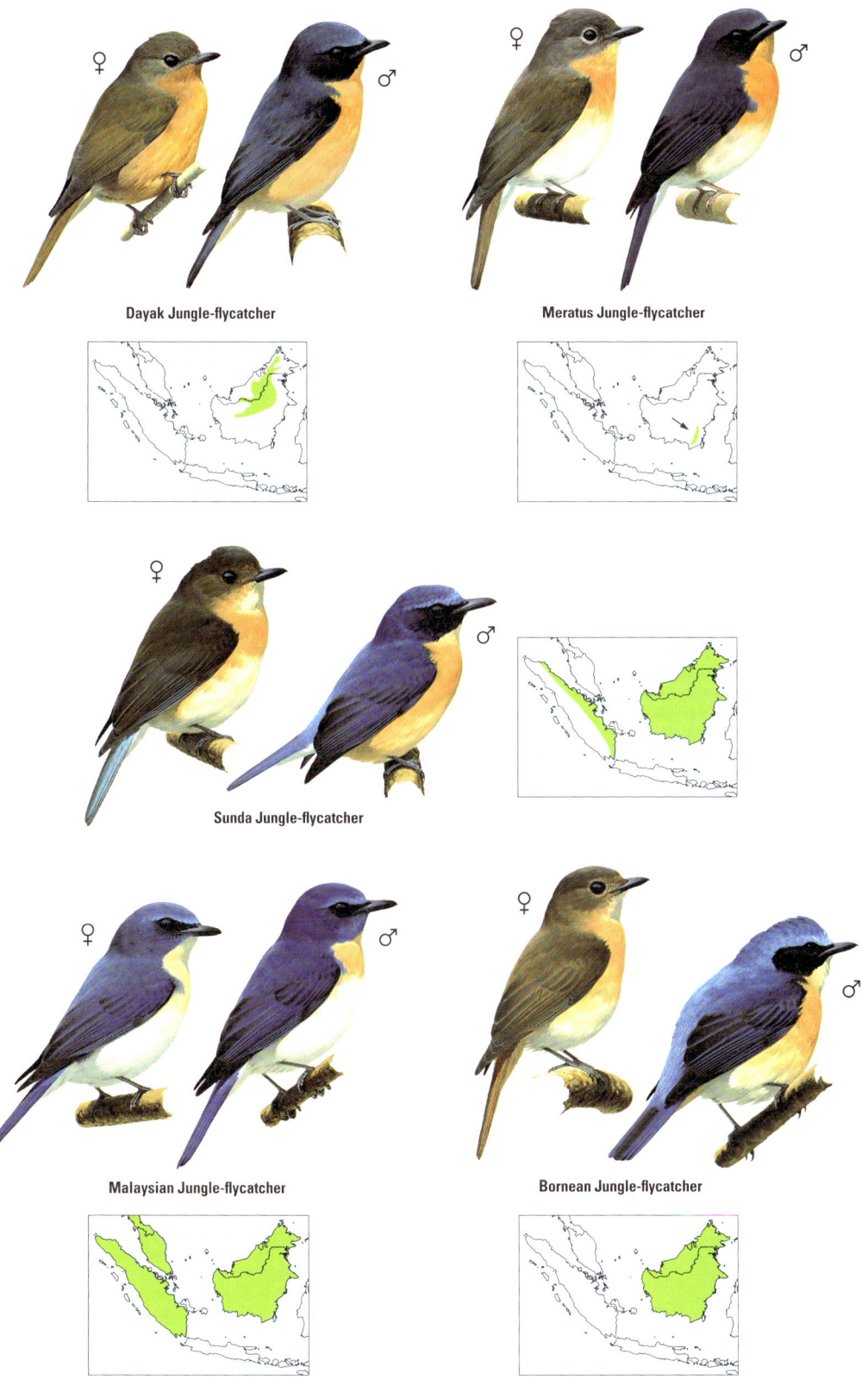

Dayak Jungle-flycatcher

Meratus Jungle-flycatcher

Sunda Jungle-flycatcher

Malaysian Jungle-flycatcher

Bornean Jungle-flycatcher

Indochinese Jungle-flycatcher *Cyornis sumatrensis*
L 14–15 cm. SE Asia. 3 ssp, 2 in region: *sumatrensis* (NE Sum, MPen); *lamprus* (Anambas). Traditionally merged with Tickell's Jungle-flycatcher *C. tickelliae* (S Asia) but differs bioacoustically and in plumage. Replaces Mangrove Jungle-flycatcher on Anambas. Its occurrence on Sum only based on single specimen reportedly from Langkat (coastal N Sum) but possibly mislabelled and from adjacent MPen where the species is common. Open dry woodlands and forest, coastal scrub, villages, bamboo. Forages in lower and mid-levels, often undergrowth of stream banks. **ID M** uniform deep blue upperparts with paler forehead and supercilium; rufous breast with sharply defined white belly. **F** grey-blue upperparts and head; underparts as male. Ssp *lamprus* larger; **M** reportedly some black on chin; **F** paler on breast. **Imm** grey-brown upperparts with buff spots; pale buff-streaked crown; buff underparts with barred and scaled throat and breast; white belly and vent. **Voc** Song: short series of up to 7 descending and then ascending, slightly slurred, metallic trilling notes, "tee-titit-wit-titoo-weee" or "whee-oo-ou-er-oo-ee"; often introduced by thin, high-pitched "seee" and followed by lower-pitched "soo see su'oo soo see see soo". Call: (i) hard "tac" or "kak"; (ii) flowerpecker-like "tik-tik"; (iii) sharp, churring "trrt-trrt". **SS** Mangrove lacks well-demarcated straight dividing line between white belly and rufous breast. See also Sunda and Malaysian Jungle-flycatchers.

Mangrove Jungle-flycatcher *Cyornis rufigastra*
L 14–15 cm. Sundaic, Phil. 8 ssp, 4 in region: *rufigastra* (Sum, Riau Is, Lingga, Bangka, Bor, Maratua, MPen); *longipennis* (Karimunjawa); *rhizophorae* (Jav–Bali); *karimatensis* (Karimata). Traditionally included Sulawesi, Kalao and Tanahjampea Jungle-flycatchers, which differ strongly in plumage, mtDNA and/or vocalisations. Locally common in mangrove forest and associated habitat, oil palm plantations. Singly or pairs; shy, forages close to the ground. **ID M** dark deep-blue upperparts with paler forehead and eyebrow; blue-black face; orange-rufous underparts sometimes slightly paler on throat and belly, but in the region always showing some orange on vent; narrow black to dark-blue chin. **F** like male but distinct whitish lores and chin. Ssp *longipennis* larger, less bright overall in both sexes; *rhizophorae* slightly smaller, brighter overall in both sexes; *karimatensis* larger with darker underparts, and vent nearly as dark as breast. **Imm** dull-brown upperparts with fine buff streaks on crown and nape, bolder on back; pale-buff underparts with dark bars and scaling; unmarked whitish vent. **Voc** Song: high-pitched series of melodious warbling notes, similar to Javan and Indochinese Jungle-flycatchers but slower and deeper. Call: (i) repeated dry "psst"; (ii) sharp staccato "chik-chik-chik..." slowing towards end. **SS** See Javan, Sunda, Meratus, Malaysian, Indochinese and Bornean Jungle-flycatchers. Male quite similar to Dayak Jungle-flycatcher, but has black (not orange) chin, and probably never overlaps elevationally.

Sulawesi Jungle-flycatcher *Cyornis omissus* E
L 14–15 cm. 3 ssp: *omissus* (Sul); *omississimus* (Togian); *per-omissus* (Selayar). Traditionally included Tanahjampea and Kalao Jungle-flycatchers, but all three differ strongly in plumage and/or vocalisations. For taxonomy, also see Mangrove Jungle-flycatcher. Common in hill and lower montane forest, 500–2300 m (Sul), but to coastal lowlands on Selayar and Togian, where it tolerates some habitat degradation. Singly or pairs, sometimes joins mixed flocks in lower forest stages and edge. **ID** Pink legs. **M** dark-blue upperparts; pale-blue supercilium; black chin; almost entirely orange-rufous underparts, deepest on breast and rufous-buff on vent. **F** dull olive-blue upperparts with orange-buff lores, chin and throat. Ssp *peromissus* **M** slightly smaller and paler overall; **F** loral streak slightly more

rufous and extending further back over eye. Ssp *omississimus* more blackish legs; **M** broader and blacker face; narrower orange throat; **F** more extensive rufous lores; rich-blue upperparts lacking olive tones. **Imm** dull-brown upperparts with fine buff streaks on crown and bolder spots on back; pale-buff underparts with dark bars on throat, scaling on breast and belly, but plain whitish vent. **Voc** Song: melodious warble of 4–6 notes, often descending, occasionally level or ascending, but mostly preceded and followed by a high-pitched sharp note, such as "tsssee jay-jer-dew-joo-joo psss"; repeated with little variation at 3–5 sec intervals, lasting 1.3 sec. Ssp *omississimus* similar but usually only has high-pitched introductory note (none at the end), and the main melodious warble is usually composed of 3–5 notes, frequently ending with a harsh jumble, such as "tsrreeet dew-dew-joojoor-whichrrew".Call: 2 dry "psst" notes. **SS** See Rufous-throated Flycatcher.

Tanahjampea Jungle-flycatcher *Cyornis djampeanus* E
L 14–15 cm. Monotypic. For taxonomy see Mangrove and Sulawesi Jungle-flycatchers. Fairly common in remnant forest patches, edge, tall scrub. Pairs, inconspicuous unless singing, tame. **ID M** as Sulawesi Jungle-flycatcher but larger bill with black malar and ear-coverts, white centre of throat. **F** orange throat. **Imm** undescribed. **Voc** Song: starting with shrill high-pitched single or double note, followed by 3–4 descending and ascending mellow notes, roughly "tsitt chew-you-werr". Call: sharp scolding.

Kalao Jungle-flycatcher *Cyornis kalaoensis* E
L 14–15 cm. Monotypic. For taxonomy see Mangrove and Sulawesi Jungle-flycatchers. Fairly common in remnant forest patches, edge, tall scrub. Pairs, inconspicuous unless singing. **ID M** white throat and breast with variable dark mottling; orange restricted to belly. **F** black chin, white throat centre. **Imm** undescribed. **Voc** Song: typical *Cyornis* song but each strophe lacks structure, constantly changing in pitch and frequency between each deliberate note, including both sombre and high-pitched notes, lasting <1 s.

Sula Jungle-flycatcher *Cyornis colonus* E
L 14 cm. Monotypic. Traditionally included Banggai Jungle-flycatcher but the two are deeply diverged genomically and vocally. These two species appear to be brownish replacements of Sulawesi Jungle-flycatcher on Sula and Banggai. Alleged ssp *subsolanus* (E Sul) only known from one lost specimen; but given the occurrence of Sulawesi Jungle-flycatcher in E Sul, this specimen was possibly mislabelled and referable to Sula or Banggai. Fairly common in primary and degraded forest, bamboo, <300 m. Singly or pairs; inconspicuous. **ID M** olive-brown upperparts with warmer brown rump and rufous tail; dirty grey-buff underparts; white throat; white centre of belly; rufous-buff vent. **F** darker grey-buff underparts. Alleged ssp *subsolanus* reported to be browner (less olive) on back and fringes to flight feathers, especially brighter reddish-brown on base of tail. **Imm** paler olive; heavily spotted buff on upperparts. **Voc** Song: soft series of 5-15 tinkling, descending, high-pitched notes "si'si'se'se'see...", lasting <1.5 s, at 3–7 kHz, interspersed with hard "teck" notes.

Banggai Jungle-flycatcher *Cyornis pelingensis* E
L 14 cm. Monotypic. For taxonomy see Sula Jungle-flycatcher. Fairly common in primary and degraded forest. Singly or pairs, occasionally small groups; inconspicuous, preferring dark areas of forest, frequents all levels up to sub-canopy. **ID M** similar to Sula, but paler or more olive (less brown) upperparts; more contrasting pattern on underparts with almost pure white lower throat and deeper buff breast, more sharply delineated from whiter mid-belly. **Voc** Song: series of 4-8 descending, medium-pitched notes with occasional rising notes, lasting <1 s, usually 2–5 kHz, rarely interspersed with "tk" notes.

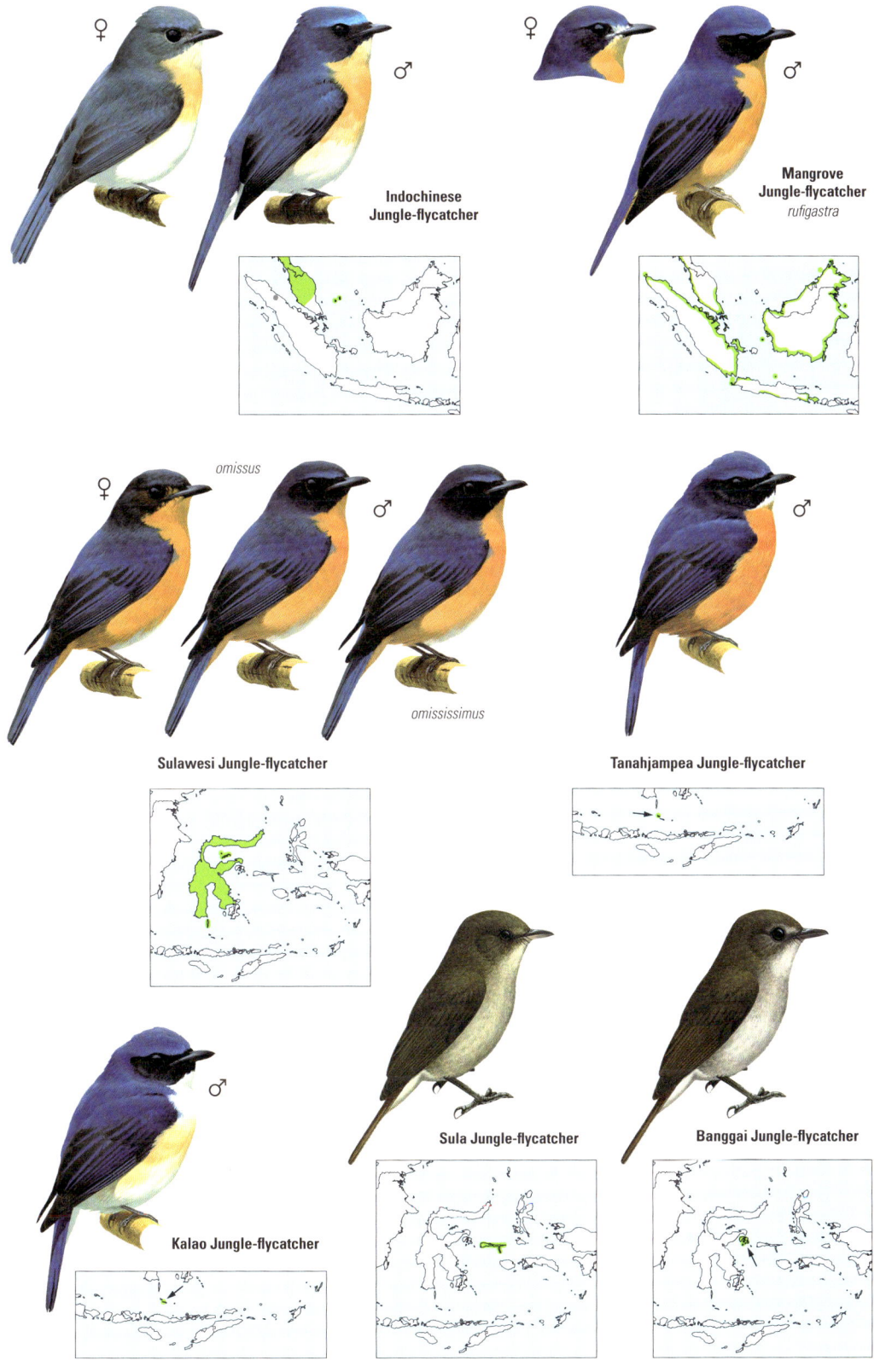

♀

♂

Indochinese Jungle-flycatcher

♀

♂

Mangrove Jungle-flycatcher
rufigastra

omissus

♀

♂

♂

omississimus

Sulawesi Jungle-flycatcher

Tanahjampea Jungle-flycatcher

♂

Kalao Jungle-flycatcher

Sula Jungle-flycatcher

Banggai Jungle-flycatcher

Rück's Jungle-flycatcher *Cyornis ruckii* **E**

L 17 cm. Monotypic. Enigmatic. Known only from two specimens of unknown provenance from trading port of Melaka (MPen, ~1880) and another two (collected 1917–1918) from two localities near Medan (N Sum) in forest, <200 m. **ID M** deep-blue overall (only lower belly grey) with pale-blue supercilium; blackish face; rump brighter electric blue; large black bill. **F** warm-brown upperparts with rich rufous rump to tail; rich rufous breast, paler belly and white vent. **Imm M** as F but upperparts bluish tinged with blue tail. **Imm F** undescribed. **Voc** Unknown. **SS** Male resembles White-tailed Flycatcher but lacks extensive white belly (has grey lower belly at most) and lacks white in tail, has darker throat and brighter blue rump. Male Pale Blue more uniformly pale-blue than Rück's, especially on throat, usually with extensive pale grey belly, longer tail and smaller bill. Indigo Warbling-flycatcher considerably smaller with white belly, black loral area (absent in Rück's) and shorter bill. Fem Rück's warmer brown on upperparts, especially tail and rump, and warmer rufous on breast than any overlapping jungle-flycatcher and lacks the white lower throat mark of White-tailed. See also Zappey's.

Pale Blue Jungle-flycatcher *Cyornis unicolor*

L 17 cm. Himalaya to SE Asia. 3 ssp, 1 in region: *cyanopolia* (Sum, Jav, Bor, MPen). Fairly common to scarce in forest, mostly hillier elevations, <1400 m. Singly or pairs; mid- to upper canopy, occasionally lower, perching inconspicuously. **ID M** bright cobalt-blue upperparts with paler forehead and eyebrow; darker-blue lores; paler blue underparts usually separated from pale grey belly by fairly straight divide. **F** grey-brown upperparts; rufous-brown tail and rump; indistinct pale eye ring (especially below eye); pale buff-grey underparts, paler on mid-belly; buff vent. **Imm** olive-brown upperparts with buff spots; buff underparts with dense dark-brown scales and barring, whiter on flanks and vent. **Voc** Song: descending, high-pitched, mournful "chee, choochichoo-choochichoo-choochee", starts hesitantly, accelerating and rising up scale, often ends with harsh "chizz", lasting 1.5–2 sec. Call: soft, rolling trill "tr-r-r-r". **SS** More horizontal stance than warbling-flycatchers: Indigo has distinct black mask (absent in Pale Blue) and – in Sum/Bor – a buff (not greyish) vent. Smaller-billed female/imm Verditer difficult to differentiate from male Pale Blue, but (1) more torquoise (less cobalt) overall, including on belly (lacking Pale Blue's straight divide to grey belly), (2) has scaled vent (plain in Pale Blue), (3) never shows Pale Blue's contrasting iridescent *Cyornis* eyebrow, and (4) often perches prominently. Fem Pale Blue confusing on her own, can be misidentified with multiple other drab or fem jungle-flycatchers, but is much drabber and greyer overall, lacks intense warm colours or breast band on underparts; shorter-billed fem Blue-and-white and Zappey's Flycatchers show some brown mottling on breast (versus uniform buff-grey underparts in Pale Blue), and their crown and mantle are more brown (lacking Pale Blue's grey tinge). See also Rück's, Fulvous-chested and Crocker Jungle-flycatchers and White-tailed Flycatcher.

White-tailed Flycatcher *Cyornis concretus*

L 18–19 cm. SE Asia. 3 ssp, 2 in region: *concretus* (Sum, MPen); *everetti* (Bor). Aberrant, genetically unique species traditionally classified as a *Cyornis* but in need of its own genus. More research into internal taxonomy needed as extralimital ssp *cyaneus* (northern SE Asia) may differ vocally. Uncommon to scarce in forest, <1700 m, but mostly 600–1200 m. Singly or pairs; in lower storey, particularly in dark gulleys, elusive. **ID M** uniform blue body with blackish face and contrasting white belly; broad white longitudinal lines on outer tail feathers, visible with tail spread; pinkish legs. **F** rather uniform warm-brown with rich-brown face; indistinct rufous-buff eyering; brilliant white lower throat patch, dull olive-brown breast; white to light-grey belly to vent; chestnut tail with white in outer feathers. Ssp *everetti* slightly smaller and duller; **M** lacks white in tail; **F** some white on inner webs of tail feathers. **Imm** brown upperparts spotted rufous; barring on breast and flanks. **Voc** Song: variable series of penetrating, sibilant, thrush-like whistles, may include short series of descending notes, and several slightly rising and some falling or slurred notes: "weEe-keekTIT-wewewe-weEekik TIT..." or "teeeTEEEwewewewewe", includes much mimicry; also short series of level, clear piping notes. Call: (i) soft "pewee"; (ii) harsh "scree". **SS** Male Zappey's and Blue-and-white have white belly extending further up breast, more clearly demarcated, brighter blue upperparts, blunt-tipped (not hooked) bill and grey (not pink) feet. Indigo Warbling-flycatcher also lacks white in tail, is smaller and has buffier vent. Male Pale Blue has greyer (not white) belly, less blackish face, lacks white in tail. Fem White-tailed's brilliant white throat spot recalls that of fem Sumatran Niltava from higher elevations, but latter has grey underparts and crown contrasting with rich-brown face (White-tailed lacks grey tones). See also Rück's Jungle-flycatcher.

Blue-and-white Flycatcher *Cyanoptila cyanomelana*

L 16–17 cm. Breeds E–NE Asia; winters to Phil, GS. 2 ssp: *cyanomelana* (breeds Japan, Kurils; winters to Phil and GS), *intermedia* (breeds NE Asia; winters to Phil and GS). For taxonomy see Zappey's. Widespread visitor, fairly common N Bor, mainly in upper hill and montane forest, <1000 m (Jav) and <1850 m (Bor). **ID M** deep cobalt-blue upperparts; glossy-black head sides, throat and breast sharply delimited from white belly and white patch on base of outer-tail feathers; *intermedia* has matte black throat and breast, upperparts more verditer-blue. **F** solid brown upperparts; indistinct white eyering; rufous-brown on wings, rump and tail; white underparts with faint to strong brown flammulations on breast and throat sides, but throat usually white. **Imm** with variable buff spotting on head and face; **M** has bluish wings, lower back and tail. **Voc** Call: (i) harsh "tchuk tchuk tchuk..."; (ii) soft "tic" and "tac" notes. **SS** See White-tailed, Narcissus and Zappey's Flycatchers. Fem Blue-and-white can be confused with several drab or fem jungle-flycatchers (for comparison see especially Pale Blue and Crocker Jungle-flycatchers), but is generally larger, exceptionally drab, lacks any strong rufous colours or distinctly delimited breast band on underparts.

Zappey's Flycatcher *Cyanoptila cumatilis*

L 16–17 cm. Breeds E Asia; winters MPen, Sum and Jav. Monotypic. Traditionally considered conspecific with Blue-and-white Flycatcher but exhibits considerable vocal, plumage and genomic differences. Scarce to rare winter visitor, perhaps more widespread (including Jav) but former taxonomic confusion has led to widespread mixing of records with Blue-and-white. **ID M** verditer-blue upperparts with bright cobalt forehead, crown and shoulders; dark verditer-blue face to breast separated by a blackish line from white belly and vent. **F/Imm** as Blue-and-white, presently not safely separable, reportedly slightly less white on throat though further study required. **Voc** Call: harsh "tchuk tchuk tchuk...". **SS** Male Blue-and-white has black (not blue) breast, lacking contrasting black line along base of breast, and darker blue upperparts. Fem Zappey's on current knowledge not safely separable from Blue-and-white. Male has much cleaner dividing line between blue breast and white belly than the smaller, darker and more superciliaried Rück's Jungle-flycatcher and Indigo Warbling-flycatcher (the latter additionally has buff vent in Bor and Sum). Fem Zappey's can be confused with multiple drab or fem jungle-flycatchers (for comparison see especially Pale Blue and Crocker Jungle-flycatchers), but is generally larger, exceptionally drab, lacks any strong rufous colours or distinctly delimited breast band on underparts. See also Narcissus and White-tailed Flycatchers.

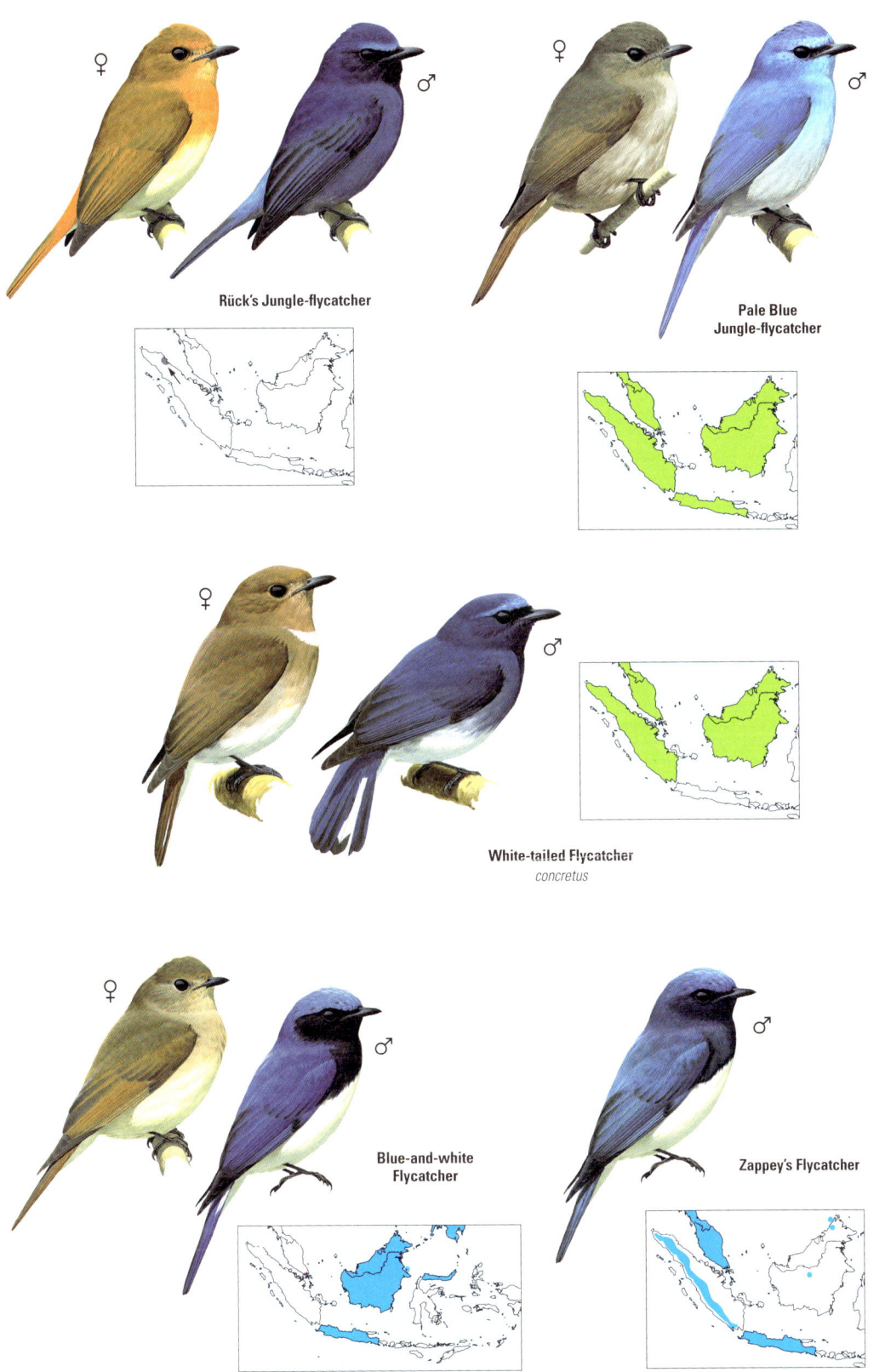

♀ ♂ **Rück's Jungle-flycatcher**

♀ ♂ **Pale Blue Jungle-flycatcher**

♀ ♂ **White-tailed Flycatcher**
concretus

♀ ♂ **Blue-and-white Flycatcher**

♂ **Zappey's Flycatcher**

Sumatran Niltava *Niltava sumatrana*

L 15 cm. Sundaic. Monotypic. Locally common in montane forest, 1000–3400 m. Singly or pairs, joins mixed flocks; in mid- and upper canopy, also in dense undergrowth, inconspicuous. **ID M** dark indigo-blue upperparts with bright iridescent crown, neck side, shoulder patches and rump; blue-black face and throat; black tail; entirely bright-orange underparts. **F** warm olive-brown upperparts with greyer crown; chestnut-brown rump and tail; pale buff-brown face and throat; white gorget; breast and belly grey becoming white lower down and orange-rufous on vent. **Imm** rusty buff spots on upperparts; black bars and scaling on underparts. **Voc** Song: (i) monotonous series of undulating clear whistles similar to Verditer Warbling-flycatcher; (ii) rapid series of up- and downslurred scratchy notes. Call: hard "chik". **SS** See White-tailed Flycatcher. **AN** Rufous-vented Niltava.

Large Niltava *Niltava grandis*

L 20–22 cm. Himalaya to SE Asia. 4 ssp, 1 in region: *decipiens* (Sum, MPen). May not include extralimital ssp *decorata* (S Vietnam; monotypic '**Dalat Niltava**') because of strong vocal differences. Fairly common in hill and montane forest, 900–1500 m, locally to 2500 m. Singly or pairs; sluggish, in undergrowth to mid-level. **ID M** entirely blackish-blue with brighter parts on crown, neck side, wing-coverts and rump; black face, wings and tail; purple-blue underparts. **F** warm olive-brown upperparts; slaty blue crown to nape; rufous edges to upperwing-coverts, flight-feathers, rump and tail; small pale blue patch on neck side; dull olive-brown underparts. **Imm** deep rufous-brown upperparts with pale buff spotting; deep rufous-brown underparts with darker bars and scalloping. **Voc** Song: simple sequence of 3 or 4 soft, rising, melancholy whistles, repeated slowly and at intervals, "oo-oo-dwee-dee" or "do ray-ray me". Call: (i) soft, unobtrusive "chu-ee", second note higher; (ii) alarm note "trr'k trr'k trr'k..."; (iii) harsh rattle.

Indigo Warbling-flycatcher *Eumyias indigo*   **E**

L 14 cm. 3 ssp: *indigo* (Jav); *ruficrissa* (Sum); *cerviniventris* (Bor). Ssp *ruficrissa* and *cerviniventris* sometimes split as '**Rufous-vented Flycatcher**' *E. ruficrissa* based on plumage, but vocal and genomic evidence required. Generally common in montane forest, 900–3000 m. Singly or pairs, joins mixed flocks; tame, often forages low in undergrowth, but also low to mid-canopy. **ID M** indigo-blue upperparts; pale blue on forehead and supercilium; black lores and chin; pale azure-blue throat; deep indigo-blue breast contrasting with whitish belly to vent. **F** less black on face. Ssp *cerviniventris* much darker blue body, brighter azure-blue on forehead to beyond eyes, rump tipped whitish-buff, belly and vent extensively warm fawn; *ruficrissa* slightly darker blue than *cerviniventris*, more extensively white at tail base, underparts as nominate but deep rufous vent. **Imm** dull blue; finely barred and buff-spotted upperparts; chin to belly buff-spotted and dark-fringed; vent white to pale-rufous. **Voc** Song: long, squeaky and ringing rambling series: "fee-fo-foo-fee-fee-fee..." or "chit chwit choo, wee toooo...". Ssp *ruficrissa* significantly shorter strophes, less monotonous series of notes. Call: (i) harsh rattling "turrr tur"; (ii) "tzit-tzit-tzit..." alarm. **SS** See White-tailed and Zappey's Flycatchers; also see Pale Blue and Rück's Jungle-flycatchers. Verditer Warbling-flycatcher lacks white belly and has more turquoise (less blue) body.

Verditer Warbling-flycatcher *Eumyias thalassinus*

L 15–17 cm. S–SE–E Asia. 2 ssp, 1 in region: *thalassoides* (Sum, Bor, MPen). Fairly common to scarce in open lowland and lower montane forest, edge, <1400 m. Singly or pairs; forages from open, fairly high perches, particularly treetops. **ID M** entirely green-blue to verditer-blue; black lores; brighter blue upperwing and tail; pale-scaled vent. **F** slightly duller and paler with grey lores; finely barred chin and upper throat. **Imm** dull turquoise, heavily speckled and spotted with pale to orange-buff. **Voc** Song from high perch: (i) prolonged series of strident, rapid, undulating notes starting hesitantly and ending abruptly, repeated at intervals; (ii) a soft jingling trill. Call: (i) short plaintive "pseeut"; (ii) longer and drier "tze-joo-jwee". **SS** See Pale Blue Jungle-flycatcher and Indigo Warbling-flycatcher.

Turquoise Warbling-flycatcher *Eumyias panayensis*

L 14 cm. Phil, Wallacea. 7 ssp, 4 in region: *septentrionalis* (N–C–SE Sul; Sula); *meridionalis* (SW Sul); *obiensis* (Obi, presumably this on Morotai); *harterti* (Seram). Extralimital Phil races were, for a long time, treated as different species based on plumage, leaving the four regional taxa as '**Wallacean Warbling-flycatcher**' *E. septentrionalis*, a treatment suggested as likely by vocal data. Locally moderately common in montane forest, regionally at lower elevations, 850–2400 m (Sul), but almost to sea level on Taliabu and >250 m on Obi and Seram. Singly or pairs, joins mixed flocks; mainly in canopy and mid-storey. **ID M** dull turquoise upperparts and throat; black lores; blue-grey breast becoming white on belly and vent. Ssp *meridionalis* largest race, throat and breast duller dark-blue; *obiensis* more azure-blue and less green-tinged plumage, belly pale-blue washed; *harterti* similar as previous but brighter blue with slight green tinge, especially on forehead, throat and edges of flight feathers, and whiter belly. **F** no black lores; duller blue forehead (to above eyes) and upper throat. **Imm** dark brown; white to golden-buff spotted on upperparts, throat and breast; blue wings and tail. **Voc** Song: (i) clear but rapid and fairly monotonous warbling series of up to 20 notes becoming more liquid in tone towards end, with much individual variation; (ii) rich medley of 5–6 notes. Call: soft wheezy whistle, repeated frequently, "swuu swee zeee swuu swee zeee swuu swee zeee...". **AN** Island Verditer Flycatcher.

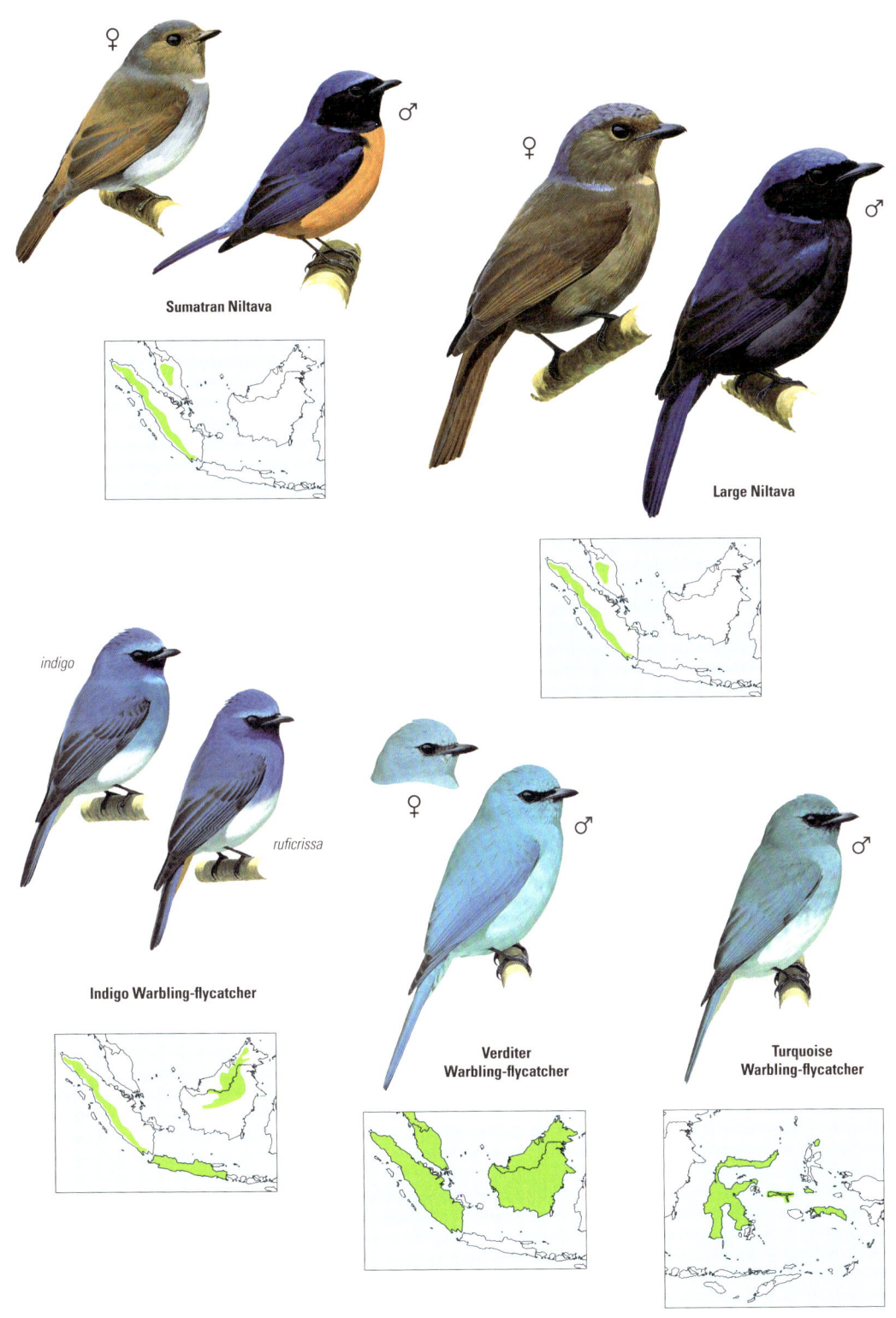

Sumatran Niltava

Large Niltava

indigo

ruficrissa

Indigo Warbling-flycatcher

**Verditer
Warbling-flycatcher**

**Turquoise
Warbling-flycatcher**

Hoevell's Warbling-flycatcher *Eumyias hoevelli* **E**
L 15 cm. Monotypic. Locally common in upper montane forest, 1400–2300 m. Singly or pairs, joins mixed flocks. **ID M** deep blue hood and breast with brighter shiny-blue forehead and eyebrow; olive-brown upperparts; deep orange belly to vent. **F** blue hood replaced by grey brown head; throat and upper breast pale greyish-buff. **Imm** buff spots on upperparts; blackish bars and scaling on underparts. **Voc** Song: (i) short, soft note followed by loud, rich series of up to 20 thrush-like notes, varying little in pitch; also shorter version of up to 5 discordant notes; (ii) loud "tsat-tsat-tsat…". Call undescribed. **AN** Blue-fronted Warbling-flycatcher/Blue-flycatcher.

Timor Warbling-flycatcher *Eumyias hyacinthinus* **E**
L 16 cm. 2 ssp: *hyacinthinus* (Timor, Semau, Rote); *kuehni* (Wetar). Fairly common in remnant monsoon forest, woodland, edge and plantations. Singly; inconspicuous in mid-storey and canopy, often close to tree trunks. **ID M** dark-blue upperparts, head and breast with brighter forehead and eyebrow; mainly black face; rufous belly. Ssp *kuehni* paler blue on head and more extensively blue on throat to breast; darker rufous on belly. **F** olive-brown upperparts; pale-blue rump and tail; rufous-orange underparts. Ssp *kuehni* more grey-brown head and upperparts (perhaps washed bluish with age); forehead and lores rufous; underparts deeper rufous. **Imm** undescribed. **Voc** Song: (i) shrill and monotonous rapid series of babbled rising-and-falling notes, lasting >30 sec; (ii) frequent subdued bubbling bulbul-like phrase. Call undescribed.

Buru Warbling-flycatcher *Eumyias additus* **E**
L 15 cm. Monotypic. Fairly common in montane forest, >500 m. Mainly in canopy and mid-storey. **ID Ad** short, flat and broad bill; dark rufous-brown upperparts with brighter rufous wings and tail, greyer head; white throat and breast with vague grey streaking; white belly to vent. **Imm** undescribed. **Voc** Song: warbling series of 20–25 alternating monosyllabic and bisyllabic fluty notes, lasting ~8 sec, rapidly repeated. **AN** Streak-breasted Jungle-flycatcher.

Flores Warbling-flycatcher *Eumyias oscillans* **E**
L 14 cm. Monotypic. Previously merged with Sumba War-bling-flycatcher into a more broadly defined '**Russet-backed Warbling-flycatcher**' *E. oscillans* (or erroneously 'Russet-backed Jungle-flycatcher' *Rhinomyias oscillans*) but vocal and plumage dif-ferences dictate break-up. Uncommon in montane forest, >1000 m, recorded down to 370 m. Singly or pairs, joins mixed flocks; skulking, quiet, in mid-storey. Easily overlooked unless singing. **ID Ad** short, blunt-tipped bill; rufous-brown upperparts with brighter rufous wings and tail, greyer head; grey underparts becoming white on belly; buff vent. **Imm** undescribed. **Voc** Song: monotonous, rapid series of jumbling, rising and falling notes, "titi'wirti'teeweertiti'titi'wirti' teeweertitit…" lasting 1–30 min. Call: harsh "tak" or "chek".

Sumba Warbling-flycatcher *Eumyias stresemanni* **E**
L 15 cm. Monotypic. For taxonomy see Flores Warbling-flycatcher. Fairly common in forest. Singly or with mixed flocks; skulking, quiet. Easily overlooked, in understorey to mid-storey but not so much in canopy when associating with mixed flocks. **ID Ad** similar to Flores but larger, longer-billed and steeper forehead; brighter rufous upperparts; buff-grey breast and sides of throat, white centre of throat; white vent. **Imm** undescribed. **Voc** Song: thrush-like quality, "toowit'toowee'toowit toowit'toowee'toowit…", in series lasting <10 sec, constantly repeated after short intervals. Call: harsh "tak" or "chek". **SS** Sumba Flycatcher is smaller, has warmer rufous-brown upperparts, whiter underparts with rufous breast sides and prefers darker forest understorey. See also Sumba Brown Flycatcher.

Matinan Warbling-flycatcher *Eumyias sanfordi* **E**
L 15 cm. Monotypic. Uncommon, local. Primary montane forest, replacing Hoevell's Warbling-flycatcher in N Sul, 1300–1780 m. Singly or pairs, joins mixed flocks; inconspicuous in undergrowth and mid-storey. **ID Ad** upperparts grey-brown, greyer crown; pale upper lores; rufous-olive rump and tail; pale brown-grey underparts with buff vent. **Imm** undescribed. **Voc** Song: series of rapid, thin and clear or subdued notes, varying in pitch, lasting ~9 sec. May give slower version with each note emphasized. Can sing repeatedly from same perch for <30 min. Call undescribed. **SS** Sulphur-bellied Whistler has brighter yellowish belly, distinct contrast between upper- and underparts.

Bornean Shade-dweller *Vauriella gularis* **E**
L 15 cm. 2 ssp: *gularis* (Sabah); *kamlae* (at least E Sarawak). Along with extralimital Philippine species, formerly associated with jungle-flycatchers (this species long called '**Eyebrowed Jungle-flycatcher**' *Rhinomyias gularis*), but now known to be more closely related to Heinrichia. Locally fairly common in montane forest, 1500–2100 m, recorded to 915–3290 m. Singly or pairs, joins mixed flocks; in understorey and on ground, tame and inquisitive. **ID Ad** rufous brown upperparts; white throat, lores and short white eyebrow; white underparts with grey breast. Ssp *kamlae* larger (may also differ in minor plumage traits). **Imm** buff-spotted upperparts with pale streaking on crown and nape. **Voc** Song: introductory high-pitched quivering note followed by 1–3 high-pitched short notes and staccato, lower-pitched "trt'trt'trt…", repeated 1–4 times in short bouts, series lasting 2–5 sec. Call: rattling "trrrrrt" in repeated short bouts. **AN** Eyebrowed Jungle-flycatcher.

♀

♂

Hoevell's
Warbling-flycatcher

kuehni ♀

hyacinthinus ♀

♂

Timor
Warbling-flycatcher

Buru Warbling-flycatcher

Flores Warbling-flycatcher

Sumba Warbling-flycatcher

Bornean Shade-dweller

Matinan Warbling-flycatcher

Heinrichia *Heinrichia calligyna* E

L 17–18 cm. >3 ssp: *calligyna* (C Sul); *simplex* (N Sul); *picta* (SE Sul). Additional unnamed populations from E Sul and possibly elsewhere. Formerly thought closely related to shortwings and usually called '**Great Shortwing**' but now known to be more closely related to Bornean Shade-dweller and extralimital Phil robins. The only well-known population in modern times, from Lore Lindu National Park (NC Sul), is for now treated as *calligyna* because females look similar in the field to specimens from SC Sul. Radical differences in fem plumage indicate likely presence of at least three monotypic species, including all three named taxa ('**Minahasa Heinrichia**' *H. simplex*, '**Latimojong Heinrichia**' *H. calligyna*, '**Mekongga Heinrichia**' *H. picta*) and additional unnamed populations, pending future bioacoustic and genetic work. Widespread and generally uncommon, more numerous at upper end of altitudinal range, 1500–3500 m. Strictly terrestrial, shy, in dense undergrowth. **ID M** deep dark-blue overall; vent rusty-brown; black lores; white base to tail feathers. **F** rusty rump; white lores; chestnut-brown throat, ear-coverts and vent; NC Sul birds show chestnut lower belly. Ssp *picta* larger, **M** base to tail feathers rufous, vent dark-blue, **F** throat to upper belly deep rufous-chestnut, belly slaty-blue; *simplex* smaller, **M** dark-blue vent, **F** mainly dark olive-brown overall, rustier on chin and throat, more olive on breast, ashy grey mid-belly. **Imm** dark brown-blue upperparts; dark brown throat with paler streaking; blue-brown breast; greyish-brown belly; dark rufous-brown on lower belly to vent. **Voc** Song: *calligyna* typically slow and strong, thrush-like, incorporating 3 melancholy, long-drawn, up-slurred and falling, tremulous notes, ending with a single shrill high-pitched note, lasting <1 min; second bird (presumably fem mate) sometimes incorporates muted harsh notes. Call: (i) thin piping; (ii) rapid thrush-like chatter, "tetetet...". Ssp *picta* significantly more variation in mournful, thrush-like notes and strophes, regularly interspersed with thin, high-pitched notes. **AN** Great Shortwing.

Lesser Shortwing *Brachypteryx leucophris*

L 11–13 cm. Himalaya to SE–E Asia. 5 ssp, 1 in region: *leucophris* (Sum–Wetar). Locally common in lower montane forest, 900–1500 m, <1800 m (Sum), <2100 m (Timor). Singly or pairs; secretive but very vocal at times. **ID** Short-tailed and short-winged brown chat. **M** warm dark-brown upperparts; short white eyebrow; paler underparts with white centre to throat and belly, breast mottled white and brown; white vent; pink legs. **F** weaker white eyebrow. **Imm** rufous-streaked upperparts; dark-brown scalloped underparts; no eyebrow. **Voc** Song: short, loud, sweet, high-pitched warble beginning with 1 to several short sibilant notes, then becoming a jumbled flourish with buzzy, rich and musical notes, lasting 2–2.5 sec, later notes typically alternating rapidly in pitch; more metallic than Javan Shortwing's song with shorter introduction. Can produce longer series, lasting <7 sec, especially in E of ssp range (but also given by excited individuals in W). Call: (i) high sibilant, slightly downslurred, short "psweet"; (ii) subdued "tack"; (iii) ringing "turr turr turr...". **SS** Other shortwings have blue-grey in plumage and are larger. Fem Javan and Sumatran Blue Robins have thinner, shorter bills and lack the white eye-brow; Javan is distinctly longer-tailed than Lesser Shortwing, whereas Sumatran has all-brown throat and breast (lacking white). See also Siberian Blue Robin.

Javan Shortwing *Brachypteryx montana* E

L 12 cm. Monotypic. Previously included Sumatran, Bornean, Flores Shortwings and numerous extralimital taxa to form more broadly-defined umbrella species, '**White-browed Shortwing**' *B. montana*. However, striking differentiation in voice and fem plumage is better accounted for by separation into multiple species. Fairly common in montane forest, 950–3000 m. Forages on the ground or on logs, moving very rapidly. **ID M** dull dark greyish-blue upperparts; short white eyebrow; paler grey underparts. **F** smaller eyebrow; rufous posterior body. **Imm** as Lesser Shortwing but more uniformly dark throat and breast, darker legs and longer tail; breast streaked buff. **Voc** Song: (i) **M** starts slowly with several jingle notes, quickens in tempo and volume to plaintive babble, lasting 10–15 sec; (ii) **F** song much shorter, slower, 6 even-spaced notes lasting ~2 sec. Call: (i) "tt-tt-tt..." with wing flicks; (ii) sharp "click" like two pebbles tapped together. **SS** See Lesser Shortwing. Javan Blue Robin is longer-tailed with white frontlet (not only eyebrow).

Sumatran Shortwing *Brachypteryx saturata* E

L 12 cm. Monotypic. For taxonomy see Javan Shortwing. Locally common in montane forest, 1400–3000 m. Singly or pairs; hopping over boulders or logs in dark gullies, not shy, but running with extreme agility when alarmed. **ID M** as Javan but richer colour and darker breast; shorter white eyebrow. **F** generally duller and less dark-blue; mid-breast and belly greyish lavender, much more extensive than **M**. **Imm** sooty blackish-brown with rusty-brown streaking and tips; in **M** mid-throat and mid-breast ashy-grey. **Voc** Song: consisting of 6–7 short, jittery, silvery notes on a descending scale, repeated ~5 times, gradually increasing in tempo and volume, stopping abruptly, with final 2 strophes more jumbled and less structured, lasting 6–9 sec. Call: single sharp "click" like two pebbles tapped together. **SS** See Lesser Shortwing. Sumatran Blue Robin less terrestrial, with white frontlet (not only eyebrow).

Bornean Shortwing *Brachypteryx erythrogyna* E

L 12 cm. Monotypic. For taxonomy see Javan Shortwing. Locally fairly common in montane forest, 900–3600 m. Forages on the ground alongside mossy fallen logs or in leaf litter; usually well-hidden but may venture out between rocks above the tree line. **ID M** dark indigo-blue; black and tail; half-concealed silky white streak from base of forehead extending to above eye. **F** indigo or slaty blue upperparts; lower back reddish-brown; deep chestnut tail; dusky black wing feathers edged with deep chestnut; head and underparts rich chestnut to chestnut-brown. **Imm** undescribed. **Voc** Song: series of loud, fluty, breezy whistles up and down the scale, first part reminiscent of Golden-bellied Gerygone, interspersed with harsh notes, final series of notes of a wider frequency spectrum, lasting 13–15 sec. Call: single sharp "click" like two pebbles tapped together.

Flores Shortwing *Brachypteryx floris* E

L 13 cm. Monotypic. For taxonomy see Javan Shortwing. Uncommon and local in montane forest, >1300 m. Singly or pairs; in dense vegetation just above the ground, elusive. **ID** Longer tail and feet than other shortwing species. **M** dull indigo-blue upperparts; narrow whitish supercilium; dark-brown ashy lores and ear-coverts; throat and mid-belly grey-white, remaining underparts ashy. **F** warm brown upperparts washed rufous on back and rump; darker crown; superciliary line as male; throat and mid-belly white; lower flanks and thighs brown; vent light rufous; chest and sides of belly pale ashy grey. **Imm** undescribed. **Voc** Song: loud, rich, explosive jangle of clear, quick, rising and falling whistles with some scratchy notes, starting and ending abruptly; individually variable, usually produced sporadically, lasting 5–15 sec. Call: loud "tack".

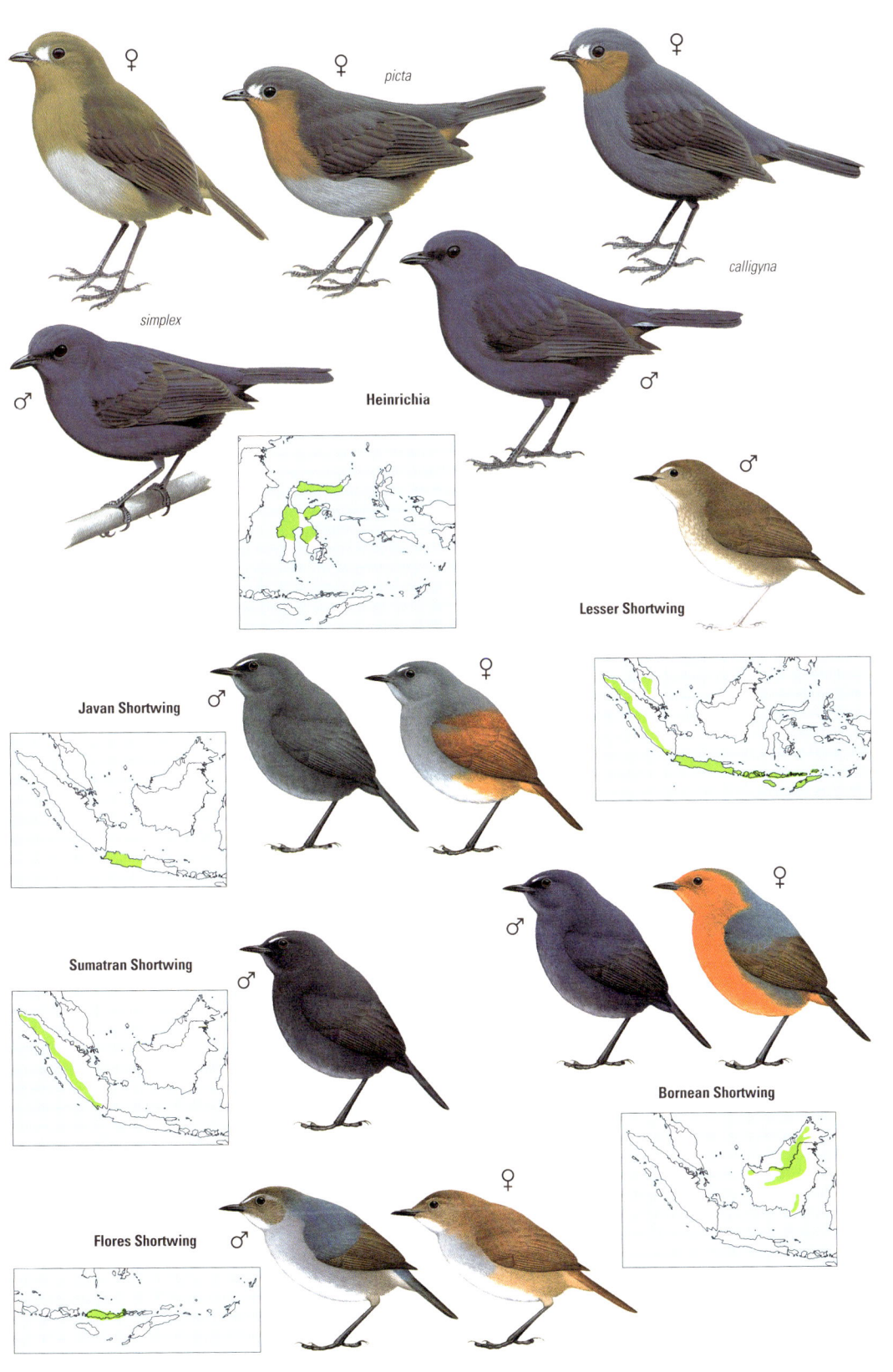

picta

calligyna

simplex

Heinrichia

Lesser Shortwing

Javan Shortwing

Sumatran Shortwing

Bornean Shortwing

Flores Shortwing

Siberian Blue Robin *Larvivora cyane*

L 13–14 cm. Breeds E Palaearctic; winters S to GS. 3 ssp: *cyane* (breeds C Siberia, N Mongolia; winters SE Asia); *bochaiensis* (breeds NE Asia; winters SE Asia); *nechaevi* (breeds Japan, Sakhalin, Kurils; probably winters to Bor). Ssp identity of birds wintering in our region difficult to assess based on clinality of plumage. Widespread winter visitor, single record Jav, to lowland and hill forest, <1700 m. Terrestrial, frequently quivers tail. **ID** Bubble-gum pink legs. **M** slaty-blue upperparts; broad black line running from lores to breast side; white underparts. Spp *bochaiensis* darker above; *nechaevi* larger, more black on neck sides. **F** grey-brown to olive-brown upperparts with blue-washed rump and tail; pale spectacles; buff-white throat to flanks; mottled throat side and breast. **Imm** dark-brown upperparts with rufous flecks; bluish (**M**) or brownish tail (**F**). **Voc** Song unlikely to be heard in region: loud, rapid, explosive trilling. Call: single sharp "tack" like two pebbles tapped together. **SS** Fem/imm told from other terrestrial drab robins and shortwings by pink (not dark) legs and tail-quivering behaviour. From Lesser Shortwing also by longer primary projection and paler plumage. Sumatran and Javan Blue Robins additionally have brighter rufous upperparts, longer tail, and more greyish belly. See also Japanese Robin.

Japanese Robin *Larvivora akahige*   V

L 14–15 cm. Breeds Japanese Archipelago; winters to E China. Monotypic. No longer includes Izu Robin *L. tanensis* (Izu Is.). One record off-shore Sabah (Nov 1978). In forest, forages on ground and low bushes. **ID M** dark red-brown upperparts; rich deep-orange face and neck to upper breast; black breast band fading into grey flanks and whiter lower belly and vent. **F** duller; orange face and throat less intense; mucky grey underparts; lacks black breast band. **Imm** pale flecking on upperparts; rufous-buff underparts with dark spotting on breast. **Voc** Song unlikely to be heard in region: series of simple, well-spaced quavering or trilled phrases. Call: (i) metallic "tsip"; (ii) short chatter. **SS** Fem Siberian Blue has distinctly paler, buffier (not grey-toned) belly and breast; pale spectacles and breast mottling (both absent in Japanese).

Siberian Rubythroat *Calliope calliope*   V

L 14–16 cm. Breeds E–C Palaearctic; winters to S–SE–E Asia, Phil. Monotypic. Recorded in N Bor (1980–1992, 2014, Feb-Mar 2015, Mar 2017). Forages on ground in dense scrub, hedges, long grass, reeds and undergrowth, <1800 m. Often has tail at least half-cocked. **ID M** olive-brown upperparts; red throat; white eyebrow and moustacial stripe; grey-brown underparts with dirty white belly. **F** white throat; supercilium and moustachial stripe sometimes more buff. **Imm** extensively mottled brown and buff. **Voc** Song unlikely to be heard in region: low, rapid warble comprising squeaky, chortling, jangly, silvery, metallic, harsh and a few clear musical notes, with much mimicry. Call: (i) short, harsh, nasal "chet" or "chakh" in mild agitation; (ii) short, musical, downslurred "svee-eek" or "chee-wee"; (iii) harsh "churr" in alarm. **SS** Combination of whitish/buff supercilium and whitish throat and moustachial is unique among robins in region.

Javan Blue Robin *Myiomela diana*   E

L 15 cm. Monotypic. Traditionally united with Sumatran Blue Robin into '**Sunda Blue Robin**' *M. diana*, but vocally and morphologically distinct. Uncommon and local in montane forest, 900–2500 m. Singly or pairs; inconspicuous, always close to ground. **ID M** indigo-blue; silvery-white forehead and spot on neck side; black wings and tail. **F** dull rufous-chestnut upperparts; greyish underparts suffused with chestnut on breast, with ill-defined white throatlet. **Imm** reddish-brown with black spotting. **Voc** Song: simple descending warble of 2–6 sweet melancholy glissading notes lasting 0.5–1 sec. Call: high-pitched whistle. **SS** See Javan and Lesser Shortwings and Siberian Blue Robin.

Sumatran Blue Robin *Myiomela sumatrana*   E

L 15 cm. Monotypic. For taxonomy see Javan Blue Robin. Scarce in montane forest, 1100–1500 m. In pairs among thick undergrowth or fallen timber, never comes to the open. **ID** As Javan Blue Robin but shorter-tailed, with **M** duller, more grey overall, with slightly larger white neck spots and frontal area; **F** darker and purer chestnut upperparts, darker chestnut throat lacks pale throatlet. **Voc** Song: series of 4–10 thin, rather weak, whistled notes on a sharply rising scale, fading out, sounding as Yellow-bellied Warbler but not all notes rising and of same strength, lasting 1.7–2 sec. **SS** See Sumatran and Lesser Shortwings and Siberian Blue Robin.

Siberian Bluetail *Tarsiger cyanurus*   V

L 13–15 cm. Breeds Palaearctic; winters SE–E Asia. Monotypic. Formerly included Himalayan Bluetail *T. rufilatus* (Himalaya, E Asia) and Gansu Bluetail *T. albocoeruleus* (N China), which differ genetically, morphologically and vocally. Single record in coastal lowlands, Sabah (Dec 1960). Winters in forest, edge, orchards and gardens, predominantly uplands. Forages on ground and low bushes, often sallying. **ID** Pinkish-black legs. **M** deep dark-blue upperparts, head and breast side; white chin to vent; rufous flanks. **F/Imm** cold-brown upperparts; buff-white throat; deeper buff breast and flanks; blue tail. **Voc** Call: (i) soft, mournful, upslurred "heed"; (ii) low throaty frog-like "tok-tok-tok..." or "kr-kr-kr...", the two often combined. **SS** See Siberian Blue Robin. **AN** Orange-flanked Bush-robin, Redflanked Bluetail.

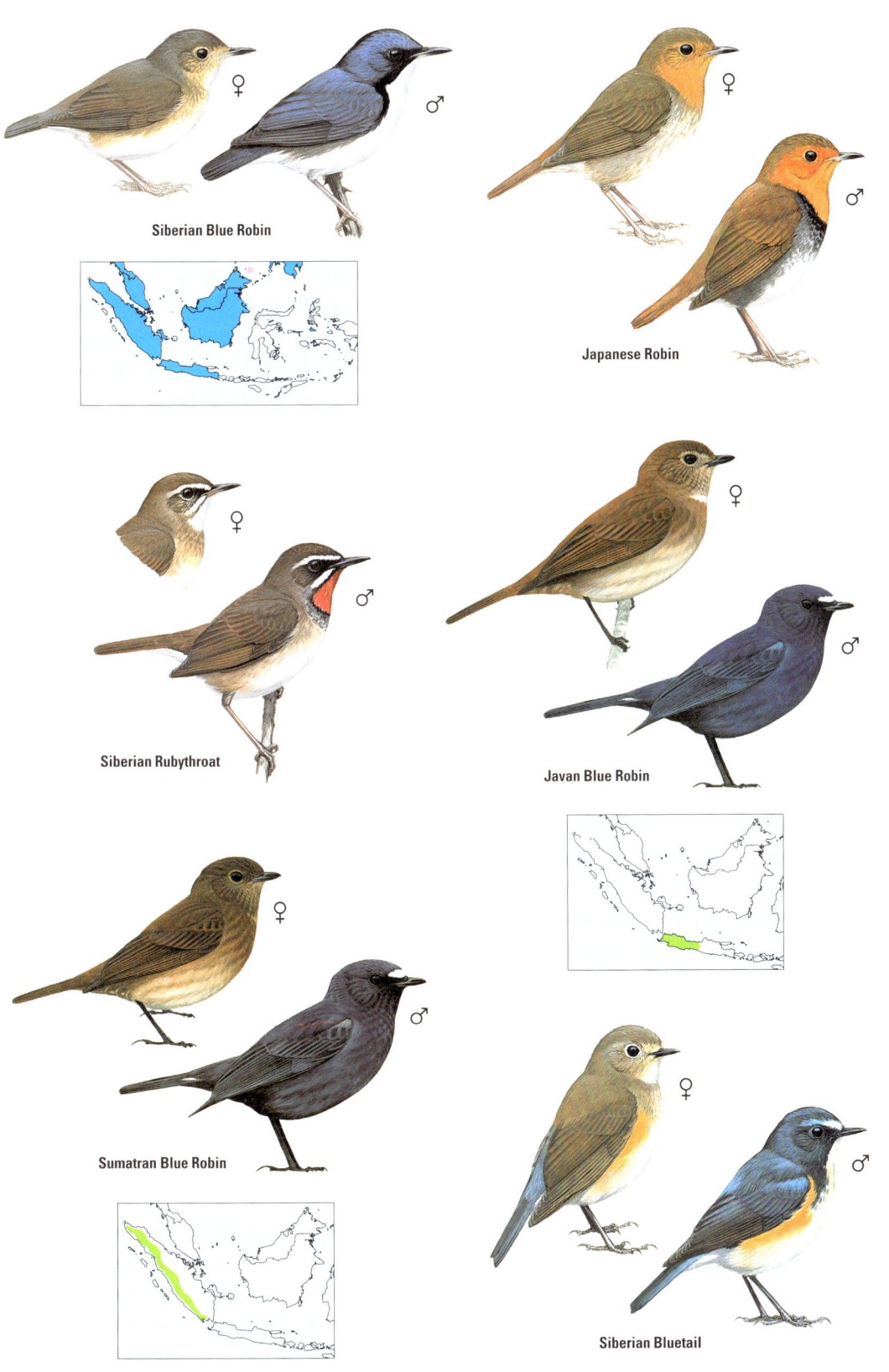

Siberian Blue Robin

Japanese Robin

Siberian Rubythroat

Javan Blue Robin

Sumatran Blue Robin

Siberian Bluetail

Sunda Forktail *Enicurus velatus* 🟩E

L 16 cm. 2 ssp: *velatus* (Jav); *sumatranus* (Sum). Fairly common (Sum) or scarce (Jav) in primary hill and lower montane forest, 600–2300 m. Forages on boulders in fast-flowing streams and rivers; shy but vocal and calling loudly when alarmed. Occasionally found on roads through forest. **ID** Pale-pink legs. **M** dark-grey upperparts with paler crown to nape; white forehead and spot behind eye; black throat; white rump and breast to belly; deeply forked black tail with white crescent-shaped bands and white outer feathers. **F** chocolate-brown crown and nape. Ssp *sumatranus* **M** larger white frontal area; **F** paler, brighter brown cap. **Imm** undescribed. **Voc** Song undescribed. Call: thin "hee" or "hee-TEE–tee (tee)", of which second note usually highest. Chestnut-naped has similar fast notes but rising in pitch. **SS** All other regional forktails are larger with strong white wing markings.

Chestnut-naped Forktail *Enicurus ruficapillus*

L 18–20 cm. Sundaic. Monotypic. Locally fairly common in lowland and hill forest, <1100 m. Forages on and among rocks along narrow streams, small shady rivers, ground near water, and occasionally secondary scrub along logging roads, very wary and calling loudly when alarmed. **ID** Pale-pink legs. **M** rich chestnut crown to nape and ear-coverts; black throat and face with white frontal area; black mantle and wings; white wingbar; white lower back to rump; long, deeply forked black tail with white crescent-shaped bands and white outer feathers; white underparts with black-scaled breast. **F** chestnut mantle. **Imm** duller head; whitish lower face to throat; greyish flanks. **Voc** Song: series of whiny, high-pitched notes barely audible, lasting >5 sec, with lots of mimicry, particularly of *Cyornis* and *Ficedula* flycatchers. Call: high-pitched, loud "teee", "teee-teee", or "teee-teee-teee...", notes rising in pitch, often in quick succession, unlike Malayan.

Javan Forktail *Enicurus leschenaulti* 🟩E

L 29 cm. Monotypic. Closely resembles Malayan but on mtDNA and vocalisations appears more closely related to different-looking Bornean. Genomic and bioacoustic research required. For taxonomy also see Bornean Forktail. Moderately common in lowland and (sub-) montane forest, <3000 m. Forages on rocks and along banks of fast-flowing rocky rivers and streams, sometimes away from running water, e.g. along roads or in forest and swampy areas. **ID Ad** black head to breast, mantle and wings; white on crown extending well beyond mid-crown; white wingbar, rump and belly; deeply forked black tail with white crescent-shaped bands; pale-pink legs. **Imm** no white crown; sooty black upperparts; white rump; slightly paler sooty breast vaguely demarcated from white belly. **Voc** Song: elaborate series of sweet, high-pitched whistles, with much mimicry. Call: (i) when alerted and taking flight, a penetrating, level "teee" or "tee-tee-tee...", all notes at equal pitch, >6 kHz; (ii) single scolding note such as dry slurred buzz, "gzuweet".

Bornean Forktail *Enicurus borneensis* 🟩E

L 28 cm. Monotypic. Previously merged with Malayan and Javan Forktails and multiple extralimital taxa to form a more broadly-defined umbrella species, '**White-crowned Forktail**' *E. leschenaulti*. However, Bornean is set apart from Malayan by deep genome-wide differentiation suggesting no gene flow despite contact. By extension, deep mtDNA divergences among most other taxa dictate separation into multiple species. Local and uncommon in (sub-) montane forest, confirmed records 500–2000 m. Forages along forest rivers and streams. **ID Ad** as Javan Forktail but slightly smaller with shorter tail; white of crown only extending to mid-crown; white on inner secondaries reportedly more restricted. **Imm** black replaced by warm dark-brown; no white crown; throat and breast with vague whitish streaking grading into whitish belly. **Voc** Song undescribed. Call: very high pitched, single, short whistle, uttered when nervous, alarmed, before taking flight, clearly downslurred ("teeeeuw") versus the flat note of Malayan ("heee"). **SS** Challenging to identify from Malayan Forktail at mid-elevations where they may overlap (see also Voc): Bornean has longer tail (with reported overlap), but best ID mark is its white forecrown only extending to mid-crown (above eye) when not erect, while Malayan (at least on Bor) has white extending noticeably beyond eye; this is harder to judge when crown erect.

Malayan Forktail *Enicurus frontalis*

L 25 cm. Sundaic. 2 ssp: *frontalis* (MPen, Sum, Nias, Bor); *chaseni* (Batu). Unnamed population in Sabah lowlands ('**Sabah Lowland Forktail**') is deeply diverged in mtDNA from populations in lowlands of Sarawak (presumably including most of Kalimantan), Sum and MPen. However, no vocal or plumage differences are known to date. More research into species boundaries required. For taxonomy also see Javan and Bornean Forktails. Uncommon, <1400 m on Sum, <1100 m on Bor although reports from higher Bornean elevational range probably refer to misidentified Bornean Forktails. Forages on rocks and along banks of fast-flowing rocky rivers and streams, sometimes away from running water, e.g. along roads or in forest and swampy areas. **ID Ad** as Javan Forktail but much smaller and shorter-tailed with more extensive white rump and belly. Ssp *chaseni* reported to have longer tail. **Imm** as Javan. **Voc** Song: as other forktails, call notes interspersed with much mimicry, particularly of *Cyornis* and *Ficedula* flycatchers. Call: high-pitched, penetrating, repeated, flat "teee", <6 kHz. **SS** See Bornean Forktail.

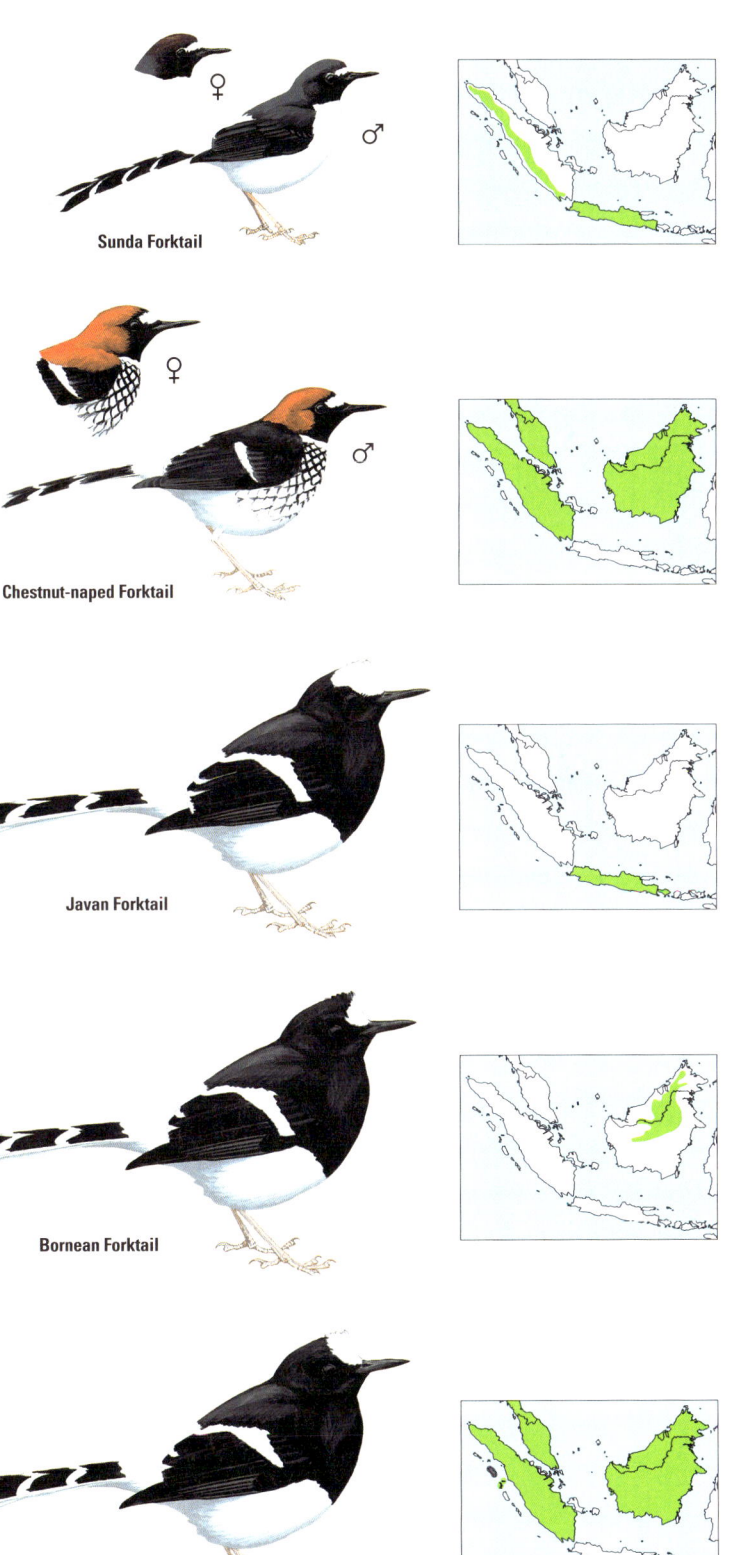

Sunda Forktail

Chestnut-naped Forktail

Javan Forktail

Bornean Forktail

Malayan Forktail

Shiny Whistling-thrush *Myophonus melanurus* **E**

L 24–29 cm. Monotypic. Common in primary hill to upper montane forest, 800–3300 m. In damp moss forest and banks of streams running through dense jungle, surprisingly arboreal, inquisitive. **ID M** velvety jet-black spangled with shiny deep-blue spots; lighter blue on supercilium and shoulder patch. **F** blacker and without body spangling. **Imm** buffish streaks on breast, flanks and forehead; metallic blue patches on mantle, scapulars and shoulder. **Voc** Song undescribed. Call: rapid, rather hoarse sputtering "ow-chrit-chrit-chrit...". **SS** See Sumatran Whistling-thrush. Blue Whistling-thrush larger with yellow (not black) bill.

Javan Whistling-thrush *Myophonus glaucinus* **E**

L 24–26 cm. Monotypic. Traditionally merged with Bornean and Sumatran but differences in plumage and vocalisations suggest separation. Common in montane forest, 800–2400 m, locally lower on Bali. Terrestrial, not always close to water, often on ridges, rather tame and inquisitive, sometimes found in mid-canopy. **ID M** bluish-black with extensive bright blue shoulder patch. **F** duller and browner. **Imm** dark-brown body finely pale-streaked, becoming bolder on lower body. **Voc** Song: series of loud clear, mournful, cascading whistles, rarely heard. Call: 2–3 loud raucous notes, not unpleasant, treeshrew-like "cheek-cheek (-cheek)". **SS** Blue Whistling-thrush much larger, with yellow (not black) bill. See also Javan Cochoa.

Bornean Whistling-thrush *Myophonus borneensis* **E**

L 25–26 cm. Monotypic. For taxonomy see Javan. Locally fairly common in (sub-) montane forest, 1000–2750 m. Forages on the ground along banks of rocky mountain streams, around limestone caves and dark ravines. **ID M** bluish-black with vestigial blue forehead and bluish sheen on throat and breast; brownish-black belly and wings; dull blue shoulder patch. **F** brownish-black with vague purplish-blue shoulder patch. **Imm** fine whitish spots on head and neck, becoming bolder from breast to belly. **Voc** Song: 3 ascending, long-drawn, slightly upslurred, shrill whistles lasting ~2 sec. Call: long chittering.

Sumatran Whistling-thrush *Myophonus castaneus* **E**

L 25 cm. Monotypic. For taxonomy see Javan. Uncommon in (sub-) montane forest, 400–1600 m. Often near watercourses or forest trails; shy. **ID M** bluish-black head and neck with metallic blue forehead band; breast bluish-black shading into dull chestnut lower belly; mantle and wings to tail chestnut with blue shoulder patch. **F** dull plain chestnut with greyish-brown head, brighter chestnut on wings; blue shoulder patch. **Imm** bluish sheen on upper nape. **Voc** Song undescribed. Call: (i) grating "waaakh"; (ii) sneezing "chreewk-chreewk-chreewk (-chreewk-chreewk)", reminiscent of Javan Whistling-thrush. **SS** Shiny Whistling-thrush and the larger, yellow-billed Blue Whistling-thrush lack brown in all plumages. **AN** Brown-winged Whistling-thrush.

Blue Whistling-thrush *Myophonus caeruleus*

L 29–35 cm. C–S–E–SE Asia. 6 ssp, 2 in region: *dichrorhynchus* (MPen, Sum); *flavirostris* (Jav). Uncommon in lowland and hill forest, 350–1300 m, locally lower. Often quite tame, hopping about on boulders in streams, edge of cultivation, around hill stations. **ID** Large yellow bill. **M** dull bluish-black; upperparts covered with metallic violet-blue spots; underparts, wings and tail deep dull-blue; sparsely silvery-spotted upperwing-coverts. **F** slightly duller. Ssp *flavirostris* darker with shorter tail; much larger bill. **Imm** sooty-black. **Voc** Song: long, disjointed string of casually melodious phrases composed of loud, clear, resonant, short, remarkably human-like whistles, rather high-pitched and wispy in tone, sometimes with mimicry. Call: (i) loud, thin, shrill "skreee" or "fweeeee", slightly downslurred, sometimes lower-pitched, shorter and more strongly downslurred; (ii) strident, far-carrying, upslurred "tzeet tze-tze-tzeet" or "bzueeet". **SS** See Javan, Sumatran and Shiny Whistling-thrushes.

Blue Rock-thrush *Monticola solitarius*

L 20–23 cm. S Palaearctic, S–SE–E Asia, Phil. 5 ssp, 3 in region: *pandoo* (breeds Himalaya to E Asia; winters to S–SE Asia including GS); *philippensis* (breeds NE–E Asia; winters to Bor, Wallacea, Phil); *madoci* (N Sum, MPen). All three ssp form a mtDNA group deeply diverged from the two extralimital ssp, which, however, greatly resemble ssp *pandoo* and *madoci* in plumage whereas *philippensis* looks different; bioacoustic and genomic study required. Rare winter visitor (*pandoo*) to N Sum and Bor, <1200 m; regular widespread winter visitor (*philippensis*) to Bor, Sul and Mol; very local resident (*madoci*) in N Sum. Singly, rarely in groups; perches on buildings and rocks in urban areas, secondary woodland, rocky sea shores; rather shy. **ID M** dull dark grey-blue body with darker and browner wings. **F** duller blue-grey, often browner upperparts; spotted and scaled buff and brown on breast, shifting to barring from lower breast to vent. Ssp *philippensis* **M** stronger blue upperparts, mid-breast to vent dull chestnut, often with indistinct narrow buff-and-black barring over body, **F** darker; *madoci* more rounded wings, smallest race, resembles all-blue plumage of *pandoo* but slightly darker upperparts, **M** slightly darker blue on throat and breast, **F** more richly suffused blue than other races, slightly richer buff on foreneck. **Imm** dark brown, more strongly marked on underparts than fem. **Voc** Song: melodious, rich, short series of individually varied phrases lasting an average 2 sec with ≥0.5 sec pause, each phrase a warble of 5–8 sweet clear slurred whistles, short churrs and rolling trills. Call: (i) deep "tak-tak"; (ii) very high "peee" and soft, liquid, but penetrating "wit-wit" as warning calls; (iii) alarm "ka-tchuc-tchuc..." or "pee-chuc-chuc...". **SS** See White-throated Rock-thrush.

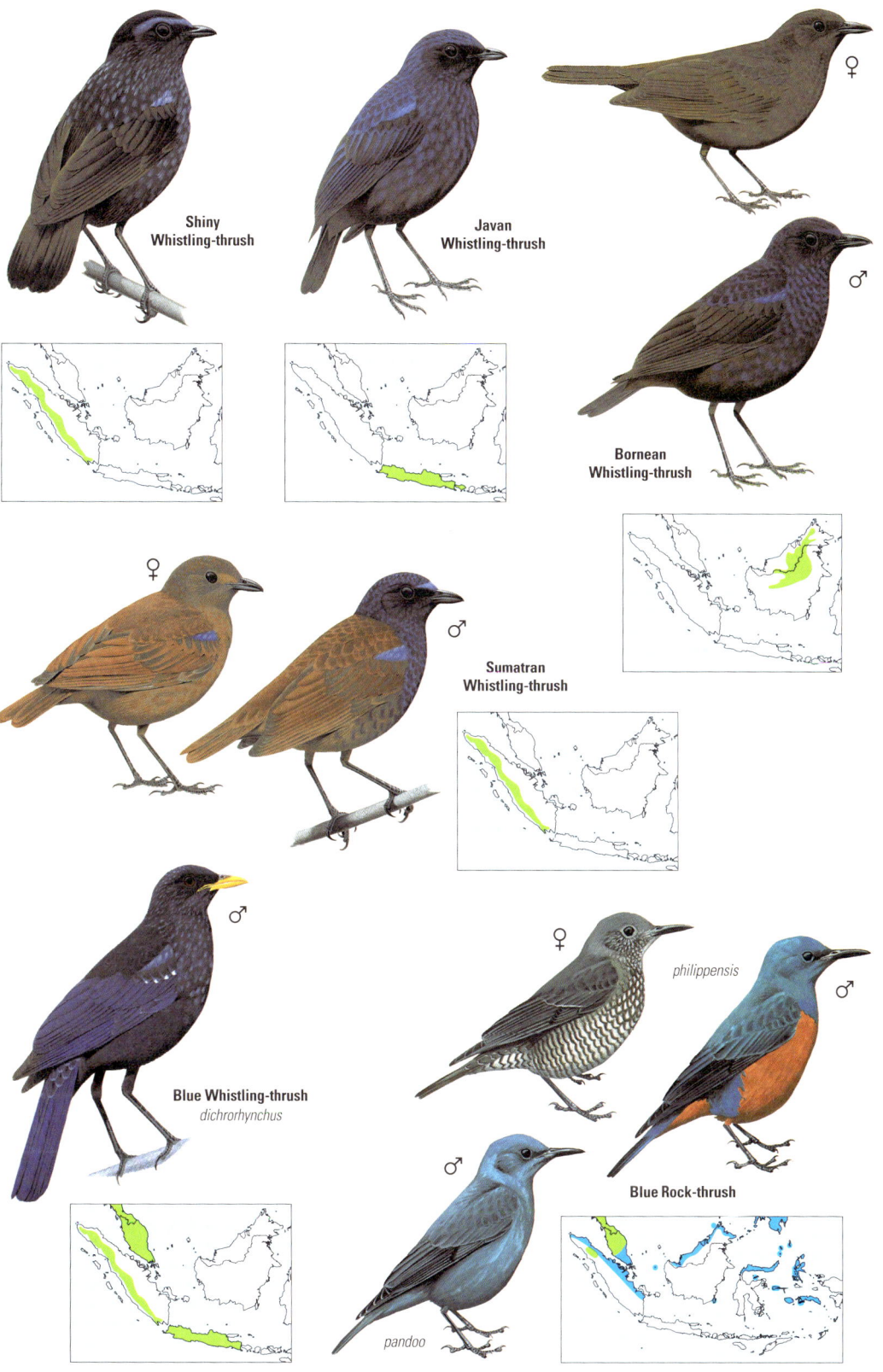

Shiny Whistling-thrush

Javan Whistling-thrush

♀

♂

Bornean Whistling-thrush

♀

♂

Sumatran Whistling-thrush

♂

Blue Whistling-thrush
dichrorhynchus

♀

philippensis

♂

♂

pandoo

Blue Rock-thrush

White-throated Rock-thrush *Monticola gularis* 〔V〕

L 16–19 cm. Monotypic. Breeds E Asia, winters to SE Asia. One record Sarawak (Nov 2015). Inconspicuous and shy in understorey of forest, woodland and secondary growth. Often flushing up, sitting motionless <2 m from ground. **ID** Pink legs; dark bill pinkish at base. **M** azure-blue crown; black ear-coverts and upperparts with striking orange rump; blue tail tipped black; chestnut-orange underparts with thin white throat line; white wing patch at base of tertials. Non-breeding shows heavy scaled appearance with pale feather fringes. **F/imm** scalloped brown upperparts; dark ear-coverts bordered by white post-auricular patch and submoustachial stripe; paler underparts with brown scalloping. **Voc** Call: sharp "tack-tack". **SS** Heavily scalloped plumage of female very different from thrushes. Horsfield's Thrush is darker, brighter plumaged with black (not brown) scalloped underparts and lacks white auricular patch. Blue Rock-thrush lacks both upperparts scalloping and distinct face pattern.

Northern Wheatear *Oenanthe oenanthe* 〔V〕

L 15 cm. Breeds Holarctic; mainly winters Africa. 3 ssp, 1 presumed in region: *oenanthe* (breeds Palaearctic, Alaska; winters Africa). As here defined, does not include Seebohm's Wheatear *O. seebohmi* (NW Africa). Vagrant with 3–4 records in Sarawak (Nov 1951, Oct 1956, Mar 1959). Forages on open ground, from perches by sallying, dropping to the ground. **ID M** pale-grey crown and mantle; broad black eyestripe broadening towards rear; thin white eyebrow; white underparts with yellowish-buff throat and breast; black wings; rump white; tail white with black tips forming an inverted T. **F** no extensive black eyestripe; browner wings. **Imm** less white in tail. **Voc** Call: (i) throaty "chack" or "tuc"; (ii) alarm call a sibilant "whit", often in combination with previous call "weet-tac". **SS** Fem Pied Bushchat darker, plainer face, all-black tail (lacking pied T pattern).

Stejneger's Stonechat *Saxicola stejnegeri* 〔V〕

L 12 cm. Breeds E Palaearctic; winters to SE–E Asia. Monotypic. Often merged with ~23 extralimital taxa into more broadly-defined umbrella species, '**Common Stonechat**' *S. torquatus* (Old World), but extensive genetic and plumage differentiation necessitates break-up. Taxonomy confused: future genomic research may show need for Stejneger's to be merged with various other Palaearctic members of the species complex. Stejneger's as here defined does not include '**Tibetan Stonechat**' *S. przewalskii* (breeds C–W China to Indochina; winters to S) because of plumage differentiation. Recorded Jambi (Sum; Jan 1976), Nias (May 1990), several records N Bor (Dec–Apr); open grass and scrub, paddyfields, reedbeds, <2500 m. Forages by dropping to the ground from perch. **ID M Ad br** brown-black upperparts with black head and throat; broad white patch on nape and neck sides; white wing patch; white rump; black tail with white tip; rufous-orange breast becoming paler on belly to white on vent. **F** dark-streaked sandy-brown upperparts; pale supercilium; buffy underparts with white throat and vent; white wing patch; rufous rump. **Ad M non-br** black-flecked head sides and throat; lores and chin often all black. **Imm** blackish-brown spotted buff on upperparts; buffish underparts with faintly spotted breast. **Voc** Call: loud grating "tsh-tsh" or "trac-trac", sometimes combined with high upslurred note becoming "whit trac-trac".

Pied Bushchat *Saxicola caprata*

L 13–14 cm. SW–C–S–SE Asia, Phil, Aus. 16 ssp, presumed 6 in region: *fruticola* (Jav–Alor; single record Sum 1991); *pyrrhonotus* (Wetar, Kisar, Sawu, Rote, Timor); *francki* (Sumba); *albonotatus* (Sul, Selayar); *cognatus* (Babar); *anderseni* (S Phil; presumably this ssp vagrant to Sabah in May 1998). Deep mtDNA divergence between *pyrrhonotus* and extralimital ssp *bicolor* (S Asia) indicates

there may be species-level differentiation within this complex, but exact boundaries unknown at present; more research required. Widespread and locally common in lowlands, <2000 m. Found in grassland, savanna, cultivation with scattered scrub and trees. Singly, pairs or small family groups; often perches in the open. **ID M** glossy black; long white shoulder patch; white axillary tips; white rump and lower belly to vent. **F** dark grey-brown upperparts; paler greyish-brown to rufous-brown underparts with variable dark streaking; variably pale-contrasting lores and throat; white vent. Ssp *pyrrhonotus* **F** more rufous-brown overall with less streaking below, throat grey-white to buff, often with faint spots; *francki* as previous but **F** more grey-brown overall; *albonotatus* **M** black fringes to white wing patch, **F** dark-fringed (partly concealed) white wing patch, dark-streaked whitish-grey underparts, white underwing-coverts; *cognatus* **F** dark fuscous overall with pronounced streaking, white rump and vent; *anderseni* (or other potential vagrant ssp from Phil) **F** paler overall, especially on breast, and – on average – less streaked on underparts than any ssp in region, usually with more well-defined pale moustachial and loral stripes. **Imm** bold buff spotting on upperparts and scaling on breast and flanks; two rufous wingbars. **Voc** Song from open perch or sometimes parachuting flight with white axillaries and rump puffed out: series of very short, hesitantly initiated but attractive whistled phrases, each repeated multiple times before changing to another slightly different phrase, each lasting ~1 sec, occasionally longer, with intervals of 5–10 sec. Call: (i) plaintive "hweet", "hew" or "seeyee", often combined with insistent scolding "tsak-tsak" or "chek-chek"; (ii) sharp downslurred clipped "spleew, spleew". **SS** See Oriental Magpie-robin and Northern Wheatear.

Timor Bushchat *Saxicola gutturalis* 〔E〕

L 16–17 cm. 2 ssp: *gutturalis* (Timor); *luctuosus* (Semau, Rote). Locally common in monsoon forest and woodland, <1200 m. Usually in pairs; foraging by gleaning and sallying in the canopy, sometimes in tall understorey scrub. **ID M** black upperparts and tail; thin, often absent, white ear streak; slightly greyish rump; white elongated shoulder patch; white bases to outer tail feathers; white underparts. Ssp *luctuosus* less white in wing; lacks white outertail base. **F** brown upperparts, more rufous on rump; white eyebrow; wings with buffy fringes; black tail with pale rufous-brown outer feathers; creamy-whitish underparts. **Imm M** as Fem but black tail with white outertail base. **Voc** Song: series of clear, sweet, unhurried phrases, each consisting of 4–5 fairly high-pitched whistled notes, the first long and upslurred, next 3–4 deliberate and alternating in pitch, lasting 2 sec. Call: subdued "tchk, tchk". **AN** White-bellied Bushchat.

Taiga Flycatcher *Ficedula albicilla* 〔V〕

L 12 cm. Breeds C–E Palaearctic; winters S–SE–E Asia. Monotypic. Traditionally included with Red-breasted Flycatcher *F. parva* (breeds W Palaearctic), but the two differ in plumage and other traits. Rare visitor to N Bor; in woodland, edge, parks. Singly; foraging in low and mid-storey; often flicks wings, cocks and flirts its black-and-white tail. **ID M** upperparts cold-brown; lores, neck sides and ear-coverts grey; tail blackish-brown; jet-black lower rump; white base to outer-tail; whitish underparts with orange-red throat completely bordered by grey breast and throat sides. **F** as M but throat whitish; breast tinged grey; belly to vent white. **Imm** as F but shows pale-tipped greater coverts. **Voc** Song unlikely to be heard in region. Call: (i) soft rattling "trrrrt"; (ii) dry clicking "tzek" notes protracted into ticking series, "tk tk tk...". **SS** Black tail with white outertail base diagnostic among little flycatchers in the region. Paleness of plumage and size could cause confusion with fem Little Pied or Asian Brown Flycatchers but note tail. **AN** Red-throated Flycatcher.

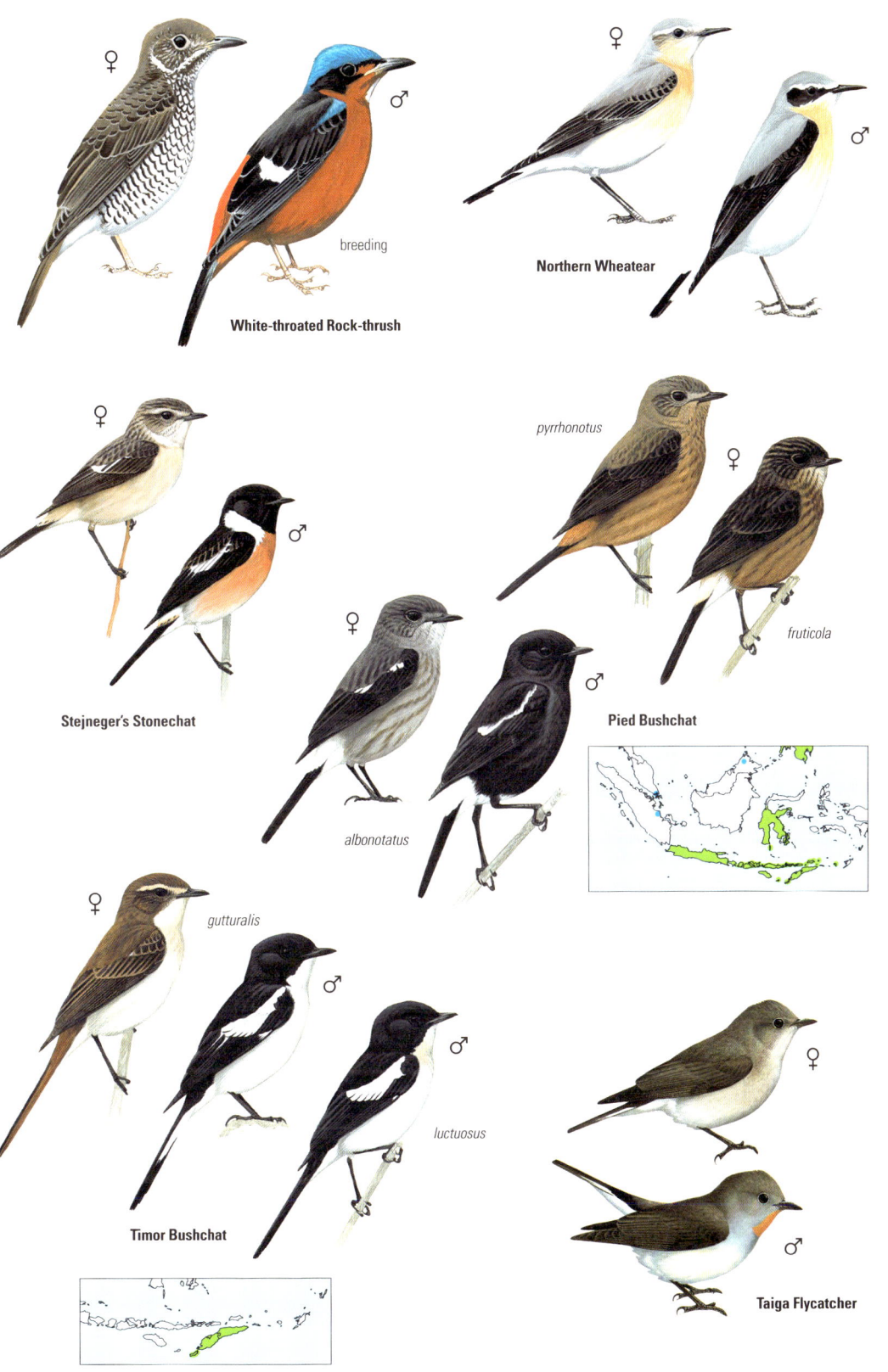

♀ ♂ breeding

White-throated Rock-thrush

♀ ♂

Northern Wheatear

♀ ♂

Stejneger's Stonechat

pyrrhonotus ♀

fruticola

Pied Bushchat

♀ ♂

albonotatus

♀ *gutturalis* ♂

♂ *luctuosus*

Timor Bushchat

♀

♂

Taiga Flycatcher

Yellow-rumped Flycatcher *Ficedula zanthopygia*

L 13 cm. Breeds NE–E Asia; mainly winters MPen, Sum–Bali. Monotypic. Few confirmed records from Bor. Fairly common in woodland, edge, but can turn up anywhere on migration. Singly; in understorey to mid-canopy, perching unobtrusively. **ID M** black upperparts; yellow lower back and rump; yellow underparts with strong orange flush on throat and breast in spring; bold white eyebrow; long white wing patch and vent. **F** dull greyish-olive upperparts; buffy loral stripe and partial eye ring; white wing patch extended along edge of tertials; yellow rump; creamy-white underparts with faint brownish-mottled throat and breast. **Imm** olive-mottled rump. **Voc** Song often heard in region before departure to breeding grounds: short phrase of low melodious thrush-like whistles. Call: repeated, loud, frog-like rattle "trtk-tk-tk", often interspersed with sweet "tee". **SS** Male Narcissus Flycatcher has yellow (not white) supercilium, more orange-tinged rump and more whitish (not yellow) belly; fem/imm has duller upperparts, dark (not yellow) rump, 1-2 pale, often faint wingbars (lacking Yellow-rumped's distinct white wing panel), and a distinct rufous tinge to outertail base. Both sexes of Green-backed Flycatcher similar to fem Yellow-rumped: Green-backed male is more strongly olive on back and head with distinct yellow supercilium (absent in fem Yellow-rumped) and has rounder white wing patch (lacking Yellow-rumped's tertial extension); fem Green-backed is more uniformly lemon-yellow (not creamy-white) across underparts, lacks yellow rump, and has yellow eye-ring (versus white or buff in Yellow-rumped). Also see Mugimaki Flycatcher.

Narcissus Flycatcher *Ficedula narcissina*

L 13 cm. Mainly breeds Japan; winters to Phil, GS. Monotypic. Previously considered conspecific with Green-backed and extralimital Ryukyu Flycatcher *F. owstoni* (Ryukyu Is.), but strong plumage, vocal and genetic differences necessitate separation. Woodland, edge, but can turn up anywhere on migration. Singly; in understorey to mid-canopy, perching unobtrusively. **ID M** black upperparts; bright yellow eyebrow and underparts (orange on throat); yellowish-white belly; extensive yellow rump; white wing panel lacks tertial extension. **F** superficially similar to Yellow-rumped: pale creamy-white underparts with mottling to throat and breast, greyish-olive upperparts, but has strong rufous tinge to outertail base and 1-2 faint whitish to buff wingbars. **Imm** more mottled appearance overall. **Voc** Song unlikely to be heard in region: rapid series of warbled phrases, "o-shin-tsuk-tsuk", followed by short, flute-like "pee-yo-kho". Call: (i) soft "tink-tink"; (ii) slightly downslurred "tee". **SS** See Yellow-rumped, Green-backed and Mugimaki Flycatchers. In migratory situations, drab fem Blue-and-white and Zappey's Flycatchers can cause confusion, but the latter two are bigger, thicker-billed, lack any pale wingbars or tertial edging, have brown tertials (blackish in Narcissus), mantle grey-brown (lacking olive tones) and tail uniformly rufous-tinged (Narcissus with rufous base but blackish towards tip).

Green-backed Flycatcher *Ficedula elisae* `V`

L 13 cm. Breeds NE Asia, winters MPen. Monotypic. For taxonomy see Narcissus. Vagrant to Sabah (Nov 2017). Likely winters to Sum/Riau Is (as annual migrant in Singapore). Inconspicuous, singly or pairs, often holding winter territory in lowland woodland, edge; favouring understorey. **ID/SS M** bright olive-green upperparts with black outerwing and conspicuous white patch on inner greater coverts; bright yellow supercilium, rump and underparts. **F** similar to Narcissus but (1) underparts usually much yellower (not creamy-

white), usually with less mottling on throat and breast; (2) eye-ring narrow yellow (not rusty-toned); (3) more intensely olive-green mantle lacking brown tinge; (4) 1-2 wingbars white (often buff and/or less conspicuous in Narcissus); (5) thicker bill than Narcissus; (6) shorter primary projection and shorter vent (reaching only halfway down tail) make for longer-tailed appearance (versus Narcissus' vent reaching well beyond halfway down tail and long primary projection). Also see fem Yellow-rumped. **AN** Elisa's Flycatcher.

Mugimaki Flycatcher *Ficedula mugimaki*

L 13 cm. Breeds E Palaearctic; winters SE–E Asia, Phil. Monotypic. Uncommon in GS, rare Sul and Mol, winters 500–2000 m, on migration in lowlands. Singly; foraging at forest edge in mid-storey to canopy. **ID** Blackish bill with pale base to lower mandible. Blackish legs (with pink hue). **M** blackish to slate-grey upperparts; short white supercilium behind eye; broad white wing patch and bases to outertail feathers; rufous-orange throat and breast becoming white on belly and vent. **F** cold-brown upperparts; 1-2 thin whitish wingbars; pale orange throat and breast; white belly and vent. **Imm** fine pale buff streaking and spots on upperparts; buffish underparts. **Voc** Song unlikely to be heard in region: loud trill. Call: (i) soft "tyoo"; (ii) <10 low "chuck-chuck-chuck..." or "tk-tk-tk...", as Yellow-rumped Flycatcher but slightly drier; (iii) metallic "turrr" or "trrrrik". **SS** Rufous-chested Flycatcher is smaller and more skulking in habits; male with both wing patch and supercilium narrower and longer than Mugimaki; fem Rufous-chested has warmer brown upperparts including uppertail base, and usually has less distinct wingbars (usually absent or buff in Sum–Bor, not whitish). Fem Yellow-rumped and Narcissus lack strong orange on throat. Various fem *Cyornis* jungle-flycatchers lack wingbars or pale edges to tertials, and have larger, all-black bills (without pale base to lower mandible); see especially Javan and Meratus Jungle-flycatchers. Also see Snowy-browed Flycatcher.

Lompobattang Flycatcher *Ficedula bonthaina* `E`

L 10–11 cm. Monotypic. Extremely local in primary montane forest, >1100 m. Scarce in dense understorey in forest interior. **ID M** olive-brown upperparts with deep chestnut-brown rump and tail; soft orange loral patch, throat and breast; belly to vent white. **F** slightly paler throat and breast. **Imm** undescribed. **Voc** Song: (i) weak, sibilant, high-pitched, rapid, rising-then-falling "tititititititit"; (ii) loud "tee-TEE (-tee)", second note higher-pitched. Call: (i) explosive "chek-chek" protracted into rattling "chechechechechek..."; (ii) quiet "tssst". **SS** Fem Snowy-browed Flycatcher has olive-brown (not contrasting chestnut-brown) tail; fem Rufous-throated Flycatcher has grey-blue (not olive-brown) crown and nape; both these species have much less contrasting orange-buff lores and breast than Lompobattang.

Sumba Flycatcher *Ficedula harterti* `E`

L 11 cm. Monopic. Fairly common in forest, edge, bushy secondary growth. Singly or pairs; inconspicuous, in low vegetation, even on ground in forest interior. **ID Ad** rufous-brown upperparts; faint grey-buff loral spot; silvery-white underparts with rufous-cinnamon breast sides. **Imm** buff tips to coverts. **Voc** Song: mournful series of 3–7 flat whistles at equal pitch, often with a single higher-pitched middle note and followed by staccato "chikik (ik)", or thin "tsitit". Call: (i) insect-like "tszzz"; (ii) "chik-ik", occasionally protracted into "chikikikik...". **SS** See Sumba Brown Flycatcher and Sumba Warbling-flycatcher.

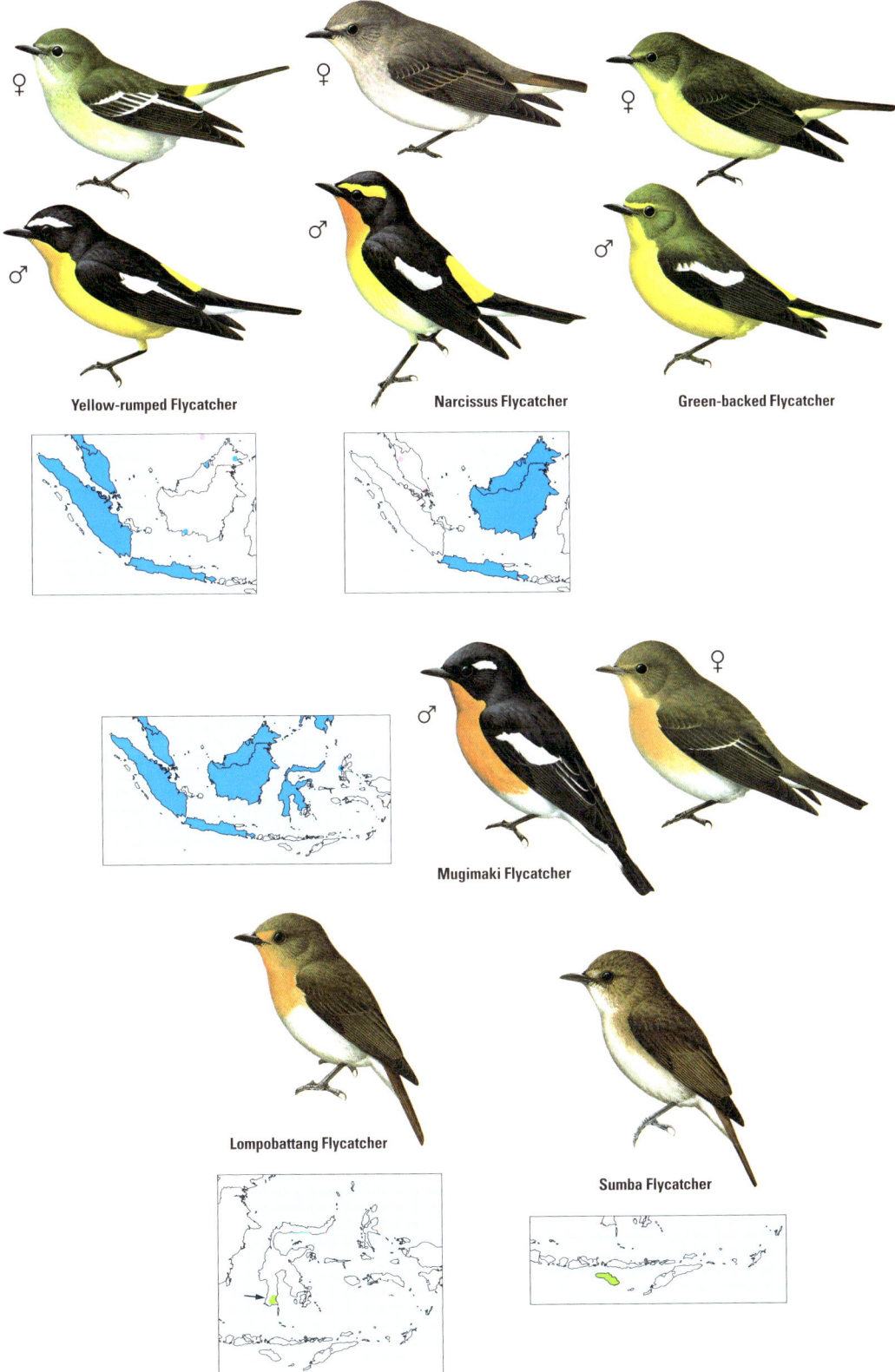

Yellow-rumped Flycatcher

Narcissus Flycatcher

Green-backed Flycatcher

Mugimaki Flycatcher

Lompobattang Flycatcher

Sumba Flycatcher

Little Pied Flycatcher *Ficedula westermanni*

L 10–11 cm. Himalaya to SE Asia, Phil. 8 ssp, 3 in region: *westermanni* (MPen, N Sum, Bor, Mindanao, N–C–E–SE Sul, Sula, Bacan, C Mol); *hasselti* (S Sum–Alor; SW Sul); *mayri* (Wetar, Timor, Rote). Current subspecific arrangement makes little geographic sense and requires revision. Fairly common in montane forest, 780–2600 m, down to sea level on Timor–Rote. Singly or pairs, joins mixed flocks; in outer canopy and mid-storey, sometimes low down at forest edge. **ID M** black upperparts with long, broad, white eyebrow; white wing and tail patches; underparts entirely white. **F** slaty bluish-grey head to mantle, russet-brown rump and tail, underparts white with grey-brown wash on breast; *hasselti* olive-grey wash to head and mantle, rich russet-brown edges of tail base; *mayri* as nominate but paler and greyer on rump and uppertail . **Imm** as F but shows pale wingbar. **Voc** Song: (i) rapidly rising and/or dropping series of thin notes (Jav); (ii) series of high-pitched, deliberate notes dropping in pitch (LS); (iii) repeated "tee-DEE" followed by warble of 6–8 notes, lasting 2 sec (Sul); (iv) soft series of 10–13 brief, thin, high-pitched, rather jerky, whistled notes ending with 3 slightly buzzy, faster notes, lasting 2–3.8 sec. Characteristic call remarkably constant throughout range and sometimes given all day, even in the heat of noon: thin, high-pitched, mellow "weet" followed by occasional lower-pitched soft rattling "trrrrt". **SS** See Asian Brown, Pygmy and Taiga Flycatchers.

Snowy-browed Flycatcher *Ficedula hyperythra*

L 11–13 cm. Himalaya to E–SE Asia. 14 ssp, 11 in region: *vulcani* (Jav–Flores); *sumatrana* (MPen, Sum, N Bor); *mjobergi* (Mt Poi in W Bor); *clarae* (Timor, Wetar); *audacis* (Babar); *jugosae* (C–SE–S Sul); *annalisa* (N Sul); *negroides* (Seram); *pallidipectus* (Bacan, perhaps Ternate); *alifura* (Buru); *betinabiru* (Taliabu). Formerly included Bundok Flycatcher *F. luzoniensis* (Phil), which is genetically and vocally distinct. Widespread and common (GS, Sul, Seram) to uncommon (LS, Buru) in hill and montane forest, 600–3000 m, to sea level on Babar. Singly or pairs; inconspicuous but tame and inquisitive, forages close to ground. **ID** Pink legs. **M** dark greyish-blue upperparts; rufous-orange throat and breast grading into white belly and vent; white eyebrow. **F** olive-brown upperparts; orange-buff breast and flanks against creamy-white rest of underparts; pale buff loral mark 'ghosting' the male's eyebrow. Ssp *sumatrana* **M** stronger rusty throat to belly, **F** slightly colder upperparts; *mjobergi* **M** resembles *vulcani*, **F** even colder (more slaty grey-tinged) upperparts than *sumatrana*, less extensive orange on underparts; *clarae* as *vulcani* but **M** paler blue-grey upperparts, narrower white eyebrow, more uniformly buff underparts, buff reaching vent, **F** more slaty-grey tinge to upperparts and uppertail, less extensive orange-buff on underparts, paler whitish (less intense buff) loral mark; *audacis* as previous but **M** darker underparts, **F** distinctly bluish-grey upperparts, almost as intense as male; *jugosae* as *vulcani* but **F** has less bright, paler, more uniformly ochraceous breast and throat; *annalisa* as previous but **F** darker-olive (more grey-tinged, less brown) upperparts, while underparts more like *vulcani*; *pallidipectus* as *vulcani* but in both sexes paler, less extensive orange-buff on underparts, more olive flanks, **F** with distinct slate-blue tinge to upperparts; *alifura* as previous but more intense orange breast in both sexes, **F** even more greyish-blue on upperparts, approaching intensity of male; *negroides* as previous but smaller and **M** darker, **F** darker with olive tinge to back; *betinabiru* as *alifura* but **M** with narrower eyebrow and less extensive rufous underparts, **F** has similarly blue upperparts as *alifura* with a washed-out male-like face pattern with a whiter (not rufous) eyebrow, a broader pale throat and extensive cold-brown mottling on breast and belly. **Imm** as female but in-

distinct buff wingbar. **Voc** Song: quiet, high-pitched and wheezing series of 2–4 mostly descending single and double notes, often with prolonged last note. Call: (i) thin, slightly upslurred "seep"; (ii) softer "sip", frequently repeated. **SS** See Lompobattang, Rufous-chested, Rufous-throated and Pygmy Flycatchers. Fem Mugimaki perches more openly (less in the undergrowth), lacks distinct pale loral mark, has more conspicuous and more whitish (less buff) wingbar, and blackish (not pink) legs.

Damar Flycatcher *Ficedula henrici*   **E**

L 12–13 cm. Monotypic. Common and widespread on single small island in lush forest. Singly or pairs; foraging below 3 m. **ID M** dark slaty-blue overall; black face; white eyebrow; white throatlet (sometimes concealed); faint white streaking on breast. **F** olive-brown upperparts with slaty tinge on wings; strong whitish eyebrow; underparts pale rusty-buff, brighter on throat and breast with fine olive streaking. **Imm** incompletely known: **M** as Ad fem but darker upperparts with rufous feather tips, and heavier streaking on underparts; **F** undescribed. **Voc** Song: (i) sibilant "tzit-tit-tsrrirree", the last part a sharply rising trill; (ii) sibilant and far-carrying song comprising variable strophes of 1 sec at 4–8 kHz, rising or descending "tzit-tit (-tit)" or "tzit-it tzititit…", very similar to Snowy-browed Flycatcher.

Cinnamon-chested Flycatcher *Ficedula buruensis*   **E**

L 11–12 cm. 3 ssp: *buruensis* (Buru); *ceramensis* (Seram); *siebersi* (Kai Besar). Likely comprises three monotypic species ('**Buru**', '**Seram**' and '**Kai Flycatcher**', respectively) based on substantial vocal and plumage differences between *buruensis* and *ceramensis*, but *siebersi* insufficiently known in life. Uncommon in lowland and hill forest, 100–1200 m, >300m on Kai Besar. Singly, pairs and in mixed flocks; shy, easily overlooked, in undergrowth and lower understorey. **ID Ad** dark ashy-brown upperparts; dark slaty-grey head; chin to breast orange-rufous becoming whitish on lower belly. Ssp *ceramensis* slaty-blue upperparts and head, uniform cinnamon-rufous underparts with wider throat; *siebersi* as previous but larger; belly possibly paler. **Imm** undescribed. **Voc** Song: *ceramensis* sibilant, scratchy, high-pitched "tsit TSIT tzit (-tzit-tzit),", last 1–3 notes descending, and "tset TSEET" or "tset TSEET tsew". Ssp *buruensis* descending series of 3-5 short, higher-pitched notes "tsit'see'sew'soo". Call: (i) "tup tup"; (ii) buzzing, nasal, downslurred "tzeeew", sometimes repeated. Ssp *siebersi* unknown.

Rufous-throated Flycatcher *Ficedula rufigula*   **E**

L 11–12 cm. Monotypic. Locally fairly common in primary and tall secondary forest, <600 m. Singly or pairs; elusive and inconspicuous in undergrowth, particularly rattan thickets. **ID M** dark blue-grey upperparts; black moustachial line; orange-rufous throat and breast; white belly to vent; bright turquoise-blue eyelid. **F** dark grey-blue upperparts and head, browner on wings and tail; extensive pale buffy lores and eyelid; rump to basal half of tail rufous-brown; underparts as male. **Imm** undescribed. **Voc** Song: 2–3 soft high-pitched, slightly scratchy notes, alternating up and down the scale "see-see-see" or "sweee-wee-seee". Call: (i) a quick "chik"; (ii) staccato chattering alarm. **SS** Male Snowy-browed Flycatcher has white eyebrow (absent in male Rufous-throated). Fem Snowy-browed is more uniformly olive-brown (not grey-blue) on upperparts, lacking contrasting rufous-brown rump and tail base. Larger-sized Sulawesi Jungle-flycatcher (typically from higher elevations) often confused, but has orange extending to belly (white in Rufous-throated); male Sulawesi has paler, bluer upperparts with narrow blackish chin (rufous in Rufous-throated), and fem has blue (not rufous) basal half of tail. See also Lompobattang Flycatcher.

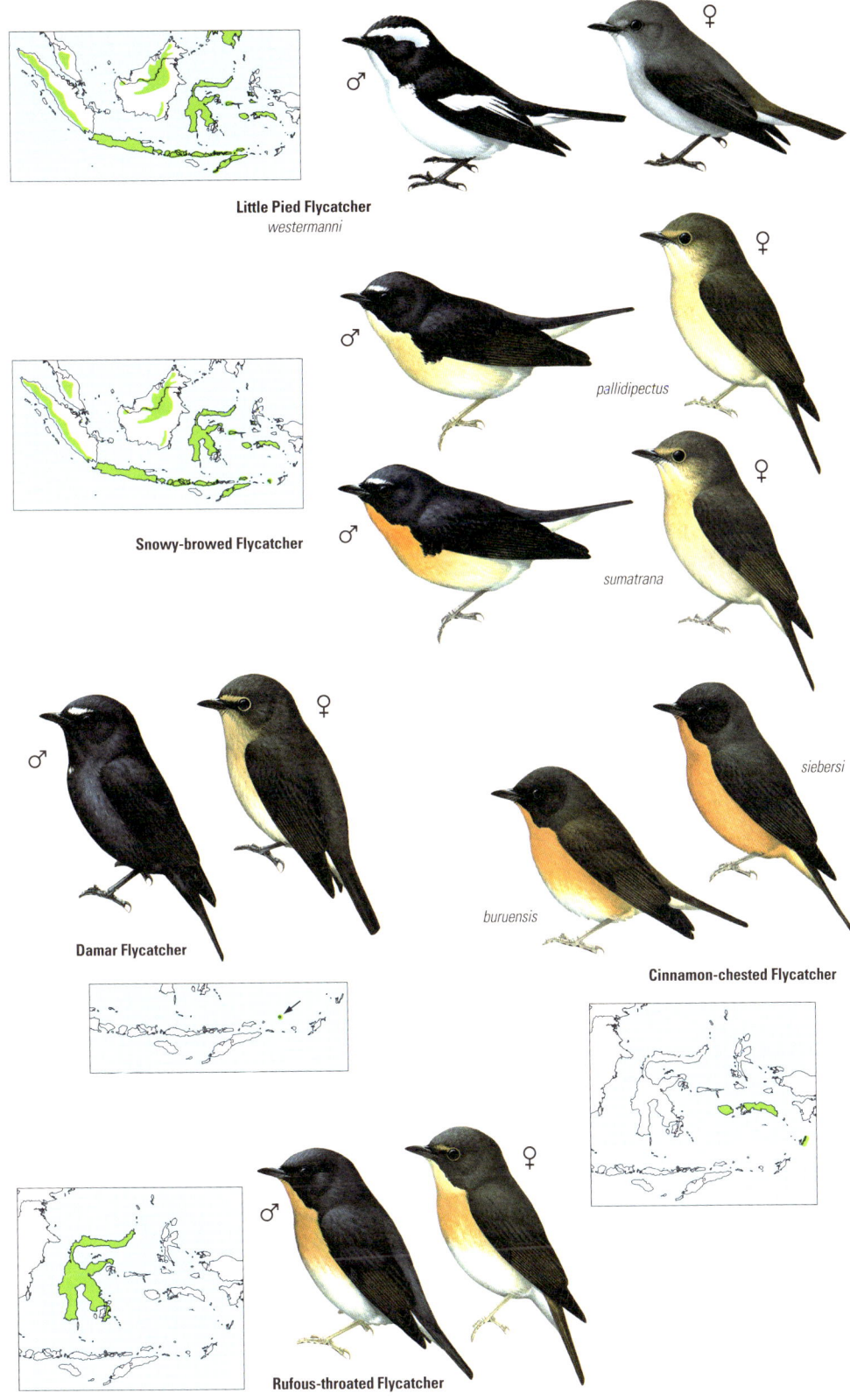

Little Pied Flycatcher
westermanni

♂ ♀

Snowy-browed Flycatcher

pallidipectus ♀

♂

sumatrana ♀

♂

Damar Flycatcher

♂ ♀

siebersi

buruensis

Cinnamon-chested Flycatcher

Rufous-throated Flycatcher

♂ ♀

Rufous-chested Flycatcher *Ficedula dumetoria*

L 11–12 cm. Sundaic, LS. 2 ssp: *dumetoria* (Jav, Lombok–Flores); *muelleri* (Sum, Bor, MPen). For taxonomy see Tanimbar Flycatcher. Fairly common (Sum–Bor) or locally common (Jav–LS) in lowland and submontane forest, <1600 m (Bor), <1500 m (Sum), 900–3000 m (Jav), 300–1900 m (LS). **ID M** black upperparts; long white supercilium; long, narrow white wing stripe from coverts down secondaries; white underparts with rufous-orange breast and throat; white base to outertail feathers. **F** cold olive-brown upperparts, warmer on wings; pale buff lores and eyering; rufous-brown rump and tail; whitish wing-covert edging (creating impression of two faint wingbars); paler orange breast and especially throat than male. Ssp *muelleri* longer and thicker bill; **M** supercilium absent in front of eye, less white in wing; **F** warmer brown upperparts (therefore less contrast with rufous-brown tail), usually no wingbar. **Imm** buff spots on coverts forming two wingbars. **Voc** Song: muted, thin and high-pitched series of 3–4 rising and falling notes, often ending on higher-pitched stressed note, lasting 1 sec per strophe. Call: (i) soft "ssit-ssit"; (ii) "ssit-truk". **SS** Fem Snowy-browed from higher elevations has (1) olive-brown (not rufous) tail and rump, (2) dusky-olive (not white) flanks, with orange-buff breast extending further down, and (3) pale supra-loral (=eyebrow) rather than pale loral area. Also see Mugimaki and Pygmy Flycatchers, Javan and Meratus Jungle-flycatchers.

Tanimbar Flycatcher *Ficedula riedeli*   **E**

L 11 cm. Monotypic. Traditionally included with Rufous-chested Flycatcher but separated based on genetic, plumage and vocal data. Fairly common in forest. Pairs, joins mixed flocks. **ID M** similar to Rufous-chested but with slightly paler upper throat, broader supercilium. **F** as M but upperparts dark brown; buff wing panel; duller orange breast. **Imm** undescribed. **Voc** Song: rather thin, very high-pitched, somewhat piercing yet moderately sweet series of 1–3 notes. Call: high-pitched sibilant "seee".

Black-banded Flycatcher *Ficedula timorensis*   **E**

L 11 cm. Monotypic. Local, uncommon in lowland forest and patches of monsoon forest, favouring bamboo, <1500 m. Singly or pairs; shy and elusive in dense undergrowth. **ID M** light rufous mantle with glossy black head, wings and tail; white underparts with broad black breast band. **F** grey crown and paler breast band. **Imm** undescribed. **Voc** Song: (i) series of 4 soft, high-pitched, thin whistles, descending and ascending, lasting 1.5 sec, repeated at regular intervals; (ii) sequence of up to 4 soft, low, short, buzzing notes, often interspersed with a piercing short downslurred whistle similar to note made by stubtail. Call: quiet, rolling trill.

Pygmy Flycatcher *Ficedula hodgsoni*

L 9–10 cm. Himalaya to SE Asia. 2 ssp, 1 in region: *sondaica* (Sum, Bor, MPen; this ssp E Timor?). Uncommon in montane forest and edge, 850–2400 m. Population in E Timor may constitute undescribed ssp. Singly or pairs, joins mixed flocks; inconspicuous, rapidly foraging in lower and mid-levels of canopy, flicking its tail and wings constantly. **ID M** bright ultramarine-blue upperparts; black mask; forecrown paler blue; deep orange-rufous underparts fading into white vent. **F** olive-brown to rich-brown upperparts, warmer brown on rump; buff throat and breast fading into white belly. **Imm** undescribed. **Voc** Song: short and fairly weak "tzzit-che-che-che-heeee" or "seet-seet-seet, brrrrrr". Call: (i) weak, high-pitched "tseep", "tip",

"pink" or "tup"; (ii) alarm or contact call a low staccato churred trill, "churrt", often combined with previous notes. **SS** Female is tricky: warmer-coloured both on upperparts and breast than similarly diminutive fem Little Pied. Fem Pygmy is most similar in plumage to larger Snowy-browed and Rufous-chested, but (1) latter two have longer tails, less horizontal posture and more skulking demeanour in undergrowth; (2) fem Pygmy usually has plainer face, lacking their extensive pale (supra-) loral marks; (3) fem Pygmy has browner (less grey-tinged) upperparts and a much warmer rump than fem Snowy-browed; (4) fem Rufous-chested sometimes has 1-2 indistinct pale wingbars (absent in Pygmy); (5) orange-buff breast colouration in Snowy-browed and Rufous-chested is more intense than in fem Pygmy (in Snowy-browed often reaching further down to belly).

IRENIDAE
Fairy-bluebird
1 species in region

Medium-sized thrush-like bird of forest and edge. Distinctive iridescent blue-black plumage. Forages conspicuously in mid- to upper storey, often in small groups at fruiting trees.

Asian Fairy-bluebird *Irena puella*

L 21–26 cm. S–SE Asia. 5 ssp, 2 in region: *crinigera* (Sum–Bor, W Sum Is.); *turcosa* (Jav). As here defined, does not include Palawan Fairy-bluebird *I. tweeddalii* (Palawan) based on mtDNA and plumage. Extralimital ssp *andamanica* (Andamans, Nicobars) sometimes separated as monotypic species '**Andaman Fairy-bluebird**' based on mtDNA divergence; more research required. Fairly common in forest, edge, <1900 m. Singly or pairs; congregates at fruiting trees in numbers. **ID M** shining deep-blue upperparts and vent; rest of body black; red iris. **F** uniform dull turquoise-green, lacking gloss. Ssp *turcosa* larger. **Imm** brownish-tinged wings; brown iris. **Voc** Song: fast, repeated series of "hwit-hwit-hwit...", usually rising in pitch and slowing in delivery, also including an irregular "do-ree" note between strophes. Call: (i) single, sharp, upslurred "h'wit"; (ii) agitated scolding "trrt".

CHLOROPSEIDAE
Leafbirds
7 species in region

Small to medium-sized birds of forest with characteristic bright green plumage. Glean for insects in foliage of mid- to upper storey but also eat fruit. Often in small groups, and typically active, vocal and conspicuous. Heavily trapped for the pet trade.

Blue-masked Leafbird *Chloropsis venusta*   **E**

L 14 cm. Monotypic. Uncommon in submontane forest including edge and clearings, 600–1500 m. Usually pairs, joins mixed flocks; favours canopy. **ID M** dark purple-blue throat to lores with mid-blue face and forecrown; breast orange edged yellow; bluish tail; grass-green upperparts; paler green underparts. **F** pale blue face and tail; yellowish tinge to breast. **Imm** undescribed. **Voc** Song: (i) thin, high-pitched mixture of trills and squeaky, upslurred chatter "tu'tu'tttrrrrut, twoo-twoi, twoo-twee..."; (ii) thin, high-pitched, descending series of 5–8 notes "si'si'swee-swee-swee'ee" lasting ~1 sec, or shortened "si'si'swee". Call: (i) thin "tsip"; (ii) harsh rattle lasting 0.5–0.8 sec.

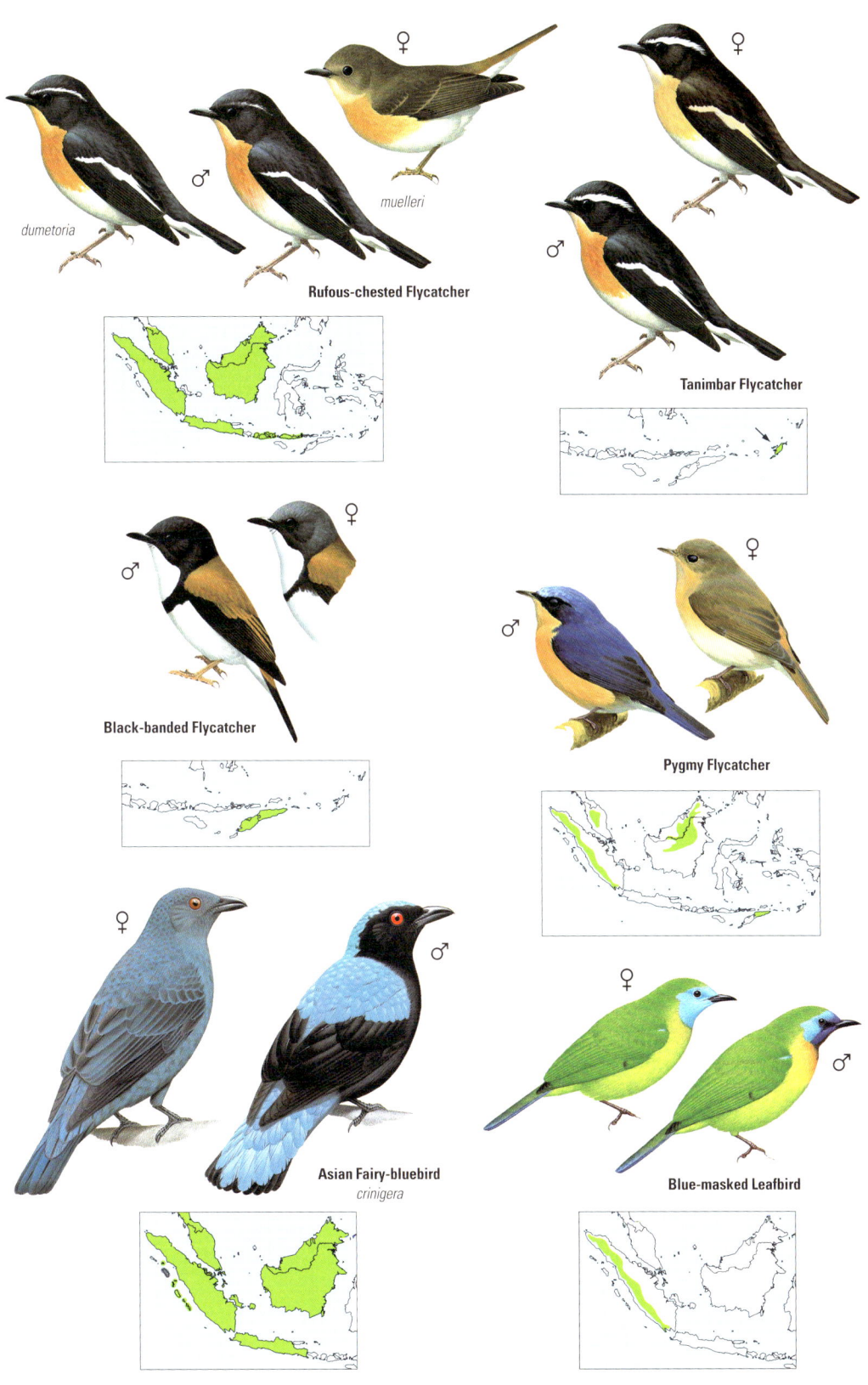

dumetoria

muelleri

Rufous-chested Flycatcher

Tanimbar Flycatcher

Black-banded Flycatcher

Pygmy Flycatcher

Asian Fairy-bluebird
crinigera

Blue-masked Leafbird

Lesser Green Leafbird *Chloropsis cyanopogon*

L 15–16 cm. Sundaic. 2 ssp, 1 in region: *cyanopogon* (Bor–Sum, S MPen). Extralimital ssp *septentrionalis* (N MPen) sometimes separated from this species based on mtDNA, but plumage and vocalisations may not suggest strong differentiation; more research required. Fairly common in forest, edge, <700 m. Singly or pairs; in mid- and upper canopy. **ID M** similar to Greater Green Leafbird but with small bill, less bulging face mask. **F** all-green plumage. **Imm** shows yellowish throat. **Voc** Song: typically a single uprising "whirr", followed by a short series of 5–20 "chip" notes at 6–8 n/s. Call: (i) single, thin, upslurred "swip, do-swip" and "do-swip-sip"; (ii) can also produce variable short, thin chattering combined with call. **SS** See Greater Green, Bornean, Blue-winged and Sumatran Leafbirds.

Greater Green Leafbird *Chloropsis sonnerati*

L 18–21 cm. Sundaic. 3 ssp: *sonnerati* (Jav); *zosterops* (Batu, Bor–Sum [incl Natuna], MPen); *parvirostris* (Nias). Uncommon, becoming locally rare because of trapping, in forest, edge, <1100 m. Singly or pairs; in mid- and upper canopy. **ID** Green overall. Large, stout, hooked bill. **M** broad black mask nearly wraps around top of eye; small turquoise patch on lesser coverts. **F** yellowish throat and eyering; faint blue malar stripe. Ssp *zosterops* less bright green; **M** has viridian-green lesser covert spot. Ssp *parvirostris* smaller bill. **Imm** as fem but lacks malar stripe. **Voc** Song: highly variable; slightly melancholy series of rich, melodious notes including "wee-woo", "wee-twit-twit", "do-twit", "chet-chet-twee", and additional chattering, ranging from a burst of 10–15 notes lasting 2–3 sec to a series of notes lasting >1 min; often includes mimicry, particularly of Asian Fairy-bluebird. Call: rich warbled "wee-choo" and "whirt". **SS** Lesser Green Leafbird is smaller-billed (lacks distinct hooked tip) and smaller-bodied with male's black mask reaching eye but not appearing to encircle it (male Greater's mask connects to outer perimeter of eye). Smaller male Blue-winged, Javan and Bornean Leafbirds have yellow or pale bright-green border around mask (green in Greater) and at least some bluish tinge to wings and tail (absent in Greater). Fem/imm of all other leafbirds are smaller than Greater Green and lack combination of yellow throat and eyering. Also see Sumatran Leafbird.

Sumatran Leafbird *Chloropsis media* 🅔

L 18–19 cm. Monotypic. Increasingly scarce in submontane forest, 600–1400 m. Singly or pairs; in mid- and upper canopy. **ID** Grass-green overall. **M** black mask bordered yellow; forecrown yellow; cobalt blue lesser covert patch. **F** has forecrown and eyelid yellow; blue lesser covert patch and indistinct blue malar stripe often bordered yellow. **Imm** all-green but with yellow eyelid. **Voc** Song: musical chattering with much interspersed mimicry: repeated "whir-whir", rolling "chee-chee-chee-chit"; continuously for 1–10 min. Call: undescribed. **SS** Both sexes of Greater (on Sum) and Lesser Green Leafbirds lack yellow forecrown and contrasting lesser covert spot. Male Greater and Lesser also lack yellow lower border to mask. Fem Lesser Green lacks Sumatran's yellow eyelid. Fem Greater Green has well-defined yellow throat (mostly green in Sumatran although can be suffused with yellow). Blue-winged has blue outerwing (green in Sumatran) with bright yellow-brassy crown and nape in both sexes (on Sumatran yellow restricted to forecrown). Imm Sumatran all-green, tricky, can look similar to imm Blue-winged or Lesser Green (with variable yellow suffusion on throat) but always shows clearer yellow eyelid.

Javan Leafbird *Chloropsis cochinchinensis* 🅔

L 16–18 cm. Monotypic. See Blue-winged Leafbird for taxonomy. Uncommon in forest, edge, <1400 m. Often in small groups (<10), joins mixed flocks; favouring canopy. **ID** Green overall; outerwing and tail (including undertail) bluish-tinged. **M** black mask bordered by bright yellowish-green except on forecrown; broad orange-yellow breast spot. **F** green (not brassy-yellow) nape; pale turquoise-blue throat. **Imm** green throat, blue restricted to malar. **Voc** Song: similar to Blue-winged, with churred notes interspersed with call notes Call: (i) whistled "tew-weet"; (ii) "tew-weet-it"; (iii) upslurred, thin "wit". **SS** See Greater Green Leafbird.

Blue-winged Leafbird *Chloropsis moluccensis*

L 16–18 cm. SE Asia. 6 ssp, 2 in region: *moluccensis* (Sum–Natuna, MPen); *viridinucha* (Bor). Traditionally merged with Javan Leafbird into an expanded '**Blue-winged Leafbird**' *C. cochinchinensis* (then often also including Bornean Leafbird), but should be separated based on mtDNA and plumage. For taxonomy see also Bornean Leafbird. Fairly common in forest, edge, <1500 m. Usually in small groups (<10), joins mixed flocks; favouring canopy. **M** black mask bordered by yellow extending over crown to brassy nape; *viridinucha* green nape. **F** blue malar; variable orange-buff crown and nape. **Imm** all-green with less blue on wing and malar; paler bill. **Voc** Song: musical, uprising "plit-we-wir" lasting 0.3 sec, regularly repeated; often with bubbly chattering notes and rattles. Call: single "chup". **SS** Compared to Lesser Green Leafbird, fem/imm Blue-winged has bluish (not green) outerwing and tail, and buff (not green) nape, although buff nape can be absent or indistinct on imm and requires close views. See also Sumatran, Greater Green and Bornean Leafbirds.

Bornean Leafbird *Chloropsis kinabaluensis* 🅔

L 17–18 cm. Monotypic. Formerly considered conspecific with Blue-winged Leafbird but overlaps in range without signs of intergradation. Fairly common in (sub-) montane forest, 550–2200 m. Usually in small groups (<10), favours canopy. **ID M** similar to Blue-winged with black mask bordered extensively by yellow; orange-buff tinge to crown; larger blue malar stripe. **F** black mask bordered by viridian. **Imm** lacks mask but otherwise not well studied. **Voc** Song: simple, melodious whistle "tooy-weet" interspersed with other call notes, lacking the rattled churred notes of Blue-winged. Call: (i) very thin, high-pitched "sip"; (ii) upslurred, thin "wit"; (iii) whistled "tew-weet-it". **SS** Difficult to separate from male Blue-winged in area of overlap: male Bornean has (1) paler-blue on outerwing, (2) longer and thicker blue malar almost reaching black throat border (shorter and less distinct rounded blue strip in Blue-winged), (3) lack of extensive yellow behind eye (variable Blue-winged tends to have much yellow or buff behind eye), and (4) slightly brighter mantle. Best identified by accompanying fem, which has unique viridian border to black mask. Male Lesser Green Leafbird lacks blue outerwing and tail, and has no paler yellow border to mask. Imm Bornean possibly indistinguishable from imm Blue-winged, and differs from imm Lesser Green in presence of variable (sometimes faint) blue tinge to outerwing and tail. Also see Greater Green Leafbird.

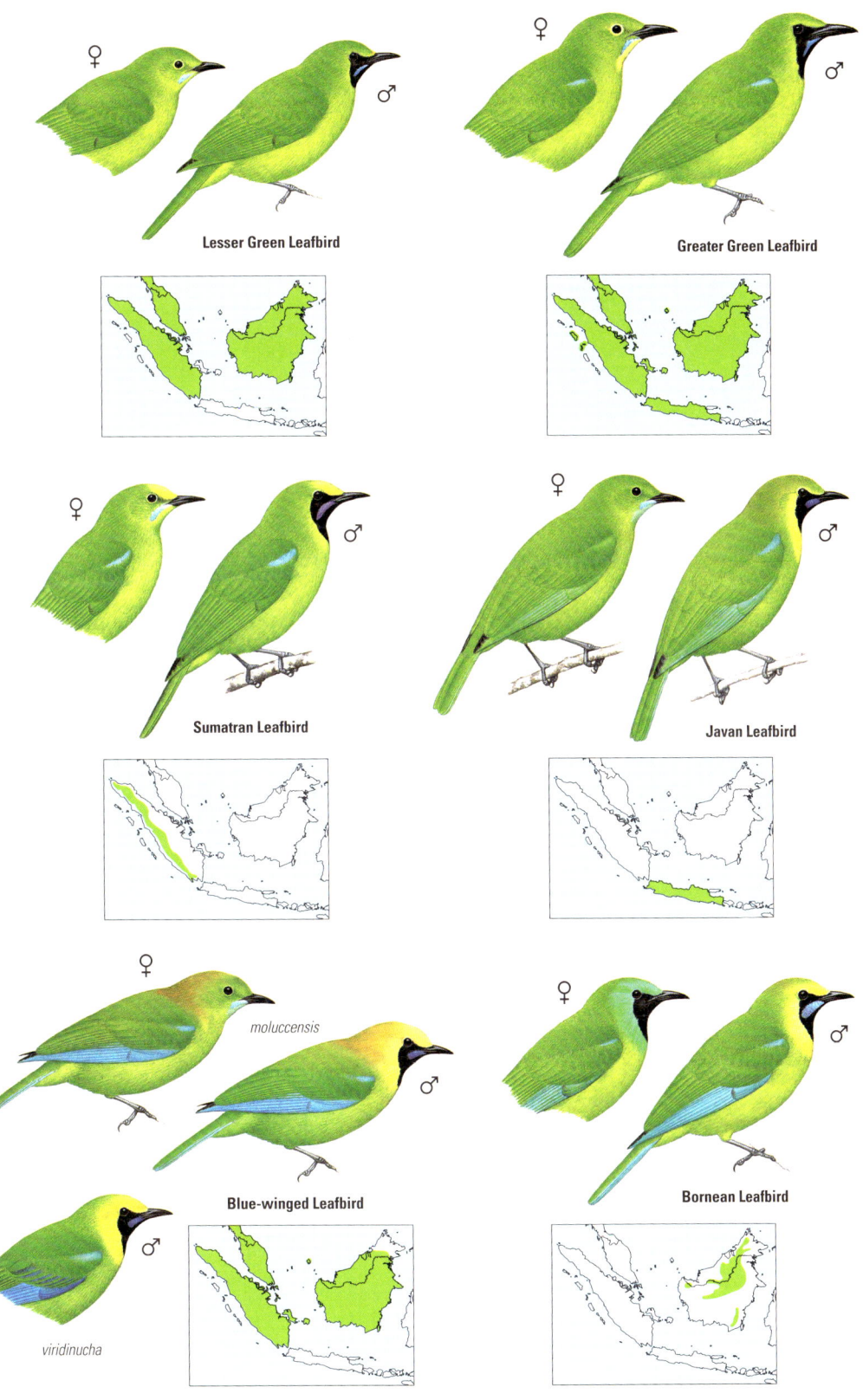

Lesser Green Leafbird

Greater Green Leafbird

Sumatran Leafbird

Javan Leafbird

moluccensis

viridinucha

Blue-winged Leafbird

Bornean Leafbird

DICAEIDAE
Flowerpeckers
29 species in region

Tiny, stocky birds that inhabit a wide range of forest and lightly wooded habitats, including agricultural and urban areas. Generally brightly coloured, active and vocal as they forage in mid- to upper storey of trees, often in groups or as part of mixed flocks.

Yellow-breasted Flowerpecker *Prionochilus maculatus*
L 10 cm. Sundaic. 4 ssp, 2 in region: *maculatus* (Sum–Bor, Nias); *natunensis* (Natuna). Fairly common in forest, edge, <900 m, rarely <1500 m. Often solitary, feeding close to ground and inside forest, joins mixed flocks. **ID Ad** greenish-olive head and upperparts; orange crown patch (often concealed); thick, black bill; yellow underparts thickly streaked green-olive; white malar and central throat. Ssp *natunensis* brighter underparts; greyer above. **Imm** orange bill; lacks streaking on more uniformly olive underparts. **Voc** Song: short, high-pitched, descending "tisisisit" lasting 0.3 sec. Call: harsh, sunbird-like di- or trisyllabic "chwit-chwit-chwit". **SS** Imm from imm Crimson-breasted by yellowish (not white) vent; Ad readily told by underparts streaking.

Scarlet-breasted Flowerpecker *Prionochilus thoracicus*
L 10 cm. Sundaic. Monotypic. Generally rare in lowland forest, locally fairly common in peatswamp forest, <1300 m. Singly or pairs; usually in canopy. **ID M** striking black hood; small scarlet crown spot; black wings and tail; large scarlet-red breast patch bordered black; mantle and belly olive-yellow. **F** grey head with paler malar stripe and throat; olive-green upperparts; brighter yellow-orange breast grading into lemon-grey belly; yellow vent. **Imm** orange bill base; underparts greyer. **Voc** Song: high-pitched, slightly buzzy 3-note "swee-zoo-swee" lasting 0.7 sec, regularly repeated. Call: harsh, scolding buzz "zik", regularly repeated. **SS** Fem Crimson-breasted Flowerpecker has olive-green (not grey) head, lacking contrast between head and rest of body. Also see Yellow-rumped Flowerpecker.

Crimson-breasted Flowerpecker *Prionochilus percussus*
L 10 cm. Sundaic. 3 ssp: *percussus* (Jav); *ignicapilla* (Sum–Bor, MPen); *regulus* (Batu). Fairly common, though local and scarce in Bor; forest, edge, <1000 m. Often in pairs; favours flowering bushes. **ID M** slate-blue head and upperparts; bright yellow underparts with small scarlet breast patch; white malar stripe; crimson crown spot; bulbous black bill. Ssp *ignicapilla* paler underparts; *regulus* underparts tinged olive, orange-red breast patch, upperparts slightly paler. **F** retains malar stripe and crown spot; upperparts olive-green; underparts washed-out yellow. **Imm** orange bill; olive-grey underparts. **Voc** (i) High-pitched "sip"; (ii) buzzy, upslurred "tit-tit". **SS** See Yellow-rumped, Yellow-breasted and Scarlet-breasted Flowerpeckers.

Yellow-rumped Flowerpecker `E`
Prionochilus xanthopygius
L 9 cm. Monotypic. Fairly common in forest, edge and bordering gardens; <1000 m, rarely <1700 m. Favours flowering bushes; often in pairs. **ID M** as Crimson-breasted Flowerpecker but breast patch more diffuse, lacks malar stripe, slate-blue extends to upper flanks; conspicuous yellow rump. **F** dull grey head with vestigial red crown spot; greyish-olive upperparts, flanks and belly; washed-out yellow

throat and breast; yellow rump. **Imm** orange bill; greyer underparts; smaller, less yellow rump. **Voc** (i) Buzzy, short "tzee-oo", regularly repeated; (ii) sharp, buzzy "tsik-tsik". **SS** Distinct yellow rump, lack of pale malar stripe and (in fem) greyer upperparts and more bluish-grey head distinguish from other *Prionochilus* flowerpeckers. Male additionally told from Crimson-breasted by blue extending onto upper flanks and more diffuse red breast patch.

Yellow-vented Flowerpecker *Pachyglossa chrysorrhea*
L 9–10 cm. Himalaya to SE Asia. 2 ssp, 1 in region: *chrysorrhea* (GS, Siberut, MPen). Fairly common in forest, <1200 m, rarely <1700 m. Singly, favouring canopy and mixed flocks. **ID** Striking: olive-green head and upperparts; white lores, malar and underparts with thick, dark streaking; bright yellow vent. **Imm** orange bill base; less bright; underparts streaking olive-green. **Voc** Song: sharp, high-pitched "tsit-TSIT, tsit-TSIT, tsit-TSIT...". Call: short, sharp, scolding buzz "dzeep".

Brown-backed Flowerpecker *Pachyglossa everetti*
L 10 cm. Sundaic. Here considered monotypic (described ssp *bungurensis* [Natuna] likely misidentified or indistinct). Rare and local in forest, particularly peatswamp and kerangas; <500 m, recorded to 1100 m. Singly or pairs, but small groups (<10) can congregate at fruiting trees. **ID Ad** head and upperparts earth-brown; greyish-buff flanks with faint, indistinct streaking on upper flanks and breast; pale creamy wash to central belly; thick, black bill, slightly paler grey base to lower mandible; creamy-yellow eye. **Imm** undescribed. **Voc** (i) Medium-pitched, short, sharp "chip"; (ii) very high-pitched, slightly ascending "zzipp". **SS** Similar Modest Flowerpecker differs in (1) white tail spots visible when tail fanned (absent in Brown-backed), (2) olive-tinged (less earth-brown) upperparts, (3) orange-red iris (not as pale creamy except in Imm), (4) slightly thinner bill, (5) more intense streaking on breast (beware Imm Modest is only faintly streaked, but still has tail spots), (6) constantly splays or wags tail sideways (not known from Brown-backed). Thicker, straighter bill and pale iris separate Brown-backed from various fem (or male Plain) *Dicaeum* flowerpeckers.

Modest Flowerpecker *Pachyglossa modesta*
L 9–10 cm. SE Asia. 4 ssp, 3 in region: *modesta* (Bor, MPen); *atjehensis* (Sum); *finschi* (Jav). Traditionally merged with Tenggara Flowerpecker and extralimital Striped *P. aeruginosa* (Phil) and Agile Flowerpecker *P. agilis* (S Asia) into more broadly-defined umbrella species, '**Thick-billed Flowerpecker**' *P. agilis*. However, some vocal differences and comparatively pronounced plumage distinctions suggest separation. Uncommon, locally common, in a variety of wooded habitats, <1000 m. Singly or pairs, but groups (<30) can congregate at fruiting trees. Characteristically wags tail from side to side. **ID Ad** olive-grey head and upperparts; pale malar; dusky flanks and indistinct brown streaking on creamy-white underparts; white tail spots; red to orange iris. Ssp *finschi* warmer olive upperparts, more distinct streaking on underparts, thinner bill; *atjehensis* as previous but more prominent tail spots and thicker bill. **Imm** orange bill; more olive upperparts; paler eye. **Voc** Song: 10-15 thin, high-pitched, descending notes "si'si'si'si...", lasting <2 s. Call: squeaky toy-like "sweep". **SS** See Brown-backed Flowerpecker. Thicker, straighter bill and streaking on underparts separate Modest from various fem (or male Plain) *Dicaeum* flowerpeckers.

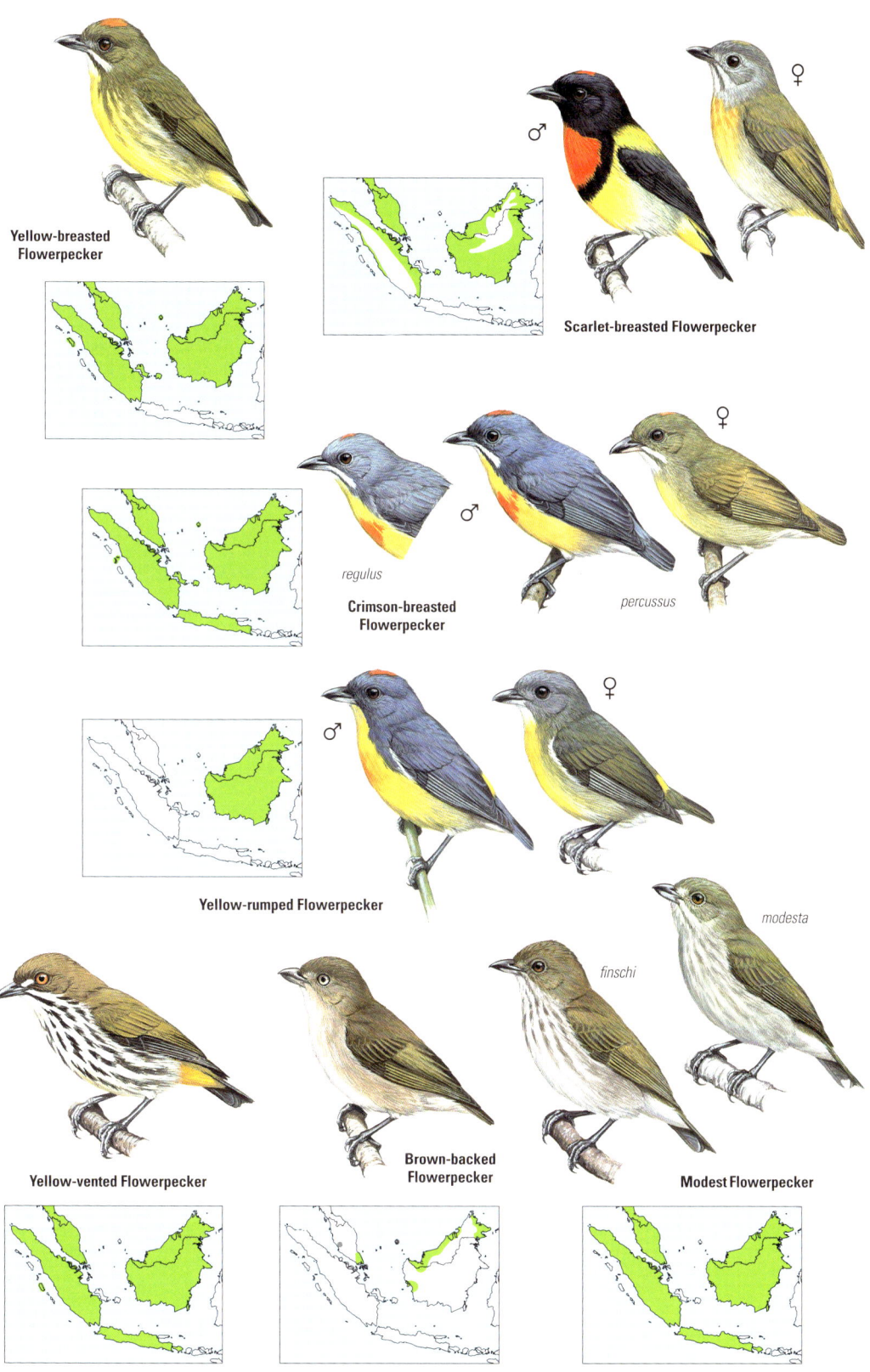

Yellow-breasted Flowerpecker

♂ ♀ **Scarlet-breasted Flowerpecker**

regulus

Crimson-breasted Flowerpecker

♂ *percussus* ♀

♂ ♀ **Yellow-rumped Flowerpecker**

modesta

finschi

Yellow-vented Flowerpecker

Brown-backed Flowerpecker

Modest Flowerpecker

Tenggara Flowerpecker *Pachyglossa obsoleta* E

L 9–10 cm. 2 ssp: *obsoleta* (Timor, Wetar); *tincta* (Flores–Alor, Sumba). For taxonomy see Modest Flowerpecker. Uncommon, locally common, in a variety of wooded habitats, <1000 m, rarely higher. Singly or pairs, but groups (<50) can congregate at fruiting trees. Characteristically wags tail from side to side. **ID Ad** olive-brown head and upperparts; pale malar; pure white underparts; white tail spots; red to orange iris. Ssp *tincta* indistinct breast streaking. **Imm** orange bill; brighter olive upperparts. **Voc** Song: thin, squeaky "chew'it, chew'it, chew'it...", regularly repeated. Call: soft, squeaky "sweep". **SS** See Golden-rumped Flowerpecker.

Golden-rumped Flowerpecker *Pachyglossa annae* E

L 9–10 cm. 2 ssp: *annae* (Flores); *sumbavensis* (Sumbawa). Common in variety of habitats: woodland, montane forest, edge, roadside scrub, villages. Singly or pairs, but small groups (<10) can congregate at fruiting trees. **ID M** olive-green head and upperparts; bright yellow feathers on rump, usually concealed; distinct pale malar stripe; dirty pale-grey streaky underparts with faint yellowish line down centre. **F** lacks yellow on rump. Ssp *sumbavensis* smaller, upperparts brighter. **Imm** less distinct underparts; orange bill base. **Voc** Song: thin, high-pitched, descending series of notes, "see-see-see...", lasting 2–4 sec at 5 n/s, gradually slowing to 3 n/s, sometimes stuttering. Call: bleating, hard series of rapid notes, "pit'pit'pit...", lasting <1 sec at 15 n/s. **SS** Tenggara Flowerpecker has less distinct malar stripe, has cleaner and whiter underparts, more brownish-tinged (less bright-olive) upperparts, white tail spots (absent in Golden-rumped), and displays unique sideways tail wagging behaviour while foraging.

Grey-sided Flowerpecker *Dicaeum celebicum* E

L 9 cm. 5 ssp: *celebicum* (Sul and satellites); *sanghirense* (Sangihe, Siau); *talautense* (Talaud); *sulaense* (Banggai, Sula); *kuehni* (Tukangbesi). Ssp *kuehni* proposed for monotypic species status ('**Tukangbesi Flowerpecker**') based on somewhat deep mtDNA divergence, but plumage and vocal differences not too pronounced. Ssp *talautense* appears to have most distinct plumage among all races and may merit monotypic species status ('**Talaud Flowerpecker**'). Comprehensive study required. Common in forest, edge, gardens, roadside bushes, <1200 m. **ID M** glossy blue-black head and upperparts; large scarlet breast patch; sooty-black flanks and central belly stripe; white chin and buff-tinged belly. Ssp *sanghirense* indistinct belly stripe, pale-grey flanks; *talautense* bluer upperparts, uniform sooty-black belly and flanks; *sulaense* greyish belly stripe, bluer upperparts, sooty-olive flanks; *kuehni* purplish-blue upperparts, grey-tinged belly and olive-grey rear flanks. **F** slate-grey head and upperparts; whitish underparts; dusky-olive flanks; *talautense* darker olive underparts. **Imm** orange bill base; yellow-tinged underparts. **Voc** Song: high-pitched, thin "soo-s'swee" lasting 0.6 sec. Call: (i) buzzy, hard "zrit"; (ii) quiet, thin "swee". **SS** See Crimson-crowned Flowerpecker.

Crimson-crowned Flowerpecker *Dicaeum nehrkorni* E

L 9 cm. Monotypic. Fairly common in (sub-) montane forest, edge, 900–2400 m, rarely lower. **ID M** scarlet crown and rump; sooty-grey head, throat and flanks; white abdomen with blackish central stripe and small scarlet breast spot; upperparts and tail glossy blue-black. **F** duller; sooty head, blue-black upperparts with red rump; underparts dusky-white. **Imm** lacks red rump; has orange bill base. **Voc** Very high-pitched, short "si'it". **SS** Fem Grey-sided Flowerpecker lacks red rump, but imm Crimson-crowned probably not safely separable from imm Grey-sided.

Yellow-sided Flowerpecker *Dicaeum aureolimbatum* E

L 9 cm. 2 ssp: *aureolimbatum* (Sul and satellites); *laterale* (Sangihe). Fairly common in woodland, edge, <2000 m. **ID Ad** olive-green crown and upperparts; darker face mask; black wings and tail; underparts white with broad, bright yellow flanks and vent. Ssp *laterale* yellow restricted to upper flanks. **Imm** pale bill base; flanks and vent less bright. **Voc** High-pitched, upslurred "sooit".

Spectacled Flowerpecker *Dicaeum dayakorum* E

L 8 cm. Monotypic. Scarce in lowland primary forest on Bor, probably <400 m. Exact habits and habitat requirements insufficiently known but possibly does not tolerate forest degradation. Has been found feeding on mistletoe in mid-canopy. **ID Ad** slate-grey head and upperparts with contrasting broken white eyering and loral line; broad white stripe down centre of underparts bordered by wide grey flanks, which can show coarse dark streaks on lower flanks (probably in **M**); quite thick, pointed bill, slightly decurved. **Imm** undescribed. **Voc** Song: Soft introductory note, followed by rapid series of ~15 high-pitched "si'si'si..." notes, gradually rising, lasting <1.5 s. Call: sharp, high-pitched "zzk". **SS** Fem Bornean Flowerpecker from higher elevations lacks white eyering and loral line and shows olive belly (white in all known photos of Spectacled) and olive mantle and rump (slate-grey in Spectacled).

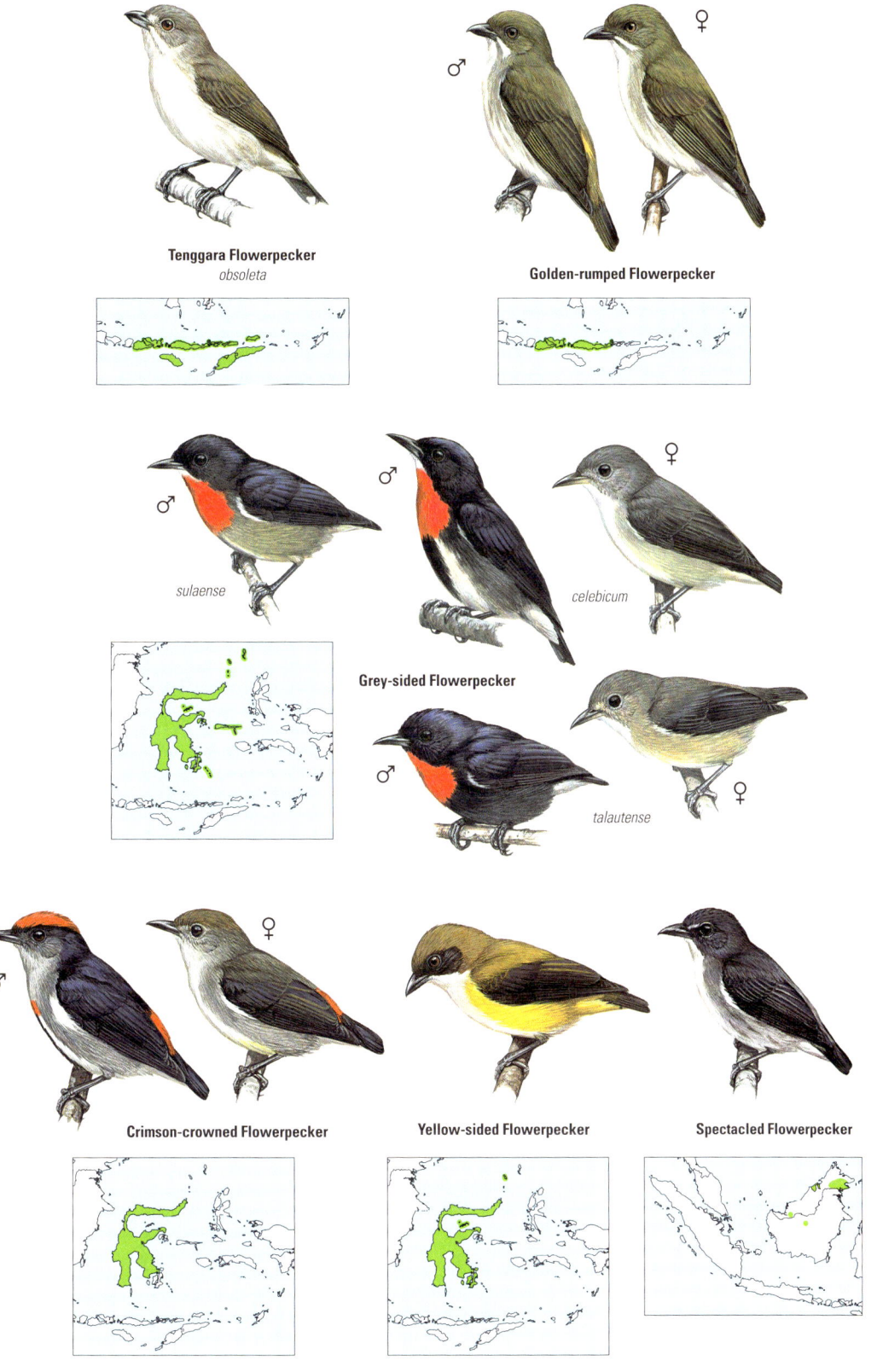

Tenggara Flowerpecker
obsoleta

Golden-rumped Flowerpecker

sulaense

celebicum

Grey-sided Flowerpecker

talautense

Crimson-crowned Flowerpecker

Yellow-sided Flowerpecker

Spectacled Flowerpecker

Orange-bellied Flowerpecker *Dicaeum trigonostigma*
L 8–9 cm. SE Asia, Phil. 17 ssp, 5 in region: *trigonostigma* (Sum and eastern satellites to Anambas and Karimata, MPen); *antioproctum* (Simeulue, Babi, Nias, Batu, Mentawai); *dayakanum* (Bor); *megastoma* (Natuna); *flaviclunis* (Jav, Bali). Complex internal taxonomy; more research required into distinctness of some races. Common in forest, woodland, edge and parkland, <1800 m. **ID** Pointed, slightly decurved, slender bill (larger in *megastoma*); *antioproctum* larger-bodied. **M** slate-blue head, wings and tail; paler throat; deep orange mantle and breast becoming paler towards vent and rump. Ssp *dayakanum* slightly darker throat, deeper orange mantle; *flaviclunis* yellower rump. **F** olive-green head and upperparts; throat, breast and flanks olive-grey; mid-belly, rump and vent brighter yellow; blackish wings and tail; pale bill base. Ssp *antioproctum* brighter rump, brighter belly; *flaviclunis* as previous but darker-yellow belly. **Imm** greener overall; orange bill base. **Voc** Song: thin series of high-pitched, deliberate notes, usually descending, sometimes level, "tsit'sit'sit'sit'sew...", lasting <1.5 sec at 6 n/s. Call: thin, hard "dzip". **SS** See Plain, Sumatran, Scarlet-backed, Scarlet-headed, Javan and Bornean Flowerpeckers.

Plain Flowerpecker *Dicaeum minullum*
L 8–9 cm. Himalaya to SE–E Asia. 5 ssp, 2 in region: *borneanum* (Bor–Sum, MPen); *sollicitans* (Jav–Bali). Often merged with Nilgiri Flowerpecker *D. concolor* (S India) and Andamans Flowerpecker *D. virescens* (Andamans) into a more broadly-defined '**Plain Flowerpecker**' *D. concolor*, but morphological differences (less so vocalisations) suggest separation. Uncommon in a variety of woodland habitats, <1200 m, rarely higher. Usually found around mistletoe. **ID Ad** olive-green head and upperparts; paler, greyer throat; usually paler loral and/or superciliary mark; olive-tinged whitish underparts; thin, decurved black bill with grey base to lower mandible. Ssp *sollicitans* less distinct lores; possibly brighter olive rump. **Imm** less olive overall; orange bill base. **Voc** Song: (i) 2–3 ascending introductory notes followed by rapid series of level notes "tsit-tsit-tsit-sis-sis-sis...", lasting 1–2 sec at 7 n/s, introductory notes sometimes absent; (ii) monotonous, thin, high-pitched "to-wit, to-wit, to-wit...". Call: short, hard "tick". **SS** Fem Scarlet-headed, Javan and Scarlet-backed Flowerpeckers have red (not olive) rump usually well visible, and a plainer face. Fem Orange-bellied has unmarked head, yellowish (not olive) belly and rump (but beware of Imm Orange-bellied which sometimes only shows yellow flush on belly). Fem Sumatran and Bornean Flowerpeckers have contrasting greyish (not olive) head (in Bornean also breast) lacking Plain Flowerpecker's paler loral/superciliary line. Fem Sumatran also has bright-buff (not olive-tinged) underparts contrasting more strongly with olive upperparts. Imm Plain Flowerpeckers (with orange bills) are probably indistinguishable from a variety of other imm flowerpeckers. Also see Brown-backed and Modest Flowerpeckers and Pygmy Heleia.

Sumatran Flowerpecker *Dicaeum beccarii* **E**
L 7–9 cm. Monotypic. Traditionally included with extralimital '**Fire-breasted Flowerpecker**' *D. ignipectus* (Himalaya to SE Asia, Phil), but separated based on distinct plumage and vocalisations. Common in (sub-) montane forest, edge, >800 m. **ID M** glossy greenish-blue head and upperparts; dusky flanks; rich buff underparts; slightly rose-tinted breast with black central belly stripe. **F** pale-grey head; olive upperparts; blackish tail; rich buff underparts. **Imm** orange bill base; greyer upperparts; more uniform overall. **Voc** Song: high-pitched, descending, 3-note "tsit-tsit-tsit" lasting 0.6 sec. Call: sharp, metallic "tsik". **SS** Fem Orange-bellied Flowerpecker is all olive-green above (lacking Sumatran's contrast between grey

head and olive back) and has yellowish belly contrasting against dirtier greyish rest of underparts (not uniform buff underparts). See also Plain Flowerpecker. Imm Sumatran might be indistinguishable from other species.

Bornean Flowerpecker *Dicaeum monticolum* **E**
L 8 cm. Monotypic. Common in (sub-) montane forest, edge, 800–2500 m, rarely to 450 m. **ID M** crown and upperparts glossy blue-black; sooty-black face, upper flanks and lower breast; large scarlet breast patch; olive-yellow belly. **F** grey head and breast; olive mantle, rump and belly; black wings and tail. **Imm** uniform olive-grey; orange bill base. **Voc** Song: high-pitched, 4-note "swee-swit-sip-sip" lasting 1 sec. Call: (i) single, upslurred "swee"; (ii) hard "chip", usually in flight. **SS** Fem Orange-bellied Flowerpecker not nearly as grey on head and breast, with yellowish (not olive) belly. See also Spectacled and Plain Flowerpeckers. Imm Bornean might be indistinguishable from other species. **AN** Black-sided Flowerpecker.

Scarlet-backed Flowerpecker *Dicaeum cruentatum*
L 7–9 cm. S–SE–E Asia. 7 ssp, 6 in region: *ignitum* (Riau Is, MPen); *sumatranum* (Sum and some satellites); *simalurense* (Simeulue); *niasense* (Nias); *batuense* (Batu, Mentawai); *nigrimentum* (Bor). Common in degraded habitat: swamp forest, edge, gardens, roadside bushes, towns and cities, but enters other woodland and forest types, <1000 m. **ID M** scarlet crown and upperparts; blackish face and breast sides; dusky flanks; glossy blue-black wings and tail; whitish underparts. Ssp *sumatranum* smaller, paler upperparts, black forehead, sooty-black face and throat; *batuense* as previous but darker face, narrow white wedge up throat and breast; *niasense* as *sumatranum* but darker colouration on throat extending to lower breast, stouter bill; *simalurense* larger, darker upperparts more scarlet than previous; *nigrimentum* has blackest face and throat extending to lower breast, darker flanks, though variable, some birds having white and scarlet areas on throat. **F** olive-grey head and upperparts; blackish wings and tail; large scarlet rump; creamy-white underparts. **Imm** orange rump; more uniform olive-brown upperparts and wings; orange bill base. **Voc** Song: thin, rising and falling "see-sip-see-sip...", 6 n/s. Call: (i) upslurred "sit"; (ii) buzzy, metallic "tzip". **SS** Fem Orange-bellied Flowerpecker never shows bright-red rump and has yellowish belly contrasting against pale-greyish rest of underparts (not uniform whitish underparts). Also see Scarlet-headed and Plain Flowerpeckers.

Scarlet-headed Flowerpecker *Dicaeum trochileum* **E**
L 8–9 cm. 2 ssp: *trochileum* (Sum–Bor–Bali); *stresemanni* (Lombok). Common (spreading N in Bor and Sum) in secondary forest, edge, mangroves, habitation, gardens, roadside bushes, <800 m. **ID M** scarlet head, upperparts and breast; glossy blue-black wings and tail; pale-grey underparts. **F** olive-brown head and upperparts; blackish wings and tail; scarlet rump; creamy-white underparts. Ssp *stresemanni* apparently shorter-billed in both sexes; **F** paler head. **Imm** browner upperparts; rump less distinct; grey-tinged underparts; orange bill base. **Voc** Song: (i) high-pitched, sharp "tsip-SI, tsip-SI, tsip-SI"; (ii) simple, high-pitched "tsoo-tsee-sit" lasting 0.6 sec. Call: short, buzzy "tzit". **SS** With practice, similar fem Scarlet-backed and Red-chested Flowerpeckers are told by slightly darker, greyer upperparts (lacking brighter olive tones) and less extensive red rump, but best identified through accompanying males. Fem Orange-bellied Flowerpecker never shows bright-red rump and has yellowish belly contrasting against pale-grey rest of underparts (not uniform whitish underparts). Also see Plain and Javan Flowerpeckers.

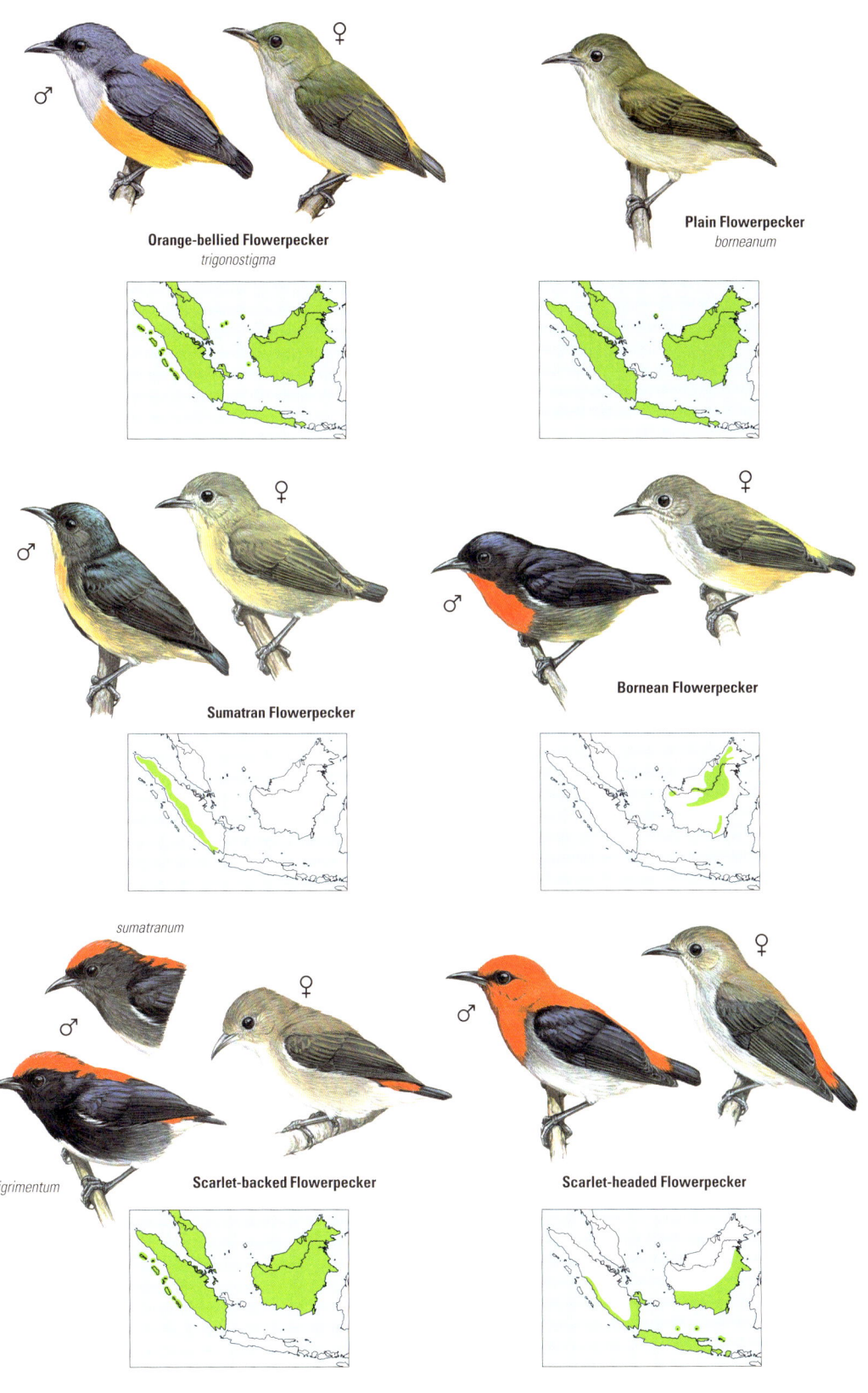

Orange-bellied Flowerpecker
trigonostigma

Plain Flowerpecker
borneanum

Sumatran Flowerpecker

Bornean Flowerpecker

sumatranum

nigrimentum

Scarlet-backed Flowerpecker

Scarlet-headed Flowerpecker

Black-fronted Flowerpecker *Dicaeum igniferum* `E`

L 9 cm. Monotypic. Common in forest, edge, gardens and roadside bushes. **ID M** black head with scarlet crown to upper mantle; scarlet rump and upper breast patch, the latter bordered black below with black line running down central abdomen; remaining upperparts glossy blue-black; white chin and remaining underparts. **F** face and throat grey; white underparts; scarlet crown and upper mantle slightly faded. **Imm** grey crown; paler bill. **Voc** Song: (i) 5–7 high-pitched "see-saw-see-saw-see..." lasting 1–1.5 sec; (ii) high-pitched "tee-tsit-tsit-tst" lasting 1 sec. Call: single, repeated "tik", usually in flight. **SS** See Flores Flowerpecker.

Red-chested Flowerpecker *Dicaeum maugei* `E`

L 9 cm. 4 ssp: *maugei* (Timor, Wetar, Romang, Damar, Sawu, Rote); *salvadorii* (Moa, Babar); *neglectum* (Nusa Penida, Lombok); *splendidum* (Salayar, Tanahjampea). Common in forest, edge, gardens and roadside bushes. **ID M** glossy blue-black head and upperparts; scarlet rump and upper breast patch; black breast band and line down belly; rest of underparts and chin white. Ssp *salvadorii* larger red breast patch, narrower black breast band; *neglectum* more slender bill, darker red breast, thicker black belly stripe; *splendidum* paler breast patch, black breast band vestigial. **F** grey head and upperparts; scarlet rump; black tail; whitish underparts. Ssp *splendidum* has reddish-flecked mantle. **Imm** orange bill base. **Voc** Song: (i) short, high-pitched "tzit-soo-see" lasting <1 sec; (ii) longer ~10 note "ta-see, ta-see, ta-see..." lasting ~2 sec. Call: short, hard "pik". **SS** See Timor and Scarlet-headed Flowerpeckers.

Javan Flowerpecker *Dicaeum sanguinolentum* `E`

L 9 cm. Monotypic. Traditionally included Flores, Sumba and Timor Flowerpeckers to form more broadly-defined umbrella species, '**Blood-breasted Flowerpecker**' *D. sanguinolentum*, but strong differences in vocalisations and plumage suggest separation. Fairly common in (sub-) montane forest, edge, roadside bushes, >800 m. **ID M** glossy dark-blue head, upperparts and upper flanks; pale-buff underparts with broad scarlet breast patch; broad black central belly stripe. **F** greyish head and upperparts with bluish tinge on wings; lemon-buff underparts; scarlet rump. **Imm** darker grey head; more yellowish underparts; orange bill base. **Voc** Five call types: (i) buzzy "whit'it'it"; (ii) repeated buzzy "whit"; (iii) buzzy "tcho-tcho-tcho..."; (iv) hard "chip"; (v) upslurred "swee". Song consists of combination of calls. **SS** Similar fem Scarlet-headed Flowerpecker from lower elevations has olive-toned (not greyish) head and mantle and more whitish (not lemon-buff) underparts. Fem Orange-bellied Flowerpecker never shows bright-red rump and has yellowish belly contrasting against greyish rest of underparts (not uniform buff underparts). Also see Plain Flowerpecker.

Flores Flowerpecker *Dicaeum rhodopygiale* `E`

L 9 cm. Monotypic. For taxonomy see Javan Flowerpecker. Fairly common in (sub-) montane forest, edge, roadside bushes, >800 m. **ID M** similar to Javan but wider breast patch; lacks blue-black upper flanks and breast sides; buffier underparts; pinkish vent. **F** similar to Javan. **Imm** darker grey head; more yellowish underparts; orange bill base. **Voc** Song: high-pitched "ta-see, ta-see, ta-see..." lasting 1–4 sec at 2 n/s, regularly interspersed with call notes. Call: (i) hard "chi'it, chi'it, chi'it...", regularly repeated; (ii) thin, downslurred "sewp"; (iii) upslurred "ti'it". **SS** Fem Black-fronted Flowerpecker has red crown.

Sumba Flowerpecker *Dicaeum wilhelminae* `E`

L 9 cm. Monotypic. For taxonomy see Javan Flowerpecker. Common in all woodland, gardens and roadside bushes. **ID** Shorter, thicker bill than Javan. **M** glossy blue-black head and upperparts; scarlet throat and breast; white chin; dirty-grey belly, darker flanks; thick black central belly stripe. **F** grey head; olive-grey upperparts; cold whitish underparts; red rump. **Imm** orange bill base. **Voc** Song: (i) short, high-pitched "tsoo-soo-see" lasting 1 sec; (ii) series of 6–10 ascending high-pitched notes "si'-sip-sip-sip..." at 6 n/s, occasionally followed by series of equally spaced descending notes; (iii) series of 10–15 descending high-pitched notes "swip-swit-swit-swit..." at 10 n/s. Call: soft "tip".

Timor Flowerpecker *Dicaeum hanieli* `E`

L 8 cm. Monotypic. For taxonomy see Javan Flowerpecker. Fairly common in montane forest, >800 m. **ID M** glossy blue-black head and upperparts; creamy-white underparts; small red breast patch; short black strip on central belly immediately below red breast patch. **F/Imm** undescribed. **Voc** Song: high-pitched "soo-sip-see" lasting 0.6 sec and similar variations. Call: high-pitched "sweree". **SS** Male Red-chested from lower elevations has red rump (absent in male Timor), whiter (less creamy) underparts, and more extensive red breast patch bordered below by black margin (only small black mid-belly strip in Timor). Females should be identified based on accompanying males on current knowledge.

Salvadori's Flowerpecker *Dicaeum keiense* `E`

L 9 cm. 2 ssp: *keiense* (Kai); *fulgidum* (Tanimbar). Traditionally included with extralimital '**Mistletoebird**' *D. hirundinaceum* (Australia, Aru) but colouration differs significantly. Common in forest, edge. **ID M** glossy blue-purple head and upperparts; pinkish-red breast, upper belly and vent; dusky olive flanks and lower belly; pinkish-white throat; relatively narrow black belly stripe. Ssp *fulgidum* slightly thicker and longer black central belly stripe; warmer, more pinkish-buff flanks and lower belly. **F** dark olive-grey head and upperparts; pink rump and vent; whitish underparts with slight greyish streaking on breast sides; *fulgidum* less olive-tinged (more greyish-brown) on upperparts, and warm-buff lower flanks on white underparts. **Imm** (*fulgidum*) orange bill base. **Voc** Song: (*keiense*) high-pitched "swee-sip" lasting 0.5 sec; (*fulgidum*) (i) series of 5–8 high-pitched "tsoo-tsoo-tsoo..." at 3–5 n/s; (ii) buzzier, more rapid series of 5–10 "tzzoo-tzzoo-tzzoo..." at 7 n/s. Call: (i) buzzy "chip"; (ii) upslurred "swee".

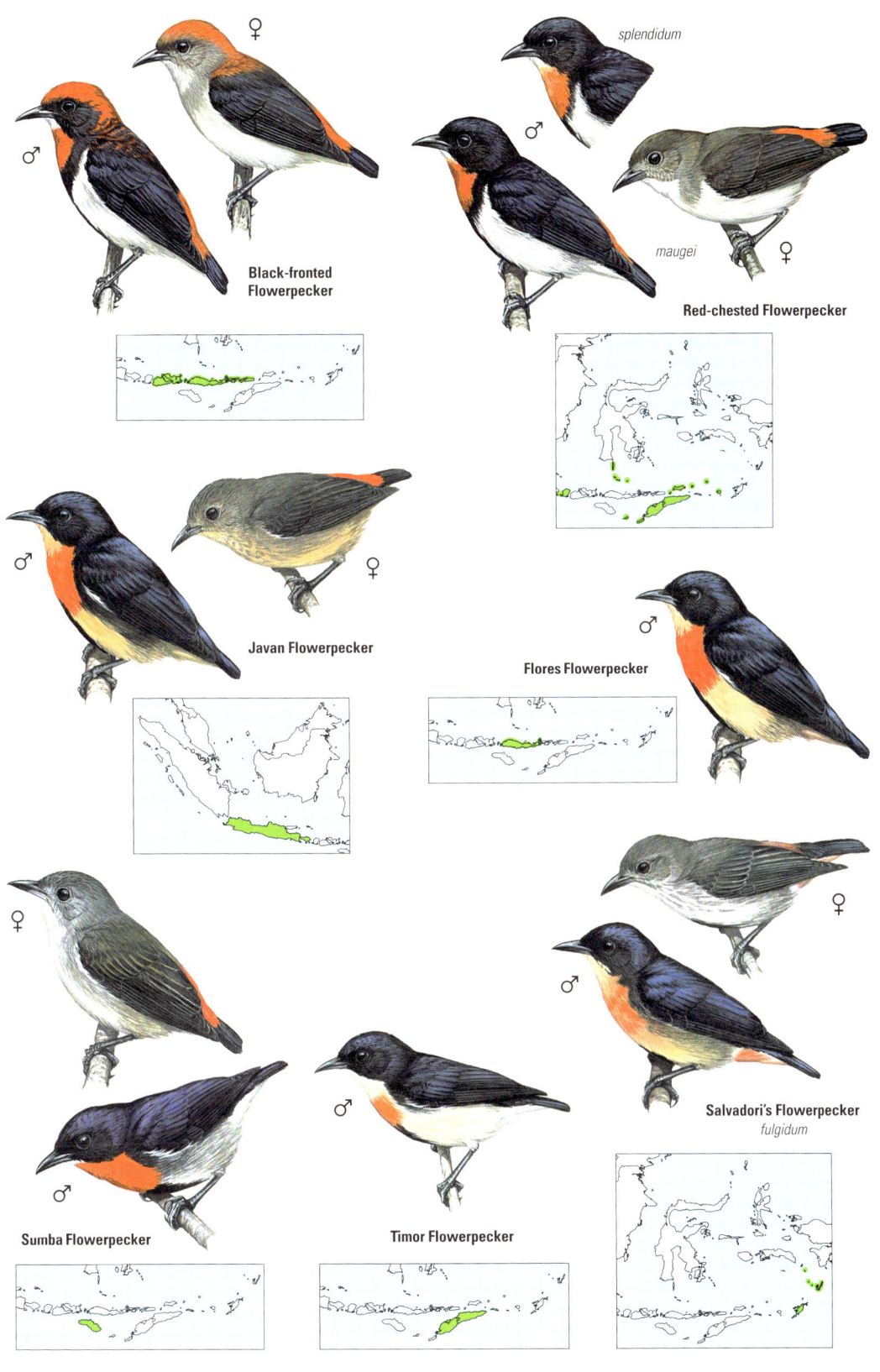

Black-fronted Flowerpecker

♀

♂

splendidum

♂

maugei

♀

Red-chested Flowerpecker

♂

♀

Javan Flowerpecker

♂

Flores Flowerpecker

♀

♂

Salvadori's Flowerpecker
fulgidum

♀

♂

Sumba Flowerpecker

♂

Timor Flowerpecker

Halmahera Flowerpecker *Dicaeum schistaceiceps* **E**

L 9 cm. Monotypic. Traditionally merged with Buru Flowerpecker into expanded '**Flame-breasted Flowerpecker**' *D. erythrothorax* but pronounced plumage differences dictate break-up. Fairly common in forest, edge. **ID M** dark grey head and throat; large scarlet breast patch; yellow-olive belly; olive upperparts. **F** broad white stripe down the mid-line of underparts; no breast patch. **Imm** more uniform dark-grey overall; orange bill base. **Voc** (i) Single, high-pitched, slightly upslurred "tseee"; (ii) single, short, sharp "peep".

Buru Flowerpecker *Dicaeum erythrothorax* **E**

L 9 cm. Monotypic. For taxonomy see Halmahera Flowerpecker. Fairly common in forest, edge, <1100 m. **ID M** dark-grey head and upper flanks; white throat; large scarlet breast patch; yellow-olive belly; olive upperparts. **F** white abdomen to throat; no breast patch. **Imm** more uniform dark-grey overall; orange bill base. **Voc** Song: ~6 high-pitched, level notes delivered at variable speed "see-see-see-see-see-see" lasting 0.5–1 sec, occasionally last note upslurred. Call: short, sharp "tik".

Seram Flowerpecker *Dicaeum vulneratum* **E**

L 9 cm. Monotypic. Common in forest, edge, <1500 m, scarcer above. **ID M** dark-grey head and upperparts; paler grey underparts; scarlet breast patch and rump. **F** white underparts; greyish flanks; lacks breast patch. **Imm** lacks red rump. **Voc** Song: series of <70 high-pitched notes, changing delivery speed "sis-sis-sis...", <6 sec at 7–13 n/s. Call: (i) hard "tuk"; (ii) high-pitched, downslurred "tsrrr". **AN** Ashy Flowerpecker.

Small, elegantly-built arboreal birds with long, decurved bills and often brightly coloured and metallic plumage. Typically feed singly or in pairs, occasionally with mixed flocks. Most species are primarily nectarivorous, although many take fruit and insects as well. Usually active and conspicuous within mid- to upper storey. Inhabit a range of wooded habitats including agricultural and urban areas.

Apricot-breasted Sunbird *Cinnyris buettikoferi* **E**

L 11 cm. Monotypic. Common in variety of wooded habitats including gardens and plantations. **ID M** iridescent purplish-green throat; orange breast patch; yellow underparts; dark olive-green upperparts; greyish-tinged crown; yellow pectoral tufts. **F** whitish throat to pale yellow belly. **Imm** undescribed. **Voc** Song: thin, high-pitched, descending "tsweet-sweet-weet-weet" lasting 1.5 sec. Call: thin "chit" and "sip".

Flame-breasted Sunbird *Cinnyris solaris* **E**

L 11 cm. 2 ssp: *solaris* (Sumbawa–Timor); *exquisitus* (Wetar). Fairly common in variety of wooded habitats including gardens and plantations, <1400 m. **ID M** iridescent blue-green forecrown and throat; orange pectoral tufts; dark olive-green upperparts; orange breast becoming yellower to vent. Ssp *exquisitus* paler pectoral tufts; heavier bill. **F** yellow underparts; some birds have thin supercilium. **Imm** greyer overall. **Voc** Song: repeated series of notes alternating in pitch, "tee-teh-teey-tee, t'tee-teh-teey..." lasting ~2 sec, regularly repeated. Call: slightly squeaky "tchew" and disyllabic "tchew-a". **SS** Fem Ornate Sunbird on average slightly brighter underparts, otherwise extremely similar, most females unidentifiable.

Ornate Sunbird *Cinnyris ornatus*

L 10–11 cm. SE Asia. 8 ssp, 2 in region: *ornatus* (MPen, GS, LS); *polyclystus* (Enggano). Traditionally united with Sahul Sunbird and extralimital Garden Sunbird *C. jugularis* (Phil) to form more broadly defined umbrella species, '**Olive-backed Sunbird**' *C. jugularis*. However, here separated because of deep differences in vocalisations and mtDNA. Fairly common in variety of habitats including woodland, parks, mangroves, urban areas and scrub, <1700 m. **ID** Olive-green upperparts, bright yellow underparts, black tail with broad white tips; *polyclystus* longer-billed, larger, with darker upperparts and deeper yellow underparts. **M** iridescent purple throat, breast and forecrown. **F** indistinct pale supercilium. **Imm** paler underparts; less bright. **Voc** Song in region: unmusical, nasal, with buzzy introductory note, "tswit chit-chit swit'swit'swit..." at 4 n/s. Call: (i) single "sweep"; (ii) buzzy "sweey". **SS** See Van Hasselt's, Purple-throated and Flame-breasted Sunbirds.

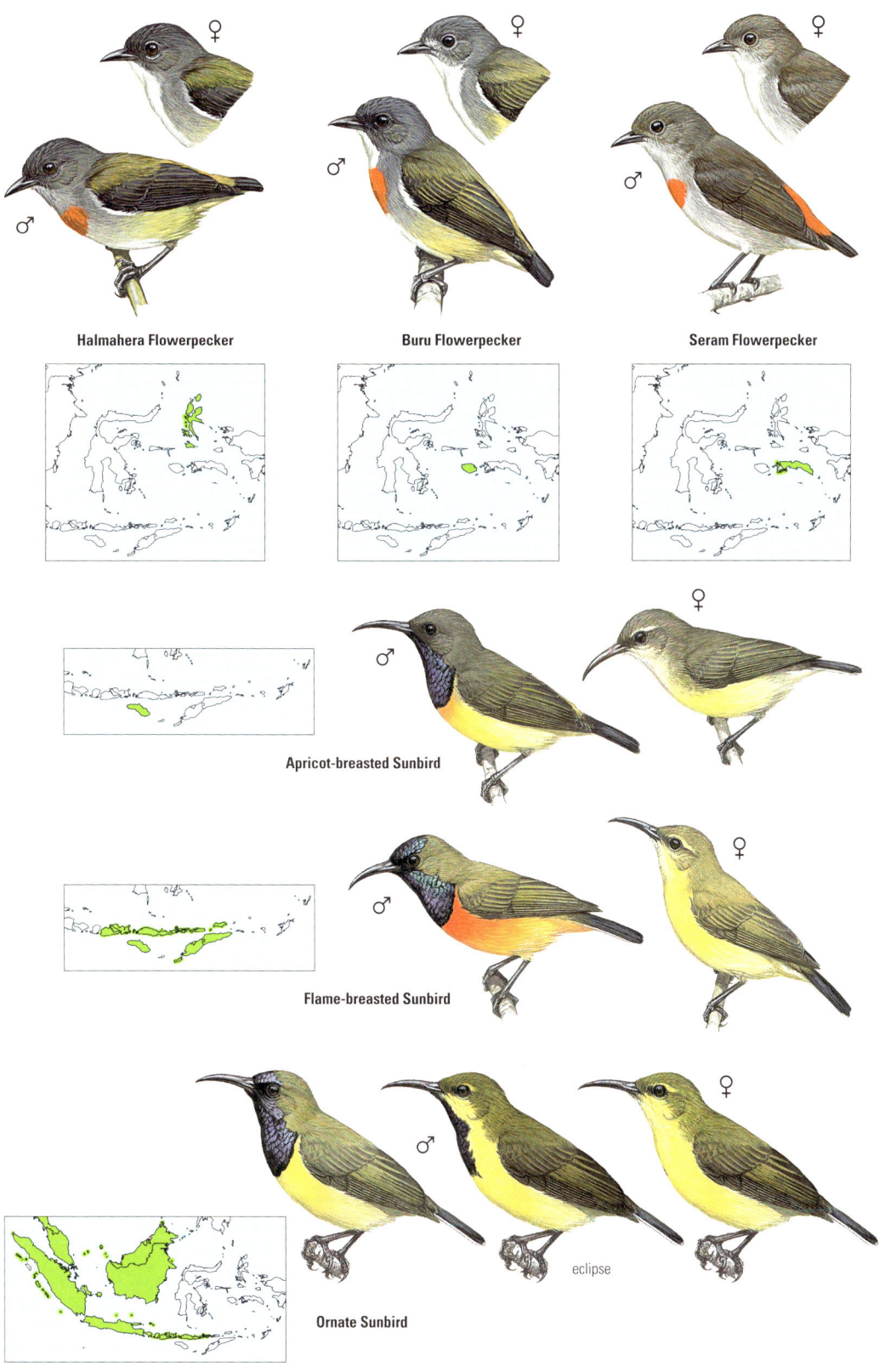

Halmahera Flowerpecker

Buru Flowerpecker

Seram Flowerpecker

Apricot-breasted Sunbird

Flame-breasted Sunbird

eclipse

Ornate Sunbird

Sahul Sunbird *Cinnyris clementiae*

L 10–11. Aus. 11 ssp, 9 in region: *clementiae* (Boano, Seram, Ambon, Watubela); *keiensis* (Kai); *buruensis* (Buru); *teysmanni* (Tanahjampea, Kalao, Bonerate, Kalaotoa, Madu); *frenatus* (N Mol; NG, Aru, Australia); *robustirostris* (Banggai–Sula); *plateni* (Talaud–Sul and satellites); *saleyerensis* (Selayar); *infrenatus* (Tukangbesi). Great morphological variation among taxa may warrant separation into ≤5 species, with a male black- versus yellow-bellied plumage emerging independently up to three times, and a male brown- versus olive-backed plumage emerging up to two independent times: '**Clementia's Sunbird**' *C. clementiae* (black-bellied and olive-backed; also including *buruensis* and *keiensis*); '**Flores Sea Sunbird**' *C. teysmanni* (black-bellied and brown-backed; monotypic); '**Tukangbesi Sunbird**' *C. infrenatus* (yellow-bellied, brown-backed and plain-faced; monotypic); '**Sahul Sunbird**' *C. frenatus* (yellow-bellied and olive-backed; also including *robustirostris*, *plateni*, *saleyerensis* and one extralimital ssp); and the extralimital '**Rand's Sunbird**' *C. idenburgi* (black-bellied and brown-backed; monotypic; NG). Genomic and bioacoustic research required. For taxonomy also see Ornate Sunbird. Fairly common in variety of habitats including woodland, cultivation, mangroves, towns and scrub, <1700 m. **ID** Black tail with broad white tips. **M** 'Clementia's' races: *clementiae* yellowish-olive upperparts (lacking pale facial stripes of some other races), purplish throat, black belly and yellow pectoral tufts; *keiensis* more golden-green upperparts, maroon lower margin to throat, flanks dark yellowish-green, dark maroon tinge to black belly; *buruensis* as previous but brighter green upperparts, lacking maroon tinge on belly. 'Flores Sea' *teysmanni* brownish upperparts; purple-green throat with green sides and bordered below by maroon band; belly glossy purple; pectoral tufts orange and yellow. 'Sahul' races: *frenatus* olive-green upperparts, extensive iridescent purple throat, yellow moustachial stripe and supercilium, yellow underparts; *robustirostris* as previous but longer-billed; *plateni* as *frenatus* but duller upperparts, purple-blue gloss to throat; *saleyerensis* distinctly paler, lemon-yellow underparts. 'Tukangbesi' *infrenatus* as *plateni* but darker and browner upperparts lacking superciliary and moustachial stripes. **F** olive-green upperparts; pale yellow underparts; indistinct yellow to whitish supercilium; *teysmanni* greyish-yellow supercilium and greyer plumage. **Imm** paler underparts, less bright overall. **Voc** Much racial variation. Ssp *clementiae* song: high-pitched trill at 8 n/s, <8 sec; call: single, hard "chip". Ssp *keiensis* song: high-pitched "chit-chit-chit..." at 5 n/s; call: *Zosterops*-like "choo". Ssp *teysmanni* song: structured jumble of rapid notes preceded by buzzy introductory note, "spzzz tchoowir'tchoowir'tchoowir..." lasting 1.5–3 sec; call: harsh "spzzz". Ssp *frenatus* song: several well-spaced introductory "sip" notes followed by long trill, "tip'tip'tip'..." lasting <1.5 sec. Ssp *plateni* song: buzzy 5–10 note "tsit'tsit'tsit..." at 7 n/s; call: (i) buzzy "sweey"; (ii) hard "chip". Ssp *infrenatus* long high-pitched trill converting halfway into lower-pitched, slower trill, preceded by 1–3 introductory notes, "chip sip-sip t't't't't't't't't't tip'tip'tip'tip'tip'tip't ip'tip'tip'tip", lasting ~3 sec; call: hard "chip". **SS** See Elegant and Black Sunbirds.

Black Sunbird *Leptocoma aspasia*

L 11 cm. Aus. 23 ssp, 9 in region: *porphyrolaema* (SW–SE–C–E Sul, Togian, Buton, Muna); *grayi* (N Sul); *sangirensis* (Sangihe, Siau); *talautensis* (Talaud); *auriceps* (Banggai–N Mol); *auricapilla* (Kayoa); *proserpina* (Buru); *aspasioides* (Seram, Ambon, Watubela; Aru); *chlorolaema* (Kai). Fairly common in forest, edge, plantations, coconut groves, <1450 m. **ID M** all black body with throat rich purple bordered greenish-blue; green crown; greenish-blue shoulder and rump. Ssp *grayi* smaller, with dark-maroon back and breast, purple-blue throat, small blue shoulder and rump; *sangirensis* throat bronzy with purple border, golden-green crown, bluish shoulder and rump; *talautensis* differs from previous by greener crown, wing-coverts violet-blue; *auriceps* blue throat, darker golden-green crown, blue shoulder and rump; *auricapilla* similar to previous but wing-coverts and rump violet or purplish-blue; *proserpina* purplish-blue throat, crown green, black wing-coverts, metallic greenish-blue scapulars and rump; *aspasioides* longer bill, purple-blue throat; *chlorolaema* dark-green throat, blue-green shoulder to rump and sides of tail. **F** pale grey head; whitish throat; olive upperparts; pale yellow underparts. Ssp *sangirensis* orange throat, pale green underparts; *talautensis* browner upperparts, orange throat, whitish underparts; *proserpina* and *aspasioides* darker grey hood, olive belly. **Imm** more uniform olive-yellow. **Voc** Song: rapid, high-pitched trill at 10 n/s, lasting 1–5 sec. Call: high-pitched, repetitive "zip, zip-zip-zip...". **SS** Similar black races of male Sahul Sunbird have dull olive-green crown and upperparts, lacking male Black's iridescent crown and shoulders. Fem Sahul shows faint supercilium, white tail tips and (compared to most Black ssp) more uniform yellow underparts (usually lacking white or orange throat). Sturdier, bigger fem Brown-throated Sunbird has distinct eyering and is drabber, more colourless overall (lacking contrast between greyish and whitish tones of hood against olive and yellow rest of body in most races of Black). See also Elegant Sunbird and Sultan's Myzomela.

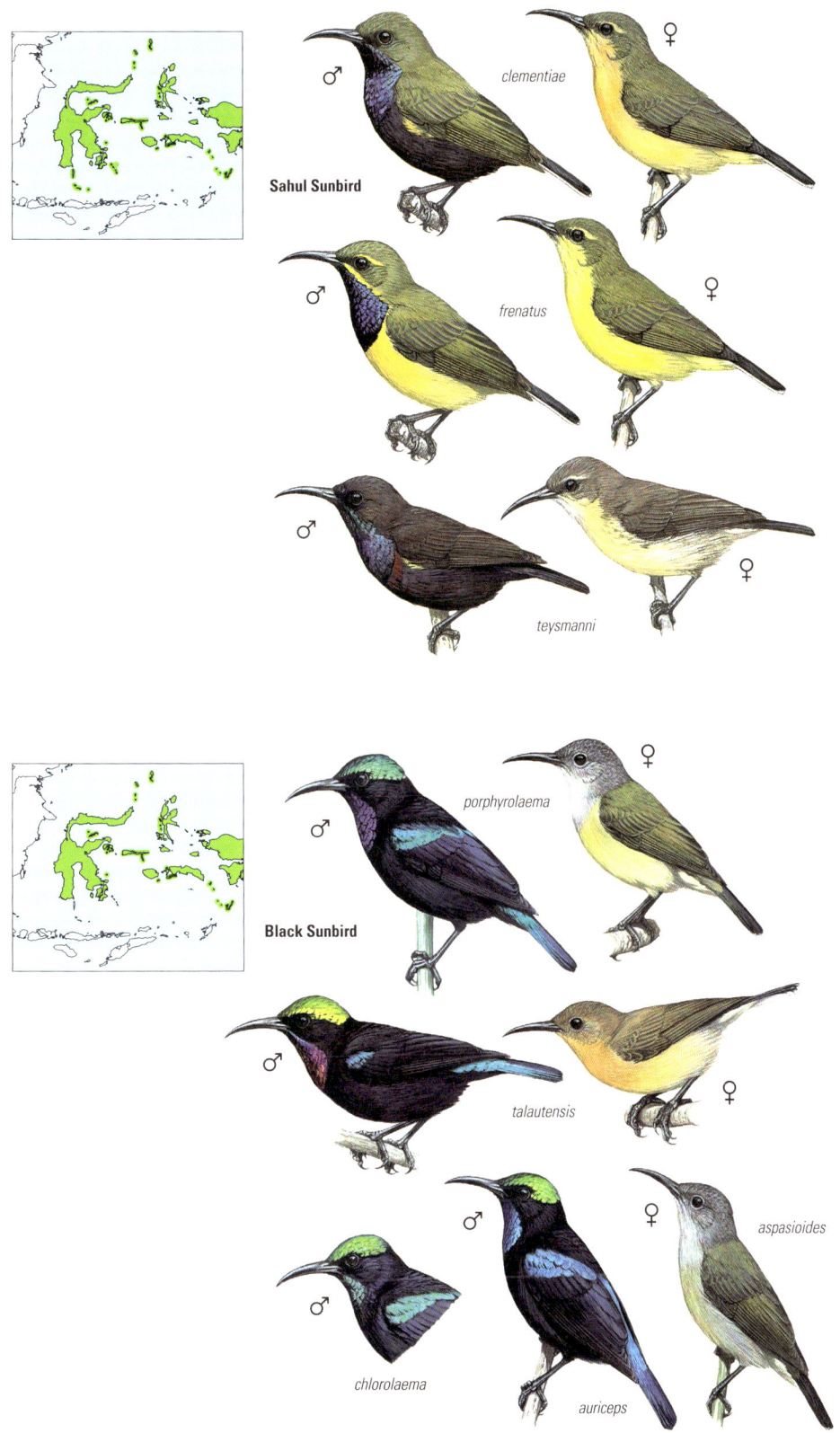

Sahul Sunbird

♂ ♀ *clementiae*

♂ *frenatus* ♀

♂ *teysmanni* ♀

Black Sunbird

♂ *porphyrolaema* ♀

♂ *talautensis* ♀

♂ *chlorolaema* ♂ *auriceps* ♀ *aspasioides*

Copper-throated Sunbird *Leptocoma calcostetha*

L 13 cm. Sundaic, Palawan. Monotypic. Highly local but fairly common where found in mangroves, coastal scrub, alluvial forest, gardens, <200 m, rarely to 900 m. **ID** Black legs. **M** overall blackish appearance; iridescent green crown, shoulder patch and rump; copper-red throat with purple sides; dull dusky flanks and belly. **F** grey head with indistinct pale broken eyering; whitish throat; yellow breast becoming paler to belly; olive upperparts; long black tail with white tips. **Imm** scaled yellowish throat. **Voc** Song: series of high-pitched rapid trills "si'si'si'..." at 6 n/s lasting 1–2 sec. Call: (i) downslurred "eh-choo"; (ii) very thin "sip". **SS** Copper-throated is larger and longer-tailed than Van Hasselt's and Purple-throated Sunbirds, male with blackish (not red) breast, fem usually looks more spectacled than Van Hasselt's and Purple-throated, with diagnostic white tail spots and distinct contrast between yellow breast and whitish throat (versus a more uniform or washed-out yellow or whitish breast and throat).

Van Hasselt's Sunbird *Leptocoma brasiliana*

L 9–10 cm. SE Asia. 5 ssp, 4 in region: *brasiliana* (SE Asia to GS); *mecynorhyncha* (Simeulue); *axantha* (Natuna); *eumecis* (Anambas). Traditionally included with Purple-throated Sunbird (under the same name) but here separated based on plumage; more research required. Locally fairly common, though recent declines in Sum–Jav due to heavy poaching pressure; forest, edge, coastal scrub, usually in high canopy (where widely overlooked), <1200 m. Singly or pairs. **ID** Black legs. **M** blackish plumage except iridescent green crown and purple throat, red breast and blue rump. Ssp *mecynorhyncha* longer bill, darker black belly; *eumecis* larger with longer bill than nominate; *axantha* larger still. **F** olive-green upperparts, slightly greyer on head; yellowish-white underparts, often paler belly and/or throat; black tail. **Imm** greyer underparts. **Voc** Song: simple, irregularly repeated, "sip-sip-chup-tiddip-sip-chup-chup-sip-tiddip-chup..." at 2–3 n/s, notes with alternating pitch. Call: (i) high-pitched, repeated "chit-chit-chit..."; (ii) low-pitched short trills. **SS** Fem Ornate Sunbird shows diagnostic but faint pale supercilium (absent in Van Hasselt's and Purple-throated), uniformly brighter yellow underparts and throat contrasting strongly with more olive (less greyish) head, and white tail tips (absent in Van Hasselt's and Purple-throated). Also see Copper-throated, Red-throated and Crimson Sunbirds. **AN** Maroon-bellied Sunbird.

Purple-throated Sunbird *Leptocoma sperata*

L 9–10 cm. Phil. 4 ssp, 1 in region: *trochilus* (Maratua, W–C–S Phil). Extralimital ssp *juliae* (W Mindanao, Sulu), perhaps deserving of monotypic species status ('**Julia's Sunbird**'), has highly distinct plumage and oddly separates Maratua population of *trochilus* from nearest population on Mindanao; more research required. For taxonomy also see Van Hasselt's Sunbird. Common in forest, edge, cultivation. **ID M** iridescent bronze-green crown; blackish face; iridescent purple throat; scarlet-orange breast; maroon mantle; iridescent blue-green pectoral spot and rump; dark-purple tail; dark olive to olive-grey lower belly to vent. **F** greyish-olive upperparts; pale lemon underparts; paler belly; black tail. **Imm** greyer underparts. **Voc** Song: high-pitched twittering, faster and more erratic than Van Hasselt's. Call: as Van Hasselt's. **SS** For differences from fem Ornate Sunbird see under Van Hasselt's. Also see Crimson and Copper-throated Sunbirds.

Brown-throated Sunbird *Anthreptes malacensis*

L 12–13 cm. SE Asia, Phil. 16 ssp, 10 in region: *malacensis* (SE Asia to most of GS); *anambae* (Anambas); *erixanthus* (Natuna); *bornensis* (NE Bor); *mjobergi* (Maratua); *heliocalus* (Sangihe, Siau); *celebensis* (Sul and satellites); *extremus* (Banggai, Sula); *convergens* (Lombok–Alor); *rubrigena* (Sumba). Has traditionally included Grey-throated Sunbird *A. griseigularis* (Phil), and some Phil races of present species may be more closely related to the latter. Common in secondary and degraded forest, edge, cultivation, especially coconut palms, mangroves and scrub, <1200 m. **ID** Robust-looking, relatively thick-billed. **M** glossy green crown and upperparts with metallic purple shoulder, rump and back; rufous-olive to chestnut upperwing-coverts; dull brownish throat and cheeks (the latter tinged greenish), otherwise underparts yellow. Ssp *anambae* paler throat and richer yellow underparts; *mjobergi* cheeks concolorous with throat; *erixanthus* greyer flanks and paler belly; *bornensis* smaller; *celebensis* drabber with greenish-tinged underparts, dull chestnut upperwing-coverts; *extremus* as previous but larger and bigger-billed, greyer on throat; *heliocalus* as *celebensis* but longer-winged with brighter, yellower underparts; *convergens* similar to *celebensis* but more greenish-yellow underparts; *rubrigena* similar to previous but lacks chestnut shoulder patch. **F** olive-green upperparts; dull yellow underparts; broad yellow broken eyering. Ssp *bornensis* duller underparts; *celebensis* pale greyish-yellow underparts; *rubrigena* greyer head. **Imm** paler bill. **Voc** Song: piercing, monotonous, up-down "wee-chew-wee-chew-wee-chew ...". Call: (i) high-pitched "tsweet" or shortened "swit"; (ii) sharp "to-wit". **SS** Females' sturdy shape and homogenous olive-yellow appearance with bright yellow eyering facilitates identification from most other female sunbirds, but see Red-throated and Black Sunbirds and Thick-billed Spiderhunter.

Red-throated Sunbird *Anthreptes rhodolaemus*

L 12 cm. Sundaic. Monotypic. Uncommon in primary and mature secondary forest, rarely plantations, <900 m. **ID** Very similar to Brown-throated Sunbird. **M** reddish throat and wing-coverts (the latter more extensive), maroon cheeks and reduced purple shoulder patch; **F** less bright on belly, sometimes tinged orange on breast, and eyering reduced to paler mark immediately below eye. **Imm** greyer underparts. **Voc** High-pitched, thin "see-choo", "see-ch'chit'it", and "sit-sit-sit-see". **SS** Brown-throated male is duller overall: (1) has dull olive-green rather than brightly maroon cheeks, (2) has less extensive and less reddish wing-coverts, and (3) has less intensely green mantle. Some individuals of fem Brown-throated very similar, but generally have more distinct eyering particularly above eye, brighter yellow belly and duller breast (always lacking orange tinge). Smaller fem Van Hasselt's and Crimson also best separated through fem Red-throated's partial pale eyering below eye (absent in the other two) and orange flush on breast (if present). Also see Thick-billed Spiderhunter.

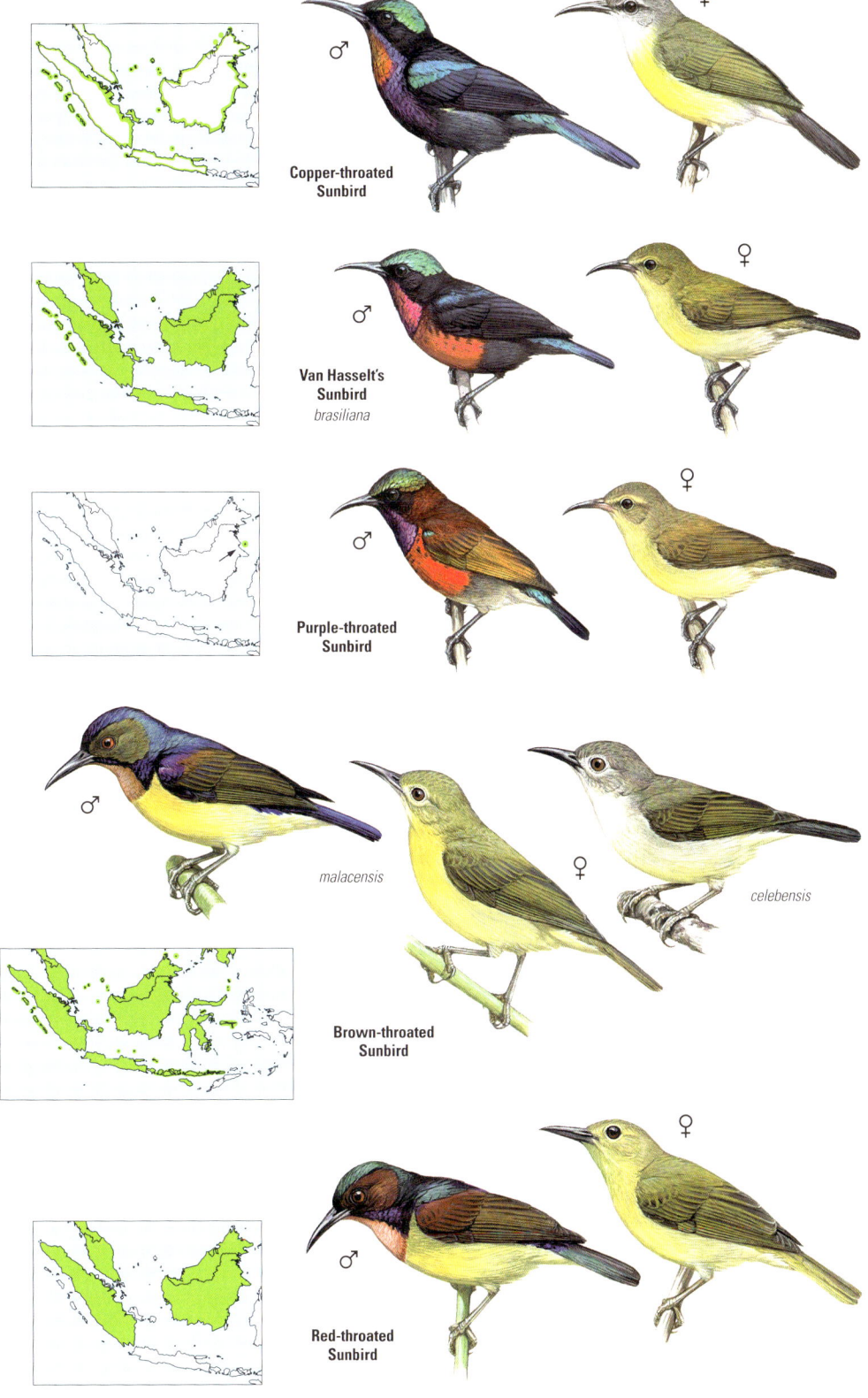

Copper-throated Sunbird

Van Hasselt's Sunbird
brasiliana

Purple-throated Sunbird

malacensis

♀ *celebensis*

Brown-throated Sunbird

Red-throated Sunbird

Plain Sunbird *Anthreptes simplex*

L 12 cm. Sundaic. Monotypic. An atypical species possibly not closely related to other *Anthreptes* sunbirds; more research required. Locally fairly common in forest, <1200 m. Singly, pairs or small groups; joins mixed flocks. **ID** Bill relatively short and straight; olive-green upperparts; pale grey underparts with olive tinge to breast and belly. **M** dark iridescent purple forehead. **Imm** browner upperparts; paler underparts. **Voc** High-pitched, upslurred "sip" and "sip-sip-sip…". **SS** Unique feeding style unlike other sunbirds, more akin to fulvetta or iora as often found in fruiting trees. Plumage lacks any bright tones; stout, quite straight bill and unique combination of sombre olive-green upperparts contrasting with grey underparts should separate from females of other sunbird species.

Crimson Sunbird *Aethopyga siparaja*

L 10–15 cm. S–SE Asia. 14 ssp, 5 in region: *siparaja* (Bor–Sum and satellites, MPen); *natunae* (Natuna); *heliogona* (Jav); *flavostriata* (N Sul); *beccarii* (remaining Sul and satellites). As here defined, does not include Magnificent Sunbird *A. magnifica* (Visayan Is in Phil) based on strong morphological and genetic differentiation. Owing to differences in fem plumage, male iridescence, presence or absence of tail extensions and mtDNA divergence, this species may be separable into three independent species: (1) '**Greater Crimson Sunbird**' *A. seheriae* (S Asia to N mainland SE Asia; 7 extralimital ssp); (2) '**Sulawesi Crimson Sunbird**' *A. flavostriata* (Sul and satellites; also including ssp *beccarii*); (3) '**Lesser Crimson Sunbird**' *A. siparaja* (Sundaic, Nicobars; also including *natunae*, *heliogona* and 2 extralimital ssp). More research required. Common in open canopy forest, edge, parkland, occasionally mangroves and gardens, <1500 m. Singly or pairs. **ID M** bright scarlet head, breast and mantle with iridescent purple forecrown and moustachial stripe; blackish belly fading to vent; yellow rump; purple tail. Ssp *natunae* paler grey belly; *heliogona* some orange on rump, belly paler grey; *flavostriata* and similar *beccarii* yellow streaking on scarlet throat, extensive red margins on upperwing, broader yellow rump, dusky belly, metallic blue forecrown, moustachial and tail. **F** dull-olive overall; slightly paler, yellower underparts and browner wings; leg colour variable, from pinkish, brownish to dark-greyish. Ssp *flavostriata* pinkish mantle; *beccarii* red-tinged upperparts. **Imm** greyer, less yellow; **M** with red spots on throat. **Voc** Song: series of staccato, squeaky notes "tsip-tsit-tsit-tsit…", and "tsit-tsoot-tsit-tsoot-tsit-tsit…", 5 n/s, can last to 5 sec. Call: harsh, squeaky "zit" and "zit-wit". **SS** Male separated from Javan and Temminck's Sunbirds by much darker grey belly, slightly darker red (less scarlet) body, shorter tail virtually lacking extended mid-rectrices; also Temminck's has red (not purple) tail. Similar fem Javan and Temminck's have paler whitish (not yellowish) belly and greyer (less olive) tones on head. Fem Temminck's additionally has orange-reddish tinge to outerwing and tail (all olive in fem Crimson). Smaller fem Van Hasselt's and Purple-throated Sunbirds superficially very similar but have shorter, blacker, square-cut tail and jet-black legs (often but not always browner or otherwise paler on Crimson); otherwise best told through accompanying males. Also see Red-throated Sunbird.

Temminck's Sunbird *Aethopyga temminckii*

L 10–13 cm. Sundaic. Monotypic. Fairly common in hill and montane forest, edge, usually >700 m, scarce in lowlands. Singly or pairs, joins mixed flocks. **ID M** strikingly scarlet with yellow and purple rump patches; silver belly; metallic purple moustachial and crown stripes; elongated scarlet tail. **F** grey head; olive-green upperparts with reddish-tinged wings and tail; underparts pale yellowish becoming whitish on belly. **Imm** like fem but greyer underparts. **Voc** Song: endless, monotonous, soft but far-carrying, grasshopper-like "ch'chit-tit, ch'chit-tit, ch'chit-tit…", 4 n/s, occasionally disyllabic. Call: 2–6 descending, thin notes "sip-sip-sip…", 6 n/s. **SS** See Crimson Sunbird.

Javan Sunbird *Aethopyga mystacalis* **E**

L 10–12 cm. Monotypic. Fairly common in submontane forest, edge, 700–1500 m, local and uncommon to sea level and to 2000 m. Singly or pairs, joins mixed flocks. **ID M** strikingly scarlet with yellow rump; slate-grey wings; silver belly; metallic purple moustachial and forecrown; elongated purple tail. **F** grey head; olive-green upperparts; underparts pale yellowish, more whitish belly. **Imm** like fem but greyer underparts. **Voc** Song: endless, monotonous, soft but far-carrying, grasshopper-like "ch'chit-tit, ch'chit-tit, ch'chit-tit…", 3 n/s. Call: (i) 1 or 2-note rising "chee-chit"; (ii) high-pitched "tsit, tsit-tsit…". **SS** Fem White-flanked Sunbird has much more distinctly contrasting white flanks, and more uniform and greyer-tinged underparts, lacking contrasting whitish belly. See also Crimson Sunbird.

White-flanked Sunbird *Aethopyga eximia* **E**

L 13 cm. Monotypic. Fairly common in montane forest, edge, clearings, 1200–3000 m, becoming more numerous at higher elevations. **ID M** iridescent blue-green crown; red throat and breast; bright olive-green upperparts; yellow rump; long, graduated blue-green tail; striking white flanks; sooty-olive belly. **F** uniform dull-olive upperparts; grey head; olive-tinged greyish underparts; white flanks. **Imm** brownish with greyer throat. **Voc** (i) Simple 3-note "chee-chee-chee", regularly repeated, interspersed with higher "teet" notes; (ii) nasal "twe-tweck". **SS** See Javan Sunbird.

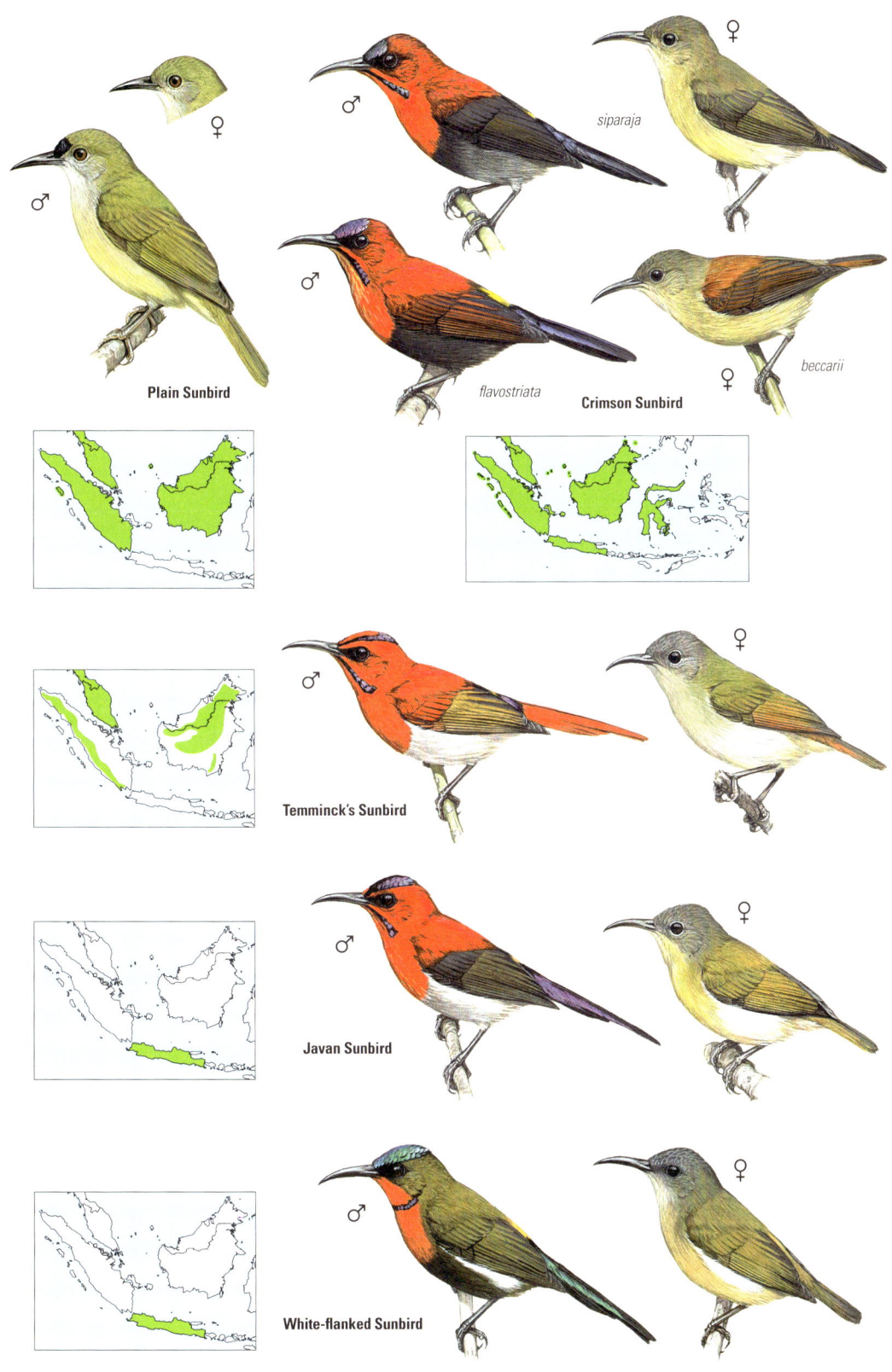

Plain Sunbird

♂

♀

Crimson Sunbird

♂ *flavostriata*

♂ *siparaja*

♀

♀ *beccarii*

Temminck's Sunbird

♂

♀

Javan Sunbird

♂

♀

White-flanked Sunbird

♂

♀

Elegant Sunbird *Duyvena duyvenbodei* `E`
L 12 cm. Monotypic. Uncommon in forest and mixed cultivation. **ID** Black bill and legs. **M** metallic green crown; maroon nape; olive-green mantle; metallic blue wings; bright yellow underparts and rump. **F** olive-green upperparts; yellowish-olive underparts. **Imm** pale bill and legs. **Voc** Song: rapid, long, repetitive series of rising and descending, high-pitched notes "sip'sip'sip…" at 10 n/s, ascending for 1 sec, then descending for 1 sec. Call: high-pitched, tremulous "sprrrt". **SS** Smaller fem Black Sunbird has orange throat contrasting somewhat with greenish-tinged rest of yellow underparts (not uniformly yellow-olive underparts). Fem Sahul Sunbird shows faint supercilium, white tail tips.

Ruby-cheeked Sunbird *Chalcoparia singalensis*
L 10–11 cm. Himalaya to SE Asia. 10 ssp, 5 in region: *panopsia* (Sum, Lingga, Belitung, Banyak, Nias, Batu); *pallida* (Natuna); *borneana* (Bor); *bantenensis* (W Jav); *phoenicotis* (C–E Jav). Uncommon in forest, <1000 m. Singly or pairs; joins mixed flocks. **ID** Short, fairly straight black bill. **M** glossy dark-green upperparts; red cheek; orange throat and breast; yellow belly. Ssp *pallida* less extensive orange throat; *borneana* darker throat and underparts; *bantenensis* brownish-tinged throat, greenish-yellow underparts; *phoenicotis* rufous throat merges gradually into belly. **F** olive-green upperparts and head. **Imm** yellow throat as underparts. **Voc** Song: (i) rapid, rising trill followed by descending, slower notes, "tirr-titit-trirrr-tir-tir-tir…"; (ii) rapid trilling, slow at end, "switit-tit-chit-choo, toosee-tit, swit-swit…". Call: thin, high-pitched "psst". **SS** Short, only slightly decurved bill is diagnostic among sunbirds (except drab Plain Sunbird).

Bornean Spiderhunter *Arachnothera everetti* `E`
L 21 cm. Monotypic. Genomic data confirm lack of gene flow with Grey-breasted from lower elevations. Bornean and Grey-breasted seem to co-occur across most of Bor with elevational displacement along main mountain range, although the more montane Bornean fully replaces Grey-breasted in lowlands at least from Sabah to Brunei. For taxonomy also see Javan Spiderhunter. Fairly common in forest, edge, < 1600 m, generally >600 m in areas of overlap with Grey-breasted. **ID Ad** bright olive-green upperparts; paler greyish underparts with fine but distinct black streaking; pink legs. **Imm** lacks streaking. **Voc** Hard, buzzy "cheet-cheet-cheet…" at 3 n/s, slightly lower-pitched than Grey-breasted. **SS** See Grey-breasted.

Javan Spiderhunter *Arachnothera affinis* `E`
L 21 cm. Monotypic. Very similar to Bornean Spiderhunter and traditionally combined with it into '**Streaky-breasted Spiderhunter**' *A. affinis*, but genetic evidence suggests Bornean's closer relationship with Grey-breasted. Specimen and field evidence indicates that this species also occurs in montane Sum, where it elevationally replaces Grey-breasted Spiderhunter from the lowlands. Fairly common in forest, edge, <1600 m, but scarce on Sum where occurs 800–1600 m. **ID Ad** bright olive-green upperparts; paler greyish underparts with fine but distinct black streaking, not as well defined as in Bornean; pink legs. **Imm** lacks streaking. **Voc** Hard, buzzy "cheet-cheet-cheet…" at 3 n/s; slightly lower-pitched than Grey-breasted. **SS** See Grey-breasted.

Grey-breasted Spiderhunter *Arachnothera modesta*
L 17–18 cm. Sundaic. 3 ssp, 2 in region: *modesta* (Bor, MPen); *concolor* (Sum, Mentawai). For taxonomy see Bornean and Javan Spiderhunters. Fairly common in forest, orchards, <1200 m. **ID Ad** bright olive-green upperparts; paler greyish underparts with fine throat and upper breast streaking; pink legs. Ssp *concolor* slightly darker upperparts. **Imm** lacks streaking. **Voc** (i) 3 buzzy, hard notes "chit-chit-chit" at 3 n/s, regularly repeated, interspersed with occasional higher-pitched "chew-chew-chew"; (ii) harsh, slightly buzzy "tee-choo". **SS** Larger Javan and Bornean from higher elevations have more distinct streaking extending to belly and harsher call. Extreme care should be taken in areas of overlap to rule out immatures, so ideally ID of Grey-breasted should not solely rely on weak streaking.

Whitehead's Spiderhunter *Arachnothera juliae* `E`
L 17–18 cm. Monotypic. Uncommon in (sub-) montane forest, 900–2100 m. Sometimes joins mixed flocks; favours canopy. **ID Ad** uniform chocolate-brown overall, boldly streaked white, particularly on belly; bright yellow rump and vent; black tail. **Imm** undescribed. **Voc** (i) Wheezy, nasal, upslurred "wirz-chir" and "chit-WHIRZZ"; (ii) in flight, single repeated "chit".

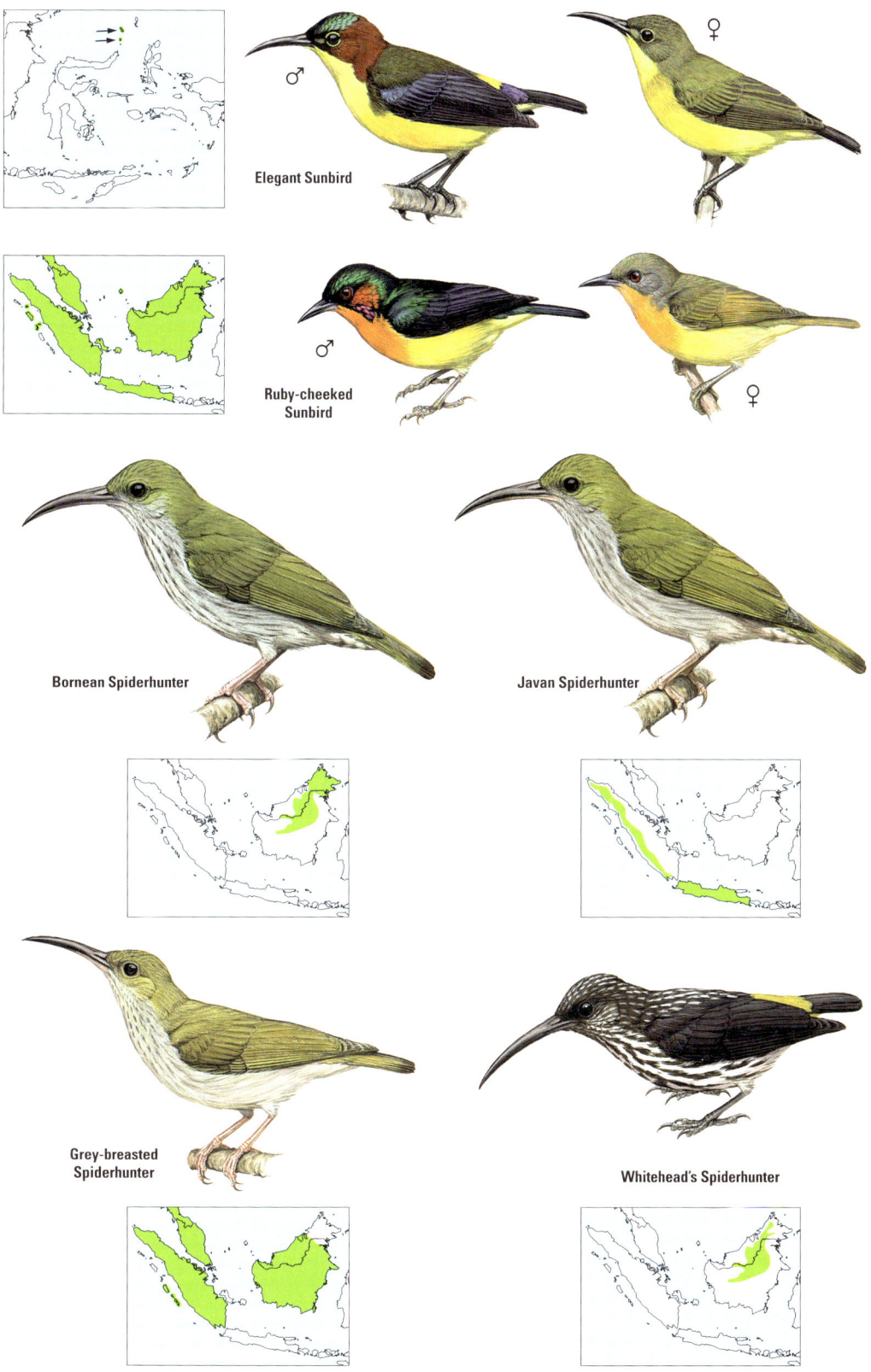

Elegant Sunbird ♂ ♀

Ruby-cheeked Sunbird ♂ ♀

Bornean Spiderhunter

Javan Spiderhunter

Grey-breasted Spiderhunter

Whitehead's Spiderhunter

Spectacled Spiderhunter *Arachnothera flavigaster*
L 21–22 cm. Sundaic. Monotypic. Fairly common in forest, edge, clearings, <1600 m. Canopy-dweller, comes lower to feed on flowers, becoming aggressive and territorial. **ID Ad** large, robust with thick, longish bill; broad yellow eyering and small yellow patch on ear-coverts; dark olive-green plumage with yellowish underparts (slightly darker olive on throat and breast). **Imm** undescribed. **Voc** Hard, far-carrying "CHIT-CHIT" and "CHIT-CHIT-CHIT", lasting 0.2 sec, usually given in flight. **SS** Smaller Yellow-eared Spiderhunter has (1) shorter, thinner bill, (2) a narrower, only partial, yellow eyering (lacking yellow below eye), (3) diffuse blackish streaking on a darker, more greyish breast (largely absent in Spectacled), and (4) a larger, more feathery yellow ear-covert patch.

Yellow-eared Spiderhunter *Arachnothera chrysogenys*
L 17–18 cm. Sundaic. 2 ssp: *chrysogenys* (W Bor–Sum and satellites, MPen; in Jav no recent records); *harrissoni* (E Bor). Fairly common in forest, edge, clearings, <1400 m; favouring upper and mid-canopy. **ID Ad** narrow, partial yellow eyering and large, feathery ear-covert patch; dark olive-green plumage with dull yellow belly and diffuse blackish streaking on greyer-tinged breast; grey pectoral tufts (absent in **F**). Ssp *harrissoni* duller mantle and wings. **Imm** lacks breast streaking. **Voc** Slightly higher-pitched than Spectacled Spiderhunter, repeated "twit-twit-twit…". **SS** See Spectacled.

Little Spiderhunter *Arachnothera longirostra*
L 13–16 cm. S–SE Asia. 8 ssp, 5 in region: *cinereicollis* (MPen, Sum and satellites); *rothschildi* (N Natuna); *atita* (S Natuna); *buettikoferi* (Bor); *prillwitzi* (Jav–Bali). As here defined, does not include Palawan Spiderhunter *A. dilutior* (monotypic; Palawan) and Orange-tufted Spiderhunter *A. flammifera* (2 ssp; S Phil) because of pronounced genetic and plumage differences. Common in forest, edge, certain cultivation, <2200 m. Singly; favours lower storey, often flying through at high speed, calling. **ID M** grey head with whitish lores and broken eyering; off-white throat; black moustachial line; yellow underparts; olive-green upperparts; white tail tips; orange pectoral tufts (visible in display). Ssp *rothschildi* bill shorter; *atita* longer-billed with deeper, brighter yellow underparts; *buettikoferi* browner and less olive overall with paler pectoral tufts; *prillwitzi* brighter yellow underparts, more orange pectoral tufts. **F** smaller; whiter throat; pale base to bill; lacks pectoral tufts. **Imm** duller; pale legs and bill. **Voc** Song: endlessly repeated, upslurred "swit-swit-swit…" at 3 n/s, also in downslurred and 2-note versions. Call: sharp, nasal "chit" and "chit-chit", often given in flight. **SS** See Thick-billed Spiderhunter.

Thick-billed Spiderhunter *Arachnothera crassirostris*
L 16–17 cm. Sundaic. Monotypic. Scarce in forest, edge, clearings, <1300 m; favouring upper and mid-canopy; can be shy. **ID Ad** dark olive-green head and upperparts with indistinct and broken yellow eyering; greyish-olive throat and breast; yellow belly; yellowish-orange pectoral tufts (absent in **F**). **Imm** duller underparts. **Voc** (i) Hard, short "chit", quickly repeated; (ii) hard, nasal "chek-chek-chek…", regularly repeated. **SS** Most nondescript spiderhunter, lacking any distinguishing features on individuals with inconspicuous broken eyering. Smaller Little Spiderhunter has greyer (not olive-green) head with contrasting white throat, black moustachial stripe (always absent in Thick-billed) and white tail tip. Female Red-throated and Brown-throated Sunbirds have shorter bill and more uniform underparts lacking duller olive tone to throat and breast.

Long-billed Spiderhunter *Arachnothera robusta*
L 21–22 cm. Sundaic. 2 ssp: *robusta* (Bor–Sum, MPen); *armata* (Jav). Generally scarce in forest, edge, clearings, <1700 m; favouring canopy of hill forest. **ID Ad** very long, decurved bill; dark olive-green head and upperparts; finely dark-streaked yellowish-olive throat and breast; yellow belly; outertail tipped white. Ssp *armata* smaller with greyish-tinged head, throat and streaking. **Imm** not well known, presumably lacks streaking, duller. **Voc** Song: rising "choy", bulbul-like, regularly repeated. Call: in flight a loud, sticky "chuk".

Purple-naped Spiderhunter *Arachnothera hypogrammica*
L 13–15 cm. SE Asia. 5 ssp, 2 in region: *hypogrammica* (Bor, Sum); *natunensis* (Natuna). Traditionally excluded from spiderhunters (then called 'Purple-naped Sunbird'), but genetic data indicates affinity with *Arachnothera*. Locally fairly common in forest, <1200 m; favours under- and mid-storey. **ID Ad** relatively short-billed; olive-green upperparts; yellow underparts boldly streaked blackish-olive; iridescent purple nape and rump patches (absent in **F**). Ssp *natunensis* has larger purple patches, finer throat streaking and larger bill. **Imm** undescribed. **Voc** Hard, rapidly repeated "tchoo-tchoo-tchoo…", 5 n/s.

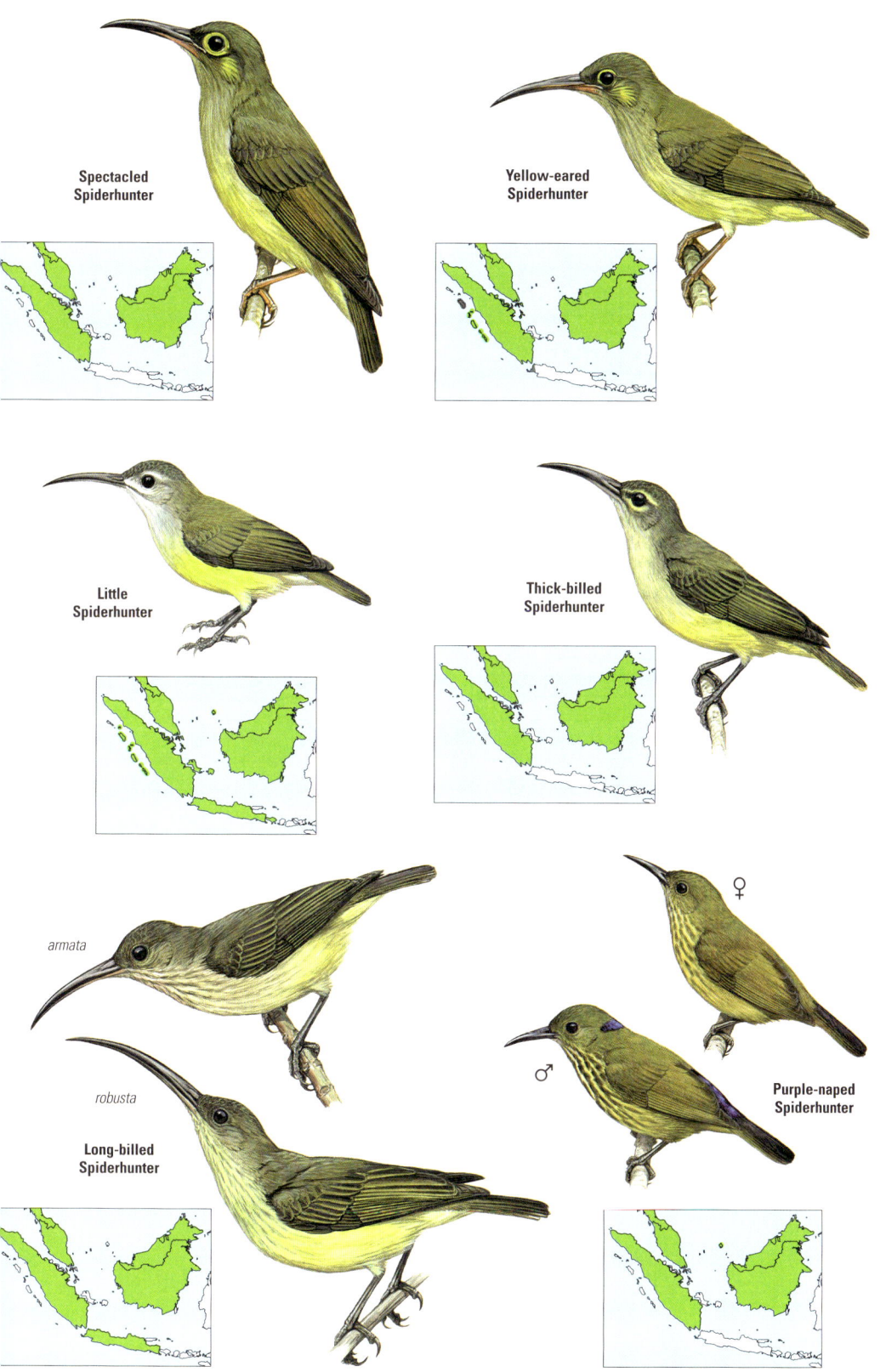

Spectacled Spiderhunter

Yellow-eared Spiderhunter

Little Spiderhunter

Thick-billed Spiderhunter

armata

robusta

Long-billed Spiderhunter

♀

♂

Purple-naped Spiderhunter

PLOCEIDAE
Weavers
3 species in region

Small, stocky, sparrow-like birds with large robust bills. Found in a variety of open grassy habitats, especially rice and cereal cultivations. Feed on the ground and in ripe crops, often in large flocks. Nest communally in elaborately constructed hanging nests.

Streaked Weaver *Ploceus manyar*
L 15 cm. S–SE Asia. 4 ssp, 1 in region: *manyar* (Jav–Bali, Bawean). Locally scarce in grassland, cultivation and marshland in native range but escaped birds have now formed thriving invasive populations elsewhere in region. Nomadic; flocks (<100) congregate around particular feeding areas, causing much crop damage. Colonial nester; builds rounded nest with short entrance funnel. **ID M br** bright yellow crown; black head; buff body with black streaking on breast and upperparts; black bill. **M non-br** as fem but shows heavier breast streaking. **F** striking: heavily streaked head with broad, yellow supercilium and moustachial stripe; streaked upperparts, breast and flanks; pinkish-horn bill. **Imm** more buffy; less heavily streaked plumage; yellow-brown bill. **Voc** Song: soft, continuous, high-pitched trill, ending in 1–5 wheezy notes, lasting <10 sec. Call: loud, flat "chirt". **SS** Female Baya and Asian Golden Weavers lack striking head pattern and strong breast streaking. See Yellow-breasted Bunting.

Baya Weaver *Ploceus philippinus*
L 15 cm. S–SE Asia. 5 ssp, 1 in region: *infortunatus* (Sum–Bali, Nias, MPen, S Indochina). Locally fairly common in grassland, cultivation, rank vegetation around rural villages. Escaped birds have now formed thriving invasive populations elsewhere in region. Flocks (<300) congregate around particular feeding areas, causing much crop damage. Colonial nester; builds elaborate retort-shaped hanging nests. **ID M br** yellow crown; blackish-brown face and throat; warm-buff underparts; streaked upperparts. **M non-br/F** streaked crown and upperparts with broad, pale supercilium; bland face and pale-buff underparts with indistinct streaks on breast side. **Imm** deeper buff underparts. **Voc** Song: (i) series of gently rising, chittering notes, accelerating then slowing in tempo, followed by a long, wheezy whistle, a buzz and finally some chirps, lasting 4–6 sec; (ii) loud, incessant chatter lasting <3 sec. Call: harsh repeated "chit". **SS** See Streaked and Asian Golden Weavers. Also see Black-headed and Yellow-breasted Buntings.

Asian Golden Weaver *Ploceus hypoxanthus*
L 15 cm. SE Asia. 2 ssp, 1 in region: *hypoxanthus* (Sum, Jav). Local and scarce in wetlands, marshland and surrounding cultivation. Escaped birds have recently been found on Bali. Small flocks (<30), often mixes with Baya Weaver, with stronger preference for wet areas. Nests in small colonies; builds small, rounded nests, usually low down in damp areas. **ID M br** bright yellow head and body including rump; black face, throat, tail and wings; greenish-black streaked mantle. **M non-br** as fem but yellow-tinged supercilium and breast; darker face. **F** as Baya but with larger bill; unmarked breast sides. **Imm** deeper buff underparts; broader crown streaking. **Voc** Song: repeated series of chattering, "chip-chip-tzeet-chip-chip-tzeet...", lasting <10 sec. Call: short, sharp "cheep". **SS** Fem not always safely separable in field from Baya unless given excellent views: both species have thick finch-like bill, but Baya's is longer and looks more slender, whereas Golden's looks extremely thick and conical; Baya has more conspicuous angled, fleshy gape-line extending beyond bill even in Ad stages, rendering aggressive facial expression, whereas Golden's bill has a punched-in expression with gape-line hardly noticeable beyond bill base in Ad (but beware Imm). Asian Golden's breast sides unstreaked, but Baya's streaking can be very faint. See also Streaked Weaver and Yellow-breasted Bunting.

ESTRILDIDAE
Munias, Parrotfinches and other estrildid finches
20 species in region

Diverse family of small, sparrow-like birds with stocky bodies and robust bills. Found in a variety of habitats from forest to open grassland and agriculture. Typically feed on the ground or in low vegetation, often in small groups, but occasionally in large flocks in ripening rice fields.

Red Avadavat *Amandava amandava*
L 9 cm. S–SE Asia. 3 ssp, 2 in region: *punicea* (Jav, Bali, S Indochina, Hainan); *flavidiventris* (Lombok–Flores, Sumba, Rote, Timor). Locally fairly common (now rare Jav, Bali) in grassland, marshland and cultivation. Flocks (<50), often mixing with munias when feeding. **ID M** bright crimson-red plumage and bill with white spotting on wings, rump and extensively on flanks. Ssp *flavidiventris* yellowish belly and white spots across breast. **F** cold grey-brown face and upperparts with white spots on coverts and tertials; creamy-buff underparts; black lores and tail; red bill and rump. **Imm** black bill; warmer brown upperparts with broad, buff double wingbar and tertial edges; buff underparts; black tail. **Voc** Song: high-pitched, descending, whistled twitter ending in quiet trill, "sweee s-s-swi' zee", lasting ~1 sec. Call: (i) high-pitched, nervous "tseet", often rapidly repeated; (ii) chirping "tsriit", perched or in flight. **SS** Imm from munias by distinct wingbars; all other plumages show red bill.

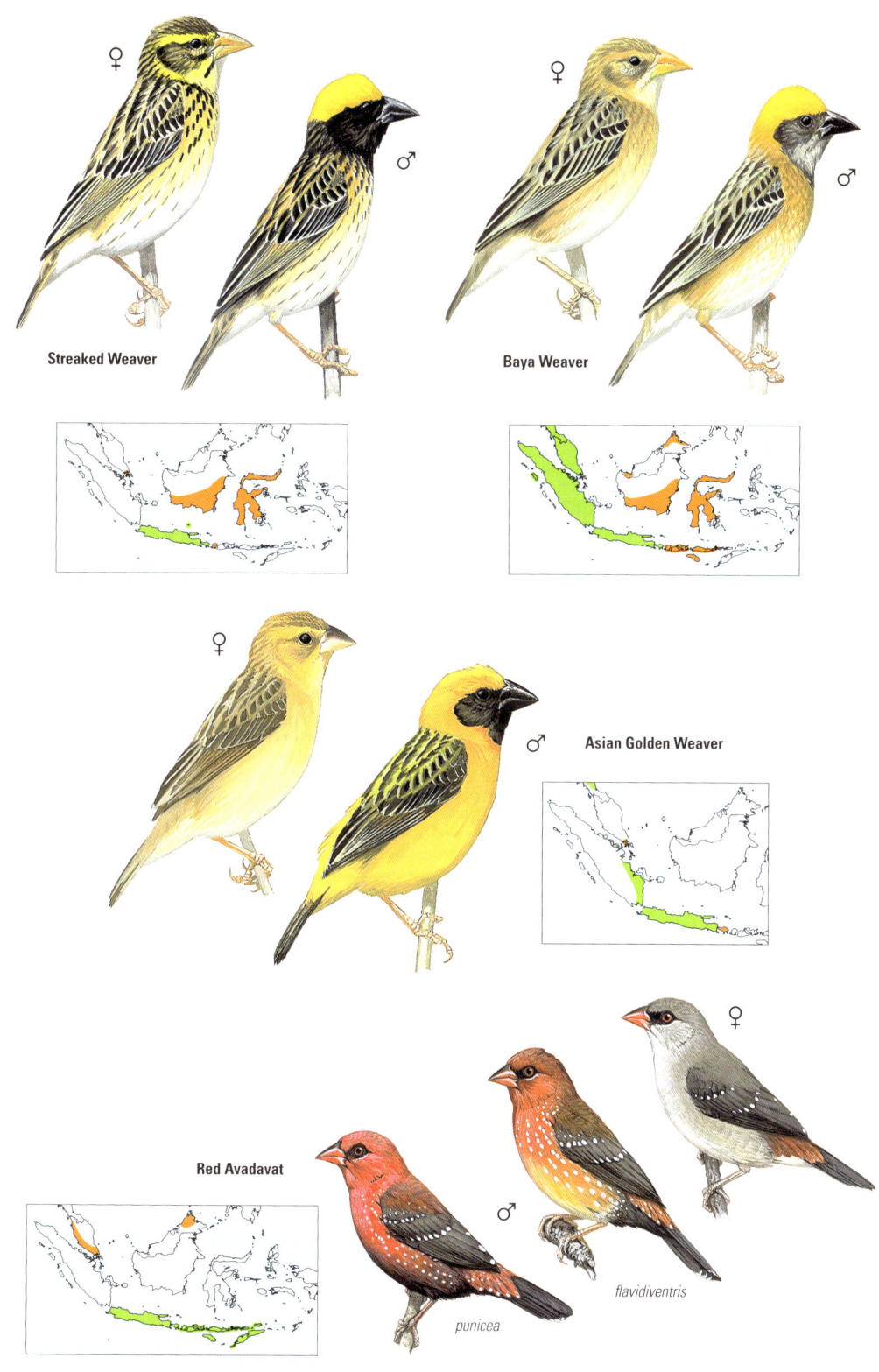

Streaked Weaver

Baya Weaver

Asian Golden Weaver

Red Avadavat

punicea

flavidiventris

Pin-tailed Parrotfinch *Erythrura prasina*

L 12–15 cm. SE Asia, Palawan. 2 ssp: *prasina* (Sum–Jav, mainland SE Asia); *coelica* (Bor, Palawan). Nomadic; locally uncommon in cultivation, edge, submontane forest, bamboo, <1500 m. Singly, pairs or small groups; joining mixed flocks in forest, feeding on flowering bamboo (<200). Eruptive; in some years can be abundant, in cultivation even with munias forming large swarms in rice fields (<1000). **ID M** blue face and throat; bright green upperparts; buffish underparts with red belly stripe; long pointed red tail. Rare **golden morph** has red tail replaced by golden yellow. Ssp *coelica* blue on throat extends to red belly. **F** duller overall; lacking red belly; pointed tail much shorter. **Imm** more washed-out; greyish-blue face; pale green upperparts; orange tail. **Voc** Song: soft, consisting of chirping and twittering strophes. Call: high-pitched, hard, thin "tsit" or "tsit-tsit", often given in flight. **SS** See Tawny-breasted Parrotfinch.

Tawny-breasted Parrotfinch *Erythrura hyperythra*

L 10 cm. Sundaic, Wallacea, Phil. 5 ssp, 4 in region: *hyperythra* (Jav); *borneensis* (N Bor, MPen); *microrhyncha* (Sul); *intermedia* (Lombok–Flores). Local, seasonally scarce (few records from Bor and Sul) in montane forest, edge, scrub, thickets, >400 m but descends into lowland rice paddies on islands where Pin-tailed Parrotfinch is absent. Singly, pairs or small groups (<5), joins mixed flocks. Inconspicuous, terrestrial to canopy. **ID M** black forehead; blue forecrown; buff face, underparts and rump contrasting with bright green crown, flanks and upperparts. Ssp *borneensis* paler buff underparts, blue extends to hindcrown; *microrhyncha* paler overall, less blue on forecrown and smaller bill; *intermedia* green-tinged crown. **F** browner forehead; reduced blue forecrown. **Imm** lacks blue forecrown; paler overall; yellow bill base. **Voc** Song: reportedly begins with long series of rhythmic crackling notes at different speeds, middle of song has series of bell-like paired notes, "dodo-doodoo-dedet-didit". Call: usually in flight, a high-pitched, hissing, downslurred, shrill "tszzit". **SS** Fem Pin-tailed has bright red (not green) tail and blue or green (not buff) face.

Tricoloured Parrotfinch *Erythrura tricolor* **E**

L 10 cm. Monotypic. Locally fairly common (uncommon Timor, common Babar), in scrub, thickets, woodland and edge, <1500 m. Singly, pairs or small groups (>20 on Babar). Inconspicuous; terrestrial to canopy. **ID M** deep-blue head and underparts contrasting with bright-green upperparts and bright red rump and tail. **F** paler blue with green extending to nape. **Imm** washed-out greyish-blue head and underparts; yellowish bill. **Voc** Song: shrill, high trill "sisisit", lasting 0.2 sec. Call: soft, thin, high-pitched "sit" and "sis-sit". **SS** See Mount Mutis Parrotfinch.

Blue-faced Parrotfinch *Erythrura trichroa*

L 12 cm. Aus. 10 ssp, 3 in region: *sanfordi* (Sul); *modesta* (N Mol); *pinaiae* (Buru, Seram). Uncommon in montane forest, edge, bamboo, >600 m. Singly, pairs or small groups (<5), joins mixed flocks. Inconspicuous; terrestrial to canopy. **ID M** deep-blue face and crown; bright-green body, slightly paler underparts with orange-tinged red rump and tail. Ssp *modesta* slightly darker green with smaller bill; *pinaiae* mantle tinged blue, greyish-blue edged secondaries. **F** with paler, less extensive blue head; plumage slightly washed-out; duller red tail. **Imm** lacks blue; uniformly dull pale-green; red tail much duller and buffish belly. **Voc** Song: very thin, high, metallic trill of 4–10 notes followed by falling whistle, lasting 1–4 sec at 4 n/s. Call: very thin, high-pitched "si'si'si'sit", usually in series of <5 descending notes.

Mount Mutis Parrotfinch *Erythrura* sp. **E**

Undescribed species currently known only from Mount Mutis (W Timor) in eucalypt forest with dense understorey, >1300 m. Singly, pairs or small groups (<5); feeding in low bushes or on ground, occasionally in eucalypt canopy. **ID M** bright red ear-coverts; sky-blue throat and forecrown with darker blue lores; bright-green body and crown; bright-red tail with slightly extended, pointed central tail feathers; black bill. Presumed **F** has indistinct blue face and red ear-covert patch. **Imm** duller green breast; buff flanks and belly; greyish-green throat; black bill. **Voc** Soft, thin, very high-pitched "sit", as Tricoloured Parrotfinch call. **SS** Imm Tricoloured shows greyish-blue (not buff-and-green) underparts.

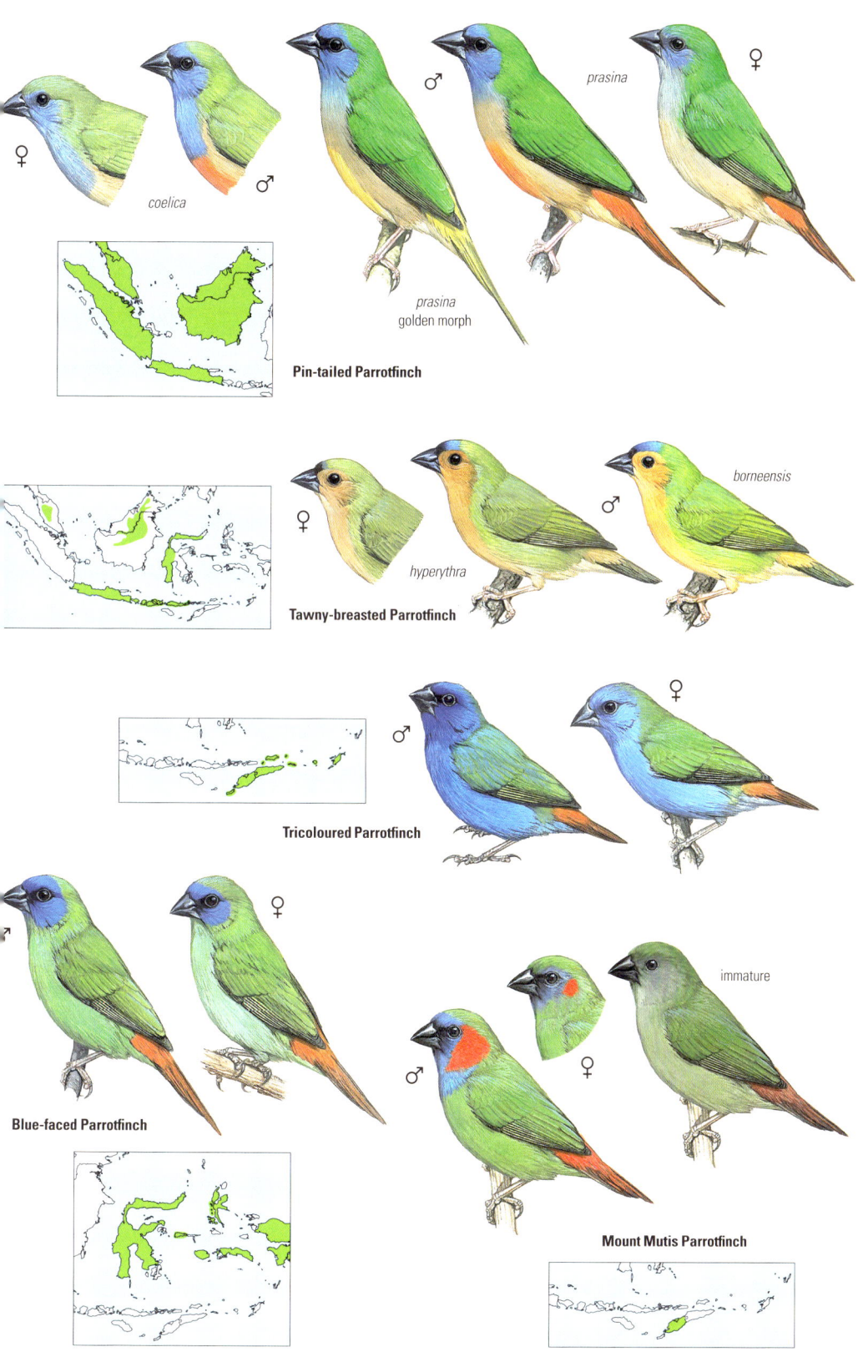

♀

coelica

♂

prasina ♂

prasina

♀

prasina
golden morph

Pin-tailed Parrotfinch

♀

hyperythra

♂

borneensis

Tawny-breasted Parrotfinch

♂

♀

Tricoloured Parrotfinch

♂

♀

Blue-faced Parrotfinch

♂

♀

immature

Mount Mutis Parrotfinch

Sunda Zebra Finch *Taeniopygia guttata* [E]
L 10 cm. Monotypic. Traditionally includes extralimital Australian Zebra Finch *T. castanotis* (Australia) but the two differ substantially in plumage and vocalisations. Locally common in arid, open habitat, cultivation, coastal areas, <2300 m. Pairs or flocks (<500); covers large areas, nomadic. **ID M** bright-orange bill; white vertical facial stripe bordered black with large orange face patch; grey head, upperparts and breast with black breast bar; buff belly; chestnut flanks with white spotting; black tail with white spots. **F** much duller; entirely lacking orange and chestnut; grey flanks; less distinct white facial stripe. **Imm** black bill. **Voc** Song: series of chattering trills. Call: squeaky "beep".

Black-faced Munia *Lonchura molucca* [E]
L 10–11 cm. 2 ssp: *molucca* (Talaud–Sul and satellites, Sula, N–C Mol, Flores Sea Is, Kai); *propinqua* (Kangean, LS, Tanimbar). Fairly common in variety of habitats: cultivation, coastal areas, villages, edge, degraded forest, <1500 m. Pairs or small groups (<20); forms smaller flocks and more arboreal than other munias. **ID Ad** black face and sharply-defined bib; underparts and rump white with black barring; mid-brown upperparts with black outerwing and tail. Ssp *propinqua* slightly paler, brighter nape; less barred underparts. **Imm** brown head and upperparts; darker wings and tail; buff underparts; black bill. **Voc** Toy trumpet-like, upslurred, squeaking "brrrrt".

Scaly-breasted Munia *Lonchura punctulata*
L 12 cm. S–SE–E Asia, Phil. 11 ssp, 7 in region: *cabanisi* (NE Bor, Phil); *fretensis* (Sum and eastern satellites, Nias, MPen); *nisoria* (S-W Bor, Jav–Sumbawa); *particeps* (Sul); *baweana* (Bawean); *sumbae* (Sumba); *blasii* (Flores–Tanimbar). Common in cultivation, gardens, open areas, scrub, <1800 m. Pairs or flocks; occasionally large swarms around seeding plants (100s). Forms huge communal roosts. **ID Ad** mid-brown upperparts; rufous face and throat; olive-brown tail; double-scaled white underparts. Ssp *fretensis* rump pale straw-coloured, underparts variably double or single-scaled; *nisoria* greyish rump, underparts double-scaled; *particeps* pale olive-grey rump, underparts rusty and single-scaled; *baweana* streaked mantle, pale-straw rump, underparts indistinctly scaled; *sumbae* as *nisoria* but warm-olive rump, underparts reddish and single-scaled, lacking marks on belly; *blasii* rump yellow. **Imm** uniform brownish-buff head and upperparts; buff to whitish underparts; black bill. **Voc** (i) Upslurred, buzzy "twit" or downslurred, buzzy "twee", continually repeated; (ii) repetitive "tit" or "tit-tit"; (iii) characteristic 2-note "pe-KING".

White-rumped Munia *Lonchura striata*
L 11–12 cm. S–SE–E Asia. 6 ssp, 1 in region: *subsquamicollis* (Sum, Lingga, Bangka, mainland SE Asia). Fairly common in scrub, grassland, edge, clearings, cultivation, <2000 m. Pairs or small flocks (<30). **ID Ad** blackish-brown body with contrasting buff-white rump and underparts; breast and vent brown. **Imm** chocolate-brown head and mantle; paler rump with black wings and tail; off-white belly and dark bill. **Voc** (i) Short, quiet, churring "pirrit", continuously repeated; (ii) louder "peep". **SS** Similar Javan and forest-dwelling White-bellied Munias lack white rump; White-bellied has white underparts restricted to central belly, not extending to flanks; Javan has black (not brown) breast and vent.

Javan Munia *Lonchura leucogastroides* [E]
L 10–11 cm. Monotypic. Common in cultivation, open areas, scrub, <1800 m. Pairs or flocks; occasionally swarms around seeding plants (100s). **ID Ad** black face to upper breast; brownish-grey crown and mantle; black rump, outerwing, vent and tail; pure white remaining underparts; pale-blue bill. **Imm** chocolate-brown head and mantle; black outerwing and tail; whitish underparts; black bill. **Voc** (i) Upslurred "wirt"; (ii) trilling "trrrt". **SS** See White-rumped and White-bellied Munias.

White-bellied Munia *Lonchura leucogastra*
L 11 cm. Sundaic, Phil. 6 ssp, 4 in region: *leucogastra* (Sum, W Jav, MPen); *palawana* (N–E Bor, Palawan); *smythiesi* (W Bor); *castanonota* (S Bor). Scarce in forest, clearings, edge; rarely strays far from forest, but occasionally found in cultivation, <700 m. Singly, pairs or small flocks (<10). **ID Ad** dark chocolate-brown overall; white belly patch not extending to flanks; olive tail; indistinct white shaft streaks from nape to mantle; pale-blue lower and darker upper mandible. Ssp *palawana* has more distinct and extensive shaft streaking; *smythiesi* streaking reduced to mantle and rump; *castanonota* crown and mantle chestnut. **Imm** upperparts paler brown; white belly still distinct; darker bill. **Voc** Song: reported "did-dib-ptcheee-ptip-ptip-tip-pteep". Call: (i) piping "too", "too-too"; (ii) soft "psing". **SS** Javan Munia (from degraded non-forest habitat) has more extensive white underparts reaching flanks and lower breast, and lacks shaft streaks. See also White-rumped Munia.

Dusky Munia *Lonchura fuscans* [E]
L 11 cm. Monotypic. Common in degraded forest, edge, clearings, scrub, cultivation, <1200 m. Pairs or small flocks (<20); larger flocks visit cultivation. **ID Ad** uniform dusky-brown overall; slight bronze sheen on upperparts; pale blue lower, darker upper mandible. **Imm** black bill; lacks bronze sheen. **Voc** (i) Cheery disyllabic "bip'bip"; (ii) shrill, upslurred "twirt".

Five-coloured Munia *Lonchura quinticolor* [E]
L 12 cm. Monotypic. Fairly common in grassland, scrub, cultivation, edge, <1800 m. Pairs or small groups; may form large flocks under optimum conditions (>1000). **ID Ad** reddish-chestnut head; chestnut-brown upperparts; orange-chestnut rump and tail contrasting with pure white underparts; massive pale-blue bill. **Imm** greyish-brown upperparts; pale-buff head and underparts. **Voc** Short, upslurred "pwi'" or more level, slightly tremulous "pee". **SS** Imm Pale-headed Munia usually has whiter head contrasting with somewhat darker underparts.

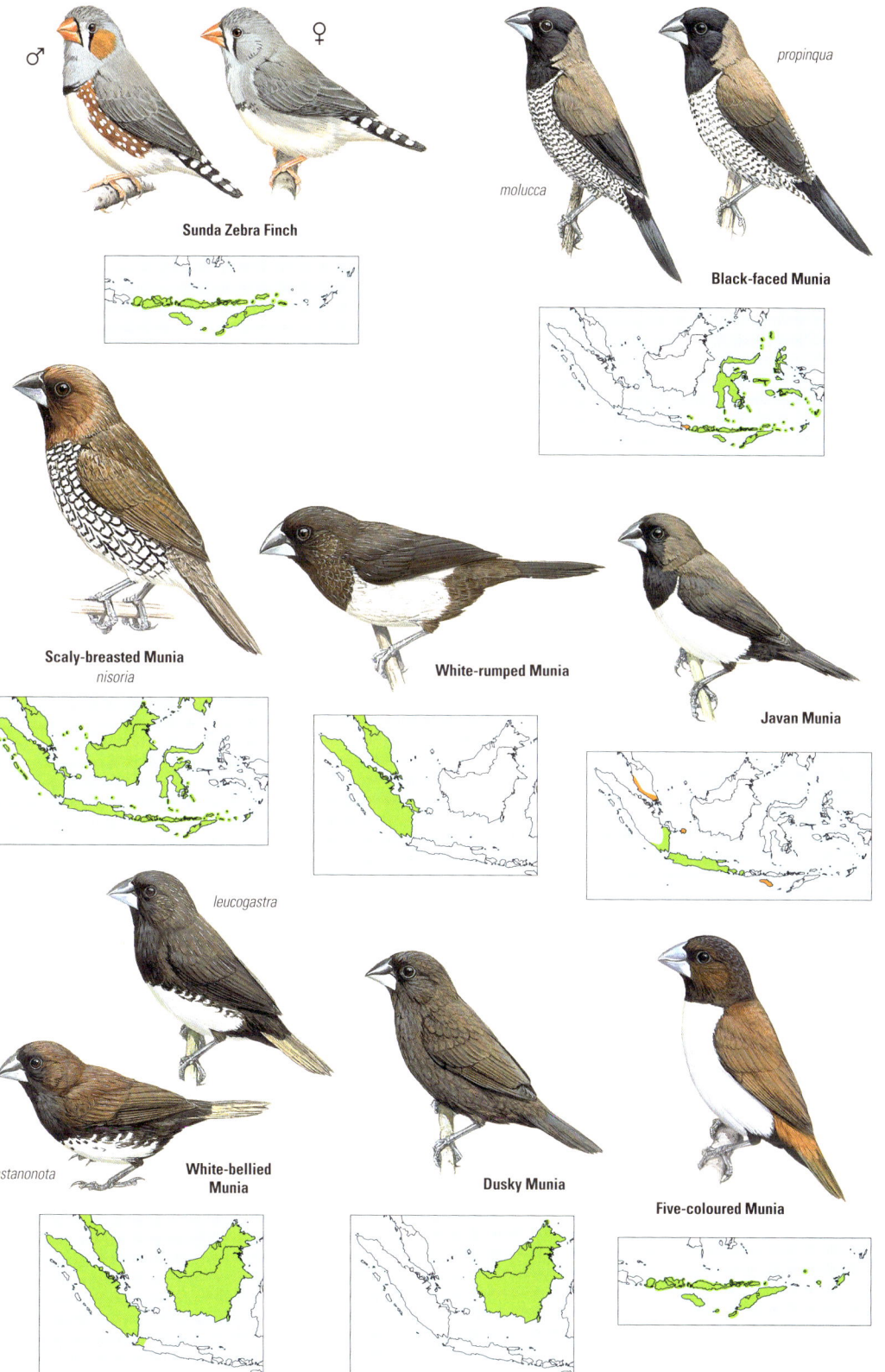

♂ ♀

Sunda Zebra Finch

propinqua

molucca

Black-faced Munia

Scaly-breasted Munia
nisoria

White-rumped Munia

Javan Munia

leucogastra

castanonota

White-bellied Munia

Dusky Munia

Five-coloured Munia

Black-headed Munia *Lonchura atricapilla*

L 11–12 cm. S–SE–E Asia, Phil. 8 ssp, 4 in region: *sinensis* (E Sum, MPen, Riau Is, Lingga); *batakana* (N Sum); *jagori* (Bor, Phil); *brunneiceps* (Sul and satellites; introduced Mol). Traditionally merged with White-capped Munia, or the two merged with extralimital Tricoloured Munia *L. malacca* (India, Sri Lanka) into expanded 'Chestnut Munia' *L. malacca*. However, extensive plumage differences suggest separation. Common in grassland, gardens, scrub, cultivation, <1800 m. Pairs or small flocks (<50). **ID Ad** black head to breast; chestnut body; reddish rump; pale-blue bill. Ssp *batakana* black belly, brighter rump; *jagori* black lower breast to belly, chestnut-orange tail; *brunneiceps* black lower breast to belly, sooty head with sooty-bronze nape. **Imm** black bill; chocolate-brown upperparts; sooty-brown head; pale buff underparts. **Voc** Sharp, downslurred "PEEP", at different pitches. **SS** Imm often not safely separable from White-capped and White-headed Munias.

White-capped Munia *Lonchura ferruginosa* **E**

L 11–12 cm. Monotypic. For taxonomy see Black-headed Munia. Scarce, locally uncommon, in larger tracts of cultivation and grassland; less tolerant of habitat degradation than other open-land munias. Pairs or small groups, but may form large flocks under optimum conditions (up to ~300). **ID Ad** white head; broad black throat and belly almost meeting each other, cut off by chestnut breast, flanks and upperparts. **Imm** whitish head; buff underparts; slightly darker buff-chestnut upperparts. **Voc** Piping "pip". **SS** See White-headed and Black-headed Munias (the latter may overlap in escapee situations).

White-headed Munia *Lonchura maja*

L 11 cm. Sundaic. 2 ssp, 1 in region: *maja* (Sum–Bali, MPen, W Sum Is.). Locally fairly common in grassland, cultivation, roadside edges, marshes, <1800 m. Often in large flocks around feeding areas (~10–300), occasionally mixing with other munias. **ID Ad** white head; pale vinous-brown breast; darker vinous-brown body with blackish belly and brighter reddish-brown tail. **Imm** uniform pale-buff gradually becoming darker on upperparts and paler on head. **Voc** Song: series of clicks, then drawn-out "weeeee heeheeeheeeheeeheee...". Call: (i) upslurred "whip"; (ii) in flight or agitated, repeated bouncing "whit". **SS** White-capped Munia has black throat; imm not safely separable from White-capped and Black-headed Munias.

Pale-headed Munia *Lonchura pallida* **E**

L 11 cm. Monotypic. Uncommon, locally fairly common, in cultivation and scrub, roosting in marshes, long grasses. Sometimes flocks around feeding areas (~10–300) mixing with other munias. Roosts in huge flocks (up to ~2000). **ID Ad** similar to White-headed Munia but underparts pale ochraceous, tail redder. **Imm** brownish-grey upperparts; whitish head and underparts gradually contrasting more with maturity. **Voc** Piping "whit-poo" and "whit". **SS** See Five-coloured Munia.

Java Sparrow *Lonchura oryzivora* **E**

L 15 cm. Monotypic. An atypical munia often erroneously separated from *Lonchura* together with Timor Sparrow. In native range, now rare or locally extinct in coastal scrub, grassland, parks, cultivation, clearings, even within cities where safe from trapping, <500 m. Widely introduced in region and globally. Pairs or small flocks (<50), joins other munias in feeding flocks. Colonial breeder. **ID Ad** pearl-grey upperparts and breast; black head and contrasting white cheeks; pink-flushed underparts; black tail; massive pink bill. **Imm** brownish-grey upperparts; paler underparts; darker crown; paler cheek patch; dusky-pink bill, eyering and legs. **Voc** A rarely heard, jangling, melodious song: several repetitions of "taktak..." as introductory notes, followed by higher-pitched, rapid "taktaktak...", repeated and smoothly passing into a "pijak-pijak-pijak...", ending with a trill "trrrrrree". Call: (i) dry, low-pitched "chuck"; (ii) metallic, thin "chip".

Timor Sparrow *Lonchura fuscata* **E**

L 12 cm. Monotypic. For taxonomy see Java Sparrow. Scarce in W, locally common in E Timor, in a variety of habitats: coastal scrub, cultivation, edge, degraded forest, clearings, plantations, <750 m. Pairs or small flocks (<30), joins larger munia flocks. **ID Ad** broad, barrel-chested with large bill; prominent white cheeks and underparts with chocolate-brown breast and upperparts; blackish crown and lower breast band; massive pale-blue bill. **Imm** paler greyish-brown upperparts; indistinct broad breast band; greyish-white underparts; hint of whitish face patch contrasting with darker crown; bill pale-blue. **Voc** Song: long series of gurgling, rattling notes, rising in pitch, "chip chip chip chip chipchipchipchip...". Call: staccato "chuck" and "chip" notes, often several birds calling simultaneously.

PASSERIDAE
Sparrows
1 species in region

Only one species in region, ubiquitous in urban environments. Found commonly throughout, almost always in close proximity to human habitation or agriculture. Generally gregarious, noisy and conspicuous, perching on buildings and foraging on the ground.

Eurasian Tree Sparrow *Passer montanus*

L 14–15 cm. Palaearctic to SE–E Asia, Phil (but widely introduced worldwide). 11 ssp, 1 in region: *malaccensis* (SE–E Asia, Phil). Abundant in and around habitation, cities, cultivation, open habitats. Pairs or flocks (up to 1000s). Primarily a terrestrial feeder. **ID Ad** chestnut crown; white face with large black cheek patch; black chin; streaked buff-and-black upperparts; pale buff underparts. **Imm** duller crown; face dirty-white with indistinct darker face patch; pale bill base. **Voc** Song: long series of evenly-spaced, fairly rapid "tsvit" notes, sometimes interspersed with higher-pitched double notes and other variations. Call: (i) hard, frequent "chip"; (ii) in flight, dry "tet-tet-tet...".

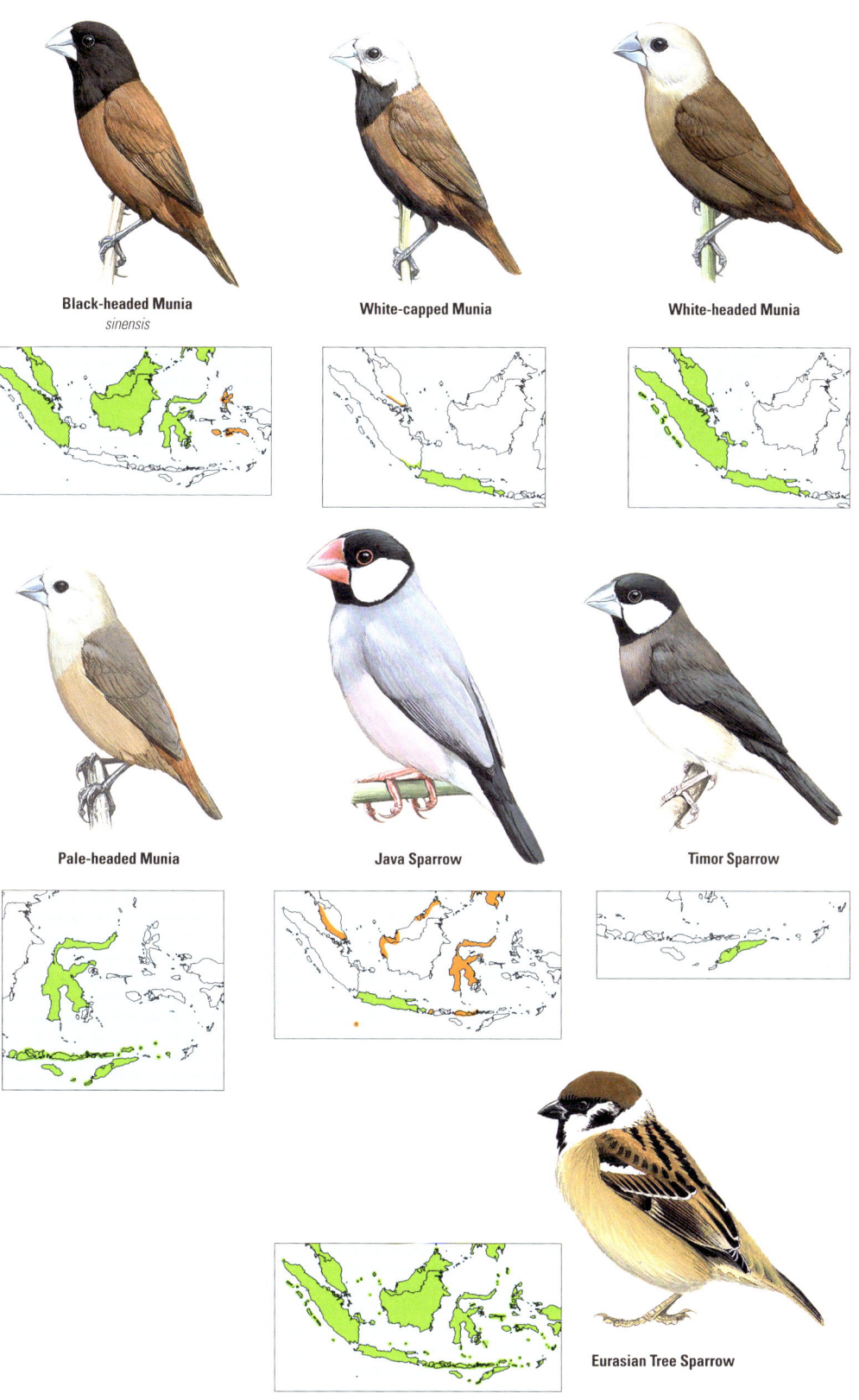

Black-headed Munia
sinensis

White-capped Munia

White-headed Munia

Pale-headed Munia

Java Sparrow

Timor Sparrow

Eurasian Tree Sparrow

MOTACILLIDAE
Wagtails and Pipits
10 species in region
With the exception of the aberrant Madanga Pipit of Buru, a family of small elegant birds with characteristically long tails and long legs. Most species forage on the ground, usually in open country, along streams and rivers, or in clearings.

Forest Wagtail *Dendronanthus indicus*
L 17–18 cm. Breeds NE–E Asia; winters S–SE–E Asia. Monotypic. Locally common winterer in Sum, rare elsewhere; forest, edge, coastal habitats, mangroves, <1500 m. Singly or small groups (<10). Terrestrial feeder in leaf-litter, flushes up to mid-canopy; can roost in large numbers (up to ~1500). **ID Ad** olive-brown crown and mantle; long white supercilium; white underparts with conspicuous double breast band; black wings with double white wingbar; long tail with white outertail; long, pink legs; conspicuous pied wing pattern visible during undulating flight. **Imm** browner, less bright upperparts; narrower breast bands. **Voc** Song, unlikely to be heard in region: repetitive see-saw series of 2–5 disyllabic "dzit-choo dzit-choo dzit-choo...". Call: metallic, far-carrying "pink", usually given in flight or when flushed.

Grey Wagtail *Motacilla cinerea*
L 17–20 cm. Breeds Palaearctic; winters Africa to Aus. 4 ssp, 1 in region: *cinerea* (most of range). First northern migrant to arrive in region (from July). Common along streambeds, road verges, open areas around woodland. Singly or small groups (<10). Terrestrial feeder. Undulating flight. **ID M br** black throat; white malar stripe; slate-grey crown, face and mantle; narrow white supercilium; blackish wings and tail with white outertail; bright yellow underparts and rump. **M non-br/F** white throat and whitish flanks and belly. **Imm** whitish to buffy underparts, but shows bright-yellow vent. **Voc** Song, sometimes heard on wintering grounds: short phrases of high-pitched notes. Call: loud, disyllabic "tittick" or "tzit-tzit"; sharper and higher-pitched than White Wagtail. **SS** See Eastern Yellow Wagtail.

Eastern Yellow Wagtail *Motacilla tschutschensis*
L 17 cm. Breeds E Palaearctic, Alaska; winters SE–E Asia, Phil, Aus. 3 ssp: *tschutschensis* (breeds NE Palaearctic, Alaska; winters SE–E Asia to Aus); *macronyx* (breeds NE Asia; winters SE–E Asia to GS, rarer east); *taivana* (breeds NE Asia; winters SE–E Asia, Phil to Sul, Mol, LS, rarest of the taxa in GS). Confused taxonomy. Traditionally merged with Western Yellow Wagtail *M. flava* (breeds W Palaearctic) into expanded 'Yellow Wagtail' *M. flava*. Current treatment largely rests on mtDNA showing substantial difference between Eastern and Western, but more recent genome-wide data refute mtDNA results as an artefact and suggest that Eastern and Western may need to be re-merged. Alternatively, the three races sometimes separated as monotypic species based on strong plumage differences: '**Green-headed Wagtail**' *M. taivana*, '**Amur Wagtail**' *M. macronyx*, and '**Bering Wagtail**' *M. tschutschensis*, although all three clearly closely-related, vocally similar and subject to intergradation. Fairly common in wetlands, cultivation, open areas, damp meadows; predominantly coastal. Flocks (up to ~200), often with pipits. **ID M br** pale grey head; long white supercilium; sometimes blackish ear-coverts; yellow throat and underparts; green-olive upperparts; little white in outertail. Ssp *macronyx* lacks supercilium though can show a trace on some individuals, slightly darker crown and mantle; *taivana* olive-green crown and ear-coverts with broad, long yellow supercilium. **M non-br/F** duller than M br on both head and underparts. **Imm** monochromatic: pale grey upperparts, conspicuous pale fringes to wings, white underparts (can show yellow tinge, particularly throat), thin white supercilium; *macronyx* almost no supercilium and darker grey crown and ear-coverts; *taivana* long, broad white supercilium, but shows traces of yellow as winter progresses, with crown starting to show green feathers. **Voc** Call: harsh, dry "tzreep", usually given in flight or when flushed. **SS** Told from any age group of Grey Wagtail by much shorter tail, different flight call and habit of frequenting meadows and open land rather than streams and rocky areas. Ad told from Grey Wagtail by olive (not grey) back. Imm told from Grey by uniformly pale underparts, lacking the contrastingly yellow vent.

White Wagtail *Motacilla alba*
L 16–18 cm. Largely breeds Palaearctic; winters to S. 11 ssp, 3 in region: *ocularis* (breeds NE Palaearctic, Alaska; winters SE Asia, Phil; few records from N Bor; vagrant Jav in Feb 2014, N Sum in Jan 2019); *lugens* (breeds NE Asia; winters E Asia; recorded Babar in Oct 2014, Sabah Nov 2012); *leucopsis* (breeds NE-E Asia, winters S-SE Asia; vagrant Bali in Nov 2015, and several records N Bor). Confused taxonomy: several races sometimes separated as independent species based on strong plumage variation, e.g. '**Black-backed Wagtail**' *M. lugens* (monotypic), '**Siberian Wagtail**' *M. ocularis* (monotypic) or '**Chinese Wagtail**' *M. leucopsis* (monotypic). However, genome-wide DNA data reveal that all subspecies form one cohesive cluster connected by much intergradation. Terrestrial feeder in wetlands, open coastal habitat, urban areas. **ID Ad M** black eyestripe, bib and hindcrown; white face, forecrown and underparts; mid-grey mantle; large white wing panel with dark bar at base of secondaries. Ssp *lugens* black mantle; white chin; large white wing panel with white secondaries; *leucopsis* as previous but lacks black eye stripe, smaller black bib, more extensive white on face, marked secondaries. **F** *ocularis* less striking head pattern; dark centred greater coverts. Ssp *lugens* greyish-black mantle (still darker than *ocularis* male); often showish blackish lesser coverts; extensive black rump; white chin; unmarked greater coverts; thick rear eye-stripe; *leucopsis* grey mantle, white throat; reduced black breast band. **Imm** grey nape, white throat, black upper breast band, dark secondaries, less conspicuous wing panel with heavily marked greater coverts; can show yellowish face; *lugens* all white wing panel; broad rear eye-stripe; lacking eye-stripe and small (sometimes absent) breast band. **Voc** Call: high-pitched, scratchy "chissik", usually in flight or when flushed.

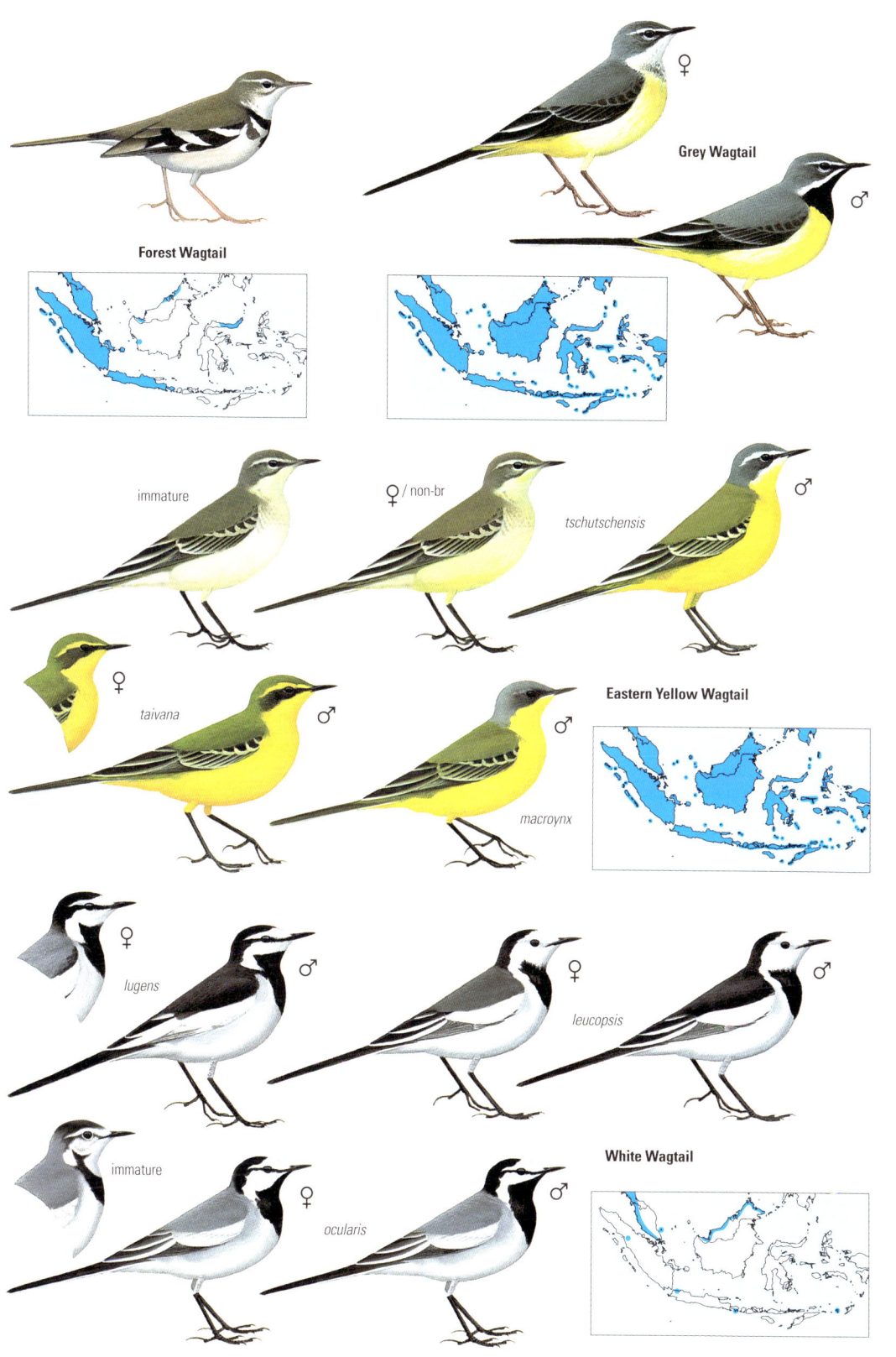

Forest Wagtail

Grey Wagtail

♀

♂

immature

♀ / non-br

♂ tschutschensis

taivana ♀

♂

♂ macroynx

Eastern Yellow Wagtail

lugens ♀

♂

♀ leucopsis

♂

immature

♀ ocularis

♂

White Wagtail

Olive-backed Pipit *Anthus hodgsoni*

L 15–17 cm. Breeds Himalaya to E Asia, C-E Palaearctic; winters S–SE–E Asia, Phil. 2 ssp: *hodgsoni* (breeds Himalaya to Japan; winters S–SE–E Asia, Phil); *yunnanensis* (breeds C-E Palaearctic; winters S–SE–E Asia, Phil). Subspecific identity of regional migrants not clear, though photos show *yunnanensis* recorded from Sabah, at least. Rare, few records, in coastal habitat, forest and edge. Singly or small groups (<20). Primarily ground feeder in leaf litter. **ID Ad** greenish-olive upperparts lightly streaked dark; buff to white supercilium; white rear ear-covert spot; thick black streaking on buff breast and flanks; white belly. Ssp *yunnanensis* plainer, indistinct streaking on mantle; slightly less marked underparts. **Imm** browner; more streaked upperparts. **Voc** Call: thin, hoarse, ringing "teez", usually in flight or when flushed. **SS** Red-throated Pipit (which is usually in more open habitat and has distinct flight call) lacks ear-covert spot, has heavy white 'braces' on back and lacks olive tinge on upperparts. See also Pechora Pipit.

Madanga Pipit *Anthus ruficollis* `E`

L 12–13 cm. Monotypic. Traditionally included with white-eyes and then called '**Rufous-throated Dark-eye**' *Madanga ruficollis* but molecular data firmly place this species within the 'olive pipit' assemblage. Rare in montane elfin forest, >1450 m. Singly or pairs, joins mixed flocks; climbing up-and-down trunks. **ID Ad** grey head, breast and belly; rufous throat; yellowish-green back and tail; yellowish-brown vent. **F** smaller. **Imm** undescribed. **Voc** High-pitched, thin, downslurred "zit". **SS** Fem/imm Buru Myzomela has decurved bill and lacks grey-olive body contrast. **AN** Madanga.

Red-throated Pipit *Anthus cervinus*

L 14–15 cm. Largely breeds N Palaearctic; winters Africa to S–SE–E Asia, Phil. Monotypic. Locally uncommon in large open cultivation, particularly ploughed fields. Terrestrial feeder, usually in flocks (~5–100s), often mixes with Eastern Yellow Wagtails. **ID Ad M br** orange-red face to breast; lightly streaked crown; boldly streaked upperparts with pale margins forming 'braces' on back; thick streaking on whitish underparts. **F br** red breast less bright and less extensive, with streaking extending to breast. **Ad non-br** white throat and breast lacking rufous on face; thick breast streaking and black malar stripe. **Imm** buffier and more heavily streaked underparts. **Voc** Call: high-pitched, thin, deflected, drawn-out "pseeee", usually given in flight or when flushed. **SS** See Pechora and Olive-backed Pipits.

Pechora Pipit *Anthus gustavi*

L 14 cm. Breeds N Palaearctic; winters Phil, Wallacea, Bor. 2 ssp, 1 in region: *gustavi* (most of range). Traditionally includes extralimital '**Menzbier's Pipit**' *A. menzbieri* (monotypic; breeds NE Asia; winter range unknown), which is here considered a different species based on distinct song and lifestyle, despite only borderline mtDNA divergence. Scarce in forest, scrub, thick cultivation, feeding in open leaf litter, often along trails. On migration can be found in coastal areas and wetlands. **ID Ad** similar to Ad non-br Red-throated Pipit: heavily black-streaked crown, mantle, breast and flanks with black malar stripe; pale supercilium (weak behind eye); black loral stripe; bold white mantle 'braces'; white underparts (breast sometimes buff); uniquely long primary projection among pipits; nape and

ear-coverts bright, often tinged buff. **Imm** underparts streaking less well-defined, extending to throat and belly. **Voc** Call: sharp, subdued "pwit", sometimes doubled. **SS** Ad non-br/imm Red-throated (which is often in more open habitat and utters different flight call) differs in the following traits: (1) has less contrasting upperparts streaking with off-white (not pure white) 'braces' and wingbars; (2) usually has shorter bill and a more yellow (not pink) base to lower mandible; (3) often has a more prominent black malar stripe; (4) has more uniformly buff underparts (versus Pechora's overall whiter underparts or contrast between buff breast and white belly); (5) usually lacks strongly warm tinge to ear-coverts; (6) typically has more distinct supercilium (especially behind eye); (7) has a much shorter primary projection; and (8) often lacks distinct black loral stripe. Olive-backed Pipit has prominent supercilium, diagnostic ear-covert spot and more olive-tinged mantle without 'braces'.

Paddyfield Pipit *Anthus rufulus*

L 15–16 cm. S–SE Asia, Phil. 6 ssp, 3 in region: *malayensis* (most of GS; MPen, S Indochina, S India, Sri Lanka); *albidus* (Sul, Bali–Alor, Sumba); *medius* (Sawu–Sermata including Timor). Common in open country: cultivation, grassland, savanna woodland, wetlands, airport runways. Singly, pairs or small groups (<20). Terrestrial feeder. **ID Ad** long creamy supercilium tapering at rear; darkish lores; prominent malar stripe; greyish-brown upperparts streaked blackish; greater-coverts paler with broad sandy edges; median coverts with dark-brownish centres and broad buff tips (forming wingbar); black-streaked breast; buff underparts, particularly flanks. Ssp *albidus* smaller, greyer mantle and whiter underparts; *medius* as previous but buffier upperparts, less white underparts. **Imm** scalloped upperparts; dark breast spotting. **Voc** Song: given in undulating flight, a wheezy series of "tseep" notes. Call: explosive but subdued "chup" or "cheep". **SS** See Richard's Pipit.

Richard's Pipit *Anthus richardi* `V`

L 17–18 cm. Breeds E Palaearctic; winters S–SE–E Asia. 5 ssp, ~1–2 in region: *ussuriensis* (breeds NE–E Asia; winters SE–E Asia) and/or *dauricus* (breeds E Siberia, NE Asia; winters S–SE Asia). Two records in coastal Sabah (Oct 2011) of unknown racial affinity. Presumed regular migrant to N Bor and N Sum. Dry grassland and meadows, often favouring taller vegetation than Paddyfield Pipit, rarely found next to urban areas or short grassy fields, and not as tame. On migration can be picked out flying high, calling. **ID/SS** Very similar to Paddyfield but larger with much longer, floppy tail nearly touching ground, often held to the side when walking; longer legs, more upright stance with a much longer hindclaw; rounder crown less flat and less wedge-shaped; stronger, thrush-like bill (versus longer and thinner in Paddyfield). **Ad** Richard's has distinctive colouration: (1) usually pale lores (typically dark in Paddyfield), (2) paler lower ear-coverts create open facial expression (versus richly coloured ear-coverts in Paddyfield creating cheek patch impression), (3) more strongly streaked crown, (4) upperparts slightly warmer brown (less grey), (5) less dense breast streaking. Ssp *ussuriensis* is darker, greyer, smaller and with relatively longer hindclaw than *dauricus*. **Imm** more sharply streaked underparts and indistinct pale wingbars. **Voc** Call: harsh, explosive "shreep", very different from weaker Paddyfield.

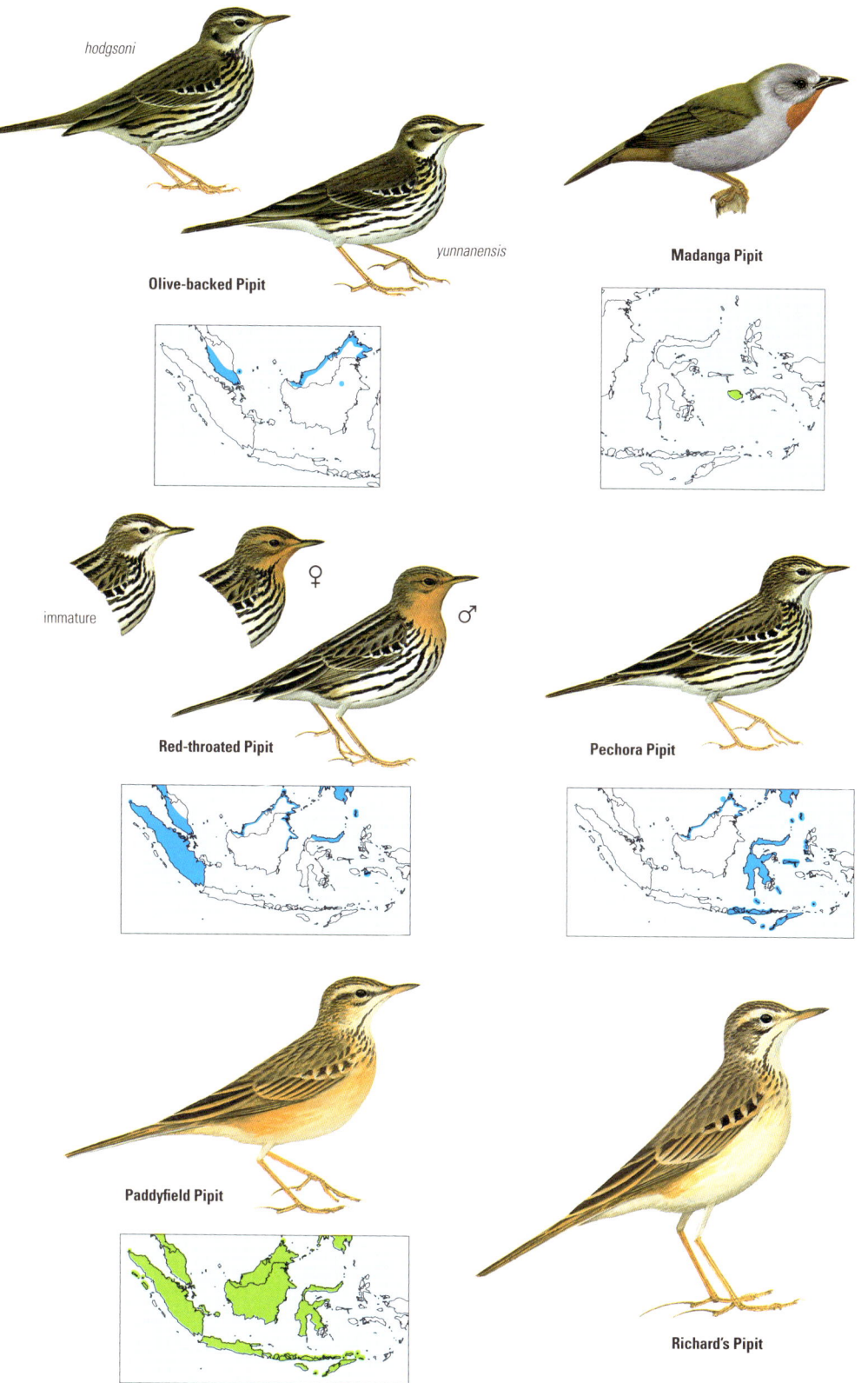

hodgsoni

yunnanensis

Olive-backed Pipit

Madanga Pipit

immature

♀

♂

Red-throated Pipit

Pechora Pipit

Paddyfield Pipit

Richard's Pipit

FRINGILLIDAE
Finches
1 species in region

Small, sparrow-like, primarily granivorous birds with stocky bodies and stout bills. Typically feed on or near the ground in forest edge and shrubby habitats, but may also forage in foliage of mid-storey. Generally quiet and unobtrusive, most often seen in flight, calling.

Indonesian Serin *Chrysocorythus estherae* **E**

L 11–12 cm. 5 ssp: *estherae* (W–C Jav); *orientalis* (E Jav); *vanderbilti* (N Sum, no confirmed sightings since 1978); *renatae* (Mt Rantekombola in SC Sul); undescribed ssp (Lore Lindu area in NC Sul). As here defined, does not include Mindanao Serin *C. mindanensis* (Mindanao), which looks substantially different. More research required into the level of morphological, vocal and genetic differentiation of *vanderbilti* and the two forms on Sul. Scarce in montane forest, edge, subalpine meadows, >1400 m. Singly or small groups (<10); feeds unobtrusively in understorey, regularly flying over canopy, calling. **ID M** black throat; yellow forecrown; yellow moustchial stripe and breast spot; yellow double wingbar and rump; greyish-brown head and upperparts; thickly streaked flanks and breast; blacker outerwing and tail; white belly; pale-blue eyering; large conical bill. Ssp *orientalis* less yellow on moustachial, narrower eyering; *vanderbilti* darker lores and throat, thicker breast pattern, narrower eyering, smaller bill; *renatae* larger cone-shaped bill, yellow restricted to small forecrown patch, yellow double wingbar, yellow rump and tertial tips; an undescribed population from NC Sul has yellow replaced by reddish wash on most individuals. **F** lacks yellow forecrown and breast; indistinct yellow wingbars. **Imm** *vanderbilti* pale collar; brown throat and breast; lacks yellow except for rump. **Voc** Song: 1–4 introductory harsh notes "twitch", followed by fast trill "tr'r'r'r'r'r't..." at 16 n/s, lasting <1.5 sec. Call: (i) constant tinkling twittering "twit-twit-twit..."; (ii) 2-note "tit-twit".

EMBERIZIDAE
Buntings
4 species in region

Small, stocky, sparrow-like birds with robust bills. In region only represented by a number of vagrant records of migratory species. Within native range typically inhabit forest edge and open country where usually found foraging on the ground or in low vegetation, sometimes in small groups.

Little Bunting *Emberiza pusilla* **V**

L 12–13 cm. Breeds N Palaearctic; winters S–SE–E Asia. Mono-typic. Recorded Sabah (Nov 1984) and Sarawak (several, between 1876–1895). Found in bushland, scrub and open woodland. Largely terrestrial feeder but regularly perches in bushes. **ID Ad** chestnut ear-coverts (bordered black) and lores; broad chestnut supercilium; blackish lateral crown stripes and moustachial stripe; broad black breast and flank streaking on clean white underparts; unmarked grey nape; streaked upperparts; white outertail feathers. **Imm** less distinct, but still shows bright face pattern; underparts buffish. **Voc** Call: short, sharp "zip".

Black-faced Bunting *Emberiza spodocephala* **V**

L 13–16 cm. Breeds E Palaearctic; winters S–SE–E Asia. 2 ssp: presumably *spodocephala* (breeds NE Asia, winters E Asia) recorded Taliabu (Oct 1991). As here circumscribed, the species does not include Masked Bunting *E. personata* (Japanese Archipelago, Kuril Is) based on morphological and genetic differences. Favours open and agricultural areas, grassland with scattered bushes. Largely terrestrial feeder but regularly perches in bushes; on Taliabu feeding with Eastern Yellow Wagtails. **ID** White outertail feathers conspicuous in flight. **M br** greyish-blue head and breast with black lores; rich brown dark-streaked upperparts; pale yellow underparts with faint flank streaking; pink bare parts. **M non-br** extensive brown on crown and ear-coverts. **F/Imm** variable streaky head colouration but usually brownish background with broad pale (often greyish) supercilium and unmarked grey nape; darker brown ear-coverts with contrasting white moustachial stripe; whitish underparts (buffier on flanks) with extensive breast and flank streaking; black-streaked brown upperparts with thin buff wingbars. **Voc** Call: quiet, slightly sibilant "tsick". **SS** Fem/imm can be dull, grey-brown, relatively featureless bunting with no obvious distinguishing field marks; specialist literature should be consulted with any vagrant bunting species.

Yellow-breasted Bunting *Emberiza aureola* **V**

L 14–15 cm. Breeds Palaearctic; winters S–SE–E Asia. 2 ssp, 1 in region: presumably *ornata* (breeds E Palaearctic, winters S–SE–E Asia). Multiple records from coastal Brunei, Sarawak and Sabah (Nov–Apr 1964–1988). Favours open areas, grassland, agricultural areas with scattered bushes. Largely terrestrial feeder but regularly perches in bushes. **ID M br** boldy marked: black mask, rich-brown upperparts to mid-crown with bold white shoulder panel and brown breast band, bright yellow underparts. **M non-br** duller markings; black mask replaced by broad yellow-buff supercilium, dark-bordered ear-coverts and yellow throat; grey-brown upperparts. **F/Imm** broad buff supercilium; darker buff-brown ear-coverts with contrasting blackish border; washed-out yellow underparts with rear flank streaking; brown crown and upperparts streaked black; broad buff wingbars; white outertail feathers conspicuous in flight. **Voc** Call: soft, sharp "tsick". **SS** Fem weavers have thicker bills, shorter tails, plumper body and less yellow underparts. Chestnut Bunting *E. rutila* (breeds E Palaearctic; winters SE–E Asia), a potential vagrant to Bor, has less contrasting face pattern and bright chestnut rump.

Black-headed Bunting *Emberiza melanocephala* **V**

L 16–18 cm. Breeds SW Palaearctic; winters S Asia. Monotypic. Recorded Mantanani (Oct 2015, Nov 2018, Oct 2019), Tiga off Sabah (several records), Kota Kinabalu (several, Jan 2018), Peleng (Dec 2015). Favours open areas, grassland, scattered bushes. Largely terrestrial feeder but regularly perches in bushes. **ID M br** boldy marked: black head, chestnut mantle, bright yellow throat, collar and underparts. **M non-br** duller markings: grey crown and blackish face mask. **F/Imm** rather uniform: plain face with black button-eye; sandy-brown head, breast and upperparts; soft yellowish tinge to underparts; brighter yellow vent; broad pale fringes to wing-coverts and tertials; large pinkish-grey bill; no white on outertail. **Voc** Call: soft, sharp "tsick". **SS** Baya Weaver has larger, brighter bill; more heavily streaked mantle; shorter tail; plumper body.

Indonesian Serin
♂
♀
♂
NC Sul ssp.

estherae
renatae

Little Bunting

♀
♂
Black-faced Bunting
spodocephala

♀
♂
Chestnut Bunting

♀
♂
breeding
Yellow-breasted Bunting
ornata

♀
♂
Black-headed Bunting

Alström, P., & Mild, K. (2010). *Pipits and wagtails of Europe, Asia and North America*. A&C Black, UK.

Alström, P., Rasmussen, P.C., Sangster, G., Dalvi, S., Round, P.D., Zhang, R., Yao, C.T., Irestedt, M., Le Manh, H., Lei, F. & Olsson, U. (2019). Multiple species within the Striated Prinia Prinia crinigera–Brown *Prinia P. polychroa* complex revealed through an integrative taxonomic approach. *Ibis* 162(3): 936–967

Alström, P., Rheindt, F.E., Zhang, R., Zhao, M., Wang, J., Zhu, X., Gwee, C.Y., Hao, Y., Ohlson, J., Jia, C., Prawiradilaga, D.M. (2018). Complete species-level phylogeny of the leaf warbler (Aves: Phylloscopidae) radiation. *Molecular Phylogenetics and Evolution* 126: 141–152.

Alström, P., Saitoh, T., Williams, D., Nishiumi, I., Shigeta, Y., Ueda, K., Irestedt, M., Björklund, M. & Olsson, U. (2011). The Arctic Warbler *Phylloscopus borealis* – three anciently separated cryptic species revealed. *Ibis* 153: 395–410.

Andersen, M.J., Hosner, P.A., Filardi, C.E. & Moyle, R.G. (2015). Phylogeny of the monarch flycatchers reveals extensive paraphyly and novel relationships within a major Australo-Pacific radiation. *Molecular Phylogenetics and Evolution* 83: 118–136.

Arndt, T., Collar, N. J. & Wink, M. (2019). The taxonomy of *Tanygnathus sumatranus*. *Bulletin of the British Ornithologists' Club* 139(4): 346–354.

Ashari, H., Prawiradilaga, D.M., Eaton, J.A., Suparno & Rheindt, F.E. (2018). New records and range extensions of birds from Timor, Alor and Rote. *Treubia* 45: 47–64.

van Balen, S., Eaton, J.A. & Rheindt, F.E. (2013). Biology, taxonomy and conservation status of the Short-tailed Green Magpie *Cissa [t.] thalassina* from Java. *Bird Conservation International* 23: 91–109.

Baveja, P., Tang, Q., Lee, J.G.H. & Rheindt, F.E. (2019). Impact of genomic leakage on the conservation of the endangered Milky Stork. *Biological Conservation* 229: 59–66.

Baveja, P., Garg, K.M., Chattopadhyay, B., Sadanandan, K.R., Prawiradilaga, D.M., Yuda, P., Lee, J.G.H., Rheindt, F.E. (2020). Using historical genome-wide DNA to unravel the confused taxonomy in a songbird lineage that is extinct in the wild. *Evolutionary Applications* 00:1–12.

Berryman & Eaton. (2020). Vocalisations and taxonomy of the Sulawesi Leaf Warbler *Phylloscopus sarasinorum* complex, including discussion of a novel undescribed taxon from Selayar, Indonesia. *Forktail* 36: 90–96.

Cai, T., Cibois, A., Alström, P., Moyle, R.G., Kennedy, J.D., Shao, S., Zhang, R., Irestedt, M., Ericson, P.G., Gelang, M. & Qu, Y. (2019). Near complete phylogeny and taxonomic revision of the world's babblers (Aves: Passeriformes). *Molecular Phylogenetics and Evolution* 130: 346–356.

Chua, V.L., Phillipps, Q., Lim, H.C., Taylor, S.S., Gawin, D.F., Rahman, M.A., Moyle, R.G. & Sheldon, F.H. (2015). Phylogeography of three endemic birds of Maratua Island, a potential archive of Bornean biogeography. *Raffles Bulletin of Zoology* 63: 259–269.

Cleere, N., Dickinson, E.C., Voisin, J–F. & Voisin, C. (2009). Case 3491 Podargus cornutus Temminck, 1822 (currently *Batrachostomus cornutus*: Aves, PODARGIDAE): proposed conservation of usage of the specific name by designation of a neotype. *Bull.Zool.Nomen.* 66 (4): 327–331.

Coates, B.J. & Bishop, K.D. (1997). *A Guide to the Birds of Wallacea*. Dove Publications, Alderley, Australia.

Collar, N. J. (2011). Species limits in some Philippine birds including the Greater Flameback *Chrysocolaptes lucidus*. *Forktail* 27: 29–38.

Collar, N.J., Eaton, J.A., & Hutchinson, R.O. (2013). Species limits in the Golden Bulbul *Alophoixus* (*Thapsinillas*) *affinis* complex. *Forktail* 29: 19–24.

Collar, N.J. & Marsden, S.J. (2014). The subspecies of Yellow-crested Cockatoo *Cacatua sulphurea*. *Forktail* 30: 23–27.

Cros, E., Chattopadhyay, B., Garg, K.M., Ng, N.S., Tomassi, S., Benedick, S., Edwards, D.P. & Rheindt, F.E. (2020). Quaternary land bridges have not been universal conduits of gene flow. *Molecular Ecology* 29(14): 2692–2706.

Cros, E., Ng, E.Y., Oh, R.R., Tang, Q., Benedick, S., Edwards, D.P., Tomassi, S., Irestedt, M., Ericson, P.G. & Rheindt, F.E. (2020). Fine-scale barriers to connectivity across a fragmented South-East Asian landscape in six songbird species. *Evolutionary Applications* 13(5): 026–1036.

Cros, E, & Rheindt, F.E. (2016). Massive bioacoustic analysis suggests introgression across Pleistocene land bridges in *Mixornis* tit-babblers. *Journal of Ornithology* 158(2): 407–419.

Eaton, J.A. & Collar, N.J. (2015). The taxonomic status of *Pycnonotus bimaculatus snouckaerti*. *Forktail* 31: 107–110.

Eaton, J.A., Mitchell, S., González Bocos, C.N. & Rheindt, F.E. (2017). A short survey of the Meratus Mountains, South Kalimantan province, Indonesia: two undescribed avian species discovered. *Birding Asia* 26: 107–133.

Eaton, J.A. & Rheindt, F.E. (2017). New avifaunal records from the Flores Sea islands, Indonesia, including novel *Phylloscopus* leaf warbler. *Birding Asia* 28: 97–106.

Eaton, J.A., Shepherd, C.R., Harris, J.B.C., Rheindt, F.E., van Balen, S., Wilcove, D.S. & Collar, N.J. (2015). Trade-driven extinctions and near-extinctions of avian taxa. *Forktail* 31: 1–12.

eBird. (2021). eBird: An online database of bird distribution and abundance [web application]. eBird, Cornell Lab of Ornithology, New York. Available: http://www.ebird.org. (Accessed: May, 2020).

Ericson, P.G., Qu, Y., Rasmussen, P.C., Blom, M.P., Rheindt, F.E. & Irestedt, M. (2019). Genomic differentiation tracks earth-historic isolation in an Indo-Australasian archipelagic pitta (Pittidae; Aves) complex. *BMC evolutionary biology* 19(1): 151.

Fabre, P.–H., Moltensen, M., Fjeldså, J., Irestedt, M., Lessard, J–P. & Jonsson, K.A. (2013). Multiple waves of colonization by monarch flycatchers (*Myiagra*, Monarchidae) across the Indo-Pacific and their implications for coexistence and speciation. *Journal of Biogeography* 41: 274–286.

Fuchs, J., Ericson, P.G.P., Bonillo, C., Couloux, A. & Pasquet, E. (2015). The complex phylogeography of the Indo-Malayan *Alophoixus* bulbuls with the description of a putative new ring species complex. *Molecular Ecology* 24: 5460–5474.

FWI/GFW. (2002). *The State of the Forest: Indonesia*. Bogor, Indonesia: Forest Watch Indonesia, and Washington DC: Global Forest Watch.

Garg, K.M., Chattopadhyay, B., Wilton, P.R., Prawiradilaga, D.M. & Rheindt, F.E. (2018). Pleistocene land bridges act as semipermeable agents of avian gene flow in Wallacea. *Molecular Phylogenetics and Evolution* 125: 196–203.

Gwee, C.Y., Christidis, L., Eaton, J.A., Norman, J.A., Trainor, C.R., Verbelen, P., & Rheindt, F.E. (2017). Bioacoustic and multi-locus DNA data of *Ninox* owls support high incidence of extinction and recolonisation on small, low-lying islands across Wallacea. *Molecular Phylogenetics and Evolution* 109: 246–258.

Gwee, C.Y., Eaton, J.A., Ng, E.Y.X., & Rheindt, F.E. (2019). Species delimitation within the *Glaucidium brodiei* owlet complex using bioacoustic tools. *Avian Research* 10(1): 36.

Gwee, C.Y., Eaton J.A., Garg, K.M., Alström, P., van Balen, S., Hutchinson, R.O., Prawiradilaga, D.M., Le, H.M., & Rheindt, F.E. (2019). Cryptic diversity in *Cyornis* (Ave: Muscicapidae) jungle-flycatchers flagged by simple bioacoustic approaches. *Zoological Journal of the Linnean Society* 186: 725–741.

Harris, J.B.C., Rasmussen, P.C., Yong, D.L., Prawiradilaga, D.M., Putra, D.D., Round, P.D. & Rheindt, F.E. (2014). A new species of *Muscicapa* flycatcher from Sulawesi, Indonesia. *PLoS ONE* 9(11): e112657. doi:101371/journal.pone.0112657.

Hartert, E. (1897). On the birds collected by Mr. Everett on the island of Savu. *Novitates Zoologicae* 4: 263–273.

Hartert, E. (1898). List of a collection of birds made in the Sula islands by William Doherty. *Novitates Zoologicae* 5: 125–136.

Hartert, E. (1898). List of birds collected in Timor by Mr. Alfred Everett. *Novitates Zoologicae* 5: 111–124.

Hartert, E. (1901). On the birds of the Key and South-east Islands, and of Ceram Laut. *Novitates Zoologicae* 8: 1–5, 93–101.

Hartert, E. (1903). The birds of the Obi Group, central Moluccas. *Novitates Zoologicae* 10(1): 1–17.

Hartert, E. (1903). On the Birds collected on the Tukang-Besi Islands and Buton, south-east of Celebes, by Heinrich Kuhn. *Novitates Zoologicae* 10(1): 18–38.

Hartert, E. (1903). On the birds of the Key and South-east Islands, and of Ceram–Laut (part 3). *Novitates Zoologicae* 10: 232–254.

Hartert, E. (1904). The birds of the South-west Islands of Wetter, Roma, Kisser, Letti and Moa. *Novitates Zoologicae* 11: 174–221.

Hoogerwerf, A. (1966–1967). Notes on the island of Bawean (Java Sea) with special reference to the birds. *The Natural History Bulletin of the Siam Society* 21: 313–340, 22: 15–103.

del Hoyo, J., Elliott, A., Sargatal, J., Christie, D.A. & de Juana, E. (eds.) (2016). Handbook of the Birds of the World Alive. Lynx Edicions, Barcelona. (retrieved from http://www.hbw.com to 6 February 2016).

Hutchinson, R., Eaton, J., Demeulemeester, B. & Rheindt, F.E. (2007). Observations of Flores Scops Owl *Otus alfredi* on Flores, Indonesia, with a first description of its vocalisations. *Forktail* 23: 184–187.

Indrawan, M. & Somadikarta, S. (2004). A new hawk-owl from the Togian Islands, Gulf of Tomini, central Sulawesi, Indonesia. *Bulletin of the British Ornithologists' Club* 124: 160–171.

Irestedt, R., Fabre, P.–H., Batalha–Filho, H., Jønsson, K.A., Roselaar, C.S., Sangster, G. & Ericson, P.G.P. (2013). The spatio-temporal colonization and diversification across the Indo-Pacific by a 'great speciator' (Aves, *Erythropitta erythrogaster*). *Proceedings of the Royal Society* B 280: 20130309.

Irham, M., Ashari, H., Trainor, C.R., Verbelen, P., Wu, M.Y. & Rheindt, F.E. (2019). A new *Myzomela* honeyeater (Meliphagidae) from the highlands of Alor Island, Indonesia. *Journal of Ornithology* 161(1): 313–324.

IUCN. (2020). *The IUCN Red List of Threatened Species.* Version 2020-2. https://www.iucnredlist.org. Downloaded on 01 December 2020.

Jarvis E. D., Mirarab S., Aberer A. J., …. Gilbert M. T. P., Zhang G. (2014). Whole genome analyses resolve early branches in the tree of life of modern birds. *Science* 346(6215): 1320–1331.

Jønsson, K.A., Irestedt, M., Christidis, L., Clegg, S.M., Holt, B.G., & Fjeldså, J. (2014). Evidence of taxon cycles in an Indo-Pacific passerine bird radiation (Aves: Pachycephala). *Proc. R. Soc. B* 281: 20131727.

Jønsson, K.A., Poulsen, M.K., Haryoko, T., Reeve, A.H. & Fabre, P.–H. (2013). A new species of masked-owl (Aves: Strigiformes: Tytonidae) from Seram, Indonesia. *Zootaxa* 3635: 51–61.

Jønsson, K.A., Blom, M.P., Marki, P.Z., Joseph, L., Sangster, G., Ericson, P.G., & Irestedt, M. (2019). Complete subspecies-level phylogeny of the Oriolidae (Aves: Passeriformes): out of Australasia and return. *Molecular phylogenetics and evolution* 137: 200–209.

Junge, G.C.A. (1953). Ornithologisch onderzoek in de Indische archipel. *Ardea* 41: 301–336.

Kennerly, P. & Pearson, D. (2010). *Reed and Bush Warblers.* Christopher Helm, London.

Kuroda, N. (1933–1936). *Birds of the Island of Java.* Volume 1 & 2. Published by the author, Tokyo.

Leader, P.J. & Carey, G.J. (2003). Identification of Pintail Snipe and Swinhoe's Snipe. *British Birds* 96: 178–198.

Leader, P.J. & Carey, G.J. (2012). Zappey's Flycatcher *Cyanoptila cumatilis*, a forgotten Chinese breeding endemic. *Forktail* 28: 121–128.

Lim, B.T., Sadanandan, K.R., Dingle, C., Leung, Y.Y., Prawiradilaga, D.M., Irham, M., Ashari, H., Lee, J.G. & Rheindt, F.E. (2019). Molecular evidence suggests radical revision of species limits in the great speciator white-eye genus *Zosterops*. *Journal of Ornithology* 160(1): 1–16.

Lim, H. C., Rahman, M.A., Lim, S.L.H., Moyle, R.G. & Sheldon, F.H. (2011). Revisiting Wallace's haunt: Coalescent simulations and comparative niche modeling reveal historical mechanisms that promoted avian population divergence in the Malay archipelago. *Evolution* 65: 321–334.

Lim, H.C., Shakya, S.B., Harvey, M.G., Moyle, R.G., Fleischer, R.C., Braun, M.J. & Sheldon, F.H. (2020). Opening the door to greater phylogeographic inference in Southeast Asia: Comparative genomic study of five codistributed rainforest bird species using target capture and historical DNA . *Ecology & Evolution:* DOI: 10.1002/ece3.5964

Lim, H. C., Sheldon, F. H. & Moyle, R. G. (2010). Extensive color polymorphism in the southeast Asian oriental dwarf kingfisher *Ceyx erithaca*: a result of gene flow during population divergence? *Journal of Avian Biology* 41: 305–318.

Lohman, D.J., Ingram, K.K., Prawiradilaga, D.M., Winker, K., Sheldon, F.H., Moyle, R.G., Ng, P.K.L., Ong, P.S., Wang, L.K., Braile, T.M., Astuti D. & Meier, R. (2010). Cryptic genetic diversity in "widespread" Southeast Asian bird species suggests that Philippine avian endemism is gravely underestimated. *Biological Conservation* 143: 1885–1890.

Manawatthana, S., Laosinchai, P., Onparn, N., Brockelman, W.Y., & Round, P.D. (2017). Phylogeography of bulbuls in the genus *Iole* (Aves: Pycnonotidae). *Biological Journal of the Linnean Society* 120(4): 931–944.

Mann, C.F. (2008). *The Birds of Borneo.* British Ornithologists' Union & British Ornithologists' Club. [B.O.U. Checklist 23].

Manthey, J.D., Moyle, R.G., Gawin, D.F., Rahman, M.A., Ramji, M.F.S. & Sheldon, F.H. (2017). Genomic phylogeography of the endemic Mountain Black-eye of Borneo (*Chlorocharis emiliae*): montane and lowland populations differ in patterns of Pleistocene diversification. *Journal of Biogeography* 44: 2272–2283.

Mees, G.F. (2006). The avifauna of Flores (Lesser Sunda Islands). *Zool. Med. Leiden* 80: 1–261.

Mees, G.F. (2010). A second contribution to the ornithology of Bangka Island, Indonesia. *Brit. Orn. Club Occas. Pubs.* 5: 137–144.

Meyer, A.B. & Wiglesworth L.W. (1898). *The Birds of Celebes and the Neighbouring Islands.* Volume 2. Friedländer, Berlin.

Mittermeier, J.C., Cottee-Jones, H.E.W., Purba, E.C., Ashuri, N.M., Hesdianti, E. & Supriatna, J. (2013). A survey of the avifauna of Obi Island, North Moluccas, Indonesia. *Forktail* 29: 128–137.

Moyle R.G., Andersen M.J., Oliveros C., Steinheimer F.D., & Reddy S. (2012). Phylogeny and Biogeography of the Core Babblers (Aves: Timaliidae). *Systematic Biology* 61(4): 631–651.

Moyle, R. G., Filardi, C. E., Smith, C. E. & Diamond J. (2009). Explosive Pleistocene diversification and hemispheric expansion of a "greater speciator". *PNAS* 106 (6): 1863–1868.

Moyle, R.G., Hosner, P.A., Jones, A.W. & Outlaw, D.C. (2015). Phylogeny and biogeography of *Ficedula* flycatchers (Aves: Muscicapidae): novel results from fresh source material. *Molecular Phylogenetics and Evolution* 82: 87–94.

Moyle R.G., Schilthuizen M., Rahman M.A., Sheldon F.H. (2005). Molecular phylogenetic analysis of the white-crowned forktail *Enicurus leschenaulti* in Borneo. *Journal of Avian Biology* 36: 96–101.

Ng, D.Y., Švejcarová, T., Sadanandan, K.R., Ferasyi, T.R., Lee, J.G., Prawiradilaga, D.M., Ouhel, T., Ng, E.Y. & Rheindt, F.E. (2020). Genomic and morphological data help uncover extinction-in-progress of an unsustainably traded hill myna radiation. *Ibis.* doi: 10.1111/ibi.12839

Ng, E.Y.X., Eaton, J.A., Verbelen, P., Hutchinson, R.O. & Rheindt, F.E. (2016). Using bioacoustic data to test species limits in an Indo-Pacific island radiation of cuckoo doves (*Macropygia*). *Biological Journal of the Linnean Society* 118 (4): 786–812.

Ng, E.Y.X., Garg, K.M., Low, G.W., Chattopadhyay, B., Oh, R.R.Y., Lee, J.G.H. & Rheindt, F.E. (2017). Conservation genomics identifies impact of trade in a threatened songbird. *Biological Conservation* 214: 101–108.

Ng, E.Y.X., Yue, A.Y., Eaton, J.A., Gwee, C.Y., van Balen, B. & Rheindt, F.E. (2020). Integrative taxonomy reveals cryptic robin lineage in the Greater Sunda islands. *Treubia* 47: 39–52.

Ng, N.S., Christidis, L., Olsen, J., Norman, J., & Rheindt, F.E. (2017). A new subspecies of Short-toed Snake-eagle from Wallacea determined from morphological and DNA comparison. *Zootaxa* 4358(2): 365–374.

Ng, N.S.R., Prawiradilaga, D.M., Ng, E.Y.X., Trainor, C., Verbelen, P. & Rheindt, F.E. (2018). A strikingly new species of leaf warbler from the Lesser Sundas as uncovered through morphology and genomics. *Scientific Reports* 8: 15646.

Ng, N.S.R. & Rheindt, F.E. (2016). Species delimitation in the White-faced Cuckoo-dove (*Turacoena manadensis*) based on bioacoustic data. *Avian Research* 7: 2.

Ng, N.S., Wilton, P.R., Prawiradilaga, D.M., Tay, Y.C., Indrawan, M., Garg, K.M. & Rheindt, F.E. (2017). The effects of Pleistocene climate change on biotic differentiation in a montane songbird clade from Wallacea. *Molecular Phylogenetics and Evolution* 114: 353–366.

Oberholser, H.C. (1912). Descriptions of one hundred and four new species and subspecies of birds from the Barussan Islands and Sumatra. *Smithsonian Misc. Coll.* 60(7): 1–22.

Oberholser, H.C. (1919). Notes on Dr. W. L. Abbott's second collection of birds from Simalur Island, Western Sumatra. *Proceedings of the United States National Museum* 55: 473–498.

Oberholser, H.C. (1932). The Birds of the Natuna Islands. *Bulletin United States National Museum* 159: 1–137.

Olsson, U. & Alström, P. (2013). Molecular evidence suggests that the enigmatic Sulawesi endemic *Geomalia heinrichi* belongs in the genus *Zoothera* (Turdidae, Aves). *Chinese Birds* 4(2): 155–160.

O'Connell, D.P., Kelly, D.J., Kelly, S.B.A., Analuddin, K., Karya, A., Marples, N.M., Rheindt, F.E. & Martin, T.E. (2020). An assessment of the avifauna of the Wakatobi Islands, Southeast Sulawesi, Indonesia: species recorded and taxonomic considerations. *Raffles Bulletin of Zoology* 68: 574–587.

Pedersen, M.P., Irestedt, M., Joseph, L., Rahbek, C. & Jønsson, K.A. (2018). Phylogeography of a 'great speciator' (Aves: *Edolisoma tenuirostre*) reveals complex dispersal and diversification dynamics across the Indo-Pacific. *Journal of Biogeography* 45(4): 826–837.

Prawiradilaga, M.D., Baveja, P., Suparno, Ashari, H., Ng, N.S., Gwee, C.Y., Verbelen, P. & Rheindt, F.E. (2017). A colourful new species of *Myzomela* honeyeater from Rote Island in eastern Indonesia. *Treubia* 44: 77–100.

Rasmussen, P. E. & Anderton, J. C. (2005). *Birds of South Asia. The Ripley Guide. Vols* 1 *and* 2. Smithsonian Institution and Lynx Edicions, Washington, D.C. and Barcelona.

Reeve, A.H., Mittermeier, J.C., Fabre, P.H., Rosyadi, I., Kennedy, J.D. & Haryoko, T. (2015). New additions to the avifauna of Obi island, Indonesia, with comments on migration and breeding seasonality of Moluccan birds. *Forktail* 31: 98–102.

Rheindt, F.E. (2010). New biogeographic records for the avifauna of Taliabu (Sula Islands, Indonesia), with the preliminary documentation of two previously undiscovered taxa. *Bulletin of the British Ornithologists' Club* 130: 33–51.

Rheindt, F.E. (2006). Splits galore: the revolution in Asian leaf warbler systematics. *Birding Asia* 5: 25–39.

Rheindt, F.E., Baveja, P., Ferasyi, T.R., Nurza, A., Rosa, T.S., Haminuddin, Ramadhan, R., & Gwee, C.Y. (2019). The extinction-in-progress in the wild of the Barusan Shama *Copsychus* (*malabaricus*) *melanurus. Forktail* 35: 28–35.

Rheindt, F.E., Christidis, L., Norman, J.A., Eaton, J.A., Sadanandan, K.R. & Schodde, R. (2017). Speciation in Indo-Pacific swiftlets (Aves: Apodidae): integrating molecular and phenotypic data for a new provisional taxonomy of the *Collocalia esculenta* complex. *Zootaxa* 4250 (5): 401–433.

Rheindt, F. E. & Eaton, J. A. (2009). Species limits in *Pteruthius* (Aves: Corvida) shrike-babblers: a comparison between the Biological and Phylogenetic Species Concepts. *Zootaxa* 2301: 29–54.

Rheindt, F.E. & Eaton, J.A. (2010). Biological species limits in the Banded Pitta *Pitta guajana. Forktail* 26: 86–91.

Rheindt, F.E., Eaton, J.A. & Verbelen, F. (2011). Vocal trait evolution in a geographic leapfrog pattern: Speciation in the *Ptilinopus subgularis* complex from Wallacea. *Wilson Journal of Ornithology* 123: 429–440.

Rheindt F.E. & Eaton J.A. (2018). Notes of the taxonomy of Cream-throated White-eye *Zosterops atriceps* and the biogeography of the Moluccas. *Birding Asia* 30: 48–53.

Rheindt, F.E. & Eaton, J.A. (2019). The taxonomy of the Blood-breasted Flowerpecker *Dicaeum sanguinolentum* complex. *Birding Asia* 31: 36–39.

Rheindt, F.E. & Eaton, J.A. (2012). Notes on the life-history and taxonomy of *Muscicapa dauurica umbrosa*, an overlooked Bornean canopy bird. *Forktail* 28: 144–146.

Rheindt, F.E. & Edwards, S.V. (2011). Genetic introgression: an integral but neglected component of speciation in birds. *Auk* 128: 620–632.

Rheindt, F.E., Gwee, C.Y., Baveja, P., Ferasyi, T.R., Nurza, A., Rosa, T.S. & Haminuddin. (2020). A taxonomic and conservation re-appraisal of all the birds on the island of Nias. *The Raffles Bulletin of Zoology* 68: 496–528

Rheindt, F.E. & Hutchinson, R.O. (2007). A photoshot odyssey through the confused avian taxonomy of Seram and Buru (southern Moluccas). *Birding Asia* 7: 18–38.

Rheindt, F.E., Norman, J.A. & Christidis, L. (2014). Extensive diversification across islands in the echolocating *Aerodramus* swiftlets. *Raffles Bulletin of Zoology: Conservation and Ecology* 62: 89–99.

Rheindt, F.E., Prawiradilaga, D.M., Ashari, H., Gwee, C.Y., Lee, G.W., Wu, M.Y., & Ng, N.S. (2020). A lost world in Wallacea: Description of a montane archipelagic avifauna. *Science* 367(6474): 167–170.

Rheindt, F.E., Prawiradilaga, D.M., Suparno, Ashari, H. & Wilton, P.R. (2014). New and significant island records, range extensions and elevational extensions of birds in eastern Sulawesi, its nearby satellites, and Ternate. *Treubia* 41: 61–90.

Rheindt, F.E., Székely, T., Edwards, S.V., Lee, P.L.M., Burke, T., Kennerley, P.R., Bakewell, D.N., AlRashidi, M., Kosztolányi, A., Weston, M.A., Liu, W.–T., Lei, W.–P., Shigeta, Y., Javed, S., Zefania, S. & Küpper, C. (2011). Conflict between genetic and phenotypic differentiation: the evolutionary history of a 'lost and rediscovered' shorebird. *PLoS ONE* 6(11): e26995.

Rheindt, F.E., Verbelen, F., Dadang Dwi Putra, Rahman, A. & Indrawan, M. (2010). New biogeographic records in the avifauna of Peleng Island (Sulawesi, Indonesia), with taxonomic notes on some endemic taxa. *Bulletin of the British Ornithologists' Club* 130: 181–207.

Richmond, C.W. (1903). Birds collected by Dr. W. L. Abbott on the coast and islands of northwest Sumatra. *Proc. US Natl. Mus.* 26: 485–524.

Sadanandan K.R.S., Tan D.J.X., Schjølberg K., Round P.D. & Rheindt F.E. (2015). DNA reveals long-distance partial migratory behavior in a cryptic owl lineage. *Avian Research* 6: 1–7.

Sadanandan, K.R., Küpper, C., Low, G.W., Yao, C.-T., Li, Y., Xu, T., Rheindt, F.E. & Wu, S. (2019). Population divergence and gene flow in two East Asian shorebirds on the verge of speciation. *Scientific Reports* 9: 8546.

Sadanandan, K.R., Low, G.W., Sridharan, S., Gwee, C.Y., Ng, E.Y.X., Yuda, P., Prawiradilaga, D.M., Lee, J.G.H., Tritto, A. & Rheindt, F.E. (2020). The conservation value of admixed phenotypes in a critically endangered species complex. *Scientific Reports* 10: 15549.

Sathiamurthy, E. V. & Voris H. K. (2006). Maps of Holocene sea level transgression and submerged lakes on the Sunda Shelf. *The Natural History Journal of Chulalongkorn University, Supplement* 2: 1–43.

Salvadori, T. (1880–1882). *Ornitologia delle Papuasia e delle Molucche*. Vols 1–3. Turin: G.B. Paravia.

Sangster, G., Alström, P., Forsmark, E. & Olsson, U. (2010). Multi-locus phylogenetic analysis of Old World chats and flycatchers reveals extensive paraphyly at family, subfamily and genus level (Aves: Muscicapidae). *Molecular Phylogenetics and Evolution* 57: 380–392.

Schlegel, H. (1863–1866). *De Vogels van Nederlandsch Indië*. AC Kruseman, Haarlem.

Shakya, S.B., Lim, H.C., Moyle, R.G., Rahman, M.A., Lakim, M., & Sheldon, F.H. (2019). A cryptic new species of bulbul from Borneo. *Bulletin of the British Ornithologists' Club* 139(1): 46–55.

Shakya, S.B., Irham, M., Brady, M.L., Haryoko, T., Fitriana, Y.S., Johnson, O., Rahman, M.A., Robi, N.J., Moyle, R.G., Prawiradilaga, D.M. and Sheldon, F.H. (2020). Observations on the relationships of some Sundaic passerine taxa (Aves: Passeriformes) previously unavailable for molecular phylogenetic study. *Journal of Ornithology* 1–14.

Sheldon, F.H., Lohman, D.J., Lim, H.C., Zou, F., Goodman, S.M., Prawiradilaga, D.M., Winker, K., Braile, T.M. & Moyle R.G. (2009). Phylogeography of the magpie-robin species complex (Aves: Turdidae: *Copsychus*) reveals a Philippine species, an interesting isolating barrier and unusual dispersal patterns in the Indian Ocean and Southeast Asia. *Journal of Biogeography* 36: 1070–1083.

Sheldon, F.H., Moyle, R.G. & Kennard, J. (2001). Ornithology of Sabah: history, gazetteer, annotated checklist and bibliography. *Ornithological Monographs* 52: 1–285.

Smythies, B.E. & Davison, G.W.H. (1999). *The Birds of Borneo.* Fourth Edition. Natural History Publications (Borneo), Kota Kinabalu.

Stresemann, E. (1939–1941). Die Vögel von Celebes. *Journal für Ornithologie* 87: 299–425, 88: 1–135, 89: 1–102.

Tan, D.J.X., Chattopadhyay, B., Garg, K.M., Cros, E., Ericson, P.G.P., Irestedt, M. & Rheindt, F.E. (2018). Novel genome and genome-wide SNPs reveal early fragmentation effects in an edge-tolerant songbird population across an urbanized tropical metropolis. *Scientific Reports* 8: 12804.

Tang, G.S.Y., Sadanandan, K.R. & Rheindt, F.E. (2016). Population genetics of the olive-winged bulbul (*Pycnonotus plumosus*) in a tropical urban-fragmented landscape. *Ecology and Evolution* 6: 78–90.

den Tex, R.–J. & Leonard, J.A. (2013). A molecular phylogeny of Asian barbets: speciation and extinction in the tropics. *Molecular Phylogenetics and Evolution* 68: 1–13.

Trainor, C.R., Verbelen, P., Johnstone, R.E. (2012). The avifauna of Alor and Pantar, Lesser Sundas, Indonesia. *Forktail* 28: 77–92.

Trainor, C.R. & Verbelen, P. (2013). New distributional records from forgotten Banda Sea islands: The birds of Babar, Romang, Sermata, Leti and Kisar, Maluku, Indonesia. *Bulletin of the British Ornithologists' Club* 133 (4): 272–317.

UNORCID, United Nations Office for REDD Coordination in Indonesia. (2015). *Forest Ecosystem Valuation*. UNORCID. Jarkata, Indonesia.

Vera, U., Päckert, M., Cibois, A., Fumagalli, L. & Roulin, A. (2018). Comprehensive molecular phylogeny of barn owls and relatives (Family: Tytonidae), and their six major Pleistocene radiations. *Molecular Phylogenetics and Evolution* 125: 127–137.

Wallace, A.R. (1862). List of birds from the Sula Islands (east of Celebes), with descriptions of the new species. *Proc. zool. Soc. Lond.* 1862: 333–346.

Wallace, A.R. (1862). On some new birds from the northern Moluccas. *Ibis* 4(16): 348–351.

Wallace, A.R. (1863). List of birds collected in the Island of Bouru (one of the Moluccas), with descriptions of the new species. *Proc. zool. Soc. Lond.* 1863: 18–36.

Wallace, A.R. (1869). *The Malay Archipelago.* Macmillan, London.

Wells, D.R. (1999). *The birds of the Thai-Malay Peninsula*, 1. San Diego and London: Academic Press.

Wells, D.R. (2007). *The birds of the Thai-Malay Peninsula*, 2. London: Christopher Helm.

White, C.M.N. & Bruce, M.D. (1986). *The Birds of Wallacea* (*Sulawesi, The Moluccas and Lesser Sunda Islands, Indonesia*). British Ornithologists' Union, London. [B.O.U. check-list No. 7].

Yue, A.Y., Ng, E.Y.X., Eaton, J.A. & Rheindt, F.E. (2020). Species limits in the Elegant Pitta (*Pitta elegans*) complex from Wallacea based on bioacoustic and morphometric analysis. *Avian Res* 11: 1–12.

LIST OF BAHASA INDONESIA BIRD NAMES

Page number	English name	Scientific name	Bahasa Indonesia name
26	Southern Cassowary	*Casuarius casuarius*	Kasuari gelambir-ganda
26	Magpie Goose	*Anseranas semipalmata*	Boha wasur
26	Spotted Whistling-duck	*Dendrocygna guttata*	Belibis totol
26	Wandering Whistling-duck	*Dendrocygna arcuata*	Belibis kembang
26	Lesser Whistling-duck	*Dendrocygna javanica*	Belibis polos
26	Plumed Whistling-duck	*Dendrocygna eytoni*	Belibis rumbai
26	Green Pygmy-goose	*Nettapus pulchellus*	Trutu hijau
26	Cotton Pygmy-goose	*Nettapus coromandelianus*	Trutu kapas
28	Radjah Shelduck	*Radjah radjah*	Umukia raja
28	Eurasian Wigeon	*Anas penelope*	Itik bungalan
28	Chinese Spot-billed Duck	*Anas zonorhyncha*	Itik paruh-totol
28	Mallard	*Anas platyrhynchos*	Itik kalung
28	Pacific Black Duck	*Anas superciliosa*	Itik alis
28	Northern Pintail	*Anas acuta*	Itik ekor-jarum
28	Eurasian Teal	*Anas crecca*	Itik sayap-hijau
30	Sunda Teal	*Anas gibberifrons*	Itik benjut
30	Grey Teal	*Anas gracilis*	Itik kelabu
30	Garganey	*Spatula querquedula*	Itik jurai
30	Northern Shoveler	*Spatula clypeata*	Itik paruh-sendok
30	Hardhead	*Aythya australis*	Kambangan australia
30	Tufted Duck	*Aythya fuligula*	Kambangan hitam
30	White-winged Duck	*Asarcornis scutulata*	Mentok rimba
32	Maleo	*Macrocephalon maleo*	Maleo senkawor
32	Moluccan Scrubfowl	*Eulipoa wallacei*	Gosong maluku
32	Tabon Scrubfowl	*Megapodius cumingii*	Gosong filipina
32	Sula Scrubfowl	*Megapodius bernsteinii*	Gosong sula
32	Tanimbar Scrubfowl	*Megapodius tenimberensis*	Gosong tanimbar
32	Dusky Scrubfowl	*Megapodius freycinet*	Gosong kelam
32	Forsten's Scrubfowl	*Megapodius forsteni*	Gosong forsten
32	Orange-footed Scrubfowl	*Megapodius reinwardt*	Gosong kaki-merah
34	Long-billed Partridge	*Rhizothera longirostris*	Puyuh siul-selanting
34	Dulit Partridge	*Rhizothera dulitensis*	Puyuh dulit
34	Roulroul	*Rollulus rouloul*	Puyuh sengayan
34	Ferruginous Partridge	*Caloperdix oculeus*	Puyuh tarun-tarun
34	Black Partridge	*Melanoperdix niger*	Puyuh hitam
34	Roll's Partridge	*Arborophila rolli*	Puyuh-gonggong roll
34	Sumatran Partridge	*Arborophila sumatrana*	Puyuh-gonggong sumatera
34	Bornean Partridge	*Arborophila hyperythra*	Puyuh-gonggong kalimantan
36	Red-billed Partridge	*Arborophila rubrirostris*	Puyuh-gonggong paruh-merah
36	Chestnut-bellied Partridge	*Arborophila javanica*	Puyuh-gonggong jawa
36	White-faced Partridge	*Arborophila orientalis*	Puyuh-gonggong timur
36	Chestnut-necklaced Partridge	*Tropicoperdix charltonii*	Puyuh-kalung melayu
36	Sabah Partridge	*Tropicoperdix graydoni*	Puyih-kalung sabah
36	Green Peafowl	*Pavo muticus*	Merak hijau
36	Great Argus	*Argusianus argus*	Kuau raja
38	Sumatran Peacock Pheasant	*Polyplectron chalcurum*	Kuau-kerdil sumatera
38	Bornean Peacock Pheasant	*Polyplectron schleiermacheri*	Kuau-kerdil kalimantan
38	Bloodhead	*Haematortyx sanguiniceps*	Puyuh kepala-merah
38	Brown Quail	*Synoicus ypsilophorus*	Puyuh coklat
38	Blue-breasted Quail	*Synoicus chinensis*	Puyuh batu
38	Red Junglefowl	*Gallus gallus*	Ayam-hutan merah
38	Green Junglefowl	*Gallus varius*	Ayam-hutan hijau
40	Salvadori's Pheasant	*Lophura inornata*	Sempidan sumatera
40	Malayan Crestless Fireback	*Iophura erythrophthalma*	Sempidan-merah melayu
40	Bornean Crestless Fireback	*Lophura pyronota*	Sempidan-merah kalimantan
40	Malayan Crested Fireback	*Lophura rufa*	Sempidan-biru melayu
40	Bornean Crested Fireback	*Lophura ignita*	Sempidan-biru kalimantan

Page number	English name	Scientific name	Bahasa Indonesia name
58	Blue-capped Fruit Dove	*Ptilinopus monacha*	Walik topi-biru
58	White-bibbed Fruit Dove	*Ptilinopus rivoli*	Walik dada-putih
58	Claret-breasted Fruit Dove	*Ptilinopus viridis*	Walik dada-lembayung
58	Grey-headed Fruit Dove	*Ptilinopus hyogastrus*	Walik kepala-kelabu
58	Carunculated Fruit Dove	*Ptilinopus granulifrons*	Walik benjol
58	Black-naped Fruit Dove	*Ptilinopus melanospilus*	Walik kembang
58	Sombre Pigeon	*Cryptophaps poecilorrhoa*	Merpati murung
60	Papuan Mountain Pigeon	*Gymnophaps albertisii*	Merpati-gunung papua
60	Buru Mountain Pigeon	*Gymnophaps mada*	Merpati-gunung buru
60	Seram Mountain Pigeon	*Gymnophaps stalkeri*	Merpati-gunung seram
60	White-bellied Imperial Pigeon	*Ducula forsteni*	Pergam tutu
60	Grey-headed Imperial Pigeon	*Ducula radiata*	Pergam kepala-kelabu
60	Moluccan Imperial Pigeon	*Ducula perspicillata*	Pergam mata-putih
60	Seram Imperial Pigeon	*Ducula neglecta*	Pergam seram
62	Cinnamon-bellied Imperial Pigeon	*Ducula basilica*	Pergam boke
62	Elegant Imperial Pigeon	*Ducula concinna*	Pergam tarut
62	Grey Imperial Pigeon	*Ducula pickeringii*	Pergam kelabu
62	Spice Imperial Pigeon	*Ducula myristicivora*	Pergam rempah
62	Green Imperial Pigeon	*Ducula aenea*	Pergam hijau
62	Pink-headed Imperial Pigeon	*Ducula rosacea*	Pergam katanjar
62	Mountain Imperial Pigeon	*Ducula badia*	Pergam gunung
62	Dark-backed Imperial Pigeon	*Ducula lacernulata*	Pergam punggung-hitam
64	Timor Imperial Pigeon	*Ducula cineracea*	Pergam timor
64	Pied Imperial Pigeon	*Ducula bicolor*	Pergam laut
64	Silver-tipped Imperial Pigeon	*Ducula luctuosa*	Pergam putih
64	Rhinortha	*Rhinortha chlorophaea*	Kadalan selaya
64	Red-billed Malkoha	*Phaenicophaeus javanicus*	Kadalan kembang
64	Chestnut-bellied Malkoha	*Phaenicophaeus sumatranus*	Kadalan saweh
64	Black-bellied Malkoha	*Phaenicophaeus diardi*	Kadalan beruang
64	Green-billed Malkoha	*Phaenicophaeus tristis*	Kadalan kera
66	Chestnut-breasted Malkoha	*Phaenicophaeus curvirostris*	Kadalan birah
66	Mentawai Malkoha	*Phaenicophaeus oeneicaudus*	Kadalan mentawai
66	Sulawesi Malkoha	*Rhamphococcyx calyorhynchus*	Kadalan sulawesi
66	Channel-billed Cuckoo	*Scythrops novaehollandiae*	Karakalo australia
66	Chestnut-winged Cuckoo	*Clamator coromandus*	Bubut-pacar jambul
66	Drongo Cuckoo	*Surniculus lugubris*	Kedasi hitam
68	Sulawesi Cuckoo	*Cuculus crassirostris*	Kangkok sulawesi
68	Indian Cuckoo	*Cuculus micropterus*	Kangkok india
68	Sunda Cuckoo	*Cuculus lepidus*	Kangkok sunda
68	Common Cuckoo	*Cuculus canorus*	Kangkok erasia
68	Himalayan Cuckoo	*Cuculus saturatus*	Kangkok ranting
68	Oriental Cuckoo	*Cuculus optatus*	Kangkok horsfield
68	Moustached Hawk-cuckoo	*Hierococcyx vagans*	Kangkok kumis
70	Northern Hawk-cuckoo	*Hierococcyx hyperythrus*	Kangkok utara
70	Malaysian Hawk-cuckoo	*Hierococcyx fugax*	Kangkok melayu
70	Whistling Hawk-cuckoo	*Hierococcyx nisicolor*	Kangkok hodgson
70	Large Hawk-cuckoo	*Hierococcyx sparverioides*	Kangkok besar
70	Bock's Hawk-cuckoo	*Hierococcyx bocki*	Kangkok gelap
72	Pallid Cuckoo	*Cacomantis pallidus*	Wiwik pucat
72	Banded Bay Cuckoo	*Cacomantis sonneratii*	Wiwik lurik
72	Plaintive Cuckoo	*Cacomantis merulinus*	Wiwik kelabu
72	Sunda Brush Cuckoo	*Cacomantis sepulcralis*	Wiwik uncuing
72	Sulawesi Brush Cuckoo	*Cacomantis virescens*	Wiwik sulawesi
72	Moluccan Brush Cuckoo	*Cacomantis aeruginosus*	Wiwik maluku
72	Australian Brush Cuckoo	*Cacomantis variolosus*	Wiwik rimba
74	Horsfield's Bronze-cuckoo	*Chrysococcyx basalis*	Kedasi australia
74	Shining Bronze-cuckoo	*Chrysococcyx lucidus*	Kedasi emas
74	Little Bronze-cuckoo	*Chrysococcyx minutillus*	Kedasi laut
74	Pied Bronze-cuckoo	*Chrysococcyx crassirostris*	Kedasi belang
74	Black-eared Bronze-cuckoo	*Chrysococcyx osculans*	Kedasi telinga-hitam
74	Asian Emerald Cuckoo	*Chrysococcyx maculatus*	Kedasi zamrud
74	Violet Cuckoo	*Chrysococcyx xanthorhynchus*	Kedasi ungu

Page number	English name	Scientific name	Bahasa Indonesia name
76	Asian Koel	*Eudynamys scolopaceus*	Tuwur asia
76	Black-billed Koel	*Eudynamys melanorhynchus*	Tuwur sulawesi
76	Pacific Koel	*Eudynamys orientalis*	Tuwur australia
76	Timor Coucal	*Centropus mui*	Bubut ayam
76	Kai Coucal	*Centropus spilopterus*	Bubut kai
78	Short-toed Coucal	*Centropus rectunguis*	Bubut hutan
78	Greater Coucal	*Centropus sinensis*	Bubut besar
78	Javan Coucal	*Centropus nigrorufus*	Bubut jawa
78	Lesser Coucal	*Centropus bengalensis*	Bubut alang-alang
78	Goliath Coucal	*Centropus goliath*	Bubut goliat
78	Bay Coucal	*Centropus celebensis*	Bubut sulawesi
80	Bornean Ground-cuckoo	*Carpococcyx radiceus*	Tokhtor kalimantan
80	Sumatran Ground-cuckoo	*Carpococcyx viridis*	Tokhtor sumatera
80	Whiskered Treeswift	*Hemiprocne comata*	Tepekong rangkang
80	Moustached Treeswift	*Hemiprocne mystacea*	Tepekong kumis
80	Grey-rumped Treeswift	*Hemiprocne longipennis*	Tepekong jambul
82	Silver-rumped Spinetail	*Rhaphidura leucopygialis*	Kapinis-jarum kecil
82	House Swift	*Apus nipalensis*	Kapinis rumah
82	Pacific Swift	*Apus pacificus*	Kapinis laut
82	Asian Palm Swift	*Cypsiurus balasiensis*	Walet-palem asia
82	Giant Swiftlet	*Hydrochous gigas*	Walet raksasa
82	Ameline Swiftlet	*Aerodramus amelis*	Walet terabai
84	Seram Swiftlet	*Aerodramus ceramensis*	Walet seram
84	Halmahera Swiftlet	*Aerodramus infuscatus*	Walet halmahera
84	Sulawesi Swiftlet	*Aerodramus sororum*	Walet sulawesi
84	Uniform Swiftlet	*Aerodramus vanikorensis*	Walet polos
84	Black-nest Swiftlet	*Aerodramus maximus*	Walet sarang-hitam
84	Edible-nest Swiftlet	*Aerodramus fuciphagus*	Walet sarang-putih
84	Volcano Swiftlet	*Aerodramus vulcanorum*	Walet kawah
86	Linchi Swiftlet	*Collocalia linchi*	Walet linci
86	Bornean Swiftlet	*Collocalia dodgei*	Walet kalimantan
86	Glossy Swiftlet	*Collocalia esculenta*	Walet sapi
86	Tenggara Swiftlet	*Collocalia sumbawae*	Walet tenggara
86	Plume-toed Swiftlet	*Collocalia affinis*	Walet bulu-kaki
86	Drab Swiftlet	*Collocalia neglecta*	Walet kusam
88	White-throated Needletail	*Hirundapus caudacutus*	Kapinis-jarum asia
88	Silver-backed Needletail	*Hirundapus cochinchinensis*	Kapinis-jarum pantat-putih
88	Brown-backed Needletail	*Hirundapus giganteus*	Kapinis-jarum gedang
88	Purple Needletail	*Hirundapus celebensis*	Kepinis-jarum ungu
88	Moluccan Owlet-nightjar	*Aegotheles crinifrons*	Atoko maluku
90	Gould's Frogmouth	*Batrachostomus stellatus*	Paruh-kodok bintang
90	Sumatran Frogmouth	*Batrachostomus poliolophus*	Paruh-kodok kepala-pucat
90	Bornean Frogmouth	*Batrachostomus mixtus*	Paruh-kodok kalimantan
90	Javan Frogmouth	*Batrachostomus javensis*	Paruh-kodok jawa
90	Blyth's Frogmouth	*Batrachostomus affinis*	Paruh-kodok melayu
90	Sunda Frogmouth	*Batrachostomus cornutus*	Paruh-kodok tanduk
92	Large Frogmouth	*Batrachostomus auritus*	Paruh-kodok besar
92	Dulit Frogmouth	*Batrachostomus harterti*	Paruh-kodok dulit
92	Spotted Nightjar	*Eurostopodus argus*	Taktarau tutul
92	Satanic Nightjar	*Eurostopodus diabolicus*	Taktarau iblis
92	Malaysian Eared-nightjar	*Lyncornis temminckii*	Taktarau melayu
92	Great Eared-nightjar	*Lyncornis macrotis*	Taktarau besar
94	Grey Nightjar	*Caprimulgus jotaka*	Cabak kelabu
94	Large-tailed Nightjar	*Caprimulgus macrurus*	Cabak maling
94	Timor Nightjar	*Caprimulgus sp.*	Cabak timor
94	Mees's Nightjar	*Caprimulgus meesi*	Cabak mees
94	Sulawesi Nightjar	*Caprimulgus celebensis*	Cabak sulawesi
94	Savanna Nightjar	*Caprimulgus affinis*	Cabak kota
96	Bonaparte's Nightjar	*Caprimulgus concretus*	Cabak kolong
96	Salvadori's Nightjar	*Caprimulgus pulchellus*	Cabak gunung
96	Talaud Rail	*Gymnocrex talaudensis*	Mandar talaud
96	Blue-faced Rail	*Gymnocrex rosenbergii*	Mandar muka-biru

Page number	English name	Scientific name	Bahasa Indonesia name
96	Bare-eyed Rail	*Gymnocrex plumbeiventris*	Mandar maluku
96	Barred Rail	*Gallirallus torquatus*	Mandar-padi zebra
96	Buff-banded Rail	*Gallirallus philippensis*	Mandar-padi kalung-kuning
98	Invisible Rail	*Gallirallus wallacii*	Mandar gendang
98	Slaty-breasted Rail	*Lewinia striata*	Mandar-padi sintar
98	Lewin's Rail	*Lewinia pectoralis*	Mandar-padi dada-kelabu
98	Snoring Rail	*Lewinia plateni*	Mandar dengkur
98	Eastern Water Rail	*Rallus indicus*	Mandar asia
98	Red-necked Crake	*Rallina tricolor*	Tikusan tukar
98	Red-legged Crake	*Rallina fasciata*	Tikusan ceruling
98	Slaty-legged Crake	*Rallina eurizonoides*	Tikusan kaki-kelabu
98	Baillon's Crake	*Zapornia pusilla*	Tikusan kerdil
100	Ruddy-breasted Crake	*Zapornia fusca*	Tikusan merah
100	Band-bellied Crake	*Zapornia paykullii*	Tikusan siberia
100	Spotless Crake	*Zapornia tabuensis*	Tikusan polos
100	White-browed Crake	*Poliolimnas cinereus*	Tikusan alis-putih
100	Watercock	*Gallicrex cinerea*	Mandar bontod
100	Sulawesi Bush-hen	*Amaurornis isabellina*	Kareo sulawesi
100	Plain Bush-hen	*Amaurornis olivacea*	Kareo talaud
100	Pale-vented Bush-hen	*Amaurornis moluccana*	Kareo zaitun
102	White-breasted Waterhen	*Amaurornis phoenicurus*	Kareo padi
102	Purple Swamphen	*Porphyrio porphyrio*	Mandar besar
102	Common Moorhen	*Gallinula chloropus*	Mandar batu
102	Dusky Moorhen	*Gallinula tenebrosa*	Mandar kelam
102	Common Coot	*Fulica atra*	Mandar hitam
102	Masked Finfoot	*Heliopais personatus*	Pedendang topeng
104	Beach Thick-knee	*Esacus magnirostris*	Wili-wili Besar
104	Pied Stilt	*Himantopus leucocephalus*	Gagang-bayam belang
104	Black-winged Stilt	*Himantopus himantopus*	Gagang-bayam timur
104	Pied Avocet	*Recurvirostra avosetta*	Avosetta belang
104	Pied Oystercatcher	*Haematopus longirostris*	Kedidir belang
104	Sooty Oystercatcher	*Haematopus fuliginosus*	Kedidir kelam
104	Far Eastern Oystercatcher	*Haematopus osculans*	Kedidir timur
106	Pacific Golden Plover	*Pluvialis fulva*	Cerek kernyut
106	Grey Plover	*Pluvialis squatarola*	Cerek besar
106	Grey-headed Lapwing	*Vanellus cinereus*	Trulek kelabu
106	Javan Lapwing	*Vanellus macropterus*	Trulek jawa
106	Red-wattled Lapwing	*Vanellus indicus*	Trulek gelambir-merah
106	Masked Lapwing	*Vanellus miles*	Trulek topeng
106	Northern Lapwing	*Vanellus vanellus*	Trulek erasia
106	Red-kneed Dotterel	*Erythrogonys cinctus*	Cerek lutut-merah
108	Oriental Plover	*Anarhynchus veredus*	Cerek asia
108	Tibetan Plover	*Anarhynchus atrifrons*	Cerek-pasir tibet
108	Siberian Plover	*Anarhynchus mongolus*	Cerek-pasir siberia
108	Greater Sand Plover	*Anarhynchus leschenaultii*	Cerek-pasir besar
108	Red-capped Plover	*Anarhynchus ruficapillus*	Cerek topi-merah
110	Malaysian Plover	*Anarhynchus peronii*	Cerek melayu
110	Kentish Plover	*Anarhynchus alexandrinus*	Ccrek tilil
110	White-faced Plover	*Anarhynchus dealbatus*	Cerek muka-putih
110	Javan Plover	*Anarhynchus javanicus*	Cerek jawa
110	Little Ringed Plover	*Charadrius dubius*	Cerek-kalung kecil
110	Common Ringed Plover	*Charadrius hiaticula*	Cerek-kalung besar
112	Long-billed Plover	*Charadrius placidus*	Cerek paruh-panjang
112	Black-fronted Plover	*Charadrius melanops*	Cerek dahi-hitam
112	Greater Painted-snipe	*Rostratula benghalensis*	Berkik-kembang besar
112	Pheasant-tailed Jaçanã	*Hydrophasianus chirurgus*	Burung-sepatu teratai
112	Comb-crested Jaçanã	*Irediparra gallinacea*	Burung-sepatu jengger
112	Bronze-winged Jaçanã	*Metopidius indicus*	Burung-sepatu picisan
114	Red-necked Phalarope	*Phalaropus lobatus*	Kaki-rumbai kecil
114	Red Phalarope	*Phalaropus fulicarius*	Kaki-rumbai merah
114	Terek Sandpiper	*Xenus cinereus*	Trinil bedaran
114	Common Sandpiper	*Actitis hypoleucos*	Trinil pantai

Page number	English name	Scientific name	Bahasa Indonesia name
114	Green Sandpiper	*Tringa ochropus*	Trinil hijau
114	Grey-tailed Tattler	*Tringa brevipes*	Trinil ekor-kelabu
114	Spotted Redshank	*Tringa erythropus*	Trinil tutul
116	Common Greenshank	*Tringa nebularia*	Trinil kaki-hijau
116	Nordmann's Greenshank	*Tringa guttifer*	Trinil nordmann
116	Lesser Yellowlegs	*Tringa flavipes*	Trinil kaki-kuning
116	Marsh Sandpiper	*Tringa stagnatilis*	Trinil rawa
116	Wood Sandpiper	*Tringa glareola*	Trinil semak
116	Common Redshank	*Tringa totanus*	Trinil kaki-merah
118	Ruddy Turnstone	*Arenaria interpres*	Trinil pembalik-batu
118	Sanderling	*Calidris alba*	Kedidi putih
118	Little Stint	*Calidris minuta*	Kedidi kecil
118	Red-necked Stint	*Calidris ruficollis*	Kedidi leher-merah
118	Temminck's Stint	*Calidris temminckii*	Kedidi temminck
118	Long-toed Stint	*Calidris subminuta*	Kedidi jari-panjang
118	Spoon-billed Sandpiper	*Calidris pygmaea*	Kedidi paruh-sendok
120	Curlew Sandpiper	*Calidris ferruginea*	Kedidi golgol
120	Dunlin	*Calidris alpina*	Kedidi belang
120	Broad-billed Sandpiper	*Calidris falcinellus*	Kedidi paruh-lebar
120	Buff-breasted Sandpiper	*Calidris subruficollis*	Kedidi dada-oker
120	Pectoral Sandpiper	*Calidris melanotos*	Kedidi dada-coret
120	Sharp-tailed Sandpiper	*Calidris acuminata*	Kedidi ekor-tajam
122	Ruff	*Calidris pugnax*	Trinil rumbai
122	Great Knot	*Calidris tenuirostris*	Kedidi besar
122	Red Knot	*Calidris canutus*	Kedidi merah
122	Common Snipe	*Gallinago gallinago*	Berkik ekor-kipas
122	Pintail Snipe	*Gallinago stenura*	Berkik ekor-lidi
122	Swinhoe's Snipe	*Gallinago megala*	Berkik rawa
124	Eurasian Woodcock	*Scolopax rusticola*	Berkik-gunung erasia
124	Sunda Woodcock	*Scolopax saturata*	Berkik-gunung merah
124	Sulawesi Woodcock	*Scolopax celebensis*	Berkik-gunung sulawesi
124	Moluccan Woodcock	*Scolopax rochussenii*	Berkik-gunung maluku
124	Long-billed Dowitcher	*Limnodromus scolopaceus*	Trinil-lumpur paruh-panjang
124	Asian Dowitcher	*Limnodromus semipalmatus*	Trinil-lumpur asia
126	Black-tailed Godwit	*Limosa limosa*	Biru-laut ekor-hitam
126	Bar-tailed Godwit	*Limosa lapponica*	Biru-laut ekor-blorok
126	Little Curlew	*Numenius minutus*	Gajahan kecil
126	Eurasian Whimbrel	*Numenius phaeopus*	Gajahan penggala
126	Far Eastern Curlew	*Numenius madagascariensis*	Gajahan timur
126	Eurasian Curlew	*Numenius arquata*	Gajahan erasia
128	Small Buttonquail	*Turnix sylvaticus*	Gemak tegalan
128	Red-backed Buttonquail	*Turnix maculosus*	Gemak totol
128	Barred Buttonquail	*Turnix suscitator*	Gemak loreng
128	Sumba Buttonquail	*Turnix everetti*	Gemak sumba
128	Australian Pratincole	*Stiltia isabella*	Terik australia
128	Oriental Pratincole	*Glareola maldivarum*	Terik asia
130	Brown Noddy	*Anous stolidus*	Camar-angguk coklat
130	Black Noddy	*Anous minutus*	Camar-angguk hitam
130	Lesser Noddy	*Anous tenuirostris*	Camar-angguk kecil
130	White Tern	*Gygis alba*	Dara-laut putih
130	Heuglin's Gull	*Larus heuglini*	Camar heuglin
130	Slaty-backed Gull	*Larus schistisagus*	Camar jelaga
130	Black-tailed Gull	*Larus crassirostris*	Camar jepang
132	Silver Gull	*Larus novaehollandiae*	Camar perak
132	Black-headed Gull	*Larus ridibundus*	Camar kepala-hitam
132	Sabine's Gull	*Xema sabini*	Camar sabine
132	Sooty Tern	*Onychoprion fuscatus*	Dara-laut sayap-hitam
132	Grey-backed Tern	*Onychoprion lunatus*	Dara-laut fiji
132	Bridled Tern	*Onychoprion anaethetus*	Dara-laut batu
132	Aleutian Tern	*Onychoprion aleuticus*	Dara-laut aleut
134	White-winged Tern	*Chlidonias leucopterus*	Dara-laut sayap-putih
134	Whiskered Tern	*Chlidonias hybrida*	Dara-laut kumis

Page number	English name	Scientific name	Bahasa Indonesia name
134	Little Tern	*Sternula albifrons*	Dara-laut kecil
134	Roseate Tern	*Sterna dougallii*	Dara-laut jambon
134	Black-naped Tern	*Sterna sumatrana*	Dara-laut tengkuk-hitam
134	Common Tern	*Sterna hirundo*	Dara-laut biasa
136	Gull-billed Tern	*Gelochelidon nilotica*	Dara-laut tiram
136	Caspian Tern	*Hydroprogne caspia*	Dara-laut kaspia
136	Great Crested Tern	*Thalasseus bergii*	Dara-laut jambul
136	Lesser Crested Tern	*Thalasseus bengalensis*	Dara-laut benggala
136	Chinese Crested Tern	*Thalasseus bernsteini*	Dara-laut cina
136	South Polar Skua	*Stercorarius maccormicki*	Skua kutub
138	Pomarine Skua	*Stercorarius pomarinus*	Camar-kejar pomarin
138	Arctic Skua	*Stercorarius parasiticus*	Camar-kejar arktik
138	Long-tailed Skua	*Stercorarius longicaudus*	Camar-kejar kecil
138	White-tailed Tropicbird	*Phaethon lepturus*	Buntut-sate putih
138	Red-tailed Tropicbird	*Phaethon rubricauda*	Buntut-sate merah
138	Red-billed Tropicbird	*Phaethon aethereus*	Buntut-sate paruh-merah
140	Cape Petrel	*Daption capense*	Petrel tanjung
140	Hawaiian Petrel	*Pterodroma sandwichensis*	Petrel hawaii
140	Barau's Petrel	*Pterodroma baraui*	Petrel barau
140	Tahiti Petrel	*Pseudobulweria rostrata*	Petrel tahiti
140	Beck's Petrel	*Pseudobulweria becki*	Petrel beck
140	Antarctic Prion	*Pachyptila desolata*	Petrel antartika
140	Streaked Shearwater	*Calonectris leucomelas*	Penggunting-laut belang
142	Flesh-footed Shearwater	*Ardenna carneipes*	Penggunting-laut kaki-merah
142	Short-tailed Shearwater	*Ardenna tenuirostris*	Penggunting-laut ekor-pendek
142	Wedge-tailed Shearwater	*Ardenna pacifica*	Penggunting-laut pasifik
142	Tropical Shearwater	*Puffinus bailloni*	Penggunting-laut tropik
142	Hutton's Shearwater	*Puffinus huttoni*	Penggunting-laut hutton
142	Heinroth's Shearwater	*Puffinus heinrothi*	Penggunting-laut heinroth
142	Bulwer's Petrel	*Bulweria bulwerii*	Petrel bulwer
142	Jouanin's Petrel	*Bulweria fallax*	Petrel hindia
144	Wilson's Storm-petrel	*Oceanites oceanicus*	Petrel-badai coklat
144	White-faced Storm-petrel	*Pelagodroma marina*	Petrel-badai muka-putih
144	Swinhoe's Storm-petrel	*Hydrobates monorhis*	Petrel-badai swinhoe
144	Matsudaira's Storm-petrel	*Hydrobates matsudairae*	Petrel-badai matsudaira
144	Little Black Cormorant	*Phalacrocorax sulcirostris*	Pecuk-padi hitam
144	Great Cormorant	*Phalacrocorax carbo*	Pecuk-padi besar
144	Little Pied Cormorant	*Microcarbo melanoleucos*	Pecuk-padi belang
144	Little Cormorant	*Microcarbo niger*	Pecuk-padi kecil
146	Oriental Darter	*Anhinga melanogaster*	Pecuk-ular asia
146	Australian Darter	*Anhinga novaehollandiae*	Pecuk-ular australia
146	Masked Booby	*Sula dactylatra*	Angsa-batu topeng
146	Brown Booby	*Sula leucogaster*	Angsa-batu coklat
146	Red-footed Booby	*Sula sula*	Angsa-batu kaki-merah
146	Abbott's Booby	*Papasula abbotti*	Angsa-batu christmas
148	Christmas Frigatebird	*Fregata andrewsi*	Cikalang christmas
148	Great Frigatebird	*Fregata minor*	Cikalang besar
148	Lesser Frigatebird	*Fregata ariel*	Cikalang kecil
150	Glossy Ibis	*Plegadis falcinellus*	Ibis rokoroko
150	Black-headed Ibis	*Threskiornis melanocephalus*	Ibis cucukbesi
150	Australian Ibis	*Threskiornis molucca*	Ibis australia
150	White-shouldered Ibis	*Pseudibis davisoni*	Ibis karau
150	Royal Spoonbill	*Platalea regia*	Ibis-sendok raja
150	Black-faced Spoonbill	*Platalea minor*	Ibis-sendok muka-hitam
152	Asian Woollyneck	*Ciconia episcopus*	Bangau sandang-lawe
152	Storm's Stork	*Ciconia stormi*	Bangau storm
152	Black-necked Stork	*Ephippiorhynchus asiaticus*	Bangau leher-hitam
152	Milky Stork	*Mycteria cinerea*	Bangau bluwok
152	Asian Openbill	*Anastomus oscitans*	Bangau nganga
152	Lesser Adjutant	*Leptoptilos javanicus*	Bangau tongtong
154	Eurasian Bittern	*Botaurus stellaris*	Bambangan erasia
154	Yellow Bittern	*Ixobrychus sinensis*	Bambangan kuning

Page number	English name	Scientific name	Bahasa Indonesia name
154	Schrenck's Bittern	*Ixobrychus eurhythmus*	Bambangan coklat
154	Cinnamon Bittern	*Ixobrychus cinnamomeus*	Bambangan merah
154	Black Bittern	*Ixobrychus flavicollis*	Bambangan hitam
156	Striated Heron	*Butorides striata*	Kokokan laut
156	Black-crowned Night Heron	*Nycticorax nycticorax*	Kowak-malam abu
156	Rufous Night Heron	*Nycticorax caledonicus*	Kowak-malam merah
156	Japanese Night Heron	*Gorsachius goisagi*	Kowak jepang
156	Malayan Night Heron	*Gorsachius melanolophus*	Kowak melayu
158	Chinese Pond Heron	*Ardeola bacchus*	Blekok cina
158	Javan Pond Heron	*Ardeola speciosa*	Blekok sawah
158	Grey Heron	*Ardea cinerea*	Cangak abu
158	Purple Heron	*Ardea purpurea*	Cangak merah
158	Great-billed Heron	*Ardea sumatrana*	Cangak laut
158	White-necked Heron	*Ardea pacifica*	Cangak pasifik
160	Great Egret	*Ardea alba*	Kuntul besar
160	Intermediate Egret	*Ardea intermedia*	Kuntul perak
160	Cattle Egret	*Ardea ibis*	Kuntul kerbau
160	Chinese Egret	*Egretta eulophotes*	Kuntul cina
160	Little Egret	*Egretta garzetta*	Kuntul kecil
162	Pacific Reef Egret	*Egretta sacra*	Kuntul karang
162	Pied Heron	*Egretta picata*	Kuntul belang
162	White-faced Heron	*Egretta novaehollandiae*	Kuntul australia
162	Great White Pelican	*Pelecanus onocrotalus*	Undan putih
162	Spot-billed Pelican	*Pelecanus philippensis*	Undan paruh-totol
162	Australian Pelican	*Pelecanus conspicillatus*	Undan kacamata
164	Osprey	*Pandion haliaetus*	Elang tiram
164	Black-winged Kite	*Elanus caeruleus*	Elang tikus
164	Jerdon's Baza	*Aviceda jerdoni*	Baza jerdon
164	Pacific Baza	*Aviceda subcristata*	Baza pasifik
166	Black Baza	*Aviceda leuphotes*	Baza hitam
166	Sulawesi Honeybuzzard	*Pernis celebensis*	Sikep-madu sulawesi
166	Oriental Honeybuzzard	*Pernis ruficollis*	Sikep-madu asia
166	Sunda Honeybuzzard	*Pernis ptilorhynchus*	Sikep-madu melayu
168	Himalayan Griffon	*Gyps himalayensis*	Nasar himalaya
168	Sulawesi Serpent-eagle	*Spilornis rufipectus*	Elang-ular sulawesi
168	Crested Serpent-eagle	*Spilornis cheela*	Elang-ular bido
168	Mountain Serpent-eagle	*Spilornis kinabaluensis*	Elang-ular kinabalu
170	Short-toed Snake-eagle	*Circaetus gallicus*	Elang-ular jari-pendek
170	Bat Hawk	*Macheiramphus alcinus*	Elang kelelawar
170	Rufous-bellied Eagle	*Lophotriorchis kienerii*	Elang perut-karat
170	Black Eagle	*Ictinaetus malaiensis*	Elang hitam
170	Flores Hawk Eagle	*Nisaetus floris*	Elang flores
170	Sulawesi Hawk Eagle	*Nisaetus lanceolatus*	Elang sulawesi
172	Javan Hawk Eagle	*Nisaetus bartelsi*	Elang jawa
172	Changeable Hawk Eagle	*Nisaetus limnaeetus*	Elang brontok
172	Blyth's Hawk Eagle	*Nisaetus alboniger*	Elang gunung
172	Wallace's Hawk Eagle	*Nisaetus nanus*	Elang wallace
174	Greater Spotted Eagle	*Clanga clanga*	Rajawali totol
174	Eastern Imperial Eagle	*Aquila heliaca*	Rajawali kaisar
174	Gurney's Eagle	*Aquila gurneyi*	Rajawali kuskus
174	Bonelli's Eagle	*Aquila fasciata*	Rajawali bonelli
174	Booted Eagle	*Hieraaetus pennatus*	Rajawali setiwel
174	Pygmy Eagle	*Hieraaetus weiskei*	Rajawali kecil
176	White-bellied Fish-eagle	*Icthyophaga leucogaster*	Elang-laut perut-putih
176	Lesser Fish-eagle	*Icthyophaga humilis*	Elang-ikan kecil
176	Grey-headed Fish-eagle	*Icthyophaga ichthyaetus*	Elang-ikan kepala-kelabu
176	Black Kite	*Milvus migrans*	Elang paria
176	Brahminy Kite	*Haliastur indus*	Elang bondol
178	White-eyed Buzzard	*Butastur teesa*	Elang mata-putih
178	Rufous-winged Buzzard	*Butastur liventer*	Elang sayap-coklat
178	Grey-faced Buzzard	*Butastur indicus*	Elang kelabu
178	Eurasian Buzzard	*Buteo buteo*	Elang buteo

Page number	English name	Scientific name	Bahasa Indonesia name
180	Western Marsh Harrier	*Circus aeruginosus*	Elang-rawa katak
180	Eastern Marsh Harrier	*Circus spilonotus*	Elang-rawa timur
180	Swamp Harrier	*Circus approximans*	Elang-rawa coklat
180	Pied Harrier	*Circus melanoleucos*	Elang-rawa tangling
182	Hen Harrier	*Circus cyaneus*	Elang-rawa biru
182	Spotted Harrier	*Circus assimilis*	Elang-rawa tutul
182	Eurasian Sparrowhawk	*Accipiter nisus*	Elang-alap erasia
182	Rufous-necked Sparrowhawk	*Tachyspiza erythrauchen*	Elang-alap maluku
182	Halmahera Goshawk	*Tachyspiza henicogramma*	Elang-alap halmahera
184	Varied Goshawk	*Tachyspiza hiogaster*	Elang-alap kelabu
184	Brown Goshawk	*Tachyspiza fasciata*	Elang-alap coklat
186	Asian Shikra	*Tachyspiza badia*	Elang-alap shikra
186	Chinese Sparrowhawk	*Tachyspiza soloensis*	Elang-alap cina
186	Japanese Sparrowhawk	*Tachyspiza gularis*	Elang-alap nippon
186	Besra	*Tachyspiza virgata*	Elang-alap besra
188	Vinous-breasted Sparrowhawk	*Tachyspiza rhodogastra*	Elang-alap dada-merah
188	Small Sparrowhawk	*Tachyspiza nana*	Elang-alap kecil
188	Spot-tailed Sparrowhawk	*Tachyspiza trinotata*	Elang-alap ekor-totol
188	Meyer's Goshawk	*Astur meyerianus*	Elang-alap meyer
190	Crested Goshawk	*Lophospiza trivirgata*	Elang-alap jambul
190	Sulawesi Goshawk	*Lophospiza griseiceps*	Elang-alap kepala-kelabu
190	Eastern Barn Owl	*Tyto javanica*	Serak jawa
190	Grass Owl	*Tyto capensis*	Serak padang
190	Minahasa Owl	*Tyto inexspectata*	Serak minahasa
192	Masked Owl	*Tyto novaehollandiae*	Serak australia
192	Oriental Bay Owl	*Phodilus badius*	Serak bukit
192	Sunda Owlet	*Taenioptynx sylvatica*	Beluk-watu gunung
192	Javan Owlet	*Glaucidium castanopterum*	Beluk-watu jawa
192	Mentawai Scops Owl	*Otus mentawi*	Celepuk mentawai
192	Simeulue Scops Owl	*Otus umbra*	Celepuk simalur
192	Enggano Scops Owl	*Otus enganensis*	Celepuk enggano
192	Mantanani Scops Owl	*Otus mantananensis*	Celepuk mantanani
194	Oriental Scops Owl	*Otus sunia*	Celepuk asia
194	Collared Scops Owl	*Otus lempiji*	Celepuk reban
194	Rajah Scops Owl	*Otus brookii*	Celepuk raja
194	Javan Scops Owl	*Otus angelinae*	Celepuk jawa
194	Reddish Scops Owl	*Otus rufescens*	Celepuk merah
194	Mountain Scops Owl	*Otus spilocephalus*	Celepuk gunung
194	Flores Scops Owl	*Otus alfredi*	Celepuk flores
196	Moluccan Scops Owl	*Otus magicus*	Celepuk maluku
196	Wetar Scops Owl	*Otus tempestatis*	Celepuk wetar
196	Rinjani Scops Owl	*Otus jolandae*	Celepuk rinjani
196	Wallace's Scops Owl	*Otus silvicola*	Celepuk wallace
196	Sula Scops Owl	*Otus sulaensis*	Celepuk sula
196	Banggai Scops Owl	*Otus mendeni*	Celepuk banggai
196	Sulawesi Scops Owl	*Otus manadensis*	Celepuk sulawesi
196	Siau Scops Owl	*Otus siaoensis*	Celepuk siau
198	Sangihe Scops Owl	*Otus collari*	Celepuk sangihe
198	Barred Eagle Owl	*Bubo sumatranus*	Beluk jempuk
198	Buffy Fish Owl	*Bubo ketupu*	Beluk ketupa
198	Short-eared Owl	*Asio flammeus*	Beluk padang
198	Spotted Wood Owl	*Strix seloputo*	Kukuk-beluk seloputo
198	Sunda Wood Owl	*Strix leptogrammica*	Kukuk-beluk coklat
200	Brown Boobook	*Ninox scutulata*	Pungguk coklat
200	Northern Boobook	*Ninox japonica*	Pungguk utara
200	Chocolate Boobook	*Ninox randi*	Pungguk kelam
200	Little Sumba Boobook	*Ninox sumbaensis*	Pungguk sumba
200	Great Sumba Boobook	*Ninox rudolfi*	Pungguk wengi
200	Seram Boobook	*Ninox squamipila*	Pungguk seram
200	Buru Boobook	*Ninox hantu*	Pungguk buru
200	Halmahera Boobook	*Ninox hypogramma*	Pungguk halmahera
200	Tanimbar Boobook	*Ninox forbesi*	Pungguk tanimbar

Page number	English name	Scientific name	Bahasa Indonesia name
202	Southern Boobook	*Ninox boobook*	Pungguk kokodok
202	Timor Boobook	*Ninox fusca*	Pungguk timor
202	Rote Boobook	*Ninox rotiensis*	Pungguk roti
202	Alor Boobook	*Ninox plesseni*	Pungguk alor
202	Ochre-bellied Boobook	*Ninox ochracea*	Pungguk oker
202	Cinnabar Boobook	*Ninox ios*	Pungguk merah-tua
202	Togian Boobook	*Ninox burhani*	Pungguk togian
202	Speckled Boobook	*Ninox punctulata*	Pungguk tutul
202	Barking Owl	*Ninox connivens*	Pungguk gonggong
204	Red-naped Trogon	*Harpactes kasumba*	Luntur kasumba
204	Diard's Trogon	*Harpactes diardii*	Luntur diard
204	Cinnamon-rumped Trogon	*Harpactes orrhophaeus*	Luntur tunggir-coklat
204	Scarlet-rumped Trogon	*Harpactes duvaucelii*	Luntur putri
204	Orange-breasted Trogon	*Harpactes oreskios*	Luntur harimau
204	Red-headed Trogon	*Harpactes erythrocephalus*	Luntur kepala-merah
206	Whitehead's Trogon	*Harpactes whiteheadi*	Luntur kalimantan
206	Javan Trogon	*Apalharpactes reinwardtii*	Luntur jawa
206	Sumatran Trogon	*Apalharpactes mackloti*	Luntur sumatera
206	Knobbed Hornbill	*Rhyticeros cassidix*	Julang sulawesi
206	Blyth's Hornbill	*Rhyticeros plicatus*	Julang papua
206	Sumba Hornbill	*Rhyticeros everetti*	Julang sumba
208	Wreathed Hornbill	*Rhyticeros undulatus*	Julang emas
208	Great Hornbill	*Buceros bicornis*	Rangkong papan
208	Rhinoceros Hornbill	*Buceros rhinoceros*	Rangkong badak
208	Helmeted Hornbill	*Rhinoplax vigil*	Rangkong gading
210	Wrinkled Hornbill	*Rhabdotorrhinus corrugatus*	Julang jambul-hitam
210	Sulawesi Hornbill	*Rhabdotorrhinus exarhatus*	Kangkareng sulawesi
210	White-crowned Hornbill	*Berenicornis comatus*	Enggang jambul
210	Bushy-crested Hornbill	*Anorrhinus galeritus*	Enggang klihingan
210	Oriental Pied Hornbill	*Anthracoceros albirostris*	Kangkareng perut-putih
210	Black Hornbill	*Anthracoceros malayanus*	Kangkareng hitam
212	Coppersmith Barbet	*Psilopogon haemacephalus*	Takur ungkut-ungkut
212	Lineated Barbet	*Psilopogon lineatus*	Takur bultok
212	Fire-tufted Barbet	*Psilopogon pyrolophus*	Takur api
212	Brown-throated Barbet	*Psilopogon corvinus*	Takur bututut
212	Black-banded Barbet	*Psilopogon javensis*	Takur tulung-tumpuk
212	Flame-fronted Barbet	*Psilopogon armillaris*	Takur tohtor
212	Blue-eared Barbet	*Psilopogon australis*	Takur tenggeret
212	Bornean Barbet	*Psilopogon eximius*	Takur leher-hitam
214	Gold-whiskered Barbet	*Psilopogon chrysopogon*	Takur gedang
214	Red-crowned Barbet	*Psilopogon rafflesii*	Takur tutut
214	Red-throated Barbet	*Psilopogon mystacophanos*	Takur warna-warni
214	Black-browed Barbet	*Psilopogon oorti*	Takur bukit
214	Mountain Barbet	*Psilopogon monticola*	Takur gunung
214	Yellow-crowned Barbet	*Psilopogon henricii*	Takur topi-merah
214	Golden-naped Barbet	*Psilopogon pulcherrimus*	Takur tengkuk-emas
216	Bornean Brown Barbet	*Caloramphus fuliginosus*	Ampis kalimantan
216	Malayan Brown Barbet	*Caloramphus hayii*	Ampis melayu
216	Sunda Honeyguide	*Indicator archipelagicus*	Pemandu-lebah asia
216	Speckled Piculet	*Picumnus innominatus*	Tukik belang
216	Rufous Piculet	*Sasia abnormis*	Tukik tikus
216	Grey-and-buff Woodpecker	*Hemicircus concretus*	Caladi cikotok
216	Buff-rumped Woodpecker	*Meiglyptes tristis*	Caladi batu
216	Buff-necked Woodpecker	*Meiglyptes tukki*	Caladi badok
218	Orange-backed Woodpecker	*Chrysocolaptes validus*	Pelatuk kundang
218	Greater Flameback	*Chrysocolaptes guttacristatus*	Pelatuk tunggir-emas
218	Javan Flameback	*Chrysocolaptes strictus*	Pelatuk jawa
218	Olive-backed Woodpecker	*Chloropicoides rafflesii*	Pelatuk raffles
218	Common Flameback	*Dinopium javanense*	Pelatuk besi
218	Rufous Woodpecker	*Micropternus brachyurus*	Pelatuk kijang
220	Banded Yellownape	*Chrysophlegma miniaceum*	Pelatuk merah
220	Checker-throated Yellownape	*Chrysophlegma mentale*	Pelatuk kumis-kelabu

Page number	English name	Scientific name	Bahasa Indonesia name
220	Greater Yellownape	*Chrysophlegma flavinucha*	Pelatuk kuduk-kuning
220	Crimson-winged Woodpecker	*Picus puniceus*	Pelatuk sayap-merah
220	Lesser Yellownape	*Picus chlorolophus*	Pelatuk jambul-kuning
220	Laced Woodpecker	*Picus vittatus*	Pelatuk hijau
222	Sumatran Woodpecker	*Picus dedemi*	Pelatuk muka-kelabu
222	Maroon Woodpecker	*Blythipicus rubiginosus*	Pelatuk pangkas
222	Ashy Woodpecker	*Dryocopus fulvus*	Pelatuk-kelabu sulawesi
222	Great Slaty Woodpecker	*Dryocopus pulverulentus*	Pelatuk-kelabu besar
222	White-bellied Woodpecker	*Dryocopus javensis*	Pelatuk ayam
224	Sulawesi Pygmy-woodpecker	*Picoides temminckii*	Caladi sulawesi
224	Sunda Pygmy-woodpecker	*Picoides moluccensis*	Caladi tilik
224	Grey-capped Pygmy-woodpecker	*Picoides canicapillus*	Caladi belacan
224	Freckle-breasted Woodpecker	*Dendrocopos analis*	Caladi ulam
224	Green-backed Kingfisher	*Actenoides monachus*	Cekakak-hutan tunggir-hijau
224	Black-headed Kingfisher	*Actenoides capucinus*	Cekakak-hutan kepala-hitam
224	Scaly Kingfisher	*Actenoides princeps*	Cekakak-hutan dada-sisik
226	Rufous-collared Kingfisher	*Actenoides concretus*	Cekakak-hutan melayu
226	Common Paradise-kingfisher	*Tanysiptera galatea*	Cekakak-pita biasa
226	Sulawesi Lilac Kingfisher	*Cittura cyanotis*	Raja-udang pipi-ungu
226	Sangihe Lilac Kingfisher	*Cittura sanghirensis*	Raja-udang sangihe
226	Banded Kingfisher	*Lacedo pulchella*	Cekakak batu
228	White-rumped Kingfisher	*Caridonax fulgidus*	Cekakak tunggir-putih
228	Stork-billed Kingfisher	*Pelargopsis capensis*	Pekaka emas
228	Great-billed Kingfisher	*Pelargopsis melanorhyncha*	Pekaka bua-bua
228	Ruddy Kingfisher	*Halcyon coromanda*	Cekakak merah
228	White-breasted Kingfisher	*Halcyon smyrnensis*	Cekakak belukar
228	Javan Kingfisher	*Halcyon cyanoventris*	Cekakak jawa
228	Black-capped Kingfisher	*Halcyon pileata*	Cekakak cina
230	Blue-and-white Kingfisher	*Todiramphus diops*	Cekakak biru-putih
230	Lazuli Kingfisher	*Todiramphus lazuli*	Cekakak lazuardi
230	Forest Kingfisher	*Todiramphus macleayii*	Cekakak rimba
230	Collared Kingfisher	*Todiramphus chloris*	Cekakak sungai
230	Talaud Kingfisher	*Todiramphus enigma*	Cekakak talaud
230	Beach Kingfisher	*Todiramphus saurophagus*	Cekakak pantai
230	Sacred Kingfisher	*Todiramphus sanctus*	Cekakak australia
232	Sombre Kingfisher	*Todiramphus funebris*	Cekakak murung
232	Cinnamon-banded Kingfisher	*Todiramphus australasia*	Cekakak kalung-coklat
232	Black-backed Dwarf-kingfisher	*Ceyx erithaca*	Raja-udang api
232	Rufous-backed Dwarf-kingfisher	*Ceyx rufidorsa*	Raja-udang punggung-merah
232	Sulawesi Dwarf-kingfisher	*Ceyx fallax*	Raja-udang sulawesi
232	Variable Dwarf-kingfisher	*Ceyx lepidus*	Raja-udang kerdil
232	Little Kingfisher	*Ceyx pusillus*	Raja-udang kecil
232	Azure Kingfisher	*Ceyx azureus*	Raja-udang biru-langit
234	Cerulean Kingfisher	*Alcedo coerulescens*	Raja-udang biru
234	Blue-banded Kingfisher	*Alcedo euryzona*	Raja-udang kalung-biru
234	Blue-eared Kingfisher	*Alcedo meninting*	Raja-udang meninting
234	Common Kingfisher	*Alcedo atthis*	Raja-udang erasia
234	Red-bearded Bee-eater	*Nyctyornis amictus*	Cirik-cirik kumbang
234	Purple-bearded Bee-eater	*Meropogon forsteni*	Cirik-cirik sulawesi
234	Chestnut-headed Bee-eater	*Merops leschenaulti*	Kirik-kirik senja
236	Blue-tailed Bee-eater	*Merops philippinus*	Kirik-kirik laut
236	Rainbow Bee-eater	*Merops ornatus*	Kirik-kirik australia
236	Blue-throated Bee-eater	*Merops viridis*	Kirik-kirik biru
236	Sulawesi Roller	*Coracias temminckii*	Tiong-lampu sulawesi
236	Common Dollarbird	*Eurystomus orientalis*	Tiong-lampu biasa
236	Azure Dollarbird	*Eurystomus azureus*	Tiong-lampu ungu
236	Hoopoe	*Upupa epops*	Hupo tunggal
238	Eurasian Kestrel	*Falco tinnunculus*	Alap-alap erasia
238	Indonesian Kestrel	*Falco moluccensis*	Alap-alap sapi
238	Australian Kestrel	*Falco cenchroides*	Alap-alap layang
238	Oriental Hobby	*Falco severus*	Alap-alap macan
238	Eurasian Hobby	*Falco subbuteo*	Alap-alap walet

Page number	English name	Scientific name	Bahasa Indonesia name
238	Australian Hobby	*Falco longipennis*	Alap-alap australia
238	Peregrine Falcon	*Falco peregrinus*	Alap-alap kawah
240	Black-thighed Falconet	*Microhierax fringillarius*	Alap-alap capung
240	White-fronted Falconet	*Microhierax latifrons*	Alap-alap dahi-putih
240	Tanimbar Cockatoo	*Cacatua goffiniana*	Kakatua tanimbar
240	Yellow-crested Cockatoo	*Cacatua sulphurea*	Kakatua jambul-kuning
240	Orange-crested Cockatoo	*Cacatua citrinocristata*	Kakatua sumba
240	Umbrella Cockatoo	*Cacatua alba*	Kakatua putih
240	Salmon-crested Cockatoo	*Cacatua moluccensis*	Kakatua maluku
242	Red-and-blue Lory	*Eos histrio*	Nuri talaud
242	Violet-necked Lory	*Eos riciniata*	Nuri halmahera
242	Scaled Lory	*Eos squamata*	Nuri kalung-ungu
242	Red Lory	*Eos bornea*	Nuri maluku
242	Blue-streaked Lory	*Eos reticulata*	Nuri tanimbar
242	Blue-eared Lory	*Eos semilarvata*	Nuri telinga-biru
242	Coconut Lorikeet	*Trichoglossus haematodus*	Perkici pelangi
242	Leaf Lorikeet	*Trichoglossus weberi*	Perkici flores
242	Marigold Lorikeet	*Trichoglossus capistratus*	Perkici oranye
244	Sunset Lorikeet	*Trichoglossus forsteni*	Perkici dada-merah
244	Olive-headed Lorikeet	*Trichoglossus euteles*	Perkici timor
244	Ornate Lorikeet	*Saudareos ornata*	Perkici dora
244	Sula Lorikeet	*Saudareos flavoviridis*	Perkici kuning-hijau
244	Meyer's Lorikeet	*Saudareos meyeri*	Perkici sulawesi
244	Iris Lorikeet	*Saudareos iris*	Perkici iris
244	Chattering Lory	*Lorius garrulus*	Kasturi ternate
244	Purple-naped Lory	*Lorius domicella*	Kasturi tengkuk-ungu
246	Buru Lorikeet	*Charmosyna toxopei*	Perkici buru
246	Red-flanked Lorikeet	*Hypocharmosyna placentis*	Perkici dagu-merah
246	Yellow-capped Pygmy-parrot	*Micropsitta keiensis*	Nuri-kate topi-kuning
246	Red-breasted Pygmy-parrot	*Micropsitta bruijnii*	Nuri-kate dada-merah
246	Blue-rumped Parrot	*Psittinus cyanurus*	Nuri tanau
246	Simeulue Parrot	*Psittinus abbotti*	Nuri simeulue
246	Red-cheeked Parrot	*Geoffroyus geoffroyi*	Nuri pipi-merah
248	Minahasa Racquet-tail	*Prioniturus flavicans*	Kringking dada-kuning
248	Sulawesi Racquet-tail	*Prioniturus platurus*	Kringking bukit
248	Buru Racquet-tail	*Prioniturus mada*	Kringking buru
248	Eclectus Parrot	*Eclectus roratus*	Nuri bayan
250	Great-billed Parrot	*Tanygnathus megalorynchos*	Betet-kelapa paruh-besar
250	Black-lored Parrot	*Tanygnathus gramineus*	Betet-kelapa buru
250	Blue-naped Parrot	*Tanygnathus lucionensis*	Betet-kelapa filipina
250	Azure-rumped Parrot	*Tanygnathus sumatranus*	Betet-kelapa punggung-biru
252	Moluccan King Parrot	*Alisterus amboinensis*	Nuri-raja ambon
252	Jonquil Parrot	*Aprosmictus jonquillaceus*	Nuri-raja kembang
252	Red-breasted Parakeet	*Psittacula alexandri*	Betet biasa
252	Long-tailed Parakeet	*Psittacula longicauda*	Betet ekor-panjang
252	Enggano Parakeet	*Psittacula modesta*	Betet enggano
254	Blue-crowned Hanging Parrot	*Loriculus galgulus*	Serindit melayu
254	Sulawesi Hanging Parrot	*Loriculus stigmatus*	Serindit sulawesi
254	Sula Hanging Parrot	*Loriculus sclateri*	Serindit sula
254	Moluccan Hanging Parrot	*Loriculus amabilis*	Serindit maluku
254	Sangihe Hanging Parrot	*Loriculus catamene*	Serindit sangihe
254	Pygmy Hanging Parrot	*Loriculus exilis*	Serindit paruh-merah
254	Javan Hanging Parrot	*Loriculus pusillus*	Serindit jawa
254	Wallace's Hanging Parrot	*Loriculus flosculus*	Serindit flores
256	Green Broadbill	*Calyptomena viridis*	Madi-hijau kecil
256	Hose's Broadbill	*Calyptomena hosii*	Madi-hijau perut-biru
256	Whitehead's Broadbill	*Calyptomena whiteheadi*	Madi-hijau whitehead
256	Black-and-red Broadbill	*Cymbirhynchus macrorhynchos*	Sempur-hujan sungai
256	Long-tailed Broadbill	*Psarisomus dalhousiae*	Madi injap
256	Silver-breasted Broadbill	*Serilophus lunatus*	Madi dada-perak
258	Banded Broadbill	*Eurylaimus javanicus*	Sempur-hujan rimba
258	Black-and-yellow Broadbill	*Eurylaimus ochromalus*	Sempur-hujan darat

Page number	English name	Scientific name	Bahasa Indonesia name
258	Dusky Broadbill	*Corydon sumatranus*	Madi kelam
258	Schneider's Pitta	*Hydrornis schneideri*	Paok schneider
258	Giant Pitta	*Hydrornis caeruleus*	Paok sintau
260	Javan Banded Pitta	*Hydrornis guajanus*	Paok jawa
260	Malayan Banded Pitta	*Hydrornis irena*	Paok melayu
260	Bornean Banded Pitta	*Hydrornis schwaneri*	Paok pancawarna
260	Blue-headed Pitta	*Hydrornis baudii*	Paok kepala-biru
260	Blue-banded Pitta	*Erythropitta arquata*	Paok kalung-biru
260	Garnet Pitta	*Erythropitta granatina*	Paok delima
260	Black-crowned Pitta	*Erythropitta ussheri*	Paok sabah
262	Graceful Pitta	*Erythropitta venusta*	Paok topi-hitam
262	Philippine Pitta	*Erythropitta erythrogaster*	Paok filipina
262	Sula Pitta	*Erythropitta dohertyi*	Paok sula
262	Sulawesi Pitta	*Erythropitta celebensis*	Paok sulawesi
262	North Moluccan Pitta	*Erythropitta rufiventris*	Paok jailolo
262	South Moluccan Pitta	*Erythropitta rubrinucha*	Paok maluku
262	Papuan Pitta	*Erythropitta macklotii*	Paok papua
264	Blue-winged Pitta	*Pitta moluccensis*	Paok hujan
264	Mangrove Pitta	*Pitta megarhyncha*	Paok bakau
264	Fairy Pitta	*Pitta nympha*	Paok bidadari
264	Wallace's Elegant Pitta	*Pitta concinna*	Paok wallace
264	Temminck's Elegant Pitta	*Pitta elegans*	Paok laus
264	Banda Elegant Pitta	*Pitta vigorsii*	Paok banda
266	Ivory-breasted Pitta	*Pitta maxima*	Paok halmahera
266	Asian Hooded Pitta	*Pitta sordida*	Paok hijau
266	Minahasa Hooded Pitta	*Pitta forsteni*	Paok minahasa
266	Lesser Myza	*Myza celebensis*	Cikarak sulawesi
266	Greater Myza	*Myza sarasinorum*	Cikarak telinga-putih
266	Scaly-crowned Honeyeater	*Sugomel lombokium*	Isap-madu topi-sisik
266	Brown Honeyeater	*Lichmera indistincta*	Isap-madu australia
268	Olive Honeyeater	*Lichmera argentauris*	Isap-madu zaitun
268	Buru Honeyeater	*Lichmera deningeri*	Isap-madu buru
268	Seram Honeyeater	*Lichmera monticola*	Isap-madu seram
268	Banda Honeyeater	*Lichmera squamata*	Isap-madu babar
268	Yellow-eared Honeyeater	*Lichmera flavicans*	Isap-madu timor
268	Black-necklaced Honeyeater	*Lichmera notabilis*	Isap-madu wetar
268	Timor Meliphaga	*Meliphaga reticulata*	Meliphaga dada-lurik
268	White-streaked Honeyeater	*Melitograis gilolensis*	Cikukua halmahera
270	Drab Myzomela	*Myzomela blasii*	Myzomela buram
270	Sultan's Myzomela	*Myzomela simplex*	Myzomela sultan
270	Red-tinged Myzomela	*Myzomela rubrotincta*	Myzomela lumuran-darah
270	Wetar Myzomela	*Myzomela kuehni*	Myzomela wetar
270	Alor Myzomela	*Myzomela prawiradilagae*	Myzomela alor
270	Sumba Myzomela	*Myzomela dammermani*	Myzomela sumba
270	Rote Myzomela	*Myzomela irianawidodoae*	Myzomela rote
270	Timor Myzomela	*Myzomela vulnerata*	Myzomela timor
272	Banda Myzomela	*Myzomela boiei*	Myzomela merah-tua
272	Tanimbar Myzomela	*Myzomela annabellae*	Myzomela tanimbar
272	Sulawesi Myzomela	*Myzomela chloroptera*	Myzomela sulawesi
272	Bacan Myzomela	*Myzomela batjanensis*	Myzomela bacan
272	Obi Myzomela	*Myzomela sp.*	Myzomela obi
272	Taliabu Myzomela	*Myzomela wahe*	Myzomela taliabu
272	Seram Myzomela	*Myzomela elisabethae*	Myzomela seram
272	Buru Myzomela	*Myzomela wakoloensis*	Myzomela wakolo
274	Timor Friarbird	*Philemon inornatus*	Cikukua timor
274	Kisar Friarbird	*Philemon kisserensis*	Cikukua kisar
274	Morotai Friarbird	*Philemon fuscicapillus*	Cikukua hitam
274	Buru Friarbird	*Philemon moluccensis*	Cikukua buru
274	Tanimbar Friarbird	*Philemon plumigenis*	Cikukua tanimbar
274	Seram Friarbird	*Philemon subcorniculatus*	Cikukua seram
274	Tenggara Friarbird	*Philemon buceroides*	Cikukua tanduk
276	Banda Sea Gerygone	*Gerygone dorsalis*	Remetuk panggul-merah

Page number	English name	Scientific name	Bahasa Indonesia name
276	Golden-bellied Gerygone	*Gerygone sulphurea*	Remetuk laut
276	Timor Gerygone	*Gerygone inornata*	Remetuk timor
276	Pied Shrike-vireo	*Pteruthius flaviscapis*	Ciu jawa
276	Blyth's Shrike-vireo	*Pteruthius aeralatus*	Ciu besar
276	Trilling Shrike-vireo	*Pteruthius aenobarbus*	Ciu kunyit
276	Erpornis	*Erpornis zantholeuca*	Yuhina perut-putih
278	Green Oriole	*Oriolus flavocinctus*	Kepudang bakau
278	Timor Oriole	*Oriolus melanotis*	Kepudang timor
278	Wetar Oriole	*Oriolus finschi*	Kepudang wetar
278	Tanimbar Oriole	*Oriolus decipiens*	Kepudang tanimbar
278	Buru Oriole	*Oriolus bouroensis*	Kepudang muka-hitam
278	Seram Oriole	*Oriolus forsteni*	Kepudang seram
278	Halmahera Oriole	*Oriolus phaeochromus*	Kepudang halmahera
278	Olive-backed Oriole	*Oriolus sagittatus*	Kepudang tunggir-zaitun
280	Black-naped Oriole	*Oriolus chinensis*	Kepudang kuduk-hitam
280	Black-hooded Oriole	*Oriolus xanthornus*	Kepudang kerudung-hitam
280	Black Oriole	*Oriolus hosii*	Kepudang hitam
280	Black-and-crimson Oriole	*Oriolus consanguineus*	Kepudang melayu
280	Javan Oriole	*Oriolus cruentus*	Kepudang jawa
282	Dark-throated Oriole	*Oriolus xanthonotus*	Kepudang hutan
282	Australasian Figbird	*Sphecotheres vieilloti*	Burung-ara hijau
282	Timor Figbird	*Sphecotheres viridis*	Burung-ara timor
282	Wetar Figbird	*Sphecotheres hypoleucus*	Burung-ara wetar
282	Sangihe Whistler	*Coracornis sanghirensis*	Kancilan sangihe
282	Maroon-backed Whistler	*Coracornis raveni*	Kancilan ungu
282	Bare-throated Whistler	*Pachycephala nudigula*	Kancilan flores
284	Mangrove Whistler	*Pachycephala cinerea*	Kancilan bakau
284	White-vented Whistler	*Pachycephala homeyeri*	Kancilan tungging-putih
284	Sulphur-bellied Whistler	*Pachycephala sulfuriventer*	Kancilan perut-kuning
284	Golden Whistler	*Pachycephala pectoralis*	Kancilan emas
284	Moluccan Whistler	*Pachycephala macrorhyncha*	Kancilan maluku
286	Tenggara Whistler	*Pachycephala calliope*	Kancilan tenggara
286	Selayar Whistler	*Pachycephala teysmanni*	Kancilan selayar
286	Babar Whistler	*Pachycephala sharpei*	Kancilan babar
286	Fawn-breasted Whistler	*Pachycephala orpheus*	Kancilan timor
288	Island Whistler	*Pachycephala phaionota*	Kancilan pulau
288	Obi Whistler	*Pachycephala johni*	Kancilan obi
288	Drab Whistler	*Pachycephala griseonota*	Kancilan tunawarna
288	Wallacean Whistler	*Pachycephala arctitorquis*	Kancilan wallacea
288	Grey Whistler	*Pachycephala simplex*	Kancilan kelabu
288	Bornean Whistler	*Pachycephala hypoxantha*	Kancilan kalimantan
288	Bar-winged Flycatcher-shrike	*Hemipus picatus*	Jingjing bukit
288	Black-winged Flycatcher-shrike	*Hemipus hirundinaceus*	Jingjing batu
290	Large Woodshrike	*Tephrodornis virgatus*	Jingjing petulak
290	Rufous-winged Philentoma	*Philentoma pyrhoptera*	Philentoma sayap-merah
290	Maroon-breasted Philentoma	*Philentoma velata*	Philentoma kerudung
290	Bristlehead	*Pityriasis gymnocephala*	Tiong-batu kalimantan
290	Common Iora	*Aegithina tiphia*	Cipoh kacat
290	Green Iora	*Aegithina viridissima*	Cipoh jantung
292	White-breasted Woodswallow	*Artamus leucorynchus*	Kekep babi
292	Ivory-backed Woodswallow	*Artamus monachus*	Kekep sulawesi
292	Black-faced Woodswallow	*Artamus cinereus*	Kekep hitam
292	Roving Cuckooshrike	*Coracina sumatrensis*	Kepudang-sungu melayu
292	Javan Cuckooshrike	*Coracina javensis*	Kepudang-sungu jawa
292	Sunda Cuckooshrike	*Coracina larvata*	Kepudang-sungu gunung
292	Slaty Cuckooshrike	*Coracina schistacea*	Kepudang-sungu kelabu
294	White-rumped Cuckooshrike	*Coracina leucopygia*	Kepudang-sungu tunggir-putih
294	Wallacean Cuckooshrike	*Coracina personata*	Kepudang-sungu topeng
294	Alor Cuckooshrike	*Coracina alfrediana*	Kepudang-sungu alor
294	Moluccan Cuckooshrike	*Coracina atriceps*	Kepudang-sungu maluku
294	Black-faced Cuckooshrike	*Coracina novaehollandiae*	Kepudang-sungu besar
294	Buru Cuckooshrike	*Coracina fortis*	Kepudang-sungu buru

Page number	English name	Scientific name	Bahasa Indonesia name
296	White-bellied Cuckooshrike	*Coracina papuensis*	Kepudang-sungu kartula
296	Pied Cuckooshrike	*Coracina bicolor*	Kepudang-sungu belang
296	Cerulean Cuckooshrike	*Coracina temminckii*	Kepudang-sungu biru
296	Stout-billed Cuckooshrike	*Coracina caeruleogrisea*	Kepudang-sungu paruh-tebal
296	Pygmy Cicadabird	*Celebesica abbotti*	Kepudang-sungu kerdil
296	Halmahera Cicadabird	*Edolisoma parvulum*	Kepudang-sungu halmahera
296	Pale-shouldered Cicadabird	*Edolisoma dohertyi*	Kepudang-sungu sumba
296	Salvadori's Cicadabird	*Edolisoma salvadorii*	Kepudang-sungu salvadori
298	Common Cicadabird	*Edolisoma tenuirostre*	Kepudang-sungu miniak
298	Tenggara Cicadabird	*Edolisoma dispar*	Kepudang-sungu kai
298	Pale Cicadabird	*Edolisoma ceramense*	Kepudang-sungu pucat
298	Lesser Cicadabird	*Lalage fimbriata*	Kepudang-sungu kecil
300	Pied Triller	*Lalage nigra*	Kapasan kemiri
300	Lesueur's Triller	*Lalage sueurii*	Kapasan sayap-putih
300	Sulawesi Triller	*Lalage leucopygialis*	Kapasan sulawesi
300	Varied Triller	*Lalage leucomela*	Kapasan alis-putih
300	Tanimbar Triller	*Lalage moesta*	Kapasan tanimbar
300	Rufous-bellied Triller	*Lalage aurea*	Kapasan halmahera
302	Ashy Minivet	*Pericrocotus divaricatus*	Sepah padang
302	Scarlet Minivet	*Pericrocotus flammeus*	Sepah hutan
302	Sunda Minivet	*Pericrocotus miniatus*	Sepah gunung
302	Flores Minivet	*Pericrocotus lansbergei*	Sepah kerdil
302	Grey-chinned Minivet	*Pericrocotus solaris*	Sepah dagu-kelabu
302	Small Minivet	*Pericrocotus cinnamomeus*	Sepah kecil
302	Fiery Minivet	*Pericrocotus igneus*	Sepah tulin
304	Sulawesi Fantail	*Rhipidura teysmanni*	Kipasan sulawesi
304	Peleng Fantail	*Rhipidura habibiei*	Kipasan peleng
304	Taliabu Fantail	*Rhipidura sulaensis*	Kipasan taliabu
304	Tawny-backed Fantail	*Rhipidura superflua*	Kipasan buru
304	Streak-breasted Fantail	*Rhipidura dedemi*	Kipasan seram
304	Charming Fantail	*Rhipidura opistherytha*	Kipasan tanimbar
304	Supertramp Fantail	*Rhipidura semicollaris*	Kipasan pengembara
304	Gilolo Fantail	*Rhipidura torrida*	Kipasan gilolo
306	Trumpeting Fantail	*Rhipidura diluta*	Kipasan flores
306	Cinnamon-tailed Fantail	*Rhipidura fuscorufa*	Kipasan ekor-coklat
306	Timor Fantail	*Rhipidura rufiventris*	Kipasan dada-lurik
306	Banda Sea Fantail	*Rhipidura hoedti*	Kipasan banda
306	Rote Fantail	*Rhipidura tenkatei*	Kipasan rote
306	Buru Fantail	*Rhipidura bouruensis*	Kipasan perut-coklat
306	Seram Fantail	*Rhipidura cinerea*	Kipasan kelabu
306	Obi Fantail	*Rhipidura obiensis*	Kipasan obi
306	Kai Fantail	*Rhipidura assimilis*	Kipasan kai
308	Spotted Fantail	*Rhipidura perlata*	Kipasan mutiara
308	Rufous-tailed Fantail	*Rhipidura phoenicura*	Kipasan ekor-merah
308	White-bellied Fantail	*Rhipidura euryura*	Kipasan bukit
308	White-throated Fantail	*Rhipidura albicollis*	Kipasan gunung
308	Sunda Pied Fantail	*Rhipidura javanica*	Kipasan belang
308	Willie Fantail	*Rhipidura leucophrys*	Kipasan kebun
308	Cerulean Silktail	*Eutrichomyias rowleyi*	Seriwang sangihe
308	Black Drongo	*Dicrurus macrocercus*	Srigunting hitam
310	Bronzed Drongo	*Dicrurus aeneus*	Srigunting keladi
310	Lesser Racket-tailed Drongo	*Dicrurus remifer*	Srigunting bukit
310	Crow-billed Drongo	*Dicrurus annectens*	Srigunting gagak
310	Greater Racket-tailed Drongo	*Dicrurus paradiseus*	Srigunting batu
312	Ashy Drongo	*Dicrurus leucophaeus*	Srigunting kelabu
312	Bornean Spangled Drongo	*Dicrurus borneensis*	Srigunting kalimantan
312	Javan Spangled Drongo	*Dicrurus jentincki*	Srigunting jawa
312	Sumatran Spangled Drongo	*Dicrurus sumatranus*	Srigunting sumatera
312	Mentawai Spangled Drongo	*Dicrurus viridinitens*	Srigunting mentawai
314	Sulu Spangled Drongo	*Dicrurus suluensis*	Srigunting sulu
314	White-eyed Spangled Drongo	*Dicrurus leucops*	Srigunting mata-putih
314	Sulawesi Spangled Drongo	*Dicrurus montanus*	Srigunting sulawesi

Page number	English name	Scientific name	Bahasa Indonesia name
314	Sula Spangled Drongo	*Dicrurus pectoralis*	Srigunting sula
314	Obi Spangled Drongo	*Dicrurus guillemardi*	Srigunting obi
314	Flores Spangled Drongo	*Dicrurus bimaensis*	Srigunting flores
314	Sumba Spangled Drongo	*Dicrurus sumbae*	Srigunting sumba
314	Lombok Spangled Drongo	*Dicrurus vicinus*	Srigunting lombok
316	Timor Spangled Drongo	*Dicrurus densus*	Srigunting timor
316	Tanimbar Spangled Drongo	*Dicrurus kuehni*	Srigunting tanimbar
316	Kai Spangled Drongo	*Dicrurus megalornis*	Srigunting kai
316	Seram Spangled Drongo	*Dicrurus amboinensis*	Srigunting seram
316	Buru Spangled Drongo	*Dicrurus buruensis*	Srigunting buru
316	Halmahera Spangled Drongo	*Dicrurus atrocaeruleus*	Srigunting halmahera
316	Bacan Spangled Drongo	*Dicrurus sp.*	Srigunting bacan
316	Morotai Spangled Drongo	*Dicrurus morotensis*	Srigunting morotai
318	Halmahera Paradise-crow	*Lycocorax pyrrhopterus*	Cendrawasih-gagak halmahera
318	Obi Paradise-crow	*Lycocorax obiensis*	Cendrawasih-gagak obi
318	Wallace's Standardwing	*Semioptera wallacii*	Bidadari halmahera
318	Pale-blue Monarch	*Hypothymis puella*	Kehicap sulawesi
318	Black-naped Monarch	*Hypothymis azurea*	Kehicap ranting
320	Blyth's Paradise-flycatcher	*Terpsiphone affinis*	Seriwang asia
320	Tenggara Paradise-flycatcher	*Terpsiphone floris*	Seriwang nusa-tenggara
320	Amur Paradise-flycatcher	*Terpsiphone incei*	Seriwang utara
320	Japanese Paradise-flycatcher	*Terpsiphone atrocaudata*	Seriwang jepang
322	Southern Rufous Paradise-flycatcher	*Terpsiphone cinnamomea*	Seriwang filipina
322	Moluccan Monarch	*Myiagra galeata*	Kehicap kelabu
322	Broad-billed Monarch	*Myiagra ruficollis*	Kehicap paruh-lebar
322	Shining Monarch	*Myiagra alecto*	Kehicap kilap
322	Island Monarch	*Monarcha cinerascens*	Kehicap pulau
324	Kai Monarch	*Symposiachrus leucurus*	Kehicap kai
324	Tanahjampea Monarch	*Symposiachrus everetti*	Kehicap tanah-jampea
324	Buru Monarch	*Symposiachrus loricatus*	Kehicap buru
324	Boano Monarch	*Symposiachrus boanensis*	Kehicap boano
324	Moluccan Spectacled Monarch	*Symposiachrus trivirgatus*	Kehicap kacamata
324	Flores Monarch	*Symposiachrus sacerdotum*	Kehicap flores
324	Australian Spectacled Monarch	*Symposiachrus melanopterus*	Kehicap sahul
324	Banda Sea Monarch	*Symposiachrus mundus*	Kehicap laut-banda
326	White-naped Monarch	*Carterornis pileatus*	Kehicap tengkuk-putih
326	Tanimbar Monarch	*Carterornis castus*	Kehicap tanimbar
326	Magpie-lark	*Grallina cyanoleuca*	Branjangan-lumpur australia
326	Tiger Shrike	*Lanius tigrinus*	Bentet loreng
326	Brown Shrike	*Lanius cristatus*	Bentet coklat
328	Long-tailed Shrike	*Lanius schach*	Bentet kelabu
328	Great Grey Shrike	*Lanius excubitor*	Bentet utara
328	Jay Shrike	*Platylophus galericulatus*	Tangkar ongklet
328	Bornean Treepie	*Dendrocitta cinerascens*	Tangkar-uli kalimantan
328	Sumatran Treepie	*Dendrocitta occipitalis*	Tangkar-uli sumatera
328	Racket-tailed Treepie	*Crypsirina temia*	Tangkar centrong
330	Malayan Black Magpie	*Platysmurus leucopterus*	Tangkar kambing
330	Bornean Black Magpie	*Platysmurus aterrimus*	Tangkar kalimantan
330	Common Green Magpie	*Cissa chinensis*	Ekek layongan
330	Javan Green Magpie	*Cissa thalassina*	Ekek-geling jawa
330	Bornean Green Magpie	*Cissa jefferyi*	Ekek-geling kalimantan
330	Long-billed Crow	*Corvus validus*	Gagak halmahera
330	Torresian Crow	*Corvus orru*	Gagak orru
332	House Crow	*Corvus splendens*	Gagak rumah
332	Large-billed Crow	*Corvus macrorhynchos*	Gagak kampung
332	Seram Crow	*Corvus violaceus*	Gagak seram
332	Sunda Crow	*Corvus enca*	Gagak hutan
332	Sulawesi Crow	*Corvus celebensis*	Gagak wokawoka
332	Banggai Crow	*Corvus unicolor*	Gagak banggai
334	Piping Crow	*Corvus typicus*	Gagak sulawesi
334	Flores Crow	*Corvus florensis*	Gagak flores
334	Rail-babbler	*Eupetes macrocerus*	Sipinjur melayu

Page number	English name	Scientific name	Bahasa Indonesia name
334	Tanimbar Flyrobin	*Microeca hemixantha*	Sikatan perut-emas
334	Grey-headed Canary-flycatcher	*Culicicapa ceylonensis*	Sikatan kepala-abu
334	Citrine Canary-flycatcher	*Culicicapa helianthea*	Sikatan matari
336	Cinereous Tit	*Parus cinereus*	Gelatik-batu kelabu
336	Australasian Bushlark	*Mirafra javanica*	Branjangan jawa
336	Eurasian Skylark	*Alauda arvensis*	Branjangan erasia
336	Sand Martin	*Riparia riparia*	Layang-layang pasir
336	Barn Swallow	*Hirundo rustica*	Layang-layang asia
336	Pacific Swallow	*Hirundo javanica*	Layang-layang batu
338	Daurian Swallow	*Cecropis daurica*	Layang-layang loreng
338	Fairy Martin	*Petrochelidon ariel*	Layang-layang bidadari
338	Tree Martin	*Petrochelidon nigricans*	Layang-layang pohon
338	Asian House Martin	*Delichon dasypus*	Layang-layang rumah
338	Sooty-headed Bulbul	*Pycnonotus aurigaster*	Cucak kutilang
338	Sunda Yellow-vented Bulbul	*Pycnonotus analis*	Merbah cerukcuk
338	Pale-faced Bulbul	*Pycnonotus leucops*	Merbah gunung
340	Orange-spotted Bulbul	*Pycnonotus bimaculatus*	Cucak gunung
340	Aceh Bulbul	*Pycnonotus snouckaerti*	Cucak aceh
340	Straw-headed Bulbul	*Pycnonotus zeylanicus*	Cucak rawa
340	Ruby-throated Bulbul	*Pycnonotus dispar*	Cucak emas
340	Bornean Bulbul	*Pycnonotus montis*	Cucak kalimantan
340	Scaly-breasted Bulbul	*Pycnonotus squamatus*	Cucak bersisik
340	Grey-bellied Bulbul	*Pycnonotus cyaniventris*	Cucak kelabu
342	Olive-winged Bulbul	*Pycnonotus plumosus*	Merbah belukar
342	Barusan Bulbul	*Pycnonotus porphyreus*	Merbah barusan
342	Cream-vented Bulbul	*Pycnonotus simplex*	Merbah corok-corok
342	Cream-eyed Bulbul	*Pycnonotus pseudosimplex*	Merbah borneo
342	Asian Red-eyed Bulbul	*Pycnonotus brunneus*	Merbah mata-merah
342	Spectacled Bulbul	*Pycnonotus erythropthalmos*	Merbah kacamata
344	Yellow-bellied Bulbul	*Alophoixus phaeocephalus*	Empuloh irang
344	Grey-cheeked Bulbul	*Alophoixus tephrogenys*	Empuloh melayu
344	Ochraceous Bulbul	*Alophoixus ochraceus*	Empuloh ragum
344	Penan Bulbul	*Alophoixus ruficrissus*	Empuloh kalimantan
344	Melodious Bulbul	*Alophoixus bres*	Empuloh jawa
346	Black-headed Bulbul	*Microtarsus melanocephalos*	Cucak kuricang
346	Black-and-white Bulbul	*Microtarsus melanoleucos*	Cucak sakit-tubuh
346	Puff-backed Bulbul	*Microtarsus eutilotus*	Cucak rumbai-tunggir
346	Hook-billed Bulbul	*Setornis criniger*	Empuloh paruh-kait
346	Finsch's Bulbul	*Iole finschii*	Empuloh leher-kuning
346	Charlotte's Bulbul	*Iole charlottae*	Brinji mata-putih
346	Buff-vented Bulbul	*Iole crypta*	Brinji sumatera
348	Hairy-backed Bulbul	*Tricholestes criniger*	Brinji rambut-tunggir
348	Cream-striped Bulbul	*Alcurus leucogrammicus*	Cucak kerinci
348	Spot-necked Bulbul	*Alcurus tympanistrigus*	Cucak mutiara
348	Cinereous Bulbul	*Hemixos cinereus*	Brinji kelabu
348	Streaked Bulbul	*Ixos malaccensis*	Brinji bergaris
348	Javan Bulbul	*Ixos virescens*	Brinji-gunung jawa
348	Sumatran Bulbul	*Ixos sumatranus*	Brinji-gunung sumatera
350	Seram Golden Bulbul	*Hypsipetes affinis*	Brinji-emas seram
350	Buru Golden Bulbul	*Hypsipetes mysticalis*	Brinji-emas buru
350	Togian Golden Bulbul	*Hypsipetes aureus*	Brinji-emas togian
350	Sangihe Golden Bulbul	*Hypsipetes platenae*	Brinji-emas sangihe
350	Halmahera Golden Bulbul	*Hypsipetes chloris*	Brinji-emas halmahera
350	Obi Golden Bulbul	*Hypsipetes lucasi*	Brinji-emas obi
350	Sula Golden Bulbul	*Hypsipetes longirostris*	Brinji-emas sula
350	Banggai Golden Bulbul	*Hypsipetes harterti*	Brinji-emas banggai
352	Chestnut-capped Babbler	*Timalia pileata*	Tepus gelagah
352	Pin-striped Tit Babbler	*Mixornis gularis*	Ciung-air melayu
352	Bold-striped Tit Babbler	*Mixornis bornensis*	Ciung-air coreng
352	Javan Tit Babbler	*Mixornis flavicollis*	Ciung-air jawa
352	Fluffy-backed Babbler	*Macronus ptilosus*	Ciung-air pongpong
352	Golden Babbler	*Cyanoderma chrysaeum*	Tepus emas

Page number	English name	Scientific name	Bahasa Indonesia name
352	Rufous-fronted Babbler	*Cyanoderma rufifrons*	Tepus dahi-merah
354	Chestnut-winged Babbler	*Cyanoderma erythropterum*	Tepus merbah-sampah
354	Bicoloured Babbler	*Cyanoderma bicolor*	Tepus kalimantan
354	Crescent-chested Babbler	*Cyanoderma melanothorax*	Tepus pipi-perak
354	Javan Scimitar Babbler	*Pomatorhinus montanus*	Cica-kopi jawa
354	Sunda Scimitar Babbler	*Pomatorhinus bornensis*	Cica-kopi melayu
354	Black Scimitar Babbler	*Melanocichla lugubris*	Cica-kopi hitam
354	Bare-headed Scimitar Babbler	*Melanocichla calva*	Cica-kopi botak
356	White-bibbed Babbler	*Stachyris thoracica*	Tepus leher-putih
356	White-necked Babbler	*Stachyris leucotis*	Tepus telinga-putih
356	Spot-necked Babbler	*Stachyris strialata*	Tepus lurik
356	Grey-headed Babbler	*Stachyris poliocephala*	Tepus kepala-kelabu
356	Grey-throated Babbler	*Stachyris nigriceps*	Tepus kepala-hitam
356	Chestnut-rumped Babbler	*Stachyris maculata*	Tepus tunggir-merah
356	Javan Babbler	*Stachyris grammiceps*	Tepus dada-putih
356	Black-throated Babbler	*Stachyris nigricollis*	Tepus kaban
358	Moustached Babbler	*Malacopteron magnirostre*	Asi kumis
358	Rufous-crowned Babbler	*Malacopteron magnum*	Asi besar
358	Scaly-crowned Babbler	*Malacopteron cinereum*	Asi topi-sisik
358	Grey-breasted Babbler	*Malacopteron albogulare*	Asi dada-kelabu
358	Sooty-capped Babbler	*Malacopteron affine*	Asi topi-jelaga
360	Büttikofer's Babbler	*Pellorneum buettikoferi*	Pelanduk buttikofer
360	Temminck's Babbler	*Pellorneum pyrrogenys*	Pelanduk bukit
360	Malayan Swamp Babbler	*Pellorneum rostratum*	Pelanduk dada-putih
360	Bornean Swamp Babbler	*Pellorneum macropterum*	Pelanduk rawa
360	Sulawesi Babbler	*Pellorneum celebense*	Pelanduk sulawesi
360	Ferruginous Babbler	*Pellorneum bicolor*	Pelanduk merah
362	Mourning Babbler	*Pellorneum malaccense*	Pelanduk ekor-pendek
362	Glissando Babbler	*Pellorneum saturata*	Pelanduk glissando
362	Leaflitter Babbler	*Pellorneum poliogene*	Pelanduk pipi-kelabu
362	Javan Black-capped Babbler	*Pellorneum capistratum*	Pelanduk topi-hitam
362	Malayan Black-capped Babbler	*Pellorneum nigrocapitatum*	Pelanduk melayu
362	Bornean Black-capped Babbler	*Pellorneum capistratoides*	Pelanduk kepala-hitam
362	Black-browed Babbler	*Malacocincla perspicillata*	Pelanduk kalimantan
364	Abbott's Babbler	*Malacocincla abbotti*	Pelanduk asia
364	Horsfield's Babbler	*Malacocincla sepiaria*	Pelanduk semak
364	Mountain Wren Babbler	*Malacocincla crassa*	Berencet gunung
364	Sumatran Rimator	*Rimator albostriatus*	Berencet sumatera
364	Eye-browed Wren Babbler	*Napothera epilepidota*	Berencet berkening
366	Striped Wren Babbler	*Kenopia striata*	Berencet loreng
366	Bornean Ground Babbler	*Ptilocichla leucogrammica*	Berencet kalimantan
366	Marbled Wren Babbler	*Turdinus marmoratus*	Berencet pualam
366	Large Wren Babbler	*Turdinus macrodactylus*	Berencet besar
366	Black-throated Wren Babbler	*Turdinus atrigularis*	Berencet leher-hitam
366	Rusty-breasted Wren Babbler	*Turdinus rufipectus*	Berencet dada-karat
366	Sunda Fulvetta	*Alcippe brunneicauda*	Wergan coklat
366	Javan Fulvetta	*Alcippe pyrrhoptera*	Wergan jawa
368	Sumatran Laughingthrush	*Leucodioptron bicolor*	Poksai sumatera
368	Sunda Laughingthrush	*Leucodioptron palliatum*	Poksai mantel
368	Javan Laughingthrush	*Garrulax rufifrons*	Poksai kuda
368	Spectacled Laughingthrush	*Garrulax mitratus*	Poksai genting
368	Chestnut-hooded Laughingthrush	*Garrulax treacheri*	Poksai kalimantan
368	Long-tailed Sibia	*Heterophasia picaoides*	Sibia ekor-panjang
368	Silver-eared Mesia	*Leiothrix argentauris*	Mesia telinga-perak
368	Javan Crocias	*Laniellus albonotatus*	Cica matahari
370	Chestnut-crested Yuhina	*Staphida everetti*	Yuhina kalimantan
370	Eyebrowed Heleia	*Apalopteron superciliare*	Opior flores
370	Crested Heleia	*Apalopteron dohertyi*	Opior jambul
370	Wallace's Heleia	*Apalopteron wallacei*	Opior wallace
370	Thick-billed Heleia	*Apalopteron crassirostre*	Opior paruh-tebal
370	Timor Heleia	*Apalopteron muelleri*	Opior timor
370	Sulawesi Heleia	*Apalopteron squamiceps*	Opior sulawesi

530

Page number	English name	Scientific name	Bahasa Indonesia name
390	Sunda Bush Warbler	*Horornis vulcanius*	Ceret gunung
390	Manchurian Bush Warbler	*Horornis canturians*	Ceret manchuria
390	Mountain Leaftoiler	*Phyllergates cucullatus*	Cinenen gunung
390	Pygmy Cupwing	*Pnoepyga pusilla*	Berencet kerdil
392	Oriental Reed Warbler	*Acrocephalus orientalis*	Kerak-basi besar
392	Australasian Reed Warbler	*Acrocephalus australis*	Kerak-basi ramai
392	Black-browed Reed Warbler	*Acrocephalus bistrigiceps*	Kerak-basi alis-hitam
392	Malia	*Malia grata*	Malia sulawesi
392	Timor Thicketbird	*Cincloramphus bivittatus*	Cica-koreng timor
394	Tawny Grassbird	*Cincloramphus timoriensis*	Cica-koreng kuning
394	Striated Grassbird	*Megalurus palustris*	Cica-koreng jawa
394	Lanceolated Warbler	*Locustella lanceolata*	Kecici lurik
394	Gray's Grasshopper Warbler	*Locustella fasciolata*	Kecici gray
394	Pallas's Grasshopper Warbler	*Locustella certhiola*	Kecici belalang
394	Middendorff's Grasshopper Warbler	*Locustella ochotensis*	Kecici siberia
396	Friendly Grasshopper Warbler	*Locustella accentor*	Kecici kinabalu
396	Sunda Grasshopper Warbler	*Locustella montis*	Kecici kuning
396	Sulawesi Grasshopper Warbler	*Locustella castanea*	Kecici coklat
396	Buru Grasshopper Warbler	*Locustella disturbans*	Kecici buru
396	Seram Grasshopper Warbler	*Locustella musculus*	Kecici seram
396	Taliabu Grasshopper Warbler	*Locustella sp*	Kecici taliabu
398	Common Tailorbird	*Orthotomus sutorius*	Cinenen pisang
398	Dark-necked Tailorbird	*Orthotomus atrogularis*	Cinenen belukar
398	Ashy Tailorbird	*Orthotomus ruficeps*	Cinenen kelabu
398	Javan Tailorbird	*Orthotomus sepium*	Cinenen jawa
398	Rufous-tailed Tailorbird	*Orthotomus sericeus*	Cinenen merah
400	Deignan's Prinia	*Prinia polychroa*	Perenjak coklat
400	Hill Prinia	*Prinia superciliaris*	Perenjak gunung
400	Bar-winged Prinia	*Prinia familiaris*	Perenjak jawa
400	Yellow-bellied Prinia	*Prinia flaviventris*	Perenjak rawa
400	Plain Prinia	*Prinia inornata*	Perenjak padi
400	Zitting Cisticola	*Cisticola juncidis*	Cici padi
400	Golden-headed Cisticola	*Cisticola exilis*	Cici merah
402	Hylocitrea	*Hylocitrea bonensis*	Kancilan buah
402	Velvet-fronted Nuthatch	*Sitta frontalis*	Munguk beludu
402	Blue Nuthatch	*Sitta azurea*	Munguk loreng
402	Metallic Starling	*Aplonis metallica*	Perling ungu
402	Tanimbar Starling	*Aplonis crassa*	Perling tanimbar
402	Moluccan Starling	*Aplonis mysolensis*	Perling maluku
404	Asian Glossy Starling	*Aplonis panayensis*	Perling kumbang
404	Short-tailed Starling	*Aplonis minor*	Perling kecil
404	Grosbeak Myna	*Scissirostrum dubium*	Jalak tunggir-merah
404	Flame-browed Myna	*Enodes erythrophris*	Jalak alis-api
404	Common Hill Myna	*Gracula religiosa*	Tiong emas
404	Tenggara Hill Myna	*Gracula venerata*	Tiong nusa-tenggara
406	White-necked Myna	*Streptocitta albicollis*	Blibong pendeta
406	Bare-eyed Myna	*Streptocitta albertinae*	Blibong sula
406	Short-crested Myna	*Basilornis celebensis*	Raja-perling sulawesi
406	Helmeted Myna	*Basilornis galeatus*	Raja-perling sula
406	Long-crested Myna	*Basilornis corythaix*	Raja-perling seram
408	Common Myna	*Acridotheres tristis*	Kerak ungu
408	Crested Myna	*Acridotheres cristatellus*	Kerak jambul
408	Javan Myna	*Acridotheres javanicus*	Kerak kerbau
408	Makassar Myna	*Acridotheres cinereus*	Kerak perut-pucat
408	Black-winged Myna	*Acridotheres melanopterus*	Jalak putih
408	Bali Starling	*Leucopsar rothschildi*	Jalak bali
408	Javan Pied Starling	*Gracupica jalla*	Jalak suren
410	Red-billed Starling	*Spodiopsar sericeus*	Jalak sutera
410	White-shouldered Starling	*Sturnia sinensis*	Jalak bahu-putih
410	Daurian Starling	*Agropsar sturninus*	Jalak cina
410	Chestnut-cheeked Starling	*Agropsar philippensis*	Jalak filipina
410	Rosy Starling	*Pastor roseus*	Jalak mawar

Page number	English name	Scientific name	Bahasa Indonesia name
410	Eurasian Starling	*Sturnus vulgaris*	Jalak eropa
412	Geomalia	*Zoothera heinrichi*	Anis geomalia
412	Everett's Thrush	*Zoothera everetti*	Anis kinabalu
412	Sunda Thrush	*Zoothera andromedae*	Anis hutan
412	White's Thrush	*Zoothera aurea*	Anis sisik
412	Horsfield's Thrush	*Zoothera horsfieldi*	Anis horsfield
412	Fawn-breasted Thrush	*Zoothera machiki*	Anis larat
412	Slaty-backed Thrush	*Geokichla schistacea*	Anis tanimbar
414	Orange-banded Thrush	*Geokichla peronii*	Anis timor
414	Chestnut-backed Thrush	*Geokichla dohertyi*	Anis nusa-tenggara
414	Chestnut-capped Thrush	*Geokichla interpres*	Anis kembang
414	Enggano Thrush	*Geokichla leucolaema*	Anis enggano
414	Red-backed Thrush	*Geokichla erythronota*	Anis punggung-merah
414	Red-and-black Thrush	*Geokichla mendeni*	Anis menden
414	Buru Thrush	*Geokichla dumasi*	Anis buru
414	Seram Thrush	*Geokichla joiceyi*	Anis seram
416	Orange-headed Thrush	*Geokichla citrina*	Anis merah
416	Siberian Thrush	*Geokichla sibirica*	Anis siberia
416	Eyebrowed Thrush	*Turdus obscurus*	Anis kuning
416	Japanese Thrush	*Turdus cardis*	Anis jepang
416	Island Thrush	*Turdus poliocephalus*	Anis gunung
418	Sulawesi Thrush	*Turdus turdoides*	Anis sulawesi
418	Fruit-hunter	*Chlamydochaera jefferyi*	Tawau dada-hitam
418	Javan Cochoa	*Cochoa azurea*	Ciung-mungkal jawa
418	Sumatran Cochoa	*Cochoa beccarii*	Ciung-mungkal sumatera
418	Oriental Magpie-robin	*Copsychus saularis*	Kucica kampung
420	Rufous-tailed Shama	*Copsychus pyrropygus*	Kucica ekor-kuning
420	White-crowned Shama	*Copsychus stricklandii*	Kucica kalimantan
420	Maratua Shama	*Copsychus barbouri*	Kucica maratua
420	Barusan Shama	*Copsychus melanurus*	Kucica barusan
420	White-rumped Shama	*Copsychus malabaricus*	Kucica hutan
422	Ferruginous Flycatcher	*Muscicapa ferruginea*	Sikatan besi
422	Asian Brown Flycatcher	*Muscicapa dauurica*	Sikatan bubik
422	Brown-streaked Flycatcher	*Muscicapa poonensis*	Sikatan asia
422	Umber Flycatcher	*Muscicapa umbrosa*	Sikatan coklat
424	Sumba Brown Flycatcher	*Muscicapa segregata*	Sikatan sumba
424	Sulawesi Brown Flycatcher	*Muscicapa sodhii*	Sikatan sulawesi
424	Grey-streaked Flycatcher	*Muscicapa griseisticta*	Sikatan burik
424	Dark-sided Flycatcher	*Muscicapa sibirica*	Sikatan sisi-gelap
424	Rufous-browed Flycatcher	*Anthipes solitaris*	Sikatan kerongkongan-putih
426	Fulvous-chested Jungle-flycatcher	*Cyornis olivaceus*	Sikatan-rimba dada-coklat
426	Grey-chested Jungle-flycatcher	*Cyornis umbratilis*	Sikatan-rimba dada-kelabu
426	Brown-chested Jungle-flycatcher	*Cyornis brunneatus*	Sikatan-rimba coklat
426	Crocker Jungle-flycatcher	*Cyornis ruficrissa*	Sikatan-rimba gunung
426	Javan Jungle-flycatcher	*Cyornis banyumas*	Sikatan-rimba jawa
428	Dayak Jungle-flycatcher	*Cyornis montanus*	Sikatan-rimba bukit
428	Meratus Jungle-flycatcher	*Cyornis sp.*	Sikatan-rimba meratus
428	Sunda Jungle-flycatcher	*Cyornis caerulatus*	Sikatan-rimba biru-langit
428	Malaysian Jungle-flycatcher	*Cyornis turcosus*	Sikatan-rimba melayu
428	Bornean Jungle-flycatcher	*Cyornis superbus*	Sikatan-rimba kalimantan
430	Indochinese Jungle-flycatcher	*Cyornis sumatrensis*	Sikatan-rimba ranting
430	Mangrove Jungle-flycatcher	*Cyornis rufigastra*	Sikatan-rimba bakau
430	Sulawesi Jungle-flycatcher	*Cyornis omissus*	Sikatan-rimba sulawesi
430	Tanahjampea Jungle-flycatcher	*Cyornis djampeanus*	Sikatan-rimba tanahjampea
430	Kalao Jungle-flycatcher	*Cyornis kalaoensis*	Sikatan-rimba kalao
430	Sula Jungle-flycatcher	*Cyornis colonus*	Sikatan-rimba sula
430	Banggai Jungle-flycatcher	*Cyornis pelingensis*	Sikatan-rimba banggai
432	Rück's Jungle-flycatcher	*Cyornis ruckii*	Sikatan-rimba aceh
432	Pale Blue Jungle-flycatcher	*Cyornis unicolor*	Sikatan-rimba biru-muda
432	White-tailed Flycatcher	*Cyornis concretus*	Sikatan-rimba besar
432	Blue-and-white Flycatcher	*Cyanoptila cyanomelana*	Sikatan biru-putih
432	Zappey's Flycatcher	*Cyanoptila cumatilis*	Sikatan cina

Page number	English name	Scientific name	Bahasa Indonesia name
434	Sumatran Niltava	*Niltava sumatrana*	Niltava sumatera
434	Large Niltava	*Niltava grandis*	Niltava kumbang-padi
434	Indigo Warbling-flycatcher	*Eumyias indigo*	Sikatan-kicau ninon
434	Verditer Warbling-flycatcher	*Eumyias thalassinus*	Sikatan-kicau hijau-laut
434	Turquoise Warbling-flycatcher	*Eumyias panayensis*	Sikatan-kicau pulau
436	Hoevell's Warbling-flycatcher	*Eumyias hoevelli*	Sikatan-kicau dahi-biru
436	Timor Warbling-flycatcher	*Eumyias hyacinthinus*	Sikatan-kicau bakung
436	Buru Warbling-flycatcher	*Eumyias additus*	Sikatan-kicau dada-loreng
436	Flores Warbling-flycatcher	*Eumyias oscillans*	Sikatan-kicau ayun
436	Sumba Warbling-flycatcher	*Eumyias stresemanni*	Sikatan-kicau sumba
436	Matinan Warbling-flycatcher	*Eumyias sanfordi*	Sikatan-kicau matinan
436	Bornean Shade-dweller	*Vauriella gularis*	Decu-lembah kalimantan
438	Heinrichia	*Heinrichia calligyna*	Decu-lembah sulawesi
438	Lesser Shortwing	*Brachypteryx leucophris*	Cingcoang coklat
438	Javan Shortwing	*Brachypteryx montana*	Cingcoang jawa
438	Sumatran Shortwing	*Brachypteryx saturata*	Cingcoang sumatera
438	Bornean Shortwing	*Brachypteryx erythrogyna*	Cingcoang kalimantan
438	Flores Shortwing	*Brachypteryx floris*	Cingcoang flores
440	Siberian Blue Robin	*Larvivora cyane*	Berkecet siberia
440	Japanese Robin	*Larvivora akahige*	Berkecet jepang
440	Siberian Rubythroat	*Calliope calliope*	Berkecet delima
440	Javan Blue Robin	*Myiomela diana*	Berkecet jawa
440	Sumatran Blue Robin	*Myiomela sumatrana*	Berkecet sumatera
440	Siberian Bluetail	*Tarsiger cyanurus*	Berkecet ekor-biru
442	Sunda Forktail	*Enicurus velatus*	Meninting kecil
442	Chestnut-naped Forktail	*Enicurus ruficapillus*	Meninting cegar
442	Javan Forktail	*Enicurus leschenaulti*	Meninting jawa
442	Bornean Forktail	*Enicurus borneensis*	Meninting kalimantan
442	Malayan Forktail	*Enicurus frontalis*	Meninting melayu
444	Shiny Whistling-thrush	*Myophonus melanurus*	Ciung-batu sumatera
444	Javan Whistling-thrush	*Myophonus glaucinus*	Ciung-batu jawa
444	Bornean Whistling-thrush	*Myophonus borneensis*	Ciung-batu kalimantan
444	Sumatran Whistling-thrush	*Myophonus castaneus*	Ciung-batu coklat
444	Blue Whistling-thrush	*Myophonus caeruleus*	Ciung-batu siul
444	Blue Rock-thrush	*Monticola solitarius*	Murai-batu tarum
446	White-throated Rock-thrush	*Monticola gularis*	Murai-batu amur
446	Northern Wheatear	*Oenanthe oenanthe*	Decu kuning
446	Stejneger's Stonechat	*Saxicola stejnegeri*	Decu jepang
446	Pied Bushchat	*Saxicola caprata*	Decu belang
446	Timor Bushchat	*Saxicola gutturalis*	Decu timor
446	Taiga Flycatcher	*Ficedula albicilla*	Sikatan kerongkongan-merah
448	Yellow-rumped Flycatcher	*Ficedula zanthopygia*	Sikatan emas
448	Narcissus Flycatcher	*Ficedula narcissina*	Sikatan narsis
448	Green-backed Flycatcher	*Ficedula elisae*	Sikatan elisa
448	Mugimaki Flycatcher	*Ficedula mugimaki*	Sikatan mugimaki
448	Lompobattang Flycatcher	*Ficedula bonthaina*	Sikatan lompobattang
448	Sumba Flycatcher	*Ficedula harterti*	Sikatan sumba
450	Little Pied Flycatcher	*Ficedula westermanni*	Sikatan belang
450	Snowy-browed Flycatcher	*Ficedula hyperythra*	Sikatan bodoh
450	Damar Flycatcher	*Ficedula henrici*	Sikatan damar
450	Cinnamon-chested Flycatcher	*Ficedula buruensis*	Sikatan buru
450	Rufous-throated Flycatcher	*Ficedula rufigula*	Sikatan leher-merah
452	Rufous-chested Flycatcher	*Ficedula dumetoria*	Sikatan dada-merah
452	Tanimbar Flycatcher	*Ficedula riedeli*	Sikatan tanimbar
452	Black-banded Flycatcher	*Ficedula timorensis*	Sikatan timor
452	Pygmy Flycatcher	*Ficedula hodgsoni*	Sikatan kerdil
452	Asian Fairy-bluebird	*Irena puella*	Kecembang gadung
452	Blue-masked Leafbird	*Chloropsis venusta*	Cica-daun sumatera
454	Lesser Green Leafbird	*Chloropsis cyanopogon*	Cica-daun kecil
454	Greater Green Leafbird	*Chloropsis sonnerati*	Cica-daun besar
454	Sumatran Leafbird	*Chloropsis media*	Cica-daun dahi-emas
454	Javan Leafbird	*Chloropsis cochinchinensis*	Cica-daun jawa

Page number	English name	Scientific name	Bahasa Indonesia name
454	Blue-winged Leafbird	*Chloropsis moluccensis*	Cica-daun sayap-biru
454	Bornean Leafbird	*Chloropsis kinabaluensis*	Cica-daun kalimantan
456	Yellow-breasted Flowerpecker	*Prionochilus maculatus*	Pentis raja
456	Scarlet-breasted Flowerpecker	*Prionochilus thoracicus*	Pentis kumbang
456	Crimson-breasted Flowerpecker	*Prionochilus percussus*	Pentis pelangi
456	Yellow-rumped Flowerpecker	*Prionochilus xanthopygius*	Pentis kalimantan
456	Yellow-vented Flowerpecker	*Pachyglossa chrysorrhea*	Cabai rimba
456	Brown-backed Flowerpecker	*Pachyglossa everetti*	Cabai tunggir-coklat
456	Modest Flowerpecker	*Pachyglossa modesta*	Cabai gesit
458	Tenggara Flowerpecker	*Pachyglossa obsoleta*	Cabai tenggara
458	Golden-rumped Flowerpecker	*Pachyglossa annae*	Cabai emas
458	Grey-sided Flowerpecker	*Dicaeum celebicum*	Cabai panggul-kelabu
458	Crimson-crowned Flowerpecker	*Dicaeum nehrkorni*	Cabai sulawesi
458	Yellow-sided Flowerpecker	*Dicaeum aureolimbatum*	Cabai panggul-kuning
458	Spectacled Flowerpecker	*Dicaeum dayakorum*	Cabai kacamata
460	Orange-bellied Flowerpecker	*Dicaeum trigonostigma*	Cabai bunga-api
460	Plain Flowerpecker	*Dicaeum minullum*	Cabai polos
460	Sumatran Flowerpecker	*Dicaeum beccarii*	Cabai perut-kuning
460	Bornean Flowerpecker	*Dicaeum monticolum*	Cabai panggul-hitam
460	Scarlet-backed Flowerpecker	*Dicaeum cruentatum*	Cabai merah
460	Scarlet-headed Flowerpecker	*Dicaeum trochileum*	Cabai jawa
462	Black-fronted Flowerpecker	*Dicaeum igniferum*	Cabai dahi-hitam
462	Red-chested Flowerpecker	*Dicaeum maugei*	Cabai lombok
462	Javan Flowerpecker	*Dicaeum sanguinolentum*	Cabai gunung
462	Flores Flowerpecker	*Dicaeum rhodopygiale*	Cabai flores
462	Sumba Flowerpecker	*Dicaeum wilhelminae*	Cabai sumba
462	Timor Flowerpecker	*Dicaeum hanieli*	Cabai timor
462	Salvadori's Flowerpecker	*Dicaeum keiense*	Cabai salvadori
464	Halmahera Flowerpecker	*Dicaeum schistaceiceps*	Cabai halmahera
464	Buru Flowerpecker	*Dicaeum erythrothorax*	Cabai buru
464	Seram Flowerpecker	*Dicaeum vulneratum*	Cabai kelabu
464	Apricot-breasted Sunbird	*Cinnyris buettikoferi*	Burung-madu sumba
464	Flame-breasted Sunbird	*Cinnyris solaris*	Burung-madu matari
464	Ornate Sunbird	*Cinnyris ornatus*	Burung-madu sriganti
466	Sahul Sunbird	*Cinnyris clementiae*	Burung-madu sahul
466	Black Sunbird	*Leptocoma aspasia*	Burung-madu hitam
468	Copper-throated Sunbird	*Leptocoma calcostetha*	Burung-madu bakau
468	Van Hasselt's Sunbird	*Leptocoma brasiliana*	Burung-madu pengantin
468	Purple-throated Sunbird	*Leptocoma sperata*	Burung-madu filipina
468	Brown-throated Sunbird	*Anthreptes malacensis*	Burung-madu kelapa
468	Red-throated Sunbird	*Anthreptes rhodolaemus*	Burung-madu leher-merah
470	Plain Sunbird	*Anthreptes simplex*	Burung-madu polos
470	Crimson Sunbird	*Aethopyga siparaja*	Burung-madu sepah-raja
470	Temminck's Sunbird	*Aethopyga temminckii*	Burung-madu ekor-merah
470	Javan Sunbird	*Aethopyga mystacalis*	Burung-madu jawa
470	White-flanked Sunbird	*Aethopyga eximia*	Burung-madu gunung
472	Elegant Sunbird	*Duyvena duyvenbodei*	Burung-madu sangihe
472	Ruby-cheeked Sunbird	*Chalcoparia singalensis*	Burung-madu belukar
472	Bornean Spiderhunter	*Arachnothera everetti*	Pijantung kalimantan
472	Javan Spiderhunter	*Arachnothera affinis*	Pijantung gunung
472	Grey-breasted Spiderhunter	*Arachnothera modesta*	Pijantung dada-kelabu
472	Whitehead's Spiderhunter	*Arachnothera juliae*	Pijantung whitehead
474	Spectacled Spiderhunter	*Arachnothera flavigaster*	Pijantung tasmak
474	Yellow-eared Spiderhunter	*Arachnothera chrysogenys*	Pijantung telinga-kuning
474	Little Spiderhunter	*Arachnothera longirostra*	Pijantung kecil
474	Thick-billed Spiderhunter	*Arachnothera crassirostris*	Pijantung kampung
474	Long-billed Spiderhunter	*Arachnothera robusta*	Pijantung besar
474	Purple-naped Spiderhunter	*Arachnothera hypogrammica*	Pijantung rimba
476	Streaked Weaver	*Ploceus manyar*	Manyar jambul
476	Baya Weaver	*Ploceus philippinus*	Manyar tempua
476	Asian Golden Weaver	*Ploceus hypoxanthus*	Manyar emas
476	Red Avadavat	*Amandava amandava*	Pipit benggala

Page number	English name	Scientific name	Bahasa Indonesia name
478	Pin-tailed Parrotfinch	*Erythrura prasina*	Bondol-hijau binglis
478	Tawny-breasted Parrotfinch	*Erythrura hyperythra*	Bondol-hijau dada-merah
478	Tricoloured Parrotfinch	*Erythrura tricolor*	Bondol-hijau triwarna
478	Blue-faced Parrotfinch	*Erythrura trichroa*	Bondol-hijau muka-biru
478	Mount Mutis Parrotfinch	*Erythrura sp.*	Bondol-hijau timor
480	Sunda Zebra Finch	*Taeniopygia guttata*	Pipit zebra
480	Black-faced Munia	*Lonchura molucca*	Bondol taruk
480	Scaly-breasted Munia	*Lonchura punctulata*	Bondol peking
480	White-rumped Munia	*Lonchura striata*	Bondol tunggir-putih
480	Javan Munia	*Lonchura leucogastroides*	Bondol jawa
480	White-bellied Munia	*Lonchura leucogastra*	Bondol perut-putih
480	Dusky Munia	*Lonchura fuscans*	Bondol kalimantan
480	Five-coloured Munia	*Lonchura quinticolor*	Bondol pancawarna
482	Black-headed Munia	*Lonchura atricapilla*	Bondol rawa
482	White-capped Munia	*Lonchura ferruginosa*	Bondol oto-hitam
482	White-headed Munia	*Lonchura maja*	Bondol haji
482	Pale-headed Munia	*Lonchura pallida*	Bondol kepala-pucat
482	Java Sparrow	*Lonchura oryzivora*	Gelatik jawa
482	Timor Sparrow	*Lonchura fuscata*	Gelatik timor
482	Eurasian Tree Sparrow	*Passer montanus*	Burung-gereja erasia
484	Forest Wagtail	*Dendronanthus indicus*	Kicuit hutan
484	Grey Wagtail	*Motacilla cinerea*	Kicuit batu
484	Eastern Yellow Wagtail	*Motacilla tschutschensis*	Kicuit kerbau
484	White Wagtail	*Motacilla alba*	Kicuit putih
486	Olive-backed Pipit	*Anthus hodgsoni*	Apung zaitun
486	Madanga Pipit	*Anthus ruficollis*	Apung buru
486	Red-throated Pipit	*Anthus cervinus*	Apung kijang
486	Pechora Pipit	*Anthus gustavi*	Apung pechora
486	Paddyfield Pipit	*Anthus rufulus*	Apung sawah
486	Richard's Pipit	*Anthus richardi*	Apung besar
488	Indonesian Serin	*Chrysocorythus estherae*	Kenari melayu
488	Little Bunting	*Emberiza pusilla*	Emberiza kecil
488	Black-faced Bunting	*Emberiza spodocephala*	Emberiza muka-hitam
488	Yellow-breasted Bunting	*Emberiza aureola*	Emberiza pundak-putih
488	Black-headed Bunting	*Emberiza melanocephala*	Emberiza kepala-hitam

BRUNEI
Sabah
Sulu Arch.

CELEBES SEA

Tarakan

Maratua

Sarawak
MALAYSIA

S u l a w e s i   Re

Minahasa Pe

Borneo

Kalimantan

Togian Is

Pelen

Makassar Strait

Sulawesi

Banggai Is

Manui

Wowoni

Laut

Buton

Muna

Matasiri

Kabaena

Masalembu

Wallace's Line

Salayar

Madura

Kangean Is

Tanahjampea

Kalao

Kalaotoa

Bonerate

Madu

BALI SEA

FLORES SEA

Lomb

Java

Bali

Lombok

Komodo

Flores

Pa

Nusa
Penida

Sumbawa

L e s s e r   S u n d a s   (N u s a   T e n g g a r a

Sumba

Semau

Sawu

Rote